B

a Lonely Planet travel survival kit

Bryn Thomas
Sean Sheehan
Pat Yale
Richard Everist
Tony Wheeler

Britain

2nd edition

Published by
Lonely Planet Publications
Head Office: PO Box 617, Hawthorn, Vic 3122, Australia
Branches: 155 Filbert St, Suite 251, Oakland, CA 94607, USA
10a Spring Place, London NW5 3BH, UK
71 bis rue du Cardinal Lemoine, 75005 Paris, France

Printed by
SNP Printing Pte Ltd, Singapore

Photographs by

Glenn Beanland	Richard Everist	Graham Imeson
Sean Sheehan	Tom Smallman	Paul Steel
Bryn Thomas	Tony Wheeler	Pat Yale

Front cover photograph by Pixel Management, The Image Bank

First Published
April 1995

This Edition
April 1997

Although the authors and publisher have tried to make the information as accurate as possible, they accept no responsibility for any loss, injury or inconvenience sustained by any person using this book.

National Library of Australia Cataloguing in Publication Data

Thomas, Bryn, 1959 -
Britain

2nd ed.
Includes index
ISBN 0 86442 518 X

1. Great Britain – Guidebooks. I. Yale, Pat, 1954 - .
II. Sheehan, Sean, 1951 - . III. Everist, Richard. Britain
IV Title. V. Title: Britain. (Series: Lonely Planet travel survival kit).

914.104859

Bryn Thomas

Born in Zimbabwe, where he grew up on a farm, Bryn contracted an incurable case of wanderlust during camping holidays by the Indian Ocean in Mozambique.

An anthropology degree at Durham University in England earned him a job polishing the leaves of pot plants in London. He has also worked as a ski-lift operator in Colorado, encyclopaedia seller in South Dakota and English teacher in Cairo, Singapore and Tokyo. Travel on five continents has included a 2500-km Andean cycling trip and 10 visits to India.

Bryn's first guide, the *Trans-Siberian Handbook*, was short-listed for the Thomas Cook Guidebook of the Year awards. He is also co-author of the LP guide to *India* and has contributed to LP's new guide, *Walking in Britain*.

Sean Sheehan

Despite what his name suggests, Sean was born and brought up in London. After teaching for a number of years, he took an escape route to South-East Asia, where he lived and worked for six years. During that time, alongside acquiring a thirst for travel, he wrote a travel guide to Malaysia and Singapore, edited Shakespeare, ran a computer column for a British publication and worked for a Japanese magazine. He co-authored the 2nd edition of the LP guide to *Ireland*, and has now returned to live in London.

Pat Yale

Pat spent several years selling holidays before throwing up sensible careerdom to head overland from Egypt to Zimbabwe. She then mixed teaching tourism with travel in Europe, Asia and Central and South America, before becoming a full-time writer.

She has worked on LP's guides to *Ireland*, *Dublin* and *Turkey*, and has contributed to *Walking in Britain*. After stints in London, Cambridge and Cirencester, she currently lives in Bristol.

Richard Everist

Richard grew up in Geelong, Australia, has travelled a bit and had a wide variety of jobs. He worked full time at Lonely Planet's head office in Melbourne before jumping the fence to become a writer. In late 1994 he was lured back into the home paddock to be Publishing General Manager.

As well as updating LP's *Papua New Guinea*, and contributing to the shoestring guides for *West Asia*, *Africa*, *Western Europe* and *Mediterranean Europe*, he has co-written LP's guides to *Nepal* and *South Africa*.

Tony Wheeler

Tony was born in England but grew up in Pakistan, the Bahamas and the USA. He returned to England to do a degree in engineering at Warwick University, worked as an automative design engineer, returned to London Business School to complete an MBA, then set out on an Asian overland trip with his wife, Maureen. That trip led to Tony and Maureen setting up Lonely Planet Publications in Australia in 1973, and they've been travelling, writing and publishing guidebooks ever since. In 1996 they moved to Paris, with their children Tashi and Kieran, for a one-year stay.

From the Authors

Bryn Thomas Thanks to everyone who has helped on the two editions of this book. For the 1st edition, Anna Jacomb-Hood, Christopher Knowles, Susy Kennard, Pauline Skyrme-Jones, Patricia Thomas, Sue Hall and Trevor Roberts made considerable contributions in research and writing.

For this new edition thanks to Anna Jacomb-Hood for help in unravelling the complexities of the fragmented British public transport system, David Else for suggestions for the walking section, and Jane Thomas for help in checking proofs. I'm also grateful to everyone at the LP office in London for their useful suggestions, in particular to clubbing gastronome Vicky Wayland, Charlotte Hindle and Diccon Bewes. Out in the field, thanks again to the patient and helpful staff of TICs in England, Scotland and Wales.

Sean Sheehan Many thanks to all the people who contributed to the book and helped with the research. At the London Lonely Planet office, thanks to Vicky Wayland, Diccon Bewes, Simon Goldsmith, Sarah Long, Helen McWilliam, Jennifer Cox and Charlotte Hindle – all of whom contributed to and enriched the London chapter.

I would like to thank Danny Gralton in Camden Town for his hospitality, help and comradeship, and Laura Furzer in Chadwell Heath for the use of her mobile phone one wet Sunday afternoon. Thanks also to the countless people who patiently and kindly dealt with my inquiries at tourist offices, bus and railway stations and assorted places around the country and, in particular, Shivah Jahangir-Tafreshi at the London Tourist Board and Bob Barton at the British Tourist Authority.

Pat Yale I'm grateful to all the friends who allowed me to milk them of relevant info, but particularly to Tony Churchill, Simon Coles, Stewart Foulkes, Sara Hayes and Roger James for allowing me to draw on their specialist knowledge, and to my mother for help with background research.

Sharon North and her family shared their insider's knowledge of York with me, while Nathan Churchill was contributing to tourism research before he was old enough to realise it.

In Scotland, I was indebted to Pietro Cecchini at Edinburgh Tourist Information Centre for finding me that elusive thing...a cheap Edinburgh B&B with a bath and space for a car! Thanks also to Drew Miller for telling me about the campaign against the Skye Bridge tolls.

Finally, thanks on behalf of all the authors to the editors and cartographers who worked on this project – particularly to Liz Filleul, Rachel Black, Cathy Oliver, Paul Harding, Tamsin Wilson and Jane Fitzpatrick.

This Book

This is the 2nd edition of LP's Britain guide. Richard Everist, Tony Wheeler and Bryn Thomas wrote the 1st edition. Bryn Thomas was coordinating author of this edition, which has been updated and restructured, particularly in the London chapter. Bryn wrote the Wales, Eastern England and Channel Islands chapters, and part of the Northern Midlands chapter. Pat Yale wrote the South-Western England and Southern Midlands chapters and part of the Northern England chapter. Bryn and Pat shared the Scotland chapters. Sean Sheehan wrote the London and South-East England chapters and part of the Northern England and Northern Midlands chapters. The three authors shared the introductory chapters.

From the Publisher

This book was edited at the Lonely Planet office in Melbourne by Liz Filleul, with invaluable help from Cathy Oliver and Paul Harding, from Chris Wyness at proofreading stage, and from Jane Fitzpatrick at layout stage. The maps were drawn by Tamsin Wilson, Rachel Black, Michael Signal, Tony Fankhauser, Dorothy Natsikas, Lyndell Taylor, Anthony Phelan and Ann Jeffree. Paul Clifton was responsible for the colour maps. Illustrations were drawn by Dorothy Natsikas and Tamsin Wilson. The book was designed by Rachel Black, and Simon Bracken designed the cover. Finally, thanks to the London Transport Museum for providing us with the London Underground map.

Warning & Request

Things change – prices go up, schedules change, good places go bad and bad places go bankrupt – nothing stays the same. So, if you find things better or worse, recently opened or long since closed, please tell us and help make the next edition even more accurate and useful.

We value all the feedback we receive from travellers. Julie Young coordinates a small team who read and acknowledge every letter, postcard and e-mail, and ensure that every morsel of information finds its way to the appropriate authors, editors and publishers.

Everyone who writes to us will find their name in the next edition of the appropriate guide and will also receive a free subscription to our quarterly newsletter, *Planet Talk*. The very best contributions will be rewarded with a free Lonely Planet guide.

Excerpts from your correspondence may appear in updates (which we add to the end pages of reprints); new editions of this guide; in our newsletter, *Planet Talk*; or in the Postcards section of our Web site – so please let us know if you don't want your letter published or your name acknowledged.

Thanks

Many thanks to the travellers who used the last edition and wrote to us with helpful hints, useful advice and interesting anecdotes. Your names follow:

Kirsten & Mils Ake-Anderson, Kelly Alexander, Kate Amos, Elwin Arens, Barbara Axon, Bonnie Baskin, Richard & Jindapon Bell, David Benson, Philip Bladon, Bert Bodecker, Bernd Bongartz, I D Booth, Sally Bothroyd, Hannah Brown, Joanna Brown, Klaus Bryn, KA Burnett, Melissa Christie, Fiona Clarke, Sandy Colburn, Pam Davidson, Chris Day, Dawn Dean, Garry Denke, Fiona Dent, Amanda Donovan, Stewart & Marie Dougan, Leanne Drummond, Michael Dudley, Mark Edebone, Tim Oliver Eynck, Jack Fitz-Simons, Fran Gale, Scott Gilmore, S Graham, D Greiling, Sarah Guy, Phillipa Hay, Doug & Mavis Haynes, Stacey Henerey, D Higbre, Colin Hill, SP Holt, Alvin Hudec, Rob Jones, Uli Kaiser, Dr John Kennedy, Kathy Kitao, Kristine Lang, Kylie Lawrence, Cherie LeLievre, Fei Chiao Liao, Jodi Lipson, Edgar Locke, Peggy Longley, John & Sheila Lough, MJ Louis, KL Marsden, V McHugh, Deb & Pete Meigs, O & D Middleton, Craig Miller, Bethan Morgan, Dan Morris, Kathryn Mumell, Toni Nash, Glenn Parsons, Janine Pike, J Ramano, M Ramsay, Silke Remmel, Dr & Mrs Jules Rossman, Winfried Ruger, Roz Russell, Michele Seigerman, Laura Shanner, Jean Davidson Sinclair, Judy Smith, Penny Smith, Jason & Jackie Staines, Andrew Stark, Rupert Stewart, Mark Stone, J Thorburn, Christine Tiscareno, Chris Truax, B van Selm, Randall van Someren, B Vazda, Hans von Tour, P R Ward, Judy Whitby, Rod Willard, Brad Wilson, Diarmuid Wilson, Barbara Wolf, John Wren, Elinor Yeo designed by Russell Black, and Simon Bracken designed the cover. Kindly thanks to the London Transport Museum for providing us with the London Underground map.

Warning & Request

Things change — prices go up, schedules change, good places go bad and bad places go bankrupt — nothing stays the same. So, if you find things better or worse, recently opened or long since closed down, please tell us and help make the next edition even more accurate and useful.

We value all the feedback we receive from travellers. Our Young coordinators read and acknowledge every letter, postcard and email and ensure that every morsel of information finds its way to the appropriate authors, editors and publishers. Everyone who writes to us will find their name in the next edition of the appropriate guide and will also receive a free subscription to our quarterly newsletter Planet Talk. The very best contributions will be rewarded with a free Lonely Planet guide.

Excerpts from your correspondence may appear in updates (which we add to the end pages of reprints), new editions of this guide, in our newsletter Planet Talk or in the Postcards section of the Web site — so let us know if you don't want your letter published or your name acknowledged.

Thanks

Many thanks to the travellers who used the last edition and wrote to us with helpful hints, useful advice and interesting anecdotes. Your names follow.

Karen & Kim Alex Aberson, Kelly Alexander, Kate Arlos, Blueprint, Ramon Axon, Deanne Baum, Reinout de Boerkam Ball, David Barton, Billy Beihl, Derek Bicker, David Bogart, JD Booth, Julia Borrowe, Hannah Brown, Linda Brown, Elisabeth, RA Brandt, Mohasir Gholub, Gerry Clarke, Shane Coleman, Paul Crayton, Chris Day, Dawn Deily, Garry Delick, Doug Dent, Amanda Dobson, Stewart & Maria Dobson, Charlie Draper, Michael Dudley, Will Embree, Jim Elliott, Jack Jack England, Frances Anne Gregors, S Graham, D Gostling, Sam, Gary Phillips, Howard, Greg, Mark Harper, Sandy Fenster, D Hilgart, John Hill, SP Holt, Alan Hudson, Tom Kress, Bill Kaner, ID, John Kennedy, David Nash, Sabine King, Kylie Levy, Diane Claud, Anderson, H, Chloe, Chao, Jean Lopez, Philip Lowes, Peggy Jennifer Acme, S Shellacom, MJ Louis, LJ Marsden, Matthew Deb & Patrick Meade, AD Monkton, Craig Miller, Lucan Mongan, Dan Morris, Kathryn Munnell, Neil Nash, Glenn Parsons, Diane Rice, Florence M Ramsay, Silk & Rommel, Dr & Mrs Jules Seamen, Michael Fogg, Rex Russell, Michael Seaman, Jim Shannon, Ian & Leon Sheridan, Roy, Ralph Tennie Smith, Samuel, Jackie Stokes, Andrew Styles, Stuart, Steven, Mark Stone, Thompson, Christine Thompson, Chris Turner, Len Visser, Sue Solomon, JB Vecchi, Hans van Trouch, F Ward, Lucy, Wade, Paul Willard, Brett Wilson, L Drummond, Wilhelm, Barbara Wolf, John Winter, Steve Yeo.

Contents

HIGHLANDS & NORTHERN ISLANDS...828

FACTS ABOUT WALES...901

FACTS FOR THE VISITOR...914

GETTING THERE & AWAY...920

Boxed Text

Map Legend

BOUNDARIES

.... International Boundary
.... Regional Boundary

ROUTES

.... Freeway
.... Highway
.... Major Road
.... Unsealed Road or Track
.... City Road
.... City Street
.... Railway
.... Underground Railway
.... Tram
.... Walking Track
.... Walking Tour
.... Ferry Route
.... Cable Car or Chairlift

AREA FEATURES

.... Parks
.... Built-Up Area
.... Pedestrian Mall
.... Market
.... Cemetery
.... Reef
.... Beach or Desert
.... Rocks

HYDROGRAPHIC FEATURES

.... Coastline
.... River, Creek
.... Intermittent River or Creek
.... Rapids, Waterfalls
.... Lake, Intermittent Lake
.... Canal
.... Swamp

SYMBOLS

✪ CAPITAL	.... National Capital	
◉ Capital	.... Regional Capital	
◍ CITY	.... Major City	
● City	.... City	
● Town	.... Town	
● Village	.... Village	

.... Embassy, Petrol Station
.... Airport, Airfield
.... Swimming Pool, Gardens
.... Shopping Centre, Zoo
... Winery or Vineyard, Picnic Site
One Way Street, Route Number
.... Stately Home, Monument
.... Castle, Tomb
.... Cave, Hut or Chalet
.... Mountain or Hill, Lookout
.... Lighthouse, Shipwreck
.... Pass, Spring
.... Beach, Surf Beach
..... Archaeological Site or Ruins
.... Ancient or City Wall
.... Cliff or Escarpment, Tunnel
.... Railway Station

.... Place to Stay, Place to Eat
.... Cafe, Pub or Bar
.... Post Office, Telephone
.... Tourist Information, Bank
.... Transport, Parking
.... Museum, Youth Hostel
Caravan Park, Camping Ground
.... Church, Cathedral
.... Mosque, Synagogue
Buddhist Temple, Hindu Temple
.... Hospital, Police Station

Note: not all symbols displayed above appear in this book

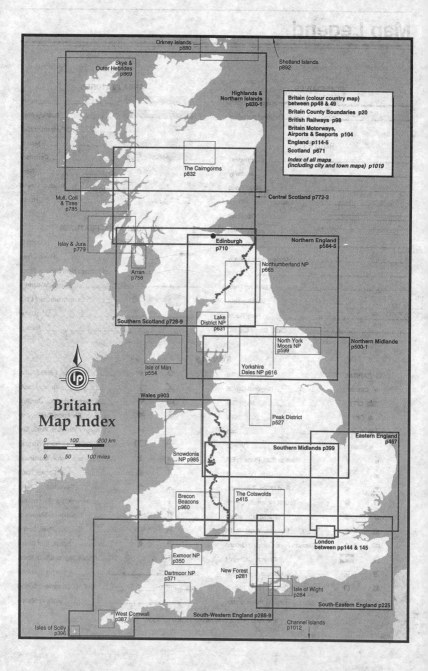

Britain
Map Index

0   100   200 km
0   50   100 miles

Orkney Islands p880

Shetland Islands p892

Skye & Outer Hebrides p869

Highlands & Northern Islands p830-1

The Cairngorms p832

Mull, Coll & Tiree p785

Central Scotland p772-3

Islay & Jura p779

Arran p756

Edinburgh p710

Northern England p584-5

Northumberland NP p665

Southern Scotland p728-9

Lake District NP p631

Isle of Man p554

North York Moors NP p599

Northern Midlands p500-1

Yorkshire Dales NP p616

Wales p903

Peak District p527

Snowdonia NP p985

Southern Midlands p399

Eastern England p467

Brecon Beacons p960

The Cotswolds p415

London between pp144 & 145

Exmoor NP p350

Dartmoor NP p371

New Forest p281

Isle of Wight p284

South-Eastern England p225

West Cornwall p387

South-Western England p288-9

Isles of Scilly p396

Channel Islands p1012

Britain (colour country map) between pp48 & 49
Britain County Boundaries p20
British Railways p98
Britain Motorways, Airports & Seaports p104
England p114-5
Scotland p671
Index of all maps (including city and town maps) p1019

Introduction

At one stage of its history this small island ruled half the world's population and had a major impact on many of the rest. For those people whose countries once lay in the shadow of its great empire a visit to Britain may almost be a cliché, but it is also essential – a peculiar mixture of homecoming and confrontation.

To the surprise of many, Britain remains one of the most beautiful islands in the world. All the words, paintings and pictures that have been produced are not just romantic, patriotic exaggerations.

In terms of area it is small, but the more you explore the bigger it seems to become. Visitors from the New World are often fooled by this magical expansion and try to do too much too quickly. JB Priestley observed of England, 'She is just pretending to be small.'

Covering it all in one trip is impossible – and that's before you start thinking of Scotland and Wales.

The United Kingdom comprises Great Britain (England, Wales and Scotland) and Northern Ireland. Its full name is the United Kingdom of Great Britain and Northern Ireland. This book confines itself to the island of Great Britain (the largest of the British Isles), the Isle of Man, the Channel Islands, and Scotland's outlying islands – the Hebrides in the west and Orkney and Shetland in the north-east.

Sometimes in summer it seems like the whole world has come to Britain. Don't spend all your time in the big, tourist-ridden towns. Do pick a small area and spend at least a week or so wandering around country lanes and villages.

Regional Facts for the Visitor

PLANNING

When to Go

Anyone who spends any extended period of time in Britain will soon sympathise with the locals' conversational obsession with the weather – although in relative terms the climate is mild and the rainfall is not spectacular (see the Climate sections in each country's Facts About chapter for more details).

Settled periods of weather – sunny or otherwise – are rare and rain is likely at any time. Even in midsummer you can go for days without seeing the sun, and showers (or worse) should be expected. To enjoy Britain you have to convince yourself that you *like* the rain – after all, that's what makes it so incredibly green!

The least hospitable months for visitors are November, December, January and February – it's cold, and the days are short (less than eight hours of daylight in December). March is marginal – although there are 12 hours of daylight and daffodils appear in the south, it can still be very cold. October is also marginal – there are nearly 11 hours of daylight, temperatures are reasonable, and weather patterns do seem to be unusually stable, which means you can get good spells of sun, or rain.

Temperatures vary around the island but, as you would expect, it's generally true to say the further north you go, the colder it gets. There's also quite a difference in the number of daylight hours. In early spring or late autumn, it's probably best to concentrate a visit in the south, especially the mild southwest.

April to September are undoubtedly the best months, and this is, unsurprisingly, when most sights and Tourist Information Centres (TICs) are open, and when most people visit. July and August are the busiest months, and best avoided if at all possible. The crowds on the coast, at the national parks, in London and in popular towns like

Oxford, Bath and York have to be seen to be believed. You're just as likely to get good weather in April, May, June, September and October, although October is getting late for the Scottish Highlands.

What Kind of Trip?

Although many people restrict their trip to Britain to a visit to London and a quick whip round the 'milk-run' towns of Oxford, Cambridge, Stratford-upon-Avon, York, Chester and Edinburgh, you'll get more out of a stay if you take the time to explore some of the less touristy towns (Glasgow, Bristol, Manchester and Leeds for example) and the wonderful countryside. The remoter parts of Wales and Scotland, in particular, are best appreciated on a longer stay. London is a great city, but it's also very expensive and

---

Whither the Weather?

It was Dr Johnson who noted that 'when two Englishmen meet, their first talk is of the weather', and two centuries later not much has changed. According to the Meteorological Office, weather reports are the third most watched television broadcasts, and in 1996 a satellite TV channel devoted entirely to the weather started beaming 24-hour forecasts into Britain.

British folklore is rich in ways of second-guessing the weather. If it snows on St Dorothea's day (6 February), we can expect no heavier snowfall. If it rains on St Swithun's day (15 July), brollies should be kept to hand for the next 40 days. The slightest tinge of evening pink and Brits are heard chanting 'A red sky at night is a shepherd's delight, a red sky at morning is a shepherd's warning' like a mantra.

Even so the weather still manages to defeat us. A few weeks without rain and hosepipe bans are rushed in; one snowflake and the railways grind to a halt. The British Rail spokesperson who attributed a delay to the 'wrong kind of snow' is still trying to live it down. ■

unrepresentative of Britain as a whole – don't let it absorb all your time.

It's easy enough to get round the country by train or bus, although it's usually much cheaper to travel by bus than by train. Alternatively there are plenty of coach tours either around the whole country from London or around specific areas. The Slow Coach also offers a hop-on, hop-off coach tour specifically designed for backpackers (see Getting Around for details).

Travellers who are planning to find work and long-term places to live should bear in mind that the peak tourist season generates casual jobs, which are often advertised in May and June. June can be a good time to look for housing as the universities and colleges close for summer and many students move back home; in addition, travellers pack their Kombis and head for the Mediterranean. Everything tightens up in October and November when people return to rebuild their finances and hibernate through winter.

Maps

The best introductory map to Britain is published by the British Tourist Authority, and is widely available in TICs (£1.20). If you plan to use the trains, you can get a useful passenger map (free) from mainline stations.

Motorists and cyclists will find a range of excellent road atlases. There's not much to distinguish them in terms of accuracy or price, but the graphics differ – pick the one you find easiest to read. If you plan to go off the beaten track, you will need one that shows at least three miles to the inch. The spiral-bound *Ordnance Survey Motoring Atlas of Great Britain* (£8.99) is recommended.

The Ordnance Survey (OS) also caters to walkers with a wide variety of maps at different scales. Their Landranger maps at 1:50,000 or about 1¼ inches to the mile are ideal. Also look out for the excellent walkers' maps published by Harveys. Unlike the OS equivalents these maps also include tourist information.

What to Bring

Since anything you think of can be bought in British cities (including Vegemite), pack light and pick up extras as you go along. Clothing in particular is good value in Britain.

A travelpack – a combination of a backpack and shoulder bag – is the most popular item for carrying gear. They're the only way to go if you plan to do any walking – a suitcase will almost certainly mean having to use expensive taxis. A travelpack's straps zip away inside the pack when not needed, making it easy to handle in airports and on crowded public transport. Most travelpacks have sophisticated shoulder-strap adjustment systems and can be used comfortably, even for long hikes.

A minimum packing list could include the following:

• underwear, socks
• two pairs of jeans or trousers
• pair of shorts or a skirt
• a few T-shirts & shirts
• a warm sweater
• a solid, comfortable pair of shoes
• thongs (flip-flops) for shared bathrooms
• a coat or jacket
• a waterproof jacket (preferably in a fabric that breathes, like Goretex)
• a medical kit
• a combination padlock
• a Swiss Army knife
• small towel
• toothpaste, toothbrush & toiletries
• neck pouch or money belt
• small daypack
• passport photos & photocopies of important documents

A tent is unlikely to be very useful; the weather hardly encourages camping and long-distance walks are well served by hostels, camping barns and B&Bs. A sleeping bag is useful in hostels and when visiting friends; get one that doubles as a quilt. A sleeping sheet with a pillow cover is necessary for staying in Scottish YHA hostels – if you don't bring one you'll have to hire or purchase one.

A padlock is handy for locking your bag to a train or a bus luggage rack, and may also be needed to secure your hostel locker. A Swiss

ORKNEY

SHETLAND

Western
Isles

Moray Firth

Moray

Highland

Aberdeenshire

Aberdeen

Perthshire
& Kinross

Angus

-1

Fife

ATLANTIC

OCEAN

Argyll
& Bute

Stirling

2

5

4

3

6 7

10 11 12

8

14

13

North
Ayrshire

East
Ayrshire

South
Lanark-
shire

Borders

South
Ayrshire

Dumfries &
Galloway

Northumberland

16 15

17

18

19

20

21 23

22

NORTH SEA

NORTHERN
IRELAND

Cumbria

Durham

NORTH
CHANNEL

Isle
of Man

North
Yorkshire

York

East Riding
of Yorkshire

24

IRISH SEA

Lancashire

See Inset

34

35

36 31

33 32

26

25

IRELAND

Anglesey

43

Cheshire

30 29

38

39

37

28

Derby-
shire

27

Lincolnshire

Caernarfonshire
& Merionethshire

44

45

46

Staffordshire

Shropshire

47

50

51

Leicestershire

Norfolk

ST GEORGE'S CHANNEL

Cardigan-
shire

Powys

48

49

52 53

70

Warwick-
shire

Cambridge-
shire

Suffolk

Pembrokeshire

Carmarthen-
shire

63

61 62

65

Hereford &
Worcester

Bedford-
shire

71

Hertford-
shire

Essex

54 55

58 60

56

64

66

Gloucester-
shire

67

Oxford-
shire

Greater
London

57

59

68 69

Berkshire

Bristol Channel

Wiltshire

Surrey

Kent

Britain
County
Boundaries

Somerset

Hampshire

West
Sussex

East
Sussex

STRAIT OF DOVER

Devon

Dorset

Isle of
Wight

Cornwall

ENGLISH CHANNEL

0   100   200 km

0   50   100 miles

LANCASHIRE INSET:

Lancashire

Bolton Bury

36

Sefton

Wigan

St
Helens

Salford

Wirral

42 41

Trafford

40

39

Cheshire

1	Dundee	25	North-East Lincolnshire	49	Sandwell
2	Clackmannan	26	North Lincolnshire	50	Walsall
3	Falkirk	27	Nottinghamshire	51	Birmingham
4	East Dunbartonshire	28	Doncaster	52	Solihull
5	Dumbarton & Clydebank	29	Rotherham	53	Coventry
6	Inverclyde	30	Sheffield	54	Swansea
7	Renfrewshire	31	Barnsley	55	Neath & Port Talbot
8	East Renfrewshire	32	Wakefield	56	Bridgend
9	Glasgow	33	Kirklees	57	Vale of Glamorgan
10	North Lanarkshire	34	Bradford	58	Rhondda Cynon Taff
11	West Lothian	35	Calderdale	59	Cardiff
12	Edinburgh	36	Rochdale	60	Caerphilly
13	Mid Lothian	37	Oldham	61	Merthyr Tydfil
14	East Lothian	38	Tameside	62	Blaenau Gwent
15	North Tyneside	39	Stockport	63	Torfaen
16	Newcastle upon Tyne	40	Manchester	64	Newport
17	Gateshead	41	Knowsley	65	Monmouthshire
18	South Tyneside	42	Liverpool	66	South Gloucestershire
19	Sunderland	43	Flintshire	67	Bristol
20	Hartlepool	44	Aberconwy & Colwyn	68	North-West Somerset
21	Stockton-on-Tees	45	Denbighshire	69	Bath & North-East Somerset
22	Middlesbrough	46	Wrexham	70	Northamptonshire
23	Redcar	47	Wolverhampton	71	Buckinghamshire
24	Kingston-upon-Hull	48	Dudley		

Army knife (or any pocketknife that includes a bottle opener and strong corkscrew) is useful for all sorts of things. For city sightseeing, a small daypack is harder for snatch thieves to grab than a shoulder bag.

Other possibilities include a compass, a torch (flashlight), an alarm clock, an adaptor plug for electrical appliances, a universal bath/sink plug, sunglasses and an elastic clothes-line.

Use plastic carrier bags to keep things organised, and dry, inside your backpack. Airlines lose bags from time to time, but there's a much better chance of getting them back if they're tagged with your name and address *inside* as well as on the outside.

SUGGESTED ITINERARIES
Depending on the time at your disposal, you might want to see and do the following:

One week
Visit London, Oxford, the Cotswolds, Bath and Wells.
Two weeks
Visit London, Salisbury, Avebury, Bath, Wells, Oxford, York and Edinburgh.
One month
Visit London, Cambridge, York, Edinburgh, Inverness, Isle of Skye, Fort William, Oban, Glasgow, the Lake District, Chester, the Cotswolds, Wells, Bath, Avebury, Oxford and Stratford-upon-Avon.
Two months
As for one month, but stay put for a week or so in one place. Explore Snowdonia (North Wales) and perhaps walk a long-distance path like the South-West Coastal Path.

HIGHLIGHTS
Islands
Colonsay
Fine sandy beaches, good walks and a mild climate with only half as much rain as on the mainland (Argyll, Scotland).
Farne Islands
Tiny, rocky islands, with amazingly tame nesting seabirds, including puffins and Arctic terns (Northumberland).
Harris
Mountainous and spectacular, with beautiful beaches and isolated crofts (Outer Hebrides, Scotland).
Iona
Very touristy during the day, but spend the night here to experience the magic of this holy island (Argyll, Scotland).
Jura
Wild and remote, with dramatic scenery, superb walks, few people and just one road (Argyll, Scotland).

Orkney
Beautiful beaches, wildflowers and the unique stone-age ruins at Skara Brae (off north coast of Scotland).

Staffa
Boat trips from Mull to see the incredible rock formations that inspired Mendelssohn's *Hebridean Overture* (Argyll, Scotland).

Coast

Beachy Head
Spectacular chalk cliffs backed by rolling downland rich in wildflowers (East Sussex).

Brighton
Tacky but vibrant resort town (East Sussex).

Ilfracombe to Lynton/Lynmouth
Hump-backed cliffs overlooking the Bristol Channel and backed by the beautiful Exmoor National Park (Devon).

Land's End to St Ives
Beautiful coast and a landscape littered with historical reminders and relics (Cornwall).

St Ives
Picturesque village and artists' haunt with two excellent sandy beaches (Cornwall).

Llandudno
Old-style seaside resort with great Victorian architecture and a beautiful site (North Wales).

Scarborough
A classic English seaside resort with a superb location (North Yorkshire).

Scarborough to Saltburn
An unspoilt coastline with beautiful fishing villages (particularly Staithes and Robin Hood's Bay) and major cliffs, backed by the North York Moors National Park (North Yorkshire).

Scotland
The Scottish coast ranges from beautiful (Berwick-upon-Tweed to John o'Groats on the east coast, and Gretna to Glasgow on the west) to extraordinary (in the north-west). From Oban to John o'Groats it is one of the world's greatest natural spectacles. Some of the most spectacular cliffs in Britain are to be found in Orkney and Shetland.

St David's to Cardigan
Unspoilt coastline in Pembrokeshire Coast National Park (South Wales).

Tintagel
A surf-battered headland, topped by a ruined castle, believed to be King Arthur's birthplace (Cornwall).

Museums & Galleries

British Museum
A great museum with amazingly comprehensive archaeological coverage of ancient civilisations (London).

Victoria & Albert Museum
A bewildering array of applied and decorative arts, including furniture, paintings, woodwork, jewellery, textiles and clothing (London).

National Gallery
The national collection of European art from the 15th to early 20th century (London).

Tate Gallery
Covering British artists from the 16th century, and modern artists (British and foreign) from the Impressionists to the present day (London).

York Castle Museum
An intriguing museum of everyday life, including reconstructed streets and authentically furnished rooms from the 17th to the 20th centuries (York).

HMS *Victory* & *Mary Rose*
The world's oldest commissioned warship and Nelson's flagship at the Battle of Trafalgar; and King Henry VIII's flagship rescued from the mud beneath Portsmouth Harbour (Portsmouth).

Ironbridge Gorge
The birthplace of the Industrial Revolution restored and recreated over a number of sites, including the world's first iron bridge (Shropshire).

Burrell Collection
A fascinating moderate-sized collection made by a wealthy shipowner, housed in a superb museum sited in parkland (Glasgow).

Historic Cities & Towns

Bath
Blessed with superb Georgian architecture, but heavily inundated with tourists (South-West England).

Beverley
An unspoilt, little-visited market town with a superb medieval church (East Riding of Yorkshire).

Cambridge
Famous university town with a compact centre. King's College Chapel is one of the most impressive buildings in Europe (Cambridgeshire).

Cockermouth
Unspoilt market town on the little-visited western edge of the Lake District (Cumbria).

Edinburgh
One of the world's greatest cities with a dramatic site and extraordinary architectural heritage (Scotland).

Helmsley
Classic Yorkshire market town, with Rievaulx Abbey, a 12th-century castle and an 18th-century mansion within easy walking distance (North Yorkshire).

Liverpool
Once a great port and industrial city, with a superb legacy of Victorian and Edwardian architecture, a strong cultural identity and vibrant nightlife (north-west England).

Melrose

A charming market town in the heart of the Borders, with a ruined abbey and good walks (Borders Region, Scotland).

Oxford

University town with evocative architecture, marred only by crowds (Oxfordshire).

Richmond

On the edge of the Yorkshire Dales, overlooking the River Swale, with a cobbled marketplace at the foot of a ruined castle (North Yorkshire).

St Andrews

An old university and golfing town, with ruined castle and harbour, on a headland overlooking a sweeping stretch of sand (Fife, Scotland).

St David's

Small town hiding an exquisite cathedral (Pembrokeshire, Wales).

Sandwich

Unspoilt and little-visited medieval township (Kent).

Shrewsbury

Interesting town with half-timbered architecture and curious medieval streets (Shropshire).

Whitby

Atmospheric fishing port on magnificent coastline (North Yorkshire).

Winchester

An ancient English capital rich in history, with a great cathedral (Hampshire).

York

A proud city with a spectacular cathedral and medieval walls, and many excellent museums (North Yorkshire).

Cathedrals & Churches

Canterbury Cathedral

The Church of England's most important cathedral, and crowded with the ghosts of the past (Kent).

Durham Cathedral

A monolithic Norman cathedral, overwhelming in scale, on a spectacular site overlooking Durham (Northern England).

Ely Cathedral

Huge building looming over the fens (Cambridgeshire).

Lincoln Cathedral

An unusual cathedral with a site surpassed only by Durham (Lincolnshire).

King's College Chapel

Perpendicular masterpiece with brilliant acoustics and one of Britain's best boys' choirs (Cambridge).

Rievaulx Abbey

Romantic abbey ruins on a beautiful site (North Yorkshire).

Salisbury Cathedral

Stylistically coherent, with Britain's tallest spire, a soaring elegance (Wiltshire).

St David's Cathedral

Tucked in a dale, a small, secretive and mystical cathedral (Pembrokeshire, Wales).

St Paul's Cathedral

Sir Christopher Wren's masterpiece, with a great view from the Dome (London).

Wells Cathedral

The centrepiece of the best medieval cathedral precinct in Britain, with brilliant medieval carving (Somerset).

Westminster Abbey

Rich in history – since King Harold, almost every monarch has been crowned here – and with an excellent boys' choir (London).

Winchester Cathedral

Architectural styles from Norman to Perpendicular in perfect harmony (Hampshire).

York Minster

The largest medieval church in Britain, incorporating Roman ruins and superb stained glass (North Yorkshire).

Historic Houses

Blenheim Palace

An enormous private house built in the Baroque style by Sir John Vanbrugh in 1704, set in parkland (Oxfordshire).

Castle Howard

Another Vanbrugh masterpiece with a dramatic setting in superb landscaped gardens (North Yorkshire).

Charleston Farmhouse

Home to Vanessa Bell, Duncan Grant and David Garnett (of the Bloomsbury Group), decorated with frescos and postimpressionist art and with a charming garden (East Sussex).

Haddon Hall

Dating from the 12th century and added to for 500 years, one of the most complete surviving medieval manor houses (Derbyshire).

Ightham Mote

A small moated manor house that has scarcely changed for 500 years (Kent).

Hampton Court Palace

Begun by Cardinal Wolsey in 1514 and a royal residence until the 18th century, an enormous, fascinating complex surrounded by beautiful gardens (London).

Knole House

An enormous house dating from the 15th century and virtually untouched (including the interior furniture) since the 17th century, set in parkland (Kent).

Royal Pavilion
An exotic fantasy, combining Indian, Chinese and Gothic elements, built by George IV in 1815 to impress his mistress (Brighton).

Tenement House
A small apartment giving a vivid insight into middle-class life at the turn of the century (Glasgow).

The Queen's House
An Inigo Jones masterpiece, built in 1635 (London).

Traquair
An extraordinary building dating from the 10th century, seemingly untouched by time (Borders Region, Scotland).

Gardens

Bodnant Garden
Famed for its rhododendrons and camellias and with fine mountain views – particularly spectacular in spring (North Wales).

Castle Kennedy Gardens
Laid out in the 18th century around castle ruins, with formal gardens and a famous rhododendron collection (Dumfries & Galloway, Scotland).

Forde Abbey
A former Cistercian abbey with wide lawns, ponds, huge trees and colourful borders (Dorset).

Great Dixter
A series of gardens begun by Sir Edwin Lutyens featuring wildflowers and brilliant spring bulbs (Kent).

Hidcote Manor Gardens
One of the most famous modern gardens in Britain (Gloucestershire).

Regents Park
Vast lawns, the spectacular Queen Mary's Rose Garden with 60,000 roses, ornamental ponds and a zoo (London).

Royal Botanic Gardens, Kew
Three hundred acres of formal gardens, woods, rock gardens, conservatories and the magnificent Palm House (London).

Sissinghurst
Magical garden created by Vita Sackville-West and Harold Nicholson of the Bloomsbury Group (Kent).

Stourhead & Stourton
Two neighbouring gardens that are very different from each other. Stourhead comprises superb landscaped parkland designed in the 1740s around a lake. The flower garden of Stourton House is in perfect contrast (Wiltshire).

Stowe Landscape Garden
An enormously influential garden started in the 17th century and now being ambitiously restored by the National Trust (Buckinghamshire).

Studley Royal & Fountains Abbey
A superb water garden on a grand scale, framing extraordinary monastic ruins (North Yorkshire).

Trelissick Garden
Rhododendrons, magnolias, hydrangeas and sub-tropical plants thrive in this area's mild climate (Cornwall).

Prehistoric Remains

Avebury & Around
More impressive than Stonehenge; extensive remains, including a stone circle (surrounded by an earth bank) and avenue, and nearby Silbury Hill and West Kennet Long Barrow (Wiltshire).

Callanish Standing Stones
A cross-shaped avenue and circle on a dramatic site (Lewis, Scotland).

Castlerigg Stone Circle
A stone circle with a beautiful location near Keswick in the Lake District (Cumbria).

Mousa Broch
The best preserved broch (defensive tower) in Britain (Shetland).

Ring of Brodgar
Well-preserved stone circle, part of an extensive ceremonial site that includes standing stones and a chambered tomb (Orkney).

Skara Brae
The extraordinarily well-preserved remains of a village inhabited 3000 years ago – including dressers, fireplaces, beds and boxes all made from stone (Orkney).

Stonehenge
An extraordinary monument, but marred by crowds and a nearby road (Wiltshire).

Roman Sites

Chedworth Villa
Well-preserved mosaic floors at this villa, built for a wealthy Roman landowner (Gloucestershire).

Fishbourne Palace
Largest Roman palace in Britain, with beautiful mosaics (near Chichester, West Sussex).

Hadrian's Wall
Now a World Heritage Site, the evocative ruins of this monumental attempt to divide the country stretch 73 miles across the north (Northumberland).

Train Journeys

Ffestiniog Line
The most scenic of the 'Great Little Trains' of Wales, runs 14 miles through Snowdonia National Park (North Wales).

Leeds-Settle-Carlisle Line
Spectacular engineering feat running through the beautiful Yorkshire Dales (North Yorkshire).

Snowdon Mountain Railway
  The lazy way to the top of Britain's second-highest mountain (Wales).
Tarka Line
  From Exeter to Barnstaple through classic Devon countryside (Devon).
Vale of Rheidol
  A spectacular 12-mile narrow-gauge steam railway between Aberystwyth and Devil's Bridge (Wales).
West Highland Railway
  Scotland's most famous railway line, with particularly dramatic sections crossing Rannoch Moor and from Fort William to Mallaig (Scotland).

Medieval Castles

Alnwick
  Dramatic castle begun in the 12th century and converted to a great house without losing its medieval character (Northumberland).
Caerlaverock
  An unusual triangular castle, surrounded by a moat (Dumfries & Galloway, Scotland).
Caernarfon
  After Windsor, the largest castle in England and Wales (North Wales).
Conwy
  One of the most interesting of the many fine castles built by Edward I to subdue the Welsh; complete with 21 towers and town walls still standing (North Wales)
Dover
  A massive fortress begun shortly after the Norman conquest, but encompassing a Roman lighthouse, Saxon church and tunnels last used in WWII (Kent).
Hermitage
  A brutal and romantic castle surrounded by bleakly beautiful countryside (Dumfries & Galloway, Scotland).
Leeds
  Extraordinarily beautiful castle in the middle of a lake, marred by large crowds (Kent).
Stirling
  The favoured royal residence of the Stewarts (Central Scotland).
Tower of London
  Begun in 1078 by William the Conqueror, a fortress, royal residence and state prison, now home to the British crown jewels (London).
Windsor
  First settled by Saxon kings, then by William the Conqueror, and still a royal residence, includes the beautiful St George's Chapel (Berkshire).

TOURIST OFFICES

The British Tourist Authority (BTA) stocks masses of information, much of it free.

Contact the BTA before you leave home because some discounts are available only to people who have booked before arriving in Britain. Travellers with special needs (be it disability, diet etc) should also contact the nearest BTA office.

In London the British Travel Centre at 12 Regent St is a good starting point for information collecting.

Local Tourist Offices

Every British town (and many villages) has its own tourist information centre (TIC) where you can get a wide range of information, particularly about places within a 50-mile radius. Most also operate a local bed-booking system and a 'book-a-bed-ahead' (BABA) scheme. In addition there are National Park Visitor Information Centres. Local libraries are also good sources of information.

Most TICs are open from 9 am to 5 pm Monday to Friday, although in popular tourist areas they may also open on Saturday and stay open later in the evening. In real honeypots like Stratford and Bath they'll be open seven days a week throughout the year. From October to March smaller TICs are often closed.

Many TICs now have 24-hour computer databases which can be accessed even when the office is closed. Others put posters with basic information about accommodation and a town plan in the window.

Tourist Offices Abroad

Overseas, the BTA represents the tourist boards of England, Scotland and Wales. Addresses of some overseas offices are as follows:

Australia
  8th floor, University Centre, 210 Clarence St, Sydney, NSW 2000 (☎ (02) 9267 4555; fax (02) 9267 4442; E-mail 100247.243@compuserve.com)
Canada
  Suite 450, 111 Avenue Rd, Toronto, Ontario M5R 3JD (☎ 416-925 6326; fax 416-961 2175)
Denmark
  Montergade 3, 1116 Copenhagen K (☎ 33 33 91 88)

France
Tourisme de Grand-Bretagne, Maison de la Grande Bretagne, 19 rue des Mathurins, 75009 Paris (entrance in les rues Tronchet et Auber) (☎ 01 44 51 56 20)

Germany
Taunusstrasse 52-60, 60329 Frankfurt (☎ 069-238 0711)

Ireland
18-19 College Green, Dublin 2 (☎ 01-670 8000; fax 670 8244)

Italy
Corso V, Emanuele 337, 00186 Rome (☎ 06-6880 6821)

Japan
Tokyo Club Building, 3-2-6 Kasumigaseki, Chiyoda-ku, Tokyo 100 (☎ 03-3581 3603)

Netherlands
Stadhouderskade 2 (5e), 1054 ES Amsterdam (☎ 020-685 50 51)

New Zealand
3rd floor, Dilworth Building, corner Queen & Customs Sts, Auckland 1 (☎ 09-303 1446; fax 09-377 6965)

Norway
Postbox 1554 Vika, 0117 Oslo 1 (☎ 095-468 212444)

Singapore
24 Raffles Place, 19-06 Clifford Centre, Singapore 048621 (☎ 535 2966)

South Africa
Lancaster Gate, Hyde Lane, Hyde Park, Sandton 2196 (☎ 011-325 0343)

Spain
Torre de Madrid 6/5, Plaza de Espana 18, 28008 Madrid (☎ 91-541 13 96)

Sweden
Klara Norra Kyrkogata 29, S 111 22 Stockholm (☎ 08-21 24 44)

Switzerland
Limmatquai 78, CH-8001 Zurich (☎ 01-261 42 77)

USA
625 N Michigan Avenue, Suite 1510, Chicago IL 60611 (personal callers only)

There are more than 40 BTA offices worldwide. Addresses are listed on their web site (http://www.bta.org.uk).

VISAS & DOCUMENTS
Passport

Your most important travel document is a passport, which should remain valid until well after your trip. If it's just about to expire, renew it before you go. This may not be easy to do overseas, and some countries insist your passport remain valid for a specified minimum period (usually three months) after your visit.

Applying for or renewing a passport can be an involved process taking from a few days to several months, so don't leave it till the last minute. Bureaucracy usually grinds faster if you do everything in person rather than relying on the mail or agents. First check what is required: passport photos, birth certificate, population register extract, signed statements, exact payment in cash, whatever.

Australian citizens can apply at post offices, or the passport office in their state capital; Canadians can apply at regional passport offices; New Zealanders can apply at any district office of the Department of Internal Affairs; and US citizens must apply in person (but may usually renew by mail) at a US Passport Agency office or some courthouses and post offices.

Citizens of European countries may not need a valid passport to travel to Britain. A national identity card can be sufficient, and usually involves less paperwork and processing time. Check with your travel agent or the British embassy.

Visas

A visa is a stamp in your passport permitting you to enter a country for a specified period of time. In 99.9% of cases, the procedure is a mere formality. Often you can get a visa at borders or airports, but not always – check first with the embassies or consulates of the countries you plan to visit.

There is a variety of visa types, including tourist, transit, business and work visas. Transit visas are usually cheaper than tourist or business visas, but they only allow a very short stay and can be difficult to extend.

In the past South Africans have had little joy travelling with their passport (the infamous Green Mamba), though this is changing rapidly now. Hong Kong residents may need visas to several countries depending on their passport endorsements. Australians need a visa to visit France or Spain – your passport may not be checked when entering these countries overland, but major problems can arise if it is requested on departure.

Visa requirements can change, and you should always check with embassies or a reputable travel agent before travelling. If you're travelling widely, carry plenty of spare passport photos (you'll need up to four every time you apply for a visa).

British Visas Visa regulations are always subject to change, so it is essential to check the situation with your local British embassy, high commission or consulate before leaving home.

Currently, if you are a citizen of Australia, Canada, New Zealand, South Africa or the USA, you are given 'leave to enter' Britain at your place of arrival. Tourists from these countries are generally permitted to stay for up to six months, but are prohibited from working. To stay longer you need an entry clearance certificate: apply to the high commission.

If you are a citizen of the European Union (EU), you may live and work in Britain free of immigration control – you don't need a visa to enter the country.

The immigration authorities have always been tough, and this can only get worse; dress neatly and carry proof that you have sufficient funds to support yourself. A credit card and/or an onward ticket will help. People have been refused entry because they happened to be carrying papers (like references) that suggested they intended to work.

Work Permits EU nationals do not need a work permit, but all other nationalities do to work legally. If the *main* purpose of your visit is to work, you basically have to be sponsored by a British company.

However, if you are a citizen of a Commonwealth country, and aged between 17 and 27 inclusive, you may apply for a Working Holiday Entry Certificate that allows you to spend up to two years in the UK and to take work that is 'incidental' to a holiday. You are not allowed to engage in business, pursue a career, or provide services as a professional sportsperson or entertainer.

You must apply to the nearest UK mission overseas – Working Holiday Entry Certificates are *not* granted on arrival in Britain. It is not possible to switch from being a visitor to a working holidaymaker, nor is it possible to claim back any time spent out of the UK during the two-year period. When you apply, you must satisfy the authorities you have the means to pay for a return or onward journey, and will be able to maintain yourself without recourse to public funds.

If you are a Commonwealth citizen and have a parent born in the UK, you may be eligible for a Certificate of Entitlement to the Right of Abode, which means you can live and work in Britain free of immigration control.

If you are a Commonwealth citizen and have a grandparent born in the UK, or if the grandparent was born before 31 March 1922 in what is now the Republic of Ireland, you may qualify for a UK Ancestry – Employment Certificate, which means you can work full time for up to four years in the UK.

Visiting students from the USA can get a work permit allowing them to work for six months; you have to be at least 18 years old and a full-time student at a college or university. It costs US$200 and is available through the Council on International Educational Exchange (☎ 212-822 2600; http://www.ciee.org), 205 East 42nd St, New York, NY 10017.

If you have queries once you are in the UK, contact the Home Office, Immigration & Nationality Department (☎ 0181-686 0688), Lunar House, Wellesley Rd, Croydon CR9 2BY (East Croydon BR).

Photocopies

It's sensible to keep photocopies of all important documents (passport, air tickets, insurance policy, travellers' cheques serial numbers) in a separate place in case of theft. It might be wise to stash £50 with the photocopies just in case. Ideally, leave a second set of copies with someone responsible in your home country.

Onward Tickets

Although you don't need an onward ticket to

be granted 'leave to enter' on arrival (see Visas above), this could help if there is any doubt that you have sufficient funds to support yourself and purchase an onward ticket in Britain.

Travel Insurance

A travel insurance policy to cover theft, loss and medical problems is a must. There are all sorts of policies and your travel agent should be able to help. The international student travel policies handled by STA Travel and other student travel organisations are usually good value. Some policies offer lower and higher medical-expense options – go for as much as you can afford, especially if you're also visiting the Channel Islands, the USA, Switzerland, Germany or Scandinavia, where medical costs can be astronomical.

Always read the small print carefully, bearing in mind that:

- Some policies specifically exclude 'dangerous activities' like scuba diving, motorcycling, skiing, mountaineering, even trekking.
- You may prefer a policy that pays doctors or hospitals directly rather than forcing you to pay on the spot and claim the money back later. If you have to claim later, make sure you keep all documentation. Some policies ask you to call back (reverse charges) to a centre in your home country where an immediate assessment of your problem is made.
- Not all policies cover ambulances, helicopter rescue or emergency flights home.
- Most policies exclude cover for pre-existing illnesses.

Driving Licence & Permit

Your normal driving licence is legal for 12 months from the date you last entered Britain; you can then apply for a British licence at post offices.

However, if you don't hold a European driving licence and plan to drive in mainland Europe, obtain an International Driving Permit (IDP) from your local automobile association before you leave – you'll need a passport photo and a valid licence. They're usually inexpensive and valid for one year only. An IDP helps Europeans make sense of your unfamiliar local licence (make sure you

take that with you, too) and can make life much simpler, especially when hiring cars and motorbikes.

While you're at it, ask your automobile association for a Card of Introduction. This entitles you to services offered by European sister organisations (touring maps and information, help with breakdowns, technical and legal advice etc), usually free of charge.

Camping Card International

Your local automobile association also issues a Camping Card International, which is basically a camping ground ID. They're also issued by local camping federations, and sometimes on the spot at camp sites. They incorporate third party insurance for damage you may cause, and many camping grounds offer a small discount if you sign in with one. Some hostels and hotels also accept carnets for signing-in purposes, but won't give discounts.

Hostel Card

If you're travelling on a budget, membership of the Youth Hostel Association (YHA)/Hostelling International (HI) is a must (£9.30 over-18, £3.20 under-18). There are around 320 hostels in Britain and members are also eligible for an impressive list of discounts. In other parts of Europe some hostels don't require you to be a hostelling member, but often charge less if you have a card. See the Accommodation section of this chapter for more information about hostelling in Britain.

Student & Youth Cards

The most useful is the International Student Identity Card (ISIC), a plastic ID-style card with your photograph. It can perform all sorts of wonders, including producing discounts on many forms of transport. Even if you have your own transport, the card will soon pay for itself through cheap or free admission to museums and sights, and cheap meals in some student restaurants.

There's a worldwide industry in fake student cards, and many places now stipulate a maximum age for student discounts or, more simply, substitute a 'youth discount' for a 'student discount'. If you're aged under 26 but not a student, you can apply for a Federation of International Youth Travel Organisations (FIYTO) card or a Euro26 Card which give much the same discounts. Your hostelling organisation should be able to help with this.

Both types of card are issued by student unions, hostelling organisations or student travel agencies. They don't automatically entitle you to discounts, but you won't find out until you flash the card.

Seniors' Cards

Discount cards for over 60s are available for rail and bus travel. See those sections in the Getting Around chapter.

International Health Card

You may need this yellow booklet if you're travelling onwards through parts of Asia, Africa and South America, where yellow fever is prevalent.

If you're a national of another EU country, Form E111 (available from post offices) entitles you to free or reduced-cost medical treatment in Britain.

Other Documents

If you're visiting Britain on a Working Holiday Entry Certificate don't forget to bring any course certificates or letters of reference that might help you find a job.

EMBASSIES

Don't expect too much from your embassy in Britain, or in any other country for that matter. They're probably not going to start worrying about you unless you get into trouble with the police or inconvenience them by expiring while on holiday. They will, however, help you replace a lost passport or offer advice on other emergencies. They won't hold mail for travellers but will help someone in your home country get in touch with you in an emergency.

UK Embassies Abroad

Some UK embassies abroad include:

Australia – High Commission
Commonwealth Ave, Yarralumla, Canberra, ACT 2600 (☎ 06-270 6666)
Canada – High Commission
80 Elgin St, Ottawa K1P 5K7 (☎ 613-237 1530)
France – Consulate
9 Ave Hoche, 8e, Paris (☎ 01 42 66 38 10)
Germany – Embassy
Friedrich-Ebert-Allee 77, 53113 Bonn (☎ 0228-23 40 61)
Japan – Embassy
1 Ichiban-cho, Chiyoda-ku, Tokyo (☎ 03-3265 5511)
New Zealand – High Commission
44 Hill St, Wellington 1 (☎ 04-472 6049)
South Africa – High Commission
255 Hill St, Pretoria (☎ 012-433 3121)
USA – Embassy
3100 Massachusetts Ave NW, Washington DC 20008 (☎ 202-462 1340)

Foreign Embassies in the UK

Countries with diplomatic representation in the UK include the following:

Austrian Embassy & Consulate
18 Belgrave Mews West, London SW1 (☎ 0171-235 3731) (tube: Hyde Park Corner)
Australian High Commission
Australia House, The Strand, London WC2 (☎ 0171-379 4334) (tube: Temple)
Canadian High Commission
Macdonald House, 1 Grosvenor Square, London W1 (☎ 0171-258 6600) (tube: Bond St)
Danish Embassy & Consulate
55 Sloane St, London SW1 (☎ 0171-333 0200) (tube: Knightsbridge)
Finnish Embassy & Consulate
38 Chesham Place, London SW1 (☎ 0171-235 9531) (tube: Hyde Park Corner)
French Consulate General
6A Cromwell Place, London SW7 (☎ 0171-838 2000) (tube: South Kensington)
German Embassy
23 Belgrave Square, London SW1 (☎ 0171-235 5033) (tube: Hyde Park Corner)
Israeli Embassy
2 Palace Green, London W8 (☎ 0171-957 9500) (tube: High St Kensington)
Italian Consulate
38 Eaton Place, London SW1 (☎ 0171-235 9371) (tube: Sloane Square)
Irish Embassy & Consulate
17 Grosvenor Place, London SW1 (☎ 0171-235 2171) (tube: Hyde Park Corner)
Japanese Embassy
101 Piccadilly, London W1 (☎ 0171-465 6500) (tube: Green Park)

Netherlands Embassy
   38 Hyde Park Gate, London SW7 (☎ 0171-584 5040) (tube: Gloucester Rd)
New Zealand High Commission
   New Zealand House, Haymarket, London SW1 (☎ 0171-930 8422) (tube: Piccadilly Circus)
South African Embassy
   Trafalgar Square, London WC2 (☎ 0171-930 4488) (tube: Charing Cross)
Spanish Embassy
   20 Draycott Place, London SW3 (☎ 0171-589 8989) (tube: Sloane Square)
Swedish Embassy & Consulate
   11 Montague Place, London W1 (☎ 0171-917 6413) (tube: Goodge St)
US Embassy
   24 Grosvenor Square, London W1 (☎ 0171-499 9000) (tube: Bond St)

CUSTOMS

Entering Britain you'll be faced with three colour-coded customs channels. If you have nothing to declare go through the green channel; if you may have something to declare go through blue if you're coming from an EU country, or red if from outside the EU.

For imported goods there's a two-tier system: the first for goods bought duty free, the second for goods bought in an EU country where tax and duty have been paid.

The second tier is relevant because a number of products (eg alcohol and tobacco) are much cheaper on the Continent. Under single market rules, however, as long as tax and duty have been paid somewhere in the EU there is no prohibition on importing them within the EU, provided the goods are for personal consumption. Consequently, a thriving business has developed with Britons making day trips to France to load their cars up with cheap beer, wine and cigarettes – the savings can more than pay for the trip.

Duty Free

If you purchase from a duty-free shop, you can import 200 cigarettes or 250 grams of tobacco, two litres of still wine plus one litre of spirits or another two litres of wine (sparkling or otherwise), 60 cc of perfume, 250 cc of toilet water, and other duty-free goods (eg

cider and beer) to the value of £136 (£75 within the EU).

Tax & Duty Paid

If you buy from a normal retail outlet, customs uses the following guidelines to distinguish personal imports from those on a commercial scale: 800 cigarettes or one kg of tobacco, 10 litres of spirits, 20 litres of fortified wine, 90 litres of wine (not more than 60 sparkling) and 110 litres of beer!

MONEY
Costs

Britain is extremely expensive and London is horrific. You can also expect prices to increase by 5 to 10% a year.

While in London you will need to budget £16 to £22 a day for bare survival. Dormitory accommodation alone will cost from £12.50 to £20 a night, a one-day travel card is £3.60, and drinks and the most basic sustenance will cost you at least £6, with any sightseeing or nightlife costs on top. There's not much point visiting if you can't enjoy some of the city's life, so if possible add another £15.

Costs will obviously be even higher if you choose to stay in a central hotel and eat restaurant meals. Hotel rates start at around £23 per person and a restaurant meal will be at least £10. Add a couple of pints of beer (£2 each) and pay entry fees to a tourist attraction or nightclub and you could easily spend £55 per day – without being extravagant.

Once you start moving around the country, particularly if you have a transport pass or are walking or hitching, the costs will drop. Fresh food is roughly the same price as in Australia and the USA. However, without including long-distance transport, and assuming you stay in hostels and an occasional cheap B&B, you'll still need around £20 per day. A country youth hostel will cost from £5.50 to £10; add £4 for food, £4 for entry charges and/or local buses, and £3 for miscellaneous items like films, shampoo, books, telephone calls...

If you hire a car or use a transport pass, stay in B&Bs, eat one sit-down meal a day and don't stint on entry fees, you'll need £30 to £40 per day (still not including long-distance transport costs). Most basic B&Bs will be from £13 to £16 per person and dinner will be from £7 to £14 (depending on whether you're eating in a pub or a restaurant and how much you drink); then add £2.50 for snacks and drinks, £3 for miscellaneous items and at least £5 for entry fees. If you're travelling by car you'll probably average a further £6 to £10 per day on petrol and parking (not including hire charges); if you travel by some sort of pass you'll probably need to average a couple of pounds a day on local transport, or hiring a bike.

Carrying Money

However you decide to carry your funds, it makes sense to keep most of it out of easy reach of snatch thieves in a money-belt or similar. You might want to stitch an inside pocket into your skirt or trousers to keep an emergency stash; certainly it makes sense to keep something like £50 apart from the rest of your cash in case of an emergency.

Take particular care in crowded places like the London Underground, and never leave wallets sticking out of trouser pockets or daypacks.

Cash

Nothing beats cash for convenience...or risk. It's still a good idea, though, to travel with some local currency in cash, if only to tide you over until you get to an exchange facility. There's no problem if you arrive at Heathrow, Gatwick or Stansted airports in London; all have good-value exchange counters open for incoming flights.

If you're travelling in several countries, some extra cash in US dollars is a good idea; it can be easier to change a small amount of cash (when leaving a country, for example) than a cheque.

Banks will rarely accept foreign coins, although some airport foreign exchanges will. Before you leave one country for the next, try to use up your change.

Travellers' Cheques

The main idea of cheques is to offer some protection from theft. American Express or Thomas Cook travellers' cheques are widely accepted and have efficient replacement policies.

Keeping a record of the cheque numbers and the cheques you have cashed is vital in case of loss. Keep this list separate from the cheques themselves.

Although cheques are available in various currencies, there's little point using US$ cheques in Britain (unless you're travelling from the USA), since you'll lose on the exchange rate when you buy the cheques and again each time you cash one. Bring pounds sterling to avoid changing currencies twice. In Britain, travellers' cheques are rarely accepted outside banks or used for everyday transactions (as they are in the USA, for example) so you need to cash them in advance.

Take most cheques in large denominations. It's only towards the end of a stay that you may want to change a small cheque to make sure you don't get left with too much local currency.

International Transfers

You can instruct your bank back home to send you a draft. Specify the city, the bank and the branch to which you want your money directed, or ask your home bank to tell you where a suitable one is, and make sure you get the details right. The whole procedure will be easier if you've authorised someone back home to access your account.

Money sent by telegraphic transfer (there will be costs involved, typically £15 or more, but ask) should reach you within a week; by mail, allow at least two weeks. When it arrives, it will most likely be converted into local currency – you can take it as it is or buy travellers' cheques.

You can also transfer money by American Express or Thomas Cook. Americans can also use Western Union although it has fewer offices in Britain from which to collect.

Plastic Cards & ATMs

If you're not familiar with the options, ask your bank to explain the workings and relative merits of credit, credit/debit, debit and charge cards.

Plastic cards are the perfect travelling companions – they're ideal for major purchases and can allow you to withdraw cash from selected banks and automatic telling machines (ATMs – known as cashpoints in Britain). ATMs are usually linked up to international money systems such as Cirrus, Maestro or Plus, so you can shove your card in, punch in a personal identification number (PIN) and get instant cash. But ATMs aren't fail-safe, especially if the card was issued outside Europe, and it's safer to go to a human teller – it can be a headache if an ATM swallows your card.

Credit cards usually aren't hooked up to ATM networks unless you specifically ask your bank to do this and request a PIN number. You should also ask which ATMs abroad will accept your particular card. Note that some European ATMs won't accept PIN numbers of more than four digits. Cash cards, which you use at home to withdraw money directly from your bank account or savings account, are becoming more widely linked internationally – ask your bank at home for advice.

Charge cards like American Express and Diners Club don't have credit limits but may not be accepted in small establishments or off the beaten track. If you have an American Express card, you can cash up to £500 worth of personal cheques at American Express offices in any seven-day period.

Credit and credit/debit cards like Visa and MasterCard (also known as Access in Britain) are more widely accepted but often have too low a credit limit to cover major expenses like car hire or airline tickets. You can get around this by leaving your card in credit when you leave home. Visa, MasterCard, Access, American Express and Diners Club cards are widely accepted, although most B&Bs require cash. MasterCard is operated by the same organisation that issues Access and Euro-cards and can be used wherever you see one or other of these signs. You can get cash advances using your Visa card at the Midland

Bank and Barclays, or using MasterCard at NatWest, Lloyds and Barclays.

If you plan to stay for a long time, and have a permanent address, it's usually straightforward to change the billing address for your card.

If you choose to rely on plastic, go for two different cards – an American Express or Diners Club with a Visa or MasterCard. Better still, combine plastic and travellers' cheques so you have something to fall back on if an ATM swallows your card or the local banks don't accept your card.

Currency

The British currency is the pound sterling (o), with 100 pence (p) to a pound. One and 2p coins are copper; 5p, 10p, 20p and 50p coins are silver; and the bulky £1 coin is gold (coloured). Like its written counterpart the word pence is usually abbreviated and pronounced 'pee'.

Notes (bills) come in £5, £10, £20 and £50 denominations and vary in colour and size. You may also come across notes issued by several Scottish banks, including a £1 note; they're legal tender on both sides of the border, though shopkeepers in England and Wales may be reluctant to accept them – in which case ask a bank to swap them for you.

Exchange Rates

Australia	A$1 =	£0.47
Canada	C$1 =	£0.45
France	FF1 =	£0.11
Germany	DM1 =	£0.40
Ireland	IR£1 =	£1.00
Japan	¥100 =	£0.54
New Zealand	NZ$1 =	£0.42
USA	US$1 =	£0.60

Changing Money

Be careful using bureaux de change, especially in London; they may offer good exchange rates but frequently levy outrageous commissions and fees. Make sure you establish the rate, the percentage commission and any fees in advance.

The bureaux at the international airports are exceptions to the rule. They charge less than most High St banks and cash sterling travellers' cheques for free. They also guarantee that you can buy up to £500 worth of most major currencies.

Bank hours vary, but you'll be safe if you visit between 9.30 am and 3.30 pm, Monday to Friday. Friday afternoons get very busy. Some banks are open on Saturday, generally from 9.30 am till noon.

Once again, the total cost of foreign exchange can vary widely. American Express offices are often cheapest, charging 1% commission, with no minimum charge. The banks are more expensive: NatWest charges 1% commission for sterling travellers' cheques, with a £4 minimum charge; Lloyds, Midland and Barclays all charge 1.5% commission, with a minimum charge of £3.

It's difficult to open a bank account, although if you're planning to work it may be essential. Building societies tend to be more welcoming and often have better interest rates. You'll need a (semi) permanent address, and it will smooth the way considerably if you have a reference or introductory letter from your bank manager at home, *plus* bank statements for the previous year. Owning credit/charge cards also helps.

Personal cheques are still widely used in Britain, but they're validated and guaranteed by a plastic card. Increasingly, retail outlets are linked to the Switch network, which allows customers to use a debit card (deductions are made directly from your current account). Look for a current account that pays interest, gives you a cheque book and guarantee card, and gives access to automated teller machines and the Switch network.

Tipping & Bargaining
In general, if you eat in a British restaurant you should leave a tip of at least 10% unless the service was unsatisfactory. Waiting staff are often paid derisory wages on the assumption that the money will be supplemented by tips.

It's legal for restaurants to include a service charge of 10 to 15% on the bill, but this should be clearly advertised. You do not add a further tip.

Some restaurants have been known to include the service charge in the total cost shown on a credit card voucher, but to leave a blank for a further tip/gratuity. This is a scam – you only have to tip once.

Taxi drivers also expect to be tipped (about 10%), especially in London. It's less usual to tip minicab drivers.

Bargaining is fine if you're buying second-hand gear but not otherwise. You can also try your Delhi delivery in the markets. Always check if there are discounts for students, young people, or youth hostel members.

Taxes & Refunds
Value-Added Tax (VAT) is a 17.5% sales tax that is levied on virtually all goods and services except food and books. Restaurant prices must by law include VAT.

It's sometimes possible to claim a refund of VAT paid on goods – a considerable saving. If you've spent *less* than 365 days out of the two years prior to making the purchase living in Britain, and if you're leaving the EU within three months of making the purchase, you are eligible.

Not all shops participate in the VAT refund scheme, and different shops will have different minimum purchase conditions (normally around £40). On request, participating shops will give you a special form/invoice; they will need to see your passport. This form must be presented with the goods and receipts to customs when you depart (VAT-free goods can't be posted or shipped home). After customs has certified the form, it should be returned to the shop for a refund less an administration fee.

Several companies offer a centralised refunding service to shops. Participating shops carry a sign in their window. You can avoid bank charges for cashing a sterling cheque by using a credit card for purchases and asking to have your VAT refund credited to your card account. Cash refunds are sometimes available at major airports.

POST & COMMUNICATIONS
Post

Post-office hours can vary, but most are open from 9 am to 5 pm, Monday to Friday, and 9 am to noon on Saturday. First-class mail is quicker and more expensive (26p per letter) than 2nd-class mail (20p).

Air-mail letters to EU countries are 26p, to non-EU European countries 31p, to the Americas and Australasia 43p (up to 10 grams) and 63p (up to 20 grams).

If you don't have a permanent address, mail can be sent to poste restante in the town or city where you are staying. American Express Travel offices will also hold mail free for card-holders.

An air-mail letter to the USA or Canada will generally take less than a week; to Australia or New Zealand, around a week.

Telephone

Since British Telecom (BT) was privatised a number of companies have started competing for its business. However, most public phone booths are still operated by BT.

The famous red phone booth survives in conservation areas. More usually you'll see glass cubicles of two types: one takes money, while the other uses prepaid, plastic debit cards and, increasingly, credit cards.

All phones come with reasonably clear instructions. If you're likely to make several calls (especially international) and don't want to be caught out, buy a BT phonecard. Ranging in values from £2 to £20, they're widely available from all sorts of retailers, including post offices and newsagents.

Most BT services are expensive; make your directory assistance calls (☎ 192) from a public telephone – they're free that way.

In this guide telephone area codes are listed at the start of the town entry or, in smaller places, with all numbers in the section.

Other codes worth knowing about are:

0345	local call rates apply
0500	call is free to caller
0800	call is free to caller
0891	premium rates apply; 39p cheap rate, 49p at other times
0990	national call rate applies

Local & National Calls Dial ☎ 100 for a BT operator. Local calls are charged by time, and national calls (including Scotland, Wales and Northern Ireland) are charged by time and distance. Standard rates are from 8 am to 6 pm, Monday to Friday; the cheap rate is 6 pm to 8 am, Monday to Friday; and the weekend rate is from midnight Friday to midnight Sunday. The latter two rates offer substantial savings.

International Calls Dial ☎ 155 for the international operator. Direct dialling is cheaper, but some shoestringers have been known to prefer operator-connected reverse-charges (collect) calls.

To get an international line (for international direct dialling) dial 00, then the country code, area code (drop the first zero if there is one) and number.

It's usually cheaper to phone overseas between 8 pm and 8 am Monday to Friday and cheapest between midnight on Friday and midnight on Sunday.

Fax & E-mail

Most hotels now have faxes. Some shops also offer fax services, advertised by a sign in the window. To collect your e-mail visit one of the growing number of cybercafés and pubs.

BOOKS

There are countless guidebooks covering every nook and cranny in Britain. When you arrive, one of your first stops should be at a good book/map shop – there are several excellent possibilities in London (see the London Bookshops section). In addition, the YHA Adventure Shop, 14 Southampton Row, Covent Garden, the British Travel Centre and the London Tourist Board's Victoria station centre stock a wide range of titles.

Lonely Planet

Lonely Planet also publishes *Walking in Britain*, which outlines all the national trails, long-distance footpaths and other interesting walking possibilities throughout Britain.

Watch out for Lonely Planet's forthcoming *London city guide*.

Guidebooks

For a preview of what you'll encounter, as well as a pretty good introduction to history and culture, the *Insight Guides* are recommended. Separate guides to *England*, *Scotland* and *Wales* cost £12.99 each.

For detailed information on history, art and architecture, the *Blue Guide* series is excellent, with a wealth of scholarly information on all the important sites, including good maps. They too have separate guides to *England* (£14.99), *Scotland* (£16.99) and *Wales* (£12.99).

If you're going to spend much time in London, it's worth buying the *Time Out London Guide* (£9.99). The *Virago Women's Guide to London* (£9.99) is good for digging out otherwise forgotten snippets of women's history.

Numerous books list B&Bs, restaurants, hotels, country houses, camping and caravan parks, and self-catering cottages but often their objectivity is questionable as the places they cover pay for the privilege of being included. Those published by the tourist authorities are reliable (if not comprehensive) and widely available in TICs. The *Which?* books produced by the Consumer's Association are good and accurate: no money changes hands before somewhere is recommended.

Walkers are very well catered for. The long-distance trails are all covered by the excellent *Countryside Commission National Trail Guide* series published by Aurum Press. The books cost from £9.99. For shorter day walks, the spiral-bound *Bartholomew Map & Guide* series is recommended. They come with good maps and descriptions; most walks described take around two to three hours.

People of literary bent might like to look at the *Oxford Literary Guide to Great Britain and Ireland* (£6.99) which details the writers who have immortalised the towns and villages.

Travel

Bill Bryson's highly-entertaining and perceptive *Notes from a Small Island* is the most recent modern travelogue covering Britain. *The Kingdom by the Sea* by Paul Theroux and Jonathan Raban's *Coasting* were both written in 1982 and so are now a little dated, but they're nonetheless very readable. Older but still readable is John Hillaby's *Journey Through Britain* which describes a walk from Land's End to John o'Groats in 1969, great for measuring the changes which have taken place over the last 30 years.

Dervla Murphy's *Tale of Two Cities*, written in 1987, offers a veteran travel writer's view of life amongst Britain's ethnic minorities in Bradford/Manningham and Birmingham/Handsworth.

History & Politics

A *Traveller's History of England* (£7.95) by Christopher Daniell offers a quick introduction to English history.

The most unexpected bestseller in 1995 was *The State We're In* (£7.99), Will Hutton's analysis of Britain's position at the close of the 20th century. *Ruling Britannia* (£7.99) by Andrew Marr also outlines the failures and possible future of British democracy. If you want to know what Britain under a Tony Blair government might be like you could try *The Blair Revolution* (£7.95) by Peter Mandelson and Roger Liddle, or Blair's own book *New Britain* (Fourth Estate).

ONLINE SERVICES

Britain is second only to the USA in its number of World Wide Web sites and there are plenty of sites of interest to cyber travellers.

Get to grips with Britain's favourite topic of conversation, the **UK Weather**, via the meteorological office on http://www.meto.gov.uk.

Many sites offer general information. The **Lonely Planet** web site (http://www.lonely planet.com.au) offers a speedy link to all the sites mentioned here. Even more comprehensive is The **Virtual Tourist** which seeks to provide a one-stop link to all travel web sites (http://wings.buffalo.edu/world). The **UK Directory** (http://www.ukdirec ry.com/travel) specialises in just British sites.

Several sites offer accommodation information. At the time of writing the **Automobile Association's** site was 'under development' but should soon offer access to the AA's database of accommodation plus its records of over 1000 places worth visiting (http://www.theaa.co.uk/theaa, or Compuserve *Go Days* or *Go Hotels*).

For a touring holiday, Farm Accommodation (http://www.webscope.co.uk/farm accom) can provide good value bed and breakfast. Should you prefer self-catering then **Holiday Rentals** (http://www.holiday rentals.co.uk) is a useful information source.

The **London Guide** has wide-ranging, if uneven, information on the capital; it even has an interactive route planner for the Underground (http://www.cs.ucl.ac.uk/misc/uk/london.html). The **Time Out** (http://www.timeout.co.uk) and **London Calling** (http://www.demon.co.uk/london-calling/content.html) pages give entertainment details and community news.

To tempt you to visit their site **Guardian Insurance** offers free pocket guides to London, Bath, Edinburgh, Oxford and York (http://www.gre.co.uk). For rail information there's Compuserve Go Railway or try http://www.rail.rz.uni-Karlsruhe.de/rail/english.html and http://www.res.bbsrc.ac.uk/plantpath/railway.

As with any venture into cyberspace there are certain things to remember. Sites vary widely in accuracy and reliability. Since some of the most interesting (opinionated?) are run by individuals they can also be ephemeral. Although accurate at the time of going to press, the web site addresses given may change. Either use the Lonely Planet site or a good web engine to check the latest details. Lycos is at http://www.lycos.com and Yahoo at http://www.yahoo.com.

NEWSPAPERS & MAGAZINES
Newspapers
The bottom end of the British newspaper market is occupied by *The Sun*, *Daily Mirror*, *Daily Star* and *The Sport*. *The Sun* is a national institution with witty headlines and nasty, mean-spirited contents. The *Daily Mirror* was once a decent newspaper with left-wing sympathies, but has slithered down-market to match *The Sun*. *The Sport* takes bad taste a step further, with a constant diet of semi-naked women of improbable proportions and stories of space invaders.

The middle-market tabloids – the *Daily Mail* and *Daily Express* – are Tory strongholds, thunderously supporting the Conservative government (although even their loyalty has faltered since the 1992 election) and reserving their spleen for anyone of liberal persuasion. *The European* makes an honourable attempt to make the British feel part of the continent.

The broadsheets can be stuffy and self-important, but are generally stimulating and well written. The *Daily Telegraph*, or 'Torygraph', far outsells its rivals and its readership remains old fogeyish despite efforts to attract a new clientele. *The Times*, once Britain's finest paper, has lost ground under Murdoch's ownership but remains conservative and influential. Started by journalists in the mid-80s, *The Independent* tries hard to live up to its title but lost readers during the early 90s and is struggling to stay afloat. The mildly left-wing *Guardian* is read by the chattering classes – it's lively and innovative.

The Sunday papers are an institution. On their day of rest, the British still sit in comfy armchairs and plough their way through endless supplements; *The Sunday Times* must destroy at least one rain forest per issue. *The Observer*, the oldest of the Sundays, was recently taken over by its soul mate, *The Guardian*. Most of the other daily papers also have a Sunday stablemate which shares its political views.

As well as all these indigenous papers, you can also buy the *International Herald Tribune* and many foreign-language papers, especially in central London.

Magazines

Walk into any high street newsagent and you'll realise that Britain boasts a magazine for almost any interest, with whole shelves of computer magazines, trainspotting magazines, heritage magazines, women's magazines and lifestyle magazines...and that's before you raise your eyes to the top shelf!

Most big towns have a listings magazine broadly along the lines of London's *Time Out*. Some are free although the best cost a pound or so and are mentioned in the relevant chapters.

Of the myriad women's magazines *Marie Claire* is probably the most stimulating and certainly the most original.

The bi-weekly satirical *Private Eye* is another British institution that retains its sharp edge even at the risk of regular run-ins with the law. The monthly *Viz* is an adult comic which appeals to those with scatological tastes.

Time and *Newsweek* are also readily available.

RADIO & TV
Radio

BBC radio just about covers all tastes. Radio 1 (275m/1089kHz and 285m/1053kHz MW; 98.8mHz FM) is the main pop music station and is undergoing a revival after some years in the doldrums. Blander Radio 2 (88-91mHz FM) plays music for old softies, while Radio 3 (247m/1215kHz MW; 91.3mHz FM) is mainly classical.

Radio 4 (1500m/198kHz LW; 417m/720kHz MW; 93.5mHz FM) offers a stimulating mixture of drama, news and current affairs; the *Today Programme* (Monday to Saturday, 6.30 to 9 am) is the quickest way to find out what's happening and what's on (part of) the nation's mind. Radio 5 Live (463m/693kHz) provides a mix of sport and current affairs. Lastly, the World Service (463m/648kHz MW) offers brilliant news coverage and quirky bits and pieces from around the world.

In the last decade, alternative radio stations have proliferated and wherever you go there's bound to be a local commercial station offering local news alongside the music. Virgin (1215kHz) is a commercial pop station. Classic FM (101.9mHz FM) does classical music with commercials, Kiss FM (100mHz) and Choice FM (96.9mHz) are the soul and dance stations, whilst the excellent Jazz FM (102.2mHz) caters for jazz and soul buffs. Viva, a station for women launched with much hype, has failed to attract an audience. The other much-hyped new arrival Talk Radio (1053kHz MW) is also struggling.

In the London area, other stations include Capital (95.8mHz FM), the commercial version of Radio 1, and Capital Gold (194m/1548kHz), which recycles golden oldies from the 60s, 70s and early 80s.

TV

Britain still turns out some of the world's best TV but the decent home-grown output is supplemented with American imports, Australian soaps, inept sitcoms and trashy chat and game shows. There are currently four regular TV channels – BBC1 and BBC2 are publicly funded by a TV licence and don't carry advertising; ITV and Channel 4 are commercial stations and do. A fifth channel, Channel 5, is poised to begin broadcasting in 1997. These are now facing competition from Rupert Murdoch's satellite TV, BSkyB, which has a variety of programming but mostly churns out rubbish, and assorted cable channels.

VIDEO SYSTEMS

With many tourist attractions now selling videos as souvenirs it's worth bearing in mind that British videos are VHS format and not compatible with NTSC or SECAM.

PHOTOGRAPHY & VIDEO
Film & Equipment

Although print film is widely available, slide film can be more elusive; if there's no specialist photographic shop around, Boots, the High St chemist chain, is the likeliest stockist. Thirty-six exposure print films cost from £4.50 for ISO 100 to £5 for ISO 400. With slide film it's usually cheapest to go for

Fourteen Million to One

Yes, that's the odds against landing the jackpot in the National Lottery, launched on an unsuspecting British public in 1994 and a success beyond the wildest dreams of its operators, Camelot.

Already the beckoning crossed finger and 'It could be you' slogan have a recognition factor with the public that it took the Association of British Travel Agents (ABTA) years of handling high-profile disasters to win. No matter that the odds on winning the big prizes must match those of being hit by a passing meteor, National Lottery outlets are mobbed with punters every Saturday and the nation tunes in in its millions to watch the BBC's over-the-top presentation of the draw, complete with Mystic Meg, the seer who never quite gets round to naming winning names.

It's easy to poke fun at the Lottery, and charities believe they have lost out as people invested in lottery tickets instead of giving. The silver lining lies in the requirement that Camelot donate some of its takings to a set of 'good causes'. It's been estimated that the next seven years will see something like £9 billion ploughed back into the community, to the benefit of everything from village halls to the planned site of the Millennium Exhibition in Greenwich.

The sting in the tail is that grant recipients have to provide 'matching funds' to benefit from their windfalls and it looks as if they may well end up fighting each other for the same resources. Indeed, the Cassandras forecast a legacy of half-completed projects as grants are withdrawn when matching funds fail to materialise.

Still, it's hard to be sniffy when your own home town (Bristol) has just been awarded £41 million towards the cost of much-needed city-centre improvements.

Pat Yale

process-inclusive versions although these will usually need to be developed in Britain: 36-exposure films cost from £7 for ISO 100 to £10.50 for ISO 400. Branches of Jessop (addresses in Yellow Pages) usually offer a discount if you buy 10 films at once.

Photography

With dull, overcast conditions common, high-speed film (ISO 200, or ISO 400) is useful. In summer, the best times of day for photography are usually early in the morning and late in the afternoon when the glare of the sun has passed.

Many tourist attractions either charge for taking photos or prohibit it altogether. Use of flash is frequently forbidden to protect delicate pictures and fabrics. Video cameras are often disallowed because of the inconvenience they can cause to other visitors.

Airport Security

You will have to put your camera and film through the X-ray machine at all British airports. The machines are supposed to be film-safe, but you may feel happier if you put exposed films in a lead-lined bag to protect them.

TIME

One hundred years ago the sun never set on the British Empire, so the British could be forgiven for thinking that London (more specifically Greenwich) was the centre of the universe. Greenwich is still the location for the prime meridian which divides the world into eastern and western hemispheres.

Wherever you are in the world, the time on your watch is measured in relation to the time at Greenwich – Greenwich Mean Time (GMT) – although strictly speaking, GMT is used only in air and sea navigation, and is otherwise referred to as Universal Time Coordinated (UTC).

Daylight-saving time (DST) muddies the water so that even Britain itself is ahead of GMT from late March to late October. But to give you an idea, San Francisco is eight hours and New York five hours behind GMT, while Sydney is 10 hours ahead of GMT. Phone the international operator on ☎ 155 to find out the exact difference.

ELECTRICITY

The standard voltage throughout Britain is 240V AC, 50Hz. Plugs have three square pins and adaptors are widely available.

WEIGHTS & MEASURES

In theory Britain has now moved to metric weights and measures although non-metric equivalents are likely to be used by much of the population for some time to come. Distances continue to be given in miles, yards, feet and inches – except on some Scottish islands where hostel distances are indicated in kilometres! In most cases this book uses miles to indicate distance.

Most liquids other than milk and beer are now sold in litres. For conversion tables, see the back of this book.

LAUNDRY

Every High St has its laundrette – with rare exceptions a disheartening place to spend much time. The average cost for a single load is £1.60 for washing, and between 60p and £1 for drying. Bring soap powder with you; it can be expensive if bought in a laundrette.

TOILETS

The toilet situation in Britain is improving. Although many city-centre facilities are still pretty grim (graffitied and with rough toilet paper), those at main stations, bus terminals and motorway service stations are generally good, usually with facilities for disabled people and those with young children. At the London rail and coach terminals you usually have to pay 20p to use the facilities but at least they're clean. You also have to pay to use the Tardis-like concrete booths in places like Leicester Square.

In theory it's an offence to urinate in the streets (and men could be arrested for indecent exposure). However, as everywhere, those who've passed the evening in the pub happily make use of underpasses and alleyways, thereby rendering them unpleasant for other people.

Many disabled toilets can only be opened with a special key which can be obtained from some tourist offices or by sending a cheque or postal order for £2.50 to RADAR (see Disabled Travellers section), together with a brief description of your disability.

HEALTH

Travel health depends on your predeparture preparations, your day-to-day health care while travelling and how you handle any medical problem or emergency that does develop.

Predeparture Planning

Health Insurance A travel insurance policy to cover theft, loss and medical problems is a good idea. See the previous Travel Insurance section for details of the types of cover available, and always read the small print.

Medical Kit It's wise to carry a small, straightforward medical kit. The kit should include:

- Aspirin or paracetamol (acetaminophen in the US) – for pain or fever.
- Antihistamine (such as Benadryl) – useful as a decongestant for colds and allergies, to ease the itch from insect bites or stings, and to help prevent motion sickness. There are several antihistamines on the market, all with different pros and cons (eg a tendency to cause drowsiness), so it's worth discussing your requirements with a pharmacist or doctor. Antihistamines may cause sedation and interact with alcohol so care should be taken when using them.
- Loperamide (eg Imodium) or Lomotil for diarrhoea; prochlorperazine (eg Stemetil) or metaclopramide (eg Maxalon) for nausea and vomiting. Antidiarrhoea medication should not be given to children under the age of 12.
- Antiseptic such as povidone-iodine (eg Betadine), which comes as a solution, ointment, powder and impregnated swabs – for cuts and grazes.
- Calamine lotion or Stingose spray – to ease irritation from bites or stings.
- Bandages and Band-aids – for minor injuries.
- Scissors, tweezers and a thermometer (note that mercury thermometers are prohibited by airlines).
- Insect repellent, sunscreen, suntan lotion, chap stick.

Health Preparations Make sure you're healthy before you start travelling.

If you wear glasses take a spare pair and your prescription. If you require a particular medication take an adequate supply, as it may not be available locally. Take the prescription or, better still, part of the packaging showing the generic rather than the brand name (which may not be locally available), as it will make getting replacements easier. It's wise to have a legible prescription or a letter from your doctor with you to show that you legally use the medication.

Immunisations Jabs are not necessary for Britain unless you're stopping over on the way and arrive from an infected area. If you're going to Europe via stopovers in Asia, Africa or Latin America, check with your travel agent and doctor. Don't leave this till the last minute, as the vaccinations may take time to become effective.

All vaccinations should be recorded on an International Health Certificate, available from your physician or government health department.

Basic Rules

Care in what you eat and drink is the most important health rule; stomach upsets are the most likely travel health problem (between 30% and 50% of travellers in a two-week stay experience this) but the majority of these upsets will be relatively minor.

Water Tap water is always safe unless there's a sign to the contrary (eg on trains). Don't drink straight from a stream – you can never be certain there are no people or cattle upstream.

Everyday Health Normal body temperature is 98.6°F or 37°C; more than 2°C (4°F) higher indicates a high fever. The normal adult pulse rate is 60 to 100 per minute (children 80 to 100, babies 100 to 140). You should know how to take a temperature and a pulse rate. As a general rule the pulse increases about 20 beats per minute for each 1°C (2°F) rise in fever.

Respiration (breathing) rate is also an indicator of illness. Count the number of breaths per minute: between 12 and 20 is normal for adults and older children (up to 30 for younger children, 40 for babies). People with a high fever or serious respiratory illness (like pneumonia) breathe more quickly than normal. More than 40 shallow breaths a minute may indicate pneumonia.

Environmental Hazards

Sunburn Even in Britain, and even when there's cloud cover, it's possible to get sunburnt surprisingly quickly – especially if you're on water, snow or ice. Use 15+ sunscreen, wear a hat and cover up with a long-sleeved shirt and pants.

Heat Exhaustion Dehydration or salt deficiency can cause heat exhaustion. In hot conditions and if you're exerting yourself make sure you get sufficient nonalcoholic liquids. Salt deficiency is characterised by fatigue, lethargy, headaches, giddiness and muscle cramps. Vomiting or diarrhoea can rapidly deplete your liquid and salt levels.

Fungal Infections To prevent fungal infections, wear loose, comfortable clothes, wash frequently and dry carefully. Always wear thongs (flip-flops) in shared bathrooms. If you get an infection, consult a chemist. Try to expose the infected area to air or sunlight as much as possible and wash all towels and underwear in hot water as well as changing them often.

Cold Hypothermia can occur when the body loses heat faster than it can produce it and the body's core temperature falls. It's surprisingly easy to progress from very cold to dangerously cold through a combination of wind, wet clothing, fatigue and hunger, even if the air temperature is above freezing.

Walkers in Britain should always be prepared for difficult conditions. It's best to dress in layers, and a hat is important as a lot of heat is lost through the head. A strong, waterproof outer layer is essential. Carry basic supplies, including food that contains simple sugars to generate heat quickly.

Symptoms of hypothermia are exhaustion, numb skin (particularly toes and fingers), shivering, slurred speech, irrational or violent behaviour, lethargy, stumbling, dizzy spells, muscle cramps and violent bursts of energy.

To treat it, get the person out of wind and rain, remove wet clothing and replace it with dry, warm clothing. Give them hot liquids – not alcohol – and some high-calorie, easily digestible food. This should be enough for the early stages of hypothermia, but if it's gone further, it may be necessary to place victims in warm sleeping bags and get in with them. Don't rub patients, or place them near a fire or remove their wet clothes in the wind. If possible, place a sufferer in a warm (not hot) bath.

Diarrhoea A change of water, food or climate can all cause the runs; diarrhoea caused by contaminated food or water is more serious.

Moderate diarrhoea, involving half-a-dozen loose movements in a day, is more a nuisance than a serious problem. Dehydration is the main danger, particularly for children, so replacing fluids is the most important treatment. Weak black tea with a little sugar, soda water, or soft drinks allowed to go flat and diluted 50% with water are all good.

With more severe diarrhoea, go straight to the casualty ward of the nearest hospital for a check-up. You may need a rehydrating solution to replace minerals and salts. Stick to a bland diet as you recover.

Motion Sickness Eating lightly before and during a trip will reduce the chances of motion sickness. If you are prone to motion sickness try to find a place that minimises disturbance – near the wing on aircraft, close to midships on boats, near the centre on buses. Fresh air usually helps; reading and cigarette smoke don't. Commercial motion-sickness preparations, which can cause drowsiness, have to be taken before the trip commences; when you're feeling sick it's too late. Ginger (available in capsule form) and peppermint (including mint-flavoured sweets) are natural preventatives.

Jet Lag Jet lag is experienced when a person travels by air across more than three time zones (each time zone usually represents a one-hour time difference). It occurs because many of the functions of the human body (such as temperature, pulse rate and empty-ing of the bladder and bowels) are regulated by internal 24-hour cycles called circadian rhythms. When we travel long distances rapidly, our bodies take time to adjust to the 'new time' of our destination, and we may experience fatigue, disorientation, insomnia, anxiety, impaired concentration and loss of appetite. These effects will usually be gone within three days of arrival, but there are ways of minimising the impact of jet lag:

• Rest for a couple of days prior to departure; try to avoid late nights and last-minute dashes for travellers' cheques, passport etc.
• Try to select flight schedules that minimise sleep deprivation; arriving late in the day means you can go to sleep soon after you arrive. For very long flights, try to organise a stopover.
• Avoid excessive eating (which bloats the stomach) and alcohol (which causes dehydration) during the flight. Instead, drink plenty of non-carbonated, nonalcoholic drinks such as fruit juice or water.
• Avoid smoking, as this reduces the amount of oxygen in the aeroplane cabin even further and causes greater fatigue.
• Make yourself comfortable by wearing loose-fitting clothes and perhaps bringing an eye mask and ear plugs to help you sleep.

Sexually Transmitted Diseases
Sexual contact with an infected sexual partner spreads these diseases. While absti-nence is the only 100% preventative, using condoms is also effective. Gonorrhoea, herpes and syphilis are the most common of these diseases; sores, blisters or rashes around the genitals, discharges or pain when urinating are common symptoms. Symp-toms may be less marked or not observed at all in women. Syphilis symptoms eventually disappear completely but the disease contin-ues and can cause severe problems in later years. The treatment of gonorrhoea and syphilis is with antibiotics.

There are numerous other sexually trans-mitted diseases, for most of which effective treatment is available. However, there is no cure for herpes and there is also currently no cure for AIDS.

HIV/AIDS HIV, the Human Immunodeficiency Virus, may develop into AIDS, Acquired Immune Deficiency Syndrome. HIV is a major problem in many countries. Any exposure to blood, blood products or bodily fluids may put the individual at risk. In many developing countries transmission is predominantly through heterosexual sexual activity. This is quite different from industrialised countries where transmission is mostly through contact between homosexual or bisexual males, or via contaminated needles shared by IV drug users. Apart from abstinence, the most effective preventative is always to practise safe sex using condoms. It is impossible to detect the HIV-positive status of an otherwise healthy-looking person without a blood test.

HIV/AIDS can also be spread through infected blood transfusions, as some developing countries cannot afford to screen blood for transfusions. In Britain, though, blood transfusions are safe. HIV can also be spread by dirty needles – vaccinations, acupuncture, tattooing and ear or nose piercing can be potentially as dangerous as intravenous drug use if the equipment is not clean.

Fear of HIV infection should never preclude treatment for serious medical conditions. Although there may be a risk of infection, it is very small indeed.

WOMEN TRAVELLERS
Attitudes to Women
The occasional wolf-whistle and groper on the London Underground aside, women will find Britain reasonably enlightened. There's nothing to stop women going into pubs alone, although this is unlikely to be a comfortable experience; pairs or groups of women blend more naturally into the wallpaper. Some restaurants still persist in assigning the table by the toilet to lone female diners, but fortunately such places are becoming fewer by the year.

Safety Precautions
Solo travellers should have few problems, although common-sense caution should be observed in big cities, especially at night, and hitching is unwise.

While it's certainly not essential, it can help to go on a women's self-defence course before setting out on your travels, if only for the increased feeling of confidence it's likely to give you.

Condoms are increasingly sold in women's toilets as well as men's. Otherwise, all chemists and many service stations stock them. The contraceptive pill is available only on prescription, as is the 'morning-after' pill (actually effective for up to 72 hours after unprotected sexual intercourse); family planning associations are listed in the phone book.

Organisations
Most big towns have a Well Woman Clinic which can advise on general health issues. Find their addresses in the local phone book or ask in the library. Should the worst come to the worst, Rape Crisis Centres can offer support after an attack.

If you'd like to stay with women while you're travelling it's worth joining Women Welcome Women, an organisation which exists to put women travellers in touch with potential hostesses. It's at 88 Easton St, High Wycombe, Bucks HP11 1LT (☎ & fax 01494-465441).

GAY & LESBIAN TRAVELLERS
In general, Britain is fairly tolerant of homosexuality. Certainly it's possible for people to acknowledge their homosexuality in a way that would have been unthinkable 20 years ago; the MP Chris Smith came out publicly without being forced to resign. That said, there remain pockets of out-and-out hostility (you only need read the *Sun*, *Mail* or *Telegraph* to realise the limits of toleration) and overt displays of affection are not necessarily wise away from acknowledged 'gay' venues.

The age of homosexual consent is currently 18, although a test case being brought in Europe could see that reduced to 16 in due course.

London and Manchester have a flourishing gay scene, and Brighton has long attracted the pink holidaymaking pound.

Organisations & Information

The Gay Men's Press has two useful pocket guides: *London Scene* and *Northern Scene*. There are several free listings magazines like *The Pink Paper*, *Boyz* or *QX*, or the *Gay Times* (£2) which also has listings. They're all available at Gay's The Word (☎ 0171-278 7654), 66 Marchmont St, near Russell Square tube. *Time Out* is also a good source of information, as are other commercial listings magazines outside London.

Another useful source of information is the 24-hour Lesbian & Gay Switchboard (☎ 0171-837 7324) which can help with most general inquiries. London Lesbian Line (☎ 0171-251 6911) offers similar help but only from 2 to 10 pm, Monday and Friday and from 7 to 10 pm on Tuesday and Thursday.

Help, advice and support are also available from the National AIDS Helpline (☎ 0800-567123) and Body Positive (☎ 0171-373 9124) which offers support to people who are HIV positive.

DISABLED TRAVELLERS

For many disabled travellers, Britain is an odd mix of user-friendliness and unfriendliness. These days few buildings go up without the need for wheelchair accessibility being acknowledged; large, new city-centre hotels and modern tourist attractions are therefore usually accessible. However, many of Britain's famous castles and stately homes offer only limited accessibility, and most B&Bs and guesthouses are in older buildings which are difficult to adapt. This means that travellers with mobility problems may end up having to pay more for accommodation than their more able-bodied fellows.

It's a similar story with public transport. Newer buses sometimes have steps that lower for easier access, as do trains, but it's always wise to check before setting out. Supermarkets and tourist attractions some-

times reserve some parking spaces near the entrance for disabled users.

Many ticket offices, banks etc are fitted with hearing loops to assist the hearing impaired; look for the symbol of a large ear.

A few tourist attractions, cathedrals etc have braille guides or scented gardens for the visually impaired.

Organisations & Information

If you have a physical disability, get in touch with your national support organisation (preferably the travel officer if there is one) and ask about the countries you plan to visit. They often have complete libraries devoted to travel, and can put you in touch with travel agents who specialise in tours for the disabled.

The Royal Association for Disability and Rehabilitation (RADAR) publishes a useful guide titled *Holidays and Travel Abroad: A Guide for Disabled People*, which gives a good overview of facilities available in Europe. Their *Access in London* (£4.10) is also required reading. Contact RADAR (☎ 0171-250 3222) Unit 12, City Forum, 250 City Rd, London EC1V 8AF.

The Holiday Care Service (☎ 01293-774535), 2 Old Bank Chambers, Station Rd, Horley, Surrey RH6 9HW, publishes a *Guide to Accessible Accommodation and Travel* for Britain (£5.95) and can offer general advice.

Rail companies in Britain theoretically offer a Disabled Persons' Railcard (£16) but some don't make it easy for people to get one. First you must fill out a form published in a booklet which you get from the Railcards Office, TRMC CP 328, 3rd Floor, The Podium, 1 Evershott Rd, London NW1 1DN. You then post it to the Disabled Person's Railcard Office, PO Box York YA1 011FB and wait.

Many TICs have leaflets with accessibility details for their particular area.

SENIOR TRAVELLERS

Senior citizens are entitled to discounts on things like public transport, museum admission fees etc, provided they show proof of their age. Sometimes they need a special pass. The minimum qualifying age is generally 60 to 65 for men, 55 to 65 for women.

Organisations & Information

In your home country, a lower age may entitle you to special travel packages and discounts (on car hire, for instance) through organisations and travel agents that cater to senior travellers. Start hunting at your local senior citizens advice bureau.

In Britain, rail companies offer a Senior Citizens Railcard (£16) for people of 60 and over, giving 30% discounts.

TRAVEL WITH CHILDREN

Successful travel with young children requires effort but can certainly be done. Try not to overdo things and consider using self-catering accommodation as a base. Include children in the planning process; if they've helped to work out where you'll be going, they'll be more interested when they get there. Include a range of activities – balance a visit to the British Museum with one to Madame Tussaud's. See Lonely Planet's *Travel with Children* by Maureen Wheeler for more information.

USEFUL ORGANISATIONS

Membership of English Heritage (EH) and the National Trust (NT) is worth considering, especially if you're going to be in Britain for a while and are interested in historical buildings. Both are non-profit organisations dedicated to the preservation of the environment, and both care for hundreds of spectacular sites.

English Heritage
    Most EH properties cost nonmembers around £2 to enter. Adult membership is £20 and gives free entry to all EH properties, half-price entry to Historic Scotland and Cadw (Wales) properties, and an excellent guidebook and map. You can join at most major sites. Ask about EH open days, when certain properties not usually open to the public can be visited.
National Trust
    Most NT properties cost nonmembers from £1 to £5 to enter. Adult membership is £26, under age 23 is £13. It gives free entry to all English, Welsh, Scottish and Northern Irish properties, and an excellent guidebook. You can join at most major sites. There are reciprocal arrangements with the National Trust organisations in Scotland, Aus-

tralia, New Zealand, Canada and the USA (the Royal Oak Foundation) – all of which are cheaper to join.
Great British Heritage Pass
    The pass gives you access to National Trust and English Heritage properties and some of the fiercely expensive private properties. It ain't cheap, but it can easily pay for itself: seven days is £25, 15 days is £36, one month is £50. It's available overseas (ask your travel agent, or contact the nearest Thomas Cook office) or at the British Travel Centre in London.
Australasian Clubs
    The London Walkabout Club (☎ 0171-938 3001), 7 Abingdon Rd W8 6AH, Deckers London Club (☎ 0171-244 8641), 35 Earl's Court Rd SW9 9RH, and Drifters (☎ 0171-402 9171), 22A Craven Terrace W2 3QH, all offer backup services like mail holding, local information, social events and cheap tours. They're mainly aimed at Aussies and Kiwis, but anyone is welcome – membership is around £15. The clubs are all associated with tour companies and their hope is that you will use them if and when you book tours.

In this book National Trust properties are indicated by the letters NT; English Heritage properties by EH.

Also see under Useful Organisations in the Scotland and Wales Facts for the Visitor chapters.

DANGERS & ANNOYANCES
Crime

Britain is remarkably safe considering its size and the disparities in wealth. However, city crime is certainly not unknown, so caution, especially at night, is necessary. Pickpockets and bag snatchers operate in crowded public places like the London Underground, although this is not a big problem.

Take particular care at night. When travelling by tube in London, choose a carriage with other people and avoid some of the deserted suburban tube stations; a bus or cab can be a safer choice.

The most important things to guard are your passport, papers, tickets and money. It's always best to carry these next to your skin or in a sturdy leather pouch on your belt. Carry your own padlock for hostel lockers. Be careful even in hotels; don't leave valuables lying around in your room. Never leave valuables in a car, and remove all luggage overnight. Report thefts to the police and ask for a statement, or your travel insurance won't pay out; thefts from cars are often excluded anyway.

Touts & Scams

Hotel/hostel touts descend on backpackers at underground and main-line stations like Earl's Court, Liverpool St and Victoria. Treat their claims with scepticism and don't accept an offer of a free lift unless you know precisely where you are going (you could end up miles away).

Never accept the offer of a ride from an unlicensed taxi driver either – they'll drive you round and round in circles, then demand an enormous sum of money. Use a metered black cab, or phone a reputable minicab company for a quote.

Every year foreign men are lured into Soho strip clubs and hostess bars and efficiently separated from their money. It's tempting to say they deserve what they don't get.

Another racket involves cardsharps who set up stalls in central London and soon attract a crowd to watch a player apparently winning large sums of money. While your attention is distracted, your pocket could well be picked...and if you're mug enough to join in the game you'll soon find that the 'luck' has suddenly switched to the other side.

Beggars

The big cities, particularly London, have many beggars; if you must give, don't wave a full wallet around – carry some change in a separate pocket. However, it's much better to give to a recognised charity. All the arguments against giving to beggars in developing countries apply in Britain too.

Shelter (☎ 0171-253 0202), 88 Old St EC1, is a voluntary organisation that helps the homeless and gratefully accepts donations; also consider buying *The Big Issue* (80p), an interesting weekly newspaper available from homeless street vendors who benefit directly from sales.

Racism

Britain is not without racial problems, particularly in some of the deprived inner cities, but in general tolerance prevails. Visitors are unlikely to have problems associated with their skin colour.

Showers

Plumbing can be woefully inadequate. In particular, the British don't understand that a good shower is one of life's basic essentials. Particularly in B&Bs or private houses you may well have to choose between a bath or a complicated contraption that will produce only a thin trickle of scalding hot or freezing cold water. Get the homeowner to explain exactly how it works if you want a half-decent shower.

LEGAL MATTERS

Drugs

Although even possession of cannabis is still illegal, drugs of every description are widely available, especially in clubs where Ecstasy is at the heart of the rave scene – some nightclubs don't even bother to sell alcohol! Nonetheless, all the usual dangers associated with drugs apply and there have been several high-profile deaths associated with Ecstasy. Possession of small quantities of cannabis usually attracts a small fine (still a criminal conviction) or a warning; other drugs are treated more seriously.

Much of Britain's crime is associated with drug dealing. Don't even think of getting caught up in it, and remember that the dodgiest bits of the cities are usually those associated with dealing.

Driving Offences

The laws against drink-driving have got tougher and are treated more seriously than they used to be. Currently you're allowed to have a blood-alcohol level of 35mg/100 ml, but there's talk of reducing the limit to a single drink. The safest approach is not to drink anything at all if you're planning to drive.

The other laws of the road most likely to catch visitors out relate to speeding and parking. The current speed limits are 30 miles per hour in built-up areas (indicated by the presence of street lighting), 60 miles per hour elsewhere and 70 miles per hour on motorways and dual carriageways. Other speed limits will be indicated by signs. Increasingly speed cameras are being installed to catch boy racers red-handed...it's hard to argue with the evidence of a film.

Parking in the wrong place may not be a criminal offence but can still cost you a lot of money, especially if your car is clamped and you have to pay to retrieve it from a pound. Car park charges may be a pain but they're cheaper than being fined.

On-the-Spot Fines

In general in Britain you rarely have to cough up on the spot for your offences. Two exceptions are trains (including London Underground trains) and buses where people who can't produce a valid ticket for the journey when asked to by an inspector can be fined there and then.

BUSINESS HOURS

Offices are generally open from 9 am to 5 pm, Monday to Friday. Shops may be open for longer hours, and most are open on Saturday from 9 am to 5 pm. An increasing number of shops also open on Sunday, perhaps from 10 am to 4 pm. In country towns, particularly in Scotland and Wales, there may be an early-closing day for shops – usually Tuesday, Wednesday or Thursday afternoon. Late-night shopping is usually on Thursday or Friday.

PUBLIC HOLIDAYS & SPECIAL EVENTS
Public Holidays

Most banks, businesses and some museums and other places of interest are closed on public holidays: New Year's Day, 2 January (Bank Holiday in Scotland), Good Friday, Easter Monday (not in Scotland), May Day Bank Holiday (first Monday in May), Spring Bank Holiday (last Monday in May), Summer Bank Holiday (first Monday in August in Scotland, last Monday in August

outside Scotland), Christmas Day and Boxing Day.

Special Events

Countless diverse events are held around the country all year. Even small villages have weekly markets, and many still enact traditional customs and ceremonies, some dating back hundreds of years. Useful BTA publications include *Forthcoming Events* and *Arts Festivals*, which list a selection of the year's events and festivals with their dates.

New Year
  Hogmanay – huge street party to greet New Year; Edinburgh
January to March
  Travel Fairs – several travel fairs aimed at the independent traveller take place nationwide. The main ones are organised by Independent Travellers' World (☎ 01179 083300)
Mid-March
  Crufts Dog Show – premier dog show; Birmingham
  Cheltenham Gold Cup – horse race meeting; Cheltenham
Last week in March
  Oxford/Cambridge University Boat Race – traditional rowing race; River Thames, Putney to Mortlake, London
First Saturday in April
  Grand National – famous horse racing meeting; Aintree, Liverpool
Early May
  FA Cup Final – deciding match in England's premier football knock-out tournament; Wembley, London
  Glasgow Mayfest – high-quality arts festival; runs for three weeks
  Brighton Festival – arts festival; runs for three weeks
Last week in May
  Chelsea Flower Show – premier flower show; Royal Hospital, London
  Bath International Festival – arts festival; runs for two weeks
First week in June
  Beating Retreat – military bands and marching; Whitehall, London
  Derby Week – horse racing and people watching; Epsom, Surrey
Mid-June
  Trooping the Colour – the Queen's birthday parade with spectacular pageantry; Whitehall, London
  Royal Ascot – more horses and hats; Ascot, Berkshire

Appleby Horse Fair – traditional Gypsy fair; Appleby, Cumbria

Late June

Lawn Tennis Championships – runs for two weeks; Wimbledon, London

Henley Royal Regatta – premier rowing and social event; Henley-on-Thames, Oxfordshire

Glastonbury Festival – huge open-air music festival & hippy happening; Pilton, Somerset

Royal Highland Show – Scotland's national agricultural show; Edinburgh

London Pride – Europe's biggest gay and lesbian march and festival

Early July

Hampton Court Palace International Flower Show – London

Mid-July

Royal Welsh Show – national agricultural show; Llanelwedd, Builth Wells

Late July

Cowes Week – yachting extravaganza; Isle of Wight

Early August

Edinburgh Military Tattoo – pageantry and military displays; runs for three weeks

Royal National Eisteddfod of Wales – Gaelic cultural festival; Neath, South Wales

Mid-August

Edinburgh International & Fringe Festivals – premier international arts festivals; run for three weeks

Late August (August Bank Holiday)

Notting Hill Carnival – enormous Caribbean carnival; London

Reading Festival – outdoor rock & roll for three days; Reading, Berkshire

Early September

Braemar Royal Highland Gathering – kilts and cabers; Braemar, Scotland

Mid-September

Farnborough International Aerospace Exhibition & Flying Display – world's largest aerospace exhibition; Farnborough, Surrey

October

Horse of the Year Show – best-known showjumping event in Britain; Wembley, London

5 November

Guy Fawkes Day – commemorating an attempted Catholic coup; bonfires and fireworks around the country

COURSES

Courses on almost any subject are available in Britain. Your local branch of the British Council should be able to provide details.

WORK

See the Visas section earlier in this chapter for details on how to go about it legally. The economic downturn has made it difficult to find jobs; however, if you're prepared to do anything and to work long hours for lousy pay, you'll almost certainly find something. Without skills, it's difficult to find a job that pays well enough to enable you to save money. You should be able to break even, but you're probably better off saving in your home country.

Traditionally, unskilled visitors have worked in pubs and restaurants and as nannies. Both jobs often provide live-in accommodation, but the hours are long, the work exhausting and the pay lousy. If you live in, you'll be lucky to get £110 per week; if you have to find your own accommodation, you'll be lucky to get £150. Before you accept a job, make sure you're clear about the terms and conditions, especially how many hours (and what hours) you will be expected to work.

In good economic times accountants, nurses, medical personnel, journalists, computer programmers, lawyers, teachers and clerical workers (with computer experience) quickly find well-paid work. Jobs have been scarce over the last few years but may now be picking up again. Even so, you'll probably need some money to tide you over while you search. Don't forget copies of your qualifications, references (which will probably be checked) and a CV.

Teachers should contact London borough councils, which administer separate education departments, although some schools recruit directly. To work as a trained nurse you have to register with the United Kingdom Central Council for Nursing, a process that can take up to three months; write to the Overseas Registration Department, UKCC, 23 Portland Place W1N 3AF. If you aren't registered you can still work as an auxiliary.

The free *TNT Magazine* is a good starting point for jobs and agencies. Bars such as All Bar One are a good bet for temporary work. For au pair and nanny work buy *The Lady*.

Also check the *Evening Standard*, national newspapers and the government-operated Jobcentres. Jobcentres are scattered around London; they're listed under the Manpower Services Commission in the telephone book, and have a branch at 195 Wardour St W1. Whatever your skills, it's worth registering with a number of temporary agencies.

Tax

As an official employee, you'll find income tax and National Insurance automatically deducted from your weekly pay packet. However, the deductions will be calculated on the assumption that you will work for the entire financial year (which runs from April 6 to April 5). If you don't work the entire year, you may be eligible for a refund. Contact the tax office, or use one of the agencies which advertise in *TNT Magazine* (but check the fee or percentage charge first). Depending on the type of work, it may be worth considering self-employment and/or starting your own company. Take professional advice first.

Anyone residing or working in Britain is also required to pay a council tax. Those on extremely low incomes *may* be partially exempt, but otherwise the tax is determined by the council's financial needs and varies only according to the value of your residence. Single householders get 25% discount.

In theory, you're obliged to register with your local council whenever you move into a permanent residence (not including hostels or hotels). In practice, the tax is very difficult to police, particularly in the case of itinerant young travellers. However, registering with a council for any reason can lead to nightmarish demands.

ACCOMMODATION

This will almost certainly be your single greatest expense. Even camping can be expensive at official sites.

For travel on the cheap, there are really only two options: youth hostels and bed & breakfasts (B&Bs). London and Scotland aside, there are few independent backpackers' hostels, although the number is growing, particularly in some of the popular hiking regions.

In the middle range, superior B&Bs are often in beautiful old buildings and some rooms will have private bathrooms with showers or baths. Guesthouses and small hotels are more likely to have private bathrooms, but they also tend to be less personal.

There are a growing number of characterless but dependable purpose-built modern hotels; the Travelodge chain, for example, offers plain, modern rooms for £39.50 each. If money's no object, there are some superb hotels, the most interesting in converted castles and mansions.

All these options are promoted by local TICs. Many charge £1 for local bookings for accommodation within the next two nights, although you may also have to pay a 10% deposit which is subtracted from the nightly price. Most TICs also participate in the book-a-bed-ahead (BABA) scheme which allows you to book accommodation for the next two nights anywhere in Britain. Most charge around £2.75 and take a 10% deposit. Outside opening hours, most TICs put a notice and map in their window showing which local places have unoccupied beds. These services are particularly handy for big cities and over weekends and the peak summer season.

The national tourist boards operate a classification and grading system; participating hotels, guesthouses and B&Bs have a plaque at the front door. If you want to be confident that your accommodation reaches basic standards of safety and cleanliness, the first classification is 'listed', which denotes clean and comfortable accommodation. One crown means each room will have a washbasin and it's own key. Two crowns means washbasins, bedside lights and a TV in a lounge or in bedrooms. Three crowns means at least half the rooms have private bathrooms and that hot evening meals are available. And so on up to five crowns.

In addition there are also gradings ('approved', 'commended', 'highly commended' and 'deluxe') which may actually

Top Left: Section of Hadrian's Wall, Northumberland
Top Right: Lock and split bridge, Stratford Canal, Warwickshire
Bottom Left: Path to Bonsall, Peak District, Derbyshire
Bottom Right: Cyclists on the Tissington Trail, Peak District, Derbyshire

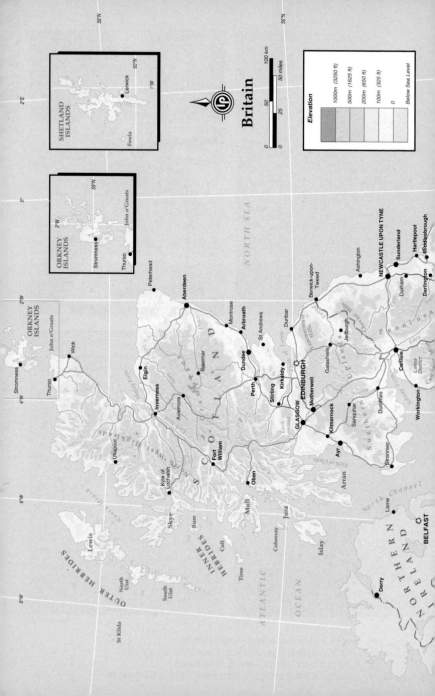

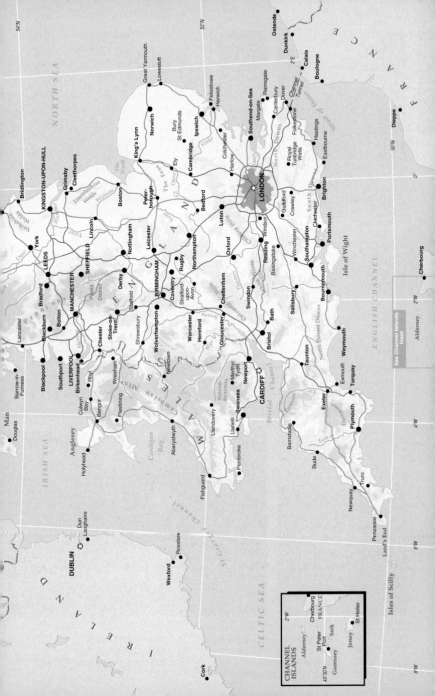

RICHARD EVERIST

TONY WHEELER

BRYN THOMAS

RICHARD EVERIST

RICHARD EVERIST

GLENN BEANLAND

A	B
C	D
E	F

A: Kissing gate, Cumbrian Way
B: Avon River narrowboat
C: Black Mountains,
   Brecon Beacons, Wales
D: Stile, Cumbrian Way
E: Stile, Cumbrian Way
F: Babbling brook, Lake District

be more significant since they reflect a subjective judgment of quality.

All this sounds useful, but in practice there's a wide range within each classification and some of the best B&Bs don't participate at all because they have to pay to do so. A high-quality 'listed' B&B can be 20 times nicer than a low-quality 'three crown' hotel. In practice, actually seeing the place, even from the outside, will give a clue as to what to expect. Always ask to look at your room before you check in.

As ever, single rooms are in short supply and many accommodation suppliers are reluctant to let a double room, even when it's quiet, to one person without charging a hefty supplement.

YHA Hostels

Membership of a Youth Hostel Association (YHA) gives you access to a network of hostels throughout England, Wales and Scotland – and you don't have to be young, or single, to use them.

There are separate, local associations for England/Wales and Scotland, and each publishes its own accommodation guide. If you plan to use hostels extensively it's *absolutely essential* to get hold of these as they include the (often complicated) opening days and hours, as well as information on price, facilities and how to reach each place.

All the British associations are affiliated with Hostelling International (HI), which has recently changed its name from International Youth Hostel Federation to move away from the emphasis on 'youth'. Some countries immediately adopted the new name, but Britain is still sticking with YHA and SYHA for the time being. It makes no difference anyway: YHA, IYHF or HI, it's all the same thing.

For England and Wales the head office is 8 St Stephen's Hill, St Albans, Herts AL1 2DY (☎ 01727-855215). Guides and membership information are available at the YHA Adventure Shop at 14 Southampton St, London WC2E 7HY (tube: Covent Garden), and branches round the country, or you can join in your home country.

National offices include:

Australia
Each state has its own Youth Hostel Association. The National Administration Office is the Australian Youth Hostels Association, Level 3, 10 Mallett St, Camperdown, NSW 2050 (☎ 02-565 1699)

Canada
Hostelling International Canada, National Office, 400-205 Catherine St, Ottawa, Ontario K2P 1C3 (☎ 613-237 7884)

New Zealand
Youth Hostels Association of New Zealand, PO Box 436, 173 Gloucester St, Christchurch 1 (☎ 03-379 9970)

USA
Hostelling International, PO Box 37613, Washington, DC 20013-7613 (☎ 202-783 6161)

All hostels have facilities for self-catering and some provide cheap meals. Advance booking is advisable, especially at weekends, bank holidays and at any time over the summer months. Booking policies vary: most hostels accept phone bookings and payment with Visa or Access (MasterCard) cards; some will accept same-day bookings, although they will usually only hold a bed until 6 pm; some participate in the book-a-bed-ahead scheme; some work on a first come, first served basis.

The advantages of hostels are primarily price (although the difference between a cheap B&B and an expensive hostel isn't huge) and the chance to meet other travellers. The disadvantages are that some are still run dictatorially, you're usually locked out between 10 am and 5 pm, the front door is locked at 11 pm, you usually sleep in bunks in a single-sex dormitory, and many are closed during winter. Official youth hostels are rarely in town centres; fine if you're walking the countryside or have your own transport, a pain if you're not.

Overnight prices depend on age: *Under 18*, you pay £3.75 to £8.20, but mostly around £5.50; *Adult*, you pay £5.50 to £19.75, but mostly around £7.45. By the time you've added £2.80 for breakfast, you can get very close to cheap B&B prices.

Throughout this book, higher hostel prices

for seniors are given first, followed by the reduced price for juniors.

Independent Hostels

The growing network of independent hostels offers the opportunity to escape curfews and lockouts for a price of around £8.50 to £9.50 per night in a basic bunkroom. Like YHA hostels these are great places to meet other travellers, and they tend to be in town centres rather than out in the sticks, which will suit the non-walking fraternity. *The Independent Hostel Guide* (£3.95) lists most independent hostels in England, Scotland, Wales and the whole of Ireland, but new places are opening fast so it's worth double-checking with the TIC.

Camping

Free camping is rarely possible, except in Scotland. Camp sites vary widely in quality, most have reasonable facilities, but they're usually ugly and inaccessible without your own transport. The RAC's *Camping & Caravanning in Britain* (£6.99) has extensive lists; local TICs also have details.

Those planning to camp extensively, or tour with a van, should join the Camping & Caravanning Club (☎ 01203-694995), Greenfields House, Westwood Way, Coventry CV4 8JH. This is the world's oldest camping and caravanning club, and it runs many British sites including club-owned sites, certificated sites with minimal facilities taking only five vans, and commercial sites which range from enormous holiday parks to quiet overnight stops for backpackers.

Many sites are open to non-members, but 2000 are not, and non-members pay higher fees. Members receive a magazine, a guide to 5000 sites and other useful services (including advice, camping carnets and insurance) for both British and European trips. Membership, which will cover one camp site and all who use it, is £30.50 – but it will quickly pay for itself.

The tourist boards rate caravan and camping grounds with one to five ticks; the more ticks, the higher the standard.

University Colleges

Many British universities offer their student accommodation to visitors during the holidays (vacations). Most such rooms are comfortable, functional single bedrooms but without single supplements. Increasingly, however, there are rooms with private bathroom, twin and family units, self-contained flats and shared houses.

University catering is usually reasonable and can range through bars, self-service cafés, takeaways and restaurants. Full-board, half-board, bed & breakfast and self-catering options are available.

Rooms are usually available from late June to late September. Bed & breakfast normally costs from £18 to £25 per person.

For more information contact BUAC (British Universities Accommodation Consortium), Box No 967, University Park, Nottingham NG7 2RD (☎ 0115-950 4571, fax 0115-942 2505)

Bed & Breakfasts, Guesthouses & Pubs

Bed & breakfasts (B&Bs) are a great British institution and the cheapest private accommodation around. At the bottom end (£12 to £17 per person) you get a bedroom in a private house, a shared bathroom and an enormous cooked breakfast (juice, cereal, bacon, eggs, sausage, baked beans and toast). Small B&Bs may only have one room to let, and you can really feel like a guest of the family – they may not even have a sign.

More upmarket B&Bs have private bathrooms and TVs in each room. Good showers are rare, however. Double rooms will often have two single beds (twin beds) rather than a double bed so you don't have to be lovers to share a room. Many B&Bs have conservative owners (which may partly explain the twin beds) so it pays to be a little careful what you say and how you act.

Guesthouses, which are often just large converted houses with half a dozen rooms, are an extension of the B&B concept. They range from £12 to £50 a night, depending on the quality of the food and accommodation. In general, they're less personal than B&Bs,

and more like the small budget hotels they really are.

Pubs and inns may also offer cheap B&B and can be good fun since they place you at the hub of the community. However, they can be noisy and are not always ideal for lone women travellers.

Hotels

The term hotel covers all sorts of accommodation, from local pubs and inns to the grand playgrounds of the hyper-wealthy.

Pubs and inns usually have a bar or two (often basic) and a lounge (with tables and chairs) where cheap meals are served; sometimes they'll also have a more upmarket restaurant as well. Increasingly in the countryside they also offer comfortable mid-range accommodation, but they can vary widely in quality.

Some hotels in large converted houses are virtually indistinguishable from guesthouses. On the coast, and in other areas that attract tourists, there are often big, old-style, residential hotels. The cheapest have sometimes been taken over by long-term homeless families who are being 'temporarily' housed by local authorities. They're not places for foreign visitors at all...which is one reason why it's wise to stick with tourist board-approved places except in rural areas.

More and more purpose-built chain hotels are appearing along the motorways and in the city centres. Most depend on business trade and offer competitive weekend rates to attract tourists; they also often have a flat rate per room (with twin or double beds and private bathroom), making them relative bargains for couples or small families. Forte Travelodges (☎ 0800-850950) charge £39.95 a room. Other such groups are Granada Lodges (☎ 0800-555300), Campanile Hotels (☎ 0181-567 6969), Comfort Inns (☎ 0800-444444), Travel Inns (☎ 01582-4144341), and Formule 1 Hotels (☎ 01302-761050).

The very best hotels are magnificent places, often with restaurants to match. If you want to splash out, pick up a copy of the *Which? Hotel Guide* (£14.99) which lists more than 1000 of the country's finest hotels, some of them in converted country-houses and castles. Recommendations are generally trustworthy because hotel owners don't have to pay to appear in the guide.

Short-Term Rental

There has been an upsurge in the number of houses and cottages available for short-term rent. Staying in one place gives you an opportunity to get a real feel for a region and a community. Cottages for four can cost as little as £100 per week; some are even let for three days.

Outside weekends and July/August, it's not essential to book a long way ahead. You may be able to book through TICs, but there are also excellent agencies who supply glossy brochures to help the decision-making. Most have agents in North America and Australasia. Among them, Country Holidays (☎ 01282-445566), Spring Mill, Earby, Colne, Lancashire BB8 6RN, has been highly recommended. English Country Cottages (☎ 01328-851155), Grove Farm Barns, Sculthorpe, Norfolk, is another large, reliable agency. It's difficult to quote average prices, but expect a week's rent for a two bedroom cottage to cost from £150 in winter,

£175 from April to June, and £250 from July to September.

The National Trust (☎ 01225-791133) also rents over 200 cottages which tend to be above average in charm, location and price. Expect a week's rent for a two-bedroom cottage to be around £175 in winter, £300 from April to June and £450 from July to September.

The most spectacular possibilities are offered by the Landmark Trust (☎ 01628-825925), Shottesbrooke, Maidenhead, Berkshire SL6 3SW, UK; and in the USA (☎ 802-254 6868) at 28 Birge St, Brattleboro, Vermont 05301. This is an architectural charity established to rescue historic buildings, which is partly funded by renting the properties after they've been restored. The trust owns 164 unusual buildings, including medieval houses, castles, Napoleonic forts and bizarre 18th-century follies (including the wonderful Pineapple near Falkirk, Scotland).

All the properties are advertised in the 280-page *Landmark Handbook* (£8.50, including postage and packing in Britain, US$19.50 including postage and packing in the USA, refundable on booking). Prices vary but average around £200 per week for a two-bedroom place in winter, around £250 from April to June, and £300 in midsummer. Four people can stay at the Pineapple, for example, for between £400 and £600 a week.

The tourist boards rate self-catering accommodation with one to five keys; the more keys, the more facilities available. One key indicates that a property is clean and comfortable, has adequate heating, lighting and seating, a TV, cooker, fridge and crockery and cutlery.

FOOD

Traditionally British food has had a dismal reputation, the result being a high incidence of obesity and heart disease. The native cuisine's most consistent success has been with the potato which shows up mashed, boiled, baked and fried.

Fortunately, things are improving fast, especially in the south. The supply of fresh fruit and vegetables has improved immeasurably. Vegetarianism has taken off in a big way, and in the main towns and cities a cosmopolitan range of cuisines is available. Particularly if you like pizza, pasta and curry you should be able to get a reasonable meal pretty well anywhere. Chain restaurants like Pierre Victoire and Caf, Rouge have also brought 'French' cuisine to most tourist-frequented high streets for reasonably moderate prices. Indeed, the one thing it may be hard to find (except in pubs) is traditional British cuisine...dishes like roast beef and Yorkshire pudding or steak & kidney pie.

Vegetarians should buy *The Vegetarian Travel Guide*, published annually by the UK Vegetarian Society and covering hundreds of places to eat and stay. Most restaurants have at least a token vegetarian dish, although, as anywhere, vegans will find the going tough. Indian restaurants offer a welcome choice.

Takeaways, Cafés & Pubs

Every high street has its complement of takeaway restaurants, from McDonald's and Pizza Hut to the home-grown and aptly named Wimpy. You may not be able to avoid them because they're relatively cheap. The best of the worst is Burger King (known as Hungry Jack's in Australia), which even serves a vegetarian beanburger.

Especially in the bigger towns, you will also find cafes, usually referred to as *caffs* or *greasy spoons*. Although they often look pretty seedy, they're usually warm, friendly, very British places and invariably serve cheap breakfasts (eggs, bacon and baked beans) and English tea (strong, sweet and milky). They also have plain but filling lunches, usually a roast with three veg, or bangers (sausages) and mash (mashed potato).

These days most pubs also do food, although Sunday can be tricky. At the cheap end pub meals are not very different from those in cafés, but at the expensive end they're closer to restaurants. Many pubs actually encompass both extremes with a cheap bar menu and a more formal restaurant that can be considerably more expensive. Chilli con carne or lasagne is often the cheapest offering on the bar menu. A filling 'ploughman's lunch' of bread, cheese and pickle rarely costs more than £3.

On a tight budget it's worth knowing that many supermarkets and department stores now have reasonable (and reasonably-priced) cafés; as supermarket opening hours lengthen, so do those of their cafés.

Self-Catering

The cheapest way to eat in Britain is to cook for yourself. Hopefully, however, you won't be forced to the extremes of an Australian shoestringer who was arrested and jailed for attempting to barbecue a Canada goose in Hyde Park! Even if you lack great culinary skills, you can buy good quality pre-cooked meals from the supermarkets (Marks & Spencer are thought to be the best but are also the priciest).

Travellers with Special Diets

If you have dietary restrictions – you're a vegetarian or require kosher food, for example – tourist organisations may be able to advise you or provide lists of suitable restaurants. Numerous vegetarian restaurants are listed in this book.

DRINKS

Takeaway alcoholic drinks are sold from neighbourhood *off-licences* rather than pubs. The best such chain is Oddbins, with branches throughout the country. Opening hours vary, but although some stay open to 9 or 10 pm, Monday to Saturday, many keep ordinary shop hours. Most close between 3 and 7 pm on Sunday. Alcohol can also be bought at supermarkets and some corner shops.

Most restaurants are licensed and their alcoholic drinks, particularly good wines, are always expensive. There are few BYO restaurants (where you can Bring Your Own bottles), although London has a few. Most charge an extortionate sum for 'corkage' – opening your own bottle for you.

Nonalcoholic Drinks

The British national drink is undoubtedly tea, although coffee is creeping up in popu-

---

The Great British Cuppa

There's no crisis too serious but the British answer will be to pop on the kettle for a nice cup of tea.

So important is tea to the British way of life that the operators of the National Grid scour the TV schedules for programmes which are likely to attract abnormally large audiences knowing that everyone will rush to turn on their kettles as soon as it ends.

The biggest electricity surge ever recorded took place after English footballer Chris Waddle kicked the ball over the crossbar in the 1990 World Cup semi-final shoot-out. The men in grey suits had expected an instant power surge. In fact it took two minutes for supporters to digest what had happened before rushing to push demand up by 2,800 megawatts. ■

---

larity and it's now fairly easy to get a cappuccino or espresso in southern towns. You can almost measure your geographical position by the strength of the tea in cafés. From a point somewhere around Birmingham the tea gets progressively stronger, the sort of brew you can stand your teaspoon up in, or so idiom would have it. Further south you're as likely to be offered Earl Grey or a herbal tea such as a traditional Indian or Sri Lankan brew.

Alcoholic Drinks

Beer British pubs generally serve an impressive range of beers – lagers, bitters, ales and stouts. What New Worlders know as beer is actually lager, and much to the distress of local connoisseurs, lagers (including Fosters and Budweiser) now constitute a huge chunk of the market. Fortunately, the traditional British bitter is fighting back, thanks to the Campaign for Real Ale (CAMRA) organisation. Look for their endorsement sticker on pub windows.

There's a wonderfully wide range of beers, ranging from very light (almost like lager) to extremely strong and treacly. They're usually served at room temperature, which may come as a shock if you've been raised on lager. But if you think of these 'beers' as something completely new, you'll discover subtle flavours that a cold, chemical lager can't match.

Ales and bitters are similar; it's more a regional name difference than anything else. The best are actually hand-pumped from the cask, not carbonated and drawn under pressure. Stout is a dark, rich, foamy drink; Guinness is the most famous brand.

Beers are usually served in pints (from £1.50 to £2), but you can also ask for a 'half' (a half pint). The stronger brews are usually 'specials' or 'extras'. Potency can vary from around 2% to 8%.

Pubs are allowed to open for any 12 hours a day from Monday to Saturday. Most maintain the traditional 11 am to 11 pm hours; the bell for last orders rings out at about 10.45 pm. On Sunday most open from noon to 3 pm and from 7 to 10.30 pm, though in London some pubs stay open all day.

Wines Good wines are now widely available and very reasonably priced (except in pubs and restaurants). In supermarkets an ordinary but drinkable bottle can still be found for less than £3.

SPECTATOR SPORT

The Brits love their games and play and watch them with fierce, competitive dedication. They've been responsible for inventing or codifying many of the world's most popular spectator sports: tennis, football (soccer) and rugby; and the Scots can claim golf. To this list add billiards and snooker, lawn bowls, boxing, darts, hockey, squash and table tennis.

The country also hosts premier events for a number of sports: Wimbledon (tennis), the FA Cup Final (football), the British Open (golf), Test Cricket, Badminton Horse Trials (equestrianism), the British Grand Prix (motor racing), the Isle of Man TT (motorcycle racing), the Derby and the Grand National (horse racing), the Henley Regatta (rowing), the Five Nations Tournament (rugby union), the Super League Final (rugby league) and the Admirals Cup (yachting).

All year round, London plays host to a myriad of sporting events. If you want to see live action, consult *Time Out* for fixtures, times, venues and ticket prices. Also see the Spectator Sports section in the London chapter.

Football

Also known as soccer to distinguish it from rugby football, this is Britain's largest spectator sport and one of the most popular participation sports.

Until recently, English football was becoming better known not for the excellence with which it is played, but for hooligan supporters pillaging their way across Europe, and for collapsing stadiums. (38 people were killed and over 400 injured at Liverpool's Heysel Stadium disaster in 1985). In the 1996 European Championships, however, the England team played brilliantly and amazed everyone by reaching the semi-finals. Football fever swept the country: in one poll 50% of teenage girls said they'd rather watch an England match than a Take That reunion!

The Football Association (FA) was formed in 1863 to establish the rules of the game and the FA Cup has been played since 1871. The Football League was originally established because professionals weren't allowed to play for the FA. The best clubs now form the Premier League, and, under a controversial televising deal, many of their matches can only be seen on BSkyB satellite TV.

Better teams include Manchester United, Liverpool, Newcastle and Arsenal. Wembley is where the English national football team play their home internationals, and also where the FA Cup Final takes place in mid-May. England plays several home internationals each season, but the prices are prohibitive, and finding yourself sitting next to English football fans for a 90-minute display of ignorance, aggression and xenophobia can be thoroughly unpleasant (as, indeed, can be finding yourself anywhere near a football stadium or even a tube station being used by supporters).

The domestic football season lasts from August to May and most matches are played at 3 pm on Saturday or 7.30 pm on Tuesday or Wednesday. Tickets cost from £7 to £20, and at all but the most popular matches there's no need to book.

The main teams in Wales are Cardiff and Swansea. Scotland has its own league, which in recent years has been dominated by Glasgow Rangers. It also has a Scottish FA Cup Final, a knock-out competition based on the English version. When Scots are playing abroad, the game unites the country; at home it serves to highlight differences and trouble can break out, especially when Catholic Celtic plays Protestant Rangers in Glasgow.

Cricket

Sometimes called the English national game, cricket is still a popular participation sport. Every summer weekend, hundreds of teams play on idyllic village greens (and city sports fields), and display all the finest English characteristics – fair play, team spirit and individual excellence (plus maiming the opposing team and abusing the umpire).

Those who are not familiar with the game will need someone to explain the rules, and may find it slow. Traditional test matches last for five days, although one-day matches are now the largest crowd pullers. At its best, cricket is aesthetically pleasing, psychologically involving, exciting and quintessentially English.

Several clubs founded in the 18th century still survive. The most famous and important is Marylebone Cricket Club (MCC), based at Lord's cricket ground in north London.

Every summer, the national side of at least one of the main cricket-playing countries (Australia, India, New Zealand, Pakistan, South Africa, Sri Lanka, West Indies) will tour and play a series of five-day test matches and a number of one-day matches. Tickets cost a fortune (£20 to £40) and tend to go fast.

Alternatively, there is a county championship with matches played at attractive grounds around the country. These are sur-prisingly low-key and relaxed. Tickets cost £5 to £10.

Rugby

It was once said that the difference between football and rugby was that football was a gentlemen's game played by hooligans while rugby was a hooligan's game played by gentlemen. Class distinctions may have fallen away, but the hooligan element lives on. A recent report listed rugby as Britain's most dangerous sport, with four times as many serious injuries per player as football.

Rugby takes its name from Rugby school in Warwickshire where the game is supposed to have originated when William Ellis picked up the ball and ran off with it during a football match in 1823. The game's full name is rugby football, but it's also known as rugger. Rugby union is played mainly in the south of England, and in Scotland and Wales.

Bath and Leicester are among the better union teams. Union fans will find south-west London the place to be, with a host of good-quality teams (including the Harlequins, Richmond and Wasps). Each year, starting in January, the Five Nations Rugby Union Championship takes place between the four nations of the British Isles and the French. This guarantees two big matches at Twickenham, the shrine of English rugby union.

Wales has always been particularly strongly associated with rugby union. During the 70s the Welsh national team was very successful, winning six out of 10 Five Nations championships. Since then, however, things haven't gone quite so swingingly. Amateur rugby union teams have also been bleeding men and talent to rugby league (although this trend could stop now that rugby union has become a professional sport too). The most successful club sides are Cardiff, Swansea, Neath and Llanelli, and you can watch their matches between September and Easter.

Played in the north of England, rugby league differs from rugby union in that there are only 13, rather than 15, players in the team. Rules and tactics also differ slightly, most notably in that possession changes from one team to the other after five tackles.

Following Rupert Murdoch's intervention in the organisation and broadcasting of rugby league, this has now become a summer game. The Super League final is held at Old Trafford in September. Teams to watch are St Helen's, Wigan and Warrington.

Golf

Although games that involve hitting a ball with a stick have been played in Europe since Roman times, it was the Scottish version that caught on. Apparently dating from the 15th century, golf was popularised by the Scottish monarchy and gained popularity in London after James VI of Scotland also became James I of England.

While St Andrews in Scotland is known as the home of golf, since the Royal & Ancient club (the recognised authority on the rules) and the famous Old Course are both there, London can boast the world's oldest golf club. James VI/I played on Blackheath in 1608 and London's Royal Blackheath takes the date of its founding from this royal teeing off.

Britain's current top golfers include Nick Faldo and Laura Davies (England), Colin Montgomerie (Scotland) and Ian Woosnam (Wales).

See the Activities chapter for information about playing golf in Britain.

Horse Racing

Ascot, which takes place for a week in late June, is such an important fixture in the racing calendar that even the Queen turns up.

The cheapest tickets are under £5; to be invited into the enclosure you must be well-dressed and expect to pay £20 to £30.

The Derby is the name of the race run at Epsom on the first Saturday in June. The Grand National is probably the best known of all the famous British horse races; this steeplechase is run at Aintree in early April.

THINGS TO BUY

Napoleon once dismissed the British as a nation of shopkeepers but today, as standardised chain stores sweep the High Streets, it would be truer to say they're a nation of shoppers. Shopping is the country's most popular sport and recreational activity.

Multinational capitalism being what it is, there are very few things you can buy that are unique to Britain. On the other hand, if you can't find it for sale in London it probably doesn't exist.

London has some of the world's greatest department stores (Harrods, Fortnum & Mason, Liberty, Harvey Nichols, Marks & Spencer), some of the best bookshops (Waterstones, Dillons, Foyles), some of the best fashion (Camden Market, Kensington Market, Covent Garden, Oxford St, Kensington), some of the best record shops (HMV, Virgin, Tower) and specialist shops of every description.

Although shop assistants can be unhelpful and few things are cheap, books and clothing can be good value – and you really don't know if you need something until you see it...

See the Excess Baggage section in the Getting There & Away chapter when you realise you've hopelessly exceeded your baggage limit.

Activities

Pursuing a favourite activity or interest is one of the best ways of escaping the beaten track. Becoming part of a country's life, and preferably an active participant, is much more rewarding than remaining an isolated spectator viewing the world through a camera lens or car window.

There's no escaping the fact that Britain is an expensive place to travel, but many activities not only open up some of the most beautiful and fascinating corners of the island, but are also well within the reach of the tightest budget. In fact, those on a shoestring budget may find themselves hiking or cycling out of necessity. Fortunately, a walk or ride through the countryside will almost certainly be a highlight – as well as the cheapest part – of a British holiday.

At the other end of the scale, those with big budgets may want to try one of the traditional British sports which are still played with enthusiasm. These activities have many variations – most involving horses, hunting, shooting or fishing – but the constant aim is to extract money from fat wallets.

Most activities are well organised and have clubs and associations that can give visitors invaluable information and, sometimes, substantial discounts. Many of these organisations have national or international affiliations, so check with local clubs before leaving home. The British Tourist Authority has brochures on most activities, which can provide a starting point for further research.

Almost every sport, activity and hobby known to humankind has obsessive British devotees. Most are pleased to meet someone who shares their interest, and their response is often generous and hospitable to a fault.

Walking

Every weekend, millions of people take to the parks and countryside. Perhaps because Britain is such a crowded island, a high premium is placed on open space and the chance to find some fresh air. In the cities, ritual weekend expeditions to the shops and markets are very often combined with a stroll in a park, ending somewhere that sells tea or beer. And the countryside is invaded every weekend by people (and dogs) taking short walks – and ending up somewhere that sells tea or beer.

Although modern developments have had a negative impact, a surprising amount of the countryside appears frozen in time, conforming to a picture of rural Britain that every movie-goer, TV-watcher and book-reader is accustomed to.

The infrastructure for walkers is excellent. Every Tourist Information Centre (TIC) has details (free or for a nominal charge) of suggested walks that take in local points of interest. Hundreds of books are available and describe walks ranging from half-hour strolls to week-long expeditions, and these are widely available in TICs, newsagents, bookshops and outdoor-equipment shops.

Every village and town is surrounded by footpaths, so all keen walkers should consider a week based in one interesting spot (perhaps in a self-catering cottage, or a youth hostel or campsite) with a view to exploring the surrounding countryside. Numerous short walks are detailed in this book.

ACCESS

Again, perhaps because Britain is such a crowded island, the rights of people to gain access to land, even privately owned land, are jealously protected. In England and Wales, the countryside is crisscrossed by a network of countless 'rights of way', most of them over private land, that can be used by any member of the public. They may traverse fields, moors, woodlands and even farmhouse yards.

These public footpaths and bridleways (the latter can be used by horse riders and mountain bikers) have existed for centuries, sometimes millennia. They are marked on maps and are often signposted where they intersect with roads. Some also have special markers at strategic points along their length (yellow arrows for footpaths, blue for bridleways, or other special markers if they are part of a particular walk). Some, however, are completely unmarked, so a good map, and the ability to use it, can be essential. If a path is overgrown or obstructed in some way, walkers are permitted to remove enough of the obstruction to pass, and to walk carefully through a crop. Discretion is advised – no farmer will appreciate damage to property.

Some rights of way cross land that is owned by the Ministry of Defence (MOD) and used occasionally by the army. When troop manoeuvres or firing are in progress access is denied and red flags are put up to warn walkers.

There are some areas where walkers can move freely beyond the rights of way, and these are clearly advertised. For instance, the National Trust (NT) is now one of the largest landowners in Britain and some of its properties are open to the public. However, land within national parks does not necessarily fit into this category.

National parks were set up in England and Wales by the Countryside Commission to protect the finest landscapes and to provide opportunities for visitors to enjoy them, but the land remains largely privately owned and farmed, and access is restricted. It is, for instance, almost always necessary to get permission from a landowner before pitching a tent.

Scotland does not have a formal system of registered rights of way, but there is a tradition of relatively free access to open country, especially in mountain and moorland areas (although there may be restrictions during the grouse and deer-hunting seasons). Nor does Scotland have national parks, although development is controlled in a number of areas that have been designated as National Scenic Areas and Nature Reserves.

In England and Wales, Areas of Outstanding Natural Beauty and Heritage Coasts are also legally protected, but again that doesn't guarantee unlimited access.

LONG-DISTANCE WALKS

The energetic, and the impecunious, should definitely consider some long-distance multi-day walks. With the exception of parts of Scotland, civilisation is never far away, so it is easy to put together walks that connect with public transport and link hostels and villages. In most cases, a tent and cooking equipment is not necessary. Warm and waterproof clothing (including a hat and gloves), sturdy footwear, lunch and some high-energy food (for emergencies), a water bottle (with purification tablets), a first-aid kit, a whistle and torch (flashlight), and a map and compass are all you need.

The best areas for long-distance walks include the Cotswolds, the Exmoor National Park, the Dartmoor National Park, the North York Moors National Park, the Yorkshire Dales National Park, the Lake District, the Pembrokeshire Coast National Park and the Scottish islands. There are many superb long-distance walks in Scotland but, in general, the potential combination of isolation and severe weather mean they require a reasonably high degree of preparation.

Over the last 30 years, a number of national long-distance trails have been developed by the Countryside Commission (a number of them traverse the national parks) and these offer walkers access to outstanding countryside. They have been created by linking existing public footpaths and bridleways and often follow routes that travellers have journeyed for thousands of years.

There are currently 15 national long-distance trails in England and Wales and three in Scotland. There are also a growing number of regional routes created by county councils, and unofficial long-distance routes devised by individuals or groups like the Ramblers' Association. Some are excellent, well organised and have good available information. On the other hand, all you need is a good map and you can plan your own!

Walkers might choose to walk the entire length of a long-distance trail (or *way*, as they are often called), which could be from 30 to 600 miles long, but many choose just a section that meets constraints of time and transport. City-bound walkers often manage to walk an entire trail over a series of weekends.

Some of the English long-distance walks, particularly along the coast, and in the Yorkshire Dales and Lake District, can be very crowded on weekends and in July/August – advance bookings for accommodation are worthwhile at these times (contact the appropriate TICs).

The countryside can look deceptively gentle, but especially in the hills or on the open moors the weather can turn very nasty very quickly at any time of the year. It is vital if you're walking in upland areas to be well equipped, and to carry (and know how to use) good maps and a compass. Always leave details of your route with someone trustworthy.

Maps, Guides & Information

Look out for Lonely Planet's new guide *Walking in Britain*, covering not only all the main long-distance walks but also a good selection of day hikes.

The Countryside Commission, in conjunction with Aurum Press and the Ordnance Survey (OS), publish excellent guides to each trail, which are widely available. They include detailed track notes, and incorporate the relevant sections from the Ordnance Survey's 1:25,000 Pathfinder maps. There are hundreds of other specialist walking guides.

The Ordnance Survey (OS) organisation publishes a wide variety of maps covering the whole country; they're widely available. For walkers, their Landranger maps at 1:50,000 – about 1¼ inches to the mile, covering about 25 x 25 miles – are usually sufficiently detailed. In some instances, where paths are unclear, the Pathfinder series at 1:25,000 – about 2½ inches to the mile, covering around 12½ x 12½ miles – is useful. There are also Pathfinder Walking

Guides (covering short walks in popular areas) and Outdoor Leisure maps (covering most national parks), both at 1:25,000.

A useful alternative to OS maps are those published by Harveys. They cover only some of the main walking areas but they also include tourist information. In some cases they may be more up to date than OS maps.

Those intent on a serious walking holiday should contact the Ramblers' Association (☎ 0171-582 6878), 1 Wandsworth Rd, London SW8 2XX. Their *Yearbook* (£4.99 plus £1 UK p&p) is widely available and itemises the information available for each walk and the appropriate maps; it also gives a list of nearby accommodation (hostels, B&Bs and bunkhouses).

South-West Coast Path

This is the longest long-distance walk in Britain, officially 594 miles long but actually 613. It follows the coast through four counties, from Minehead in Somerset, around Devon and Cornwall, to Poole in Dorset. The path is also known as the South-West Way and the South-West Peninsula Coastal Path.

The South-West Coast Path is based on the trails used by coastguards to patrol the area in search of smugglers, so it mostly sticks to the edge of the coast and a considerable amount of walking up and down hills is involved.

Few people walk the whole path in one go, since this takes about six to seven weeks. The most scenic and popular part is the route that runs from Padstow to Falmouth around Land's End, a distance of 163 miles entirely within Cornwall. This section is a medium to easy walk and it could easily be done in two weeks. There's plenty to see – secret coves, wrecks, the remains of cliff castles, tumuli, settlements, disused mines and quarries, a wide range of birdlife, seals etc – so a pair of binoculars is a good idea.

This section could be walked as follows: Padstow to Treyarnon Bay (10½ miles); Treyarnon Bay to Newquay (12½ miles); Newquay to Perranporth (11 miles); Perranporth to Portreath (11 miles); Portreath to St Ives (17 miles); St Ives to Pendeen (13 miles); Pendeen to Sennen Cove (nine miles); Sennen Cove to Porthcurno (six miles); Porthcurno to Penzance (11 miles); Penzance to Porthleven (13 miles); Porthleven to The Lizard (13 miles); The Lizard to Coverack (11 miles); Coverack to Helford (13 miles); Helford to Falmouth (10 miles).

Accommodation is not a problem, although you should book in advance in summer. There are hostels, camping grounds and B&Bs on or very near the path.

The South-West Way Association (☎ 01752-896237) publishes an annual guide with trail descriptions and accommodation details (£3.99, plus 55p for UK postage), as well as detailed descriptions of 37 short sections (75p each). These are available from Mrs M Macleod (☎ 01803 873061), 1 Orchard Drive, Kingkerswell, Devon TQ12 5DE. The official Aurum Press guides cover the South-West Coast Path in four sections – *Padstow to Falmouth* is £10.99.

Cotswold Way

The Cotswold Way follows the western edge of the Cotswold Hills from Chipping Campden, just south of Stratford-upon-Avon, to Bath. The countryside and Cotswold villages are a delight but the way is also a walk through England's history, with numerous prehistoric hill forts and ancient burial barrows. There are Saxon and Civil War battle sites, reminders of the Romans, some fine stately homes, the ruins of a magnificent medieval monastery and many historical markers and monuments. The path itself winds through fields and woods and over hills, and through a patch of England that is at its most affluent. The pretty-as-a-picture postcard villages exude a heady aroma of solid bank accounts and expensive public schools.

The Cotswold Way is about 100 miles long and can be done in five days, although a week is better. A seven-day walk could be broken up as follows: Chipping Campden to Broadway (6 miles); Broadway to Winchcombe (12 miles); Winchcombe to Cheltenham (11 miles); Cheltenham to Painswick (19 miles); Painswick to Dursley (16 miles); Dursley to Old Sodbury (20 miles); Old Sodbury to Bath (19 miles).

Mark Richards' *The Cotswold Way* (Reardon, £3.95) is a step-by-step account of the route with informative hand-drawn maps. The *Cotswold Way Handbook* (the Ramblers' Association, £1.50 plus 25p p&p) is updated annually and has a variety of itinerary suggestions. It is available from the Cotswold Warden Service (☎ 01452-425674), County Planning Department, Gloucestershire County Council, Shire Hall, Gloucester GL1 2TN.

The Cotswold Way is less than ideal for walkers on a tight budget – B&Bs are often pricier than usual, and there are few convenient youth hostels or camping grounds.

Cleveland Way

The 108-mile-long Cleveland Way is the second-oldest National Trail, and unquestionably one of the greatest walks in Britain, showing a cross section of the best scenery in Yorkshire and a region rich in history, geology and wildlife.

It loops around the North York Moors National Park, passing through small Yorkshire villages and farmland, past the ruins of Rievaulx Abbey and over heather-covered moors. It then follows a spectacular coastline through fishing villages and seaside resorts. There is a rich assortment of relics that include Bronze-Age burial sites, Iron-Age forts, Roman signal stations, medieval abbeys and castles, and industrial relics from the 17th and 18th centuries. The region is also closely associated with Captain James Cook and there are a number of monuments and museums commemorating his life.

The full walk is undeniably challenging and takes about a week, although the way is never more than a couple of miles from a sealed road, so there are numerous potential cut-out points. There are many options for tackling shorter sections, especially along the coast. Daily sections for the full walk could be as follows: Helmsley to Kilburn (10 miles); Kilburn to Osmotherley (14 miles);

Osmotherley to Kildale (20¼ miles); Kildale to Saltburn (14¾ miles); Saltburn to Whitby (20 miles); Whitby to Scarborough (18 miles); Scarborough to Filey (8 miles).

The best guidebook, because it includes OS maps at 2½ inches to one mile, is *Cleveland Way* (Aurum Press, £9.99) by Ian Sampson. The *Cleveland Way*, published by Footprint, has strip maps at scales between 1¾ inches and one inch to the mile, plus useful track notes and information about available facilities. The national park authorities publish the *Cleveland Way – Accommodation & Information Guide* (50p), which is available from visitor centres and local TICs or free if you write to Cleveland Way Project Officer (☎ 01439-770657), North York Moors National Park, The Old Vicarage, Bondgate, Helmsley, York Y06 5BP.

Cumbria Way

The Cumbria Way is a 70-mile walk that traverses the county of Cumbria and the incomparable landscape of the Lake District first popularised for walkers by Wordsworth and Coleridge. Most of the way lies within the Lake District National Park, and most of it follows valleys at relatively low altitudes, so bad weather is not a major issue (although it also traverses several high passes and gives a dramatic taste of the mountains). A number of peaks are within easy reach.

If the weather does remain good (a day or so of rain is virtually inevitable and *cannot* be considered bad weather!), it is impossible to imagine a more beautiful walk. It takes in a full cross section of the best of the Lake District – from the little-visited southern valleys to the shores of Coniston Water, the great peaks of the Langdale Pikes, Derwent Water, the flanks of Skiddaw, and another forgotten backwater between Keswick and Carlisle. As an introduction to the Lake District it is definitely unsurpassed.

It is an easy walk logistically: it travels south-north between Ulverston, on Morecambe Bay, and Carlisle, near Hadrian's Wall. A suggested itinerary is: Ulverston to Coniston (16 miles); Coniston to Dungeon Ghyll (11 miles); Dungeon Ghyll to Keswick (16 miles); Keswick to Caldbeck (14 miles); Caldbeck to Carlisle (13 miles).

The Ordnance Survey Landranger 1:50,000 series (£4.75) is *almost* detailed enough and covers the walk on three sheets (Nos 85, 90 and 97). A couple of sections are quite tricky to navigate, however, and most people will find the appropriate map from the Ordnance Survey Pathfinder 1:25,000 series useful. The section from Ulverston to Coniston Water is one (Pathfinder No 626), and the other (Pathfinder No 576).

Two guidebooks are *The Cumbria Way* (Dalesman, £4.95) by John Trevelyan and the more recently-published *Guide to the Cumbria Way* by Philip Dubcock (Miway Publishing, £3.75).

Hadrian's Wall

Hadrian's Wall runs for over 70 miles across the north of England from Newcastle upon Tyne to Bowness-on-Solway, west of Carlisle. Much of the Wall has disappeared completely or is in ruins but, in theory, the route would make an excellent long-distance trail, and an extra five miles would make it a coast-to-coast walk. Currently, however, this would involve quite a bit of walking along roads and through towns – the best way to experience the Wall is on a series of day hikes, totalling 27 miles. A National Trail is being developed but it won't be completed until the year 2001!

To walk the most interesting sections of the Wall you could base yourself in or around Haltwhistle or at Once Brewed, and make use of the good local public transport system. Alternatively, there are places to stay along the route at Greenhead, Gilsland and Brampton. The three day hikes are as follows: Once Brewed to Once Brewed (circular walk; 7½ miles), Once Brewed to Greenhead (seven miles), and Greenhead to Brampton (12½ miles). As well as the Wall itself, this route takes in several Roman forts, including Housesteads and Vindolanda, various turrets and temples, and also passes through Northumberland National Park, where the scenery is at its finest.

Hadrian's Wall: The Wall Walk by Mark Richards (Cicerone Press, £7.99) is an excellent guide describing a route that roughly follows the route of the Wall, taking in the good parts and giving detours through the countryside to avoid the less interesting sections. The OS *Historical Map & Guide – Hadrian's Wall* covers the Wall in strip-mat format at scales of 1:25,000 and 1:50,000, and is adequate for finding your way, with the route of the original Wall superimposed on the modern information. The OS Landranger 1:50,000 sheet 86, *Haltwhistle*, goes beyond this strip and covers the walks mentioned here.

The Pennine Way

The 250-mile Pennine Way can claim to be the granddaddy of British long-distance walks as it was first conceived back in 1935, although not 'officially' recognised until the 1960s. If the weather is uncooperative it can also be one of the toughest walks in Britain as it follows the mountainous spine of northern England into Scotland, often crossing long stretches of unprotected high country. Careful planning, good equipment and caution are all essential requisites for walking the Pennine Way. Completing the whole walk in two weeks is a real endurance test; allowing three weeks is far more realistic.

The walk starts at Edale, in the north of the Peak District, and immediately makes the tough climb up to the 2000-foot-high Kinder Scout plateau. This 'in the deep end' approach on the first day is followed by a long spell of 'bog hopping' across the exposed moors of the Dark Peak. Continuing north through Brontë country, the route goes right through the Yorkshire Dales National Park then joins Hadrian's Wall for a pleasant jaunt along the most interesting section of this ancient barrier. The final stretch of the walk crosses the full length of the Northumberland National Park before bringing weary walkers to a well-earned rest at

Kirk Yetholm, just over the border in Scotland.

There are numerous books on the Pennine Way, including the two-volume *Pennine Way* by T Hopkins (Aurum Press, £9.99 each). Classic British walking writer Alfred Wainwright also describes the route in his *Pennine Way Companion* (Michael Joseph, £9.99). The Pennine Way Council, 29 Springfield Park Avenue, Chelmsford, Essex CM2 6EL, publishes the *Pennine Way Accommodation and Catering Guide* (90p plus 20p p&p). These publications are available from the Peak Park Joint Planning Board, National Park Office, Aldern House, Baslow Road, Bakewell, Derbyshire DE45 1AE.

Peddars Way & Norfolk Coast Path

This is an undemanding 94-mile trail that follows a Roman road across the middle of Norfolk from Knettishall Heath to the beautiful north Norfolk coast at Holme-next-the-Sea. It follows this coastline through a number of attractive, untouched villages like Wells-next-the-Sea and Cromer.

Although the trail ends at Cromer, it's possible to continue for another 40 miles to Great Yarmouth. The start of the trail (Knettishall Heath) is also the end of another path, the Icknield Way, which runs for 105 miles across England from Ivinghoe Beacon. Ivinghoe Beacon also happens to be the end of the Ridgeway (see following section), so these three paths could be linked together into a long march of 284 miles from Avebury to Cromer.

The Peddars Way Association (☎ 01603-623070), 150 Armes St, Norwich NR2 4EG, publishes a guide and accommodation list for £2.10 (plus 25p UK p&p). There are several guidebooks, including *Peddars Way & Norfolk Coast Path* by Bruce Robinson (Aurum Press, £9.99).

The Ridgeway

The remains of a prehistoric track that is Britain's oldest road, the Ridgeway, is now a National Trail beginning near Avebury (Wiltshire) and running north-east for 85 miles to Ivinghoe Beacon near Aylesbury (Buckinghamshire). It follows the high open ridge of the chalk downs and then descends to the Thames Valley before finally winding through the Chiltern Hills. The western section (to Streatley) can be used by mountain bikes, horses, farm vehicles and recreational 4WDs. Unfortunately, recreational 4WDs have recently become very fashionable in Britain; for peace and quiet, walk during the week.

The best guide is *The Ridgeway* by Neil Curtis (Aurum Press, £9.99). A range of useful publications including an excellent *Information & Accommodation Guide* (£1.50 plus 40p for UK postage) is available from the Ridgeway Officer (☎ 01865-810224), Countryside Service, Department of Leisure & Arts, Holton, Oxford OX33 1QQ. Cyclists should get a copy of *The Mountain Biker's Guide to the Ridgeway* by Andy Bull & Frank Barrett (Newspaper Publishing, £5.99).

Friends of the Ridgeway is a voluntary organisation that aims to preserve the trail for quiet recreational use. Contact Nigel Forward (☎ 0171-794 2105), 90 South Hill Park, London NW3 2SN for information.

Thames Path

The path that runs the length of the River Thames, 180 miles from the river's source in Gloucestershire to the Thames Barrier in London, is the newest National Trail, officially designated in 1996. This famous waterway rises at Thames Head, south of Cirencester, and flows through a varied landscape that includes quintessentially English villages, peaceful meadowland and ugly suburban sprawl around the capital.

There are few youth hostels along the route, but B&B is available in many towns and villages. Contact the Countryside Commission (☎ 01242-521381), John Dower House, Crescent Place, Cheltenham, Gloucestershire GL50 3RA, for more information. *The Thames Walk* (Ramblers' Association, £3.95 plus 70p p&p) by David Sharp covers the trail in 19 sections.

South Downs Way

The South Downs Way National Trail is a bridleway, which means it can be walked, ridden or cycled. It covers 99 miles between the coastal resort of Eastbourne and Winchester, a cathedral city and the ancient capital of England.

It's an easy walk, readily accessible from London, so parts can be busy, especially on weekends. It covers a beautiful cross-section of classic English landscapes, beginning with spectacular chalk cliffs at Beachy Head, then traversing an open chalk ridge (the Downs) with great views, before entering rolling, wooded country as you approach Winchester.

The chalk downs are amongst the longest continuously inhabited parts of the island and the way itself follows an ancient ridgeway track that dates back 4000 years. It passes numerous prehistoric remains, and some charming medieval villages. You are never far from a comfortable B&B and a good pub; there are also six youth hostels on or near the way, although they are all in the section between Eastbourne and Arundel.

The way could be walked in a week, although most guides break it up into nine or 10 sections. There are numerous guidebooks, and some annually produced accommodation guides. The Eastbourne TIC (see the Eastbourne section in the South-Eastern England chapter) is particularly helpful, and has a good supply of information. The *South Downs Way* by Paul Millmore (Aurum Press, £9.99) has route descriptions and maps.

Dales Way

The Dales Way links two of England's greatest national parks – the Yorkshire Dales and Lake District – and although it is not an official National Trail, it is a popular and well-organised route. Some parts are not signposted, however, so you need good maps.

Officially it begins at Ilkley, which is accessible from Leeds with regular trains, in a densely populated corner of West Yorkshire famous for its mill towns.

Alternatively, you could start at Bolton Priory or Grassington (see the Yorkshire Dales National Park section in the Northern England chapter), which are both on the way. Much of the walk follows river banks through the Yorkshire Dales, so the walking is easy, although there are some open expanses of moorland between one dale (valley) and the next. The walk ends with a spectacular descent to Bowness on the shores of Lake Windermere, the main town in the Lake District National Park.

The way mostly follows ancient trails, passing through or near many villages, so B&B accommodation is not a problem (although booking is still advised). There are also a number of youth hostels along the way (including at Grassington), as well as camping barns. It would be an easy seven-day walk, or just four or five days from Grassington to Windermere. Distances are as follows: Ilkley to Barden (12 miles); Barden to Grassington (seven miles); Grassington to Buckden (12 miles); Buckden to Dentdale (16 miles); Dentdale to Sedbergh (11 miles); Sedbergh to Burneside (15 miles); Burneside to Bowness (eight miles).

There are numerous guidebooks, including *The Dales Way* by Colin Speakman (Dalesman, £5.95), which is supplemented by the *Dales Way Companion* by Paul Hannon (Hillside Publications, £4.50), with excellent detailed maps. The TICs at Leeds, Grassington and Windermere are all good sources of information, as is the Ramblers' Association (see under Maps, Guides & Information at the start of the Walking section), which produces an accommodation brochure, the *Dales Way Handbook* (90p plus 70p p&p).

Coast to Coast

The Coast to Coast walk was devised by the near-legendary walker and creator of superb illustrated walking guides, Alfred Wainwright. It's an unofficial trail covering 190 miles from St Bees Head on the west coast to Robin Hood's Bay on the east. It traverses three national parks – the Lake District, Yorkshire Dales and North York Moors – and

covers a range of England's most spectacular scenery, from sea cliffs to mountains, dales and moors.

It's a hard walk, since it crosses the grain of the land. It has been divided into 14 daily stages, largely defined by the availability of overnight accommodation: St Bees to Ennerdale Bridge (14 miles); Ennerdale Bridge to Rosthwaite (15 miles); Rosthwaite to Grasmere (10 miles); Grasmere to Patterdale (eight miles); Patterdale to Shap (16 miles); Shap to Kirkby Stephen (20 miles); Kirkby Stephen to Keld (13 miles); Keld to Reeth (11 miles); Reeth to Richmond (11 miles); Richmond to Ingleby Cross (23 miles); Ingleby Cross to Clay Bank Top (12 miles); Clay Bank Top to Blakey (nine miles); Blakey to Grosmont (13 miles); Grosmont to Robin Hood's Bay (16 miles).

The walk is serviced by the innovative Coast to Coast Packhorse (☎ 01768-371680), which is based at Kirkby Stephen (see that section in the Northern England chapter). This is a minibus (daily from April to late September) that runs the length of the walk and carries backpacks (and bodies where appropriate). Backpacks (and bodies) are delivered to a pick-up point at the next stop on the walk. Packs cost £3.50 per stop, or £51 all the way from St Bees to Robin Hood's Bay.

The guidebook to use is *A Coast to Coast Walk* by Alfred Wainwright (Michael Joseph, £9.95). There's also Paul Hannon's *A Coast to Coast Walk* (Hillside Publications, £7.99) which includes maps. An accommodation pamphlet is available – for £2 plus a large stamped, self-addressed envelope – from Mrs Whitehead (☎ 01748-886374), East Stonesdale Farm, Keld, Richmond, North Yorkshire DL11 6LJ.

West Highland Way

This 95-mile hike through the Scottish Highlands runs from Milngavie (pronounced mullguy), seven miles from the centre of Glasgow, north along Loch Lomond to Fort William.

The route passes through a tremendous range of landscape that includes some of the most spectacular scenery in the country. It begins in the Lowlands, but the greater part of this trail is amongst the mountains, lochs and fast-flowing rivers of the Highlands. In the far north the route crosses wild Rannoch Moor and reaches Fort William via Glen Nevis, in the shadow of Britain's highest peak, Ben Nevis.

The path is easy to follow and it uses the old drove roads along which cattle were herded in the past, the old military road (built by troops to help control the Jacobites in the 18th century) and disused railway lines.

Best walked from south to north, the walk can be done in about six or seven days, in the following sections: Milngavie to Drymen (12 miles); Drymen to Rowardennan (14 miles); Rowardennan to Inverarnan (13 miles); Inverarnan to Tyndrum (12 miles); Tyndrum to Kingshouse (18 miles); Kingshouse to Kinlochleven (9 miles); Kinlochleven to Fort William (14 miles).

You need to be properly equipped with good boots, maps, a compass, and food and drink for the northern part of the walk. Midge repellent is also worth bringing.

Accommodation should not be too difficult to find, though between Bridge of Orchy and Kinlochleven it's quite limited. In summer you should book B&Bs in advance. There are some youth hostels on and near the path, as well as bunkhouses. It is also possible to camp in some parts.

The new Harveys map, *West Highland Way* (£5.95), is currently the most accurate map and also contains tourist information. *The West Highland Way* by Robert Aitken (HMSO, £14.95) comes with a 1:50,000 Ordnance Survey route map and is the most comprehensive guide available. *West Highland Way* (Aurum Press, £10.99) by Anthony Burton is cheaper, newly published and also contains OS maps. A free accommodation list is available from TICs and from the path manager (☎ 01389-758216).

Pembrokeshire Coast Path

This 186-mile clifftop trail includes some of the finest beaches in Britain and offers the best coastal scenery in Wales.

Lying entirely within the Pembrokeshire Coast National Park in south-west Wales, the coast path passes through tiny fishing villages, skirts secluded coves and crosses some sparsely populated regions. The only towns of any size on the route are Pembroke, Milford Haven and Fishguard but there are, nevertheless, numerous places to stay that are conveniently located along the path.

As well as being renowned for its superb coastal scenery, the area is of particular interest to birdwatchers – only parts of the Scottish coast attract more varied seabird life. Although there are a number of steep climbs and descents along its route, the path is not hard going if you take it slowly. And there are numerous worthwhile distractions along the way: St David's (the smallest city in Britain, with its fine cathedral), several ruined castles, Iron-Age forts, beaches and nature reserves – not to mention the pubs.

The path is best walked from south to north and you should allow 13 to 15 days. Suggested route divisions are: Amroth to Tenby (seven miles); Tenby to Manorbier (8 miles); Manorbier to Bosherston (13 miles); Bosherston to Angle (15 miles); Angle to Pembroke (11 miles); Pembroke to Milford Haven (10 miles); Milford Haven to Marloes Sands (17 miles); Marloes Sands to Newgale (19 miles); Newgale to Whitesands Bay (18 miles); Whitesands Bay to Trevine (11 miles); Trevine to Fishguard (19 miles); Fishguard to Newport (11 miles); Newport to St Dogmael's (15 miles).

The Pembrokeshire Coast National Park (☎ 01437-764636) publishes an accommodation guide for the walk. *The Pembrokeshire Coast Path* by Brian John (Aurum Press, £9.99), includes Ordnance Survey maps.

Offa's Dyke Path

Offa's Dyke was a grand earthwork project, conceived and executed in the 8th century by the King Offa, to separate his kingdom of Mercia from Wales. The border between England and Wales has been defined roughly by the dyke ever since.

This 168-mile trail runs from Chepstow in

the south through the beautiful Wye Valley and Shropshire Hills to end on the north Wales coast at Prestatyn. Rather than sticking religiously to the dyke, which is overgrown in some places and built over in others, the trail makes many detours along quiet valleys and ridges. The route offers a tremendous range of scenery, possibly the most varied of any long-distance trail. Another path, Glyndwr's Way, leaves Offa's Dyke Path at Knighton, following a 120-mile route west across central Wales to Machynlleth then back to Welshpool.

There are two guidebooks to the walk (*Chepstow to Knighton* and *Knighton to Prestatyn*) by Ernie & Kathy McKay & Mark Richards (Aurum Press, £9.99 each). A guide including accommodation and transport details is available (£1.80 including UK p&p) from the Offa's Dyke Association (☎ 01547-528753), Offa's Dyke Centre, West St, Knighton, Powys LD7 1EN.

Cycling

Travelling by bicycle is an excellent way to explore Britain. Away from the motorways and busy main roads there's a vast network of quiet country lanes leading through peaceful villages. Bring your own bike or hire one when you arrive. Cycle routes have been suggested throughout this book.

INFORMATION

The British Tourist Authority publishes a useful free booklet, *Cycling*, with some suggested routes, lists of cycle holiday companies and other helpful information. Many regional TICs have information on local cycling routes and places where you can hire bikes. They also stock cycling guides and books – look out for the range of route map/guides produced by the Ordnance Survey.

The Cyclists' Touring Club (CTC) (☎ 01483-417217, fax 01483-426994), 69 Meadrow, Godalming, Surrey GU7 3HS, is a membership organisation providing comprehensive information (free of charge to members) about cycling in Britain and overseas. They can provide suggested routes (on and off-road), lists of local cycling contacts and clubs, recommended accommodation, organised cycling holidays, a cycle hire directory, and a mail-order service for Ordnance Survey maps and books for cyclists.

Annual membership fees are currently £12.50 for under 18s (or unemployed), £16.50 for senior citizens (currently 60 for women and 65 for men), and £25 for other adults. Some cycling organisations outside Britain have reciprocal membership arrangements with the CTC.

Country Lanes (☎ 01425-655022), 9 Shaftesbury St, Fordingbridge, Hampshire SP6 1JF, is a small company that runs a range of cycling trips in southern England. These range from bicycle hire and self-guided itineraries for those who prefer to travel independently, to five-day group trips. There are numerous other companies offering cycling trips.

Taking Cycles by Air or Train

Air Most airlines will carry a bike free of charge, so long as the bike and panniers don't exceed the per-passenger weight allowance (usually 20 kg/44 lb). Hefty excess baggage charges may be incurred if you do, and this applies to both internal and international flights. Note that some charter-flight companies do make a charge for the carriage of bikes.

Inform the airline that you will be bringing your bike when you book your ticket. Arrive at the airport in good time to remove panniers and pedals, deflate tyres and turn handlebars around – the minimum dismantling usually required by airlines.

Train Bikes can be taken on most train journeys in Britain. However, the current privatisation of rail services in Britain means that each of the 25 train companies can decide their own policy about bikes on trains.

Generally, bikes can be taken on local services free of charge on a first-come-first-served basis – though some train companies do not carry bikes on certain routes or during peak hours. On most long-distance routes (particularly InterCity services) it is necessary to make a reservation for your bike. Reservations will almost always incur a charge – usually around £3 for a single or day return journey.

To be sure that you can take your bike you should make your reservation (and get your ticket) at least 24 hours before travelling – this is because some trains carry only one or two bikes.

To ensure you have no problems check bike-carriage details for the whole of your planned journey at least 24 hours before you travel. You should also check if there are going to be engineering works on the line because bikes cannot be carried on replacement bus services.

Roads, Lanes & Tracks

Bikes are not allowed on motorways, but you can cycle on all other roads (on the left!) unless the road is marked 'private'. A-roads tend to be busy and are best avoided. B-roads are usually quieter and many are pleasant for cycling.

The best roads for the cyclist are the unclassified roads, or 'lanes' as they are called. Linking small villages together, they are not numbered: you simply follow the signposts from village to village. There is a whole network of lanes throughout lowland Britain, meandering via picturesque villages through quiet countryside. Lanes are clearly shown on Ordnance Survey maps.

In England and Wales, cycles can be ridden on any unmade road (track) which is identified as a public right of way on OS maps. A right to cycle does not usually exist on a footpath, however. In Scotland the rules for off-road riding are different, and it's best to inquire locally about whether cyclists can use a particular track. The surface condition of tracks, however, varies considerably: some are very poor and slow going.

WHERE TO CYCLE
South-Eastern England

The south-east corner of England has more traffic than other parts of the country, but with careful route planning you can find quiet roads and tracks and forget how close you are to the busy city of London. Northwest of London, the Chiltern Hills offer scenic cycling. The area to the south and east of London is characterised by the North and South Downs, two ridges of higher land running east-west, and the Weald in between – undulating, often wooded terrain. The landscape is beautiful in places and offers plenty of opportunities for good cycling. The south coast is heavily populated and the main roads here are busy and best avoided by cyclists.

You should also avoid cycling in London if possible; traffic is heavy and road surfaces can be poor. If you must cycle in the city, contact the London Cycling Campaign (☎ 0171-928 7220) for maps and information.

South-Western England

The counties of Somerset, Dorset and Wiltshire have a varied landscape, with a combination of easy valley routes and steeper climbs in the hill ranges. Many parts of this region are popular with cyclists. The ancient woodland and open heath of the New Forest offer easy cycling.

Cornwall and Devon, with their steep country lanes, can be challenging. In the north, the coastline is rugged and sometimes inaccessible. Small roads drop steeply to pretty fishing villages nestling in the coves along the coast. The bleak, upland landscapes of Dartmoor, Bodmin Moor and Exmoor contrast starkly with the seaside towns on the south coast of Devon. The coast enjoys the best of the British climate but suffers its share of tourist traffic during the summer months.

Southern Midlands

In the Southern Midlands, the Cotswolds area of Gloucestershire and Oxfordshire is particularly attractive. It's a great place to cycle but there's a shortage of budget accommodation here.

Further north, the dense network of motorways and heavily trafficked roads serving the industrial centres means that any extensive tour of the region would require careful planning in order to avoid these busy arteries. There are pockets of quiet roads with pretty villages and some forests, lakes and canals worth exploring – Charnwood Forest, for example, and many parts of Hereford and Worcester, and Northamptonshire. The land is relatively low-lying and the cycling is gentler than in the north of England.

Eastern England

This is an excellent area for a first cycle tour and for those seeking an easy-going cycling holiday. East Anglia is generally low-lying and flat, with small areas of gently undulating country and woodland, particularly in Suffolk. Much of the area is characterised by arable farmland dissected by rivers, lakes (broads), marshes (such as the Fens) and many small and picturesque settlements.

Norfolk and Suffolk have a good network of quiet country roads. There are, however, two things to watch out for. First, breezes off the North Sea can sometimes be strong, especially in the Fens. Second, whilst the area is well served with bridges, roads sometimes run parallel to a river or canal and you may have to travel a little further than expected to find a bridge. It pays to have a good map and to plan your route in advance.

Northern Midlands

The Peak District (Derbyshire) is one of the most popular cycling areas in the country and marks the southern tip of the Pennines. There's challenging terrain, steep hills, rewarding scenery and a fairly good network of quieter roads, plus some excellent cycling/walking tracks along disused railway routes.

The area around Manchester and Liverpool, built-up and crisscrossed with motorways and other busy roads, is far less attractive to cyclists.

Northern England

This region offers some superb cycling, much of it strenuous, especially high up in the Pennines where you're exposed to the elements.

There are some exhilarating rides in the wild North York Moors. Take plenty of warm clothes and food for these exposed areas. To the west, the Yorkshire Dales offer tough cycling over the tops of the moors and gentler riding in the valleys themselves. The scenery is superb, there's plenty of interest and some excellent pubs.

The Lake District of Cumbria is best explored by cyclists outside the months of July and August, when its rather limited network of roads is crammed with tourist traffic. Use the smaller roads where possible and be prepared for some steep, long climbs in this magnificent region of mountains and lakes.

In the far north of England, there are quiet roads and plenty of historical interest in Northumberland. There are some very attractive sections of coastline in this area. Inland, the Cheviot Hills and Kielder Water and Forest offer many rough tracks – great for the off-road rider to explore, but it's easy to get lost. Take good maps and a compass.

Scotland

Cyclists in search of the wild and remote will enjoy north-west Scotland. Its majestic Highlands and mystical islands offer quiet pedalling through breathtaking mountainscapes. There are fewer roads in this part of Scotland and generally less traffic. Roads are well graded, but sometimes very remote, so carry plenty of food with you. Of the isles, Skye now has a bridge to the mainland and suffers the worst of seasonal traffic; good ferries between all the islands offer easy escape routes.

For the less intrepid cyclist, the beautiful forests, lochs, glens and hills in the central and southern areas of Scotland are more easily accessible and have a more intimate charm. Cyclists can seek out the smaller roads and tracks to avoid the traffic.

Beware the Scottish midge, prevalent during summer and early autumn, and especially annoying if you're camping.

Wales

The varied landscape of the country and the warm welcome you get from the people make Wales an excellent place to cycle.

In the north, the rugged peaks of Snowdonia National Park rise to over 3000 feet, providing a dramatic backdrop to any cycling trip. During the summer the main roads can get busy with holiday traffic, so it's best to visit this area early or late in the season. Alternatively, head further east towards the Clwydian and Berwyn hills, where less rugged but more peaceful cycling can be found.

The Cambrian mountains through mid-Wales offer quiet cycling both on and off-road. In south Wales, the scenic Black Mountains and Brecon Beacons National Park are popular cycling areas. Much of Wales is hilly, and some low gears will be appreciated. For a less strenuous tour, the English/Welsh border is an area of gently undulating hills. The Isle of Anglesey in the far north-west and the Pembrokeshire coast in the far south-west are also popular with cyclists seeking to avoid the hills.

SOME SUGGESTED CYCLING ROUTES

The CTC provides useful touring sheets (free to members) for every cycling region in Britain, with accommodation suggestions. They can also help you plan a long-distance cycling trip.

Land's End to John o'Groats

The best known long-distance route on the island runs from the extreme south-west tip, Land's End, to the north-east corner, John o'Groats. Along quiet roads, this is a distance of some 1000 miles, hopefully with the wind behind you. The ride is a classic British favourite, but not only with cyclists. Along the route you'll meet such eccentric characters as bed-pushers and three-legged pub-crawlers, all being sponsored per mile, raising money for charitable causes.

The route is challenging and goes via the scenic western side of England, crossing to the east once in Scotland. Many cyclists do the ride in two to three weeks, following one of the CTC's three recommended routes. The main road route runs via Exeter, Cheddar, Shrewsbury, Carlisle, Dumfries, Fort William and Bonar Bridge. The 14-day youth hostel route follows quiet roads via Exeter, Wells, Leominster, Chester, Slaidburn, Windermere, Dumfries, Glasgow, Loch Lomond, Fort William and Loch Ness. The B&B route also follows quiet roads through North Devon, Cheddar, Ludlow,

Sustrans & the National Cycle Network

Sustrans is a civil-engineering charity whose goal is the creation of a 6500-mile network of cycle paths that will pass through the middle of most major towns and cities in Britain.

When Sustrans announced this objective in 1978 the charity was barely taken seriously but increasingly congested roads have now made the public reconsider the exalted place given to the car in modern Britain. The government's massive road building programme has been cut back and £42 million has been donated to Sustrans by the Millenium Commission to ensure that 2500 miles of routes will be open by the end of the century. The whole network will be complete by 2005.

Half the network is to be on traffic-free paths (including disused railways and canal-side towpaths), the rest of the system along quiet minor roads. Cyclists will share the traffic-free paths with wheelchair users and walkers. Many useful sections are open now – the 16-mile path between Bath and Bristol, for example, is the ideal way to visit these two places. In 1996 Lôn Las Cymru, the Welsh National Cycle Route stretching north-south across the country, was opened. The Scotland National Cycle Route runs 425 miles from Carlisle to Inverness.

Maps are available from Sustrans covering all the routes (free for the shorter paths, £3-4.95 for map-guides for the national routes). For more information contact Sustrans (☎0117-929 0888), 35 King Street, Bristol BS1 4DZ, or visit their web site: http://www.sustrans.org.uk. ■

Slaidburn, Brampton, Peebles, Edinburgh, Crieff, Dunkeld and Inverness.

Furthest East to Furthest West

This is another coast-to-coast challenge through some of the best of Britain's varied scenery. The route starts at Lowestoft Ness in Suffolk and ends at the lighthouse at Ardnamurchan Point, on the west coast of Scotland. It's worth taking two to three weeks for this 700-mile route, although the CTC has details of a 10-day trip with accommodation in youth hostels.

The route crosses the flat fenlands of Norfolk, passing through the Lincolnshire and Yorkshire Wolds into the beautiful Yorkshire Dales. From here northwards it's low gears as the route climbs high into the Pennines, with spectacular views of the dales below. After a few hairpin bends, the road sweeps down to Barnard Castle, then up again over the moors. Once into Northumberland you pass Kielder Water, then ride through the forest and over the border into Scotland.

Passing through Ettrick Forest and the Moorfoot Hills, you descend to the capital, Edinburgh. From here, follow the cycle path over the Forth Bridge and head westwards, passing Lake Menteith. The route goes through the Trossachs beside some of the famous Scottish lochs before heading north into the Grampian range, over breathtaking Rannoch Moor to Glencoe. A short ferry hop across Loch Linnhe and the Ardnamurchan peninsula with its lighthouse is soon in sight. This is an exhilarating ride through some spectacular scenery.

Other Coast-to-Coast Routes

There are many other coast-to-coast variations undertaken by cyclists. You could go from Cumbria to Whitby, staying in youth hostels; from St David's Head (south Wales) to Great Yarmouth (Norfolk); follow the 'Opposite Diagonal' – the opposite route to Land's End-John o'Groats – from Dover (Kent) to Durness and Cape Wrath (northwest Scotland); or ride across Scotland, from Aberdeen to the Isle of Mull and back.

Wye Valley

The River Wye meanders some 130 miles from the Cambrian Mountains in Wales to the Severn estuary. It is usually possible to follow quiet roads near the river. A week to 10 days could easily be spent exploring the area.

The southern part of the Wye Valley is densely wooded and forms the border between the south-east corner of Wales and Gloucestershire in England. Chepstow, situated on the northern reaches of the Severn estuary, is an ideal and accessible starting point. The main road (A466) follows an attractive course alongside the river, but this road can be busy during the tourist season. Climb the steep valley sides onto quieter country roads and enjoy the expansive views out over the Severn estuary. It's undulating terrain, with some steep hills.

A detour east into the Forest of Dean provides opportunities for family cycle rides and day excursions, many of the forest tracks being open to cyclists. Back by the Wye, Monmouth and Ross-on-Wye are pleasant towns worth visiting.

Yorkshire Dales

A week-long cycle tour through this beautiful national park is an exhilarating experience, and Skipton is a convenient starting point. Cycle northwards to Linton (Wharfedale) and Hubbersholme. Climb north-west over Fleatmoss to Hawes; roads are steep but the scenery is superb. Take quiet roads eastwards along Wensleydale to Askrigg and Aysgarth, then north to Reeth.

For the intrepid, a detour over Tan Hill and back to Keld may be attempted. Alternatively, follow Swaledale westwards, then head north-west to Kirkby Stephen. From here, cycle south to Sedbergh and then through beautiful Dentdale. Head south to Horton-in-Ribblesdale, Stainforth and then east, passing Malham Tarn to Malham and back to Skipton.

This route covers about 130 miles but there are plenty of opportunities for scenic detours.

Hebridean Islands

The Hebridean Islands off the west coast of Scotland, linked by a comprehensive ferry system, provide superb cycling opportunities. You need to allow two to three weeks to give yourself time to enjoy the scenery in this enchanting region. Interesting circular routes are possible on most islands. This route comprises some 280 miles of cycling, and any tour will need to be planned around the timings of the ferry crossings; some are summer only.

Ardrossan, near Ayr, is a good starting point since the ferry to the Isle of Arran leaves from here. On Arran, cycle north to Lochranza for another ferry to the Kintyre peninsula. You can cycle north to Lochgilphead and Oban to catch the ferry to Tobermory on the Isle of Mull.

Mull is worth exploring before taking the ferry across to Kilchoan. Cycle eastwards along the Ardnamurchan peninsula to Salen, then north to Mallaig. Ferries leave from here to Armadale on the Isle of Skye. You can then cycle north to Uig, or follow numerous other routes around the island.

From Uig, take a ferry to Tarbert (Isle of Harris) in the Outer Hebrides. These outer isles are wild and remote places with very quiet lanes to explore. Cycle south to Benbecula and onto South Uist where you can catch the ferry back to Oban.

Golf

Britain, and in particular Scotland, is the home of golf. There are, in fact, more courses per capita in Scotland than in any other country in the world. The game has been played here for centuries and there are currently over 1900 courses in Britain, both private and public.

All courses are tested for their level of difficulty, and most are playable all year round. Some of the private clubs only admit members, friends of members, or golfers who have a handicap certificate or a letter of introduction from their club, but the majority welcome visitors.

Note that most clubs give members priority in booking tee-off times; it's always advisable to book in advance. It should be easier to book a tee-off time on a public course but weekends, on all courses, are usually busy. You should also check whether there's a dress code, and whether the course has golf clubs for hire (not all do) if you don't have your own.

INFORMATION

Tourist boards have information leaflets; the BTA has a useful *Golfing Holidays* booklet giving lists of hotels and golfing events. For Scotland, *Golf in Scotland* is a free brochure listing 400 courses and clubs with details of where to stay. Contact the Scottish Tourist Board (☎ 0131-332 2433), 23 Ravelston Terrace, Edinburgh EH4 3EU, for a copy.

The Golf Club of Great Britain (☎ 0181-390 3113) is based at 3 Sage Yard, Douglas Rd, Surbiton, Surrey KT6 7TS.

COSTS

A round of golf on a public course will cost about £6. Private courses are more expensive with green fees ranging from £12 to £20 – and up to £40 on championship courses. However, many clubs offer a daily or weekly ticket. For example, a Golf Ticket in Scotland costs between £40 and £70 for five days (Monday to Friday) depending on the area. The Mid Wales Golf Card costs £60 and allows you to play on different courses in the area for up to seven days.

A set of golf clubs is about £5 (per round) to hire.

Tracing your Ancestors

Many visitors to Britain have ancestors who once lived in this country. Your trip would be a good chance to find out more about them and their lives; you may even discover relatives you never knew about. There is, however, no one central record office – records for England and Wales are kept in

London, and those for Scotland are kept in Edinburgh.

ENGLAND & WALES

The two most important places to find records for England and Wales are St Catherine's House and the Public Record Office.

For records of births, marriages and deaths since 1 July 1837, contact the **Office of Population Censuses & Surveys** (OPCS), General Register Office, St Catherine's House, 10 Kingsway, London WC2B 6JP. The public search room is open from Monday to Friday, 8.30 am to 4.30 pm. It is not possible to telephone St Catherine's House. The OPCS publishes a very useful leaflet called *Tracing Records of Births, Marriages & Deaths*. For this and further details contact the General Register Office (☎ 0151-471 4800), OPCS, PO Box 2, Southport, Merseyside PR8 2JD.

The **Public Record Office** (PRO) has records from 1086 (the Domesday Book) to the present day. It's based at two sites: Ruskin Ave, Kew, Richmond, Surrey TW9 4DU, and Chancery Lane, London WC2A 1LR, but the phone number for both is the same (☎ 0181-876 3444). The PRO's Internet page on the World Wide Web is http://www.open.gov.uk/pro/prohome.htm. The search rooms are open from Monday to Friday, 9.30 am to 5 pm, but are closed for two weeks a year, usually in October, but you should check before you visit. You should also ring the PRO to check which site to go to – many documents and records are in the process of being moved from the Chancery Lane site to Kew. Take your passport or another form of identification if you want to see original records. Remember that documents referring to individuals are closed for 100 years to safeguard personal confidentiality. It is also not possible to see documents or records until the PRO has preserved them, even though they may have been officially released.

The PRO has a guide, *The Current Guide*, to help you find your way round the records, but it's quite a complex task. If you'd like someone to do the search for you (for a fee), the PRO, and the Association of Genealogists & Record Agents (no telephone), 1 Woodside Close, Stanstead Rd, Caterham, Surrey CR3 6AU, can send you a list of professional record agents and researchers. The association can also supply the name of an agent who will search for living relatives.

SCOTLAND

If your ancestors were Scottish you should first go to the **General Register Office** (GRO) (☎ 0131-314 4433), New Register House, 3 West Register St, Edinburgh EH1 3YT. This office holds birth, marriage and death records since 1855, the census records and old parochial registers. Contact the GRO for leaflets giving details of its records and fees. The office is open Monday to Friday, from 9 am to 4.30 pm. Before you go, contact the office to reserve a search-room seat, particularly if you have limited time in Edinburgh.

Next door to this is part of the **Scottish Record Office** (☎ 0131-535 1314), HM General Register House, 2 Princes St, Edinburgh EH1 3YY. There are two search rooms: the historical search room, which is where you should go to research ancestors (no charge), and the legal search room, where you can see records for legal purposes (a fee is payable). Staff will answer simple inquiries, by correspondence, if precise details are given. If you wish more research to be done for you (perhaps before you come), the office will send you a list of professional searchers. All correspondence should be addressed to: The Keeper of the Records of Scotland, Scottish Record Office, and sent to the above address.

BOOKS

If you're serious about ancestry research, it may be worth buying a copy of *Tracing Your Ancestors in the Public Record Office*, by Amanda Bevan and Andrea Duncan (HMSO, £7.95), or *Tracing Your Scottish Ancestors* by Cecil Sinclair (HMSO, £6.95).

Surfing & Swimming

Most overseas visitors do not think of Britain as a place to go for a beach holiday – and there are good reasons for this. The best ones are the climate and the water temperature. You definitely have to be hardy, or equipped with a wetsuit, to do anything more than take a quick dip. On the other side of the equation, Britain has some truly magnificent coastline and some wonderful sandy beaches. And the British have been taking holidays by the seaside since the 18th century, so there is a fascinating, sometimes bizarre, tradition to explore.

Visiting a British seaside resort should be high on the list of priorities for anyone wishing to gain an insight into British society. The resorts vary from staid retirement enclaves like Eastbourne, to vibrant cultural centres like Brighton and cheerful family resorts like Hastings. And then there's Blackpool, which pretty much defies categorisation. One thing remains common to them all, however, and that is that the fun happens on shore and it's done fully clothed!

Summer water temperatures are roughly equivalent to winter temperatures in southern Australia (around 55° F). Winter temperatures are about 10° F colder, giving a temperature range not dissimilar to that in northern California. So getting in the water, at least in summer, is definitely feasible if you have a wetsuit. A 3 mm full suit (steamer) plus boots will be sufficient in summer, while winter requires a 5 mm suit, plus boots, hood and gloves.

The best beaches, with the best chance of sun and surf and the genuine possibility of luring you into the water, are in Cornwall and Devon. Newquay, on the west Cornish coast five or six hours by road from London, is the capital of a burgeoning British surf scene, and it has a plethora of surf shops and all the appropriate paraphernalia and trappings, from Kombis to bleached hair. The boards and wetsuits sold are good quality and competitively priced in international terms.

Sadly, many British beaches, including those in Cornwall, suffer from pollution, often thanks to local towns draining their storm water and sewage offshore. It's worth checking with a local before taking the plunge.

For most visiting surfers, the most unusual aspect of surfing in Britain is the impact of the tides. The tidal range is huge, which means there are often a completely different set of breaks at low and high tides. As is usually the case, the waves tend to be biggest and best on an incoming tide. Sadly, the waves in spring, autumn and winter tend to be bigger and more consistent than in summer. The conditions in summer are pretty unreliable.

The entire west coast of Cornwall and Devon is exposed to the Atlantic and there is a string of surf spots from Land's End to Ilfracombe. The shallow continental shelf, however, means the waves rarely get over five feet. Spring and autumn are the best times. There are a number of good breaks around Newquay, including Fistral, England's premier surfing beach and home to the main surfing contests. There are similar conditions on the Gower Peninsula and the south-west corner of Wales from Tenby to Fishguard.

Northern Scotland has the island's biggest and best surf, and although the outside temperatures are considerably lower than in the south, the water temperatures are only marginally lower. The entire coast has surf but it's the north, particularly around Thurso, that has outstanding world-class possibilities. The west coast is mainly sheltered by islands, and although there are no doubt untapped possibilities on the islands, they are difficult and expensive to get to. Islay is occasionally surfed. The east coast is easily accessible, but the swells are unreliable and short-lived.

There's quite a large surfing community in Thurso, thanks to several famous breaks. There are two breaks, one in front of the harbour wall with lefts and rights, known as Reef, and one at Beach. Thurso East (Castle Reef) is the big one: a huge right that works up to 15 feet.

Fishing

Angling, as a sport and pastime, was obviously well established in England by medieval times. A *Treatyse of Fysshnge With an Angle*, published in 1496, described fishing flies which are still in use today. The 17th century saw great improvements in equipment and also brought Izaak Walton's classic book.

Fishing is divided into several distinct categories, topped by dry-fly fishing which is considered, by its proponents, to be the highest form of the sport. An artificial lure, made to imitate a small insect, must be gently dropped on the surface in order to deceive and catch the fish. Fly fishing is used for that most cautious of game fish, the trout. Fish are described as coarse fish or game fish, the latter because they vigorously struggle against capture. Curiously, fishing is an activity with widely differing vocabularies between English and American usage.

Fishing is enormously popular in Britain but also highly regulated. Many prime stretches of river are privately owned, and fishing there can be amazingly expensive. The Environment Agency (formerly the National Rivers Authority – NRA) administers licences for rod fishing in England and Wales. A one-year licence (valid from 1 April to 31 March) for coarse fishing costs £15 (£7.50 for those over 65 or for children aged 12 to 16). An eight-day licence costs £4.50 and a one-day licence £1.50. Salmon and sea trout licences cost £55/£27.50 for one year (1 April to 31 March), £15 for an eight-day licence and £5 for a one-day licence.

Rod licences are available from every post office in England and Wales, bankside agents and Environment Agency Regional Offices. Contact the Environment Agency (☎ 01454-624400), Rivers House, Waterside Drive, Aztec West, Almondsbury, Bristol BS12 4UD for details. Tackle shops are also good places to make fishing inquiries. Before fishing anywhere in England and Wales you must have the correct licence and the permis-

Izaak Walton

Angling has a patron saint in the person of Izaak Walton (1593-1683), author of *The Compleat Angler*. Walton was modestly educated but widely read and scholarly and became the friend of many eminent men, particularly among the clergy. His treatise on the pleasures of fishing has gone through hundreds of editions and its title has become a household phrase. Walton commenced his working life as an ironmonger but made his name as a writer, first with biographies, including one of John Donne, the poet and preacher. He spent his final years at Winchester, with his friend the Bishop of Winchester, and the Cathedral has a Walton window. ■

sion of the owner or tenants of the fishing rights.

There is a statutory close season (15 March to 15 June) when coarse fishing is banned on all rivers and streams – different rules apply on canals, lakes, ponds and reservoirs. The actual dates for close seasons vary according to the region and need to be checked in advance – the Environment Agency will be able to advise.

The fishing situation in Scotland, where there is a dense thicket of regulations on salmon fishing, is even more complicated. Fishing in Scotland is also amazingly expensive. An article in *The Economist* on fishing in Scotland revealed that purchasing a 'timeshare' right to fish a river in Scotland costs about £6000 per year per fish caught by the average angler!

Horse Riding & Pony Trekking

Seeing the country from the saddle is highly recommended, even if you're not an experienced rider. There are riding schools catering to all levels of proficiency, many of them in national park areas.

Pony trekking is a popular holiday activity: a half-day should cost around £10, and hard hats are included. Many pony trekkers are novice riders so most rides are at walking speed with the occasional trot. If you're an experienced rider there are numerous riding schools with horses to rent – TICs have details.

We've listed some riding schools and pony trekking centres in the Activities section of national park chapters where appropriate. For more information contact the British Horse Society (☎ 01203-414288), British Equestrian Centre, Stoneleigh Park, Kenilworth, Warwickshire CV8 2LR. They publish *Where to Ride* (£5.99) which lists places throughout the UK. They can also send you lists specific to a particular area (eg the Cotswolds).

Canal & Waterway Travel

Britain's surprisingly extensive network of canals and waterways spread rapidly across the country at the same time as the Industrial Revolution transformed the nation. As a method of transporting freight (passengers were always secondary), they were a short-lived wonder, trimmed back by railways and killed off by modern roads. By WWII, much of the waterway system was in terminal decline; the once-bustling canals had become long, stagnant channels of no economic significance. Today, however, the canals are booming once again, but now as part of the leisure industry.

Exploring Britain by canal can be immensely rewarding. Narrowboats (barges carried coal, longboats carried Vikings) can be rented from numerous operators around Britain and for a family or a group they can provide surprisingly economical transport and accommodation. They also allow you to explore a hidden side of Britain. Travelling the waterways, it's easy to forget that the Britain of motorways and ring roads even exists. Canals lead you to a Britain of idyllic villages, pretty countryside and convenient and colourful waterside pubs. More surprisingly, they can show you a very different side of some otherwise unremarkable cities. Birmingham from its canals is quite different to Birmingham from the ring road.

The canal system is also a wonderful example of the power and vision of the Industrial Revolution's great engineers. No obstacle stood in the way of these visionaries, who threw flights of locks up steep hillsides or flung amazing aqueducts across wide valleys. They built to last as well – the lock equipment which you 'work' as you travel along the canals is often well over a century old.

The canals are not restricted to narrowboat users. The canal towpaths have become popular routes for walkers and cyclists who can enjoy the same hidden perspective as people actually out on the waterways. There are over 3000 miles of navigable canals and rivers in Britain, so there is plenty to explore. Contact TICs for more information.

HISTORY
As the Industrial Revolution swept across Britain, a growing need developed for means of transporting goods ranging from coal and iron to fine Wedgwood pottery. The first serious canals appeared in the 1760s, led by James Brindley's Bridgewater Canal, used for conveying coal to the burgeoning factories in Manchester. The development of canal locks, enabling the canal boats to go up and down hills, facilitated the spread of canals. Thomas Telford pioneered more modern canals, which took the shortest route from A to B, even when it involved multiple locks, tunnels, embankments and other complex engineering work. The Birmingham & Liverpool Junction was an example of this more advanced type of canal.

Some of the most interesting examples of canal engineering include the nearly two-mile-long Blisworth Tunnel near Stoke Bruerne. For particularly long inclines, locks were sometimes arranged in flights, where the top gate of one lock was also the bottom gate of the next. Ingenious attempts were made to design alternatives to canal locks. The inclined plane at Foxton, near Market Harborough, Leicestershire, dating from 1900, moved boats 75 vertical feet, the equivalent of a flight of 10 locks. The 1875 Anderton Lift near Northwich, Cheshire, simply floated the boats into a tank which was then lifted 50 feet. When a valley or river intervened, some canal engineers carried their canals right across in aqueducts, the most famous of which is the 1007-foot-long Pontcysyllte Aqueduct in Wales.

For an interesting offshoot of the canals, visit the High Peak Trail in the Peak District. This early railway line has now been recycled to become a walking and bicycle track, but it was originally constructed by canal engineers still thinking in canal terms. Instead of engineering the long gentle inclines so they would be suitable for railway engines, they built the line with short steep rises up which the trains would have to be hauled, a dry-land equivalent of a canal's lock system.

Early canal boats were pulled by horses, walking on the towpaths alongside the canals, but by the mid-1800s steam power was starting to supersede horsepower. Later, diesel power replaced steam. Modern narrowboats for cruising still follow the traditional style but come equipped with all mod-cons, from refrigerators to televisions.

Even if you don't get out on the canals, it's fascinating to visit one of the canal museums around Britain. They can be found at Stoke Bruerne near Northampton, at Devizes in Wiltshire, at Ellesmere Port near Chester and right in the centres of Nottingham and Gloucester.

THE WATERWAYS

Britain's boating waterways consist of both natural rivers and lakes and artificial canals. In all there are over 3000 miles of navigable waterways; about half are canals and half of those are 'narrow' canals, where the locks are just seven feet wide.

A narrowboat trip can vary from lazy relaxation to surprisingly hard work. When you're chugging down a wide river with only the occasional lock to be worked, it's the easiest means of transport imaginable. On the other hand, on a steep section of canal where one lock is followed immediately by another, narrowboat travel can be a combination of aerobics (keys to be wound, paddles to be raised and lowered), weight lifting (heavy lock gates to be pushed open and closed) and jogging (the lock crew runs on ahead to prepare the lock before the boat gets there). Canal travel is great if you have children and they're often exhausted by the end of the day!

Locks

A lock enables boats to go up or down a hill. It's a bathtub-shaped chamber with a single door at the top end and a double door at the bottom. *Sluices* in the doors let water flow into or out of the lock when the *paddles* over the sluices are opened. A winding handle or *key* is used to open or close the paddles and this is one of the essential pieces of equipment for narrowboat travel. The process of going through a lock is known as *working* the lock.

On narrow canals the locks are usually wide enough and long enough for just one boat at a time. On rivers or wider canals they may be large enough for two or more boats. In a wider lock it's essential to keep your boat roped to the side to prevent it yawing around as the water flows in or out of the lock. But don't tie it up tightly – the ropes will need to be shortened or lengthened as the water level changes.

Narrowboats

There are over 200 firms renting narrowboats in Britain. Typically, a narrowboat will be 40 to 70 feet in length and no more than seven feet wide. Narrowboats are usually surprisingly comfortable and well equipped with bunks and double beds, kitchen and dining areas, a fridge, cooker, flush toilet, shower and other mod-cons. Usually they are rented out by the week, although shorter periods are sometimes available.

As narrowboats usually come so well equipped for everyday living, food supplies are all you need to worry about and there are plenty of shopping opportunities along the waterways. Alternatively, careful planning can see you moored at a riverside pub or restaurant for most meals.

Boats can accommodate from two or three people up to 10 or 12. Costs vary with the size of boat, the standard of equipment and the time of year. At the height of the summer season, a boat for four would vary from around £500 to £1000 per week. Larger boats work out cheaper per person; a boat for eight might cost £1000 per week. This means canal travel can cost not much over £100 per person for a week's transport and accommodation, a terrific travel bargain.

Although there are independent boat operators scattered all over the country, there are also centralised booking agencies who handle bookings for many of the individual companies. One of the biggest is Hoseasons Holidays (☎ 01502-501010), Sunway House, Raglan Rd, Lowestoft, Suffolk NR32 3LW.

If you only want a brief introduction to the canal system, there are over 50 firms operating day trips from various centres. A number of operators offer hotel boat trips where you simply come along for the ride.

Travelling the Waterways

No particular expertise or training is needed, nor is a licence required to operate a narrowboat. You're normally given a quick once over of the boat and an explanation of how things work, a brief foray out onto the river or canal and then you're on your way. Proceed with caution at first, although you'll soon find yourself working the locks like a veteran. There are a variety of rules and suggestions that will make narrowboat travel easier for you and other waterway users:

Travel at an appropriate speed
    Narrowboats are not made for high-speed travel and if your speed is too fast for the waterway your wake will break along the bank and cause damage. Slow down when passing moored boats.
Keep your narrowboat neat and shipshape
    If you need to quickly tie up by the bank, hammer in a mooring peg, or fend off another boat with a pole, it will be much easier if ropes are neatly

coiled, hammer and pegs are kept in the right place and equipment is all to hand.
Don't drop the key into the water!
    Without the key you cannot work the paddles to open and close the locks. A surprising number of keys get dropped into canals so ensure you always have a spare. Fortunately, if you do lose a key a replacement can usually be purchased quite cheaply at a boatyard. Fishing keys out of locks is a popular children's moneyraiser, just like fishing golf balls out of water traps.
Get a good guidebook for the waterway you're exploring
    A good guide will point out lunchtime pubs, overnight mooring spots and interesting attractions along the way.
Conserve water
    Canals are artificial creations and ensuring a steady supply of water at the top of the system is not always straightforward. Every time you use a lock, thousands of gallons flow downhill. You can help to conserve the water by sharing locks and waiting for oncoming boats if the lock is already *set* in their direction.

More information on the canal system is available from the Inland Waterways Association (☎ 0171-586 2510), 114 Regent's Park Rd, London NW1 8UQ. They publish the *The Inland Waterways Guide* (£2.75), a general guide to holiday hire with route descriptions. Approximately two-thirds of the waterways in Britain are operated by the British Waterways Board (☎ 01923-226422), Willow Grange, Church Rd, Watford, Hertfordshire WD1 3QA. The British Waterways Board publishes *The Waterways Code for Boaters*, a free handy booklet packed with useful information and advice. They also publish a complete list of hire-boat and hotel-boat companies. Nicholsons/OS *Guide to the Waterways* is a useful guide that comes in three sections: South, Central and North (for England and Wales only) – each one is £9.99.

Skiing

No one comes to Britain to ski. Indeed, some may be surprised to learn that there are ski resorts here. There are actually five main ski centres, all in Scotland, but the slopes are far less extensive and the weather considerably less reliable than anything you'll find in the Alps. On a sunny day, however, and with good snow, it can be very pleasant.

Scotland offers both alpine (downhill) and nordic (cross-country) skiing as well as other snow-related sports. The high season is from January to April, but it's sometimes possible to ski from as early as November to as late as May. Package holidays are available but it's very easy to make your own arrangements, with all kinds of accommodation on offer in and around the ski centres.

INFORMATION

Contact the Scottish Tourist Board (☎ 0131-332 2433) for its detailed *Ski Scotland* brochure and accommodation list. Alternatively, you can phone the skiing information centre for each area: Nevis Range (☎ 01397-705825); Glencoe (☎ 01855-851226); Glenshee (☎ 013397-41320); The Lecht (☎ 01975-651440); and Cairngorm (☎ 01479-861261 ext 201). There's an answerphone service for calls outside business hours.

The Ski Hotline weather-report service can be useful. Phone ☎ 0891-654 followed by 654 (for all centres); 660 (for Nevis Range); 658 (for Glencoe); 656 (for Glenshee); 657 (for The Lecht); and 655 (for Cairngorm).

COSTS

It's easy to hire ski equipment and clothes when you arrive but you should book lessons, if you want them, in advance. The prices vary in each centre but on average expect to pay £9 to £11 per day for skis, sticks and boot hire; and £6 to £10 per day for ski clothes.

Lift passes cost £11 to £17 per day, or £41 to £68 for a five-day pass (photo required). In a group, ski lessons cost £14 to £20 for a day, and £45 to £75 for five days; private lessons are £18 to £30 per hour.

Packages including ski-hire, tuition and pass cost from about £75 for three days (midweek). Two, four or five day, and weekend packages are also available.

All charges are reduced for juniors – 18 and under (Nevis Range); under 16 (Glencoe, Glenshee, The Lecht); and under 18 (Cairngorm).

RESORTS

Glenshee (3019 feet) and **Cairngorm** (3600 feet) are the biggest ski centres. Glenshee offers the largest network of lifts and selection of runs in Scotland. It also has snow machines for periods when the real thing doesn't appear. Cairngorm has almost 30 runs spread over an extensive area. Aviemore is the main town and there's a ski bus service from here and from the surrounding villages to the slopes.

Glencoe (3636 feet) is the oldest of the resorts and it is now open seven days a week. The **Nevis Range** (4006 feet) offers the highest ski runs, the only gondola in Scotland to take you to the foot of the main skiing area, and a dry (plastic) ski slope. **The Lecht** (2600 feet) is the most remote centre. However, it's good for beginners and families, as well as for nordic skiers.

Access to the centres is probably easiest by car – there are plenty of car parks. Slopes are graded in the usual way, from green (easy) through blue and red to black (very difficult); and each centre has a ski patrol. You should ensure that your travel insurance covers you for winter sports.

All the ski resorts have facilities for snowboarding. The Lecht is best for beginners and the other four resorts are best for intermediates. They are all OK for advanced snowboarders.

Steam Railways

The invention of the steam engine and the subsequent rapid spread of the railway to almost every corner of Britain transformed life in the 19th century. In 1963 the Beeching Report led to the closure of many rural lines and stations, and in 1968 British Rail stopped using steam trains. For many people these two events brought the first century of rail travel in

Britain to a sad end. It wasn't long, however, before rail enthusiasts reopened some of the lines and stations and restored many of the steam locomotives and rolling stock used in the proverbial 'golden age of rail'.

There are now nearly 500 private railways in Britain, many of them narrow gauge, using steam or diesel locomotives from all over the world. The main lines are detailed

in the appropriate sections of this book. A useful guide to private steam railways is *Railways Restored* (Ian Allan, £9.99). The guide is published annually and lists the major preserved railways, museums and preservation centres in the British Isles. It also gives details of opening times and includes a locomotive stocklist for most centres.

Getting There & Away

London is one of the most important air transport hubs in the world, and in these days of severe competition between the airlines there are plenty of opportunities to find cheap flights.

Forget about shipping, unless by 'shipping' you mean the many ferry services from Europe. Only a handful of ships still carry passengers across the Atlantic; they don't sail often and are very expensive, even compared with full-fare air tickets.

Some travellers arrive or leave through Europe, and some head on to Africa, the Middle East and Asia, and what used to be the Soviet Union. The trans-Siberian and Mongolian express trains could well begin to carry more people to and from Europe as Russia opens up to tourism.

Whichever way you're travelling, make sure you take out travel insurance. This not only covers you for medical expenses and luggage theft or loss, but also for cancellation of or delays in your travel arrangements. Ticket loss is also covered, but make sure you have a separate record of all the details – or better still, a photocopy of the ticket. Buy insurance as early as possible. If you buy it the week before you fly, you may find, for instance, that you're not covered for delays to your flight caused by strikes or other industrial action that may have been in progress before you took out the insurance.

Paying for your ticket with a credit card often provides limited travel accident insurance, and you may be able to reclaim the payment if the operator doesn't deliver. In the UK, credit card providers are required by law to reimburse consumers if a company goes into liquidation and the amount in contention is more than £100. Ask your credit card company what it's prepared to cover.

For travel to/from Europe, buses (as always) are the cheapest and most exhausting method of transport, although discount rail tickets are competitive, and budget flights (especially stand-by and last-minute offers) can be very good value. Bear in mind a small saving on the fare may not adequately compensate you for an agonising two days on a bus that leaves you completely exhausted for another two days. And when making an assessment, don't forget the hidden expenses: getting to and from airports, departure taxes, and food and drink consumed en route.

Until the opening of the Channel Tunnel, most people going to/from Europe bought combined rail/ferry or coach/ferry tickets between London and European capitals like Paris, Brussels and Amsterdam. New rail and bus options via the Tunnel should be competitive. The ferry companies and airlines are optimistic they will be able to compete, particularly on the basis of price, if not on time. The increased competition, however, could mean that prices drop.

See the Land section for information on combined tickets and the Tunnel. Of course, it is also possible to get to and from the ferry ports under your own steam and just pay for the ferry itself.

AIR

There are international air links with London, Manchester, Newcastle, Edinburgh and Glasgow, but most cheap flights wind up in one of the four London airports: Heathrow is the largest, followed by Gatwick, Stansted and Luton.

London is Europe's major centre for discounted long-haul airfares. There are countless travel agents, some of dubious reliability; the good ones include Trailfinders and all the main 'student' travel services. They understand what a tight budget is, they are competitive and reliable, and you don't have to be a student to use their services. See the Information section in the London chapter for details.

The listings magazine *Time Out*, the Sunday papers, and the *Evening Standard* carry ads for cheap fares. Also look out for

TNT Magazine (recommended) and *Southern Cross* – you can often pick them up free outside the main train and tube stations.

Make sure the agent you use is a member of some sort of traveller-protection scheme, such as that offered by ABTA (Association of British Travel Agents). If you have paid an ABTA-registered agent for your flight and they go out of business, ABTA will guarantee a refund or an alternative. Unregistered bucket shops are riskier but sometimes cheaper.

Linehaul Express (☎ 0181-759 5969) offers very cheap flights in exchange for carrying documents. The Globetrotters Club (BCM Roving, London WC1N 3XX) publishes a newsletter called *Globe* which covers obscure destinations and can help in finding travelling companions.

Buying Tickets

The plane ticket may well be the single most expensive item in your budget, and buying it can be an intimidating business. There will be a multitude of travel agents hoping to separate you from your money, and it's always worth researching the current state of the market. Start early: some of the cheapest tickets have to be bought months in advance, and some popular flights sell out early.

Cheap tickets are available in two distinct categories: official and unofficial. Official ones are advance-purchase tickets, budget fares, Apex, super-Apex, or whatever other brand name the airlines care to use.

Unofficial tickets are discounted tickets that the airlines release through selected travel agents. Airlines can supply information on routes and timetables, and their low-season, student and senior citizens' fares can be competitive, but they do not sell discounted tickets. Bear in mind that normal, full-fare airline tickets sometimes include one or more side trips to Europe free of charge, and/or fly-drive packages, which can make them good value.

Return tickets usually work out cheaper than two one-ways – often *much* cheaper. In some cases, a return ticket can even be cheaper than a one-way. Round-the-World (RTW) tickets can also be great bargains, sometimes cheaper than an ordinary return ticket. RTW prices start at about UK£900, A$1800 or US$1300 depending on the season.

Official RTW tickets are usually put together by two airlines, and permit you to fly anywhere on their route systems so long as you don't backtrack. There may be restrictions on how many stops you are permitted, and on the length of time the ticket will remain valid. Travel agents put together unofficial RTW tickets by combining a number of discounted tickets.

Discounted tickets are usually available at prices as low as or lower than the official Apex or budget tickets. When you phone around, find out the fare, the route, the duration of the journey, the stopovers allowed and any restrictions on the ticket (see the Air Travel Glossary at the end of this chapter), and ask about cancellation penalties.

You are likely to discover that the cheapest flights are 'fully booked, but we have another one that costs a bit more'. Or the flight is on an airline notorious for its poor safety standards and liable to leave you confined in the world's least favourite airport for 14 hours in mid-journey. Or the agent claims to have the last two seats available, which he or she will hold for you for a maximum of two hours. Don't panic – keep ringing around.

If you are travelling from the USA or South-East Asia, or leaving Britain, you will probably find that the cheapest flights are advertised by small and obscure agencies. Many such firms are honest and solvent, but there are a few rogues who will take your money and disappear. If you feel suspicious about a firm, leave a deposit (no more than 20%) and pay the balance when you get the ticket. You could phone the airline direct to check you actually have a booking before you pick up the ticket. If the travel agent insists on cash in advance, go somewhere else or be prepared to take a very big risk.

You may decide to pay more than the rock-bottom fare by opting for the safety of a better known travel agent. Firms such as STA Travel, which has offices worldwide, Council Travel in the USA, Travel CUTS in

Air Travel Glossary

Apex Apex, or 'advance purchase excursion' is a discounted ticket which must be paid for in advance. There are penalties if you wish to change it.

Baggage Allowance This will be written on your ticket: usually one 20 kg item to go in the hold, plus one item of hand luggage.

Bucket Shop An unbonded travel agency specialising in discounted airline tickets.

Bumped Just because you have a confirmed seat doesn't mean you're going to get on the plane – see Overbooking.

Cancellation Penalties If you have to cancel or change an Apex ticket there are often heavy penalties involved; insurance can sometimes be taken out against these penalties. Some airlines impose penalties on regular tickets as well, particularly against 'no show' passengers.

Check In Airlines ask you to check in a certain time ahead of the flight departure (usually two hours on international flights from Britain). If you fail to check in on time and the flight is overbooked the airline can cancel your booking and give your seat to somebody else.

Confirmation Having a ticket written out with the flight and date you want doesn't mean you have a seat until the agent has checked with the airline that your status is 'OK' or confirmed. Meanwhile you could just be 'on request'.

Discounted Tickets There are two types of discounted fares – officially discounted (see Promotional Fares) and unofficially discounted. The lowest prices often impose drawbacks like flying with unpopular airlines, inconvenient schedules, or unpleasant routes and connections. A discounted ticket can save you other things than money – you may be able to pay Apex prices without the associated Apex advance booking and other requirements. Discounted tickets only exist where there is fierce competition.

Full Fares Airlines traditionally offer first class (coded F), business class (coded J) and economy class (coded Y) tickets. These days there are so many promotional and discounted fares available from the regular economy class that few passengers pay full economy fare.

Lost Tickets If you lose your airline ticket an airline will usually treat it like a travellers' cheque and, after inquiries, issue you with another one. Legally, however, an airline is entitled to treat it like cash and if you lose it then it's gone forever. Take good care of your tickets.

No Shows No shows are passengers who fail to show up for their flight, sometimes due to unexpected delays or disasters, sometimes due to simply forgetting, sometimes because they made more than one booking and didn't bother to cancel the one they didn't want. Full fare passengers who fail to turn up are sometimes entitled to travel on a later flight. The rest of us are penalised (see Cancellation Penalties).

On Request An unconfirmed booking for a flight; see Confirmation.

Open Jaws A return ticket where you fly out to one place but return from another. If available this can save you backtracking to your arrival point.

Canada and Trailfinders in London offer good prices to most destinations, and are competitive and reliable.

Use the fares quoted in this book as a guide only. They are likely to have changed by the time you read this.

Travellers with Special Needs

If you have special needs of any sort – you've broken a leg, you require a special diet, you're taking the baby, or whatever – let the airline people know as soon as possible so that they can make arrangements. Remind them when you reconfirm your booking and again when you check in at the airport.

Children aged under two travel for 10% of the standard fare (or free on some airlines) if they don't occupy a seat, but they don't get a baggage allowance either. 'Skycots', baby food and diapers should be provided if requested in advance. Children aged between two and 12 usually get a seat for half to two-thirds of the full fare, and do get a baggage allowance.

Excess Baggage

Many people, but especially those who spend time working, accumulate considerably more baggage than the 20 kg allowed by airlines (note that the routes to/from, or

Overbooking Airlines hate to fly empty seats and since every flight has some passengers who fail to show up (see No Shows) airlines often book more passengers than they have seats. Usually the excess passengers balance those who fail to show up but occasionally somebody gets bumped. If this happens guess who it is most likely to be? The passengers who check in late.

Promotional Fares Officially discounted fares like Apex fares which are available from travel agents or direct from the airline.

Reconfirmation At least 72 hours prior to departure time of an onward or return flight you must contact the airline and 'reconfirm' that you intend to be on the flight. If you don't do this the airline can delete your name from the passenger list and you could lose your seat. You don't have to reconfirm the first flight on your itinerary or if your stopover is less than 72 hours. It doesn't hurt to reconfirm more than once.

Restrictions Discounted tickets often have various restrictions on them – advance purchase is the most usual one (see Apex). Others are restrictions on the minimum and maximum period you must be away, such as a minimum of 14 days or a maximum of one year. See Cancellation Penalties.

Standby A discounted ticket where you only fly if there is a seat free at the last moment. Standby fares are usually only available on domestic routes.

Tickets Out An entry requirement for many countries is that you have an onward or return ticket, in other words, a ticket out of the country. If you're not sure what you intend to do next, the easiest solution is to buy the cheapest onward ticket to a neighbouring country or a ticket from a reliable airline which can later be refunded if you do not use it.

Transferred Tickets Airline tickets cannot be transferred from one person to another. Travellers sometimes try to sell the return half of their ticket, but officials can ask you to prove that you are the person named on the ticket. This is unlikely to happen on domestic flights; on an international flight tickets may be compared with passports.

Travel Agencies Travel agencies vary widely and you should ensure you use one that suits your needs. Some simply handle tours while full-service agencies handle everything from tours and tickets to car rental and hotel bookings. A good one will do all these things and can save you a lot of money but if all you want is a ticket at the lowest possible price, then you really need an agency specialising in discounted tickets. A discounted ticket agency, however, may not be useful for other things, like hotel bookings.

Travel Periods Some officially discounted fares, Apex fares in particular, vary with the time of year. There is often a low (off-peak) season and a high (peak) season. Sometimes there's an intermediate or shoulder season as well. At peak times, when everyone wants to fly, not only will the officially discounted fares be higher but so will unofficially discounted fares or there may simply be no discounted tickets available. Usually the fare depends on your outward flight – if you depart in the high season and return in the low season, you pay the high-season fare. ■

---

through, the USA often have much more generous allowances than those to the east). The most economic solution is to contact one of the many shipping companies that advertise in *TNT Magazine* or *Traveller Magazine* and arrange to have the surplus either shipped or airfreighted home. This should not be a last-minute decision since the companies will often need a couple of days notice to arrange, first, the delivery of cartons or tea chests and, second, a pick-up time.

It is also worth giving yourself time to phone around for quotes. Be immediately suspicious of a company that offers rates that are substantially cheaper than the average.

Check that the company you choose is either a bonded member of an overseas division of the British Association of Removers, or the Association of International Removers. The shipping business does not have standard safeguards for its customers and in recent years a number of companies have collapsed or disappeared. This can mean losing possessions entirely, having bags stuck in Britain, or, if you're lucky, just paying twice.

Shipping is considerably slower and cheaper than airfreight and delivery dates are approximate at best. Most companies will quote eight to 12 weeks for shipping to Australasia, but the reality can be 16 to 20 weeks.

Airfreight generally takes from one to two weeks. For shipping, the charges are based on volume; for airfreight, both weight and volume.

There are generally two other alternatives: door to door, or door to port/airport. Most companies deliver boxes and packing materials and pick up free in London, but you can elect whether you pick up goods from the port or airport at the goods' destination. The additional cost of having a tea chest delivered door to door can add £50 to the charge (providing you live less than 30 miles from the port – more otherwise), but in most cases this is money well spent. It's easy to waste at least a day battling with bureaucracy and there are substantial fees you cannot avoid (port and unloading charges, plus customs charges).

Your goods cannot be released until they are cleared by customs. Generally, import duty will not be levied if the goods have been privately used for a reasonable period of time, but the wise will check regulations with their embassy or high commission in advance. If your goods are subject to import duty, you should make sure you're home before they are so you can provide the appropriate documentation.

If you will arrive after your goods, make sure a friend or relative can answer customs inquiries on your behalf. They'll need a photocopy of your passport, the date you left and plan to return, a list of contents and a letter authorising them to obtain the goods. In New Zealand, if a friend or relative clears the goods, import duty will automatically be levied, although you will be able to claim a refund when you get home.

If you plan to pick your goods up from the port or airport yourself, bear in mind that once the goods arrive you generally have only a couple of days grace before hefty storage charges are levied. Fortunately, most companies will store baggage in London (usually for a nominal charge) and ship it on a nominated date.

Insurance is recommended. Check (and that means reading the small print) that it covers loss, theft and breakage of individual items, not just the entire package, that claims can be settled at your destination and that the goods are insured for full replacement value.

The USA

The North Atlantic is the world's busiest long-haul air corridor and the flight options are bewildering. The *New York Times*, the *LA Times*, the *Chicago Tribune*, the *San Francisco Chronicle* and the *San Francisco Examiner* all produce weekly travel sections in which you'll find any number of travel agents' ads. Council Travel and STA Travel have offices in major cities nationwide. You should be able to fly New York-London return for around US$400.

Airhitch (☎ 212-864 2000) is worth contacting for one-way tickets and can get you to London (one way) for around US$330/450 from the east coast/west coast of the USA.

Another option is a courier flight, where you accompany a parcel or freight to be picked up at the other end. A New York-London return can be had for around US$360 or less. You can also fly one way. The drawbacks are that your stay in Europe may be limited to one or two weeks, your luggage is usually restricted to hand luggage (the parcel or freight you carry comes out of your luggage allowance), and you may have to be a resident and apply for an interview before they'll take you on (dress conservatively). Find out more about courier flights from As You Like It Travel (☎ 212-779 1771), 18 East 41 St, NY 10017.

The *Travel Unlimited* newsletter, PO Box 1058, Allston, MA 02134, publishes monthly details of the cheapest airfares and courier possibilities for destinations all over the world from the USA and other countries, including the UK. It's a treasure trove of information. A year's subscription is US$25 (US$35 abroad).

Canada

Travel CUTS has offices in all major cities. Scan the budget travel agents' ads in the *Toronto Globe & Mail*, the *Toronto Star* and the *Vancouver Province*.

See the previous USA section for general

information on courier flights. For courier flights originating in Canada, contact FB On Board Courier Services (☎ 905-612 8095) in Toronto. A courier return flight to London or Paris will set you back between C$375 and C$450 from Toronto or Montreal, around C$475 from Vancouver.

Australia

STA Travel and Flight Centres International are major dealers in cheap airfares. Check the travel agents' ads and ring around.

The Saturday travel sections of the *Sydney Morning Herald* and Melbourne's *The Age* newspapers have many ads offering cheap fares to London, but don't be surprised if they happen to be sold out when you contact the agents: they're usually low-season fares on obscure airlines with conditions attached.

Discounted return fares on mainstream airlines through a reputable agent like STA Travel cost between A$1600 (low season) and A$2500 (high season). Flights to/from Perth are a couple of hundred dollars cheaper. A Britannia charter service also operates between Britain and Australia/New Zealand. Between November and March, prices can drop as low as £499 return from London to Sydney and £698 return from Sydney to London. Contact Aus Extras (☎ 02-9251 1299), level 6, 201 George St, Sydney, or, in the UK, Austravel (☎ 0171-838 1011), 152 Brompton Rd, London SW3 1HX, or ☎ 0171-734 7755 at their Knightsbridge office.

New Zealand

As in Australia, STA Travel and Flight Centres International are popular travel agents. Not surprisingly, the cheapest fares to Europe are routed through the USA, and a Round-the-World ticket can be cheaper than a return.

Africa

Nairobi, Kenya, is probably the best place in Africa to buy tickets to Britain, thanks to the many bucket shops and the strong competition between them. A typical one-way/return fare to London would be about US$550/800.

If you are thinking of flying to London from Cairo, it's often cheaper to fly to Athens and to proceed with a budget bus or train from there.

South Africa Student Travel, Rosebank, Johannesburg (☎ 011-447 5551; Cape Town, 021-418 6570), is primarily aimed at students and has youth fares to London from R3200 (low season) to R3500 (high). The Africa Travel Centre (☎ 021-235555), cnr Military Rd and New Church St, Tamboerskloof, Cape Town, also has keen prices.

Asia

Hong Kong is the discount plane-ticket capital of Asia, and its bucket shops are at least as unreliable as those of other cities. Ask the advice of other travellers before buying a ticket. Many of the cheapest fares from South-East Asia to Europe and London are offered by Eastern European carriers. STA Travel has branches in Tokyo, Singapore, Bangkok and Kuala Lumpur.

To/from India, the cheapest flights tend to be with Eastern European carriers like LOT and Aeroflot, or with Middle Eastern airlines such as Syrian Arab Airlines and Iran Air. Bombay is the air transport hub, with many transit options to/from South-East Asia, but tickets are slightly cheaper in Delhi.

Europe

Excellent discount charter flights are often available to full-time students aged under 30 and all young travellers aged under 26 (you need an ISIC card or an official youth card) and are available through the large student travel agencies.

Typical low season one-way/return flights from London bucket shops start at: Amsterdam £69/74, Athens £85/129, Frankfurt £65/104, Istanbul £99/119, Madrid £75/89, Paris £50/69 and Rome £77/128. Official tickets with carriers like British Airways can cost a great deal more.

Ireland Dublin is linked by a variety of airlines to a variety of cities in Britain including all the major London airports. There are also flights to various regional centres in the Republic of Ireland. The standard one-way economy fare from London to Dublin is £75, but advance-purchase fares are available offering return tickets for as low as £70. These must be booked well in advance as seats are often limited.

Regular connections between Belfast and the rest of Britain include the British Airways shuttle service from London's Heathrow. Costs on the shuttle range from £77 for a regular one-way ticket to £131 for an advance-purchase return. British Midland Airways offers similar fares. Jersey European Airways has a £55 return fare from Gatwick or Stansted and BA Express has a £99 advance-purchase return from Luton.

LAND
Overland Route

After the heady 1970s, the overland trail to/from Asia lost much of its popularity – the Islamic regime in Iran made life hard, and the war in Afghanistan effectively closed that country. Now that Iran is rediscovering the merits of tourism, the Asia route has begun to pick up again, though unpredictable instabilities – eg Pakistan – may prevent the trickle of travellers turning into a flood for the time being.

A new overland route through what used to be the Soviet Union could become important over the next few years. At this stage the options are more or less confined to the trans-Siberian/Mongolian railway lines to/from Moscow (see the following Train section), but other modes of transport are likely to become available beyond the Urals as the newly independent states open up to travellers.

Going to/from Africa will involve a Mediterranean ferry crossing (discounting the complicated Middle East route). Unfortunately, due to problems in Africa (trouble in Algeria and Morocco and civil war in Sudan in the east), the most feasible Africa overland routes of the past have all but closed down.

Travelling by private transport beyond Europe requires plenty of paperwork and other preparations, and a detailed description is beyond the scope of this book. Following sections tell you what's required within Europe.

Morocco and most of Turkey lie outside Europe, but the rail systems of both countries are still covered by Inter-Rail (though only the 26+ version is valid in Turkey) – see under Inter-Rail Passes later in this section. If you don't have an Inter-Rail pass, the price of a cheap return train ticket from London to Morocco compares favourably with equivalent bus fares – it's worth keeping in mind.

Trans-Siberian Trains To/from central and eastern Asia, a train can work out at about the same price as flying, depending on how much time and money you spend along the way, and it can be a lot more fun. There are three routes to/from Moscow across Siberia: the trans-Siberian to/from Vladivostok, and the trans-Mongolian and trans-Manchurian, both to/from Beijing. There's a fourth route south from Moscow and across Kazakhstan, following part of the old Silk Route to/from Beijing. Prices can vary enormously, depending on where you buy the ticket and what is included. For full details see the *Trans-Siberian Handbook* (Trailblazer, 1997) by Bryn Thomas.

The trans-Siberian takes just under seven days from Moscow via Khabarovsk to Vladivostok, from where there is a boat to Japan (Niigata) or Hong Kong. The boats only run from May to September.

The trans-Mongolian passes through Mongolia to Beijing and takes about 5½ days. A 2nd-class sleeper in a four-berth compartment would cost US$200 to US$250 if purchased in Moscow or Beijing. If you want to stop off along the way or spend some time in Moscow, you'll need 'visa support' – a letter from a travel agent confirming that they're making your travel/accommodation bookings required in Russia or Mongolia. Locally based companies that do all-inclusive packages (with visa support) that can be arranged from abroad include the Travellers Guest House (☎ 0095-971 40 59, fax 280 97 86) in Moscow and Monkey Business (☎ 2723 1376, fax 2723 6653) in Hong Kong, with an

Getting There & Away – Land 87

information centre in Beijing. There are a number of other budget operators.

The trans-Manchurian passes through Manchuria to Beijing and takes six days.

The fourth route runs from Moscow via Almaty in Kazakhstan, crosses the border on the new line to Ürümqi (north-western China) and follows part of the old Silk Route to Beijing. At present you can't buy through tickets.

There are countless travel options between Moscow and the rest of Europe. Most people will opt for a train, usually to/from Berlin, Helsinki, Munich or Vienna.

Bus

Even without using the Tunnel, you can still get to Europe by bus or train – there's just a short ferry/hovercraft ride thrown in as part of the deal. Eurolines (☎ 01582-404511), a division of National Express (the largest UK bus line), has an enormous network of European destinations, including Ireland and Eastern Europe.

You can book through any National Express office, including Victoria Coach Station, London, which is where coaches depart and arrive, and at many travel agents. They also have agents around Europe, including: Paris (☎ 1-49 72 51 51); Amsterdam (☎ 020-267 5151); Frankfurt (☎ 069-79 03240); Madrid (☎ 91-530 7600); Rome (☎ 06-88 40840); and Budapest (☎ 1-1172 562).

Youth fares are available for holders of National Express Discount Coach Cards (see the following Getting Around chapter). In fact, the discount is quite disappointing in most cases.

The following single/return prices and journey times are representative: Amsterdam £36/49 (12 hours); Athens £126/218 (56 hours); Frankfurt £52/88 (18½ hours); Madrid £76/137 (27 hours); Paris £36/49 (10 hours); and Rome £85/129 (36 hours).

Eurolines also have some good-value explorer tickets that are valid up to six months and allow travel between a number of major cities. For example, you can visit Amsterdam, Barcelona, Rome and Paris and return to London for £227.

Hoverspeed (☎ 01304-240241) claim the fastest coach service to Europe on their SeaSprint service with a 6½ hour London-Paris journey from £39 return. London to Brussels or Amsterdam is also available.

Eurobus (☎ 0181-991 1021; in the US (800) 727-2437) travels a pre-determined route around Europe and around Britain with a hop on and hop off reservation service. A ticket costs from £100 for two weeks to £240 for three months and those over 26 pay a little more.

Train

Trains are a deservedly popular mode of transport: they are good meeting places, comfortable, frequent, generally reliable, and rail passes make them affordable.

If you plan to travel extensively by train, consider buying the *Thomas Cook European Timetable*, which gives a complete listing of train schedules and indicates where supplements apply or where reservations are necessary. It is updated monthly and is available from Thomas Cook outlets worldwide. You can also get train times from all over the world on the Internet.

Although the Tunnel service (see below) is now well under way, the most popular of the old rail/ferry and rail/hovercraft services to/from Europe continue relatively unchanged; many prices have actually gone down.

For inquiries concerning Rail International's European trains, call ☎ 0171-834 2345.

Non-tunnel rail options depend on whether you cross the Channel on a hovercraft or ferry, or from Bologne/Folkestone or Newhaven. The cheapest option to Paris is 2nd class via Newhaven and the Sealink ferry; adult singles/returns are £39/65 and the journey takes nine hours. If you travel via Dover and Hoverspeed the fares change to £45/59, but the journey time drops to six hours.

Direct trains to Rome and Madrid travel via Dover and Stena Line. Adult singles/

returns for Madrid are £125/212 (34 hours), to Rome £108/176 (23 hours).

For Holland, Belgium and Germany you cross the Channel from Harwich or Ostend. From Harwich, adult singles/returns to anywhere in Holland are £55/69 (13 hours), to Berlin £122/174 (19½ hours). From Ostend the fare to Holland changes to £49/75 and to Berlin it changes to £127/213.

European Rail Passes There are several passes for use on European rail systems but the most important point to note is that they're not valid on the railways of Britain!

The **Eurail Pass** can only be bought by residents of non-European countries, and is supposed to be purchased before arriving in Europe. In fact, it can be bought within Europe as long as your passport proves you've been there for less than six months, but the outlets where you can do this are limited and it's cheaper to buy the pass outside Europe. French Railways (☎ 0345-30003) 179 Piccadilly, London, is one such outlet. There's a range of Eurail Passes: a one-month pass (under 26) costs £479, for example. Passes for those aged 26 or over are for 1st class travel only but you can get good discounts if you're travelling with one other person (two other people from April to September).

The **Europass** is a new rail pass for non-Europeans that gives between five and 15 days of unlimited travel within a two month period. It's a little cheaper than the Eurail Pass because it covers fewer countries.

The **Inter-Rail Pass** is similar to the Eurail Pass but is available only to residents of European countries. Within the UK, Inter-Rail Passes can be purchased only by people who have been resident for at least six months. For those under 26, there are seven passes each covering a different zone and costing £185 for 15 days travel. Zone E, for example, includes France, Belgium, the Netherlands and Luxembourg. Multi-zone passes are better value and are valid for one month: all seven zones costs £275.

The **Euro-Domino Pass** (called a Freedom Pass in Britain) is for single countries. It's available for three, five or 10 days. Prices for under 26/over 26 range from £79/99 (for the Netherlands) to £189/239 (for Spain).

The Rail Europe Senior Card is worth investigating for travellers aged over 60.

For the full story on travel in Europe, see Lonely Planet's *Western Europe on a shoestring* or their other European guides.

Cheap Tickets European rail passes are only worth buying if you plan to do a fair amount of travelling within a short space of time.

When weighing up options, you should consider the cost of other cheap-ticket deals. Travellers aged under 26 can pick up BIJ (Billet International de Jeunesse) tickets which cut fares by up to 50%. Unfortunately, you can't always bank on a substantial reduction. The £120 return from London to Zürich represents a £17 saving on the normal fare; in contrast, London to Munich return saves £39 on the full fare of £203.

Various agents issue BIJ tickets in London, including Campus Travel (☎ 0171-730 3402), 52 Grosvenor Gardens, London SW1 0AG (tube: Victoria), which sells Eurotrain (BIJ) tickets. Eurotrain options include circular Explorer tickets, allowing a different route for the return trip: London to Madrid, for instance, takes in Barcelona, Paris and numerous other cities. The fare for this Spanish Explorer ticket is £175, valid for two months. Rail International (☎ 0171-834 2345) and Wasteels (☎ 0171-834 7066), Platform 2, Victoria Station, London SW1, also sell BIJ tickets.

Channel Tunnel For the first time since the ice ages, Britain has a land link (albeit a tunnel) with mainland Europe. Two services operate through the Tunnel: Eurotunnel operates a rail shuttle service (Le Shuttle) for motorbikes, cars, buses and freight vehicles, using specially designed railway carriages, between terminals at Folkestone in the UK and Calais in France; and the railway companies of Britain, France and Belgium operate a high-speed passenger service, known as Eurostar, between London, Paris and Brussels.

Le Shuttle Specially designed shuttle trains run 24 hours a day, departing every hour in each direction between 7 am and 11 pm and every two hours between 11 pm and 7 am.

Eurotunnel terminals are clearly signposted and connected to motorway networks. British and French Customs and Immigration formalities are carried out before you drive on to Le Shuttle. Inside the train you can stay with your car, listen to the radio, use the toilet facilities or stretch your legs.

Eurotunnel claims the total time from motorway to motorway, including loading and unloading, is one hour; the shuttle itself takes 35 minutes. This sounds impressive, but the total time if you travel by hovercraft is under two hours, and ferries only take 2½ hours.

Price is obviously an important factor; a car and up to five passengers costs £126. You can buy prepaid tickets (☎ 0990-353535) or simply pay by cash or credit card at a toll booth. The shuttle operates on the basis of first come, first served; reservations for particular services are not possible.

Eurostar Eurostar runs a service between London and Paris (up to fifteen a day), and London and Brussels (up to eight a day). There are now direct Eurostar services from Glasgow and Manchester to both Paris and Brussels, and from Birmingham to Paris. There are easy onward connections from London to Wales and from Brussels to Germany and the Netherlands. A new overnight service offers evening departures from UK stations to give morning arrivals on the continent.

In England, trains arrive at and depart from the international terminal at Waterloo station (the name, commemorating a certain battle, being a wonderful example of British sensitivity to their neighbours). Some trains stop at Ashford International station in Kent, and at Frethun (near Calais) or Lille. Immigration formalities are completed on the train, but British Customs are at Waterloo.

The London to Paris journey takes three hours (which will drop to an amazing 2½ hours when the British get it together to build a high-speed track through Kent). From London to Brussels takes three hours and 15 minutes (which will eventually drop to two hours and 10 minutes).

Get tickets from travel agents and major railway stations. The normal single/return fare to Paris is £77/155 but various special offers and advance purchase may reduce this.

Car & Motorcycle

See the preceding Channel Tunnel section for information on the Tunnel shuttle and the following Sea section for details on ferry charges for cars. See the Getting Around chapter for information on buying a car or van.

Paperwork & Preparations Proof of ownership should always be carried (a Vehicle Registration Document for British-registered cars) when driving in Europe. Also carry your national licence and an International Driving Permit (IDP) from your motoring organisation (see under Documents in the Regional Facts for the Visitor chapter).

Third party motor insurance is a minimum requirement. Most UK motor insurance policies automatically provide this for EU countries and some others. Get your insurer to issue a Green Card (which may cost extra), an internationally recognised proof of insurance, and check that it lists all the countries you intend to visit. You'll need this in the event of an accident outside the country where the vehicle is insured. Also ask your insurer for a European Accident Statement form.

Taking out a European breakdown assistance policy, such as the AA Five Star Service or the RAC Eurocover Motoring Assistance, is a good investment. Both of these include a bail bond for Spain, which is also recommended. Ask your motoring organisation for a Card of Introduction, which entitles you to free services offered by affiliated organisations around Europe.

Every vehicle which travels across an

international border should display a nationality plate of its country of registration. A warning triangle, to be used in the event of breakdown, is compulsory almost everywhere (although not in Britain). Recommended accessories are a first-aid kit (compulsory in Austria, Slovenia, Croatia, Yugoslavia and Greece), and a fire extinguisher (compulsory in Greece and Turkey). Contact the RAC (☎ 0181-686 0088) or the AA (☎ 01256-20123) for more information.

SEA

There are a bewildering array of alternatives between Britain and mainland Europe. This chapter outlines the main alternatives, but it does not give a complete listing.

Competing companies operate on the main routes, and the resulting service is comprehensive but complicated. The same ferry company can have a whole host of different prices for the same route, depending upon the time of day or year, the validity of the ticket, or the size of a vehicle. Return tickets may be much cheaper than two single fares, and vehicle tickets may also cover a driver and passenger. There are very cheap day-return tickets available (like Dover-Calais for £8), but they are strictly policed.

It is worth planning (and booking) ahead where possible as there may be special reductions on off-peak crossings. Unless otherwise stated, the prices quoted for cars do not include passengers. The ferries/hovercraft all carry cars and motorcycles.

Passenger Ships

The days of earning your passage on a freighter to or from Britain have well and truly passed. Even if you have a mariner's ticket, a shipping company is unlikely to want to sign you up for a single trip.

Regular long-distance passenger ships disappeared with the advent of cheap air travel to be replaced by a small number of luxury cruise ships. The grand lady of them all, Cunard's *Queen Elizabeth II*, sails between New York and Southampton 28 times a year; the trip takes five nights each way and a return ticket costs from UK£1025,

though there are also one-way and 'fly one way' deals.

The standard reference for passenger ships is the *ABC Cruise & Ferry Guide* published by the Reed Travel Group (☎ 01582-600111), Church St, Dunstable, Bedfordshire LU5 4HB.

A more adventurous (though not necessarily cheaper) alternative is as a paying passenger on a freighter. Freighters are far more numerous than cruise ships and there are many more routes from which to choose. With a bit of homework, you'll be able to sail between Britain and just about anywhere else in the world, with stopovers at exotic ports which you may never have heard of. The previously mentioned *ABC Cruise & Ferry Guide* is a good source of information.

Passenger freighters typically carry six to 12 passengers (more than 12 would require a doctor on board) and, though less luxurious than dedicated cruise ships, give you a real taste of life at sea. Schedules tend to be flexible and costs vary but seem to hover around US$95 a day; vehicles can often be included for an additional fee.

France

On a clear day, one can actually see across the Channel. A true budget traveller would obviously swim – it's only seven hours and forty minutes if you can match the record.

Dover/Folkestone/Newhaven The shortest ferry link to Europe is from Dover and Folkestone to Calais and Boulogne.

Dover is the most convenient port for those who plan onward travel (in England) by bus or train. P&O (☎ 0990-980980), Stena Line (☎ 0990-707070) and Hoverspeed (☎ 01304-240241) all operate between Dover and Calais every one to two hours. It is worth checking prices for all three.

Stena Line charges one-way adult/student passengers £24/20; cars and drivers, depending on the date and time, from £52 to £140 including the driver; from £62 to £162 for up to four passengers; motorcycles and riders from £44 to £52. These fares are for their fast

45-minute catamaran service and the 90-minute ferry.

Prices for P&O and Hoverspeed are generally similar to those of Stena Line – special offers can make a big difference, however. The hovercraft operated by Hoverspeed only take 35 minutes to cross the Channel rather than the 90 minutes taken by ferries.

Stena Line also operates seven or eight services a day between Newhaven and Dieppe, a four-hour journey by ferry, roughly half that by catamaran. Fares start at £24 single for a foot passenger and £52 single for a car plus driver.

In response to increasing competition from the Channel Tunnel, Stena Line and P&O have announced plans to create a new merged company, P&O-Stena Line, which will operate their Dover to Calais and Newhaven to Dieppe routes. At the time of going to press, they were awaiting EU approval for this merger. Should they get it, their fleets are likely to be cut back and price rises on the short sea crossings to France are a distinct possibility.

Ramsgate Another short, cheap hop worth investigating is the Sally Ferries (☎ 0990 595522) route to Dunkerque. There are five sailings a day that take 2½ hours; a single costs £22 and a car costs from £71 to £106.

Portsmouth P&O (☎ 0990-980555) operate three or four ferries a day to/from Cherbourg and Le Havre. The day ferries take five to six hours and the night ferries take from seven to eight hours. A single is from £18 to £28 and a car costs from £63 to £148. Brittany Ferries (☎ 0990-360360) has at least one sailing a day to/from Caen and St Malo. Portsmouth-Caen takes six hours and costs the same as the P&O routes. The Portsmouth route, unlike the St Malo route which costs a little more, only runs from mid-November to mid-March. Brittany also has a ferry from Plymouth to Roscoff.

Spain
From Plymouth, Brittany Ferries (☎ 0990-360360) operates at least one ferry a week to Santander, which is on the north coast of Spain. The journey time is 24 hours; a single is from £46 to £76 and a vehicle costs from £146 to £254. Brittany also operates a service between Santander and Portsmouth that takes 30 hours. P&O (☎ 0990-980555) operates a service between Portsmouth and Bilbao at similar rates.

Scandinavia
Until one looks at the ferry possibilities, it's easy to forget how close Scandinavia and Britain are to each other, and why the Vikings found English villages so convenient to pillage.

Aberdeen & Shetland One of the most interesting possibilities is the summer-only link between Shetland, Norway, the Faroes, Iceland and Denmark. The agent is P&O (☎ 01224-572615), but the operator is the Smyril Line.

First you have to get to Shetland from Orkney, or from Aberdeen, Scotland. P&O (☎ 01224-572615) has daily sailings from Aberdeen to Lerwick (Shetland) from Monday to Friday. A reclining seat will cost £42/47 depending on the season.

The Smyril boat operates from 3 June to 28 August. The sailing order is Denmark (Saturday), to the Faroes (Monday), to Shetland (Monday), to Norway (Tuesday), to Shetland (Wednesday), to the Faroes (Wednesday), to Iceland (Thursday), to the Faroes (Friday), to Denmark (Saturday) and so on. Depending on the season, one-way couchette fares (a couchette is a sleeping berth) from Shetland to Norway are £40/52, to the Faroes £47/62, to Denmark £94/124, and to Iceland £100/133.

Newcastle The Norwegian Color Line (☎ 0191-296 1313) operates ferries all year to Stavanger and Bergen in Norway. They depart on Saturday and Tuesday from January to May and September to December, and on Saturday, Monday and Wednesday from mid-May to mid-September. They're overnight trips, and the high-season fare for a reclining chair is £83; a car and four people costs £230.

During summer, Scandinavian Seaways (☎ 0191-296 0101) operates ferries to Esbjerg (Denmark) and Gothenburg (Sweden).

Esbjerg ferries depart on Friday and Sunday from mid-June to mid-August; it's an overnight journey taking around 20 hours. A couchette is from £102 to £120; a car costs an extra £57.

Gothenburg ferries depart on Sunday from mid-June to mid-August; it's an overnight journey taking around 24 hours. A couchette is from £130 to £149; a car costs an extra £57.

Harwich Harwich is the major port linking southern England and Scandinavia. Scandinavian Seaways (☎ 01255-240240) has ferries to Esbjerg (Denmark) and Gothenburg (Sweden). In summer ferries leave every two days; the trip to Esbjerg takes 20 hours, to Gothenburg 24 hours. Travelling to Esbjerg, a single in a four-berth couchette is from £74 to £102; a car costs from £36 to £47 extra. Travelling to Gothenburg, a single in a four-berth couchette is from £90 to £130; a car costs from £36 to £47 extra.

Belgium, the Netherlands & Germany
There are two direct links with Germany but many people prefer to drive to/from the Dutch ferry ports.

Harwich & Felixstowe Scandinavian Seaways (☎ 01255-240240) has ferries to Hamburg (Germany) every two days; the trip takes 21 hours. A single in a four-berth couchette is from £65 to £83; a car costs from £36 to £47 extra.

Stena Line (☎ 0990-707070) has two ferries a day to the Hook of Holland, the Netherlands; the day ferry takes 7½ hours and the night ferry takes 9½ hours. A single is £36 and a car plus passengers costs from £88 to £156.

Note that Felixstowe is now used only by freight traffic; P&O's passenger ferry service has been discontinued.

Newcastle Scandinavian Seaways (☎ 0990-333000) has a twice-weekly ferry to Hamburg from late-March to October, taking 20 hours. A single in a four-berth couchette is from £72 to £110 and a car is from £42 to £64.

Ramsgate Sally Ferries (☎ 0990-595522) has six ferries and a number of jet foils to Ostend every day. The ferry takes four hours and the jet foil (passengers only) takes 95 minutes. A single on the ferry costs £22, on the jet foil £26.50. A car plus passengers costs from £50 to £170.

Ireland
There is a great variety of ferry services from Britain to Ireland using modern car ferries. Figures quoted are one-way fares for a single adult, for two adults with a car and for four adults with a car. There are often special deals, return fares and other money savers worth investigating.

Want to travel free? On some routes the cost for a car includes up to four or five passengers at no additional cost. If you can hitch a ride in a less than full car, it costs the driver nothing extra.

There are services from eight ports in England, Scotland and Wales (and from the Isle of Man) to six ports in Ireland. From south to north, interesting possibilities include:

Swansea to Cork The 10-hour crossing costs £29/179/179 at peak times but it operates only from mid-March to early January. In Britain, contact Swansea Cork Ferries (☎ 01792-456116), Ferry Port, Kings Dock, Swansea SA1 5RU.

Fishguard & Pembroke to Rosslare This popular short crossing takes 3½ hours (Fishguard) or 4½ hours (Pembroke) and costs as much as £30/199/199 (Fishguard) or £27/189/189 (Pembroke) on peak-season weekends; at other times of the year the cost can drop as low as £20/79/79. A 99-minute catamaran crossing from Fishguard costs from £36/209/209 down to £24/94/94. Stena Line (☎ 01233-647047), Charter House, Ashford, Kent TN24 8EX, operates Fishguard-Rosslare. Irish Ferries (☎ 0171-491 8682), 150 New Bond St, London W1Y 0AQ, operates Pembroke-Rosslare.

Holyhead to Dublin & Dun Laoghaire The 3½-hour crossing between Holyhead and Dublin costs £27/189/189 at peak seasons, down to £20/89/89 in the off season. The regular ferry between Holyhead and Dun Laoghaire takes 3½ hours and costs from £24/204/204 down to £20/109/109. There is also a fast 99-minute service that costs from £30/204/204 down to £26/99/99. Stena Line (☎ 01233-647047), Charter House, Ashford, Kent TN24 8EX, operates Holyhead-Dun Laoghaire. Irish Ferries (☎ 0171-491 8682), 150 New Bond St, London W1Y 0AQ, operates Holyhead-Dublin.

Liverpool to Belfast The Norse Irish overnight service is not heavily promoted but it's easy to get to Liverpool from London. The trip costs £95 for a car only and £47 for each passenger, including dinner, breakfast and cabin accommodation. Contact Norse Irish Ferries (☎ 0151-944 1010), North Brocklebank Dock, Bootle, Merseyside L20 1BY, for details

Stranraer to Belfast The glamorous new SeaCat service uses an Australian-made high-speed catamaran to race across in just 1½ hours at a cost of £25/189/1208 at peak times. Call SeaCat (☎ 0345-523523) for bookings.

Stranraer & Cairnryan to Larne There are as many as 15 sailings daily on this route which takes about 2½ hours and costs £36/158/165 at peak times, down to as low as £29/63/68 at other times. Stena Line (☎ 01233-647047), Charter House, Ashford, Kent TN24 8EX, operates Stranraer-Larne. P&O (☎ 01581-200276), Cairnryan, Stranraer, Wigtownshire DG9 8RF, operates Cairnryan-Larne.

Liverpool and Heysham via Douglas (Isle of Man) to Belfast It takes 3¾ hours between Heysham and Douglas, 4½ hours between Douglas and Liverpool, and four hours between Belfast and Douglas. Peak time fares to/from the Isle of Man from Belfast, Heysham or Liverpool are £52/220/334. Isle of Man Steam Packet Company (☎ 01624-661661), PO Box 5, Douglas, Isle of Man IM99 1AF operates these services.

LEAVING BRITAIN

People taking flights from Britain have to pay an Air Passenger Duty. Those flying domestically and to countries in the European Union will pay £10; those flying beyond the EU will pay £20. At present, there is no departure tax if you leave by sea or tunnel.

See under Money in the Regional Facts for the Visitor chapter for details on how to reclaim Value Added Tax when you depart.

WARNING

This chapter is particularly vulnerable to change – prices for international travel are volatile, routes are introduced and cancelled, schedules change, special deals come and go, and rules and visa requirements are amended.

Airlines and governments seem to take a perverse pleasure in making price structures and regulations as complicated as possible. You should check directly with the airline or travel agent to make sure you understand how a fare (and any ticket you may buy) works.

The upshot of this is that you should get opinions, quotes and advice from as many airlines and travel agents as possible before you part with your hard-earned cash. The details given in this chapter should be regarded as pointers and are not a substitute for careful, up-to-date research.

Getting Around

Public transport in Britain is generally of a high standard, but it can be expensive. Over the last 18 years, government policy has favoured car ownership, and some local rail and bus services have been reduced. This is bad news for visitors without their own wheels since they're going to want to get to the national parks and small villages where transport is worst.

It's certainly worth considering car rental for at least part of your trip. However, even if you're not driving, with a mix of local buses, the occasional taxi, plenty of time, walking and occasionally hiring a bike, you can get almost anywhere.

Buses are nearly always the cheapest way to get around. Unfortunately they're also the slowest (sometimes by a considerable margin), and on main routes you are confined to major roads which screen you from the small towns and landscapes that make travelling in Britain worthwhile in the first place. With discount passes and tickets bought in advance (Apex and SuperApex), trains can be competitive; they're quicker and often take you through beautiful countryside that is relatively unspoilt by the 20th century.

Ticket types and prices vary considerably. For example, a standard single rail ticket from London to Edinburgh is £61, but a SuperApex return ticket is £34! A standard bus ticket from London to Edinburgh is £20.50 for a single, but with a small company you might find a return ticket for £20.

See the bus and train fare tables in this chapter to get a full picture of the way the different tickets stack up. If you know how far you are travelling (even if your planned journey is not specifically covered) you can get a *rough* idea of costs by working from the mileage columns.

The BTA distributes an excellent brochure, *Getting about Britain for the Independent Traveller*, which gives details of bus, train, plane and ferry transport around Britain and into Europe.

See the Scotland and Wales Getting Around chapters for information specific to those countries.

AIR

Most regional centres and islands are linked to London. However, unless you're going to the outer reaches of Britain, in particular northern Scotland, planes are only marginally quicker than trains if you include the time it takes to get to/from airports. Note that there is now a £5 airport departure tax added to the quoted price of tickets.

Domestic Air Services

The main operators are British Airways (☎ 0345-222111), British Midland (☎ 0345-554554), and Air UK (☎ 0345-666777). There are several other smaller companies. Most airlines offer a range of tickets including full fare (very expensive but flexible), Apex (for which you must book at least 14 days in advance) and special offers on some services (British Airways calls these Seat Sale fares and also has occasional World Offer fares which may be even cheaper). There are also youth fares (for under 25s) but Apex and special-offer fares are usually cheaper.

Prices vary enormously. For example, a return ticket from London to Edinburgh on BA costs £240 full fare, £117 Apex, £99 to £109 Seat Sale, £79 on World Offer fare. Their cheapest one-way fare is £94. Air UK and British Midland charge £58 return but you must stay for one Saturday night and there are restrictions on when you can fly out and back. EasyJet (☎ 01582-445566) now offers no-frills flights for £29 one-way between London (Luton) and Edinburgh, Glasgow and Aberdeen but tickets are only sold direct, by phone, not through a travel agent. Tickets are sold on a first-come-first-served basis – when the £29 tickets are sold the price goes up to £39 and so on up to £59. Return flights can be booked.

Examples of other BA Apex/Seat Sale return fares include Inverness for £133/68, Aberdeen for £128/68, Jersey (Channel Islands) for £107/69, Kirkwall (Orkney) for £246/193, and Lerwick (Shetland) for £262/214. One-way tickets are about the same price as Seat Sale fares.

Air Passes

If you're flying into the UK on BA you may be eligible for a UK Airpass. This costs an additional £52 per internal flight between each zone in the country, and must be arranged at least seven days prior to arrival in the UK.

BUS

Road transport in Britain is almost entirely privately owned and run. National Express (☎ 0990-808080) runs the largest national network – it completely dominates the market and is a sister company to Eurolines – but there are often smaller competitors on the main routes.

In Britain, long-distance express buses are usually referred to as coaches, and in many towns there are separate terminals for coaches and buses. Over short distances, coaches are more expensive (though quicker) than buses.

A number of counties operate telephone inquiry lines which try to explain the fast-changing and often chaotic situation with timetables; wherever possible, these numbers have been given. Before commencing a journey off the main routes it is wise to phone for the latest information.

Another useful, though somewhat hefty (1000 pages), source of information is the GB Bus Timetable (£11) published three times a year by Southern Vectis (☎ 01983-522456; fax 01983-524961), Nelson Road, Newport, Isle of Wight TO30 1RD. The timetable lists all main bus services in Britain and also gives the best way of reaching places that are not served by rail – the nearest rail station and the frequency of bus services to that particular place are listed.

Unless otherwise stated, prices quoted in this chapter are for economy single tickets; see the bus fare table in this section.

Passes & Discounts

The National Express Discount Coach Card can be bought from all National Express agents and is available to students studying full-time in the UK, to all young people between 16 and 25 and to people aged 60 and over. A passport photo is required; ISIC cards are accepted as proof of student status, and passports for date of birth.

The National Express Britexpress Card is available to all overseas visitors on presentation of a passport. It can be bought overseas, at Heathrow or Gatwick, or at the National Express/Eurolines office (☎ 0990-808080), 52 Grosvenor Gardens, London (tube: Victoria).

There are four National Express Tourist Trail Passes available to UK and overseas citizens, which can be bought overseas through travel agents, or at any National Express agent in the UK.

For more information on prices and what these passes provide, see the table in this chapter.

Slowcoach

Slowcoach (☎ 01249-891959) is an excellent bus service designed especially for those staying in youth hostels, but useful for all budget travellers. Buses run on a regular circuit between London, Windsor, Bath, Stratford, Manchester, the Lake District, Edinburgh, York, Nottingham, Cambridge, and London, calling at youth hostels. You can get on and off the bus where you like (there's no compulsion to stay at a hostel). See the Scotland Getting Around chapter for information on other similar operations, and the table in this chapter for price details.

Postbus

Many small places can only be reached by postbuses – minibuses that follow postal delivery routes. These are circuitous routes through many of the most beautiful areas of England, Wales and Scotland. For the free

British Transport Passes

Pass Name	Cost (Prices for adults/ discount card holders)	Bus/train/ferry services offered
National Express Tourist Trail Pass	£49/39 for 3 days; £79/65 for 5 days in a 10-day period; £119/95 for 8 days in a 16-day period; £179/145 for 15 days in a 30-day period	Unlimited travel on all National Express bus services, and Scottish Citylink.
National Express Discount Coach Card (full-time students; under 26; over 60)	£7	30% off adult fares on National Express buses and Scottish Citylink.
National Express Britexpress Card	£12	30% off National Express and/or Scottish Citylink bus journey nominated in a 30-day period.
Slowcoach	£89	Jump on, jump off circuit bus travel linking youth hostels; no time limit.
BritRail Pass (must be bought outside Britain)	US$165/135 (adult/youth) for 4 days; US$235/189 for 8 days; US$365/289 for 15 days; US$465/369for 22 days; US$545/435 for 31 days	Unlimited rail travel throughout Britain.
Flexipass (must be bought outside Britain)	US$199/160 for 4 days per month; US$280/225 for 8 days per month; US$425 (adult) for 15 days per month; US$340 (youth) for 15 days per 2 months	Unlimited rail travel throughout Britain.
BritRail/Drive	(Prices for small car) US$265 for 3 days' car hire plus 3 days' train; US$490 for 7 days' car hire plus 6 days' train	Combines Flexipass (above) with Hertz car hire.
BritRail Rovers	£220/145 for 7 days; £360/238 for 14 days.	Domestic version of BritRail pass: unlimited train travel in Britain.
Regional Rovers		Train travel in particular regions only.
Young Person's or Senior's Railcard	£16 per annum	34% off rail travel throughout Britain.

See also the Disabled Railcard and the Family Railcard decribed in the text.

Postbus Guide to England & Wales contact Postbus Services (☎ 0171-490 2888), Post Office HQ, 130 Old Street, London EC1V 9PQ; for the Scottish postbus timetable contact Postbus Services (☎ 01463-256273) Royal Mail, 7 Strothers Lane, Inverness IV1 1AA.

Sightseeing Buses

Several companies operate bus tours in tourist towns around England. They have regular buses circulating on a fixed route and your one-day ticket lets you get on and off the bus as many times as you like for the day. Guide Friday is the largest company.

TRAIN

Despite the cutbacks of the last decade, and the privatisation programme which is now in full swing, Britain still has an impressive rail service – if you're using it as a tourist rather than a commuter, that is. There are several particularly recommended trips on beautiful lines through sparsely populated country, the most famous being in Wales and Scotland.

Unfortunately, Eurail passes are not recognised in Britain. There are local equivalents, but they aren't recognised in the rest of Europe.

Rail Privatisation

British Rail is no more. The former company's three main operating regions – Network South East (covering the entire south-east of England), Regional Railways (the rest of England and Wales) and ScotRail (Scotland) – have been split into 25 train operating companies (TOCs). A separate company, Railtrack, owns the track and stations. The government hopes to complete the sell-off by 1997 but, so far, only half of the TOCs have been sold. This transport section is therefore likely to change considerably – visitors must get up-to-date information.

A condition of the privatisation process is that main railcards will still be issued, and travellers must be able to buy a ticket to any destination from any railway station. When privatisation is complete, passengers will only be able to travel on services provided by the company who issued their ticket and each company will be free to set whatever fare they choose. Currently, companies using the same route must charge the same fare but if they use a different route they can charge what they like. Thus, between some stations, passengers can buy a cheaper ticket for a more roundabout journey or pay more for a direct route.

The main routes are served by excellent InterCity trains that travel at speeds of up to 140 mph and whisk you from London to Edinburgh in just over four hours.

If you're planning a long journey (over 150 miles) and do not have a rail pass, the cheapest tickets on offer must be bought two weeks in advance. Phone InterCity (☎ 0800-450450, free call) for credit-card bookings (8 am to 10 pm daily). For shorter journeys, it's not really necessary to purchase tickets or make seat reservations in advance. Just buy them at the station before you go.

Rail Classes

There are two classes of rail travel: 1st, and what is now officially referred to as standard (although in class-conscious Britain this will always be called 2nd class). First class costs 30 to 50% more than 2nd and, except on very crowded trains, is not really worth the extra money.

On overnight trains (between London and Plymouth, Exeter, Bristol, and on the routes to Scotland) there are sleeping compartments, with one berth in 1st and two in 2nd. The additional cost for these berths is £30/25 for 1st/2nd class. It's essential to reserve these in advance.

Unless stated otherwise, the prices quoted in this book are for 2nd-class adult single tickets.

BritRail Passes

BritRail passes are the most interesting possibility for visitors, but they are *not available in Britain* and must be bought in your country of origin. Contact the BTA in your country for details. For further information on the passes, see the table on the opposite page.

It's possible to combine BritRail's Flexipass (see the British Transport Passes table) with a single or return Eurostar trip to Paris or Brussels. A return four/eight-day pass costs $363/445; only adult fares are available and the ticket cannot be bought in Europe.

BritRail/Drive

BritRail/Drive combines a Flexipass with the use of a Hertz rental car for side trips. See the British Transport Passes table in this chapter for details. For further information, contact the BTA in your country.

Rail Rovers

The domestic version of the passes are BritRail Rovers: a seven-day All Line Rover is £220/145, and 14 days is £360/238. There are also regional Rovers and some Flexi Rovers to Wales, north and mid-Wales, the North Country, the north-west coast and Peaks, the south-west, and Scotland. Details have been given in the appropriate sections.

Railcards

You can get discounts of up to 34% on most off-peak fares (except Apex and SuperApex – see the following Tickets information) if you're aged 16 to 25, or over 60, or studying full-time, or disabled – but you must first buy the appropriate railcard. There are also railcards for families.

The cards are valid for one year and most are available from major stations. You'll need two passport photos, and proof of age (birth certificate or passport) or student status.

Young Person's Railcard – Costs £16 and gives you 34% off most tickets and some ferry services; you must be aged 16 to 25, or a student of any age studying full-time in the UK

Senior Citizen's Railcard – Available to anyone over 60, this card costs £16 and gives a 34% discount

Disabled Person's Railcard – Costs £14 and gives a 34% discount to a disabled person and one person accompanying them; available through post offices or by writing to British Rail, PO Box 28, York YO1 1FB. It can take up to three weeks to process this card so you should apply early

Family Railcard – Costs £20 and allows discounts of 34% (20% off Saver and SuperSaver tickets) for up to four adults travelling together, providing one of the card-holders is a member of the party. Up to four accompanying children pay a flat fare of £2 each. A couple of journeys can pay for the card

Network Card – If you're planning to do a lot of rail travel in the south of England, a Network card may be worth considering. This is valid for the region previously known as Network South East – London and the entire south-east of England, from Dover to Weymouth, Cambridge to Oxford. It costs £14, or £10 for holders of the Young Person's Railcard. Discounts apply to up to four adults travelling together providing one of the card-holders is a member of the party. Children pay a flat fare of £1. Travel is permitted only after 10 am Monday to Friday and at any time on the weekend. A couple of journeys can pay for the card.

Tickets

If the various train passes and railcards aren't complicated enough, try making sense of the different tickets.

Children under five years old travel free; aged between five and 15 they pay half-price for most tickets, and full fare for Apex and SuperApex tickets. See the train fare table for ticket prices.

Single ticket – Valid for a single journey at any time on the day specified; expensive

Day Return ticket – Valid for a return journey at any time on the day specified; relatively expensive

Cheap Day Return ticket – Valid for a return journey on the day specified on the ticket, but there may be time restrictions and it is usually only available for short journeys; often about the same price as a single. You're not usually allowed to travel on a train that leaves before 9.30 am

Open Return – For outward travel on a stated day and return on any day within a month

Apex – A very cheap return fare, rivalling National Express prices; for distances of more than 150 miles; you must book at least seven days in advance, but seats are limited so book ASAP

SuperApex – Cheapest return fare for journeys to and from north-east England or Scotland; you must book at least 14 days in advance, but seats are limited and not available on all trains so book ASAP

SuperSaver – A cheap return ticket with up to 50% savings; not available in south-eastern England; cannot be used on Friday, Saturday in July and August, nor in London before 9.30 am or between 4 and 6 pm

SuperAdvance – For travel on Friday, and also Saturday in July and August; similarly priced to the SuperSaver, but must be bought before midday on the day before travel, or earlier

Saver – Higher priced than the SuperSaver, but can be used any day and there are fewer time restrictions

AwayBreak ticket – For off-peak travel in the old Network South East region (south-eastern England). Valid for four nights (five days) for journeys over 30 miles or 40 miles from London

StayAway ticket – As above but valid for one month

On a return ticket it's currently possible to stop off at up to three places on the line with the return portion of the ticket. As the new rail companies become established, however, this may not continue. Check when you buy the ticket.

Telephone Bookings

The InterCity National Sales Freephone (☎ 0800-450450) is open from 8 am to 10 pm every day, and bookings can be paid for with MasterCard (Access), Visa, American Express, Diners Club and Switch. Tickets are sent by post and must be ordered five days before travel.

For other advance ticket telephone sales ring ☎ 0345-225225. The service is open from 7.45 am to 10.15 pm.

✦✦✦

Coach/Bus Fares from London

The sample fares below are for single/return travel from London on the National Express coach (bus) system. To qualify for the discount fares you must have a Discount Coach Card (£8 – see Bus in this section for details). The discount is applicable on nonadvance-purchase fares only.

If you're not eligible for a Discount Coach Card you'll need to buy your ticket at least seven days in advance and avoid travelling on a Friday (or Saturday in July and August) to avoid paying the full fares.

Fares below have been rounded up to the next pound.

			Nonadvance Purchase				7-Day Advance	
			Not Fri✦ (Economy)		Fri (Standard)		Not Fri✦	Fri
miles	to	hours	Adult sgl/rtn(£)	Discount sgl/rtn(£)	Adult sgl/rtn(£)	Discount sgl/rtn(£)	Adult rtn(£)	Adult rtn(£)
23	Windsor✳	1	(serviced by other operators – see text)					
51	Brighton✳	1¾	7/10	5/7	7/10	5/7	7/10	5/7
54	Cambridge	2	7/9	5/7	7/9	5/7	7/9	5/7
56	Canterbury	2	10/11	7/8	12/13	8/9	10	12
57	Oxford✳	1¾	3/6	3/5	3/6	3/5	3/6	3/6
71	Dover	2½	11/12	8/8	14/14	10/10	11	13
83	Salisbury	2¾	13/14	9/10	16/17	11/12	13	15
92	Stratford	2¾	13/14	9/10	16	11/12	12	15
106	Bath✳	3	17/19	12/13	21/22	15/16	17	20
110	Birmingham	2½	14/15	10/10	16/17	11/12	13	16
115	Bristol✳	2¼	18/19	13/14	22/23	16/17	17	21
131	Lincoln	4¾	22/23	16/17	26/28	16/17	21	25
150	Shrewsbury	4½	17/18	12/13	20/21	14/15	16	19
155	Cardiff	3¼	20/22	14/16	25/26	18/19	20	23
172	Exeter✳	3¾	23/25	17/18	28/30	20/21	22	27
184	Manchester	4	21	15	21	15	18	18
188	York✳	4	26	18	26	18	20	20
193	Liverpool	4¼	21	15	21	15	18	18
211	Aberystwyth	7¼	20/22	14/16	25/26	18/19	20	23
215	Scarborough	5¾	30	21	37	26	24	24
255	Durham	4¾	26	18	26	18	20	20
259	Windermere	7	30/33	22/23	37/39	26/28	30	35
280	Penzance	6	33/35	23/25	40/42	28/30	32	38
290	St Ives	7	33/35	23/25	40/42	28/30	32	38
299	Carlisle	5½	21/26	20/24	21/26	20/24	26	26
350	Galashiels	8	33/35	23/25	39/42	28/30	31	31
375	Edinburgh✳	8	21/26	20/24	21/26	20/24	26	26
397	Glasgow✳	7	21/26	20/24	21/26	20/24	26	26
434	Dundee	8¼	36/43	26/30	36/43	26/30	34	34
450	Perth	8¼	36/43	26/30	36/43	26/30	34	34
489	Oban	12	46/54	32/38	46/54	32/38	41	41
503	Aberdeen	10½	41/49	29/34	41/49	29/34	40	40
536	Inverness	12	41/49	29/34	41/49	29/34	40	40
590	Ullapool	14	48/60	34/42	48/60	34/42	51	51
652	Thurso	15½	40/50	33/45	40/50	33/45	50	50

✦ Not on Friday or Saturday in July and August.
✳ Other companies also operate this route and are often cheaper. See main text for more information. National Express may have some special EarlyBird fares but they are usually only applicable for the journey into London.

✦✦✦

✛✛✛

Rail Fares from London

Rail travel is faster than coach travel but usually more expensive. The sample fares below are for 2nd-class single/return travel from London.

A Eurail pass cannot be used in Britain. If you're studying full-time in the UK, or are under 25, or are over 60, or are disabled, or have children, you can purchase a railcard which allows a discount (usually 34%) on all standard class fares except Apex and SuperApex.

If you don't have a BritRail pass and are not eligible for a railcard you can still save money by buying your ticket in advance, though these tickets are usually available only on journeys of more than 150 miles. Cheap tickets include Apex, which must be bought seven days in advance, SuperApex (14 days in advance) and SuperAdvance (see note below). Even cheaper promotional fares are sometimes available.

Fares below have been rounded up to the next pound. Where two routes are available between London and the station below, the fare for the cheaper route has been listed.

| | | | Nonadvance Purchase | | | | | 7/14-Day Advance | |
| | | | Peak | Saver (Off Peak✱) | | SuperSaver (Not Fri✦) | | Apex | SuperApex |
miles	to	hours	Adult sgl/rtn(£)	Adult sgl/rtn(£)	Railcard sgl/rtn(£)	Adult sgl/rtn(£)	Railcard sgl/rtn(£)	Adult sgl/rtn(£)	Adult sgl/rtn(£)
23	Windsor	½	6/6	5/5	3/3	–		–	
51	Brighton	¾	13/15	12/13	8/8	(Awaybreak £17)		(Stayaway £20)	
54	Cambridge	1	15/16	12/14	8/9	(Awaybreak £17)		–	–
56	Canterbury	1½	15/15	13/14	9/10	–		–	–
57	Oxford	¾	15/28	13/14	8/9	(Awaybreak £17)		–	–
71	Dover	1¼	19/20	17/18	11/12	(Awaybreak £20)		–	–
83	Salisbury	1¼	21/21	19/19	13/13	(Awaybreak £24)		(Stayaway £28)	
92	Stratford	2¼	15/29	15/21	10/14	(Cheap day return £18)		–	–
106	Bath	1¼	18/22	18/19	12/12	18/22	12/15	15/15	–
110	Birmingham	1½	17/34	16/23	–	17/20		14/14	–
115	Bristol	1½	18/22	18/32	12/22	18/19	12/12	16/17	–
131	Lincoln	1¾	33/66	33/39	22/26	31/32	20/21	–	–
150	Shrewsbury	2½	38/69	36/37	24/24	29/29	19/19	18/18	–
155	Cardiff	2	28/37	28/37	18/24	28/28	18/19	23/23	–
172	Exeter	2	39/40	34/35	22/23	34/35	22/23	24/25	–
184	Manchester	2½	53/96	44/45	29/29	34/35	22/23	26/26	19/19
188	York	2	51/102	51/56	34/37	45/46	30/30	34/35	–
193	Liverpool	2½	51/93	44/45	29/29	34/35	22/23	26/26	19/19
211	Aberystwyth	5¼	50/91	45/46	29/30	36/37	24/25	25/25	–
215	Scarborough	2¾	53/106	53/61	35/40	50/51	33/34	40/41	–
255	Durham	2¾	64/128	64/70	42/46	56/57	37/38	38/39	28/28
259	Windermere	3¾	62/112	56/57	37/38	46/47	30/31	33/34	–
280	Penzance	5	50/99	50/55	33/36	46/47	30/31	30/31	–
290	St Ives	5½	50/99	50/56	33/37	47/48	31/32	31/32	–
299	Carlisle	3½	64/118	62/63	41/42	50/51	33/34	37/38	29/29
350	Galashiels	6	69/129	69/71	46/47	58/59	38/39	–	–
375	Edinburgh	4	68/72	68/72	45/48	61/62	40/41	45/46	33/34
397	Glasgow	5	68/72	68/72	45/48	61/62	40/41	45/46	33/34
434	Dundee	5¾	68/76	68/76	45/50	62/63	41/42	52/53	–
450	Perth	6	68/76	68/76	45/50	62/63	41/42	52/53	–
489	Oban	9½	79/90	79/90	52/60	75/76	50/50	59/60	–
503	Aberdeen	6½	76/83	76/83	50/55	70/71	47/47	57/58	–
536	Inverness	8¼	76/83	76/83	50/55	70/71	47/47	57/58	–
590	Ullapool		(No rail service – bus from Inverness)						–
652	Thurso	13	84/96	84/96	55/63	83/84	55/55	70/71	–

✱ You may travel back on a peak-time train, but not on your outward journey.
✦ Not on Friday or Saturday in July and August, but you can travel on these days for this price if you buy a SuperAdvance ticket. This must be bought before 2 pm on the day before (ie Thursday for Friday travel).

✛✛✛

✝✝✝

Rail Itineraries

The following itineraries include tourist highlights as well as some of the most scenic rail trips. Journey times are approximate. Most of the suggested stops are on British Rail InterCity lines so services are fairly frequent. Pick up a copy of the *Guide to InterCity Services*, available at most main railway stations, which gives timetables.

Britain (14 Days)
Journey Times

London	to York	(two hours)
York	to Durham	(50 minutes)
Durham	to Edinburgh	(1¾ hours)
Edinburgh	to Glasgow	(one hour)
Glasgow	to Windermere	(2½ hours via Oxenholme)
Windermere	to Chester	(3½ hours via Oxenholme and Crewe)
Chester	to Conwy	(1¼ hours)
Conwy	to Cheltenham	(3½ hours via Crewe and Birmingham)
Cheltenham	to Bath	(50 minutes via Bristol)
Bath	to Oxford	(1¼ hours via Didcot)
Oxford	to London	(one hour)

Route From London's King's Cross, it's only two hours to York. With Roman walls, medieval streets and the largest Gothic cathedral in England, York is high on every visitor's list of priorities. Under an hour north is Durham, tiny in comparison to York but with a magnificent cathedral, rising high above the River Wear.

From Durham, continue north and cross the border to Edinburgh, Scotland's capital, with its famous castle and even more famous festival, the world's largest. Completely different in atmosphere, and with superb galleries and a lively arts scene, Glasgow is under one hour to the west.

To reach the Lake District from Glasgow, you need to change trains in Oxenholme. Stay two nights in Windermere so that you can spend at least one full day taking in the superb scenery that inspired Wordsworth and many other poets and artists. To get to the walled city of Chester, with its black and white Tudor buildings, you need to change trains in Oxenholme and Crewe.

From Chester, follow the north coast of Wales to Conwy to visit one of Edward I's magnificent castles, built to subdue the Welsh. Travel back and change at Chester or Crewe and again at Birmingham for Cheltenham, the grand Regency town on the edge of the Cotswolds. From Cheltenham, move on to the beautiful city of Bath, a 12-minute train journey beyond Bristol.

Bath to Oxford requires a change at Didcot. Spend two nights at Britain's oldest university town, allowing time for an excursion to nearby Blenheim Palace. The trip back to London takes only one hour by train.

Scotland (4 Days)
Journey Times

Edinburgh	to Glasgow	(one hour)
Glasgow	to Fort William	(3¾ hours)
Fort William	to Mallaig	(1½ hours)
Mallaig	to Kyle of Lochalsh	(two hours by boat, summer only)
Kyle of Lochalsh	to Inverness	(2½ hours)
Inverness	to Perth	(2½ hours)
Perth	to Edinburgh	(1½ hours)

Route This route includes the West Highland Line, arguably the most scenic rail journey in the country, and the Kyle Line across the Highlands from Kyle of Lochalsh to Inverness. The ScotRail Flexi Rover ticket (£60) allows travel on this route for four days out of eight.

It takes less than one hour from Edinburgh to Glasgow's central station. Nearby, from Queen St station, trains depart on the West Highland Line. The route passes Loch Lomond on the way to Crianlarich, then climbs over wild Rannoch Moor, with views of Ben Nevis, Britain's highest peak. From Fort William, the train crosses the River Lochy. There are superb views of Loch Shiel and, after Glenfinnan station, Loch Eilt. The rails run through tunnels along the edge of the sea lochs to Arisaig, Britain's most westerly railway station, then north to Morar with views across to the islands of Skye, Rhum and Eigg. The line follows the coast from Morar to Mallaig.

✝✝✝

In the summer there are ferry services for the two-hour voyage to Kyle of Lochalsh, the terminus of the Kyle Line from Inverness. From Inverness there are frequent departures south to Perth, where it's worth stopping to see nearby Scone Palace before continuing to Edinburgh.

Wales (3 Days)
Journey Times

Shrewsbury	to Dovey Junction	(1¾ hours)
Dovey Junction	to Porthmadog	(1½ hours)
Porthmadog	to Blaenau Ffestiniog	(1¼ hours)
Blaenau Ffestiniog	to Llandudno Junction	(1¼ hours)
Llandudno Junction	to Shrewsbury	(two hours via Chester)

Route Wales is known for its Great Little Trains, narrow-gauge railways passing through some spectacular countryside. This route links several of them with the mainline network to make an enjoyable three-day trip around North Wales, starting and ending in Shrewsbury (England). It might just be possible to do the whole journey in one day, but spending a couple of nights in Wales would allow time to appreciate the superb scenery of Snowdonia National Park. The North & Mid Wales Flexi Rover ticket (£22) allows travel anywhere on this route for three days out of seven.

From Shrewsbury you travel west to Dovey Junction to join the Cambrian coast railway that follows the coast north. You could stop at Harlech to see the 13th-century castle. From Porthmadog, the narrow-gauge Ffestiniog Railway takes you in steam-hauled carriages through Snowdonia to Blaenau Ffestiniog. Another small railway continues through Betws-y-Coed to Llandudno Junction to connect with the coastal railway. Follow the coast east back to England. Connecting trains for Shrewsbury leave from Chester. ∎

CAR & MOTORCYCLE

Travelling by private car or motorcycle enables you to get to remote places, and to travel quickly, independently and flexibly. Unfortunately, the independence you enjoy does tend to isolate you and cars are nearly always inconvenient in city centres.

There are five grades of road. Motorways are triple or dual carriageways and deliver you quickly from one end of the country to another. In general, they are a fairly unpleasant experience. You miss the most interesting countryside, and the driving is fast and aggressive. Be particularly careful if you use them in foggy or wet conditions. Unfortunately, the primary routes (main A-roads) are often very similar.

Minor A-roads are single carriageways and are likely to be clogged with slow-moving trucks, but life on the road starts to look up once you join the B-roads and minor roads. Fenced by hedgerows, these wind through the countryside from village to village. You can't travel fast, but you won't want to.

If you can, avoid bringing a car into London. Traffic moves slowly and parking is expensive. Traffic wardens and wheel clampers operate with extreme efficiency and if your vehicle is towed away it'll cost you over £100 to get it back.

At around 57p per litre (equivalent to £2.16 for a US gallon), petrol is expensive by American or Australian standards; and diesel is a only few pence cheaper. Distances, however, aren't great.

Road Rules

Anyone using the roads should get hold of the *Highway Code* (99p), which is often available in TICs. A foreign driving licence is valid in Britain for up to 12 months from the time of your last entry into the country. If you're bringing a car from Europe make sure you're adequately insured.

Briefly, vehicles drive on the left-hand side of the road; front-seat belts are compulsory and if belts are fitted in the back they must be worn; the speed limit is 30 mph (48 kph) in built-up areas, 60 mph (96 kph) on single carriageways, and 70 mph (112 kph)

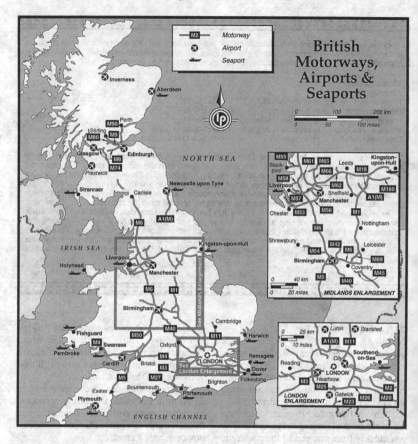

M2		Motorway
⊗		Airport
		Seaport

British Motorways, Airports & Seaports

0   100   200 km
0   50   100 miles

Inverness

Aberdeen

Perth
M90
Stirling
M80 M9
Glasgow
M8   Edinburgh
Prestwick
M74

NORTH SEA

Stranraer
Carlisle
Newcastle upon Tyne

M6
A1(M)

IRISH SEA

Liverpool
Kingston-upon-Hull
Holyhead
Manchester

See Midlands Enlargement

M6   M1

Birmingham

Cambridge
M40
M11
Fishguard   M50
Swansea   Oxford   Harwich
M4   M4
Pembroke   Ramsgate
Cardiff   Bristol   LONDON
M3   Dover
M5   M27   *See London Enlargement*   Folkestone
Exeter   Bournemouth   Brighton
Plymouth   Portsmouth

ENGLISH CHANNEL

MIDLANDS ENLARGEMENT

M55   M61 M65   Leeds   Kingston-upon-Hull
Black-pool   M66   M18
M58   Liverpool   M62   M180
M57   Sheffield   A1(M)
Chester   M53   Manchester
M56   M1
M6   Nottingham
Shrewsbury   M42   Leicester
M54   M6   M69
Birmingham   Coventry   M45
M5   M40

0   40 km
0   20 miles

LONDON ENLARGEMENT

0   25 km
0   10 miles

Luton   Stansted
A1(M)   M11
City   Southend-on-Sea
Reading   LONDON
M3   Heathrow   M2
M25   M20
Gatwick   M26
M23

---

on dual or triple carriageways; you give way to your right at roundabouts (traffic already on the roundabout has the right of way); and motorcyclists must wear helmets.

See Legal Matters in Facts for the Visitor for information on drink-driving rules.

Car Parking

Many places in Britain, big and small, could easily be overrun by cars. As a result, there are often blanket bans on, or at least active discrimination against, bringing cars into the centre. It's a good idea to go along with it even if, sometimes, you will have to walk

further. The parking will be easier and you'll enjoy the places more if it's not cluttered up with cars, yours and others. This particularly applies in small villages – park in the car parks, not on the street.

In bigger cities there will often be 'short-stay' and 'long-stay' car parks. Prices will often be the same for stays of up to two or three hours, but for lengthier stays the short-stay car parks rapidly become much more expensive. The long-stay car parks may be slightly less convenient but they're much cheaper.

A yellow line painted along the edge of the road indicates there are parking restrictions.

The only way to establish the exact restrictions is to find the nearby sign that spells them out. A single line means no parking for at least an eight-hour period between 7 am and 7 pm, five days a week; a double line means no parking for at least an eight-hour period between 7 am and 7 pm, more than five days a week; and a broken line means there are some restrictions.

Rental

Rates are expensive in the UK; often you will be best off making arrangements in your home country for some sort of package deal. The big international rental companies charge from around £150 a week for a small car (Ford Fiesta, Peugeot 106).

The main companies include Avis (☎ 0990-900500), British Car Rental (☎ 01203-716166), Budget (☎ 0800-181181), Europcar (☎ 0345-222525), Eurodollar (☎ 01895- 233300), Hertz (☎ 0345-555888) and Thrifty Car Rental (☎ 01494-442110).

Holiday Autos (☎ 0990-300400) operates through a number of rental companies and can generally offer excellent deals. A week's all-inclusive hire starts at £129 for a very small Fiat. For other cheap operators check the ads in TNT Magazine. TICs have lists of local car-hire companies.

If you're travelling as a couple or a group, a camper van is worth considering. Sunseeker Rentals (☎ 0181-960 5747) has four-berth and two-berth vans for £200 to £300 per week.

Purchase

It is possible to buy a reasonable vehicle for around £1000; a reliable van (see following section) could be up to twice as much. Check Loot (every weekday), Autotrader (Friday; includes photos) and the Motorists' Guide (monthly; lists models and average prices).

In Britain all cars require a Ministry of Transport safety certificate (MOT), valid for one year and issued by licensed garages; full third party insurance – shop around but expect to pay at least £300; registration – a standard form signed by the buyer and seller, with a section to be sent to the Department of Transport; and tax (£140 for one year, £77 for six months) – from main post offices on presentation of valid MOT, insurance and registration documents.

You are strongly recommended to buy a vehicle with valid MOT and tax. MOT and tax remain with the car through a change of ownership; third party insurance goes with the driver rather than the car, so you will still have to arrange this (and beware of letting others drive the car). For further information about registering, licensing, insuring and testing your vehicle, contact a post office or Vehicle Registration Office for leaflet V100.

Van

Vans provide a popular method of touring Britain and Europe, particularly for shoe-string travellers. Often three or four people will band together to buy or rent a van. Look at the adverts in the TNT Magazine if you wish to form or join a group.

TNT Magazine carries ads for vans, as does Loot. The Van Market in Market Rd, London N7 (near Caledonian Rd tube station), is a long-running institution where private vendors congregate on a daily basis. Some second-hand dealers offer a 'buy-back' scheme for when you return from Europe, but buying and reselling privately is better if you have the time.

Vans usually feature a fixed high-top or elevating roof and two to five-bunk beds. Apart from the essential camping gas cooker, professional conversions may include a sink, fridge and built-in cupboards. You will need to spend at least £1000 to £2000 for something reliable enough to get you around Europe.

An eternal favourite is the VW Kombi; they aren't made any more but the old ones seem to go on forever, and getting spares isn't a problem. Once on the road you should be able to keep budgets lower than by using trains, but don't forget to set some money aside for emergency repairs.

The main advantage of going by van is flexibility: with transport, eating and sleeping requirements all taken care of in one unit, you are tied to nobody's timetable but your own. The main disadvantage is that you'll

Driving Itineraries

If you're only visiting Britain for a short holiday, you can pack in a lot more if you have your own set of wheels and plan your itinerary carefully.

Visitors used to left-hand drive vehicles, and who find the prospect of driving on the 'wrong' side of the road daunting, should avoid driving in the cities. On the following route around England, you could travel from the airport to London and from London to Cambridge by train or bus, pick up your rental car there, tour round the country and return the car to the airport as you leave, without going back to London.

England (12 Days)
Road Distances

London	to Cambridge	(61 miles)
Cambridge	to Lincoln	(94 miles)
Lincoln	to York	(81 miles)
York	to Durham	(75 miles)
Durham	to Windermere	(115 miles)
Windermere	to Chester	(113 miles)
Chester	to Stratford-upon-Avon	(65 miles)
Stratford-upon-Avon	to Bath	(99 miles)
Bath	to Salisbury via Avebury	(59 miles)
Salisbury	to Windsor	(75 miles)
Windsor	to London	(23 miles)

Route Leave London on the M11, which leads directly to Cambridge. Spend the day in this ancient university town and take a punt out on the river. From Cambridge, take the A604 to Huntingdon to join the A1, stopping at Stamford for a quick look at this unspoilt old town. Continue along the A1, turning off onto the A46 for Lincoln. This old Roman city has a superb Norman cathedral and castle.

Leave Lincoln on the A15, the Roman road known as Ermine St, heading north. Join the M180 for seven miles, then take the A15 over the Humber Bridge. Immediately after crossing the bridge, take the A63 for seven miles, then the A1034 to Market Weighton, following signs for York via the A1079. York Minster is the largest Gothic cathedral in England, and York is a fascinating place.

Head west out of York on the A59 to join the A1. Leave the A1(M) and get on the A690 to Durham, an easier route than the A177. Durham is a World Heritage Site with one of the finest cathedrals in the country.

From Durham, take the A691 to Consett, and then the A692 four miles south-west to join the A68 going north. The A69 leads west through Haydon Bridge to Bardon Mill, where signposts direct you for the three-mile journey to Housesteads Fort, part of Hadrian's Wall. After stopping to see the fort, continue west along the B6318 to rejoin the A69, following signposts for Carlisle. Two miles east of Carlisle, take the M6 south to the A66, which you follow west for a mile. Turn left onto the scenic A592, which leads into the heart of the Lake District, past Ullswater to Windermere. Stay two nights in Windermere to give yourself time for a good walk in this beautiful area.

From Windermere take the A591 south-east to join the M6 south, eventually taking the M56 to Chester. Spend the night in Chester before taking the A41 and A442 south to join the M54 near Telford. You may wish to stop at nearby Ironbridge Gorge to see this cradle of the Industrial Revolution and its interesting museums, or at Warwick, south of Birmingham, to see its impressive castle. Bypass Birmingham on the M6 and join the M40 (watch the signs as this is an easy exit to miss). Take the A3400 to Stratford-upon-Avon for a quick look at Shakespeare's birthplace and to see a play by the Royal Shakespeare Company in the evening.

The following day, visit Blenheim Palace, one of the most impressive stately homes in the country, and drive through Cotswold villages to the beautiful town of Bath. The A3400 and the A44 lead you to Woodstock, and Blenheim stands on the edge of the town. From Blenheim, take the A4095 to Witney, the A40 to the village of Burford, the B4425 through Bibury to Cirencester, and the A433, then the A46, to Bath.

From Bath, follow the A4 to the prehistoric complex of Avebury, less well known but more atmospheric than Stonehenge. Continue east along the A4 to join the A346 and A338 south to Salisbury, well known for its cathedral.

Leave Salisbury on the A360 north to join the A303 near Stonehenge, continuing east onto the M3. At Basingstoke, take the A33 to join the M4, stopping at Windsor to see the castle. Heathrow airport is only about 10 miles from Windsor, so you could stay the night in the Windsor area and drop off your rental car at the airport as you leave.

Scotland (7 Days)
Road Distances

Edinburgh	to St Andrews	(58 miles)
St Andrews	to Aberdeen	(83 miles)
Aberdeen	to Inverness	(106 miles)
Inverness	to Fort William	(65 miles)
Fort William	to Glasgow	(102 miles)
Glasgow	to Stirling	(26 miles)
Stirling	to Edinburgh	(35 miles)

Route Take the A90 out of Edinburgh over the Forth Road Bridge. The A90 becomes the M90 soon after the bridge, and you should turn onto the A91 north of Kinross, following signs to St Andrews. It's worth spending the night in this interesting seaside town, best known as the home of golf.

From St Andrews, turn off the A91 along the A919 and A92 following signs for Tay Bridge and Dundee. Stop to see Scott's Antarctic research ship *Discovery*, conveniently moored beside the bridge in Dundee. Continue on the A929 and the smaller A928 to Glamis Castle, one of the most famous of Scotland's many castles. From Glamis take the A94 to the affluent granite city of Aberdeen.

You could take one of several routes from Aberdeen to Inverness. The direct route is along the A96 via Elgin, a distance of 106 miles. Alternatively, and if you have an extra day to spare, consider taking the route through the Grampian Mountains, via the A93, A939, A95 and A9 – about 150 miles. Balmoral Castle, the Queen's Scottish residence, which can be visited when the royal family is not at home, is a short distance off this route.

From Inverness, follow Loch Ness on the A92, stopping at Urquhart Castle and the nearby Loch Ness Monster Exhibition. Continue on the A82 to Fort William, leaving yourself time for an evening walk in Glen Nevis. To climb Ben Nevis, Britain's highest peak, you'd need to allow a whole day.

Take the A82 south from Fort William, stopping in Glen Coe and then continuing past Loch Lomond to Glasgow. Spend the following day in this lively city before taking the M80 to Stirling, a drive of under one hour. Look around Stirling's magnificent castle the next day before returning to Edinburgh.

Wales (5 Days)
Road Distances

Cardiff	to Brecon	(35 miles)
Brecon	to St David's	(85 miles)
St David's	to Machynlleth	(77 miles)
Machynlleth	to Llanberis	(60 miles)
Llanberis	to Llandudno via Caernarfon	(27 miles)
Llandudno	to Chester	(47 miles)

Route Cardiff is about 30 miles from the River Severn and the border with England. Spend half a day in the Welsh capital to see the castle or the folk museum before taking the A470 north to Brecon.

After a morning's walk in the Brecon Beacons National Park, drive west on the A40 to St David's. Situated in the heart of the Pembrokeshire Coast National Park, this is Britain's smallest cathedral town.

Follow the coast road, the A487, to the seaside town of Aberystwyth and the village of Machynlleth, on the southern edge of Snowdonia National Park. Located just outside Machynlleth, the Centre for Alternative Technology is an interesting place to visit.

Get an early start the next day and take the quickest route to the foot of Mt Snowdon, the second-highest peak in Britain. From Machynlleth, follow the A487 to Dolgellau, then the A470 and A487, turning off at Penrhyndeudraeth onto the A4085 to Beddgelert. From here take the A498 and the A4086, following signs for Llanberis. To walk up Snowdon, stop by the youth hostel on the pass before Llanberis; if you're going to cheat and take the mountain railway to the top, continue into Llanberis. There are numerous B&Bs in this area.

From Llanberis it's about seven miles to Caernarfon, a run-down town dominated by a magnificent castle. Take the A487 and A55 east to Conwy, where there's another interesting castle, and spend the night in Llandudno, four miles north. This is a classic British seaside resort with rows of welcoming B&Bs.

To return to England, the A55 provides fast access to Chester, just over an hour's drive east. ■

often have to leave your gear unattended inside. They're also expensive to buy in spring and hard to sell in autumn. As an alternative, consider a car and tent.

Motorcycle Touring
Britain is made for motorcycle touring, with winding roads of good quality and stunning scenery to stimulate the senses. Just make sure your wet-weather gear is up to scratch. Crash helmets are compulsory.

The International Motorcyclists Tour Club (£19 per annum plus a £3 joining fee) organises European (and worldwide) biking jaunts, and members regularly meet to swap information. Contact James Clegg (☎ 01484-664868), Membership Secretary, 238 Meltham Road, Netherton, Huddersfield, Yorks HD4 7HL.

Motoring Organisations
Consider joining a motoring organisation for 24-hour breakdown assistance. The two largest in the UK are the AA (☎ 0800-919595) and the RAC (☎ 0800-550550). One year's membership starts at £44 for the AA and £36 for the RAC. Both these companies can also extend their cover to include Europe.

If you're a member of a motoring organisation back home, you should check to see if it has a reciprocal arrangement with an organisation in Britain.

BICYCLE
See under Cycling in the Activities chapter.

HITCHING
Hitching is never entirely safe in any country in the world, and we don't recommend it. Travellers who decide to hitch should understand that they are taking a small but potentially serious risk. However, many people do choose to hitch, and the advice that follows should help to make their journeys as fast and safe as possible.

Hitching is reasonably easy in Britain, except around the big cities and built-up areas, where you'll need to use public transport. It's against the law to hitch on motorways or the immediate slip roads; make a sign and use approach roads, nearby roundabouts, or the service stations. On some of the Scottish islands, where public transport is infrequent, hitching is so much a part of getting around that local drivers may stop and offer you lifts without your even asking.

Although hitching in Britain is probably safer than hitching in many other Western countries, it's obviously not without its dangers, and it's certainly not advisable for a woman to hitch alone. Two women will be reasonably safe but a man and a woman travelling together is probably the best combination.

If you don't like the look of someone who stops for you, don't get in the car. Likewise, if you're a driver, take care over who you pick up. The brother of one of the authors was stabbed by a hitchhiker he stopped for on the M1 motorway.

A lift-share agency, Freewheelers (☎ 0191-222 0090), has been set up recently. This matches passengers with drivers for a £3 pick-up charge and a fee of 3.5p per mile. It's easier to get lifts along the most popular routes, eg London to Birmingham, Manchester and Liverpool. For further information and membership details, contact Freewheelers, 25 Low Friar St, Newcastle upon Tyne NE1 5UE, or on e-mail: freewheelers@freewheelers.co.uk.

WALKING
See under Walking in the Activities chapter.

BOAT
See the Getting There & Away and Getting Around sections of regional chapters, and the Activities chapter.

ORGANISED TOURS
Since travel is so easy to organise in Britain, there is very little need to consider a tour. Still, if your time is limited and you prefer to travel in a group, there are some interesting possibilities. The BTA has information.

Companies with trips pitched at a young crowd include Top Deck (☎ 0171-370 4555), 131 Earls Court Rd SW5; Drifters (☎ 0171-262 1292), 10 Norfolk Place W2; Contiki, (☎ 0171-637 0802) c/o Royal

National Hotel, Russell Square, Bedford Way WC1 – all in London; and Tracks (☎ 02303-814949), 8 Evesgate Park Barn, Smeeth, Ashford, Kent TN25 6SX.

If you don't fit into this category, try Shearings Holidays (☎ 01942-824824), Miry Lane, Wigan, Lancashire, WN3 4AG. They have a very wide range of four to twelve-day coach tours covering the whole country. They also offer Club 55 holidays for the more mature holiday-maker – on their West Country tour you can expect resident entertainers, bingo every evening and wrestling one evening per week!

For the over 60s, Saga Holidays (☎ 0800-300500), Saga Building, Middleburg Square, Folkestone, Kent CT20 1AZ, offers holidays ranging from cheap coach tours and resort holidays to luxury cruises around Britain and abroad. Saga also operates in the USA (☎ 617-262 2262) at 222 Berkeley St, Boston, MA 02116, and in Australia (☎ 02-957 5660) at Level 1, 10-14 Paul St, Milsons Point, Sydney 2061.

TAXI

See the London chapter for info on the famous London taxis and their minicab competitors. Outside London, taxis are usually reasonably priced. In the country you could expect to pay around £1.20 per mile, which means they are definitely worth considering to get to an out-of-the-way hostel, sight, or the beginning of a walk. A taxi over a short distance will often be very competitive with a local bus, especially if there are three or four people to share the cost.

ENGLAND

Facts about England

England dominates both the political entity that is the United Kingdom and the geographical entity that is the island of Great Britain. Although the Scots and Welsh made an enormous contribution to the British Empire it was, and in some ways remains, an English empire.

England's position on the edge of Continental Europe, removed but in many ways an integral part, has always provided unique opportunities and problems. The pendulum has swung from isolation to integration and back again a number of times. In this era of the European Union and the Channel Tunnel, England is probably more European than it has been for 700 years.

Despite this, travellers will find a country where the institutions and symbols that had

England Chapter Divisions

ATLANTIC OCEAN

IRISH SEA

NORTH SEA

ENGLISH CHANNEL

SCOTLAND

WALES

Northumberland

Cumbria

Durham

NORTHERN ENGLAND

Isle of Man

North Yorkshire

Lancashire

East Riding of Yorkshire

NORTHERN MIDLANDS

Cheshire

Derby-shire

Notting-hamshire

Lincolnshire

Staffordshire

Leicester-shire

Shropshire

Warwick-shire

Northampton-shire

Hereford & Worcester

SOUTHERN MIDLANDS

Norfolk

Cambridge-shire

EASTERN ENGLAND

Suffolk

Bedford-shire

Gloucester-shire

Oxford-shire

Buckinghamshire

Hertfordshire

Essex

LONDON

Wiltshire

Berkshire

Surrey

Kent

SOUTH-EASTERN ENGLAND

Somerset

Hampshire

W Sussex

E Sussex

SOUTH-WESTERN ENGLAND

Devon

Dorset

Isle of Wight

Cornwall

0   75   150 km
0   40   80 miles

UNITARY AUTHORITIES
1 York
2 Sefton
3 Liverpool
4 Knowsley
5 St Helens
6 Wigan
7 Bolton
8 Salford
9 Trafford
10 Bury
11 Manchester
12 Rochdale
13 Oldham
14 Tameside
15 Stockport
16 Calderdale
17 Bradford
18 Leeds

19 Kirklees
20 Wakefield
21 Barnsley
22 Sheffield
23 Rotherham
24 Doncaster
25 Kingston-upon-Hull
26 North Lincolnshire
27 North-East Lincolnshire
28 Wolverhampton
29 Walsall
30 Sandwell
31 Birmingham
32 Dudley
33 Solihull
34 Coventry
35 South Gloucestershire
36 Bristol
37 North-West Somerset
38 Bath & North-East Somerset

ENGLAND ..... Chapter
Norfolk........... County

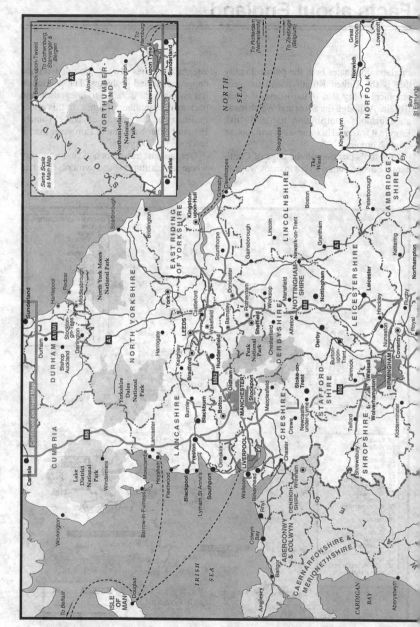

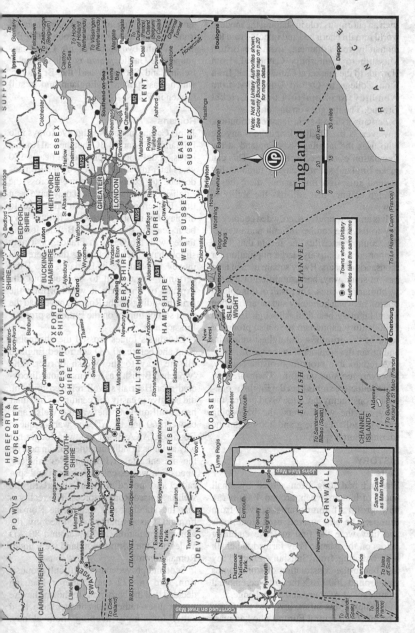

England

such an enormous role in shaping the modern world remain cherished and intact – from the monarchy to Parliament, from the British Museum to Canterbury Cathedral, from Harrods to the market at Camden Lock, from Eton College to Oxford University, from Wembley Stadium to Lord's Cricket Ground. The list goes on and on.

Perhaps its most significant contribution, however, is the English language – anyone who uses the language has England at the foundation of their consciousness. This can make England seem strangely familiar, but beyond this first impression, there lies a foreign country that still has the ability to bewilder.

It is an overpopulated, crowded country so day-to-day life can be difficult and intense. The country's fertility has meant that it has supported a (relatively) large population for thousands of years. Every square inch of land has, in some way, been modified or altered by human activities. The result of this collaboration between humanity and nature is often breathtakingly beautiful, although 19th and 20th-century capitalism have also produced some of the grimmest and ugliest industrial and urban developments in the world.

A remarkable proportion of the country, however, remains unspoilt. There are few more seductive sights than the English countryside on a sunny day – the vivid greens, the silky air, the wildflowers, the ballooning trees, the villages, the grand houses and the soaring church spires.

HISTORY
Celts

England had long been settled by small bands of hunters when, around 4000 BC, a new group of immigrants arrived from Europe. The new arrivals used stone tools and they were the first to leave enduring marks on the island. They farmed the chalk hills radiating from Salisbury Plain. They also began the construction of stone tombs and, around 3000 BC, the great ceremonial complexes at Avebury and Stonehenge.

The next great influx involved the Celts, a people from central Europe who had mas-

tered the smelting of bronze and, later, of iron. They started arriving around 800 BC and brought two forms of the Celtic language: the Gaelic, which is still spoken in Ireland and Scotland, and the Brythonic, which was spoken in England and is still spoken in Wales.

Romans

Julius Caesar made investigative forays into England in 55 and 54 BC, but the real Roman invasion did not take place until nearly 100 years later in 43 AD. Quite why the Romans decided to extend their power across the English Channel is unclear. It may have been that Emperor Claudius felt the need to display his military prowess, it may have been fear of the Celts in Britain joining forces with the Gauls in France, or it may simply have been the feeling that there was money to be made in England. The latter certainly turned out to be true, but the expense of obtaining it was horrible; the British holdings of the Romans never had the right sort of impact on the Empire's profit & loss account.

Claudius's forces crossed the channel to Kent and before 50 AD controlled England all the way to the Welsh border. The 'wretched British', as a Roman note discovered near Hadrian's Wall referred to them, did not give in easily and centurions had their hands full quelling the warlike Welsh and, between 60 and 61 AD, the warrior queen Boudicca (AKA Boadicea), who fought her way as far as Londinium, the Roman port on the present site of London. Nevertheless, opposition was essentially random and sporadic and posed no real threat to the well-organised Roman forces. The reality is that the stability and wealth the Romans brought was probably welcomed by the general population, and by around 80 AD Wales and the north of England were under Roman control.

Scotland proved a more difficult proposition, and in 122 the Emperor Hadrian decided that the barbarians to the north were a lost cause – rather than conquer them, he'd settle for simply keeping them at bay.

Accordingly, he ordered a wall to be built right across the country; to the south would be civilisation and the Roman Empire, to the north would be the savages. Only 20 years later, the Romans made another attempt at bringing the unruly northerners into line and constructed the Antonine Wall, further north, but it was soon abandoned and for nearly 300 years Hadrian's Wall marked the outermost limit of the Roman Empire. Paved roads radiated from London to important regional centres – Ermine St ran north to Lincoln, York and Hadrian's Wall, and Watling St ran north-west to Chester.

The Romans brought stability and also considerable economic advance to Britain and, after it was recognised by the Emperor Constantine in 313, they also brought Christianity. By this time the Empire was already in decline but the Romans were not driven out by the British, nor did they withdraw to fight fires closer to home. Britain was simply abandoned. Money stopped coming from Rome and, although the outposts stumbled on for some time (control of the garrisons had been slowly shifting from soldiers to farmers in any case), eventually they crumbled and were deserted. The end of Roman power in Britain is generally dated at around 410.

Anglo-Saxons & Viking Invasions

As Roman power faded, England went downhill. The use of money, once supplied by Rome, dwindled – as a result, trade declined, rural areas lost their population, travel became unsafe and local fiefdoms developed. Heathen Angles, Jutes and Saxons – Teutonic tribes originating from north of the Rhine – began to move into the vacuum created by the Roman departure. During the 5th century, these tribes advanced across what had been Roman England, absorbing the Celts so thoroughly that today most place names in England have Anglo-Saxon origins.

By the end of the 6th century, England had split into a number of Anglo-Saxon kingdoms, and by the 7th century these kingdoms had come to think of themselves collectively as English. The Celts, particularly in Ireland, kept Latin and Roman Christian culture alive. Christianity, a fragile late-Roman period import, may have declined at first but the arrival of St Augustine in 597 was followed by the swift spread of Augustinian missions.

As memories of Rome faded and the Celts merged with the Anglo-Saxons, England was divided into three strong kingdoms. In the 7th century, Northumbria was the dominant kingdom, extending its power far across the border into Scotland. In the 8th century, Mercia became stronger and King Offa marked a clear border between England and Wales, delineated by Offa's Dyke, which walkers can still follow today. Mercia's power eventually withered, to be replaced by that of King Egbert of Wessex, who was the first to rule all of England. At the same time, a new round of attacks was inflicted on the country, this time by fierce northerners, the Vikings.

By the mid-9th century, the Vikings were becoming invaders rather than raiders and in 865 an occupying army moved in to conquer the Anglo-Saxon kingdoms. The Norwegian Vikings took northern Scotland, Cumbria and Lancashire, while the Danes conquered eastern England, making York their capital. They spread across England until, in 871, they were confronted by Alfred the Great of Wessex.

England was divided between the northern Danelaw and southern Wessex, the old Roman Watling St approximating the border. Alfred's successor, Edward the Elder, ended up controlling both Wessex and the Danelaw, but in subsequent generations control of England seesawed from Saxon (Edgar, king of Mercia and Northumberland) to Dane (Canute and his hopeless sons) and back to Saxon (Edward the Confessor).

Edward the Confessor had been brought up in Normandy – a Viking duchy in France – alongside his cousin Duke William, the future Conqueror. Edward's death left two contenders for the crown: Harold Godwineson, his English brother-in-law, and William, his Norman cousin. Harold eventually gained the throne but ruled less than a year, during which time he marched north to defeat a Viking invasion, then turned south to meet another.

Normans & Plantagenets

The year 1066 is of enormous importance in English history because the Norman invasion in that year capped a millennium of invasions and since then there have been none, although Mr Hitler came very close. In that year William, soon to be subtitled the Conqueror, landed with 12,000 men and defeated Harold at the Battle of Hastings. The conquest of England by the Northmen/Normans was completed rapidly; English aristocrats were replaced by French-speaking Normans, dominating castles were built and the feudal system was imposed.

The Normans were efficient administrators; already by 1085-86 the *Domesday Book* had provided a census of the country, its owners, its inhabitants and its potential. William I was followed in 1087 by William II and, when a mysterious arrow killed him in the New Forest, he was succeeded by Henry I. Intermarriage between Normans and Saxons was already becoming common, Henry himself marrying a Saxon princess.

A bitter struggle for the succession followed Henry I's death, and was not finally determined until Henry II (the Count of Anjou and grandson of Henry I) took the throne as the first of the Plantagenet Norman kings in 1154. Henry II had inherited more than half of modern France and the extent of his power clearly surpassed that of the king of France.

Not only was the enduring English habit of squabbling between royalty becoming established, but an almost equally enduring habit of squabbling between royalty and the church was also under way. Henry II blotted his copybook by having Thomas Becket, that 'turbulent priest', murdered in Canterbury Cathedral in 1170. Richard I, the Lionheart, was too busy crusading around the Holy Land to bother much about governing Britain and by the end of his brother John's reign, much of the Norman land in France

had been lost, disputes with the church in Rome were never-ending, and the powerful barons were so fed up they backed John into a corner and forced him to sign the Magna Carta in 1215.

This first real bill of human rights may have been intended purely as an agreement between lords and their king but its influence was to spread far further afield.

The Magna Carta did not end the power struggle between the king and his barons. In 1265 the barons held both Henry III and Prince Edward, but Edward escaped, defeated the barons and followed Henry III as Edward I in 1272. Further agreements were forged between the king and his noblemen during his reign and English control was extended across the Welsh and Scottish borders.

Edward II ascended the throne in 1307 but his lack of military success (he led his army to an horrendous defeat at the hands of Robert the Bruce of Scotland), his favouring of personal friends over his barons and, it is said, his homosexuality brought his reign to a grisly end when his queen and her lover had him imprisoned in Berkeley Castle and then murdered.

Things were scarcely better during Edward III's 50-year reign. His long rule saw the start of the Hundred Years' War with France in 1337 and the arrival of the Black Death in 1349. The plague, after a series of return bouts, eventually carried off one and a half million people, more than a third of England's population of four million. The young Richard II had barely taken the throne before he was confronted with the Peasants' Revolt in 1381 and its brutal suppression spread a wave of unrest across an already deeply unsettled country.

As well as this clash between the peasantry and the ruling class, the 14th century also saw considerable changes in society, exemplified by the rise of English and the decline of French, the language of the nobility. Chaucer's *Canterbury Tales*, first published around 1387, was not only one of the first books to be written in English, it was also one of the first printed books. In 1380,

John Wycliffe made the first English translation of the Bible, but 150 years later William Tyndale was burnt at the stake for daring to *print* the Bible in English.

The struggle to retain English control over territory in France had been a dominant concern of the Plantagenet and later Lancastrian kings. It was a prime cause of the Hundred Years' War and, to finance these adventures, the Plantagenet kings had to concede a considerable amount of power to Parliament, which jealously protected its traditional right to control taxation.

Houses of Lancaster & York

Richard II was an ineffectual king and in 1399 Henry IV seized the throne as the first of the House of Lancaster. His father, John of Gaunt, one of the younger sons of Edward III, was not only the power behind the throne during Edward III's last years, but had also been the major influence on Richard II. Henry IV was followed by Henry V, who decided it was time to stir up the dormant Hundred Years' War.

He defeated the French at Agincourt and Shakespeare later ensured his position as one of the most popular English kings. Henry VI ascended the throne as an infant and rather than warfare, devoted himself to architectural advances (King's College Chapel in Cambridge and Eton Chapel near Windsor) tempered by bouts of insanity. The Hundred

Years' War ground to a halt in 1453, the English forces straggled back from France and the Wars of the Roses popped up as an instant outlet for their skills.

Once again it was a question of succession, with Henry VI represented by the red rose of Lancaster and Richard, Duke of York, as the white rose of York. Henry VI may have been helpless, but his wife, Margaret of Anjou, was made of different mettle and in 1460 her forces defeated and killed Richard, only for Richard's son Edward to turn the tables on her and her king a year later. As Edward IV, he was the first Yorkist king but he now had to contend with Richard Neville, the scheming Earl of Warwick. Labelled 'the kingmaker', the earl teamed up with Margaret of Anjou to bring Henry VI back to the throne and shuttle Edward IV into exile in 1470, but in 1471 Edward IV came bouncing back to defeat and kill the earl and capture Margaret and Henry. Soon after, Henry was mysteriously dispatched in the Tower of London.

Edward IV was a larger-than-life king but his 12-year-old son Edward V reigned for only two months in 1483 before being murdered, with his younger brother, in the Tower of London. Whether or not Richard III, their uncle and the next king, was their killer has been the subject of much conjecture, but few tears were shed when he, crying out for a horse in exchange for his kingdom,

---

Wars – a Hundred Years & the Roses

Wars are rarely what they seem. In recent times, WWI was the 'Great War' until WWII came along to give it a number. The Hundred Years' War was an on-again, off-again affair which effectively lasted for 116 years, from the first English success at Crécy to the final English realisation that they could not hold France as well as England. It's been suggested that the war was as much a French civil war as an Anglo-French conflict but the struggle really resulted from the entangled English and French royal family lines and their conflicting spheres of control. The Black Death, shortage of funds and other 14th-century catastrophes combined to provide plentiful interruptions.

The Wars of the Roses were a similarly stop-and-start dispute, which only got their name nearly 400 years later, courtesy of romantic novelist Sir Walter Scott. It's been estimated that over the 30 years from 1455 until Henry VII grabbed the throne, actual 'war' only occupied 60 weeks. Medieval warfare was nothing like later blood-and-death struggles; damaging a rival economically by destroying villages and crops was as likely to be the policy as full-on fighting. ∎

according to Shakespeare, was tumbled from the throne by Henry Tudor, first of the Tudor dynasty, in 1485.

Tudors

Henry VII, a Lancastrian descended on his mother's side from John of Gaunt, patched things up with the York side by marrying the daughter of Edward IV and arranged strategic marriages for his own children.

Matrimony may have been a more useful tool than warfare for Henry VII but the multiple marriages of his successor, Henry VIII, were a very different story. Fathering an heir was Henry VIII's immediate problem and the church's unwillingness to cooperate with this quest led to the split with Catholicism. Parliament made Henry the head of the Church of England and the Bible was translated into English. In 1536 Henry VIII 'dissolved' the smaller monasteries in Britain and Ireland, a blatant takeover of their land and wealth as much as another stage in the struggle between church and state. There was little sympathy for the wealthy and often corrupt monasteries from the general population and in 1539-40 another monastic land grab swallowed the larger ones as well. The property was sold or granted to various members of the nobility, raising money for the king's military campaigns and ensuring the loyalty of his followers.

Nine-year-old Edward VI followed Henry VIII but only ruled for six years, during which Catholicism declined and Protestantism grew stronger. His devoutly Catholic sister Mary I reversed that pattern, but she too only ruled for five years.

Elizabeth I, the third child of Henry VIII, seemed to have inherited a nasty mess of religious strife and divided loyalties, but her 45-year reign oversaw a period of boundless English optimism epitomised by the defeat of the Spanish Armada, the global explorations of English seafarers, the expansion of trade, the literary endeavours of William Shakespeare and the scientific pursuits of Francis Bacon.

Stuarts & the Commonwealth Interlude

The one thing the Virgin Queen failed to provide was an heir and she was succeeded

Queen Elizabeth I

by James I, first of the inflexible Stuart dynasty. Since he was already James VI of Scotland, he effectively brought England, Scotland and Wales together as one country. His attempts to smooth relations with the Catholics were set back by the anti-Catholic outcry that followed Guy Fawkes' Gunpowder Plot, an attempt to blow up Parliament and the king in 1605. The power struggle between monarchy and Parliament became even more bitter during the reign of Charles I, eventually degenerating into the Civil War which pitched the king's Royalists (Cavaliers) against the Parliamentarians (Roundheads). Catholics, traditionalist members of the Church of England and the old gentry supported Charles I, whose power base was the north and west. The Protestant Puritans and the new rising merchant class based in London and the towns of the south-east, supported Parliament.

The 1644-9 struggle resulted in victory for the Parliamentary forces, the execution of Charles I and establishment of the Commonwealth, ruled by Oliver Cromwell, the brilliant Parliamentary military leader. A rampage around Ireland starting in 1649 failed to exhaust his appetite for mayhem.

By 1653 he had also become fed up with Parliament and as the 'Protector' assumed near dictatorial powers. Oliver Cromwell laid the foundation for the British Empire by modernising the army and navy and was followed half-heartedly by his son, but in 1660 Parliament decided to re-establish the monarchy as the alternatives were proving far worse.

Charles II proved to be an able, though often utterly ruthless, king who brought order out of chaos, and the Restoration foreshadowed a new burst of scientific and cultural activity after the strait-laced Puritan ethics of the Commonwealth. In this period of expansion, colonies stretched down the American coast and the East India Company established its headquarters in Bombay.

Unfortunately, James II was not so far-sighted and his attempts to ease restrictive laws on Catholics ended with defeat at the hands of William III, better known as William of Orange (the Dutch husband of Mary II, the Protestant daughter of James II). To take their joint throne, however, William and Mary had to agree to a Bill of Rights, and with the later Act of Settlement Britain was established as a constitutional monarchy with clear limits on the powers of the monarchy and a ban on any Catholic or even anyone married to a Catholic ascending the throne.

Although William and Mary's Glorious Revolution of 1688 was relatively painless in Britain, the impact in Ireland, where the Protestant ascendancy dates from William's victory over James at the Battle of the Boyne, was nowhere near as straightforward.

Mary died before William, who was followed by Anne (the second daughter of James II), but the Stuart line died with her.

Empire & Industry

In the 18th century, the Hanoverian kings increasingly relied on Parliament to govern the kingdom, and from 1721 to 1742 Sir Robert Walpole became Britain's first prime minister in all but name. This period of tranquillity was shattered in 1745 by Bonnie Prince Charlie's attempt to seize the throne but this Jacobite Rebellion, ended in disaster for Scotland at the Battle of Culloden.

Stronger English control over the British Isles was mirrored by even greater expansion overseas, where the British Empire absorbed more and more of America, Canada and India, and the first claims were made to Australia after Captain James Cook's epic voyage. The Empire's first major reverse came when the American colonies won their independence in 1782.

This setback led to a period of isolationism. During this time, Napoleon rose to power in France before naval hero Nelson and military hero Wellington curtailed, then ended, his expansion.

Meanwhile, at home, Britain was becoming the crucible of the Industrial Revolution. Canals (following the Bridgewater Canal in 1765), steam power (patented by James Watt in 1781), steam trains (launched by George Stephenson in 1830), the development of coal mines and water power transformed the means of production and transport, and the rapidly growing towns of the Midlands became the first industrial cities. Medical advances led to a dramatic increase in the population but the rapid change from an agricultural to an industrial society caused great dislocation. Nevertheless, by the time Queen Victoria took the throne in 1837, Britain was the greatest power in the world. Britain's fleets dominated the seas, linking an enormous empire, and its factories dominated world trade.

Under prime ministers Disraeli and Gladstone, the worst excesses of the Industrial Revolution were addressed, education became universal, trade unions were legalised and the right to vote was extended to most men, although women did not get the vote until after WWI.

Edwardian Era to WWII

Queen Victoria died in 1901, right on the threshold of the new century, and the ever-expanding Britain of her era died with her. It was not immediately evident that a century of relative decline was about to commence

✱✱✱

Kings & Queens of England

Nobody glancing at England's tempestuous story could ever claim that the country's history was dull. The position of king or queen of England (or perhaps worse, *potential* king or queen) would probably rank with being a drug dealer in a present-day American ghetto as one of history's least safe occupations. They've died in battle (an arrow through the eye for Harold II), been beheaded (Charles I), murdered by a wicked uncle (Edward V at the age of 12) or been knocked off by their queen and her lover (Edward II, for whom a particularly horrible death was concocted as 'punishment' for his homosexuality).

The English monarchs have often been larger-than-life characters: wife abusers of the very worst kind like Henry VIII, sufferers from insanity like George III, even stutterers like George VI. And as for scandal, the current royal family's inability to keep their clothes on or learn how to use cellular phones is only a fleeting shadow of what their predecessors got up to.

Nor has it been left solely to the men. England has been led by some powerful women, from the day Queen Boudicca charged her chariot through the Romans, right down to Maggie Thatcher, who projected herself as a queen even if she wasn't one. The two most successful monarchs in English history were probably Queen Elizabeth I and Queen Victoria, and the hapless Henry VI was lucky to be married to Margaret of Anjou, who seemed to have a private army which she led with much greater aplomb than her husband.

Saxons & Danes
Alfred the Great 871-99
Edward the Martyr 975-79
Ethelred II (the Unready) 979-1016
Canute 1016-35
Edward the Confessor 1042-66
Harold II 1066

Normans
William I (the Conqueror) 1066-87
William II (Rufus) 1087-1100
Henry I 1100-35
Stephen 1135-54

Plantagenet (Angevin)
Henry II 1154-89
Richard I (Lionheart) 1189-99
John 1199-1216
Henry III 1216-72
Edward I 1272-1307
Edward II 1307-27
Edward III 1327-77
Richard II 1377-99

Lancaster
Henry IV (Bolingbroke) 1399-1413
Henry V 1413-22
Henry VI 1422-61 & 1470-71

York
Edward IV 1461-70 & 1471-83
Edward V 1483
Richard III 1483-85

Tudor
Henry VII (Tudor) 1485-1509
Henry VIII 1509-47

Edward VI 1547-53
Mary I 1553-58
Elizabeth I 1558-1603

Stuart
James I 1603-25
Charles I 1625-49

Commonwealth & Protectorate
Oliver Cromwell 1649-58
Richard Cromwell 1658-59

Restoration
Charles II 1660-85
James II 1685-88
William III (of Orange) 1689-1702
& Mary II 1689-94
Anne 1702-14

Hanover
George I 1714-27
George II 1727-60
George III 1760-1820
George IV 1820-30
William IV 1830-37
Victoria 1837-1901

Saxe-Coburg-Gotha
Edward VII 1901-10

Windsor
George V 1910-36
Edward VIII 1936
George VI 1936-52
Elizabeth II 1953-

✱✱✱

when Edward VII, so long in waiting to become king, ushered in the relaxed new Edwardian era. In 1914 Britain bumbled into the Great War (WWI), a war of stalemate and horrendous slaughter which not only wrote trench warfare into the dictionary but also dug a huge trench between the ruling and working classes.

The old order was shattered and by the war's weary end in 1918 one million Britons had died and 15% of the country's accumulated capital had been spent. The euphoria of victory brought with it an extension of the right to vote to all men aged 21 and over, and voting rights were finally extended to women, but only to those aged 30 and over, and with other restrictive qualifications. It was not until 1928 that women were granted the same rights as men, despite Churchill's opposition.

Political changes also saw the eclipse of the Liberal Party. It was replaced by the Labour Party which won power, albeit in coalition with the Liberals, for the first time in the 1923 election. James Ramsay Mac-Donald was the first Labour prime minister. A year later the Conservatives were back in power, but the rankling 'us and them' mistrust which had developed during the war, fertilised by soaring unemployment, flowered in the 1926 General Strike. Over half a million workers hit the streets – the heavy-handed government response included sending in the army and set the stage for the labour unrest which was to plague Britain for the next 50 years.

In the mid-20s it did, however, look like Britain had finally solved one centuries-old problem. The war had no sooner ended than Britain was involved in another struggle, the bitter Anglo-Irish War, which commenced in 1919 and ground to a halt in mid-1921, with Ireland finally achieving independence. Unhappily, the decision to divide the island into two was to have long-term repercussions.

The unrest of the 1920s, with a population often at odds with its government, worsened in the 1930s as the world economy slumped, ushering in a decade of misery and political upheaval. Even the royal family came in for

its share of shake-ups in the 1930s, with the 1936 abdication of Edward VIII. This followed his decision to marry a woman who was not only twice divorced but also American; it's hard to guess which was the worse crime.

The less-than-charismatic George VI followed his brother Edward, but the scandal was a hint of the prolonged trial by media which the royal family would undergo 50 years later.

Britain dithered through the 20s and 30s with mediocre and visionless government conspicuously failing to confront the problems the country faced. Meanwhile on the Continent, the 30s saw the rise of imperial Germany under Adolf Hitler and by the time the Prime Minister, Neville Chamberlain, returned from Munich in 1938 with a promise of 'peace in our time', the roller-coaster was already heading downhill towards disaster. On 1 September 1939, Hitler invaded Poland and two days later Britain declared war – WWII had commenced.

WWII

German forces swept through France and pushed a British expeditionary force back to the beaches of Dunkirk in May/June 1940. Only an extraordinary flotilla of rescue vessels turned a total disaster into a brave defeat. By mid-1940, the other countries of Europe were either ruled by or under the direct influence of the Nazis, Stalin had negotiated a peace agreement, the USA was neutral, and Britain, under the stirring leadership of Winston Churchill, was virtually isolated. Neville Chamberlain, reviled for his policy of appeasement, had stood aside to let Churchill lead a wartime national coalition government.

Between July and October 1940, the Royal Air Force withstood the bomber raids of the Luftwaffe and won the Battle of Britain. Churchill's extraordinary exhortations inspired a never-say-die mood in the country and Hitler's invasion plans were blocked, although 43,000 Britons had died in the bombing raids.

As in WWI a stalemate ensued, although this time the English Channel was the trench between the opposing forces. Also, as in WWI, bringing the USA into the conflict would tip the balance. In December 1941, Japanese forces invaded Malaya and, just hours later, bombed the US fleet in Pearl Harbor.

The British colony of Hong Kong fell within days and Singapore fell by mid-February, but in Europe the arrival of American forces and the bitter fighting in Russia, which Hitler had invaded in June 1941, began to tip the balance. In late 1942, German forces were defeated in North Africa and the German bomber raids on England in 1940 and 41 were answered with Allied raids on Germany in 1942 and 43. Tragically, the German decision to bomb cities rather than military targets was mirrored in the Allied raids, which caused huge civilian losses without coming close to crippling Hitler's war machine.

By 1944 Germany was in retreat, the Allies had complete command of the skies and the long-awaited D-day invasion took place on the Normandy beaches in June 1944. Meanwhile, the Red Army was pushing back the Nazi forces from the east and in May 1945 it was all over for the Nazis. Hitler was dead, Germany was a smoking ruin, and Europe was to suffer new divisions which would last for nearly 50 years. Three months later, two atomic bombs forced the surrender of Japan and WWII was over.

Postwar Reconstruction

Fortunately there was greater postwar wisdom in 1945 than in 1918. The Marshall Plan, which helped rebuild an economically strong Europe, was a stark contrast to the post-WWI demands for reparations which created the misery and resentment which nurtured the Third Reich's rise. An electorate hungry for change tumbled Churchill from power and ushered in the Labour Party's Clement Attlee and a strong policy of nationalisation.

In the 1930s the artistic Bloomsbury Set had included not only writers and artists, but also the brilliant economist John Maynard Keynes. His belief that government could and should influence the economy added the words Keynesian Economics to the dictionary; his ideas on economics were also a factor in the much lower levels of unemployment which followed the war. Nationalisation of key industries, government manipulation of the economy and the institution of the National Health Service were all part of the creation of the post-war welfare state, but rebuilding after the damage of the war was to be a long and slow process.

The postwar baby boomers, flesh and blood evidence of the huge upward blip in the birth statistics which followed the war, experienced rationing and belt-tightening for many years after hostilities ceased. Britain's depleted reserves also had to cope with the retreat from the empire as one by one the colonies became independent: India in 1947, Malaya in 1957 and Kenya in 1963.

Postwar Britain was a less powerful nation but the recovery was still sufficiently strong for Prime Minister Harold Macmillan to boast in 1957 that most people in Britain had 'never had it so good'.

Swinging 60s to the Thatcher Years

By the 1960s the wartime recovery was really complete, the last vestiges of the Empire had been cast off and the Beatles era suddenly made grey old England a brighter and livelier place. The economy also looked, on the surface, to be stronger and more resilient, but even though Harold Wilson's Labour Party seemed to be doing the right things it was all built on shaky foundations. The 1970s brought the oil crisis, inflation and increased international competition, a combination which quickly revealed the British economy's inherent weaknesses.

Everything in Britain eventually comes down to class and the long struggle between a disgruntled working class and an inept ruling class finally boiled over in the 70s.

Neither Labour, under Wilson and Callaghan, or the Conservatives, under Heath, proved capable of controlling the country and the industrial strife of 1974, and its repercussions later in the decade, finally tipped the balance. In the 1979 election, the iron lady, Margaret Thatcher, led the Conservatives to power and introduced the tough new policy of Thatcherism.

Her solutions were brutal and the consequences, whether for better or worse, are still being debated. British workers and their unions were obstructive and Luddite? She broke them. British companies were inefficient and unimaginative? She drove them to the wall. The postwar nationalised companies were a mistake? Like Henry VIII dissolving the monasteries, she sold them off.

The new harder working, more competitive Britain was also a polarised Britain, with a new trench dug between the many people who prospered from the Thatcher years and the many others who found themselves not only jobless but jobless in a far less gentle environment. Despite the evident dislike a large slice of the population held for her, by 1988 Thatcher was the longest serving British prime minister of the 20th century. Her repeated electoral victories were aided by the Labour Party's long period of destructive internal struggles.

At the same time as the excesses of socialism were becoming more and more unpopular with an ever-growing percentage of the population, the Labour Party's 'loony left' tried to drag the party ever further from the centre. The chaos spawned a short-lived Social Democratic Party, revitalised the Liberals as a real third-party alternative, and ensured a spell on the opposition benches for the Labour Party which, at the time of writing, has stretched for more than 17 years.

Britain in the 90s

The Thatcherite shift to the right reached even her own party's limits of tolerance with her unpopular poll tax, and in 1990 she was dumped by her party in favour of the amazingly dull John Major. Unfortunately for the Labour Party, the immense reserves of suspicion they had managed to bank up were enough to ensure Major's election in 1992. All the opinion polls suggest that at the next election, which must be held before May 1997, a Labour government will be formed under Tony Blair.

Britain appears to be emerging from the late 80s/early 90s recession a little more powerfully than other countries in the European Union. Britain is still a wealthy and influential country, but it's no longer a superpower and no longer able to maintain that it is anything more than an island, just off the mainland.

GEOGRAPHY

Covering 50,085 square miles, England is the largest of the three political divisions within the island of Great Britain. Bound by Scotland to the north and Wales to the west, England is no more than 18 miles from France across the narrowest part of the English Channel. Now that the Channel Tunnel has been completed, however, it's no longer completely cut off from mainland Europe.

Much of England is flat or low-lying. The highest point (Scafell Pike in Cumbria) is only 3210 feet above sea level; Scotland and Wales, however, have more mountains and higher peaks.

England can be divided into four main geographic areas. In the north of the country a range of limestone hills and valleys, known as the Pennines, stretches in a central ridge from Derbyshire 250 miles north to the border with Scotland. To the west are the Cumbrian Mountains and the Lake District, one of the most scenic and best known of Britain's national parks.

South of the Pennines is the central area known as the Midlands, heavily populated and an industrial heartland since the 19th century. At its centre is Birmingham, Britain's second-largest city after London. The Black Country is the northern part of this region, stretching from just north of Birmingham through Staffordshire to Wolverhampton.

The south-west peninsula, known as the West Country and including Cornwall, Devon and parts of Somerset, is a plateau with granite outcrops and a rugged coastline.

A high rainfall and rich pastures provide good dairy farming – Devon cream is world-famous. The numerous sheltered coves and beaches, and the mild climate, make the West Country a favourite holiday destination for the British. The wild grass-covered moors of Dartmoor and Exmoor are popular with walkers.

The rest of the country is known geographically as the English Lowlands, which are a mixture of farmland, low hills, an industrial belt and densely populated cities that include the capital. The eastern part of this region, including Lincolnshire and East Anglia (Norfolk, Suffolk and Cambridgeshire), is almost entirely flat and at sea level. The Fens are the rich agricultural lands, once underwater but drained in the 18th century, that extend from Lincoln to Cambridge.

London is in the south-east of the country, on the River Thames. Further south are hills of chalk known as downs. The North Downs stretch from south of London to Dover where the chalk is exposed as the famous white cliffs. The South Downs run across Sussex, parallel to the south coast.

CLIMATE

Climatologists classify England's climate as temperate maritime, for which read mild and damp.

Despite the country being fairly far north, temperatures in England are moderated by light winds that blow in off seas warmed by the Gulf Stream. In winter, when the sea is warmer than the land, this stops temperatures inland falling very far below 0°C; in summer, when the sea is cooler than the land, it keeps summer temperatures from rising much above 30°C. The average high in London for June to August is 21°C; the average low 12°C.

Variations in the weather across England are not as great as across Britain as a whole. It tends to be colder in the north but not as cold as in Scotland. London, the south-east and the West Country are the warmest regions.

Rainfall is greatest in hilly areas (the Lake District and the Pennines) and in the West

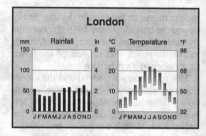

Country. Some of these areas can get up to 4500 mm of rain a year. The eastern side of England gets the lowest amount of rain in the whole of the UK. Some parts of Essex and Kent have recorded an annual rainfall of less than 600 mm.

You can, however, expect some cloudy weather and rain anywhere in Britain at any time. An umbrella or raincoat are recommended. A large plastic cycling cape can be useful even if you're not on a bike, since it can be worn over a backpack. Come prepared and you needn't find the weather as depressing as the locals appear to. The climate was the main reason given by the 50% of Brits who said in a recent survey that they'd emigrate if given the chance.

ECOLOGY & ENVIRONMENT

In a place as small as Britain, with its long history of human occupation, it is hardly surprising that the way the countryside looks today is largely the result of human interaction with the environment. As the population has grown, so too have the demands made upon the land to yield food, firewood and building materials – this has led to the extinction of unknown numbers of plant and wildlife species.

Since WWII the pattern of land use in Britain has changed dramatically, with a similarly dramatic effect on wildlife. Modern farming methods have changed the lay of the land in some places from a cosy patchwork of small fields separated by thick hedgerows to vast open areas of cultivation. As well as protecting fields from erosion, hedgerows provide habitat for wildlife and shelter for other plant species. Tens of thousands of miles of hedgerows have been destroyed and their destruction continues – since 1984, over 25% of hedgerows have disappeared.

The general reduction in biodiversity in Britain over the last 50 years has numerous other causes, including the increased use of pesticides, blanket planting of conifers (see the Plants section) and massive road-building schemes. Government policy has for many years favoured road over rail, allocating billions of pounds each year to the construction of new roads, and encouraging private car ownership. Vehicle numbers have nearly quadrupled over the last thirty years. Parts of the country, however, are protected as nature reserves and national parks, and as important natural habitats (Sites of Special Scientific Interest – SSSIs).

The environment is also reeling under the impact of tourism. In the New Forest, for example, eight million day-trippers flock annually into England's oldest parkland eroding the soil, churning up meadows and generally disturbing the wildlife. Most of them come by car and other motorists cannot leave the M27 because the sliproads are jammed with visitors to the forest. Curbs are inevitable and already restrictions have been introduced affecting camping and cycling. Similar problems are faced by authorities in other parts of the country.

There are literally hundreds of wildlife and environmental groups in Britain. For more information try: World Wide Fund for Nature (☎ 01483-426444), Panda House, Weyside Park, Godalming, Surrey, GU7 1XR; Greenpeace (☎ 0171-354 5100), Canonbury Villas, London N1 2PN; Friends of the Earth (☎ 0171-490 1555), 26 Underwood St, London N1 7JQ; or the RSNC Wildlife Trusts Partnership (☎ 01522-544400), The Green, Witham Park, Waterside South, Lincoln LN5 7JR, which has links with numerous regional groups.

Wildlife Walks & Holidays

In national parks it's often worth joining nature walks led by the park warden. Many are free; ask at information centres for details. Seashore rambles can also be an enjoyable and enlightening experience if led by an expert.

A number of companies in England offer wildlife holidays ranging from weekend breaks to longer residential courses, and with activities ranging from basic nature rambles to watching birds, foxes and badgers from special hides. Ask at TICs or try the Countryside Education Trust (☎ 01590-612340), Out of Town Centre, Palace Lane, Beaulieu, Brockhurst SO42 7YG; Wildlife Breaks (☎ 01926-842413), Oaktree Farm, Buttermilk Lane, Yarningale Common, Claverdon, Warwickshire CV35 8HW; or Peak National Park Centre (☎ 01433-620373), Losehill Hall, Castleton, Derbyshire S30 2WB. Also see Flora & Fauna in the Scotland and Wales sections.

If you want to volunteer to work on an environmental project, contact any of the organisations listed earlier in the Ecology & Environment section. Earthwatch (☎ 01865-311600), Belsyre Court, Observatory Rd, Oxford OX2 6HU, can put you on scientific expeditions to several parts of Britain (as well as worldwide). Costs, however, are usually at least £500.

FLORA & FAUNA
Flora

England was once almost entirely covered with woodland, but tree cover has now fallen to a mere 7.3%, the lowest figure for any country in Europe after Ireland. Italy has 22% tree cover, France 27%.

As long ago as 1919, a government agency known as the Forestry Commission was established to halt this decline with a long-range plan to plant five million acres (two million hectares) of trees by the year 2000. Substantial grants for landowners ensured that this target was achieved by the early 1980s. The environmental problems caused by planting the fast-growing conifers that were recommended by the Forestry Commission became obvious only in the last few decades. Very little can grow beneath conifers and large areas of ancient peatland have been destroyed by plantations. In recent years, however, there has been a switch to establishing new broadleaf woods.

Apart from vast areas of conifers (mainly in the north of England, Scotland and Wales), other trees common in England include the oak, elm, chestnut, lime (not the citrus variety), ash and beech.

Despite the continued destruction of plant habitat, there is still a wide variety of wildflowers, particularly in spring. Small white snowdrops are the first to flower, sometimes as early as February. Around Easter (late March or early April), parks around the country are bright with yellow daffodils. In woodlands there are purple carpets of bluebells; yellow primroses, buttercups and cowslips are common in meadows. Tall purple foxgloves flower from June to September.

In the summer, cultivated fields may be edged with red poppies. A flowering crop that you cannot fail to notice is oilseed rape and expanses of this brilliant yellow crop are becoming more common.

Gorse bushes are abundant on heathland and other rough sandy places. They have small yellow flowers and a mass of sharp spines instead of leaves. Found in the same habitat, broom is very similar, though lacking the prickles. Fern-like bracken is also common.

On the moors there are several varieties of flowering heathers, bracken and whortleberries (also known as bilberries) growing on small shrubs, one and a half feet in height. These tiny blue-black berries are good to eat when they ripen in the summer.

There are many plant identification books. One of the classics is *The Concise British Flora in Colour*, with 1486 beautifully accurate paintings of different species by artist-vicar William Keble Martin.

Fauna

There are 116 protected animal species in Britain; animals such as the beaver, wolf and reindeer, once common, are extinct.

The red deer is the largest British mammal, with herds found on Exmoor and Dartmoor, in the Lake District and in such large numbers north of the border that culling is required. Fallow deer, introduced long ago by the Romans, live in small herds of 20 or so animals and can still be seen in the New Forest and Epping Forest. Roe deer are smaller, about the size of a large goat, and are quite common in forest areas where they do considerable damage to young trees. Other species that have been introduced include the Asian muntjac and the Chinese water deer.

Despite the fox corpses that line Britain's roads, this animal is prospering, having adapted well to suburban life. Although it's nocturnal, the fox can often be seen before dark, and even on the edges of cities, scavenging around dustbins. Badgers are much more shy and although their setts (burrows) may be seen in woods, they come out only at night. Another animal that you're more likely to see as a roadside casualty is the hedgehog.

The grey squirrel, introduced from North America, is very common and has almost entirely replaced the smaller red squirrel. Also introduced from abroad, and having escaped from fur farms, the mink is prospering. Otter numbers are also growing, despite competition from mink in some areas. Once very rare, the pine marten is again being seen in some forested regions. Stoats and weasels are rarely encountered.

Rabbits are extremely common; the brown hare, with longer legs and ears, is found in parts of England. There are several small rodent species including the brown rat

The shy badger is rarely seen in Britain – however, some wildlife organisations run nocturnal badger-spotting events aimed at nature lovers.

(originally from Asia), the tiny shrew and harvest mouse (once common in the hedgerows), and the water vole (or water rat). At dusk, bats are often seen.

Two species of seal frequent the coasts around England: these are the grey seal and the common seal, which is actually less common than the grey.

England's only venomous snake is the adder, also known as the viper. Usually less than one and a half feet in length, it inhabits dry places on heaths and moors. Numbers fell from hundreds of thousands to less than 20,000 before it was added to the list of protected species. Other reptiles include the harmless grass snake, the slowworm, the common lizard, and amphibians such as frogs, toads and newts.

Amongst the various fish species found in England, salmon and brown trout are best known. See the Activities chapter for information on fishing.

Birds Birdwatching is a popular pastime in Britain; a wide range of species can be observed thanks to the mild climate.

While the numbers and diversity of coastal bird species do not appear to be in great danger, the same cannot be said for other British birds. A number of species that were quite common only 25 years ago are rapidly dwindling. The breeding population of the tree sparrow, for example, is now 15% of the 1971 figure. The destruction of habitat is largely to blame.

The gardens of urbanised England support the easily recognisable red-breasted robin, sparrow, thrush, blackbird and blue tit (yellow front, blue/white head). Pigeons are so abundant that they're now considered a pest, particularly in cities. Crows are very common, likewise the black and white magpie, also a member of the crow family.

Skylarks are becoming less common each year, but you can still hear their twittering song high above open ground. At dusk you may see the tawny owl or, very occasionally, the rarer barn owl.

Lakes and inland waterways support a variety of birdlife. The mute swan is Britain's biggest bird. All swans, except for two groups on the Thames, are said to belong

to the monarch, but it's unlikely that they'd now make much of a feast to set before a king or queen. On rivers where fishing is popular some of the swans have died from lead poisoning, having swallowed discarded fishing weights while foraging.

Populations of Canada geese, introduced 300 years ago, have increased dramatically. Bold and aggressive, large numbers of them can strip fields of their crops.

There are several varieties of duck, the mallard being common. The male, with green head and narrow white collar, is easily recognisable.

The pheasant was introduced from Russia over 900 years ago and, while reared on large estates for shooting, now also breeds in the wild. Other gamebirds include the partridge and grouse.

Raptors are now rare. There are a few heavily protected golden eagles in the Lake District. Kestrels and sparrowhawks are sometimes seen, especially hunting near motorways.

Around the coast are large populations of seagulls, terns, cormorants, gannets, shags, razorbills and guillemots. The comical puffin, with its massive, red-and-yellow bill, is a member of the auk family. It comes to land only to breed, which it does in numerous colonies across the length of the British Isles from the Isle of Wight to Shetland.

Twitchers (or birdwatchers) should contact the Royal Society for the Protection of Birds (☎ 01767-680551), The Lodge, Sandy, Bedfordshire SG19 2BR, which runs over 100 bird reserves. They publish *Enjoying Wildlife*, a guide to their reserves (£4.95). Membership of the Wildfowl and Wetlands Trust (☎ 01453-890333), Slimbridge, Gloucestershire GL2 7BT, gives entry to its nine reserves and a magazine twice a year.

Amongst the shelves of books for birdwatchers, look for the *Where to Watch Birds* regional series published by Christopher Helm (£12.99).

Cruelty to Animals
The English, it has been said, love their animals more than their children. In fact the

Royal Society for the Prevention of Cruelty to Animals was established before the National Society for the Prevention of Cruelty to Children and the former charity still earns more in donations than the latter.

However, there can scarcely be a sport more redolent of England, whether it's the English countryside, the English class system or the English landed gentry, than fox hunting. Nor, in the closing years of the 20th century, can there be a sport more ideologically unsound. Oscar Wilde summed it up 100 years ago as 'the unspeakable in pursuit of the inedible'.

Remarkably, fox hunting does survive and, even more remarkably, foxes do too. These days it's estimated that Britain's 200-odd hunts kill about 20,000 foxes a year, but 40,000 are killed by vehicles and over 100,000 are trapped or shot. In fact many foxes may actually owe their existence to the hunters since it is believed that many field-side stretches of hedge and small woods are there due to fox-hunting farmers intent on providing more living quarters for foxes.

Hunting may not kill that many foxes and the fox population may actually be encouraged in order to provide more hunting prey, but it's undeniably a cruel sport. Anti-hunting sentiment in England runs strong and polls have revealed that two-thirds to three-quarters of the population would support a hunting ban. It's also undeniably a sport of the upper class or at least of the wealthy. Annual membership of a hunt is typically around £400 and a day out hunting can be as low as £10, but for a classy hunt like the Quorn it can run to over £100. The curious attire, starting with a 'pink' (which in fox-hunting parlance means red!) jacket, can cost thousands from a London tailor. And then there are the horses; most fox hunters, a survey by the NT revealed, own two or more horses in part because different hunts require different types of horse.

National Parks

England's national parks cover about 7% of the country and include Dartmoor, Exmoor, the Lake District, the Peak District, the Yorkshire Dales, the North York Moors and Northumberland. The New Forest and the Broads were recently also given national park status.

The term national park is misleading. Unlike national parks in some countries, these are not wilderness areas where humans have been excluded. They include places of outstanding natural beauty that have been given special protection through an act of Parliament passed in 1949. National parks are not owned by the nation; most of the land within them is in private ownership or belongs to charitable trusts such as the National Trust.

National park status does not give the visitor any special rights of access. It does, however, mean that development within the park is controlled through planning committees. Information centres and recreational facilities are provided for visitors.

GOVERNMENT & POLITICS

The United Kingdom does not have a written constitution but operates under a mixture of Parliamentary statutes, common law (a body of legal principles based on precedents that go back to Anglo-Saxon customs) and convention.

The monarch is the head of state, but real power has been whittled away to the point where the current Queen is a figurehead who acts almost entirely on the advice of 'her' ministers and parliament.

Parliament has three separate elements – the Queen, the House of Commons and the House of Lords. In practice, the supreme body is the House of Commons, which is directly elected every five years. An earlier election can be called at the request of the party in power, or if the party in power loses a vote of confidence.

Voting is not compulsory, and candidates are elected if they win a simple majority in their constituencies. There are 650 constituencies (seats) – 523 for England, 38 for Wales, 72 for Scotland and 17 for Northern Ireland.

The House of Lords consists of the Lords Spiritual (26 senior bishops of the Church of England) and more than 1100 Lords Temporal

✚✚

A Great British Republic?

The Queen of England remains a popular figure in Britain but the same cannot be said for most other members of the royal family. A recent opinion poll showed that for the first time the number saying the monarchy will disappear within the next 50 years is greater than the number who expect it to survive.

Even more alarming – or welcoming – is the fact that less than 20% of people under 25 think that Britain would be worse off without a monarchy. If the Labour party gains power and carries out its reform of the House of Lords, the Windsors would be the last family in Britain with the privilege of political power by accident of birth.

So is it goodbye to the Queen's opening of parliament, the Christmas broadcast, the royal presence at the Cup Final and the familiar profile on postage stamps and coins?

If so, it will be an astonishing royal act of self-destruction because apart from a few brave souls like the Labour politician Tony Benn, few voices have dared to question the monarchy in Britain. Partly due to the Queen's untainted image, the monarchy remained a sacrosanct institution until other members of the Windsor family began to provide the public with a soap opera to rival *Coronation Street*. Now the unthinkable has begun to be thinkable and, for the first time, a leading newspaper in 1996 called for the abolition of the monarchy.

Revelations about the undignified marital troubles of the Prince and Princess of Wales and the lifestyle of other family members like the Duchess of York led another newspaper to dub the Windsors the most dysfunctional family in Britain. ■

✚✚

(all hereditary and life peers), and the Lords of Appeal (or 'law lords'). None are elected by the general population. If the Lords refuse to pass a bill, but it is passed twice by the Commons, it is sent to the Queen for her automatic assent. In addition, any 'money' bill, a bill which involves the raising of revenue, automatically becomes law one month after the Commons passes it on to the Lords, regardless of whether or not the Lords have passed it.

The Prime Minister is the leader of the majority party in the House of Commons and is technically appointed by the Queen. All other ministers are appointed on the recommendation of the Prime Minister, most of them coming from the House of Commons. Ministers are responsible for government departments. The senior 20 or so ministers make up the Cabinet, which, although answerable to Parliament, meets confidentially and in effect manages the government and its policies.

For the last 150 years a predominantly two-party system has operated. Since 1945 either the Conservative Party (also known as the Tory party) or the Labour Party has held power, the Conservatives drawing their support mainly from suburbia and the countryside, Labour from urban industrialised areas, Scotland and Wales.

Put crudely, the Conservatives are right-wing, free-enterprise supporters, and Labour is left-wing in the social-democratic tradition. In recent years, however, the Labour Party has shed most of its socialist credo, and the Conservatives have softened their hard-right approach. In the 1992 general election, John Major led the Conservatives to their fourth consecutive victory. Tony Blair is expected to win the 1997 general election and form a moderate Labour government.

ECONOMY

Until the 18th century, England's economy was based on agriculture and the manufacture of woollen cloth. In the late 18th century, the Empire and the Industrial Revolution allowed Britain to become the first industrialised trading nation and the populations of south Wales, the Midlands, York-shire and the Scottish Lowlands expanded rapidly as the drastically changing economy stimulated the opening of mines, factories and canals. Conditions for the workers were often appalling, although there were examples of paternalistic and far-sighted factory owners who tried to provide model working conditions for their employees.

Britain dominated 19th-century world trade but the 20th century dawned with slow decline already under way. Britain had been the pioneering influence in many of the 19th century's leading engineering fields, from railways to ocean liners, but it did not enjoy the same utterly dominant role in new 20th-century developments like automobiles and aircraft. Following WWII, a considerable proportion of industry was nationalised as first railways, gas and electricity services, coal mines, steel manufacturing and ship-building, and later (although probably reluctantly) even cars, came under government control. If anything, public ownership only accelerated the decline until the world-wide upheavals in manufacturing in the 1970s and 80s changed the gradual fall into a precipitous drop.

Under Margaret Thatcher, the nationalisation process was reversed and many areas were sold off, some of them with dramatic success. The standard adjectives used to describe British Airways, for example, switched from huge, money-losing and demoralised to huge, money-making and efficient. Meanwhile, many traditional areas of activity, like mining and engineering, simply disappeared and only North Sea oil saved Britain from a horrendous economic crunch. Although manufacturing continues to play an important role (particularly in the Midlands), service industries like banking and finance have grown rapidly (particularly in London and the south-east).

A survey of the British economy in the influential magazine *The Economist* pinned the blame for Britain's weak 20th-century economy on its strong 19th-century one. The level of investment in Britain has consistently been far lower than that of competitive nations, and in comparison to the Victorian era it has been truly awful. For too long Britain has been living off its 19th-century inheritance and as a result growth rates and productivity improvements have been low. The elitist education structure, which accounts for the shortage of trained technicians and craftspeople, has compounded the problem, and that old British bugbear, the class system, has also played its deleterious part.

Maggie took a serious bite out of the power of the old-school-tie brigade, but for far too long British business consisted of poorly trained and shortsighted management, which seemed to be in permanent conflict with an equally poorly trained workforce, who were dragged back further by the large chips on their collective shoulders.

England enters the last years of the 20th century with many problems but also with a much greater awareness of their causes. London continues to develop as one of the world's major financial centres, and all over the country the sweeping aside of old management and workforce attitudes has revolutionised many businesses, from newspapers to car manufacturing. In late 1996, the economy seemed to be emerging from a long recession and although unemployment was still high (well over 2 million), inflation was low (under 2.5%).

POPULATION

Britain has a population of over 55 million, or around an average of 600 inhabitants per sq mile, making the island one of the most crowded on the planet. The majority of the population is concentrated in England (which has a population of 48 million) in and around London, and in the Midlands around Birmingham, Manchester, Liverpool, Sheffield and Nottingham.

To these figures you can factor in an annual influx of nearly 20 million tourists.

PEOPLE

The Brits are a diverse bunch, as one would expect given the variety of peoples who have made this island their home (see the previous history section for more information). To generalise, however, the dominant Anglo-Saxons, as they are sometimes referred to, are predominantly Germanic/Scandinavian.

Particularly since the Industrial Revolution, England has attracted large numbers of people from Scotland, Wales and Ireland. In the 18th, 19th and 20th centuries there were

The Decline & Fall of the British Car Industry

In 1968, clutching my degree in engineering, I joined the engineering department of Rootes Cars in Coventry, a company on a one-way street to oblivion. In retrospect it was like being present for the death throes of a dinosaur.

Rootes neatly summed up everything that was wrong with British manufacturing. In the 1950s, Lord Rootes assembled a collection of lesser British automotive brand names like Singer, Sunbeam, Humber and Hillman under the Rootes umbrella. In the early 1960s, Rootes belatedly tried to liven up their staid model line-up with the Hillman Imp, a first-rate automotive disaster. The poor little Imp was actually a delight to drive but every step of the way it was a mistake. When European car manufacturing was moving towards larger and roomier cars, the Imp was a minicar. When smaller manufacturers were realising that high-value niche production was the only way to make money (BMW were the epitome of this discovery) the Imp was a bare-bones economy vehicle. When front-wheel drive was about to become the wave of the future (the Mini pioneered the change in 1958), the Imp was one of the last rear-engined cars like the old VW Beetle. Worse, when Britain was about to establish a solid reputation for building not-yet-production-ready cars, the unfortunate Imp, with its high-tech but underdeveloped die-cast aluminium engine, was a paragon of unreliability.

If all this wasn't bad enough, the British government, intent on decentralising British industry (little realising it was going to self-destruct in the next few decades), persuaded Rootes to build the Imp in Scotland, where the factory was plagued with labour unrest and poor-quality work. Rootes was soon haemorrhaging red ink and in 1967 Chrysler stepped in to take it over. My 1½ years at Rootes/Chrysler saw the US firm try to apply to their British offshoot the same genius that would soon lead them to the brink of disaster in the USA.

The engineering division was full of weirdly archaic British systems, such as the separation of employees into 'works' and 'staff'. Works started and finished 45 minutes earlier than staff. As a result, at the start of the day they had to wait for the staff to arrive and tell them what to do, and at the other end the staff sat around because there was nobody around to do the things that needed doing. Of course, there were plenty of 'works' activities which 'staff' could easily manage themselves (and vice versa) but stepping over rigidly drawn demarcation lines was a recipe for disaster.

In 1970 the car I was working on (later to pop up in Australia as the Chrysler Centura) was dropped and me with it. Soon afterwards Chrysler started to fall through the floor and their European divisions (Simca in France and Rootes in England) were both taken over by the French firm Peugeot. Today, Peugeots are assembled at the old Rootes/Chrysler factory at Ryton-on-Dunsmore. Ramshackle old Rootes did, however, provide some of the inspiration that led me to setting up Lonely Planet. Soon after I joined the company, a Hillman Hunter was entered in the London-Sydney Marathon car rally; remarkably it won. Poring over maps of Afghanistan and Iran used by the team sparked my interest in making the Asia overland trip and led to Lonely Planet's first guidebook.

Tony Wheeler

Hillman Imp

also significant influxes of refugees. Huguenots (French Protestants) arrived in the 18th century, and Jews arrived in the 19th and, of course, the first half of the 20th century.

The big cities are multicultural – since WWII there has been significant immigration from many ex-colonies, especially the West Indies, Pakistan and India. Outside of London and the big Midlands cities, however, the population is overwhelmingly Anglo-Saxon, although the immigrant influence can be seen in the Chinese and Indian restaurants that can be found in even the smallest of towns. In recent years, population growth has been virtually static or even negative, and emigrants have often outnumbered immigrants. See also the later Culture section.

ARTS

The greatest artistic contributions of the English have been in theatre, literature and architecture. Although there are notable individual exceptions, there is not an equivalent tradition of great painters, sculptors or composers.

Perhaps the most distinctive phenomenon is the huge number of extraordinary country houses. Aristocrats of the 18th and 19th centuries knew quality when they saw it, and they surrounded themselves with treasures in the most beautiful houses and gardens of Europe. Waited-on hand and foot, the elite of a mighty empire, they believed with certainty they were at the absolute pinnacle of civilisation.

Fortunately, although their successors have often inherited arrogance intact, inheritance taxes have forced many to open their houses and priceless art collections to the public. England is a treasure house of masterpieces from every age and continent. The architectural heritage is superb but, with a few notable exceptions, the 20th century has failed to add anything more inspiring than motorways, high-rise housing estates and tawdry suburban development.

British publishers churn out 80,000 books a year, and the range and quality of theatre, music, dance and art is outstanding by any measure.

Literature

Anyone who has studied 'English' literature will find that to some extent the landscapes and people they have read about can still be found. Travelling in the footsteps of the great English, Scottish and Welsh writers, and their characters, can be one of the highlights of visiting Britain. There is a phenomenal wealth of books that capture a moment in time, a landscape, or a group of people. This guide only gives a few suggestions of where to start.

In the beginning was Chaucer with his *Canterbury Tales*. This book may be responsible for more boring lectures than any other, but in its natural environment it comes to life, giving a vivid insight into medieval society, in particular into the lives of pilgrims on their way to Canterbury. Neville Coghill has written a good modern translation.

The next great figure to blight schoolchildren's lives was Shakespeare. Nonetheless, many will be tempted to follow in his footsteps – to Stratford-upon-Avon where he lived and the site of the Globe Theatre in London where his works were dramatised.

The most vivid insight into 17th-century life, particularly in London, is courtesy of *Samuel Pepys' Diary*. In particular, he gives the most complete account of the plague and the Great Fire of London.

The popular English novel, as we know it, did not really appear until the 18th century with the upsurge of the literate middle class. If you plan to spend time in the Midlands, read Elizabeth Gaskell's *Mary Barton*, which paints a sympathetic picture of the plight of the workers during the Industrial Revolution. This was also the milieu about which Charles Dickens wrote most powerfully. *Hard Times* is set in fictional Coketown and paints a brutal picture of the capitalists who prospered in it.

Jane Austen wrote about a very different social class – a prosperous, provincial middle class. The intrigues and passions boiling away under the stilted constraints of 'propriety' are beautifully portrayed in *Emma* and *Pride and Prejudice*.

If you visit the Lake District, you will find constant references to William Wordsworth, the romantic poet who lived there for the first half of the 19th century. Modern readers may find him difficult, but at his best he has an exhilarating appreciation of the natural world.

More than most writers, Thomas Hardy depended heavily on a sense of place and on the relationship between place and people. This makes his best work an evocative picture of Wessex, the region of England centred on Dorchester (Dorset) where he lived. *Tess of the D'Urbervilles* is one of his greatest novels.

Moving into the 20th century, DH Lawrence chronicled life in the Midland coal-mining towns in the brilliant *Sons & Lovers*. Joseph Conrad's *The Secret Agent* explores a murky world of espionage in London.

Written in the 1930s in the middle of the Depression, George Orwell's *Down & Out in Paris & London* describes Orwell's destitute existence as a temporary vagrant. Some travellers in the 1990s may find they can identify with him. At about the same time, Graham Greene wrote of the seamy side of Brighton in *Brighton Rock*.

Doris Lessing painted a picture of London in the 1960s in *The Four Gated City*, a part of her 'Children of Violence' series. One of the funniest and most vicious portrayals of Britain in the 1990s is by Martin Amis in *London Observed*, a collection of stories set in the capital. There are many other interesting perspectives: Hanef Kureishi writes about the lives of young Pakistanis in London in *The Black Album*, and Caryl Phillips writes of the Caribbean immigrants' experience in *The Final Passage*.

Theatre
The historical legacy stretches back to Shakespeare and medieval times, and London is still one of the theatre capitals of the world.

> ✿✿✿✿✿✿✿✿✿✿✿✿✿✿✿✿✿✿✿✿
>
> **The Mousetrap**
> Described by *The Guardian* as 'Cluedo dramatised for the theatre', Agatha Christie's *The Mousetrap* has been pulling punters into the theatre for a record-breaking 44 years and yet still they keep coming to watch a play that Christie herself said was 'not really frightening...not really horrible...not really a farce.'
> And who was left with egg on their face? Well, the people who took up the film rights in 1956 on the understanding that no movie should be released until six months after the play closed. ■
>
> ✿✿✿✿✿✿✿✿✿✿✿✿✿✿✿✿✿✿✿✿

The recession and the unsupportive Conservative government have combined to make life hard, especially for innovative new theatre. Financial demands and the need for proven reliability explains a depressing growth in the theatrical art of playing safe – be it Agatha Christie's *Mousetrap*, now in its fifth decade and the longest running play in history, or Andrew Lloyd Webber's *Cats*, now into a second decade.

The National Theatre in London is the nation's theatre flagship and offers a cocktail of revived classics, contemporary plays and appearances by radical young companies. The Barbican in London, and Stratford-upon-Avon are home to the Royal Shakespeare Company, which can be fusty but is usually excellent. And most regional cities have at least one world-class company and the facilities to stage major touring productions.

At any time of the year London's many fringe-theatre productions offer an eccentric selection of the amazing, the boring, the life-changing and the downright ridiculous. See the London Entertainment section.

Film
A constant complaint from film-makers is that if only there was sufficient funding and support within the country then British directors and actors (Alan Rickman, Tim Roth, Emma Thompson, Mike Figgis...) would not constantly have to look to Hollywood for

work. Even film-makers who mostly work within the country cannot always be assured of support. Mike Leigh, who won the Palme D'Or in 1996 for his *Secrets & Lies*, has made a number of compelling movies about contemporary Britain which were considered too political to be supported.

It's a pity really because there is a wealth of talent and tradition associated with film in England, borne out by the British Tourist Authority's free map and brochure that highlights numerous places around the country with a film connection. The good news is that Elstree Studios, where the clever bits in *Star Wars* were made, is open again and the BBC has now joined Channel Four *(Four Weddings and a Funeral)* in making movies.

Popular Music

Over the years, English musicians have had an enormous impact on popular music – much greater, strangely, than their influence on 'serious' music.

We could begin a survey with Gilbert & Sullivan's light operas – but we won't. The swinging 60s produced The Beatles, The Rolling Stones, The Who and The Kinks; the late 60s and the glam years of the early 70s had stardust-speckled heroes like David Bowie, Marc Bolan and Bryan Ferry, and bands like Fleetwood Mac, Pink Floyd, Deep Purple, Led Zeppelin and Genesis; they were followed by punk's best known spokesmen, The Sex Pistols and The Clash.

The turbulent, ever-changing music scene of the 80s saw the new romantics, left-wing 'agit-pop', and the development of a chaotic club and rave scene featuring house and techno music. New bands that made it big included the Police, the Eurythmics, Wham, Duran Duran, Dire Straits, UB40 and The Smiths.

Of late, the Americans have dominated rock music with grunge (which has more than a passing resemblance to punk). However, recent times have seen the rise of post-grunge music and the renaissance of the quintessentially English Indie pop band with the likes of Blur, Elastica, Pulp, Suede and above all Oasis.

These new bands, and many others, prove that recent reports of the death of English popular music have been seriously exaggerated – especially by nostalgic fortysome-

---

Britpop Rules the Airwaves

Since the 1960s, British rock music has shown an astonishing ability to reinvent itself at regular intervals, with psychedelia giving way to heavy metal, and glam rock to punk.

The mid-1990s were the turn of something rock journos had no sooner christened 'Britpop' than they were comprehensively savaging it. Not that that would have bothered its most prominent representatives, Blur, Pulp and, most of all, Oasis, whose members have been laughing all the way to the bank.

'Britpop' is characterised by the sort of whistleable tunes even oldies can relate to and lyrics that evoke everyday experience in a way that has had the bands labelled the offspring of the Kinks and the Beatles. Noel Gallagher, lyricist for Oasis, makes no bones about his debt to the Beatles.

Of course, the pop world being what it is, it's not enough for the bands to pump out great tunes and memorable lyrics. At the 1996 music-industry-sponsored Brit awards, the Gallagher brothers insulted both prize-giver and audience, and Jarvis Cocker, lead singer of Pulp, jumped on stage to protest against Michael Jackson's presentation of himself in quasi-religious light and wound up under arrest. To cap it all, in 1996 Liam and Noel Gallagher arrived separately on their US tour, only to row so badly that it was cancelled halfway through. Funnily enough, it's Blur, whose music sounds most rough-edged, who keep the lowest profile, despite efforts to talk up singer Damon Albarn's rivalry with the Gallaghers.

Seminal 'Britpop' albums are Oasis's *(What's The Story) Morning Glory?*, Blur's *Parklife* and Pulp's *Different Class*. ∎

things. In all the major cities there is an enormous variety of music on offer. See the London Entertainment section.

Classical Music & Opera

London is quite probably the classical music capital of Europe, and most of the major companies undertake countrywide tours. There are five symphony orchestras, various smaller outfits, a brilliant array of venues, reasonable prices and high standards of performance. The biggest dilemma faced by the concertgoer is an enviable one: that of picking from the sheer embarrassment of riches on offer.

Opera tends to be more of a problem, and the problem is that it costs so much to produce. The Royal Opera House, the flagship company in London, is constantly beset by money difficulties, but it maintains its five-star rating, regularly nabbing opera superstars. If you want a good seat, be prepared to take out a mortgage. The recent boom in the popularity of opera in England is partly thanks to Pavarotti scoring a massive hit with Puccini's 'Nessum Dorma'. The English love a good tune.

See the London Entertainment section.

Visual Arts

As a repository of art, England's museums and stately homes are unmatched. They're stuffed with fine examples of painting and sculpture from every age and corner of the globe. The National Gallery in London, in particular, should not be missed.

English artists have never dominated an historical epoch (in the way that Italian, French and Dutch schools have, for instance), but there are a sprinkling of geniuses that visitors should look for. The Tate Gallery, London, is the place to start for a survey of British painting.

Perhaps it's encouraged by the quality of English light, but there is a fine tradition of water-colourists, beginning with William Blake. Nineteenth-century artists like Turner, Constable and some of the pre-Raphaelites (Holman Hunt, Millais, Burne-

Jones) succeeded brilliantly in capturing their native countryside.

The big names post-WWII include Francis Bacon and Lucien Freud, both of whom have concentrated on painting human figures, David Hockney with his pop-art realism and Damien Hurst with his sensational formaldehyde creations. The private Saatchi Gallery in London often has the most exciting contemporary painting.

ARCHITECTURE

Britain's vast architectural endowment reaches back more than 5000 years to the remarkable 'cathedral' of Stonehenge and the village of Skara Brae in Orkney. Although the record is sometimes sparse, there are survivors from that time on. Every group of invaders has left its mark (especially if they built in stone) – often unquestionably building for posterity; in other words, for us.

Roman and Saxon work is rare, which is not so surprising considering the Roman legacy is getting close to 2000 years old. Complete Norman buildings are also rare, but there are still many examples of 900-year-old craftsmanship in everyday use. The great houses that are scattered so profusely through the countryside are very often based on Norman castles, and churches and cathedrals also often incorporate Norman elements.

Survivors from the 16th and 17th centuries are progressively more common, and at this age – around 400 years – quite mundane and ordinary domestic architecture survives. For someone to live in an 18th-century house – a mere 200 or 300 years old – is totally unremarkable.

Monumental British architecture has always been outstanding, and domestic vernacular architecture was certainly visually appealing up to the Industrial Revolution. With some notable exceptions, since then it seems the guiding principle for builders and architects has been to spend as little money as possible. Aesthetic considerations were for those who could afford them – the rich. Post WWII, most building has also been disappointing, with a particular lack of regard for the overall fabric of the cities. There have been, nonetheless, some outstanding new buildings, particularly in the last 10 years.

Fortunately, there has been a strong and successful campaign to protect the island's architectural heritage (thanks in particular to the National Trust and English Heritage organisations). This nostalgic obsession does sometimes go to extreme lengths, and popular British architecture and design can seem very conservative.

Church Terminology

Britain's rich collection of churches is of great interest for history and architecture but it's often very confusing. You're admonished to inspect ceilings in chancels, inscriptions in naves, misericords in choirs, monuments in chapels, or tombs in transepts. Furthermore, the church might be Saxon or Norman or Early English or Perpendicular or more likely a combination of two or more of these styles. It may not even be a church you're in. Perhaps it's really an abbey, a minster or a cathedral. What does it all mean?

Basically a church is a church, is a church; they're all places for Christian worship. Technically, a cathedral is the principal church of a diocese and contains the bishop's throne. A diocese is the district for which a bishop is responsible. In practice a cathedral is usually larger and grander than a church, although there are some large churches and some small cathedrals. In contrast, a church is usually a more local affair; the term 'parish church' indicates that local nature.

The term abbey can mean a monastery of monks or nuns or the buildings they used. The abbey church was a church intended principally for use by the monks or nuns, not for the general population.

When Henry VIII dissolved the monasteries in the 1530s, many of the abbeys in England and Ireland were destroyed or converted into private homes, although some survived as churches. Thus there are abbey churches which were taken over by the general populace (like Malmesbury Abbey

in Wiltshire) and also stately homes which are known as abbeys (like Beaulieu Abbey in Hampshire).

A minster (like Wimborne Minster in Dorset) refers to a church at one time connected to a monastery. A collegiate church is another specialised term; think of it as almost a cathedral!

Church Architectural Styles

What makes old churches especially interesting in a totally secular sense is that they expressed the very highest levels of human endeavour. In our age it's computers, space capsules and aircraft which are at the cutting edge of technology. During the Industrial Revolution it was railways, ships and huge bridges which symbolised humanity's greatest achievements. In the medieval era it was churches. These great churches were often built to the outermost limits of building technology and it wasn't unusual for catastrophic collapses to occur even during construction.

English churches are fascinating to wander around, especially once you've learnt a little about the various periods, styles and design elements, but it's even more interesting to go backstage and inspect the church construction.

A tour of the roof or tower of Salisbury Cathedral is a real time-machine trip to a medieval building site. When construction finished nearly 700 years ago, the builders simply downed tools and left; some of their equipment is still sitting there. These time-travel tours take place several times a day and only cost a pound or two.

Very few English churches are uniformly of one style. Usually the design of one period has been piled on another and, like a Russian toy, there are churches within churches. When decay, subsidence or other actions brought part of a church down, the reconstruction was often in whatever was the current style. As a result a church may, for example, have opposite walls in entirely different styles. Alternatively, a growing congregation or increased wealth often inspired extensions or a more magnificent tower or spire, inevitably in a more recent style.

Political changes also affected churches and their design. Between 1536 and 1540, Henry VIII 'dissolved' the monasteries. This was both the final step in an ongoing power struggle between church and state and a straightforward takeover of monastic wealth.

The riches Henry VIII shared out to friends and supporters after this great land grab established the fortunes of much of Britain's nobility. The Reformation of the 16th and 17th centuries saw an attack on imagery in churches and huge numbers of statues and images were destroyed then, particularly during the attack on 'Popish' influence during the reign of Mary I.

The main design periods for British churches are listed below.

Saxon The earliest churches in England were built during the Saxon era from around 700 to 1050. They were generally small, squat, solid and unembellished and were characterised by round arches and square towers. Since most Saxon churches were built of wood, few survive. However St Lawrence's in Bradford-on-Avon, Wiltshire, and St Martin's in Wareham, Dorset, are both predominantly from Saxon times.

All Saints at Brixworth and All Saints at Earls Barton are near Northampton in Northamptonshire, and both have very clear Saxon origins. The style is also known as Early Romanesque or pre-Conquest Romanesque on the grounds that the design derived from Roman influence.

Norman After the Norman invasion in 1066, Saxon architecture gave way to Norman, a style known as Romanesque in Continental Europe. As in Saxon churches, rounded arches and squat, square towers were utilised. The easily visible difference in appearance is due to detailing and decoration.

The Norman style lasted only about a century, but surviving Norman churches (or churches with much Norman influence) are generally larger in scale than their Saxon

predecessors. Squat, square, massive, thick and bulky are all descriptive adjectives applied to the Norman style. There is no purely Norman church in England but Southwell Minster, Norwich Cathedral and Durham Cathedral are all predominantly Norman.

Early English Norman design gave way to a Transitional style and then to Early English from around 1150 to 1280. The rounded arches started to be supplanted by pointed ones in the transitional period while Early English made greater use of pointed arches and added ribbed vaults and flying buttresses.

Early English was the first phase of Gothic design (the Gothic tag was not dreamt up until the 17th century) and is also known as Early Pointed, aptly describing the change from the earlier rounded designs. Salisbury Cathedral is the prime example of this style and Lichfield Cathedral is mostly Early English. Churches from the Gothic periods look much lighter and more delicate than their solid and heavy predecessors.

Decorated The mid-Gothic or Decorated period followed Early English from 1280 to 1380. As the name indicates, Decorated was marked by ornate window tracery and other elaborate design elements. Examples of the style include the chapter houses of Salisbury Cathedral and Southwell Minster, the naves of Lichfield Cathedral and Exeter Cathedral, the Angel Choir at Lincoln Cathedral and the chapter house of York Minster.

Perpendicular The third Gothic phase lasted from around 1380 to 1550 and saw the ornate tracery of Decorated give way to more regular and rectilinear (an alternative name) designs. The nave of Canterbury Cathedral is a good example. More use was made of stained glass and elaborate fan vaults appeared, notably at King's College Chapel in Cambridge and Henry VII's Chapel in Westminster Abbey.

Few churches were built from the time of the monastic dissolution in the 1530s until

Typical English cathedral

the beginning of the Stuart period in 1603 and the throes of the Reformation between 1550 and 1660 were not kind to churches.

Later Designs There was little religious building during the 17th century apart from Sir Christopher Wren's magnificent St Paul's Cathedral (and other London churches), which did not follow on from any preceding English designs. The 18th and early 19th centuries saw little new building. However, from 1818 onwards many new churches went up in the industrial cities while there was also in phase of heavy-handed restorations and Victorian 'improvements'. Some of these were so unsympathetic that the Society for the Protection of Ancient Buildings was formed in 1877.

The new religious buildings of this period were frequently in Gothic Revival, an unimaginative rehash of earlier periods. The constructing of cathedrals has not been a popular activity during the 20th century, but Coventry Cathedral is certainly a notable design.

Church Architectural Glossary
The following is a list of definitions and terminology to help you in your exploration of Britain's churches:

Abbey
A monastery of monks or nuns or the buildings they used. When Henry VIII dissolved the monasteries between 1536 and 1540, many of the abbeys in England and Ireland were destroyed or converted into private homes, although some survived as churches. Thus an abbey today may be a church or a home.

Aisle
Passageway or open space along either side of the nave and/or down the centre.

Alignment
Churches are almost always aligned east-west, with the altar, chancel and choir towards the east end and the nave towards the west.

Ambulatory
Processional aisle at the east end of a cathedral, behind the altar.

Apse
Semicircular or rectangular area for clergy, at east end of church in traditional design.

Baptistry
Separate area of a church used for baptisms.

Barrel Vault
Semicircular arched roof.

Boss
Covering for the meeting point of the ribs in a vaulted roof, often colourfully decorated so bring binoculars.

Brass
A type of memorial common in medieval churches consisting of a brass plate set into the floor or a tomb, usually with a depiction of the deceased but sometimes simply with text.

Buttress
Vertical support for a wall; see Flying Buttress.

Campanile
Free-standing belfry or bell tower; Westminster Cathedral and Chester Cathedral have modern ones.

Canon
Priest who is a member of a cathedral's chapter.

Carrel
Small 'cells' where monks sat to study or meditate, usually found around the cloister.

Cathedral
Principal church of a diocese containing the bishop's throne. From the Latin *cathedra* or seat.

Chancel
Eastern end of the church, usually reserved for choir and clergy. The name comes from the Latin word for lattice because of the screen which once separated the two parts of the church.

Chantry
Chapel established by a donor for use in his or her name after death.

Chapel
Small, more private shrine or area of worship off

the main body of the church. In some British cathedrals, chapels were also established by the different craftsmen's guilds.

Chapel of Ease
Chapel built for those who lived too far away from the parish church.

Chapter House
Building in a cathedral close where the dean meets with the chapter, the clergy who run the cathedral.

Chevet
Chapels radiating out in a semicircular sweep, first found in France but also seen at Westminster and Canterbury in England.

Choir
Area in the church where the choir is seated, usually to the east of the transepts and nave; sometimes used interchangeably with chancel or presbytery.

Clerestory
Also *clearstory*, wall of windows above the triforium.

Cloister
Covered walkway linking the church with adjacent monastic buildings.

Close
Buildings grouped around a cathedral, also known as the *precincts*.

Collegiate
Church with a chapter of canons and prebendaries, but not a cathedral.

Corbel
Stone or wooden projection from a wall supporting a beam or arch.

Crossing
Intersection of the nave and transepts.

Dean
Head of a chapter of canons, and cathedral or collegiate church administrator.

Flying Buttress
Supporting buttress in the form of one side of an open arch.

Font
Basin used for baptisms, usually towards the west end of the building, often in a separate baptistry.

Frater
Common room or dining area in a medieval monastery.

Garth
Open central area within a cloister.

Lady Chapel
Chapel, usually at the east end of a cathedral, dedicated to the Virgin Mary.

Lancet
Pointed window in Early English style.

Minster
Name applied to certain larger churches which were originally attached to a monastery.

Misericord
Hinged choir seat with an often amusingly carved bracket which could be leant against.

Nave
Main part of the church at the western end, where the congregation gather.

Parson
Parish priest.

Piscina
Basin for priests to wash their hands.

Prebend
Allowance paid to a canon or member of the chapter or the position for which that allowance is paid.

Presbytery
Eastern area of the chancel beyond the choir, where the clergy operate.

Priory
Religious house governed by a prior, inferior to an abbey.

Pulpit
Raised box where priest gives sermon. From the Roman term for a raised platform or stage from which an actor recited. Pulpits for preachers were not common until 1603 when they were made compulsory.

Quire
Medieval term for choir.

Refectory
Monastic dining room.

Reredos
Literally 'behind the back'; backdrop to an altar.

Romanesque
European term for the architectural styles known in Britain as Saxon and Norman.

Rood Screen
A screen carrying a *rood* or crucifix, which separated the nave from the chancel.

Squint
Angled opening in a wall or pillar to allow a view of the altar.

Transepts
North-south projections from the nave, often added at a later date and giving the whole church a cruciform cross-shaped plan. Some medieval English cathedrals (Canterbury, Lincoln, Salisbury) feature smaller second transepts.

Triforium
Internal wall passage above the arcade and below the clerestory; behind it is the 'blind' space above the side aisle.

Undercroft
Vaulted underground room or cellar.

Vault
Roof with arched ribs, usually in a decorative pattern.

Vestry
Robing room, where a parson's clerical robes are kept and where he puts them on.

Secular Architecture

Perhaps one of the most distinctive features of the English countryside and of English culture is the ongoing love affair between the rich and their enormous – and quite beautiful – country houses. No other country has a comparable number. As is the case with churches, many have evolved over time and incorporate a variety of architectural styles and fashions.

Secular Architectural Styles

A number of the architectural styles previously described for churches were echoed in the construction of castles (in particular the Normans' massive Romanesque style) which are the basis for many great houses. Gradually, however, the strategic importance of living in a large and utilitarian pile of stones was negated by the development of effective artillery and, finally, by more peaceful times.

From the 16th century on, most architectural innovations were applied in houses – the great age of cathedral building was over. Often the English nobility adopted, and adapted, various European styles. Sometimes castles were completely abandoned. At others, they were incorporated into a new and improved version.

Tudor Gothic The extensive use of brick and glass was first popularised from the end of the 15th century, and was influenced by Perpendicular church architecture. It is characterised by graceful tracery in broad windows, and elegant vertical lines. Hampton Court Palace and Knole House are early examples, and Longleat House, Montacute House and Hardwick Hall are outstanding representatives of the mature style.

Many half-timbered houses also survive from this time – with great oak beams infilled with brick and other materials. Many examples can be found in Kent, and there are outstanding examples in Shrewsbury.

Palladianism In the late 16th and early 17th centuries, English architects were heavily influenced by Greek and Roman designs that were repopularised by Italian Renaissance designers, in particular by Andrea Palladio. The style was austere, with strict adherence to rules of proportion and symmetry, and often included classical elements like columns and porticos.

The earliest and most famous proponent in England was Inigo Jones, who built his masterpieces, the Banqueting Hall (Whitehall, London) and Queen's House (Greenwich), around 1620. The style survived well into the 18th century in the hands of John Wood the Elder and John Wood the Younger in Bath, and Robert Adam in Edinburgh, although in its later incarnation it is often described as Georgian.

Baroque The Baroque style (sometimes also described as Classicism) developed out of Palladianism from the late 17th to mid-18th centuries. This style is, as the name suggests, characterised by its exuberant use of decorative features. Although the severe lines of Palladianism were softened by curves and decoration, the underlying principles of proportion and balance remained.

The greatest and most influential proponent of this style was Sir Christopher Wren who, in the aftermath of the Great Fire of 1666, changed the face of London. His masterpiece is St Paul's Cathedral, but he was responsible for no less than 53 churches. The secular style is most famous in the work of Nicholas Hawksmoor and Sir John Vanbrugh, who collaborated on Castle Howard and Blenheim Palace.

Greek & Gothic Revival In the 18th, 19th and early 20th centuries, there were revivals of severe Greek classicism, with architects like Sir John Soane and buildings like St George's Hall (Liverpool) and the British Museum. An opposite reaction was manifested by the highly decorative Gothic revival movement, championed by Sir Gilbert Scott, Augustus Pugin and Sir Charles Barry, the architect for the Houses of Parliament.

20th Century London, although seriously battered by the 20th century, is also home to a number of outstanding modernist and post-modernist buildings. Designed for the Festival of Britain in 1951 by Sir Robert Mathew and Sir Leslie Martin, the Royal Festival Hall is an outstanding building that still seems fresh, despite its age.

More recent, and even more controversial, additions to the scene include the London Ark by Ralph Erskine, the Sackler Galleries (Royal Academy) and Stansted airport by Norman Foster, the Waterloo International train terminal and Financial Times Print Works by Nicholas Grimshaw, and Lloyd's Insurance Market & Offices by Richard Rogers.

CULTURE

It is difficult to generalise about the English and their culture, but there is no doubt they are a creative, energetic and aggressive people who have had an impact on the world that is entirely disproportionate to their numbers. They are a diverse bunch and they have created a diverse society.

Many visitors have strong preconceptions about English culture and characteristics but, if you do, you would be wise to abandon them.

The most common is that the English are reserved, inhibited and stiflingly polite. Remember, however, that this is one of the most crowded, tourist-inundated countries on the planet and that some of these characteristics are a protective veneer developed in response to dealing with a constant crush of people. Remember also, that although regional and class differences have shrunk, accents and behaviour still vary widely depending on where you are and with which class you are mingling.

Terms like 'stiff-upper-lip', 'cold' and 'conservative' might apply to some elements of the middle and upper classes, but in general they do not apply to the working class, or the northerners. Visit a nightclub in one of the big cities, a football match, an historic steam train run by volunteers, a good local pub, or a country B&B and other terms might spring to mind: uninhibited, tolerant, exhibitionist, passionate, aggressive, obses-

sive, humorous, sentimental, hospitable and friendly.

No country in the world has more obsessive hobbyists, who very often teeter on the edge of complete madness – train *and* bus spotters, twitchers (or birdwatchers), sports fanatics, fashion victims, royalists, model-makers and collectors of every description, steam preservationists and historical society members, ramblers, pet owners, gardeners...

England is a country of sceptical individualists who deeply resent any intrusion on their privacy or freedom, so it is not surprising their flirtation with state socialism was brief. Change happens slowly, and only after proceeding through endless consultations, committees, departments and layers of government.

As a result, most things (including the cities) have developed organically and chaotically. This is a country where the streets are not straight and the trains do not run on time.

There are some cynics who proclaim that England is in a state of terminal decline, but there is no doubt the major cities are still cultural powerhouses. You can only wonder what they will incubate next – perhaps a new tribe at the cutting edge of popular culture (like New-Age travellers, punks, hippies and mods), or perhaps a political or economic movement (like industrialisation, imperialist capitalism, parliamentary democracy, socialism and Thatcherism).

RELIGION

The Church of England, a Christian church that became independent of Rome in the 16th century (see The Tudors under History earlier in this chapter), is the largest, wealthiest and most influential in the land. It is an 'established' church (along with the Church of Scotland), meaning it is officially the national church, and it has a close relationship with the state: the queen or king appoints archbishops and bishops on the advice of the prime minister.

Attendances at Sunday services average only 1.2 million and continue to decrease. It is difficult to generalise about the form of worship. It varies from High church, which is full of pomp and ceremony, and close in many ways to Roman Catholicism, to Low church, which is less traditional and has been more influenced by Protestantism and, most recently, the evangelical movement. Evangelical and charismatic churches are the only Christian ones to show a recent increase in attendance.

The Church of England has traditionally been aligned with the ruling classes, but over recent years has been critical of the Conservative government's social policies. In 1994, after many years of debate, the first women were ordained as priests.

Other significant Protestant churches, the 'free' churches with no connection to the state, include Methodists, Baptists, the United Reformed Church and the Salvation Army. Women have been priests in all these churches for some years.

Roman Catholics have at times since the 16th century been terribly persecuted; one modern legacy is the intractable problem of Northern Ireland. They did not gain political rights until 1829 or a formal structure until 1850, but today about one in 10 Britons considers themselves Catholic.

Recent estimates suggest there are now well over one million Muslims, and there are also significant numbers of Sikhs and Hindus. The fact is that nowadays more non-Christians in England visit a place of worship than do Christians.

LANGUAGE

English is perhaps England's most significant contribution to the modern world. The English, of every class and background, take enormous pleasure in using their language and idiom inventively (nowhere, for instance, are there more crossword fanatics). The language continues to evolve and to be used and exploited to the full. See the Glossary at the back of this book for examples.

English as it is spoken in England is sometimes incomprehensible to overseas visitors – even to those who assume they have spoken it all their lives. Regional dialects have disappeared, but significant variations, especially in accent, survive. Some accents can be virtually impenetrable. It's OK to ask someone to repeat what they have said, but try not to laugh.

Big Ben and the Union Flag, London

RICHARD EVERIST

TOM SMALLMAN

TOM SMALLMAN

Top: Royal Naval College, Greenwich
Left: Deck chairs in Hyde Park, London
Right: Sculpture at British Museum, London

MAP 1

Greater London

Scale: 0 — 2.5 — 5 km / 0 — 1.5 — 3 miles

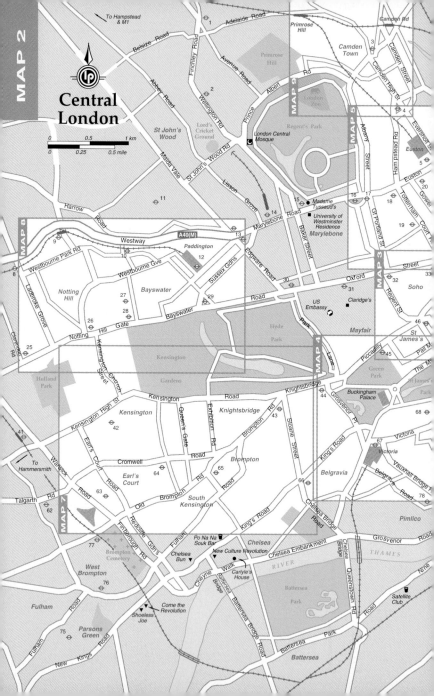

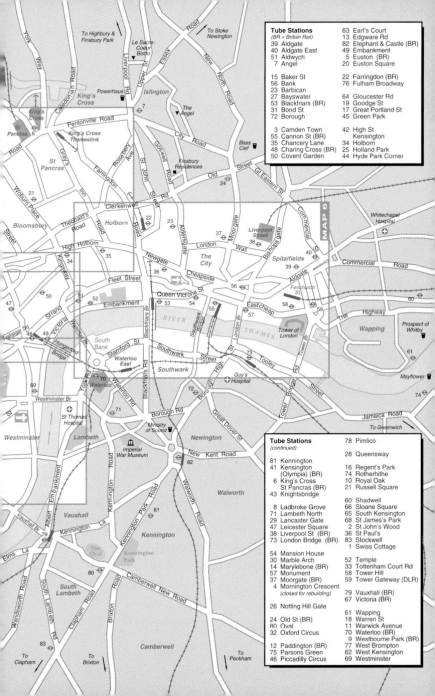

MAP 3

MAP 6

West End

Southbank

To the City

Melbourne

Waterloo Bridge

Lincoln's Inn Fields

Kingsway

Aldwych

Strand

Lancaster Place

Savoy Street

See South Bank Arts Complex Map

Thames

200 m
200 yards

100
100

River

Hungerford Bridge

Great Queen Street

Newton Street

Drury Lane

Macklin Street

Museum Street

Bloomsbury St

New Oxford Street

Tottenham Court Rd

High Holborn

St Giles High Street

Denmark St

Charing Cross Road

Cambridge Circus

Shaftesbury Avenue

Earlham Street

Monmouth Street

Neal Street

Endell Street

Drury Lane

Bow Street

Floral Street

Russell Street

Catherine Street

Wellington Street

Bow St

Tavistock St

Southampton Street

Maiden Lane

King Street

Garrick St

Bedford Street

Chandos Place

William IV Street

Duncannon St

Charing Cross

St Martin's Lane

Upr St Martin's La.

Bedfordbury

New Row

Garrick St

Cranbourn St

St Martin's Pl

Trafalgar Square

Charing Cross Station

Villiers Street

Craven Street

Northumberland Avenue

Whitehall

To Westminster

Victoria Embankment Gardens

Embankment

Charing Cross

Admiralty Arch

To Buckingham

The Mall

Cockspur St

Pall Mall

Leicester Square

Bear St

Cranbourn Street

Newport Street

Gerrard Street

Lisle Street

Wardour Street

Coventry Street

Whitcomb St

Haymarket

Regent Street

Waterloo Place

Charles II Street

Pall Mall

ST JAMES'S

St James's Square

Jermyn Street

Duke of York Street

Duke Street

St James's Street

King Street

Piccadilly

Piccadilly Circus

Glasshouse Street

Regent Street

Sackville Street

Vigo Street

Old Bond Street

Burlington Arcade

Cork Street

Savile Row

New Bond Street

Conduit Street

Clifford Street

Dover Street

Albemarle Street

MAP 4

Green Park

Hyde Park Corner

Piccadilly

To Hyde Park Corner

MAYFAIR

Maddox St

Hanover St

To Marble Arch

Oxford Circus

Regent Street

Great Portland Street

Great Titchfield Street

Margaret Street

Mortimer Street

Wells Street

Berners Street

Newman Street

Eastcastle Street

Oxford Street

Poland Street

Great Chapel St

Hollen St

Soho Street

Dean Street

Frith Street

Greek Street

Sutton Row

Falconberg Mews

Meard St

Bateman St

Old Compton Street

Brewer Street

Berwick Street

Berwick St Market

Wardour Street

D'Arblay Street

Broadwick Street

Lexington Street

Marshall Street

Great Pulteney Street

Beak Street

Warwick Street

Ganton Street

Carnaby Street

Kingly Street

Marlborough Street

Foubert's Place

Argyll Street

Ramillies Place

Restricted access, 7am–7pm, Monday to Friday

SOHO

To Bloomsbury

Denmark Place

Litchfield St

New Oxford Street

Manette Street

Sherwood Street

Air St

Glasshouse Street

Brewer Street

Rupert Street

Rupert St

Winnett St

Great Windmill Street

Shaftesbury Avenue

Denman Street

Archer Street

Smith's Court

PLACES TO STAY
7 Oxford St Youth
   Hostel
14 Hazlitts
26 High Holborn
52 Fielding Hotel
77 The Hampshire
93 Ritz Hotel

PLACES TO EAT
9 Pizza Express
10 Nusa Dua
11 dell'Ugo
15 Mildred's
16 Gay Hussar
22 Neal's Yard
23 Food for Thought
24 Belgo Centraal
25 Rock & Sole
   Plaice
27 Diana's Diner
28 Designer
   Sandwiches
31 Wagamamas
32 Melati
34 Freedom Café
35 Mezzo
36 French House
   Pub & Dining Room
37 Patisserie Valerie
39 Chiang Mai
40 Living Room &
   Gopals of Soho
41 Bar Italia
42 Compton St Café
44 Pollo
46 Bunjies
47 The Ivy
50 Café des Amis
   du Vin
59 Atlantic Bar & Grill
60 New Piccadilly
62 The Criterion
63 Rock Island Diner
67 Wong Kei
70 Planet Hollywood
   & Fashion Café
71 Chuen Chen
   Ku/Jade Garden
72 Poons

74 Tokyo Diner
78 Mr Wu
79 Cafe Pelican
81 Calabash
   Restaurant
85 Chez Gerard
86 Rules
88 Joe Allen
89 Orso
94 Quaglino's
96 The Wren at St
   James
99 Football, Football
100 Sports Café

PUBS & CLUBS
2 100 Club
4 Hanover Grand
5 Flamingo Bar
12 Dog & Duck
13 Riki Tik
17 Astoria
18 Velvet
   Underground
19 Borderline
21 Marquee
30 Emporium
33 Village Soho &
   The O' Bar
38 Ronnie Scott's
43 Three
   Greyhounds
45 Coach & Horse
48 Lamb & Flag
53 Browns
56 Legends
65 Thunder Drive
66 Bar Rumba
68 Café de Paris
73 Polar Bear
76 Hippodrome
82 Gardening Club
110 Heaven
111 Gordon's Wine
   Bar

OTHER
1 HMV Records
3 Virgin Megastore
6 Liberty

8 Black Market
   Records
20 Foyle's Bookshop
29 Hamley's
49 Stanfords
51 Royal Opera
   House
54 Peacock Theatre
55 Royal Arcade
57 Museum of
   Mankind
58 Royal Academy
   of Arts
61 Tower Records
64 Rock Circus
69 Trocadero
75 Prince Charles
   Cinema
80 English National
   Opera
81 The Africa Centre
83 St Paul's Church
84 Covent Garden
87 YHA Adventure
   Shop
90 India House
91 Courtauld
   Institute Gallery
92 Australia House
95 Fortnum & Mason
97 New Zealand
   House
98 British Travel
   Centre
101 American
102 Scottish Tourist
   Board
103 Canada House
104 Nelson's Column
105 National Gallery
106 National Portrait
   Gallery
107 Trafalgar
   Post Office
108 St Martin's in
   Fields & Café in
   Crypt
109 South Africa
   House
112 ICA

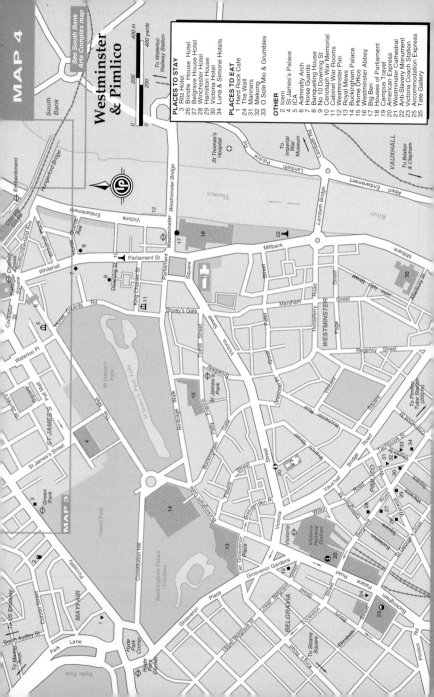

MAP 4

Westminster & Pimlico

See South Bank Arts Complex map

0   100   200   300   400 m
0   100   200   300   400 yards

PLACES TO STAY
3   Ritz Hotel
26 Brindle House Hotel
27 Belgrave House Hotel
28 Winchester Hotel
29 Hamilton House
30 Victoria Hotel
34 Luna & Simone Hotels

PLACES TO EAT
1   Hard Rock Café
21 The Well
31 Manners
32 Mekong
33 O Sole Mio & Grumbles

OTHER
2   Iceni
5   St James's Palace
6   ICA
7   Admiralty Arch
8   Admiralty Guards
9   Banqueting House
10 No 10 Downing St
11 Cenotaph War Memorial
12 Cabinet War Rooms
13 Westminster Pier
14 Buckingham Palace
15 Royal Mews
16 Westminster Abbey
17 Home Office
18 Houses of Parliament
19 Big Ben
20 Campus Travel
21 American Express
22 Westminster Cathedral
23 Anti-Slavery Monument
25 Victoria Coach Station
24 Accommodation Express
35 Tate Gallery

To Waterloo Railway Station

South Bank

Thames

St Thomas's Hospital

To Imperial War Museum

VAUXHALL

To Brixton & Clapham

Charing Cross

Embankment

Hungerford Bridge

Victoria Embankment

Westminster Bridge

Lambeth Bridge

Albert Embankment

River

Millbank

Whitehall

Parliament St

Downing St

King Charles St

Parliament Square

Storey's Gate

Millbank

Marsham Street

Horseferry Road

Page Street

Regency Street

WESTMINSTER

Cockspur St

Trafalgar Square

Northumberland Ave

Craven St

Northumberland Place

Horse Gds Ave

Horse Guards Rd

St James's Park

St James's Park Lake

Birdcage Walk

The Mall

Green Park

ST JAMES'S

St James's Square

Pall Mall

St James's Street

Waterloo Pl

MAP 3

To Marble Arch

US Embassy

Curzon Street

South Audley St

Park Lane

To Hyde Park Corner

Hyde Park Corner

MAYFAIR

Piccadilly

Constitution Hill

Buckingham Palace Gardens

Grosvenor Place

Grosvenor Gardens

Lwr Grosvenor Place

Buckingham Gate

Buckingham Palace Rd

Palace St

Victoria St

Broadway

Tothill Street

Victoria Street

Petty France

Caxton Street

Victoria Street

Vandon St

Strutton Ground

Greycoat Place

Rochester Row

Vincent Square

Vauxhall Bridge Road

Vauxhall Bridge Road

Francis Street

Bressenden Pl

Victoria Railway Station

Wilton Road

Belgrave Road

Warwick Way

Eccleston Bridge

St George's Drive

Ebury Bridge Road

Gillingham St

Hugh St

Guildhouse St

Warwick Way

Belgrave Rd

Charlwood St

Denbigh St

Tachbrook St

Moreton St

Lupus St

Rampayne St

PIMLICO

To Pimlico Tube Station (200 m)

Wilton Rd

BELGRAVIA

Lower Belgrave Street

Eccleston Street

Ebury Street

Elizabeth Street

St George's Drive

Buckingham Palace Rd

To Sloane Square

To Chelsea

Pimlico Rd

MAP 5

Holborn, Bloomsbury & Marylebone

PLACES TO STAY
3   International Students House
6   John Adams Hall
7   Passfield Hall
8   JAH's Hotel
9   Crescent Hotel
13 Rosebery Avenue Hall
15 Carr Saunders Hall
17 Arran House Hotel
18 Hotel Cavendish
20 Royal Hotel
28 Museum Inn
29 Ruskin Hotel
31 St Margaret's Hotel
36 YMCA

PLACES TO EAT
8   Ravi Shankar
10 North Sea Fish Restaurant
14 Ravi Shankar
25 Cyberia Café
26 The Greenhouse
27 Mille Pini
33 Mille Pini
34 Victoria Gallery Café
37 Wagamama
38 Museum Street Café

PUBS & CLUBS
1   Central Station Nightclub
22 Lamb
32 Queens Larder
39 Leisure Lounge

OTHER
4   UCL Hospital
5   University College London
11 Gay's The Word Bookshop
12 Royal Free Hospital
16 Telecom Tower
19 Dillons the Bookstore
21 London Taxi Centre
23 Dickens House Museum
24 Middlesex Hospital
30 British Museum
35 Gray's Inn
40 Sir John Soane's Museum
41 Lincoln's Inn Court

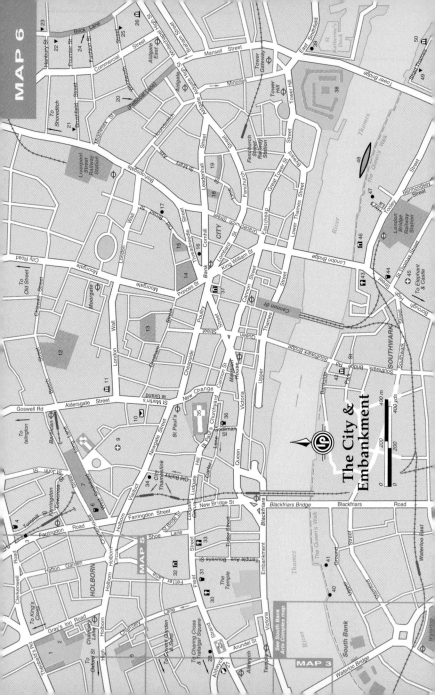

MAP 6

The City & Embankment

MAP 5

MAP 3

To Shoreditch
Brick Lane
Hanbury St
Commercial Street
Spitalfield Street
To Old Street
City Road
To Islington
Goswell Rd
HOLBORN
To King's Cross
Clerkenwell
Gray's Inn Road
Chancery Lane
To Covent Garden & Soho
To Charing Cross & Trafalgar Square
To Oxford St
High Holborn
Liverpool Street Railway Station
Bishopsgate
Moorgate
London Wall
Barbican
Farringdon Road
Aldersgate Street
St Martin's le Grand
Newgate Street
Holborn Viaduct
Old Bailey
Ludgate Hill
Fleet Street
Temple
The Temple
Arundel St
Strand
Aldwych
Aldgate
Aldgate East
Whitechapel
Mansell Street
Minories
Tower Gateway
Tower Hill
Tower Bridge
East Smithfield
St Katherine's Dock
Leadenhall Street
Cornhill
Threadneedle Street
Bank
CITY
Lombard Street
King William St
Cannon Street
Cheapside
Queen Victoria Street
Upper Thames Street
Lower Thames Street
Great Tower St
Byward
Fenchurch Street
Fenchurch Street Railway Station
Eastcheap
London Bridge
Southwark Bridge
Blackfriars Bridge
Blackfriars
New Bridge St
Farringdon Street
St John Street
Tooley Street
London Bridge Railway Station
Bermondsey Street
St Thomas Street
Borough High Street
SOUTHWARK
To Elephant & Castle
The Queen's Walk
Thames
River Thames
South Bank
See South Bank Arts Complex map
Waterloo Bridge
Waterloo East
Blackfriars Road
The Queen's Walk
Mansion House
St Paul's
St Paul's Churchyard
Godliman St
New Change
Bread Street
Queen Street
Poultry
Princes St
Moorgate
Wall
London Wall
Coleman St

400 m
400 yds
200
200
0
0

PAUL STEEL

Tower Bridge, London

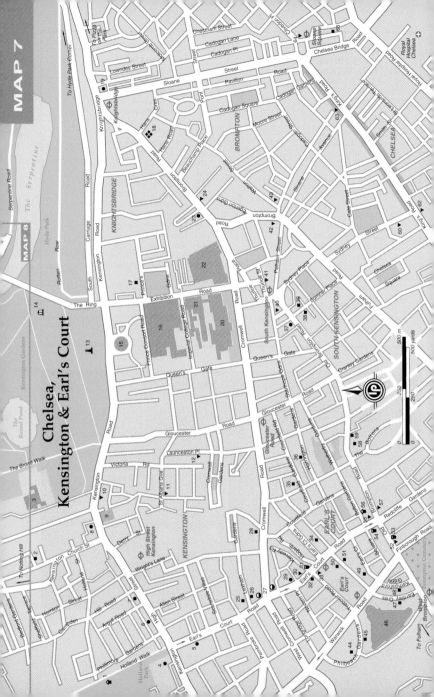

MAP 7

Chelsea, Kensington & Earl's Court

MAP 8

Serpentine Road

The Serpentine

Hyde Park

Rotten Row

South Carriage Drive

The Ring

Kensington Gardens

The Round Pond

The Broad Walk

Kensington Gore

Kensington Road

To Hyde Park Corner

To Pizza on the Park

Chestham Street

Cadogan Lane

Cadogan Pl

Lowndes Street

Sloane Street

Pavilion Road

Cadogan Gardens

Cadogan Square

Sloane Square

Chelsea Bridge Road

Chelsea Bridge

Royal Hospital Chelsea

Royal Hospital Road

St Leonard's Terrace

King's Road

CHELSEA

Smith Street

Smith Terrace

Tedworth Square

Moore Street

Pont Street

Cadogan Gardens

Sloane Street

BROMPTON

Beauchamp Place

Walton Street

Brompton Road

Pelham Street

Brompton

Egerton Gdns

Pelham Street

Sydney Street

Chelsea Square

Cale Street

King's Road

KNIGHTSBRIDGE

Knightsbridge

Hans Crescent

Hans Road

Hans Place

Sloane Avenue

Draycott Avenue

Fulham Road

Exhibition Road

Prince's Gate

Prince Consort Road

Imperial College Road

Queen's Gate

Thurloe St

Thurloe Place

Sydney Place

Onslow Gardens

Sumner Place

Cranley Gardens

SOUTH KENSINGTON

Old Brompton Road

South Kensington

Harrington Road

Queen's Gate

Gloucester Road

Cornwall Gardens

Stanhope Gdns

Victoria Rd

Launceston Pl

Cornwall Gardens

Gloucester Road

Cromwell Road

Grenville Place

Ashburn Gardens

Courtfield Gardens

The Boltons

Gilston Road

Tregunter Road

Redcliffe Gardens

Brompton Road

Cathcart Road

Finborough Road

Brompton Cemetery

Earl's Court Gardens

Bramham Gardens

Kempsford Gdns

Eardley Cres

Warwick Road

Philbeach Gardens

Pembroke Road

EARL'S COURT

Earl's Court Square

Earl's Court Road

Earl's Court Gardens

Trebovir Road

Nevern Square

Nevern Place

Penywern Road

Hogarth Rd

Earl's Ct Gdns

Kenway Rd

Kenway Rd

KENSINGTON

High Street Kensington

Wright's Lane

Derry St

Kensington Church St

Allen Street

Scarsdale Villas

Marloes Road

Pembroke Road

Earl's Court Road

Abingdon Road

Phillimore Gardens

Holland Walk

Holland Park

Campden Hill Road

Argyll Road

Hornton Street

Stafford Terrace

Phillimore Gardens

Bedford Gardens

To Notting Hill

To Fulham

West Cromwell Road

Warwick Road

Pembroke Gardens

Pembroke Road

500 m
500 yards
0 250
0 250

1 ▲
2 ■
3
4 ▲
5
6 ●
7
8 ■
9 ■
10 ■
11 ■
12 ▲
13 ▲
14 ⌂
15
16
17 ■
18 ✦
19 ■
20
21
22
23 ▲
24 ▲
25 ■
26 ●
27 ●
28 ■
29 ●
30 ●
31 ●
32
33
34 ■
35 ■
36 ■
37 ●
38 ■
39 ●
40 ●
41 ■
42 ■
43 ■
44 ▲
45 ▲
46
47
48 ■
49 ●
50 ●
51 ●
52 ●
53 ●
54 ●
55 ■
56 ■
57 ▲
58 ▲
59 ▲
60 ▲
61 ●
62
63 ▲
64 Φ
65 ●
66

RICHARD EVERIST

Hyde Park

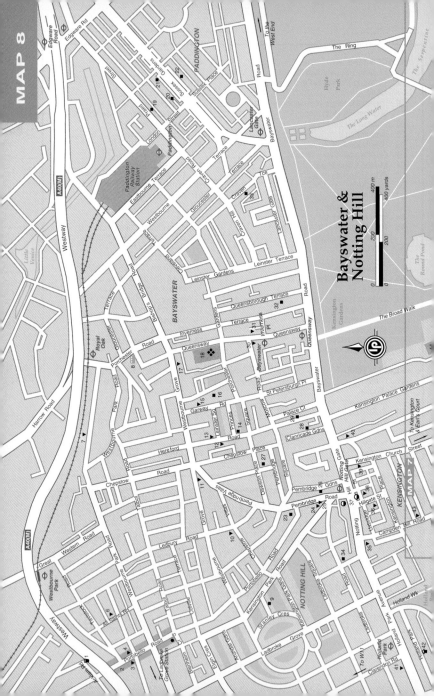

MAP 8

Bayswater & Notting Hill

400 m

400 yards

PADDINGTON

Edgware Rd

Edgware Road

To the West End

The Ring

The Serpentine

Hyde Park

The Long Water

Westway

A40(M)

Paddington Railway Station

London Street

Praed Street

Paddington Street

Sussex Place

Sussex Gardens

Kenson Street

Gloucester Terrace

Eastbourne Terrace

Westbourne Terrace

Bishop's Bridge Road

Craven Road

Craven Terrace

Craven Hill

Lancaster Gate

Lancaster Gate

Bayswater

Leinster Terrace

Leinster Gardens

Craven Hill Gdns

BAYSWATER

Porchester Terrace

Porchester Gardens

Queensborough Terrace

Inverness Terrace

Inverness Pl

Queensway

Queensway

Bayswater Road

Kensington Gardens

The Broad Walk

The Round Pond

Royal Oak

Porchester Road

Bishop's Bridge Road

Westbourne Terrace

Westbourne Grove

Garway Rd

Leinster Sq

Princes Square

Queensway

Moscow Road

St Petersburgh Pl

Palace Ct

Kensington Palace Gardens

Harrow Road

Bourne Terrace

Westbourne Park Road

Hereford Road

Chepstow Place

Ledbury Road

Chepstow Road

Dawson Place

Pembridge Square

Pembridge Villas

Pembridge Road

Clanricarde Gdns

Pembridge Gdns

Notting Hill Gate

Kensington Church Street

Hillgate St

Notting Hill Gate

To Kensington & Earl's Court

KENSINGTON

MAP 7

Westbourne Park

Great Western Road

Tavistock Road

Westbourne Park Road

Talbot Road

Westbourne Park Villas

Portobello Road

Colville Terrace

Kensington Park Road

NOTTING HILL

Ladbroke Grove

Stanley Cres

Elgin Cres

Arundel Gdns

Blenheim Cres

Ladbroke Grove Station

Lancaster Road

Westbourne Park Road

Campden Hill Road

Holland Park Avenue

Holland Wk

Holland Park

Ladbroke Grove

Clarendon Rd

To W11

Hyde Park Gate

Westway

A40(M)

Little Venice

RICHARD EVERIST

Little Venice, London

PAUL STEEL

London cab

MAP 9

Camden Town

To Tufnell Park & Archway

PLACES TO EAT
1 Lemonia
2 Primrose Brasserie
4 Marine Ices
5 Marathon
7 Belgo Noord
8 Nando's
9 Cottons Rhum Shop
12 Silks & Spice
13 Thanh Binh
14 Bintang
15 Primates
21 Arizona

26 Jazz Café
30 Ruby in the Dust
31 Café Delancey
32 The Raj
33 El Parador

PUBS & CLUBS
3 Lansdowne
10 Lock Tavern
11 Dingwalls & HQ Club
22 Bar Gansa
27 World's End/Underworld
28 Black Cap
29 Crown & Goose

OTHER
6 Roundhouse
11 Stables
16 Camden Lock Market -
    West/Middle/East Yards
    & Indoor Market Hall
18 Camden Canal Market
19 London Waterbus
    Company
20 Compendium Bookshop
23 Camden Market
24 Electric Market
25 Laundrette

KENTISH TOWN

Kentish Town West

To Hampstead Heath

Chalk Farm

Adelaide Road

To Swiss Cottage

Primrose Hill

PRIMROSE HILL

Primrose Hill

To Lords & Edgware Rd

London Zoo

Regent's Park

CAMDEN TOWN

Camden Town

Mornington Crescent (Closed for rebuilding)

To Bloomsbury & Soho

To King's Cross

REGENT'S PARK

MAP 5

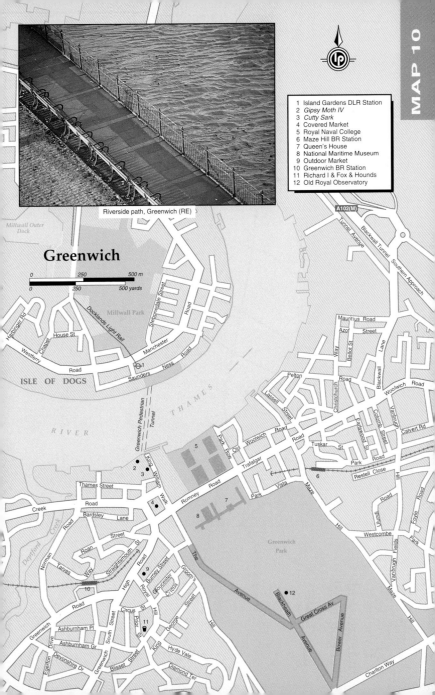

MAP 10

1 Island Gardens DLR Station
2 *Gipsy Moth IV*
3 *Cutty Sark*
4 Covered Market
5 Royal Naval College
6 Maze Hill BR Station
7 Queen's House
8 National Maritime Museum
9 Outdoor Market
10 Greenwich BR Station
11 Richard I & Fox & Hounds
12 Old Royal Observatory

Riverside path, Greenwich (RE)

Greenwich

0   250   500 m
0   250   500 yards

Millwall Outer Dock

Millwall Park

Docklands Light Rail

ISLE OF DOGS

THAMES

RIVER

Greenwich Pedestrian Tunnel

Greenwich Park

Blackheath

MAP 12

London Underground-Geographical

Note: Bakerloo line between Piccadilly Circus and Elephant & Castle closed until July 1997

Bakerloo
Central
Circle
District
Hammersmith & City
Jubilee
Metropolitan
Northern
Piccadilly
Victoria
Docklands Light Rail
British Rail

0   0.25   0.5   0.5 mile
0   0.5   1 km

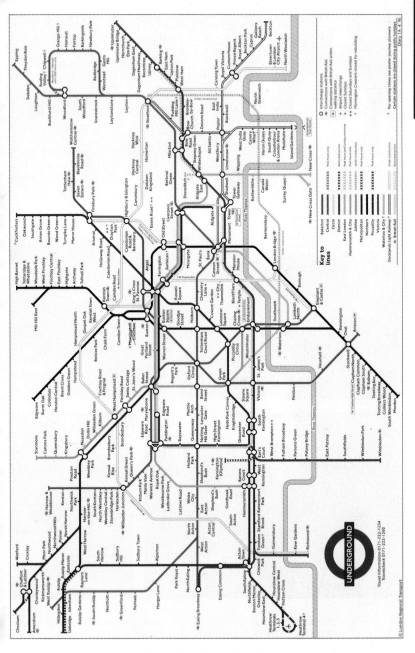

UNDERGROUND

Travel Information 0171-222-1234
TravelCheck 0171-222-1200

© London Regional Transport

Diary 1A 4 96

Key to lines

Bakerloo
Central
Circle
District
East London
Hammersmith & City
Jubilee
Metropolitan
Northern
Piccadilly
Victoria
Waterloo & City †
British Rail

Peak hours only

Restricted service

Peak hours and Sundays mornings

Peak hours only

Under construction

Peak hours only

Under construction

Restricted service

○ Interchange stations
● Connections with British Rail
⊖ Connections with British Rail within walking distance
✈ Airport interchange
+ Closed Sundays
× Closed Saturdays and Sundays
† Mornington Crescent closed for rebuilding

* For opening times see poster journey planners
Certain stations are closed during public holidays

LRT REG'D USER NO 96/2501

GRAHAM IMESON

TONY WHEELER

RICHARD EVERIST

RICHARD EVERIST

TONY WHEELER

A	B
C	
D	E

A: Horse guard, London
B: Changing of the Guard, Buckingham Palace
C: Hampton Court Palace
D: 'And 'alf a pound of tomahtas, guv', Kilburn High St, London
E: Flower seller, London

London

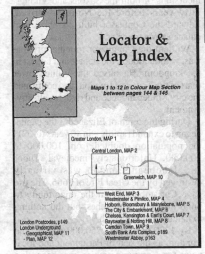

Locator & Map Index

Maps 1 to 12 in Colour Map Section between pages 144 & 145

Greater London, MAP 1

Central London, MAP 2

Greenwich, MAP 10

West End, MAP 3
Westminster & Pimlico, MAP 4
Holborn, Bloomsbury & Marylebone, MAP 5
The City & Embankment, MAP 6
Chelsea, Kensington & Earl's Court, MAP 7
Bayswater & Notting Hill, MAP 8
Camden Town, MAP 9
South Bank Arts Complex, p189
Westminster Abbey, p163

London Postcodes, p149
London Underground
- Geographical, MAP 11
- Plan, MAP 12

Once the capital of the greatest empire the world has ever known, London is still the largest city in Europe. It is embedded in the culture, the vocabulary and the dreams of every English speaker. At times it will be more grand, evocative, beautiful and stimulating than you could have imagined; at others it will be colder, greyer, dirtier and more expensive than you believed possible.

It is a cosmopolitan mixture of the Third World and First World, of chauffeurs and beggars, of the establishment and the avant-garde. There are seven to 12 million inhabitants depending on the count, and 20 million visitors a year. As you will soon discover, an amazing number are extremely wealthy. Fortunately, however, the majority are not. It will soon become clear what side of this divide you are on, and you will also discover a London that caters to those who work long hours for lousy wages.

For the budget traveller, London is a challenge. Money has a way of mysteriously evaporating every time you move. If you have limited funds it's necessary to plan, to book ahead and to prioritise. There's little point in putting up with the crowds, the underground and the pollution if you can't budget to take advantage of at least some of the theatre, the exhibitions, the shops, the pubs and clubs, the cafés and restaurants. A peg or two above desperation, you can find reasonable value. And some of the very best is very cheap, sometimes free.

Unlike comparable European capitals, much of London looks unplanned and grubby. It is, but that is part of its appeal. Two thousand years of architecture is piled and jumbled together. This was the world's first industrial mega-city, and even today, problems dating from the 19th century remain. Sections of the population are still shockingly deprived.

London can be slovenly, sometimes outrageous, but usually in a comfortable sort of way. It can also be heart-stoppingly beautiful. And there are very few cities in the world that do not seem provincial by comparison.

HISTORY

Although a Celtic community settled around a ford across the River Thames, it was the Romans who first developed the square mile now known as the City of London. They built a bridge and an impressive city wall, and made the city an important port and the hub of their road system.

LONDON

The Romans left, but trade went on. Few traces of London dating from the Dark Ages can now be found, but London survived the incursions of both the Saxons and Vikings. Fifty years before the Normans arrived, Edward the Confessor built his abbey and palace at Westminster.

William the Conqueror found a city that was, without doubt, the richest and largest in the kingdom. He raised the White Tower (part of the Tower of London) and confirmed the city's independence and right to self-government.

During the reign of Elizabeth I the capital began to expand rapidly – in 40 years to 1603 the population doubled from 100,000 to 200,000. Unfortunately, medieval, Tudor and Jacobean London was virtually destroyed by the Great Fire of 1666. The fire gave Christopher Wren the opportunity to build his famous churches, but did nothing to halt the city's growth.

By 1720 there were 750,000 people, and London, as the seat of Parliament and focal point for a growing empire, was becoming ever richer and more important. Georgian architects replaced the last of medieval London with their imposing symmetrical architecture and residential squares.

The population exploded in the 19th century, creating a vast expanse of Victorian suburbs. As a result of the Industrial Revolution and rapidly expanding commerce, it jumped from 2.7 million in 1851 to 6.6 million in 1901.

Georgian and Victorian London was devastated by the Luftwaffe in WWII – huge swathes of the centre and the East End were totally flattened. After the war, ugly housing and low-cost developments were thrown up on the bomb sites. The docks never recovered – shipping moved to Tilbury, and the Docklands declined to the point of dereliction. They were rediscovered by developers in the 1980s, though development lost its momentum with the recession of the early 1990s.

Riding on a wave of Thatcherite confidence and deregulation, London boomed in the 1980s. The new wave of property developers proved to be only marginally more discriminating than the Luftwaffe, although there are some outstanding modern buildings amongst the dross. There are ambitious plans to rebuild parts of the South Bank with proceeds from the National Lottery, and Greenwich (pronounced Grenitch) will undergo a facelift now that it has been chosen as Britain's official site for ushering in the third millennium.

ORIENTATION

London's main geographical feature is the Thames, a tidal river that enabled an easily defended port to be established far from the dangers of the English Channel. Flowing around wide bends from west to east, it divides the city into northern and southern halves.

London sprawls over an enormous area. Fortunately, the underground system, the 'tube', makes most of it easily accessible, and the ubiquitous (though geographically misleading) underground map is easy to use. Any train heading from left to right on the map is designated as eastbound, any train heading from top to bottom is southbound. Each line has its own colour.

Most important sights, theatres, restaurants and even some cheap places to stay lie within a reasonably compact rectangle formed by the tube's Circle line, just to the north of the river. All the international airports lie some distance from the city centre but transport is easy. See the Getting Around section later for details on airport transport.

Although London's relatively few skyscrapers stick out like sore thumbs, they are not easily accessible to sightseers. The best and most central lookout to help you orient yourself is, surprisingly, over 300 years old: the Golden Gallery at St Paul's Cathedral.

London blankets mostly imperceptible hills, but there are also good views from Primrose Hill (adjoining Regent's Park), Hampstead Heath (north of Camden), and Greenwich Park (downriver east of central London).

Throughout this chapter, the nearest tube station has been given with addresses; the

London map shows the location of tube stations and the areas covered by the detailed neighbourhood maps. The London Postal Areas map in this chapter will also be helpful, especially with outlying suburbs.

Maps

A decent map is vital. First, get a single-sheet map so you can see all of central London at a glance; the British Tourist Authority (BTA) produces a good one. Even if you only plan to stay for a night or two, buy a copy of the *London A-Z* street directory (black & white £2.95, colour £3.95, extra-large central London £3.75) as soon as possible. A compass could be handy. It is easy to be totally disoriented when you emerge from a tube station.

Terminology

'London' is an imprecise term used loosely to describe nearly 800 sq miles of Greater London enclosed by the M25 ring road.

London is not administered as a single unit, but divided into widely differing boroughs run by local governments with significant autonomy. A borough (or town) with a cathedral was traditionally a city, so traditionally there were two cities in Greater London: Westminster and London! It is the City of London that is known simply as 'the City'.

Boroughs are further subdivided into districts (or suburbs, or precincts if you prefer), which, to a large degree, tally with the first group of letters and numbers of the postal code. The letter(s) correspond to compass directions from the centre of London, which according to the post office must lie somewhere not too far from St Paul's Cathedral: EC means East Central, WC means West Central, W means West, NW means North West, and so on. The numbering system after the letters is less helpful: 1 is the centre of the zone, further numbers relate to the alphabetical order of the postal district names, which are not always in common use.

Districts and postal codes are often given on street signs, which is obviously vital when names are duplicated (there are 47 Station

Rds), or cross through a number of districts. To further confuse visitors, many streets change name (Holland Park Ave becomes Notting Hill Gate, which becomes Bayswater Rd, which becomes Oxford St...), or duck and weave like the country lanes they once were. Street numbering can also bewilder: on big streets the numbers on opposite sides can be way out of kilter (315 might be opposite 520) or, for variation, they can go up one side and down the other.

To add to the confusion, some London suburbs – well within the M25 – do not give London as a part of their addresses, and do not use London postal codes. Instead they're considered part of a county.

The City & the East

The City refers to the area that was once the old walled city, before the inexorable colonisation of the surrounding towns and villages had begun. Although it lies in the south-eastern corner of the Circle line, it is regarded as the centre. As you may have guessed, the West End (much more the tourist centre) lies to the west.

The City is still one of the most important financial centres in the world. Full of bankers during the working week, it is deserted outside work hours. The same is not true of its most famous sights: the Tower of London, St Paul's Cathedral and the market at Petticoat Lane.

To the east, beyond the Circle line, is the East End, once the exclusive habitat of the cockney, now a cultural melting pot. This incorporates districts like Smithfields, Hackney, Shoreditch and Bethnal Green. There are some lively corners, and cheap rents, but in general it is blighted by traffic and urban decay. Much of the East End was flattened during WWII and it shows.

Farther east again lie the Docklands. Once part of the busiest port in the world, thousands of acres of prime real estate fell into disuse after WWII, mirroring the decline of the empire. In the early 1980s, a light railway (an interesting excursion from Tower Gateway) was built and property developers were unleashed.

Across the river (accessible by foot tunnel) is beautiful Greenwich, which is home to the *Cutty Sark* ship, and contains superb architecture, open space and the Prime Meridian.

The West

West of the City, but before the West End proper, are Holborn and Bloomsbury. Holborn (pronounced hoeburn) is Britain's sedate legal heartland, the home of Rumpole and common law. Bloomsbury is still synonymous with the literary and publishing worlds. There are dozens of specialist shops, and it has the incomparable British Museum, stuffed to the seams with loot from every age and every corner of the globe.

The West End proper lies west of Tottenham Court Rd and Covent Garden, which is trendy and tourist-ridden but fun, and south of Oxford St, an endless succession of department stores packed with vicious, bargain-hunting shoppers. It includes such icons as Trafalgar Square, the restaurants and clubs of not-so-seedy Soho, the famous West End cinemas and theatres around Piccadilly Circus and Leicester Square, and the elegant shops of Regent and Bond Sts – not forgetting Mayfair, the most valuable property on the Monopoly board.

St James's and Westminster are southwest, SW1 to be precise. Would this square mile be a nuclear target? Well, in no particular order, it includes Whitehall, No 10 Downing St, the Houses of Parliament, Westminster Abbey and Buckingham Palace.

To the south of Victoria station, lies Pimlico, not a particularly attractive district but central, and with a good supply of cheapish, decentish hotels.

Kensington, Earl's Court, South Kensington and Chelsea are in the south-west corner formed by the Circle line.

Earl's Court, once infamous as Kangaroo Valley and home to countless expatriate Australians, now has a strong Middle Eastern influence. It's pretty tacky, and seems to get tackier by the year, but there are still some cheap hotels, a number of backpackers'

hostels and a couple of Australian pubs, plus cheap restaurants and travel agents. It is not a bad place to start your visit.

South Kensington is more chic and trendy, and there is a clutch of interesting museums (the Victoria & Albert, Science, Natural History and Geological). Chelsea has abandoned the bohemian for comfort, and Kings Rd has bid farewell to the punks, but it is still an interesting centre for young fashion.

The North

Accessible from Notting Hill Gate, but more easily reached from Ladbroke Grove, Notting Hill is a lively, interesting district, with a large West Indian population. It gets trendier by the day, but the Portobello Rd market is still good value and there are pubs, trendy bars and interesting shops.

North of Kensington Gardens and Hyde Park, Bayswater and Paddington are pretty much tourist ghettos, but there are plenty of hostels, cheap and mid-range hotels, good pubs and interesting restaurants (particularly along Queensway and Westbourne Grove).

From west to east, the band of suburbs to the north of the Central line include Kilburn, Hampstead, Camden Town, Kentish Town, Highgate and Highbury. Kilburn is London's Irish capital and bedsit land; not a bad place to live. Hampstead, with its great views, is fashionable, quiet and civilised, while Camden Town, although well advanced on the road to gentrification, still has some ordinary people and a gaggle of trendy but very enjoyable weekend markets.

The South

Cross the Thames from Central London and you could be excused for thinking you've arrived in a different country. This is working-class London and it seems a long way from the elegant, antiseptic streets of Westminster. Much of South London is very poor, very dirty, but very alive.

For the short-term visitor there may be few pressing reasons to visit, although there are cultural oases like the South Bank Centre (a venue for interesting exhibitions and con-

London Postcodes

To read a postcode from this map:
Determine lettered prefix (SE), and
add numbered suffix (9)

For instance, postcode for Eltham is SE9

- - - - Prefix boundary
——— Suffix boundary

certs), Kew with its superb gardens, and
Wimbledon with its tennis courts.

If you stay for any length of time,
however, there's a fair chance you will end
up living in suburbs like Clapham, Brixton,
Camberwell or even farther out.

Brixton was notorious for racial problems
in the early 1980s, but it is definitely no
Harlem, even though unemployment is high
and the crumbling buildings and piles of
rubbish may look the part. You'll enjoy its
tatty market and arcades whatever your skin
colour. Most of the district is as safe as
anywhere else, but don't wander too far off
the main streets until someone locates the
'front line' for you – an area around Railton
Rd which is best left to the locals.

INFORMATION
There's no shortage of information; the
problem is wading through it.

Look out for Lonely Planet's forthcoming
London city guide. Time Out (a listings magazine, issued every Tuesday, £1.70) is a
mind-bogglingly complete listing of everything happening and is recommended for
every visitor. The same company publishes
the *Time Out London Guide* (paperback,

£8.99). It also publishes the *Time Out Guide to Eating & Drinking in London* (magazine format, £7.50) which lists over 1700 restaurants and bars, although only some are cheap. *The Guardian* newspaper on a Saturday features a very useful guide to what's happening during the week, and Thursday's *Evening Standard* (30p) has its own weekly what's on magazine.

If you balk at paying, there are free magazines available from pavement bins, especially in Earl's Court, Notting Hill and Bayswater: *TNT Magazine*, *Southern Cross* and *Traveller* and *SA Times*. They have Australian, New Zealand and South African news and sports results, but they're invaluable for every budget traveller, with entertainment listings, excellent travel sections, and useful classifieds covering jobs, cheap tickets, shipping services and accommodation. The pocket-sized *Footloose in London* is also useful. *TNT* is the glossiest and most comprehensive of the bunch; phone ☎ 0171-373 3377 for the nearest distribution point.

Loot (£1.30) is a daily paper made up entirely of classified ads that are placed free by sellers. You can find everything from second-hand wrestling magazines to kitchen sinks and cars, as well as an extensive selection of flats and house-share ads. Also worth considering, if you're planning some serious shopping, is the *Time Out Guide to Shopping & Services* (magazine format, £6).

For information on buses, trains and the tube, see the Getting There & Away and Getting Around sections at the end of this chapter; for connections further afield, see the Getting There & Away and Getting Around chapters.

Tourist Offices

London is a major travel centre, so aside from information on London there are also offices that deal specifically with England, Scotland, Wales, Ireland, most European countries and many others.

British Travel Centre The British Travel Centre, 12 Regent St, Piccadilly Circus

SW1Y 4PQ (tube: Piccadilly Circus), is two minutes walk from Piccadilly Circus. This chaotic and comprehensive information and booking service offers tours, *bureau de change*, theatre tickets, train, air and car travel, accommodation, map and guidebook shop, and the Wales and Irish Tourist Boards. It's very busy and open every day: Monday to Friday from 9 am to 6.30 pm, Saturday and Sunday from 10 am to 4 pm (Saturday, 9 am to 5 pm between May and September). For general inquiries telephone 0181-846 9000.

London Tourist Information Centres There are Tourist Information Centres (TICs) in Heathrow terminals 1 to 3, and at Gatwick, Luton, and Stansted airports. The main centre on the Victoria station forecourt has a number of services including accommodation bookings, information, and a book and map shop. They're open Monday to Saturday from 8 am to 6 pm, Sunday from 8.30 am to 4 pm, and can be extremely busy. There is also a TIC at the Arrivals Hall in Waterloo International Terminal and one in the Liverpool St underground station. Send written inquiries to 26 Grosvenor Gardens SW1W 0DU (☎ 0171-730 3488).

Accommodation Bookings It is possible to make same-day accommodation bookings at the TICs at Victoria and Heathrow, although they charge £5 for a hotel or B&B booking and £1.50 for hostels; ☎ 0171-824 8844 for bookings.

Alternatively, at Victoria there are a couple of private hotel reservation centres (one on the main concourse, one outside near the steps to the underground) that charge £3 for a booking.

Backpackers can seek out Accommodation Express, a free service for backpackers to be found outside the Victoria railway and tube station on Buckingham Palace Rd. They have a courtesy bus to the Chelsea Hotel (see Private Hostels under Places to Stay later) and other budget hostels.

Foreign Consulates

With a few notable exceptions (Iraq, for

instance) London is an excellent place to gather information and visas. See the Facts for the Visitor chapter.

Money

Whenever possible, avoid using *bureaux de change* to change your money. For more info, see the Facts for the Visitor chapter at the beginning of this book.

There are 24-hour bureaus in Heathrow Terminals 1, 3 and 4. Terminal 2's bureau is open daily from 6 am to 11 pm. Thomas Cook has branches at Terminals 1, 3 and 4. There are 24-hour bureaus in Gatwick's South and North Terminals and one at Stansted. The airport bureaus are actually good value; they don't charge commission on sterling travellers' cheques, and on other currencies it's 1.5% with a £3 minimum.

At Victoria railway station near the tourist office, Thomas Cook has a bureau that's open daily from 6 am to 11 pm.

The main American Express office (☎ 0171-930 4411), 6 Haymarket (tube: Piccadilly), is open for currency exchange Monday to Friday from 9 am to 5.30 pm, Saturday from 9 am to 6 pm, and Sunday from 10 am to 5 pm. Other services are available weekdays from 9 am to 5 pm and Saturday from 9 am to noon.

The main Thomas Cook office (☎ 0171-499 4000), 45 Berkeley St (tube: Green Park), is open from 9 am (10 am on Thursday) to 5.30 pm Monday to Friday, from 9 am to 4 pm on Saturday. There are many branches scattered around the centre of London.

Post & Communications

Poste Restante Unless otherwise specified, poste restante mail is sent to London Chief Office (☎ 0171-239 5047), King Edward Building, King Edward St ECI (tube: St Paul's). It's open from 9 am to 6.30 pm, Monday to Friday. It's more convenient to have your mail sent to Poste Restante, Trafalgar Square Branch Office, London WC2N 4DL. The physical address is 24-28 William IV St (tube: Charing Cross). Mail will be held for four weeks; ID is required.

Telephone London telephone numbers have two codes (0171 or 0181) before a seven-digit number. To get a telephone operator, call ☎ 100; for telephone directory inquiries, ☎ 192; international, ☎ 153. For the international operator (for collect/reverse charges) phone ☎ 155.

CallShop etc. is a private company with cheaper rates than British Telecom for international calls and you can find them at 181a Earls Court Rd (☎ 0171-390 4549) and 88 Farringdon Rd (☎ 0171-837 7788), open until midnight.

Fax CallShop etc. (see the previous section) is the best place to use when sending or receiving faxes. The rate for receiving a fax is 25p a page.

E-mail See the information on Internet cafés in the Entertainment section.

Travel Agencies

London has always been a centre for cheap travel. Refer to the Sunday papers (especially the *Sunday Times*), *TNT Magazine* and *Time Out* for listings of cheap flights, and watch out for sharks.

The long-standing and reliable firms include:

Trailfinders
194 Kensington High St W8 (tube: High St Kensington). A complete travel service, including a bookshop, information centre, visa service and immunisation centre (☎ 0171-938 3939). There are also branches at 215 Kensington High Street and 42-50 Earls Court Road, Kensington W8
STA Travel
74 Old Brompton Rd SW7 (tube: South Kensington). The largest worldwide student/budget agency (☎ 0171-361 6262)
Campus Travel
52 Grosvenor Gardens SW1 (tube: Victoria). It also has offices in large YHA Adventure Shops (☎ 0171-730 8111)
Council Travel
28A Poland St W1 (tube: Oxford Circus). The USA's largest student and budget travel agency (☎ 0171-437 7767)

Bookshops

All the major chains are good sources for

guidebooks and maps, but there are also a number of specialist travel bookshops. Also see the boxed aside on bookshops.

Stanfords
12 Long Acre WC2 (tube: Covent Garden). This contains one of the largest and best selections of maps and guides in the world (☎ 0171-836 1321)

Travellers' Bookshop
32 St George St W1 (tube: Oxford Circus). It has a good collection of guides, and an interesting selection of literature (☎ 0171-493 0876).

Travel Bookshop
13 Blenheim Crescent, Notting Hill W11 (tube: Ladbroke Grove). It's across the road from Books for Cooks and has all the new guides, plus a selection of out of print and antiquarian gems (☎ 0171-229 5260)

Daunt Books
83 Marylebone High St W1 (tube: Baker St). A wide selection of travel guides in a beautiful old shop (☎ 0171-224 2295)

Laundry

There are countless laundrettes and there should be one within walking distance of your accommodation. Try Forco at 60 Parkway in Camden Town; Bendix at 395 Kings Rd in Chelsea; Notting Hill Laundrette at 12 Notting Hill Gate.

Medical Services

Reciprocal arrangements within the EU and with Australia and New Zealand mean that citizens of these countries do not pay for emergency medical treatment. Non-EU residents, however, would have to pay if admitted to a hospital ward. Regardless of nationality, anyone should receive free emergency treatment if it's a simple matter like bandaging a cut.

Hospitals with 24-hour emergency departments include:

Guy's Hospital
St Thomas St, SE1; tube: London Bridge (☎ 0171-955 5000)

St Bartholomew's Hospital (Barts)
West Smithfield, EC1; tube: Farringdon Rd (☎ 0171-601 8888)

St Thomas' Hospital
Lambeth Palace Rd, SE1; tube: Waterloo (☎ 0171-928 9292)

University College Hospital
Gower St, W1; tube: Euston Sq (☎ 0171-387 9300)

Emergency dental treatment is also available at Guy's Hospital.

A number of companies have visa and medical (immunisation) services; a few advertise in *TNT Magazine*. Charges can differ widely. Trailfinders (☎ 0171-938 3999), 194 Kensington High St W8, has both a visa service and an immunisation centre. The International Medical Centre (☎ 0171-486 3063) has two branches, including one at the Top Deck (Deckers) headquarters, 131 Earl's Court Rd SW5. Top Deck also hosts the Rapid Visa Service (☎ 0171-373 3026). Nomad (☎ 0181-889 7014), 3 Turnpike Lane N8, sells travel equipment and medical kits, and gives immunisations (Saturday only).

☎ 0800-567123 is a free AIDS helpline number and the Terrence Higgins Trust (☎ 0171-242 1010) is also a worthwhile source of advice.

Emergency

Dial ☎ 999 (free) for fire, police or ambulance. The local police station (see phone book) can advise you of the nearest late-night pharmacy.

WALKING TOUR

As always, walking is the best way to discover a new city. The centre of London can easily be explored on foot. The following tour could be covered in a day, but it does not allow you the chance to explore any of the individual sights in detail. It will, however, give you an introduction to the West End and Westminster. See the separate sections on all these sights later in the chapter.

Start at **St Paul's Cathedral**, Christopher Wren's masterpiece that was completed in 1710, and climb to the top of the Golden Gallery for one of the best views of London. Unless you're feeling very energetic, catch a tube from St Paul's station to Covent Garden (west on the Central line to Holborn, then west on the Piccadilly line).

✿✿

London in a Hurry
The most famous sights in London can be visited (or at least viewed) in a flying visit without feeling too much like you're on a roller-coaster ride. Here are a few suggestions to help you make the most of your time.

Two days
If you're only in London for a couple of days, consider using one of the hop-on-hop-off tourist sightseeing buses (see Bus Tours). Visit Trafalgar Square, Buckingham Palace (Changing of the Guard), Big Ben, the Houses of Parliament and Westminster Abbey. Then head for Tower Bridge and the Tower of London (for the Crown Jewels) or St Paul's Cathedral (climb to the top of the dome for a superb view of the city).

Wander around the West End, particularly Soho and Covent Garden, Piccadilly Circus and Harrods department store. If you've still got time visit the British Museum. In the evening take in a show at a West End theatre, and visit one of London's many pubs.

Four days
As well as the above sights, take a cruise from Charing Cross Pier to Greenwich, where you can visit the Royal Observatory, the Royal Naval College, the Queen's House and the Cutty Sark (allow at least a full afternoon).

Camden Town and Portobello Rd are excellent weekend maket places. Also good is a canal cruise, the most popular being from Little Venice to Camden Lock (for the market). For a bit of greenery visit Hyde Park (try to get to Speaker's Corner on a Sunday) and Regent's Park. You could also visit one of London's tourist traps – such as Madam Tussaud's waxworks or Rock Circus.

Day trips can be made to Windsor Castle in Berkshire, and Leeds Castle in Kent.

One week
You should be able to see all of the above, as well as adding a few more galleries and museums (the Tate, National Gallery and Imperial War Museum). Take a ride on the Docklands Light Railway to see the developing London Docklands area. Visit Kew Gardens (it can be reached by boat from Westminster Pier) and Hampton Court Palace.

If you've still got time and wish to include sights beyond London, day trips are possible to many places in southern England – Oxford, Cambridge, Winchester and Bath among them. ■

✿✿✿

Covent Garden, once London's fruit and vegetable market, has been restored to a bustling piazza. It's one of the very few places in London where pedestrians rule, and you can watch the buskers for a few coins and the tourists for free. The opera house is on the north-east corner, and the main YHA Adventure Shop is on Southampton St off the south side.

Return to the tube station and turn left into Long Acre (look for Stanfords bookshop on your left) and continue across Charing Cross Rd into **Leicester Square** with its cinemas and franchise food. Note the Leicester Square Theatre Ticket Booth, which sells half-price tickets on the day of performance.

Continue along Coventry St, past the Trocadero and Madame Tussaud's Rock Circus, until you get to **Piccadilly Circus**,

with Tower Records, one of the best music shops in London. Shaftesbury Ave enters the circus at the north-eastern corner, with the cheap kebab/pizza counters. This is the street of theatres and runs back into Soho, with its myriad restaurants. Regent St curves out of the north-west corner up to Oxford Circus.

Continue west along Piccadilly to St James church (with its excellent cheap restaurant) and the Royal Academy. Detour into the extraordinary **Burlington Arcade**, just after the academy; beware the arcade Burties (private 'police') who, amongst other things, are supposed to stop you whistling.

Return to Piccadilly and continue until you get to St James's St on your left (south). This takes you down to **St James's Palace**, the royal home from 1660 to 1837 until it was judged insufficiently impressive. Skirt around its east side and you come onto The Mall.

Trafalgar Square is to the east (left), **Buckingham Palace** (commonly referred to as Buck House) is to the west. From 3 April to 3 August the changing of the guard happens daily at 11.30 am; from August to April it is at 11.30 am on alternate days. The best place to be is by the gates of Buck House, but the crowds are awesome. Cross back into St James's Park, the most beautiful in London, and follow the lake to its east end. Turn right onto Horse Guards Rd. This takes you past the **Cabinet War Rooms**, £4 admission, which give an extraordinary insight into the dark days of WWII.

Continue south along Horse Guards Rd, then turn left on Great George St, which takes you through to beautiful Westminster Abbey, the Houses of Parliament and Westminster Bridge. **Westminster Abbey** is so rich in history you need half a day to do it justice. The coronation chair where all but two monarchs since 1066 have been crowned is behind the altar, and many greats – from Darwin to Chaucer – have been buried here. The best way to soak in the atmosphere, however, is to attend Evensong (5 pm on Monday, Tuesday, Thursday and Friday; 3 pm on Saturday and Sunday).

The **Houses of Parliament** and the St Stephen's tower, better known by the name of the famous bell within it, **Big Ben**, were actually built in the 19th century in mock medieval style. The best way to get into the building is to attend the Commons or Lords visitors' galleries during a Parliamentary debate. Phone ☎ 0171-219 4272 for information.

Walking away from Westminster Bridge, turn right into Whitehall (Parliament St). On your left, Downing St has an ordinary-looking house at **No 10** that offers temporary accommodation to prime ministers. Farther along on the right is the Inigo Jones-designed Banqueting House, outside which Charles I was beheaded. Continue past the Horse Guards, where you can see a changing of the guard (less crowded than at Buck House) at 11 am Monday to Saturday and 10 am on Sunday.

Big Ben

Finally, you reach **Trafalgar Square** and Nelson's Column. The National Gallery and National Portrait Gallery are on the north side.

OTHER WALKS

Although central London is blighted by heavy traffic, there are some places where you can escape.

You can follow the Grand Union Canal from Little Venice to the Thames eight miles away. Start at Blomfield Rd, near Warwick Ave tube station. Except for a few breaks where it disappears underground, the canal runs around Regent's Park, through the Camden Lock Market, past grubby but interesting warehouses and industrial areas, and enters the river at Limehouse in the East End. From there you can catch the Docklands Light Railway back to Tower Gateway, which links with the Tower Hill tube station. See the Canal Tour section later if you want to catch a boat part of the way.

All visitors should make the most of London's glorious parks. A long walk starting at St James's and continuing through Green, Hyde, Kensington and Holland parks will banish any urban blues.

London Walks (☎ 0171-624 3978) has daily two-hour guided walks for £4 that begin and end outside underground stations.

RIVER TOUR – EAST

If walking doesn't seem like a good idea, consider catching a boat from Westminster Pier (beside Westminster Bridge) down the river to Greenwich (every half hour from 10 am, single/return £5.30/6.30). You pass the site of Shakespeare's Globe Theatre, stop at the Tower of London, and continue under Tower Bridge and past many famous docks.

Greenwich can absorb the best part of a day. Start with the **Cutty Sark**, the only surviving tea and wool clipper and one of the most beautiful ships ever built. Wander around the Greenwich market, then visit the **Queen's House**, a masterpiece designed in 1616 by Inigo Jones. If you're interested in boats and naval history, continue to the **National Maritime Museum**. The **Royal Naval College**, beside the river, was designed by Wren.

Climb the hill behind the museum to the **Old Royal Observatory**. A brass strip in the observatory courtyard marks the prime meridian that divides the world into eastern and western hemispheres. There are great views over Docklands – with the massive Canary Wharf development just over the river – and back to London.

Walk back down the hill and through the Greenwich foot tunnel (near the *Cutty Sark*) to Island Gardens. From the other side of the river there is a superb view of the Naval College and the Queen's House – a classic arrangement of buildings. The Docklands Light Railway whisks above ground from Island Gardens back to Tower Gateway, and there are good views of the new Docklands developments. Unfortunately, it only runs on weekdays; buses run on weekends. Zone 1 & 2 Travelcards are valid.

If you are still raring to go, you could dash into the **Tower of London**. The tower dates from the 1070s when William the Conqueror began the White Tower. The castle was turned into an enormous concentric fortress by Henry III and has been a fortress, royal residence and prison. It now houses the crown jewels and royal armoury, and there are inevitably large crowds (visit during the week). Or, on Sunday, visit Petticoat Lane market a short walk north up the Minories.

RIVER TOUR – WEST

River boats also run west from Westminster Pier, an enjoyable excursion, although it takes considerably longer and is not as dramatic and interesting as the trip to the east.

There are two possible destinations: Kew Gardens and Hampton Court Palace, both of which are highlights of a London visit. It's not really feasible to see both in the same day, if you plan to travel by boat.

Kew Gardens, the Royal Botanic Gardens, are a beautiful, restful escape from the real world. Ferries sail from Westminster Pier every 30 minutes from 10.15 am to 2.30 pm (from the Monday before Easter until the end of September). They take 1½ hours and a single/return costs £5/7. While you're out here, cross Kew Bridge and walk to the right along the (left) bank of the Thames; there are a number of pleasant riverside pubs. It's possible to return by tube (tube: Kew Gardens, Zone 3). Admission to the Gardens is £5/3.

Hampton Court Palace is the grandest Tudor house in the country. Built by Cardinal Wolsey in 1514 and 'adopted' by Henry VIII, it is a beautiful mixture of architectural styles – from Henry's splendid Great Hall to the State Apartments built for King William III and Queen Mary II by Wren. The superb palace grounds, near the Thames, include deer and a 300-year-old maze. Ferries leave from Westminster Pier. They operate from April to October at 10.30 and 11.15 am and noon, take 3½ hours and cost £7. There are also trains every half hour from Waterloo station (£3.90 return, Zone 6). Admission to the Palace is £7.50/5.60.

CANAL TOUR

The London Waterbus Company (☎ 0171-482 2550) runs regular 90-minute trips between Camden Lock and Little Venice, via London Zoo and Regent's Park. From 1 April to the end of October boats depart from the locks at Camden and Little Venice every hour between 10 am and 5 pm; the last return trip departs at 3 pm, the last one-way trip at 3.45 pm. There is a reduced service, weekends only, from November to March. One-way tickets are £3.50/2.10, return tickets £4.50/2.70.

BUS ROUTES

One of the best ways to explore London is to buy a Travelcard and jump on some of the regular double-decker buses. From north to south, or vice versa, the No 24 is good. Beginning in Hampstead, it travels through Camden and along Gower St (passing London University and Dillons Bookshop) to Tottenham Court Rd. From Tottenham Court Rd it travels along Charing Cross Rd, past Leicester Square to Trafalgar Square, then along Whitehall, past the House of Commons, Westminster Abbey and Westminster Cathedral. It reaches Victoria station and then carries on to Pimlico, which is handy for the Tate Gallery.

From east to west, take the No 8. This is a 'routemaster' bus (red, open-backed and with a conductor) and comes from Bethnal Green Market. It passes or runs close to the Whitechapel Art Gallery, Petticoat Lane Market, Liverpool St station, the City, the Guildhall and Old Bailey. It then crosses

Holborn and enters Oxford St, travelling along through Oxford Circus, passing Bond St, Selfridges and the largest Marks & Spencer store. Get off at Hyde Park Corner unless you wish to continue north up Edgware Rd to Willesden Green.

BUS TOURS

A number of companies offer tours around the main sights in double-decker buses. They're all expensive and are really only worth considering if you've got plenty of money or you're only going to be in London for a day or two.

Trafalgar Square in front of the National Gallery, and in front of the Trocadero on Coventry St between Leicester Square and Piccadilly Circus, are convenient starting points.

The Original London Sightseeing Tour (☎ 0171-222 1234) has a 1½-hour tour departing from Victoria St near Victoria station (as well as a number of other stops). They have a system where you can buy a ticket from Piccadilly and Oxford Circus TICs for £8; other TICs charge £9 and on the bus you pay £10. London Plus has a more extensive route and you can hop on and off the buses at a number of major attractions. Tickets are the same prices.

WEST END

The West End of London is a heady, incredible mixture of consumerism and culture. A number of outstanding museums and galleries rub shoulders with a far larger number of tacky tourist traps while world-famous places and monuments share the streets with some of the capital's best shopping and entertainment possibilities.

Trafalgar Square

Trafalgar Square (tube: Charing Cross) is the closest you'll get to finding the heart of the city, where great marches and rallies take place, and where the new year is seen in by thousands of crushed, drunken revellers.

The square was designed by Nash, and executed by Barry, who was also partly responsible for the Houses of Parliament. It's a rather boastful affair, mostly commemorating England's colonial and military past. Nelson's Column commemorates the naval defeat of Napoleon in 1805. The 165-foot-tall phallic erection attracts tourists and pigeons in equal numbers.

National Gallery The porticoed front of the National Gallery (☎ 0171-839 3321) takes up most of the north side of the square. Though old and lacking funds for new acquisitions, with over 2000 paintings it is by far the best gallery in London, and one of the best in the world.

There are at least a dozen amazing pictures to look at, from *The Annunciation* by Lippi, Raphaelo's *Pope Julius*, through van Eyck's *Arnolfini Wedding*, Titian's *The Killing of Actaeon*, and on to Velasquez's *Rokeby Venus* and *The Bathers* by Cezanne. That's without even mentioning priceless works by Leonardo da Vinci, Holbein, Bosch, Breughel, Poussin, Bellini, Vermeer, Caravaggio and Seurat.

The true marvel of the National Gallery is that it's right in the heart of London and entry is free. Therefore if you're in the mood for only one or two great paintings, you can view them at your leisure and move on, without feeling pressured to make the most of a once-only opportunity. There's even a rather pleasant basement café.

The gallery is open Monday to Saturday from 10 am to 6 pm (8 pm on Wednesday), Sunday from 2 pm to 6 pm.

National Portrait Gallery This gallery (☎ 0171-306 0055) has the same opening hours as the National Gallery, and is opposite St Martin's. It has an array of paintings of the famous and the not-so-famous; admission is free.

St Martin's in the Fields (☎ 0171-930 1862), occupies a prime site at the north-eastern corner of Trafalgar Square. An influential masterpiece by James Gibbs, dating from the early 18th century, there is something intrinsically likeable about this church. The slightly silly wedding-cake spire is offset by the splendid visual harmony of white stone linking St Martin's and the National Gallery. When floodlit this becomes one of the great vistas of London.

During the day, St Martin's continues its long tradition of tending to the poor and homeless, running amongst other things a soup kitchen. In fact this is a social church all round, with an adjoining craft market, and brass rubbing centre, bookshop and a reasonable café in the crypt. What's more, all year round from Monday to Thursday there are concerts at 1.05 pm which provide the perfect opportunity to enjoy the church interior, a restrained mixture of plain and ornate decorative effects. There are also evening concerts at 7.30 pm on Thursday, Friday and Saturday with admission rates that vary from £6 to £15.

It's open Monday to Saturday from 10 am to 6 pm, Sunday from noon to 6 pm.

Leicester Square
A few years ago Leicester Square was a gruesome example of London's seediness and general disrepair. Now that it's been enlarged and tarted up it has quite an enjoyable buzz. It's London's bustling, brightly lit centre for overpriced, middle-of-the-road entertainment, containing four huge cinemas, various nightclubs and plenty of nearby pubs. On a warm summer's night when the square is full of buskers and crowds it's definitely worth strolling through – on your way to somewhere else.

Piccadilly Circus
Piccadilly Circus is the world-famous, neon-lit home of the statue Eros. It used to be the hub of London, the empire even, where flower girls flogged their wares and people arranged to meet or simply bumped into each other. It is now fume-choked and pretty uninteresting – surrounded by the Rock Circus, Tower Records and a disappointing Japanese department store.

Don't believe what the other guidebooks tell you; Londoners most certainly do not use the Circus as a starting point for a fun-packed night out. It's young, weary tourists who come to

Piccadilly Circus and sit beside Eros waiting for something to happen. Invariably, it doesn't.

Rock Circus Rock Circus (☎ 0171-734 8025), London Pavilion, Piccadilly Circus W1 (tube: Piccadilly Circus), is one of the most enjoyable and popular attractions in London. What's bad about the Rock Circus is its incredible tackiness, which is also what makes it so good.

Motorised wax versions of Madonna, Hendrix, Prince, George Michael and bags of other rock icons sing and gyrate comically and quite spookily. Though some of the visual and aural special effects are rather haphazard, the whole experience sustains a weird and dreamlike appeal.

It's open daily from 10 am to 10 pm from late June to early September. Outside of summer it's open Monday, Wednesday, Thursday and Sunday 11 am to 9 pm; Tuesday from noon to 9 pm; Friday and Saturday from 11 am to 10 pm; £7.50/6.95.

Trocadero The Trocadero (☎ 0990-50 50 40), Piccadilly Circus W1 (tube: Piccadilly Circus), first opened as a men's tennis court in 1744, but now it's an indoor entertainment complex with a number of hi-tech attractions, anchored by Segaworld.

The £12/9 admission charge to Segaworld includes unlimited access to the six rides, but the queues can be very long and other interactive games cost £1 or 50p a shot.

Royal Academy of Arts
The Royal Academy of Arts (☎ 0171-439 7438), Burlington House, Piccadilly W1 (tube: Green Park), tends to be the poor cousin to the Hayward Gallery, with international exhibitions that aren't quite as sexy and high profile. This doesn't mean that the displays can't be excellent, or that the crowds won't flock here.

Past displays have included the excellent American Art in the 20th century and drawings by Goya and Modigliani. Each summer, as is the tradition, the academy holds its Summer Exhibition, an open show that

anyone can enter. The quality can be mixed, but on the right day, amidst the glorious setting of one of London's few remaining 18th-century mansions, nobody seems to mind that much.

It's open daily from 10 am to 6 pm; £5.50/4.

Museum of Mankind
The Museum of Mankind (☎ 0171-437 2224), 6 Burlington Gardens W1 (tube: Piccadilly Circus), is the ethnographic department of the British Museum transplanted to the middle of Piccadilly. At any time, only one-sixth of the museum's possessions are on display.

Masks from Africa, musical instruments from Asia, carvings from America, tribal skirts, totems, talismans and so on from just about everywhere tell of a complex and varied world. Unless you stumble on something in which you have a particular interest, the museum can fail to capture the imagination. It has a smart and pleasant café.

The museum is open Monday to Saturday from 10 am to 5 pm, Sunday from 2.30 to 6 pm; free.

Burlington & Royal Arcades
Built in 1819, Burlington Arcade, off Piccadilly (tube: Piccadilly Circus), recalls a bygone age – selling the kinds of things that only the very rich could want or imagine that they need. It's more than slightly shocking to find that these customers still exist.

Watch out for the beadles, the uniformed guards who patrol the arcade, with a brief to prevent high spirits, whistling and the thoroughly inelegant popping of bubble gum. Surprisingly, there's a low-key atmosphere, and this polite and genteel arcade is well worth a short visit.

The Royal Arcade runs off Old Bond St, which runs into Piccadilly just past the Royal Academy and Burlington Arcade. Built in 1879, it reflects that era's love affair with Gothic style. It's a covered thoroughfare lined with extremely expensive shops selling quintessential English ware, like hunting jackets, pipe tobacco, cashmere jumpers and golfing knickerbockers.

Fortnum & Mason

Fortnum & Mason (☎ 0171-734 8040), 181 Piccadilly W1 (tube: Piccadilly Circus), is noted for its exotic, old-world food hall, but it also carries plenty of overpriced and stuffy fashion wear. All kinds of strange foodstuffs can be purchased here, along with the famous food hampers that cost an arm and a leg. This is where Scott of the Antarctic stocked up before heading off to the wilderness. These days you'd be better advised buying your travel provisions elsewhere and settling for a small, gift-wrapped box of chocolates for a show-off present. It's open Monday to Saturday from 9.30 am to 6 pm.

Oxford St

What was once London's premier shopping street has lost a lot of its lustre. From Oxford Circus to Tottenham Court Rd, the feel is distinctly tatty, featuring permanent 'closing down' sales and spivs - shopfront salesmen who draw in tourists by offering dubious bargains, usually on electrical goods. From Oxford Circus to Marble Arch, the tone is classier – there's a string of department stores, including Debenhams, John Lewis and massive Selfridges, which although battling to keep up with Harrods, is still a place for everything you might conceivably want.

Beside the flagship HMV and Virgin record stores, Oxford St's other great shopping institution is the big Marks & Spencer store near Marble Arch. The well-priced clothes, though not the height of fashion, are not nearly as uncool as they used to be.

Wallace Collection

The Wallace Collection (☎ 0171-935 0687), Hertford House, Manchester Square W1 (tube: Bond St), is London's finest small gallery. It has a treasure trove of high-quality paintings from the 17th and 18th centuries, including Rubens, Titian, Poussin, Frans Hals' *Laughing Cavalier* and Rembrant's *Titus*, excellent porcelain and a collection of

armour – all housed in a splendidly Italianate mansion.

The collection was bequeathed to the nation towards the end of the last century with the proviso that it be kept intact and open to the general public. It tends to be something of a well-kept secret and the kind of gallery you might overlook. This would be a mistake.

It's open Monday to Saturday from 10 am to 5 pm, Sunday from 2 to 5 pm; free.

Hamleys

Hamleys (☎ 0171-734 3161), 188 Regent St W1 (tube: Oxford Circus), is an enormous toy shop. It's the place to go if you want to see every imaginable toy in the universe, or to commence your second childhood. Prices can be high, however, and you may well be able to buy more cheaply elsewhere. It's open Monday to Wednesday and Friday from 10 am to 7 pm, Thursday from 10 am to 8 pm, Saturday from 9.30 am to 7 pm, and Sunday from noon to 6 pm.

Liberty

Liberty (☎ 0171-734 1234), Regent St W1 (tube: Oxford Circus), is as unique and amazing as Harrods, with high fashion, great modern furniture, a unique fabrics department and those inimitable silk scarves. It was born at the turn of the century out of the influential arts & crafts movement – in Italy Art Nouveau was called Liberty Style, after the store. Both its appealing interior design and the helpful sales staff add to the pleasure of shopping and browsing here. It's particularly good during the January and summer sales. It's open Monday to Wednesday, Friday and Saturday from 10 am to 6.30 pm; Thursday from 10 am to 7.30 pm.

Carnaby St

Carnaby St, behind Oxford Circus tube station near Liberty, was the centre of the world in the swinging 60s, but it's now a sleazy joke (it's currently up for sale at £79 million). There's nothing to be said for the place, although there are still crowds of misguided young tourists. Adjoining Carnaby St

LONDON

Shopping in London

Londoners are the greatest shoppers in the world, so it is not surprising that London has some of the world's greatest shops. Shopping is regarded as part science, part sport, part entertainment, part recreation. It's a serious business. To get any feeling of London life you have to abandon anti-consumerist principles and throw yourself into the fray.

Covent Garden combines shopping with entertainment and a visit there is recommended. The most famous big store is Harrods in Knightsbridge but Liberty at Oxford Circus is equally interesting. From there a walk up Oxford St to Marble Arch takes you past some classy department stores. Alternatively, hop down Regent St to look in at Hamleys toy store and snobby Fortnum & Mason at Piccadilly Circus.

Markets

The markets are where you see London life at its best: they're bustling, interesting and full of character(s).

Berwick St in Soho is one of the last strongholds of real life in the West End and the fruit and vegetables are among the best and the cheapest in London (stock up for a picnic). Camden attracts huge crowds all weekend. It's trendy and a lot of fun – don't confuse it with Camden Passage near the Angel which specialises in antiques. The East End markets are a bargain-hunter's paradise – cheap and chaotic. Portobello Rd has fruit and vegetables during the week and general goods – mostly trendy and not very cheap – on Friday and Saturday. Brixton has barrows piled high with fruit and vegetables, and there are lively arcades that *must* be explored – the Caribbean comes to London.

Fashion

It's easy to be intimidated by London's indoor fashion markets – to believe that these places are central HQ for the fashion police, and only the most trendy fashion victims will be made welcome. However, designers at Hyper-Hyper (☎ 071-938 4343), 26-40 Kensington High St W8, and the Garage (☎ 0171-352 8653), 181 King's Rd SW3, are mostly struggling types, more than a little keen to sell you their imaginative glad rags. So, mosey along and see the great, the ridiculous and the eminently wearable, and note the bloody cheap price tags.

Kensington Market (☎ 0171-938 4343), 49-53 Kensington High St W8, is a rather different kettle of fish. It's something of a dinosaur, a shambles – and a lot of fun. It's more leather and patchouli oil than high fashion – the place for second-hand Levis, army jackets, hippy dippy rags and hand-made jewellery.

Kensington Market is open Monday to Saturday from 10 am to 6 pm. Hyper-Hyper is open Monday to Wednesday, Friday and Saturday from 10 am to 6 pm; Thursday from 10 am to 7 pm. The Garage is open Monday to Saturday from 10 am to 6 pm.

Music

There are the three goliath-sized music shops in London: Tower Records (☎ 0171-439 2500), 1 Piccadilly Circus; HMV (☎ 0171-631 3423), 150 Oxford St W1; and Virgin Megastore (☎ 0171-631 1234), 14-30 Oxford St W1.

Tower Records is easiest to find and stays open the latest. Its jazz, world music and soundtrack sections are pretty good, but overall the shop is hectic, and difficult to negotiate. This is no place to browse. The Tower chain is a lot more composed and user-friendly in the States. They seem to think the British record-buying public will settle for less – and they do.

HMV is great for orders, classical music and specialist categories, but again the shop is loud and crowded. The Virgin Megastore near Tottenham Court Rd is by far the most pleasant and relaxed of the rival giants. The layout is a tad bewildering but worth persevering with; there are some excellent bargains.

London also has a range of excellent specialist stores. Ray's Jazz Shop (☎ 0171-240 3969), 180 Shaftesbury Ave WC2, speaks for itself. There's rare and recent jazz and the staff are helpful and knowledgeable.

A trip around Honest Jon's (☎ 0181-969 9822), 278 Portobello Rd W10; their new jazz shop next door; Dub Vendor (☎ 0171-223 3757), 274 Lavender Hill SW11; Trax (☎ 0171-734 0795), 55 Greek St W1; and Black Market (☎ 0171-437 0478), 25 D'Arblay St W1, should get you well stocked. They have dance and every kind of modern black music, from House, Dub, Acid, Hip-Hop, Rare Groove, Swing, Rap, Techno, Reggae and all the other mutant music forms that make London the dance capital of the world.

Reckless Records (☎ 0171-437 4271),at 30 Berwick St W1, UFO Music (☎ 0171-636 1281), at 18

✛✛✛

Hanway St W1, and assorted music stalls at Kensington Market (☎ 0171-938 4343), 49-53 Kensington High St W8, will keep the second-hand and rare-vinyl hunter happy for quite a while.

Books
For those who read the book or saw the movie *84 Charing Cross Rd*, Charing Cross Rd will need no introduction. This is where to go when you want reading matter.

Foyle's (☎ 0171-437 5660), 119 Charing Cross Rd W1, is the biggest and by far the messiest and most confusing. It has to be seen to be believed, but then head for Waterstones (☎ 0171-434 4291)), 121-131 Charing Cross Rd, or Books Etc (☎ 0171-379 6838) which is next door. The Waterstones chain has transformed the book-buying experience in London. Their many stores are well stocked, smartly appointed and the staff are knowledgeable and keen to help. Books Etc tends to lag a bit behind its neighbour, but it does have a slight edge where alternative and avant-garde titles are concerned.

There are also plenty of specialist book shops in the area, from the self-explanatory Sportspages (☎ 0171-240 9604), 94-96 Charing Cross Rd; to the broadest selection of crime and detective fiction at Murder One (☎ 0171-734 3485), 71-73 Charing Cross Rd; and Zwemmer (☎ 0171-379 7886), 24 Litchfield St, for all kinds of art books. The ever-expanding Silver Moon (☎ 0171-836 7906), 64-68 Charing Cross Rd, has women's and feminist titles. Helter Skelter (☎ 0171-836 1151), 4 Denmark St, focuses on popular music.

Further afield, Dillons (☎ 0171-636 1577), 82 Gower St WC1, has the edge on academic titles. Gay's the Word (☎ 0171-278 7654), 66 Marchmont St, Russell Square WC1 stocks, unsurprisingly, male gay writing; Compendium (☎ 0171-485 8944), 234 Camden High St NW1, serves as the focus for left-wing, alternative and hard-to-find titles. Books for Cooks (☎ 0171-221 1992), 4 Blenheim Crescent W11, has an enormous collection of cookery books; there's also a small attached café where you can sample some of the recipes.

A number of shops specialise in travel. Stanfords (☎ 0171-836 1321), 12 Long Acre WC2 (tube: Covent Garden), has one of the largest and best selections of maps and guides in the world. The Travellers' Bookshop (☎ 0171-493 0876), 32 St George St W1, has an interesting selection, including antiquarian books. The Travel Bookshop (☎ 0171-229 5260), 13 Blenheim Crescent W11, across the road from Books for Cooks, has all the new guides, plus a selection of out-of-print and antiquarian gems. Daunts Books (☎ 0171-224 2295), 83 Marylebone High St W1, has a wide selection of travel guides and other subjects all arranged under each country in a beautiful old shop. ■

✛✛✛

is west Soho, a decidedly more salubrious neck of the woods, with plenty of groovy bars, restaurants and outlets for hip designers such as Pam Hogg and the Duffer of St George.

COVENT GARDEN
Ever since the fruit-and-vegetable market was uprooted and moved across the river to Nine Elms, Covent Garden (tube: Covent Garden) has been an ever-burgeoning shopping and entertainment hub.

What was once Covent Garden, a vegetable field attached to Westminster Abbey, and later the haunt of writers like Pepys, Fielding and Boswell looking for somewhat shady nightlife, is now a triumph of conservation and commerce. Beyond the piazza are

streets of clothes shops and bars, restaurants, and designer gift shops. Covent Garden can be overcrowded, but it's also one of the few parts of London where pedestrians rule, and there's always a corner of relative peace where you can watch the world go by.

Stall holders once flogged fresh produce in the arcaded piazza; now they sell antiques, clothes and overpriced bric-a-brac. Jubilee Market, the weekend crafts fair at the corner of the piazza and Southampton St, is where you can find toys and artistic bumph. Continue down Southampton St for the main YHA Adventure Shop, which has a good range of guidebooks and outdoor equipment, and where you can join the YHA.

Facing out on to the piazza on the western side is the famous porticoed rear of St Paul's

Church – the actors' church. Here, on most evenings, you can find street theatre and buskers. If you're looking for a quiet escape, walk down either King St or Henrietta St and look for the narrow entrances into the churchyard. There are trees, flowers, some patches of grass and very little noise. Originally designed by Inigo Jones, the simple church is little more than a stone rectangle with a pitched roof.

For all things African, turn left down King St after leaving St Paul's and find the Africa Centre (☎ 0171-836 1973), 38 King St WC2, the best place in London for news and arts from a continent that only ever seems to be remembered when there's a famine or a war. There are often African bands, and there's an excellent well-priced African restaurant, the *Calabash* – see Places to Eat for details.

Parallel to the north, you'll find Floral St, where swanky designers like Paul Smith, Jigsaw, Jones and Agnes B have their main outlets. One street further north, Long Acre has Emporio Armani, Woodhouse, The Gap, and Flip (a true thrift shop selling 50s American clothing). There are also bookshops (including Waterstones, for guidebooks and maps) and St Martin's College of Fashion & Design.

Neal St, leading from Long Acre all the way down to Shaftesbury Ave, is a narrow lane lined with interesting shops selling hats, beads, leather, unusual footwear and strange teas. This, along with Floral St and the streets nearby such as Mondaymouth, Shelton, Earlham and the Seven Dials crossroads is the best of Covent Garden. (See the Places to Eat section later for details on Neal's Yard, another attractive escape.)

WESTMINSTER

A British city is traditionally a town with a cathedral and so traditionally there were two cities in London: Westminster and London! It is the City of London that is known simply as 'the City' but Westminster is the centre of political power and most of its places of interest are defined by their association with royal and/or parliamentary power. By way of cultural power, two notable institutions lie to the north and south; the ICA and the Tate Gallery respectively.

Westminster Abbey

Westminster Abbey (☎ 0171-222 7110), Dean's Yard SW1 (tube: St James's Park or Westminster), is one of the most visited churches in the Christian world. It has played an important role in the history of the English church and since 1066 every sovereign apart from Edward V and Edward VIII has been crowned here.

It is world-famous as the resting place of monarchs and the venue for other great pageants. Also within its walls is Britain's largest collection of tombs and monuments to the famous, which can distract attention from the beauty of the building itself.

There are guided tours lasting about $1\frac{1}{2}$ hours (£7), or you can take a portable tape-recorded commentary, which you can stop and start at your leisure (£6). Access to the chapels costs £4/2 so both tour options are good deals as they include admission. There is half price admission on Wednesday from 6 pm to 7.10 pm and this is the only time when photographs may be taken.

Access to the nave is free at all times; it's open Tuesday to Thursday from 7.30 am to 6 pm, Wednesday from 7.30 am to 7.45 pm. The royal chapels and transepts are open Monday to Friday from 9 am to 3.45 pm, and Saturday from 9 am to 1.45 pm and 4 to 4.45 pm, Sunday is for services only.

The Chapter House, Pyx Chamber and Abbey Museum (☎ 0171-222 5897; EH) are open 10 am to 6pm from April to September, closing at 4 pm between October and March; £2.50/1.90. The College Garden is open April to September, Tuesday and Thursday from 10 am to 6 pm; October to March, Tuesday and Thursday from 10 am to 4 pm. The Brass Rubbing Centre (☎ 0171-222 4589) is open Monday to Saturday from 9 am to 5.30 pm.

One of the best ways to visit the abbey is to combine it with a service, particularly evensong when the choir fills the abbey with the music of angels. The atmosphere and the acoustics will send shivers down your spine.

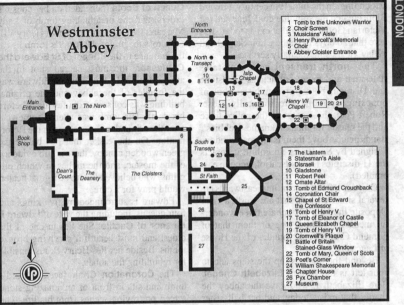

Westminster Abbey

North Entrance

North Transept

Islip Chapel

Main Entrance

The Nave

Book Shop

Dean's Court

The Deanery

The Cloisters

South Transept

St Faith

Henry VII Chapel

1. Tomb to the Unknown Warrior
2. Choir Screen
3. Musicians' Aisle
4. Henry Purcell's Memorial
5. Choir
6. Abbey Cloister Entrance

7. The Lantern
8. Statesman's Aisle
9. Disraeli
10. Gladstone
11. Robert Peel
12. Ornate Altar
13. Tomb of Edmund Crouchback
14. Coronation Chair
15. Chapel of St Edward the Confessor
16. Tomb of Henry V
17. Tomb of Eleanor of Castile
18. Queen Elizabeth Chapel
19. Tomb of Henry VII
20. Cromwell's Plaque
21. Battle of Britain Stained-Glass Window
22. Tomb of Mary, Queen of Scots
23. Poet's Corner
24. William Shakespeare Memorial
25. Chapter House
26. Pyx Chamber
27. Museum

Evensong lasts less than an hour; Monday, Tuesday, Thursday and Friday at 5 pm; Saturday and Sunday at 3 pm; free.

The main entry is at the west door, above which are two towers built by Sir Christopher Wren and his Baroque pupil Hawksmoor. Entering the nave can be alarming; on first sight the whole place is crowded, not only with people but with an enormous number of memorials. In the centre of the floor, surrounded by poppies, is a **Tomb to the Unknown Warrior**; brought back from the battlefields of WWI. Nearby is a stone commemorating the life of Winston Churchill.

At the east end of the nave is the **screen** separating it from the choir; built in 1834, it is the fourth screen to be placed here. Against this are monuments to Sir Isaac Newton and Lord Stanhope, by Rysbrack. Above the screen is the magnificent organ, dating from 1730. Look skyward to the beautiful stone

vaulted ceiling in the nave, and the fan vaulted aisles.

Before the gates (where you have to pay to proceed) on the right, there's a pulpit, from where, every hour, a priest offers a prayer. Once through the blue-and-gold gates you pass organ pipes as you walk east. This is the **musicians' aisle**, with memorials commemorating musicians who served the abbey. In a very appropriate setting, at the second pillar on the right after the organ pipes, is **Henry Purcell's memorial**. He was once organist at the abbey, and died in 1695.

Make your way eastwards to the Lantern, the heart of the abbey, where coronations take place. Standing in the centre, if you face east, the sanctuary, where the high altar stands, is before you. The **ornate altar**, designed by Sir Gilbert Scott in 1897, depicts the last supper.

Turn around and take a breath – the **choir**, where the monks once worshipped, is quite astounding. In the mid-19th century, Edward Blore created the stunning gold, blue and red Victorian Gothic choir that exists today. It is here that 20 boys from the Choir School and 12 lay vicars sing the daily services.

The **north transept** commemorates statesmen and many politicians. Gladstone and Disraeli, both prime ministers but of opposing opinions, are ironically close. Robert Peel, the creator of the police force and the reason for their nickname 'Bobbies', stands near. Above them is the rose window, designed by Sir James Thornhill; it depicts the 11 disciples (Judas Iscariot, of course, is omitted).

On your left as you continue eastwards are several small chapels that are worth a visit. Opposite the Islip Chapel are three wonderful medieval **tombs**, one of them that of Edmund Crouchback, founder of the House of Lancaster.

Beyond the chapels, up the steps and to your left is the **Queen Elizabeth Chapel**. Here Elizabeth I, who gave the abbey the charter that exists today, and her half-sister Mary I share an elaborate tomb. In life, they did not get on, which may be why there is no effigy of Mary.

The most easterly part of the abbey is **Henry VII's Chapel** (added in 1503), an outstanding example of late Perpendicular architecture. The magnificently carved wooden stalls, reserved for the Knights of the Order of the Bath, feature a colourful headpiece bearing the chosen personal statement of its occupant. Recent members of the order include Ronald Reagan and Norman Schwarzkopf.

Behind the altar, from which hangs a 15th-century *Madonna and Child* by Vivarini, is the black-marble **sarcophagus** of Henry VII and his queen, Elizabeth of York. All are housed under an amazing fan-vaulted Tudor ceiling. Beyond this is the **Battle of Britain stained-glass window**. At its entrance a **plaque** marks the spot where Oliver Cromwell's body lay until the restoration, whereupon it was disinterred, hanged at Tyburn and beheaded.

In the south aisle is the **tomb of Mary Queen of Scots** (beheaded on her cousin's orders) and the breathtaking tomb of Lady Margaret Beaufort, the mother of Henry VII.

Across the bridge, **Henry V's tomb** lies at the entrance to the **Chapel of St Edward the Confessor**, the most sacred spot in the abbey, behind the high altar. St Edward was the founder of the abbey and the original building was consecrated a few days before his death. His tomb was altered somewhat after the original was destroyed in the Reformation. On the casket that lies below the green wooden canopy, there is still evidence of the mosaic, and the niches in which pilgrims, who believed him to be a great healer, would pray for a cure.

Edward is surrounded by five kings and four queens, including the wife of Edward I, **Eleanor of Castile**. She lies in one of the oldest and most beautiful surviving bronze tombs. Beside her lies Henry II, responsible for rebuilding the abbey.

The **Coronation Chair** faces Edward's tomb and sits in front of an amazing stone screen portraying scenes from his life. The chair dates from around 1300 and is made of oak. Below its seat used to lie the Stone of Scone (pronounced skoon) – the Scottish coronation stone pilfered in 1297 by Edward. The stone was finally moved back to Scotland – but to Edinburgh Castle, not to Scone – in 1996, though the Scots had to agree to return it for any future coronations.

In the **south transept** is **Poet's Corner**, where several of England's finest writers are buried, a precedent that was established with Geoffrey Chaucer, although he was actually buried here because he had been Clerk of Works to the Palace of Westminster, not because he had written *The Canterbury Tales*. The practice actually began in earnest in 1700.

In front of two medieval wall paintings on the south wall stands the **memorial to William Shakespeare**, who, like TS Eliot, Byron, Tennyson, William Blake (whose bronze head by Sir Jacob Epstein has very unnerving eyes) and various other luminaries, is not actually buried here. There are memorials for Handel, holding a score of the

Messiah, Edmund Spenser, Lord Tennyson and Robert Browning, as well as the graves of Charles Dickens, Henry James, Lewis Carroll and Rudyard Kipling.

One of the chapels reserved for private prayer is St Faith's. Scraps of skin belonging to a thief who attempted to rob the abbey in the 16th century remain on the door; he didn't get far and was flayed for his crime.

The entrance in the north-east corner of the abbey's cloister dates from the 13th century, the rest of it from the 14th. The **Chapter House**, east down a passageway off the cloister, has one of the best preserved medieval tile floors in Europe and is octagonal in shape. On the eight walls can be seen remains of religious paintings. It was used by the king's council as its chamber, and the House of Commons used it as a meeting place in the 16th century. To this day it is the government that runs the Chapter House and the adjacent **Pyx Chamber**, once the Royal Treasury but now displaying the abbey's plate, and boasting the oldest altar in the building.

The **museum** exhibits the death masks of generations of royalty and there are wax effigies representing Charles II and William III (who is on a stool to make him as tall as his wife Mary).

To reach the 900-year-old College Garden, the oldest in England, enter Dean's Yard and the Cloisters on Great College St.

Houses of Parliament

The Houses of Parliament (☎ 0171-219 4272), Parliament Square SW1 (tube: Westminster), include the House of Commons and House of Lords. Jointly built by Barry and Pugin during the Victorian neo-Gothic frenzy, the original golden brilliance of the edifice was revealed after a thorough cleaning.

There is restricted access to both chambers when they're in session. Members of parliament can give constituents tickets, or you turn up and hope for the best. To avoid the worst of the crowds and queues it's best to turn up any weekday evening around 5 or 6 pm for access to the galleries. Parliamen-

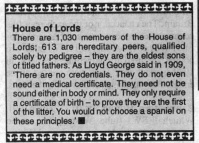

House of Lords
There are 1,030 members of the House of Lords; 613 are hereditary peers, qualified solely by pedigree – they are the eldest sons of titled fathers. As Lloyd George said in 1909, 'There are no credentials. They do not even need a medical certificate. They need not be sound either in body or mind. They only require a certificate of birth – to prove they are the first of the litter. You would not choose a spaniel on these principles.' ■

tary holidays tend to be long and unpredictable, so it's best to ring in advance to check when the houses are in session. At the moment it's free admission but there is a proposal to charge £5.

Whitehall

This wide, short avenue leads from Trafalgar Square to Parliament Square. The flanking buildings house government offices, the administrative heart of the nation and, once upon a time, of the empire: from the Admiralty and the Ministry of Defence at the north end to Downing St and The Treasury at the south.

The buildings are fine, but the only exceptional edifice is Inigo Jones' splendid Banqueting House. Opposite is Horse Guards Parade where the mounted guard is changed twice daily, offering a more accessible version of the ceremony than the one held outside Buckingham Palace. See the Buckingham Palace section for times. The Cenotaph, near the Parliament Square end of Whitehall, commemorates those who gave their lives in WWI and II.

Downing St Sir George Downing was a Dublin diplomat who was, legend has it, the second man ever to graduate from Harvard. After his glory years in the American colonies, Downing came to London and built a row of sturdy-looking houses off Whitehall. Four remain.

Since 1732, when George II made a gift of No 10 to Robert Walpole, it has been the

LONDON

official residence of the prime minister of Britain. The chancellor of the exchequer (the country's senior economic and financial minister) lives next door at No 11. The other two houses are used for government offices. In 1989 massive iron gates were erected at the entrance to guard against IRA terrorist attacks.

Banqueting House (☎ 0171-930 4179), Whitehall SW1 (tube: Westminster), is the only surviving building from the old Whitehall palace that burnt down in 1698, and the first Renaissance structure in London.

In the early 17th century, Inigo Jones went to northern Italy, saw what Palladio had done with porticoes and pilasters, and returned to London to build the Banqueting House. Unless you're a big fan of Rubens and his allegorical work, you'd be better off sparing yourself the admission price and admiring this much neglected and ignored jewel from outside.

It's open Monday to Saturday from 10 am to 5 pm; £3/2.25.

Cabinet War Rooms

The Cabinet War Rooms (☎ 0171-930 6961), Clive Steps, King Charles St SW1 (tube: Westminster), was where the British Government hid for five years, beneath more than three feet of concrete, to conduct wartime business. It is from here that Winston Churchill made his stirring speeches. Fifty years later, and fully restored to its 1940s state, the bunker is an eerie and disquieting place to visit.

Part of the burgeoning war-nostalgia industry it may be, but the practical details, the trivia of daily life on display, from toothbrush mugs to grey army standard bed blankets, have the spooky capacity to make you connect with recent history more viscerally than most museum exhibits ever manage.

It's open daily from 10 am to 5.15 pm; £4/3.

ICA

The Institute for Contemporary Arts (☎ 0171-930 3647), The Mall SW1 (tube:

Charing Cross), has, ever since its inception after WWII, managed to hang on to its reputation for being at the cutting edge of all kinds of arts. Good films, dance, photography, art, theatre, music, lectures, video and book readings; all of these things and more go on in any given week.

The complex includes a small bookshop, an art gallery, cinema, bar, café and theatre. There is invariably something worthwhile to see, the bar and restaurant are good value, and there's an interesting and relaxed crowd. At its best the ICA is a truly stimulating and enjoyable place to hang out.

It's open daily from noon to 1 am; a day pass is £1.50, £1 with any ticket purchase, 50p after 9 pm.

St James's Park & Green Park

St James's Park (☎ 0171-930 1793), The Mall SW1 (tube: St James's Park), is the neatest and most royal of London's royal parks, and it also has the best vistas: of Westminster, Buckingham Palace, St James's Palace, Carlton Terrace and Horse Guards Parade. The flower beds are sumptuous and colourful, but if a criticism is possible it is that everything is a little too genteel, too pretty and too artificial.

St James's Palace is not open to the public. The striking Tudor gatehouse is best approached from St James's St. Building was initiated by the palace-hungry Henry VIII in 1530, but besides the gatehouse none of the original edifice survives. It's never really been much used, although all foreign ambassadors are still accredited to the court of St James.

Green Park adjoins St James's just across The Mall, and is a less fussy, more naturally rolling park, with trees and open space, sunshine and shade. Once a duelling ground and, like Hyde Park, a vegetable field during WWII, Green Park tends to be less crowded than its illustrious neighbour.

The parks are open daily from 6 am to midnight.

Buckingham Palace

Buckingham Palace (☎ 0171-930 4832) SW1 (tube: Victoria or Green Park) is when St James's Palace was judged to be too old-fashioned and insufficiently impressive. Eighteen rooms (out of 661) are open for viewing, including the Throne Room and State Dining Room. Glimpses of royal domestic life and living quarters, the kind of stuff we'd really like a look at, are strictly off the menu.

No doubt, true believers will feel a frisson of excitement to walk such hallowed halls, but those looking for an insight into royal life, or for artistic excellence (give or take a Rembrandt or two) will be disappointed. The interiors range from bad kitsch to tasteless opulence – there's a lot of red plush, fancy wallpaper, gold and chandeliers. Some have likened the experience to being trapped in a chocolate box.

Basically, there are many great houses in Britain that are both considerably more beautiful and much more interesting. The entry price (£8.50/6) is high, and the queues can be daunting. Tickets are available on the day from 9 am at the ticket office on the south side of Green Park; opening times are 8 August to the end of September, daily, from 9.30 am to 5.30 pm.

Royal Mews The Royal Mews (☎ 0171-930 4832), Buckingham Palace Rd SW1, behind the palace, is home to all the flash vehicles the royals use for getting around on ceremonial occasions.

If you have an interest in horse livery, ornately painted coaches, luxurious stables (considerably better than most London hotels), customised Rollers and glass-topped limos, then this is the place for you. Basically, you get to see the trappings of pomp close-up, which is an intriguing diversion, although not worth a special journey.

The Royal Mews is open from 2 April to the end of September, Tuesday to Thursday, from noon to 4 pm; from 5 August also on Monday; the rest of the year open Wednesday only; £3.50/2.50.

Changing the Guard This is one of those quintessentially English events visitors to London must see, although you'll probably

Queen Victoria Monument outside Buck House

located at the end of The Mall, where St James's Park and Green Park meet at a giant traffic roundabout. In 1993, the Queen opened Buckingham Palace (or Buck House as it is sometimes known) to the public for the first time, to raise money for repairs to fire-damaged Windsor Castle. Apparently, in five years time, once sufficient money has been raised, it will be closed again.

Buckingham Palace was built in 1803 for the Duke of Buckingham. It has been the London home for the royal family since 1837 go away wondering what all the fuss was about. The old guard comes off duty and is replaced by the new guard in the forecourt of Buckingham Palace. There are plenty of bright red uniforms and funny hats, shouting, marching and some loud military music – and that's it. If you arrive early, grab a prime spot by the railings; more likely than not, however, you'll be 10 rows back and hardly see a thing. You could try a similar ceremony at the Whitehall.

Buckingham Palace
    From 3 April to 3 August daily at 11.30 am;
    August to April alternate days at 11.30 am.
Whitehall
    From Monday to Saturday at 11 am, Sunday at
    10 am.

Westminster Cathedral

Westminster Cathedral (☎ 0171-834 7452), Ashley Place SW1 (tube: Victoria), is the headquarters for the Catholic Church in Britain, and the only prime example of neo-Byzantine architecture in the city (completed in 1903). Its distinctively striped red-brick and white-stone tower features prominently in the West London skyline. The interior is part splendid marble and mosaic work and part bare brick – the money ran out. The highly regarded stone carvings of the 14 Stations of the Cross by Eric Gill and the marvellously sombre atmosphere make this a cherished haven from the booming traffic of Victoria St.

Never a place likely to be overrun by hordes fresh off the tour bus, the cathedral is open daily from 7 am to 7 pm. There are eight masses daily from Monday to Friday; seven masses on Saturday. Sunday services are at 7, 8, 9, 10.30 am, noon, 5.30 and 7 pm.

An Organ Festival (☎ 0171-798 9055) is held every second Tuesday at 7 pm, from 18 June to 10 September; admission is £6/4.

Tate Gallery

The Tate Gallery (☎ 0171-887 8000), Millbank SW1 (tube: Pimlico), is a confusing gallery that pleases and frustrates in equal measure. The confusion stems from its dual role as keeper of the nation's international modern art collection, and the nation's historical archive of British art. This means you can spend pleasurable hours viewing high quality Picasso, Matisse, Cezanne, Johns, Rothko and Pollock, and then find yourself surrounded by weak modern British paintings, or stuffy Victorian work featuring endless paintings of thoroughbred race-horses.

Frustration stems from the fact that the Tate only has hanging space for one-quarter of its treasures at any given time – so the paintings you want to see might not be on show.

Adjoining the pleasantly airy main building is the **Clore Gallery**, James Stirling's quirky stab at acceptable, post-modern architecture, where the bulk of JMW Turner's paintings can be found. Turner is perhaps the only British artist who would consistently and universally be counted among the all-time greats. Though a lot of Turner can be too much, the Clore, like the main gallery, is a must-see.

The galleries are open Monday to Saturday from 10 am to 5.50 pm, Sunday from 2 to 5.50 pm; free. Major special exhibitions, usually two a year, have a separate admission rate from £4 to £7.

BLOOMSBURY

Bloomsbury is an area of central London, east of Tottenham Court Rd and north of Holborn, that contains both the British Museum and London University. It's an area of elegance and learning with a seamless merging of fine Victorian terraces and tranquil Georgian squares.

Between the world wars Bloomsbury was home to a number of elitist intellectuals and artists who named their loose clique after the area. The novelists Virginia Woolf and EM Forster, who lived in Tavistock Square and Brunswick Square respectively, and the economist Maynard Keynes were the main, still-noted members of a rather low-octane, but interminably celebrated, bunch.

Until recently, lovely Bedford Square was home to many of London's publishing houses, before they were swallowed up by American conglomerates and shipped to West London. These included Jonathan Cape, Chatto and Bodley Head (set up by Woolf and her husband Leonard). These publishers were part-conspirators in launching and sustaining the Bloomsbury Group myth and industry, regularly churning out collections of letters, memoirs and biographies.

Other well-known members included the biographer Lytton Strachey; the art critic Roger Fry, who organised the first-ever London show of the French Impressionists, and has been rather dubiously credited with coining the movement's name; and Vanessa Bell, sister of Virginia Woolf, and Duncan Bell who painted mediocre pictures.

British Museum

The British Museum (☎ 0171-636 1555), Great Russell St WC1 (tube: Holborn or

Russell Square), is one of the oldest museums in the world, the largest museum in Britain, and the most visited attraction in London.

The collection is vast, diverse and amazing, but because of this the museum can also be a daunting place. It's full of so much stuff, most of it so unfamiliar, that to enjoy it requires time, effort and discretion. See as much as you'd like to see, not as much as you believe you should.

So get yourself a free guide to the rooms, and fix upon a few 'must see' exhibits, such as the weird Assyrian treasures and Egyptian mummies; the Elgin Marbles; the Rosetta Stone; the Magna Carta; the Sutton Hoo treasure; the exquisite pre-Christian Portland Vase and the 2000-year-old corpse found in a Cheshire Bog, fondly known as Lindow Man. And then make time for some personal fancies, be it Saxon weaponry, Hindu sculptures, or Japanese teahouses.

London's Museums & Art Galleries

London has so many great museums and art galleries, the first problem is deciding which to visit. The next problem is that most of them are so large you cannot possibly see everything.

Museums

The greatest of them all is the British Museum, with its unparalleled Egyptian, Mesopotamian, Greek and Roman collections. Next on the list should be the Victoria & Albert Museum, with the world's greatest collection of decorative arts, including clothes. The Museum of London deals with the history of London, from Roman times on. The Imperial War Museum has an extraordinary collection and some amazing recreations (the 'Blitz Experience' is recommended). And the Museum of the Moving Image (MOMI) deals with the history of film and TV with interactive displays.

The other two big museums in South Kensington, the Science and the Natural History museums, are enormously popular but if you seek out lesser-known ones like the Museum of Mankind or the Sir John Soane's Museum you will not have to suffer the crowds. New museums include the Rugby Museum at Twickenham and the Cannabis Museum in Bethnal Green in east London.

The London White Card is a three-day (£15) or seven-day (£25) pass that offers unlimited access to most of the museums. They are available from the participating museums.

Art Galleries

A visit to the National and Tate galleries is a must, but there are also likely to be interesting exhibitions at, among many others, the Saatchi Collection, Hayward Gallery (South Bank Centre), the ICA, Riverside Studios and the Royal Academy of Arts. Check *Time Out* for current shows.

The National Gallery covers all leading European schools from the 13th to 20th centuries; the Tate Gallery features the history of British art, especially Turner, and international modern art.

Lesser known galleries include the Courtauld Institute and, well worth a visit, the Wallace Collection. It is also worth checking to see what's on at the Whitechapel Gallery in east London. Finally, don't forget the paintings permanently exhibited at Kenwood House in Hampstead Heath. ■

✛✛✛✛✛✛✛✛✛✛✛✛✛✛✛✛✛✛✛✛✛✛

Cultural Theft?

As you wander through the British Museum, you might mull over the thorny issues of cultural theft. Much of what you're looking at wasn't just 'picked up' along the way by Victorian travellers and explorers, but stolen, or purchased, with the assistance of musket and cannon. It's the largest pirate treasure in the world. From time to time, this becomes a real political issue: during the 80s the Greek government made a vigorous, though unsuccessful, bid for the return of the so-called Elgin Marbles to their original home on the Parthenon in Athens. ■

✛✛✛✛✛✛✛✛✛✛✛✛✛✛✛✛✛✛✛✛✛✛

If you happen to be at the museum at 2, 3, or 4 pm, Monday to Friday, pay a quick visit to the **British Library**, a grand structure where folks like Bernard Shaw, Gandhi and Karl Marx once studied. Film buffs should note that the villain in Alfred Hitchcock's *Blackmail*, the first British talking picture, came crashing through the massive glass dome in the movie's climax. Over the next few years, the British Library will be moving to its new building at St Pancras.

The museum is open Monday to Saturday, from 10 am to 5 pm, Sunday from 2.30 to 6 pm. Admission is free, but donations are strenuously welcomed.

Dickens' House

Charles Dickens' House (☎ 0171-405 2127), 49 Doughty St WC1 (tube: Russell Square), is the only surviving residence of the many the great Victorian novelist occupied before moving to Kent. Here he wrote *Pickwick Papers*, *Nicholas Nickleby* and *Oliver Twist*, between bouts of worry concerning various debts, deaths and the burden of an ever-growing family.

The Charles Dickens Society saved this standard Victorian terraced house from demolition in 1925 and turned it into a museum, which to this day is stuffed full with fusty old first editions and assorted mementos.

It's open Monday to Saturday from 10 am to 5 pm; £3/2.

HOLBORN & EMBANKMENT

Of the millions of tourists who flood London every year, relatively few seek out the select places of interest in the Holborn and Embankment area. There is a beautiful church, a museum and an art gallery, and this most interesting corner of London is also the lair of lawyers.

Inns of Court

There are four Inns of Court all clustered near to Holborn and Fleet St: **Lincoln's Inn** (☎ 0171-405 1393), Lincoln's Inn Fields WC2 (tube: Holborn); **Gray's Inn** (☎ 0171-405 8164), Gray's Inn Rd WC1 (tube: Holborn or Chancery Lane); **Inner Temple** (☎ 0171-797 8250), King's Bench Walk EC4 (tube: Temple); and **Middle Temple** (☎ 0171-353 4355), Middle Temple Lane EC4 (tube: Temple).

All London barristers work from within one of the inns, which can boast a roll call of former members ranging from Oliver Cromwell to Mahatma Gandhi, from Charles Dickens to Margaret Thatcher. Britain might be an increasingly classless society, but the aloof and complacent mood of invulnerability and permanence that you see here suggests some things haven't changed all that much.

It would take a lifetime spent working here to fully grasp the intricacies and subtleties of the arcane protocols of the inns – they're a lot like the Freemasons (both organisations date back to the 13th century) and, needless to say, a lot of barristers are indeed Freemasons.

Despite being rather inaccessible to the outsider, both Gray's Inn and Lincoln's Inn have peaceful and picturesque lawns and quadrangles. These make for a delightful walk, especially early on weekday mornings before the legal machine has cranked into action, and the hordes of self-important barristers in funny gowns and wigs have started to rush around.

All four inns suffered considerable damage during the war. Lincoln's Inn is relatively intact, with original 15th-century buildings, including the Tudor Chancery Lane Gatehouse – although the archway leading from the adjoining park, Lincoln's Inn Fields, is in fact mock. Inigo Jones helped plan the chapel at Lincoln's Inn, which was built in 1621 and remains pretty well preserved.

Not far from the inns, at the bottom of the Strand, are the Royal Courts of Justice, a gargantuan melange of Gothic spires and pinnacles, and burnished Portland stone. Here civil cases are tried – often involving politicians and actresses contesting libel cases with the tabloid newspapers. The gangsters and serial killers stand trial at the Old Bailey, near St Paul's.

Lincoln's Inn Grounds are open Monday to Friday from 9 am to 5 pm; Lincoln's Inn Chapel is open Monday to Friday from 12.30 to 2.30 pm; Gray's Inn is open Monday to Friday from 10 am to 4 pm; Inner Temple is open Monday to Friday from 10 am to 4 pm; Middle Temple is open Monday to Friday from 10 am to 4 pm.

Sir John Soane's Museum

Sir John Soane's Museum (☎ 0171-405 2107), 13 Lincoln's Inn Fields, WC2 (tube: Holborn), is partly a beautiful, if quirky, house and partly a small collection of diverse and interesting objects.

Sir John Soane was a leading early 19th-century architect (he also designed the Bank of England). He married into a lot of money which he spent on customising a couple of houses in Lincoln's Inn Fields, close to the Inns of Court. The building itself is a curiosity, with a glass dome bringing light to the basement, a lantern room filled with statuary, and a picture gallery where each painting folds away if pressed to reveal another one behind. Nothing is quite how it seems here, which, along with Soane's Victorian ragbag collection, is its charm.

Soane's Egyptiana predated the massive Victorian flirtation with all things pharaonic. His collection includes a sarcophagus of Seti I, as well as, on a completely different plane, the original *Rake's Progress*, William Hogarth's cartoon burlesques of late 18th-century London lowlife.

The museum is open Tuesday to Saturday from 10 am to 5 pm and also from 6 to 9 pm on Tuesday; free.

Courtauld Institute

The Courtauld Institute (0171-873 2526), Strand WC2 (tube: Aldwych), following its move to the splendid riverside site of Somerset House, is now able to hang a much larger proportion of its eclectic haul of paintings. Exhibits include work by Rubens, Bellini, Velasquez and Botticelli, though the main emphasis is on top-drawer post-impressionist paintings by Van Gogh, Renoir, Degas and Monet.

It's open Monday to Saturday from 10 am to 6 pm, Sunday from 2 to 6 pm; £3/1.50.

Temple Church

Temple Church (☎ 0171-353 1736), Inner Temple, King's Bench Walk EC4 (tube: Temple, not on Sunday), was originally planned and built by the secretive, sinister Knights Templar between the 12th and 13th centuries. Though the Knights Templar were ultimately suppressed for being too powerful, stone effigies of notable knights adorn the floors of the light and airy nave of this most beautiful but seldom-visited place of worship. Heavily damaged during the last war, but sensitively restored, it is London's only round church, modelled on the Church of the Holy Sepulchre in Jerusalem.

It's open Monday to Saturday from 10 am to 4 pm, Sunday from 12.45 to 4 pm.

Fleet Street

Fleet St used to be known as the Street of Shame, where clapped-out printing presses and equally clapped-out journalists filled the nation's newspapers with gossip, opinion, speculation, lies and, on an especially bad day, an honest story or two.

Since the time of Caxton, people have had ink on their fingers in this neck of the woods – until Rupert Murdoch, new technology and the Docklands redevelopment finally brought the curtain down in the middle of the 80s. Now all that remains are ghosts, *El Vino's*, the journos' No 1 watering hole, and the former *Daily Express* building, a dashing medley of chrome, glass and nautical curves, London's finest Art-Deco building.

St Bride's

St Bride's (☎ 0171-353 1301), Fleet St EC4 (tube: Blackfriars), is a small, but perfect church designed by Sir Christopher Wren. The soaring spire may have been the original inspiration for the design of the traditional English wedding cake.

It was once the journalists' church, before newspapers departed for Dockland sites to the east, and presently houses a museum of printing and the foundations of seven churches in its crypt. These also contain some Roman remains found during renovations made following WWII bombing. St Bride's choir is one of the best in London.

It's open Monday to Friday from 8 am to 5 pm, Saturday from 9 am to 5 pm, Sunday 9 am to 7.30 pm.

Dr Johnson's House

Dr Johnson's House (☎ 0171-353 3745), 17 Gough Square (tube: Blackfriars), is Johnson's well-preserved Georgian town house where he lived from 1748 to 1759. Johnson was a lexicographer who, along with six full-time assistants working in the attic upstairs, compiled the first-ever English dictionary.

Johnson is also famous for his witty, scathing aphorisms, all written down by his amanuensis and fellow Scot, James Boswell. 'Life is everywhere a state in which much is to be endured and little to be enjoyed' – which may account for the rather austere interiors of the house. Or have the curators failed to collect sufficient artefacts? A nice house, but not a must-see.

It's open April to September, Monday to Saturday from 11 am to 5.30 pm; October to April, Monday to Saturday from 11 am to 5 pm; £3/2.

MARYLEBONE & REGENT'S PARK

Marylebone Rd is north of Oxford St and home to the capital's number one tourist trap, Madam Tussaud's. Fortunately, it is also close to Regent's Park which provides a haven of peace in the city as well as being close to the hustle and bustle of Camden Town which lies just to the east.

Madame Tussaud's

Madame Tussaud's (☎ 0171-935 6861), Marylebone Rd NW1 (tube: Baker St), is one of London's most visited sights, which certainly means one of the most hideously crowded, and, in this case, one of the most overrated.

It's basically for kids, school parties and rainy days – unless of course you're a devotee of ghoulish bad taste, in which case a visit to the creepy Chamber of Horrors is recommended. If you're tickled by the idea of a waxwork Madonna in her basque, you're better off going to the Rock Circus.

It's open May to September, daily from 9 am to 5.30 pm; October to June, Monday to Friday from 10 am to 5.30 pm, Saturday and Sunday from 9.30 am to 5.30 pm; £8.75/5.75. Arrive early in the morning or late in the afternoon to avoid the worst of the queues.

Regent's Park

Regent's Park (tube: Baker St or Regent's Park), north of Marylebone Rd and west of Camden was, like all other London parks, once used as a royal hunting ground, subsequently farmed and then revived as a place for fun and leisure during the 18th century.

Soon after, John Nash was employed by the Prince Regent to do something grand and architectural. Nash's architectural brief was the closest London has ever come to a grand plan, with Regent St carving its way from the park all the way down to the Mall. Most of Regent St was torn down by the Victorians, but Nash's contribution – immaculate, stuccoed terraces around the perimeter of Regent's Park – survives.

With its **mosque, London Zoo**, the **canal** at the northern end, an **open-air theatre** where Shakespeare is performed during the summer months, ponds and colourful flower beds, football pitches and summer softball games, Regent's Park is a lively but serene, local but cosmopolitan haven in the heart of the city. The **Queen Mary Rose Gardens,** which lie at the heart of the park, are particularly spectacular; there is an adjoining café.

To the north-east of Regent's Park, across Prince Albert Rd, is **Primrose Hill,** which, besides being less touristy and conventionally pretty, also has a spectacular view over London.

London Zoo This zoo (☎ 0171-722 3333), Regent's Park NW1 (tube: Camden Town), was once the most scorned of tourist sites in the whole metropolis: decrepit, Victorian, cruel and under constant threat of closure. A recent much-needed cash injection and major image overhaul – with the stress upon conservation and education – has seen something of an improvement. Moreover, the elegant and cheerful Penguin House offers architectural buffs a view of one of London's foremost Modernist structures.

It's open March to the end of October, daily from 10 am to 5.30 pm; November to March, daily from 10 am to 4 pm; £7.80/ 6.70. A visit can easily be combined with a canal boat ride to Little Venice, or a walk down the canal to the markets at Camden Lock.

THE CITY

This is where the Romans built a walled community 2000 years ago and the boundaries of today's City of London have not changed much. There is plenty to see and lots to do and a quiet stroll on a Sunday offers a unique chance to appreciate the architectural richness of its many famous buildings.

St Paul's Cathedral

St Paul's Cathedral (☎ 0171-236 4128) (tube: St Paul's or Mansion House) was built, amidst much controversy, by Sir Christopher Wren between 1675 and 1710. It stands on the site of two previous cathedrals, the first of which dated back to 604.

St Paul's was one of the 50 commissions that Wren was given after the Great Fire of London. Plans for alterations had already been made, but the fire gave him the opportunity to build from scratch. Several plans

were spurned before the authorities accepted the current design.

Despite being surrounded by some less-than-pleasant architecture (a subject close to Prince Charles' heart), the dome still dominates the City and is only exceeded in size by St Peter's in Rome. The pictures of the cathedral miraculously surrounded by the devastation of WWII bombing are well known; fortunately, the dome survived virtually unharmed, although other parts of the cathedral were not entirely unscathed. The windows were blown out (hence the clear glass in the majority of the cathedral) and various other parts were also damaged.

In 1981 it featured in acres of newsprint as the venue for the wedding of Prince Charles and Lady Diana Spencer. They broke with royal tradition, partly because Charles thought the acoustics were much better than those in Westminster Abbey. Time your visit to coincide with a service and judge for yourself.

The cathedral is open Monday to Saturday from 8.30 am to 4 pm. Admission is £3.50/3, or £6/5 if you wish to visit the galleries. Recorded tours that last 45 minutes are available for £2.50, and guided tours leave the tour desk at 11, 11.30 am, 1.30 and 2 pm. These last 1½ hours.

Visitors who enter the west door are greeted by attendants waiting for admission fees, but things improve once you negotiate this obstacle. Proceed up the nave until you reach the dome; 100 feet above is the **Whispering Gallery** (the lower part of a triple dome) so called because if you talk close to the wall it carries your words around to the other side.

This gallery, and the **Stone** and **Golden** galleries can be reached by a staircase in the south transept, but give them a miss if you suffer from claustrophobia or vertigo. All in all there are 530 narrow steps as you ascend and 543 narrow steps when you descend. The reward is a stunning view from the Stone Gallery – one of the best views of London. You can continue up to the Golden Gallery, if you feel like climbing further.

When you get back down to earth, look at the ornately carved **choir stalls** by Grinling

Gibbons, and the **iron screens** by Jean Tijou. Walk around the altar, with its outrageous canopy, to the **American Chapel**, a memorial to Americans who were killed during WWII.

At the west side of the south transept, close to a memorial to the painter JMW Turner, there's a staircase leading down to the **Crypt** and the **Treasury**. The Crypt has memorials to a number of military demigods including Wellington, Kitchener and Nelson, who is below the dome in a black sarcophagus. There are also effigies rescued from the previous cathedral that look a bit the worse for wear – not surprisingly as they were saved from the fire. There is also a niche that exhibits Wren's controversial plans and his 'great' model.

The most poignant memorial of them all is to Sir Christopher Wren, adorned by his son's famous epitaph: *Lector, si monumentum requiris, circumspice* – Reader, if you seek his monument, look around you.

The Museum of London

The Museum of London (☎ 0171-600 3699), 150 London Wall EC2 (tube: Barbican), is one of London's newest and freshest museums, telling the history of a city from the Ice Age to the mobile-phone age.

It's well designed, and the displays are imaginative and clear, starting with prehistoric times. The sections on Roman Britain and Roman Londinium make full use of the nearby ruins of a Roman fort discovered during road construction. Models and audiovisual displays show events like the Fire of London and allow the viewer to gain an understanding of a city evolving and developing.

The focus is on people, just as much as buildings and streets; the times of Dickensian London, of mass prostitution, sweat-shop labour, unionisation and the suffragettes are particularly poignant moments. The entrance ticket lasts three months, so visitors to the city might wish to come here at the start of their stay and just before they leave. It's well worth a second visit.

The museum is open Tuesday to Saturday from 10 am to 6 pm, Sunday from noon to 6 pm; £3.50/1.75.

Barbican

The Barbican (☎ 0171-638 8891), Silk St EC2 (tube: Moorgate or Barbican), was built in the heart of the City of London, on a large bomb site left over from WWII. The ambitious plan was to do something terribly modern and smart, by providing a complex for offices, housing and the arts.

The result was a forbidding series of byzantine wind tunnels, no shops, plenty of expensive high-rise apartments and an enormous cultural centre. Here you'll find the well-designed London home for the Royal Shakespeare Company (RSC), the London Symphony Orchestra and the London Classical Orchestra. There are also two cinemas, smaller theatrical auditoria, and ample gallery space, with possibly the best photographic shows in London.

With all the talent, space and money that was at its disposal, the Barbican should have become London's version of the Pompidou Centre in Paris, or the Lincoln Centre in New York – instead it feels more like a local arts centre in Communist Poland, incongruously populated by overfed rich bods from the City. It's worth a visit, however, both for the RSC, and the free concerts and exhibitions given in the foyer.

St Bartholomew-the-Great

St Bartholomew-the-Great (☎ 0171-606 5171), West Smithfield EC1 (tube: Barbican), is a stone's throw from the Barbican arts centre, and is more than worth a fleeting visit. One of London's oldest churches, adjoining one of London's oldest hospitals (presently threatened with closure) the authentic Norman arches and detailings lend this holy space a kind of rustic calm.

Approaching from nearby Smithfield's Market through the 13th-century archway is like walking into history. Film buffs might note the climactic wedding scene from *Four Weddings & A Funeral* was filmed in St Bart's.

From mid-February to mid-November it's open Monday to Friday from 8.30 am to 5 pm, Saturday from 10.30 am to 1.30 pm, Sunday from 8 am to 8 pm. The rest of the year it closes an hour earlier during weekdays.

Smithfield Market

Smithfield Market, West Smithfield EC1 (tube: Farringdon), is the last-surviving produce market in Central London. Billingsgate (fish) and Covent Garden (fruit and vegetables) have long since moved to the hinterlands. Supposedly Europe's largest wholesale meat market, this is certainly no place for faint hearts or vegetarians.

They stopped selling livestock here a century ago, around the same time that the main buildings were erected by Horace Jones, the man responsible for Leadenhall market. Early weekday mornings Smithfield is a hive of activity. Many of the local pubs open from the middle of the night to cater for the stall-holders' unsociable work hours and, assuming you can pass yourself off as a cockney meat seller, there's always the chance of an early-morning pint with your fried breakfast. It's open Monday to Friday from 5 am to 10.30 am.

Tower of London

The Tower of London (☎ 0171-709 0765), Tower Hill EC3 (tube: Tower Hill), is a beautifully preserved monument to cruelty. This may seem an odd description, but from 1078, when William the Conqueror laid the first stone of the White Tower, until well into this century, the Tower of London has been much more than an ancient tourist attraction.

When Rudolf Hess' 1941 peace mission turned into a fiasco, it was at the Tower that he commenced his long years of incarceration. No visitor will forget the Bloody Tower, where the young princes, sons and heirs of Edward IV, were allegedly slaughtered by their wicked uncle Richard III. Thomas More, Anne Boleyn, Lady Jane Grey and Walter Raleigh are also amongst the notable ex-residents. Other blood-curdling attractions include Traitor's Gate, the river

entrance through which condemned prisoners arrived to face their death, and the Martin Tower with its display of torture implements.

Historically, the tower has served as both castle and palace. Though never the royal seat, which has either been in Winchester, or Westminster, it was where all of Henry VIII's wives set up home, even before it turned into a prison for some of them prior to death by execution. There are some remnants of royal residence from long ago, the most impressive being the Chapel of St John, with its beautiful stone Romanesque arches and magical golden light.

Dwarfed as it is by the high-rise blocks of the nearby City business district, and spic and span thanks to years of restoration, it is rather difficult to take the Tower seriously as a fortress. The ramparts and battlements look like a movie set for Camelot. Nevertheless in its time the 90-foot-high White Tower was the tallest building in London, in a prime position to see off any invasionary force that sailed up the Thames, and well situated to keep an eye on the notoriously restive populace of the city.

Several arduous and time-consuming armament displays punctuate the average visit to the tower. Some would say that there are too many shields, pikes and lancets, and even too many jewels. There's a lot to be said for rationing yourself, otherwise castle fatigue is likely to set in.

Start with a quick peak at the famous **ravens** on the green. Their wings are clipped because legend says the day they desert the Tower, London shall fall to its enemies. Next, a snapshot of one of the famous Beefeater guards is acceptable, if not essential. Take in the **Bloody** and **White Towers**. See a few weapons, torture racks and some rare and highly expensive glittering objects in the recently opened, purpose-built **Jewel House**. And that's really quite enough to be going on with – and easily your money's worth. As with quite a few London sights, you sometimes have to remind yourself that the object is fun and not sheer endurance.

The tower is open March to October, Monday to Saturday from 9.30 am to 6 pm,

Sunday from 10 am to 6 pm; November to February, Monday to Saturday from 9 am to 5 pm. Admission is £8.30/6.25.

Tower Bridge

Tower Bridge (☎ 0171-407 0922), on the Thames SE1 (tube: Tower Hill), was built late last century when London was still a thriving port. Access to the upper river was imperative, hence the ingenious drawbridge mechanism which can clear the way to oncoming ships in under two minutes.

Now that London is a dead port you rarely see the bridge do its stuff (except in American movies). Although it's slightly off the tourist's beaten track, Tower Bridge affords excellent views across the City and Docklands. There's also an excellent 20th-century museum with robots and interactive displays.

It's open April to October, daily from 9.30 am to 6.30 pm; November to March, daily from 10 am to 4.45 pm. Museum entry is £5.50/3.75.

Lloyd's of London

Lloyd's of London, (☎ 0171-327 6210), 1 Lime St EC3 (tube: Aldgate), the most famous house of insurance brokers in the world, where everything from planes to film stars' legs is insured, wouldn't be much of a tourist mecca if it weren't for the building it is housed in.

Richard Rogers, high-tech doyen of postmodern architecture and architect of the Pompidou Centre, created one of London's most spectacular new buildings – and was roundly slagged for it. Britain has produced some of the best modern architects practising today but, sadly, most of their best buildings are constructed elsewhere. Lloyd's, with its external pipes and ducts, is a triumphant exception, especially at night when it becomes a spectacular, illuminated riot of yellow and blue.

Access to the equally excellent interior is restricted to groups from recognised organisations who book in advance.

Leadenhall Market

There's been a market on this site in Whittington Ave, Gracechurch St EC1 (tube: Bank), since the year dot. It began life as a Roman forum, and in the 15th century Richard Whittington, the Lord Mayor of London, made it an official food market. Nowadays the Leadenhall arcades serve food and drink to hard-working City folk. Naturally, the prices aren't cheap but the selection is excellent. And the Victorian glass-and-iron structure is an architectural treat. It's open Monday to Friday from 7 am to 3 pm.

Guildhall

The Guildhall (☎ 0171-606 3030), Gresham St EC2 (tube: Bank), remains a striking example of grand 15th-century architecture, despite serious fire damage during the 17th century and WWII, and restoration of mixed quality.

The seat of government for the City for nearly 800 years, with open meetings still held every third Thursday of each month (except August), the Guildhall also hosts an annual flower show and various ceremonial banquets including the Booker Prize awards – the leading British literary prize which, more often than not, is won by natives of other Commonwealth nations.

It's open daily from 10 am to 5 pm, closed on Sunday between October and April; free.

THE EAST END

The East End is within walking distance of the City, but what a change of style! This is working-class London and while it bears all the signs of being neglected there is the compensation of a fascinating mix of cockney/Indian/Bangladeshi/Jewish culture. Other attractions include some interesting, offbeat museums and the best-value Asian cuisine in London.

Geffrye Museum

The Geffrye Museum (☎ 0171-739 9893) Kingsland Rd, Dalston E2 (tube: Old St; leave by exit 2 and take bus No 243), was built on land bequeathed by Robert Geffrye, a late 16th-century mayor of London who made a fortune out of the slave trade. Maybe it was guilt that inspired this small but perfectly formed museum devoted to the history of family life and interior design.

Originally it was a school for carpenters and artisans. Now each room is decked out in the interior design of different epochs from the Elizabethan age, running through to the present Elizabeth's coronation in 1953. No effort has been spared and the attention to detail is amazing. Some will find this museum a slight bore, others a fund of fascinating domestic knowledge.

It's open Tuesday to Saturday from 10 am to 5 pm, and Sunday from 2 to 5 pm; free.

Bethnal Green Museum of Childhood

The Bethnal Green Museum of Childhood, (☎ 0181-983 5200), Cambridge Heath Rd E2 (tube: Bethnal Green), has the ability to bring memories of childhood rushing back. Set in a 19th-century building in the East End, exhibits include an enormous number of dolls, dolls' houses (those on the ground floor must be seen), trains, cars, children's clothes, books and puppets.

It's open Monday to Thursday and Saturday from 10 am to 5.50 pm, Sunday 2.30 to 5.50 pm, closed Friday; free.

Cannabis Museum

The Cannabis Museum (☎ 0171-613 5166), 31 Redchurch St, E2 (tube: Bethnal Green), has just opened and visitors should telephone to check the hours of opening. The law circumscribes the nature of the exhibits but there is some interesting material on the history of hemp and the museum functions alongside an information centre that champions the legalisation of marijuana.

Whitechapel Art Gallery

Whitechapel Art Gallery (☎ 0171-522 7878), 80-82 Whitechapel High St E1 (tube: Aldgate East) has been renovated beautifully, creating light and airy exhibition spaces on two floors which are a temporary home for a vast variety of contemporary shows. There are plenty of lectures, often

instigated by the artist-in-residence of the time, and a good café which is a welcome relief from culture-vulturing.

It's open Tuesday to Sunday from 11 am to 5 pm, (8 pm on Wednesday), closed on Monday; admission is £4/2.60, free on Tuesday.

East End Markets

Petticoat Lane Market (tube: Aldgate, Aldgate East or Liverpool St) is East London's celebrated Sunday morning market on Middlesex St, which borders the City and Whitechapel, between the hours of 9 am to 2 pm. What exactly it's celebrated for isn't so clear anymore.

Who wants to pay over the odds for a batch of broken chocolate bars, undesirable trinkets and dubious looking household goods and fabrics? Close enough to the Tower of London to be a bit of a tourist con, Petticoat Lane cashes in on the fact that many people are a bit bleary on Sunday morning, and aren't necessarily as discerning as they would normally be.

Brick Lane Market Near Petticoat Lane is Brick Lane Market (tube: Aldgate East), another Sunday-morning market, open from 5 am to 2 pm, and a far better experience. This is the real East End.

On the streets off Brick Lane and along Bethnal Green Rd, you'll find the junk stacked high, with items as diverse as gold, antique books, second-hand (stolen?) bikes and dodgy furniture. And you haggle.

Avoid Brick Lane (which is pretty dull) until lunchtime, then try one of the numerous Bengali and Bangladeshi restaurants and cafés. These are the best places in town for cheap curries. Forget roast meat and three vegetables – a curry makes an excellent Sunday lunch.

Columbia Rd Market (tube: Shoreditch or Old St), rounds off the East London Sunday morning open-market experience. It's a short walk from Brick Lane, and is the most in-vogue of the three contenders. It's a plant-and-flower market, which means you might not actually buy much, despite enjoying the sights and consuming a bagel or two.

DOCKLANDS

The Docklands was once the greatest port in the world – at the hub of the British Empire and its enormous worldwide trade. First the Luftwaffe flattened the area during WWII, then technological and political change finished it off. The empire evaporated, and enormous new bulk carriers and container ships demanded deepwater ports and new loading and unloading techniques.

During the 80s it was decided that so much land and space so close to the city should be put to good speculative use. New offices nobody needed were quickly and shoddily built. New toy-town houses for yuppies were thrown up beside new marinas. Places like the beautiful **Tobacco Dock** (☎ 0171-702 9681), The Highway E1 (tube: Wapping), were transformed into shopping malls where yuppies could buy delicatessen food and designer clothes. A lot of money was spent, but very little filtered down to the disenfranchised local population who watched with awe and irritation.

But money doesn't necessarily stick, and when a recession arrived in the 90s the boom was punctured. The offices stood empty, the yuppies lost their jobs, their apartments wouldn't sell, and the trendy shops hung out For Sale signs. Tobacco Dock went into receivership and although it has now shuddered back into life the area is not as busy with shops as was once predicted.

Some see the Docklands, and its failure, as a parable for the free-enterprise 80s. It certainly represents a tragic lost opportunity for London. Nonetheless, the architecture, weird urban spaces and socio-economic contrasts offer an engrossing experience.

Getting around can be difficult, however – a problem that has always been the Docklands' Achilles heel. In the Thatcherite 80s, it was philosophically unsound for government to underwrite development by providing decent transport infrastructure. Critics point to comparable developments at

La Défense in Paris – a tremendous success, thanks in part to its efficient transport links.

The London Docklands Visitor Centre (☎ 0171-512 1111), 3 Limeharbour, Isle of Dogs (DLR: Crossharbour), has information but individual explorers should start on the south bank, between London Bridge and Tower Bridge, with **Hays Galleria** (tube: London Bridge). This features the obligatory atrium, and is topped with a fake Victorian iron-and-glass roof. It houses a mix of office space, shops and cafés selling overpriced mineral water. Nearby, **St Olave's House** is one of London's finest Art-Deco buildings, a diminutive riverside office block built in 1932 and fronted with gold mosaic lettering and bronze relief sculptures.

Continue eastwards along the south bank a short distance past Tower Bridge to Butler's Wharf and the Design Museum.

The **Design Museum** (☎ 0171-407 6261), Shad Thames SE1, is a dinky modernist structure filled with objects that range from superb to downright silly. Complementing the permanent collection, there's a small space for temporary exhibitions. Though rather outflanked by the modern design wing at the Victoria & Albert Museum, the Design Museum is still worth a visit. It's open Monday to Friday from 11.30 am to 6 pm, Saturday and Sunday from noon to 6 pm; £4.50/3.50.

Return to Tower Bridge and cross the river, turning right to the ugly World Trade Centre and **St Katherine's Dock**, the first of the rejuvenated docks – once at the vanguard of change and a symbol of Docklands optimism.

Walk east along the river from St Katherine's Dock to **Wapping** and Wapping High St, home to Rupert Murdoch's media empire, and the *Prospect of Whitby* (☎ 0171-481 1095), 57 Wapping Wall, an ancient, very popular riverside pub. Return to Tower Gateway to catch the DLR across the Isle of Dogs.

The second DLR station from Tower Gateway is at Limehouse Basin, the centre of London's Chinatown in the last century. The only reminders are street names like

Ming and Mandarin St. It's easy to forget the long history of the Docklands especially when it is buried by enormous developments like Canary Wharf, three stops further on,

Canary Wharf (DLR: Canary Wharf), until recently the largest building site in Europe, is dominated by Cesar Pelli's tower – a square prism with a pyramidal top. When building stopped there were more than two million sq yards of unlet office space in London, and over 500,000 of them were in Canary Wharf. Continue on the DLR to reach Island Gardens, across the river from Greenwich.

Change at West India Quay station for a northbound DLR to All Saints station. The **Financial Times Print Works**, 240 East India Dock Rd E14 (DLR: All Saints), is one of London's most beautiful modern buildings. It's a brilliant creation of metal and glass designed by Nicholas Grimshaw. The huge printing presses are showcased and illuminated as they roll each night.

Further east is the Thames Flood Barrier, built to save London from the great tidal river that made this city what it is. The massive floodgates are supported by a row of concrete piers capped with gleaming metal, like an extraordinary sculpture. The Victoria, Albert and George VI docks that are close by were the largest and last docks to be built and the last to capitulate. This is the location for the new Short Take Off and Landing (STOL) London airport – it caters to jet-set business folks from the City.

Getting There & Away
Tourist boats from Westminster Bridge run past part of the Docklands but don't necessarily stop where you'd want them to. The commuter riverbus service went out of business in 1993. So budget travellers, along with everyone else, have to use their feet, buses, and the inefficient but entertaining Docklands Light Railway (DLR); Zone 1 & 2 Travelcards are valid, but it only operates on weekdays from 5.30 am to 9.30 pm.

The DLR starts at Tower Gateway, which is linked to Tower Hill tube station, and continues across the Isle of Dogs through Canary Wharf to Island Gardens, across the river from Greenwich. Greenwich is linked to the Isle of Dogs by foot tunnel. For an interesting loop, cross the river and return by boat or train from Greenwich (see the upcoming Greenwich section).

CHELSEA, KENSINGTON & EARL'S COURT
Chelsea still cashes in on its avant-garde fashion image but the reality is quite disappointing. The best shops are found a little to the north in Kensington and here too is a cluster of top notch museums that will do less damage to your budget than nearby Harrods or Harvey Nichols.

Carlyle's House
Carlyle's House (☎ 0171-352 7087, NT), 24 Cheyne Row SW3 (tube: Sloane Square), is

---

High in the Sky?
The relative modesty of London's skyline – in terms of height anyway – has as much to do with practicalities as with aesthetics. The dense subterranean web of sewers and tunnels poses an engineering problem, and heritage pressure groups can make use of a complex planning bureaucracy to prevent the demolition of old buildings. A lack of finance also comes into play; the latest proposal to construct a 1,265-feet transparent skyscraper is estimated to cost at least £400 million.

The proposed skyscraper, named the Milennium Tower by its designer Norman Foster, would dwarf the 50-storey, 800-feet-high Canary Wharf, which is currently Britain's tallest building. Before Canary Wharf, the capital's skyline was dominated by the 40-storey, 600-feet-high NatWest Tower (1981). The gangly Telecom Tower (1965) is 580 feet tall, though its mast tops it to 620 feet.

In 1711 when Christopher Wren rebuilt St Paul's Cathedral, London had the tallest spire in Europe – the cross on top of the Dome reached 365 feet above street level. ■

the Queen Anne residence where the great essayist and historian came to live in 1834. Here he wrote, amongst many other things, his famous history of the French Revolution. Legend has it that when the manuscript was complete, a maid mistakenly threw it on the fire, and the good and diligent Thomas duly wrote it all again.

This is a charming house and it's not hard to see how it became an artists' hang-out, attracting such people as Mill, Thackeray and Dickens. Chopin often played the piano here, and the easy-going staff will permit you to sit at it by yourself.

It's open from 30 March to the end of October, Wednesday to Sunday from 11 am to 4.30 pm; £3.

National Army Museum

The National Army Museum (☎ 0171-730 0717), Royal Hospital Rd SW3 (tube: Sloane Square), has a tendency to pander to the war-bore minority. Various displays on the history of weapons, armies, artillery and tactics, turn quite quickly from being potentially interesting to dull and repetitious. Though recent additions to the exhibits include scorched weaponry fresh from the Gulf War, the predominant sensation is of being stuck in a rather plodding time warp.

It's open daily from 10 am to 5.30 pm; free.

South Kensington Museums

Victoria & Albert Museum The Victoria & Albert Museum (☎ 0171-938 8441), Cromwell Rd SW7 (tube: South Kensington), is stuffed full with all kinds of booty collected together under the umbrella identity of a museum of decorative art and design.

You can see ancient Chinese ceramics and modernist architectural drawings, Korean bronze and Japanese swords, samples from William Morris' 19th-century arts & crafts movement, cartoons by Raphael and Asian watercolours, sculpture by Rodin, gowns from the Elizabethan era and dresses straight from this year's Paris fashion shows, ancient jewellery, a 1930s radio wireless set, an all-wooden Frank Lloyd Wright study, and a pair

of Doctor Martens boots. Everything is here, plus a bit more.

During the last decade this massive, fragmentary museum underwent a series of changes in order to make sense of what it was doing and to modernise. The changes were supposed to have been seismic, but seem pretty skin deep. Though it's far more streamlined than previously, a walk around the V&A is closer to a walk round a humungous Victorian junk shop than a late 20th-century museum. The rambling, sprawling shapelessness of the V&A is a strong part of its appeal, however.

All you can do is pick out something from the free guide pamphlet that catches your eye and chase it down. Although, amazingly, most of the V&A's four-million-piece collection is actually on display, you'll never ever get to see everything. And that's how it should be.

The museum is open Monday from noon to 5.50 pm, Tuesday to Sunday from 10 am to 5.50 pm; admission is £5/3.

Science Museum The Science Museum (0171-938 8008), Exhibition Rd, South Kensington SW7 (tube: South Kensington), was once a dreary destination for school excursions – today it's a place to have fun and, yes, learn something. The curators have fully absorbed the changing world of computer games and interactive technology, and the need for a museum to be live and interesting. So there are plenty of buttons to press, launch pads, flight simulators, rocket cabins and hot-air balloons.

Flight is the thing here, making the less-busy but quietly absorbing rooms concerning meteorology, food and medicine good places to find a bit of peace and space. An early start is advised for this often packed museum.

It's open daily from 10 am to 6 pm; £5/2.60; free after 4.30 pm.

Natural History Museum The Natural History Museum (☎ 0171-938 9123), Cromwell Rd, South Kensington SW7 (tube: South Kensington), is one of London's finest

Gothic revival buildings, with its grand cathedral-like main entrance, the gleaming brick and terracotta frontage, the thin columns and articulated arches, and the detailed stone carvings of all plant and animal life on earth.

This museum can be inundated by a sea of screaming schoolkids, but they are generally fascinated by the dinosaurs so the crowd thins out on the wondrous mammal balcony, at the Blue Whale exhibit, or in the spooky ecology gallery (a moonlit replica rainforest). For a complete escape, you can go upstairs to the more stuffy, traditional exhibits.

The best idea is to visit early in the morning or the late afternoon. That way you get a shot at seeing the dinosaurs and the excellent multimedia displays – if you're lucky. The museum is open Monday to Saturday from 10 am to 5.50 pm, Sunday from 11 am to 5.50 pm. It costs £5.50/2.80, but is free after 4.30 pm on weekdays and after 5 pm on weekends.

Holland Park

Holland Park lies west of Notting Hill and High St Kensington. It's both a residential district, with elegant pastel-painted town houses, and a well-wooded park which was once the grounds to Holland House, a sprawling, pinnacled mansion destroyed during WWII. Besides having a big and tiring hill, the park possesses a youth hostel, a playground and restaurant, and some delightful formal gardens.

Nearby is **Leighton House** (☎ 0171-602 3316), 12 Holland Park Rd W14. A jewel of a house, it was once the home of Lord Leighton, a pre-Raphaelite painter of the last century, who decked out parts of his house with Arab-style interiors, including mosaic floors, Islamic tiles, carved wooden screens and a small fountain. It's a little-known house and it contains some notable pre-Raphaelite paintings – well worth a short visit. It's open Monday to Saturday from 11 am to 5.30 pm; free.

Knightsbridge & Kensington Shopping

Harrods This famous store (☎ 0171-730 1234), Knightsbridge SW1 (tube: Knightsbridge), is like nothing else in London. It's a pain because it is so crowded, and because the security staff tell you how to carry your daypack. On the other hand, the toilets are fab, the food hall is enough to make you swoon, and if they haven't got what you want, it probably doesn't exist. No other store has such a sense of sheer, outrageous abundance. Don't miss it, although you may be wise to leave your credit cards somewhere safe. It's open on Monday, Tuesday and Saturday from 10 am to 6 pm, Wednesday to Friday from 10 am to 7 pm.

Harvey Nichols Harvey Nichols (☎ 0171-235 5000), 109-125 Knightsbridge SW1 (tube: Knightsbridge), is the high-fashion heart of the city; a class act. There's a great food hall, an extravagant perfume department and jewellery to save up for. But it's fashion that Harvey Nichols does better than the rest: from Miyake to Lauren, Hamnett to Calvin Klein, and a whole floor of up-to-the-minute menswear. The selection is unrivalled and the prices high, although during sales there are some great bargains, and the store's own clothing line is reasonable. It's open Monday, Tuesday, Thursday and Friday from 10 am to 7 pm; Wednesday from 10 am to 8 pm; Sunday from 2 to 5 pm.

The Conran Shop The Conran Shop (☎ 0171-589 7401), Michelin House, 81 Fulham Rd SW3 (tube: South Kensington), is the brainchild of Terence Conran, who was behind Habitat, and is still behind a number of classy London restaurants. Now his retrostyle farmhouse interiors, furniture and kitchenware are available more exclusively, with more exclusive prices to match. Though never actually out of fashion, his designer's vision of good taste is currently in vogue again.

The great appeal of Conran's is partly due to its setting. Michelin House, built pre-WWI, is a mosaic-and-tiled wonder, an unusual and appealing building that has been impeccably restored. It's open Monday, Thursday and Friday from 9.30 am to 6 pm,

Tuesday from 10 am to 6 pm, Wednesday from 9.30 am to 7 pm, Saturday from 10 am to 6.30 pm, Sunday from noon to 5.30 pm.

HYDE PARK, NOTTING HILL & BAYSWATER

The growing popularity of the Notting Hill Carnival (in late August) reflects the multi-cultural appeal of this area of West London. Notting Hill became a focus for immigrants from Trinidad in the 1950s and today it is a thriving and vibrant corner of London with the expanse of Hyde Park separating it from the West End.

Hyde Park

Hyde Park is the largest royal park in central London. Acquired from the church by Henry VIII, it was first the hunting ground of kings and aristocrats, and subsequently a venue for duels, executions, horse racing, the 1851 Great Exhibition, an enormous potato field during the war and, more recently, the site for music concerts by the likes of Queen, the Rolling Stones and Pavarotti. The park is a riot of colour during the spring, and full of lazy sunbathers in the summer. Boating on the Serpentine Lake is an option for the energetic.

Besides parkside sculptures by Henry Moore and Jacob Epstein, Hyde Park boasts its own permanent art gallery. The **Serpentine Gallery** (☎ 0171-402 6075), beautifully sited just south of the lake and west of the main road that cuts through the park, specialises in contemporary art (entrance is free).

Hyde Park's sheer size and creative landscaping gives a strong sense of variety – from bustle to perfect tranquillity. **Speaker's Corner** (near Marble Arch) is a long-standing London tradition where every Sunday anyone with a soapbox can hold forth on whatever subject takes their fancy. Though rather overrated and not the spectacle it once was, it can still be entertaining.

On the southern edge of the park, the **Albert Memorial** is an over-the-top monument to a rather ordinary man. Albert was the German husband of Queen Victoria. His monument looks like a great fat altar piece. Due to smog and neglect the memorial has been under wraps for some time, and, since the refurbishment money has run out, it could remain shrouded for some time to come.

Adjoining Hyde Park is **Kensington Gardens**, with its fountains, statue of Peter Pan, Round Pond and a more formal manicured appearance. This is the location for **Kensington Palace** (☎ 0171-937 9561), once the London home of Prince Charles and Princess Diana. It's now all Diana's, and is where, according to the royal watchers, the triumphantly liberated princess holds unofficial court. The 17th-century palace is also partially open to the public. There's a charming sunken garden and a collection of royal dresses, culminating in Princess Diana's wedding dress.

Like all big-city parks, Hyde Park/Kensington Gardens can be rather less pleasant and welcoming at night. Although it's not nearly as bad as New York's Central Park, you should stay well away once darkness falls.

Those who don't suffer from vertigo might round off a visit with a pricey drink at *Windows on the World* (☎ 0171-493 8000), the 28th-floor bar on top of London's Hilton Hotel, Park Lane W1. The prices are steep (£3.50 for a bottle of lager), the interior is tacky, the clientele sad and dull, but the bar is open until late and the view out over the park and across to the river is superb. (Tucked away behind the Hilton is Shepherd's Market, a small square that at night becomes an upmarket red-light area servicing customers at the posh hotels.)

Hyde Park and Kensington Gardens are open daily from 5 am to midnight. Kensington Palace is open daily from 9.45 am to 3.30 pm; £5.50. The Serpentine Gallery is open daily from 10 am to 6 pm; free. *Windows on the World* is open Monday to Friday from noon to 3 pm, and 5.30 pm to 1 am, Saturday 5.30 pm to 1 am; smart attire is required.

Portobello Market

Along with Camden Market, Portobello Rd (tube: Notting Hill or Ladbroke Grove) is

London's most famous weekend street market. Starting from groovy Notting Hill it wends its way northwards, changing markedly in character, and eventually finishes past the Westway flyover in Ladbroke Grove.

The start of the route is made up of over-priced antiques, the obligatory hand-made jewellery, paintings, ethnic stuff, and other things you can't afford, don't need and will regret having purchased. Later the stalls drop a little down-market with fruit and veg, second-hand clothing, cheap household goods and bric-a-brac. This is where you *might* find a bargain.

Portobello has character and colour and it's an enjoyable place to take a stroll on Saturday morning before people-gridlock sets in.

At the Ladbroke Grove end, there are fruit and vegetables for sale Monday to Saturday (except Thursday afternoon) from 8 am to 5 pm. The general-goods market is open Friday from 8 am to 3 pm and Saturday from 8 am to 5 pm.

CAMDEN TOWN & NORTH LONDON

From the Gothic splendour of St Pancras station one can walk along to Euston station and up Eversholt St to Camden Town, a tourist mecca that is especially lively at weekends. Up to twenty years ago Camden Town was home to a large Irish community, but yuppiefication has changed all that and nowadays parts of it blend in more harmoniously with the sedate middle class character of Hampstead further to the north.

St Pancras Station

Together with Barry and Pugin's Houses of Parliament, St Pancras station, Euston Rd NW1, is the pinnacle of the Victorian Gothic revival. Whether you like the style or not, St Pancras is something special: there's a dramatic glass-and-iron train shed at the back, engineered by the great Brunel, and an absurd pinnacled hotel, designed by Gilbert Scott, at the front.

Though the railway station is still active, the hotel has been empty and disused for a long time now, which means only the occasional TV show gets in to see the immense central staircase and superb detailing. Next door is the new British Library building.

Camden Passage

This art and antiques area (tube: The Angel) runs parallel with Upper St just north of the tube station and should not be confused with Camden Market in Camden Town. The best time to pay a visit is on a Saturday when a multitude of stalls sell more affordable items than the serious shops that specialise in heavy duty antiques, including a converted tramshed renamed The Mall.

Camden Market

In over twenty years Camden Market has developed into a major tourist attraction. It's grown from a small collection of stalls by Camden Lock (on the Grand Union Canal) and now extends virtually from Camden Town tube station northwards to Chalk Farm tube station. On your first visit it is hard to believe there is any system to the chaos.

To get the real essence of the market the best time to go is at the weekend – Sunday is particularly busy. If the crowds and mayhem are not your idea of fun, however, a lot of the stalls function through the week, increasing in number as you get to Thursday and Friday.

If you arrive at Camden Town tube station, take the right-hand exit and turn right again on to Camden High St (which becomes Chalk Farm Rd).

Your first option is the **Electric Market**, a busy studenty club on Friday and Saturday nights, housed in an old ballroom. On Sunday it is transformed into a market. Sometimes there are record sales, but 60s clothes dominate. Opposite is a covered area with stalls selling a mish-mash of leather goods, army-surplus stuff and a café. Next is **Camden Market** (open from Thursday to Sunday), which houses stalls for fashion, clothing and jewellery.

By this time you may already be needing sustenance. There are a variety of counters selling fast food, and numerous alternatives.

The *Arizona* (☎ 0171-284 4730), 2A Jamestown Rd, has a lively atmosphere, outside tables, the normal Mexican fodder and mobile tequila-slammer-serving girls/boys. Main dishes are around £7.

Continue north past the bootleg music sellers and hair plaiters, and over the bridge. If you need to escape the crowds, the canal is a lovely walk, especially heading west past London Zoo to Little Venice in Maida Vale. You can also take a boat trip with the London Waterbus Company (☎ 0171-482 2660) or one of the private narrowboat operators.

Over the bridge and on the right, is the **Camden Canal Market**, which has bric-a-brac from around the world. On the left, and beyond the indoor market, which is quite a recent development, is the small section where the market originated. This area, right next to the canal lock, houses a diverse range of food, ceramics, furniture, oriental rugs, musical instruments, designer clothes and so on. A number of shops are housed in the surrounding buildings.

From this area you can walk along the **Railway Arches**, which mainly contain second-hand furniture. A slow meander will eventually lead you to **The Stables**, the northernmost part of the market, where it is possible to find antiques, eastern artefacts, rugs and carpets, pine furniture, and 50s and 60s clothing. If you want to get straight to The Stables there is an entrance on Chalk Farm Rd; this route passes *Thanh Binh*, 14 Chalk Farm Rd, which serves delicious noodles from the street for £1.50.

Saatchi Gallery

The Saatchi Gallery (☎ 0171-624 8299), 98a Boundary Rd NW8 (tube: St John's Wood), is the private collection of contemporary art owned by Charles Saatchi, until recently co-chairman of what was once the biggest advertising agency in the world, and advertising guru to the British Tory party.

Saatchi is a serious collector with, some say, an unhealthy influence on the fortunes of new artists. When Saatchi buys a batch of Julian Schnabel, Schnabel becomes a big star with a bigger bank balance. But, when

Saatchi unloads his Schnabel collection on the cheap, Schnabel looks like a has-been.

Alternating with the ever-fluid permanent collection are shows promoting Saatchi's new purchases, masquerading as debut exhibitions for epoch-making new movements. Recent hot shots have included Damien Hirst, king of formaldehyde, and the eloquent sculpture of Rachel Whiteread. Despite the quibbles, the exhibition space is excellent, light, airy and large, and can be well worth a visit.

It's open from Thursday to Sunday from noon to 6 pm; admission is £3.50, free on Thursday.

Hampstead & Highgate

Perched on a hill four miles north of the City, Hampstead is a pretty Georgian village attached to an enormous, rambling heath. You can lose yourself on Hampstead Heath and truly forget that you're still in one of the largest, noisiest cities in the world. This is something you can't forget when walking up Hampstead High St, or Heath St, which are both inundated with pricey shops and bumper-to-bumper traffic.

Nonetheless, Hampstead retains its charm and character – part left-wing intelligentsia, part arty bohemia. Many famous people have made this suburb their home: poets like Coleridge, Keats and Pope; Charles II's mistress, Nell Gwyn; General de Gaulle; Freud; and the painters John Constable and William Hogarth.

Architecturally, Hampstead is a harmonious balance of Georgian and early Victorian, speckled with a few rare and notable examples of modernist architecture. If you wish to delve deeper into the pleasures of Church Row and Admiral's Walk, Lauderdale House, Burgh House, Fenton House and so on, it's worth picking up a local guide to the village from one of the many second-hand bookshops in Flask Walk.

There are woods, meadows, hills and bathing ponds on the heath and, most important of all, there is space. Also you'll find **Kenwood House** (☎ 0181-348 1286; EH), a magnificent house rejigged by Robert

Adam in the middle of the 17th century, stuffed with fine paintings by the likes of Rembrandt, Vermeer and Van Dyck.

Keats House This house (☎ 0171-435 2062), Keats Grove, Hampstead NW3 (tube: Hampstead), was home to the golden boy of the Romantic poets. Never short of generous pals, Keats was persuaded to find a refuge here by Tom Armitage Brown during the years 1816-21. In this garden, under a plum tree, Keats wrote his most celebrated poem, *Ode to a Nightingale*.

Apart from many preserved mementos, plenty of original Keats manuscripts, and Keats' collection of Shakespeare and Chaucer, the visitor can get to take a peak at some of his love letters. This house serves as a charming tribute to a short, but productive, poet's life.

It's open April to October, Monday to Friday from 10 am to 1 pm and 2 to 6 pm, Saturday from 10 to 1 pm and 2 to 5 pm, Sunday from 2 to 5 pm; November to March, Monday to Friday from 1 to 5 pm, Saturday from 10 am to 1 pm and 2 to 5 pm, Sunday from 2 to 5 pm. Admission is free but there's a box for voluntary donations.

Freud's House This house (☎ 0171-435 2002), 20 Maresfield Gardens NW3 (tube: Hampstead), was the great man of Vienna's final resting place after he escaped the Nazis and came to London in 1938. He only lived here a year before dying, but the many Greek and oriental artefacts, the library and the famous couch that launched a thousand psychoanalytical sessions give a sense of greater permanence.

Freud's daughter Anna elected to preserve the study and library in the exact state he left them, so the place feels a bit spooky, like a chapel or a morgue. Freud's museum in Vienna is better, but Freud buffs will still enjoy a tour.

It's open Wednesday to Sunday from noon to 5 pm; £3/1.50.

Highgate Cemetery This is the final resting place for Karl Marx, the novelist George Eliot and lots of dull, ordinary people that lie beneath eccentric and extraordinary tombs. Highgate Cemetery (☎ 0181-340 1834), Swain's Lane N6 (tube: Highgate), has wild, hectic acres of absurdly decorated Victorian tombs, catacombs, family plots linked in a ring and based on ancient Egyptian burial sites, all topped off by spooky cypresses.

It's divided into two parts. The only way to see the western section is by tour: Saturday and Sunday all year on the hour from 11 am to 4 pm; Monday to Friday, March to November, at noon, 2 and 4 pm; £3.

Marx's tomb can be found in the comparatively uninteresting eastern part, which is open daily from 10 am to 4 pm (to 5 pm from April to October); £1.

GREENWICH

Greenwich (BR: Greenwich) has strong connections to royalty, the sea and to science. It lies to the east of London, where the Thames widens and deepens, and there is a sense of space rare in the big city. Packed with beautiful architecture, with the magnificent *Cutty Sark*, and quaint and villagey in its own right, Greenwich is a London highlight. It can be reached by boat, rail or the Docklands Light Railway. The boat trip, at least one way, is recommended.

Greenwich is home to an extraordinary, interrelated cluster of classical buildings – all the great architects of the enlightenment have made their mark, largely thanks to royal patronage. Henry VIII and his daughters Mary and Elizabeth I were all born here. Charles II was particularly fond of the area and had Christopher Wren build both the Royal Observatory and part of the Royal Naval College, which was added to and finished by Vanbrugh in the early 17th century.

The Naval College was built upon the site of the old Greenwich palace, and was designed in two separate halves in order to maintain a view of the river from the Queen's House, Inigo Jones' miniature masterpiece of neo-Palladian harmony.

There's a foot tunnel under the river from Greenwich to the Isle of Dogs, a mixed area combining new office developments, stalled yuppiefication and inner-city neglect. The Isle of Dogs is home to a large immigrant community and there is considerable racial disharmony. Local government elections have seen limited but notable success for local neo-fascist candidates.

You might not wish to spend a lot of time in the Isle of Dogs, but from the entrance to the foot tunnel there are brilliant views of Greenwich's architectural collection. This is one of London's most magnificent vistas.

Cutty Sark

The *Cutty Sark* (☎ 0181-858 3445), King William Walk SE10, was the fastest sailing ship that had ever sailed the seven seas and it remains one of the most beautiful ever built.

Launched in 1869, it is the only surviving example of the clipper ship, which dominated mid-19th-century trade, especially in tea and wool, across both the Pacific and Atlantic. The *Cutty Sark* sailed its last journey in 1938 and came to Greenwich in the 50s to be put on permanent display. When it's not crowded, wandering around it can be a rewarding experience. You don't have to be a salty old sea dog to find this sleek and graceful thoroughbred of ships captivating.

It's open April to September, Monday to Saturday from 10 am to 6 pm, Sunday from noon to 6 pm; October to March, Monday to Saturday from 10 am to 5 pm, Sunday from noon to 5 pm; £3.25/2.25.

Gipsy Moth IV

Gipsy Moth IV (☎ 0181-853 3589), also in King William Walk SE10, was the boat used by Francis Chichester during 1966-7 when he completed the first solo circumnavigation of the world by an Englishman. The guy was 66 at the time and endured 226 days in this pokey, bath-sized craft. Later, he was given a knighthood and various civic plaudits. It's open Spring to October, Monday to Saturday from 10 am to 6 pm, Sunday from noon to 6 pm; 50/30p.

National Maritime Museum

Further along King William Walk is the National Maritime Museum (☎ 0181-858 4422), Romney Rd SE10, a massive collection of boats and naval relics. There are maps, charts, uniforms and miscellaneous bits and pieces designed to tell the long and pickled history of Britain as a seafaring nation. A royal barge and Nelson's blood-stained uniform from the Battle of Trafalgar are the star attractions. But this isn't really enough, and it doesn't take long before the experience starts to pall. If you've enjoyed the *Cutty Sark*, that's probably enough sea lore for one day. The best thing about the museum is the building itself. Designed by Inigo Jones and completed by Wren, it is a vital component in Greenwich's architectural collection.

The museum is open March to October, Monday to Saturday from noon to 6 pm, Sunday from 2 to 6 pm; November to February, Monday to Saturday from 10 am to 5 pm, Sunday from 2 to 5 pm; £5.50/4.50.

Royal Naval College

The Royal Naval College (☎ 0181-858 2154) is mostly closed to the public. Only the chapel, which was rebuilt following a fire in 1779, and the Painted Hall can be seen. Both interiors are extravagantly painted, opulent and rococo – they're unrestrained and utterly non-utilitarian in a way that's unknown these days. The college is open daily from 2.30 to 4.45 pm. Admission is free.

Queen's House

The Queen's House (☎ 0181-858 4422), Romney Rd SE10 (BR: Greenwich or Maze Hill), is a stunning example of the Palladian style of architecture transported to 17th-century London courtesy of Inigo Jones. Some may find it impressive but rather dull, others may find the grace, restraint and symmetry quite stirring. Completed in 1637, it become the home of Henrietta, wife of Charles I, and she adored it. Now that it has been fully restored and refurbished it isn't hard to see why.

It's open daily from 10 am to 5 pm; £5.50/4.50 (which includes a second visit within 12 months).

Greenwich Market

On Saturday and Sunday Greenwich hosts an antique and crafts market. Needless to say this comes with the obligatory mix of stalls selling second-hand clothes and handmade jewellery. Some books, plants and household bric-a-brac can also be found. As with most of London's weekend markets, some stuff is good, but most of the true discoveries and amazing bargains went five years ago. However, Greenwich Market is far better than some.

The surrounding streets are studded with bars, cafés and pubs. The *Trafalgar* pub on the riverside is big and crowded but fairly authentic and the views of the river are excellent.

Greenwich Park & Old Royal Observatory

Greenwich Park, which continues into Blackheath at the top of the hill, is one of London's loveliest parks – there's a grand avenue, wide open spaces, and rambling picturesque walks. It is partly the work of Le Nôtre who landscaped the palace gardens of Versailles.

The Old Royal Observatory (☎ 0181-858 4422), in the middle of the park, was inaugurated in 1675 by Charles II in order to properly establish, through astronomy, longitude at sea. The Octagon Room, designed by Wren, is where the first astronomer-royal made his observations and calculations.

Thereafter Greenwich became accepted as Prime Meridian, or zero hour, and from 1884 onwards the whole world – even the French – accepted Greenwich Mean Time as the universal measurement of standard time. Here the globe divides between east and west and you can place one foot either side of the meridian line and straddle the two hemispheres.

The observatory is open daily from 10 am to 5 pm; £5.50/4.50.

There's a fine view over Greenwich and the river from the observatory – taking in the city and the new Dockland sights, including Pelli's Canary Wharf tower, one of the largest structures in Europe, looming prominently in the middle distance.

Getting There & Away

The best way to get to/from Greenwich is by boat. Alternatively, there are trains from Charing Cross station, which are both quicker and cheaper, or you can catch the Docklands Light Railway on the north side of the river.

The boats drop you off at Greenwich pier close to both the *Cutty Sark* and *Gipsy Moth IV*. They leave from Westminster Pier (beside Westminster Bridge) every half hour from 10 am; single/return costs £4.40/5.40.

To get to the Docklands Light Railway (DLR), cross the river through the Greenwich Foot Tunnel (from near the *Cutty Sark*). On the other side there is a superb view back to Greenwich, and there's also the Island Gardens terminal for the DLR. The railway whisks above ground to Tower Gateway (connecting with the Tower Hill tube station) – there are good views of the new Docklands developments. Unfortunately the railway only runs on weekdays from 5.30 am to 9.30 pm; buses run on weekends; Zone 1 & 2 Travelcards are valid. See the Docklands section earlier in the chapter.

SOUTH LONDON

It's unlikely that you will spend much time in South London but there are a number of interesting places that make a journey across or under the Thames well worthwhile.

Imperial War Museum

The Imperial War Museum (☎ 0171-416 5000), Lambeth Rd SE1 (tube: Lambeth North), is one of London's most popular museums. Try to go early morning or late afternoon to dodge the inevitable crowds.

What was a rather dry series of war exhibits has been radically overhauled to meet the needs of political soundness and the demands of the modern museum-goer. Though military buffs are still more than pleased with what's on show, stress is placed on the social cost of war: the Blitz, food shortages, propaganda, and war paintings by the likes of Henry Moore.

The horrible life of an average soldier during wartime is brilliantly recreated in

***

Bedlam

The Imperial War Museum's thoroughly sane treatment of the horrors and exhilaration of human conflict is ironically housed in what was once The Royal Bethlehem Mental Hospital, from which the term 'bedlam' was coined. The museum is situated in the rather grand-sounding Geraldine Mary Harmsworth Park, but the locals refer to it simply as Bedlam Park. ∎

***

exhibits such as The Trench Experience. These exhibits have been updated to include recent conflicts such as the Falklands and Gulf wars.

It's open daily from 10 am to 6 pm; £4.10/3.

Shakespeare Globe Centre

The Shakespeare Globe Centre (☎ 0171-928 6406), Bear Gardens, Bankside SE1 (tube: London Bridge), presently consists of the new Globe Theatre and a new Shakespeare exhibition opened in the shell of an Inigo Jones indoor theatre that is being built. A visit to the exhibition includes a guided tour of the Globe Theatre itself. The exhibition is open daily from 10 am to 5 pm; £5/3.

The new Globe Theatre officially opens in June 1997.

HMS Belfast

HMS *Belfast* (☎ 0171-407 6434), Morgan's Lane, Tooley St SE1 (tube: Tower Hill or London Bridge), a cruiser that fought in WWII and was involved in the sinking of the *Scharnhorst* in 1943, is now moored peacefully in the Thames. There is a tendency to glorification, but there's no getting away from the great fun to be had exploring the ship, and pretending you're Jack Hawkins in *The Cruel Sea*, stalking Jerry through the North Sea.

Open March to October, from 10 am to 6 pm daily; November to March, from 10 am to 5 pm daily; £4.40/3.30.

South Bank

The South Bank is a crush of arts venues, roughly situated between Hungerford Railway Bridge and Waterloo Bridge on what is traditionally known as the wrong side of the river (tube: Waterloo). A stunning architectural spectacle of brightly lit concrete cubes at night, it tends to be rather grey and forbidding by day.

The **Hayward Gallery** caters for large-scale, over-subscribed mainstream modern

***

All's Well That Ends Well

The original Globe Playhouse was built in 1598-99, burnt down in 1613 and was immediately rebuilt. In 1642 (26 years after Shakespeare's death) the Globe theatre was closed for good by the Puritans. End of play – until 1949 when the American actor/producer Sam Wanamaker came to London for the first time, expecting to find a Globe theatre.

By then the original site was part of a listed Georgian terrace, but Wanamaker was determined to see a new Globe and in 1970 the Globe Playhouse Trust he established was offered a site 200 yards from the original location. Work on the new site began in 1987 and when Wanamaker died in 1993 his much cherished dream was becoming a reality.

June 1997 sees the official opening of the rebuilt Globe, accommodating an audience of some 1500, which includes 500 standing. The standing audience is just one feature of the theatre which reflects the original as closely as possible. Performances will take place in daylight (though artificial light will be used when necessary to replicate daylight conditions).

The new Globe will be at the heart of an incredible cultural facelift that is reshaping the south bank of the Thames opposite St Paul's Cathedral. Before the year 2000 there will be an indoor theatre as designed by Inigo Jones in 1617 and the nearby, disused Bankside Power Station will become an extension to the Tate Gallery, housing its collection of international 20th-century art. ∎

***

art exhibitions. The brilliant **Festival Hall** complex hosts classical, opera, jazz and choral music, all at very competitive rates. There are also free recitals in the foyer most early evenings and a range of cafés and restaurants. There are three theatres at the **National Theatre**, home of the great British dramatic tradition. There's also the under-attended **National Film Theatre** and the Museum of the Moving Image (MOMI).

Adjoining the South Bank is the rebuilt **Gabriel's Wharf**, a pint-sized monument to Prince Charles' notion of community architecture, featuring plenty of chintzy shops selling cushions, jewellery and odd-looking clothes. The best thing is the view – you look across the river to St Paul's, Lloyds, Canary Wharf and so on – like Manhattan-on-Thames.

Just to the east of Gabriel's Wharf is the delightful **Oxo Tower**. It was built in 1928 by the beefstock company and cunningly cut round a prevailing ban on outdoor advertising by incorporating its name into the building's design.

Museum of the Moving Image The Museum of the Moving Image (MOMI) (☎ 0171-401 2636), South Bank SE1 (tube: Waterloo), is tucked away amongst the arts venues on the South Bank. MOMI is a marvellous museum experience, sensitively mixing showbiz and educational needs, fun and information.

From the very first days of film, of zoetropes, cinematography and magic lanterns, the displays move smoothly forward through the hazy days of silent Hollywood and the glamour and glory era of the 30s and onwards. Along the way studious reference is made to the pioneers of European cinema such as Gance and Eisenstein, as well as to TV, documentaries and newsreels. There are actor-guides for added entertainment and plenty of opportunities for audience participation whether making your own animations, interviewing stars, or acting in your own movie.

MOMI is open daily from 10 am to 6 pm; £5.95/4.85.

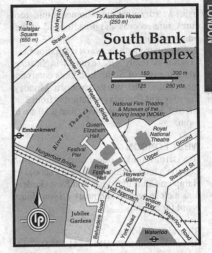

Hayward Gallery The Hayward Gallery (☎ 0171-928 3144), Belvedere Rd SE1 (tube: Waterloo), is London's senior exhibition space for major international art shows. Some love the grey concrete building, an integral part of the South Bank arts centre, others can't say a nice thing about it. Whatever, it's an excellent space in which to display contemporary and 20th-century art. And there's no denying its pulling power, which is its foremost problem: the crowds. If the media have cranked up the hype, it's best either to arrive early – or pack a picnic and join the queue.

The gallery can close for up to two months between exhibitions so check before turning up. It's open Monday and Thursday to Sunday from 10 am to 6 pm, Tuesday and Wednesday from 10 am to 8 pm; £5/3.50.

Brixton Market
Brixton Market (tube: Brixton) is a cosmopolitan treat made up of diverse parts: the rainbow coalition, The Body Shop, reggae music, slick Muslim preachers, halal meat, fruit and vegetables... On Electric Ave and in the covered Granville Arcade you can buy wigs, exotic foodstuffs from goat to tilapia

LONDON

fish, weird spices and homeopathic root cures, rare records and dreadful end-of-the-line furnishings.

The suburb with the worst reputation in all London is really OK, even at night-time, when it's one of South London's entertainment hubs. The market is open Monday, Tuesday and Thursday to Saturday from 8.30 am to 5.30 pm; Wednesday from 8.30 am to 1 pm.

WEST LONDON

If visitors make one short foray into London's hinterland, then it really should be Hampton Court they visit. But Kew Gardens runs a close second and nearby Syon House is not far behind.

Riverside Studios

Riverside Studios (☎ 0181-741 2255), Crisp Rd W6 (tube: Hammersmith), is West London's equivalent of the ICA, a mixed-media arts centre with two good-sized auditoria which cater to film, theatre, modern dance, and about a dozen art shows per year featuring the occasional 'name' overseas artist. The problem with Riverside is that it feels a bit low key and cut off. Both the studios and Hammersmith itself aren't always that easy to reach. On the plus side, there is a good set of river-front pubs nearby on the Chiswick side of Hammersmith Bridge, a popular haunt on summer evenings. The centre is open Monday to Saturday from 9 am to 11 pm, Sunday from noon to 11pm.

Kew Gardens

Kew Gardens (☎ 0181-940 1171), Kew Rd, Richmond, Surrey (tube: Kew Gardens), is one of the most visited sights on the tourist itinerary, which means it can get very crowded during summer. Spring is the best time to visit, but at any time of year this expansive array of lawns, formal gardens and botanical greenhouses has space and delights to offer.

There are two soaring Victorian conservatories, the Palm House and the Temperate House, made of glass and iron and housing an exotic variety of plant life. There's also the Princess of Wales Conservatory, opened in 1987, which houses plants from 10 different climate zones. Kew isn't just a park but an important botanical research centre and it maintains its reputation as the most exhaustive botanical collection in the world.

Kew Palace, once a royal residence dating from the early 1600s, is an unexceptional structure when compared with Syon House across the river.

Kew Gardens, or the Royal Botanic Gardens, is open November to January, daily from 9.30 am to 4.30 pm; February, daily from 9.30 am to 5 pm; March, daily from 9.30 am to 6 pm; April to August, Monday to Saturday from 9.30 am to 6.30 pm, Sunday from 9.30 am to 8 pm; September to mid-October, daily from 9.30 am to 6 pm; £4.50/3.

Kew Palace is open April to September daily from 11 am to 5.30 pm; £1.50/75p.

As an alternative to the tube to Kew Gardens station (Zone 3), ferries sail from Westminster Pier every 30 minutes from 10.15 am to 2.30 pm (from the Monday before Easter until end of September). They take 1½ hours and single/return costs £5/7.

Richmond

Nearby Richmond is a pleasant riverside village, and **Richmond Park** is the largest and most rural of the royal parks. It can be reached on foot from Kew by following the river towards Twickenham. There are good places to eat and drink in Richmond, including the *White Swan* pub-restaurant adjoining Richmond Theatre, where you can go before taking the tube back to central London. Alternatively, cross Kew Bridge and turn right along the river bank for some pleasant riverside pubs.

Syon House

Syon House (☎ 0181-560 0881), Syon Park, Brentford, Middlesex (tube: Gunnersbury, BR: Syon Lane) is a superb example of the English stately home. The house where Lady Jane Grey ascended to the throne for her nine-day-long monarchy in 1554 was remodelled by Robert Adam in the 18th century, and possesses plenty of Adam furniture and oak panelling. The interior was designed along gender-specific lines, with pastel pinks and purples for the ladies' gallery, and mock Roman sculptures for the men's dining room. The gardens, including an artificial lake, were landscaped by Capability Brown.

This small but perfectly formed house can be easily reached from Kew. It's open April to September, Wednesday to Sunday from 11 am to 5 pm; October, Sunday from 11 am to 5 pm; £5.50/4.

Hampton Court Palace

Hampton Court Palace (☎ 0181-781 9500), East Molesey, Surrey (BR: Hampton Court), by the River Thames, is the largest and grandest Tudor structure in England, but is surprisingly compact and undaunting. It's knee deep in historical circumstance, close to London and yet very much removed, with superb gardens, and a famous 300-year-old maze.

Cardinal Wolsey built the original palace. He gave it to Henry VIII as a peace offering in 1525, and shortly afterwards had his head chopped off. In the late 17th century, William and Mary employed Christopher Wren to build extensions. As a result it is a beautiful mixture of architectural styles. Unexpectedly, Tudor chimneys and gables and Wren's classical style go well together.

It's open April to October, Monday from 10.15 am to 6 pm, Tuesday to Sunday from 9.30 am to 6 pm; October to March, Monday from 10.15 am to 4.30 pm, Tuesday to Sunday from 9.30 am to 4.30 pm; £8/5.75.

There are trains every half-hour from Waterloo station (£3.90 return, Zone 6), or the palace can be reached by river boat from Westminster Pier to Hampton Court Pier. Ferries depart from April to October at 10.30 am, 11.15 am and noon; they take 3½ hours and cost £7.

PLACES TO STAY

Whichever way you cut it, accommodation in London is ridiculously expensive. Despite this, demand can still outstrip supply, so it is worth booking a night or two's accommodation, especially in July and August. The official TICs at the airports and at Victoria station can arrange last-minute bookings, but they charge £5.

In summer the Victoria station office has enormous queues, but there are also slightly cheaper, less-busy, private operators that charge up to £5. Outside the station on Buckingham Palace Rd towards the coach station, Accommodation Express (☎ 0171-233 8139) has free bookings and a courtesy bus for the Chelsea Hotel and a number of other private hostels.

Hostel dorm accommodation will cost from £10 to £19.75. You can expect to pay £25/30 for very basic singles/doubles without bathroom, £25/35 with. You'll be lucky to find anything really pleasant for much less than £35/50. There are, of course, some superb hotels in London, but they are *very* expensive. If you have enough money for one or two splurges, wait until you get into the countryside, where you will get much better value.

Camping

Tent City (☎ 0181-743 5708), Old Oak Common Lane W3 (tube: East Acton), is the cheapest option in London, short of sleeping rough. There are dormitory-style tents with beds for £5.50. It's open from June to September and you are advised to book. It also has tent sites but doesn't take caravans or camper vans. They also have a place in Hackney in East London – Millfield Rd E5 – where a pitch for a tent or van is £5.

Lee Valley Park, Picketts Lock Sport & Leisure Centre (☎ 0181-345 6666), Picketts Lock Lane, Edmonton N9, has 200 pitches for tents or caravans. It's open all year and the nightly charge is £4.75 per person plus £2.20 for electricity.

YHA Hostels

There are presently seven YHA hostels in London, with a new one about to open, but they are crowded during summer. Sometimes they can't even accept advance bookings. If they have room, they all take advance bookings by phone (if you pay by Visa or MasterCard). They do hold some beds for those who wander in on the day, but wander in early, and be prepared to queue. All but one offer 24-hour access and all of them provide a bureau de change. Adults will have to pay £12.25 to £19.75, juniors £8.50 to £16.55.

You can join the association at the YHA London headquarters (☎ 0171-836 8541), 14 Southampton St WC2 (tube: Covent Garden), where there's also a bookshop, excellent outdoor equipment and a branch of Campus Travel.

Enquire at the headquarters about the new 150-bed hostel, *St Pancras International*, which should be open by the time you read this. It will be in Euston Rd opposite the new British Library, conveniently located close to the Kings Cross, Euston and St Pancras rail links.

Rotherhithe (☎ 0171-232 2114), Salter Rd SE16 (tube: Rotherhithe), is an impressive, purpose-built hostel. Unfortunately, it's a bit far out, and the area is not great; transport is fair. On the other hand, the hostel is good; rooms are mainly six-bed, although there are some fours and a few doubles; all have attached bathroom. There's a licensed restaurant as well as kitchen facilities. Rates for seniors/juniors are £19.75/16.55.

Carter Lane (☎ 0171-236 4965), 36 Carter Lane EC4 (tube: St Paul's), is virtually next door to St Paul's Cathedral in an intelligently restored old building, which was the cathedral choir's school. The position and the hostel are excellent, although this end of town does get pretty quiet outside working hours. Rooms are mainly four, three or two beds. There's a licensed cafeteria but no kitchen. Rates are £19.75/16.55.

Earl's Court (☎ 0171-373 7083), 38 Bolton Gardens SW5 (tube: Earl's Court), is an old townhouse in a tacky, though lively, part of town; it is not the best equipped of the hostels, however. Rooms are mainly 10-bed dorms. There's a cafeteria and kitchen. Rates are £17.70/15.55.

Hampstead Heath (☎ 0181-458 9054/7196), 4 Wellgarth Rd NW11 (tube: Golders Green), is in a beautiful setting with a well-kept garden, although it is a bit isolated. The dorms are comfortable, and each room has a basin with hot and cold water. There's a rather average, though licensed, cafeteria and a kitchen. Rates are £14.40/12.30.

Highgate Village (☎ 0181-340 1831), 84 Highgate West Hill N6 (tube: Archway), is in an attractive Georgian house close to Hampstead Heath; once again it is a bit isolated. There are kitchen facilities, but no evening meals and the absence of 24-hour staffing means you need to be in by midnight. It's the cheapest YHA option in London with rates at £12.25/8.50.

Holland House (☎ 0171-937 0748), Holland Walk, Kensington W8 (tube: High St Kensington), has a great location in the middle of Holland Park and is close to everything. It's large, very busy and rather institutional, but the position really can't be beaten. There's a cafeteria and kitchen. Rates are £17.70/15.55.

Oxford St (☎ 0171-734 1618), 14-18 Noel St W1 (tube: Oxford Circus), is the most basic of the London hostels, but it is right in the centre of town. There's a large kitchen, but no meals. Rates are £17.30/14.10.

Epping Forest hostel (☎ 0181-508 5161), High Beach, Loughton, Essex (tube: Loughton), is over 10 miles from central London and a good two-mile walk from the nearest tube station, but it may be worth considering if all else is full. Rates are £6.75/4.60 (but allow for the tube fares).

University Colleges

University halls of residence are let to non-students during the holidays, usually from the end of June to mid September. They're somewhat more expensive than the youth hostels, but you usually get a single room (there are a small number of doubles) with shared facilities, plus breakfast. Bookings are coordinated by the British Universities Accommodation Consortium (BUAC) (☎ 0115-950 4571), Box 653, University Park, Nottingham NG7 2RD, although you can also contact the colleges direct.

The London School of Economics (Room

B508, LSE, Houghton Street, WC2A 2AE) has a number of its halls available at Easter and summer. *Carr Saunders Hall* (☎ 0171-323 9712), 18-24 Fitzroy St W1 (tube: Great Portland St), is not the greatest part of town, but it's central enough; open Easter and summer holidays; singles/doubles with full breakfast are £17.50/30 over Easter, £22/42 in the summer. Self-catering flats of different sizes are also available on a weekly basis in the summer only, ranging from £238 for a two person flat to £539 for five persons. *High Holborn* (☎ 0171-379 5589), 178 High Holborn WC1 (tube: Holborn), is centrally located and has self-catering singles/doubles for £25/43, with continental breakfast, in the summer only. *Passfield Hall* (☎ 0171-387 3584), Endsleigh Place WC1 (tube: Euston), consists of ten late-Georgian houses in the heart of Bloomsbury. A bed and full breakfast is £17.50/30 at Easter, £19/35 in the summer. Similar rates apply at *Rosebery Avenue Hall* (☎ 0171-278 3251), 90 Rosebery Avenue EC1 (tube: Angel).

Imperial College of Science & Technology (☎ 0171-589 5111), 15 Prince's Gardens SW7 (tube: South Kensington), is in a brilliant position near the Kensington museums; open Easter and summer; B&B £25/40.

Regent College (☎ 0171-487 7483), Inner Circle, Regent's Park NW1 (tube: Baker St), is a converted Regency manor right in the middle of beautiful Regent's Park, convenient to Camden and central London; open May to September; singles/doubles £25/36.

John Adams Hall (☎ 0171-387 4086), 15-23 Endsleigh St WC1 (tube: Euston), is central and facilities include a swimming pool; open Easter and summer; B&B is £19 per night for more than seven nights, £21.40 for less.

King's Campus Vacation Bureau (☎ 0171-351 6011), 552 Kings Rd SW10 0UA, administers bookings for a number of central King's College residence halls. Rates range from £14 to £23 per person, include access to excellent facilities, and most include a continental breakfast.

Finsbury Residences (☎ 0171-477 8811), Bastwick St EC1 (tube: Old Street), comprises two modern halls belonging to City University. A bed and continental breakfast is £19.50 per person, £97.50 a week; available over Christmas, Easter and the summer; evening meals are available on request.

University of Westminster (☎ 0171-911 5000), 35 Marylebone Rd NW1 (tube: Marylebone), has singles and doubles for £15.70 per person under 26, £21.50 over 26, and £3 for an optional continental breakfast.

Independent Hostels

There are a number of hotels/hostels that operate on the simple principle that if you squash six people in a room and charge them £10 each you make more profit than if you have a couple at £20 per person. They are not suitable for fastidious, anti-social claustrophobics.

In terms of facilities offered, most of the hostels don't vary much. Most have three or four small bunk-beds jammed into a room, a small kitchen and some kind of lounge room. Some have budget restaurants and some even have a bar. They are cheaper and much more relaxed than the official YHA hostels, but the standards are more hit and miss. Problems with theft are relatively unusual, but be careful with your possessions and deposit your valuables in the office safe. In the past, some hostels have had an irresponsible attitude to fire safety – check fire escapes are accessible.

Apart from noise levels, safety and cleanliness, the most important variable is the atmosphere. This can change by the week, as to a certain extent it is dependent on the people who happen to be staying. If you're not happy with your first pick, try somewhere new.

The largest number of private hostels are in Earl's Court (SW5), which consequently has the biggest backpacker scene, but there are some in Paddington and Bayswater (W2), Notting Hill and Holland Park (W11), Bloomsbury (WC1) and Pimlico (SW1). With the possible exception of Notting Hill and Bloomsbury, all these areas are pretty seedy. Notting Hill and Bayswater are central and close to Hyde Park; Notting Hill, in particular, is a great part of London.

Notting Hill The *Palace Hotel* (☎ 0171-221 5628), 31 Palace Court W2 (tube: Notting Hill Gate), has dorm beds for £10. It has a pleasant and convenient location and isn't quite as run down and manic as some of the others.

The *London Independent Hostel* (☎ 0171-229 4238), 41 Holland Park W11 (tube: Holland Park) is on an elegant street and is well positioned. It's also good value (all things being relative) with dorms for £8, quads for £9, triples for £10, doubles for £11 per person.

The *Centre Français* (☎ 0171-221 8134), 61 Chepstow Place W2 (tube: Notting Hill Gate), is like a cross between a YHA hostel and a college residence. It's immaculately maintained, comfortable in an institutional sort of way, and only about half the clientele are French. A continental breakfast is included. A bed in a bright and cheery dorm of eight beds is £11.70, in a three/four bed dorm £15. The singles/doubles (£22.50/36) are spartan, but do include washbasins and desks.

Bloomsbury The *Museum Inn* (☎ 0171-580 5360), 27 Montague St WC1 (tube: Holborn), has an excellent position opposite the British Museum. There's a party atmosphere and the management are friendly. Quite a few rooms have colour TVs, there are decent kitchen facilities, and a basic breakfast is included in the price: £17 per person in the one double; £15 in a four-bed dorm; £13 in a nine-bed dorm.

The *International Students House* (☎ 0171-631 8300), 229 Great Portland St W1 (tube: Great Portland St), is really in a different class, more like a university residential college. For a start you get singles or doubles; they're ordinary, but clean. There are excellent facilities and a friendly atmosphere – you don't have to be a student. It's open all year. B&B ranges from £23.40 for a single to £14 for a quad. Book in advance.

Earl's Court The *Curzon House Hotel* (☎ 0171-581 2116), 58 Courtfield Gardens SW5 (tube: Gloucester Rd), is one of the better private hostels – much loved by Let's Go researchers, but don't hold that against it. There's a relaxed and friendly atmosphere. Dorms are £13 per person, singles/doubles with facilities are £23/36.

The *Chelsea Hotel* (☎ 0171-244 6892), 33 Earl's Court Square SW5 (tube: Earl's Court), is a classic hostel. There's a restaurant with meals for £3, and hundreds of cheery backpackers wandering around. They have some good-value singles and doubles as well as dorms. A dorm bed is £10, a twin is £27 and a single is £16.

Regency Court Hotel (☎ 0171-244 6615), 14 Penywern Rd SW5 (tube: Earl's Court), is in need of renovation and some travellers have a low opinion of the place. Dorms are £10; doubles £20; triples £40 and quads £50. A better bet is *Windsor House* (☎ 0171-373 9087) next door at 12 Penywern Rd. A dorm bed is £10, a single £28, a double £38 and triples £48, all including breakfast.

The *Court Hotels* (tube: Earls Court), at 194-196 Earls Court Rd SW5 (☎ 0171-373 0027) and 17-19 Kempsford Gardens (☎ 0171-373 2174), are under Australasian management and have well-equipped kitchens and TV in most rooms. A dorm bed is £11, singles/doubles are £21/24, and weekly rates are available.

Paddington & Bayswater The *Palace Court Hotel* (☎ 0171-727 4412, 221 9228), 64 Princes Square W2 (tube: Bayswater), is in a good position, has clean rooms and a good atmosphere. The bar is open late to guests, and there's a budget restaurant. Arrive early if you can. You'll pay £9 for a quad, £12 for a twin. Prices drop outside summer. Ring for details on their free minibus from Victoria.

The *Quest Hotel* (☎ 0171-229 7782), 45 Queensborough Terrace W2 (tube: Bayswater), is just around the corner from all the action on Queensway and is a minute from Hyde Park. It has a friendly atmosphere and a pool table, but gets pretty crowded. There are kitchen facilities; dorms are £11.50 and £12.50 and a limited number of beds are available on a weekly basis for about £2 less per night.

Next door, the *Royal Hotel* (☎ 0171-229 7225), 43 Queensborough Terrace W2 (tube: Bayswater), is much like many other hostels, but they do make an effort not to overcrowd the rooms. As a result, many people stay for quite long periods of time. A very basic double is £9 per person, and quads are £8 per person.

Pimlico The *Victoria Hotel* (☎ 0171-834 3077), 71 Belgrave Rd SW1 (tube: Victoria), is a 15-minute walk from Victoria station. It has been criticised for being overcrowded and poorly maintained but it may be worth considering if you arrive in London late at night, or have to leave early in the morning. Reception is open 24 hours. Beds are around £14.

Hotels & B&Bs

Bloomsbury (WC1), Bayswater (W2), Paddington (W2), Pimlico (SW1) and Earl's Court (SW5) are the centres for budget hotels. Each area has advantages and disadvantages, but the prices remain pretty consistent. If you want an attached bathroom you will be lucky to find anything for less than £25, even in winter.

Outside the high season, prices are nearly always negotiable; don't be afraid to ask for the 'best' price and for a discount if you are either staying more than a couple of nights or don't want a cooked breakfast. In July, August and September prices can jump by 25% or even more, and it is definitely worth phoning ahead. Many of the cheapies don't take credit cards.

B&Bs in Londoners' private houses can be good value; double-room prices range from £15 to £30 per person per night. At £15 you would be quite a distance out and share a bathroom, at £16 a little closer, at £18 you should be in a central location like Bloomsbury, and from £25 to £30 in a central area with private bathroom. Bookings (minimum three days) can be made free in advance through London Homestead Services (☎ 0181-949 4455, 24 hours), Coombe Wood Rd, Kingston-upon-Thames, Surrey KT2 7JY. Bed & Breakfast (GB) (☎ 01491-578803), PO Box 66, Henley-on-Thames RG9 1XS, specialises in central London. Primrose Hill B&B (☎ 0171-722 6869), 14 Edis St NW1 8LG, is a small agency with select properties in or near Hampstead. Guests get their own latchkeys and rates are between £20 and £30. Or contact the BTA or local TICs.

Good-quality hotels are scattered around, but there are some excellent places in Notting Hill, Marble Arch, the West End and Bloomsbury.

Notting Hill Notting Hill is one of the most interesting, attractive and convenient parts of London. It has become increasingly trendy and expensive over the last few years, but it's still home to a wide variety of Londoners, and a large West Indian community. Portobello Market is fun, and several interesting bars and restaurants have sprung up at the Ladbroke Grove end of Portobello Rd.

Holland Park Hotel (☎ 0171-792 0216), 6 Ladbroke Terrace W11 (tube: Notting Hill Gate), has a great position on a quiet street near Holland Park and the hubbub of Notting Hill. The rooms are very pleasant and it's particularly good value; singles/doubles without bathroom are £40/54, with bathroom £54/72.

At the beginning of Portobello Rd, the *Gate Hotel* (☎ 0171-221 2403), 6 Portobello Rd W11 (tube: Notting Hill Gate), has classic frilly English décor in an old town house. Rooms are well equipped and all have bathroom. Singles/doubles are £38/70.

Hillgate Hotel (☎ 0171-221 3433), 6 Pembridge Gardens W2 (tube: Notting Hill Gate), has a great position and rooms with all the facilities you'd expect in a good hotel. Singles/doubles are £50/60.

Portobello Hotel (☎ 0171-727 2777), 22 Stanley Gardens W11 (tube: Notting Hill Gate), is a superb small hotel – embodying everybody's dream of what a great London hotel should be. It has a great location and is beautifully appointed, friendly and peaceful. It's not cheap, but you won't begrudge the expense. Singles/doubles are £95/135.

Earl's Court Earl's Court has been a hangout for refugees from the far-flung corners of the empire for a long time. At one stage it was infamous as Kangaroo Valley, but now Australians are less conspicuous than Africans, Arabs and Indians. Most people seem to be in transit, and it shows in the grubby, unloved streets. It's relatively convenient, although not quite as convenient as the other districts in this guide – it's not really within walking distance of many places you will want to be, so you're heavily dependent on the tube.

The *St Simeon* (☎ 0171-373 0505), 38 Harrington Gardens SW7 (tube: Gloucester Rd), is within walking distance of the South Kensington museums. They have dorms as well as singles and doubles; prices are around £14 per person but seem to be negotiable.

The *Boka Hotel* (☎ 0171-370 1388), 33 Eardley Crescent SW5 (tube: Earl's Court), is a relaxed place where guests have the use of a kitchen. Most rooms don't have bathroom. Singles/doubles start at £22/35 and there's also a dorm from £12.

Shellbourne Hotel (☎ 0171-373 5161), 1 Lexham Gardens W8 (tube: Gloucester Rd), is tatty but clean, and the rooms are well equipped for their price – TVs, showers, direct-dial telephones – and you get a full breakfast. Singles/doubles/triples are £26/37/60.

York House Hotel (☎ 0171-373 7519), 27 Philbeach Gardens SW5 (tube: Earl's Court), is relatively cheap, but you get what you pay for. The rooms are basic, although some have showers. Singles/doubles without bath are £26/42; doubles/triples with bath are £58/68.

Philbeach Hotel (☎ 0171-373 1244), 30 Philbeach Gardens SW5 (tube: Earl's Court), is a pleasant, well-decorated hotel, popular with a male and female gay clientele. There's a decent restaurant and bar and a nice

garden. Rooms without bathroom are £45/55, with bathroom they are £50/65.

The *London Tourist Hotel* (☎ 0171-370 4356), 15 Penywern Rd SW5 (tube: Earl's Court), is a pleasant mid-range hotel. Singles/doubles with bathroom are £39/54.

The *Merlyn Court Hotel* (☎ 0171-370 1640), 2 Barkston Gardens SW5 (tube: Earl's Court), is an unpretentious place with a nice atmosphere. The rooms are clean, small and reasonable value. Singles/doubles with bathroom are £45/55, without they're £30/45. Triples and quads with/without bathroom are £65/70.

Pimlico Pimlico is not the most attractive part of London to stay in, but you are very close to the action, even if there's not much happening immediately around you. For an area that sees a large transient population, the quality of the hotels is reasonably good. In general the cheap hotels (around £30 per person) are better value than their counterparts in Earl's Court.

If only all London's budget hotels were like the *Luna & Simone Hotels* (☎ 0171-834 5897), 47 Belgrave Rd SW1 (tube: Victoria). They're central, spotlessly clean, comfortable and they don't have offensive décor. Doubles without bathroom are from £38, with bathroom from £54. Facilities vary from room to room, but a full English breakfast is included. There are free storage facilities if you want to leave some bags behind while you go travelling.

The *Belgrave House Hotel* (☎ 0171-828 1563), 32 Belgrave Rd SW1 (tube: Victoria), is another pleasant hotel that doesn't have a doss-house atmosphere. Singles/doubles are £30/40, including breakfast, and weekly rates are available.

The *Brindle House Hotel* (☎ 0171-828 0057), 1 Warwick Place North SW1 (tube: Victoria), is in an old building off the main thoroughfares. Although the décor is a mess, the rooms are much more pleasant than the foyer suggests – they're light and clean. Singles are £30 (shared facilities), doubles are £45/40 (with/without facilities).

A step up in quality and price, *Hamilton*

House (☎ 0171-821 7113), 60 Warwick Way SW1 (tube: Victoria), has singles/doubles with private bathroom, TV and telephone for £56/68. The doubles are worth considering.

The *Winchester Hotel* (☎ 0171-828 2972), 17 Belgrave Rd SW1, (tube: Victoria), is clean, comfortable and welcoming. For the area, which is definitely convenient, it's pretty good value. All rooms have private bathroom, TV and phone. Doubles and twins are £60.

Sloane Square, Chelsea & Kensington

Sloane Square, Chelsea and Kensington are trendy and expensive districts, but they are convenient, especially for museums and shopping, and they don't feel like tourist ghettoes.

The *Magnolia Hotel* (☎ 0171-352 0187), 104 Oakley St SW3 (tube: South Kensington), has a good position, and is remarkably good value. The only drawback is a bit of a hike to the nearest tube station. The rooms are pleasant, but if possible get one at the back, away from traffic noise. There's colour TV in all rooms. Singles with/without bathroom are £43/33, doubles with bathroom are £48 and £56 and without are £43. Triples are £60.

The *Swiss House Hotel* (☎ 0171-373 2769), 171 Old Brompton Rd, is a clean, good-value hotel, on the edge of Earl's Court. Singles/doubles without shower and toilet are £36/53 and doubles with a shower are £68, which is a bit steep since they only give you a continental breakfast. It is a nice place, however, and you do get a TV and a direct dial phone.

The *Vicarage Private Hotel* (☎ 0171-229 4030), 10 Vicarage Gate W8 (tube: High St Kensington), is in a good location near Hyde Park between Notting Hill and Kensington. It's a pleasant, well-kept place with good showers and some charm. Singles/doubles are £36/58. This place is recommended in a number of guidebooks so you have to book ahead.

Abbey House (☎ 0171-727 2594), 11 Vicarage Gate W8 (tube: High St Kensington), is a particularly good-value small hotel; it

modestly describes itself as a B&B. The décor is decent, the welcome is warm, and it's on a quiet residential road between Notting Hill and Kensington. Singles/doubles are £36/68. Booking is recommended.

Hotel 167 (☎ 0171-373 0672), 167 Old Brompton Rd SW5 (tube: Gloucester Rd), is a small and stylish hotel. It's immaculately kept and has (for England) an unusually uncluttered and attractive décor. All rooms have private bathroom. Singles are £60, doubles range from £75 to £82.

Midway between Kensington and Earl's Court, the *Amber Hotel* (☎ 0171-373 8666), 101 Lexham Gardens W8 (tube: Earl's Court), is pretty good value for London with fully equipped rooms from £75/85. Across the road, the *London Lodge Hotel* (☎ 0171-244 8444), 134 Lexham Gardens W8 (tube: Earl's Court), has nice rooms and an excellent breakfast. All rooms are fully equipped; singles £75, doubles at £90.

In Kensington proper (a good location, especially for museums) there are two excellent places on Sumner Place, neither of which advertise themselves with signs. There's not a great deal to separate the two, but *Five Sumner Place* (☎ 0171-584 7586), 5 Sumner Place SW7 (tube: South Kensington), has won a number of awards and is the cheaper. The rooms are comfortable and well equipped (all have bathroom, TV, phone, drinks cabinet – and more) and there's an attractive conservatory and garden. Singles range from £81 to £92, doubles £116.

Number Sixteen (☎ 0171-589 5232), 16 Sumner Place SW7 (tube: South Kensington), shares all the attributes of No 5. Singles range from £80 to £105, doubles from £140 to £145, but they also have weekend specials from £50 per person.

Annandale House Hotel (☎ 0171-730 5051), 39 Sloane Gardens, Sloane Square SW1 (tube: Sloane Square), is a discreet, traditional small hotel in a fashionable part of London. Expect real linen napkins and tablecloths. All rooms have phone and TV and some have private bathroom. Singles/doubles from £40/75.

Paddington Paddington is even seedier than Earl's Court, and although there are lots of cheap hotels (or is it *because* there are lots of cheap hotels?), single women in particular will probably feel more comfortable elsewhere. It is convenient, however, and there are some decent places at decent prices.

Right in the centre of the action, *Norfolk Court & St David's Hotel* (☎ 0171-723 4963), 16 Norfolk Square W2 (tube: Paddington), is a friendly place with the usual out-of-control décor, but it's clean and comfortable. Basic singles/doubles have washbasin, colour TV and telephone and cost £28/40. With shower and toilet, prices jump to £50 for a double.

Sussex Gardens is lined with small hotels and, unfortunately, is also a major traffic route. Most places aren't inspiring, but there are some gems among the dross. The *Balmoral House* (☎ 0171-723 7445), 156 Sussex Gardens W2 (tube: Paddington), is an immaculate and very comfortable place with singles with/without bathroom for £40/30 and doubles with facilities for £52. All rooms have TVs and a full English breakfast is served.

The *Europa House* (☎ 0171-723 7343), 151 Sussex Gardens W2 (tube: Paddington), is clean, quiet and well equipped. All rooms have bathroom, TV and telephone. Singles/doubles cost £45/60.

The *Gresham Hotel* (☎ 0171-402 2920), 116 Sussex Gardens W2 (tube: Paddington), is a stylish, small hotel, with well-equipped rooms. Expect to pay £60 for a single and £75 for a double

Bayswater Bayswater is extremely convenient and, as a result, some parts feel as if they are under constant invasion. Some of the streets immediately to the west of Queensway – which has an excellent selection of restaurants – are depressingly run down.

The *Oxford Hotel* (☎ 0171-402 6860), 13 Craven Terrace (tube: Lancaster Gate), is reasonable value. All rooms have TV; singles and doubles cost £65 and this goes down to £48 if they are rented for eight days.

Sass House (☎ 0171-262 2325), 11 Craven Terrace (tube: Lancaster Gate), is fairly basic and threadbare and there are only doubles at £46, including continental breakfast. One of the best options in Bayswater is the *Garden Court Hotel* (☎ 0171-229 2553), 30 Kensington Gardens Square W2 (tube: Bayswater). It's a well-run, well-maintained family hotel, with well-equipped rooms. They all have telephone and TV. Breakfasts are good. Singles/doubles without bathroom are £32/48, with bathroom £45/65.

Manor Court Hotel (☎ 0171-792 3361), 7 Clanricarde Gardens (tube: Queensway), is off Bayswater Rd – a good location. It may not be spectacular, but you could do a lot worse for the money. Singles with private showers are £30, and doubles with private bathroom are £50.

Marble Arch Marble Arch, at the western end of Oxford St, is a rather bland area – a mix of comfortable hotels and offices, but lacking real life. It is definitely convenient, however.

Glynne Court Hotel (☎ 0171-262 4344), 41 Great Cumberland Place W1 (tube: Marble Arch), is fairly typical. All rooms have TV and telephone. Singles/doubles are £42/60, but you only get a continental breakfast.

Wigmore Court Hotel (☎ 0171-935 0928), 23 Gloucester Place, Portman Square W1H (tube: Marble Arch), has pretty horrible décor, although someone must love it. On the other hand, this is a thoughtful, well-organised place, and very comfortable. All rooms have bathroom, are well equipped, and guests have access to a kitchen and self-serve laundry. All in all, it's good value. Singles/doubles are £45/79 in peak season, about 10% cheaper out of season.

The *Edward Lear Hotel* (☎ 0171-402 5401), 28 Seymour St W1H (tube: Marble Arch), was formerly the home of Victorian painter and poet Edward Lear. It's a small, comfortable hotel. All rooms have TV, tea and coffee facilities and telephone. Singles/doubles without bathroom range from £39 to £60, with bathroom from £49 to £85.

Durrants Hotel (☎ 0171-935 8131), George St W1H (tube: Marble Arch), just behind the Wallace Collection, is a large hotel that, amazingly, was once a country inn. It's smart and luxurious with a great position for shoppers. Singles/doubles with bathroom start at £87/105, but breakfast is extra.

Bryanston Court Hotel (☎ 0171-262 3141), 55 Great Cumberland Place W1H (tube: Marble Arch), has something of the atmosphere of a gentlemen's club with leather armchairs and a formal style. It's particularly aimed at business people, and all rooms have private bathroom, TV and phone. It's expensive during the week at £73/90, but has a special offer, available at weekends and between December and February, of doubles for £75.

West End There are tremendous advantages to staying in the centre of town – as the real estate agents say, location, location and location. Unfortunately this is a privilege that doesn't come cheap.

Soho has a reputation for sleaze, but although there are still some dubious clubs and shops, it is now the thriving centre for London's nightlife. It has an enjoyable European atmosphere, with countless restaurants, busy pubs and numerous trendy cafés spilling onto the streets.

Hazlitt's (☎ 0171-434 1771), 6 Frith St, Soho Square W1V (tube: Tottenham Court Rd), is one of the finest hotels in London. Needless to say, it's not cheap. Built in 1718, it comprises three linked Georgian houses. All the rooms have names and are individually decorated with antique furniture and prints. It's right in the heart of London and has efficient personal service. There are only 23 rooms and booking is advisable. Singles/doubles are £126/162.

The *Fielding Hotel* (☎ 0171-836 8305), 4 Broad Court, Bow St WC2 (tube: Covent Garden), is remarkably good value considering where it is – on a pedestrian walk, almost opposite the Royal Opera House. The hotel

looks like an old pub, but the rooms are clean and well run. Most have private bathroom, TVs and telephones. Singles/doubles with bathroom are £63/80.

You can't get more central than *The Hampshire* (☎ 0171-839 9399), Leicester Square. It's a part of the Radisson Edwardian group, which has a number of other luxury hotels scattered around London. All of them are only for people for whom money is not an issue. The Hampshire tends to be full of rich, retired Americans and top-flight business people. Singles/doubles are £219/261.

Claridges (☎ 0171-629 8860), Brook St W1, is one of the greatest of London's five-star hotels. It's a hotel from a bygone era where you could easily bump into people you last saw in *Hello* magazine. The Art-Deco suites were designed in 1929 and have log fires in winter. Expect to pay £258/348 for singles/doubles.

The *Ritz* (☎ 0171-493 8181), 150 Piccadilly W1, is the most famous of London's hotels, and has a spectacular position overlooking Green Park. If you need to know the price, you can't afford to stay there!

Hampstead *La Gaffe* (☎ 0171-794 7526), 107 Heath St NW3 (tube: Hampstead) is in Hampstead, which retains a villagey atmosphere and can seem a long way from London, although it is still handy by tube. La Gaffe is a small, rather eccentric, but nonetheless comfortable hotel in an 18th-century cottage. Singles/doubles with bathroom are £42/65.

Bloomsbury Bloomsbury is very convenient, especially for the West End. It's a peculiar mix made up of London University, the British Museum, beautiful squares, Georgian architecture, traffic, office workers, students and tourists. It's definitely worth considering.

Tucked away to the north of Russell Square, around Cartwright Gardens, there is a group of the most comfortable, attractive and best value hotels in London, still within easy walking distance of the West End. They're on a crescent around a leafy garden, and although they aren't the cheapest places in London, they are worth it if you have the money to spend.

Jenkin's Hotel (☎ 0171-387 2067), 45 Cartwright Gardens WC1 (tube: Russell Square), has attractive, comfortable rooms with style. All have washbasin, TV, telephone and fridge, and prices include English breakfast. Singles/doubles are £39/52; doubles with private facilities are £62. Guests can even use the tennis courts in the gardens across the road.

The *Crescent Hotel* (☎ 0171-387 1515), 49 Cartwright Gardens WC1 (tube: Russell Square), is a bigger place, but is still a family-owned operation of a high standard, with basically the same prices as Jenkin's. The *Euro Hotel* (☎ 0171-387 4321) and *George Hotel* (0171-387 8777), both in Cartwright Gardens, are also good and are around the same price.

There's a row of places along Gower St, and they all seem to be pretty fair value. Not all of them have double glazing on the front windows, which is essential if you are sensitive to traffic noise. Insist on one of the back rooms overlooking the garden, which happen to be the nicest anyway.

The *Arran House Hotel* (☎ 0171-636 2186), 77 Gower St WC1 (tube: Goodge St), is a friendly, welcoming place with a great garden. Singles range from £31 to £41 (with shower and toilet), doubles from £46 to £61, and there are also triples and quads. They have sound-proofing on their front rooms, and all have colour TV and telephone. There are also laundry facilities.

The *Hotel Cavendish* (☎ 0171-636 9079), at No 75, and the *Jesmond Hotel* (☎ 0171-636 3199), at No 63, are fairly basic, but clean and entirely adequate. They have singles/doubles for £28/42. You share a bathroom, although all rooms have washbasin and you get a full English breakfast.

The *Repton Hotel* (☎ 0171-436 4922), 31 Bedford Place WC1 (tube: Russell Square), is pretty good value considering its position – Bedford Place is not nearly as busy as Gower St. There's a TV and telephone in every room; singles/doubles are £48/60.

They also have one dorm with six beds at £14 per person.

If all you want is a room, and you don't mind noise and primitive facilities, you'll be happy with the *Royal Hotel* (☎ 0171-636 8401), Woburn Place WC1 (tube: Russell Square). There certainly aren't many cheaper options, and it is clean enough. Singles/doubles are £18/36.

St Margaret's Hotel (☎ 0171-636 4277), 26 Bedford Place WC1B (tube: Russell Square), is in a classic Bloomsbury townhouse. It's not particularly inspirational, but it's very clean, family-run, the location is good, and it's not bad value. There's a TV and telephone in all rooms and some rooms have a private bathroom. Singles/doubles are £40/50.

The *Ruskin Hotel* (☎ 0171-636 7388), 23 Montague St WC1B , and its sister hotel *Haddon Hall Hotel* (☎ 0171-636 2474), 39 Bedford Place WC1B (tube: Holborn), are both fairly basic places with ordinary décor, but they have good locations and are entirely adequate (many rooms have private bathroom). Doubles with bathroom are £67; singles/doubles without are £39/55.

Short-Term Rental

Prices for rental accommodation are high and standards are low, but on the plus side, most places are fully furnished (including linen and crockery) so there aren't many things you have to buy.

At the bottom end of the market there are bedsits – a single furnished room, usually with a shared bathroom and kitchen, although some have basic cooking facilities. Expect to pay £50 to £100 per week. The next step up is a studio, which normally has a separate bathroom and kitchen, for between £75 and £120. One-bedroom flats average between £90 and £135. Shared houses and flats are the best value, with a bedroom for between £40 and £60 plus bills. Most landlords demand a security deposit (normally one month's rent) plus a month's rent in advance.

Rooms and flats are advertised at the *New Zealand News* UK office in the Royal Opera

Arcade behind New Zealand House, in *TNT Magazine*, *Time Out*, the *Evening Standard* and *Loot*. If you decide to use an agency, check that it doesn't charge fees to tenants; Jenny Jones (☎ 0171-493 4381) and Derek Collins (☎ 0171-930 2773) are free.

PLACES TO EAT

London is the culinary capital of the country. Virtually every national cuisine and cooking style is on offer – but at a price. In general, you'll be lucky to get a decent meal and a glass of wine for less than £10 per head, except in pubs where the food is usually very average. If you want to keep costs down, resist the temptation of alcohol, which is always expensive.

Restaurant chains such as Café Rouge, Café Flo, Dôme, Prêt à Manger, Café Pasta, Pizza Express, Nacho's and the Stockpot are popping up all over town and combine good-value food with pleasant, stylish surroundings. Indian restaurants are consistently good value; unfortunately they often tone down their spices for the English palate. Pasta places can be good, especially if they're run by Italians (a lot aren't). Chinese restaurants are also worth considering. It's very difficult to find good-quality English cuisine at a reasonable price.

There's a surprising lack of good guides to London restaurants; the best is the *Time Out Eating & Drinking in London Guide* (£7.50), but it doesn't have much for shoestringers and it's difficult to wade through. Harden's *Good Cheap Eats* (£4.95) is an annual guide to budget establishments.

There are a number of hunting grounds in the West End: around Covent Garden, especially north-east between Endell St and St Martin's Lane; around Soho, especially north-west of the intersection of Charing Cross Rd and Shaftesbury Ave (including Old Compton St and Frith St); north of Leicester Square on Lisle and Gerrard Sts (the main centre in London for Chinese restaurants).

Camden Town (NW1) has a cosmopolitan range of restaurants and cafés that can become very crowded at the weekend. The

✥✥✥✥✥✥✥✥✥✥✥✥✥✥✥✥✥✥✥✥✥✥✥

Time for Tea?
A great English tradition that still survives is 'afternoon tea'. It's a ritual in which every visitor should partake, although you'll need respectable clothes for the places mentioned below. A traditional tea includes a selection of delicate sandwiches (cucumber is a favourite), biscuits, gooey cakes, scones (with cream and jam) and pots of tea. Just a snack really.

The two most famous venues are Fortnum & Mason and the Ritz. *Fortnum's Fountain* (☎ 0171-734 8040), 181 Piccadilly W1 (tube: Piccadilly Circus), has afternoon tea for £10.50, and a champagne tea (!) for £15. These are served between 3 and 5 pm (not Sunday). *The Ritz* (☎ 0171-493 8181), Piccadilly W1 (tube: Piccadilly Circus), has afternoon tea between 2 and 6 pm for a bargain £17.50 per person. Booking is advised. ■

✥✥✥✥✥✥✥✥✥✥✥✥✥✥✥✥✥✥✥✥✥✥✥

hotel zone around Bayswater (W2) is well served by moderately priced restaurants along Queensway and Westbourne Grove. There are some interesting possibilities around Notting Hill. Earl's Court (SW5) is full of uninspiring budget eateries.

There are several places serving Indian food. Brick Lane (E1) in the East End, has a number of cheap but good Bangladeshi restaurants; in Stoke Newington, Church St (N16) has a row of interesting restaurants, some of which are Indian; and for South Indian menus, which are particularly good for vegetarians, there are some excellent places on Drummond St (NW1).

The Americanisation of British restaurants continues and theme restaurants are currently very popular. A family atmosphere and plenty of distractions are the main ingredients for their success, as well as good old American burgers, salads, fries, ice cream and shakes. The best-known places are Planet Hollywood on Leicester Square and the Hard Rock Café by Green Park.

Covent Garden
Budget Conscious Neal's Yard is a peaceful escape from the West End bustle. There are some good-value and healthy takeaway

places, all grouped around a flower-bedecked courtyard. *Neal's Yard Bakery & Tea Room* (☎ 0171-836 5199), 6 Neal's Yard (tube: Covent Garden), is the star performer, however. It has limited, but very good, wholefood vegetarian offerings around £3. Unfortunately, it's only open until 4.30 pm. Neal's Yard is signposted from Neal St, and is off Short's Gardens and Monmouth St.

Food for Thought (☎ 0171-836 0239), 31 Neal St WC2 (tube: Covent Garden), is a small and reliable vegetarian place. The menu features dishes like spinach and mushroom South Indian bake for £2.90, stir-fried vegetables for £2.70. It's nonsmoking, but you can bring your own bottle.

Diana's Diner (☎ 0171-240 0272), 39 Endell St (tube: Covent Garden), is very basic, but it's also very cheap. The food is not inspiring, but it's OK. Spaghetti is from £3.50 and you'll find a range of grills and roasts around £4.50. A few doors down at 27, *Designer Sandwiches* dishes up award-winning sandwiches for under £3.

Rock & Sole Plaice (☎ 0171-836 3785), 47 Endell St WC2 (tube: Covent Garden), is a no-nonsense fish & chip shop with basic formica tables. The average price is £7 and the fish is delicious. It is unlicensed but you can BYO.

Café in the Crypt (☎ 0171-839 4342), St Martin-in-the-Fields Church, on Trafalgar Square (tube: Charing Cross), is in an atmospheric crypt under the church. The food is good and there are plenty of offerings for vegetarians, but it can be a bit noisy and hectic. Most main dishes are from £5 to £6. Dinner is served daily between 5 and 7 pm.

Splashing Out *Café des Amis du Vin* (☎ 0171-379 3444), 11-14 Hanover Place WC2 (tube: Covent Garden), is very handy for pre or post-theatre meals. Each of its three floors has a different price range. The ground-floor brasserie is reliable and offers all the favourites: steak frites, quiches and omelettes cost between £4 and £7.50. Upstairs, in the more expensive eatery, a set meal, lunch or dinner, is £15.95.

Café Pelican (☎ 0171-379 0309), 45 St Martin's Lane WC2 (tube: Leicester Square), functions as a restaurant, brasserie and café bar. Its location, close to the English National Opera, is fantastic and it's a great people-watching spot, particularly in fine weather when you can sit at pavement tables. Inside it is rather like an ocean liner. There are reasonably priced snacks in the brasserie. More substantial French dishes are available from the restaurant where confit de canard, for example, is £9.25 and a good, complete meal costs around £20.

Calabash (☎ 0171-836 1976), in the Africa Centre, 38 King St WC2 (tube: Covent Garden), serves food from all over Africa. The menu describes dishes to the uninitiated; a typical dish is yassa (£6.50), chicken marinated with lemon juice and peppers, that hails from Senegal. There are beers from all over Africa and wines from Algeria, Zimbabwe and South Africa. A glass of house wine costs £1.60 and an average price for a meal is £15.

Chez Gerard (☎ 0171-379 0666), The Market, The Piazza WC2 (tube: Covent Garden), offers traditional French fare such as steak frites. The restaurant has a balcony overlooking the opera house but tables can't be reserved. Main dishes range from £9-15.

Joe Allen (☎ 0171-836 0651), 13 Exeter St WC2 (tube: Covent Garden), is a star-spotter's paradise. Theatre posters adorn the walls and the tables are covered by gingham at lunchtime and white table cloths and candles at night. There is a jolly buzz to the atmosphere here and it gets crowded, so book. Starters and main dishes (lamb chops, grilled halibut, vegetarian, etc) are varied. A three-course meal will come to at least £20.

Rules (☎ 0171-836 5314), 35 Maiden Lane WC2 (tube: Covent Garden), is very British; there's an Edwardian interior and waiters proudly wear starched white aprons. The menu is very meat orientated but fresh-water fish is also available. Puddings are traditional: trifles, pies and an abundance of custard. Prices are steep (main courses start from £13) but the quality and feel of the place make up for it.

The Ivy (☎ 0171-836 4751), 1 West St

WC2 (tube: Leicester Square), is showbizzy and an event in itself. The menu is modern British and lists dishes such as steak tartare, cumberland sausages, onions and mash. Some Mediterranean dishes also feature: grilled haloumi with roast peppers and tapenade, tomato and basil galette. Desserts include tiramisu and sticky toffee pudding. It is a pricey outing (expect to pay £30 per person) but it's ideal for a special occasion.

Taking the huge elevator down to the basement and walking through the immense kitchens is all part of the appeal at *Belgo Centraal* (0171-813 2223), 50 Earlham St WC2 (tube: Covent Garden). The waiters at this Belgian restaurant are dressed as monks and the décor is steel. Moules, spit-roasts and lager are the speciality and this is the only restaurant in town to have a menu of 100 different flavoured lagers including banana, peach and cherry. Set menus range from £5 to £12; 'Beat the Clock' runs Monday to Friday from 6 to 8 pm and means that the time you sit down is the price you pay for your main dish.

Soho

Soho is the gastronomic centre of London with numerous restaurants and numerous cuisines to choose from. There are also some interesting cafés that spill out onto the street, especially around the corner of Frith and Old Compton Sts.

Two old-timers, veritable institutions in fact, are *Bar Italia* (☎ 0171-437 4520), 22 Frith St W1 (tube: Tottenham Court Rd), which is crowded and boisterous, and the home of London's first decent coffee; and *Patisserie Valerie* (☎ 0171-823 9971), 44 Old Compton St W1 (tube: Tottenham Court Rd), which is famous for its artistic and calorie-busting cakes.

Budget Conscious You can get a 10-course all-you-can-eat Chinese lunch or dinner buffet for £4.50 at *Mr Wu* (☎ 0171-839 6669) 6-7 Irving St WC2 (tube: Leicester Square). Even if the price goes up a little, this is still a good deal for anyone with an appetite.

Poons (☎ 0171-437 4549), 27 Lisle St WC2 (tube: Leicester Square), is where the upmarket Poons empire started. It's tiny, with classic laminex tables and fluorescent lights, but it has exceptional food at very good prices. They specialise in superb wind-dried meats. The dried duck is heavenly, and the steamed chicken is equally sensational. If you're hungry, start with soup and order perhaps two dishes and rice – you'll pay around £9 per person. Be prepared to queue at busy times, and to be hustled out the door pretty quickly.

Wong Kei (☎ 0171-437 6833), 41 Wardour St W1 (tube: Leicester Square), is famous for the rudeness of the waiters. Some find this adds to the experience, but even if you don't, you might be tempted by the food, which is cheap and good Cantonese. Set menus start at £5 for a minimum of two people.

Nusa Dua (☎ 0171-437 3559), 11 Dean St W1 (tube: Tottenham Court Rd), is a rather garish Indonesian restaurant, but the prices are very reasonable and the food is superb. Share a few main courses and you'll spend around £10 each. The tofu and tempeh are excellent and there are plenty of vegetarian offerings.

Pizza Express (☎ 0171-437 9595), 10 Dean St W1 (tube: Tottenham Court Rd), might not sound very appealing, but it is in fact unusually good. At street level you get cheap, good-quality pizzas from £3.40 to £7 and a glass of wine for £2.10; downstairs you eat to the accompaniment of excellent jazz (admission downstairs is between £8 and £20).

Tokyo Diner (☎ 0171-287 8777), 2 Newport Place WC2 (tube: Leicester Square), is great place to stop off for a quick bowl of noodles or plate of sushi before the cinema or theatre. It's good value.

Pollo (☎ 0171-734 5917), 20 Old Compton St W1 (tube: Leicester Square), attracts an art-student crowd with numerous pastas for around £3. It can be very busy.

Stepping into the *New Piccadilly* (☎ 0171-437 8530), 8 Denman St (tube: Piccadilly Circus), is like stepping into a time warp – nothing, except the prices, has changed since it first opened in the 1950s. Even the prices haven't changed as much as you would expect: pastas and pizzas are around £3.50, chicken and steaks weigh in at around £4.50.

Melati (☎ 0171-437 2745), 21 Great Windmill St W1 (tube: Piccadilly Circus), is a highly acclaimed South-East Asian restaurant with excellent food and a good range of options for vegetarians. Various noodle and rice dishes are around £5. You'll probably spend around £12.

Mildred's (☎ 0171-494 1634), 58 Greek St W1 (tube: Tottenham Court Rd), is only small, so you may well share a table. The chaos is worth it, however, because the vegetarian food is both good and well priced. Expect to pay around £4.50 for a main meal with delicious fresh flavours, £2.10 for a glass of wine.

The *Living Room*, Bateman St between Frith and Greek Sts W1 (tube: Tottenham Court Rd), is a unique oasis and, although it is favoured by the young and the hip of Soho, it's not intimidating. It's basically a coffee shop with meat and vegetarian sandwiches under £4, but there are comfortable sofas at the back.

Gopal's of Soho (☎ 0171-434 1621), 12 Bateman St W1 (tube: Tottenham Court Rd), is quite cramped but offers delicately spiced food at affordable prices. Thalis (set meals) are good value; £10.75 for vegetarian and £1 more for the meat equivalent. A glass of house wine is £1.95.

Bunjies (☎ 0171-240 1796), 27 Litchfield St WC2 (tube: Leicester Square), is a folk club tucked away off Charing Cross Rd where you can also get cheap and reasonable vegetarian food. Most main dishes are around £4.

Wagamamas (☎ 0171-292 0990), 10A Lexington St W1 (tube: Piccadilly Circus) is not the place to go for a quiet dinner. Loud and fun with great Japanese food, you have to share tables and may have to queue. Main dishes range from £4 to £7.

The Sports Café (☎ 0171-839 8300), 80 Haymarket SW1 (tube: Piccadilly Circus) is a multi-sports theme bar. There's a restaurant, dance floor and acres of memorabilia. You can't get away from sport here: a TV on your table keeps you occupied while you await your burger and chips for around £8. Not far away, at 57-60 Haymarket, is *Football, Football* (☎ 0171-839 9317). No prizes for guessing the theme here. There's a bar and 330-seat restaurant. It's a fun place to go but the Anglo-American food is quite expensive at around £9 for most main dishes.

Arnie, Bruce and Sly's adventure into the restaurant world has been an international success. Be prepared to queue at *Planet Hollywood* (☎ 0171-287 1000), 13 Coventry St W1 (tube: Leicester Sq). There's standard American fare at Beverly Hills prices.

Nearby at 5-6 Coventry St the girls are fighting back at the newly opened *Fashion Café* (☎ 0171-287 5888). It's owned by supermodels Naomi Campbell, Claudia Schiffer, Christy Turlington and Elle MacPherson.

Splashing Out The *French House Dining Room* (☎ 0171-437 2477), 49 Dean St W1 (tube: Tottenham Court Rd), is on the 1st floor of a typically old-fashioned Soho pub. Upstairs is a tiny, high-ceilinged room with a convivial atmosphere. There is a short, changing-daily menu which offers robust English food. Typical examples are roast duck for £12 and grilled lamb chump and lentils for £9.50. They have an excellent range of British cheeses. Booking is advised.

The *Atlantic Bar & Grill* (☎ 0171-734 4888), is at 20 Glasshouse St W1 (tube: Piccadilly Circus). High ceilings, a large dining area and two bars make the Atlantic a very buzzy and atmospheric place to eat. Food is expensive (£14 for a main course) and you must book at the weekend. Last booking is for 11.30 pm; a cheaper bar menu is available until 2 am.

Chiang Mai (☎ 0171-437 7444), 48 Frith St W1 (tube: Tottenham Court Rd), is a top-class Thai restaurant with a separate vegetarian menu and a wide range of soups. Meat eaters should try kratong tong (curried meat wrapped in cases of batter). There are set menus from £40/30 for two people.

Dell 'Ugo (☎ 0171-734 8300), 56 Frith St W1 (tube: Tottenham Court Rd), has had fluctuating reports on its food, but the atmosphere appeals to many customers. It is on three floors: a café and bar on the ground floor, then a bistro on the second floor and a restaurant on the third level. The menu is the same throughout: Mediterranean in flavour; expect to pay around £25 for a meal.

The Gay Hussar (☎ 0171-437 0973), 2 Greek St W1 (tube: Tottenham Court Rd), keeps to a familiar format which makes it a regular haunt for many. It is now in its fifth decade and offers a wide range of Hungarian dishes. There are firm favourites, like the veal goulash which costs £14.75 (vegetables are extra). The extras could make this an expensive trip, but it is a unique gastronomic experience within a rich and decorous setting.

A particularly good way to sample the best of Chinese cuisine is to partake in Cantonese dim sum. This consists of selecting numerous small dishes and relaxing with a pot of jasmine tea. If you feel unsure of what to choose, the *Chuen Cheng Ku* (☎ 0171-437 1398), 17 Wardour St W1 (tube: Leicester Square), is ideal. Open daily from 11 am to midnight, all the dishes – dumplings, paper-wrapped prawns and numerous other delicacies – are trundled around on heavily laden trolleys. The same kind of fare can be found next door at the *Jade Garden* (☎ 0171-439 7851), 15 Wardour St W1. Here you order from the menu. A set meal for two at both places is around £20.

Mezzo (☎ 0171-314 4000), 100 Wardour St W1 (tube Piccadilly Circus) is another of Terence Conran's successful ventures which attracts London's media crowd – and those with aspirations. Nevertheless, it's a fun place to eat. Upstairs is more casual and better value: about £6 for a main course. It can be very busy: at a weekend they often do over 1000 covers per evening.

St James's
Budget Conscious *The Wren at St James* (☎ 0171-437 9419), 35 Jermyn St SW3

(tube: Piccadilly Circus), is the perfect escape from the West End, but it is only open during the day. It adjoins St James church (which often has free lunch-time concerts) and in summer it spills out into the shady churchyard. There are plenty of vegetarian dishes for around £3.50, and excellent home-made cakes.

Fans of *Grease* will enjoy the *Rock Island Diner* (☎ 0171-287 5500), 2nd Floor, London Pavilion W1 (tube: Piccadilly Circus). A resident DJ plays 60s and 70s hits. The food is typically American and there's dancing in the aisles!

Splashing Out Also right on Piccadilly Circus, *The Criterion* (☎ 0171-930 0488) has a spectacular interior and quite an atmosphere, so you won't feel comfortable if you look like a scuzzball. The menu offers fashionable Mediterranean-style food like sauteed goat's cheese and roasted peppers, but there are also some British classics like fish & chips. Main courses are from £10.50 to £15.

The original *Hard Rock Café* (☎ 0171-629 0382), 150 Old Park Lane W1 (tube: Hyde Park Corner) is now over 25 years old and as popular as ever.

Quaglino's (☎ 0171-930 6767), 16 Bury St W1 (tube: Piccadilly Circus) has remained constantly popular since its relaunch back in 1993. The food is good but still manages to be outdone by the atmosphere which is busy, fun and glamorous. Main dishes start at £13.

Bloomsbury & Holborn
Budget Conscious *Wagamama* (☎ 0171-323 9223), 4 Streatham St off Coptic St WC1 (tube: Tottenham Court Rd), is a deservedly successful Japanese restaurant. It's spartan and people share long tables. The food is generous, delicious and cheap. Main dishes cost around £5.

The Greenhouse (☎ 0171-637 8038), 16 Chenies St WC1 (tube: Goodge St), is part of the Drill Hall complex. It's busy, so expect to share a table. The reason it's busy is the excellent vegetarian food, with main courses for £3.95. The paintings on the wall are for sale.

The *North Sea Fish Restaurant* (☎ 0171-387 5892), 7 Leigh St WC1 (tube: Russell Square), sets out to cook fresh fish and potatoes well – a limited ambition, but one that British fish & chip shops rarely achieve. The North Sea does. The fish (deep-fried or grilled) and a huge serving of chips will set you back from £6 to £7.

Mille Pini (☎ 0171-242 2434), 33 Boswell St WC1 (tube: Holborn), is a true Italian restaurant with reasonable prices. You'll waddle out, but you'll only spend about £10 if you have two courses and coffee.

October Gallery (☎ 0171-242 7367), 24 Old Gloucester St WC1 (tube; Russell Square), is, as the name suggests, based within a small gallery. It is only open for lunch and has a varied daily menu catering to both meat-eaters and vegetarians. On warm days, take advantage of the courtyard. Meals are around £6.

If you think you can pass yourself off as a taxi driver, try the *London Taxi Centre* at 7 Herbrand St WC1 (tube: Russell Square). The cafeteria is on the second floor and serves classic meals like pie, mashed potatoes and eggs for around £4. Tea is only 25p and sandwiches and salads are also available.

Splashing Out The *Museum Street Café* (☎ 0171-405 3211), 47 Museum St WC1 (tube: Tottenham Court Rd), is packed at lunchtimes and less busy in the evening. Cooking, like the interior, is straightforward. Freshly cooked ingredients combine to offer char-grilled fish and snappy salsas. Lunch set meals are cheaper but a three-course meal in the evening will cost £21.50. It is licensed but you can BYO for a £5 corkage charge.

Bayswater
There are literally dozens of places on Queensway and Westbourne Grove – from cheap takeaways to good quality restaurants. Surprisingly, there are even some decent restaurants on the 2nd floor of Whiteley's

shopping centre, although they are not particularly cheap.

Budget Conscious The cheapest pit-stop on Queensway is *Quick* at No 92, near the intersection with Moscow Rd, which has fish & chips with salad for £3.50 and pizza with salad for £1.

For something more interesting, try *The Mandola* (☎ 0171-229 4734), 139 Westbourne Grove W2 (tube: Bayswater), which offers vegetarian Sudanese dishes like tamiya, a kind of felafel, for £3.50 and meat dishes for £6. The portions are small so it would be better value if a couple were sharing dishes.

Micro-Kalamaris (☎ 0171-727 9122), 66 Inverness Mews W2 (tube: Bayswater), is the cheaper, unlicensed sibling of the licensed Mega-Kalamaris in the same mews, parallel to Queensway. Conditions are a bit micro, but the food is macro. A set menu is £25.

Khan's (☎ 0171-727 5420), 13 Westbourne Grove W2 (tube: Bayswater), is one of the largest and best Indian restaurants – it's authentic, the décor is smart and it's good value. They have vegetarian dishes and a selection of meat curries for around £4.

Nachos (☎ 0171-792 0954), 147 Notting Hill Gate W11 (tube: Notting Hill Gate), is a large and popular Mexican joint with better than average quality at decent prices.

Splashing Out *Inaho* (☎ 0171-221 8495), 4 Hereford Rd W2 (tube: Bayswater), is a tiny Japanese restaurant. A tempura set dinner consists of an appetiser, soup, mixed salad, yakitori, sashimi, tempura, rice and seasonal fruits. This costs £20. There is also a teriyaki equivalent for £22.

L'accento (☎ 0171-243 2201), 16 Garway Rd W2 (tube: Bayswater), has a stylish interior and offers a two-course set menu for £10.50. This could include mussel stew in white wine and fresh herbs, followed by grilled pork chop filled with sundried tomatoes and leeks. If you step away from this menu it is quite expensive.

Veronica's (☎ 0171-229 5079), 3 Hereford Rd W2 (tube: Bayswater), is trying to establish that England does have a culinary heritage and, at the same time, promote healthy eating. This might sound like a dull proposition, but there are some fascinating dishes and the restaurant has won many awards. A three-course set menu is £15.

Notting Hill & Ladbroke Grove

Budget Conscious Portobello has plenty of trendy bars and restaurants; *Café Grove* at the Ladbroke Grove end of Portobello, with a verandah overlooking the action has cheap and cheerful vegetarian food at around £5.

Costa's Grill (☎ 0171-229 3794), 14 Hillgate St W8 (tube: Notting Hill Gate), is a reliable Greek place, with dips at £1.50 and mains like souvlaki for £4.50.

Prost (0171-727 9620), 35 Pembridge Rd W11 (tube: Notting Hill Gate), is a small one-up one-down restaurant serving traditional German cuisine. Main courses are under £10; venison in red wine with blueberry sauce, for example, is £8.25 but between 5.30 and 11 pm any two courses are £8.95. Dinner is served daily but it's only open for lunch on Saturday and Sunday.

Modhubon (☎ 0171-243 1778), 29 Pembridge Rd W11 (tube: Notting Hill Gate), has been recommended for its inexpensive Indian food. Main dishes are under £5 and a set lunch is £3.90.

All Saints (☎ 0171-243 2808), 12 All Saints Rd W11, is a café especially popular on Saturday during the Portobello Rd Market.

Across the road, *Geales* (☎ 0171-727 7969), 2 Farmer St W8 (tube: Notting Hill Gate), is a very popular fish restaurant in the old-fashioned English style. The fish is priced according to weight and season, and is always fresh. Fish & chips average out at about £7 a person, which is a lot more than you'd pay in a fish shop, but worth it. It's closed on Sunday.

Splashing Out *Kensington Place* (☎ 0171-727 3184), 201 Kensington Church St W8 (tube: Notting Hill Gate), has an impressive glass front and a design-conscious interior – providing the perfect backdrop for a special meal. Starters start at £4 and main courses from £9. A wide range of dishes (meat, fish and vegetarian) are available as well as daily specials. The average price for a meal is about £25.

W11 (☎ 0171-229 8889), 123a Clarendon Rd W11 (tube: Holland Park), produces a menu of excellent modern British/European food – despite the weird Egyptianish interior. An average meal, including a bottle of house wine, will set you back £20 to £25 per person.

The Ark (☎ 0171-229 4024), 122 Palace Gardens Terrace W8 (tube: Notting Hill), is an old survivor, but with a relaxed and pleasant atmosphere. The food is French – good quality, simple, and reasonably priced. Most mains are from £8 to £10. Booking is recommended.

Pomme d'Amour (☎ 0171-229 8532), 128 Holland Park Ave W11 (tube: Holland Park), is a charming, sophisticated French restaurant with main courses priced at around £9.

Hammersmith & Fulham

Splashing Out *Deals* (☎ 0181-563 1001), The Broadway Centre W6 (tube: Hammersmith Broadway), offers good value food (£8 for a main dish) and a menu for everyone. There's some seating outside, a cocktail bar upstairs and a happy hour in the early evening.

Kartouche (☎ 0171-823 3515), 329 Fulham Rd SW10, (tube; South Kensington), is Fulham Rd's most popular restaurant for the 20-40s age group. Food and service are both good and there's a downstairs bar for pre or post-dinner drinks. Main courses average £10.

The River Café (☎ 0171-381 8824), Thames Wharf, Rainville Rd W6 (tube: Hammersmith) has a fabulous location on the Thames, and serves what is probably the best nouvelle Italian cuisine in London. It's not cheap – main dishes start at £17.

Pimlico

Budget Conscious *Manners* (☎ 0171-828 2471), 1 Denbigh St SW1 (tube: Victoria), offers a decent range of dishes at a very good price: starters are £2, and a three-course £8 set dinner is £5 between 5.30 and 8 pm. Lunch is £5. Closed Sunday.

O Sole Mio (☎ 0171-976 6887), 39 Churton St SW1 (tube: Victoria), is a standard, decent-value Italian restaurant with pizzas and pastas under £6. Next door, *Grumbles* is a pleasant wine bar with, amongst other things, vegetable risotto for £5.95, kebabs for £6.25, entrecote steak £9.95.

Splashing Out *Mekong* (☎ 0171-834 6896), 46 Churton St SW1 (tube: Victoria), is reputed to be one of the best Vietnamese restaurants in London. They have a set meal for £12 for a minimum of two persons, and house wine is reasonable at £1.70 per glass. Booking is advised.

Knightsbridge
Budget Conscious There's a definite Continental feel to *Patisserie Valerie* (☎ 0171-823 9971), 215 Brompton Rd SW5 (tube Knightsbridge), a wonderful place to stop for a coffee and pastry or light snack. Breakfast is popular at the weekend (£4.80 for full English) and newspapers are provided.

Pizza on the Park (☎ 0171-235 5273), 11 Knightsbridge SW5 (tube: Hyde Park Corner), is really popular for its pizzas and jazz in the basement. There's also a spacious restaurant upstairs and, if you're lucky, a few tables overlooking Hyde Park. Pizzas average £6.50.

Splashing Out *The Fifth Floor at Harvey Nichols* (☎ 0171-235 5250), Knightsbridge SW1 (tube: Knightsbridge) is the perfect place to drop after you've shopped. It's expensive – main courses cost between £10 and £15.

Chelsea & Kensington
Budget Conscious The *Chelsea Kitchen* (☎ 0171-589 1330), 98 King's Rd SW3 (tube: Sloane Square), has some of the cheapest food in London – and it ain't half bad. The surroundings are pretty spartan,

however. Minestrone soup is 70p, spaghetti is £2 and apple crumble is 80p.

At 5 Kings Rd, *New Culture Revolution* (☎ 0171-352 9281) (tube: Sloane Square) is a trendy but good-value dumpling and noodle bar. Top to bottom windows at the front mean that the restaurant is bright – you eat in full view of passers-by. Main dishes cost around £6.

If the weather is decent make for the Chelsea Farmers' Market on Sydney St. There are a number of small stalls that spill out into a pleasant outdoor area. Among them, the *Sydney St Café* has burgers and steak sandwiches for around £6. The *Il Cappuccino* has coffee for £1.

Popular with the 20-35s, *Henry J Bean's* (☎ 0171-352 9255), 195 King's Rd SW3 (tube: Sloane Square), is an American bar and restaurant, one of the few London places to have a garden. Music and a happy hour give this place a fun atmosphere. Main dishes are from £5 to £8.

Wodka (☎ 0171-937 6513), 12 St Albans Grove W8 (tube: High St Kensington), lies in a quiet residential area away from the hustle and bustle of High St Ken. Its décor is plain and the food is Polish. Blinis range from £4.90 to £6.50. A large array of vodkas is available.

A British version of the American diner, the *Chelsea Bun* (☎ 0171-352 3635), Limerston St SW10 (tube: Earl's Court) is brilliant value. Breakfast is served all day, and there's seating on the upstairs veranda. Main dishes cost between £4 and £7.

Owned by members of the England rugby team, *Shoeless Joes* (☎ 0171-384 2333), 555 King's Rd SW5 (tube: Fulham Broadway) is another sports-theme restaurant.

Cuba (☎ 0171-938 4137), 11 Kensington High St (tube: High St Kensington), offers a wide selection of tapas, steak sandwiches – even roasts, all reasonably priced. It's a trendy, friendly restaurant. Downstairs there's a live band or a DJ every night and dancing until 2 am. A three-course meal with wine for two people is about £35.

Spago (☎ 0171-225 2407), 6 Glendower Place SW7 (tube: South Kensington), is the best value restaurant in the vicinity, which can be reflected in queues. The reason? A good range of pastas and pizzas from £4.

Daquise (☎ 0171-589 6117), 20 Thurloe St SW7 (tube: South Kensington), is very close to the museums. It's a Polish place, rather shabby-looking but with a good range of vodkas and good food. A set lunch is £6.60.

Splashing Out *Oriel* (☎ 0171-730 2804), 50 Sloane Sq SW1 (tube: Sloane Square), is a perfect place to meet before you go shopping in King's Road. The Brasserie has tables overlooking the square. Main dishes are £7.

The Canteen (☎ 0171-351 7330), Chelsea Harbour SW10, is Michael Caine's well-known restaurant. There's a good traditional British and French menu. The décor may not be to everyone's taste but the location and service are good.

The Collection (☎ 0171-225 2641), 64 Brompton Rd SW3 (tube: South Kensington), is in a great location in a converted gallery. The main restaurant is on a balcony overlooking the bar where you can also have a snack for about £5 although drinks are expensive. This is one for people who want to see and be seen.

In a very pretty setting in the heart of South Kensington, *Daphne's* (☎ 0171-589 4257), 110-112 Draycott Ave (tube: South Kensington), is small enough to be cosy but not claustrophobic. They do delicious Mediterranean-style food; booking is a must. It's very popular with the who's who crowd.

Launceston Place (☎ 0171-937 4912), 1A Launceston Place W8 (tube: High St Kensington), is tucked away in the back streets of Kensington. It's a pretty and intimate restaurant which has no pretence. The food is Continental and quite expensive, although they do set dinners for £14.50 and £17.50. Perfect for dinner à deux.

Earl's Court
Budget Conscious *Benjy's*, 157 Earl's Court Rd SW5 (tube: Earl's Court), is an institution. It's really nothing more than a

fairly traditional café, but it's always busy and although the food is nothing to write home about, it is cheap and filling. Serious breakfasts with as much tea or coffee as you can drink are around £3.50. There are grills for around £4.

Nando's (☎ 0171-259 2544), 204 Earl's Court Rd SW5 (tube: Earl's Court) serves Portuguese-style cooking concentrating on chicken dishes, all flame-grilled. A meal with a drink costs around £5.

Krungtap (☎ 0171-259 2314), 227 Old Brompton Rd SW10 (tube: Earl's Court), is a busy, friendly Thai restaurant. Most dishes are £3 to £4. Portions are generous although beer is expensive.

The *Troubadour* (☎ 0171-370 1434), 265 Old Brompton Rd (tube: Earl's Court), has an illustrious history as a coffee shop and folk venue. Amongst others it has hosted Dylan, Donovan and Lennon. These days they still occasionally have bands, and they also have good-value food. Service is slow, but the wait is worthwhile; order at the counter. Vegetable soup is £1.85, pasta is £4.

Splashing Out *Mr Wing* (☎ 0171-370 4450), 242-244 Old Brompton Rd (tube: Earl's Court) is one of London's best Chinese restaurants. Make sure you get a seat in the jungle-styled basement. The food is expensive but very good.

Camden
Budget Conscious A quiet place is the *El Parador* (☎ 0171-387 2789), 245 Eversholt St (tube: Camden Town). There's a good vegetarian selection including quesos (cheese dish) for £3.50, with meat and fish dishes just a little more expensive.

The Raj (☎ 0171-388 6663), 19 Camden High St (tube: Camden Town) is a small Indian place with all-you-can-eat lunch and dinner buffets for £3.50 and £3.75 respectively.

Ruby in the Dust (☎ 0171-485 2744), 102 Camden High St (tube: Camden Town), is a cheerful and atmospheric bar/café. There isn't a huge menu, but it's interesting:

Mexican snacks, soup for £2.85 and mains like mussels and noodles for £5.45.

Silks & Spice (☎ 0171-267 5751), 28 Chalk Farm Rd, is a Thai/Malay restaurant with main dishes around £5.

Marine Ices (☎ 0171-485 3132), 8 Haverstock Hill NW3 (tube: Chalk Farm), as the name suggests, started as an ice-cream parlour but has been successful on the savoury front for quite some time. The options are pizzas and pastas at around £5. There are also meat dishes which cost more, but it is imperative that you try one of the amazing ice creams to round off the meal.

Primrose Brasserie (☎ 0171-483 3765), 101 Regents Park NW1 (tube: Chalk Farm) serves good value Polish food, such as salt beef. Starters cost from £2 and mains dishes from £4.50, and it's BYO.

Lemonia (☎ 0171-586 7454), 89 Regent's Park Rd NW1 (tube: Chalk Farm), is always busy and it is advisable to book. It is close to the delights of Primrose Hill and offers good-value food and a lively atmosphere. Meze costs £10.50 per person and both the vegetarian and meat moussakas for £6.60 are particularly tasty.

Bar Gansa (☎ 0171-267 8909), 2 Inverness St NW1 (tube: Camden) is an arty but fun tapas bar with dishes around £3. There's a £10 a head set menu for groups. The service is good and the staff friendly.

Bintang (☎ 0171-284 1640), 93 Kentish Town Rd NW1 (tube: Camden Town), is a small and tackily decorated South-East Asian restaurant. This may not sound too promising but the food is generally delicious and reasonably priced. The service leaves something to be desired but at an average of £10 a head and BYO it is worth experiencing. If the décor does offend there is always the option of a takeaway service. Open Tuesday to Sunday from 6 to 11.30 pm.

You can enjoy potent £4 Caribbean cocktails at *Cottons Rhum Shop, Bar & Restaurant*, 55 Chalk Farm Rd NW1. The *Marathon* is an infamous late night source of kebabs and beer.

Splashing Out *Belgo Noord* (☎ 0171-267 0718), 72 Chalk Farm Rd NW1 (tube: Chalk Farm), is a beautifully designed Belgian fish restaurant/bar. Waiters wear monks' habits and despite the place's trendiness and popularity the food is really good value. If you're unsure, go for the set menu: a starter, a beer, a bowl of mussels and chips for £12. They have three sittings, but it is still necessary to book in advance. There's another branch in WC2.

Café Delancey (☎ 0171-387 1985), 3 Delancey St NW1 (tube: Camden Town), offers the opportunity to get a decent cup of coffee, accompanied (or not) by a snack or a full meal in a relaxed European-style brasserie. There is a supply of newspapers on hand. The menu runs from breakfast to supper, with daily specials on the blackboard. Main dishes are from £7 to £12 and wine starts at £6.50.

Primates (☎ 0171-284 1059), 257 Royal College St NW1 (tube: Camden Town), is a quirky restaurant, slightly off the beaten track. It is not inexpensive, with prices around £20, but the food is both good and generous. Closed Sunday.

Vegetarian Cottage (☎ 0171-586 1257), 91 Haverstock Hill NW3 (tube: Chalk Farm), is a good-quality vegetarian restaurant. The cottage special is particularly delicious: it combines mushrooms, lotus roots, Buddha's cushion fungus, nuts and vegetables, all wrapped in a lotus leaf. Expect to pay a total of around £15.

Hampstead & Islington

Budget Conscious *Coffee Cup* (☎ 0171-435 7565), 74 Hampstead High St NW3 (tube: Hampstead), is a popular café with a wide-ranging menu from bacon and eggs to pasta. There's something for every taste and every time of day. Good value.

The *Everyman Café* (☎ 0171-431 2123), Holly Bush Vale NW3 (tube: Hampstead), is attached to the cinema of the same name. If you're looking for a quiet place to eat in Hampstead, with reasonable food, this is a good choice. The three-course set menu is £7.

If shopping for arts and antiques in Camden Passage, consider a meal at *Le*

Sacre-Coeur Bistro (☎ 0171-354 2618), 18 Theberton St, a turning off the other side of Upper St a little north of the Business Design Centre. A set lunch is £6, mussels and pancake dishes are £3.95.

East End & The Docklands
Budget Conscious *Ravi Shankar* (☎ 0171-833 5849), 422 St John St EC1 (tube: Angel), is a small but inexpensive restaurant favoured by vegetarians – their all-you-can-eat lunch-time buffets for £4.50 are extremely popular. They have another branch at 133 Drummond St NW1 (tube: Warren St).

There are a number of cheap Bangladeshi restaurants on Brick Lane, including *Aladin* (☎ 0171-247 8210) at 132 and *Nazrul* (☎ 0171-247 2505) at 130 (tube: Aldgate East). Both are unlicensed, but you should eat for around £7. Many people believe this is the best subcontinental food in London.

Brick Lane Beigel Bake (☎ 0171-729 0616), 159 Brick Lane E1 (tube: Liverpool St), is at the Bethnal Green Rd end of Brick Lane – and open 24 hours. You won't find bagels better, fresher or cheaper.

Splashing Out Terence Conran, furniture retailer and restaurateur, who helped to set up the Design Museum in the Docklands, has located some of his excellent, expensive restaurants in the vicinity. These include the *Blueprint Café* (☎ 0171-378 7031), which is actually on top of the Design Museum. Expect to pay around £35 for a meal here with wine.

The Apprentice (☎ 0171-234 0254), 31 Shad Thames SE7 (tube: Tower Hill), is so named because trainee chefs practice here. Prices are lower than the neighbouring Conran restaurants, with main dishes between £7 and £15 and a set lunch for £9.50.

Waterloo & Brixton
Budget Conscious *The Fire Station* (☎ 0171-401 3267), 150 Waterloo Rd SE1 (tube: Waterloo) is in a part of town that has long been a culinary desert. The Fire Station

(and it once was) is convenient for the South Bank. There's a lively atmosphere and the bar is pleasant enough to make the wait for a table enjoyable. There's a varied menu with reasonable prices (£7 to £10 for a main meal).

For a quieter, more intimate atmosphere try the *Bar Central* (☎ 0171-928 5086) at 131 Waterloo Rd E1 (tube: Waterloo). Despite the name, this is actually a restaurant with a small bar. Main courses cost around £7 and the service is efficient.

Try *Pizzeria Franco* (☎ 0171-738 3021), 4 Market Row, Brixton for the best pizzas and cappuccinos in south London; and the *Phoenix*, 441 Coldharbour Lane, Brixton for a classic and reliable caff.

ENTERTAINMENT
The essential tool is *Time Out* (£1.70), which is published every Tuesday and covers a week of events. The only danger is that there is so much happening you'll be paralysed with indecision.

The biggest problem is transport. The last underground trains leave between 11.30 pm and 12.30 am (depending on the station and line), so you either have to figure out the night buses or pay for a minicab. The second-biggest problem is that most pubs close at 11 pm – that's not a misprint! Fortunately, there are clubs where you can continue partying, although you'll have to pay to enter (£5 to £10) and the drinks are always expensive.

Late-night venues often choose to have a 'club' licence, which means you have to be a member to enter. In practice, they usually include the membership fee as part of the admission price. Many venues have clubs that only operate one night a week, and have a particular angle – whether it be the style of music they play or the kind of people they attract.

They can change with bewildering speed – and they sometimes use the membership requirement to exclude people they don't think will fit in. In some places you'll be excluded if you wear jeans, runners (trainers) and a T-shirt; in others you'll be excluded if you don't. It's not a bad idea to phone in advance to get an idea of cost and membership policy.

London theatre, music and dance are extraordinarily diverse, high quality (at their best) and extremely reasonably priced by world standards. It would be a crime not to organise yourself tickets for one or two of the best productions, even if you don't normally go to the theatre. The National Theatre puts on consistently good performances, often with some of the best young actors and directors around, and the Royal Shakespeare Company is also consistently excellent. Numerous cheap ticket offers are listed in *Time Out*. See the Theatre section later for information on the Leicester Square Theatre Ticket Booth, which sells half-price tickets for West End productions on the day of performance.

Pubs & Bars

Pubs are perhaps the most distinctive contribution the English have made to urban life – and nothing really compares to a good one. Traditionally the 'local' has been at the hub of the community, and in many parts of London this tradition is very much alive.

Perhaps partly because of the cramped and low-quality housing many people live in, the pub becomes a virtual extension of their homes – a combination lounge room, and long-running, though usually low-key, party. The 'regulars' become members of an extended gregarious family, although, curiously, relationships often do not extend beyond the door of the pub. Finding a local where you feel comfortable is the first step to being a real Londoner.

These days, a 'traditional' London pub is likely to have antipodean bar staff, and noisy 'fruit' (slot) machines competing with a TV and a juke box. Most will sell a good range of beers, and some sort of cheap and filling bar food, although in the traditional pub this will be, at best, limited. Their main aim is to sell beer. When you fall out of the pub at 11 pm, you adjourn to the nearest curry house for more beer and some real sustenance.

Bars are starting to outnumber pubs in some parts of London. You pay more for a drink (beer may not be on tap) and the fridges are full of designer drinks. However, the stylish décor, late opening hours and more upmarket atmosphere attract the upwardly-mobile 20-35s. Some bars have a DJ at weekends and make a door charge. Pitcher & Piano and All Bar One are fast-growing chains. Dôme and Café Rouge are more like continental brasseries – you can just drink, have a snack or eat a decent meal.

Sampling a range of pubs and bars is an essential duty for every visitor to London. The following brief list of suggestions will be no substitute for careful individual research!

West End & Soho

Coach & Horses, 29 Greek St W1 (tube: Leicester Square) – a small, busy pub that has a regular clientele, but is nonetheless hospitable to visitors; made famous by alcoholic *Spectator* columnist Jeffrey Bernard.

Dog & Duck, 18 Bateman St W1 (tube: Tottenham Court Rd) – tiny, but it retains much of its old character and has loyal locals.

Riki Tik, 23 Bateman St W1 (tube: Leicester Square) – famous for its flavoured vodka shots (Rolo and Toblerone are to die for) and half-price jugs of cocktails before 8 pm during the week. No suits allowed.

The French House 49 Dean St W1 (tube: Leicester Square) – very popular; they only serve halves, which is strange, but there is an enjoyable atmosphere.

Three Greyhounds, 25 Greek St W1 (tube: Tottenham Court Rd) – since being refurbished this pub has become more continental in style; good food and several varieties of ale.

The Flamingo Bar, Hanover St W1 (tube: Oxford Circus) – Latin American theme bar. Often has live sets. Good for pre-Hanover Grand drinks (see Clubs section).

The '0' Bar, 83-85 Wardour St W1 (tube: Piccadilly Circus) – two main drinking floors with a DJ downstairs at the weekend (£5 cover charge). Best during the week for half-price pitchers of cocktails before 8 pm. Good meeting point.

Covent Garden

Lamb & Flag, 33 Rose St WC2 (tube: Covent Garden) – tucked down a narrow alleyway between Garrick and Floral Sts stands this pleasantly unchanged pub; food available.

Outback Inn, 11 Henrietta St (tube: Covent Garden) – a popular Australiana-themed bar with live music and cheap midweek drink specials; packed to the hilt from Thursday to Sunday.

LONDON

★★

Gay & Lesbian London

When starting to explore the London gay scene, you could easily feel overwhelmed by the number of places to visit. Gay London has a livelier, more eclectic scene than most other European cities.

The best starting point is to pick up a free listings magazine – *The Pink Paper, Boyz* or *QX* – available from most gay cafés, bars and clubs. Magazines like *Gay Times* (£2) and the lesbian *Diva* (£2) also have listings. *Time Out* is another excellent source of information.

London's bars and clubs cater for every predilection, but there's a growing trend towards mixed gay/straight clubs. There are also men or women-only nights; check the press for details.

In Soho, recently labelled the 'gay village', there's a cluster of bars and cafés. Walk down Old Compton St, from Charing Cross Rd. On your right at No 34 is the friendly, sometimes frantic, 24-hour *Compton St Café. Balaans*, at No 60, is a moderately-priced, popular, continental-style café. Further up the street are numerous gay-owned bars, shops and eateries. *Soho Men*, above *Clone Zone* at No 64 offers a 90-minute facial for £35. Further into Soho you'll find *The Freedom Café*, 60 Wardour St, serving food and drink for a mixed clientele, and at 57 Rupert St is *The Yard*, with a pleasant courtyard where you can eat and drink. There's also *Village Soho*, 81 Wardour St, a popular two-level bar and a young, stylish crowd.

Near Tottenham Court Rd tube, the long-established, friendly *First Out*, 52 St Giles High St, is a mixed lesbian-gay café serving vegetarian food and with periodic exhibitions.

Café de Paris, 3 Coventry St (tube: Leicester Square), is an intimate club playing mainly house and garage. Just beyond Long Acre is Europe's largest gay bar, *The Base*, 167 Drury Lane (tube: Covent Garden). There's also the *Gardening Club*, 4 The Piazza (tube: Covent Garden), where the most popular nights are Club for Life (Saturday) and Queer Nation (Sunday).

The further you go from the West End, the more local the clientele becomes. *The Black Cap*, 171 Camden High St (tube: Camden Town), is a late-night bar with a good drag reputation. Further out on Hampstead Heath, a popular cruising spot, *The King William IV*, 75 Heath St (tube: Hampstead Heath), is a friendly pub with sofas and log fires. Also in north London, *The Central Station*, 37 Wharfdale Rd (tube: King's Cross) has a bar with special one-nighters, including a women-only night called the Clit Club – depending on the night it's very popular. Further east at the Angel tube station, *The Angel*, open from midday, is a vegetarian café/bar tucked away at 65 Graham St, also good for women.

Earl's Court, now somewhat eclipsed by Soho, still has a few places of interest. There's the excellent *Wilde About Oscar* restaurant in the *Philbeach Hotel*, 31 Philbeach Gardens, and *The Coleherne*, 261 Old Brompton Rd, one of London's oldest pubs.

Love Muscle at the *Fridge*, Town Hall Parade, Brixton Hill (tube: Brixton), has dance music on Saturday nights with a mixed crowd. *Heaven*, Villiers St (tube: Charing Cross), in the West End, is London's most famous gay club with three dance floors. Every night has a different slant, so check the press for details.

Turnmills, 55B Clerkenwell Rd EC1 (tube: Farringdon), has three gay nights. From 10 pm to 3 am on Saturday it's Pumpin Curls, a women's club. From 3 am onwards it's called Trade – London's first all-nighter, which goes until 12.30 pm on Sunday. Breakfast is served at 6 am. On Sunday, at the same venue, ff runs until 8 am on Monday with techno and trance music.

Before hitting the clubs, it's worth picking up advertising flyers (available in most bars), which will give you a reduced entry price. Any saving is worthwhile, because clubbing can be expensive. Places tend to be packed at the weekends, but you can party nonstop from Friday into Monday.

If the club scene's not for you, you can also make new friends at the myriad social, sport and dance groups and classes. *Time Out* and the gay press have the details. ■

★★

The Polar Bear, 30 Lisle St WC2 (tube: Leicester Square) – West End pub popular with Australasians.

ICAfé, The Mall SW1 (tube: Piccadilly Circus) – in the ICA arts centre, but friendly and interesting; licensed to 1 am.

Gordon's, 47 Villiers St WC2 (tube: Embankment) – an old wine bar in ancient vaults beneath the street, but spilling out into the Embankment Gardens in summer.

Chelsea & Fulham

Po Na Na Souk Bar, 316 King's Rd SW3 (tube: Sloane Square) – African-style fun bar where you can drink in little tented alcoves, seated on leopard skin sofas or chairs, playing backgammon. Even the cigarette machine is painted like a zebra.

Come The Revolution, 541 King's Rd SW6 (tube: Fulham Broadway) – Italianate interior with murals and wrought-iron tables and chairs; this bar is large but can get very crowded, though there's also a garden.

The Fez Bar, 222 Fulham Rd SW6 (tube: South Kensington) – cave-like bar in the livelier part of the Fulham Rd. Open until 2 am at the weekend; £5 cover charge.

Bloomsbury & Holborn

Lamb, 94 Conduit St WC1 (tube: Russell Square) – a well-preserved Victorian interior of mirrors, old wood and 'snob screens'.

The Queen's Larder, 1 Queen's Square WC1 (tube: Russell Square) – a handy retreat on the corner of the square, with outside benches and pub grub.

Notting Hill

Beach Blanket Babylon, 45 Ledbury Rd W11 (tube: Notting Hill Gate) – extraordinary Gaudi-esque décor, and a great place for watching Notting Hill trendies; expensive food.

Market Bar, 240A Portobello Rd W11 (tube: Ladbroke Grove) – interesting décor, interesting crowd, and a relaxed atmosphere.

Windsor Castle, 114 Campden Hill Rd W11 (tube: Notting Hill Gate) – pleasant garden and good pub food: half a dozen oysters and a half bottle of champagne for £15.

The Westbourne, 101 Westbourne Park Villas W2 (tube: Westbourne Park) – trendy pub where the Notting Hill crowd congregate. Large forecourt is great in the summer and there's good-value bar food.

Camden & Primrose Hill

Crown & Goose, 100 Arlington Rd NW1 (tube: Camden Town) – new-style pub attracting a youngish crowd with good no-nonsense food.

Lock Tavern, Chalk Farm Rd NW1 (tube: Camden Town) – convenient for the market, with a roof terrace ideal for people-watching; decent pub fare.

Lansdowne, 90 Gloucester Ave NW1 (tube: Chalk Farm) – new-style pub with bohemian style and excellent, reasonably pricey food. On Sunday there's a pricey set menu at £15 but it's very popular, so book if you feel inclined to spoil yourself.

Hampstead

Flask, 14 Flask Walk NW3 (tube: Hampstead) – handy for the tube, with real ale and good food; a friendly local.

Holly Bush, 22 Holly Mount NW3 (tube: Hampstead) – idyllic pub with a good selection of beers; ordinary food.

Spaniards Inn, Spaniards Rd NW3 (tube: Hampstead) – dating from 1585; in winter you can warm up around an open fire, in the summer you can enjoy the garden; food available.

Earl's Court

Prince of Teck, 161 Earl's Court Rd SW5 (tube: Earl's Court) – infamous Australasian pub.

Blanco's, 314 Earl's Court Rd SW5 (tube: Earl's Court) – lively, authentic Spanish tapas bar serving Spanish beer. Open until midnight.

Hammersmith

Dove, 19 Upper Mall W6 (tube: Ravenscourt Park) – a small 17th-century building close to the Thames; good food and fine ales.

The Ship, 41 Jews Row SW18 (BR: Wandsworth Town) – tricky to get to, but worth the struggle; sit with a drink and some pleasant food and enjoy the river.

Chiswick

The City Barge, 27 Strand on the Green, Chiswick W4 (tube: Kew Gardens) – built in 1484 and perched dangerously close to the river's edge; basic English food.

Richmond

White Cross Hotel Water Lane Riverside, TW9 (tube: Richmond) – popular thanks to riverside location, good food and fine ales.

City

Eagle, 159 Farringdon Rd EC1 (tube: Farringdon) – one of the first of the new-style pubs, with delicious food and a good range of beers; busy.

Smithfield

The Cock Tavern (☎ 0171-248 2918), The Poultry Market, Smithfield Market EC1 (tube: Farringdon) – a local for those working in Smithfield meat market; a 40 oz steak is the house speciality (£16.50) and there's a free bottle of wine for anyone who finishes it (the record is 13 minutes!). Open from 5.30 am for breakfast.

London Bridge

George Inn, 77 Borough High St SE1 (tube: London Bridge) – London's only surviving galleried coaching inn surrounding a courtyard; beautiful, but busy after-work drinking hole.

Rotherhithe

Mayflower, 117 Rotherhithe St SE16 (tube: Rotherhithe) – sit on the jetty and watch the Thames at this pub that has survived surrounding new development.

Wapping

Prospect of Whitby, 57 Wapping Wall E1 (tube: Wapping) – one of the oldest surviving drinking houses in London; on the tourist trail, but good terrace overlooking the Thames.

Greenwich

Richard I, Royal Hill SE10 (BR: Greenwich) – off the main tourist route; good beer and a garden make it an ideal retreat; or try the *Fox & Hounds* next door.

Internet Cafés

Being online is more than a hobby for some, with the electronic world now almost part of everyday life.

Cyberia Café (☎ 0171-209 0983), 39 Whitfield St W1 (tube: Goodge St), was the first Internet café in London. They have full Internet access with 10 terminals in the café (£2.50 for half an hour) and 12 in the training room. Weekday training costs £30 for two hours and needs to be booked in advance. The food's good with specials at £4 to £5. Another branch, the New Broadway Café, is in Ealing W5 (tube: Ealing Broadway).

Check out Lonely Planet's award-winning World Wide Web site: http://www.lonely planet.com.

Popular Music

London offers an enormous variety of music, whether it be megastars raking in the cash at Wembley, Earl's Court and similar hangar-sized venues, or hot new bands at the Astoria in Charing Cross Rd, Subterranea in Notting Hill, the Brixton Academy in Brixton or The Forum in Kentish Town.

There's new and happening jazz at Ronnie Scott's and the Camden Jazz Café, or folk and country & western at Harlesden's Mean Fiddler, with pub rock featuring loud and kicking at Islington's Powerhaus or Garage.

Capital FM radio station has a useful ticket hotline (☎ 0171-420 0958). *i-D* is a lifestyle/fashion mag with good coverage of the hot and the hip.

The major venues for live, contemporary music include:

Astoria 157 Charing Cross Rd WC2 (tube: Tottenham Court Rd) – dark, sweaty and atmospheric, with good views of the stage. Cheap gay nights (£1) on Monday and Thursday (☎ 0171-434 0403).

Brixton Academy 211 Stockwell Rd SW9 (tube: Brixton) – enormous venue with good atmosphere (☎ 0171-924 9999).

Hackney Empire 291 Mare St E8 (tube: Bethnal Green) – superb Edwardian theatre; an excellent venue (☎ 0181-985 0171).

Labatts Apollo Hammersmith Queen Caroline St W6 (tube: Hammersmith) – formerly the Hammersmith Odeon, legendary venue, although the cinema-style layout keeps punters in their seats (☎ 0171-416 6080).

Shepherd's Bush Empire Shepherd's Bush Green W12 (tube: Shepherd's Bush) – one of the best venues in London (☎ 0181-740 7474).

The Forum 9-17 Highgate Rd NW5 (tube: Kentish Town) – formerly the Town & Country club, and still an excellent roomy venue (☎ 0171-344 0040).

The Grand St John's Hill SW11 (BR: Clapham Junction) – converted cinema with a balcony (☎ 0171-738 9000)

Wembley Arena Empire Way, Middlesex (tube: Wembley Park) – huge venue with little to recommend it (☎ 0181-900 1234)

Smaller places with a more 'club-like' atmosphere that are worth checking for interesting bands include:

Borderline Orange Yard, off Manette St WC2 (tube: Tottenham Court Rd) – small relaxed venue, with a reputation for big-name bands playing under pseudonyms (☎ 0171-734 2095).

Rock Garden The Piazza WC2 (tube: Covent Garden) – small basement venue, often packed with tourists, but also hosting good bands (☎ 0171-240 3961).

Subterrania 12 Acklam Rd W10 (tube: Ladbroke Grove) – atmospheric and showcasing up-and-comers (☎ 0181-960 4590).

Underworld 174 Camden High St NW1 (tube: Camden Town) – beneath the World's End pub, a small venue with up-and-coming bands (☎ 0171-482 1932).

Jazz London has historically had a thriving jazz scene and, with its recent resurgence thanks to acid-jazz, hip-hop, funk and swing, it's stronger than ever:

Jazz Café 5 Parkway NW1 (tube: Camden Town) – very trendy restaurant/venue; best to book a table (☎ 0171-916 6060).

Pizza Express 10 Dean St W1 (tube: Leicester Square) – beneath the main restaurant, a small basement venue (☎ 0171-437 9595).

Ronnie Scott's 47 Frith St W1 (tube: Leicester Square) – operating since 1959; seedy and expensive if you're not a member (£45 a year); £12 between Monday and Thursday and £14 at weekends. There's no obligation to drink or eat but wine is from £12.50 a bottle, £1.25 for half a pint of beer, and food from £5 (☎ 0171-439 0747).

100 Club 100 Oxford St W1 (tube: Oxford Circus) – legendary London venue, beginning with the Stones and at the centre of the Punk revolution, now concentrating on jazz (☎ 0171-636 0933).

Blues & Folk Three places worth checking out are:

Biddy Mulligans 205 Kilburn High Rd NW6 (tube: Kilburn) – a traditional Irish pub, with live music at weekends (☎ 0171-624 2066).

Bunjies 27 Litchfield St WC2 (tube: Leicester Square) – a legendary folk club with a good-value restaurant (☎ 0171-240 1796).

Mean Fiddler Acoustic Room 24 High St, Harlesden NW10 (tube: Willesden Junction) – top-quality acoustic folk (☎ 0181-961 5490).

Clubs

It's not uncommon for a London club to be remembered more for the evening it hosts than for the venue. A club can change from night to night, depending on the DJ. If you want to know what's going on get a copy of *Time Out* or *Mixmag*. Alternatively, a few of the record shops around Soho, like Black Market Records, 25 D'Arblay St W1, have flyers and details of events. Many clubs have a gay night (see Gay & Lesbian London section).

Entry prices vary from £10 to £15 for most clubs, plus about £3 for an alcoholic drink. The very happening clubs don't kick off until midnight and are usually open until 4 or 5 am. Dress can be smart (no suits) or casual; the more outrageous you look the better chance you have of getting in!

Bagleys Studios Kings Cross Freight Depot, off York Way N1 (tube: Kings Cross) – a huge converted warehouse with five dancefloors, four bars and an outside area for the summer. The music varies from room to room and the atmosphere is excellent (☎ 0171-278 2777).

Bar Rumba 36 Shaftesbury Ave W1 (tube: Piccadilly Circus) – varied nights including Salsa. Small but very popular club; Thai food served all night (☎ 0171-287 2715).

Blue Note 1 Hoxton Square N1 (tube: Old St) – relaxed club with live sets, funk, jazz and soul (☎ 0171-729 8440).

Browns 4 Great Queen's St WC2 (tube: Holborn) – the stars' after-party hangout. Though slightly pretentious it's a lively, fun club – if you can get in (☎ 0171-831 0802).

Café de Paris 3 Coventry St W1 (tube: Piccadilly) – completely revamped, this is London's newest dining bar. If you'd rather just be a spectator, this immense building has a galleried restaurant overlooking the dancefloor (☎ 0171-734 7700).

The Cross Good Ways Depot, off York Way N1 (tube: Kings Cross) – one of London's leading venues, hidden under the arches. Brilliant DJs and a great ambience guarantee a good night (☎ 0171-837 0828).

Emporium 62 Kingly St W1 (tube: Oxford Circus) – very popular with the beautiful set, Emporium is one of the trendiest clubs in town (☎ 0171-734 3190).

The End 16A West Central St WC1 (tube: Holborn) – modern industrial décor; free water fountain. For serious clubbers who like their music underground (☎ 0171-419 9199).

The Fridge Town Hall Parade SW2 (tube: Brixton) – a wide variety of club nights in an excellent venue which is not too big, not too small. Saturday is gay night (☎ 0171-326 5100).

Gardening Club 4 The Piazza WC2 (tube: Covent Garden) – a varied crowd; this cave-like club tends to attract fun-loving out-of-towners (☎ 0171-497 3154).

The Grand St John's Hill SW11 (BR: Clapham Junction) – always a laugh if you want somewhere with less of an attitude, the Grand has established its reputation with retro evenings (☎ 0171-738 9000).

Hanover Grand 6 Hanover St W1 (tube: Oxford Circus) – voted 'Best Club in London' two years running. There are two very different floors. You may have to queue but it's definitely worthwhile (☎ 0171-499 7977).

The Hippodrome Hippodrome Corner WC2 (tube: Leicester Square) – notorious for its glitzy dancefloors and bright lights. Expensive and very popular with tourists (☎ 0171-437 4311).

Iceni 11 White Horse St, off Curzon St W1 (tube: Green Park) – three floors of contrasting music and a friendly atmosphere make this one of the more accessible clubs (☎ 0171-495 5333).

Legends 29 Old Burlington St W1 (tube: Green Park) – very suave-looking interior and separate bars mean that Legends is more social than other clubs. Good for meeting people (☎ 0171-437 9933).

Leisure Lounge 121 Holborn EC1 (tube: Chancery Lane) – if you enjoy sweating, being shoved around and listening to some serious music, you'll love it here (☎ 0171-242 1345).

Ministry of Sound 103 Gaunt St SE1 (tube: Elephant & Castle) – now renowned internationally, this cavernous club attracts hard-core clubbers as well as people who just want to chill out. Open until 9 am. Don't expect to do any talking in the box room (☎ 0171-378 6528).

Thunder Drive 24 Shaftesbury Ave W1 (tube: Piccadilly Circus) – dance floor down a sweeping staircase but there are plenty of other distractions to keep you amused all night. Décor and menu intended to take you on a journey through America (☎ 0500-734616).

Velvet Underground 143 Charing Cross Rd WC2 (tube: Tottenham Court Rd) – an intimate, friendly club swathed in red velvet (☎ 0171-734 4687).

Dingwalls, The East Yard, Camden Lock NW1 (tube: Camden Town) – comedy acts at weekends, music during the week and club nights every night. Upstairs there's a terrace bar which gives you an aerial view of the lock and the market; food is available (☎ 0171 267 0545).

HQ Club, West Yard, Camden Lock NW1 (tube: Camden Town) – soul and funk on Friday nights, salsa on Saturday night and club nights during the week. The cover charge averages around £5, depending on the day of the week (☎ 0171 485 6044).

Classical Music & Opera

London is the classical music capital of Europe – with five symphony orchestras, various smaller outfits, a brilliant array of venues, reasonable pricing, and high standards of performance.

The biggest dilemma facing the concert goer is how to pick from the riches on offer. On any night of the year the choice will range from traditional crowd-pleasers to new music and 'difficult' composers.

Venues include the *Wigmore Hall* (☎ 0171-935 2141), 35 Wigmore St W1 (tube: Bond St), which offers intimacy and variety – the Sunday-morning recitals are particularly good. The *South Bank* provides innovation and diversity in its three main auditoria. The *Royal Albert Hall* (☎ 0171-589 8212), Kensington Gore SW7 (tube: South Kensington) is a splendid old concert hall that, from mid-July to mid-September, plays host to the Proms – one of the biggest and most democratic classical-music festivals in the world.

Opera tends to be more of a problem; the problem is, it is costly to produce and costly to attend. The *Royal Opera House* (ROH) (☎ 0171-304 4000), Covent Garden WC2 (tube: Covent Garden), is constantly beset by money difficulties, as well as repeated allegations of mismanagement and elitism. In spite of all this the ROH maintains its reputation for excellence, regularly bagging opera superstars like Pavarotti and Domingo for performances. If you want a good seat be prepared to take out a mortgage; fortunately a really bad seat can be had for as little as £2 and the cheapest seats with clear views of the stage are from £7.50 to £29.

The *London Coliseum*, home of the English National Opera (☎ 0171-632 8300), St Martin's Lane WC2 (tube: Leicester Square), is more reasonably priced, if rather variable in its quality and programming. From 10 am on the day of performance there are balcony seats for £5. Expect a long queue.

On Hampstead Heath, **Kenwood** holds a series of free evening musical recitals during the summer, when people sit out on the grass and eat strawberries, drink chilled white wine and listen to classical music – a highlight of summer in London.

Theatre

Despite all the stories of gloom and doom, London theatre continues to thrive. There are few cities in the world with comparable variety, quality and such reasonable prices.

The *National Theatre* (☎ 0171-928 2252), the nation's theatre flagship, has three auditoria in the South Bank complex (the Olivier, the Lyttleton and the Cottesloe) and uses them effectively to show classics, contemporary plays, and guest appearances by the best young companies from around the world. Good tickets for matinees start at £7 and there are cheaper student standby tickets.

The *Barbican* is the London home to the Royal Shakespeare Company (☎ 0171-638 8891); it's undoubted excellence can sometimes be disappointingly conservative. Matinee tickets start at £6, and there are cheap student standby tickets.

The *Royal Court* (☎ 0171-730 1745), operating temporarily out of two other theatres until its own Sloane Square theatre has been rebuilt, tends to favour the new and the anti-establishment – various enfants terribles from John Osborne to Caryl Churchill got their first break here. Phone for details.

Don't forget the new Globe theatre (see

South London section) which should be up and running by the time you read this.

Then there's the West End, with every summer bringing a new crop of plays. If this isn't enough, at any time of the year, London's many off-West End and fringe-theatre productions offer a selection of the amazing, the boring, the life-changing and the downright ridiculous. London has many theatre agencies which will sell you tickets, especially for the popular performances like *Cats*. Most of them charge a hefty commission so it's always worth checking with the theatre first to see if you can get a ticket for the original price.

The Leicester Square Theatre Ticket Booth, on the south side of Leicester Square sells half-price tickets (plus £2 commission) for West End productions on the day of performance. They open Tuesday to Sunday from noon to 3.30 pm for matinee tickets only and from 1 to 6.30 pm, Monday to Saturday, for evening tickets only. Beware of booths nearby, like the one opposite the Hippodrome on Cranbourne St, which advertise half-price tickets but fail to mention that a hefty commission has first been added to the price of the ticket.

Ballet & Dance

London is home to five major dance companies and a host of small and experimental companies. The *Royal Ballet* (☎ 0171-240 1066) shares the Royal Opera House in Covent Garden, and presents the best classical ballet in Britain. Tickets can be enormously expensive, but rear amphitheatre tickets are on sale cheaply on the day of performance (phone ☎ 0171-836 6903).

Sadler's Wells has a long dance history, but its theatre in Rosebury Ave will be closed for rebuilding until 1998. The *Peacock Theatre* (☎ 0171-312 1996), Portugal St WC2 (tube: Aldwych), will now host the London Contemporary Dance Theatre and London City Ballet. The Royal Sadler's Wells Ballet is now the Birmingham Royal Ballet.

The *Riverside Studios* and *ICA* (see the Cultural Centres section earlier in this chapter) have the most important venues for small experimental companies.

Cinema

During the 50s and 60s many of London's great Art-Deco and Art-Nouveau cinema houses shut down. In the late 80s there was a resurgence, and a number of characterless multi-screen complexes were opened. The boom continues to this day, but this is not altogether good news: the new complexes are expensive and thrive on mainstream American fare. Full-price tickets are around £7, but afternoon shows are usually cheaper, and on Monday quite a few places offer half-priced tickets all day.

Nevertheless, you can still see an awful lot of movies in London. Every year, in November, the National Film Theatre comes out of hiding from its South Bank bunker to play host to the London Film Festival.

The last bastions of diversity and creative programming are Hampstead's *Everyman* (☎ 0171-435 1525), Holly Bush Vale NW3 (tube: Hampstead), with its uncomfortable, ancient chairs, and the *National Film Theatre* (☎ 0171-928 3232), South Bank (tube: Embankment).

The *Notting Hill Coronet* (☎ 0171-727 6705), Notting Hill Gate W11 (tube: Notting Hill), is an attractive old theatre and possibly the last cinema in the politically correct Western world where smoking is permitted.

The *Prince Charles Cinema* (☎ 0171-437 8181), Leicester Place WC2 (tube: Leicester Square), is the cheapest in London with tickets for new-release films from only £1.99. They have a number of films each day so check the programme carefully.

SPECTATOR SPORT

All year round London plays host to myriad events, and the TV is constantly chocka with coverage of every kind of sport. As always *Time Out* is the best source of information on fixtures, times, venues and ticket prices.

Football

Wembley (☎ 0181-902 8833) is the home of English football. This is where the English national side plays international matches and where the FA Cup final takes place in mid-May. A tour of Wembley Stadium includes the opportunity to walk down the players' tunnel onto the pitch, as well as going up to receive the Cup to the (taped) roar of the crowd. Tours take place daily (☎ 0181-902 8833) between 10 am and 4 pm (3 pm in winter) and cost £6.95/4.75.

There are a dozen league teams in London. Big teams like Tottenham (☎ 0171-365 5050) and Arsenal (☎ 0171-704 4040) play in the top-flight Premier League, meaning that any weekend of the season, from August to April, good-quality football is just a tube ride away. Hooliganism isn't much of a problem these days. Since the Hillsborough stadium tragedy in 1989 most stadia have gone all-seater, and the mood at most matches has cooled accordingly. The only thing that holds people back these days is the exorbitant prices, which start at £11 per game.

Cricket

Cricket continues to flourish, despite the dismal fortunes of the England team. Test matches take place at Lord's (☎ 0171-289 8979) and the Oval (☎ 0171-582 6660) cricket grounds. Sadly, tickets cost a fortune and tend to go fast. You're better off looking out for a county fixture: Middlesex play at Lord's, Surrey play at the Oval.

There are daily tours of Lord's, including the famous Long Room, at noon and 2 pm, as well as one at 10 am on county match days (no tours when major matches are on). Cost is £5.50/4 (☎ 0171-432 1033).

Rugby Union

For rugby union fans south-west London is the place to be. There are a host of good-quality teams like Harlequins, Richmond and Wasps. Each year, starting in January, the Five Nations Rugby Union Championship takes place between the four nations of the British Isles, and the French. This guarantees two big matches at Twickenham (☎ 0181-892 8161), the shrine of English union football. There is now a Museum of Rugby

at Twickenham which can include a tour of the stadium. The cost is £4 for the museum and tour, £2.50 for just the museum. Advance booking is essential (☎ 0181-892 2000).

Rugby League

Rugby league fans would be advised to get on a train and head for the north of England, or settle for watching the London Crusaders, the only rugby league side in southern England. In May, the rugby Challenge Cup final is held at Wembley.

Tennis

Tennis and Wimbledon (☎ 0181-946 2244) are synonymous, but queues, exorbitant prices, limited ticket availability and cramped conditions can turn a Wimbledon dream into a nightmare. Wimbledon has sold its soul (and most of its seating) to corporate entertainers; the rest of the world has to make do with the leftovers.

If you haven't a show court ticket and you don't want to camp out all night, go along in the late afternoon and take your chances on buying a returned ticket for £5. Otherwise you might try the pre-Wimbledon tournament at Queen's (☎ 0171-381 7000) which attracts many of the top male players.

Athletics

Athletics meetings take place regularly throughout the summer at Crystal Palace (☎ 0181-778 0131), attracting major international and domestic stars. Tickets are from £10.

Racing

If you're looking for a cheap and thrilling night out, consider going to 'The Dogs'. Greyhounds run at Harringay, Wimbledon, Wembley and Catford and entry is as little as £3.50 for a 12-race meeting. A few small bets will mean guaranteed excitement, and you'll rub shoulders with a London subculture that is gregarious, and more than slightly shady.

Alternatively, there's horse racing with plenty of top-quality courses lying just south of the city. Ascot in June can be nice if rather posh; Epsom on Derby Day can be a crushing experience in more ways than one. Windsor, by the River Thames, is an idyllic spot for a summer evening picnic. Sandown is another top racing course.

GETTING THERE & AWAY

London is the major gateway to Britain, so transport information is in the Getting There & Away and Getting Around chapters. Look up your proposed British destination for prices and possibilities to/from London; in particular see the tables in the Getting Around chapter.

Airports

Heathrow Heathrow is one of the largest, busiest airports in the world. In true British style, it has grown organically and now has four terminals, each an airport in itself. There are also two tube stations. It is, therefore, important to check from which terminal your flight is departing – when you reconfirm your ticket is a convenient time.

Although the place appears chaotic and it is impossible to find anywhere pleasant to have a farewell drink (though there are pubs or bars in all four terminals), it is pretty well organised. Duty-free facilities are not impressive (they're particularly weak on photographic and electronic equipment), but each terminal has excellent, competitive currency-exchange facilities, and good information counters. There are also a number of accommodation booking counters.

There are some large 'international' hotels nearby which are served by courtesy buses; these may be necessary to consider if you're leaving or arriving at a peculiar time, but none are cheap, or particularly noteworthy. Even if the tube isn't running, those on a budget will do better to catch a minicab for cheaper accommodation in central London (perhaps Earl's Court, which is on the right side of town).

Baggage Hold has left-luggage facilities in Terminal 1 (☎ 0181-745 5301) and Terminal 4 (☎ 0181-745 7460) from 6 am to 11 pm. The charge is £2 per item up to 12 hours

and £3 per item up to 24 hours. Excess Baggage (☎ 0181-759 3344) offers a similar service in Terminals 2 and 3. Both companies also have a baggage forwarding service.

For general inquiries and flight information (except British Airways) phone ☎ 0181-759 4321. For British Airways ring ☎ 0181-759 2525. Other useful numbers are:

Car Park Information ☎ 0800-844844
London Underground ☎ 0171-222 1234
Hotel Reservation Service ☎ 0181-759 2719

Be warned that theft is a growing problem at Heathrow.

Getting There & Away The airport is accessible by bus and underground, but the underground is the cheapest, most reliable method (between 5.30 am and 11.30 pm). The station for Terminals 1, 2 and 3 is directly linked to the terminal buildings; there is a separate station in Terminal 4. Check which terminal your flight uses when you reconfirm. The adult single fare is £3.20, or use an All Zone Travelcard which is £3.90. The journey time from central London is about an hour.

The Airbus (☎ 0171-222 1234) services are also useful; there are two routes, the A1 which runs along Cromwell Rd to Victoria, and the A2 which runs along Notting Hill Gate and Bayswater Rd to Russell Square. Buses run every half-hour and cost £6.

A minicab to/from central London will cost from around £20; a metered black cab around £30. Airport Transfers (☎ 0171-403 2228) is a minicab company that will both deliver to and pick up from the airport – a lifesaver if you've got a lot of baggage, but not much cash.

Gatwick Gatwick is a large airport, but much smaller than Heathrow, so in many ways it's easier and more pleasant. Its only drawback is the relative expense of the rail link to Victoria, but this, too, is more pleasant than the tube to Heathrow.

There are two terminals, north and south, linked with an efficient monorail service; it's still best to check which terminal you will use when you reconfirm your ticket. There are all the predictable stores, and several eating and drinking areas.

Accommodation options close to the airport are expensive and unremarkable. If you need more information phone the central Gatwick Directory (☎ 01293-535 3530). This number will connect you to Thomas Cook who deal with hotel reservations.

Excess Baggage plc (☎ 01293-569 9900), in both the North and South terminals, has left-baggage facilities available daily from 6 am to 10 pm. The charge is £2 per item up to 12 hours and £3 per item up to 24 hours. They also have a baggage forwarding service.

Getting There & Away The Gatwick Express runs nonstop between the main terminal and Victoria station from 4.30 am to 11 pm. Singles are £8.90 and the journey time is half an hour. The regular service takes just a little longer, runs all day and all night and costs £7.50. BA customers can check in at Victoria station.

A minicab to central London will cost around £35, a metered black cab around £70. Airport Transfers (☎ 0171-403 2228) is a minicab company that will deliver to and pick up from the airport.

Stansted It is anticipated that eight million passengers a year will pass through the terminal by the end of this century, and there will be space to accommodate 15 million in the future. At the moment this is hard to believe, but if you are offered a ticket that arrives or departs from here don't be put off. It is 45 minutes from London's Liverpool St station and you arrive under the airport building and are then whisked up to the main concourse by escalator.

The building then becomes apparent – designed by Foster Associates, it is simplicity itself and one of the best recent buildings in Britain. Everything was designed for maximum ease of travel.

There is one number (☎ 01279-680500) for general inquiries, hotel reservations and rail information.

Getting There & Away There is a direct train link to Liverpool St, which takes 45 minutes and costs £10.10. You can change at Tottenham Hale for the West End and other Victoria Line stations, including Victoria. There are trains every half hour.

Minicabs to/from central London will cost about £35, a black cab around £75. Airport Transfers (☎ 0171-403 2228) is a minicab company that will deliver to and pick up from the airport.

Luton Luton is, by London standards, a small airport, mainly catering to cheap charter flights.

Getting There & Away Catch the airport-station Luton Flyer bus outside the arrivals hall for a 15-minute trip to the railway station then take the train for King's Cross or St Pancras, another 45 minutes; the all-in price is £9.90. There are regular services approximately every 20 minutes, starting early and finishing late.

London City Airport Business travellers account for almost all the passengers using the London City Airport (☎ 0171-474 5555). There are flights from here to nearly 20 European destinations, including Edinburgh and Dublin.

Getting There & Away The airport is to the east of the Blackwall Tunnel in east London. A shuttle bus runs between the airport and both Liverpool St tube station (£4 single) and Canary Wharf (£2 single) on the DLR, between 6 am and 9 pm. An alternative would be to take the DLR to Prince Regent Lane and catch the No 473 bus from there.

Bus
Bus travellers arrive and depart from Victoria Coach Station, Buckingham Palace Rd, about 10 minutes walk south of the Victoria railway and tube station. If you have to wait around, head to *The Well* across Ecclestone Place – it's a clean, peaceful oasis with cheap food. It closes at 5 pm and on Sunday.

Train

There are eight major railway stations in London, and all are connected by tube. For those of you with a combined rail/ferry ticket, if your train goes via South-East England (to/from France, Belgium, Spain or Italy), Victoria is the station; to/from Harwich and Felixstowe (for Germany, the Netherlands and Scandinavia), Liverpool St is your station; to/from Newcastle (for Scandinavia), King's Cross is your station. There's a superb international terminal at Waterloo from which all services that use the Channel Tunnel depart.

There are information centres at all the main stations. For rail information by phone, one inquiry number now covers all destinations in Britain; ☎ 0345 484950.

GETTING AROUND
Bus & Underground

London Regional Transport is responsible for the buses and the underground trains (the 'tube'). It has a number of information centres providing free maps, tickets, and information on night buses. Amongst others, there are centres in each Heathrow terminal, and at Victoria, Piccadilly and King's Cross stations; or phone ☎ 0171-222 1234.

Buses are much more interesting and pleasant to use than the tube, although they can be frustratingly slow. There are four types of tickets: one-journey bus tickets sold on the bus (minimum 50p), daily and weekly bus passes, single or return tube tickets (sold at stations, sometimes from vending machines, minimum £1.20) and Travelcards.

Travelcards are the easiest and cheapest option, and they can be used on all forms of transport (Network SouthEast trains in London, buses and tubes) after 9.30 am. London is divided into concentric rings, or zones, and the travelcard you need will depend on how many zones you cross. Most visitors will find that a Zone 1 & 2 card will be sufficient (£3.20). If you plan to start moving before 9.30 am you can buy a Zone 1 & 2 LT Card (London Transport Card) for £4.30. Weekly Travelcards are

also available; they require an identification card with a passport photo (Zone 1 & 2 is £15.70). Weekend Travelcards for Saturday and Sunday are 25% cheaper than two one-day cards. Family Travelcards are also available.

Times of the last tube trains vary from 11.30 pm to 12.30 am depending on the station and the line. A reasonably comprehensive network of night buses runs from or through Trafalgar Square – get to the square and ask. London Regional Transport publishes a free timetable, *Buses for Night Owls*, which lists them all. One Day Travelcards cannot be used, but Weekly Travelcards can.

Train

Several rail companies now run passenger trains in London; most lines interchange with the tube. Travelcards can be used.

Taxi

The classic London black cabs (☎ 0171-253 5000, 0171-272 0272) are excellent, but not cheap. A cab is available for hire when the yellow sign is lit. Fares are metered and a 10% tip is expected. They can carry five people.

Minicabs are cheaper freelance competitors to the black cabs; anyone with a car can work, but they can only be hired by phone. Some have a very limited idea of how to get around efficiently (and safely). They don't have meters, so it is essential to get a quote before you start. They can carry four people.

Small minicab companies are based in particular areas: ask a local for the name of a reputable company, or phone one of the large 24-hour operators (☎ 0171-272 2612, 0171-383 3333, 0171-602 1234, 0181-340 2450, 0181-567 1111). Women travelling by themselves at night can choose Ladycabs (☎ 0171-272 3019), which has women drivers. Gays and lesbians can choose Freedom Cars (0171-734 1313).

Car & Motorcycle

If you're blessed/cursed with private transport, avoid peak hours (7.30 to 9 am, 4.30 to 7 pm), and plan ahead if you will need to park in the centre. Cars parked illegally will be clamped, which is as agonising as it sounds. A clamp is locked on a wheel and in order to have it removed you have to travel across town, pay an enormous fine, then wait most of the day for someone to come and release you. Phone National Car Parks (☎ 0171-499 7050) for car-park addresses; rates vary. You're best to forget this option and stick with the public transport – you don't need the aggro.

Bicycle

All the hire places listed below offer mountain or hybrid bikes in mint condition. Each demands at least £150 deposit (credit-card slips are accepted), however long you intend to hire for. Particularly in London it is advisable to wear a helmet.

Bikepark
 14 ½ Stukeley St WC2 – minimum charge is £4 for four hours; £10 for the first day, £5 the second day and £3 for subsequent days; helmets, racks, lights and panniers are £1.50 a day, child seats also available (☎ 0171-430 0083).

Dial-a-Bike
 18 Gillingham St SW1 – £6.99 per day and £29.90 per week; helmet hire is £1 and panniers are £5 a side; insurance is available (☎ 0171-828 4040).

Boat

There's quite a range of services on the river. See the Greenwich, Kew Gardens and Hampton Court Palace sections for two popular trips. The main starting points are at Westminster Bridge and Charing Cross. For information on downriver trips (towards Greenwich) phone ☎ 0171-515 1415; for information on upriver trips (towards Kew) phone ☎ 0171-930 4721.

South-Eastern England

Locator & Map Index

LONDON

Windsor & Eton p227
St George's Chapel p228

Canterbury p233
Canterbury Cathedral p235

Dover p242

Winchester p270
Winchester Cathedral p271

Around Folkestone p246

Rye p251

Portsmouth p276

Chichester p268

Lewes p259

Brighton p262

Hastings p254

Isle of Wight p284

New Forest p281

While many of the towns and villages of Berkshire, Surrey, Kent, East and West Sussex and Hampshire are virtual dormitories for London workers, this is still a region exceptionally rich in beauty and history. This has always been Britain's front line, a mere 22 miles from the French coast, and names like Hastings, Dover and Portsmouth inevitably evoke images of invasion and war. A controversial new invasion began in 1994 when the Channel Tunnel finally opened. Those bold enough to travel underwater from France pop up near Folkestone. Those brave enough to use the ferries also find this coastline is their landfall, as it was for the Romans and Normans, amongst many others.

Whatever images you have of England, you can find them in this region: picturesque villages and towns with welcoming old pubs (Chilham, Sandwich, Rye, Lewes and Winchester among many others), spectacular coastline (the famous white cliffs of Dover), impressive castles (Dover, Hever, Leeds and Ightham Mote), great houses (Chartwell, Knole), gardens (Sissinghurst), great cathedrals at Canterbury and Winchester and, finally, the kitsch and vibrant seaside resort of Brighton.

ORIENTATION & INFORMATION

The main roads and railway lines radiate from London like spokes in a wheel, linking the south-coast ports and resorts with the capital. Chalk country runs through the region along two hilly east-west ridges, or downs.

The North Downs curve from Guildford towards Rochester, then to Dover where they become the famous white cliffs. The South Downs run from north of Portsmouth to end spectacularly at Beachy Head near Eastbourne. Lying between the two is the Weald, once an enormous stretch of forest, now orchards and market gardens.

PLACES TO STAY

Among others, there are youth hostels in Canterbury, Broadstairs, Dover, Hastings, Brighton, Portsmouth, Winchester and several on the Isle of Wight.

There is a B&B booking service covering the entire south-east and costing £3, plus the nightly charge. From April to September there's a free number (☎ 0800-212653); at other times phone ☎ 01865-727562.

GETTING AROUND
Bus

Fast, regular buses follow the spokes out

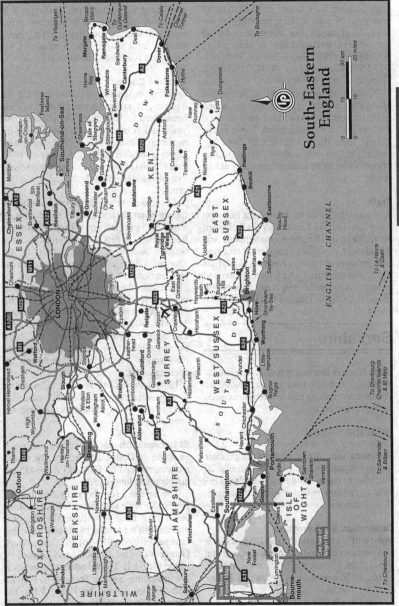

from London, but it is very difficult to travel east-west by bus without resorting to the slow, local buses. For information on all public transport options in Kent, ring ☎ 0800-696996, West Sussex ☎ 01243-777556, East Sussex ☎ 01273-474747, Hampshire ☎ 01962-868944.

Virtually all services in Kent, Sussex and Hampshire accept Explorer Tickets, which give unlimited travel and cost around £6.10/4.30 for adults/children. These can be bought from the bus drivers or from bus stations and are nearly always the best value option if you are travelling reasonably extensively.

Train

It is possible to do an interesting rail loop from London via Canterbury East, Dover, Rye, Hastings, Brighton, Portsmouth and Winchester. If you are considering this kind of extensive rail travel, a Network SouthEast Card (see the introductory Getting Around chapter) is essential. For train information phone the national number ☎ 0345-484950.

Berkshire

Berkshire has one major tourist attraction – Windsor and its famous castle. After Windsor, everything else in Berkshire comes a very distant second.

WINDSOR & ETON
- *pop 31,000* • ☎ *01753*

Windsor Castle is one of Britain's premier tourist attractions and since it is only 20 miles from central London, and easily accessible by rail and road, it crawls with tourists. If at all possible, avoid weekends.

Orientation & Information

Windsor Castle overlooks the Thames River and the town of Windsor spreading out to the west. Eton is essentially a small village, linked to Windsor by a pedestrian bridge over the Thames.

The TIC (☎ 852010) is at 24 High St. It's

open daily, 9.30 am to 5 pm; closing at 6.30 pm in July and August. The main post office is on Peascod St and, like the TIC, has a bureau de change. The Laundro-Coin laundrette is at 56 St Leonards Rd.

Windsor Castle

Standing on chalk bluffs overlooking the Thames, Windsor Castle (☎ 831118) has been home to British royalty for over 900 years and is one of the greatest surviving medieval castles. It was built in stages starting as a wooden motte and bailey in 1070, then rebuilt in stone in 1165 and successively extended and rebuilt right through to the 19th century.

Castle areas to which the public are admitted are generally open March to October, 10 am to 5.15 pm (last entry 4 pm), closing an hour earlier the rest of the year. In summer, weather and other events permitting, the changing of the guard takes place at 11 am (not on Sunday). The State Apartments are closed when the royal family is in residence, the most regular occasion being during the annual Ascot horse racing meeting in June. The Union Jack flying over the castle does not mean the Queen's at home; the Royal Standard flying from the Round Tower is the busy signal. Phone for variations on the opening hours.

Entry to the castle is £8.50/4.50, except on Sunday when entry is £6.50/3.50 because St George's Chapel, a prime attraction, does not open until 2 pm.

St George's Chapel One of Britain's finest examples of Gothic architecture, the chapel was commenced by Edward IV in 1475 but not completed until 1528.

The nave is a superb example of the Perpendicular style with beautiful fan vaulting arching out from the pillars. The chapel is packed with the **tombs of royalty** including George V (ruled 1910-36) and Queen Mary, George VI (ruled 1936-52) and Edward IV (ruled 1461-83). The **wooden oriel window** is a fine example of the Tudor style, built for Catherine of Aragon by Henry VIII. The **garter stalls** are the chapel's equivalent of

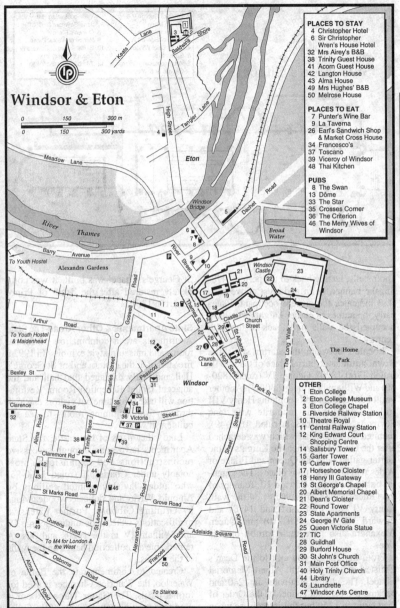

Windsor & Eton

SOUTH-EASTERN ENGLAND

PLACES TO STAY
4 Christopher Hotel
6 Sir Christopher Wren's House Hotel
32 Mrs Airey's B&B
38 Trinity Guest House
41 Acorn Guest House
42 Langton House
43 Alma House
49 Mrs Hughes' B&B
50 Melrose House

PLACES TO EAT
7 Punter's Wine Bar
9 La Taverna
26 Earl's Sandwich Shop & Market Cross House
34 Francesco's
37 Toscano
39 Viceroy of Windsor
48 Thai Kitchen

PUBS
8 The Swan
13 Dôme
33 The Star
35 Crosses Corner
36 The Criterion
46 The Merry Wives of Windsor

OTHER
1 Eton College
2 Eton College Museum
3 Eton College Chapel
5 Riverside Railway Station
10 Theatre Royal
11 Central Railway Station
12 King Edward Court Shopping Centre
14 Salisbury Tower
15 Garter Tower
16 Curfew Tower
17 Horseshoe Cloister
18 Henry III Gateway
19 St George's Chapel
20 Albert Memorial Chapel
21 Dean's Cloister
22 Round Tower
23 State Apartments
24 George IV Gate
25 Queen Victoria Statue
27 TIC
28 Guildhall
29 Burford House
30 St John's Church
31 Main Post Office
40 Holy Trinity Church
44 Library
45 Laundrette
47 Windsor Arts Centre

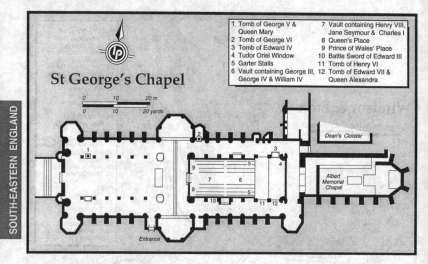

St George's Chapel

1 Tomb of George V & Queen Mary
2 Tomb of George VI
3 Tomb of Edward IV
4 Tudor Oriel Window
5 Garter Stalls
6 Vault containing George III, George IV & William IV
7 Vault containing Henry VIII, Jane Seymour & Charles I
8 Queen's Place
9 Prince of Wales' Place
10 Battle Sword of Edward III
11 Tomb of Henry VI
12 Tomb of Edward VII & Queen Alexandra

choir stalls. Dating back to the period 1478-85, the banner, helm and crest above each stall indicates the current occupant. Plates carry the names of earlier knights who have occupied the stalls right back to the 14th century.

Located between the garter stalls the **Royal Vault** is the burial place of George III (ruled 1760-1820), George IV (ruled 1820-30) and William IV (ruled 1830-37). Another **vault** between the stalls contains Henry VIII (ruled 1509-47), his favourite wife Jane Seymour, and Charles I (ruled 1625-49), reunited with his head which was detached after the Civil War. When the Knights of the Garter gather here the Queen and Prince of Wales will also take their places. The gigantic **battle sword** of Edward III, founder of the Order of the Garter, hangs on the wall. Henry VI (ruled 1422-61 and 1470) and Edward VII (ruled 1901-10) and Queen Alexandra also have their **tombs** on this side.

From the chapel you exit to the Dean's Cloister and the adjacent Albert Memorial Chapel. The chapel originated in 1240 and became the original chapel of the Order of the Garter in 1350 but fell into disuse when

St George's Chapel was built. It was completely restored after the death of Prince Albert in 1861.

State Apartments & Other Areas The State Apartments are a combination of formal rooms and museum-style exhibits. In 1992 a fire started at the eastern end of St George's Hall and badly damaged that hall and the adjacent Grand Reception Room. Restoration will take some time but visitors can look through from adjoining rooms to see the builders at work.

Like other parts of the castle, the State Apartments have gone through successive reconstructions and expansions, most notably under Charles II (ruled 1660-85) who added lavishly painted ceilings by Antonio Verrio and delicate woodcarvings by Grinling Gibbons. Further extensive modifications were made under George IV and William IV in the 1820s and 30s. A remarkable art collection hangs on the walls of the rooms.

Created to commemorate the Battle of Waterloo, the Waterloo Chamber is used for formal meals. The Garter Throne Room is used for investing new Knights of the Order of the Garter. The King's Drawing Room is also known as the Rubens Room, after the three paintings hanging there. The King's State Bedchamber has paintings by Canaletto and Gainsborough but Charles II actually slept in the adjacent King's Dressing Room. Some of the finest paintings at Windsor are hung here including works by Van Dyck, Holbein, Rembrandt, Rubens and Dürer. The King's Closet was used by Charles II as a study and has works by Canaletto, Reynolds and Hogarth.

From the king's rooms the route continues into the queen's rooms. The Queen's Ballroom has a remarkable collection of Van Dyck paintings. Only three of the 13 Antonio Verrio ceiling paintings from Charles II's time survive, one of them in the Queen's Audience Chamber. More Gobelins tapestries and another Verrio ceiling can be found in the Queen's Presence Chamber.

Queen Mary's Dolls' House was the work of architect Sir Edwin Lutyens and was built in 1:12 scale in 1923. It's complete in every detail down to running water to the bathrooms. Entry to the Dolls' House is an additional £1.

Around the Town

Windsor's fine **Guildhall** stands on High St beside Castle Hill. It was built between 1686-9, the construction completed under the supervision of Christopher Wren. Note that the central columns in the open area do not actually support the 1st floor; the council insisted upon them despite Wren's conviction that they were unnecessary. The inch or two of clear air proved his point.

Some of the oldest parts of Windsor are found along the cobbled streets behind the Guildhall. The visibly leaning **Market Cross House** is right next to the Guildhall. Charles II kept Nell Gwyn, his favourite mistress, in **Burford House** on Church St.

Eton College

Cross the Thames by the pedestrian Windsor Bridge to arrive at another enduring symbol of Britain's class system: Eton College, a famous public (meaning private) school that has educated no less than 18 prime ministers, and is now educating Prince William. A number of buildings date from the mid-15th century when the school was founded by Henry VI.

The museum (☎ 671177) is open to visitors during term from 2 to 4.30 pm, during the Easter and summer holidays from 10.30 am. Entry is £2.20/1.50. Guided tours of the school cost £3.20 to £5.80. Thinking of sending your son to join the 1200 to 1300 boys at Eton? Set aside £12,888 per year for the basic fees; you can shop for the top hat and tails uniform as you walk back along High St to Windsor.

Places to Stay

Hostel The *Windsor Youth Hostel* (☎ 861710) is a mile west from the Central railway station at Edgworth House, Mill Lane, Clewer. Follow Arthur Rd or Barry Ave out from the centre; you can walk along the riverbank. It's open from 2 January to 23 December and the nightly cost is £9.10/6.15.

B&Bs & Hotels The Windsor TIC charges a hefty £2.50 to make accommodation bookings. Cheaper, but centrally located, B&Bs include *Mrs Hughes'* (☎ 866036) at 62 Queens Rd. The rate is £20 per person. Nearby is *Langton House* (☎ 858299) at 46 Alma Rd, with doubles at £34 to £45, and *Alma House* (☎ 862983) at No 56, with similar prices. The rooms have a sink and shower but no toilet.

Melrose House (☎ 865328) at 53 Frances Rd has rooms from £35/45. *Suffolk Lodge* (☎ 864186), at 4 Bolton Ave, costs £29 for a single, £52 for a double and all rooms have attached bathroom. The *Acorn Guest House* (☎ 840692) is right by the Holy Trinity Church at 14 Trinity Place. *Mrs Airey* (☎ 855062) at 48 Clarence Rd is another straightforward B&B with rooms at £24 to £42. *Cobweb Corner* (☎ 852372) at 115 Clarence Rd costs from £19 per person.

On Thames St, just south of Windsor Bridge, *Sir Christopher Wren's House* (☎ 861354) costs from £100 to £129 although there is a walk-in rate of £80/89 if rooms are available. It was built by Christopher Wren in 1676. Across the river at 110 Eton High St, the *Christopher Hotel* (☎ 852359) dates from 1511 and has rooms from £66/73.

Places to Eat

Perhaps it's time to double-check the strength of the castle fortifications: the full line-up of pizza, burger and ice cream culinary imperialism is arrayed along Thames St, facing the castle walls. McDonald's to Baskin Robbins are all here.

Right next to the Guildhall on High St the *Earl's Sandwich Shop* turns out excellent sandwiches, French sticks and the like (for £2 to £3) from the tiny and precarious-looking Market Cross House.

Peascod St and its extension St Leonards Rd are good restaurant hunting grounds. *Francesco's* (☎ 863773) at 53 Peascod St is a very popular pizza, pasta and cappuccino specialist. Meals are around £6 and there's a take-away service. The *Crosses Corner* (☎ 862867) at 73 Peascod St is a pub and wine bar with interesting food which also attracts the crowds. Just past the Victoria St junction at 5 St Leonards Rd, *Toscano* (☎ 857600) is a wine bar and restaurant with a set lunch menu for £8.75, dinner £11.75. The *Viceroy of Windsor* (☎ 858005) is a flashy tandoori restaurant at 27 St Leonards Rd with £6 dishes and a vegetable thali for £9.25. The *Thai Kitchen* (☎ 833899) at 83 St Leonards Rd is a little cheaper.

The cobbled streets of Old Windsor shelter numerous restaurants behind the Guildhall, particularly along Church St and Church Lane. Going away from the centre *Dôme* (☎ 864405) at 5 Thames St is a noisily convivial French brasserie-style bar, part of a London chain. *La Taverna* (☎ 863020) at 2 River St is a popular Italian restaurant with a set meal for £12.50. *Punter's Wine Bar* on Thames St near the bridge to Eton is a good place for lunches and light meals and has a pre-theatre dinner for £11.50. There are more restaurants along Eton High St; in fact premises along this road are seemingly equally divided between restaurants, pubs and antique shops.

Entertainment

Popular pubs include the *Merry Wives of Windsor* on St Leonards Rd, *Crosses Corner* and the *Criterion* on the Peascod St/Victoria St corners and the *Star*, further up Peascod St towards the castle. *Dôme* at 5 Thames St looks across to the castle. On Thames St, near the Windsor Bridge to Eton, the *Swan* is a noisy, crowded and rowdy bar.

The *Windsor Arts Centre* (☎ 859336) on the corner of St Leonards Rd and St Marks Rd contains a bar, theatre and live music venue and attracts a young crowd. The *Theatre Royal* (☎ 853888) is the town's main theatre.

Getting There & Away

It's 20 miles by road or rail from central London. It only takes about 15 minutes by car between Windsor and Heathrow airport. See also the fares tables in the Getting Around chapter.

Bus Bus Nos 700, 701, 702 or 718 for Windsor depart from London's Victoria coach station about every hour. No 192 (Monday to Saturday) or No 170 (Sunday) connects Windsor with Heathrow airport. On Sunday the No 701 London service also goes via Heathrow.

Train There are two Windsor and Eton railway stations – Central station on Thames St, directly opposite the Windsor Castle entrance gate, and Riverside station near the bridge to Eton. In the Victorian era both lines faced some difficulties in negotiating a route into Windsor. The line into Windsor Central eventually obtained permission to cross the fields west of Eton College on the condition that the Brunel-designed viaduct across the meadows had arches high enough to allow an Eton boy to walk underneath without removing his top hat.

From London trains run to the Riverside station from Waterloo every half-hour (hourly on Sunday) and take 50 minutes.

Services from Paddington to Central require a change at Slough, five minutes from Windsor, but take about the same time. The fare is £5.20 one way, £5.40 day return on either route. Travelling further west to Bath or Oxford, go to Slough to pick up the main westbound trains.

Getting Around

Guide Friday open-top double-decker bus tours of the town cost £6.50/2. French Brothers (☎ 851900) operate boat trips from Windsor and Runnymede (where the Magna Carta was signed in 1215) and there are also trips from other Thames-side towns. A half-hour trip costs £2.80/1.40.

Surrey

Surrey has some lovely corners and if you're desperate to escape London, a walk on the North Downs – which start near Farnham and extend into Kent – is worth considering. A considerable amount of Surrey, however, is really almost a part of Greater London, lying within the M25 ring road. Even beyond the M25, most of the towns and villages are home to large numbers of people who commute to the city. Guildford, an affluent town with an attractive High St and an ugly modern cathedral, is the administrative centre.

AROUND SURREY

Epsom Downs Racecourse, near Epsom, has operated since the days of James I and is home to the Derby, one of Britain's premier races.

Five miles north-west of Dorking off the A246 Leatherhead-Guildford road, **Polesden Lacey** (☎ 01372-458203; NT) is a regency villa with an attractive garden and good views. Also on the A246, but on the eastern outskirts of Guildford, **Clandon Park** (☎ 01483-222482; NT) is a Palladian-style house (designed by a Venetian architect) built about 1730.

Kent

The history of the coastal towns is long and interesting, but with the exception of Sandwich, most of the towns were wrecked by the arrival of the railway and mass 19th-century tourism.

The inland area, however, has some of the country's loveliest countryside and most attractive villages. Between the North and South Downs lies an area known as the Weald, much of it designated an Area of Outstanding Natural Beauty.

The fertile rolling hills are now home to hop gardens (and the distinctive cone-shaped roofs of oast houses used for drying hops), orchards and well-off London commuters. It is still possible to see woods that are being managed with traditional coppicing techniques. And the area is still leafy and beautiful.

GETTING AROUND

Reflecting the fact that it is both densely populated, and home to many London commuters, Kent has a good network of public transport. The county council has a public transport information freephone (☎ 0800-696996) and also publishes an excellent public transport map (ask for it at bus stations and TICs).

Bus

For the purposes of bus transport, Kent is divided into east and west – draw a line north-south through Ashford to get the rough dividing point. Stagecoach East Kent (☎ 01227-472082 for inquiries throughout Kent) has quite an efficient and comprehensive set of services. In the west, one of the main operators is Maidstone & District (☎ 01634-832666), based in Chatham.

Explorer Tickets (£6.10/4.30 for adults/children) are accepted by all the main companies and on Sunday the Kent Sunday Ranger is even better value (£7.50/3.75/2.25 for families/adults/children).

CANTERBURY

- *pop 36,000*   • ☎ *01227*

Canterbury's greatest treasure is its magnificent cathedral, the successor to the church St Augustine built after he began converting the English to Christianity in 597. After the martyrdom of Archbishop Thomas à Becket in 1170, the cathedral became the centre of one of the most important medieval pilgrimages in Europe, a pilgrimage that was immortalised by Geoffrey Chaucer in *The Canterbury Tales*.

Although it is not the most beautiful cathedral, it is certainly one of the most impressive and evocative – the ghosts of saints, soldiers and pilgrims seem to crowd around. Not even baying packs of children can completely destroy the atmosphere although, if you can, go late in the day to avoid school groups.

Canterbury was severely damaged by bombing during WWII and parts, especially to the south of the cathedral, have been rebuilt insensitively. However, there's still plenty to see and the bustling centre is atmospheric and alive. The town crawls with tourists, but that simply means all is well with the world – they've been coming for a very long time.

Canterbury can easily be visited on a day trip from London and it makes an ideal stopover on the way to/from Dover. There are a couple of interesting places nearby (particularly Chilham and Sandwich), but it's too far north and east to use as a base for more than a night or two.

History

The first settlement on the site of Canterbury dates to the 1st century BC when there was a Celtic community on either side of the River Stour. It became an important place under the Romans. After the Romans left, the Jutes (from southern Scandinavia) resettled the city. In 597 St Augustine arrived, beginning his mission at the court of Ethelbert, whose wife Bertha was already Christian. Augustine (and Bertha?) successfully converted the king and many of his subjects.

Augustine founded a Benedictine monastery and abbey, and the city was established as the centre of the English church. It thrived, both under the Anglo-Saxons and those great cathedral builders, the Normans. The cathedral's fame, however, did not eclipse that of St Augustine's Abbey until after the murder of Archbishop Thomas à Becket.

In 12th-century England, the natural tension between church and state reached breaking point when Henry II refused to accept the independence of the Roman church and the authority of a foreign pope.

Before Henry made him archbishop, Becket had been a loyal and worldly courtier, a close friend of the king, famed for his brilliance and luxurious lifestyle. Henry thought Becket would be an ally in his battle against the pope – but he was wrong. From the time he became archbishop in 1162, Becket completely renounced his old lifestyle and friend.

In 1170 the personal and political conflict reached a tragic culmination when knights, apparently without Henry's knowledge, cut down and killed the archbishop in the cathedral.

Within hours of the murder rumours of miracles spread, and a few years after his death Thomas was made a saint. His jewel-encrusted shrine became the most important place of pilgrimage in England, and was famous throughout Europe. As Chaucer observed, however, for many the pilgrimage quickly became a good excuse for a holiday and Canterbury's merchants thrived on the pilgrim/tourist trade.

Becket once again became a victim of the battle between church and state when Henry VIII acted to dissolve the increasingly corrupt monasteries. In 1538 St Augustine's Abbey was demolished and St Thomas' shrine, remains and relics were totally destroyed.

Orientation

The centre of Canterbury is enclosed by a medieval city wall and a modern ring road. The centre is easy to get around on foot, virtually impossible to get around by car.

SOUTH-EASTERN ENGLAND

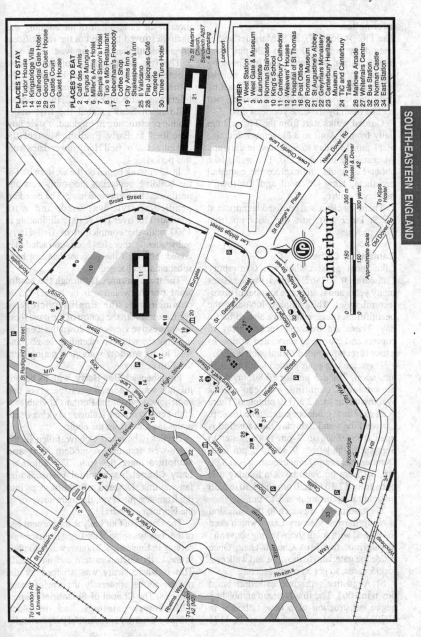

PLACES TO STAY
13 Tudor House
14 Kingsbridge Villa
18 Cathedral Gate Hotel
29 Georgian Guest House
31 Castle Court Guest House

PLACES TO EAT
2 Café des Amis
4 Fungus Mungus
6 Miller's Arms Hotel
8 Simple Simon's Hotel
17 Tuo e Mio Restaurant
  Debenham's Freebody
  Coffee Shop
19 City Arms Inn &
  Shakespeare's Inn
25 Il Vaticano
28 Flap Jacques Café
  Creperie
30 Three Tuns Hotel

OTHER
1 West Station
3 West Gate & Museum
5 Laundrette
9 Norman Staircase
10 King's School
11 Canterbury Cathedral
12 Weavers' Houses
15 Hospital of St Thomas
16 Post Office
20 Roman Museum
21 St Augustine's Abbey
22 Greyfriars Monastery
23 Canterbury Heritage
  Museum
24 TIC and Canterbury
  Tales
26 Marlowe Arcade
27 Whitefriars Centre
32 Bus Station
33 Norman Castle
34 East Station

Canterbury

To St Martin's Church, Sandwich A257 & Camping

Longport

New Rd

To Youth Hostel & Dover A2

To Kipps Hostel

Old Dover Rd

Approximate Scale

Lower Chantry Lane

St George's Place

St George's Street

Upper Bridge Street

Lwr Bridge Street

Broad Street

To A28

To A28

Northgate

Burgate

The Borough

Palace Street

King Street

St Radigund's Street

Mill Lane

The Borough

Sun Street

Mercery Lane

High Street

St Margaret's Street

Best Lane

St Peter's Street

Pounds Lane

St Peter's Place

St Dunstan's Street

To London Rd & University

Stour Street

Castle Street

Watling Street

Beer Cart Lane

Rosemary Lane

St George's Lane

CNV Trail

Footbridge

Pin Hill

Castle Way

Winchep

Rheims Way

River Stour

To London Rd A2 (M2)

To London Rd A2 (M2)

300 m
300 yards

0   150   300 m
0   150   300 yards

Information

The TIC (☎ 766567), 34 St Margaret's St, is open daily from 9.30 am to 5.30 pm. They have a bureau de change and free booking service for local B&Bs and ferry tickets. Inquire about the new Great Stour Museum, dedicated to the history of local brewing, that will be open by the time you read this.

Guided walks start from the TIC at 2 pm daily from 6 April to 3 November and also at 11 am, Monday to Saturday, in July and August. The cost is £2.50. The walks take about 1½ hours and explore the cathedral precincts, King's School and the town's medieval centre.

There's a clean and civilised laundrette at 36 St Peter's St, just one door up from Fungus Mungus.

Canterbury Cathedral

Like most great cathedrals, Canterbury Cathedral (☎ 762862) evolved in stages over many years and it reflects a number of architectural styles. The complex, including the beautiful cloisters, can easily absorb half a day. There are treasures tucked away in corners and a trove of associated stories, so a tour is recommended. Admission is £2/1.

There are one-hour guided tours at 10.30 am, noon, 2 and 3 pm for £2.80, or, if the crowd looks daunting, you can take a Walkman tour for £2.50 (30 minutes). There is an excellent guidebook available for 95p. On weekdays and Saturday the cathedral is open from 9 am to 7 pm from Easter to September, and from 9 am to 5 pm from October to Easter; choral evensong is at 5.30 pm, 3.15 pm on Saturday. On Sunday it is open from 12.30 to 2.30 pm and 4.30 to 5.30 pm; choral evensong is at 3.15 pm.

The traditional approach to the cathedral is along narrow Mercery Lane, which used to be lined with small shops selling souvenirs to pilgrims, to Christ Church Gate. Once inside the gate, turn to the right and walk east for 55 yards, to get an overall picture.

St Augustine's original cathedral burnt down in 1067. The first Norman archbishop began construction of a new cathedral in 1070, but only fragments remain. In 1174 most of the eastern half of the building was again destroyed by fire but the magnificent crypt beneath the choir survived.

The fire presented the opportunity to create something in keeping with the cathedral's new status as the most important pilgrimage site in England. In response, William of Sens created the first major Gothic construction in England, a style now described as Early English. Most of the cathedral east of Bell Harry tower dates from this period.

In 1391 work began on the western half of the building, replacing the south-west and north-west transepts and nave. The new Perpendicular style was used, and work continued for over 100 years, culminating in 1500 with the completion of Bell Harry. Subsequently, more has been subtracted than added, although the exterior has not been substantially changed.

The main entrance is through the **south-west porch**, which was built in 1415 to commemorate the English victory at Agincourt. From the centre of the nave there are impressive views east down the length of the church, with its ascending levels, and west to the **window** with glass dating from the 12th century.

From beneath **Bell Harry**, with its beautiful fan vault, more impressive glass that somehow survived the Puritans is visible. A 15th-century screen, featuring six kings, separates the nave from the choir.

Becket is believed to have fallen in the north-west transept. A modern **altar and sculpture** mark the spot. The adjoining **Lady Chapel** has beautiful Perpendicular fan vaulting. Descend a flight of steps into the Romanesque crypt, the main survivor of the Norman cathedral.

The Chapel of Our Lady at the western end of the crypt has some of the finest Romanesque carving in England. St Thomas was entombed in the Early English eastern end until 1220. This is where Henry was whipped for the murder and is apparently the site of many miracles. The **Chapel of St Gabriel** features 12th-century paintings, and the **Black Prince's Chantry** is a beautiful Perpendicular

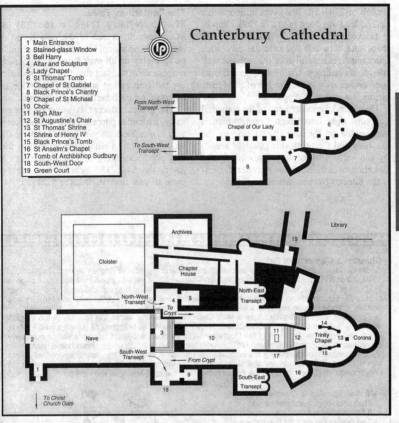

Canterbury Cathedral

1 Main Entrance
2 Stained-glass Window
3 Bell Harry
4 Altar and Sculpture
5 Lady Chapel
6 St Thomas' Tomb
7 Chapel of St Gabriel
8 Black Prince's Chantry
9 Chapel of St Michael
10 Choir
11 High Altar
12 St Augustine's Chair
13 St Thomas' Shrine
14 Shrine of Henry IV
15 Black Prince's Tomb
16 St Anselm's Chapel
17 Tomb of Archbishop Sudbury
18 South-West Door
19 Green Court

chapel, donated by the prince in 1363, now used by Huguenots (French Protestants).

Exit the crypt to the south-west transept. The **Chapel of St Michael** includes a wealth of tombs, including that of Archbishop Stephen Langton, one of the chief architects of the Magna Carta. The superb **12th-century choir** rises in stages to the **High Altar** and Trinity Chapel. The screen around the choir stalls was erected in 1305 and evensong has been sung in this inspiring space every day for 800 years. **St Augustine's Chair**, dating from the 13th century, is used to enthrone archbishops.

The stained glass in Trinity Chapel is mostly 13th century and celebrates the life of St Thomas and miracles attributed to him. **St Thomas' shrine** no longer exists, but it is still possible to see the alabaster shrine of Henry IV, buried with his wife **Queen Joan of Navarre**, and the **Black Prince's tomb** with its famous effigy along with the prince's shield, gauntlets and sword.

Opposite **St Anselm's Chapel** is the **tomb for Archbishop Sudbury** who, as Chancellor for the Exchequer, was held responsible for a hated poll tax – he was beheaded by a mob during the Peasants'

Revolt of 1381. His body was buried with a ball of lead; his head is in a Suffolk church.

Leave the cathedral by the **south-west door** and turn left towards the city wall. Queningate is a small door through the wall which, according to tradition, Queen Bertha used on her way to the Church of St Martin, before the arrival of Augustine.

Go around the eastern end of the cathedral and turn right into Green Court, which is surrounded on the east (right) side by the Deanery and the north side (straight ahead) by the early 14th-century Brewhouse and Bakehouse. In the north-west corner (far left) is the famous Norman Staircase (1151).

The Canterbury Tales

The Canterbury Tales (☎ 454888), St Margaret's St, is one of the new breed of automated historical recreations that seem to be springing up all over Britain. This one is redeemed by the fact that Chaucer's stories are the centrepoint and it does provide an entertaining introduction to the classic.

The general concept, however, is strange: jerky, hydraulic puppets seem an inefficient way to recreate history. Why not have a really well-done film? Perhaps the promoters feel they need something in three dimensions to justify the £4.75/3.95 ticket. The centre is open all year from 9.30 am to 5.30 pm.

Chaucer's *Canterbury Tales*

Geoffrey Chaucer is considered to be one of the first and greatest of English writers. Born around 1340, the son of a middle-class London vintner, Chaucer had a varied career. He began as a page to the Duke of Clarence, fought in France, held a number of middle-ranking political posts, and was court poet under Edward III and Richard II. He was, therefore, well positioned to observe medieval England and his writing brilliantly captures a wide cross-section of people.

For many, English literature begins with Chaucer. His writing marks the triumph of the English language over the Latin of the Church, which had dominated all branches of learning, and French, which had been the language of the Normans and their court. Indeed, Chaucer's early works were translations from French, and even his later work was strongly influenced by French and Italian.

To many readers describing his language as English is to stretch the definition somewhat, but although quite a few words are now strange to us and the spelling is abominable, the original is still understandable (concentrate on the sound rather than the appearance of the word):

'A clerk ther was of Oxenford also
That unto logyk hadde longe ygo
As leen was his hors as is a rake
And he nas nat right fat I undertake...'

The *Canterbury Tales*, his most popular work, consists of a collection of some 24 stories told by a party of pilgrims on their journey to the shrine of Becket at Canterbury. Chaucer paints a lively, ironic picture of the pilgrims and although the world has changed, the personalities he describes are still easily recognisable. Most 20th-century readers will find a modern translation a good deal more enjoyable to deal with than the original, however. The Canterbury Tales recreation in St Margaret's St also provides an entertaining introduction. ■

Chaucer's Clerk from *Canterbury Tales*

Weavers' Houses

These heavily restored, but still charming, Tudor houses were once home to Huguenot refugees who established a silk weaving industry in Canterbury.

West Gate & Museum

The West Gate, dating from the 14th century, is the only remaining city gate. It survived because it was used as a prison; it is now a small museum featuring arms and armour. It's open all year, Monday to Saturday, from 11 am to 12.30 pm and 1.30 to 3.30 pm; 60p/40p. A combined ticket that includes the Heritage Museum and the Roman Museum saves a little money.

Greyfriars Monastery

This was the first Franciscan (the Grey Friars) monastery in England, founded in 1267. The picturesque building spans a small branch of the River Stour, and includes an upstairs chapel that is open to the public from mid-May to September, Monday to Saturday from 2 pm to 4 pm. Eucharist is celebrated every Wednesday at 12.30 pm.

Canterbury Heritage Museum

The Canterbury Heritage Museum (☎ 452747), Stour St, in a converted 14th-century building, gives good, though rather dry, coverage of the city's history. The building, once the Poor Priests' Hospital, is worth visiting in its own right. It's open all year from 10.30 am to 5 pm, but Sunday only from June to October and only from 1.30 to 5 pm; £1.70/1.10.

Roman Museum

The days of mud-coloured objects in glass cases are well and truly over. At the Roman Museum (built underground around the remains of a Roman town house, in Butchery House, opposite the Shakespeare Inn) you get to smell the smells of a Roman kitchen, visit the marketplace, handle artefacts and take a computer-generated tour of the town house.

It's open all year, Monday to Saturday, from 10 am to 5 pm, and on Sunday from June until the end of October, 1.30 to 5 pm; £1.70/1.10.

St Augustine's Abbey

Henry VIII acted with thoroughness when St Augustine's Abbey (☎ 767345; EH) was demolished in 1538 – only foundations remain. Admission is £1.50/75p.

Places to Stay

Hostels The *Youth Hostel* (☎ 462911), 54 New Dover Rd, is a half-mile or so from the eastern railway station. Continue on St George's St (the continuation of High St) which becomes New Dover Rd. The hostel is in an old Victorian villa and is closed from late December to the end of January; the nightly charge is £9.10/6.15. You can camp here in the summer for £4.35, but only when the hostel is full!

Kipps (☎ 786121), 40 Nunnery Fields off Old Dover Rd, is an independent hostel with beds for £10 and single/twin/family rooms for £12.95/12/11 per person.

Camping *St Martin's Caravan Site* (☎ 463216), Bekesbourne Lane, is a Camping & Caravanning Club site, open from March to October. It's a huge site about two miles from the town and facilities include hot showers and laundry. A non-member backpacker pays £5.85 per person.

B&Bs & Hotels Most Canterbury accommodation is quite expensive, particularly in July and August. In a couple of cases, prices almost double; ring ahead to avoid nasty surprises.

You can stay in the heart of the city, right by the cathedral at the *Cathedral Gate Hotel* (☎ 464381), 36 Burgate. Although the walls are on the thin side and some of the floors slope alarmingly, the rooms are comfortable and the views of the cathedral are magnificent. It's a fantastic location, with the possible drawback that cars have to be parked about 500 yards away. Rooms are from £21/40 to £46/70.

Kingsbridge Villa (☎ 766415), 15 Best Lane, also in the centre of town just off High

St, is a comfortable B&B with colour TVs in rooms, some of which have their own bathrooms. Singles are £18, doubles from £30 to £42. Parking is available.

The nearby *Tudor House* (☎ 765650), 6 Best Lane, has canoes and boats to hire to guests. Rooms are from £17/28.

The *Castle Court Guest House* (☎ 463441), 8 Castle St, is a straightforward B&B with prices around £16 per person, and there is limited parking.

There are a number of cheapish B&Bs on London Rd, still within walking distance of the centre, but not in the heart of the old city, like those that have already been covered. *Ann's House* (☎ 768767), 63 London Rd, is pretty good value and, as a result, is often full. There's parking and rooms with bathroom start at £18/34.

Yorke Lodge (☎ 451243), 50 London Rd, across the road from Ann's, is a little dearer; rooms have private bathrooms. The *Derwent Guest House* (☎ 769369), 62 London Rd, has three rooms (shared bathrooms) at £34 each.

There's another batch closer to the intersection with St Dunstan's St (and therefore town), including the *London Guest House* (☎ 765860), 14 London Rd, with rooms around £18 per person, and *Courtney Guest House* (☎ 769668), 4 London Rd, with rooms from £20/30.

The more upmarket hotels mainly cluster on New Dover Rd; there are a number with doubles around £50. The *Ebury Hotel* (☎ 768433), 65 New Dover Rd, has rooms from £41/59. The *Ersham Lodge Hotel* (☎ 463174), 12 New Dover Rd, nearer town, is a bit cheaper with prices from £38/52.

Four miles away, the *Thruxted Oast* (☎ 730080), Mystole, Chartham, is an excellent B&B in converted oast houses (where hops were dried). The buildings have loads of character. Rates are £75 for luxurious twin accommodation. Book in advance, because there are only three rooms.

Places to Eat
There's a good range of reasonably priced eating places in Canterbury. If you want to

do some window-menu shopping start in St Margaret's St and then walk down High St to West Gate. There are also a couple of interesting places just outside the gate.

Il Vaticano (☎ 765333), 35 St Margaret's St, has excellent Italian food, in particular a wide range of pastas from £4.25 to £7.95.

The *Three Tuns Hotel* at the end of St Margaret's serves good-value pub meals from around £4.

Tuo e Mio Restaurant (☎ 761471), 16 The Borough, is considered by some to be the best restaurant in Canterbury. It serves high-quality Italian food with main dishes around £8.

Fungus Mungus (☎ 781922), 34 St Peter's St, has good-value and interesting vegetarian dishes around £5 but it may be closing down.

Café des Amis just beyond the West Gate serves authentic Mexican cuisine – which is very different from the usual repetitive combinations of beans, cheese and chilli. There's a great atmosphere, the food is both delicious and interesting, and the prices are reasonable. Most starters are from £3 to £4, mains from £5 to £8. Try mole poblano – roast loin of pork in a sauce made of chillies, spices, nuts, seeds and tomato with rice and salad for £6.95. Reserve a table at weekends.

Debenham's Freebody Coffee Shop is classically twee – the sort of place where the local matrons are likely to be found. It's close to the cathedral, however, and good value. Coffee is 85p for a mug, scones 75p.

Flap Jacques Cafe Creperie, 71 Castle St, opposite the Castle Court Guest House, serves French-style pancakes from £1.80 to £4.95. Open seven days a week, the café also has live music and offers a 10% student discount. It's small but has a sunny atmosphere.

Entertainment
Get hold of a copy of *What & Where When*, a free guide to what's on in Canterbury, available from the TIC.

There are quite a few lively pubs, thanks in no small part to the student population. Two on St Radigund's St worth checking out are *Simple Simon's*, which has a beer garden and usually features some sort of folk music in the evening, and the *Miller's Arms*, which is a classic student hang-out.

Other possibilities are *The City Arms Inn* and *Shakespeare's Inn*, close to the main gate to the cathedral on Butchery Lane.

Getting There & Away
Canterbury is 58 miles from London and approximately 15 miles from Margate, Ramsgate, Sandwich, Dover, Folkestone and Ashford. See also the fares tables in the Getting Around chapter.

Bus The bus station is just within the city walls at the east end of High St.

Stagecoach East Kent has a good network around the region. There are numerous buses from London with National Express (☎ 0990-808080).

National Express also has buses linking Dover, Folkestone, Hythe, Ashford and Canterbury. Canterbury to Dover is £3.10.

Train There are two railway stations: East (for the youth hostel), accessible from London's Victoria, and West, accessible from London's Charing Cross and Waterloo. The journey takes about 1¾ hours and costs £13 for a day return. There are regular trains between Canterbury East and Dover Priory (45 minutes, £3.70).

Getting Around
Taxi Try Laser Cars (☎ 464422) or Linx Taxis (☎ 464232) – expect to be charged around £1 per mile.

Bicycle You can hire sturdy mountain bikes from Canterbury Cycle Mart (☎ 761488), 19-23 Lower Bridge St, for £10 per day or £50 per week.

MARGATE
• *pop 39,000* • ☎ *01843*
Margate was one of the earliest and most popular seaside resorts in England, with Londoners travelling down by boat. A kinder guidebook than this says Margate 'enjoys fresh sea breezes off the North Sea'. We'll call it a freezing wind and add, quite gratuitously, the sea is grey. There are hundreds of B&Bs and hotels, and a number of tacky entertainment centres. Looking at Margate, God got so depressed she created Torremolinos. There's a TIC (☎ 220241) on Marine Drive.

BROADSTAIRS
• *pop 21,600* • ☎ *01843*
Broadstairs developed later than Margate, in late Regency/early Victorian times, with the coming of the railway. It has remained much smaller, and still has the peculiar fascination of a real English resort that has not gone completely to seed.

Charles Dickens lived in Broadstairs from 1830 to 1851, writing much of *David Copperfield* and *Bleak House* in a house on top of the cliff above the pier, now a local history museum. The nearby **Dickens House Museum** (☎ 862853), 2 Victoria Pde, has a trove of Dickens' personal possessions; open daily, 2.30 to 5.30 pm; £1/50p.

The TIC (☎ 862242) is on High St.

Places to Stay & Eat
There's a wide range of places to eat (with plenty of fish & chips on offer) in the narrow old streets running down to the harbour.

Broadstairs has a recommended youth hostel which is convenient for the Sally Line Ramsgate-Dunkerque ferry (three miles away). The *Thistle Lodge Youth Hostel* (☎ 604121), 3 Osborne Rd, is run by a helpful couple; the overnight charge is £8.25/5.55. From the station, turn right under the railway and continue for 30 yards to a crossroads with traffic lights, then turn left into The Broadway leading to Osborne Rd. Ferry tickets are on sale.

There are plenty of B&Bs. There are some good-quality places, all with sea views, some with rooms with private bathrooms, on the Eastern Esplanade. The *East Horndon Private Hotel* (☎ 868306), at 4 Eastern Esplanade, *Gull Cottage Hotel* (☎ 861936), at No 5, and *Bay Tree Hotel* (☎ 862502), at No 12, charge around £20 per person.

Getting There & Away

There are hourly Eastonways (☎ 588033) buses to Ramsgate (No 29) for the ferry (sometimes Sally Line runs a courtesy bus), and regular buses to Canterbury (No X81), although only hourly to Canterbury on Sunday.

There are regular trains to/from London's Victoria station (via Chatham), Canterbury West, and Dover Priory.

RAMSGATE

- *pop 38,000*   • ☎ *01843*

Ramsgate was a fashionable Victorian resort, but although it has been hit by recession and the decline in English seaside holidays it's still just kicking thanks to Sally Line ferries and a large yacht marina.

The harbour is attractive and overlooked by some impressive Regency crescents.

There are some interesting narrow streets with some unusual buildings further behind. Near the marina, there's a **Maritime Museum** (☎ 587765) that charts the seafaring history of Ramsgate back to Roman times. A visit to nearby Begwell Bay could take in a free tour of a replica Viking ship.

The TIC (☎ 591086) is on Queen St and is open Monday to Saturday from 9.30 am to 5 pm.

Ramsgate is 74 miles from London, 16 from Canterbury. See the introductory Getting There & Away chapter for details of destinations from Ramsgate.

SANDWICH

- *pop 4500*   • ☎ *01394*

Sandwich is literally a backwater. Once a thriving Cinque Port on the sheltered Wantsum Channel, it has been deserted by

---

Cinque Ports

Kent juts into the Channel – it's a mere 17 miles between Dover and Cap Gris Nez – so it's not surprising its past is a mixed story of war and trade. The Romans had important ports at Regulbium (Reculver), Rutupiae (Richborough), Dubrae (Dover) and Anderida (Pevensey), and a naval fleet and chain of forts defending what they called the Saxon Shore against German raiders.

When the German raiders (the Jutes, Angles and Saxons, otherwise known as the Anglo-Saxons) succeeded the Romans they exploited the region's natural advantages by trading and fishing. In the absence of a professional army and navy, however, their thriving east-coast towns were the front line against Viking raids and invasions and were frequently called upon to defend themselves, and the kingdom, at land and sea.

In 1278, King Edward I formalised this already ancient arrangement by legally defining the Confederation of Cinque (pronounced sink) Ports. The five Head Ports – Sandwich, Dover, Hythe, Romney (now New Romney) and Hastings – were granted numerous privileges in exchange for providing the king with ships.

As the ports became more powerful and the demands of trade and defence increased the confederation expanded to include Rye and Winchelsea, and each Head Port incorporated Limbs, or supporting towns and villages. At times there were up to 30 Limbs of the confederation, in addition to the Head Ports.

By the end of the 15th century most of the Cinque Ports' harbours had become largely unusable thanks to the shifting coastline, and a professional navy was based at Portsmouth. Only Dover now remains an important port.

As is often the case in Britain, while real importance and power has evaporated, the pomp and ceremony remains. The Lord Warden of the Cinque Ports is a prestigious post now given to faithful servants of the crown – they get an apartment at Walmer Castle, and a chance to wear funny clothes and a big gold chain. The current warden is the Queen Mother, but amongst the previous incumbents was Sir Robert Menzies, the Prime Minister of Australia from 1949 to 1966. Sir Robert earned his reward with uninhibited grovelling, including his famous speech to Elizabeth II where he quoted a medieval poet:

'I did but see her passing by
and yet I love her 'til I die' ■

the sea and pretty much forgotten by the world. As a result the town is a remarkable medieval time capsule that has not been substantially altered since the 16th century.

Because it is two miles from the sea it has escaped the horrible fate of most Cinque Ports that were 'developed' as seaside resorts in the 19th century. More remarkably, the town has managed to avoid being turned into Ye Cute Olde Englishe Village in the 20th.

Orientation & Information

The town is on the south bank of the River Stour and is still mostly surrounded by an earthen embankment (dating from the 14th century). Everything is within easy walking distance.

The TIC (☎ 613565), on the New St side of the Guildhall, is open from May to 9 September, daily from 11 am to 3 pm. The TIC sells a fascinating official guidebook for 60p, and provides information on a town walking trail and some pleasant short walks in the surrounding countryside.

Things to See & Do

Sandwich is not renowned so much for outstanding individual buildings as for the overall impact of unspoilt medieval streetscapes. **Strand St** is said to have more half-timbered houses than any other in England. Elsewhere, a number of buildings have Dutch or Flemish characteristics (note the stepped gables in some buildings), the legacy of Protestant Flemish refugees who settled in the town in the 16th century.

The exterior of the **Guildhall** (☎ 617197) was substantially altered in 1910, but the interior is little changed since the 16th century. It's open Tuesday to Saturday from 10.30 am to 4 pm, Sunday from 2 to 4 pm, closed Monday; £1/80p.

The **Church of St Clement** has one of the finest surviving Norman towers in the country – designed as much for defensive purposes as for anything else.

Places to Stay & Eat

The range of places to stay is quite limited, so you may be forced to make a day trip –

which is easily done from Canterbury, Ramsgate or Dover.

The *Bell Hotel* (☎ 613388), The Quay, overlooking the river, is the town's posh hotel with rooms for £70/90; *Magnums* is a café belonging to the hotel and has a wide range of meals under £5. The *New Inn* (☎ 612335), Harnet St, near the Guildhall, has considerably more reasonable rooms with private bathrooms for £20 per person. There are very few cheap B&Bs but you could try *Mrs Rogers* (☎ 612772), 57 St George's Rd, who charges £15 per person.

The *Sandwich Leisure Park* (☎ 612681), Woodnesborough Rd, is open from March to October and has tent and caravan sites.

Getting There & Away

Sandwich is about 15 miles from Canterbury and about 10 from Dover. Buses leave from the Guildhall, and the railway station is south of the town wall off New St (which becomes Dover Rd).

Stagecoach East Kent Buses has an hourly service between Deal and Canterbury via Sandwich (X11, X12), but not on Sunday, as well as a daily two-hourly service (No 613/614, 40 minutes). The 611 bus is an irregular service between Deal and Sandwich. There is a daily, hourly service to/from Folkestone and Dover (No 93/94, 1½ hours). The X70 goes hourly, except on Sunday, to Broadstairs, where the hostel will reimburse the bus fare if you are staying there.

Thanet Bus (☎ 01227-722263) has an hourly service to/from Ramsgate.

Sandwich is on the railway line between Margate, Dover Priory and Folkestone Central; there are regular trains.

DOVER

- *pop 37,000* • ☎ 01304

Dover has two things going for it: the world's busiest passenger harbour and a spectacular medieval castle. It's the only Cinque Port that hasn't yet sunk, although it will come under increasing pressure from the Channel Tunnel – and no-one can say with confidence whether or not it will actually go down the plug hole.

Dover is sited along the River Dour which created a safe harbour on a stretch of coast dominated by the famous white cliffs. There is evidence of an Iron Age settlement, and the Romans unquestionably identified the strategic importance of the site. Dubrae, as Dover was known, was a fortified port in the chain of defences along the Saxon Shore.

The Normans, needless to say, immediately built a castle. The existing building dates to 1181 and was known as the Key of England. It has played an important military role, most recently in WWII.

The foreshore of Dover is basically an enormous, complicated (though well-signposted) and unattractive vehicle ramp for the ferries. The town itself was badly damaged during WWII and today, under siege from heavy traffic, has no charm. The feeling that everyone is en route to somewhere much more interesting – as soon as possible – doesn't help.

Orientation & Information

Dover is dominated by the looming profile of the castle to the east. The town itself runs

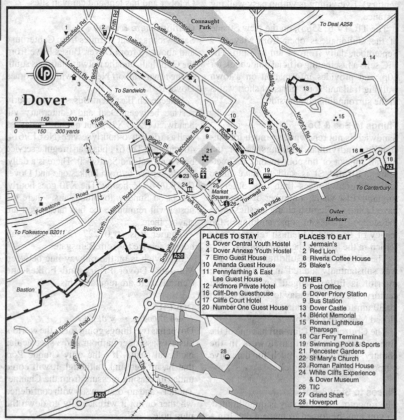

PLACES TO STAY
3 Dover Central Youth Hostel
4 Dover Annexe Youth Hostel
7 Elmo Guest House
10 Amanda Guest House
11 Pennyfarthing & East Lee Guest House
12 Ardmore Private Hotel
16 Cliff-Den Guesthouse
17 Cliffe Court Hotel
20 Number One Guest House

PLACES TO EAT
1 Jermain's
2 Red Lion
8 Riveria Coffee House
25 Blake's

OTHER
5 Post Office
6 Dover Priory Station
9 Bus Station
13 Dover Castle
14 Blériot Memorial
15 Roman Lighthouse Pharosgn
18 Car Ferry Terminal
19 Swimming Pool & Sports
21 Pencester Gardens
22 St Mary's Church
23 Roman Painted House
24 White Cliffs Experience & Dover Museum
26 TIC
27 Grand Shaft
28 Hoverport

back from the sea along a valley formed by the unimpressive River Dour (in Roman times, this formed a navigable estuary).

The TIC (☎ 205108) is on Townwall St near the seafront and is open daily from 9 am to 6 pm. It has an accommodation and ferry-booking service.

The Mangle, on Worthington St, is a convenient laundrette just near the Riveria Coffee House and not far from the Roman Painted House.

Dover Castle

Dover's main attraction is a well-preserved medieval fortress with a beautiful location and spectacular views across the Channel. To add to its fascination, there are the remains of a Roman lighthouse, or Pharos within the fortifications, as well as a restored Saxon church.

The **Pharos** is possibly the oldest standing building in England (dating from 50 AD), and certainly one of the most intriguing. Built as a lighthouse by the Romans, it guided ships into the estuary of the Dour below.

The **keep** was built on the orders of Henry II between 1181 and 1187 and its walls are up to 22 feet thick in places. The castle survived sieges from rebellious barons in 1216 and the French in 1295, was captured by the Parliamentarians in 1642, was the headquarters for operations against German submarines in WWI, and the command post for the evacuation of Dunkerque in 1940.

The excellent tour of **Hellfire Corner** covers the castle's history during WWII, and takes you through the tunnels which burrow through the chalk beneath the castle.

The castle (☎ 201628; EH) is open daily from 10 am to 6 pm; between October and March, from 10 am to 4 pm. Entry is £6/3, including a 55-minute guided tour of Hellfire Corner; there is a worthwhile audio tour of the keep for an additional £1.50.

White Cliffs Experience & Dover Museum

An enormous amount of money has been spent on this new-breed museum, which is

tricked out with robots, dioramas, and light and sound shows. If you are a history buff, the museum is actually very interesting. If you've got kids in tow and it's wet outside, the Experience will be a lifesaver.

From April to October the electronic bit – the Experience (☎ 210101) – and the museum are open daily from 10 am to 5 pm; admission is £4.99/3.50 for both, or £1.50/75p for the museum only.

Roman Painted House

The most remarkable aspect of these remains is that they have survived at all. Unless you're a keen archaeologist, however, you may be disappointed. There's little to see beyond the foundations, and the painting is fragmentary.

The house (☎ 203279), New St, is open April to October, Tuesday to Sunday from 10 am to 5 pm (Monday also in July and August); £1.50.

Grand Shaft

Beginning at Snargate St, there's a 140-foot triple staircase which was cut into the white cliffs as a short cut to town for troops stationed on the Western Heights during the Napoleonic Wars. According to tradition, one staircase was for officers and their ladies, the second for the NCO's and their wives, and the third for soldiers and their women!

Cycle Route

It is possible to follow an interesting route between Dover, Deal, Sandwich and Canterbury. The countryside is mostly flat, and there are plenty of quiet country lanes. Depending on how circuitous the route, it would be approximately a 35-mile ride. Pick up a 'Cycling in East Kent' pack, which details several routes, from the TIC.

Places to Stay

There are two youth hostels, both of which can fill up very quickly in summer; one or the other may close during winter. Finding any accommodation can be tough in high summer, so making a booking is advisable.

The TIC has a booking service and there's accommodation information on ☎ 01839-401571.

The main hostel, *Dover Central Youth Hostel* (☎ 201314), 306 London Rd, charges £9.10/6.15 per night. The *Dover Annexe* (☎ 206045), 14 Godwyne Rd, is also comfortable, although a bit cramped. The overnight charge, including breakfast, is £11.90.

B&Bs are mainly strung along Folkestone Rd (the A20) but there is another batch on Castle St and Maison Dieu Rd in town.

The *Elmo Guest House* (☎ 206236), 120 Folkestone Rd, is reasonable value at £12 to £19 per person.

The *Valjoy Guest House* (☎ 212160), 237 Folkestone Rd, has only three rooms and charges £15 per person in July, £17 in August; bed only is from £15.

Tucked under the castle, near the Eastern Docks (ideal if you have an early ferry), the *Cliffe Court Hotel* (☎ 211001), 25 East Cliff, Marine Pde, is an elegant Regency hotel with parking. Most rooms have sea views and private bathrooms and the rate is from £15 to £22 per person. Across the road, *Cliffe-den* (☎ 202418), 63 East Cliff, Marine Pde, is quiet and pleasant with a per-person rate from £14 to £18.

The popular *Number One Guest House* (☎ 202007), 1 Castle St, has private bathrooms, and breakfasts are served in your room. There's a lock-up garage. B&B is £17 to £21 per person.

There are a number of places along Maison Dieu Rd. Two worth considering are *Pennyfarthing* (☎ 205563), at 109, and *East Lee Guest House* (☎ 210176), at 108. They are both comfortable places with private bathrooms. Room-only rates are from £17 to £21 per person.

Harold St – a quiet cul-de-sac that runs parallel to Maison Dieu Rd – has the *Amanda Guest House* (☎ 201711), at No 4, which has B&B from £13 to £17. The *Ardmore Private Hotel* (☎ 205895), 18 Castle Hill Rd, is a comfortable and civilised hotel in a gracious old house. Guests have private bathrooms and B&B ranges from £16 to £22.50.

Those looking for a modern comfortable hotel and who have a vehicle should try the *Forte Posthouse* (☎ 821222), Singledge Lane, Whitfield, a short drive away on the A2; £56 per person.

Places to Eat

There's not a lot of joy for gourmets in Dover, despite (or because of?) the proximity to Calais. There are a number of restaurants and fast-food outlets around Market Sq, but you will probably do best with a pub meal. On King St, *Topo Gigio*, closed on Sunday evening, has pasta for around £4, pizzas from £5 to £6.

The *Red Lion*, just off Frith Rd, has excellent filling meals for around £5, and is convenient to both youth hostels. It has a pleasant garden and a skittle alley. Also convenient for the hostel, *Jermain's* is a clean, efficient place with a range of good-value traditional meals like roast beef for £3.30.

Blakes (☎ 202194), 52 Castle St, in the centre of town, is a Victorian pub with a garden and good-value food, closed Sunday. *The Britannia* (☎ 203248), on Townwall St, is a bright and airy pub with good-value meals.

The *Riveria Coffee House* (☎ 201303), 9 Worthington St (the continuation of Pencester Rd) is a busy little café with pink menus, pink tablecloths and pink-cheeked waitresses. Toasted sandwiches are from £1.30; enormous baked potatoes are from £1.70; a scone, jam and cream is £1.10 and decent filter coffee is 75p.

Getting There & Away

Dover is 75 miles from London and 15 from Canterbury. See the fares tables in the Getting Around chapter.

Ferry departures are from the Eastern Docks (accessible by bus) below the castle, but the Hoverport is below the Western Heights. The train station is a short walk to the west of the town centre. The ferry companies run complimentary buses from Dover Priory (some even link the Central Youth Hostel). The bus station is in the centre of town.

Bus National Express has numerous buses to Dover, and most stop at Canterbury. London to Dover is £11.25 return. Stagecoach East Kent Buses (☎ 240024) has an office on Pencester Rd. Canterbury is the bus hub for the region; there is no direct link, for instance, between Dover and Brighton, which makes a bus loop around the coast a little complicated. There is one bus per day from Canterbury to Brighton and an hourly service to/from Folkestone (No 90/93/94, half an hour).

Train There are over 40 trains a day from London's Victoria and Charing Cross to Dover Priory (two hours, £18.50).

There's an enjoyable hourly service that runs across the rich Romney Marsh farmlands from Ashford to Rye and Hastings (£6.50). There are hourly trains from Hastings to Battle (15 minutes, £2.20). Hastings to Brighton is another hour and costs £8.

Boat For information on ferries to/from Dover see the introductory Getting There & Away chapter. For information on day trips and special offers phone ☎ 401575.

Getting Around
Bus Fortunately, the ferry companies run complimentary buses between the docks and railway station. They're a long walk apart, especially if you've got some heavy bags.

There are infrequent East Kent buses to the Eastern Docks from the Pencester Rd bus station (D25, D15 or D15A for 49p).

Taxi Central (☎ 240441) and Britannia (☎ 204420) have 24-hour services. One way to Folkestone or Deal would cost about £6.50. Local trips start at £1.40 plus 50p per mile.

Bicycle You can hire a range of bicycles from Andy's Cycle Shop (☎ 204401), 156 London Rd.

FOLKESTONE
- *pop 46,280* • ☎ *01303*

With no particular sights of note, Folkestone is a ferryport with SeaCat services to

Boulogne. The Channel Tunnel begins (or ends) just outside Folkestone: Le Shuttle's car-carrying rail services (no foot passengers) use the terminal two miles north-west of the town.

Folkestone is a considerably more pleasant place to stay than Dover. There's a classic beachside funfair and, above on the cliffs, The Leas, a unique garden promenade lined by substantial Victorian hotels with great views.

The TIC (☎ 258594), Harbour St, near the inner harbour, is open daily from 9 am to 5.30 pm, later in summer for evening arrivals of the SeaCat. There's also a TIC (☎ 270547) at the Channel Tunnel Terminal where you can make accommodation bookings.

There are numerous places to stay. The *Chilton House Hotel* (☎ 249786), 14 Marine Pde, is a clean, decent place with rooms with bathroom for £20/35, without for £16/28. Near The Leas, the *Salisbury Hotel* (☎ 252102), 30 Clifton Gardens, has rooms with bathrooms, some with sea views, from £25 per person. The *Westward Ho! Hotel* (☎ 221515), 13 Clifton Crescent, has views, but is only £18.50. The pleasant *Rhodesia Hotel* (☎ 253712), 2 Clifton Crescent, doesn't have the views so is only £15.

For information on ferries to/from Folkestone, see the introductory Getting There & Away chapter.

ASHFORD
- *pop 45,500* • ☎ *01233*

Despite the fact that the new international railway station is the only passenger boarding point between London and the Continent for trains using the Channel Tunnel, Ashford looks like a depressed town.

Orientation & Information
The TIC (☎ 629165), 18 The Churchyard, is open Monday to Saturday from 10 am to 4.30 pm and to 5.30 pm in summer.

Places to Stay & Eat
There are plenty of B&Bs. *Quantock House* (☎ 627596), Quantock Drive, is within walking distance of the town centre, bus and

SOUTH-EASTERN ENGLAND

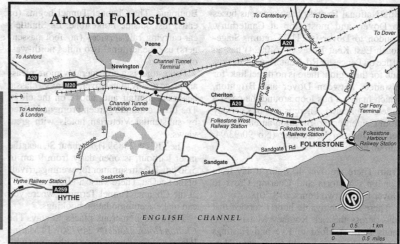

Around Folkestone

To Canterbury   To Dover   To Dover

Peene
To Ashford
Newington   Channel Tunnel Terminal
A20   Ashford Rd   A20
M20
To Ashford   Channel Tunnel   Cheriton   Churchill Ave
& London   Exhibition Centre   A20   Cheriton Rd   Car Ferry Terminal
Folkestone West   Cherry Garden Ave   Dover Rd   Folkestone Harbour Railway Station
Blackhouse Hill   Railway Station   Folkestone Central Railway Station   FOLKESTONE
Sandgate Rd
Sandgate
Hythe Railway Station   Seabrook   Road
A259
HYTHE

ENGLISH CHANNEL

0   0.5   1 km
0   0.5 miles

Network SouthEast stations. The charge per person including breakfast is from £17 to £18. *Hamlee House* (☎ 634429), 2 Earls Ave, Willesborough, has a single, a double and a twin from £15 per person.

You certainly should be able to eat well for under £10 at any of the following: *Trattoria Romana* (☎ 638033), 32 Bank St; *Royal Mandarin* (☎ 620347), 9 North St; *Tandoori Nights* (☎ 636681), 9 Torrington Rd. If you find yourself depressed and down on your luck in Ashford, try a breakfast special at *Brannigan's Bistro*, 30 Bank St, for 99p!

Getting There & Away
Ashford is 70 miles from London, 15 from Canterbury, seven from Dover, about 25 from Rye and Tenterden.

Bus Stagecoach East Kent Buses (☎ 01233-472082), Station Rd, has an interesting service (No 400) between Canterbury and Rolvenden via Ashford. From Rolvenden there's a service, No 340 on South Coast Buses (☎ 0345-581457), to Hastings.

Train See the introductory Getting There & Away chapter for information on the interna-

tional rail service. There are frequent Network SouthEast services to Rye and Hastings; to Canterbury, Ramsgate and Margate; to Folkestone, Dover Priory, Ramsgate and Margate; to Maidstone and London's Victoria; and to Tonbridge and London's Charing Cross.

Getting Around
Taxi Try Arrow Taxis (☎ 630222), or United Taxis (☎ 629291/2/3).

SISSINGHURST CASTLE GARDEN
Sissinghurst Garden (☎ 01580-715330; NT), off the A262 between Biddenden and Cranbrook, is an enchanted place. Vita Sackville-West and her husband Harold Nicholson (of the infamous Bloomsbury Group) discovered a ruined Elizabethan mansion in 1930 and created a superb garden in and around the surviving buildings. The castle and gardens are surrounded by a moat, and rolling wooded countryside. All the elements come together to create an exquisite, dreamlike English beauty. Anyone who has ever doubted the rich seductiveness of the English landscape has not been to Sissinghurst in spring or summer.

The gardens are open from 2 April to 15 October – Tuesday to Friday from 1 to 6.30 pm, and on Saturday and Sunday from 10 am to 5.30 pm; it's closed on Monday. The ticket office opens at noon from Tuesday to Friday. Admission is £5/2.50.

Place to Stay

It is possible to stay in the substantial estate manager's house, 100 yards from Sissinghurst Castle. Every room (including the bathroom) has stunning views over the famous gardens and the surrounding countryside. *Sissinghurst Castle Farm* (☎ 01580-712885) is deservedly popular and costs from £22.50 per person; booking is advised.

Getting There & Away

The nearest railway station is Staplehurst on the line between Tonbridge and Ashford. Maidstone & District's Maidstone to Hastings bus service (No 4/5) passes the station and Sissinghurst.

HEVER

Idyllic Hever Castle (☎ 01732-865224) near Edenbridge, a few miles west of Tonbridge, was the childhood home of Anne Boleyn, mistress to Henry VIII and then his doomed queen. The moated castle was built in the 13th and 15th centuries and restored in the early 1900s by William Waldorf Astor. The exterior is unchanged from Tudor times, but the interior now has superb Edwardian woodwork. The castle is surrounded by a garden, again the creation of the Astors, that incorporates a number of different styles, including a formal Italian garden with classical sculpture.

It's open from March to late November daily from noon to 6 pm; admission to the castle and gardens is £6/3, to the gardens only £4.40/2.60. The nearest railway station is Hever on the Uckfield line, a mile from the castle itself (£5.60 from London's Victoria station).

CHARTWELL

Chartwell (☎ 01732-866368) is the large country house just north of Edenbridge that Winston Churchill bought in 1922 and which remained the family home until his death. The house is filled with important memorabilia.

The house (only) is open in March and November on Saturday, Sunday and Wednesday from 11 am to 4.30 pm. The house, garden and studio are open from April to October; Tuesday, Wednesday and Thursday from 11 am to 4 pm, Saturday and Sunday from 11 am to 5.30 pm. Entry to the house only is £2/1, to the house and garden £4.50/2.25.

KNOLE HOUSE

In a country that is full of extraordinary country houses, Knole (☎ 01732-450608; NT), just south of Sevenoaks, is outstanding. It may be exceeded in size by Blenheim, but its graceful Elizabethan/Jacobean simplicity is more beautiful. Substantially dating from 1456, it is not as old as some of the great houses that incorporate medieval fortresses, but it is more coherent in style.

It seems as if *nothing* substantial has been changed since early in the 17th century, including the furniture. It is the Sackville family, who have owned the house since 1566, who can take credit for somehow resisting the temptation to rebuild and redecorate according to 'modern' fashions. After all, there are some things that just cannot be improved.

Vita Sackville-West, co-creator of Sissinghurst, was born in the house in 1892, and her friend Virginia Woolf based the novel *Orlando* on the history of the house and family.

The house is vast, with seven courtyards, 52 staircases and 365 rooms, so the excellent guidebook (£1.50) is recommended. There is public access from April to October; Wednesday, Friday, Saturday and Sunday from 11 am to 5 pm, Thursday from 2 to 5 pm; admission is £4.50 and last entry is at 4 pm. Parking is £2.50 (free for NT members). The grounds are open all year.

Places to Stay

Nearby Sevenoaks is not particularly exciting, but it's not bad, and there are plenty of

Winston Churchill – Warmonger or War Hero?

Modern historians have fallen over themselves to debunk the myths that surround Churchill, and many people now have mixed feelings about the man. Those too young to have heard his great speeches are now likely to have a better knowledge of his mistakes than of his strengths and achievements. Those on the left remember his conservative beliefs, Australians remember the tragedy of Gallipoli in WWI and the abandonment of Australia in WWII, and East Europeans remember betrayal at the Yalta Conference.

By any objective assessment, however, Churchill was an extraordinary man and one of the greatest leaders that the British have ever had.

Winston Churchill was born at Blenheim Palace in 1874, the son of a cabinet minister and his American wife, and a direct descendant of the Duke of Marlborough. He was sent to Harrow School, which he hated, later saying, 'I would far rather have been apprenticed as a bricklayer's mate...it would have taught me more; and I should have done it better!'

At the age of 18 he entered the army and over the next few years fought on the north-west frontier of India and actually participated in a cavalry charge in the Sudan. In 1899 he sailed to South Africa to report on the Boer War. He was taken prisoner, but later escaped, a feat that transformed him into a popular hero in Britain.

Churchill became a Conservative member of parliament in 1900 at the age of 25. In 1911 he became First Lord of the Admiralty, with responsibility for the navy. During the early days of WWI, he was held responsible for the Gallipoli debacle in Turkey. As a result, in November 1915, he resigned from Cabinet and went to the Western Front in France where he commanded a Scottish battalion in the front-line trenches. In December 1916 he was brought back into the government as Minister for Munitions and finally, at the end of the war, was put in charge of the massive task of demobilisation.

Over the next five years, Churchill was involved in negotiating the post-Ottoman Empire boundaries in the Middle East and the Irish Treaty which led to formation of the Irish Free State. From 1924 to 1929 he was Chancellor of the Exchequer, with responsibility for the government's economic policies. In June 1929, however, the Conservatives were defeated, and for the next 10 years Churchill found himself in the political wilderness. He spent his time writing, painting and attempting to alert the world to the Nazi danger.

On 1 September 1939 Germany invaded Poland and within days Churchill was recalled as First Lord of the Admiralty. In May 1940, at the age of 65, he became prime minister. At the time, Europe was either ruled by or under the direct influence of the Nazis, Stalin had negotiated a peace, the USA was neutral, and by September Britain was being bombed in what appeared to be a prelude to invasion. Churchill later wrote, 'I was conscious of a profound sense of relief. At last I had the authority to give directions over the whole scene. I felt as if I were walking with destiny, and that all my past life had been but a preparation for this hour and this trial'.

Documents released from German archives show that Hitler and his best advisers saw Britain as riven by class jealousy and bitter political divisions. They were convinced that large-scale resistance would swiftly collapse – as it had done throughout western Europe. Their assessment was probably right, but their prognosis did not bargain on the extraordinary performance of Churchill, who rallied the British when the situation looked almost hopeless: 'We shall defend our island, whatever the cost may be, we shall fight on the beaches, we shall fight on the landing grounds, we shall fight in the fields and in the streets, we shall fight in the hills; we shall never surrender...'

Following the defeat of Germany, the British people went to the polls, and the Conservative Party and Churchill were defeated. He remained the Leader of the Opposition but managed to find time for writing and painting. He was once again prime minister from 1951 to 1955 and in 1953 he was awarded the Nobel Prize for Literature. He died in 1965 at the age of 90. Almost 20 years earlier at the end of WWII, he had said, 'The road has been long and terrible. I am astonished to find myself here at the end of it.' ∎

Winston Churchill

B&Bs. The TIC (☎ 01732-450305) is on Buckhurst Lane, just to the east of High St. *Mrs Lloyd* (☎ 01732-453236), and *Beech Combe* (☎ 01732-741643), Holly Bush Lane, are both central and both have rooms for £15/33. The *Sevenoaks Park Hotel* (☎ 01732-454245), Seal Hollow Rd, has a three-acre garden and a swimming pool; most rooms have bathrooms and cost from £50/60.

Getting There & Away

Knole is to the south of Sevenoaks, east of the A225. The town's railway station, which is on the line from London's Charing Cross to Tonbridge, is a 1½-mile walk from the house.

IGHTHAM MOTE

For six and a half centuries Ightham Mote (☎ 01732-810378; NT) has lain hidden in a narrow wooded valley in the Weald. Not only has it survived, it has grown more beautiful – as the stone mellowed, a wing was added here, a room converted there...

Somehow it has survived wars, storms, changes in ownership, and generation after generation of occupants. This is all the more remarkable since it is not an aristocratic mansion full of priceless treasures, just a small medieval manor house surrounded by a moat.

Although parts date from around 1340, the building of today is like an architectural jigsaw puzzle, and you need a detailed guide to unravel which bit belongs to what century. Some of the additions and alterations seem haphazard, but the materials (wood, stone, clay), the building's scale, and the frame of water somehow create a harmonious whole.

The location is picturesque, the building is extraordinary. It's six miles east of Sevenoaks off the A25, 2½ miles south of Ightham off the A227. It's open from April to October, daily except Tuesday and Saturday, from noon to 5.30 pm, Sunday from 11 am to 5.30 pm; £4.

LEEDS CASTLE

Just east of Maidstone, Leeds Castle (☎ 01622-765400) is justly famous as one of the world's most beautiful castles. Like something from a fairy tale, it stands on two small islands in a lake surrounded by rolling wooded hills. The building dates from the 9th century, but Henry VIII transformed it from a fortress into a palace. It is overrun by families, especially at the weekend, and stunning though the surroundings undoubtedly are, the atmosphere is more hysterical than historical.

It's open daily. Admission is £7/4.80. National Express (☎ 0990-808080) has one bus a day direct from Victoria station (leaving at 10 am); it must be prebooked and the combined cost of admission and travel is £15/11.25. The nearest railway station is Bearsted on the Kent Coast Line to Ashford. British Rail has a combined admission/travel ticket for £15.90/7.90 from London's Victoria or Charing Cross stations.

East Sussex

East Sussex has some of the most spectacular coastal scenery in Britain, superb countryside along the spine of the South Downs, and a variety of towns and sights – all within easy reach of London.

Although they are touristy, Rye and Battle have a definite magic. Lewes is as historically interesting, but seems to be bypassed by the crowds.

Hastings and Brighton are two of England's largest and most interesting seaside towns, but for an extraordinary mix of class and tackiness Brighton is in a category of its own.

GETTING AROUND

East Sussex has a good network of public transport, and rail is particularly good from a traveller's point of view. The county council operates a very helpful public transport information line (☎ 01273-474747) from Monday to Friday, 9 am to 4.30 pm, and also publishes an excellent public transport map (ask for it at bus stations and TICs).

Bus

There's quite a bit of overlap between Kent and East Sussex bus operators. In particular, Stagecoach East Kent Buses (☎ 01277-472082) helps operate several routes. In Sussex itself, the major operators are Eastbourne Buses (☎ 01323-416416), South Coast Buses (☎ 0345-581457), which cover Hastings and Southdown as well, Lewes Coaches (☎ 01273-479123), and Brighton & Hove Buses (☎ 01273-886200).

Explorer Tickets (£6.10/4.30 for adults/children) are accepted by all the main companies, and are also accepted by some companies in Kent.

Train

Most people without their own transport will find that rail will serve them best in East and West Sussex. There are fast regular services from London to Hastings, Brighton and Chichester on the coast, and a line that runs the length of the Sussex coast linking these three main towns and many smaller in-between.

RYE
- *pop 5400*   • ☎ *01797*

Rye, once a Cinque Port, is a picturesque medieval town with half-timbered buildings, winding cobbled streets and a number of literary associations.

Rye is sometimes claimed to be the most beautiful town in Britain and, as a result, is inundated with tea shops and tourists. Because it is so popular and because it so perfectly meets expectations for Ye Olde English Town, it can seem strangely unreal – as if all you see is a façade and real life has long since fled. If you do visit – and the town would make a good base – avoid summer weekends.

Orientation & Information

Rye is only small, so it can easily be covered on foot. Cars are completely impractical and it is best to park in one of the large car parks on the outskirts of town. The railway and bus stations are adjacent to each other on the north side of town.

The Rye Heritage Centre & TIC (☎ 226696), Strand Quay, is south-west of the railway station on the River Tillingham. During summer the TIC is open daily from 9 am to 5.30 pm, in winter weekdays from 11 am to 1 pm and at the weekend from 10 am to 4 pm. The post office is on the corner of Wish St and the road to the railway station.

Things to See & Do

The Heritage Centre, home to the **Rye Town Model Sound & Light Show**, which gives a theatrical half-hour introduction to the town's history (open daily, £2/1.50), is a good place to start. From the Heritage Centre, walk up cobbled Mermaid St, one of the most famous streets in England, with timber-framed houses dating from the 15th century. The **Mermaid Inn** was a notorious smuggler's haunt and in the 18th century the Hawkhurst Gang, one of the most feared gangs in the country, used the pub to openly celebrate successful runs.

Turn right at the T-intersection for **Lamb House** (☎ 224982; NT), West St, mostly dating from 1722 and Georgian in style. It was the home of the American writer Henry James from 1898 to 1916. It's open from April to October, on Wednesday and Saturday from 2 to 5.30 pm; £2.20.

Continue around the dogleg until you come out at Church Square, which is surrounded by a variety of attractive houses, including the Friars of the Sack on the south side at No 40, which was part of a 13th-century friary. The **Church of St Mary the Virgin** is sited on the highest point in Rye and incorporates a mixture of ecclesiastical styles. The turret clock is the oldest in England (1561), still working with its original mechanism; the two gilded cherubs, known as the Quarter Boys, strike bells on the quarter-hour only.

Turn right at the eastern corner of the square for **Ypres Tower** (pronounced wiper), which is part of the 13th-century town fort that survived French raids. It now houses a small local museum relating to the Cinque Ports; it's presently being refur-

SOUTH-EASTERN ENGLAND

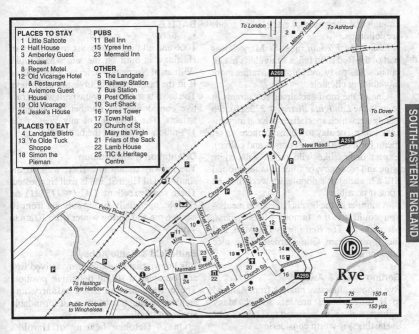

PLACES TO STAY
1 Little Saltcote
2 Half House
3 Amberley Guest House
8 Regent Motel
12 Old Vicarage Hotel & Restaurant
14 Aviemore Guest House
19 Old Vicarage
24 Jeake's House

PLACES TO EAT
4 Landgate Bistro
13 Ye Olde Tuck Shoppe
18 Simon the Pieman

PUBS
11 Bell Inn
15 Ypres Inn
23 Mermaid Inn

OTHER
5 The Landgate
6 Railway Station
7 Bus Station
9 Post Office
10 Surf Shack
16 Ypres Tower
17 Town Hall
20 Church of St Mary the Virgin
21 Friars of the Sack
22 Lamb House
25 TIC & Heritage Centre

Rye

bished but should be open from April to October. Admission was £1.50/50p. There are good views from the Gun Garden – a nice picnic spot.

Places to Stay

There's a good range of places to stay. There are several small places on New Rd (the A259 to Dover), including the *Amberley* (☎ 225693) at No 5, with B&B starting at £15.50 per person. Military Rd also has some good-value places, including *Little Saltcote* (☎ 223210) and *Half House* (☎ 223404); prices are from £15 to £20 per person.

The *Aviemore Guest House* (☎ 223052), 28 Fishmarket Rd, is close to the town centre and has rooms from £15 to £20 per person, some with bathroom. *The Windmill Guest House* (☎ 224027), Mill Lane, off Ferry Rd, has rooms with bathroom for £16 per person.

Prices tend to be higher in the centre of town, and parking can be difficult. One

exception to the rule is *Regent Motel* (☎ 225884), 42 Cinque Ports St, which has private parking, and double rooms with bathroom for £30.

The *Old Vicarage* (☎ 222119), 66 Church Square, and *Jeake's House* (☎ 222828), Mermaid St, are atmospheric old houses with comfortable, attractive rooms with bathroom and rates from £20 to £29.50 per person. They're recommended.

The *Old Vicarage Hotel & Restaurant* (☎ 225131) is a Queen Anne house on East St, with spacious attractive rooms, some with four-poster beds, all with bathroom; £28 to £42 per person.

Places to Eat

There's a surprisingly diverse range of choice for a small English town. During the day, if you're looking for something for a picnic, try *Ye Olde Tuck Shoppe*, opposite the Town Hall. The building dates from the 14th century and although the name is enough to make you choke, the baked goods are delicious.

Simon the Pieman, near St Mary's, was part of the Red Lion Inn, a smuggler's haunt, but now has pasty and chips for a rather more law-abiding clientele.

One of the most acclaimed restaurants in town is the *Landgate Bistro* (☎ 222829), 5/6 Landgate, which specialises in local ingredients. From Tuesday to Thursday there's a set menu for £14.90 (three courses and coffee). Expect dishes like wild rabbit with white wine and rosemary, or fillet of lamb (around £12 à la carte). It's popular on weekends, so book if possible.

A number of the hotels have good meals – you could try the famous old *Mermaid*, Mermaid St. The *Bell Inn* in The Mint, and the *Ypres Inn* in Gun Gardens have nice outdoor areas.

Getting There & Away
Rye is on an attractive rail link from Ashford to Hastings; buses are less useful. Many sights are close, so a shared taxi (about £12 to Hastings) is worth considering.

Bus Stagecoach East Kent runs an hourly service (No 711) between Folkestone and Brighton via Hythe, Rye and Hastings. Monday to Saturday, Eastbourne Buses (☎ 01323-416416) has a thrice-daily service (No 30) to Brighton via Eastbourne, Battle and Bodiam Castle.

Train Rye is only 1½ hours from London's Charing Cross, via Ashford. Trains leave Ashford hourly from Monday to Saturday and there are five services on Sunday.

Getting Around
Taxi Try Rye Motors Taxis (☎ 223176) or Rother (☎ 224554).

Bicycle The rather incongruous, and definitely optimistic, Surf Shack (☎ 225746), Market Rd, hires Marin mountain bikes at £2 per hour and £10 per day. Book ahead on weekends. They can suggest and provide maps for some pleasant day trips.

BATTLE
- *pop 5000*   •   ☎ 01424

1066 and all that...Battle, six miles north of Hastings, is built on the site where Duke William of Normandy defeated King Harold II in the last successful invasion of Britain. The town is surprisingly unspoilt and attractive considering the number of visitors it attracts. The highlight of any visit is the 1½-mile walk around the battlefield.

Orientation & Information
The railway station is a short walk to the south-east of High St, but is well signposted. There's an excellent TIC (☎ 773721) on High St, open daily during summer from 10 am to 6 pm and during winter from 10 am to 4 pm.

Battlefield & Battle Abbey
It is known that Harold's army arrived first and occupied a strong defensive position. There were around 7000 infantry and archers, making one of the most formidable armies of the time.

On 14 October, hearing of Harold's arrival, William marched north from Hastings and took up a position about 400 yards south of the English. His army also numbered around 7000 men, but included 2000 to 3000 cavalry.

William's forces made several unsuccessful uphill attacks against the English shield wall, then the knights feigned retreat drawing many English after them. Volleys of arrows caused more English casualties and, finally, Harold was struck in or near the eye. While he tried to pull the arrow from his head he was struck down by Norman knights. At the news of his death the final English resistance collapsed.

Construction of the abbey began in 1070 and it was occupied by Benedictines until the Dissolution in 1539. Only foundations of the church can now be seen and the altar's position is marked by a plaque, but quite a few monastic buildings survive. There's an interesting museum in the gatehouse relating to the daily life of a monastery.

Battle Abbey and Battlefield (☎ 773792;

The Scandinavian Invasions

Like most historical events, the invasion of England by Duke William of Normandy can look very different depending on which side you sympathise with, in this case the English or the Normans. The romantic tendency is to identify with the valiant losers, the rustic and easy-going English, rather than the proud and ruthless Normans – a perspective embodied in the myth of Robin Hood.

From the 9th century, the primary challenge facing England, and indeed, much of Christian Europe, was how to deal with the barbarian Vikings who swept out of Scandinavia. With complete mastery of the seas and rivers, the Danish and Norwegians first raided with appalling ferocity, then seized land and established their own kingdoms – in north-eastern England, Ireland, Germany and France.

In England, by 871 only Wessex – the half-Saxon, half-Celtic country south of the Thames and the Cotswolds – was under English control. At this low point, King Alfred the Great succeeded in neutralising the Vikings' military superiority and began a process of assimilation. Many Vikings became Christian and gradually English kings reasserted their authority over all of England. But raiding continued and during the disastrous reign of Ethelred the Unready (978-1016) the invasions reached a new peak. Finally, in 1017, Canute, the king of Denmark and later of Norway, was crowned king of England.

Canute and his sons failed to establish a dynasty, and the kingship passed to St Edward the Confessor, the son of Ethelred the Unready and his second wife, Emma of Normandy, who was also the great-great-aunt of a certain Duke William of Normandy. Edward was partly brought up in the Duchy of Normandy and was close friends with Duke William. When he became king, many resented the favouritism he showed to Norman friends; he had a particularly stormy relationship with the most powerful noble in his kingdom, Earl Godwin.

Godwin persuaded the king to marry his daughter Edith, and pushed his son, Harold, as a possible successor. In 1051, however, Edward promised the throne to Duke William, a promise confirmed by the Archbishop of Canterbury, and reinforced in 1064 when Harold Godwineson undertook to support William's claim and swore an oath of fealty.

Despite these oaths, when Edward died on 5 January 1066, Harold claimed the dying king had bequeathed him the kingdom and the lords of Wessex duly elected him king. In doing so they ignored the claims of William of Normandy, the King of Norway and the grandson of Edmund Ironside in favour of a man without a drop of royal blood.

We can only speculate on what led to this coup. There is no doubt, however, that Harold II had command of the army and widespread support, especially in the south. This implies that the prospect of a Norman – a French-speaking Viking – king did not appeal to the leading English nobles, which is not surprising. On the other hand, neither is it surprising that Duke William decided he would take by force what he believed to be rightfully his.

The first person to contest Harold II's claim, however, was the King of Norway, Harold Hardraada. On 20 September, Hardraada entered York, a former Viking capital, and apparently had no trouble convincing many of its citizens to join him on a march south. Harold II marched swiftly to meet the threat and on 24 September he defeated Hardraada's forces at Stamford Bridge. Duke William landed his forces at Pevensey on 28 September. Not knowing which Harold he would face in battle – Hardraada or Godwineson – he marched to Hastings. Harold II heard of William's landing on 2 October while he was celebrating his victory at Stamford Bridge. He chose to respond as quickly as possible, marched south, and sometime on Friday 13 October reached a ridge to the north of Hastings now known as Battle. ■

EH) has tape tours (£1.50/75p), and an excellent guidebook (£2.25) is available. Entry, including the abbey, is £3.50/1.80.

Places to Stay & Eat

There are not many cheap places to stay within easy walking distance, so it may be preferable to use Hastings as a base. If you do choose to stay in Battle, you'd be wise to consult the TIC.

High Hedges (☎ 774140), 28 North Trade Rd, is about a 10-minute walk from the TIC, and has a twin, a double and a single at £15 per person. *Little Croft* (☎ 773524), London Rd, is also reasonably close, and similarly priced.

Two miles north-west of Battle at Netherfield (on the B2096), *Netherfield Hall* (☎ 774450), opposite the church and one mile from the village inn, has comfortable double rooms; £40 to £45. *Senlac Park* (☎ 773969), Main Road, Catsfield, is a camping site within sight of the abbey; tents or vans are £6.50 a night.

Getting There & Away

Battle is on the main railway line between London's Charing Cross and Hastings; there are numerous services. National Express also has a London to Hastings service (No 067) which passes through.

Battle is on Eastbourne Buses' irregular service between Brighton (No 30, one hour) and Bodiam (1½ hours). Maidstone & District runs hourly buses (No 4/5) to Hastings.

HASTINGS
- *pop 82,000*   • ☎ *01424*

When people think of English seaside towns, Hastings is unlikely to spring to mind in the same way that places like Brighton, Eastbourne, Scarborough and Blackpool do, but it is nonetheless a classic. It still attracts

3½ million people a year – so there must be something going for it. It is a very English place, a down-to-earth family resort with lots of touristy things to do, and, perhaps what is most surprising, a peculiar charm.

It can seem a schizophrenic place, partly because several different Hastings, from several historical periods, survive. Along the coast there's a long stretch of tackiness – mostly run-down Regency/Victorian guest-houses, the inevitable fun parks and a pier. At the eastern end of town, below the castle, you'll find an atmospheric old town and the Stade, a beach that is tangled with nets, winches and working fishing boats.

Orientation & Information

In response to the new fad for the seaside, St Leonards was founded to the west of Hastings in 1827. It's a planned resort, with some impressive, if crumbling, architecture. Moving eastwards, there's a pier, with the

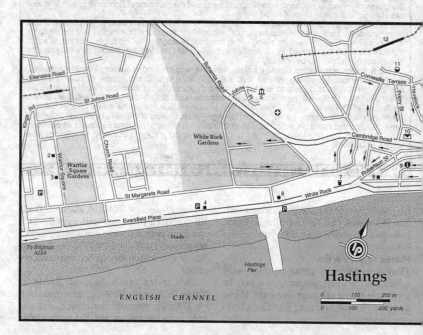

Hastings

SOUTH-EASTERN ENGLAND

inevitable attractions, the town centre, with the railway station and main bus stops, West Hill, with the ruined castle, the old town and Stade and, finally, East Hill, with good walks in the Country Park.

The TIC (☎ 718888), 4 Robertson Terrace, is open Monday to Saturday from 10 am to 5 pm; there's another branch on the foreshore near the Stade, but it's open weekends, and a third branch at the train station between May and September. There's a laundrette on High St, opposite the Old Town Hall Museum.

Stade

The bustling activity on the Stade creates one of the most memorable sights on the south coast. Fishing has increasingly become a high-tech industry requiring ocean-going vessels, so a large fleet of small boats is a rarity. There have been several failed attempts to build a harbour, so the fishermen must still haul their luggers onto the Stade. Winches, housed in small shacks, now do the hard work.

Further behind the Stade are the unique three-storey, wood-and-tar sheds, known as net shops. Dating from the 16th century, although most are now modern constructions, they were built high to minimise the ground rent the fishermen were required to pay. There are now a number of shops selling fresh fish and crabs and, along Rock-A-Nore Rd, places selling traditional delicacies like jellied eels, cockles, whelks and mussels.

Hastings Castle & 1066 Story

It is believed William erected a prefabricated wooden castle here before the Battle of Hastings. The surviving fragmentary remains date from after the battle, but there are good views and an audiovisual presentation. The West Hill Cliff Railway (see Getting Around) gives easy access. The castle

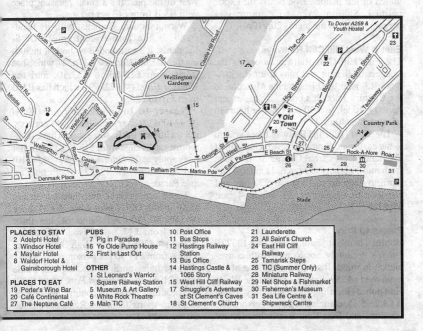

PLACES TO STAY
2 Adelphi Hotel
3 Windsor Hotel
4 Mayfair Hotel
8 Waldorf Hotel & Gainsborough Hotel

PLACES TO EAT
19 Porter's Wine Bar
20 Café Continental
27 The Neptune Café

PUBS
7 Pig in Paradise
16 Ye Olde Pump House
22 First in Last Out

OTHER
1 St Leonard's Warrior Square Railway Station
5 Museum & Art Gallery
6 White Rock Theatre
9 Main TIC
10 Post Office
11 Bus Stops
12 Hastings Railway Station
13 Bus Office
14 Hastings Castle & 1066 Story
15 West Hill Cliff Railway
17 Smuggler's Adventure at St Clement's Caves
18 St Clement's Church
21 Launderette
23 All Saint's Church
24 East Hill Cliff Railway
25 Tamarisk Steps
26 TIC (Summer Only)
28 Miniature Railway
29 Net Shops & Fishmarket
30 Fisherman's Museum
31 Sea Life Centre & Shipwreck Centre

(☎ 717963) is open all year, from Easter to September, 10 am to 5.30 pm, and from October to April, 11 am to 3.30 pm; £2.60/1.80. Combined entry to the Smuggler's Adventure, a high-tech holiday experience, is £5.50/3.60.

Fishermen's Museum

The museum (☎ 461446), Rock-A-Nore Rd, is housed in what was the fishermen's chapel, built in 1854. Exhibits include the *Enterprise*, a clinker lugger built in 1909. It's open May to September, Monday to Friday, 10.30 am to 5 pm, Saturday and Sunday from 2.30 to 5 pm; free.

The Pier

Hastings Pier is an honest, unpretentious pier, and electric fruit machines and laser games aside, it hasn't made much effort to keep up with the 20th century. It may be a tad decrepit, but standards are maintained. As the sign says: 'No baiting up or fish to be gutted or left inside'. Don't miss the exotic palmist, Sharon; even your future is a bargain. Entry to the pier is 20p/10p.

East & West Hill Cliff Railways

The East Hill Cliff Railway is one of the steepest in Britain and runs from Rock-A-Nore Rd, near the Fishermen's Museum, to the Country Park. It's open all year except January, 10 am to 5.30 pm (shorter hours in winter); 60p/40p.

The West Hill Cliff Railway takes you up to the castle and Smuggler's Adventure in St Clement's Caves from George St. It's open from mid-February to March, 11 am to 4 pm, April to September, 10 am to 5.30 pm, and October to December, 11 am to 4 pm; 55p/35p.

Places to Stay

Hostel There's a *Youth Hostel* (☎ 812373), but it's definitely not located with convenience in mind. It's on the west side of the main road (A259) to Rye, north of the White Hart pub at Guestling Hill; the nightly charge is £8.25/5.55, camping is £4 per person. The Hastings and East Kent hourly bus service

(No 11/12) from Hastings to Rye and Folkestone passes it; they leave from bus stop C near the Hastings railway station. Buses stop after 6 pm and there are no buses on Sunday.

Camping *ShearBarn Holiday Park* (☎ 423583) has a great location in the hills to the east of town, about 1½ miles from the old town. It's a large park and there are sites from £4 to £12 per night.

B&B & Hotels When in Hastings, the name of the game is to get a sea view, but bear in mind the coastal esplanade changes name from east to west: East Pde, Marine Pde, Pelham Place, Denmark Place, Carlisle Pde, White Rock St, Eversfield Place, Grand Pde, Marina St...

With this in mind, the *Marina Lodge Guest House* (☎ 715067), 123 Marina St, St Leonards, is on the coast, but about a mile west of the pier. It's a small pleasant place with B&B from £13 per person.

Warrior Square Gardens, with its bandstand, is the formal centrepiece of St Leonards. It's surrounded by hotels, including the *Adelphi Hotel* (☎ 437622), which has B&B from £16.50 to £23.50, and the *Windsor Hotel* (☎ 422709), which has B&B from £16 to £25.

Nearer to town, the *Mayfair Hotel* (☎ 434061), 9 Eversfield Place, St Leonards, is a traditional B&B; some rooms have bathrooms; rates range from £16 to £25. Similar rates apply at the *Gainsborough* (☎ 434010) and the *Waldorf* (☎ 423771), both on Carlisle Parade.

There are several guesthouses tucked away in the Old Town. *Lavender & Lace* (☎ 716290), 106 All Saints St, has three rooms from £15 per person. *Lionsdown House* (☎ 420802), 116 High St, has three rooms, from £17.50 per person.

Three miles north of Hastings on Battle Rd (A2100), the *Beauport Park* (☎ 851222) is a beautiful Georgian country house with excellent sports facilities. Rates per person are around £45.

Places to Eat

Fresh seafood is the most appropriate choice, and there are plenty of places selling fish & chips, particularly in the Old Town and along towards Rock-A-Nore Rd. Try *The Neptune Cafe* on Rock-A-Nore Rd, opposite the TIC. While near the net shops, you'll never have a better chance to try mussels, whelks and cockles (50p a plate). Be brave!

There are a number of interesting old pubs on George St in the Old Town: the 400-year-old *Anchor Inn* has live music in the evening and *Ye Olde Pump House* has classic bar meals (try the sausages for £4.45!). *The First In Last Out*, on High St, is one of the most popular pubs in town. Known as the Filo, it brews its own beer and serves interesting lunches.

There are a few restaurants along George St and several on High St. *Porters Wine Bar* (☎ 427000), 56 High St, has reasonably priced meals; starters from £2.50 and main courses around £5. They also have jazz in the evening. *Café Continental*, at No 53, specialises in crêpes which start at £1.70.

Entertainment

There's plenty of live music in Hastings. *The Crypt* club (☎ 444675), Havelock Rd (near the railway station), has interesting music nearly every night. *The Street Cafe Bar*, Cambridge Rd, (☎ 01424-424458) has live jazz every Tuesday evening and a varied mix for the rest of the week. *The Pig in Paradise* pub, White Rock, and *The Carlisle*, Pelham St, both regularly host live music.

Getting There & Away

The countryside east to Rye is attractive and the coast has some dramatic cliffs. To the west it's basically a flat and continuously developed strip of beach without much interest.

Bus Maidstone & District runs buses (Nos 4/5) to Battle, and Stagecoach East Kent runs a service (No 711) between Brighton and Folkestone via Hastings and Rye.

Train Hastings is well served by rail, with regular trains to/from London's Charing Cross (1½ hours) via Battle, and to/from London's Victoria via Gatwick airport, Lewes and Eastbourne. There are regular services to/from Ashford (45 minutes) via Rye, and heading west around the Sussex coast you can hop from Hastings to Pevensey, Eastbourne, Glynde, Lewes, Brighton, Chichester, Fishbourne and Portsmouth.

Getting Around

Bus There's quite an efficient local bus service. The TIC has a bus map.

Taxi Try Crown Taxis (☎ 855855) or Thomas Taxis (☎ 424216)

CHARLESTON FARMHOUSE

Charleston (☎ 01323-811265) is a fascinating memorial to the Bloomsbury Group. It's a Tudor/Georgian farmhouse at the foot of the South Downs, just south of the A27 between Lewes and Eastbourne. Vanessa Bell (Virginia Woolf's sister, and an important painter) moved into the farmhouse in 1916 with Duncan Grant (another painter) and the writer David Garnett.

Vanessa and Duncan embarked on decorating and painting the house, a process that continued into the '60s. Clive Bell added his collection of furniture and paintings in 1939. Every surface is painted with murals, and the house is full of decorative textiles, pictures, ceramics and furniture. There's also a lovely garden and interesting outbuildings, including a medieval dovecote.

The house is managed by the Charleston Trust; opening hours are fairly weird, so ring ahead. Admission is £4.50/3. The No 125 runs, infrequently and not on Sunday, past the Charleston turn-off from Lewes bus station. The nearest railway station is at Berwick, on the Brighton to Eastbourne line, a two-mile walk from the farmhouse.

GLYNDEBOURNE

Located two miles east of Lewes, Glyndebourne (☎ 01273-812321) is a remarkable English phenomenon. In 1934,

Smuggling on the South Coast

Smuggling in England has a long history, presumably beginning in the 13th century when Edward I first imposed duties on exported wool and imported wine. His motives were straightforward – he wanted the money. Enterprising sailor/merchants, especially those placed close to the coast of France in Kent and Sussex, immediately seized the opportunity to make profits by avoiding the Crown's tax.

A system of enforcing the customs laws was not established until 1680, when sloops were introduced to patrol the coast. The customs officers were, however, poorly paid, especially in comparison to the fortunes being earned by smugglers, so there was soon widespread corruption.

The general public was inclined to look on smugglers at worst as honest thieves, at best as romantic heroes who provided struggling folk with cheap goods. They called the smugglers *owlers*, since they often used imitation owl calls to communicate at night. Whole communities cooperated by building tunnels to link cellars and trapdoors to join attics so that contraband could be whisked from one end of a village to the other under the noses of the law.

In Elizabethan times, wool and guns from the Wealden fields and foundries were smuggled out and wine was smuggled in. As the taxes broadened, so did the smugglers' shopping lists, until they finally included spirits, tobacco, tea, coffee, chocolate and silk. From 1614 to 1825 the export of wool was actually forbidden, which was a great boost to business.

The smugglers used small swift craft to transport their goods and to outpace the law. In East Kent, Deal Galleys (powered by oarsmen) were famous for their speed. Such was Prime Minister William Pitt's frustration that in 1784 – and again in 1812 – he ordered all Deal Galleys to be burnt.

Large-scale community-sanctioned smuggling dwindled after 1832 when a new and more efficient coastguard was established and the newfangled idea of free trade led to reduced duties. It is difficult to say what the current situation is. Certainly, the bales of marijuana that occasionally wash up on the coast are not figments of anyone's imagination. The demand is there, and if someone has a boat and the right contacts, so is the ability.

Corruption, at least in some countries, is rife. And amongst a fairly wide section of society the smuggler is likely to be seen, at worst, as an honest thief...

'Them that asks no questions isn't told a lie,
Watch the wall, my darling, while the Gentlemen go by' ■

John Christie, a science teacher from Eton, inherited a large Tudor mansion and indulged both his, and his opera singer wife's, love of opera by building an opera house – in the middle of nowhere. It is now internationally famous; seats start at £10 to £100 in summer, £3 to £46 in the autumn.

The season runs from May until October, with performances beginning around 6 pm. There is a long supper interval when patrons have champagne picnics on the lawns (you can bring your own or there is a buffet). Private transport is essential.

NEWHAVEN

Most British ferry ports are unpleasant, depressing places and Newhaven has the unfortunate distinction of being one of the worst. Since it is linked by train to London (58 miles, 1¼ hours), by boat to Dieppe, France (65 miles, four hours), and by bus to

Brighton (eight miles) and Eastbourne (12 miles), there is absolutely no need to eat there, let alone stay.

Getting There & Away

See the introductory Getting There & Away chapter for information on ferries to/from Newhaven. Frequent trains link Newhaven Harbour, where they connect directly with the ferry, to London's Victoria station. Brighton & Hove and Southdown buses have frequent buses (No 712, Explorer tickets accepted) between Brighton and Eastbourne via Newhaven.

LEWES

• *pop 15,376*   • ☎ *01273*

Lewes is an attractive old town that occupies a ridge above the River Ouse. An important Norman castle was constructed soon after the invasion, but it fell into disuse in the mid-14th century.

From 1768 to 1774, Thomas Paine, the author of *The Rights of Man* and *The Age of Reason*, lived in The Bull on High St (now Bull House, opposite St Michael's), and married the daughter of the publican. Paine was eventually sacked from his job as an excise officer, his marriage collapsed and he went to America. His books advocated universal voter franchise, a progressive income tax, old age pensions, family allowances and a national system of education!

Much of the town is Georgian, but there are also much older styles (sometimes hidden behind Georgian facades). A large variety of materials have been used – timber beams, brick, flint, stone, weatherboards and wooden tiles – creating an absorbing architectural mosaic.

Orientation & Information

Lewes was an important river port, and there are still warehouses (and Harvey's, the last working brewery in East Sussex) along the river. The town is built on a steep ridge between the river and the castle ruins, with High St climbing the spine and a number of steep streets and passages *(twittens)* running off it. Driving around narrow Lewes streets and negotiating the one-way system is not fun; forget the central car park (try the one on North St) and put on your walking shoes.

The TIC (☎ 483448), 187 High St, is open Monday to Friday, 9 am to 5 pm, Saturday from 11 am to 3 pm and Sunday 10 am to 2 pm; there are reduced hours in winter.

Lewes Castle & Museum of Sussex Archaeology

The ruins of the castle date back to the 12th century. There isn't much left, but the views

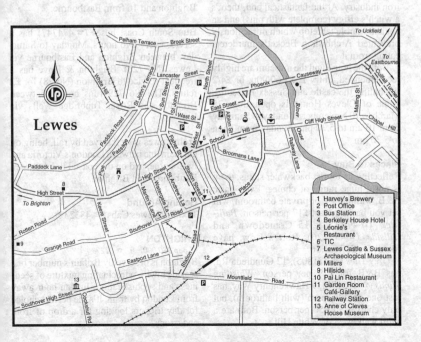

Lewes

To Uckfield
To Eastbourne
Pelham Terrace
Brook Street
Lancaster Street
North Street
Phoenix
Causeway
St John's Terrace
St John's St
Sun Street
East Street
Albion St
West St
Market St
Cliff High Street
Mailling St
Cuilfail Tunnel
River Ouse
Chapel Hill
White Hill
Paddock Road
Fisher St
School Hill
Railway Lane
Paddock Lane
Pipe Passage
High Street
Broomans Lane
St Andrew's Lane
Station Street
Lansdown Place
High Street
Watergate La
Martin's Lane
Keere Street
To Brighton
Rotten Road
Southover
Road
Grange Road
Eastport Lane
Southover High Street
Cockshut Rd
Mountfield Road

1 Harvey's Brewery
2 Post Office
3 Bus Station
4 Berkeley House Hotel
5 Léonie's Restaurant
6 TIC
7 Lewes Castle & Sussex Archaeological Museum
8 Millers
9 Hillside
10 Pai Lin Restaurant
11 Garden Room Café-Gallery
12 Railway Station
13 Anne of Cleves House Museum

make a visit memorable. The adjacent museum portrays the impact on the region by various invaders and has a well-displayed collection of prehistoric, Roman, Saxon and medieval objects and oddities.

The complex (☎ 486290) is open all year from Monday to Saturday, 10 am to 5.30 pm, Sunday from 11 am to 5.30 pm; £3/1.50. It is possible to buy a combined ticket that includes Anne of Cleves House Museum for £4/2.

Anne of Cleves House Museum

Anne of Cleves House (☎ 474610), Southover High St, dates back at least to the early 16th century; it was given to Anne of Cleves by Henry VIII as part of the settlement for their divorce.

It now houses a folk museum that includes all sorts of amazing things. At the prosaic end of the spectrum there's furniture, toys, musical instruments, odds 'n' ends, and an extensive collection relating to the Sussex iron industry. At the fantastical end, there's a witch's effigy (complete with pins) and an ancient marble tabletop which miraculously prevented Archbishop Becket's murderers eating from it.

Both the house and the museum are highly recommended; entry is £1.60/90p, or £4/2 (including the castle and Sussex museum). Anne of Cleves House is open from 25 March to 10 November, Monday to Saturday from 10 am to 5.30 pm; Sunday from noon to 5.30 pm.

Places to Stay

Reflecting its tourist backwater status, there is not a huge range of choice. Even basic B&B, without TV or private bathroom, will set you back at least £17 per person. *Bailiwick* (☎ 474377), 15 Cranedown, and *Hillside* (☎ 473120), Rotten Row, have rooms for £17 to £36.

Grey Tiles (☎ 471805), 12 Gundreda Rd, has B&B for £17 per person. *Whistling Winds* (☎ 475170), 9 Hawkenbury Way, has just one double room (with bathroom), but only charges £13.50 per person. Both are a short walk west of White Hill.

The choice is more interesting if you can afford to pay a little more. The *Berkeley House Hotel* (☎ 476057), 2 Albion St, is a carefully restored Georgian town house; £30 per person. *Millers* (☎ 475631), 134 High St, is a 16th-century timber-framed town house with two doubles (£48; non-smoking).

Places to Eat

Léonie's Restaurant (☎ 487766), 197 High St, a former gentleman's club dating from 1770, serves coffee and sandwiches during the day, and imaginative meals in the evening; two courses for £12, three for £15.

The *Pai Lin Restaurant* (☎ 473906), 20 Station St, serves delicious Thai food, with most curries around £5. *The Garden Room Café-Gallery* (☎ 478636), 14 Station St, is a relaxed place for coffee and light meals but it closes at 5 pm.

Getting There & Away

Lewes is 50 miles from London, nine from Brighton and 16 from Eastbourne.

Bus South Coast buses (☎ 474747) has a service every two hours, Monday to Saturday, between Brighton and Eastbourne via Lewes (No 728). Brighton & Hove has a frequent service to Brighton (No 28) for £2 return. The No 729 runs hourly between Brighton and Royal Tunbridge Wells via Lewes.

Train Lewes is well served by rail, being on the main line between London's Victoria and Eastbourne, and on the coastal link between Eastbourne and Brighton.

Getting Around

Taxi Try Lewes Cabs (☎ 483232).

BRIGHTON

• *pop 180,000* • ☎ *01273*

Brighton is deservedly Britain's number one seaside town – a fascinating mixture of seediness and sophistication. Just an hour away from London by train, it's the perfect choice for day trippers looking for a drop of froth and ozone.

The essential flavour of the town dates from the 1780s when the dissolute, music-loving Prince Regent (later King George IV) built his outrageous summer palace for lavish parties by the sea. Brighton still has some of the hottest clubs and venues outside London, including the largest gay club on the south coast, a vibrant population of students, excellent shopping, a thriving arts scene, and countless restaurants, pubs and cafés.

Orientation & Information

Brighton railway station is a 15-minute walk north of the beach. When you leave the station, go straight down the hill along Queen's Rd. The interesting part of Brighton lies to the left. When you reach the major intersection at the clocktower, turn left into North St, which will take you down towards the Royal Pavilion. To get to the briny and unmistakable Palace Pier, continue down North St and turn right into Old Steine (it's a road and it's pronounced steen).

The bus station is tucked in a small square sandwiched between the beach and Palace Pier (south) and the main traffic roundabout (north) formed by the Old Steine. There's an information/booking office for buses on Old Steine.

The TIC (☎ 333755), 10 Bartholomew Square, has public transport maps, and should also have copies of Brighton's listings magazine, *The Punter* (70p). If not, pick up a copy from any good newsagent.

There is a branch of American Express at 82 North St (☎ 321242).

Bubbles Laundrette, 75 Preston St, even has cute pictures on the wall.

Royal Pavilion

The Royal Pavilion (☎ 603005) is an extraordinary fantasy; an Indian palace on the outside, a Chinese brothel on the inside. It all began with a seaside affair, when the Prince Regent, aged 21, came to the fishing village of Brighthelmstone to hang out with his wayward uncle, the Duke of Cumberland. He fell in love with both the seaside and a local resident, Maria Fitzherbert, and decided that this was the perfect place to party.

The first pavilion, built in 1787, was a simple classical villa. It wasn't until the early 1800s, when everything Eastern became the rage, that the current creation began to take shape. The final Indian-inspired design was produced by John Nash, architect of Regent's Park and its flanking buildings, and was built between 1815 and 1822. George is said to have cried when he first saw the Music Room, which confirms that he was a very strange man indeed. The whole edifice is over the top in every respect and is not to be missed.

It's open June to September every day from 10 am to 6 pm, October to May to 5 pm; price £3.75. The *Queen Adelaide Tea Rooms* are on the top floor, and are a very pleasant spot to rest and recuperate. A pot of tea is 80p, sandwiches are around £1.60, and salads and simple meals like a ploughman's lunch are around £2.80.

The Royal Pavilion

SOUTH-EASTERN ENGLAND

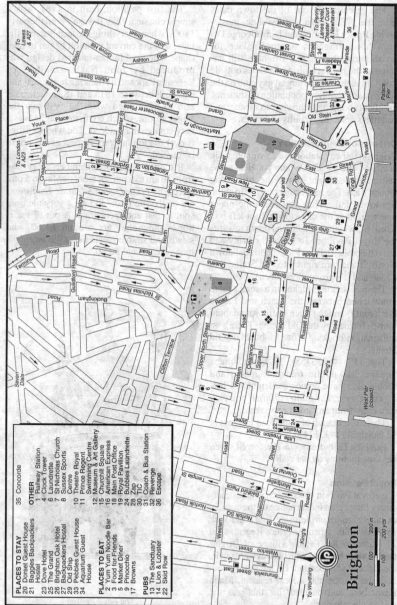

PLACES TO STAY
20 Dorset Guest House
21 Baggies Backpackers Hostel
23 Dove Hotel
25 The Grand
26 Brighton Oak Hotel
27 Backpackers Hostel
33 Pebbles Guest House
34 Aquarium Guest House

PLACES TO EAT
2 Yum Yum Noodle Bar
3 Food for Friends
5 Market Diner
9 Pinocchio
17 Browns

PUBS
13 The Sanctuary
14 Lion & Lobster
22 Skid Row

35 Concorde

OTHER
1 Railway Station
4 Clock Tower
6 Laundrette
7 St Nicholas Church
8 Sussex Sports
10 Theatre Royal
11 Prince Regent Swimming Centre
12 Museum & Art Gallery
15 Churchill Square
16 American Express
18 Main Post Office
19 Royal Pavilion
24 Bubbles Laundrette
28 TIC
31 Coach & Bus Station
32 Revenge
36 Escape

Brighton

0   100   200 m
0   100   200 yds

Brighton Museum & Art Gallery

The Brighton Museum & Art Gallery (☎ 603005), built originally as an indoor tennis court, houses a quirky collection of Art-Deco and Art-Nouveau furniture, archaeological finds, surrealist paintings and costumes. The most famous exhibit is Salvador Dali's sofa in the shape of lips, but it's often away on loan. Entry is free, and it's open daily (except Wednesday) from 10 am to 5 pm, 2 to 5 pm on Sunday.

Palace Pier

The Palace Pier is the very image of Brighton, with its Palace of Fun. In this case, fun is taken to mean takeaway food and 1000 machines, all of which have flashing lights, and all of which take your money. This is *the* place to stick your head in a cardboard cutout of Prince Charles or Princess Diana, and the best spot to buy sticks of famous Brighton Rock candy – check out the E numbers (Brilliant Blue FCF sounds especially delicious). It's open daily and the deckchairs are free.

Further along the beach you'll see the derelict West Pier. Though it's closed to the public, its red neon name still lights up at night. After the 1987 storms, the landward section had to be demolished.

St Nicholas

St Nicholas, above town at the top of Dyke Rd, is the old parish church. Parts date from around 1370 and it contains a beautifully carved Norman font. The churchyard is the resting place of Phoebe Hessel who, in order to be with her lover, dressed as a man and served for 17 years as a soldier in the West Indies. She died in 1821 at the age of 108.

Special Events

Brighton hosts the largest arts festival outside Edinburgh for three weeks every May; though mostly mainstream, there are fringe events too. During the festival there's an information point at the Dome box office, Church St, from 10 am to 6 pm daily.

Places to Stay

Hostels Brighton has two independent hostels, which are more convenient alternatives to the YHA hostel which is a long bus ride from the centre of town. *Baggies Backpackers* (☎ 733740), 33 Oriental Place, is a spacious place with wonderful décor and truly excellent showers. Beds are £8 per night and there are three double rooms for £23.

Brighton Backpackers Hostel (☎ 777717), 75 Middle St, is in a listed building, and many of the internal spaces have been decorated with murals painted by visiting travellers. Beds are £9 per night and, if full up, floor space is £5. There are also double rooms for £25. There's also a new annexe 50 metres away on the seafront with dorms, doubles with bath, and a roof-terrace. There are discounts for residents at the watersports centre opposite.

B&Bs & Hotels There's no shortage of hotels, guesthouses and B&Bs. The main cluster of cheap B&Bs is to the east of the Palace Pier. Cross the Old Steine roundabout and walk up St James St; there are several streets with B&Bs, particularly Madeira Place and Charlotte St.

Pebbles (☎ 684898), 8 Madeira Place, is comfortable and costs £18/30. Also worth trying is the *Aquarium Guest House* (☎ 605761), 13 Madeira Place, which has rooms from £16 per person, and *Madeira House* (☎ 681115), at No 14, with rooms from £11 to £16. The *Dorset Guest House* (☎ 694646), 17 Dorset Gardens, is recommended and costs £17 per person.

Brighton's hotels are located further west, with many overlooking the sea. The *Dove Hotel* (☎ 779222), 18 Regency Square, is close to restaurant-filled Preston St and the ghost of the West Pier. All bedrooms have attached bathroom, and singles/doubles cost from £35/58.

The *Brighton Oak Hotel* (☎ 220033), West St, was built in the 1930s in Art-Deco style and offers singles/doubles for £50/60.

The elegant *Grand* (☎ 321188), Kings Rd, was built in the 1860s and completely refurbished following the IRA bombing during the Tory party conference of October 1984. Prices are hefty, with singles/doubles from £130/165. Special offers are available.

The immense and slightly shabby *Old Ship* (☎ 329001), also on Kings Rd by the seafront, is the doyen of Brighton's hotels. In the 1830s, Thackeray stayed there whilst writing *Vanity Fair*. It costs from £30/60 (minimum of two nights stay in July and August).

Places to Eat

Brighton is jam-packed with good-value eating places. Wander around the Lanes or head down to Preston St, which runs back from the seafront near West Pier, and you'll turn up all sorts of interesting, affordable possibilities. If you can't afford to eat well for around £7, buy a hot dog at the pier, or throw yourself off the end.

Food for Friends (☎ 202310), 17 Prince Albert St, is Brighton's most enduring vegetarian haunt. Main meals are around £5 and there are takeaways and snacks as well.

The *Dorset Street Bar* (☎ 605423), 28 North Rd, is a friendly pub in the heart of the buzzy North Laine area. Meals start at around £5. It has a good selection of wines and bottled beers and excellent coffee.

The *Yum Yum Noodle Bar* (☎ 606777), 22 Sydney St, has good-value Chinese, Malay, Thai and vegetarian specials from £3.50. Downstairs, the Yum Yum Oriental Market has more steamers, woks, pickles and dried things in bags than you can poke a stick at.

Black Chapati (☎ 699011), 12 Circus Pde, New England Rd, is in an unpleasant part of town, and the décor has been described as a cross between a Bangkok noodle house and an airport caff. But the food is deservedly famous – a brilliant blend of Indian cuisines. Starters are from £5 and main meals are around £9.

Browns (☎ 323501), 3 Duke St, is a popular brasserie with branches around the country. It's not cheap, but not expensive either, and there's a pleasant atmosphere. A grilled goat's cheese salad is £7.15, fisherman's pie is £7.65.

Pinocchio (☎ 677676), 22 New Rd, near both the theatre and the Pavilion, offers a full range of Italian fare at very reasonable prices – a three-course meal is £9.95. Always busy, it's usually possible to be squeezed in.

The Sanctuary (☎ 770002), 51 Brunswick St East, is a pub and café. With its sunny laid-back atmosphere, flowers and comfy chairs, it's *the* place to hang out and discover what's really happening in Brighton. Downstairs is a cosy bar/venue open late for music, poetry and performance, while upstairs you can choose light meals from an excellent vegetarian menu (most offerings from £2 to £5).

Entertainment

Brighton is literally jumping with pubs, bars and clubs, but as always fashion is fickle – check *The Punter* and bar and café walls for places of the moment.

The *Greys* (☎ 680734), 105 Southover St, which runs between Richmond Terrace and Queen's Park Rd due east of the station, is a very pleasant pub with a studenty feel. There's live music on some nights.

Some of the long-standing clubs worth investigating include the *Zap* (☎ 821588), Kings Rd Arches, midway between the two piers; the *Escape* (☎ 606906), 10 Marine Pde; the *Concorde* (☎ 606460), Madeira Drive; and the more laid-back *Jazz Rooms* at 10 Ship St.

Revenge (☎ 606064), 32 Old Steine St, is a mostly male gay club with a big sound system, two dancefloors, two bars and lots of cabaret.

Things to Buy

Just south of North St (and north of the TIC) you'll find **The Lanes**, a maze of narrow alleyways crammed with antique, jewellery and fashionable clothes shops. Some of the best restaurants and bars are around here too. But for trendier, cheaper shops, good cafés and a slightly less touristy feel, explore **North Laine**, a series of streets north of North St, including Bond, Gardner, Kensington and Sydney Sts. Check out the flea market on Upper Gardner St on Saturday morning. There's also a massive market of second-hand stuff every Sunday from 7 am to 1 pm in the Brighton station car park.

Getting There & Away

Transport to and from Brighton is fast and frequent. See the fares tables in the introductory Getting Around chapter. London is 53 miles away.

Bus National Express has numerous buses from London and there's a coast link west to Cornwall.

Local bus companies include Brighton & Hove (☎ 886200) and Stagecoach Coastline (☎ 237661). The No 28 runs every 15 minutes from Churchill Square to Lewes (£2 return).

Train There are over 40 fast trains a day from London's Victoria and King's Cross (one hour). There are plenty of trains between Brighton and Portsmouth (1½ hours, £10.30). There are also frequent services to Eastbourne, Hastings, Canterbury and Dover.

Getting Around

Taxi Try Brighton & Hove Radio Cabs (☎ 204060), Southern Taxis (☎ 324555), or Hove Streamline (☎ 202020); rates are £2 for the first mile, £1.30 thereafter.

Bicycle You can hire from Sunrise Cycles (☎ 748881) by West Pier, or Alpine Cycles (☎ 625647), 7 Beaconsfield Rd. Their rates start at £10 a day but Locate a Bike (☎ 624422) at 76 North Rd charges only £5 a day.

West Sussex

West Sussex is not as densely packed with castles and great houses as East Sussex and Kent, but it has some superb countryside and some lovely small villages. Chichester makes a good base for exploring the rolling hills and the small villages that are tucked away within them.

GETTING AROUND

Bus

The major bus operators are Brighton & Hove (☎ 01273-821111), Stagecoach Hants & Surrey (☎ 01252-512513), Stagecoach Hampshire Bus (☎ 01256-464501), Sussex Coastline (☎ 01903-237661), South Coast (☎ 01273-474747) and Hastings Buses (☎ 01424-433711).

Explorer Tickets are accepted by all the main companies, and are also accepted in East Sussex and by some companies in Kent.

Train

Chichester is served by the main line from London's Victoria to Portsmouth (via Gatwick airport). Chichester is also on the Sussex coast line that runs west from Hastings to Portsmouth.

ARUNDEL

Arundel is a pleasant little tourist trap, at the foot of a romantic-looking castle. Despite its ancient appearance and history, however, most of the town dates from Victorian times. Although neither the town nor the castle are particularly interesting, the town does make a good base (best avoided on summer weekends). The countryside north along the Arun valley and west along the South Downs is amongst the most beautiful in England.

The TIC (☎ 01903-882268), 61 High St, is open daily in summer. There are numerous B&Bs and hotels. *Arundel Youth Hostel* (☎ 882204) is 1½ miles from the town.

Rail is definitely the efficient way of getting to/from Arundel; it's 55 miles from London, 20 from Brighton and 11 from Chichester.

CHICHESTER

• *pop 28,000* • ☎ *01243*

Chichester is the thriving administrative centre for West Sussex, but it has been an important town since the time of the Romans. It lies on the flat meadows between

SOUTH-EASTERN ENGLAND

the South Downs and the sea and was once a port.

East, West, North and South Sts were laid out by the Romans for their town, Noviomagus, and the foundations for an enormous Roman villa, and its beautiful mosaics, survive at Fishbourne on the town outskirts. The Norman castle has long disappeared, but the cathedral survives. The City Cross at the centre of town dates from 1501 (built by Bishop Story for the 'comfort of the poore people there') and is one of the finest in the country. A substantial part of the town centre is dominated by classic Georgian architecture.

Orientation & Information

Chichester is a busy shopping town, so it has had to come to grips with a traffic problem – which it has done well. There's a bypass and an inner ring road outside the old city walls with a number of long-stay parking areas along it, all of which are within easy walking distance of the town centre. Vouchers can be bought at the TIC for on-street parking in the centre.

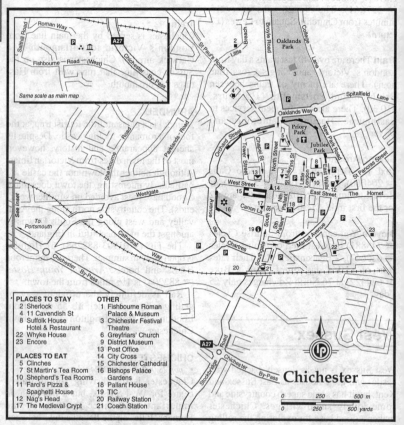

PLACES TO STAY		OTHER	
2	Sherlock	1	Fishbourne Roman
4	11 Cavendish St		Palace & Museum
8	Suffolk House	3	Chichester Festival
	Hotel & Restaurant		Theatre
22	Whyke House	6	Greyfriars' Church
23	Encore	9	District Museum
		13	Post Office
PLACES TO EAT		14	City Cross
5	Clinches	15	Chichester Cathedral
7	St Martin's Tea Room	16	Bishops Palace
10	Shepherd's Tea Rooms		Gardens
11	Farci's Pizza &	18	Pallant House
	Spaghetti House	19	TIC
12	Nag's Head	20	Railway Station
17	The Medieval Crypt	21	Coach Station

Chichester

The TIC (☎ 775888), 29A South St, is open from Monday to Saturday, 9.15 am to 5.15 pm, and, from April to September, on Sunday from 10 am to 4 pm.

Chichester Cathedral

The Chichester Cathedral of today has evolved over 900 years, but it remains substantially Norman, or Romanesque, and is more harmonious in appearance than most other churches of similar antiquity. It is also smaller than some of the more famous cathedrals, but though it is less awe-inspiring, it is also more intimate.

Work began in 1075, continuing for over 100 years – the nave survives; at the beginning of the 13th century the inside of the clerestory, the retrochoir, sacristy and porches were built in the Early English Gothic style; the side chapels and Lady Chapel date from the beginning of the 14th century and are in the Decorated style; and, finally, the cloisters, bell tower and unique detached belfry were built in Perpendicular style around the turn of the 15th century.

There are a number of treasures on display in the cathedral, and the story of the cathedral is best revealed by an expert: guided tours operate from Easter to October, Monday to Saturday at 11 am and 2.15 pm. In particular, don't miss the 16th-century paintings by Lambert Barnard, the exquisite 12th-century stone carvings, said to be among the finest masterpieces of Romanesque sculpture, the shrine of St Richard, the window designed by Marc Chagall, and the poignant tomb of the Earl of Arundel and his countess. The two are shown holding hands, with their feet resting on their pet dogs (this in 1376) – which inspired Philip Larkin to write *An Arundel Tomb*, but also shows the English have been peculiar about dogs for a long time.

Chichester has a fine choir, which sings daily at evensong. Evensong is at 5.30 pm from Monday to Saturday, 3.30 pm on Sunday. Admission to the cathedral is free but there is a suggested donation of £2/1.

Pallant House

Of the many fine Georgian houses in the town, Pallant House (☎ 774557), 9 North Pallant, is outstanding. It was built by a wealthy wine merchant who spared no expense. It has been carefully restored and now houses an excellent collection of mainly modern, mainly British art. It's open all year, Tuesday to Saturday, 10 am to 5.30 pm; £2.50/1.

Church of the Greyfriars

The Franciscans established a church here in 1269, on the old site of the castle – now Priory Park in the eastern corner of the town. The simple, but quite beautiful, building which remains was their choir and now overlooks the local cricket pitch. After dissolution in 1538, the building became the guildhall and later a court of law, where William Blake was tried for sedition in 1804.

Special Events

Chichester's Festival Theatre (☎ 781312), built in 1962, is a striking modern building in parkland to the north of the ring road. Sir Laurence Olivier was the theatre's first director, Duncan C Weldon has recently been appointed to the position, and it is now at the centre of an important arts festival, the Chichester Festivities (☎ 785718), held every July.

Places to Stay

Camping The *Southern Leisure Lakeside Village* (☎ 787715), Vinnetrow Rd, takes family tents and vans between Easter and October at £7.50 plus £1.50 per person. It is also possible to camp at the *Goodwood Racecourse* (☎ 774486) from Easter to September, except during race meetings!

B&Bs & Hotels *Encore* (☎ 528271), 11 Clydesdale Ave, is a short walk from the centre. The rate is from £17 to £21 per person. *Sherlock* (☎ 787128), 20 Little Breach, is particularly convenient for the theatre. There's one double and one twin from £14 to £16 per person. Or there's *11 Cavendish St* (☎ 527387), a non-smoking B&B, with one double and one single at £16 per person.

SOUTH-EASTERN ENGLAND

Whyke House (☎ 788767), 13 Whyke Lane, is run by a helpful couple who live next door to the guesthouse, which means you can use the fully equipped kitchen if you choose. They have one single room, one double, two twins and a family room, and serve a continental breakfast. With private facilities the rate is £19.50 per person, with shared facilities it's £17.50.

Suffolk House Hotel & Restaurant (☎ 778899), 3 East Row, is a Georgian house in the heart of the city with a range of comfortable single/double rooms from £37 to £48.50 per person.

Places to Eat

Chichester is well endowed with good restaurants; most are within an easy walk of each other in the city centre, so it's not difficult to check them out. The two main restaurant zones are on South St and on St Pancras St (off East St). It's worth booking at any time during the Chichester Festivities and if you wish to eat after theatre performances.

Clinchs Coffee Shop & Restaurant (☎ 789915), 4 Guildhall St, is a good-value place close to the theatre. In the evening, main courses start at around £6.50 and include simple dishes like seafood bake and nut roast. A school dinnery sticky pudding is £2.25 and coffee is 90p. *The Medieval Crypt* (☎ 537033), 12 South St, is a brasserie/bar in a fascinating old building. Prawns in garlic are £4.95, steak and kidney pie £6.95.

St Martin's Tea Room (☎ 786715), 3 St Martin's St, serves excellent, mainly organic vegetarian food in a Georgian house. There's a garden for summer and a log fire for winter. Most main dishes are around £3. It's open Monday to Saturday from 9 am to 6 pm and is recommended for its teas and cakes.

Shepherd's Tea Rooms (☎ 774761), 35 Little London, is a traditional tea room in a period house that has won a clutch of awards, including the Tea Council Award of Excellence in 1995. The cakes are delicious (from £1 to £3) and there are also light meals (around £6). It's open Monday to Friday

from 9.15 am to 5 pm, Saturday from 8 am to 5 pm.

Farci's Pizza and Spaghetti House (☎ 537979), 5 St Pancras St, has a good range of antipasto for around £5.50, and pasta and pizzas from £5.50.

For a pub meal try the bar in the *Nag's Head Hotel* on the corner of St Pancras St and East St.

Getting There & Away

Chichester is 60 miles from London, 11 from Arundel and 18 from Portsmouth.

Bus Chichester is served by the Coastline Express (No 700/701) which runs between Brighton (two hours) and Portsmouth (one hour), from Monday to Saturday every half-hour; on Sunday every hour. It's slow.

Train Chichester is on the Sussex Coast line between Brighton (one hour; twice as fast as the bus) and Portsmouth (30 minutes). Trains are frequent during the week, at least hourly on Saturday and Sunday. Chichester can also be reached easily from London's Victoria, via Gatwick airport and Arundel (an hourly service; 1¾ hours).

Getting Around

Taxi Try Dunnaway's Taxis (☎ 782403).

AROUND CHICHESTER

To the south of Chichester lies the popular Chichester Harbour, with a huge marina and several attractive fishing villages such as Bosham. To the north lie the beautiful South Downs, and several more unspoilt villages – like East and West Dean and Charlton (which is six miles from Chichester). *The Fox Goes Free* and *Woodstock House* in Charlton and the *Hurdlemakers* in East Dean are pubs worth looking for.

Fishbourne Roman Palace & Museum

Discovered in 1960, the palace at Fishbourne (☎ 01243-785859), Salthill Rd, is believed to have been built for a local king who allied himself to the Romans. The palace was built and altered in several stages, but the main construction began around 75 AD. It was spectacular in size and luxury – its bathing facilities would still put most contemporary British arrangements to shame. Although all that survives are foundations and some extraordinary mosaic floors, the ruins still convey a vision of 'modern' style and comfort.

The pavilion that shelters the site is an ugly creation, but there are some excellent reconstructions and the garden has been replanted as it would have been in the 1st century. The museum is open all year, with variable hours – May to September from 10 am to 5 pm; admission is £3.60/1.60.

Getting There & Away The museum is sited just to the west of Chichester, to the north of the A259, off Salthill Rd, signed from Fishbourne village. Regular buses (No 66/266, hourly from Monday to Saturday) leave from outside the cathedral and stop at the bottom of Salthill Rd (a five-minute walk away). The museum is also within a 10-minute walk of Fishbourne railway station, on the line between Chichester and Portsmouth.

Petworth House & Park
Twelve miles north-east of Chichester, Petworth House dates primarily from 1688. The architecture is impressive (especially the west front), but the art collection is extraordinary. JMW Turner was a regular visitor and the house is still home to the largest collection (20) of his paintings outside the Tate Gallery. There are also many paintings by Van Dyck, Reynolds, Gainsborough, Titian and Blake. Petworth is, however, most famous for its park, which is regarded as the supreme achievement of Lancelot (Capability) Brown's natural landscape theory.

The house (☎ 01798-342207; NT) is open April to October, daily except Monday and Friday, from 1 to 5.30 pm; £4.20/2. The car park and Pleasure Ground, part of the landscaped grounds featuring a number of classical follies, are open noon to 6 pm. The

park is open daily throughout the year from 8 am to sunset; entry is free.

Petworth is six miles from the railway station at Pulborough. There is a limited bus service (No 1/1A) from the station to Petworth Square, Monday to Saturday.

Hampshire

Hampshire has plenty to slow down visitors on their way to the West Country. First there's Winchester with its important cathedral, then the important maritime centres of Portsmouth and Southampton, and finally the beautiful New Forest, the largest remaining relict (ie still original) area of forest in England.

For bus information in Hampshire dial ☎ 100 and ask for Freephone County Bus Line.

WINCHESTER
• *pop 37,000* • ☎ *01962*
Winchester is a beautiful cathedral city with a lovely river and water meadows surrounded by rolling chalk downland. If one place lies at the centre of English history and embodies the romantic vision of the English heartland, it is Winchester. Despite this it seems to have escaped inundation by tourists – certainly by comparison to nearby Salisbury and to theme parks like Bath and Oxford.

An Iron Age hill fort overlooks the city. The Romans built Venta Bulgarum on the present-day site; part of their defensive wall can still be seen incorporated into a later medieval defence. Alfred the Great and many of his successors, including Canute and the Danish kings, made Winchester their capital, and William the Conqueror came to the city to claim the crown of England. The Domesday Book was also written here but much of the present-day city dates from the 18th century, by which time history had bypassed Winchester and the town had settled down as a prosperous market centre.

SOUTH-EASTERN ENGLAND

There are lots of good walks in the surrounding countryside. Winchester can be covered in a day trip from London, but it could also be a base for exploring the south coast or the country further west towards Salisbury.

Orientation & Information

The city centre is compact, easily negotiated on foot, and there's a good system of signposts. The railway station is a 10-minute walk to the west of the city centre while the bus and coach station is right in the centre,

directly opposite the Guildhall and TIC. High St, partly pedestrianised, is the main shopping street.

The TIC (☎ 840500), the Guildhall, Broadway, is open Monday to Saturday, 10 am to 6 pm and Sunday 11 am to 2 pm during the June to September peak season. They produce the excellent *Winchester Visitor's Guide* (£1), which includes info on sights, and places to stay and eat. Regular guided walking tours (£2/50p) operate from April to October and on Saturday only between November and March.

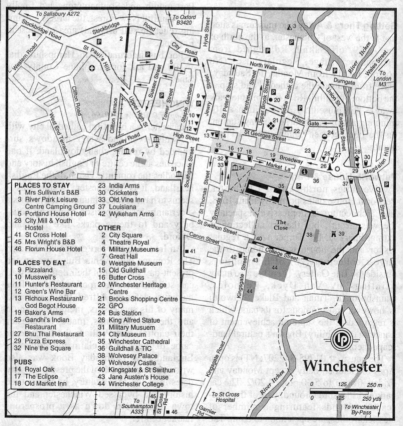

PLACES TO STAY
1   Mrs Sullivan's B&B
3   River Park Leisure
     Centre Camping Ground
5   Portland House Hotel
28 City Mill & Youth
     Hostel
41 St Cross Hotel
45 Mrs Wright's B&B
46 Florum House Hotel

PLACES TO EAT
9   Pizzaland
10 Musswell's
11 Hunter's Restaurant
12 Green's Wine Bar
13 Richoux Restaurant/
     God Begot House
19 Baker's Arms
25 Gandhi's Indian
     Restaurant
27 Bhu Thai Restaurant
29 Pizza Express
32 Nine the Square

PUBS
14 Royal Oak
17 The Eclipse
18 Old Market Inn

23 India Arms
30 Cricketers
33 Old Vine Inn
37 Louisiana
42 Wykeham Arms

OTHER
2   City Square
4   Theatre Royal
6   Military Museums
7   Great Hall
8   Westgate Museum
15 Old Guildhall
16 Butter Cross
20 Winchester Heritage
     Centre
21 Brooks Shopping Centre
22 GPO
24 Bus Station
26 King Alfred Statue
31 Military Musuem
34 City Museum
35 Winchester Cathedral
36 Guildhall & TIC
38 Wolvesley Palace
39 Wolvesey Castle
40 Kingsgate & St Swithun
43 Jane Austen's House
44 Winchester College

Winchester

Winchester Cathedral

Winchester's first church, the Old Minster, was built by King Kenwalh in 648. Its site, with subsequent enlargements, is marked out in the churchyard adjacent to the current Winchester Cathedral (☎ 853137). Old Minster was supplanted by New Minster, where Alfred the Great (871-99) was eventually interred after a short period in Old Minster. By around 1000 Old Minster was one of England's largest Saxon churches but the Norman conquest in 1066 brought sweeping changes and the foundations for a new cathedral were laid in 1079.

By 1093 the cathedral was nearly complete; the remains of St Swithun, whose name was attached to the associated monastery, were transferred to the new building and the very next day demolition orders were served on the Old Minster. The New Minster was also demolished around 1110. The completed cathedral was the longest in Britain at the time but it faced problems, in part due to the soggy ground upon which its inadequate foundations were laid. Plans for towers at the transept ends were soon abandoned and in 1107 the central tower collapsed.

In the 13th century the east end of the cathedral was enlarged and extended in the Early English style to make the retrochoir. The central choir and presbytery were next rebuilt and from the mid-14th century the Norman nave, suffering from severe subsidence, was completely rebuilt in the Perpendicular style. The Priory of St Swithun was demolished at the time of the dissolution of the monasteries and the cathedral suffered some damage during the Civil War, but there have been no further major changes.

The cathedral is entered from the west end into the towering nave which has been described as 'fudged Gothic'. In the north aisle is the **grave of Jane Austen**, who died a stone's throw from the cathedral in 1817. Her inscription gives no hint of her literary achievements! The transepts are the most original part of the cathedral and the **Holy Sepulchre Chapel** has wall paintings dating from 1120 and 1240. Crypt tours normally commence from the north transept but are often suspended if the crypt is flooded. They take place Easter to September, Monday to Saturday, at 10.30 am and 2.30 pm. As an

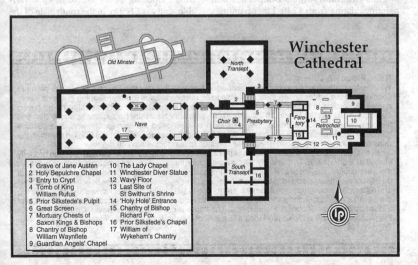

Winchester Cathedral

Old Minster

North Transept

Nave

Choir

Presbytery

Feretory

Retrochoir

South Transept

1 Grave of Jane Austen
2 Holy Sepulchre Chapel
3 Entry to Crypt
4 Tomb of King William Rufus
5 Prior Silkstede's Pulpit
6 Great Screen
7 Mortuary Chests of Saxon Kings & Bishops
8 Chantry of Bishop William Waynflete
9 Guardian Angels' Chapel
10 The Lady Chapel
11 Winchester Diver Statue
12 Wavy Floor
13 Last Site of St Swithun's Shrine
14 'Holy Hole' Entrance
15 Chantry of Bishop Richard Fox
16 Prior Silkstede's Chapel
17 William of Wykeham's Chantry

alternative, try the **unmarked door** which gives access to a part of the crypt where a modern statue is displayed.

The choir features amusingly carved wooden choir stalls, the work of William Lyngwode from 1307. The **tomb of King William Rufus** stands in the choir. The presence of the unpopular king's tomb was cited as a reason for the collapse of the tower in 1107. The **pulpit** was provided by Prior Silkstede around 1520 and the carved folds of silk are a visual pun on his name!

At the end of the presbytery is the magnificent 15th-century **Great Screen**. At the Reformation the figures in the screen were removed and broken up. The current figures are 1890 replacements, which is how Queen Victoria (2nd level, 3rd row from right of minor figures) has managed to sneak in with the Saxon royalty. **Mortuary chests**, high up under the arches on both sides of the presbytery, contain the bones of Saxon royalty and bishops.

The retrochoir has a number of **chantry chapels**, small chapels devoted to one person such as Bishop William Waynflete, Chancellor of England and founder of Magdalen College, Oxford. The particularly original **Guardian Angels Chapel** has wall paintings dating from 1240. Later paintings can be seen in the **Lady Chapel**, and just outside this chapel is a small **statue of William Walker**, the diver who spent five years shoring up the submerged cathedral footings early this century. The **wavy floor** of the south side of the retrochoir is a reminder of the subsidence problems the cathedral faced at this end.

In the middle of the retrochoir is the last **site of St Swithun's shrine**. After his rainy arrival the saint toured around the cathedral in subsequent centuries before Henry VIII's Commission for the Destruction of Shrines got rid of him in 1538. From 1150 to 1476 St Swithun's shrine featured a **Holy Hole**, a tunnel beneath the shrine for keen pilgrims to crawl through. The entrance can still be seen. The **chantry of Bishop Richard Fox** has a skeletal effigy.

In the south transept, **Prior Silkstede's Chapel** has the grave of Izaak Walton (1593-1683) and a window dedicated to this patron saint of the pastime of fishing and author of *The Compleat Angler*. The south transept Library and Triforium Gallery house a display of cathedral treasures including damaged figures from the Great Screen and the illuminated 12th-century Winchester Bible. Opening hours are somewhat variable; entry is £1/50p. In the south aisle of the

Rain, Floods & Divers

Winchester Cathedral is a curiously waterlogged place; to this day the church's crypts are prone to flooding and the subterranean tours are liable to be suspended due to water seeping in after a heavy rainfall. According to legend St Swithun is the cause of the problem. He insisted that he be buried outside the Old Minster but on 15 July 971, 109 years after his death, his request was forgotten and his remains were moved inside. The deceased saint showed his displeasure with an awesome rainstorm and ever since he has been reputed to have special powers over the English weather. If it rains on 15 July, so the legend goes, it will continue to rain for the next 40 days.

All this rainfall led to serious problems with the cathedral's foundations, which had not been properly seated at the east end. By the early 1900s it was clear there were major problems and it was feared the walls could actually collapse. Since it was impossible to drain out the foundations or to shore them up underwater, it was decided to bring in a deep-sea diver who would dig out the beech-log foundations and repack the area with sacks of cement. From 1906 to 1911 William Walker worked away at rebuilding the waterlogged foundations and the success of his labours is commemorated with a small statue of a diver by the Lady Chapel at the east end. The figure is not of Walker, however. Due to a mix up in the photographs the sculptor produced a likeness of the project's engineer, Francis Fox, rather than the diver! ■

nave is the **chantry of Bishop William of Wykeham**, founder of New College, Oxford, and of Winchester College and also responsible for the nave, although he died in 1404 when it was still under construction.

Tours of the cathedral are run by enthusiastic local volunteers and it's worth going to evensong at 5.30 pm Monday to Saturday or 3.30 pm on Sunday. There are tower tours on Wednesday at 2.15 pm, Saturday at 11.30 am and 2.15 pm (£1.50). The cathedral is open daily, 7.15 am to 6.30 pm and a £2.50 donation is requested.

City Mill
The first bridge across the Itchen at the end of Broadway is credited to St Swithun. Right over the river the City Mill (☎ 870057; NT), which once ground grain for the local bakers, was rebuilt in 1743 although an earlier mill had stood here in medieval times. The mill is open April to September, Wednesday to Sunday, 11 am to 4.45 pm; £1. The building is shared by the youth hostel; check the old print of the hostel bathing facilities in 1938.

City Museum
The museum (☎ 863064) on The Square has interesting displays on Roman ruins on the top floor, a collection of Winchester shopfronts on the middle floor, and the story of Saxon and Norman Winchester on the ground floor. It's open April to September, Monday to Saturday, 10 am to 5 pm (closed from 1 pm to 2 pm on Saturday), and Sunday from 2 to 5 pm. The rest of the year it closes on Monday. Entry is free.

Heritage Centre
The Winchester Heritage Centre (☎ 851664) at 30-32 Upper Brook St tells the story of Winchester. It's open April to October, Tuesday to Saturday, 10.30 am to 1 and 2 to 4.30 pm, and Sunday from 2 to 4.30 pm; £1/50p.

Westgate & Great Hall
The Westgate Museum (☎ 869864) on High St is in the old medieval gateway, at one time a debtors' prison. The displays include a macabre set of gibbeting irons, last used to display the body of an executed criminal in 1777. It's open April to September, Monday to Saturday, 10 am to 5 pm (closed between 1 and 2 pm on Saturday) and Sunday from 2 to 5 pm. The rest of the year, apart from November to January when it's closed completely, it closes on Monday. Entry is 30p/20p.

Little remains of Winchester Castle, which was begun by William the Conqueror and was the site of many dramatic moments in English history, including the trial of Sir Walter Raleigh in 1603. The Great Hall (☎ 845610) was the only part Oliver Cromwell did not destroy and it houses King Arthur's Round Table, now known to be a fake at 'only' 600 years old. It's open all year, daily from 10 am to 5 pm and to 4 pm at weekends in winter; free.

Wolvesey Castle & Palace
Wolvesey Castle's (☎ 854766; EH) name, so the story goes, comes from a Saxon king's demand for an annual payment of 300 wolves' heads. Commenced in 1107, the castle was completed by Henry de Blois, grandson of William the Conqueror, over half a century later. In the medieval era it was the residence of the Bishop of Winchester when this was the richest bishopric in England. It was largely demolished in the 1680s and today the bishop lives in the adjacent Wolvesey Palace; £1.50/80p.

A beautiful walk runs alongside the River Itchen to Wolvesey Castle with attractive flower-decked gardens backing the houses on the other side of the river.

Winchester College
Winchester College (☎ 868778) on College St was founded in 1382 by Bishop Wykeham and students are still known as Wykehamists. It was the model for the great public (meaning private) schools of England. The chapel and cloisters are open to visitors from 10 am to 1 pm and 2 to 5 pm (except Sunday morning). From April to September, one-hour guided tours leave at 11 am (except Sunday) and 2 and 3.15 pm (£2.50/2).

Water Meadow Walk & St Cross Hospital
From the college there's a beautiful one-mile walk to the Hospital of St Cross (☎ 851375), which was founded in 1136. The hospital is the oldest charitable institution in the country and is open April to October, Monday to Saturday from 9.30 am to 12.30 pm and 2 pm to 5 pm; the rest of the year the hours are 10.30 am to 3.30 pm with the same break for lunch. Entry is £2/50p, which entitles you to the Wayfarer's Dole (a crust of bread and horn of ale), sustenance doled out to any itinerant passer-by. St Catherine's Hill, topped by an Iron Age hill fort site, looks across to the hospital over the bypass and river.

Special Events
An annual Winchester highlight is the early July Hat Fair, a two-day festival of street theatre, taking its name from the practice of 'hatting' the audience – passing the hat around for contributions. Earlier in the year in May there's a Folk Festival.

Places to Stay
Hostel The *Youth Hostel* (☎ 853723), City Mill, 1 Water Lane, is in a beautiful 18th-century restored water mill. From the centre of town walk down High St, which becomes The Broadway, cross the River Itchen and take the first left into Water Lane. The nightly cost is £7.45/5.

Camping There are camping facilities a 10-minute walk north from the centre of town. The *River Park Leisure Centre* (☎ 869525), Gordon Rd, North Walls, is open from June to September and has tent sites for £8.25.

B&Bs & Hotels There are plenty of small B&Bs in the £15 to £18 bracket, most with only one or two rooms. St Cross Rd and parallel Christchurch Rd are good hunting grounds.
Mrs B Sullivan (☎ 862027), 29 Stock-bridge Rd, near the railway station, has three rooms at £15 per person. *Mrs R Wright* (☎ 855067), 56 St Cross Rd, also has three rooms from £18 per person. Across the road

at No 47 is *Florum House Hotel* (☎ 840427) with singles/doubles from £30/46.
St Cross Hotel (☎ 854819) at 17 St Cross Rd has a range of rooms with and without attached bathrooms. In summer they start at £27/44. *Portland House Hotel* (☎ 865195) is centrally located at 63 Tower St and has rooms with attached bathroom from £36/48. The *Wykeham Arms* (☎ 853834), near the college at 75 Kingsgate St, has some fine rooms at £67/77.

Places to Eat
Fast Food, Cafés & Pubs The standard assortment of international fast fooderies can be found around the centre. The *Abbey Bar* in the Guildhall offers lunch and snacks daily and there's also a good café in the *Cathedral Visitors Centre*. The *Richoux Restaurant* (☎ 841790) in God Begot House at 101 High St is a genteel café and restaurant open till early evening. Located at 4 Jewry St, *Green's Wine Bar* is a good place for a light meal. Try the *Baker's Arms* on Market Lane for sandwiches.

Pubs are a good bet for cheap meals; the colourful *Wykeham Arms* (☎ 853834), at 75 Kingsgate St near the college, has restaurant dishes at £9 to £12 and a cheaper bar menu. *Nine the Square* (☎ 864004) at 9 Great Minster St is a pleasant wine bar.

Restaurants The ever reliable *Pizza Express* (☎ 841845), 1 Bridge St, near the old mill and overlooking the river, serves excellent pizzas (£4 to £6). At the other end of town, *Pizzaland* (☎ 840037) serves similar food at 16 Jewry St.

The *Bhu Thai Restaurant* (☎ 844424) at 3 Eastgate St, right by the King Alfred statue, has main dishes for around £5. *Gandhi Indian Cuisine* (☎ 863940) is at 163 High St opposite the Guildhall.

The bright and cheerful *Muswell's* (☎ 842414) at 8 Jewry St offers burgers, salads, Mexican food and other dishes. *Hunter's Restaurant* (☎ 860006) at 5 Jewry St is a slightly upmarket restaurant, closed on Sunday.

Entertainment

The *Wykeham Arms* at 75 Kingsgate St looks very authentically old English with school desks as tables and tankards like stalactites hanging from the ceiling. The *Royal Oak* on High St is yet another claimant for the oldest bar in England title. Close to the City Museum there's the minute but atmospheric *Eclipse*, the popular *Old Vine* and the *Old Market Inn*, on the corner with Market St.

The *India Arms* is opposite the Guildhall, while by the river on Bridge St the *Louisiana* is a bare studenty pub with pool tables; the *Cricketers* is just across the road and river.

The *Theatre Royal* (☎ 843434) is on Jewry St.

Getting There & Away

Winchester is 65 miles from London by the M3 and only 15 miles from Southampton.

Bus National Express buses stop by the King Alfred statue on Broadway and other buses go to the bus station opposite the Guildhall. There are regular National Express buses to London via Heathrow (two hours, £9), and less frequent ones to Oxford (2½ hours, £8) and Southampton (30 minutes, £2.10).

Stagecoach/Hampshire Bus (☎ 01256-464501) has a good network of local buses linking Salisbury (No 68, 1½ hours, £2.90), Southampton (X64, 45 minutes, £1.60), Portsmouth (No 69, 1¾ hours, £2.90) and other centres in the south-east. Their Explorer Ticket (£4.25/2.90) is also good on most Wilts & Dorset buses which serve the region further to the west. There is also a similar but less useful Getaway Ticket at the same price. In summer there are buses to the Motor Museum at Beaulieu (see under Beaulieu in the New Forest section).

Train There are fast links with London's Waterloo, the south coast and the Midlands. There are two or more departures most hours to London, taking less than 1½ hours and costing £15.10 one way. The fare to Southampton is £3.20, to Portsmouth it's £6.10.

Getting Around

Bus Buses from City Rd by the railway station run to the main bus station on Broadway, opposite the tourist office.

Bicycle Mike's Bikes (☎ 885651) rents bikes for £14 a day.

AROUND WINCHESTER
Chawton

In this small village north-west of Winchester, one mile from Alton, is the **Jane Austen House** (☎ 01420-83262), where the author lived from 1809 until her death in 1817, although she actually died in Winchester. The house has a variety of Austen memorabilia and is open daily from 11 am to 4.30 pm and more restricted days the rest of the year; £1.50/50p.

Bishop Waltham Palace

Constructed between the 12th century to the 14th century, and ruined in the Civil War, Bishop Waltham Palace (☎ 01489-892460; EH) was another imposing residence of the powerful Bishop of Winchester. The palace is between Winchester and Portsmouth and you can get there on a Winchester-Southsea bus No 69. Admission is £2/1.

PORTSMOUTH

- *pop 183,000*   •   ☎ *01705*

For much of British history, Portsmouth has been the home of the Royal Navy and it is littered with reminders that this was, for hundreds of years, a force that shaped the world. Portsmouth's major attractions are the historic ships in the Naval Heritage Area but it is still a busy naval base and the sleek, grey killing machines of the 20th century are also very much in evidence.

Largely due to bombing during WWII, Portsmouth is not a particularly attractive place but Old Portsmouth, around the Camber, has some interesting spots, and the adjoining suburb of Southsea is a lively seaside resort.

Orientation

The bus station, Portsmouth Harbour

railway station, the harbour and the passenger ferry terminal for the Isle of Wight are conveniently grouped together, a stone's throw from the Naval Heritage Area and the TIC. The quay is known as The Hard.

Southsea, where most accommodation and restaurants are concentrated, is about a mile south of Portsmouth Harbour. The Isle

PLACES TO STAY
13 Keppel's Head Hotel
16 The Saltings
17 Fortitude Cottage
24 University of Portsmouth
39 Turret Hotel
40 Southsea Lodge Hostel
41 Solent Hotel

PLACES TO EAT
18 Seagull Restaurant
29 Osborne Rd Restaurants & Café's
30 L'Escargot Restaurant
31 Country Kitchen
33 Bistro Montparnasse

PUBS
 7 The Ship Anson
12 Lady Hamilton
14 The Still & West
15 Spice Island Inn
19 Bridge Tavern
34 The Parade
36 Jolly Sailor

OTHER
 1 HMS *Victory*
 2 *Mary Rose*
 3 Royal Museum
 4 HMS *Warrior*
 5 Mary Rose Exhibition Centre
 6 TIC
 8 Gosport Ferry
 9 Isle of Wight Passenger Ferry
10 Portsmouth Harbour Railway Station
11 Bus Station
20 Isle of Wight Vehicle Ferry
21 Round Tower
22 Square Tower
23 Cathedral of St Thomas of Canterbury
25 Royal Garrison Church
26 City Museum
27 Isle of Wight Hovercraft Slipway
28 War Memorial
32 Sea Life Centre & Summer TIC
35 D-day Museum
37 Southsea Castle
38 Pyramid Centre
42 South Parade Pier

of Wight vehicle ferry and Old Portsmouth are both on the old harbour known as the Camber, midway between Portsmouth Harbour and Southsea.

Information

The TIC (☎ 826722) on The Hard provides guided tours, an accommodation service and plenty of brochures. In summer the office is open daily from 9.30 am to 5.45 pm. There are also TIC offices at the Continental Ferryport (☎ 838635), at 102 Commercial Rd (☎ 838382) and, in the summer, at Southsea (☎ 832464).

Naval Heritage Area

The Royal Navy has often shown a fairly flexible attitude to fund-raising techniques, so at the end of a day in Portsmouth you should not be surprised to find you have been separated from many gold coins. The Naval Heritage Area (☎ 839766) has three classic ships which you can visit as a group or individually. Entry is £5.15/3.25 for one ship or £10/6 for all three. Tickets are bought just inside the Victory Gate entrance to the area and entry to any of the ships includes admission to the Royal Navy Museum; separately it costs £3/2. The area is open March to October, daily from 10 am to 6 pm, and November to February, daily from 10.30 am to 5 pm.

The Ships HMS *Victory* was Lord Nelson's flagship at the Battle of Trafalgar in 1805; Nelson died on board the ship during the battle. Commissioned in 1765, the *Victory* was already 40 years old at the time of its great battle and it was still afloat, though in tatty condition, when it was converted to museum use in 1922.

Exploring HMS *Victory*, and walking in the footsteps of Lord Nelson and his multi-cultural crew of ruffians and gentlemen, is about as close as you can get to time travel – an extraordinary experience. This is a very popular tourist attraction, however, and to handle the crowds the tours are conducted at high speed although with considerable humour. Even the gruesome story that the

ship's surgeon amputated 54 limbs during the course of the battle is recounted with a grin.

Adjacent to the *Victory* are the carefully conserved remains of the hull of Henry VIII's favourite ship, the *Mary Rose*. Built in 1509, the 700-ton *Mary Rose* sank offshore from Portsmouth in 1545. Its time-capsule contents were raised to the surface in 1982, after 437 years underwater. Finds from the ship are displayed in the Mary Rose Exhibition Centre, which also recounts the discovery and salvage of the ship.

Dating from 1860, HMS *Warrior* was a transition ship, as wood was forsaken for iron and sail for steam. The ship illustrates life in the navy in the Victorian era.

Royal Navy Museum The museum, housed in five separate galleries, has an extensive collection of ship models, dioramas of naval battles, displays relating to Lord Nelson and a mass of other equipment, plus exhibits on the history of the Royal Navy (for times and costs see above).

Old Portsmouth to Southsea

On a sunny day it's very pleasant to sit at **The Point**, beside the cobbled streets of Old Portsmouth, and sip a pint from one of the pubs while watching the car ferries and navy ships enter or depart the harbour.

Only fragments of the **Cathedral of St Thomas of Canterbury** in Old Portsmouth date back to its foundation in 1180. The nave and tower were rebuilt around 1690 and further additions and extensions were made in 1703 and 1938-39. Immediately south of Old Portsmouth is the **Round Tower**, originally built by Henry V, a stretch of old fort walls and the **Square Tower** of 1494.

Continue south to the ruins of the **Royal Garrison Church**, which started life in 1212, was closed in 1540, then reopened in its new role and restored in 1866-68 before being damaged in a WWII air raid in 1941. A **moat** runs beside the waterfront before an amusement park and the Isle of Wight hovercraft slipway. Harbour cruises also operate

SOUTH-EASTERN ENGLAND

from here and the anchor of HMS *Victory* is on display.

At the Southsea end of the waterfront there's a cluster of attractions, old and new, on Clarence Esplanade. The **Sea Life Centre** (☎ 734461) has aquarium displays and is open in summer, daily from 10 am to 5 pm; £4.50/3.50. Portsmouth was a major departure point for the Allied D-Day forces in 1944 and the **D-Day Museum** (☎ 827261) recounts the story of the Normandy landing with the 272-ft Overlord Tapestry and other exhibits. It's open daily, 10 am to 5.30 pm; £4/2.30.

Henry VIII's **castle** (☎ 827261) dates from 1544-45 and is open daily, 10 am to 5.30 pm; £1.60/95p. It's said that he saw the *Mary Rose* sink from this point. The **Pyramid Centre** is a pool and waterslide complex, costing £4. **South Parade Pier** is a typical British seaside pier with amusements.

Other Things to See

The 'Story of Portsmouth' is recounted in the **City Museum** (☎ 827261) on Museum Rd. It's open daily from 10 am to 5.30 pm; free. Beyond the South Parade Pier in Southsea is the **Natural History Museum** (☎ 827261) on Eastern Pde and the **Royal Marines Museum** (☎ 819385) on Barracks Rd.

The **Charles Dickens Birthplace** (☎ 827261) is at 393 Old Commercial Rd, north of the Portsmouth & Southsea railway station. It's furnished in a style appropriate to 1812, the year of his birth, but the only genuine piece of Dickens' furniture is the couch on which he died in 1870! The house is open April to October, daily from 10 am to 5.30 pm; entry is £1.60/65p.

Organised Tours

Guide Friday tours of the city (☎ 01789-294466) cost £5/1.50.

Places to Stay

The main concentration of B&Bs is in Southsea, about a mile south of the Naval Heritage Area.

Hostels The *Youth Hostel* (☎ 375661), Old Wymering Lane, Cosham, is well to the north, about four miles from the main sights. The nightly cost is £8.25/5.55 and bus No 12 operates to Cosham from the harbour bus station. Far more convenient is the friendly *Southsea Lodge* (☎ 832495) at 4 Florence Rd in Southsea, an independent hostel charging £8 a night.

During the summer the *University of Portsmouth* (☎ 843178) offers B&B-style accommodation overlooking Southsea Common from £14 per person or flats at the Nuffield Centre, St Michael's Rd, which accommodate up to six people and cost from £156 per week.

Camping The *Harbour Side Site* (☎ 663867 on weekdays) takes vans and tents. It's on the waterfront at Eastern Rd, two miles east of the town.

B&Bs & Hotels Although most accommodation is in Southsea there are a couple of alternatives. If you want to be close to the Naval Heritage Area the *Lady Hamilton* (☎ 870505) at 21 The Hard does B&B at £14 to £25 per single, £28 to £35 per double. Also on The Hard, the *Keppel's Head Hotel* (☎ 833231) charges from £30 per person.

There are a couple of handy B&Bs on The Point in Old Portsmouth, both costing from £28/40. The *Saltings* (☎ 821031) is at 19 Bath Square West while *Fortitude Cottage* (☎ 823748), with doubles only, is at 51 Broad St.

In Southsea there are a great many B&Bs with cheaper places costing from £14 to £19 per person. Close to South Parade Pier, there are numerous places along Waverley Rd, Granada Rd, St Ronan's, Malvern Rd and Beach Rd. See the map for this B&B happy hunting ground. It's easy just to wander around checking vacancy signs but a few names to start with are the *Quetta Guest House* (☎ 734414) at 53 St Ronan's Rd, *St Ann's Guest House* (☎ 827173) at 17 Malvern Rd and the *Albatross Guest House* (☎ 828325) at 51 Waverley Rd (with navy-inspired rooms).

Slightly more expensive places, between £30 and £50 per person, with sea views and attached bathrooms for most rooms are found along Clarence Pde and South Pde. Try the *Turret Hotel* (☎ 291810) on Clarence Pde or the *Solent Hotel* (☎ 875566) at 14-17 South Pde.

Places to Eat

There's a café in the Naval Heritage Area and another above the bus station on The Hard. Sandwiches and snacks or pub food at the *Ship Anson* and the *Lady Hamilton* can also be found on The Hard. At The Point in Old Portsmouth there are several popular pubs (see Entertainment) while the *Seagull Restaurant* (☎ 824866) at 13 Broad St specialises in seafood.

Osborne Rd in Southsea is the restaurant centre with a variety of cafés, pubs and restaurants, including Thai, Indian and Chinese places. *Snookies Café* at No 82 is an old-fashioned sandwich bar and bakery, while *La Croissanterie* at No 54 is a more modern place with excellent French-bread rolls. The *Osborne* is popular for pub food while *Fatty Arbuckle's* (☎ 739179) at No 61 has burgers and pasta. *Barnaby's* (☎ 821089) at No 56 is a glossier restaurant with main courses at £5 to £8.

Nearby at 59A Marmion Rd, *Country Kitchen* is a wholefood restaurant, open for lunch weekdays and Saturday. Also close to Osborne Rd is the *Bistro Montparnasse* (☎ 816754) at 103 Palmerston Rd and *L'Escargot* (☎ 812761) at 7 Stanley St bring French cuisine to Portsmouth: an eight-course feast is £17, at weekends it's £20.

The main fast food outlets are found around Osborne St or along Commercial Rd, by the Portsmouth & Southsea railway station.

Entertainment

Old Portsmouth has some of the most popular pubs including the *Still & West* and the *Spice Island Inn* on the harbour side and the *Bridge Tavern* overlooking the Camber. There's a variety of discos, clubs and pubs like the *Parade* and *Jolly Sailor* along Clarence Pde in Southsea.

Concerts are staged at the *Guildhall* (☎ 824355) on Guildhall Square while theatrical productions take place at the *Kings Theatre* (☎ 828282) on Albert Rd in Southsea or the *New Theatre Royal* (☎ 649000) on Guildhall Walk.

Getting There & Away

Portsmouth is 75 miles south-west of London and is well connected to the rest of the country.

Bus National Express has a daily service between Brighton and Portsmouth (£6.75). There are numerous buses to London, some via Heathrow airport (2½ hours, £12.50). One bus a day heads west as far as Penzance in Cornwall (11 hours, £31). The bus station is right on The Hard by the Portsmouth Harbour railway station.

Train There are over 40 trains a day from London's Victoria and Waterloo (faster from Waterloo, 1½ hours, £16.80). There are plenty of trains between Brighton and Portsmouth (1½ hours, £10.30), trains about every hour to Winchester for £6.10. Portsmouth can make a good first or final night in England if you're arriving or departing Gatwick airport as there are direct trains for £13.36 on the Victoria-Gatwick-Portsmouth line.

For the Naval Heritage Area get off at the final stop, Portsmouth Harbour.

Boat There are a number of ways of getting to the Isle of Wight, but the most convenient for those without vehicles is the Wightlink Portsmouth Harbour-Ryde or the Hovertravel Southsea-Ryde hovercraft. Wightlink also operates the Portsmouth-Fishbourne car ferry. See the Isle of Wight section for more information.

See the introductory Getting There & Away chapter for information on services to France. P&O (☎ 827677) has several ferries a day to Cherbourg and Le Havre in France and less frequent services to Bilbao in Spain.

Brittany Ferries (☎ 827701) operate to Caen and St Malo in France. The Continental Ferryport is further north from the Naval Heritage Area.

Getting Around
Bus A No 6 bus operates between the Portsmouth Harbour bus station, right beside the railway station, and South Parade Pier in Southsea. Bus No 17 or 6 will take you from the station to Old Portsmouth. The fare is 70p or you can get a day pass for £2.15. Admiral minibuses can be hailed anywhere (except Commercial Rd in the centre); you don't have to find a bus stop.

Taxi A taxi from Portsmouth Harbour to Southsea costs £3.50; there's a taxi rank beside the railway and bus station.

Boat Ferries shuttle back and forth between The Hard and Gosport. It's free from The Hard, £1.10 from Gosport. Bicycles are free. There are harbour cruises to see the navy ships in port from The Hard and from Southsea, by the hovercraft landing place. Typical costs are around £2.50 for a 50-minute voyage.

SOUTHAMPTON
- *pop 211,000* • *☎ 01703*

Southampton is a fairly large city and port of only mild interest. It developed as a major medieval trading centre with important connections to France and other European countries. Its trading role gradually declined but Southampton took up a new life as an important shipbuilding and then aircraft manufacturing centre.

These pursuits were its downfall in WWII when two nights in late 1940 saw over 30,000 bombs rain down on the city. Nearly 4000 buildings were destroyed, but Southampton bounced back to be the major centre for the D-Day departures when over two million US troops set out for the Normandy beaches. There's a surprising amount of the medieval city remaining, despite the wartime destruction, and a well-signposted circuit walk around the walls.

The TIC (☎ 221106) is at the northern end of the pedestrian stretch of Above Bar St and is open Monday to Saturday.

Getting There & Away
From Southampton airport at Eastleigh there are connections to centres in Britain, the Channel Islands, Paris and Amsterdam.

National Express (☎ 0990-808080) has bus services to major centres all over Britain including to Heathrow and London. From Southampton Central station services to London's Waterloo (80 minutes) operate twice-hourly for much of the day.

See the Getting There & Away chapter for details about ferries operating from Southampton.

NEW FOREST
The New Forest is not a national park, but outside the Highlands of Scotland this is the largest area of relatively natural vegetation in Britain. It's been that way since 1079 when William the Conqueror gave the area its name.

A variety of ancient traditions survive in the New Forest. The wild ponies for which the forest is famed are each owned by a *commoner*; it's one of the New Forest rights for commoners to graze their stock on the Open Forest. The forest is managed by 10 *verderers* who meet six times a year at the Verderers' Court in Lyndhurst.

The New Forest covers 145 sq miles, of which 105 sq miles is forest and woodland; the rest is occupied by villages and farmland. It's a pretty area to drive through but the New Forest is even better when you get off the roads and onto the cycling and walking tracks.

Information
The New Forest Visitor Centre (☎ 01703-282269) in Lyndhurst is open daily from 10 am to 6 pm and has a wide variety of information on the New Forest. Visitors are requested to follow some basic rules in the New Forest, most of them simple good sense:

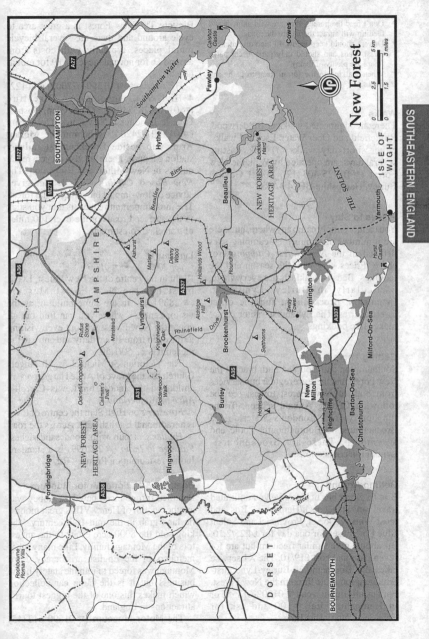

- Don't feed the ponies; they are wild animals and feeding will attract them onto the roads.
- Drivers should keep below 40 mph on unfenced forest roads and should only park in car parks (there are plenty of them).
- When walking in the forest, keep to paths and tracks.

Walks

There are signposted walks at Bolderwood, Rhinefield and Ober Water. Escorted walks, either short day walks or walks lasting several days, are operated by Walk the New Forest (☎ 01425-403412), Forest Garden, Burley, Hampshire BH24 4AR.

Places to Stay

You cannot simply camp anywhere, but there are a number of commercial camping sites detailed in the *New Forest Camping* brochure. Prices vary with the season and the facilities. Bed & breakfasts are everywhere, particularly in Burley, Lyndhurst, Lymington, Brockenhurst and the other forest centres. The Lyndhurst visitor centre makes free bookings.

Getting There & Away

Southampton and Bournemouth bracket the New Forest and there are regular bus services from both to New Forest towns; see the following Getting Around section. Trains run hourly from London's Waterloo via Brockenhurst to Bournemouth, Poole and Weymouth. There are Brockenhurst-Lymington connections.

Getting Around

Bus Explorer bus tickets give you unlimited travel on Stagecoach/Hampshire Bus and most Wilts & Dorset, Provincial and Solent Blue Line buses for one day for £4.25/2.10. Busabouts give similar freedom but are for seven days and cost £19/10. The X1 service takes the Bournemouth-Burley-Lyndhurst-Southampton route through the New Forest. For bus information call ☎ 01202-673555 or in Hampshire dial ☎ 100 and ask for Freefone County Bus Line.

Bicycle The New Forest is a great area to cycle around and there are several bicycle rental places, typically with costs from around £6 for normal bicycles, £9 for mountain bikes.

HE Figgures (☎ 01590-672002) is at 122-4 High St, Lymington. AA Bike Hire (☎ 01703-283349) is at Fern Glen, Gosport Lane in Lyndhurst. New Forest Cycle Hire (☎ 01590-624204) is behind the Morant Arms pub beside Brockenhurst railway station car park. There are also bicycle rental outlets in New Milton and Ringwood. The *New Forest Cycling Code* leaflet gives advice on low-impact bicycling in the forest. The most important request is that you stick to the surfaced roads or the over 100 miles of gravelled forest roads.

Lyndhurst

- *pop 3000*   • ☎ *01703*

Right in the centre of the New Forest, Lyndhurst has the New Forest Museum (☎ 283914) – in the same building as the visitor centre – where you can find out all about the New Forest without even visiting it. It's open from 10 am daily and entry to the museum is £2.50/1.50.

The Victorian St Michael & All Angels Church has the grave of Alice Hargreaves, in childhood the model for Lewis Carroll's *Alice in Wonderland*.

Forester's on High St in the centre of town is a traditional English café. Across the road is *Hunter's*, a pub with good sandwiches. *Passage to India* (☎ 282099) is a standard Indian restaurant on Romsey Rd.

Beaulieu & National Motor Museum

Beaulieu (pronounced bew-lee) Abbey was another victim of Henry VIII's great monastic land grab in the mid-16th century. The king sold the 8000-acre estate to the ancestors of the Montagu family. Like many other members of the English aristocracy, Lord Montagu was forced to join the stately home business but it is the large car collection which makes this one of the biggest tourist attractions in England.

The **Motor Museum** (☎ 01590-612345)

has a diverse collection of cars including a number of land speed record-holders, like the 1927 Sunbeam, which was the first car to exceed 200 mph, and the jet-powered Bluebird, which raised the record past 400 mph in 1964. From the museum area visitors can walk or choose between a replica 1912 double-decker bus or a monorail to get to the Palace House and the Abbey ruins.

The **Palace House** was once the abbey gatehouse and displays various family mementos. Only the foundations of the Abbey church remain. The **Monk's Frater** was not destroyed at the dissolution and has been the Beaulieu parish church since 1538. Other monastic buildings have exhibits on life in the monastery.

The Beaulieu attractions are open Easter to September, daily from 10 am to 6 pm, and the rest of the year to 5 pm. Entry to the whole complex is £8/5.50.

Getting There & Away To get to Beaulieu from Southampton, take a Waterfront Ferry or a Solent Blue Line bus No 38/39 to Hythe, from where bus No 112 (No 34 on summer Sundays) operates to the village and on to Lymington.

Isle of Wight

• *pop 124,000* • ☎ *(01983)*

The Isle of Wight covers 147 sq miles, stretches 23 miles long by 13 miles wide and lies only a couple of miles off the Hampshire coast. It makes a popular day trip from the mainland (try to avoid summer weekends) although there's enough of interest to justify a longer stay.

The relatively uncrowded roads, particularly along the south coast, are an attraction for cyclists, and there are walking paths almost the whole way around the 65-mile coastline.

ORIENTATION & INFORMATION
The island is a bit like a parallelogram with north-east, north-west, south-west and south-east sides. Newport is the main town, in the middle of the island. Other towns are mainly along the north-east and south-east coasts; the south-west coast is less developed. Isle of Wight Tourism (☎ 524343) is at Quay House, Town Quay, Newport but also has information centres at Cowes, Ryde, Sandown, Shanklin, Ventnor and Yarmouth.

NEWPORT & CARISBROOKE CASTLE
The island's major town is Newport, with a Roman villa (☎ 529720) on Cypress Rd and nearby Carisbrooke Castle (☎ 522107; EH). The ridgetop castle is two miles south-west of Newport and dates from Norman times although the site is Saxon. Charles I was imprisoned here in 1647-8 before his trial and execution in London. The window in which he got stuck while trying to escape can still be seen; £3.80/1.90.

COWES & OSBORNE HOUSE
Located at the northern tip of the island, Cowes is a major yachting centre and the late July/early August Cowes Week is an important international yachting event. Naturally the town has a Maritime Museum.

Since the time of King George III, British royalty have been fond of the seaside (see the Weymouth section in the South-Western England chapter); the Isle of Wight's resort status was confirmed when Queen Victoria shifted her beach allegiance from Brighton to **Osborne House** (☎ 200022; EH) in East Cowes. The house was built from 1845-51 and Queen Victoria died here in 1901. The rooms she was using at that time were left virtually untouched from her death until 1954 when the house was opened to the public. The Indian-inspired Durbar room is of particular interest. Admission to the house is £4.50/3.

Osborne House has an antipodean connection: Victoria's Government House in Melbourne's Botanic Gardens is a copy, built in 1872.

RYDE TO VENTNOR
Located on the eastern side of the island, Ryde, Sandown, Shanklin and Ventnor are

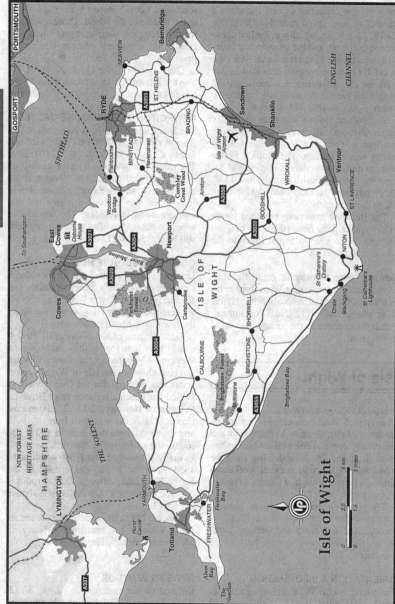

Isle of Wight

typical English seaside resorts. **Ryde** is the most important entry point to the island and the busiest of these resort towns. **Quarr Abbey** at Binstead near Ryde was founded in 1132 and destroyed in 1536. A Benedictine monastery was built here in 1908. Steam trains operate on Havenstreet Railway (☎ 884343), starting just south of Ryde. The round-trip costs £5.50/3.50.

Brading has a Roman villa (☎ 406223) with fine mosaic floors. It's open April to September, Monday to Saturday, 10 am to 5.30 pm, and Sunday from 10.30 am to 5.30 pm; £1.50/85p. The town also has two interesting old houses – Morton Manor and Nunwell House – and a wax museum (yes, there's a chamber of horrors).

Located at the easternmost tip of the island, **Bembridge** has a Shipwreck Centre & Maritime Museum (☎ 872223), open March to October, daily from 10 am to 5 pm; £2.10/1.50. The only windmill on the island (☎ 873945; NT), dating from 1700, can also be seen here. It's open April to October, Sunday to Friday, 10 am to 5 pm, and Saturday in July and August only; £1.20/60p. A fine five-mile coastal walk leads from Bembridge to Sandown.

VENTNOR TO ALUM BAY

The south coast from Ventnor to Alum Bay is the quietest stretch of the island circuit. The southern point of the island is marked by **St Catherine's Lighthouse**, which was built in 1837-40 and is usually open to the public Easter to mid-September, Monday to Saturday, 1 to 6 pm. At Niton Undercliff the *Buddle Inn* (☎ 730243) is a popular pub.

Looking like a stone rocketship, **St Catherine's Oratory** is a lighthouse dating from 1314 marking the highest point on the island. It's perched on a hilltop overlooking Blackgang Chine. The *Wight Mouse Inn* (☎ 730431) at Chale is a good place for a pub meal and has a garden.

St Agnes Church at Freshwater has a thatched roof – it cost £600 to rethatch it in 1962, £9000 in 1981. The Tennyson Trail runs across High Down Ridge, past Tennyson's Monument to the Needles, from

Freshwater Bay; Lord Tennyson, son of the poet, lived near here.

THE NEEDLES & ALUM BAY

Located at the western tip of the island, the **Needles** are three towering rocks which rise out of the sea to form the postcard symbol of the island. A lighthouse, topped by an ugly helicopter landing pad, stands at the end of the final rock. At one time there was another rock which really was needle-like but the 120-ft-high spire collapsed into the sea in 1764.

The road and bus service to this end of the island ends at **Alum Bay**, famed for its coloured sands. There's an unappealing melange of amusement park rides and souvenir shops at Alum Bay and a chairlift to take you down to the beach. From Alum Bay a walking path leads a mile (buses every hour, every half-hour in peak season) to the **Needles Old Battery** (☎ 754772; EH), a fort established in 1862 and used as a lookout during WWII. The fort directly overlooks the Needles and there's a café where you can sip tea and enjoy the view. The fort is open April to October, Sunday to Thursday, 10.30 am to 5 pm; July and August it opens daily; £2.40/1.20.

PLACES TO STAY

There are two youth hostels on the island – *Sandown Youth Hostel* (☎ 402651) on the eastern end (£7.45/5, but £9.10/6.15 in July/August) and *Totland Bay Youth Hostel* (☎ 752165) on the western end (£8.25/5.55, but also rising to £9.10/6.15 at the peak season).

There are more than 20 camping grounds and a brochure is available from Isle of Wight Tourism. A tent site typically costs £5 to £12 in the high season, £4 to £7 in the low. There's a huge range of B&B and hotel accommodation and the tourist information centres will make bookings. Self-catering accommodation and farm holidays are also popular.

GETTING THERE & AWAY

There is a wide variety of passenger or car and passenger ferry services from the mainland, although if you're bringing a car it's

SOUTH-EASTERN ENGLAND

wise to book ahead at busy times of year. Standard fares are listed but there are all sorts of special deals available.

Portsmouth to Ryde & Fishbourne

Wightlink (☎ 01705-827744) operates a passenger catamaran ferry from The Hard to Ryde (15 minutes) and a car ferry (35 minutes) to Fishbourne. The day return fare is £5.80/2.90 to Ryde, standard return is £6.80/3.40 to Fishbourne. A host of car fares are quoted, starting from £39 for the cheapest summer return.

Hovertravel (☎ 01705-811000) hovercrafts zoom back and forth between Southsea (near Portsmouth) and Ryde. The 10-minute crossing costs £7.70/3.85 for a day return. Connecting buses operate between the Portsmouth & Southsea railway station and the terminal.

Southampton to Cowes

Red Funnel (☎ 01703-330333) operates car ferries from Southampton to East Cowes (£4.50, day return £6) and high-speed passenger ferries from Southampton to West Cowes (£6, day return £9). Children travel for half-price.

Lymington to Yarmouth

The passenger day return on the Wightlink (☎ 01705-827744) car ferry is £4.80/2.40. A return ticket for car and passengers costs from £39. The trip takes 30 minutes.

GETTING AROUND
Bus & Train

Southern Vectis (☎ 522456) is the island bus operator and their 7 and 7A Island Explorer route does a complete circuit of the island. There's a short railway line from Ryde to Shanklin with a steam railway line branching off from Havenstreet. Rover Tickets give you unlimited use of bus and trains for £5.95/3 for a day or £24/12 for a week. Fares are lower in winter. Southern Vectis, and other companies, also operate round-the-island tour buses.

Bicycle

Bicycles can be rented in Cowes, Freshwater Bay, Ryde, Sandown, Shanklin, Ventnor and Yarmouth. Typical costs are around £8 per day. Several publications are available on suggested bicycle rides around the Isle of Wight.

South-Western England

HIGHLIGHTS

- Walking the streets of Georgian Bath
- Exploring Avebury and the surrounding prehistoric monuments
- The Swannery at Abbotsbury
- Listening to Wells Cathedral choir by candlelight
- Eating in Padstow's Fish Restaurant
- The Tate Gallery at St Ives
- Fossil-hunting at Lyme Regis
- Watching a play at Minack Theatre
- Day tripping to Lundy Island
- Walking on Dartmoor
- St Just-in-Roseland churchyard in spring

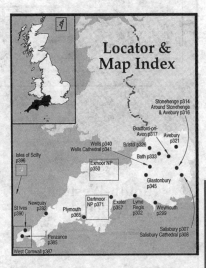

The counties of Dorset, Wiltshire, Somerset, Devon and Cornwall include some of the most beautiful countryside and spectacular coastline in Britain. They are littered with the evidence of successive cultures and kingdoms that have been swept away by one invader after another.

The region can be divided between Devon and Cornwall, out on a limb to the far west, and Wiltshire, Dorset and Somerset in the east, which are more central and so more easily accessible.

Devon and particularly Cornwall were once Britain's Wild West and rife with smuggling. Cornwall even had its own language although the last Cornish speaker probably died in the 1770s. The weather in this part of England is milder than elsewhere and some of the beaches boast golden sand and surfable surf. Despite the competition from cheap holidays in Spain and Greece, the 'English Riviera' still seethes with sunburnt suburbanites every summer. It's wise to steer clear of the coastal towns in July and August, not least because the narrow streets are choked with traffic.

Some people find Cornwall disappointing. You'll certainly feel cheated if you expect the extreme south-western tip of the island to be full of untouched, undiscovered hideaways. Thanks to thoughtless development, Land's End – a veritable icon – has been reduced to a commercially-minded tourist trap, and inland much of the peninsula has been devastated by generations of tin and china-clay mining. However, many of the coastal villages retain their charm, especially if you visit out of season.

The South West Coast Path, a long-distance walking route, follows the coastline from Minehead in Somerset, around the peninsula to Poole, near Bournemouth in Dorset, giving spectacular access to the best and most untouched sections of the coastline. The Dartmoor and Exmoor national parks are equally popular with walkers.

Further east, some truly great monuments flag up the story of English civilisation: the Stone Age left Stonehenge and spellbinding Avebury; Iron Age Britons created Maiden Castle, just outside Dorchester; the Romans (and the later Georgians) developed Bath;

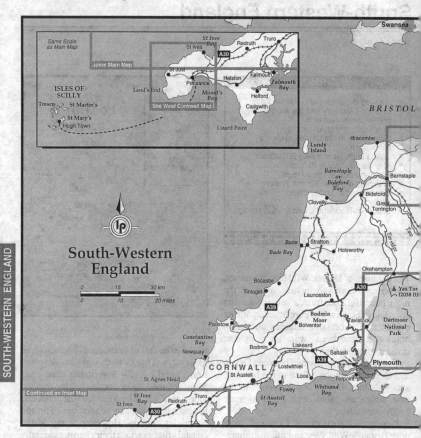

SOUTH-WESTERN ENGLAND

the legendary King Arthur is supposedly buried at Glastonbury; the Middle Ages left the great cathedrals at Exeter, Salisbury and Wells; and the 16th and 17th-century landed gentry left great houses like Montacute and Wilton. The east is densely packed with things to see, and the countryside, though varied, is a classic English patchwork of hedgerows, thatched cottages, stone churches, great estates and emerald green fields.

Towns like Bath and Salisbury are honeypot tourist attractions on every first-time visitor's hit list. The charms of Dorset, Somerset and North Devon are more low-

key, and you can happily wander around without too many plans and without stumbling over too many people.

ORIENTATION & INFORMATION

The chalk downs centred on Salisbury Plain run across Wiltshire and down through central Dorset to the coast. Granitic Dartmoor and Exmoor dominate the Devon landscape. The railways converge on Exeter, the west's most important city, then run round the coast, skirting the granite *tors* (outcrops) of Dartmoor to Truro, Cornwall's uninspiring administrative centre, and Penz-

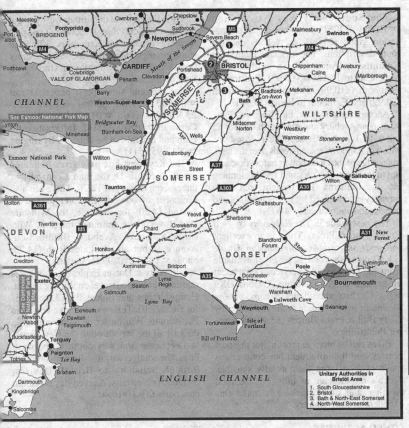

ance. Bristol and Salisbury are other important transport hubs.

There are several YHA youth hostels in the Dartmoor and Exmoor national parks, and at Salisbury, Bath, Bristol, Exeter, Plymouth, Penzance, Land's End, Tintagel and Ilfracombe.

WALKS & CYCLE ROUTES

The south-west has plenty of beautiful countryside, but walks in the Dartmoor and Exmoor national parks, and round the coastline, are the best known. The barren, open wilderness of Dartmoor can be an acquired

taste, but Exmoor covers some of the most beautiful countryside in England, and the coastal stretch from Ilfracombe to Minehead is particularly spectacular. See the separate sections on Dartmoor and Exmoor later in this chapter for more information.

The South West Coast Path, the longest national trail, is not a wilderness walk – villages with food, beer and accommodation are generally within easy reach. It follows truly magnificent coastline. Completing a section of the path should be considered by any keen walker; if possible, avoid busy summer weekends.

The South West Way Association (☎ 01803-873061) publishes an accommodation guide (£3.99), as well as detailed route descriptions. The official Countryside Commission/Aurum Press guides cover Minehead to Padstow (£9.99), Padstow to Falmouth (£10.99), Falmouth to Exmouth (£9.99) and Exmouth to Poole (£7.95).

Another famous walk, the Ridgeway Path, starts near Avebury and runs north-east for 85 miles to Ivinghoe Beacon near Aylesbury. Much of it follows ancient roads over the high, open ridge of the chalk downs before descending to the Thames Valley and finally climbing into the Chilterns. The western section (to Streatley) can be used by mountain bikes and horses (and, unfortunately, 4WDs).

The best guide is *The Ridgeway* by Neil Curtis (Aurum Press). There is an excellent *Information and Accommodation Guide* (£1.50 plus 40p for UK postage) available from the Countryside Service, Department of Leisure & Arts, Holton, Oxford OX9 1QQ. Cyclists should get a copy of *The Mountain Biker's Guide to the Ridgeway* by Andy Bull & Frank Barrett (£5.99, Newspaper Publishing).

Bikes can be hired in most major regional centres, and the infrequent bus connections make cycling more than usually sensible. There's no shortage of hills, but the mild weather and quiet backroads make this excellent cycling country.

OTHER ACTIVITIES
Surfing
The capital of British surfing is Newquay on the west Cornish coast which comes complete with surf shops, bleached hair, Kombis and neon-coloured clothing. The surfable coast runs from Porthleven (near Helston) in Cornwall, west around Land's End and north to Ilfracombe. The most famous reef breaks are at Porthleven, Lynmouth and Milbrook; though good, they are inconsistent.

GETTING AROUND
Bus
National Express buses provide reasonable connections between the main towns, particularly in the east, but the further west you go, the more difficult things become. Transport around Dartmoor and Exmoor is difficult in summer, nigh on impossible at any other time. This is territory that favours those with their own transport.

For regional timetables, phone Dorset ☎ 01305-224535; Somerset ☎ 01823-255696; Devon ☎ 01392-382800; and Cornwall ☎ 01872-322142. Information for Bath and Bristol can be obtained by ringing ☎ 0117-955 5111.

The Key West bus pass gives unlimited travel in South Devon and Cornwall for three/seven days for £12/20. There are also a number of one-day Explorer passes for around £4.50; for example, the Wiltshire Day Rover gives unlimited travel in Wiltshire (Salisbury, Avebury, Bradford-on-Avon etc), but also includes Bath (£4.75; phone ☎ 0345-090899 for details).

The Wilts & Dorset Explorer ticket gives one day's unlimited travel on Wilts & Dorset, Hampshirebus and Solent Blue Line buses for £4.25/2.10. This pass will take you from Portsmouth, Winchester or Southampton in the east all the way through the New Forest to Dorchester and Weymouth in the west. From the south coast, it will take you north through Salisbury to Bristol, Devizes, Swindon or Newbury. A seven-day Busabout pass costs £19.10/10.40.

Train
Train services in the east are reasonably comprehensive, linking Bristol, Bath, Salisbury, Weymouth and Exeter. Beyond Exeter, a single line follows the south coast as far as Penzance, with spurs to Barnstaple, Gunnislake, Looe, Falmouth, St Ives and Newquay. The line from Exeter to Penzance is one of Britain's most beautiful. For more information, phone the British Rail national inquiry line, ☎ 0345-484950.

The Freedom of the Southwest Rover allows seven days unlimited travel west of a line drawn through (and including) Salisbury, Bath, Bristol and Weymouth for £47/33.

Dorset

Despite its natural beauty and attractive towns and villages, most of Dorset manages to avoid inundation by tourists. The impressively varied coast includes the large resort towns of Bournemouth and Weymouth, as well as Lyme Regis, a particularly attractive spot with famous literary connections. The Dorset Coastal Path, part of the longer 613-mile South West Coast Path, runs for most of the length of the coast.

Inland is Dorchester, the heart of Thomas Hardy's fictional Wessex. Dorset also boasts famous earthworks (Maiden Castle), castles (Corfe Castle), stately homes (particularly Kingston Lacy), a string of Lawrence of Arabia connections, some fine churches (Christchurch Priory, Wimborne Minster and Sherborne Abbey) and one of England's best known chalk hill figures (the Cerne Giant).

ORIENTATION & INFORMATION

Dorchester makes a good base for exploring the best of Dorset, but Lyme Regis, Bridport or Weymouth will suit those who prefer the coast. One of the reasons for Dorset's backwater status is that no major transport routes cross it. A rail loop runs west from Southampton to Dorchester, then north to Yeovil, and the main westbound InterCity trains stop at Axminster (East Devon).

BOURNEMOUTH & POOLE

- *pop 265,000* • ☎ *01202)*

Technically two separate towns, Bournemouth and Poole are virtually continuous. A popular beach resort since the mid-19th century, Bournemouth continues to exude an air of Victorian seaside prosperity. The medieval port of Poole is now a container dock and yachting centre.

Orientation & Information

Bournemouth's TIC (☎ 451700) is on Westover Rd. Poole TIC (☎ 253253) is at the Quay.

Things to See

Bournemouth is noted for its beautiful chines, sharp-sided valleys running down to the sea. The wonderful **Russell-Cotes Art Gallery & Museum** (☎ 452800) looks out to sea from Russell-Cotes Rd in Bournemouth and has a varied collection, much of it garnered from its namesake's travels. The museum is open, free, Tuesday to Sunday, 10 am to 5 pm.

In Shelley Park, Beechwood Ave, in Boscombe, the **Shelley Rooms** (☎ 303571) house a collection of Shelley memorabilia. They're open Tuesday to Sunday, 2 to 5 pm, and entry is free. *Frankenstein* author Mary Shelley is buried at St Peters.

Compton Acres (☎ 700778) is a cluster of gardens in a sheltered cliff chine. They're open March to October, daily from 10.30 am to 5.45 pm. Entry is £4.20/1. Bus Nos 150/1 go there from the centre.

Poole Old Town has attractive 18th-century buildings, including a wonderful Customs House. The **Waterfront Museum** (☎ 683138) recounts the town's history, including the prosperity brought by its Newfoundland fishing trade. **Scaplen's Court Museum** is housed in a nearby medieval merchant's house. Both museums are open Monday to Saturday, 10 am to 5 pm, and Sunday from 2 to 5 pm. Entry to the Waterfront Museum is £1.50/90p, to Scaplen's Court 75p/50p; a combined ticket costs £1.95/1.25.

Brownsea Island is a NT nature reserve at the mouth of Poole Harbour where the first Boy Scout camp was held in 1907. From April to October boats from Poole Quay cost £3.15/2.15 return, plus a landing fee of £2.20/1.10. During winter the RSPB operates sporadic Birdboats to watch the harbour birdlife; phone ☎ 666226 for boat information.

Places to Stay & Eat

Bournemouth and Poole are full of places to stay and the TICs make free bookings. There are also plenty of camping grounds around the towns.

In Bournemouth, check out *Sandhurst* (☎ 423748), 16 Southern Rd, Southbourne, with beds from £17 per person, or *Parklands Hotel* (☎ 552529), 4 Rushton Crescent, with rooms from £19-25.

Amid the fish & chip shops are more interesting, if pricier, places to eat. Try *Sophisticats* (☎ 291019) at 43 Charminster Rd, Bournemouth, or *Corkers Restaurant, Bistro and Café, Bar* (☎ 681393) at 1 High St, The Quay, Poole.

Getting There & Away
Trains take about two hours from London Waterloo. There are also regular bus connections, including National Express (☎ 0990-808080). A ferry shuttles across from Sandbanks to Studland (pedestrians 80p, car and passengers £2). This is a short cut from Poole to Swanage, Wareham and the west Dorset coast, but summer queues can be horrendous.

Getting Around
Wilts & Dorset Red Buses (☎ 0345-090899) serve the Bournemouth-Poole-Swanage area. A day Explorer ticket costs £4.25/2.10, while a seven-day Busabout ticket costs £19.10/10.40.

Green Machines (☎ 0585-112220) at Rockley Park, Poole, hires out mountain bikes.

AROUND BOURNEMOUTH & POOLE
Christchurch
* *pop 30,000*   * ☎ *01202*

Five miles east of Bournemouth is Christchurch, an attractive small town which might make a pleasant alternative base to Bournemouth. The TIC (☎ 471780) is at 23 High St.

Magnificent **Christchurch Priory** (☎ 485804) stands between the Avon and Stour rivers. The Norman nave had a new choir added to it in the 15th century, when the tower was also built. Among the wonderful misericords in the choir, look for a carving of Richard III and another of a fox 'friar' preaching to a flock of geese. In summer you can climb the tower for views and learn about priory life in the St Michael's Loft Museum. Guided tours can be arranged

by phoning ☎ 485804. Visitors are asked for a £1 donation.

Opposite the Priory is the **Red House Museum & Gardens** (☎ 482860), a workhouse now accommodating a local history museum. It's open Tuesday to Saturday, 10 am to 5 pm and Sunday 2 to 5 pm. Admission costs £1/60p.

Wimborne
* *pop 14,000*   * ☎ *01202)*

The attractive small town of Wimborne is centred around its interesting old church, or minster. The TIC (☎ 886116) is on High St, near the minster.

Wimborne Minster Founded around 1050, the minster was considerably enlarged in Decorated style in the 14th century and became the parish church in 1537 when Henry VIII began attacking monasteries. It's notable for its twin towers and for the varied colours of its stonework. The mid-15th-century Perpendicular-style west tower was added when there were fears for the strength of the simpler Norman-style 12th-century central tower. Those fears were realised when the crossing spire fell in 1600.

Inside, the nave columns, the piers of the central tower and the north and south transepts are the main Norman survivors. Traces of 13th to 15th-century painted murals can be seen in a Norman altar recess in the north transept. In the presbytery is a 1440 brass of King Ethelred who was killed in battle in 871, the only brass commemorating a king in England.

In Holy Trinity Chapel is the tomb of Ettricke, the 'man in the wall'. A local eccentric (but obviously one with some influence), he refused to be buried in the church or in the village and was interred in the church wall. Confidently expecting to die in 1693, Ettricke also had his memorial engraved. When he survived his prediction by 10 years, the 1693 was rechiselled to 1703.

Above the choir vestry is a chained library established in 1686.

Around Town The 16th-century **Priest's House** (☎ 882533), near the minster, now houses the Museum of East Dorset Life with a series of reconstructed period rooms. It's open April to October, Monday to Saturday, 10.30 am to 5 pm, and June to September on Sunday from 2 to 5 pm. Entry is £1.95/75p.

Kingston Lacy

Two miles north of Wimborne is Kingston Lacy (☎ 01202-883402; NT), a fine 17th-century house with 18th-century landscaped gardens. It's unusual in that it didn't decline into genteel poverty and then have to be completely refurnished. The last occupant lived in the house until 1981 without selling a thing, so the house is dense with furniture and art, much of it collected by William Bankes, who was responsible for major renovations in the 1830s.

The house is open April to October, Saturday to Wednesday from noon to 5.30 pm. Entry is £5.20/2.60; gardens only £2/1.

SOUTH-EAST DORSET

The south-eastern corner of Dorset – the Purbeck peninsula – is crowded with pretty thatched villages and crumbling ruins. The Dorset Coastal Path, part of the 613-mile South West Coast Path, runs through wonderful scenery along this stretch. The Wareham TIC can supply a free leaflet describing the 47-mile Purbeck Cycleway which starts from the town. There are plenty of camping grounds around and B&Bs in almost every village.

Tolpuddle

Tolpuddle, on the A35, played a historic role in the development of trade unions. In 1833, a group of farm workers met to discuss a cut in their wages and were promptly arrested, convicted of holding an illegal meeting (striking was not illegal) and sentenced to transportation to Australia. Public support for the 'Tolpuddle Martyrs' resulted in their pardon in 1836.

A memorial stands by a tree under which they probably gathered. A small museum on the western outskirts recounts the tale. It's open, free, Tuesday to Saturday, 10 am to 5.30 pm, and Sunday from 11 am to 5.30 pm.

Wareham

- *pop 2800*   • ☎ *01929*

The pretty village of Wareham forms a neat square, bounded by the River Frome on its southern side and by a remarkably intact Saxon wall on the other three sides. To complete the pattern, North, East, South and West Sts run in the four cardinal directions from The Cross in the centre. The museum and TIC (☎ 552740) by The Cross stock an excellent walking-tour map. The village was badly damaged by a succession of fires, most disastrously in 1762, after which thatched buildings were banned.

Wareham Museum (☎ 553448), on East St, adjacent to the Town Hall, is open Easter to mid-October, daily from 11 am to 1 pm and 2 to 4 pm. A Lawrence of Arabia collection supplements the usual local items.

You can rent rowing boats from **Abbots Quay**, once a busy port on the River Frome. The sturdy **earth banks** around the town were built after a Viking attack in 876. A stretch on the West Wall is known as Bloody Bank, after Monmouth rebels were executed here in 1685 following the Bloody Assizes (see the Dorchester section).

Standing on the wall beside North St is Saxon **St Martin's Church**, which dates from about 1020. Although the porch and bell tower are later additions, and larger windows have been added over the centuries, the basic structure is unchanged. Inside, there's a 12th-century wall painting on the northern wall and a marble effigy of Lawrence of Arabia. The Saxon origins of **St Mary's Church** on the other side of the village, near The Quay, were obliterated when it was rebuilt in 1842.

Places to Stay & Eat Several camping grounds can be found around Wareham. Convenient B&Bs include *Belle Vue* (☎ 552056), on West St, right on top of West Wall, which costs £19 a head. The *Black Bear Hotel* (☎ 553339), at 14 South St, is fronted by a lifesize figure of a bear. Rooms with attached bathroom cost from £25/40. The picturesque *Old Granary* (☎ 552010)

Lawrence of Arabia

The green fields and pretty villages of Dorset are a long way from the sandy wastes of Arabia but there are numerous Lawrence connections to this area. The TIC in Wareham even produces *The Lawrence of Arabia Trail* leaflet (10p).

Born in 1888 in Wales, TE Lawrence was the son of Sir Thomas Chapman, who had abandoned his first wife and their daughters in Ireland to run off with the girls' governess. As Mr and Mrs Lawrence they had five boys; Thomas Edward was the second. Lawrence studied history at Oxford University, specialising in the Middle East. He travelled extensively in the region between 1909 and 1914, and his expertise led to a Cairo army posting at the outbreak of WW I.

Turkey, still known as the Ottoman Empire at the time, was allied with Germany and, as Arab unrest began to develop, Lawrence led a brilliant guerrilla campaign against the Ottoman forces, culminating in the capture of Aqaba in mid-1917. After the war, he was disgusted to find his Arab visions discarded at the bargaining table as the old Ottoman Empire was carved up between Britain and France. Refusing military honours, he spent several years shuttling between Europe and the Middle East, while at the same time revelations of his dramatic exploits earned him the epithet 'Lawrence of Arabia'.

Lawrence was always an enigmatic character and in 1922 he clandestinely joined the Royal Air Force as a low-ranking enlisted man under the assumed name of John Hume Ross. At the same time he published, in a very limited edition, his immense work, *Seven Pillars of Wisdom*. Newspapers soon broke the story of his RAF hideaway but a year later he joined the army as Private TE Shaw, a name he later assumed legally. He was stationed at Bovington Camp in Dorset and bought Clouds Hill; a nearby cottage. In 1925 he transferred to the RAF and spent the next 10 years in India and England before his discharge in 1935. Retiring to Clouds Hill at the age of 46, he was killed two months later in a motorbike accident.

Lawrence connections in Dorset include Bovington Camp, where the tank museum has a small Lawrence display. He died at Bovington Military Hospital six days after his accident, which took place between the camp and Clouds Hill, only a mile away. His grave is in the cemetery of St Nicholas Church, Moreton. The Wareham Museum houses more Lawrence memorabilia, and the small Saxon church in Wareham has a stone effigy of Lawrence. ■

on The Quay has rooms from £19.50 to £32.50 per person and a pleasant restaurant.

Bovington Camp Tank Museum

The Tank Museum (☎ 405096) houses an extensive collection from the earliest WWI prototypes, through to WWII tanks from both sides, and on to examples from Cold War days. From more recent times, there's also a collection of Iraqi tanks from the Gulf War. It's open daily from 10 am to 5 pm, and entry is £5/3. Lawrence of Arabia was stationed here in 1923 and there's a small museum in the shop.

Clouds Hill

Lawrence of Arabia's former home (☎ 405616; NT) is open April to October, Wednesday to Friday and Sunday, noon to 5 pm. Entry to the tiny house is £2.20.

Corfe Castle

Corfe Castle's magnificent ruins tower above the pretty stone village at its base, offering wonderful views over the surrounding countryside. Even by English standards, the 1000-year-old castle had a dramatic history. In 978, 17-year-old King Edward was greeted at the castle gate by his step-

SOUTH-WESTERN ENGLAND

mother, Queen Elfrida, proffering a glass of poisoned wine; even before the poison could take effect he was stabbed to death. His half-brother, Ethelred the Unready, succeeded him, as the wicked queen had planned, but the martyred boy king was canonised as St Edward in 1001.

The castle (☎ 01929-481294; NT) was besieged twice during the Civil War, being reduced to the present picturesque ruin after the second assault, in 1646. It's now open February to October, daily from 10 am to 5.30 pm (4.30 pm in March; 11 am to 3.30 pm the rest of the year). Entry is £3/1.50.

Places to Stay & Eat The village has several pubs and B&Bs, and there are several camping grounds nearby. The NT has a pleasant tearoom overlooking the castle.

Swanage

In Victorian times local quarryman John Mowlem made a fortune supplying stone from Swanage for the huge rebuilding projects in booming London. The firm bearing his name is still a major building contractor. He also judiciously chose buildings in London which were due for demolition and shipped material back to Swanage. As a result, there are City of London bollards dotted around town, the Wellington Clock Tower was rescued from London Bridge and stands on the pier, and the Town Hall has a grandiose stone front removed from the Wren-influenced Cheapside Mercers Company building.

The TIC (☎ 01929-422885) is on Shore Rd. There's a centrally located youth hostel (☎ 01929-422113) and lots of B&Bs to confirm Swanage's popularity as a beach resort.

Lulworth Cove & the Coast

The lovely Dorset coast is at its most spectacular (and crowded) between Lulworth Cove and Durdle Door. Lulworth Cove is almost perfectly circular and nearly enclosed by towering cliffs. Durdle Door has a fine beach, a dramatic cove and an impressive natural archway. It's about a mile west of

Lulworth Cove with fine clifftop walks in both directions.

Places to Stay The *Durdle Door Caravan Park* (☎ 01929-400200) on the fields above the cliffs has tent sites. There are a number of places to stay at Lulworth Cove, and more just back from the coast in West Lulworth. The *youth hostel* (☎ 01929-400564) is on School Lane, West Lulworth, and costs £8.25/5.55 in the peak July/August season, £7.45/5 the rest of the year.

DORCHESTER
• *pop 14,000* • ☎ *01305*

Dorset's county town was chosen as the site of the Bloody Assizes in 1685 and the Tolpuddle Martyrs were tried here in 1834. But despite its fame as the home of novelist Thomas Hardy, modern Dorchester is a sleepy place and brash Weymouth or pretty Cerne Abbas would make equally good bases for exploring the local attractions.

Orientation & Information

Most of Dorchester's action takes place along South St which runs into pedestrianised Cornhill and then emerges in the High St, divided into East and West parts at St Peter's church. The TIC (☎ 267992) is in Trinity St alongside the Antelope Walk shopping arcade. It sells the *Historical Guide*

The Bloody Assizes

In 1685 the Duke of Monmouth, illegitimate son of Charles II, landed at Lyme Regis intending to overthrow James II and become king. His rebellion ended in defeat at the Battle of Sedgemoor in Somerset, and the duke was beheaded in the Tower of London – it took four swings of the axe to sever his head. Judge Jeffreys, the chief justice, tried the rebels in Dorchester in a barbaric trial known as the Bloody Assizes. Over 300 rebels were hanged and their gruesome drawn-and-quartered remains were displayed in towns and villages all over the region. Nearly 1000 more rebels were transported to Barbados and many more were imprisoned, fined or flogged. ∎

✚✚✚

Hardy's Heart

In the graveyard of St Michael's church in Stinsford a graveslab reads 'Here lies the heart of Thomas Hardy, son of Thomas and Jemima Hardy', an unexceptional epitaph behind which lies a quite exceptional story.

When author Thomas Hardy died in 1928 his will stated that he wished 'to be buried in Stinsford churchyard unless the nation strongly desires otherwise.' Since the nation desired that he should be buried in Poets' Corner in Westminster Abbey, a compromise solution was agreed: Hardy's ashes would go to Westminster but his heart would be buried in Stinsford.

So far so good, but then the tale takes a curious turn. Rumour has it that the heart was removed, wrapped in a tea towel and put in a biscuit tin to await the funeral. Unfortunately when the undertaker arrived to collect it, he found the tin open on the floor with a contented-looking cat sitting beside it. Not to be thwarted, he killed the cat, wrapped it in the tea towel and put it into the tin which was then buried in the churchyard according to plan.

Did it happen? Well, a contemporary description of the undertaker's behaviour on the day in question might suggest that something out of the ordinary had happened. But without digging up the grave we will never know for sure. ■

✚✚✚

– *Dorchester* (50p) with interesting walks around town, and lots of Hardy literature including a set of leaflets which retrace the scenery of individual novels.

Museums

Dorset County Museum (☎ 262735), on High West St, houses the study where Hardy did his writing. There are also sections on the archaeological excavations at Maiden Castle, fossil finds from Lyme Regis and a rural craft collection. It's open Monday to Saturday, 10 am to 5 pm (in July and August on Sunday too) and entry is £2.35/1.20.

There's a small **Dinosaur Museum** (☎ 269880) and a **Hardy's Wessex** (☎ 250525) exhibit in Icen Way, and a **Tutankhamun Exhibit** (☎ 269571) in High West St. The **Dorset Military Museum** (☎ 264066), beyond the Bridport Rd roundabout, traces Dorset military valour overseas.

St Peter's Church

Beside the County Museum, St Peter's has been heavily restored but still boasts a 12th-century doorway. After the Bloody Assizes, the heads of Judge Jeffreys' victims were impaled on the church railing.

Thomas Hardy Associations

The **Barclay's Bank building** at No 10 South St provided the fictional home for Thomas Hardy's *Mayor of Casterbridge*. Hardy himself worked for a time at an architect's office at No 62. A **statue** of Hardy watches the traffic from a seat by the West Gate roundabout.

Poundbury

Those interested in the wranglings between Britain's modernist and traditionalist architects should drop in on **Poundbury**, the modern town designed to immortalise Prince Charles' conservative ideals, in Dorchester's western outskirts.

Places to Stay

Dorchester has several reasonably priced B&Bs. In quiet Cornwall Rd, *Thornhill House* (☎ 260007) at No 14 and *Clovelly* (☎ 266689) at No 19 charge from £15 a head for rooms opposite the well-kept Borough Gardens. *Maumbury Cottage* (☎ 266726), at 9 Maumbury Rd and convenient for the stations, also charges from £15.

Casterbridge Hotel (☎ 264043), at 49 High East St, is a luxurious small hotel where B&B costs from £22 to £42 a head in rooms with attached bathrooms. In High St West the *Westwood House Hotel* (☎ 268018) at No 29 and *Wessex Royale Hotel* (☎ 262660) at No 32 are fine Georgian hotels in the same price bracket.

Places to Eat

An atmospheric place to take tea or a bigger meal, provided you're not squeamish about the gruesome historical associations, is the half-timbered *Judge Jeffreys' Lodgings* (☎ 264369) at 6 High West St. Sensitive souls might prefer the coffee lounge in *Napper's Mite*, an early 17th-century almshouse in South St, the *Horse with the Red Umbrella* on High West St or the *Potter Inn* on Durngate St.

The *Royal Oak* on High West St does good pub food, as does the nearby *Old Ship Inn*, the oldest pub in town.

Allow around £20 a head for a three-course meal at the *Mock Turtle Restaurant* (☎ 264011) on High West St. *The Old Tea House* across the road is cheaper.

If you're waiting for a train, the *Full Moon* (☎ 268365) at Dorchester West station does Chinese and Vietnamese food, including a Sunday eat-as-much-as-you-like buffet for £9.50.

Getting There & Away

There are two railway stations, Dorchester South and unstaffed Dorchester West, both south-west of the town centre. Dorchester South is linked seven or eight times daily to London (three hours, £27) via Bournemouth (£6) and Southampton (£12). There are numerous services to Weymouth (10 minutes, £2.10). Dorchester West has connections to Bath (two hours, £8.50) and Bristol.

Bus connections tend to be much slower...the buses from London take four hours! Local bus operators include Southern National (☎ 01305-783645), Wilts & Dorset (☎ 01202-673555) and Dorchester Coachways (☎ 01305-262992) who run to Weymouth, Lyme Regis, Taunton and Salisbury.

Getting Around

Dorchester Cycles (☎ 268787), at 31B Great Western Rd, rents bikes for £10 a day.

AROUND DORCHESTER
Maiden Castle

One and a half miles south-west of Dorchester, the earthwork ramparts of Maiden Castle stretch for three miles and enclose nearly 50 acres. The site has been inhabited since Neolithic times but the first fort was built here around 800 BC. It was subsequently abandoned, then rebuilt around 500 BC. The earth walls were later extended and enlarged in 250 and 150 BC. Despite the addition of more defences, the Romans still captured it in 43 AD, finally abandoning it in the 4th century. The sheer size of the walls and ditches and the area they enclose is stunning, and there are wonderful views. Dorchester Museum displays finds from the site.

Hardy's Cottage

The cottage where Thomas Hardy was born and where he wrote *Far from the Madding Crowd* is at Higher Bockhampton, about three miles north-east of Dorchester and reached by a 10-minute walk from the car park. Despite the absence of Hardy memorabilia, the house (☎ 01305-262366; NT) may be visited by prior appointment for £2.50; otherwise, you can view the garden from April to October (except Thursday), 11 am to 6 pm.

Cerne Abbas & the Cerne Giant

Eight miles north of Dorchester, delightful little Cerne Abbas has several fine 16th-century houses and a medieval church. The much rebuilt abbey house is now a private residence, although the ruins behind the house can be inspected (entry £1/20p). The Abbot's Porch (1509) was once the entrance to the whole complex.

Just north of the village is the Cerne Giant, one of Britain's best known chalk figures. The giant stands 180 feet tall and hefts a 120-foot-long club, but he's particularly renowned for his more eyecatching 40-foot penis.

With several B&Bs, Cerne Abbas would make a good alternative to staying in Dorchester (20 minutes by bus). The *Old Market House* and *Singing Kettle* are pleasant tearooms and there's pub food at the *Red Lion* and *New Inn*.

WEYMOUTH

- *pop 40,000* • ☎ *01305*

Only eight miles south of Dorchester, this bustling seaside resort makes a good alternative to Dorchester as a base for exploring Hardy country – Weymouth was 'Budmouth' in the novels. It was George III's experimental dip in Weymouth waters in 1789 which sparked the British passion for the seaside. Despite the shock of emerging from his 'bathing machine' to hear a band strike up in his honour, the king revisited Weymouth 13 times. In 1810, local residents erected the colourful statue on The Esplanade in his honour.

Orientation & Information

The main part of Weymouth, between the beach and the Inner Harbour, is only a few blocks wide. The Esplanade is the main walk along the beach, but each block of the road has a different secondary name. St Mary St is the pedestrianised shopping centre but Hope Square, on the far side of the pretty Old Harbour, is more inviting. The TIC (☎ 785747) is on The Esplanade.

Esplanade & Old Harbour

Weymouth is a fine example of the archetypal English seaside resort and a summer walk along The Esplanade will reveal garish beach-equipment stands, deck chairs for hire, donkey rides and Punch & Judy shows. Look for the brightly painted Jubilee Memorial Clock of 1888 and the equally vivid statue of King George III, patron saint of Weymouth tourism.

The less brash Old Harbour inlet is lined with attractive old buildings used as shops, restaurants and pubs, and packed with fishing trawlers and fancy yachts from around the world.

Deep Sea Adventure

The Deep Sea Adventure (☎ 760690), in an old grainstore at 9 Custom House Quay, traces the history of diving, with exhibits on local shipwrecks, the *Titanic* and the £40 million gold recovery from HMS *Edinburgh*, sunk while part of a convoy from Russia. William Walker, the Winchester Cathedral diver (see Winchester in the South-Eastern England chapter) plays his part, as does the intriguing story of John Lethbridge and his pioneering 'diving engine' of 1715. The exhibit is open daily, 10 am to 5.30 pm (closes 4.30 pm November to February and 10 pm in July and August). Entry is £2.75/2.25.

Brewer's Quay & the Timewalk

Brewer's Quay on Hope Square has a shopping centre and plentiful attractions, including the excellent Timewalk (☎ 777622) which takes you through the town's early history as a trading port, the disaster of the Black Death plague years, the drama of the Spanish Armada, and its development as a resort. You even see a figure of the portly George III emerging from his famous bathing machine. The Timewalk ends with the story of the Devenish brewery, in which it is housed. It's open daily, 9.30 am to 5.30 pm (later in July and August). Entry is £3.50/2.50.

Tudor House

When Tudor House (☎ 782925) at 3 Trinity St was built around 1600, the waterfront would have lapped the front door. Furnished in Tudor style, it's open June to September, Tuesday to Friday, 11 am to 3.45 pm; Sunday afternoons only from October to May. Entry, including a guided tour, is £1.50/50p.

Nothe Fort

Perched on the end of the promontory, 19th-century Nothe Fort (☎ 787243) houses a museum on Britain's coastal defence system. It's open from 10.30 am daily, from early May to late September (Sunday from 2 pm only in winter). Entry is £2.50 (children free).

Places to Stay

Camping There are caravan parks between Overcombe and Preston, north along the Dorchester Rd and south near Sandsfoot Castle and Chesil Beach.

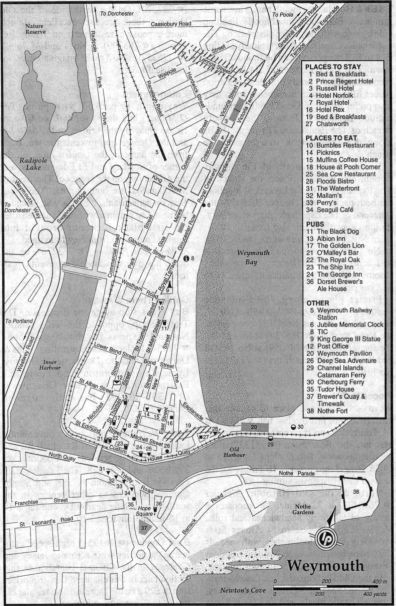

SOUTH-WESTERN ENGLAND

PLACES TO STAY
1 Bed & Breakfasts
2 Prince Regent Hotel
3 Russell Hotel
4 Hotel Norfolk
7 Royal Hotel
16 Hotel Rex
19 Bed & Breakfasts
27 Chatsworth

PLACES TO EAT
10 Bumbles Restaurant
14 Picnics
15 Muffins Coffee House
18 House at Pooh Corner
25 Sea Cow Restaurant
28 Floods Bistro
31 The Waterfront
32 Mallam's
33 Perry's
34 Seagull Café

PUBS
11 The Black Dog
13 Albion Inn
17 The Golden Lion
21 O'Malley's Bar
22 The Royal Oak
23 The Ship Inn
24 The George Inn
36 Dorset Brewer's
Ale House

OTHER
5 Weymouth Railway
Station
6 Jubilee Memorial Clock
8 TIC
9 King George III Statue
20 Weymouth Pavilion
26 Deep Sea Adventure
29 Channel Islands
Catamaran Ferry
30 Cherbourg Ferry
35 Tudor House
37 Brewer's Quay &
Timewalk
38 Nothe Fort

Weymouth

| 0 | 200 | 400 m |
| 0 | 200 | 400 yards |

B&Bs & Hotels Weymouth has an awesome number of B&Bs and small hotels, lined up side by side with the pricier places along The Esplanade. Cheaper B&Bs, typically costing £14 to £18 per person, can be found all over town. The sheer number of B&Bs makes recommendations pretty pointless, but good places fill fast in summer when owners may also prefer long lets. Good hunting grounds include Brunswick Terrace, the northern stretch of The Esplanade. The pretty B&Bs along this stretch look straight over the beach.

Lennox St, just north of the railway station, and Waterloo Place, the stretch of The Esplanade from the Lennox St junction, are both packed with cheaper B&Bs. At the other end of The Esplanade, just before Weymouth Quay, there are also ranks of B&Bs from Nos 1 to 34. *Chatsworth* (☎ 785012), at No 14, looks out to sea in one direction and across the Old Harbour in the other. Rooms with attached bathroom are £24 to £28 per person.

Pricier places along The Esplanade include the *Hotel Rex* (☎ 760400) at No 29, with nightly charges from £31 per person, the *Hotel Norfolk* (☎ 786734) at No 125-26, the *Russell Hotel* (☎ 786059) at No 135-38 and the *Prince Regent Hotel* (☎ 771313) at No 139.

Places to Eat
Weymouth is a good place to sample that most British of fast foods – fish & chips. At 14 Trinity Rd, on the southern side of the harbour, the *Waterfront* (☎ 781237) does popular takeaway fish & chips for £3.25 to £4.35. Round the corner at 10 Trinity St, the *Seagull Café* dispenses similar fare.

North of the Old Harbour, *Picknics* (☎ 761317), at 31 Maiden St, prepares a variety of takeaway sandwiches and rolls. *Muffins Coffee House* in St Albans St is extremely popular for lunches, with specials chalked on boards outside. Try also *Bumbles Restaurant* in St Thomas St for light lunches.

In the Old Harbour, the *Sea Cow Restaurant* (☎ 783524), at 7 Custom House Quay, turns out hearty meals, as does *Floods Bistro*

(☎ 722270). On the south side of the Old Harbour, there are two excellent, though more expensive, restaurants on Trinity Rd. *Perry's* (☎ 785799) at No 4 and *Mallam's* (☎ 776757) at No 5 make imaginative use of local seafood.

Entertainment
Weymouth is packed with pubs. Try *O'Malley's* and the *Royal Oak*, on Custom House Quay by the bridge, or the *Ship Inn* and the *George Inn*, towards the sea. Back from the harbour, the *Golden Lion*, on the corner of St Mary and St Edmund Sts, and the *Albion Inn*, on the corner of Thomas and St Alban Sts, are both popular. The *Black Dog*, on pedestrianised St Mary St, is said to be the oldest pub in town, and is named after the first black Labrador brought into England on a ship from Newfoundland.

Weymouth Pavilion (☎ 783225), on the quay, has a busy schedule of events year-round.

Getting There & Away
Bus Buses stop along the Esplanade. The Travel Shop, opposite the TIC, handles National Express bus bookings. Phone ☎ 783645 for local bus information. Wilts & Dorset operates to Dorchester, Salisbury, Lyme Regis, Taunton, and Poole and Bournemouth. Dorchester Coachways (☎ 01305-262992) has daily buses to London for £12.50.

Train Weymouth station is conveniently located at the junction of Ranelagh Rd and King St. Hourly services to London take $3\frac{1}{2}$ hours and cost £28. The London train goes via Bournemouth (£7.30) and Southampton. Services to other centres in the south-west include nearby Dorchester, a 10 to 15-minute run for £2.10.

Boat Condor (☎ 761551) high-speed catamaran car ferries whiz across to Jersey and Guernsey in the Channel Islands (see that section later in this chapter). Day-trip prices start at £29 a head. There are also regular car ferries to Cherbourg in France.

WEYMOUTH TO LYME REGIS
Portland

South of Weymouth, Portland is joined to the mainland by the long sweep of Chesil Beach. Many famous buildings have been made from locally quarried Portland stone. **Portland Castle** (☎ 820539; EH) is one of the finest examples of the defensive castles constructed during Henry VIII's castle-building spree, spurred by fear of an attack from France. Entry costs £2/1.

There are superb views from the lighthouse at the end of **Portland Bill**. A £1 donation is suggested for climbing the 134-foot-high tower. An earlier, smaller lighthouse acts as a bird observatory.

Chesil Beach

Chesil Beach is a long curving sandbank (except that it's made of stones rather than sand) stretching along the coast for 10 miles from Portland to Abbotsbury. The bank encloses the slightly stagnant waters of the Fleet Lagoon, a haven for water birds, including the famed Abbotsbury swans. The stones vary from pebble size at Abbotsbury in the west to five to seven inches in diameter at Portland in the east; local fishermen can supposedly tell their position along the bank by gauging the size of the stones. In places, the stone bank reaches 50 feet high. Although winter storms can wash right over the top, it has never been broken up. The bank is accessible at the Portland end and from just west of Abbotsbury.

Abbotsbury

Pretty little Abbotsbury boasts several attractions. The huge **tithe barn**, at one time a communal storage site for farm produce, is 272 feet long and was used for a harvest supper scene in Polanski's *Far from the Madding Crowd*. It houses an interesting country museum and is open April to October, daily, 10 am to 6 pm, Sunday only the rest of the year. Entry is £2.50/1.

On the coast, and offering fine views of the Fleet Lagoon, is **Abbotsbury Swannery** (☎ 871130). Swans have been nesting here for 600 years and the colony can number up to 600, plus cygnets. The walk through the swannery and reed beds will tell you all you ever wanted to know about swans. Come in May for the nests, in late May and June for the cygnets. It's open daily, 10 am to 6 pm (to dusk in winter), and entry is £4.50/1.50.

The swannery was founded by Abbotsbury's Benedictine monastery, which was destroyed in 1541. Traces of the monastery remain by the tithe barn. The energetic can walk up to 14th-century **St Catherine's Chapel**, overlooking the swannery, the village and Chesil Beach.

Places to Stay & Eat Abbotsbury has several B&Bs and places to eat. The *Swan Inn* on the Weymouth side of town does pub food and has a pleasant garden. The *Ilchester Arms* (☎ 871243), right in the village, has rooms at £41.50 a head.

LYME REGIS
• *pop 4600*   • ☎ 01297

The attractive seaside town of Lyme Regis marks the end of Dorset – Devon begins just beyond the pier known as the Cobb. The Cobb is a famous literary spot: not only did Louisa Musgrove's accident in Jane Austen's novel *Persuasion* take place here, but it was also where *The French Lieutenant's Woman* stood and stared out to sea in John Fowles' novel (and where Meryl Streep stood in the film version).

The town's other claim to fame is prehistoric. The limestone cliffs on either side of town are some of Britain's richest sources of fossils, and the first dinosaur skeletons were discovered here.

In 1685, the Duke of Monmouth landed on Monmouth Beach, west of the town, to start his abortive rebellion against James II. See Dorchester earlier in this chapter for more details.

Orientation & Information

The A3052 drops precipitously into Lyme Regis from one side and climbs equally steeply out on the other. From Bridge St, where the A3052 meets the coast, Marine Parade runs west to the harbour. The TIC

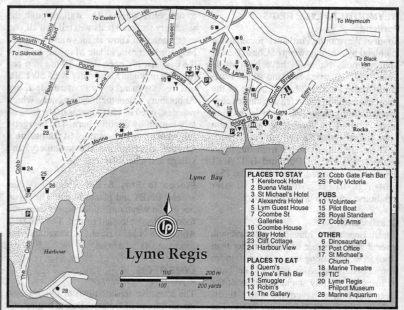

PLACES TO STAY
1 Kersbrook Hotel
2 Buena Vista
3 St Michael's Hotel
4 Alexandra Hotel
5 Lym Guest House
7 Coombe St Galleries
16 Coombe House
22 Bay Hotel
23 Cliff Cottage
24 Harbour View

PLACES TO EAT
8 Quern's
9 Lyme's Fish Bar
11 Smuggler
13 Robin's
14 The Gallery

21 Cobb Gate Fish Bar
25 Polly Victoria

PUBS
10 Volunteer
15 Pilot Boat
26 Royal Standard
27 Cobb Arms

OTHER
6 Dinosaurland
12 Post Office
17 St Michael's Church
18 Marine Theatre
19 TIC
20 Lyme Regis Philpot Museum
28 Marine Aquarium

Lyme Bay

Lyme Regis

Harbour

The Cobb

Rocks

To Black Ven

(☎ 442138) is where Bridge St becomes Church St.

Museums
Lyme Regis Philpot Museum (☎ 443370), in Bridge St, has displays on fossils and local history. The cliffs west of the harbour and Monmouth Beach are still prone to fossil-exposing landslips; the museum has details of the Dowlands Landslip on Christmas Day 1839, when a stretch of clifftop 400 feet wide and three quarters of a mile long slid away, taking with it farms and houses. It's open daily, 10.30 am to 5 pm (closed noon to 2.30 pm on Sunday); entry is £1/40p.

Dinosaurland (☎ 443541), on Coombe St, is an eclectic mix of science, fossils and local folklore. It's open Easter to November, daily, 10 am to 5 pm; entry is £3.20/2.90.

The Cobb
The Cobb is a 600-foot-long stone jetty-cum-breakwater. The small **Marine**

Aquarium (☎ 443678) has interesting displays of local marine life. It's open April to October, Monday to Friday, 10 am to 5 pm, and later on weekends. Entry is £1.20/70p.

Places to Stay
Lyme Regis has plenty of hotels, guesthouses and B&Bs. Two people with a tent can camp at *Uplyme Touring Park* (☎ 442801) at Hook Farm, Uplyme, for £6. To get there, walk up Silver St/Uplyme Rd (towards Exeter) for about 15 minutes.

Lym Guest House (☎ 442164), 1 Mill Green, at the junction of Hill Rd and Sherbourne Lane, has B&B from £15 to £22 per person. *Coombe House* (☎ 443849), 41 Coombe St, costs £15 to £16 for rooms with attached bathroom. *Coombe St Galleries* (☎ 442924), 33 Coombe St, has beds from £12.50. On Cobb Rd, up from the harbour, there's *Harbour View* (☎ 443910) and *Cliff Cottage* (☎ 443334), both with beautiful views and both in the £15 to £17 range.

St Michael's Hotel (☎ 442503), on Pound St, has nice views and costs £20 to £25 per person for rooms with attached bathroom. Nearby is the *Alexandra Hotel* (☎ 442010), one of the town's finest hotels, which charges £45 to £135 per person. Round the corner on Pound Rd, the *Kersbrook Hotel* (☎ 442596) costs from £33 to £38. The *Bay Hotel* (☎ 442059), on Marine Parade, costs from £30 to £36 per person.

Places to Eat

For fish & chips try *Lyme's Fish Bar* at 34 Sherborne Lane or the *Cobb Gate Fish Bar* on the waterfront.

Many of the pubs do food – try the *Cobb Arms* or the *Royal Standard*, both on Marine Parade by the Cobb. The *Pilot Boat* on Bridge St and the *Volunteer* on Broad St are other possibilities.

Quern's (☎ 442988), on Mill Lane by the river, offers everything from pizza and pasta to vegetarian dishes and fish. Traditional fare can be found at *Polly Victoria* (☎ 442886), at the Cobb end of Marine Parade. The *Smuggler* in Broad St does all-day breakfast for £4.50, cream teas for £2.85, pizza for £4.50 and stays open until 8 pm.

Getting There & Away

Lyme Regis makes a convenient midway point between Dorchester or Weymouth and Exeter. National Express connects with Exeter, a one hour 45-minute trip. Southern National Bus No 31 links Lyme Regis to Taunton and Weymouth via Axminster.

AROUND LYME REGIS
Parnham

Parnham (☎ 01308-862204) is both a home and a showroom for owner John Makepeace's contemporary furniture. You might pick up a chair for £600 but most pieces are in the £3000 to £10,000 range. It's near Beaminster, five miles north of Bridport, and is open April to October, Wednesday and Sunday, 2 to 5 pm. Entry is £4/2.

Forde Abbey

Set in 30 acres of magnificent gardens, Forde Abbey (☎ 01460-220231) is a monastery converted into a private home. It's open April to October, Wednesday and Sunday, 1 to 4.30 pm. Entry is £4.80 (children free), which includes admission to the gardens. The gardens are open 10 am to 4.30 pm, daily year-round, and entry is £3.50 (children free).

SHERBORNE
• *pop 7500* • *☎ 01935*

Sherborne has a wonderful abbey church with a long, colourful history. On the edge of town, the remains of the Old and New Castles face each other across Sherborne Lake. The TIC (☎ 815341) is at 3 Tilton

SOUTH-WESTERN ENGLAND

Finding Fossils

Lyme Regis is still popular with fossil hunters, although these days you would have to be up very early to get there ahead of the professionals. They follow weather reports assiduously, waiting for heavy rain or storms to bring the cliff slides which expose new finds.

Prime fossil areas are east of Lyme Regis under the Black Ven Cliffs and right on to Stonebarrow and Golden Cap (4½ miles away), or west of town along Pinhay Bay. Small ammonites are the most likely find, although they can be over three feet across, and two or three ichthyosauruses are found in a typical year. *Finding Fossils in Lyme Bay* or other locally available booklets give more details. Take care when fossil hunting. At high tide, the sea comes right up to the cliffs (check tide times before departing) and the cliffs can be very unstable (don't attempt to climb them).

The Lyme Regis Fossil Shop (☎ 01297-442088), at 4 Bridge St, and the Old Forge Fossil Shop (☎ 01297-445977), at 15 Broad St, have extensive fossil collections. Dinosaurland (☎ 01297-443541), on Coombe St, conducts 1½-hour fossil walks for £3.50/2.10. ■

Court, Digby Rd, opposite the abbey entrance.

Sherborne Abbey

The abbey started life as a small Saxon church early in the 8th century, and became a Benedictine abbey in 998. After further expansion and decoration, it was seized by the Crown in 1539 whereupon the townsfolk clubbed together and bought it as their parish church.

Simmering unrest between monastery and town flared up in 1437. At that time, the monks used the chancel of the church while the townspeople used the nave. When the monks attempted to narrow a doorway between the abbey and the connected All Hallows Church (now gone), a pitched battle broke out and a flaming arrow shot across the church from town end to monastery end and set the roof alight.

The abbey is entered via a Norman porch built in 1180. Immediately on the left is the Norman door, built in 1140, which was the cause of the 1437 riots and fire. The remains of All Hallows are to the west of the Saxon wall; a Saxon doorway from 1050 survives. The superb fan vault above the choir dates from the early 15th century and is the oldest ceiling of this type and size in the country. The similar vault over the nave is from later in the century. Solid Saxon-Norman piers support the abbey's soaring central tower.

The monk's choir stalls also date from the mid-15th century and are carved with amusing figures.

Other Abbey Sights The abbey has a cathedral-like close where you'll find the 1437 **St John's Almshouses**, open to the public May to September on Tuesday and Thursday to Saturday from 2 to 4 pm; entry costs 50p. The **museum** (☎ 812252) in Half Moon St has a model of the Old Castle before it was slighted. It's open April to October, Tuesday to Saturday, 10.30 am to 4.30 pm, and on Sunday from 2.30 to 4.30 pm; entry is 50p/15p. **Sherborne School**, a boy's private school, dates back to 1550 and utilises various buildings from the monastery.

Old Castle

East of the town centre stand the ruins of the Old Castle (☎ 812730; EH), originally constructed from 1107. In the late 16th century, Sir Walter Raleigh took a fancy to the castle and Queen Elizabeth I negotiated its purchase for him. Before Sir Walter could move in, he incurred the queen's displeasure by marrying one of her ladies-in-waiting and Sir Walter and his new bride paid a short visit to the Tower of London. Later he spent large sums of money modernising the castle, before deciding it wasn't worth the effort and moving across the River Yeo to start work on the new castle.

Cromwell destroyed the castle after a 16-day siege in 1645. 'A malicious and mischievous castle, like its owner,' (the Earl of Bristol) he thundered. Admission costs £1.30/70p.

Sherborne Castle

Sir Walter Raleigh commenced his New Castle (☎ 813182) in 1594 but by 1608 he was back in prison, this time at the hands of James I. The king first gave the castle away, then took it back, and in 1617 sold it to Sir John Digby, the Earl of Bristol. It's been the Digby family residence ever since. The castle is open Easter to September, Thursday, Saturday and Sunday, 1.30 to 5.30 pm; entry is £3.60/1.80.

Places to Stay

Centrally located, cheaper B&Bs costing £16 or £17 per person include *Netherleigh* (☎ 813339) and *Bay Trees* (☎ 816527) on Bristol Rd, or the *Old Poste* (☎ 813404) and the slightly more expensive *Tudor Lodge* (☎ 816009) on Long St.

The *Antelope Hotel* (☎ 812077) on Greenhill costs from £22.50 to £30 per person. The *Quinns* (☎ 815008) on Marston Rd costs from £21 to £28 per person in rooms with attached bathroom. The *Britannia Inn* (☎ 813300) on Westbury St costs from £18 to £21 per person.

Places to Eat

The *Three Wishes Coffee Shop & Restaurant*

at 78 Cheap St does soup and a roll for £2.25. Similar fare is marginally pricier a few doors away at *Tips Bistro*. The *Cross Keys Hotel* (☎ 812492), at the junction of Cheap and Long Sts, right by the abbey, has an extensive pub-food menu.

SHAFTESBURY
• *pop 4900* • ☎ *01747*

Situated on an 800-foot-high ridge, **Shaftesbury Abbey** (☎ 852910) was founded in 888 by Alfred the Great and was at one time England's richest nunnery. Today, only scant signs of the foundations remain, situated off Park Walk with fine views over the surrounding countryside. St Edward (see Corfe Castle under South-East Dorset earlier in this section) was said to have been buried here, and King Canute died at the abbey in 1035. It's open from April to October, daily, 10 am to 5 pm and entry is 90p/30p.

The picturesquely steep cobbled street known as **Gold Hill** tumbles down the ridge from beside the abbey ruins. **Shaftesbury Museum** (☎ 852157) at the top of the hill is open from Easter to September, daily, 11 am to 5 pm; entry is 75p/10p.

The TIC (☎ 53514) at 8 Bell St has a board outside listing local B&Bs and other accommodation. The *Ship Inn* and *King's Arms*, by the central car park, have pub food, or try *The Salt Cellar*, a cosy café at the top of Gold Hill.

Wiltshire

Wiltshire boasts wonderful rolling chalk downs, Britain's most important prehistoric sites at Stonehenge and Avebury, arguably the country's finest cathedral in Salisbury and a number of the stateliest of stately homes at Wilton, Stourhead and Longleat. The Ridgeway Path, taking walkers along a crest of the downs, has its western end in Wiltshire.

WILTSHIRE CYCLEWAY
Wiltshire boasts six circular cycle routes. The longest is a 160-mile circuit encircling almost the whole county. TICs stock the *Wiltshire Cycleway* brochure which details the routes and lists cycle shops and rental

---

Chalk Figures
Wiltshire's rolling fields are a green cloak over a chalk substructure, and the practice of cutting pictures into the hillsides has a long history. The technique is simple: mark out your picture and cut away the green grass and topsoil to reveal the white chalk below. The picture will need periodic maintenance, but not much – some of the chalk figures may date back to prehistoric times, although the history of the oldest figures is uncertain. Although Wiltshire has more chalk figures than any other county, the best are probably the 180-foot-tall Cerne Giant (with his even more notable 40-foot penis) in Dorset and the 365-foot-long Uffington White Horse in Oxfordshire (which really requires a helicopter or hot-air balloon for proper inspection).

Horses were particularly popular subjects for chalk figures in the 18th century and noteworthy ones can be seen in Wiltshire at Cherhill near Calne, Alton Barnes and Hackpen, and at Osmington near Weymouth in Dorset.

During WWI a series of regimental badges were cut into a hillside outside Fovant in Wiltshire. A New Zealand WWI regiment left a gigantic kiwi on a hillside at Bulford, near Amesbury in Wiltshire. Get a copy of Kate Bergamar's *Discovering Hill Figures* (Shire Publications) for the complete lowdown on England's chalk figures. ∎

Chalk figure in Wiltshire – the Cherhill Horse

outlets. *Wiltshire Cycleway Campsites* lists camping grounds along the routes.

KENNET & AVON CANAL

Stretching from Bristol to Reading, the 87-mile-long Kennet & Avon Canal was reopened in 1990 after standing derelict for 40 years. Built by the brilliant engineer John Rennie between 1794 and 1810, it's now used by narrow boats and has some fine stretches of towpath. The stretch from Bath to Bradford-on-Avon passes a notable aqueduct. The flight of 29 locks just outside Devizes is an engineering marvel. The Kennet & Avon Canal Museum (☎ 01380-721279) on the wharf in Devizes has information on the canal.

SALISBURY

- *pop 37,000*   •   ☎ *01722*

Salisbury is justly famous for its cathedral and its close, but it's still very much a bustling market town, not just a tourist trap. Markets have been held in the town centre twice weekly for over 600 years and the jumble of stalls still draws a cheery crowd. The town's architecture mixes every style since the Middle Ages and includes some beautiful, half-timbered black-and-white buildings.

Salisbury makes a good base for visiting attractions throughout Wiltshire and for excursions to the coast.

Orientation & Information

The town centre is a 10-minute walk to the east of the railway station or just a couple of minutes down Endless St from the bus station. Everything is within easy walking distance of Market Square, the town centre, with its impressive guildhall.

The TIC (☎ 334956) in Fish Row, directly behind the guildhall, sells *Seeing Salisbury* (80p), a useful pamphlet which outlines walks around the town and across the water meadows for classic views of the cathedral.

Salisbury Cathedral

The Cathedral Church of the Blessed Virgin Mary (☎ 328726) is one of the most beauti-

ful and cohesive in Britain, an inspiration to the artist John Constable (1776-1837) who painted it from across the water meadows. It was built in uniform Early English (or Early Pointed) Gothic, a style characterised by the first pointed arches and flying buttresses and a feeling of austerity. The uniformity is a result of the speed with which the cathedral was built between 1220 and 1258 and to the fact that it has not subsequently undergone major rebuilding. The sole exception is the magnificent spire, at 404 feet the highest in Britain, an afterthought added between 1285 and 1315.

Salisbury cathedral had its origins two miles further north with a Norman cathedral at Old Sarum (see that section later in this chapter). In 1217, Bishop Poore petitioned the pope for permission to move the cathedral to a better location, complaining that the water supply on the hilltop was inadequate, the wind drowned out the singing, the weather gave the monks rheumatism, the crowded site meant the housing was inadequate and, worst of all, the soldiers were rude. His request was granted and in 1220 a new cathedral was constructed on the plains, conveniently close to three rivers.

Starting at the eastern end, Trinity Chapel was completed by 1225, the main part of the church by 1258 and the whole thing by 1266. The cloisters were added at about the same time and a few years later it was decided to add the magnificent tower and spire. Because this had not featured in the original plans the four central piers of the building were expected to carry an unexpected extra 6400 tons. Some fast thinking was required to enable them to do this.

The highly decorative West Screen was the last part of the cathedral to be completed and provides a fine view from across the close. The cathedral is entered via the cloister passage and the **south-west door**. The 230-foot-long nave, with its beautiful Purbeck marble piers, was 'tidied up' by James Wyatt in 1789-92; amongst other things he lined up the tombs in the nave neatly. At the south-western end of the nave is the **grave slab of**

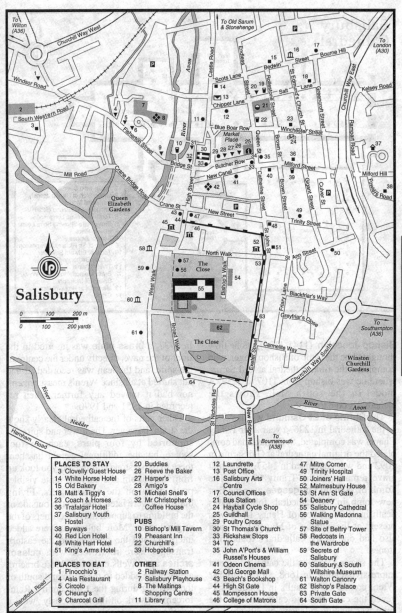

Salisbury

0   100   200 m
0   100   200 yards

PLACES TO STAY		20 Buddies	12 Laundrette	47 Mitre Corner
3 Clovelly Guest House		26 Reeve the Baker	13 Post Office	49 Trinity Hospital
14 White Horse Hotel		27 Harper's	16 Salisbury Arts	50 Joiners' Hall
15 Old Bakery		28 Amigo's	Centre	52 Malmesbury House
18 Matt & Tiggy's		31 Michael Snell's	17 Council Offices	53 St Ann St Gate
23 Coach & Horses		32 Mr Christopher's	21 Bus Station	54 Deanery
36 Trafalgar Hotel		Coffee House	24 Hayball Cycle Shop	55 Salisbury Cathedral
37 Salisbury Youth			25 Guildhall	56 Walking Madonna
Hostel		**PUBS**	29 Poultry Cross	Statue
38 Byways		10 Bishop's Mill Tavern	30 St Thomas's Church	57 Site of Belfry Tower
40 Red Lion Hotel		19 Pheasant Inn	33 Rickshaw Stops	58 Redcoats in
48 White Hart Hotel		22 Churchill's	34 TIC	the Wardrobe
51 King's Arms Hotel		39 Hobgoblin	35 John A'Port's & William	59 Secrets of
			Russel's Houses	Salisbury
PLACES TO EAT		**OTHER**	41 Odeon Cinema	60 Salisbury & South
1 Pinocchio's		2 Railway Station	42 Old George Mall	Wiltshire Museum
4 Asia Restaurant		7 Salisbury Playhouse	43 Beach's Bookshop	61 Walton Canonry
5 Circolo		8 The Maltings	44 High St Gate	62 Bishop's Palace
6 Cheung's		Shopping Centre	45 Mompesson House	63 Private Gate
9 Charcoal Grill		11 Library	46 College of Matrons	64 South Gate

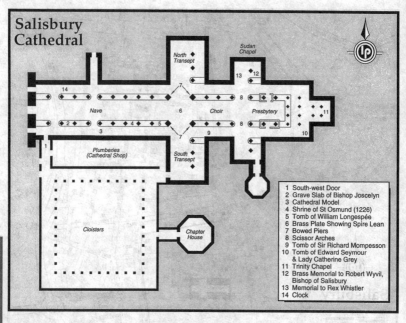

Salisbury Cathedral

Bishop Joscelyn (1141-1184), at one time thought to be the tomb of Bishop Roger, who completed the final cathedral at Old Sarum where he was bishop from 1107 to 1139. A **model** in the south aisle shows the cathedral's construction.

The **Shrine of St Osmund** was installed in the cathedral in 1226, a year after Trinity Chapel was completed. St Osmund had completed the original cathedral at Old Sarum in 1092 and was canonised in 1457. His actual grave remains in the Trinity Chapel. The **Tomb of William Longespée** was the first new tomb in the cathedral, following his death in 1226. A son of Henry II, he was present at the signing of Magna Carta and also laid one of the cathedral's foundation stones.

The soaring spire is the cathedral's most impressive feature. In 1668, Sir Christopher Wren, creator of St Paul's in London, surveyed the cathedral and calculated that the spire was leaning sideways by 29½ inches.

In 1737, a **brass plate** was inserted in the floor of the nave, directly under the centre of the spire, and the lean was recorded. It had not shifted at all since Wren's measurement, nor had it moved any further when re-recorded in 1951 and 1970.

Other parts of the cathedral clearly show the strain, however. The tower and spire are supported by four **piers**, each six-foot square, but the additional weight has bent these massive stone columns. If you look up from the bottom, the curve is quite visible, particularly on the eastern piers. Flying buttresses were later added to the outside of the building to support the four corners of the original tower. More buttresses were added internally and the openings to the eastern transepts were reinforced with **scissor arches** as in Wells cathedral. More bracing arches were added to the north and south of the crossing during the 15th century. Reinforcement work on the notoriously 'wonky spire' continues to this day.

Not everything in the cathedral requires looking upwards. The **tomb of Sir Richard Mompesson**, who died in 1627, and his wife Catherine, is a brilliantly colourful work. The grandiose **tomb of Edward Seymour** (1539-1621) and **Lady Catherine Grey**, sister of Lady Jane Grey, is at the east end of the ambulatory. The first part of the cathedral to be built, **Trinity Chapel**, at the eastern end, has fine Purbeck marble pillars; the vivid blue *Prisoners of Conscience* stained-glass window was installed in 1980.

The Sudan chapel contains a magnificent 14th-century **memorial brass** to Bishop Robert Wyvil showing him praying in Sherborne castle, and a **prism memorial** to artist Rex Whistler who lived in The Close. The **clock** displayed in the north aisle is the oldest in England and one of the oldest in the world. It was certainly in existence in 1386 when funds were provided for maintenance of a 'clocke'. It originally stood in the separate bell tower, but when that was demolished in 1790 (part of Wyatt's spring-clean) the clock and bell were moved to the cathedral's tower until a new clock was installed in 1884. Restored in 1956, it continues to operate, maintaining the the 600-year-old tradition of having a clock in this position.

The cloisters lead to the beautiful **Gothic Chapter House** of 1263-84 which houses one of the four surviving original versions of Magna Carta, the agreement made between King John and his barons in 1215. The delicate fan-vaulted ceiling is supported by a single central column. A frieze around the room recounts Old Testament tales.

The cathedral is open June to September, 8 am to 8.30 pm, and the rest of the year until 6.30 pm; a donation of £2.50/50p is requested. The Chapter House (30p) is open Monday to Saturday, 9.30 am to 4.45 pm, and Sunday from 1 to 4.45 pm. Monday to Saturday there are roof tours (£1) up to four times daily and tower tours to the base of the spire (£2) at 11 am and 2 pm. Both offer unique opportunities to get to grips with medieval building practices and are highly recommended.

Cathedral Close

Salisbury Cathedral has England's largest, and arguably most beautiful, cathedral close. Many of the buildings were constructed at the same time as the cathedral although it owes most of its present appearance to Wyatt's late 18th-century clean-up of the cathedral. The Close was actually walled in, physically separating it from the town, in 1333, using the old cathedral at Old Sarum as a source of building material. To this day it remains an elite enclave, with the gates in the wall still locked every night. Residents have their own gate keys. The most famous current resident is former prime minister Edward Heath.

Wyatt also cleared the close grounds of gravestones and demolished the late 13th-century external belfry, by then in a ruinous condition. Striding across the close lawns on the western side of the cathedral is Elizabeth Frink's **Walking Madonna** (1981).

The Close has several museums and houses open for inspection, most of them with café facilities. The **Salisbury & South Wiltshire Museum** (☎ 332151) in the King's House has exhibits on local prehistory, including Stonehenge and Old Sarum. It's open year-round, Monday to Saturday, 10 am to 5 pm. In July and August, it's also open on Sunday from 2 to 5 pm. Entry is £3/75p. A half-hour audio-visual performance, **'Secrets of Salisbury'**, is on show in the Medieval Hall (4122472) which is open daily from 10 am to 5.30 pm, for £1.50/1. The **Redcoats in the Wardrobe** exhibit (☎ 414536) is open April to October, daily from 10 am to 4.30 pm and shows military paraphernalia. In November, February and March, it is open only on weekdays. Entry is £1.80/£1.

Built in 1701, **Mompesson House** (☎ 335659; NT) is a fine Queen Anne house with a walled garden. It's open April to October, Saturday to Wednesday, noon to 5.30 pm. Entry is £3.10/1.55. **Malmesbury House** (☎ 327027) was originally a 13th-century canonry and later the residence of the Earls of Malmesbury. It's open April to September, Tuesday to Saturday, 11 am to 5.30 pm; entry is £3 (£4 on Saturday).

From High St, The Close is entered by the narrow High St Gate. Just inside is the **College of Matrons**, founded in 1682 for widows and unmarried daughters of clergymen. South of the cathedral is the **Bishop's Palace**, now the Cathedral School, parts of which date back to 1220. The **Deanery** on Bishop's Walk mainly dates from the 13th century. Izaak Walton, patron saint of fishermen (see under Winchester Cathedral in the South-Eastern England chapter), lived for a time in the **Walton Canonry**, and no doubt dropped a line in the nearby Avon.

St Thomas's Church
Were it not for Salisbury cathedral, splendid St Thomas's Church would attract much more attention. The light airy edifice you see today dates mainly from the 15th century and its principal drawcard is the superb 'doom', or judgement day, painting which spreads up and over the chancel arch. Painted around 1475, it was whitewashed over during the Reformation and uncovered again in 1881. In the centre, Christ sits in judgment astride a rainbow with scenes of heaven on the left and hell on the right; hell is supervised by a hairy devil whose foot pokes out onto the chancel arch. On the hell side look out for a bishop and two kings, naked except for their mitre and crowns, and for a miser with his moneybags and a female alehouse owner, the only person allowed to hang on to her clothes.

On the south-western wall a carved oak panel of 1671 commemorates one Humphrey Beckham. The inscription note that it was 'His own Worke...' led to Beckham's name becoming a byword for boasting in Salisbury. Note also the lovely Lady Chapel with 18th-century woodwork and older monuments painted brown to match it.

Market Square
Markets were first held here in 1219 and since 1361 have been held every Tuesday and Saturday. The market once spread much further than the present car-park area and street names like Oatmeal Row, Fish Row or Silver St indicate their medieval specialities.

The square is dominated by the late 18th-century guildhall.

Facing the guildhall are two **medieval houses**: John A'Port's of around 1425 and William Russel's of 1306. Russel's looks newer because of a false front, but inside its age is revealed. The present shop owners, Watson's of Salisbury, are used to sightseers and produce a leaflet about what is probably the town's oldest house.

Immediately behind Market Square look out for Fish Row, with some fine old houses, and for the 15th-century **Poultry Cross**.

Places to Stay
The TIC has a comprehensive list and will make free bookings for visitors.

Hostels The *youth hostel* (☎ 327572), Milford Hill, is an attractive old building in two acres of garden, an easy 10-minute walk along Milford St from the centre of Salisbury, just beyond the ring road. Nightly cost is £9.10/6.15 for an adult/child.

Close to the bus station, *Matt & Tiggy's* (☎ 327443) at 51 Salt Lane is an independent hostel-like guesthouse with simple dorm rooms and no curfew. It's a pleasant old house with a café attached. A bed costs £8.50, breakfast another £2.

Camping The *Coombe Nurseries Park* (☎ 328451) is about three miles west of Salisbury at Netherhampton. A tent site for two costs £7.50. There are other sites in the vicinity.

B&Bs & Hotels Castle Rd, the A345 continuation of Castle St north from Salisbury, has a wide choice of B&Bs between the ring road and Old Sarum. *Leena's* (☎ 335419) at No 50 has six singles/doubles from £17.50/32. *Victoria Lodge* (☎ 320586) at No 61 is a larger guesthouse with 21 rooms, most with attached bathroom, from £27.50/40.

Follow Milford St out of the centre and, just beyond the ring road and the youth hostel, turn right to *Byways* (☎ 328364) at 31 Fowlers Rd. Rooms cost from £22/39, almost all of them with attached bathrooms.

This is a pleasantly quiet area but only a short walk from the centre of town. On the other side of the centre, near the railway station, *Clovelly Guest House* (☎ 322055), at 17-19 Mill Rd, has rooms from £22/40, most with attached bathroom.

Just north of the centre, the *Old Bakery* (☎ 320100), at 35 Bedwin St, is a small B&B in a 16th-century house with rooms from £18/34 a single/double. The *Coach & Horses* (☎ 336254), on Winchester St, has rooms at £40/50.

More expensive but historically interesting places include the *Red Lion Hotel* (☎ 323334), on Milford St, which has rooms from £62/98 (it looks superb in autumn when the creeper draping the courtyard turns red), and the *King's Arms Hotel* (☎ 327629), at 9-11 St John's St, which has rooms from £50/95. Five hundred years old (but modernised!), the *Trafalgar Hotel* (☎ 338686), at 33 Milford St, has 18 rooms, all with attached bathroom, costing £40/50.

Flashiest of all is the newly refurbished *White Hart Hotel* (☎ 327476), 1 St John's St, with 68 rooms for £90/105 a single/double concealed behind a grand portico near the cathedral close.

Places to Eat
Restaurants Upstairs on Market Square, *Harper's* (☎ 333118) prepares trad English food but with some imagination. It's open every day. Also looking out on the square is *Amigo's* (☎ 328923), which offers Mexican food and tapas. *Buddies* (☎ 331166), at 11-13 Salt Lane, specialises in burgers.

Fisherton St, between the centre and the station, features a choice of reasonably priced ethnic restaurants. Just across the bridge, the *Charcoal Grill* (☎ 322134), at No 18, is a bright, cheerful, authentic Turkish restaurant with all sorts of kebabs for about £5. Further along, *Cheung's* (☎ 327375), at No 60-64, is a popular Chinese restaurant, while the *Asia Restaurant* (☎ 327628) at No 90 is good for spicy Indian food.

Cafés & Pubs In Market Square in the centre, *Reeve the Baker* has an upstairs tearoom, popular for lunch and snacks. *Michael Snell's* and *Mr Christopher's*, near St Thomas's Church, both do light lunches and teas, while *Circolo* in Fisherton St is a glossy, modern café/bar serving soup and a roll for £1.75.

The *Pheasant Inn* (☎ 327069), an old pub on the corner of Salt Lane and Rollestone St, attracts a young crowd and serves lunches for around £4. The *Coach & Horses* (☎ 336254), on Winchester St, is also popular, with burgers for £3 and other pricier pub-style dishes.

Entertainment
There is often interesting live entertainment including high-quality contemporary music and performances in the *Salisbury Arts Centre* (☎ 321744), a converted church in Bedwin St. It's open Tuesday to Saturday 10 am to 4 pm, and houses a café.

The *Salisbury Playhouse* (☎ 320333) is on Malthouse Lane. The *Odeon Cinema* on New Canal must be one of the few cinemas in the world with a medieval foyer.

Churchill's, on Endless St, just north of Market Square, features live music while *Hobgoblin*, on Milford St, is a noisy, smoky pub with a young clientele. The *City Arms* and the *Market Inn* are dead central on Market Square, while *Bishop's Mill Tavern* has an outdoor area with river views.

Getting There & Away
See the fares tables in the Getting Around chapter. Just beyond the northern edge of the New Forest, Salisbury is 88 miles west of London, 52 miles east of Bristol and 24 miles from Southampton.

There are excellent walking and cycling routes to and from Salisbury; Hayball Cycle Shop (see Getting Around) sells the useful *Cycling Around Salisbury* for £1. The Clarendon Way is a 26-mile walking route to Winchester.

Bus National Express has a daily Portsmouth-Salisbury-Bath-Bristol service, but it's more expensive than local operators Wilts & Dorset (☎ 336855) and Badgerline

(☎ 01722-553231); Salisbury-Bath costs about £6 with National Express, £3 with the local operator. There are roughly hourly services to Bath via Wilton and Bradford-on-Avon (X4, two hours), to Bournemouth and Poole (X3, 1½ hours) and to Southampton (X7, 1¼ hours).

Wiltshire Bus (☎ 0345-090899) can provide information on all Wiltshire's numerous bus operators. Their Wiltshire Day Rover ticket costs £4.85/3.60 and gives unlimited bus travel for one day. A 7-day Busabout ticket allows unlimited travel on Wilts & Dorset, Hampshire Bus and Solent Blue Line buses for £19.10/10.40. Wilts & Dorset operates bus No 3 to Stonehenge; Nos 5 (Monday to Saturday) and 6 (Sunday only) to Avebury, Marlborough and Swindon; and Nos 184/5 (and X84 in summer) to Dorchester. Hampshire Bus operates No 68 to Winchester.

There are three daily National Express buses (☎ 0990-808080) to London via Heathrow (three hours, £13).

Train Salisbury is linked by rail to Portsmouth (numerous, 1¼ hours, £10.10), Bath (numerous, two hours, £9) and Exeter (10 per day, two hours, £18.70). There are 30 trains a day from London's Waterloo station (1½ hours, £19.10). To get to Winchester (£8.60) requires a change at Basingstoke or Southampton. The Railair service takes you from Salisbury to Woking by train, with regular buses from there to Heathrow for £21.20 one way.

Getting Around

Bikes can be hired from Hayball Cycle Shop (☎ 411378) on Winchester St for £7.50 per day. A more novel way to get around is to pick up a City Rickshaw from Poultry Cross or Queens St; a short tour of the centre costs £2; a longer tour with the return by horse-drawn omnibus is also available in summer. At noon a rickshaw picks up from the railway station and drops off at Mompesson House in The Close; the £2 fare includes a discount off admission to the house.

Excellent one-hour walking tours of Salis-

bury leave from the TIC at 6 pm from May to September for £2/1.

AROUND SALISBURY
Old Sarum

Once an Iron Age hillfort, Old Sarum (☎ 01722-335398; EH) became a town with its own cathedral in the Middle Ages. Today, the 56-acre site consists of impressive earthworks offering fine views of Salisbury, with ruins of the Norman fortifications and the foundations of the old cathedral nestling inside.

Bishop Osmund completed the first 173-foot-long cathedral in 1092 but it was immediately struck by lightning and badly damaged. Around 1130, it was rebuilt and extended, but this second cathedral was abandoned with the shift to Salisbury and finally demolished in 1331 to provide building material for the walls of the cathedral close.

By 1540 the last house had disappeared but Old Sarum continued to elect two members to Parliament until 1833 – a classic example of the sort of 'rotten borough' the 1832 Reform Act was designed to abolish.

Old Sarum is two miles north of Salisbury, and from Monday to Saturday there are up to four buses an hour. Entry costs £1.70/90p.

Wilton House

Henry VIII gave Wilton House (☎ 01722-743115) to William Herbert in 1541. Herbert became the Earl of Pembroke in 1551, a title the colourful family has held since. After a fire destroyed most of the house it was redesigned by Inigo Jones and completed when the fifth Earl took over. The present Earl of Pembroke is the seventeenth.

A visit to Wilton House and its 21 acres of grounds starts with a video, followed by a tour of the kitchen and laundry. The hall has a statue of Shakespeare, who dedicated the first folio edition of his plays to the third Earl. Inigo Jones was responsible for the Single and Double Cube Rooms, with their magnificent painted ceilings, elaborate plaster work and paintings by Van Dyck.

Wilton House is 2½ miles west of Salisbury on the A30 and buses depart up to six times hourly. It's open April to October from 11 am to 6 pm (last admission 5 pm). Admission to the house is £6.20/3.80.

While in Wilton you might also visit the **Wilton Carpet Factory** (☎ 01722-744919) in King St which is open all year round (except 10 days over Christmas and the New Year) Monday to Saturday 9 am to 5 pm and Sunday 11 am to 5 pm. Entry costs £3.50/1.50.

Old Wardour Castle

Just north of the A30 between Salisbury and Shaftesbury, the Old Castle (☎ 01747-870487; EH) was built around 1393 and suffered severe damage during the Civil War. Entry to the picturesquely-sited ruins is £1.50/80p.

STONEHENGE

Stonehenge (☎ 01980-624715; EH/NT) is Europe's most famous prehistoric site. It consists of a ring of enormous stones (some of which were brought from Wales), built in stages beginning 5000 years ago. Reactions vary, some feeling that the car park, gift shop and crowds of tourists swamp the monument, and that the two roads surging past rob it of atmosphere. Avebury, 19 miles to the north, is more isolated and recommended for those who would like to commune with the ley lines in relative peace (see Avebury section later).

The Site

Stonehenge was built and rebuilt over a 1500-year period. Construction started around 3000 BC when the outer circular bank and ditch were constructed. An inner circle of granite stones, known as bluestones from their original colouring, was erected 1000 years later. The stones weighed up to four tons each and were brought from the Preseli Mountains in South Wales, nearly 250 miles away.

Around 1500 BC, the huge stones which make Stonehenge instantly recognisable were dragged to the site, erected in a circle and topped by equally massive lintels to make the sarsen (the type of sandstone) tri-lithons (the formation of vertical and horizontal stones). The sarsens were cut from an extremely hard rock found on the Marlborough Downs about 20 miles from the site. It's estimated that dragging one of these 50-ton stones across the countryside to Stonehenge would require about 600 people.

Also around this time, the bluestones from 500 years earlier were rearranged as an inner horseshoe. In the centre of this horseshoe went the altar stone, a name given for no scientific reason in the 18th century. Around the bluestone horseshoe was a sarsen horseshoe of five trilithons. Three of these trilithons are intact, the other two have just a single upright. Then came the major circle of 30 massive vertical stones, of which 17 uprights and six lintels remain.

Further out was another circle delineated by the 58 Aubrey Holes, named after John Aubrey who discovered them in the 1600s. Only a handful of the stones remain in this circle. In the same circle are the South Barrow and North Barrow, each originally topped by a stone. Between them are two other stones, though not quite on the east-west axis. Outside the Aubrey Holes circle was the bank and then the ditch.

The inner horseshoes are aligned along the sun's axis on rising in midsummer and setting in midwinter. From the midsummer axis, approximately NNE, the Avenue leads out from Stonehenge and today is almost immediately cut by the A344. The gap cut in the bank by the Avenue is marked by the Slaughter Stone, another 18th-century name tag. Beyond the ditch in the Avenue, the Heel Stone stands on one side, and recent excavations have revealed that another Heel Stone stood on the other. Despite the site's sun-influenced alignment, little is really known about Stonehenge's purpose.

The site is open April to October, daily from 9.30 am to 6 pm (7 pm from June to August), and to 4 pm the rest of the year. Entry is £3/1.50. Some feel that it is unnecessary to pay the entry fee because you can get a good view from the road, and even if you do enter you are kept at some distance from the stones.

SOUTH-WESTERN ENGLAND

SOUTH-WESTERN ENGLAND

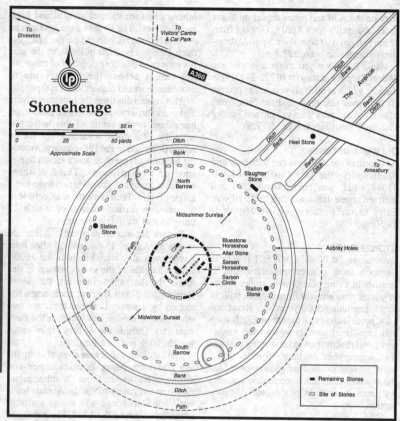

Stonehenge

0   25   50 m
0   25   50 yards
Approximate Scale

To Shrewton

To Visitors' Centre & Car Park

A360

The Avenue

Ditch
Bank
Bank
Ditch

Ditch
Bank
Bank
Ditch

Heel Stone

To Amesbury

Ditch
Bank

Slaughter Stone

North Barrow

Midsummer Sunrise

Station Stone

Path

Bluestone Horseshoe
Altar Stone
Sarsen Horseshoe
Sarsen Circle

Aubrey Holes

Station Stone

Midwinter Sunset

South Barrow

Bank
Ditch

Path

■ Remaining Stones
□ Site of Stones

Getting There & Away
Stonehenge is two miles west of Amesbury
on the junction of the A303 and A344/A360.
It's nine miles from Salisbury (the nearest
railway station). Buses leave Salisbury bus
station for Stonehenge, picking up at the
railway station, up to nine times a day in
summer from 10 am. A ticket costs £2.70 or
£4.25 return. Consider a Wilts & Dorset
Explorer for £4.25.

Guide Friday (☎ 01722-336855) operates
two-hour tours to Stonehenge from Salisbury. They depart up to four times daily in
midsummer and cost £10.50/5, including

entry to the site. There are various minibus
tours to Stonehenge, including some that
also go to Avebury.

AROUND STONEHENGE
Stonehenge is surrounded by a collection of
mysterious prehistoric sites, several of them
only recently revealed by aerial surveys.
Only the sites within the NT boundaries are
open to the public; others are on private
property. The *Stonehenge Estate Archaeological Walks* leaflet details walks around
these sites.

Three miles east of Stonehenge and just

The Battle for Stonehenge

'A national disgrace' is how the Public Accounts Committee of the House of Commons described the situation at Stonehenge in 1992. Despite its World Heritage Site status, the 20th century hasn't been kind to Stonehenge, which is hemmed in by the busy A303 to the south and the quieter A344 to the north. Instead of being encouraged to let their imaginations rip, visitors have to put up with being funneled through a tunnel under the A344 and then staring at the stones from behind a barbed-wire barricade with a constant backdrop of roaring traffic.

For a relatively small site, Stonehenge has always received a daunting number of visitors...700,000 at the last count. To make matters worse, in the 1980s latterday Druids and New Age travellers began to descend on Stonehenge for the summer solstice en masse, often lingering for weeks afterwards. Archaeologists claimed that they would damage not just the stone circle but the lesser monuments in the surrounding fields as well. The ensuing police clampdown on solstice visits turned into an annual stand-off, culminating in the infamous Battle of the Beanfield when television viewers were treated to pictures of women and children being tipped out of a motley assortment of ancient vehicles in a none too gentle fashion. The barbed wire is one legacy of the clash; the 1994 Criminal Justice and Public Order Act, aimed at making it harder for convoys to assemble, is another.

So what hope for a brighter future? Ideally English Heritage and the National Trust would like to see both roads moved back from the site. However, in 1996 the government deemed the estimated £300 million required to reroute the A303 through a tunnel a bill too high and shunted the scheme into a siding labelled longer term.

Undaunted, the NT and EH are pressing on with plans for a Stonehenge Millennium Park which would at least see the A344 closed and the visitor centre repositioned a mile away to give the site back some of its mystique by the year 2000. ■

Stonehenge

---

north of Amesbury is **Woodhenge**, where concrete posts mark the site of a concentric wooden structure which predates Stonehenge.

North of Stonehenge and running approximately east-west is the **Cursus**, an elongated embanked oval, once thought to have been a Roman hippodrome; in fact it is far older, although its purpose is unknown. The **Lesser Cursus** looks like the end of a similar elongated oval. Other prehistoric sites around Stonehenge include a number of burial mounds, like the **New King Barrows**, and **Vespasian's Camp**, an Iron Age hillfort.

STOURHEAD

Stourhead (☎ 01747-841152; NT) is another of England's fine stately homes, but here the house is merely an adjunct to the stunning garden. If you have to choose between house and garden, opt for the outdoors.

Wealthy banker Henry Hoare built the house between 1721 and 1725, while his son, Henry Hoare II, created the garden in the valley beside the house. Subsequent Hoares enlarged and enriched the house: traveller and county historian Sir Richard Colt Hoare added wings between 1790 and 1804, and the house was rebuilt after a fire in 1902. Landscapes by Claude and Gaspard Poussin

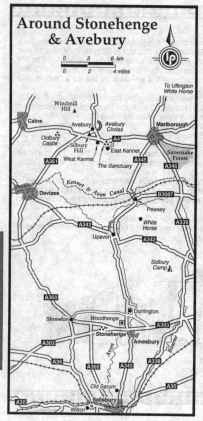

Around Stonehenge & Avebury

15th-century **Bristol Cross**, acquired from the city of Bristol in 1765, past **St Peter's Church** and the **Spread Eagle Inn** back to the starting point. From near the Pantheon, a 3½-mile side trip can be made to **King Alfred's Tower**, a 160-foot-high folly overlooking Wiltshire, Somerset and Dorset.

The garden is open daily from 9 am to 7 pm (or sunset). The house is open April to October, Saturday to Wednesday, noon to 5.30 pm. Entry costs £4.20/2.20 to the house, another £4.20/2.20 to the garden (£3.20/ 1.50 in winter). A combined house and garden ticket costs £7.50/3.50. King Alfred's Tower is another £1.50/ 70p.

LONGLEAT

Longleat (☎ 01985-844400) is the English stately home turned circus act. Following Henry VIII's monastic land grab, Sir John Thynne picked up the priory ruins and Longleat's 900 acres for the princely sum of £53 in 1541. Having acquired the 13th-century Augustinian priory, he turned 16th-century architecture on its head to produce a house that looked out onto its magnificent park rather than in towards its courtyards. It was still under construction when he died in 1580, but although its external appearance hasn't changed since, there have been many internal alterations. The rooms are sumptuously furnished and feature seven libraries with 40,000 books. Capability Brown landscaped the surrounding park in 1757-62, planting woods in the background and creating the Half Mile Pond.

After WWII, taxation started to nibble away at the English nobility's fortunes, just as maintenance costs skyrocketed and servants became scarce and expensive. The sixth Marquess of Bath responded by pioneering the stately home business at Longleat, going on to add new, less serious attractions in the grounds. These days Longleat boasts a pub, a narrow-gauge railway, a Dr Who exhibit, a pet's corner, a butterfly garden and a safari park with lions, as well as the magnificent old house. The eccentric 7th Marquess has even added a series of murals,

betray the inspiration for the Stourhead gardens.

A two-mile circuit takes you around a garden and a lake created by Henry Hoare II out of a series of medieval fish ponds. From the house, the walk leads by an **ice house**, where winter ice would be stored for summer use. At the **Temple of Flora** it continues around the lake edge, through a **grotto** and past a **Gothic cottage** to the **Pantheon**. There's a climb up to the **Temple of Apollo**, copied from a temple at Baalbek in Lebanon, which has fine views down the length of the lake. From the temple, you descend to the some depicting his numerous 'wifelets', in his private apartments.

Longleat House is open daily, 10 am to 4 pm (6pm from Easter to September). The safari park is open mid-March to November, 10 am to 5.30 pm; the other attractions open an hour later. Entry to the grounds costs £2/50p, to the house £4.80/3.50, to the safari park £5.50/4, and there are entry charges to 13 other features. An all-inclusive ticket costs £11/9. Buses run to the park's entrance gate, a 2½-mile walk from Longleat House through marvellous grounds.

BRADFORD-ON-AVON
- pop 9000   • ☎ 01225

Bradford-on-Avon is a beautiful, small town with fine stone houses and factories rising like a series of terraced paddy fields from the river. It's only eight miles by road from Bath, where the range of accommodation and restaurants is much wider, so a day trip is a good alternative to staying here.

Orientation & Information
The Town Bridge with its lock-up is Bradford-on-Avon's most important landmark. The crowded buildings rise up from the river on the northern side. The TIC (☎ 865797) is across the bridge from the railway station. The Kennet and Avon Canal passes through Bradford-on-Avon.

Around Town
Although Bradford-on-Avon dates back to Saxon times, it reached its peak in the 17th and 18th centuries as a weaving centre. The magnificent factories and imposing houses were the showpieces of the town's wealthy clothing entrepreneurs. The soothing honey colour of the solid stone buildings encourages wandering. Start at the **Shambles**, the original marketplace, inspect adjacent **Coppice Hill** and wander up Market St to the terrace houses of **Middle Rank** and **Tory**. Across the river, by the Town Bridge, is **Westbury House**, where a riot against the introduction of factory machinery in 1791 led to three deaths.

The first bridge across the Avon at the

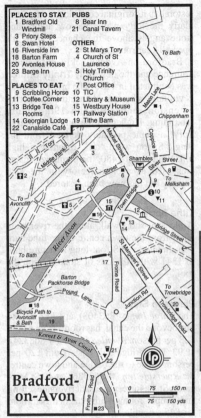

PLACES TO STAY
1 Bradford Old Windmill
3 Priory Steps
5 Swan Hotel
16 Riverside Inn
18 Barton Farm
20 Avonlea House
23 Barge Inn

PLACES TO EAT
9 Scribbling Horse
11 Coffee Corner
13 Bridge Tea Rooms
14 Georgian Lodge
22 Canalside Café

PUBS
8 Bear Inn
21 Canal Tavern

OTHER
2 St Marys Tory
4 Church of St Laurence
6 Holy Trinity Church
7 Post Office
10 TIC
12 Library & Museum
15 Westbury House
17 Railway Station
19 Tithe Barn

Bradford-on-Avon

Town Bridge site was constructed around the 12th century but the current bridge dates from 1610. The small room jutting out was originally a chapel and then a lock-up. The **Bradford-on-Avon Museum** (closed Monday and Tuesday) is in the library by the river.

Churches
Tiny **St Laurence** is one of Britain's finest Saxon churches, probably dating from around 700 AD. Later it was put to secular use and by the 19th century was no longer even recognised as a church. It has now been

SOUTH-WESTERN ENGLAND

restored to its original condition; note particularly the lofty walls, narrow arches and stone angels above the chancel arch. It's open all year round.

Bradford-on-Avon quickly outgrew St Laurence and the new **Holy Trinity Church** was completed in 1150. The original church is virtually submerged beneath 14th-century extensions and 15th and 19th-century rebuilding. Higher up the hill is **St Marys Tory**, a name probably derived from the Anglo-Saxon word 'tor', meaning a high hill. Built about 1480, the hermitage chapel was used as a cloth factory in the 18th century but has now been restored.

Tithe Barn

A pleasant short walk along the river bank leads from the town centre to the tithe barn – an immense 168-foot-long structure built in 1341 with 100 tons of stone tiles on the roof.

Places to Stay

The *Barge Inn* (☎ 863403), at 17 Frome Rd just beyond the canal, has rooms from £18 to £28 per person. *Avonlea House* (☎ 868324), at 93 Trowbridge Rd, costs from £20 per person. Close to the bridge and town centre, the *Riverside Inn* (☎ 863526), at 49 St Margarets St, has a very pleasant riverside setting and simple rooms with attached bathroom for £45 a double.

If you can afford more, this is a good town for a splurge. *Priory Steps* (☎ 862230), at Newtown, is only a few minutes walk from the town centre but has wonderful views from its hillside position. Rooms, all with attached bathroom, are £42/58. The *Bradford Old Windmill* (☎ 866842), at 4 Masons Lane, is a beautifully converted old windmill overlooking the town with singles for £39 to £55 and doubles for £39 to £69. The *Swan Hotel* (☎ 868686), at 1 Church St, right in the town centre, has singles at £40 to £50, doubles at £50 to £65. In a quiet, atmospheric spot by the canal is *Barton Farm*, a 14th-century farmhouse beside the tithe barn which charges from £35 a room.

Places to Eat

The olde-worlde *Bridge Tea Rooms* beside the Town Bridge serves excellent lunches and teas: stilton and celery soup with a roll for £2.75, cream tea for £3.95. Other possibilities for lunch or tea include the tiny *Coffee Corner* behind the TIC and the *Scribbling Horse* beside it. The *Canalside Café* in the Lock Inn Cottage, near where Frome Rd crosses the canal, is also good for snacks.

The *Swan Hotel* in the centre does bar food for £3 to £5 and has a restaurant with set meals. Other pub food possibilities include the *Bear Inn*, at 26 Silver St, and the *Canal Tavern*, at 49 Frome Rd. The *Georgian Lodge* beside the Town Bridge is a bit flashier with dishes like wild boar and apple sausages for £6.50.

Getting There & Away

There are hourly trains and buses (No X4) to Bath. Once a week there are also buses to Devizes and Chippenham.

Getting Around

Bicycles can be hired for £10 a day from the Lock Inn Cottage (☎ 868068), at 48 Frome Rd by the canal.

CHIPPENHAM & AROUND

Chippenham itself (population 22,000) is an unexceptional market town which might make a touring base for several nearby attractions.

The TIC (01249-657733) stocks a town trail and can advise on accommodation costing from £15 a head. The museum in the 15th-century **Yelde Hall** is open March to October from 10 am to 12.30 pm and 2 to 4.30 pm (closed Sunday).

Castle Combe

A Cotswold village that's strayed, Castle Combe is as close to the dream English village as you can get. There's a 13th-century market cross and a pack bridge with weavers' cottages reflected in a pool, and the main street is lined with flower-covered stone cottages, pubs and tasteful shops. Pretty medieval St Andrew's Church also contains a remarkable 13th-century monument of Sir Walter de Dunstananville.

Gates Tea Shop (☎ 01249-782111), by the market cross, has two double rooms costing £40 or £45 depending on the bed. During the day you can get a cream tea here for £3.40. At the opposite end of the price spectrum, the cheapest bed at the grand *Manor House Inn* (☎ 782206) is £50. Both the *Castle Inn* and the *White Hart* do pub lunches.

One bus a day (7 am) leaves Chippenham railway station for Castle Combe.

Corsham Court
An Elizabethan mansion dating from 1582, Corsham Court (☎ 01249-701610) was enlarged and renovated in the 18th century to house the art collection accumulated by Paul Methuen and his descendants. The house is open Easter to September, Tuesday to Sunday, 2 to 5 pm; shorter hours and days the rest of the year. Entry is £3.50/2.

Lacock
An astonishingly attractive village, Lacock lays claim to being the birthplace of photography and has many buildings from an extensive medieval monastic complex. The village dates back to the Saxon era, well before the foundation of Lacock Abbey. Many of the buildings date from medieval times and are owned by the NT; few were built after the 18th century.

The NT's *Lacock Village* leaflet (25p) plots a route round the most interesting buildings. King John's **Hunting Lodge** dates in part from the 13th century and the adjacent **St Cyriac's Church** is mainly late 15th century but its origins are Norman, possibly even Saxon; note the 1501 brass in the south transept to Robert and Elizabeth Baynard and their 18 children. The **Sign of the Angel Hotel** dates from 1480. W H Fox Talbot of Lacock Abbey founded the village **primary school** on High St in 1824. His **grave** is in the village cemetery. Note also the 14th-century **tithe barn**.

Lacock provided the setting for many scenes in the BBC's acclaimed 1995 production of *Pride and Prejudice*.

Lacock Abbey Lacock Abbey (☎ 01249-730227) was established as a nunnery in 1232, then sold to William Sharington by Henry VIII in 1539. Sharington converted the nunnery into a home, demolished the church, tacked a tower onto the corner of the abbey building and added a brewery, but he retained the abbey cloister and other medieval features. Despite three marriages he had no children and the house passed to the Talbot family, who eventually handed the whole village over to the NT in 1944. Two Talbots still live in part of the house.

In the 19th century, William Henry Fox Talbot, a prolific inventor, conducted crucial experiments in the development of photography; an 1835 image of the abbey's oriel window may be the first photograph ever taken.

The abbey is open April to October, Wednesday to Monday, from 1 to 5.30 pm. The grounds open an hour earlier. Entry is £4.20/2.10; £2.10/1 for the cloister and grounds only.

Fox Talbot Museum of Photography 'I think 1839 may fairly be considered as the real date of the birth of the Photographic Art,' said WH Fox Talbot. At the entrance gate to the abbey is a museum (☎ 01249-730459) detailing his pioneering photographic work in the 1830s, at the same time as Louis Daguerre was working in France. His particular contribution was the photographic negative, from which further positive images could be produced rather than the photograph being a one time, one image process.

The museum is open April to October, daily, 11 am to 5.30 pm; entry is £2.30/1.10.

Places to Stay & Eat Lacock makes a wonderful place to stay although accommodation is both limited and relatively pricey. *King John's Hunting Lodge* (☎ 730313) at 21 Church St has two lovely rooms with exposed beams costing £45/55 for B&B. It also houses a weekend and summer-season tearoom. At 1 The Tanyard, *Lacock Pottery* (☎ 730266) has beds available from £20 a head, with good healthy breakfasts thrown in. You can also join a pottery course here. Pricier but highly atmospheric are rooms in the 15th-century *Sign of the Angel* (☎ 730230); beds beneath exposed beams cost from £50/75.

All three village pubs do food. At the *Sign of the Angel* (☎ 730230) a three-course meal costs a hefty £37.50. The *George* is cheaper and hugely popular. The *Carpenter's Arms* is the most reasonably priced and most spacious.

Getting There & Away Monday to Saturday bus Nos 234/237 operate a roughly hourly service from Chippenham (10 minutes).

DEVIZES
• *pop 12,500* • ☎ *01380*

An attractive market town, Devizes was once an important coaching stop and a number of Market Place's old inns survive. The TIC (☎ 729408) is at 39 St John's St, right by the market square. Interesting buildings around Market Place include the **Corn Exchange**, topped by a figure of Ceres, goddess of agriculture, and the **Old Town Hall** of 1750-52.

Just beyond the TIC, **St John's Alley** has a wonderful collection of Elizabethan houses with the upper floors cantilevered over the street. The new **Town Hall**, dating from 1806, is at this end of St John's St.

St John's Church displays elements of its original Norman construction, particularly the solid crossing tower. **Devizes Museum** (☎ 727369), at 41 Long St, has interesting displays on the development of Avebury and Stonehenge, a brand-new section on Roman history and an upstairs social history room. It's open Monday to Saturday, 10 am to 5 pm (closed on Saturday from 1 to 2 pm). Entry is £1.75/40p.

The **Kennet & Avon Canal Centre** (☎ 729489), just north of the town centre, is open Easter to Christmas, daily, 10 am to 5 pm; entry is £1, children free. The **Caen Hill** flight of 29 successive locks is just outside Devizes.

Places to Stay & Eat
In nearby Rowde, *Lakeside* (☎ 722767) has

tent sites for £6 and £7. The small camping ground at *Lower Foxhangers Farm* (☎ 828254) is cheaper at £5.

Pinecroft (☎ 721433) in Potterne Rd has rooms for £20/34 and hires out mountain bikes as well. The *Bear Inn* (☎ 722444), on Market Place, is a nice 17th-century establishment with rooms for £50/75. The 18th-century *Black Swan Inn* (☎ 723259), also on Market Place, costs £33/50. The *Castle Hotel* (☎ 729300), on New Park St, has rooms for £34/47.

The popular *Wiltshire Kitchen* (☎ 724840), at 11/12 St John's St, does light lunches. Otherwise the pubs around Market Place are your best bet for reasonably-priced fare, especially on market days.

Getting There & Away
Bus Nos 33/233 run a service from Chippenham except on Sundays.

AVEBURY
• ☎ *01672*

Avebury stands at the hub of a prehistoric complex of ceremonial sites, ancient avenues and burial chambers. It's a bigger site and less visited than Stonehenge and you may well find it more atmospheric. The impact of Neolithic people on the environment is so dramatic you can almost feel them breathing down your neck. In addition to the enormous stone circle, Avebury itself is a pretty village and nearby sites include Silbury Hill and West Kennet Long Barrow. The Ridgeway Path has its western end at Avebury.

Orientation & Information
The Avebury stones encircle much of the village, but don't drive into it as the car park on the A4361 is only a short stroll from the circle. The TIC (☎ 539425) is in the Great Barn. The NT has a shop near St James Church.

Stone Circle
The stone circle dates from around 2600 to 2100 BC, between the first and second phase of construction at Stonehenge. Its diameter

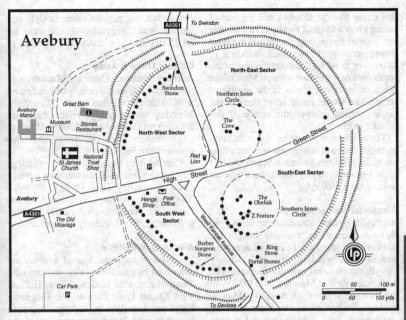

Avebury

To Swindon

A4361

North-East Sector

Swindon Stone

Northern Inner Circle

Great Barn

Avebury Manor

Museum

Stones Restaurant

North-West Sector

The Cove

Green Street

St James Church

National Trust Shop

Red Lion

High Street

South-East Sector

Avebury

A4361

The Old Vicarage

Henge Shop

Post Office

South West Sector

West Kennet Avenue

The Obelisk

Z Feature

Southern Inner Circle

Barber Surgeon Stone

Ring Stone

Portal Stones

Car Park

0   50   100 m
0   50   100 yds

To Devizes

SOUTH-WESTERN ENGLAND

of about 380 yards makes the circle is one of the largest in Britain. The site originally consisted of an outer circle of 98 standing stones from 10 to 20 feet in length, many weighing up to 20 tons. They had been selected for their size and shape, but had not been worked to shape like those at Stonehenge. The stones were surrounded by another circle formed by an 18-foot-high earth bank and a 20 to 30-foot-deep ditch. Inside were smaller stone circles to the north (27 stones) and south (29 stones).

The circles remained largely intact through the Roman period. A Saxon settlement grew up inside the circle from around 600 but in medieval times, when the church's power was strong and fear of paganism even stronger, many of the stones were deliberately buried. Worse was to come in the late 17th and early 18th century when the village expanded and stones were broken up for building material. Fortunately, William Stukeley (1687-1765) surveyed the site

around this time. In 1934, under the supervision of Alexander Keiller, buried stones were located and resurrected, and markers were placed where stones had disappeared. The wealthy Keiller actually bought Avebury in order to restore 'the outstanding archaeological disgrace of Britain'.

Modern roads into Avebury neatly dissect the circle into four sectors. Start from High St, near the museum and car park, and walk round the circle in a counter-clockwise direction. There are 12 standing stones in the south-west sector, one of which is known as the **Barber Surgeon Stone**, after the skeleton of a man found under it; from the equipment buried with him, he appeared to have been a medieval travelling barber-surgeon, killed when a stone accidentally fell on him.

The south-east sector starts with the huge **portal stones** which marked the entry to the circle from West Kennet Ave. The **southern inner circle** stood in this sector and within this circle was the **Obelisk** and a group of stones known as the **Z Feature**. Just outside this smaller circle, only the base of the **Ring Stone** remains. Few stones, standing or fallen, are to be seen around the rest of the south-east or north-east sectors. Most of the northern inner circle was in the north-east sector. The **Cove**, made up of three of the largest stones, marked the centre of this smaller circle.

The north-west sector has the most complete collection of standing stones, including the massive 65-ton **Swindon Stone**, the first stone encountered and one of the few never to have been toppled.

Alexander Keiller Museum

Alexander Keiller, whose fortune came from Dundee marmalade, not only bought the Avebury Circle but most of the village, West Kennet Ave, Windmill Hill and virtually everything else that was up for sale. The Alexander Keiller Museum (☎ 539250), in the former stables of Avebury Manor, explains the history of the Avebury Circle and houses finds from the sites. It's open April to October, daily from 10 am to 6 pm (from 10 am to 4 pm in winter). Entry is £1.50/80p.

The Village

St James Church has Saxon origins, Norman features and an unusual rood loft. The late 17th-century **Great Barn** (☎ 539555) houses the Museum of Wiltshire Rural Life. It's open mid-March to October, daily, 10 am to 5.30 pm; winter weekends only, from 11 am to 4 pm. Entry is 95p/50p.

Having narrowly escaped exploitation as a Tudor theme park, graceful **Avebury Manor** (☎ 01672-539388; NT) is now under restoration. It's open from April to October, Tuesday, Wednesday and Sunday from 2 to 5.30 pm. Admission costs £3.50/1.75.

Places to Stay & Eat

B&B is available at *The Old Vicarage* (☎ 539362) for £20 a head, or at *The Red Lion* (☎ 539266) where doubles cost £37.

Adjacent to the Great Barn, the *Stones*

Restaurant is a popular cafeteria-style restaurant with 'megaliths' (hot dishes) for £4.95 and 'mason's lunches' for £3.95.

Getting There & Away

Avebury is between Calne and Marlborough, just off the A4, and can easily be reached by a Wilts & Dorset Bus (three times daily, Monday to Saturday; twice daily on Sunday), which operates Salisbury-Marlborough-Avebury-Swindon. Tour buses also operate from Salisbury.

Coming from Bath, you'll have to change buses at Devizes; check connections with the county inquiry line (☎ 0345-090899). Thamesdown operates Swindon-Avebury-Devizes or Marlborough regularly Monday to Saturday, less frequently on Sunday.

AROUND AVEBURY

Several important sites around Avebury are connected by excellent walks, starting with the stroll across the fields to Silbury Hill and West Kennet Long Barrow. The Ridgeway Path starts near Avebury and runs westward across Fyfield Down, where many of the sarsen stones at Avebury (and Stonehenge) were collected.

Windmill Hill

The earliest site around Avebury, dating from about 3700 BC, Windmill Hill was a Neolithic enclosure or 'camp'. Ditches confirm its shape.

The Avenue & Sanctuary

The 1½-mile-long West Kennet Ave, lined by 100 pairs of stones, connects the Sanctuary with the Avebury Circle. Today, the B4003 road runs along the same route and at its southern end the A4 virtually overrides the avenue. The stone shapes along the avenue alternated between column-like stones and triangular-shaped ones, and Keiller suggested they may have been intended to signify male and female.

Only the site of the Sanctuary remains, although the post and stone holes indicate there was a wooden building surrounded by a stone circle. The possible route of Beck-hampton Ave, a similar route into Avebury from the south-west, is mainly speculative.

Silbury Hill
Rising abruptly from the surrounding fields, Silbury Hill is one of the largest artificial hills in Europe, similar in size to the smaller Egyptian pyramids. Like a truncated cone, its 130-foot-high summit ends in a flat top that is 100 feet in diameter. It was constructed in stages from around 2500 BC but its purpose is a mystery.

West Kennet Long Barrow
Across the fields south of Silbury Hill stands West Kennet Long Barrow, the finest burial mound in England. The barrow dates from around 3500 BC and is 340 feet long by 75 feet wide. Its entrance is guarded by huge sarsens, massive sandstone stones like those at Stonehenge, and its roof is constructed of gigantic overlapping capstones. About 50 skeletons were found when it was excavated. The finds are displayed in Devizes Museum.

MARLBOROUGH
• *pop 5400*   • ☎ *01672*
Marlborough started life as a Saxon settlement at The Green, and the main street extended westward from there to a 60-foot-high prehistoric mound. The Normans erected a motte and bailey fortification on the mound. Later the town grew as a trading centre and, to make more room for the market, the houses along High St were pushed back until the road reached its present extraordinary width. High St today makes an interesting stroll, particularly on Wednesday and Saturday, which are market days. Marlborough College, an exclusive private school, now occupies the site of the old Norman castle. Just west of the college is a small white horse cut into the hillside by schoolboys in 1804.

The TIC (☎ 513989) is in George Lane car park off High St. There's plenty of accommodation along High St and George Lane. Pubs with good food along High St include the *Green Dragon*, the early 17th-century

Sun Inn and the *Wellington Arms*. *Café René* is a pleasant lunch spot in Hughenden Yard arcade off the west end of High St.

MALMESBURY
• *pop 4300*   • ☎ *01666*
Perched on top of a hill, Malmesbury has a superb semi-ruined abbey church, a late 15th-century market cross and several pleasant pubs and restaurants. The TIC (☎ 823784) in the Town Hall on Market Lane gives away a good *Town Trail*. It's round the corner from the small **Athelstan Museum**.

Malmesbury Abbey
Malmesbury Abbey is a wonderful mix of ruin and active church. The church was begun in the 12th century and by the 14th was a massive construction 320 feet long with a tower at the western end and a tower and spire at the crossing. In 1479, a storm brought down the tower and spire, and its fall destroyed the crossing and the eastern end of the church.

Worse was to come when the monastery was suppressed in 1539 and the abbey sold to a local clothier. Initially he moved looms into the nave but changed his mind in 1541 and gave it to the town because the adjacent parish church of St Paul's was in ruins. In about 1662, the west tower fell, destroying three of the west bays of the nave. Today's church consists of the remaining six bays, about a third of the original church, framed by ruins at either end.

The church is entered via the magnificent south porch, its doorway a Norman work with stone sculpture illustrating Bible stories. The huge carved Apostles on each side of the porch are some of the finest Romanesque carvings in Britain. Looking out over the nave from the south side is the watching loft, a lookout box whose purpose is obscure. In the north-eastern corner of the church is a medieval cenotaph (empty tomb) commemorating Athelstan, king of England from 925 to 939 and grandson of Alfred the Great. Some of the original roof bosses from the collapsed roof are on display.

Steps lead up to the parvis, a small room above the porch (50p requested), which contains a collection of books, including a four-volume illuminated manuscript Bible of 1407, and pictures of the abbey. A window at the western end of the church shows Elmer the Flying Monk. In 1010, he strapped on wings and jumped from the tower. Remarkably, he survived, and blamed his crash-landing on aerodynamic problems.

In the south-western corner of the churchyard, the 14th-century steeple of St Paul's, the parish church prior to 1541, is now the abbey's belfry. Towards the south-eastern corner of the churchyard is the unfortunate **Hannah Twynnoy's gravestone**. She died in 1703 at the age of 33 and her headstone recounts: 'For tyger fierce, Took life away, And here she lies, In a bed of clay'. How did this fate befall a Wiltshire woman? The tiger belonged to a visiting circus and she was killed in the White Lion pub where she was a serving maid.

The abbey is open 10 am to 4 pm daily. A £1 donation is requested.

Places to Stay & Eat
A 10-minute riverside walk from the centre, the *Burton Hill Camping Park* (☎ 822585) has sites for £6.

The *King's Arms Hotel* (☎ 823383), on High St, is an old coaching inn with rooms from £18 per person. *Bremilham House* (☎ 822680), on Bremilham Rd, an easy walk from the town centre, costs £17.50/30. The historic *Old Bell Inn* (☎ 822344), on Abbey Row by the abbey, charges £70/105 for luxurious rooms.

The cheerful *Whole Hog* (☎ 825845) is a restaurant and wine bar right behind the market cross. A hogburger costs £3.95 (vegetarian version available), a pigwitch sandwich from £2.75.

Getting Around
Bikes can be rented from CH White (☎ 822330), 51 High St, for £5 a day.

Bristol & Bath

The small, unloved county of Avon, cobbled together by border commissioners in 1974, is no more. It has now been disbanded into the four unitary authorities of Bristol, North West Somerset, Bath & North East Somerset and South Gloucestershire – but from the visitor's point of view, the most interesting places to see remain Bristol and Bath.

BRISTOL
* *pop 414,000* • ☎ *0117*
Bristol is south-western England's largest city, and if you approach by coach or through the unlovely southern suburbs, you might wonder what you're getting into. Second World War bombing raids destroyed much of the centre, which was rebuilt with scant regard for aesthetics in the 1950s and 60s. The city does, however, have pockets of magnificent architecture, docks and warehouses that have been rescued from ruin, and plenty of pubs and restaurants.

Although it's six miles from the Severn estuary, Bristol is most famous as a port. By the late 19th century, however, changing trading needs rendered the docks obsolete; early this century they were relocated from the city centre to nearby Avonmouth and Portishead. The aerospace and finance industries brought renewed prosperity in the early 1980s, but later defence cutbacks dealt the city a devastating blow. Although Bristol is still relatively affluent, don't be surprised to be approached by beggars in the city centre.

The mainly Afro-Caribbean suburb of St Paul's, just north-east of the centre, remains a run-down, occasionally tense part of town with a heavy drug scene, best not visited alone at night. However, St Paul's Carnival over the first weekend of July is a must if you're passing through.

Bristol is an important transport hub, with connections north to the Cotswolds and the Midlands, south-west to Devon and Cornwall, and east to Bath (an easy day trip). South Wales is linked to Bristol across the Severn Bridge. The Second Severn Crossing from Sudbrook Point in Gwent to Severn Beach opened in 1996.

History

Little is known about Bristol until the 10th century, but in the Middle Ages a town grew up around a castle near what is now Bristol Bridge. The centre of town was then around Wine, High, Broad and Corn Sts.

Several religious houses were established on high ground above the marshes, commemorated in the name of Temple Meads station. The importance of choosing high ground is shown by a look at Bristol's own leaning tower, attached to Temple Church in Victoria St.

It was a wealthy merchant, William Canynges, who paid for the original church on the site of St Mary Redcliffe. Soon Bristol's wealth was dependent on the triangular trade in slaves, cocoa, sugar, tobacco and manufactured goods with Africa and the New World. It was from Bristol that John Cabot sailed to discover Newfoundland in 1497, an event which will be commemorated on its 500th anniversary in 1997.

By the 18th century, the city was suffering from competition from Liverpool in particular, and the Avon Gorge made it hard for large ships to reach the city-centre docks. By the 1870s, when new docks were opened at Avonmouth and Portishead, Britain's economic focus had shifted northwards.

Orientation

The city centre is to the north of the Floating Harbour. The central area is compact and easy to get around on foot but very hilly. Clifton lies to the north-west, accessible by bus from the centre. Bristol's main shopping centre is Broadmead, with the new undercover Galleries shopping mall, but the shops lining Park St, Queens Rd and Whiteladies Rd, and those in Clifton, are more interesting.

The main railway station is Bristol Temple Meads, one mile to the south-east of the centre and linked to it by regular buses. Some trains use Bristol Parkway, five miles to the north, just off the M4, which is accessible from the centre by bus and train. A taxi will cost about £7.

The bus and coach station, currently in Marlborough St to the north of the city centre pending possible relocation, serves National Express coaches and Badgerline buses to surrounding towns and villages.

Information

The TIC (☎ 926 0767) is impressively housed in St Nicholas Church, St Nicholas St, which has a magnificent 18th-century altarpiece by William Hogarth. The comprehensive *Visitors Guide* (£1.50) is worth buying, as is the booklet describing the 2¾-mile Bristol Heritage Trail.

Venue, a fortnightly listings magazine (£1.70), gives details of what's happening in Bristol. *Bristol Books* (☎ 924 5458), 180B Cheltenham Rd, is excellent for second-hand books.

The City Museum sells a £3 passport ticket giving admission to the Industrial Museum, the Georgian House and the Red Lodge. These museums also offer half-price admission after 4 pm. Children under 16 and full-time students get in free at any time.

St Paul's Carnival, a smaller version of London's Notting Hill Carnival, livens up the first Saturday of each July. There's a regatta in the harbour in July, and not-to-be-missed hot-air balloon and kite festivals in Ashton Court, across Clifton Suspension Bridge, in August and September.

St Mary Redcliffe

Described as 'the fairest, goodliest and most famous parish church in England' by Queen Elizabeth I in 1574, St Mary Redcliffe (☎ 929 1487) outdoes the cathedral in splendour. It's a stunning piece of Perpendicular architecture with a grand hexagonal porch. Plans to move the main road in front of the church would give it back some of its original tranquillity.

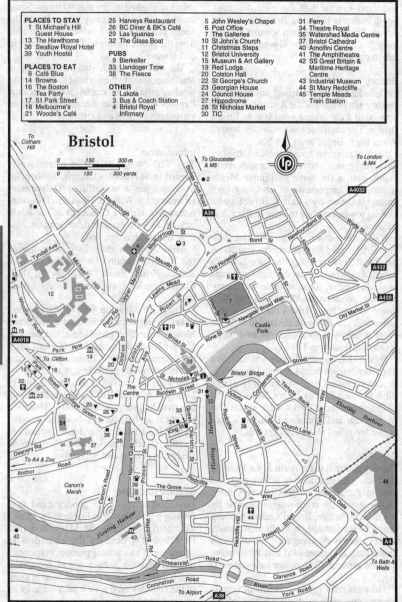

PLACES TO STAY
1 St Michael's Hill
  Guest House
13 The Hawthorns
36 Swallow Royal Hotel
39 Youth Hostel

PLACES TO EAT
8 Café Blue
14 Browns
16 The Boston
  Tea Party
17 51 Park Street
18 Melbourne's
21 Woode's Café

25 Harveys Restaurant
26 BC Diner & BK's Café
29 Las Iguanas
32 The Glass Boat

PUBS
9 Bierkeller
33 Llandoger Trow
38 The Fleece

OTHER
2 Lakota
3 Bus & Coach Station
4 Bristol Royal
  Infirmary

5 John Wesley's Chapel
6 Post Office
7 The Galleries
10 St John's Church
11 Christmas Steps
12 Bristol University
15 Museum & Art Gallery
19 Red Lodge
20 Colston Hall
22 St George's Church
23 Georgian House
24 Council House
27 Hippodrome
28 St Nicholas Market
30 TIC

31 Ferry
34 Theatre Royal
35 Watershed Media Centre
37 Bristol Cathedral
40 Arnolfini Centre
41 The Amphitheatre
42 SS Great Britain &
  Maritime Heritage
  Centre
43 Industrial Museum
44 St Mary Redcliffe
45 Temple Meads
  Train Station

Bristol

To Cotham Hill

0   150   300 m
0   150   300 yards

To Gloucester & M5

To London & M4

Lord Mayor's Chapel

Once the chapel of St Mark's Hospital, the Lord Mayor's Chapel (☎ 929 4350) is a medieval gem squeezed in between shops opposite the cathedral and packed with stained-glass windows, medieval monuments and ancient tiles. The church-loving poet John Betjeman dubbed it 'for its size one of the very best churches in England...'. It's open daily except Monday, 10 am to noon and 1 to 4 pm.

Cathedral

Originally founded as the church of an Augustinian monastery in 1140, Bristol Cathedral (☎ 926 4879) gained cathedral status in 1542. One of its most striking features is its Norman chapter house. The choir dates back to the 14th century but much of the nave and the west towers were designed by George Street in 1868. Look out for a rare Saxon carving of the 'Harrowing of Hell' in the south transept.

New Room

Tucked away in Broadmead Shopping Centre, the New Room (☎ 926 4740) was the world's first Methodist chapel when it opened in 1739. John Wesley, whose equestrian statue stands in the courtyard, preached from its double-decker pulpit. Upstairs, you can visit the old living quarters, with rooms for John and Charles Wesley and Francis Asbury.

The chapel (☎ 926 4740) is open, free, from 10 am to 1 pm and from 2 to 4 pm daily except Sunday (and Wednesdays in winter).

City Museum & Art Gallery

The gallery (☎ 922 3571) houses a mixed bag of exhibits, ranging from Egyptian mummies through natural history and local history to fine art; check with the TIC or in *Venue* for details of temporary exhibitions. It's open daily, 10 am to 5 pm; admission is £2 (children free).

Georgian House

The Georgian House (☎ 921 1362) at 7 Great George St was home to 18th-century sugar merchant John Pinney, and retains complete period fixtures and fittings. It's open Tuesday to Saturday, 1 to 5 pm; entry is £1 (children free).

Red Lodge

This Elizabethan house (☎ 921 1360) with walled garden was much altered in the 18th century. One room is preserved as a memorial to Mary Carpenter who set up the first women's reformatory here in 1854. It's open Tuesday to Saturday, 1 to 5 pm; admission is £1 (children free).

SS Great Britain

Bristol was home to the Victorian engineering genius Isambard Kingdom Brunel (1806-59), best known for the Clifton Suspension Bridge (see below). In 1843, he designed the first ocean-going iron ship, the SS *Great Britain*, the first large ship to be driven by a screw propeller.

For 43 years the ship served as a cargo vessel and a liner, carrying passengers as far as Australia, then in 1886 it was badly damaged passing Cape Horn. The cost of repairs was judged too high, so it was sold for storage. In 1970, it was returned to Bristol where it has been undergoing restoration in the dry dock where it was originally built.

The ship (☎ 926 0680) is open daily from 10 am to 6 pm (5 pm in winter); tickets are £2.90/1.90.

Entrance is via the **Maritime Heritage Centre**, which celebrates Bristol's shipbuilding past (same opening hours as the ship; admission free).

Bristol Old Station

Before rushing for their train, visitors to Temple Meads station should pause to look at what is the oldest surviving major railway terminus in the world, built to yet another Brunel design in 1839-40. The original terminus stands to the left of the modern one; the Great Train Shed, with its mock hammerbeam roof, last saw a train in 1966 – try the door of the Brunel Centre and you may be able to look round.

Parts of the old station now house the

SOUTH-WESTERN ENGLAND

Exploratory (☎ 922 5944), Bristol's hands-on science exhibition. It's open daily from 10 am to 5 pm and costs £4/2.

Clifton & the Suspension Bridge

The northern suburb of Clifton boasts some splendid Georgian architecture, including the Cornwallis and Royal York crescents, as well as some of Bristol's most attractive shopping streets. Bus Nos 8/9 and 508/9 run to Clifton from the centre of Bristol.

The spectacular 245-foot-high **Clifton Suspension Bridge**, designed by Brunel, spans a dramatic stretch of the Avon Gorge. Work on the bridge began in 1836 but wasn't completed until 1864, after Brunel's death. The bridge is an inevitable magnet for stunt artists. More poignantly, it's also a favoured suicide spot. A famous story relates how Sarah Ann Hedley jumped from the bridge in 1885 after a lovers' tiff. Her voluminous petticoats parachuted her safely to earth and she lived to be 85.

On Durdham Downs, overlooking the bridge, an **Observatory** houses a fascinating camera obscura. Nearby is **Bristol Zoo** (☎ 970 6176), open daily from 9 am to 6 pm (5 pm in winter). Admission costs £5.90/2.80.

Blaise Castle House Museum

In the northern suburb of Henbury lies Blaise Castle (☎ 950 6789), a late 18th-century house which contains a fine museum of West Country rural and urban life. Admission is free and it's open Tuesday to Sunday, 10 am to 1 pm and 2 to 5 pm.

On a hill in grounds laid out by Humphrey Repton stands a mock castle. Across the road is **Blaise Hamlet**, a cluster of thatched cottages (NT) designed for estate servants in 1811 by John Nash; with its neatly-kept green and flower-filled gardens, it's everyone's fantasy of a 'medieval' English village.

Bus Nos 1/501 pass this way from the city centre.

Organised Tours

From June to the end of September, hop-on, hop-off open-top bus tours circle 14 points in Bristol every day except Saturday. Tickets (£5/3) can be bought on board the bus or from the TIC.

Places to Stay

Hostels Bristol has very little cheap accommodation, but the 124-bed *Bristol Youth Hostel* (☎ 922 1659), 14 Narrow Quay St, is an excellent place to stay. It occupies a converted warehouse five minutes from the centre of town. The nightly charge is £10.90/7.45.

Outside term time, the university also lets out rooms; cheapest are in *Hiatt Baker Hall* (☎ 968 1512) in Parry's Lane, Stoke Bishop; pricier but more central are those in *The Hawthorns* (☎ 923 8366), Woodland Rd, Clifton.

Camping The small *Baltic Wharf Caravan Club* (☎ 926 8030) site in Cumberland Rd, 1½ miles from the centre, charges £10.50 for a tent space for two people. It's near the A370, A369, A4 and A3029 junctions. Advance booking is essential, especially at weekends.

B&Bs & Hotels *St Michael's Hill Guest House* (☎ 973 0037), 145 St Michael's Hill, is well situated and good value, for £13/19 without breakfast, £15/22 with. The *Lawns Guest House* (☎ 973 8459), 91 Hampton Rd, is in the leafy suburb of Redland and offers singles for £23 and doubles from £38.

Most of the other cheap B&Bs tend to be a fair distance from the centre. There are several on Bath Rd (the A4) and Wells Rd (the A37). *Kensington Hill Guest House* (☎ 977 6566), at No 578 Bath Rd, has nine rooms, all with bathroom attached, for £20/30. The *A4 Hotel* (☎ 971 5492), at 511 Bath Rd, is a little nearer the centre but is more expensive. During the week, rooms are £38.50/60; at weekends, they come down to £28/50.

Clifton, 1½ miles from the centre, is a very attractive suburb and a good place to stay, but most of the B&Bs here cost £20-25 per person. On Oakfield Rd (off Whiteladies Rd), the *Oakfield Hotel* (☎ 973 5556) has rooms for £26/37. In Tyndalls Park Rd the *Alandale* (☎ 973 5407) charges from £30/45.

The *Washington Hotel* (☎ 973 3980), St Paul's Rd, is midway between the city centre and Clifton Suspension Bridge. During the week, rooms are £43/59 with attached bathroom, £25/42 without. At weekends, they're £36/46 with bath, £23/43 without.

About a mile north of the centre, *Courtlands Hotel* (☎ 942 4432), 1 Redland Court Rd, Redland, is a family-run place with a bar and restaurant. There are 26 rooms, most with bathroom attached, for £38/48.

Going more upmarket, try the *Avon Gorge Hotel* (☎ 973 8955), Sion Hill, Clifton, which has a terrace overlooking the suspension bridge. Popular with business people, it's expensive during the week, but at the weekend prices drop to £50/76 for B&B or £61/98 for B&B and dinner, provided you stay two nights.

Berkeley Square Hotel (☎ 925 4000), 15 Berkeley Square, Clifton, is in a Georgian building just off Park St. Prices start at £49/69 without breakfast.

The *Grand Hotel* (☎ 929 1645), Broad St, is a Victorian hotel in the heart of the city. During the week, rooms are £89/99 and breakfast is extra. At weekends, B&B costs £39 a head, or £50 if you also have dinner and stay two nights.

Flashiest of all is the 19th-century *Swallow Royal Hotel* (☎ 925 5100), on College Green beside the cathedral. Swish B&B costs £110/125 during the week, £60/95 at weekends.

Places to Eat

If you're dining on a short shoestring, *BC Diner* and *BK's* next door, on the corner of College Green (opposite the Watershed), provide hot competition for each other. Slightly pricier but in infinitely more pleasant surroundings are the café/bars in the *Watershed Media Centre* (☎ 921 4135) and the *Arnolfini Centre* (☎ 937 9330), both overlooking the waterfront; quick, tasty lunches in either cost around £5.

At the bottom of Christmas Steps, black and white half-timbered *Pellegrino's* dispenses scrumptious fish & chips. Nearby, *The Three Sugar Loaves* is a pub with a series of cosy cubby holes.

Across the road from the TIC, *Las Iguanas* (☎ 927 6233), 10 St Nicholas St, offers Mexican and South American food – three-course lunches for £4.95. Tucked away in a side street just off Broadmead is the excellent, stylish *Café Blue* (☎ 940 5626) in what was the old Silver St fire station. Here you can have a drink or a coffee over the papers, or move up a step to the rear for a proper meal. Lunch need cost no more than £4, although a two-course set meal costs £9.99.

Heading towards Clifton, Park St is lined with reasonably priced pizzerias: try *Pastificio* or *Vincenzo's*, where there's rooftop dining. *Woode's Café*, at the bottom of Park St, sells excellent sandwiches. *The Boston Tea Party* (☎ 929 8601) at No 75 also does tasty sandwiches while *51 Park St* (☎ 926 8016) has everything from Sunday brunches to cream teas. *Melbournes* (☎ 922 6996), 74 Park St, keeps prices down with a bring-your-own-bottle policy. *Browns* (☎ 930 4777), 38 Queens Rd, serves excellent pasta for around £6 in the classy surroundings of the neo-Venetian ex-university refectory.

A 20-minute walk from the centre and running off Queens Rd, Whiteladies Rd now boasts so many flashy restaurants that it has been dubbed Bristol's Golden Mile. See and be seen at *Henry J Bean's* American diner (☎ 974 3794) at No 95, or at Henry Africa's Hothouse (☎ 923 8300) at No 65.

Rocinantes (☎ 973 4482), at No 85, is a lively tapas bar with good choices for vegetarians. *Johnny Yen's Wok Diner* (☎ 973 0730), at No 113, is an entertaining Japanese-Malay-Thai-Chinese DIY diner. You pay £4.95 for a three-course lunch. At No 119, *Pierre Victoire* (☎ 973 0716) serves good cheap French food – £4.90 for a three-course lunch. Just off Whiteladies Rd, bargain Indian Baltis are on offer at a number of Cotham Hill Balti Houses; prices start at around £3.

For a splurge, the place to go is *Harveys Restaurant* (☎ 927 5034), above Harveys Wine Museum on 12 Denmark St; four-course dinners cost £29. In a prettier setting is *The Glass Boat* (☎ 929 0704), a converted barge on Welsh Back, where dinner will cost around £20.

Entertainment

Venue (see Information section) gives details of theatre, music, gigs – the works.

Of the theatres, the *Hippodrome* (☎ 929 9444), St Augustine's Parade, hosts ballet, musicals and pantomimes, while the *Theatre Royal* (☎ 987 7877) sticks with straight drama. The *Colston Hall* (☎ 922 3686), Colston St, stages everything from concerts to wrestling bouts, and *St George's Church* (☎ 923 0359), on Brandon Hill (off Park Street) offers regular musical recitals.

Most interesting cinema programmes tend to be at the *Watershed Media Centre* (☎ 925 3845), the *Arnolfini Centre* (☎ 929 9191) and the King's Square *Arts Centre* (☎ 942 0195).

Most pubs in and around St Augustine's Parade (the city centre) are best avoided, especially at weekends. Instead, head down King St to the *Llandoger Trow* or the *Old Duke* which hosts nightly jazz sessions. Popular student hang-outs include *The Albion*, in Boyces Ave, Clifton, and the *Highbury Vaults* on St Michael's Hill, which has a courtyard for alfresco tippling. Cider-lovers shouldn't miss *The Coronation Tap* in Sion Place, Clifton.

The *Fleece* (☎ 927 7150), St Thomas St, hosts world-music sessions and live bands, as does the legendary *Bierkeller* (☎ 926 8514), All Saints St, which has played host to plenty of rock luminaries; entry costs from £1 to £12 depending on the night of the week and who's playing.

Trendy nightspots come and go with alarming frequency. The popular *Lakota* (☎ 942 6208), 2 Upper York St, stays open until 4 or 6 am, whereupon you can move on to *Club Loco* (☎ 942 6208), in Hepburn Rd, off Stokes Croft, which has a 24-hour licence. *Yum Yum* on Saturday night at Club Leo (☎ 929 2420), in St Nicholas St which

leads to Bristol Bridge, is the place for gay clubbers.

Getting There & Away

See the fares tables in the Getting Around chapter. Bristol is 115 miles from London, 75 from Exeter and 50 from Cardiff.

Air Bristol airport (☎ 01275-474444) is eight miles south-west of town, off the A38.

There are buses to the airport from Marlborough St bus station and less frequently from Temple Meads railway station.

Bus Bristol offers excellent bus connections. Every 1½ hours National Express (☎ 0990-808080) sends coaches to Heathrow airport (2½ hours, £22.50) and Gatwick airport (three hours, £25). Services into central London are equally regular (2½ hours, £9.75), but Turners (☎ 0117-955 5333) currently sells the cheapest tickets to London – just £4.95/9.50 for a single/return; buy a ticket from the driver. Bakers Dolphin (☎ 961 4000) also sells cheap tickets on this route. Their Flyer ticket costs £13.95 return, and is sold in Bakers Dolphin travel agencies around town.

National Express also has frequent buses to Cardiff (1¼ hours, £6). There are a couple of buses a day to Barnstaple (2¾ hours, £14) and regular buses south to Cornwall (Truro – 4½ hours, £26) and Devon (Exeter – 1¾ hours, £9.50), Oxford (2½ hours, £12.50) and Stratford-upon-Avon (2½ hours, £13).

Local Badgerline buses (☎ 955 3231) also operate out of Marlborough St bus station; buy a ticket when you board. There are frequent services to Bath, Wells and Glastonbury. Hourly buses to Bath can also be picked up outside Temple Meads railway station. There are also services to Salisbury and north to Gloucester. Day Rambler tickets (£4.60) let you use Badgerline and City Line buses all day.

Train Bristol is an important rail hub, with regular connections to London Paddington (1½ hours). Most trains (except those to the south) use both the Temple Meads and Parkway stations.

Bath is only 20 minutes away, so it's an easy day trip (£4.30 day return). There are frequent links to Cardiff (¾ hour, £6.10), Exeter (1 hour, £13.90), Fishguard (3½ hours, £19.40), Oxford (1½ hours, £18) and Birmingham (1½ hours, £12).

Boat Between July and October you can travel by boat along the Bristol Channel from Bristol to Clevedon, Penarth, Ilfracombe, Barry and Lundy Island. Sailings are on the SS *Balmoral* or the SS *Waverley*, the world's last sea-going paddle steamer. Prices start at £5.95 to Clevedon. Full details from Waverley Excursions on ☎ 01446-720656.

Getting Around
Bus City Line (☎ 955 3231) bus fares aren't cheap, but Dayrider tickets, available on the bus after 9 am, Monday to Friday, and at any time at the weekend, let you make six City Line rides for £2.60.

Clifton is a long walk from the town centre. Catch bus Nos 8/9 (508/509 at weekends) from bus stop 'Cu' on Colston Ave, or from Temple Meads railway station. In summer, half-hourly bus No 511 loops from Baltic Wharf to Broadmead, through Clifton Triangle and Hotwells, and back to Baltic Wharf, linking many of the major attractions and shopping centres.

Taxi There's a taxi rank on St Augustine's Parade but this is not a place to hang around late at night. To call a cab free, ring 1A Premier Cabs on 0800 716777. A taxi to the airport costs around £12.

Car Bristol suffers atrocious traffic congestion and parking spaces are hard to find and/or expensive, although the TIC provides a free map with details of city-centre car parks. If you're visiting from Bath, there's a Park & Ride scheme (not Sunday) on the A4 from Keynsham. Parking is free; a return bus ticket to the centre costs £1.30.

Boat The nicest way to get around is the ferry which, from April to September, plies the Floating Harbour, stopping at the SS *Great*

Britain, Hotwells, the Baltic Wharf, the Centre, Bristol Bridge (for Broadmead shopping centre) and Castle Park. The ferry (☎ 927 3416) runs every 40 minutes; a short hop is 80p/50p, a complete circuit £2.50/1.50.

BATH
* *pop 84,400*   * ☎ 01225*
Beautiful Bath is one of the 'must sees' on any first-time visitor's list. For more than 2000 years, the city's fortune has revolved around its hot springs and the tourism linked to it. It was the Romans who first developed a complex of baths and a temple to Sulis-Minerva on the site of what they called Aquae Sulis. Today, however, Bath is just as famous for its glorious Georgian architecture, which has won it World Heritage Site status from UNESCO.

Throughout the 18th century, Bath was the most fashionable and elegant haunt of English society. Aristocrats flocked here to gossip, gamble and flirt. Fortunately, they had the good sense and fortune to employ a number of brilliant architects who designed the Palladian terraced housing, the circles, crescents and squares, that dominate the city.

Like Florence in Italy, Bath is an architectural gem. It too has a much-photographed, shop-lined bridge, and like Florence, the town can sometimes seem little more than an upmarket shopping mall for wealthy tourists. However, when sunlight brightens the honey-coloured stone, and buskers and strollers fill the streets and line the river, only the most churlish would deny its charm. Head up some of the steep hills and you can even find pockets of Georgiana that only the residents seem to appreciate.

Bath looks wealthier than Bristol, in part because its beauty attracts monied residents, in part because the sheer crush of visitors ensures the good life to those involved in tourism. The best known sites in and around Abbey Courtyard receive too many visitors for their own good. Away from the centre, however, smaller museums fight for the droppings from their more famous neighbours' tables and are genuinely pleased to see those who trouble to seek them out. Inevitably, Bath also has its share of residents for whom affluence is somebody else's success story. For all the glitzy shops, you'll see beggars on the streets. The legacy of 1980s boom-bust economics also lingers in abandoned shops and hotels even in the city centre.

History

Prehistoric camps on the hills around Bath indicate settlement before the Romans arrived, and legend records King Bladud founding the town after being cured of leprosy by a bath in the muddy swamps. The Romans seem to have established the town of Aquae Sulis (named after the Celtic goddess Sul) in 44 AD and it was already a spa, with an extensive baths complex, by the reign of Agricola (78-84).

When the Romans left, the town declined and was captured by the Anglo-Saxons in 577. In 944, a monastery was set up on the site of the present abbey and there are still traces of a medieval town wall in Borough Walls St. Throughout the Middle Ages, Bath served as an ecclesiastical centre and a wool trading town. However, it wasn't until the 18th century that the city came into its own, when the idea of taking spa water as a cure for assorted ailments led to the creation of the beautiful city visitors see today. Those were the days when Ralph Allen developed the quarries at Coombe Down and employed the Woods (father and son) to create the glorious crescents and terraces; when Doctor William Oliver created the Bath General Hospital for the poor and gave his name to the Bath Oliver biscuit; and when the gambler Richard 'Beau' Nash became the arbiter of fashionable taste.

By the mid-19th century, sea bathing had become more popular than visiting spas and Bath fell from favour as a place to stay. Curiously, even in the 1960s few people appreciated its architecture and many houses were pulled down to make way for modern replacements before legislation was introduced to protect what remains.

Orientation

Although hemmed in by seven hills, Bath still manages to sprawl quite a way (as you'll discover if you stay at the youth hostel). Fortunately, the centre is compact and easy to get around.

The railway and bus stations are both south of the TIC at the end of Manvers St. The most obvious landmark is the abbey, across from the Roman Baths and Pump Room. Guided tours and open-top bus tours leave from Terrace Walk nearby.

Information

From mid-June to mid-September, the TIC (☎ 462831), Abbey Chambers, Abbey Churchyard, is open until 7 pm from Monday to Saturday, and until 6 pm on Sunday. For the rest of the year, it closes at 5 pm, and 4 pm on Sunday. It has an American Express bureau de change. Advance booking for accommodation over holiday periods is essential. Free walking tours (highly recommended) leave from the Abbey Churchyard at 10.30 am (except Saturday). Bath's hilly terrain makes life difficult for disabled visitors but the TIC supplies a free guide with helpful information.

Bath has a bad traffic problem and parking space is hard to find. In the city centre, you must display a parking disc bought from a local shop in your windscreen; they cost 50p for half an hour.

From mid-May to early June the Bath Festival is in full swing with events in all the town's venues, including the abbey. *Venue*, the Bristol and Bath listings magazine, publishes full programme details, although popular events are booked up well in advance. Details are available from the Festival Box Office (☎ 462231), Linley House, 1 Pierrepont Place, from February each year. Accommodation is likely to be particularly hard to find during the festival.

Much of the city centre, including the maze of passageways just north of Abbey Churchyard and Shire's Yard off Milsom St, is given over to shops, frequently of the pricey 'novelty' kind, but the flea market (antiques and clothes) is a popular place for

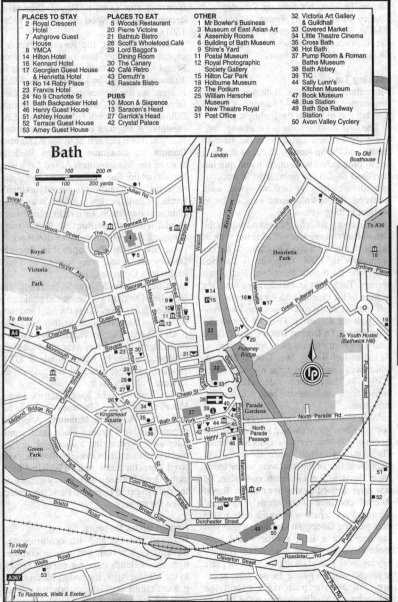

PLACES TO STAY
2 Royal Crescent Hotel
7 Ashgrove Guest House
8 YMCA
14 Hilton Hotel
16 Kennard Hotel
17 Georgian Guest House & Henrietta Hotel
19 No 14 Raby Place
23 Francis Hotel
24 No 9 Charlotte St
41 Bath Backpacker Hotel
46 Henry Guest House
51 Ashley House
52 Terrace Guest House
53 Arney Guest House

PLACES TO EAT
5 Woods Restaurant
20 Pierre Victoire
21 Bathtub Bistro
26 Scoff's Wholefood Café
29 Lord Baggot's Dining Room
30 The Canary
40 Café Retro
43 Demuth's
45 Rascals Bistro

PUBS
10 Moon & Sixpence
13 Saracen's Head
27 Garrick's Head
42 Crystal Palace

OTHER
1 Mr Bowler's Business
3 Museum of East Asian Art
4 Assembly Rooms
6 Building of Bath Museum
9 Shire's Yard
11 Postal Museum
12 Royal Photographic Society Gallery
15 Hilton Car Park
18 Holburne Museum
22 The Podium
25 William Herschel Museum
28 New Theatre Royal
31 Post Office

32 Victoria Art Gallery & Guildhall
33 Covered Market
34 Little Theatre Cinema
35 Cross Bath
36 Hot Bath
37 Pump Room & Roman Baths Museum
38 Bath Abbey
39 TIC
44 Sally Lunn's Kitchen Museum
47 Book Museum
48 Bus Station
49 Bath Spa Railway Station
50 Avon Valley Cyclery

Bath

0   100   200 m
0   100   200 yards

To London

To Old Boathouse

Julian Rd

Royal Crescent

Brock Street

Bennett St

The Circus

Paragon

Walcot Street

River Avon

Henrietta Rd

Bathwick Street

To A36

Royal Victoria Park

Royal Ave

George Street

Milsom Street

Broad Street

Henrietta Park

Henrietta St

Sydney Place

Great Pulteney Street

To Bristol

Charlotte St

Queen Square

Barton St

Monmouth Place

Midland Bridge Rd

Kingsmead Square

Bath St

Stall St

York

Henry St

Charles Street

To Youth Hostel (Bathwick Hill)

Pulteney Bridge

Grand Pde

Pulteney Road

Parade Gardens

North Parade Rd

North Parade Passage

Green Park

Green Park Rd

River Avon

St James's Parade

Corn Street

Manvers Street

Broad Quay

Lower Bristol Road

Dorchester Street

Railway Street

Claverton Street

Rossiter Rd

Pier Park Rd

To Holly Lodge

Wells Road

To Radstock, Wells & Exeter

SOUTH-WESTERN ENGLAND

bargain hunters. It's held on Saturday and Sunday mornings on Walcot St, near the YMCA. There's also a covered market with excellent second-hand bookstalls next to the Guildhall in High St.

Walking Tour

Much more than Bristol, Bath was designed for wandering around – you need at least a full day just to take in the highlights.

The best starting point is the **abbey**, conveniently situated across from the **Roman Baths** and **Pump Room**. Ahead of it, you'll see a colonnade – walk under it and turn left into Stall St. On the right, Bath St has convenient arcading so bathers could walk between the town's three sets of baths without getting wet.

Walk down Bath St. At the end stands the **Cross Bath** where Mary of Modena, wife of James II, erected a cross in gratitude for her pregnancy in 1688. Opposite is the **Hot Bath**, the third bath built over Bath's hot springs. Turn right and walk down the alley in front of the cinema into Westgate St. Turn left and follow the road round into Barton St and past the Georgian **Theatre Royal** and **Lord Baggot's Dining Room**, where Beau Nash lived with his mistress Juliana Popjoy. At the end of Barton St is **Queen Square**, which was designed by John Wood the Elder (1704-54); the northern side, where seven houses form one cohesive unit, is especially attractive.

Walk round the square and leave it by the north-western corner which leads into Royal Avenue. On the right is Queen's Parade Place; the two small, stone kiosks on the right-hand side of the road were where sedan chair carriers, the Georgian equivalent of taxi drivers, used to wait for custom. Royal Avenue continues northwards into Royal Victoria Park; a path skirting the eastern side runs past the **Georgian Garden**, where you can see what a Bath garden would have looked like during the town's 18th-century heyday, with gravel taking the place of grass to protect women's long dresses from staining. Follow the path right round the perimeter and you'll emerge on the lawn in front of the famous **Royal Crescent**, designed by John Wood the Younger (1728-1801).

After inspecting the Royal Crescent's superb architecture, turn right along Brock St and walk down to the **Circus**, a circle of 30 houses designed by John Wood the Elder. Plaques on the houses commemorate their famous residents, among them Thomas Gainsborough, Clive of India and David Livingstone. A left turn out of the Circus will take you down Bennett St to the **Assembly Rooms** and **Costume Museum**. Walk in front of the Museum into Alfred St, where houses retain fine 18th-century metal fittings, including snuffers to put out footmen's torches. Continue down Alfred St and turn right into Bartlett St, then right into George St and left down Milsom St, Bath's main shopping drag. About halfway down you'll pass the **Royal Photographic Society Gallery** in what was once Thomas Lightoler's Octagon Chapel.

At the bottom of Milsom St, bear right into New Bond St until you reach the grand colonnaded post office. Cross the road and turn right along busy Northgate St, then left along Bridge St (passing the **Victoria Art Gallery** on the right), to the River Avon and **Pulteney Bridge**, designed by Robert Adam in 1774. From the bridge, you can look down on terraced Pulteney Weir.

Continue straight ahead across Laura Place and along Great Pulteney St. At the far end is the **Holburne Museum**. A plaque opposite, at No 4 Sydney Place, commemorates Jane Austen, the author who did so much to immortalise Georgian Bath and who lived here for three years. Walking back along Great Pulteney St, take any turning on the right to get to Henrietta Park, the perfect place for a rest.

Roman Baths Museum

Between the 1st and 4th centuries, the Romans built a bath and temple complex over one of Bath's three natural hot springs. In the Middle Ages, the baths crumbled and it wasn't until the 17th century that anyone paid the spring much more heed. However, by the end of the century, Mary of Modena was only one of a growing number of visitors coming to 'take the cure' in Bath. In 1702, the visit of Queen Anne set the seal on the trend and the town began to expand.

Nowadays, a raised walkway gives visitors their first glimpse of the Great Bath, complete with Roman paving and lead base and surrounded by 19th-century arcading. A series of excavated passages and chambers beneath street level lead off in several directions and let you inspect the remains of other smaller baths and hypocaust (heating) systems. One of the most picturesque corners of the complex is the 12th-century King's Bath, built around the original sacred spring; through a window you can see the pool, complete with niches for bathers and rings for them to hold on to; 1.5 million litres of hot water still pour into the pool every day. The museum outlines the history of the baths and exhibits finds made during excavations, including the fine gorgon head found on the site of the temple of Sul and the gilt bronze head from the cult statue.

The Roman Baths (☎ 477000) are one of England's most popular attractions and can be uncomfortably congested in summer, when the museum's enclosed corridors can also feel very claustrophobic. Visit early on a midweek morning and you'll probably have a much better time. The baths are open daily from 9 am to 6 pm (5 pm in winter and on Sunday) and you should allow an hour to get round. Tickets are £5.60/3.30, but a combined ticket giving entry to the Costume Museum as well (see below) costs £7.50/4.

Pump Room

The elegant 18th-century Pump Room is attached to the Roman Baths Museum and a fountain from the King's Bath dispenses tepid spa water which is on sale in the classy restaurant. Since Georgian times, diners here have been serenaded by a Palm Court trio, a tradition which continues today. Pictures on the wall depict Georgian luminaries, including Sir Robert Walpole and Ralph Allen, whose quarries at Coombe Down provided much of the Bath stone used to build the town's squares and crescents. There's also a statue of Richard 'Beau' Nash (1674-1761), the uncrowned 'king' of Georgian Bath, a gambler who laid down the rules of etiquette for the town's fashionable visitors. The Pump Room is open for stylish dining from 9.30 am to 5 pm (4.30 pm in winter).

Bath Abbey

Edgar, the first king of united England, was crowned in a church in Abbey Courtyard in 973, but the present abbey, more glass than stone, was built between 1499 and 1616, making it the last great medieval church raised in England. The nave's wonderful fan vaulting was erected in the 19th century. Cleaning of the interior is expected to continue well into 1997.

Perhaps the most striking feature of the abbey's exterior is the west facade, where angels climb up and down stone ladders, commemorating in stone a dream of the founder Bishop Oliver King. The abbey boasts 640 wall monuments, the second-largest collection after Westminster Abbey; among those buried here are the Reverend Thomas Malthus, the Victorian philosopher famous for his views on population control; Sir Isaac Pitman, who devised the Pitman method of shorthand; and Beau Nash, who is buried at the eastern end of the south aisle.

Bath Abbey (☎ 422462) is open Monday to Saturday, 9 am to 6 pm (4.30 pm in winter) and Sunday afternoon only; a donation of £1.50 is requested.

On the abbey's southern side, steps lead down to a vault in which a small **museum** describes the abbey's history and its links with the baths and fashionable Georgian society. It's open Monday to Saturday, 10 am to 4 pm; entry is £2/1.

Assembly Rooms & Museum of Costume

The Assembly Rooms were where fashionable late 18th-century Bath visitors gathered to play cards, dance and listen to music. The basement museum displays costumes from 1590 to the present day, including alarming crinolines that would have forced women to approach every doorway sideways.

The Museum (☎ 461111) is open daily from 10 am (11 am on Sunday) to 6 pm (5 pm in winter); tickets are £3.20/2. Combined tickets with the Roman Baths Museum are cheaper (see above).

No 1 Royal Crescent

Superbly restored to its 1770 magnificence, down to the minutest detail, this town house on the beautiful Royal Crescent is well worth visiting to see how people lived during Bath's glory days.

The grand Palladian house (☎ 428126) is open from March to October, Tuesday to Sunday, 10.30 am to 4.30 pm (3.30 pm November to mid-December). Tickets cost £3.50/2.50.

Other Things to See

Building of Bath Museum Housed in the 18th-century chapel of the Countess of Huntingdon in the Paragon, this museum (☎ 333895) details how Bath's Georgian splendour came into being, a more interesting story than you might imagine. The museum is open March to November, Monday to Sunday, 10.30 am to 5 pm; entry is £2.50/1.50.

Holburne Museum & Crafts Study Centre This is another fine 18th-century building originally designed for a different purpose. The former Sydney Hotel now houses Bath's collections of porcelain and antiques, as well as paintings by great 18th-century artists like Gainsborough and Stubbs. On Great Pulteney St, the museum (☎ 466669) is open from Easter to November, Monday to Saturday, 11 am to 5 pm, and on Sunday from 2.30 to 6 pm. Tickets are £3.50/1.50.

Mr Bowler's Business Tucked away in Julian Rd, Bath's industrial heritage centre (☎ 318348) is housed in what was originally an 18th-century 'real' tennis court. Most of the fittings belonged to Jonathan Burdett Bowler's 19th and 20th-century mineral-water bottling plant and brass foundry. It's

open daily from 10 am to 5 pm (weekends only in winter); entry is £3/2.

Sally Lunn's Kitchen Museum Round the corner from the abbey in North Parade Passage, this small basement museum (☎ 461634) consists mainly of exposed foundation stones, but a commentary describes how Sally Lunn, a 17th-century Huguenot refugee, used to bake brioches. Similar brioches are still on sale in the café upstairs. It's open Monday to Saturday, 10 am to 6 pm and on Sunday from noon to 6 pm. Entry costs 30p.

Victoria Art Gallery Opposite Pulteney Bridge, Bath's small art gallery (☎ 477772) contains two Thomas Rowlandson cartoons belonging to a series entitled 'The Comforts of Bath'. It also has paintings by Walter Sickert who lived nearby. Admission is free, and it's open on weekdays from 10 am to 5.30 pm, and Saturday from 10 am to 5 pm.

RPS National Photographic Gallery In Milsom St, this gallery (☎ 462841) contains exhibits illustrating the history of photography, a bookshop and the excellent *In Focus* café. It's open daily from 9.30 am to 5.30 pm; entry is £3/1.75.

Museum of East Asian Art This museum (☎ 464640), at 12 Bennett St, contains more than 500 jade, bamboo, porcelain and bronze objects from China, Korea, Cambodia, Thailand and Japan. It's open daily from 10 am to 6 pm (5 pm on Sunday). Entry is £3.

Organised Tours

Free two-hour walking tours of Bath leave from outside the Pump Room daily (except Saturday in winter); phone ☎ 477786 for details.

Guide Friday (☎ 444102) runs open-top, hop-on, hop-off bus tours daily from 9.25 am to 5 pm, Easter to October; shorter hours for the rest of the year. The buses pass Terrace Walk behind the abbey, and Bath bus station. Tickets cost £6.50/2.

Two-hour ghost walks depart from the

Nash Bar in the Garrick's Head pub at 8 pm Monday to Friday, May to October; Friday only in winter (£3). Bizarre Bath comedy walks (£3) leave nightly from the Huntsman Inn in North Parade Passage at 8 pm.

Places to Stay

Hostels The new *Bath Backpackers Hotel* (☎ 446787) at 13 Pierrepont St is Bath's most convenient budget accommodation, less than 10 minutes walk from the bus and train stations. B&B in dorm rooms with up to eight beds costs £9.50. There's a lounge and cooking facilities and even a spa bath.

The *YMCA International House* (☎ 460471) is also central, takes men and women and has no curfew, but is often full, especially in summer. Approaching from the south along Walcot St, look out for an archway and steps on the left about 200 yards past the post office. Singles/doubles with continental breakfast are £12.50/23, dorms are £10.

Bath Youth Hostel (☎ 465674) is out towards the University of Bath, a good 25-minute walk, or catch Badgerline bus No 18 (75p return) from the bus station. There are compensatory views and the building is magnificent. It's open all day, all year, and charges £9.10/6.15 in July and August.

Camping About three miles west of Bath, at Newton St Loe, is the *Newton Mill Touring Centre* (☎ 333909), which has space for tents and charges £7.95 for a tent and two people. It's open year-round. To reach it, take the B3310 off the A4.

B&Bs & Hotels Staying in Bath doesn't come cheap. In summer, most places charge at least £18/32. The main areas are along Newbridge Rd to the west, Wells Rd to the south, and around Pulteney Rd in the east. Bath is a popular place to spend the weekend and prices reflect this.

Henry Guest House (☎ 424052), 6 Henry St, is a bargain at £16 per person considering its central location. It's just a few minutes walk from the bus and railway stations. The eight rooms all have shared baths. *No 9*

Charlotte St (☎ 424193) is also dead central, and good value from £30 for a double.

There are numerous B&Bs on and around Pulteney Rd. *Ashley House* (☎ 425027), 8 Pulteney Gardens, has eight rooms, some with attached shower, from £20 to £25 per person. *No 14 Raby Place* (☎ 465120), off Bathwick Hill just after you turn off Pulteney Rd, is a non-smoking establishment charging £18 to £21 per person. Continue along Bathwick Hill over the canal to *No 14 Dunsford Place* (☎ 464134), a two-room B&B that charges from £15 per person.

There are several places along Henrietta St, near Henrietta Park. At No 34, the *Georgian Guest House* (☎ 424103) has a range of rooms from £20 for a single with shared bathroom to £35/45 for rooms with attached shower. The *Henrietta Hotel* (☎ 447779) is next door at No 32. During the week, rooms cost from £25/35; at weekends, the price rises to £35/55 or more. All rooms have attached bathrooms and a buffet breakfast is included. On the other side of the same street is the *Kennard Hotel* (☎ 310472), at No 11, which has rooms for £30/54 with bathrooms attached.

In an idyllic location beside the River Avon, the *Old Boathouse* (☎ 466407), Forester Rd, is an Edwardian boating station within walking distance of the centre. Comfortable non-smoking rooms with attached bathrooms cost from £20 per person.

There's a string of B&Bs west of the centre along Upper Bristol Rd (A4). Most cost at least £20 a head. On Crescent Gardens, try *Lamp Post Villa* (☎ 331221) at No 3, or *Waltons Guest House* (☎ 426528) at No 17.

Wells Rd (A367) also harbours B&Bs. At No 99, *Arney Guest House* (☎ 310020) has three rooms and charges from £20/30 with shared bath. There are numerous other places nearby.

Bath also has several luxurious small hotels. *Somerset House* (☎ 463471), 35 Bathwick Hill, is a comfortable non-smoking Georgian restaurant with rooms with views over Bath. Rooms cost from £43/100 at weekends. *Holly Lodge*

(☎ 424042), 8 Upper Oldfield Park, is a 10-minute walk from the centre and has views over the city. Rooms in this non-smoking award-winning hotel are from £46/75.

Bath's top place to stay is on the grandest of the grand crescents. The *Royal Crescent Hotel* (☎ 319090), 15-16 Royal Crescent, has 46 rooms in the two central houses here. There's a garden behind the hotel and an excellent restaurant. Decorated with period furnishings, rooms are officially from £98/120, but if it's low season and midweek you can negotiate a lower price. In historic Queen Square the *Francis Hotel* (☎ 424257) has 94 rooms in what were originally six separate houses. Rooms cost from £80/100 a single/double.

Places to Eat
With so many visitors passing through, Bath overflows with pleasant eating and drinking places.

In Manvers St near the bus station *Bloomsburys Café-Bar* (☎ 311955) has a good choice of vegetarian dishes (vegetable stroganoff for £3.95) alongside the chicken curry, scampi etc.

Near the abbey *Café Retro* (☎ 339347) in York St does three-course meals for around £10, although you can snack for much less. *Demuth's* (☎ 446059) in North Parade Passage serves vegetarian/vegan meals like pesto toast from about £4.50. In Union Passage, *Ben's Cookies* does home-made soups with a roll for £1.30.

Pierre Victoire (☎ 334334) at 16 Argyle St does a popular three-course set lunch for £4.90. Also in Argyle St is *Maxson's Diner* (☎ 444440), a small, cosy diner featuring Cajun and North American dishes. Nearby, at 2 Grove St, *Bathtub Bistro* (☎ 460593) is a good-value place serving interesting dishes like black bean moussaka for £5.50. *Rascals Bistro* (☎ 330201), at No 8 Pierrepont St, is a popular basement restaurant serving three-course lunches for £6.95. The scenery is more inviting at *Woods* (☎ 314812), 9 Alfred St where prices for two-course lunches start at around £5.

Right in the centre of town, on Walcot Rd,

there are several restaurants upstairs in the modern Podium shopping complex; choose from Tex-Mex at *Footlights* (☎ 480366), spicy Szechuan-style Chinese at *Just Duck* (☎ 481333), or Italian at *Caffe Piazza* (☎ 429299). There's also a very popular branch of *Carwardine's Coffee House*.

In an attractive cobbled street, *The Canary* (☎ 424846), 3 Queen St, has an interesting menu with a range of main dishes for around £5.50; cream teas cost £3.50. The real place for cream teas, however, is the *Pump Room*. Here one sips one's tea and heaps one's scones with jam and cream while being serenaded by the Pump Room Trio. It's not cheap at £5.10, but it's very much part of the Bath experience. Alternatively, pop into *Sally Lunn's* (see Other Things to See above) which has been baking brioches for over 300 years.

The *Moon & Sixpence* (☎ 460962), 6 Broad St, is a pleasant pub which offers two-course eat-all-you-can lunches for £5. Pubs will probably be your best bet for cheap evening meals, too. *The Crystal Palace* (☎ 423944), Abbey Green (south of Abbey Churchyard), has a beer garden, traditional ale and meals like lasagne and salad for £4.55.

Entertainment
The sumptuous *Theatre Royal* (☎ 448844) in Barton St often features shows on their pre-London run. *Bath Abbey* has a regular programme of lunchtime recitals; tickets are £2 on the door. There's also a *Puppet Theatre* under Pulteney Bridge.

Bath has a good range of atmospheric pubs. As well as those mentioned above (Places to Eat), you could also try the intimate *Coeur de Lion* (off the High St at 17 Northumberland Place), the *Bell* on Walcot St, or the *Saracen's Head*, the city's oldest pub, on Broad St. To work up a thirst, follow the canal north-east 1½ miles out of Bath to the village of Bathampton, where the *George* is beside the towpath. Food here is good but not particularly cheap.

Getting There & Away
See the fares tables in the Getting Around chapter. Bath is 106 miles from London, 19

miles from Wells and only 12 from Bristol. The Bristol and Bath Railway Path links these two towns.

Bus There are National Express (☎ 0990-808080) buses every two hours from London (three hours, £17.50) but Turners (☎ 0117-955 5333) currently sells the cheapest tickets – just £6.50/12.50 for a single/ return. Bakers Dolphin (☎ 0117-961 4000) charges £8.50/13.95 for a single/return.

There's one bus a day between Bristol and Portsmouth via Bath and Salisbury (see the Salisbury section for details). There's also a link with Oxford (two hours, £9.50), and Stratford-upon-Avon via Bristol (2½ hours, £14).

Some excellent map-timetables are available from the bus station (☎ 464446). The Badgerline Day Rambler (£4.60) gives you access to a good network of buses in Bristol, Somerset (Wells, Glastonbury), Gloucestershire (Gloucester) and Wiltshire (Lacock, Bradford-on-Avon, Salisbury).

Train There are numerous trains from London Paddington (1½ hours, £25). There are also plenty of trains to Bristol for onward travel to Cardiff, Exeter or the north. Hourly trains link Portsmouth and Bristol via Salisbury and Bath. A single ticket from Bath to Salisbury is £8.70; Bath to Portsmouth is £19.30.

Getting Around
Bicycle Bikes can be hired from Avon Valley Cyclery (☎ 461880), behind the railway station, from £9 per day. Cyclists can use the Bristol and Bath Railway Path which runs for 12 miles along the route of a disused railway, passing through several villages on the way.

Boat Hourly passenger boats (£3) leave from beneath Pulteney Bridge and sail to Bathampton from April to October. Alternatively, you can hire canoes, punts or rowing boats to propel yourself along the Avon from £3.50 an hour; try Bath Boating station (☎ 466407) in Forester Rd.

AROUND BATH
American Museum
Claverton Manor (☎ 460503), three miles south-east of Bath, is an 1820s mansion housing re-created 17th to 19th-century American home interiors, a collection of quilts and other American memorabilia. The grounds contain galleries of folk art and antique maps, as well as a tepee, a herb garden and several shops.

Bus No 18 to the University drops you half a mile from the entrance. The house is open daily except Monday, from 2 to 5 pm, the grounds from 1 to 6 pm. Tickets cost £5/2.50, although you can buy a gardens-only ticket for £2/1.

Dyrham Park
Twelve miles east of Bristol on the A46, Dyrham Park is a 263-acre deer park surrounding the fine 17th-century house of William Blathwayt, secretary of state to William III.

The house (☎ 891364; NT) is open April to October, Friday to Tuesday, noon to 5 pm; tickets cost £5/2.50. The park can be visited daily year-round, from noon to 5.30 pm; entry is £2.60. A Ryan's coach leaves Bath for Dyrham at 1 pm on Saturday and returns at 5.30 pm for £1.90 return.

Somerset

Somerset is a largely agricultural county, known for its cider-making, cricket club and Cheddar cheese. The two towns of most interest to visitors are Wells, with its superb cathedral, and Glastonbury, a mystical place – particularly if you're a Druid or New Age hippy.

Somerset offers some good walking country. The Mendip Hills are cut by gorges where caves have been inhabited since prehistoric times. The Quantocks to the west are less cultivated, while to the far west of the county, the wilder Exmoor National Park (see the next section) spans the border with Devon.

GETTING AROUND

The Somerset transport inquiry line is
☎ 01823-255696 but you can also phone the
bus companies direct: the region is roughly
split between Badgerline (☎ 01934-416851)
north of Bridgwater, and Southern National
(☎ 01823-272033) to the south.

The 613-mile South West Coast Path
begins in Minehead and follows the West
Country coast round to Poole in Dorset. See
the Activities chapter for information. TICs
stock *Cycle Round South Somerset* describing a 100-mile cycle route from Yeovil.

WELLS

- *pop 9400*   • ☎ *01749*

Taking its name from three springs that
emerged near the medieval Bishop's Palace,
Wells is England's smallest cathedral city. It
has managed to hang on to much of its medieval character and the cathedral is one of
England's most beautiful, with one of the

best surviving examples of a full cathedral
complex.

Wells is 22 miles south-west of Bath, on
the edge of the Mendip Hills. As well as
being a good base for touring the Mendip
Hills, it's within easy reach of Cheddar,
Wookey Hole and Glastonbury.

Orientation & Information

The city centre is compact and easy to get
around. The TIC (☎ 672552) is in the Town
Hall in picturesque Market Place near the
cathedral. City Cycles (☎ 675096), 80 High
St, has bikes for hire from £7.50 per day, and
there are lots of interesting walking and
cycling routes nearby; the TIC has details.
Markets are held in Market Place on
Wednesday and Saturday.

Wells Cathedral

The cathedral was built in stages from 1180
to 1508 and incorporates several Gothic

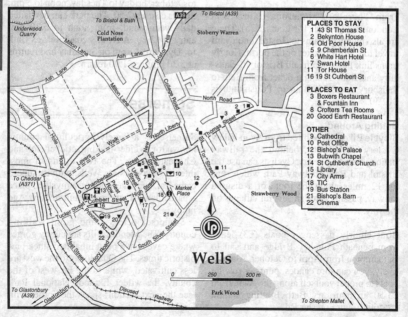

PLACES TO STAY
1   43 St Thomas St
2   Bekynton House
4   Old Poor House
5   9 Chamberlain St
6   White Hart Hotel
7   Swan Hotel
11 Tor House
16 19 St Cuthbert St

PLACES TO EAT
3   Boxers Restaurant
    & Fountain Inn
8   Crofters Tea Rooms
20 Good Earth Restaurant

OTHER
9   Cathedral
10 Post Office
12 Bishop's Palace
13 Bubwith Chapel
14 St Cuthbert's Church
15 Library
17 City Arms
18 TIC
19 Bus Station
21 Bishop's Barn
22 Cinema

Wells

styles. Its most famous feature is the wonderful **west front**, an immense sculpture gallery with over 300 figures, which was built between 1230 and 1250 and restored to its original splendour in 1986. Apart from the figure of Christ, installed in 1985 in the uppermost niche, all the other figures are original.

Inside, the most striking feature is the pair of **scissor arches**, separating the nave from the choir, a brilliant solution to the problem posed by the subsidence of the central tower; they were added in the 14th century, shortly after the tower's completion. Just before the hour, make sure you're standing in front of the intriguing **mechanical clock** in the north transept.

Among other things to look out for in the cathedral are the elegant **Lady Chapel** at the eastern end; the seven **effigies** of Anglo-Saxon bishops ringing the choir; and the **chained library** upstairs from the south transept. The library is open from April to September, Monday to Friday, 2.30 to 4.30 pm; entry is 40p.

Reached by worn steps leading off the north transept is the glorious mid-13th-century **Chapter House**, the ceiling ribs of

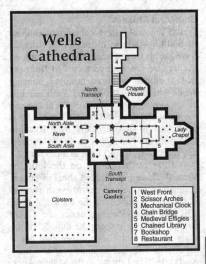

Wells Cathedral

1 West Front
2 Scissor Arches
3 Mechanical Clock
4 Chain Bridge
5 Medieval Effigies
6 Chained Library
7 Bookshop
8 Restaurant

which sprout like a palm from a central column.

Externally, look out for the **Chain Bridge** built from the northern side of the cathedral to Vicars' Close to enable clerics to reach the cathedral without getting their robes wet. The **cloisters** on the southern side surround a pretty courtyard.

The cathedral (☎ 674483) is open daily from 7.15 am to 6 pm (8.30 pm in July and August); visitors are asked to donate £2.50. Guided tours cost £1, as do photography permits.

Bishop's Palace

Beyond the cathedral is the moated Bishop's Palace (☎ 678691), a private residence dating back to the 13th century, which has beautiful gardens. It's open Tuesday, Thursday and bank holidays, 10 am to 6 pm; Sunday from 2 am to 6 pm; and daily in August; entry is £2.50/free. It's to be hoped that a penny-pinching scheme to close off the view from the gate to non-fee-payers will be nipped in the bud.

After a decade during which no swans knew the trick, a new generation of birds has now learnt to ring a bell outside one of the windows when it wants to be fed.

Wells Cathedral Clock

High up in the north transept is a wonderful mechanical clock dating from 1392, the second oldest surviving in England after the one in Salisbury Cathedral.

The complex-looking dial shows the hours in two sets of 12 on the outer circle, with the sun rotating round the earth to mark the hours. The minutes are shown on the inner circle, each indicated by a rotating star.

The clock also shows the position of the planets and the phases of the moon, but it's the entertaining cabaret act performed above it by jousting knights on horseback that draws a small crowd on the hour (the quarter-hour in summer).

Quarterjacks in the shape of 15th-century knights use poleaxes to hit a bell to mark the time on the clock's exterior face. ■

Cathedral Close

Wells Cathedral is the focal point of a cluster of buildings whose history is inextricably linked to its own. Facing the west front, on the left are the 15th-century **Old Deanery** and a salmon-coloured building housing **Wells Museum** (☎ 673477), with exhibits about caving in the Mendips, local life and the cathedral architecture. The museum is open April to October, daily, from 10 am to 5.30 pm; and November to April, Wednesday to Sunday, from 11 am to 4 pm for £2.

A little further along on the left, the **Vicars' Close** is a cobbled street of houses dating back to the 14th century with a chapel at the end; members of the cathedral choir still live here. Passing under the Chain Bridge, you can inspect the outside of the Lady Chapel and a lovely medieval house called The Rib, before emerging at a main road called The Liberty. In the Middle Ages, this marked the boundary of the cathedral precincts within which a refugee could take sanctuary.

St Cuthbert's Church

Wells Cathedral is such a major draw that many visitors never venture beyond its beautiful close. However, it's worth dropping by stately **St Cuthbert's Church** to admire its splendid 15th-century Perpendicular tower and brilliantly coloured nave roof. Look out for the boss of a sow suckling five piglets in the south porch.

Places to Stay

The nearest youth hostel is at Street near Glastonbury (see the upcoming Glastonbury section) but there are plenty of B&Bs with prices around £15 per person. The one at *9 Chamberlain St* (☎ 672270) is very central and charges £17 per person. The B&B at *19 St Cuthbert St* (☎ 673166) overlooks the cathedral in a quiet part of town and charges £14 a bed.

The *Old Poor House* (☎ 675052), at 7A St Andrew St, is a comfortable 14th-century cottage just outside the cathedral precincts. The nightly charge is £16.50 per person. Slightly further out, at 7 St Thomas St,

Bekynton House (☎ 672222) has beds from £19. Further along, *43 St Thomas St* (☎ 677137) is a former inn with a garden and beds from £16. Nearby *Tor House* (☎ 672322) at 20 Tor St charges from £24.

There's a cluster of hotels in Sadler St near the cathedral. The *White Hart Hotel* (☎ 672056) has rooms for £45/60 with bathrooms attached. The *Swan Hotel* (☎ 678877) is a fine 15th-century inn with some four-poster beds; some of the rooms look straight onto the cathedral's west front. They quote a room price of £65/86, but ask about special deals.

Places to Eat

The most atmospheric place to eat is the restaurant in the cathedral cloisters where you can lunch on soup and a roll from £1.80, overlooked by 18th-century monuments; it's open Monday to Saturday, 10 am to 5 pm, and Sunday, 12.30 to 5 pm. Near the bus station is the *Good Earth Restaurant* (☎ 678600) at 4 Priory Rd which does three-course lunches for £4.65 and some excellent pizzas and quiches. *Crofters Tea Rooms*, upstairs at 3 Market Place, does lunches and cream teas.

The *City Arms* (☎ 673916), 69 High St, serves good pub grub, and also has a restaurant with main dishes from around £5. Part of the pub used to be a jail in Tudor times.

The town's best restaurant is probably *Boxers* (☎ 672317), upstairs in the Fountain Inn at 1 St Thomas St, where you'll pay about £15 for a three-course meal.

Entertainment

A year-round programme of lunchtime recitals and evening concerts offers the chance to hear the historic cathedral choir in full voice. For details, phone ☎ 674483.

Getting There & Away

Badgerline (☎ 673084) operates hourly buses from Bristol and Bath. No 163 runs from Wells to Taunton (for Exmoor) via Glastonbury and Street. Bus Nos 161/2 travel via Shepton Mallet to Frome. Heading for the coast, bus Nos 126 and 826 travel to

Weston-super-Mare via Cheddar, while the No 170 service heads for Burnham-on-Sea. There's no railway station in Wells; the nearest is 15 miles away at Castle Cary, linked to Wells by bus No 168.

MENDIP HILLS

The Mendip Hills are a ridge of limestone hills about 25 miles long and five miles wide in northern Somerset. These are not lofty hills – their highest point is Black Down (1068 feet) to the north-west – but they stand out in an area which is otherwise very flat, giving way in the south to the Somerset Levels where roads often run on causeways above flood level.

Nowadays, the Mendip Hills form a densely cultivated agricultural area, but in the past they were more famous for coal mining, traces of which can be seen round Radstock and Midsomer Norton to the east. The Romans are known to have mined for lead around Charterhouse and Priddy; lead mining continued throughout the Middle Ages and right up until the turn of this century. Pubs which seem to be in the middle of nowhere are survivors from a time when mining brought plenty of thirsty drinkers. You can see the remains of St Cuthbert's lead mines near Priddy, and scruffy hollows around Charterhouse mark the sites of shallow mine workings. Quarrying for stone is an important – and controversial – industry to this day.

The A371 skirts the southern side of the Mendip Hills and any of the towns along it – Axbridge, Cheddar, Wells or Shepton Mallet – would make good touring bases, though Wells is probably best.

Getting There & Away

Badgerline buses (☎ 673084) serve this area, although don't expect services to be very frequent off the major roads. Apart from the buses to Wells and Glastonbury (see above), Nos 126/826 run between Wells, Cheddar and Axbridge. Nos 160/162 regularly link Wells with Shepton Mallet, while No 173 runs between Bath, Radstock, Midsomer Norton and Wells.

Coming by car, the Mendip Hills are squeezed in between the A38 Bristol to Burnham-on-Sea and A37 Bristol to Wells roads.

Wookey Hole

Wookey Hole, the site of a sequence of caves carved out by the River Axe, one of them containing a spectacular lake, is just two miles east of Wells. The striking shape of one particular stalagmite gave rise to the legend of the Witch of Wookey. Nowadays, the caves are the focal point of a series of other attractions, including an ancient handmade paper mill, an Edwardian fairground, a maze of mirrors and an arcade of vintage amusement machines.

The Wookey Hole (☎ 01749-672243) attractions are open daily April to September from 9.30 am to 5.30 pm; 10.30 am to 4.30 pm in winter; entry is £6/3.50. Bus No 172 offers an hourly service between Wells and Wookey Hole (10 minutes, 85p). A three-mile walk to Wookey is signposted from New St in Wells.

Cheddar Gorge

The Mendips' most dramatic scenery can be found along its southern side where the Cheddar Gorge cuts a one-mile swathe through the landscape, exposing great sweeps of 450-foot-high grey stone cliff. Approaching on foot from the north or walking along the clifftop paths, it's possible to imagine how wild and spectacular Cheddar must have been before the stalactite and stalagmite-filled Cox's and Gough's caves started to suck in the crowds; however, the area immediately around the caves can be very offputting in summer when the place heaves with visitors. It's probably best to visit out of season, bearing in mind that most of the teashops (with the exception of the *Hillside Cottage Tea Rooms*) and fish & chip shops only open over winter weekends.

The **Cheddar Showcaves** (☎ 742343) are open daily, Easter to September, 10 am to 5.30 pm; and from October to Easter, 10.30 am to 4.30 pm. Entry is £6/4 which

SOUTH-WESTERN ENGLAND

Cheddar Cheese

The country's most famous cheese only began to become widely known when people started visiting Cheddar Gorge and taking home some of the local cheese. Cheddar was just one of many Somerset villages that produced this type of cheese.

Over the years, and with mass production not only all over Britain but in several other countries as well, Cheddar has become a generic name for any pale yellow, medium-hard cheese. The name covers a wide range of qualities, from soapy supermarket Cheddar to the delicious farmhouse variety, which is mature and tangy.

If you're interested in the process for making genuine Cheddar Cheese, the Cheddar Gorge Cheese Company (☎ 01934-742810) is open daily. It's just off the B3135. ■

covers entry to the heritage centre, lookout tower and clifftop walk.

The TIC (☎ 01934-744071) in the Gorge is only open from May to October.

Cheddar village, to the south-west of the gorge, has an elegant church and an ancient market cross but is otherwise disappointing. *Cheddar Youth Hostel* (☎ 01934-742494) is one mile from the caves on Hillfield, a road off The Hayes on the western side of the village. It's open daily in July and August, daily except Sunday from mid-February to June, and except Sunday and Monday in September and October. The nightly charge is £4.60/6.75.

Badgerline bus Nos 126/826 run between Wells (9 miles) and Weston-super-Mare via Cheddar (20 minutes, £1.85), hourly from Monday to Saturday and every two hours on Sunday.

Axbridge
• ☎ *01934*

Just 1½ miles from Cheddar, the pretty village of Axbridge is light years away from its tackiness and makes a much nicer, albeit pricier, place to stay. One corner of the central square is dominated by the striking half-timbered **King John's Hunting Lodge**

(☎ 732012; NT), a Tudor merchant's house now housing the local museum. It's open daily 2 to 5 pm from Easter to 30 September. Another corner is occupied by the huge late Gothic church of St John with 17th-century plaster ceiling. The rest of the square is ringed with hotels and restaurants.

For somewhere to stay, try the *Axbridge Wine Vaults* (☎ 732228) or *The Lamb* (☎ 732253) where doubles cost £35, or *The Oak House* (☎ 732444) where they cost from £40. To eat, choose between the *Spinning Wheel Restaurant* (☎ 732476), where a three-course dinner midweek costs £13.95, and the 15th-century *Almshouse Bistro* (☎ 732493).

You can walk or cycle to Axbridge from Cheddar. Badgerline bus No 126 from Cheddar to Burnham-on-Sea also passes through the centre.

Mendip Villages

The Mendip villages are not renowned for particularly striking buildings, although you might be interested in the huge church of 19th-century **Downside Abbey**, established by English monks driven from France by the French Revolution. Downside is now a famous Roman Catholic boys' school.

Otherwise, many of the villages are pretty, in a low-key way, and several have fine Perpendicular church towers. Especially impressive is that at **Chewton Mendip** (on the A37 from Bristol to Wells), where there's an attractive medieval churchyard cross. The village of **Compton Martin** has a Norman church with a 15th-century tower. One mile to the east, **West Harptree** is a prettier village with two 17th-century former manor houses. Near **East Harptree** are the remains of Norman Richmont Castle, which was captured from supporters of Matilda by those of King Stephen in 12th-century skirmishing.

GLASTONBURY
• *pop 6900*   • ☎ *01458*

Although it's little more than a large village, Glastonbury is England's unofficial New Age capital – the place to come if you want your runes read, if you want to find out about

English paganism or if you just want to buy crystals, candles or made-to-measure shoes.

Myths and legends about Glastonbury abound. One story tells how Jesus came here with his great-uncle Joseph of Arimathea, while another reports Joseph bringing the chalice from the Last Supper with him. Later legends also made Glastonbury the burial place of King Arthur and Queen Guinevere, and the tor (the nearby hill), the Isle of Avalon. Finally, the tor was thought to guard a gateway to the underworld. Over time, these different tales became entangled with each other in a potent mixture which has left Glastonbury important to Christians and atheists alike, as a glimpse at the various bookshops confirms.

Whatever you choose to believe, Glastonbury has the ruins of a 14th-century abbey, a couple of museums, mystic springs and superb views from the tor to make it well worth a day of your time.

Orientation & Information

The main bus stop is opposite the Town Hall in Magdalene St, within sight of the market cross and the abbey ruins.

The TIC (☎ 832954), in the Tribunal, 9 High St, stocks free maps and accommodation lists, and sells leaflets describing local walks (10p each) and village trails (25p each). From Easter to October you can hire bikes for £6/25 a day/week at Pedalers (☎ 831117), opposite the abbey entrance. There's a market on Tuesday.

The Glastonbury Festival, a three-day summer extravaganza of music, theatre, circus, mime, natural healing etc, is a massive affair with over 1000 acts, which doesn't always go down too well with the locals. It takes place at Worthy Farm, Pilton, eight miles from Glastonbury. Admission is by advance ticket only and costs in excess of £60 for the whole festival. Phone ☎ 668899 for details.

Glastonbury Abbey

Legend suggests that there has been a church on this site since the 1st century, but the first definite traces date back to the 7th century when King Ine gave a charter to a monastery here. The first abbey church seems to have reached the height of its importance under the abbacy of St Dunstan, later an archbishop

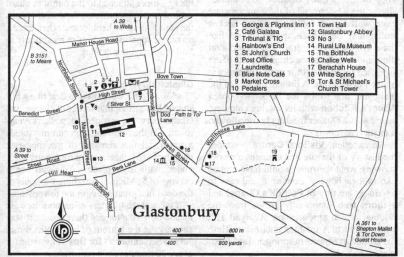

Glastonbury

of Canterbury. During his time in office, King Edgar, the first king of a united England, died and was buried at Glastonbury.

In 1184, the old church was destroyed by fire; reconstruction began in the reign of Henry II. In 1191, monks claimed to have had visions confirming hints in old manuscripts that the 6th-century warrior-king Arthur and his wife Guinevere were buried in the grounds. Excavations to the south of the old church uncovered what was said to be their tomb, and a lead cross recording that fact, which has since disappeared. The couple were reinterred in front of the high altar of the new church in 1278 and the tomb survived until 1539 when Henry VIII dissolved the monasteries.

The last abbot was hanged, drawn and quartered on the tor. After that, the abbey complex gradually collapsed, its component parts scavenged to provide building materials. It wasn't until the 19th century that Romanticism brought renewed interest in King Arthur and the sites associated with him.

The ruins you see at Glastonbury today are mainly of the church built after the 1184 fire. They include a **Lady Chapel**, built, unusually, at the western end of the church; some nave walls; parts of the crossing arches which may have been scissor-shaped like those in Wells Cathedral; some **medieval tiles**; and remains of the choir. The site of the supposed **tomb of Arthur and Guinevere** is marked in the grass. A little to the side of the main site, don't miss the flagstone-floored **Abbot's Kitchen** with its soaring chimney; later use as a Quaker meeting house allowed it to survive intact.

An excellent **Visitors Centre** describes the history of the site and contains a model showing what the ruins would have looked like in their heyday. Behind it, and easy to overlook, are tiny **St Patrick's Chapel** and a **thorn tree** supposedly grown from the original which sprouted on Wearyall Hill when Joseph of Arimathea stuck his staff into the ground. It flowers in spring and at Christmas.

The site (☎ 832267) is open daily from 9.30 am (9 am from June to August) to 6 pm or dusk; entry is £2.50/1. There's a small car park (60p) at the site.

Lake Village Museum

A small museum devoted to the prehistoric village that flourished near Glastonbury when the surrounding lowlands had not yet been drained is upstairs in the Tribunal, the medieval courthouse which dates back to 1400 and now houses the TIC. Wet conditions have allowed an unusually large quantity of wooden artefacts to survive – even a dugout canoe (in a separate room at the back). The museum (☎ 832949; EH) is open April to September, Sunday to Thursday, 10 am to 5 pm (5.30 pm on Friday and Saturday; 4.30 pm from October to March). Admission costs £1.50/75p.

St John's Church

Set back from the High St is this stunning open-plan Perpendicular church which has a spectacular 15th-century wooden roof and pillars so thin it's hard to believe they can support the weight of the walls. Look out for the egg-timer attached to the pulpit to guard against overlong sermons. Vandalism means the church must be kept locked when there's no one to supervise it. You're most likely to find it open on market day.

Glastonbury Tor

'Tor' is a Celtic word used to describe a hill shaped like a triangular wedge of cheese, and Glastonbury tor is open to walkers year-round. On the 525-foot-high summit stands a tower, all that remains of the medieval church of St Michael, a saint frequently associated with high places. You can see a carving of St Michael weighing the souls of the dead in a giant scale on the tower front.

It takes three-quarters of an hour to walk up and down the tor and there are short-stay car parks at the bottom of both paths. From July to September a 'Tor Bus' runs to the tor every 20 minutes (40p return).

White Spring

This spring flows out into a cave at the foot of the tor in Wellhouse Lane, and has been dressed up with a café and mock medieval and Tudor house facades; atmospheric or Disneyfied depending on your mood and the number of other visitors.

Chalice Well

The Chalice Well has become entwined in Glastonbury myths and legends, even though its name probably relates to its site in Chilkwell St rather than to real links with the Holy Grail. The well has a long association with traditions of healing and you can drink from it as the water pours out through a lion's head spout. It then runs through brick channels into the gardens below, eventually cascading down a series of ceramic dishes into two interlocking basins surrounded by flowers. It's a beautiful, peaceful spot to spend a few hours and is open daily March to October from 10 am to 6 pm, November to February from 1 to 4 pm; entry is £1/50p.

Rural Life Museum

Partially housed in a fine late 14th-century tithe barn, the Rural Life Museum in Bere Lane exhibits artefacts associated with farming, cider-making, cheese-making and other aspects of country life in Somerset. In the grounds, you can see rare breeds of sheep and chicken, and apple trees. Upstairs, don't miss the three-seater toilet, with holes for Mum, Dad and Junior.

The barn itself has fine carvings on the gables and porch and an impressive timber roof; it now houses a collection of old agricultural machinery. The museum (☎ 831197) is open from Easter to October, weekdays except Monday 10 am to 5 pm, weekends 2 pm to 6 pm; for the rest of the year it's open 11 am to 4 pm on Saturday and closed on Sunday and Monday. Entry is £1.50/40p.

Places to Stay

The nearest hostel is in Street, two miles to the south. *Street Youth Hostel* (☎ 01458-442961) is open April to October, daily

except Tuesday; every day in July and August. Beds cost £7.45/5 for adults/children. Bus No 376 from Glastonbury stops at Marshalls Elm, from where the hostel is a 500-yard walk.

Glastonbury has B&Bs from around £14 a night and many establishments offer vegetarian meals, muesli breakfasts, aromatherapy etc. The TIC has a complete list.

There are several camping grounds in and around Glastonbury. *Ashwell Farmhouse* (☎ 832313), Ashwell Lane, is the nearest. It's below the tor, just off the A361, and is open year-round. A tent site costs £2.50.

Tor Down Guest House (☎ 832287), at No 5 Ashwell Lane, has rooms from £12/25 for singles/doubles and does vegetarian meals. *The Bolthole* (☎ 832800), at 32 Chilkwell St, is near the foot of the tor, and has just two rooms, from £13.50 per person. There are a couple of similar B&Bs nearby in the same street.

Berachah (☎ 834214) in Well House Lane is convenient for the tor and the wells and has beds from £15.

The *George & Pilgrims Inn* (☎ 831146), 1 High St, has a history dating back to the reign of Edward III. Rooms cost from £50/65 but two-night special breaks including dinner are better value.

Travellers may be interested in peaceful *No 3 Magdalene St* (☎ 832129) whose owners have seen a bit of the world themselves, hence the Indian fabrics and wall hangings. Comfortable rooms with private bathrooms cost £50/65.

Places to Eat

If you've ever considered becoming a vegetarian, Glastonbury would be a good place to start since it's one of the few places in England where nut roasts are more common than pot roasts.

The *Blue Note Café*, 4A High St, has tables in a courtyard; soup and bread costs £1.50, Greek cheese and mushroom pie £3. Across the street, at 5A, *Café Galatea* serves delicious leek and broccoli buckwheat pancakes for £3.85 and doubles as a sculpture gallery and cybercafé (£3 for half an hour on the Internet).

Rainbow's End, 17A High St, does amazing mushroom curry (£2.70) and huge chunks of chocolate cake (£1.20). It's down an alley with shops selling second-hand books and shoes, and is open from 10 am to 4 pm.

A three-course lunch at the *George & Pilgrims Inn* (☎ 831146), 1 High St, costs £9.50.

Getting There & Away
There's a daily National Express bus from London (4¼ hours, £13), and also to Bath. Badgerline runs buses from Bristol (No 376) to Wells, Glastonbury and Street. Glastonbury is only six miles from Wells, a 15-minute bus journey (every half hour, £1.55). Bus No 163 from Wells continues to Taunton, from where there are buses to Minehead (for Exmoor). Bus No 376 continues to Ilchester and Yeovil.

QUANTOCK HILLS
The Quantocks, in western Somerset, are a ridge of red sandstone hills, 12 miles long, not much more than three miles wide and running down to the sea at Quantoxhead. Like the Mendips, these are lowly hills – just 1262 feet high at their highest point – but they're less cultivated and can look much more bleak. The narrow country lanes and woody dells make this enjoyable walking country.

Some of the most attractive country is owned by the NT, including the Beacon and Bicknoller hills which offer views of the Bristol Channel and Exmoor to the northwest. In 1861, red deer were introduced to these hills from Exmoor and there's a thriving local tradition of stag hunting.

A road runs across the bleaker part of the Quantocks from Over Stowey to Crowcombe, and there's a walkers' track as well. At Broomfield, six miles north of Taunton, Fyne Court houses a visitors centre (☎ 01823-451587), open daily from 9 am to 6 pm, where you can pick up information. The Quantocks Information Centre in Nether Stowey library (☎ 01836-794835) provides a series of circular walk leaflets. Bridgwater or Taunton would make passable bases for exploring the Quantocks, but it's more atmospheric to stay in one of the villages.

Getting There & Away
To appreciate the lanes and woods of the Quantocks at their peaceful best, aim to arrive on a weekday when the Bridgwater and Taunton weekend visitors are back at their desks. Coming by car, the M5 linking Bristol and Exeter skirts the eastern edge of the Quantocks. The A358 then runs along the western side of the hills, linking Taunton to Williton in the north.

Trains from Bristol, Bath and Exeter call at Taunton and Bridgwater, and infrequent Southern National (☎ 01823-272033) buses serve the main roads. Badgerline bus No 29A from Bristol continues on to Bridgwater and Taunton after Wells and Glastonbury on Sunday and bank holidays only.

Nether Stowey & Holford
One of the Quantocks' most famous visitors was the poet Coleridge, who lived at **Nether Stowey** from 1769 to 1796. You can visit Coleridge Cottage (☎ 01278-732662; NT) where he wrote *The Ancient Mariner*; it's open April to October, Tuesday to Thursday and Sunday, 2 to 5 pm; entry is £1.60/80p.

Coleridge's friend Wordsworth, and Wordsworth's sister Dorothy, also spent 1797 at nearby Alfoxden House in **Holford** – a pretty village near a wooded valley. *Lyrical Ballads*, published in 1798, was the joint product of Coleridge's and Wordsworth's stays.

Two miles west of Holford is the *Quantock Hills Youth Hostel* (☎ 01278-741224), set in a wooded area. It's open from April to August, daily except Sunday and Monday from April to July; the nightly charge is £6.75/4.60. Southern National bus No 15 from Bridgwater gets you to Nether Stowey, No 28 from Taunton or Minehead will drop you at Williton; in either case it's then a 3½ to four-mile walk.

West Somerset Railway

Trains on Britain's longest privately run railway steam between Bishops Lydeard and Minehead, the seaside town 20 miles away. There are stops along the line at Crowcombe, Stogumber, Williton, Doniford Beach, Watchet, Washford, Blue Anchor and Dunster.

Trains run daily from June to September, and at winter weekends. A ticket from Bishops Lydeard to Minehead costs £4/7.50 for an adult single/return; children are half-price. There's a bus link to Taunton railway station. Phone ☎ 01643-707650 for 24-hour talking timetables.

Crowcombe

One of the prettiest Quantock villages, Crowcombe still has cottages built of stone and cob (a mixture of mud and straw), many with thatched roofs. There's a pleasant church with 16th-century bench ends, and part of its spire still in the churchyard where it fell when struck by lightning in 1725. The 16th-century Church House has mullioned windows and a Tudor door. Crowcombe Court is a fine Georgian house.

Crowcombe Heathfield Youth Hostel (☎ 01984-667249), Denzel House, is two miles from the village and half a mile from Crowcombe station on the West Somerset Railway. It's a seven-mile hike over the Quantocks from the hostel in Holford. You can also get here on bus No 28C from Taunton station, getting off at Triscombe Cross and walking about three-quarters of a mile. The hostel is open daily from mid-July to August. At other times phone in advance. Beds cost £6.75/4.60 for adults/children.

TAUNTON

- *pop 35,000*   • ☎ *01823*

Coming to the Quantocks by bus or train you're likely to arrive in Taunton, Somerset's disappointing administrative centre. **Somerset County Museum** (☎ 255504), in part of the castle, is open Monday to Saturday, 10 am to 5 pm. The **Church of St Mary Magdalene** has one of Somerset's finest towers, and an impressive oak Tudor roof in

the nave. The TIC (☎ 336344) is in the library in Paul St.

Taunton is on a main National Express coach route, with services to London (3½ hours, £9), Bridgwater (20 minutes), Bristol and Exeter. It's also on the main West Country rail line.

MONTACUTE HOUSE

Twenty-two miles south-east of Taunton, and four miles west of the market town of Yeovil, Montacute House (☎ 01935-823289; NT) is an impressive Elizabethan mansion built in the 1590s for Sir Edward Phelips, a Speaker of the House of Commons. The house has survived with very little alteration, apart from the addition of the west front in the 18th century. The Long Gallery displays Tudor and Jacobean portraits on loan from London's National Portrait Gallery. Formal gardens and a landscaped park surround the house.

It's open from April to October, daily except Tuesday, noon to 5 pm; £5/2.50.

Exmoor National Park

Covering parts of West Somerset and North Devon, Exmoor is a small national park (265 sq miles) enclosing a wide variety of beautiful landscapes. Along the coast, the scenery is particularly breathtaking with hump-backed headlands giving superb views across the Bristol Channel. Exmoor's cliffs are the highest in England, rising in places to 1200 feet.

A high plateau rises steeply behind the coast, but is cut by steep, fast-flowing streams. The bare hills of heather and grass run parallel to the coast; the highest point is Dunkery Beacon at 1703 feet. On the southern side the two main rivers, the Exe and Barle, wind their way along wooded valleys.

Horned sheep, Exmoor ponies (descended from ancient hill stock) and England's last wild red deer still roam the moors. The symbol of the park is the antlered head of a stag, and depending on the season you may see people hunting. Although the sport is supported by local farmers, who see the deer as a pest, it's equally strongly opposed by others, causing conflict in the hunting season. You'll need a strong stomach to take all the trappings of the hunt – stag heads, sets of antlers, meaty menus – offered up in Exmoor pubs.

There are several particularly attractive villages: Lynton and Lynmouth, joined by a water-operated railway; Porlock, on the edge of the moor in a beautiful valley; Dunster, dominated by its partly-medieval castle; and Selworthy, with traditional thatched cottages.

Arguably the most dramatic section of the South West Coast Path is between Minehead and Padstow.

ORIENTATION
From west to east the park measures only about 21 miles and north to south just 12 miles. It's accessible from the west through Barnstaple, from the south through Tiverton, and from the east through Minehead.

Within the park boundaries, the main centres are Dulverton on the southern edge;

Exford in the centre; Dunster in the east; and Porlock, Lynton and Lynmouth on the coast.

There are over 600 miles of public footpaths and bridleways, most of them waymarked.

INFORMATION
The National Park Authority (NPA) has five information centres in and around the park, but it's also possible to get information in the TICs at Barnstaple, Ilfracombe, Lynton and Minehead. The NPA centres at Dunster (☎ 01643-821835), Lynmouth (☎ 01598-752509), County Gate (☎ 01598-741321), and Combe Martin (☎ 01271-883319) are open daily from the end of March to October. For the rest of the year, some of these offices are closed or operate limited opening hours. The main visitors centre and the Exmoor NPA headquarters (☎ 01398-323841) in Dulverton is open all year but for limited hours in winter.

The *Exmoor Visitor* is a free newspaper listing useful addresses, accommodation and a programme of guided walks and bike rides from the villages offered by the NPA and local organisations. Most walks are in the

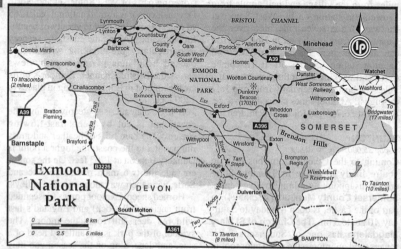

summer but there are some throughout the year.

The visitors centres and TICs stock a wide range of walking guides and Ordnance Survey maps.

WALKS

Although over 70% of Exmoor is privately owned, there are numerous waymarked paths. The best known routes are the Somerset and North Devon Coast Path (part of the South West Coast Path) and the Exmoor section of the Two Moors Way, which starts in Lynmouth and follows the River Barle through Withypool and on to Dartmoor.

Part of the 180-mile Tarka Trail (based on the countryside that inspired Henry Williamson's *Tarka the Otter*) is in the park. Join it in Combe Martin and walk to Lynton/Lynmouth, and then inland to Brayford and Barnstaple.

Exmoor's main walking centres are Lynton, Porlock, County Gate, Oare, Horner, Exford, Simonsbath, Withypool and Dulverton. In spring or autumn, you may glimpse Britain's only poisonous snake, the adder, sunning itself by the path. It's a shy reptile whose venom is usually only life-threatening to babies and small dogs.

CYCLE ROUTES

Cyclists are not allowed on public footpaths or the open moor, and horse riders and walkers have priority on public bridleways and roads used as public paths. Official places for cyclists include a coastal route – along the old Barnstaple railway line, parts of the Tarka Trail, the Brendon Hills and Crown Estate woodland. The visitors centres will be able to advise on where you can go.

OTHER ACTIVITIES
Pony Trekking & Horse Riding

Exmoor is popular riding country and stables scattered round the park offer ponies and horses for all abilities for rides from a few hours to a full day. Wet weather gear is recommended – it can turn cold and rainy very quickly. Charges are from about £6.50 per hour.

Contact Pine Lodge Riding & Holidays

(☎ 01398-323559), Higher Chilcott Farm, Dulverton; or Burrowhayes Farm (☎ 01643-862463), West Luccombe, Porlock.

Red Deer Tracking

Several companies offer Exmoor safaris tracking wild red deer. Try Exmoor Safari (☎ 01643-851318) which has departures from Exford, Minehead or Dulverton. Charges are from £6 to £9 per person.

Fishing

To fish for salmon and trout, you need a licence, usually obtainable from the main shop or village post office. Sea fishing is possible from the harbour walls, and boats can be hired in the larger coastal villages.

PLACES TO STAY & EAT

There are youth hostels in Minehead and Ilfracombe (outside the park) and Lynton and Exford in the park. Camping is allowed with the landowner's permission; local shops will usually know who owns the surrounding land. Along the coast, there are regular camping grounds with all the usual facilities.

There's no shortage of B&Bs and hotels in this holiday area. To stay on a working farm (either in a self-catering cottage or on a B&B basis) contact the Farm Holiday Bureau (☎ 01643-841249), Little Quarme, Wheddon Cross, near Minehead, Somerset TA24 7EA.

There are plenty of places to eat in Exmoor – old country pubs with low beams to hit your head on and log fires in the winter, little shops serving cream teas, as well as more upmarket restaurants.

GETTING THERE & AWAY

National Express coaches go from London to Barnstaple and Ilfracombe daily. There are also buses from Plymouth and Bristol to Barnstaple.

Southern National (☎ 01823-272033) and Scarlet Coaches (☎ 01643-704204) run services from Taunton to Minehead, Dunster, Watchet and Williton. You could also do part of this journey on the privately run West Somerset Railway (see Somerset section).

From London Paddington, InterCity services stop at Taunton, Tiverton Parkway and Exeter. These places can also be reached from Bristol (on the Bristol-Plymouth line). From Exeter, the scenic Tarka Line runs to Barnstaple; the journey takes about 1½ hours and there are about four trains a day.

For Dulverton and the southern part of the park, Kingdom's Tours (☎ 01884-252373) operates a service from Tiverton bus station. Buses run from Barnstaple along the northern coast of the park to Lynton and Minehead.

GETTING AROUND
It's easiest to get around with your own transport, on foot or horseback, because bus services are limited. Some services are based on school runs, some are operated by volunteer drivers, most are seasonal and few operate on Sunday. On the other hand the narrow streets of Exmoor villages quickly clog up in peak season and parking can be tricky.

Bus The *Exmoor Bus Timetable* is available free from TICs. You could also phone Devon County Council's bus inquiry line (☎ 01392-382800) or Somerset County Council's Public Transport Department (☎ 01823-255696).

Details of local bus services to and from Exmoor towns and villages appear in the appropriate sections following. A Southern National/Red Bus Day-Out Explorer Pass costs £4.50/2.75 and gives discounts on West Somerset Railway services too.

Bicycle Tarka Trail Cycle Hire (☎ 01271-24202), Railway Station, Barnstaple, and Exmoor Downhill (☎ 01643-706912), 1 Warden Rd, Minehead, have all kinds of bikes for hire. Since Exmoor is hilly, a mountain bike would be advisable. Charges start from £8 per day rising to £46 for seven days.

DULVERTON
• *pop 1300*   • ☎ *01398*
This attractive village, south of the moor in the Barle Valley, is the local 'capital' and home to the park's head office. The Exmoor National Park Visitors Centre (☎ 323841) is at 7-9 Fore St.

Dulverton's narrow streets get choked with traffic in summer so try to visit out of season.

Walks
The four-hour circular walk along the river from Dulverton to Tarr Steps – an ancient stone clapper bridge across the River Barle – is recommended. Add another three or four hours to the walk by continuing from Tarr Steps up Winsford Hill for distant views over Devon.

Places to Stay & Eat
You get breakfast in bed at *Town Mills* (☎ 323124) from £16 per person. Their driveway is just off the High St. *Springfields Farm* (☎ 323722) is four miles from Dulverton on the Exford road; B&B costs £21.50/32 with bath. Evening meals are served but only from mid-May, when the lambing season is over.

Highercombe (☎ 323616), two miles north of Dulverton at the end of a no-through road, offers B&B from £18. It's 1½ miles from Highercombe to Tarr Steps.

Crispins Restaurant (☎ 323397), 26 High St, serves decent vegetarian food. *The Lion Hotel* in Bank Square has good bar food.

Getting There & Away
Ridler's (☎ 323398) runs a twice-daily Dulverton to Minehead school service, Monday to Friday during term time. Kingdom's Tours (☎ 01884-252373) runs a service from Tiverton to Dulverton (35 minutes, £1.20) from Monday to Friday, and tours in the Exmoor area.

DUNSTER
• *pop 800*   • ☎ *01643*
Possibly the most attractive Exmoor village, Dunster can be packed with people in summer. The main attraction is the castle but there's also St George's Church, a working water mill, an old packhorse bridge, the

Top: Dartmoor, Devon
Middle: St Ives, Cornwall
Bottom: Castle Combe, Wiltshire
Right: On the beach, Lyme Regis, Dorset

Left: Warwick Castle, Warwickshire
Right: Corfe Castle, Dorset
Bottom: Hermitage Castle, Borders, Scotland

nearby beach and the 17th-century octagonal Yarn Market – relic of a time when the people of Dunster made their living from weaving, rather than tourism.

An Exmoor National Park Visitors Centre (☎ 821835) is on Dunster Steep.

Dunster Castle

Heavily restored to the Victorian ideal of how castles should look – turrets, crenellations etc – Dunster Castle (☎ 821314; NT) dates back to Norman times although only the 13th-century gateway of the original structure survives. Inside are Tudor furnishings and portraits of the Luttrell family, including a bizarre 16th-century portrait of Sir John skinny-dipping.

It's open from April to October, Saturday to Wednesday, 11 am to 5 pm (4 pm in October). Entry is £5/2.60. The surrounding garden and park are open most of the year. It's a short, steep walk up from the village.

Places to Stay

The nearest youth hostel is two miles away at Minehead (see below).

Woodville House (☎ 821228) in West St charges from £16 for B&B. *The Old Priory* (☎ 821540) is a medieval house in walled gardens opposite the dovecote. It's open all year and charges from £17.50 per person for B&B (£40 for a room with a four-poster bed). *Dollons House* (☎ 821880) in Church St does luxury B&B from £22.50 in non-smoking rooms.

Exmoor House Hotel (☎ 821268), 12 West St, is a very comfortable, non-smoking hotel which charges from £26.50 per person for B&B in rooms with attached bathroom.

Places to Eat

The *café* (☎ 821759) at Dunster Watermill, Mill Lane, is a good place to go for lunch or tea in summer; for £1.60/75p you can watch wholemeal flour being ground in the mill. *The Tea Shoppe* (☎ 821304), 3 High St, does morning coffee, lunches and cream teas in its 15th-century tearooms. If it's full there are several other places along the High St.

The Luttrell Arms (☎ 821555) opposite the Yarn Market does pleasant bar snacks.

Getting There & Away

Southern National runs a Monday-Saturday shuttle bus service (No 39) between Minehead and Dunster. You can also get here on the West Somerset Railway (see Somerset section).

MINEHEAD
• *pop 8500* • ☎ *01643*

Somerset's largest seaside resort is just outside the park's eastern border. During summer, it's packed with British holiday-makers, many of them escaped from Butlin's Somerwestworld, a vast holiday camp. Come in May, however, and the town still enacts medieval May Day ceremonies with a Hobby Horse performing a fertility dance through the streets.

The South-West Coast Path begins/ends in Minehead.

The TIC (☎ 702624) at 17 Friday St has a list of B&Bs if you want to stay. Two miles south of Minehead, in a secluded spot, is *Minehead Youth Hostel* (☎ 702595) at Alcombe Combe. It's open daily in July and August, daily except Monday from April to June, and also except Monday and Tuesday in September and October. The nightly charge is £7.45/5.

Lyn Valley Transport has Tuesday and Friday services to Porlock (more frequent in summer). Ridler's has one bus a day Monday to Friday to Dulverton. Southern National runs to Dunster and Taunton. Lyn Valley has buses to Lynton/Lynmouth but only a few days a week. Minehead is the northern terminus for the West Somerset Railway.

EXFORD

This tiny village in the centre of the park makes a good base for walks, especially to Dunkery Beacon, the highest point on Exmoor, four miles from Exford.

Places to Stay & Eat

Exford Youth Hostel (☎ 01643-831288) is in a Victorian house by the River Exe in the village centre. A bed costs £8.25/5.55 and the hostel is open daily in July and August; daily except Sunday in April, May and June. Phone for other opening hours.

There are two camping grounds just outside Exford, off the Porlock road. *Downscombe Farm* (☎ 01643-831239) charges £6 for two people. *Wester Mill Farm Campsite* (☎ 01643-831238) is open from April to October and charges £3 per person.

Exmoor House Hotel (☎ 01643-831304) in Chapel St does B&B from £18 a head.

The *White Horse Inn* (☎ 01643-831229), a 16th-century inn right by the bridge, does B&B from £30 per person in rooms with attached bathroom. There's bar food during the week and a carvery on Sunday.

Getting There & Away
From May to October Lyn Valley (☎ 01598-753320) runs buses a few times a week from Lynton/Lynmouth. Over the moor, it's a seven-mile walk to Exford from Porlock, 10 from Minehead Youth Hostel, 12 from Dunster and 15 from Lynton.

PORLOCK
• *pop 1500*   •   ☎ *01643*
This attractive village of thatched cottages lies in a deep valley, reached by a steep lane. Two miles further west is the charming harbour, Porlock Weir.

The picturesque NT-owned village of **Selworthy** is 2½ miles east of Porlock. Its cream-painted cob and thatch cottages make this a popular movie location; in 1994 Thomas Hardy's *The Return of the Native* was filmed here.

Places to Stay & Eat
Most places are on the High St. For B&B, cosy, thatched *Myrtle Cottage* (☎ 862978) charges from £16 per person and is open all year. The *Lorna Doone Hotel* (☎ 862404) offers B&B from £18. All rooms have bathroom attached.

The Ship Inn (☎ 862507) is a 13th-century thatched hostelry mentioned in *Lorna Doone*. B&B is from £19.50 per person and

the pub serves real ale as well as country wines – try the local damson wine or cider.

Piggy in the Middle (☎ 862647) does good steak and seafood but is not particularly cheap...lobster for around £16. There are several tearooms in the High St which serve lunch as well.

Getting There & Away
Southern National (☎ 01823-272033) runs a two-hourly Minehead to Porlock service Monday to Saturday throughout the year (20 minutes, £1.30). The service is extended to Lynton and Lynmouth in the summer months.

LYNTON & LYNMOUTH
• *pop 2075*   •   ☎ *01598*
A water-operated cliff railway links the village of Lynton with Lynmouth, 600 feet below it. The picturesque, steeply wooded gorge of the West Lyn River, which meets the sea at Lynmouth, can be delightful out of season. This is a good base for walks along the coast and in the northern part of the park.

In 1952, storms caused the East and West Lyn rivers to flood, destroying 98 houses and claiming the lives of 34 people. The disaster is recorded at the **Lyn and Exmoor Museum** (☎ 752317), in haunted St Vincent's Cottage, Market St, Lynton. From late March to late October, the museum is open daily (afternoon only on Sunday) but closes from 12.30 to 2 pm for lunch.

The **cliff railway** is a simple piece of environmentally friendly Victorian engineering. Two cars linked by a steel cable descend or ascend the slope according to the amount of water in their tanks. For 40p/20p it's the best way to get between the two villages between Easter and November (8 am to 7 pm daily).

There's a TIC (☎ 752225) in Lynton Town Hall and a National Park Visitors Centre (☎ 752509) by Lynmouth harbour.

Walks
Lynton TIC and Lynmouth Visitors Centre have information about the many local walks. The South West Coast Path and the Tarka Trail pass through the villages, and the

Two Moors Way, linking Exmoor with Dartmoor, starts in Lynmouth.

As you leave Lynmouth you'll see signs to **Glen Lyn Gorge** which is open year-round and has a small exhibition centre, open in summer only. It costs £2/1 to walk along the gorge.

The **Valley of the Rocks**, which is believed to be where the River Lyn originally flowed, was described by the poet Robert Southey as 'rock reeling upon rock, stone piled upon stone, a huge terrifying reeling mass'. It's just over a mile west of Lynton and makes a pleasant walk along the coastal footpath. East of Lynmouth, the lighthouse at **Foreland Point** is another good focus for a walk.

Watersmeet, two miles along the river from Lynmouth, makes another popular hike. The old hunting lodge houses a NT teashop.

Places to Stay & Eat

Lynton Youth Hostel (☎ 753237) is at Lynbridge, roughly a mile outside Lynton. It's a Victorian house in the gorge, open daily in July and August; daily except Sunday from April to June; phone for other times. The nightly charge is £7.45/5.

The Retreat (☎ 753526), 1 Park Gardens, Lydiate Lane, Lynton, has B&B from £15 per person. Lydiate Lane is parallel to the main street. *Orchard House Hotel* (☎ 753247), Watersmeet Rd, Lynmouth, charges from £15, as does *Oakleigh* (☎ 752220), 4 Tors Rd, Lynmouth. In Lynbridge Rd virtually side by side and with stunning views are *Woodlands* (☎ 752324) and *Valley House* (☎ 752285), charging from £16 and £18 respectively.

The *Rising Sun* (☎ 753223) is a 14th-century inn beside Lynmouth harbour. The poet Shelley brought his 16-year-old bride here for their honeymoon, and you can stay in their rose-clad cottage for £55/110. Cheaper rooms cost from £39.50 per person, and they also do two-night packages including dinner. This is an excellent place for a pub lunch or evening meal.

Getting There & Away

Red Bus (☎ 01271-45444) has a service five times a day from Barnstaple to Lynton/Lynmouth (one hour, £2), Monday to Saturday. In the summer, Monday to Friday, the service is extended once a day through to Minehead.

Lyn Valley Bus (☎ 753320) runs an infrequent service four days a week from Lynton to Taunton. They also have services to Minehead, Doone Valley and other places – phone for further details.

Driving from Porlock note that Porlock Hill is notoriously steep; look out for the old AA box at the top where motorists could phone to report overheated radiators. There are two alternative toll roads (75p or £1), both of them scenic and both of them less steep.

Devon

Devon's tourist attractions are no secret. For the British, the county has long been a popular place for a traditional family holiday by the seaside and the coastal resorts are still crowded in summer. The county's history is inextricably bound up with the sea; from Plymouth, Drake set out to fight the Spanish Armada and the Pilgrim Fathers sailed to America. Exeter Cathedral has the longest stretch of Gothic vaulting in the world. Little country lanes lead to idyllic villages of thatched cottages; tearooms serve traditional cream teas and you can buy rough cider from local farms. Inland, there's superb walking country in two national parks – wild Dartmoor in the centre and Exmoor in the north, which extends into Somerset (see separate sections).

GETTING AROUND

Contact the Devon County Public Transport Help Line (☎ 01392-382800) weekdays from 8.30 am to 5 pm for information. They can send you the invaluable *Devon Public Transport Map*, listing the 50 bus companies now operating within the county and the useful *Dartmoor Bus Services Timetable*.

Devon's rail network skirts along the south coast through Exeter and Plymouth to Cornwall. There are some picturesque stretches where the line travels right beside the sea. Two branch lines run north – the 39-mile Tarka Line from Exeter to Barnstaple, and the 15-mile Tamar Valley Line from Plymouth to Gunnislake.

EXETER

- *pop 89,000*   • ☎ *01392*

The West Country's largest city, with one of the finest medieval cathedrals in the region, Exeter is the main transport hub for Devon and Cornwall, and a good starting point for Dartmoor.

Many of the older buildings were destroyed in the air raids of WWII and much of Exeter is modern and architecturally uninspiring. It is, however, a thoroughly livable university city with a thriving nightlife.

Until the 19th century, Exeter was an important port, and the waterfront (which includes a large boat museum) is slowly being restored.

History

Exeter was founded by the Romans in about 50 AD to serve as the administrative capital for the Dumnonii of Devon and Cornwall. There was, however, a settlement on the banks of the Exe long before the arrival of the Romans.

By the 3rd century, the city was surrounded by a thick wall, parts of which can still be seen although most of it has either been buried or incorporated into buildings.

The fortifications were battered by Danish invaders in the Middle Ages and by the Normans in the 11th century. In 1068 William the Conqueror took 18 days to break through the walls. He appointed a Norman seigneur to construct a castle, the ruins of which can still be seen in Rougemont Park.

Exeter was a major trading port until Isabel, Countess of Devon built a weir across the river, halting river traffic. It was not until 1563, when the first ship canal in Britain was

dug to bypass the weir, that the city began to re-establish itself as a trading centre.

Exeter has been closely involved in many of England's greatest battles. Three of the ships sent to face the Spanish Armada were built here and some of the greatest sea captains of the time, Drake, Raleigh and Frobisher, lived in the area for part of their lives. In 1942 heavy air raids reduced large areas of Exeter to rubble.

Orientation

The old Roman walls enclose a hill in a bend of the River Exe, and the cathedral's great square towers still dominate the skyline. Most of the sights are accessible on foot; long-stay car parks are well signposted.

There are two railway stations (Central and St David's); most InterCity trains use St David's, 20 minutes walk west of the city centre.

Information

The TIC (☎ 265700), Civic Centre, Paris St, is just across the road from the bus station, a short walk north-east of the cathedral.

Guided tours led by the volunteer Exeter 'Redcoats' are well worth joining. They last 1½ to two hours, cost £1.30 a head and cover a range of subjects, from a standard walking tour (daily) to a ghost walk (Tuesday, 7 pm). Tours leave from outside the Royal Clarence Hotel or from Quay House. Ask at the TIC for details.

Exeter Cathedral

Exeter's jewel is the Cathedral Church of St Mary and St Peter, a magnificent building that has stood largely unchanged for the last 600 years. Unlike many of the cathedrals in the country, it was built within a relatively short time, which accounts for its pleasing architectural unity.

There's been a church on this spot since 932. In 1050, the Saxon church was granted cathedral status and Leofric was enthroned as the first Bishop of Exeter. Between 1112 and 1133 a Norman cathedral was built in place of the original church. The two transept towers were built at this time – an unusual

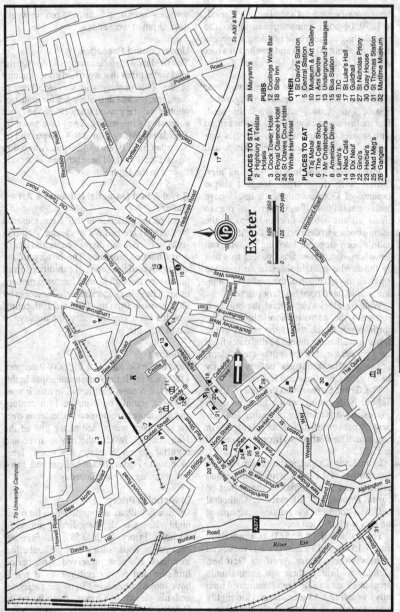

PLACES TO STAY
2 Highbury & Telstar
3 Hotels
3 Clock Tower Hotel
20 Royal Clarence Hotel
24 St Olaves Court Hotel
29 White Hart Hotel

PLACES TO EAT
4 Taj Mahal
6 The Cake Shop
7 Mr Christopher's
8 American Diner
9 Lamb's
14 Next Café
19 Dix Neuf
21 Gino's
23 Herbie's
25 Mad Meg's
26 Ganges
28 Maryam's

PUBS
12 Coolings Wine Bar
18 Ship Inn

OTHER
1 St David's Station
5 Central Station
10 Museum & Art Gallery
11 Arts Centre
13 Underground Passages
15 Bus Station
16 TIC
17 St Luke's Hall
21 Guildhall
27 St Nicholas Priory
30 Quay House
31 St Thomas Station
32 Maritime Museum

Exeter

design for English cathedrals of the period. In 1270, Bishop Bronescombe instigated the remodelling of the whole building, a process that took about 90 years and resulted in a mix of Early English and Decorated Gothic styles.

You enter through the impressive Great West Front, with the largest surviving collection of 14th-century sculpture in England. The niches around the three doors are filled with statues of Christ and the Apostles surrounded by saints and angels, kings and queens.

Inside, the cathedral is light and airy, roofed with the world's longest single expanse of Gothic vaulting. It might have been even brighter if a controversial plan to clean all the stonework and repaint the ceiling bosses in their original bright colours hadn't been stopped. Looking up, you can see where restoration was brought to a halt by those who thought the scheme over the top even though much of the medieval cathedral would have been brightly painted.

Walking clockwise around the building, you pass the **astronomical clock** in the north tower, which shows the phases of the moon as well as the time. The dial dates from the 15th century but the works are modern. Opposite is the **minstrels' gallery**, used by the choir at Christmas and Easter.

The **Great Screen** was erected in 1325. Behind is the choir, which features some interesting misericords including the earliest representation of an elephant in England. The **Bishop's Throne** was carved in 1312.

In the Lady Chapel, at the eastern end, are the **tombs** of bishops Bronescombe and Leofric, and a memorial to the author of *Lorna Doone*, RD Blackmore. Cathedral staff will point out the famous sculpture of the lady with two left feet.

The cathedral (☎ 55573) is open daily from 7.15 am and a £2 donation is requested from visitors. From April to October, Monday to Friday, there are guided tours (free) at 11 am and 2.30 pm (Saturday 11 am only) which last 45 minutes and are highly recommended. It's also worth attending a

service – evensong is at 5.30 pm on weekdays, 3 pm at weekends.

Underground Passages
The medieval maintenance passages for the lead water pipes that were laid under the city in the 14th century still survive. They're dark, narrow and definitely not for claustrophobes but the guided tours (☎ 265887) are surprisingly interesting. They take place on Tuesday to Friday from 2 to 4 .30 pm and on Saturday from 10 am to 4.30 pm. Admission costs £2.50/1.25. The entrance is beside Boot's in the High St.

Royal Albert Memorial Museum & Art Gallery
Most of the galleries in this large museum (☎ 265858) are laid out in classic Victorian style, with crowded display cases and lots of dusty hunting trophies. The history of the city is covered in a series of exhibitions from prehistory, through Roman Exeter to modern times. The gallery upstairs includes works by Devon artists from the 18th and 19th centuries. It's open, free, Monday to Saturday, 10 am to 5.30 pm.

Guildhall
Parts of the Guildhall (☎ 265500) date from 1160, making it the oldest municipal building in the country that is still in use. It was, however, mainly built in the 14th century and the impressive portico that extends over the pavement was added at the end of the 16th century. Inside, the city's silver and regalia are on display. It's open, free, Monday to Friday, 10 am to 1 pm and 2 to 4 pm; morning only on Saturday.

St Nicholas Priory
Originally built as accommodation for overnight visitors to the Benedictine priory, St Nicholas Priory (☎ 265858), off Fore St, became the house of a wealthy Elizabethan merchant. It's now preserved, with period furniture and plaster ceilings, as it might have looked when lived in by the merchant and his family. It's open, free, Easter to October, Monday to Saturday, 10 am to 5 pm.

Quay House Interpretation Centre

Down by the river, this display and audiovisual presentation offers a painless resumé of the city's history and its commercial reliance on the river. There's no charge, and it's open daily from Easter to October, 10 am to 5 pm.

Maritime Museum

Across the river from Quay House, this museum exhibits more than a hundred craft, including a Chinese junk, Venetian gondola, Danish icebreaker and famous dinghies like the one in which Captain Bligh was set adrift from the *Bounty*. *Bertha* is the world's oldest surviving working steamship, built in 1844 to a design by Isambard Kingdom Brunel.

This is very much a 'hands on' museum (☎ 58075) and visitors are free to climb over most of the exhibits. It's open daily, 10 am to 5 pm (4 pm in winter); £4.25/2.50.

Walks & Cycle Routes

The 11-mile walk to the *Steps Bridge Youth Hostel* on Dartmoor follows country lanes through Shillingford St George and Doddiscombleigh (where you should stop at the *Nobody Inn*, one of the south-west's best pubs). A 30-mile cycle tour of Dartmoor takes you from Exeter through Doddiscombleigh and Bovey Tracey to Widecombe-in-the-Moor and back to Exeter.

Places to Stay

Hostels In a large house overlooking the River Exe, *Exeter Youth Hostel* (☎ 873329), 47 Countess Wear Rd, is two miles southeast of the city towards Topsham. It's open all year round and the nightly charge is £9.10/6.15 in July and August, and £8.25/5.55 at other times. From High St, catch minibuses K or T (10 minutes, 80p) and ask for Countess Wear post office. Bus Nos 57 or 85 will get you there from the bus station.

The best value accommodation in Exeter is the university's *St Luke's Hall* (☎ 211500) – just £12.50 per person including breakfast. The catch is that it's available only in March, April, July, August and September (college vacations).

B&Bs & Hotels The cheapest B&Bs are on the outskirts of the city. The *Old Mill* (☎ 59977), Mill Lane, Alphington, is in a quiet residential suburb and has B&B from £10 a head. It's easy to reach by bus.

Most B&Bs and cheaper hotels lie in the area east of St David's station and north of Central station. There are several reasonable B&Bs on St David's Hill. The *Highbury* (☎ 434737), 85 St David's Hill, is good value from £15/25 with attached bath. *Telstar Hotel* (☎ 72466), at No 77, has rooms from £14/25; £30 for a double with attached shower. *Glendale Hotel* (☎ 74350), at No 8, has rooms from £16 per head, some with attached showers.

The *Clock Tower Hotel* (☎ 424545), 16 New North Rd, has singles from £15, doubles from £25 or £19/33 with attached bathroom. There are several other places along this road and more on Blackall Rd and Howell Rd. *Rhona's* (☎ 77791), 15 Blackall Rd, has beds from £12 each. *Raffles Hotel* (☎ 70200), 11 Blackall Rd, is more upmarket; all rooms have an attached bathroom and charges are from £28/40.

The *Claremont* (☎ 74699) is a comfortable B&B for non-smokers at 36 Wonford Rd, quite a drive out on the eastern side of the city. Rooms are £24/34 with attached bathrooms.

The *White Hart Hotel* (☎ 79897), South St, is an old coaching inn, and the cobbled courtyard through which the coachmen drove their horses is still the focal point. It's an interesting place to stay, with rooms with attached bath from £38/48 at weekends, £56/80 during the week.

The centrally located *St Olaves Court Hotel* (☎ 217736), Mary Arches St, has 15 comfortable rooms each with attached bathroom and complimentary decanter of sherry. Prices are from £50/60 during the weekend, £65/80 during the week.

Dating back to the 14th century, the *Royal Clarence Hotel* (☎ 319955) has the best location of all, right in Cathedral Yard. Their weekend B&B deals are good value at £44 a head; pay the extra £10 for a front room with a superb view of the cathedral. During the week, these rooms cost £69/89; breakfast is extra. Former guests include Tsar Nicholas I and Lord Nelson.

Places to Eat

Exeter has some more interesting fast-food places to give Burger King a run for its money. Across the road from Central station, *The American Diner* plays the part with Mom's meatloaf on its menu for £4.95.

Strains of Edith Piaf and the smell of freshly baked bread drift out across Cathedral Yard from *Bread Stix*. A baguette, filled with anything from brie to smoked salmon, makes a delicious lunchtime snack. For a cream tea, or something more substantial, try *Hanson's*, also in Cathedral Yard.

The most popular bakery with students is the *Cake Shop*, on Longbrook St, run by a French woman. Everything from the Danish pastries to the sugar buns seems to be over-sized and underpriced.

There are several bistro-style places around Gandy St. *Coolings Wine Bar* (☎ 434184), at No 11, is popular and has a good range of main dishes (from about £4) and an extensive wine list. *Dix Neuf* (☎ 422606) does tasty tuna sandwiches for £3.95. There's live music here on Monday, Wednesday and Friday nights.

Herbies (☎ 58473), 15 North St, is an excellent vegetarian restaurant. Its home-made soups, chillies and apple pie are highly recommended.

Italian restaurants include *Maryam's* (☎ 496776), South St; pizzas from £4.50.

The *Ganges* (☎ 72630), Fore St, is reputed to be the best of the Indian restaurants, but the *Taj Mahal* (☎ 58129), 50 Queen St, is good value and does an all-you-can-eat Sunday buffet for £5.95.

Said to have terrorised the kitchens of the Sheriff of Exeter, Mad Meg now lends her name to a Middle Ages theme restaurant with long wooden tables and bare flagstones. *Mad Meg's* (☎ 221225) serves English baronial fare steaks – ribs, pheasant, rabbit etc. Main courses range from £7.95 to £14.45, but students get a 20% discount on Monday nights

and special prices (from £3.95 for main courses) on Wednesdays.

The city's top restaurants include *Lamb's* (☎ 54269), 15 Lower North St, under the old iron bridge. It's surprisingly good value with main dishes from £9.50 to £15.50. The restaurant at *St Olaves Court Hotel* is also recommended but more expensive.

Sir Francis Drake's favourite local is said to have been the *Ship Inn* (☎ 70891), Martin's Lane – the alley between the High St and the Cathedral. The place trades heavily on its famous customer, but it's convenient and the food's good value. The *Tap Bar* at the White Hart Hotel feels more authentic with sawdust on the floor and half-gallon jugs of real ale. Bar food includes chicken and chestnut pie, £5.95.

The *Double Locks* (☎ 56947) is a popular pub right beside the Exeter Shipping Canal, with good food, great puddings and daily barbecues in summer. It's a 20-minute walk south along the canal from the Maritime Museum.

Entertainment

The *Arts Centre* (☎ 421111), in Gandy St, stages dance, theatre, film and music events and is open daily except Sunday. Exeter has three theatres, the *Theatre Royal* (☎ 267222), the *Northcott* (☎ 493493), on the university campus, and the smaller *Barnfield* (☎ 71808), which feature programmes from touring companies and local groups.

There's live music each night in the subterranean *Cavern* (☎ 495370), 83 Queen St. Entry is free on Saturday but there are charges for gigs on other nights.

Nightclubs come and go. Down on the Quay are *Volts* and *Boxes*, both popular with students. Student ID is required for discos at the students' union on Friday and Saturday.

Getting There & Away

See the fares tables in the Getting Around chapter. Exeter is 172 miles from London, 75 from Bristol, 45 from Plymouth and 120 from Land's End. If you're driving down from London, follow the M3 and then the A303, not the congested A30. It's even faster to take the M4 to Bristol and then the M5 south to Exeter.

Air Scheduled services run between Exeter airport (☎ 367433) and Ireland, the Channel Islands and the Isles of Scilly.

Bus The booking office at the bus station (☎ 427711 for information) is open daily from 7.45 am to 6.30 pm.

National Express runs coaches between Exeter and numerous towns in Britain, including London (four hours, £22) via Heathrow airport (three hours), Bath (2¾ hours, £12), Bristol (1½ hours, £13.40), Salisbury (two hours, £17.40) and Penzance (five hours, £16). There's a daily south-coast service between Brighton and Penzance (via Portsmouth, Weymouth, Dorchester, Bridport, Exeter and Plymouth) departing Exeter for Brighton (seven hours, £23 if you don't travel on Friday) at 12.40 pm.

Devon General runs the hourly No X38 to Plymouth (1¼ hours, £4.15) and also has buses to Okehampton (one hour, £2.19) and Torquay.

Train The fastest trains between London and Exeter use London Paddington and take 2½ to three hours (£34), leaving hourly. Trains from London's Waterloo also leave hourly but take three hours, following a more scenic route via Salisbury.

Exeter is at the hub of lines running from Bristol (1½ hours, £13.90), Salisbury (two hours, £16.50) and Penzance (three hours, £18.50).

The 39-mile branch line to Barnstaple (1½ hours, £8.70) is promoted as the Tarka Line, following the river valleys of the Yeo and Taw and giving good views of traditional Devon countryside with its characteristic, deep-sunken lanes. There are 11 trains a day, Monday to Friday, nine on Saturday and four on Sunday. A reduced service operates during the winter.

Most InterCity trains use St David's station.

Getting Around

Bus Exeter is well served by public transport

with an efficient fleet of minibuses (appropriately named Nippers) and buses. A one-day Freedom ticket on the Exeter bus system costs £2.35. Bus N links St David's station with Central station and passes near the coach station.

Taxi There are taxi ranks outside the railway stations. Alternatively, try Capital Taxis (☎ 433433).

Bicycles & Canoes St David's Leisure Hire Centre (☎ 213141), Preston's Yard, Ludwell Lane, rents bicycles (as well as camping equipment and canoes). Three-speeds cost £5 a day, mountain bikes cost £12 and a tandem £25.

Saddles & Paddles (☎ 424241), on the quay, rents bikes and Canadian canoes (£6 per hour or £20 per day). They organise nightly paddling parties, with a barbecue at the Double Locks Hotel.

AROUND EXETER
Powderham Castle
The castle (☎ 01626-890243) is on the estuary of the River Exe, eight miles from Exeter. It dates from the 14th century but was considerably altered in the 18th and 19th centuries. The home of the Courtenay family, it contains collections of French china and Stuart and Regency furniture and features some garish rococo ceilings. It's open from April to September, daily except Saturday, 10 am to 5.30 pm; entry is £4.50/2.95.

A la Ronde
Jane and Mary Parminter planned to combine the magnificence of the Church of San Vitale, which they'd visited in Ravenna, with the homeliness of a country cottage, to create the perfect dwelling place. The result is an intriguing 16-sided house (☎ 01395-265514; NT) whose bizarre interior decor includes a shell-encrusted room, a frieze of feathers and sand and seaweed collages.

It's open April to October, Sunday to Thursday, 11 am to 5 pm; entry is £3.10/1.50. It's two miles north of Exmouth on the A376;

Devon General bus No 57 runs close by en route to Exeter.

SOUTH DEVON COAST

Devon's south coast is dotted with traditional seaside resorts, which are crowded in summer. They are linked by the South West Coast Path which follows the length of the coast.

Sidmouth
• *pop 11,000*   •   ☎ *01395*

A busy fishing port in the Middle Ages, Sidmouth became a fashionable holiday resort when the future Queen Victoria visited with her parents in 1819. The town still retains a certain grandeur, with many gracious Regency buildings. To the east, a steep path climbs Salcombe Hill, with superb views from the top.

Sidmouth is best known for its folk festival which has grown from a small gathering to a major event on the international folk scene. The festival take over the town for a week in late July or early August. Tickets for all the events cost £98/49, plus £20 to camp; a day's ticket is £22 plus £4 if you're camping. Phone ☎ 01296-393293 for information.

The TIC (☎ 516441) shares a home with the public swimming pool in Ham Lane.

The nearest hostel is the *Beer Youth Hostel* (☎ 01297-20296), Bovey Combe, Townsend, in a large house half a mile west of the village of Beer. It's open daily in July and August, daily except Sunday from April to June, and also except Monday in September and October. The nightly charge in summer is £8.25/5.55.

There are two buses an hour from Exeter (45 minutes, £2.60) to Sidmouth. Bus No 899 runs to Beer village, from where it's a half-mile walk.

Torbay Resorts

The three towns set around Torbay – Torquay, Paignton and Brixham – describe themselves as the English Riviera, but while it's true that the climate here is one of the most equable in the country, if you're expecting Cannes, forget it.

Torquay, with a population of over 60,000, is the largest and brashest of the three. There's a long seaside promenade, hung with coloured lights at night, and streets of hotels and cheap B&Bs, all trying to vanquish the ghost of *Fawlty Towers* which took Torquay as its location. Most of the hotels now seem to be staffed by Liverpudlian rather than Spanish Manuels.

The TIC (☎ 01803-297428) is on Vaughan Parade, near the harbour.

Agatha Christie was born here and Torquay Museum (☎ 293975), 529 Babbacombe Rd, has a display on the author. It's open Monday to Saturday from 10 am to 4.45 pm in summer, weekdays only in winter; entry is £2/1.25. Torre Abbey (☎ 293593), in the park set back from the beach, was a monastery converted into a country house. It now houses a collection of furniture, glassware and more Agatha Christie mementos. It's open daily, April to October, from 9.30 am to 5 pm. Entry is £2.50/1.50.

To the south around the bay, Torquay merges into **Paignton**, which promotes itself as a seaside resort for the family. Roundham Head separates the two main beaches; there's a zoo and aquarium. The TIC (☎ 01803-558383) is on the Esplanade.

Brixham is a fishing town crowded round a small harbour. In the middle of the 19th century, this was the country's busiest fishing port and is still the place to come for a fishing expedition. Kiosks line the harbour touting boat trips. It costs around £18 to fish for conger, ling and coalfish around the wrecks in the bay, less to fish for mackerel. Before parting with your money, it's worth asking whether there are any mackerel shoals about. To arrange a trip, contact the skippers directly – *Sea Spray* (☎ 851328), *Calypso/Gemini* (☎ 851766) or *Our Jenny* (☎ 854444). The TIC (☎ 01803-852861) is on the quay.

Four miles from Brixham and across the water from Dartmouth, the attractively located *Maypool Youth Hostel* (☎ 01803-842444) is one mile south-west of Galmpton. Beds are £7.45/5 and it's open every day from April to August. Bus No 100 stops at Churston Pottery, one mile away beside Churston train station.

Getting There & Away The No X46 bus service runs hourly from Exeter to Torquay (one hour, £3.55). Service No 100 operates every 12 minutes along the coast from Torquay to Paignton (15 minutes, £1.10) and Brixham (25 minutes, £1.65).

A branch rail line runs from Newton Abbot, via Torquay to Paignton. The Paignton & Dartmouth Steam Railway (☎ 555872) runs from Paignton along the coast on the scenic seven-mile trip to Kingswear on the River Dart, linked by ferry (six minutes) to Dartmouth. A combined rail/ferry ticket to Dartmouth costs £5.30/3.50 for an adult/child, one way.

Dartmouth
- *pop 5300* • ☎ *01803*

On the River Dart estuary, Dartmouth is an attractive port with a long history. The deep natural harbour has sheltered trading vessels since Norman times, fishing boats for many more centuries, the Pilgrim Fathers in 1620 on their way to Plymouth, and D-day landing craft bound for France in 1944. Today, it's filled with yachts, but naval associations continue with the Royal Navy's officers' training college located on the edge of town.

Narrow streets wind through the town. In the centre, the Butterwalk is a row of timber-framed houses built in the 17th century, with a museum featuring a large collection of model boats. **Dartmouth Castle** (☎ 833588), ¾ of a mile outside the town, dates from the 15th century and was designed so that a chain could be placed to the companion castle at Kingswear to block off the estuary. The castle is open daily in summer; entry is £1.80/90p.

The TIC (☎ 834224) is on Mayor's Ave.

Places to Stay & Eat The youth hostel (see under Brixham) is across the river at Maypool, about five miles away. There are cheap B&Bs along Victoria Rd; try *Pickwick*

(☎ 833415) at No 75 and *Galleons Reach* (☎ 834339) at No 77 – both around £13 per person. Near the waterfront is the *Captain's House* (☎ 832133), 18 Clarence St, with rooms from £24/34, all with bathroom attached.

Dartmouth has something of a reputation for gourmet dining. The *Royal Castle Hotel* (☎ 833033), on the quay, has a popular restaurant, but better known is the *Carved Angel* (☎ 832465) on South Embankment, where a memorable meal will set you back around £30 a head. *Billy Budd's* (☎ 834842) at 7 Foss St offers bistro-style main courses from £3.50; fish is a speciality. The *Exchange* (☎ 832022) in a half-timbered building in Higher St is also promising.

The *Cherub* (☎ 832571), also in Higher St, claims to be the town's oldest building and is a good place for a pint.

Getting There & Away The best way to approach Dartmouth is by boat, either on the ferries across from Kingswear (six minutes, £1.90 for a car and four people, 40p for a foot passenger) or downstream from Totnes (1¼ hours, £4.20). River Dart Cruises (☎ 832109) is one operator. From Exeter, take a train to Totnes and a boat from there.

Totnes
- *pop 6300* • ☎ *01803*

Nine miles inland from Torquay and 10 miles upriver from Dartmouth, Totnes was once one of the most prosperous towns in Britain, a centre for the tin and wool industry. It's now a trendy market town ('the Glastonbury of the west') with a thriving arts community.

This is a pleasant place to wander around, with interesting shops, numerous Elizabethan buildings and a busy quay. There are cruises on the river with frequent departures to Dartmouth in summer.

Totnes Museum, Fore St, contains an exhibition on the history of computers – Charles Babbage, who made the first plans for the calculator in the 19th century, grew up here. It's open Monday to Saturday; entry is 50p. Totnes Castle (☎ 864406; EH) is open daily in summer; entry is £1.50/80p.

The TIC (☎ 863168) is in The Plains.

Places to Stay & Eat *Dartington Youth Hostel* (☎ 862303), Lownard, is two miles from Totnes off the A385 near Week. It's open daily except Monday from April to October (daily in July and August); the nightly charge is £7.45/5. Western National bus No X80 from Torquay to Plymouth via Totnes passes close by.

Five minutes walk from the Totnes railway station, you can stay at *Mrs Park's* (☎ 862555), 1 Castle View, from £14 per person (non-smoking), or *Mrs Allen's* (☎ 862638), 7 Antrim Terrace, from £16 per person. The 600-year-old *Old Forge* (☎ 862174) in Seymour Place is more atmospheric and even has its own old lock-up. At 3 Plymouth Rd, off the High St, *Alison Fenwick* (☎ 866917) offers B&B for £14 per person, and can arrange private tours of Dartmoor.

There's good food at the *Kingsbridge Inn* (☎ 863324), Leechwell St; interesting local dishes include rabbit and prune pie, and most main courses are around £6. Totnes High St is lined with interesting places to eat. *Willow Vegetarian Restaurant* (☎ 862605), 87 High St, does soups from £1.20 and main dishes for around £2.50, while *Rumour* (☎ 864682), 30 High St, is the nearest thing to an Amsterdam brown café that you'll find in England.

Getting There & Away Buses run only a few times a week to Exeter, but National Express coaches stop here. There are frequent rail connections to Exeter (45 minutes, £6.30) and Plymouth (25 minutes, £4.80). The railway station is a 15-minute walk from the town centre.

A short walk from Totnes mainline railway station, the private South Devon Railway (☎ 642336) runs to Buckfastleigh (25 minutes, £5.90 return; £5.40 if you book at the TIC) on the edge of Dartmoor.

PLYMOUTH

- *pop 239,000* • ☎ *01752*

Plymouth was renowned as a maritime centre long before Drake's famous game of bowls on Plymouth Hoe in 1588, but this history is difficult to appreciate as you approach through the extensive modern suburbs of Devon's largest city. Devastated by WWII bombing raids, most of Plymouth has been rebuilt, although the Barbican (the old quarter by the harbour where the Pilgrim Fathers set sail for the New World) has been preserved.

History

Plymouth really began to expand in the 15th century, with the development of larger ships; the Plymouth Sound provided a perfect anchorage for warships.

The seafarer most commonly associated with Plymouth is Sir Francis Drake who achieved his knighthood through an epic voyage around the world; setting out from Plymouth in 1577 in the *Golden Hind*, he returned three years later.

In 1588, Drake played a prominent part in the defeat of the Spanish Armada, the fleet sent to invade England by Philip II who wanted to restore Catholicism to this country. On the way home from a Caribbean raid in 1586, Drake had taunted the Spanish king with an attack on some ships in Cadiz harbour.

Whether Drake really was playing bowls on the Hoe at the time is debatable, but the English fleet certainly did set sail from here. Drake was vice admiral and John Hawkins (who had sailed with him on the 1586 raid) was rear admiral. The Armada was chased up the English Channel to Calais, where the troops they were supposed to collect for the planned invasion of Britain failed to arrive. The English then attacked the fleet with fire ships. Many of the Spanish vessels escaped but were blown off course and wrecked off Scotland. Losses were England nil, Spain 51.

Thirty-two years later, the Pilgrim Fathers' two ships, the *Mayflower* and the *Speedwell*, put into Plymouth. Because the second ship was badly damaged, only the

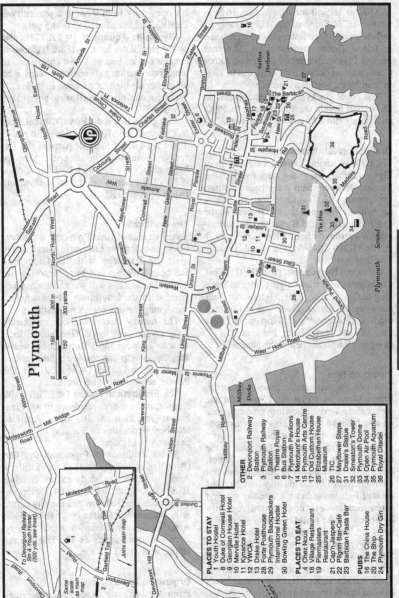

Plymouth

SOUTH-WESTERN ENGLAND

PLACES TO STAY
1   Youth Hostel
8   Duke of Cornwall Hotel
9   Georgian House Hotel
10   Merville Hotel
11   Kynance Hotel
12   YWCA
13   Drake Hotel
28   Forte Posthouse
29   Plymouth Backpackers
      International Hostel
30   Bowling Green Hotel

PLACES TO EAT
4   Chez Nous
18   Village Restaurant
19   Piermasters
      Restaurant
21   Cap'n Jaspers
22   Pilgrim Bar-Café
23   Barbican Pasta Bar

PUBS
16   The China House
20   The Ship
24   Plymouth Dry Gin

OTHER
2   Devonport Railway
      Station
3   Plymouth Railway
      Station
5   Theatre Royal
6   Bus Station
7   Plymouth Pavilions
14   Merchant's House
15   Plymouth Arts Centre
17   Old Custom House
25   Elizabethan House
      Museum
26   TIC
27   Mayflower Steps
31   Drake's Statue
32   Smeaton's Tower
33   Plymouth Dome
34   Open Air Pool
35   Plymouth Aquarium
36   Royal Citadel

Mayflower set sail for America on 16 September 1620. Some of the 102 passengers and crew spent their last night on English soil in Island House, now the TIC. Another famous Plymouth mariner is Captain James Cook, who set out from the Barbican in 1768 in search of a southern continent.

The royal dockyard was established at Devonport beside the Tamar River in 1690, and there's still a large naval base here.

Orientation & Information

The railway station is about a mile north of Plymouth Hoe, the grassy park overlooking the sea. Between them is the pedestrianised city centre, with shopping streets branching off Armada Way, and the bus station. To the east of the Hoe is the Barbican, the interesting old quarter, by Sutton Harbour.

The TIC (☎ 264849) is in Island House, 9 The Barbican.

Plymouth Boat Cruises (☎ 822797) offers a number of boat trips ranging from an hour-long harbour cruise (£3/1.50) to a four-hour cruise up the Tamar. The cruise to Calstock can be combined with a rail trip on the Tamar Line. Boats leave from Phoenix Wharf, along the Barbican (below the citadel).

Plymouth Hoe

This famous promenade gives wonderful, breezy views over Plymouth Sound. In one corner there's even a bowling green; the one on which Drake finished his game was probably where his statue now stands.

The Hoe's most obvious landmark is the red-and-white-striped **Smeaton's Tower**, originally the Eddystone Lighthouse but rebuilt here in 1882. This may look like just another lighthouse but it's actually the first scientifically-designed jointed masonry lighthouse in the world. Open in summer, it costs 75p/40p to climb the 93 steps.

The **Plymouth Dome** (☎ 603300), below Smeaton's Tower, details Plymouth's history through high-tech audiovisual shows. There's also a Tudor street with rowdy locals to liven things up, and a harbour observation deck with interactive computers and radar.

It's open daily from 9 am to 6 pm; entry is £3.50/2.30. Last admission is at 5 pm.

Plymouth Aquarium (☎ 222772), also by the Hoe, dates back to 1888. It claims to contain one of Europe's best collections of temperate marine fish but may seem a bit tame after the high-tech Dome. Entry is £2/1 and it's open daily from 10 am to 6 pm (5 pm in winter).

East of the Hoe is the **Royal Citadel**, built by Charles II in 1670 and still in military use. There are guided tours of parts of the fortress, including the chapel, May to September, daily at 2 and 3.30 pm. Tickets (£2.50/1.50) can be purchased at Plymouth Dome or at the TIC.

The Barbican

To get an idea of what Plymouth must have been like before the Luftwaffe redesigned it, visit the Barbican with its Tudor and Jacobean buildings and busy Victorian fish market. Americans will want to make a pilgrimage to the **Mayflower Steps** where a sign listing the passengers marks the spot.

The narrow streets harbour interesting galleries and craft shops. One famous local artist to look out for is Beryl Cook, whose naughty, plump figures fetch high prices. The Barbican Gallery (☎ 661052), 15 The Parade, sells prints of her work.

The **Elizabethan House** (☎ 253871), 32 New St, is the former residence of an Elizabethan sea captain. It's open April to October, Wednesday to Sunday, 10 am to 5 pm; entry is £1/50p.

At 60 Southside St, **Plymouth Dry Gin** (☎ 667062) has daily tours of the distillery, April to September, daily except Sunday, 10.30 am to 4 pm; tickets are £1.75/95p.

Between the Barbican and the city centre is the **Merchant's House** (☎ 264878), 33 St Andrews St, a museum of social history, open the same times as the Elizabethan House; entry is £1.05/30p.

Organised Tours

From April to early October, Guide Friday (☎ 222221) runs a hop-on, hop-off, open-top bus tour passing the main sights every 30 minutes. Tickets cost £4.50/1.

Places to Stay

Hostels *Plymouth Youth Hostel* (☎ 562189), Belmont Place, Stoke, is in a Grecian-style mansion two miles from the centre. In summer beds cost £9.10/6.15 for adults/children. The hostel is open daily from March to October. Western National bus Nos 14, 15 and 81 and Citybus Nos 33/4 pass this way from the city centre. Devonport railway station (50p from Plymouth) is a quarter of a mile from the hostel.

Plymouth Backpackers International Hostel (☎ 225158), at 172 Citadel Rd, the Hoe, has 48 beds for £7.50 a night.

Plymouth YWCA (☎ 660321) is also well-located, by the Hoe on 9 Lockyer St, but most accommodation tends to be taken by long-term residents. A bed in a dorm costs £6.80, and rooms are £10.75/18.50. A returnable £10 key deposit is payable and breakfast is included. Men can also stay here.

Camping The nearest camping ground is *Riverside Caravan Park* (☎ 344122), which is four miles from the centre on Longbridge Rd (off Plympton Rd). It costs £8.50 for a tent and two people.

B&Bs & Hotels B&Bs and hotels cluster round the north-western corner of the Hoe and are generally good value, from around £12 per person.

Citadel Rd is lined with places to stay. At No 73, *Merville Hotel* (☎ 667595) charges £11/24 for a single/double, but there's only one single. *West Winds* (☎ 601777), 99 Citadel Rd, charges £18/28; the doubles have a shower attached.

The large, friendly *Kynance Hotel* (☎ 266821), 107 Citadel Rd, has rooms from £21.50/38 with attached bath. A continental breakfast is provided if you're leaving early on the ferry. Slightly more upmarket is the *Georgian House Hotel* (☎ 663237), 51 Citadel Rd, where rooms with bath cost from £27/36.

Bowling Green Hotel (☎ 667485), 9 Osborne Place, Lockyer St, is, as the name suggests, located right beside the Hoe bowling green. It's a small, comfortable place run by friendly people. Rooms with attached shower (shared toilet) cost £28/36. Also on Lockyer St is the *Drake Hotel* (☎ 229730), 1 Windsor Villas, with rooms for £42/52 with attached bathroom, £29/42 without. Nearby is the *Imperial Hotel* (☎ 227311) with rooms from £29.95/45.

Most of the modern business hotels near the Hoe are characterless concrete blocks where prices drop at weekends. The *Forte Posthouse* (☎ 662828), the Hoe, is probably the best value, charging from £32.45 for a double at weekends. It has good views over Plymouth Sound.

The *Duke of Cornwall* (☎ 266256), Millbay Rd, is an impressive Victorian Gothic hotel situated between the Hoe and the ferry terminal. B&B costs from £69.50/79.50.

Places to Eat

The Barbican area makes the best hunting ground for interesting places to eat, especially along Southside St and New St behind the TIC. At 40 Southside St the *Barbican Pasta Bar* offers pizza from £3.75. Across the road *Piermasters* (☎ 229345) does two-course set lunches for £9.90, while the *Village Restaurant* (☎ 667688) specialises in seafood; scallops mornay costs £11.50. Cheaper is the *Pilgrim Bar-Café* right beside the TIC which does chicken and chips for £2.95. Cheaper still is *Cap'n Jasper's*, a popular snack stand that does breakfasts and burgers near the Mayflower Steps.

The Ship (☎ 667604), beside the marina in the Barbican, offers bargain-priced carvery meals for £5.50 (one course), £8.50 (two courses) or £10.49 (three courses).

The city's top restaurant is the predominantly French *Chez Nous* (☎ 266793), 13 Frankfort Gate (a short walk from the Theatre Royal). Seafood is a speciality, and main courses are around £18; a three-course set lunch or dinner is £28.50. Booking is advisable.

Entertainment

Plymouth's *Theatre Royal* (☎ 267222), Royal Parade, attracts surprisingly big names for a regional theatre. *Plymouth Arts Centre* (☎ 660060), 38 Looe St, has a cinema, art galleries and a vegetarian restaurant. Outside is the giant mural by local artist Robert Lenkiewicz. The *Pavilions* (☎ 229922) in Millbay Rd hosts everything from Tom Jones to the Bolshoi Ballet.

The Barbican is a good place to drink in the evening; the *Dolphin*, on Southside St, and the *Ship*, on the Barbican, are both popular. The *China House* (☎ 260930), Marrowbone Slip, off Exeter Rd, overlooking Sutton Harbour, is a popular pub in a converted warehouse. There's live music most evenings (jazz/blues).

Getting There & Away

Plymouth is 211 miles from London, 90 from Land's End and 46 from Exeter.

Bus National Express (☎ 0990-808080) has direct connections to numerous cities including London (4½ hours, £16.50) and Bristol (2½ hours, £18). Stagecoach runs the cheapest buses to/from Exeter (¾ hours, £4.15).

Western National (☎ 01752-222666) runs an hourly service to Yelverton (35 minutes, £1.35), but there are no buses on Sunday or bank holidays. A one-day Western National Explorer ticket costs £4.

Train The fastest way to get to London is by train (3½ hours, £40). There are also direct services to Bristol (1½ hours, £23.50) and Penzance (two hours, £9.50).

There's a scenic route to Exeter (one hour, £8.90) – the line follows the Exe estuary, running beside the sea for part of the way. The Tamar Valley Line, through Bere Ferrers, Bere Alston and Calstock to Gunnislake, is another scenic route. In summer, it's possible to travel to Calstock by train (£3.60) and return by boat (see Information above).

Boat Brittany Ferries (☎ 0990-360360) sails from Millbay Docks to Roscoff in France (up

to three departures a day in summer, six hours, £20 to £30) and Santander in Spain (Monday and Wednesday in summer, 24 hours, £52 to £76).

Getting Around

Bus Plymouth Citybus is the main local bus operator. Service No 25 runs between the city centre (Royal Parade), the Barbican and the Hoe. Bus No 30 links Royal Parade with the railway station. For local bus information phone ☎ 222221.

AROUND PLYMOUTH
Mount Edgcumbe

The 400-year-old home of the Earls of Mount Edgcumbe lies across the water in Cornwall. Although the house is open to the public and filled with 18th-century furniture, it's the French, Italian and English gardens that draw visitors. The gardens are open daily, free; you get to them from Plymouth on the Cremyll foot ferry.

Buckland Abbey

Eleven miles north of Plymouth, Buckland Abbey (☎ 01822-853607; NT) was a Cistercian monastery, transformed into a family residence by Sir Richard Grenville and bought in 1581 by Sir Francis Drake. Among the memorabilia is Drake's Drum, used to summon sailors onto the deck of the *Revenge* before battle with the Armada. When Britain is in danger of being invaded, the drum is said to beat by itself.

It's open daily except Thursday from April to October, 10.30 am to 4.45 pm; and 2 to 5 pm at weekends in winter; entry is £4.20. Bus No 83 from Plymouth connects with the No 55 from Yelverton.

NORTH DEVON
Barnstaple

• *pop 24,500*   • ☎ *01271*

Barnstaple is a large town and transport hub – a good starting point for North Devon and Exmoor (see separate section). The Museum of North Devon (☎ 46747) in The Square aside, there's little reason to stay. Contact the TIC (☎ 388583), North Devon Library, Tuly

St, for B&Bs. The nearest youth hostel is six miles away at Instow.

Barnstaple is at the north-western end of the Tarka Line from Exeter and connects with a number of bus services around the coast. Filers (☎ 01271-863819) runs a bus along the A39, south of Bideford, to Lynton, but the most interesting option is the excellent No 300 scenic service (late May to late September only) that crosses Exmoor from Barnstaple, through Woolacombe and Lynton to Minehead (£4.50 for a one-day Explorer Pass).

Mountain bikes are available from Tarka Trail (☎ 24202) at the railway station for £8 per day.

Ilfracombe
• *pop 10,471* • ☎ *01271*

Rising above its little harbour, Ilfracombe is North Devon's largest seaside resort, although the best beaches are five miles west at Woolacombe, and at Croyde Bay, two miles beyond. Both are popular with surfers.

The TIC (☎ 863001) is on the Promenade, and the town is packed with B&Bs. *Ilfracombe Youth Hostel* (☎ 865337), 1 Hillsborough Terrace, stands above the town, overlooking the harbour. The nightly charge is £8.25/5.55, and it's open from April to September, daily except Sunday (every day in July and August).

There are frequent Filers buses between Ilfracombe and Barnstaple (35 minutes, £1.50).

Lundy Island
Ten miles out in the Bristol Channel, Lundy is a granite mass, three miles long, half a mile wide and up to 400 feet high. There's a resident population of just 13 people, one pub (the *Marisco Tavern*), one church and no roads.

People come to climb the cliffs, watch the birds, dive in the marine nature reserve or escape from the world in one of the 23 holiday homes.

Interesting properties that can be rented include the lighthouse and the castle but they need to be reserved months in advance. For

---

Puffin Pence

Martin Harman, owner of Lundy Island from 1925 to 1954, was a typical English eccentric. Not satisfied with owning the remote island, he was determined to make it independent from the rest of the UK, closing the Post Office and issuing his own stamps. Given that Lundy took its name from the old Norse word for puffin, the stamps were denominated in 'puffinage' instead of sterling.

The stamps were ignored but in 1930 Harman carried things a step further and issued a Lundy coinage, with his own head in place of the king's and a puffin on the reverse. These, too, were denominated in 'puffins' instead of shillings and pence. Such defiance couldn't be overlooked and Harman was duly convicted of counterfeiting under the 1870 Coinage Act.

Sadly, Lundy's once-common puffins are now a thoroughly endangered species; you'll be lucky to see any at all. ■

---

information, phone ☎ 01237-431831. Otherwise you can day trip from Ilfracombe or Bideford (two hours, £23/11.50 for adults/children). There are between two and five sailings a week from these ports. For bookings, phone ☎ 01237-470422.

Bideford
• *pop 14,000* • ☎ *01237*

Charles Kingsley based his epic novel *Westward Ho!* on the town of Bideford, not on the nearby seaside resort of the same name – that was actually named after the book. Bideford's a pleasant enough place but there's no need to stay here. Several useful bus services pass through the town, though, and the boat to Lundy Island leaves from the quay.

The TIC (☎ 477676) is on the quay. Bicycles can be hired from Bideford Bicycle Hire (☎ 424123), Torrington St, from £7.50 a day.

There are frequent buses to Barnstaple (30 minutes, £1.10). Service No 2A runs to Appledore (15 minutes, £1.30).

Appledore
This attractive little town with its narrow streets and olde-worlde charm is the complete

antithesis of tacky Westward Ho! nearby. Appledore was long associated with boat-building, but the industry declined in the early part of this century. Revived in 1963, it has managed to continue through the recession. The North Devon Maritime Museum (☎ 01237-422064) tells the story of local boatbuilding, shipwrecks and smuggling.

The *Seagate Hotel* (☎ 01237-472589) is a friendly waterside pub that does B&B from £25 per person.

Foot passengers can cross to Instow on the ferry (£1) in summer; half a mile east is *Instow Youth Hostel* (☎ 01271-860394), Worlington House, New Rd. Beds are £8.25/5.55 for adults/juniors; it's open daily from May to August; other opening days are complex so phone ahead. It's close to the Tarka Trail and accessible by bus No 301 from Barnstaple and a ¾-mile walk.

Clovelly

Clinging to a steep slope above a picturesque harbour, Clovelly must be Devon's most photographed village. It's now so popular with visitors that it has built itself a visitors centre (☎ 431288) and you now have to pay £1.80/60p to get in from the car park above. From Easter to October Land-Rovers ferry visitors up the slope between 9.30 am and 5.30 pm.

The tiny village, with its one cobbled street (flat shoes advisable), is certainly attractive and the best way to appreciate it is to stay here. Several places do B&B. Try *Temple Bar* (☎ 01237-431438) or Mrs Golding's (☎ 01237-431565), 104 High St, both around £14 per person. Right by the harbour, the *Red Lion* (☎ 01237-431237) charges £35 for a double.

There are several departures a day on Filers No 319 service to Bideford (40 minutes, £1.35).

Dartmoor National Park

Although the park is only about 365 square miles in area, it encloses some of the wildest, bleakest country in England – suitable

terrain for the Hound of the Baskervilles (one of Sherlock Holmes' more famous opponents). The landscape and weather (mist, rain and snow) can make this an eerie place to be.

Dartmoor lies within the county of Devon and is named after the River Dart, which has its source here; the West and East Dart rivers merge at Dartmeet. The park covers a granite plateau punctuated by distinctive tors (high rocks), which can look uncannily like ruined castles, and is cut by deep valleys, or combes, and fast-flowing rivers and streams. Some tors, such as Vixen Tor, are almost 100 feet high. The moorland is covered by gorse and heather, and is grazed by sheep, cattle and semi-wild Dartmoor ponies. The countryside in the south-east is more conventionally beautiful, with wooded valleys and thatched villages.

There are plenty of prehistoric remains – Grimspound is possibly the most complete Bronze Age village site in England and the many cairns and tumuli mark the burial places of ancient chieftains.

The area was once rich in minerals such as tin, copper, silver, lead and china clay and the remains of old mines and quarries are scattered about. Most of Dartmoor's prehistoric monuments are built of rough grey local granite. The quarries at Haytor produced stone for Nelson's Column, London Bridge and many other monuments. The wealth generated by these enterprises has left the moor's small communities with attractive churches and buildings. Dartmoor's best known building, however, is the high-security prison at Princetown.

Most of the park is around 2000 feet high. The highest spot is High Willhays at 2038 feet, near Okehampton. About 40% of Dartmoor is common land but 15% of the park (the north-western section, including High Willhays and Yes Tor) is leased to the Ministry of Defence (MOD) and closed for firing practice for part of the year.

This is wonderful hiking country, but you won't be alone in summer on the most popular routes. It's still essential to have a good map since it's easy to get lost, particularly if the mist comes down.

ORIENTATION

Dartmoor is ringed by a number of small market towns and villages, including Ashburton, Buckfastleigh, Tavistock and Okehampton. It's 10 miles from Exeter and seven from Plymouth. Buses link these towns with Princetown, Postbridge and Moretonhampstead on the moor itself. The two main roads across the moor meet near Princetown, the only village of any size on Dartmoor.

Two Bridges, with its medieval clapper bridge, is the focal point for car and coach visitors, and can be extremely crowded in summer. Most of the places to see are on the eastern side; the western side is for serious walkers.

INFORMATION

You can get information about Dartmoor at the TICs in Exeter and Plymouth, and there are other visitors centres in and around the park. The NPA's High Moorland Visitors Centre (☎ 01822-890414), Old Duchy Hotel, Princetown, is open daily all year.

The other visitors centres are generally open daily from April to October, 10 am to

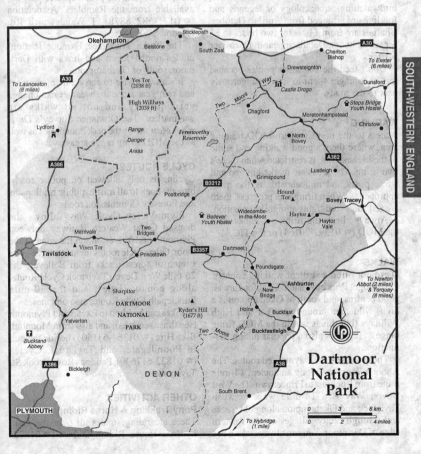

SOUTH-WESTERN ENGLAND

Dartmoor National Park

5 pm, and are at Bovey Tracey (☎ 01626-832093); Haytor (☎ 01364-661520); Postbridge (☎ 01822-880272); New Bridge (☎ 01364-3303); Okehampton (☎ 01837-53020); Ivybridge (☎ 01752-897035); and Tavistock (☎ 01822-612938).

These information centres have useful publications, including the *Dartmoor Visitor* and *Guide to Dartmoor*, both of which are free and are updated annually. They also stock walking guides and Ordnance Survey maps. The *Bus & Walks* leaflet shows walks linked to bus routes.

Guided walks focusing on local wildlife, birdwatching, archaeology or legends and folklore are arranged from April to October. Charges are from £1.50 for two hours to £3 for seven hours. Details appear in *Dartmoor Visitor*.

Don't feed the Dartmoor ponies because this encourages them to move dangerously near to the roads.

WARNING

Access to the north-western MOD training area, where there's good walking and some of the highest tors, is restricted when there's live firing. The areas are marked by red and white posts and noticeboards at the main approaches. When firing is in progress, there are red flags (red lights at night) in position.

Always check the firing schedules with the MOD (☎ 01392-70164) or the TIC.

WALKS

Dartmoor offers excellent walking country. Postbridge, Princetown and Chagford are all good centres, and south of Okehampton is a high, wild area around Yes Tor and High Willhays (but this is within the MOD firing range). Haytor is also a popular hiking destination.

There are several waymarked routes. The Abbot's Way runs along an ancient 14-mile route from Buckfast to Princetown. The West Devon Way is a 14-mile walk between Tavistock and Okehampton along old tracks and through pretty villages on the western edge of Dartmoor. You can always take a bus

for part of this route since the walk runs parallel to the No 187 bus route.

Youth hostels are conveniently placed a day's walk apart across the moor, so a five-day circuit from Exeter is possible.

The Templer Way is an 18-mile hike from Teignmouth (on the south coast) to Haytor, following the route originally designed to transport Dartmoor granite down to the docks.

The Two Moors Way runs from Ivybridge, on the southern edge of the moor, 103 miles north to Lynmouth in Exmoor. The *Two Moors Way* (£2.70, plus 70p UK p&p) is available from the Ramblers' Association (☎ 0171-582 6878), 1 Wandsworth Rd, London SW8 2XX.

The Tarka Trail (see Exmoor section) circles north Devon and links with Dartmoor, south of Okehampton.

It's always wise to carry a map, compass and rain gear since the weather can change very quickly and not all walks are waymarked. The Ordnance Survey's *Dartmoor Map* shows the park boundaries as well as the MOD firing range areas.

CYCLE ROUTES

Cycling is only allowed on public roads, byways open to all traffic, public bridlepaths and Forestry Commission roads.

Plym Valley Cycle Way follows the disused Great Western Railway between Plymouth and Yelverton, on the edge of the moor. Other cycle routes include a three-mile stretch of forest tracks from Bellever; the 26-mile West Devon Tavistock Cycle Route, along country lanes; and the 30-mile Sticklepath Cycle Route, also on lanes.

Bikes can be hired in Exeter and Plymouth (see those sections), and also from Mountain Bike Hire (☎ 01364-631505) beside the pub in Poundsgate, and Tavistock Cycles (☎ 01822-617630), Paddons Row, Brook St, Tavistock.

OTHER ACTIVITIES
Pony Trekking & Horse Riding

There are riding stables all over the park. Lydford House Riding Stables (☎ 01822-

820321), Lydford House Hotel, Lydford, charges from £8 per hour.

Near Widecombe-in-the-Moor, Babery Farm Stables (☎ 01364-631296) offers half-day rides and pub rides (two hours riding, one hour in the pub) from £16. Shilstone Rocks Riding & Trekking Centre (☎ 013642-281) charges £16 for two hours.

Climbing
Rock climbing can only be done where there is a right of access – on private land you must ask the owner's permission first. Popular climbing areas are at Haytor, owned by the NPA, and Dewerstone, owned by the NT. Groups need to book in advance. Ask at a visitors centre or TIC for details.

Fishing
You can fish on certain stretches of the East and West Dart (with a Duchy of Cornwall permit), on the Tavy, Walkham, Plym, Meavy and Teign, as well as on seven reservoirs in the park. A permit is usually needed; phone the Environment Agency (☎ 01392-444000, ext 2052) for information.

PLACES TO STAY & EAT
If you're backpacking, the authorities and owners of unenclosed moorland don't usually object to campers who keep to a simple code: don't camp on moorland enclosed by walls or within sight of roads or houses; don't stay on one site for more than two nights; don't light fires; and leave the site as you found it. With large tents, however, you can only camp in designated camping grounds. There are several camping and caravan parks around the area, many on farms.

There are youth hostels at Postbridge, bang in the middle of the moor, and at Steps Bridge, near Dunsford (between Moretonhampstead and Exeter), as well as at Exeter, Plymouth and Dartington.

Princetown, Postbridge and Holne have camping barns: 'stone tents' which sleep up to about 15 people. Cooking and shower facilities and a wood burner are provided. You sleep on the floor or on a bunk bed; bring your own bedding. For more information, phone ☎ 01722-337494.

The larger towns on the edge of the park (like Okehampton and Tavistock) all have plentiful supplies of B&B and hotel accommodation. Within the park itself, accommodation is sometimes limited, so you need to book ahead in summer. There are also several comfortable country-house hotels in the park.

Dartmoor Tourist Association (☎ 01822-890567) produces an accommodation guide; there's a service charge of £2.75 if you book rooms through any of the National Park Visitors Centres. TICs have details of farm B&Bs.

The old pubs and inns provide a focus for local communities and are sometimes the only places you can get anything to eat in small villages.

GETTING THERE & AWAY
Exeter or Plymouth are the best starting points for the park, but Exeter has the better transport connections to the rest of the country. Totnes, Exeter, Newton Abbot and Plymouth all have InterCity train services to London, Bristol and the Midlands. National Express has coach services between London and Exeter, Newton Abbot, Okehampton and Plymouth.

The only railway stations near the park are at Ivybridge and South Brent on the Exeter/Plymouth line. Ivybridge is useful for people who want to walk the Two Moors Way. The single fare from Exeter is £7.80 (40 minutes).

The most useful bus that actually crosses Dartmoor is DevonBus No 82, the Transmoor Link, running between Exeter and Plymouth via Steps Bridge, Moretonhampstead, Warren House Inn, Postbridge, Princetown, Sharpitor and Yelverton. It runs daily in summer (late May to late September), but there are only three buses each way. For more information phone ☎ 01752-382800.

DevonBus No 359 follows a circular route from Exeter through Steps Bridge, Moretonhampstead and Chagford to

Drewsteignton, and then back to Exeter (Monday to Saturday, three times a day each way). The No X39 (operated by Devon General) goes along the A38 between Plymouth and Exeter, stopping at Buckfastleigh and Ashburton. Western National Nos 83/84 operates from Plymouth via Yelverton to Tavistock every 20 minutes.

The summer-only Dartmoor Sunday Rover ticket (£3.50) entitles you to unlimited travel on most bus routes within the area and to rail travel on the Tamar Valley Line from Plymouth to Gunnislake.

On summer Sundays, DevonBus No 187 loops round from Plymouth, through Gunnislake, Tavistock, Mary Tavy, Lydford, Okehampton and Sticklepath, on its way to Exeter; you could do part of this journey on the Tamar Valley Line or even by boat (see Plymouth section).

Since buses are infrequent and subject to change, it's best to work out what you want to do, then contact the Devon County Public Transport Help Line (☎ 01392-382800) weekdays from 8.30 am to 5 pm. They will send you the *Dartmoor Bus Services Timetable* with suggestions for walks connected to bus routes.

PRINCETOWN
- ☎ 01822

At 1377 feet, Princetown is England's highest settlement and Dartmoor's largest community. With the infamous prison located here, it's not Dartmoor's most beautiful town but is close to excellent walking country.

The town was created in the late 18th century by Thomas Tyrwhitt, who wanted to convert large areas of the moorland into arable farmland. When this failed, he came up with another plan to create employment for the people who had moved into the area, suggesting that a prison be built to house prisoners of war. In the first half of the 19th century, the prison housed both French and American POWs. When hostilities with these countries ceased, British prisoners were transferred here. There are now about 600 inmates in the maximum-security prison.

The High Moorland Visitors Centre (☎ 890414) was once the Duchy Hotel. It has displays on Dartmoor and an information centre which stocks maps.

Places to Stay & Eat
The *Plume of Feathers* (☎ 890240), Princetown's oldest building, is a pub near the visitors centre, with all sorts of cheap accommodation. The camping ground (from £2.50 per person) is open year-round, the stone tent costs from £3.50 and there's bunkhouse accommodation from £5.50 (including rooms for two and four people). You need to book well in advance.

The *Devil's Elbow* (☎ 890232), Two Bridges Rd, across from the visitors centre, is a pub offering B&B from £12.50 per person.

Getting There & Away
DevonBus No 82 (Transmoor Link) runs here from either Exeter or Plymouth (both 50 minutes). The service operates daily between July and late September, and on Saturday, Sunday and bank holidays between May and June. A £3.50 Sunday Rover ticket allows a day's travel on the system. The No 170 links Princetown with Tavistock and Newton Abbot.

POSTBRIDGE
- ☎ 01822

Right in the middle of the park, Postbridge makes a popular starting point for local walks. It's known for its granite clapper bridge which crosses the East Dart River. Clapper bridges date from the 13th century and are made of large slabs of granite supported at each end by short, stone pillars.

Local legend tells of the landlady of an 18th-century temperance house who took to serving alcohol – much to the horror of her husband who poured it into the river. A dog which paused to quench its thirst was driven mad by the potent mixture and died. Its tormented spirit is still said to haunt Dartmoor, one version of the story that gave Conan Doyle the idea for *The Hound of the Baskervilles*.

From April to October, there's a NPA Visitors Centre in the car park. There's also a post office and shop in the village.

Places to Stay & Eat

Bellever Youth Hostel (☎ 880207) is one mile south-east of Postbridge on the western bank of the river. It's open daily in July and August, daily except Sunday from April to June, and also except Monday in September and October. A bed costs £8.25/5.55 for adults/juniors.

Runnage Farm (☎ 880222) has a camping barn – the nightly charge is £4 per person. To reach the farm, take the small road off the B3212 just before you reach Postbridge coming from the Moretonhampstead side.

East Dart Hotel (☎ 880213) is 100 yards from the clapper bridge and has beds from £20. In summer, it has a restaurant called *221B Baker St* after Sherlock Holmes' London address. Cream teas are also served (£2.95).

The *Lydgate House Hotel* (☎ 880209) is a quarter of a mile from the village centre in an attractive, sheltered valley. It's an excellent place to stay with beds from £26; they also do a good three-course dinner for £15.

Two miles north-east of Postbridge, along the B3212 towards Moretonhampstead, is the *Warren House Inn* (☎ 880208). It's a good place to come after a walk, and you can warm yourself by a fire they claim has been burning continuously since 1845. There's real ale, and pub food including steak and ale pie (£5.75).

Headland Warren Farm (☎ 880206) is a farm on the moor, five miles from Postbridge. B&B is from £20 per person and it's convenient for walkers since it's by the Two Moors Way.

Getting There & Away

The Transmoor Link (DevonBus No 82) runs through Postbridge between Plymouth and Exeter.

BUCKFASTLEIGH
* ☎ 01364

On the park's south-eastern edge, Buck-

fastleigh is an old market town near the Upper Dart Valley. Nearby is Buckfast Abbey, Britain's last working monastery.

For centuries, Buckfastleigh was a centre for the manufacture of woollen cloth. Above the town is the parish church, and in the graveyard, in a heavy tomb built by villagers to ensure he could not come back to life, lies Sir Richard Cabell, the most hated man in Dartmoor. When this evil landowner died in the 17th century, it's said that black phantom hounds were seen speeding across the moor to howl beside his grave.

Buckfast Abbey

Buckfast Abbey, two miles north of Buckfastleigh, was founded in 1016 and flourished in the Middle Ages through its involvement in the wool trade. With the Dissolution, it was abandoned in 1539. In 1806, the ruins were levelled and a mock-Gothic mansion erected; the house was purchased in 1882 by a group of exiled French Benedictine monks. The abbey church was built between 1906 and 1932 by the monks, and an impressive, modern stained-glass figure of Christ dominates the eastern end chapel.

The abbey (☎ 01364-642519) is a popular tourist attraction. Entry is free, except for the exhibition (74p) and the charge for the car park in summer. The monks augment their income by keeping bees and making tonic wine.

Places to Stay & Eat

About three miles north-west of Buckfastleigh, in Holne, there's budget accommodation in a stone barn at *Holne Court Farm* (☎ 01364-631271) from around £3 per person.

In Buckfastleigh, *Woodholme Guest House* (☎ 01364-643350), 113 Plymouth Rd, offers B&B for £16 a head with shared bath. The *Dartbridge Inn* (☎ 01364-642214), Totnes Rd, offers B&B from £50 for a double with attached bath. The restaurant and tearooms at *Buckfast Abbey* are good for lunch or tea.

Getting There & Away

Bus No X39 runs from Buckfastleigh to Exeter (one hour, £3.10) or Plymouth (40 minutes, £3.10), from Monday to Saturday about four times a day. Bayline No 88 goes hourly from Newton Abbot to Buckfastleigh, Monday to Saturday for £2.50.

The South Devon Railway (☎ 01364-642336) links Totnes and Buckfastleigh (every 1½ hours, 25 minutes, £5.90 return) with a seven-mile journey beside the River Dart on a steam-operated country branch line. The service operates daily from mid-May to September. In April and October, trains run on Wednesday, Saturday and Sunday, and in May every day except Monday, Thursday and Friday.

WIDECOMBE-IN-THE-MOOR

Uncle Tom Cobbleigh and all still flock to this popular little Dartmoor village, and not just on the second Tuesday of September when the fair, commemorated in the famous folk song, takes place. The fine 14th-century granite church, known as the Cathedral in the Moor, was funded by prosperous tin miners and has a 120-foot-high tower.

There's a Visitor Information Point at Sexton's Cottage, adjacent to the Church House. Built in 1537 as a brewhouse, the Church House is now the village hall.

Cockingford Farm Campsite (☎ 013642-258) is 1½ miles south of Widecombe, five miles from Ashburton. It costs £3.50 per person to camp here.

MORETONHAMPSTEAD & STEPS BRIDGE

Moretonhampstead, a market town at the junction of the B3212 and the A382, is on the Transmoor Link bus route, 14 miles from Princetown.

Just inside the park's north-eastern border, 4½ miles east of Moretonhampstead, along the B3212, is *Steps Bridge Youth Hostel* (☎ 01647-252435). In summer beds cost £6.75/4.60 and it's open daily from April to September. It's a 10-mile walk from here to the hostel in Exeter.

You can camp at *Clifford Bridge Park* (☎ 01647-24226), Clifford, from Easter to September, from £3.70 a person and tent. The site is by the River Teign, three miles west of Steps Bridge, and there's even a heated swimming pool.

CHAGFORD

• *pop 1500* • ☎ *01647*

This delightful country town by the Teign River makes a more attractive base for the park's north-eastern area than nearby Moretonhampstead. In the 14th century, it was a Stannary town where the tin mined on the moor was weighed and checked, and the taxes paid. It's an excellent walking and riding centre.

Places to Stay & Eat

Lawn House (☎ 433329) in Mill St offers B&B from £16.50 per person. *Glendarah House* (☎ 432404) is a six-minute walk from the church and has rooms with attached bath from £27 per person.

The pretty *Three Crowns Hotel* (☎ 433444), in the High St opposite the church, dates from the 13th century. Beds cost from £25.

Evelyn Waugh stayed at *Easton Court Hotel* (☎ 433469) while writing *Brideshead Revisited*. It's a lovely thatched 15th-century building, just off the A382 at Easton, on the opposite side from the turning to Chagford. B&B is from £36 per person.

Getting There & Away

From Exeter (one hour, £2.20), Red Bus No 359 goes via Moretonhampstead. From Okehampton, there are buses daily except Monday and Thursday.

CASTLE DROGO

Just over a mile from Chagford is **Castle Drogo** (☎ 01647-433306; NT), a medieval-looking granite fortification that was designed by Sir Edwin Lutyens, and constructed between 1910 and 1930 for a wealthy businessman, Julius Drewe, who died shortly after moving in. It overlooks the wooded gorge of the River Teign with fine views of Dartmoor. Once you've been round what must be the most comfortable castle in the kingdom, you can rent croquet sets for a game on the lawn. It's open from April to October, daily except Friday, 11 am to 5.30 pm; entry is £4.80.

OKEHAMPTON
• *pop 4200* • ☎ *01837*
The A30, the main route to Cornwall, divides bustling Okehampton from Dartmoor. Some of the wildest walking on the moor lies south of Okehampton, but since it's within the MOD's firing area, you should phone in advance to check that it's open. The part of the park that is south of Belstone is also good, and is outside the MOD zone.

Okehampton has several attractions to delay hikers. The ruined castle (☎ 52844; EH) above the town charges £2/1.50 for admission. The Museum of Dartmoor Life (☎ 52295), West St, has interactive exhibits, displays and photographs about the moor and its inhabitants. It's open daily from June to September, 10 am to 5 pm; phone for other opening times; entry is £1.60/80p.

It's a pleasant three to four-hour walk along part of the Tarka Trail from Okehampton to Sticklepath, where the Finch Foundry (☎ 840046; NT) has three working water wheels. It's open April to October, daily except Tuesday, 11 am to 5 pm; entry is £2.40. The *Two Museums Walk* leaflet has information on this hike. Bus No 629 (daily) links Sticklepath with Okehampton.

The Visitors Centre (☎ 53020) is at 3 West St.

Places to Stay & Eat
Yeritz Caravan & Camping Park (☎ 52281) is three-quarters of a mile east of Okehampton on the B3260. They charge £2.50 for one person and a tent. *Oldditch Caravan & Camping Park* (☎ 840734) is on the edge of Sticklepath, four miles east of Okehampton.

The *Fountain Hotel* (☎ 53900), Fore St, has rooms for £15/30 with shared bathrooms. *Heathfield House* (☎ 54211), Klondyke Rd, does B&B with bathroom from £22 per person.

You can get basic lunches and teas at the *Victorian Pantry* opposite the Visitors Centre.

Getting There & Away
Okehampton is 23 miles west of Exeter, 29 miles north of Plymouth. There are numerous Jennings buses (☎ 01288-352359) to Exeter (one hour, £1.80) and Tavistock, with connections to Plymouth.

The Tarka Trail passes through Okehampton and Sticklepath on a 180-mile route through north Devon.

LYDFORD
• *pop 1800* • ☎ *01822*
This picturesque village on the western edge of the moor is best known for the 1½-mile **Lydford Gorge**. An attractive but strenuous riverside walk leads to the 90-foot-high White Lady waterfall and past a series of bubbling whirlpools, including the Devil's Cauldron. It's owned by the NT and is open daily from April to October, 10 am to 5.30 pm; entry is £3.

There's evidence of both Celtic and Saxon settlements here, and the ruins of a Norman castle. Lydford was the administrative centre for the Stannary towns (see Chagford). Courts trying recalcitrant tin workers were particularly harsh; it was said that perpetrators of offences punishable by death would be hanged in the morning and tried in the afternoon.

Places to Stay & Eat
The 16th-century *Castle Inn* (☎ 820242), which featured in *The Hound of the Baskervilles*, is right beside the castle and 150 yards from Lydford Gorge. It's a good place to stay, as well as an atmospheric place for a pint and an excellent place to eat, offering interesting dishes like burgundy fish stew or Malaysian vegetarian stew. B&B costs £37.50/49 with bathroom attached, £27/40 without.

By the main entrance to the White Lady waterfall, *Manor Farm Tea Rooms* serves cream teas and light lunches.

Lydford House Hotel (☎ 820347), on the edge of the village, offers B&B from £34 per person. There's a riding stable in the grounds (£8 per hour, or two hours from £15).

Getting There & Away

Red Express (DevonBus No 86) crosses Devon from Ilfracombe to Plymouth via Lydford, three times a day on Friday, Saturday, Sunday and Monday. Service No 187 operates between Exeter, Tavistock and

Plymouth five times a day on Sunday in the summer.

TAVISTOCK
- *pop 8700*   • ☎ *01822*

Tavistock's glory days were in the late 19th century, when it was one of the world's largest copper producers. Until the Dissolution, Tavistock Abbey controlled huge areas

---

Letterboxing

If you see a walker acting furtively and slipping an old Tupperware box into a tree stump or under a rock, you may be witnessing someone in the act of letterboxing. This wacky pastime has more than 10,000 addicts and involves a never-ending treasure hunt for several thousand 'letterboxes' hidden all over Dartmoor.

In 1844 the railway line reached Exeter, and Dartmoor started to receive visitors, for whom this was a chance to imagine themselves as great explorers. One guide for these intrepid Victorian gentlefolk was James Perrott of Chagford. In 1854, he had the idea of getting them to leave their calling cards in a glass jar at Cranmere Pool – the most remote part of the moor accessible at that time. It was not until 1938 that the second 'box' was established, and the idea really took off after WWII. Originally, people left their card with a stamped addressed envelope in a box and if someone else found it they would send it back.

There are now about 4000 boxes, each with a visitors' book for you to sign and a stamp and inkpad (if they haven't been stolen) to stamp your record book. Although it's technically illegal to leave a 'letterbox' because in effect you're leaving rubbish on the moor without the landowner's permission, as long as the boxes are unobtrusive, most landowners tolerate them. Now there are even German, French, Belgian and American boxes, not to mention 'mobile boxes', odd characters who wander the moors waiting for a fellow letterboxer to approach them with the words 'Are you a travelling stamp?'!

Once you've collected 100 stamps, you can apply to join the '100 Club' whereupon you'll be sent a clue book with map references for other boxes. Contact Godfrey Swinscow (☎ 015488-21325), Cross Farm, Diptford, Totnes, Devon TQ9 7NU, for more information.

Inevitably, as more people go letterboxing, a downside (other than general nerdiness) has been identified. A code of conduct now prohibits letterboxers from disturbing rocks, vegetation or archaeological sides in their zeal. Even so there have been mutterings about the disturbance caused to nesting golden plovers and ring ouzels... ∎

Cartoon by Peter Morris

of Devon and Cornwall; only slight ruins remain.

On the outskirts of town is a statue of Sir Francis Drake, who was born in Crowndale, just over a mile from Tavistock. Buckland Abbey, the mansion he bought after circumnavigating the globe, can be visited (see the Devon section).

There's a National Park Visitors Centre (☎ 612938) in the Town Hall. Bikes can be rented from Tavistock Cycles (☎ 617630), Paddons Row, opposite Goodes Cafe, Brook St, for £12 a day.

DevonBus No 118 runs every two hours to Okehampton. The Sunday No 187/8 service links Exeter and Tavistock with Gunnislake railway station for Plymouth.

Cornwall

At the country's extreme south-western tip, Cornwall has been described as a beautiful frame around a plain picture. The metaphor is a good one, for the coastline is wonderful – a mix of high, jagged cliffs and pretty inlets sheltering little fishing villages. The interior, however, is much less attractive, even desolate in places.

Cornwall likes to emphasise its separateness from the rest of the country and the county's cultural roots are indeed different, for this was the Celts' last bastion in England after they were driven back by the Saxons. The Cornish language survived until the late 19th century. Efforts are being made to revive it, but Cornish mainly lives on in place names – every other village name seems to be prefixed with *tre-* (meaning settlement).

In the 18th and 19th centuries Cornwall dominated the world's tin and copper markets. Most of the mines have now closed but the industrial past has left scars on the landscape. China clay is still mined around St Austell but tourism has largely replaced the mining industry. Unfortunately though, it offers mainly low-paid, seasonal work and Cornwall is now one of the poorest parts of Britain.

Mebyon Kernow...A Regional Assembly for Cornwall?

The Scottish and Welsh nationalist parties have a reasonably high political profile but away from its Cornish heartland few people would have heard of Mebyon Kernow ('the Sons of Cornwall'), the Cornish nationalist party which plans to fight the next general election with a call for a Cornish regional assembly.

The omens aren't great. In the 1979 and 1983 general elections MK failed to win a single seat. However, it has had more success in local elections and currently holds seven local council seats. Now it hopes to ride the crest of a wave of renewed interest in what it means to be Cornish, with a few people speaking the Cornish language for the first time since the 19th century. ■

In summer, Cornwall's seaside resorts are packed but don't let this put you off, since the holiday-makers tend to congregate around the larger resorts of Bude, Newquay, Falmouth, Penzance and St Ives, and even at the height of the season some of these towns are still worth a visit. Newquay is Britain's surfing capital, and you can't fail to be impressed by beautiful St Ives.

Cornish churches lack the splendour of those in Devon and Somerset and even Truro cathedral is a relative newcomer. However, the names of the churches speak loudly of Cornwall's separateness. Where else would you cross paths with St Non, St Cleer, St Keyne and the many others whose lives are detailed in *The Cornish Saints* by Peter Berresford Ellis?

WALKS & CYCLE ROUTES

The Cornwall Coast Path is the most scenic section of the long-distance South-West Coast Path. The Saints' Way is a 26-mile waymarked trail that runs from Fowey across the centre of the county to Padstow on the northern coast. It was used in the 6th century as a route for Celtic missionaries between Brittany (France) and Wales or

Ireland, saving a long sea trip around Land's End.

Youth hostels are well placed along the coast for stops on a walk or cycle ride around Cornwall. In the north, the 17-mile Camel Trail follows an old railway line from just outside Padstow through Bodmin and along the River Camel. You can rent bikes from Bridge Bike Hire (☎ 01208-813050) in Wadebridge.

GETTING AROUND

For information about buses, there's an efficient helpline (☎ 01872-322142). The main bus operator is Western National (☎ 01209-719988); an Explorer ticket gives a day's travel on its system for £4/2 and there are several other passes.

For rail information, phone ☎ 01872-76244. The main rail route from London terminates in Penzance, but there are branch lines to St Ives, Falmouth, Newquay and Looe. A Cornish Regional Rover ticket costs £32 for seven days, or £23 for three days in seven.

The TICS sell the county council's annual *Public Transport Timetable* (with a map), listing all the air, bus, rail and ferry options in Cornwall.

SOUTH-EAST CORNWALL

Southern Cornwall is very different in character to the wild north and central parts of the county. This is a more gentle area of farms, wooded inlets and pretty fishing villages – some overrun by tourists in the summer but worth visiting at quieter times.

The mild climate favours many plants that thrive nowhere else in Britain and there are several gardens worth visiting, with rhododendron trees growing almost as tall as in their natural Himalayan habitat. TICs stock the free *Gardens of Cornwall* map and guide with full details.

The best gardens in the area are **Heligan** (☎ 01726-844157), four miles south of St Austell, and **Trelissick Garden** (☎ 01872-862090; NT), four miles south of Truro, beside King Harry's Ferry.

Cotehele

Seven miles south-west of Tavistock, on the west bank of the Tamar, the river that forms the boundary between Devon and Cornwall, the Cotehele estate comprises a small stately home with splendid garden, a quay with a museum, and a working water mill.

One of Britain's finest Tudor manor houses, Cotehele has been the Edgcumbe family home for centuries. The hall is particularly impressive, and many rooms are hung with great tapestries; because of their fragility, there's no electric lighting. Visitor numbers are limited, so you may have to wait. Pick up a timed ticket when you arrive.

Cotehele Quay is part of the National Maritime Museum and has a small museum with displays on local boat-building and river trade. The *Shamrock*, the last surviving Tamar barge, is moored nearby.

Cotehele Mill is a 15-minute walk away and can be seen in operation; there's also an adjoining cider press.

The estate (☎ 01579-351346; NT) is open daily except Friday from April to October, 11 am to 5.30 pm; entry is £5.60; £2.80 for the garden and mill only. You can get here by boat from Plymouth with Plymouth Boat Cruises (☎ 01752-822797) in summer – phone for days and times, or by bus from Tavistock to Calstock, one mile from Cotehele, on Western National bus No 99.

East & West Looe

A bridge connects these twin towns, on either side of the river. They make up the county's second largest fishing port, the place to come if you're into shark fishing. Contact the Tackle Shop (☎ 01503-262189) for trips from £25 per day.

East Looe is the main part of the town, with narrow streets and little cottages; the wide, sandy beach is to the east. There are boat trips from the quay to tiny Looe Island, a nature reserve, and to Fowey and Polperro. The TIC (☎ 01503-262072) is in the Guildhall on Fore St.

British Rail trains travel the scenic Looe Valley Line from Liskeard (30 minutes,

£2.10), on the main London-Penzance line, at least five times a day.

Walk An excellent five-mile walk links Looe to the nearby village of Polperro via beaches, cliffs and the old smuggling village of Talland. You should allow around two hours; buses connect the villages every day in summer.

Polperro

Much prettier than Looe, Polperro is an ancient fishing village around a tiny harbour, best approached along the coastal path from Looe or Talland. Unfortunately, it's very popular with day-trippers so you should try to visit in the evening or during low season.

The village is a picturesque jumble of narrow lanes and fishing cottages, and was once heavily involved in pilchard fishing by day and smuggling by night – there's a small smugglers' museum in the centre. There's no TIC.

Fowey

- *pop 2535*   • ☎ *01726*

Pronounced foy, unspoilt Fowey lies on the estuary of the same name. The town has a long maritime history and in the 14th century conducted its own raids on coastal towns in France and Spain. This led to the Spanish launching an attack on Fowey in 1380. The town later prospered by shipping Cornish china clay, which it still does, although yachts mainly fill its harbour today. Although there are no specific sights (apart from a small museum and aquarium), Fowey is a good base for walks around the estuary. The TIC (☎ 833616) is in the post office, 4 Custom House Hill.

Walk Fowey is at the southern end of the Saints' Way (see Walks & Cycle Routes at the start of this section). Ferries operate across the river to Bodinnick (40p a foot passenger, another £1 for a car) to access the four-mile Hall Walk to Polruan. You can catch a ferry from Polruan back to Fowey.

Places to Stay & Eat *Golant Youth Hostel* (☎ 833507), Penquite House, is four miles north of Fowey in Golant. It's open daily from February to August and daily except Friday from September to early November. The nightly charge is £9.10/6.15. Western National's bus No 24 from St Austell to Fowey stops in Castle Dore, 1½ miles from the hostel.

There's B&B at *The Odd Spot* (☎ 832527), 34 Station Rd, from around £16 per person. The delightful *Marina Hotel* (☎ 833315) is right on the waterfront on the Esplanade. Rooms with sea view and attached bath are around £50. It also has an excellent restaurant. Recommended pubs in Fowey include the big *King of Prussia*, on the quay, and the *Ship* and the *Lugger*, back from the water on Lostwithiel St.

When did Cornish Die?

A Celtic language akin to Welsh, Cornish was spoken west of the Tamar until the 19th century. Written evidence indicates that it was still widely spoken at the time of the Reformation, but after a Cornish rising against the English in 1548, the language was suppressed. By the 17th century only a few western people living in the peninsula's remote western reaches still spoke nothing but Cornish.

Towards the end of the 18th century linguistic scholars foresaw the death of Cornish and fanned out round the peninsula in search of people who still spoke it. One such scholar, Daines Barrington, visited Mousehole in 1768 and recorded an elderly woman called Dolly Pentreath abusing him in Cornish for presuming she couldn't speak her own language.

Dolly died in 1769 and has gone down in history as the last native speaker of Cornish. However, Barrington knew of other people who continued to speak it into the 1790s, and an 1891 tombstone in Zennor commemorates one John Davey as 'the last to possess any traditional considerable knowledge of the Cornish language'.

Recently efforts have been made to revive the language. Unfortunately there are now three conflicting varieties of 'Cornish' – Unified, Phonemic and Traditional – and no sign that it can regain its former importance. ■

Getting There & Away There are frequent departures from St Austell (50 minutes, £1.50) on Western National's service No 24, which also passes Par, the closest railway station to Fowey.

Lanhydrock House
Amid parkland above the Fowey River, 2½ miles south-east of Bodmin, this grand country house (☎ 01208-73320; NT) was rebuilt after a fire in 1881. The impressive gallery, with its fine plaster ceiling, survived the fire, but the house is mainly of interest for its portrayal of the 'Upstairs Downstairs' divisions of life in Victorian England. The kitchens are particularly interesting, complete with all the gadgets that were mod cons 100 years ago.

The house is open daily except Monday from April to October, 11 am to 5.30 pm. Entry is £5.90; £3 for the gardens only. The garden is open year-round. Bodmin Parkway railway station is 1¾ miles from the house.

Charlestown
Despite its size, St Austell is not particularly exciting and most people will pass straight through. However, it's worth making a detour south to visit the port of Charlestown, a marvellously picturesque village and harbour built by Charles Rashleigh between 1790 and 1815. On the best days the harbour will be filled with magnificent square-rig ships. However, these are sometimes away taking part in worldwide film assignments. The **Shipwreck and Heritage Centre** (☎ 01792-69897) has exhibits on many aspects of Cornish sea life, with animated models illustrating 19th-century village life. It's open March to October from 10 am to 5 pm (6 pm in high summer) and costs £3.25. The attached *Bosun's Bistro* does teas, coffees and lunches.

If you'd like to stay, *T'Gallants* (☎ 01726-70203) is a fine Georgian house doing B&B for £36 to £38 a double. Alternatively, the *Pier House Hotel* (☎ 01726-67955) right on the quayside charges from £30/50 a single/double.

TRURO
• *pop 18,000* • ☎ *01872*

Truro was once the distribution centre for Cornwall's tin mines and its prosperity dates from this time. Lemon St has some fine Georgian architecture, and the cathedral is worth a visit if you're passing through, even though it only dates back to the late 19th century. Built in neo-Gothic style, it was the first new cathedral to be built in Britain since St Paul's in London.

The TIC (☎ 74555) is in the municipal buildings on Boscawen St, near the covered market. The **Royal Cornwall Museum** (☎ 72205) in River St has exhibits on Cornish history, archaeology and minerology. It's open every day except Sunday from 10 am to 5 pm.

Places to Stay & Eat
There's no hostel but cheap B&Bs near the railway station can be found on Treyew Rd. Try *The Fieldings* (☎ 262783), at No 35, which charges from £14/26. There are more upmarket B&Bs on Tregolls Rd, including *Karenza* (☎ 74497), at No 72, which charges £16 per person.

The *Royal Hotel* (☎ 70345) in Lemon St is a fine Georgian building convenient for the cathedral. Beds cost from £32/50.

In Pannier Market near the TIC, *Fodders* (☎ 74384) does quiches from £3.35, filled jacket potatoes from £1.30 and cakes from 80p. *Upstairs, Downstairs* in pretty Cathedral Lane does sandwiches for £2.95 or tea and cake from £1.30.

Getting There & Away
Truro is 246 miles from London, 26 from St Ives and 18 from Newquay.

National Express (☎ 0990-808080) has buses to numerous destinations, sometimes requiring a change at Plymouth. There are four direct daily services to London (6½ hours, £31.50), St Ives (one hour, £4.65) and Penzance (1½ hours, £4.65). Western National (☎ 01209-719988) covers many local bus routes.

Truro is on the main rail line between London Paddington (4¾ hours, £45) and

Penzance (45 minutes, £5.60). There's a branch line from here to Falmouth (20 minutes, £2.10) and to St Ives (£5.30, change trains at St Erth).

ROSELAND PENINSULA

South-west of Truro, the Roseland peninsula gets its intriguing name not from flowers (although there are plenty of them) but from the Cornish word *ros*, meaning promontory. Villages worth visiting include **Portloe**, a wreckers' hangout on the Coastal Path, **Veryan** which is awash with daffodils in spring, **St Mawes** with a castle (☎ 01326-270526; EH) built by Henry VIII to guard the Fal estuary and **St Just-in-Roseland** which boasts what must be one of the most beautiful churchyards in the country, full of flowers and tumbling down to a creek with boats and wading birds.

SOUTH-WEST CORNWALL

Falmouth

- *pop 18,000* • ☎ *01326*

Falmouth is not Cornwall's most exciting town, but has an interesting castle with a youth hostel in its grounds. There are also several worthwhile boat trips from the pier.

The port came to prominence in the 17th century as the terminal for the Post Office Packet boats which took mail to America. The dockyard is still important for ship repairs and building.

Pendennis Castle (☎ 316594; EH), on the end of the promontory, is Cornwall's largest fort, worth visiting for the displays inside and the superb views from the ramparts. Entry costs £2.20/1.10.

The TIC (☎ 312300) is at 28 Killigrew St, by the bus station in the town centre. From the Prince of Wales pier below, there are ferries to St Mawes. In summer, boat trips travel to Truro and there are excursions to a 500-year-old Smuggler's Cottage upriver. For information, contact Enterprise Boats (☎ 374241) or St Mawes Ferries (☎ 313201).

Places to Stay & Eat *Pendennis Castle Youth Hostel* (☎ 311435) is at the castle, ¾

of a mile from Falmouth railway station. It's open daily from mid-February to September, and daily except Sunday and Monday in October and November; a bed costs £8.25/5.55.

There are cheap B&Bs lining Melvill Rd, convenient for the railway station. *Wayside Lodge* (☎ 317260), 5 Melvill Rd, has a range of rooms and charges from £14 per person.

Bon Ton Roulet (☎ 319290), in pretty cobbled Church St, is a good place for a meal, with pasta from £4.25 and more exotic dishes such as king prawns for £9.15. There's pub food in the *Kings Head*, also on Church St.

Getting There & Away National Express has buses from Falmouth to numerous destinations, including London (6¼ hours, £31.50). There are two-hourly buses to Penzance (one hour, £2.10). For St Ives, you must change at Penzance or Truro; this also applies to Newquay (except on Sunday).

Falmouth is at the end of the branch line from Truro (20 minutes, £2). In summer, you can also travel by boat to Truro (one hour, £2.50); at low tide, when boats can only get as far as Malpas, there's a bus service to Truro.

The Lizard

The Lizard peninsula is Britain's most southerly point and good walking country since much of the coastline is owned by the National Trust. The mild climate guarantees that several rare plant species flourish, and there are stretches of unusual red-green serpentine rock.

In 1901 Marconi transmitted the first transatlantic radio signals from Poldhu. The Lizard is still associated with telecommunications and the centre is dominated by the white satellite dishes of the Goonhilly Earth Station.

Across the north of the Lizard is the beautiful **Helford River**, lined with ancient oak trees and hidden inlets – the perfect smugglers' hideaway. Daphne du Maurier's Frenchman's Cove can be reached on foot from the car park in **Helford** village. Helford is so pretty that its houses are quickly snapped up by the rich and famous: Tim Rice and Pete Townsend have houses here, as does Peter de Savary, the man responsible for the commercialisation of Land's End.

On the northern bank of the river is **Trebah Garden** (☎ 01326-250448), dramatically situated in a steep ravine filled with giant rhododendrons, huge Brazilian rhubarb plants and Monterey pines. It's open daily from 10.30 am to 5 pm; entry is £2.90/1. Near Gweek, at the western end of the river, is the **Cornish Seal Sanctuary** (☎ 01326-221361), which treats injured marine animals and is open to visitors every day from 9 am to 5.30 pm; entry is £4.75/3.25.

Cadgwith is the quintessential Cornish fishing village, with thatched, whitewashed cottages and a small harbour. *Cadgwith Cove Inn* usually serves delicious crab sandwiches. Lizard Point is a 3½-mile walk along the coast path from here. It's about eight miles in the opposite direction to *Coverack Youth Hostel* (☎ 01326-280687) which is open from April to October.

The Lizard's transportation hub is Helston, served by Truronian buses (☎ 01872-73453). Bus No 320 runs from Truro via Helston to the village of Lizard (1¾ hours, £2.30); there are four buses daily, Monday to Saturday. It's just under a mile from the village to Lizard Point.

St Michael's Mount

In 1070 St Michael's Mount was granted to the same monks who built Mont St Michel off Normandy. Though not as dramatically sited as the French model, St Michael's Mount is still impressive. High tide cuts the island off from the mainland, and the priory buildings (☎ 01736-710507; NT) rise loftily above the crags.

St Michael's Mount was an important place of medieval pilgrimage. Since 1659 the St Aubyn family have lived in the ex-priory buildings.

At low tide, you can walk across from Marazion, but at high tide in summer a ferry (☎ 01736-710265) lets you save your legs

for the stiff climb up to the house. There's an introductory video in the building by the harbour, but the best way to appreciate the house is to use the Walkman tour. The house is open from April to October, Monday to Friday, 10.30 am to 5.30 pm; entry is £3.70. Phone for other opening times.

Western National's bus Nos 2 and 2A pass Marazion from Penzance and continue to Falmouth.

PENZANCE
• *pop 19,000* • ☎ *01736*

At the end of the line from London, Penzance is a very pleasant small town in which to linger (and shop) with a curious mix of seaside holiday-makers, locals, artists and New Age hippies. Newlyn, on the western edge of Penzance, was the centre of a community of artists in the late 19th century; some of their handiwork can be inspected in **Newlyn Museum and Art Gallery**, New Rd, which is open Monday to Saturday 10 am to 5 pm.

Orientation & Information

The harbour spreads along Mount's Bay, with the ferry terminal to the east, the train and bus stations just to the north and the main beach to the south. The town itself spreads uphill towards the domed Lloyds Bank building with a statue of local man, Humphrey Davy, inventor of the miner's lamp, in front. Part of the bank now houses craft shops.

The TIC (☎ 62207) is in the car park by the railway and bus stations.

Things to See

Penzance has some attractive Georgian and Regency houses in the older part of town around Chapel St, where you'll also find the exuberant early 19th-century **Egyptian House**. Further down towards the harbour is the **Maritime Museum**.

The **National Lighthouse Centre** (☎ 60077), Wharf Rd, relates the history of the lighthouses that have helped keep ships off this dangerous coast. It's open daily from March to October, 11 am to 5 pm; entry is

PAT YALE

PAT YALE

RICHARD EVERIST

Left: Egyptian house in Penzance, Cornwall
Right: 'Tall Ships' in dock, Charlestown, Cornwall
Bottom: A spot of croquet at Bishop's Palace, Wells, Somerset

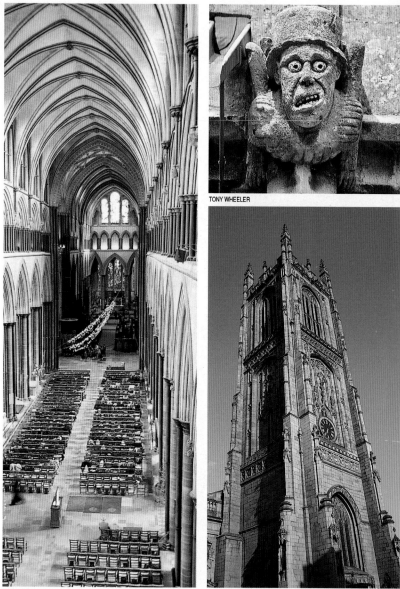

TONY WHEELER

TONY WHEELER

TONY WHEELER

Left: Salisbury Cathedral, Wiltshire
Top Right: Gargoyle, St Peter's, Winchcombe, Gloucestershire
Bottom Right: Derby Cathedral, Derbyshire

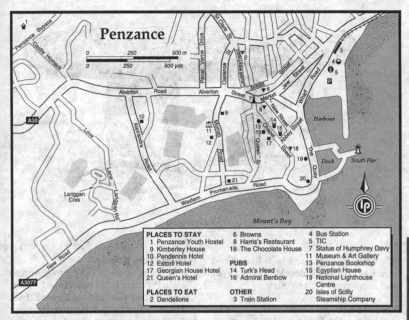

PLACES TO STAY
1 Penzance Youth Hostel
9 Kimberley House
10 Pendennis Hotel
12 Estoril Hotel
17 Georgian House Hotel
21 Queen's Hotel

PLACES TO EAT
2 Dandelions

6 Browns
8 Harris's Restaurant
18 The Chocolate House

PUBS
14 Turk's Head
16 Admiral Benbow

OTHER
3 Train Station

4 Bus Station
5 TIC
7 Statue of Humphrey Davy
11 Museum & Art Gallery
13 Penzance Bookshop
15 Egyptian House
19 National Lighthouse
   Centre
20 Isles of Scilly
   Steamship Company

£2.50/1. Some examples of the Newlyn school of painting are exhibited in the **Penzance Museum & Art Gallery** (☎ 63625), on Morrab Rd. It's open daily except Sunday 10.30 am to 4.30 pm (Saturday 10.30 am to 12.30 pm, free) for £1/50p.

Walks

The 25-mile section of the Coast Path around Land's End to/from St Ives is one of the most scenic parts of the whole route. It can be broken at the youth hostel at St Just (near Land's End), and there are plenty of other cheap farm B&Bs along the way. See Lonely Planet's *Walking in Britain* for more information.

Places to Stay

Penzance Youth Hostel (☎ 62666), Castle Horneck, Alverton, is an 18th-century mansion on the outskirts of town. Walk west through town on the Land's End road (Market Jew St) until you get to a thatched cottage opposite the Pirate Inn, turn right and cross the A30 bypass road until you get to the signposted lane. Bus Nos 5B, 6B or 10B run from the railway station to the Pirate Inn. The nightly charge is £9.10/6.15 for adults/ juniors.

Penzance has lots of B&Bs and hotels, especially along the Promenade, Alexandra Rd and Morrab Rd. *Pendennis Hotel* (☎ 63823), on Alexandra Rd, charges around £13 per person and has some rooms with attached bath.

In Morrab Rd, *Kimberley House* (☎ 62727), at No 10, has nine bathless rooms and charges £15 per person. The more upmarket *Estoril Hotel* (☎ 62468), at No 46, charges from £24 to £26 a head for rooms with a bath.

In the older part of Penzance, the *Georgian House Hotel* (☎ 65664), 20 Chapel St, has beds from £25 with bathroom attached, from £17 without.

The *Queen's Hotel* (☎ 62371), on the

Lanyon Coit, near Penzance

Promenade, is Penzance's best. Rooms cost from £44/76 a single/double, with a £5 per head supplement for a sea view.

Places to Eat

Dandelions, 39A Causeway Head, is a vegetarian café and takeaway which usually has a daily special like vegetable and cheese ratatouille for £2.50. *Browns* in Bread St is similar.

Chapel St has several cheap places to eat as well as two well known pubs. The kitschy *Admiral Benbow* (☎ 63448), on the corner of Chapel St and Abbey St, is crowded with figureheads and other nautical decor. The *Turk's Head* (☎ 63093), also on Chapel St, has a better reputation for its food. The crab soup is excellent value at £1.70 as are crab salads for £7.50. The *Chocolate House*, at 44 Chapel St, also serves delicious food, including crab sandwiches.

For a splurge, head for *Harris's Restaurant* (☎ 64408), at 46 New St, a narrow, cobbled street opposite Lloyds Bank. It's open Monday to Saturday for lunch and dinner and specialises in English cuisine using local ingredients. Try John Dory, a delicious fish found in local waters. Main dishes in the evening are from £9.50 to £12.50.

Getting There & Away

See the fares tables in the Getting Around chapter. Penzance is 281 miles from London, nine from Land's End and eight from St Ives.

There are five buses a day from Penzance to London (five hours, £30 if you book a week ahead) and Heathrow airport, one direct bus a day to Exeter (five hours, £16.50) and three buses a day to Bristol via Truro and Plymouth. To St Ives (20 minutes, £2.50) there are at least two services an hour. There are daily Western National services to Land's End (one hour, £2.20), hourly during the week, less frequently at weekends.

The train offers an enjoyable if pricey way to get to Penzance from London. There are five trains a day from London Paddington (five hours, £30 if you buy your ticket a week in advance). There are frequent trains from Penzance to St Ives between 7 am and 8 pm (20 minutes, £2.60).

For ferries to the Scilly Isles, see that upcoming section.

WEST CORNWALL
Mousehole

Mousehole (pronounced mowsel) is another idyllic fishing village that's well worth seeing outside the height of the season. It was once a pilchard fishing port, and tiny cot-

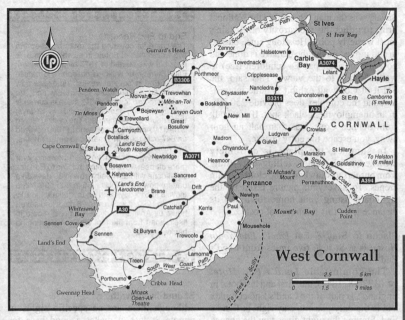

West Cornwall

tages cluster round the edge of the harbour. Like St Ives, the village attracts artists and there are several interesting craft shops.

The excellent *Ship* (☎ 01736-731234) does good seafood and fresh fish; beds cost £20 per person. The *Lobster Pot* (☎ 01736-731251) is more upmarket and charges £23.50 for lobster; rooms overlooking the harbour cost £40 per person. *Annie's Eating House* serves cream tea for £2.75.

Infrequent Sunday to Friday buses run the 20-minute journey to Penzance.

Minack Theatre

Probably the world's most spectacularly located open-air theatre, Minack perches on the edge of the cliffs overlooking the bay. It was built by Rowena Cade, an indomitable local woman who did much of the construction with her own hands, continuing until her death in 1983. The idea came to her when her family provided the local theatre group with an open-air venue for a production of *The*

Tempest. The place was so well suited that annual performances were instituted.

There are performances at the theatre (☎ 01736-810181) from late May to late September; tickets cost £6/2.50. Seats are hard, so bring a cushion or hire one here. There's also an exhibition centre open daily from Easter to October, 9.30 am to 5.30 pm (sometimes closed when there's a performance taking place); tickets are £1.70/50p.

The theatre is below the village of Porthcurno, three miles from Land's End and nine miles from Penzance. Western National's bus No 1 (01209-719988) from Penzance to Land's End stops at Porthcurno, Monday to Saturday.

Land's End

The coast on either side of Land's End is some of the most spectacular in Britain, but the theme park development (☎ 01736-871501) is a Thatcherite monument to the elevation of commerce over all else. Peter de

Savary was the man who outbid the National Trust to inflict this monstrosity on Britain's most westerly point. He's long since cashed in and moved on but the damage is done and now we must all pay £4 (children free) to walk through to the views. That said, the Spirit of Cornwall exhibit is quite interesting, and the complex does provide 250 jobs in an unemployment black spot. If you walk from Sennen Cove, less than half an hour away, you escape the entry charge.

In summer, the place is extremely crowded, with stands selling everything from burgers to strawberry and clotted cream crêpes. To have your picture taken by the signboard listing your home town and its distance from this famous spot costs £5.

Places to Stay & Eat *Land's End Youth Hostel* is at St Just, five miles from Land's End.

The comfortable *Land's End Hotel* (☎ 01736-871844), the 'first and last hotel in England', is part of the Land's End complex and is the only place to stay right at Land's End. Staying the night gives you the chance to stroll around the headland in the evening after the crowds have gone. B&B costs from £32.50 to £55. You can eat here too, in the *Atlantic Restaurant* or in the bar.

Just over a mile north of Land's End, Sennen Cove boasts a beautiful, sandy beach. There are good pub lunches at the *Old Success Inn* (☎ 01736-871232), where you can also stay from £32 per person. *Myrtle Cottage* (☎ 01736-871698) serves cream teas and light lunches. You can stay for £13.50 per person, and there's also a fish & chip shop.

Getting There & Away Land's End is 3147 miles from New York, 886 miles from John o'Groats and nine miles from Penzance. There are buses along the coast to St Ives, from Sunday to Friday; and daily buses to Penzance.

Westward Airways (☎ 01736-788771) offers flights over Land's End in Cessnas; a five-minute hop costs £16/14, 10 minutes is £25/17 and half an hour is £50/40.

End to End Records

The craze for covering the route between the two extremities of Britain in as short a time as possible was started in 1875 by an American, Eliuh Burritt, who walked from John o'Groats to Land's End in 'several weeks'. Times are now measured a little more accurately and the walking record for the 886⅓ miles is currently held by Malcolm Barnish, who did it in 12 days, three hours and 45 minutes. The cycling record is held by Andy Wilkinson, who in 1990 covered an 847-mile route in a mere one day, 21 hours, two minutes and 19 seconds.

Recently, people have been devising ever more off-beat ways of doing the End to End. It's been done with a wheelbarrow in 30 days, in a battery-powered Sinclair C5 in 80 hours, on a tricycle in 5½ days and on rollerskates in 9½ days. In 1990, it was run in 26 days and seven hours by Arvind Pandya – no great record in itself, apart from the fact that he was running backwards! ■

St Just-in-Penwith

Although there are no specific sights in remote St Just, it makes a good base for walks west to Cape Cornwall or south along the Coast Path to Land's End.

In Victorian times St Just was a centre for local tin and copper mining. **Geevor Tin Mine** (☎ 01736-788662), at Pendeen, north of St Just, finally closed in 1990 and is now open to visitors (in sensible shoes) daily from 10.30 am to 5.30 pm.

Alongside the abandoned engine houses from old tin and copper mines, the area between St Just and St Ives is littered with standing stones and other mysterious ancient remains. If prehistory's your thing, it's worth tracking down **Lanyon Quoit**, the **Mên-an-Tol** and **Chysauster Iron Age Village** (☎ 01736-61889; EH).

Land's End Youth Hostel (☎ 01736-788437) is about half a mile south of the village at Letcha Vean. It's closed from January to mid-February; the nightly charge is £5/7.45. You can also stay at the independent *Whitesands Lodge* (☎ 01736-871776) backpackers hostel in Sennen village; dorm beds cost £8. Even cheaper is the *Kelynack*

Bunkbarn (☎ 01736-787633), one mile south of St Just; a bunk bed costs £5 but with only 10 beds, advance booking is wise.

There are several B&Bs in the area. Recommended is the *B&B* at 2 Fore St, beside the *Star* pub, where you pay £15 per person with a hearty breakfast. Head on to Botallack for *Manor Farm* (☎ 01736) 788525), a stone farmhouse offering B&B with big breakfasts for £40 a double.

ST IVES
• *pop 9500*   •   ☎ *01736*

St Ives is an exceptionally beautiful little town. The omnipresent sea, the extraordinary brightness of the light, the harbour, the beautiful sandy beaches, the narrow alleyways, steep slopes and hidden corners are all captivating. Artists have been coming here since Turner visited in 1811, and in 1993 a branch of London's Tate Gallery opened here. These days countless galleries and craft shops line its narrow streets. No one could visit the New Craftsman at 24 Fore St (☎ 795652) and not want to buy something.

Unfortunately in summer St Ives is unbelievably crowded – avoid July and August weekends.

Orientation
The area above St Ives' harbour is very built up and merges into Carbis Bay. Fore St, the main shopping street, is set back from the wharf and crammed with eating places. The north-facing section of the town, overlooking Porthmeor Beach, comprises the Tate Gallery and many guesthouses. The railway station is by Porthminster Beach, with the bus station nearby, up Station Hill.

Information
The TIC (☎ 796297) is in The Guildhall in Street-an-Pol.

In summer, a Park & Ride service operates from the Park Avenue car park above the town. Windansea (☎ 796560), on Fore St, rents wet suits, seven-foot boards (£5 per day) and mountain bikes (£10 per day).

St Ives Tate
Opened in 1993 in a £3 million building designed by Evans and Shalev (architects of the award-winning Truro Law Courts), the Tate is a showcase for the St Ives school of art. The impressive building (☎ 796226) replaced an old gasworks, and has wide central windows framing the surfing scene on Porthmeor Beach below.

Inside, the collection is small and exclusive, with works by Ben Nicholson, Barbara Hepworth, Naum Gabo, Terry Frost and other local artists.

It's open April to September, Monday to Saturday, from 11 am to 7 pm (to 9 pm on Tuesday and Thursday); October to March, Tuesday to Sunday, 11 am to 5 pm. Entry is £3; a £3.50 ticket includes admission to the Barbara Hepworth Museum. The café on the roof is almost as popular as the Gallery itself.

Barbara Hepworth Museum
Barbara Hepworth was one of the 20th century's greatest sculptors. In the 1930s, with Henry Moore and Ben Nicholson (her then husband), she was part of the leading group of artists with an interest in abstraction. While Moore's sculpture remains close to the human form, Hepworth avoided representational works.

She moved to Cornwall in 1939 and lived here from 1949 until her death in a fire in 1975. The beautiful garden forms a perfect backdrop for some of her larger works. The museum (☎ 796226) is on Ayr Lane, across town from the Tate, and is open the same times.

Leach Pottery
Bernard Leach travelled to Japan in 1909 to teach etching, but soon discovered a talent for pottery. When he returned in 1920, his Japanese-inspired work had a profound influence on British ceramics. He died in 1979 but the pottery he established is still used by several craftspeople, including his wife, Janet Leach. The showroom (☎ 796398) is open from 10 am to 5 pm on weekdays. It's along the road to Zennor, on the outskirts of St Ives.

SOUTH-WESTERN ENGLAND

St Ives

0   100   200 m
0   100   200 yards

Porthmeor Surf Beach

St Ives Bay

Harbour

PLACES TO STAY
3 Penclawdd & Gowerton
   Guest Houses
6 The Anchorage
12 Palm Trees Guest House
20 Kandahar
21 Pedn-Olva Hotel
22 Toby Jug Guest House

PLACES TO EAT
2 Pig 'n' Fish
7 Bay View Café
8 Joseph's Restaurant
13 Hoi Tin Chinese
   Restaurant
16 Hunters

PUBS
4 The Sloop Inn
5 The Grey Mullet

OTHER
1 Tate Gallery St Ives
9 Windansea
10 New Craftsman
11 Barbara Hepworth
   Museum
14 Lifeboat Station
15 St Andrew's Church
17 Post Office
18 TIC
19 Bus Station
23 Railway Station

Porthminster Beach

SOUTH-WESTERN ENGLAND

Beaches

There are several excellent, clean beaches in the area. **Porthmeor** is the surfing beach to the north of the town, below the Tate. Just east is the tiny, sandy cove of **Porthgwidden**, with a car park nearby.

There are sandy areas in the sheltered St Ives Harbour, but most families head south to **Porthminster**, which has half a mile of sand and a convenient car park. **Carbis Bay**, to the south-west, is also good for children. **Porthkidney Sands**, the next beach along, is only safe for swimming between the flags. It's dangerous to swim in the Hayle estuary.

Walks

There's a superb four-hour walk along the coast path from St Ives to the little village of Zennor, where DH Lawrence wrote part of *Women in Love*. The interesting church has a mermaid carved on one of its bench ends, the *Tinners Arms* serves good food and cream teas, and there's a small museum. Buses link St Ives with Zennor every day except Saturday.

Places to Stay

The nearest hostel is in Penzance. There's no camping ground by the beach, but *Ayr*

Holiday Park (☎ 795855) is only half a mile above the town in Higher Ayr. It costs from £8.50 for a tent and car.

The main road into St Ives from Penzance, above Carbis Bay, is lined with B&Bs in the £14 to £16 bracket, but the closer you are to the town centre the better.

The *Toby Jug Guest House* (☎ 794250), convenient for the bus station at 1 Park Ave, is good value with B&B from £13 per person. There are 10 rooms, each with a toby jug as a teapot.

Across the other side of town, *Palm Trees Guest House* (☎ 796109), 2 Clodgy View, is a friendly place above Porthmeor Beach. There are six rooms and they charge from £15 per person. There are several similar places in this area.

On Sea View Place, in an excellent location right by the sea, there's *Penclawdd* (☎ 796869), at No 1, charging £13 to £16 per person; and *Gowerton* (☎ 796805), at No 6, for around £14 per person.

There's B&B at the *Sloop Inn* (☎ 796584), by the harbour, although this location could be noisy in summer. B&B costs from £20.

The Grey Mullet (☎ 796635), 2 Bunkers Hill, is an excellent guesthouse in the old part of town, close to the harbour. Rooms cost from £17 to £21 per person; some have bath attached. Opposite is an attractive cottage called the *Anchorage* (☎ 797135) with B&B prices slightly lower than at the Grey Mullet.

Kandahar (☎ 796183), 11 The Warren, is right on the rocks by the water. It charges £24 per person for a room with attached bath, £16 per person without. It's ideally located for the bus and railway stations. Nearby is the more upmarket *Pedn-Olva Hotel* (☎ 0796222), Porthminster Beach, which has a similar waterside location. Beds cost from £40 and there's a small swimming pool and sun deck.

To the south, overlooking Porthminster Beach, is the comfortable *Longships Hotel* (☎ 798180), on Talland Rd where rooms with sea views and bathrooms cost from £17 to £25 per person.

Places to Eat

Best of the pubs is the 14th-century *Sloop Inn* next to the harbour where the bar is hung with paintings by local artists. Its seafood is very popular; fresh fish (cod, sole, plaice) costs £6 to £8. There are several other places to eat along the Wharf, including *Hoi Tin Chinese Restaurant* (☎ 797814) and the *Bay View Café*.

Hunters (☎ 797074), on St Andrews St, is a seafood and game restaurant; you can bring your own bottle here, which keeps prices down. Nearby is *Wilbur's Café* (☎ 796663) which features US cooking.

The top place to eat is the *Pig'n'Fish* (☎ 794204), Norway Lane, which is renowned for its seafood. To justify the 'Pig' part of the name, you get pork scratchings (grilled pig skin – much tastier than it sounds) to nibble while you look at the menu. Main dishes range from about £11 to £15, with turbot, monkfish, bass, red mullet and mussels usually featuring on the menu. Prior notice needs to be given for vegetarian meals.

Getting There & Away

See the fares tables in the Getting Around chapter. St Ives is 277 miles from London and eight from Penzance. National Express (☎ 0990-808080) has three buses a day to London (7½ hours, £32). There are also buses to Newquay (1¼ hours, £3.85), Truro (one hour, £2.85) and Plymouth (three hours, £5.25). For Exeter, you must change at Plymouth.

There's a bus service from St Ives to Land's End via Zennor, St Just-in-Penwith and Sennen Cove every day in summer (just once a day on Saturday). There are three buses a day, and an Explorer ticket allowing a day's travel on the route is £4. In winter, you must go via Penzance.

St Ives is easily accessible by train from Penzance and London via St Erth.

NEWQUAY
* *pop 14,000*   *   ☎ *01637*

If you're keen on surfing you'll love Newquay, Britain's surfing capital. If not your best bet is to pass through as quickly as possible.

Little that predates the 19th-century survives in Newquay, but on the cliff north of Towan Beach stands the whitewashed **Huer's House**, where a watch was kept for approaching pilchard shoals. Every Cornish fishing village had a watchtower like this and the netting operation was directed by the huer. Until they were fished out early in this century, these shoals were enormous – one St Ives catch of 1868 netted a record 16½ million fish.

Orientation & Information

The TIC (☎ 871345) is on Marcus Hill near the bus station in the town centre.

The **Sea Life Centre** (☎ 872822) on Towan Promenade is open daily from 10 am to 5 pm. Admission costs £4.50/2.95.

The surf shops on Fore St and Cliff Rd all hire fibreglass boards and wet suits for £5 to £6 each per day. If you don't know how to surf, contact Offshore Surfing (☎ 877083), on Tolcarne Beach, for an all-inclusive, half-

day beginner's lesson (£18). The Sunset Surf Shop (☎ 877624) at 106 Fore St also runs in-shop 'soft' tuition.

Beaches

Fistral Beach, to the west of the town round Towan Head, is the most famous British surfing beach. There are fast hollow waves, particularly at low tide, and good tubing sections when there's a south-easterly wind. This is where the World Surfing Championships take place in the last week of July and first week of August.

Watergate Bay is a two-mile-long sandy beach on the east side of Newquay Bay. At low tide it's a good place to learn to surf. A mile south of Newquay, **Crantock** is a small north-west-facing sheltered beach, where the waves are best at mid to high tide.

Places to Stay

Hostels Several independent hostels cater

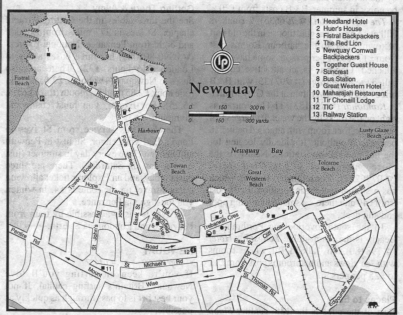

1 Headland Hotel
2 Huer's House
3 Fistral Backpackers
4 The Red Lion
5 Newquay Cornwall Backpackers
6 Together Guest House
7 Suncrest
8 Bus Station
9 Great Western Hotel
10 Maharajah Restaurant
11 Tir Chonaill Lodge
12 TIC
13 Railway Station

Newquay

for surfers in particular. The nearest to Fistral Beach is *Fistral Backpackers* (☎ 873146) at 18 Headland Rd, a well-equipped place with a clean kitchen, satellite TV and computer games, together with a wide range of surf maps and videos. Beds in 6-bed dorms cost £5. *Newquay Cornwall Backpackers* (☎ 874668), in an excellent central position overlooking Towan Beach at Beachfield Ave, has dorm beds for £6.50 a night or £39 per week.

Camping There are several large caravan parks/camping grounds in the area. *Trenance Caravan & Chalet Park* (☎ 873447), at the southern end of Edgcumbe Ave, has 50 spaces for tents. It charges £4.75 per person.

B&Bs & Hotels Newquay is so crammed with cheap B&Bs that it makes little sense to recommend some above others. Bear in mind that you still need to book ahead in July and August. Prices vary greatly according to season, particularly at the larger hotels. Trebarwith Crescent, Mount Wise, Dane Rd, Tower Rd, Cliff Rd and Narrowcliffe are all packed with places to stay and the TIC has full details.

The eyesore *Headland Hotel* (☎ 872211) is the best located of Newquay's large hotels. As the name suggests, it's out on the headland, above Fistral Beach. Rooms cost from £30 to £50 per person. The imposing *Great Western Hotel* (☎ 872010), across from the railway station, charges £25.50 per person in rooms with bath.

Places to Eat

There are numerous greasy spoons, tearooms, burger bars and pubs, but nothing for the gastronome. For tea and cakes, try *The Old Print House* (☎ 0871326), just off Bank St.

The top Indian place is *Maharajah* (☎ 877377), 39 Cliff Rd, near the Great Western Hotel. A chicken curry costs £3.95.

At the junction of Fore St, Tower Rd and Beacon Rd, near the backpacker places, a couple of cafés do breakfasts to suit surfing appetites for around £3.

The larger hotels have three-course set dinners. The *Headland Hotel* (see Places to Stay) charges £14.95.

Entertainment

At the same junction of Fore St, Tower Rd and Beacon Rd the *Red Lion* pub is a surfers' hangout. Head there to find out what's going on.

Getting There & Away

Newquay is 252 miles from London, 32 from St Ives. National Express provides connections through Plymouth to most places in Britain and has two direct buses daily to London (six hours, £30.50). There are four buses to Plymouth (1¼ hours, £4.35) and one direct service to Exeter.

There are four trains a day between Par and Newquay on the main London-Penzance line.

NORTH CORNWALL

Some of Britain's best beaches face the Atlantic along the North Cornwall coast but getting around this area without your own transport can be tricky.

From Newquay, the coastal road passes **Bedruthan Steps**, a series of rock stacks along a sandy beach. There's a NT teashop here. At **Constantine Bay**, there's a wide, sandy beach, good for surfing.

Padstow

- *pop 2300*   •   ☎ *01841*

On the Camel River estuary, Padstow is an attractive fishing village best known for its Hobby Horse, really a man dressed up in an enormous tent-like dress and mask. As he dances through the streets, he is taunted by the local women; if he catches one, he pulls her under the tent, and pinches her – to ensure future motherhood, of course.

The poet John Betjeman is buried at St Enodoc Church, across the water and north of Rock. Above the village is Prideaux Place (☎ 532411), built in 1592 by the Prideaux-Brune family. It's open from Easter to September, Sunday to Thursday, 1.30 to 5 pm; entry is £4/1.

The TIC (☎ 533449) is on the North Quay.

Padstow has one restaurant worth a detour. The *Seafood Restaurant* (☎ 532485) on the harbourfront serves, inevitably, all manner of fish dishes; expect to pay at least £25 a head. When it's closed on Sunday you can eat bistro-style but with less choice at its sister hotel at 4 New St, *St Petroc's House* (same telephone number).

Tintagel & Boscastle
* *pop 1750* * *☎ 01840*

Tintagel has sold its soul to the great god Tourist for whom innumerable car parks and tacky tea shops have been provided. That said, even the summer crowds and the grossly commercialised village can't entirely destroy the surf-battered grandeur of Tintagel Head. The scanty ruins are not King Arthur's castle, since they mainly date from the 13th century; but there's no reason to disbelieve the theory that he was born here in the late 5th century. The ruins (☎ 770328; EH) are open from April to October daily from 10 am to 6 pm (4 pm in winter); entry costs £2.20/1.70. There are exhilarating walks along the cliffs.

Back in the village, **Tintagel Old Post Office** (☎ 770024; NT) is a higgledy-piggledy 14th-century house turned post office. It's open from April to October, daily from 11 am to 5.30 pm; entry is £2/1.50.

A couple of miles along the coast, Boscastle can also get overcrowded but is still absurdly picturesque. In particular, hunt out Minster church in a wonderful wooded valley. There's a well-stocked visitors centre in the car park (☎ 250010).

Places to Stay *Tintagel Youth Hostel* (☎ 770334) is in a spectacular setting on the Coast Path, ¾ of a mile west of the village. It's open daily except Wednesday from April to mid-May, daily from mid-May to September; beds cost £7.45/5. Alternatively, *Boscastle Youth Hostel* (☎ 250287) is open from mid-March to October (closed Monday and Tuesday from mid-March to mid-May, and in October) for the same price. It's perfectly sited right on the edge of the harbour.

The *Cornishman Inn* (☎ 770238) in the centre of Tintagel charges from £20 to £25 a head in rooms with bath. With a car, you might prefer to follow the signs to Trebarwith to stay in the *Old Millfloor* (☎ 770234), a B&B in a delightful setting charging from £36. Or there's *Sunnyside* (☎ 250453) right beside Boscastle harbour, with beds from £14 without bath.

Getting There & Away Western National's Nos 52/B run from Bodmin Parkway, and the X4 comes from Bude. There are occasional buses from Plymouth.

Bodmin Moor
Cornwall's 'roof' is a high heath pockmarked with bogs and with giant tors like those on Dartmoor rising above the wild landscape – Brown Willy (1375 feet) and Rough Tor (1311 feet) are the highest.

The A30 cuts across the centre of the moor from **Launceston**, which has a castle perched above it like the cherry on a cake (☎ 01566-772365; EH) and a granite church completely covered in carvings. At **Bolventor** is *Jamaica Inn* (☎ 01566-86250), made famous by Daphne du Maurier's novel of the same name. Stop for a drink on a misty winter's night and the place still feels atmospheric. In summer, it's full of day-trippers queuing to view the author's desk and the bizarre Mr Potter's Museum of Curiosity, a collection of stuffed kittens and rabbits in the best of Victorian bad taste.

Bolventor is a good base for walks on Bodmin. About a mile to the south is **Dozmary Pool**, said to have been where Arthur's sword, Excalibur, was thrown after his death. It's a four-mile walk north of Jamaica Inn to Brown Willy.

Bude
* *pop 2700* * *☎ 01288*

Five miles from Devon, Bude is another resort that attracts both families and surfers. Crooklets Beach is the main surfing area, just north of the town. Nearby Sandymouth is good for beginners, and Duckpool is also

---

The Daphne du Maurier Trail

Daphne du Maurier, author of a number of best-selling thriller romances set in Cornwall, has probably done more to publicise the county than anyone else. For many years she lived on the Fowey estuary, originally in Ferryside (a house in Bodinnick) and later in Menabilly.

Her first big success was *Jamaica Inn*, an entertaining tale of a smuggling ring based at the famous inn. The idea for the story is said to have come when she and a friend got lost in the mists of Bodmin Moor, eventually stumbling upon the inn. The local vicar entertained them with gripping yarns of Cornish smugglers. Jamaica Inn has a small display about the author. The vicar was from nearby Altarnun, where the church receives a steady flow of du Maurier fans.

The author's next book was *Rebecca*, written in 1938. Manderley, the house in the book, was based on Menabilly, where the author lived – it's not open to the public. *Frenchman's Creek* was set around the inlet of the same name on the Helford River. Lanhydrock House and Falmouth's Pendennis Castle both feature in *The King's General*.

The West Country Tourist Board produce a useful *Daphne du Maurier in Cornwall* leaflet. ■

---

popular. Summerleaze Beach, in the centre of Bude, is a family beach.

The Bude Visitors Centre (☎ 354240) on the Crescent has lists of B&Bs.

Bude is well served by buses, including a daily National Express coach to London (6½ hours, £30).

ISLES OF SCILLY
- *pop 2000*   • ☎ *01729*

Twenty-eight miles south-west of Land's End, the Scilly Isles comprise a group of 140 rocky islands with an extremely mild climate caused by the warm Gulf Stream that allows plants and trees that grow nowhere else in Britain to flourish. One of the main objectives for visitors is the subtropical garden at Tresco Abbey. Growing flowers for the mainland is an important industry.

St Mary's, Tresco, St Martin's, St Agnes and Bryher are inhabited. St Mary's is the largest (three miles by two) and has most of the population. Most of the islands have white, sandy beaches and gin-clear water that attracts divers. The pace of life is slow and gentle – forget any idea of a wild nightlife.

Information
The Isles of Scilly Tourist Board (☎ 01720-422536) is at Porthcressa Bank, on St Mary's.

Accommodation should be booked in advance, particularly in summer, and tends to be more expensive than on the mainland. All the islands except Tresco have camping grounds which charge from £2.50 to £4 per person. The TIC will send you an accommodation list.

Every Friday evening, and on some Wednesdays in summer, you can watch gig racing – traditional six-oar boats (some over 100 years old) originally used to race out to wrecked ships.

St Mary's
The capital is Hugh Town, on an isthmus that separates the Garrison area from the main part of the town, where boats from the mainland dock. The TIC and most of the places to stay are here.

There are several enjoyable walks on St Mary's. The hour-long Garrison Walk offers good views of the other islands and you pass Star Castle, once an Elizabethan fort, now a hotel. There's a two-hour walk to Peninnis headland, where numerous ships have been wrecked, and a three-hour Telegraph Walk via assorted ancient historical sites and burial chambers. The TIC has details.

The *camping ground* (☎ 422670) is at Garrison Farm. Cheaper B&Bs in Hugh Town include *Lyonnesse Guest House* (☎ 422458), which costs around £20, and *The Wheelhouse* (☎ 422719) from £22.50.

The *Atlantic Hotel* (☎ 422417) is right by

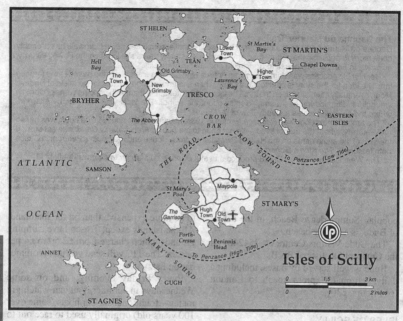

Isles of Scilly

the water in Hugh Town, and has a good restaurant. It costs from £47.50 per person for B&B and dinner.

The top place to stay is the *Star Castle Hotel* (☎ 422317). Luxuries include a heated swimming pool and four-poster beds. Rooms are from £40 per person for B&B and dinner.

Tresco

The second largest island is best known for the Abbey Garden, laid out in 1834 on the site of a 10th-century Benedictine abbey. There are more than 5000 subtropical plants and a display of figureheads from the many ships that have been wrecked off these islands.

There's no camping ground or budget accommodation on the island, just the *New Inn* (☎ 422844), which charges £48 to £75 per person including dinner, and the upmarket *Island Hotel* (☎ 422883), from £70 per person.

Bryher

The smallest of the inhabited islands is wild and rugged; Hell Bay in an Atlantic gale is a powerful sight. There are good views over the islands from the top of Watch Hill. From the quay, occasional boats cross to deserted Samson Island.

There's a *camping ground* (☎ 422886) in Jenford, and very comfortable accommodation at the *Hell Bay Hotel* (☎ 422947) for around £65 per person including dinner.

St Martin's

Known for its beautiful beaches, St Martin's is the most northerly island. There's cliff scenery along the north shore, a good walk on Chapel Downs up to the Day Mark and long stretches of sand on both north and south coasts.

The *camping ground* (☎ 422888) is near Lawrence's Bay. B&Bs include *Polreath* (☎ 422046), which has rooms from £18.50 to £22 per person. The only hotel is *St*

Martin's (☎ 422092) on Tean Sound with twins from £80.

St Agnes
A disused lighthouse overlooks the bulb fields of Britain's most southerly community. To the west are striking granite outcrops, including one that resembles Queen Victoria. At low tide, you can walk across the sand to the neighbouring island of Gugh.

The *camping ground* (☎ 422360) is near the beach at Troy Town Farm. There's B&B at *Covean Cottage* (☎ 422620) for £20 to £22 per person.

Getting There & Away
Air Isles of Scilly Skybus (☎ 0345-105555) is the islands' airline. It has frequent flights in summer (daily except Sunday) between Land's End aerodrome and St Mary's. The flight takes 15 minutes and for an adult/child costs £42.50/21.75 one way (£34/17 standby), £53/26.50 for a day return and £50/25 for a short break of one to three nights. There's a free car park at the Land's End aerodrome, or a free shuttle bus from Penzance railway station, which should be booked in advance. There are also flights from Exeter (Monday to Saturday), Newquay (Tuesday and Thursday), Plymouth (Monday, Wednesday and Friday) and Bristol (Monday, Tuesday, Thursday and Friday).

British International Helicopters (☎ 01736-63871) has daily flights, Monday to Saturday, year-round, from Penzance heliport. The journey takes 20 minutes and costs £44/22 in each direction, £57/28.50 for a day return, £67/33.50 for a five-day excursion and £50/25 for a late saver return for a one to three-night stay (bookable only one day in advance). There are also flights to Tresco (for the gardens), Monday to Saturday, from Penzance; prices are the same as those for St Mary's. It costs £2 per day to leave your car at the heliport and there's a bus link to Penzance railway station.

Boat From April to October, the Isles of Scilly Steamship Company (☎ 0345-105555) has one departure a day, Monday to Friday, and occasional sailings at weekends, between Penzance and St Mary's. The trip takes 2¾ hours and costs £65/32.50 in high season for an adult/child return ticket. One to three-night breaks cost £44/22.50 return. A day trip costs £30/15 and allows you 4½ hours ashore. In Penzance, the reservations office is by the south pier. Students with a student card qualify for the child fare.

Getting Around
There are regular departures to the other four islands from St Mary's harbour. A return trip to any island costs £3.80. Daily boat trips to see the seals and sea birds cost £5.

On St Mary's, you can hire bikes from Buccabu Hire (☎ 422289), near the TIC, from £3.50 per day. There's also an infrequent circular bus service, and tours of St Mary's by minibus.

SOUTH-WESTERN ENGLAND

Southern Midlands

Locator & Map Index

Birmingham p454
Coventry p442
Stratford-upon-Avon p448
Warwick p445
Cheltenham p421
Gloucester p429
Oxford p401
The Cotswolds p415
LONDON

Sometimes known as the Heart of England, this patchwork of small counties contains some of the country's best and worst. The worst can be found in a wide corridor either side of the M1 motorway. But although Hertfordshire, Bedfordshire and Buckinghamshire are a graveyard for modern town planning (see, for example, Milton Keynes), there are still occasional gems – Hatfield House is one instance.

London's uninspiring suburban sprawl continues to advance into the Chilterns, and Birmingham and Coventry – never famous for their beauty – struggled to weather WWII and the industrial decline of the 1970s and 80s.

To the west, however, it's a different story. Despite the usual modern suburban problems, Oxford is still extremely beautiful. The south-west Chilterns remain largely unspoilt and accessible to walkers of the Ridgeway, the 85-mile trail that starts in Avebury and runs north-east to Ivinghoe Beacon, near Aylesbury.

The Cotswolds embody the popular image of the English countryside. The prettiness can be forced, and most villages are no strangers to mass tourism, but there will be moments when you'll be transfixed by a combination of golden stone, flower-draped cottages, church spires, towering chestnuts and oaks, rolling hills and green fields that seems almost too good to be true.

The Cotswolds Way follows the western escarpment overlooking the Bristol Channel for 100 miles from Chipping Campden to Bath, but it's quite feasible to tackle a smaller section.

To the west lies the Bristol Channel and the wide Severn Valley, a natural border with Hereford & Worcester county and the region known as the Welsh Marches. Hereford & Worcester has rich, agricultural country with orchards and market gardens. The Wye Valley (see also the Southern Wales chapter) is a famous beauty spot, popularised by the 18th-century Romantic poets.

The southern Midlands boast some of England's most popular tourist sites including Blenheim Palace, Warwick Castle, Stratford-upon-Avon and Oxford.

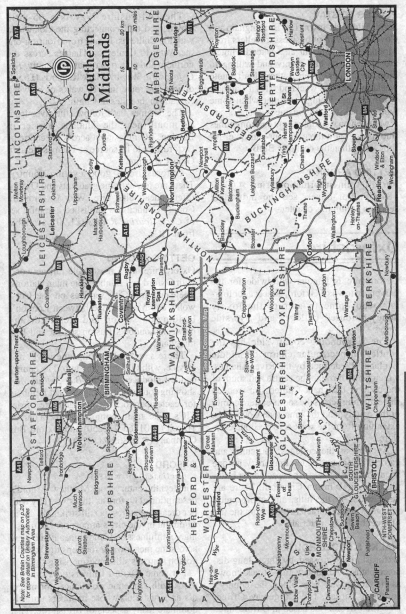

Southern Midlands

PLACES TO STAY

South Midlands' towns like Birmingham and Coventry are full of business travellers from Monday to Friday but at weekends, hotels are likely to be half-empty and willing to drop their rates. Even if they don't quote weekday rates and weekend rates it's always worth asking. In high summer when some factories close and business visitors are fewer even on weekdays, you can sometimes find a room at a three or four-star hotel for little more than the cost of a B&B.

GETTING AROUND

For all train information, ring ☎ 0345-484950. For buses, see the individual sections within this chapter.

Oxfordshire

Oxfordshire is famous worldwide for the university town of Oxford, a mecca for tourists who come to admire the lovely honey-coloured colleges and riverside views.

The surrounding countryside has the gentle, unspectacular charm of middle England. It's defined by the River Thames, which flows through the centre and south of the county; the chalk Chilterns, a wooded ridge running across the south-eastern corner of the county; and the limestone Cotswolds, extending from the west across Gloucestershire.

As well as the colleges, museums and gardens of Britain's oldest university, no-one should miss Blenheim, the spectacular birthplace of Sir Winston Churchill. There are good walks in the hills, and many pretty villages whose character stems from the use of local building materials.

WALKS & CYCLE ROUTES

Oxfordshire is crossed by three long-distance paths. The ancient ridge track known as the Ridgeway runs along the county's southern border. The Ridgeway Officer (☎ 01865-810224) is based in Oxfordshire.

The Oxfordshire Way is a 65-mile waymarked trail connecting the Cotswolds with the Chilterns. It runs from Bourton-on-the-Water to Henley-on-Thames across the northern and eastern parts of the county. *The Oxfordshire Way* by Mark Richards (£6.99) divides the route into 16 walks of between two and eight miles in length.

The Thames Path follows the river from its mouth near the Thames Barrier in London, 175 miles west across the centre of Oxfordshire to its source at Thames Head in Gloucestershire.

Oxfordshire is good cycling country. There are few extreme gradients and Oxford offers cheap bike hire. West Oxfordshire County Council has published a helpful set of *Cycle Touring Routes* (£1.90), available from TICs.

GETTING AROUND

Oxfordshire has a reasonable rail network, with Oxford and Banbury the main stations. There are InterCity services on the Cotswolds and Malvern line between London's Paddington station and Hereford, and between London's Euston station and Birmingham.

There's a fairly comprehensive bus service, with Oxford as the hub. The county council produces a useful *Bus & Rail Map* showing routes and giving contact numbers for each operator; it's available free from TICs. The main companies are Thames Transit (☎ 01865-772250) and Oxford Bus Company (☎ 01865-711312).

OXFORD

• *pop 115,000*   •   ☎ *01865*

Nineteenth-century poet Matthew Arnold's description of Oxford as 'that sweet city with her dreaming spires' is still strikingly apt in summing up the city's atmosphere of questing youthfulness and erudition; and the view across the meadows or rooftops to Oxford's golden spires is still a mesmerising sight.

For some, Oxford University is synonymous with academic excellence, for others it's an elitist club whose members unfairly dominate many aspects of British life. That

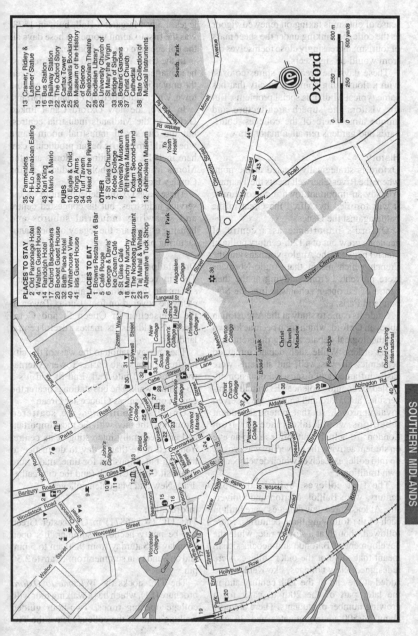

PLACES TO STAY
2 Old Parsonage Hotel
4 Walton Guest House
14 Randolph Hotel
17 Oxford Backpackers House
20 Becket Guest House
32 Bath Place Hotel
40 Whitehouse View
41 Isis Guest House

PLACES TO EAT
1 Browns Restaurant & Bar
6 Café Rouge
9 George & Davis' Ice Cream Café
9 St Giles Café
18 Munchy Munchy
21 The Nosebag Restaurant
23 Taj Mahal & Whites
31 Alternative Tuck Shop

35 Parmentiers
42 Hi-Lo Jamaican Eating House
43 Karl King
44 Mario & Mario

PUBS
10 Eagle & Child
34 Kings Arms
34 Turf Tavern
39 Head of the River

OTHER
3 St Giles Church
8 Keble College
8 University Museum & Pitt Rivers Museum
11 Bodtam Second-hand Bookshop
12 Ashmolean Museum
13 Cramer, Ridley & Latimer Statue
15 TIC
16 Bus Station
19 Railway Station
22 The Oxford Story
24 Carfax Tower
25 Blackwell's Bookshop
26 Museum of the History of Science
27 Sheldonian Theatre
28 Bodleian Library
29 University Church of St Mary the Virgin
33 Bridge of Sighs
36 Botanic Gardens
37 Christ Church Cathedral
38 Bate Collection of Musical Instruments

Oxford

SOUTHERN MIDLANDS

sense of elitism is taking on renewed vigour as the colleges, sinking under the sheer mass of tourism, increasingly close themselves off from would-be sightseers.

These days the dreaming spires co-exist with a flourishing commercial city that has some typical Midlands social problems. But for visitors the superb architecture and unique atmosphere of the colleges, court-yards and gardens remain a major draw.

History
Oxford is strategically located at the point where the River Cherwell meets the Thames. Already an important town in Saxon times, it was fortified by Alfred the Great in the battle against the Danes.

Oxford's importance as a centre of academe grew out of a 12th-century political quarrel between the Anglo-Normans and the French which meant that Anglo-Normans were prevented from studying at the then centre of European scholastic life, the Sorbonne in Paris.

Students came to study at the Augustinian abbey in Oxford, which soon became known for theological debate among different religious orders. While such debate remained academic, all was well, but students were easily inflamed and discussion occasionally spilled over into violence. Eventually universities at Oxford and Cambridge received royal approval, so that potential student rebellions would take place far from London. To help the authorities keep an eye on student activity, the university was broken up into colleges, each of which developed its own traditions.

The first colleges, built in the 13th century, were Balliol, Merton and University. At least three new colleges were built in each of the following three centuries. More followed, though at a slower rate, while the development of Baroque and neoclassicism meant that some of the older colleges were redesigned. New colleges, like Keble, were added at the end of the 19th century and in the later part of the 20th to cater for a growing number of students. There are now about 14,500 undergraduates and 36 colleges. Lady Margaret's Hall, built in 1878, was the first to admit women. These days all the colleges are open to both sexes.

In the Civil War, Oxford was the royalist headquarters, and the city was split between the university, on the side of the king, and the town, which supported the Parliamentarians.

In 1790, the new Oxford Canal linked Oxford to the Midlands industrial centres, but the city's real industrial boom came when William Morris began producing cars here in 1912. The Bullnose Morris and the Morris Minor were both produced in the Cowley factories.

These days Oxford depends more on the service industries, but its congested centre and sprawling industrial suburbs and housing estates are the legacy of the manu-facturing past.

Orientation
The city centre is surrounded by rivers and streams to the south, east and west and can easily be covered on foot. Carfax Tower, at the intersection of Queen St and Corn-market/St Aldates Sts, makes a useful central landmark.

The railway station to the west of the city has frequent buses to Carfax Tower. Alternatively, turn left into Park End St and it's a 15-minute walk. The bus station is nearer the centre, on greenless Gloucester Green.

University buildings are scattered throughout the city, with the most important and architecturally interesting at its centre. You need more than a day to do justice to them all but, if pushed for time, make sure you visit Christ Church (and the city cathedral), New and Magdalen colleges.

Information
The TIC (☎ 726871) in Gloucester Green can be pretty hectic in summer. It's open Monday to Saturday from 9.30 am to 5 pm, and on Sunday in summer from 10 am to 3.30 pm.

The TIC stocks the *Welcome to Oxford* brochure (£1), which has a walking tour with college opening times. Two-hour guided walking tours of the colleges leave the TIC at 10.30 and 11 am and 1 and 2 pm; they cost £4/2.50.

College opening hours are increasingly restrictive; some don't open at all, some only accept guided groups, many close in the morning and others charge for admission.

Carfax Tower

In the heart of the city at the top of the street known as St Aldates, Carfax Tower, with its quarterjacks, is all that remains of medieval St Martin's Church. There's a fine view from the top, good for orientating yourself. It's open daily from March to October; admission is £1.20/60p.

Museum of Oxford

This museum (☎ 815559) introduces the city's history. It's open Monday to Saturday, 10 am to 4 pm (5 pm on Saturday); entry is free, but there's a good tour for £1.50.

Pembroke College

Pembroke College (☎ 276444) in St Aldates was founded in 1624. Sir Roger Bannister, the man who first ran a mile in under four minutes, is a past Master, and Dr Samuel Johnson a former student.

Christ Church

Opposite Pembroke is the grandest of all Oxford colleges, Christ Church (☎ 276150), founded in 1525 by Cardinal Wolsey, and refounded by Henry VIII in 1546. The roll call of illustrious former students includes John Wesley, William Penn, W H Auden and Lewis Carroll.

The main entrance is below Tom Tower, so called because it was dedicated to St Thomas of Canterbury. The upper part of the tower, designed by Christopher Wren in 1682, rests on a Tudor base. The tower bell, Great Tom, chimes 101 times each evening at 9.05 pm, the time when the original 101 students were called in. Since Oxford is five minutes west of Greenwich, this is actually 9 pm Oxford time. For visitors, entry into the college is further down St Aldates, via the Memorial Gardens. It's open daily from 10 to 11.30 am and 2 to 4 pm (2 to 5 pm Sunday).

The Great Hall is closed between noon and 2 pm, the cathedral closes at 4.45 pm and the Chapter House at 5 pm. There's an admission charge of £3/2.

The cloisters lead to **Christ Church Cathedral**, England's smallest cathedral, which has been the city's Anglican cathedral since the reign of Henry VIII. It was founded on the site of the nunnery of St Frideswide, whose shrine was a focus of pilgrimage until it was partly destroyed on Henry VIII's orders. The shrine was reconstructed in the 19th century. Beside it is a Watching Loft so a guard could ensure that the faithful did not walk off with the saint's relics. The Lady and Latin chapels boast some particularly fine windows.

From the cathedral, you can enter **Tom Quad** with a central pond that served as a water reservoir in case the college caught fire. To the south side is the **Hall**, the college's grand dining room, with an impressive hammerbeam roof. You can also explore another two quads and visit the **Picture Gallery**.

Merton College

Merton College (☎ 276310) in Merton St was founded in 1264 as one of the original three colleges and represents the earliest form of collegiate planning. The 14th-century **Mob Quad** was the first of the college quadrangles. The **library** leading off the quad is the oldest medieval library still in use, with some of the books still chained as they used to be to prevent theft. The library possesses a number of 15th-century astrological instruments, and an astrolabe that may have been used by Chaucer. Former students include TS Eliot and Kris Kristofferson.

Merton's squat naveless **chapel** of 1290 was the first of many in Oxford. It contains finely decorated windows dating from around 1300. It's usually closed to the public.

Magdalen College

Magdalen (pronounced maudlen) College is in the High St, near the handsome bridge

SOUTHERN MIDLANDS

over the River Cherwell. One of Oxford's richest colleges, it has the most extensive and beautiful grounds, including a deer park, river walk, three quadrangles and superb lawns. It's also a popular location for movie-makers and part of *Shadowlands*, the story of CS Lewis, was filmed here.

The college was founded in 1458 by William of Waynflete, the Bishop of Winchester. The chapel dates from the late 15th century and its 144-foot-high bell tower was built around 1500. At 6 am on 1 May each year, the college choir ushers in May Day with a hymn sung from the top of the tower to the crowds below. Pubs open before breakfast ensuring that this is a very well supported tradition.

Former Magdalen students include Oscar Wilde, Sir John Betjeman and Dudley Moore. The college (☎ 276000) is open every afternoon, and from 11 am to 6 pm from late June to September. There's an entry charge of £2/1 from April to September.

Botanic Gardens

Opposite Magdalen is the Botanic Gardens (☎ 276920), founded in 1621 by Henry Danvers for the study of the use of plants in medicine. It's open daily 9 am to 5 pm and there's a £1.50 entry charge from mid-June to September.

St Edmund Hall

St Edmund Hall (☎ 279000) is where the Mohawk chief, Oronhyatekha, studied in 1862. Its little chapel was decorated by William Morris and Edward Burne-Jones.

Queen's College

Queen's College (☎ 279121) in High St was founded in 1341 but the current buildings are all in Classical style. Like most of the colleges, Queen's preserves some idiosyncratic traditions: students are summoned to meals with a trumpet call and at Christmas a boar's head is served to commemorate the occasion when a scholar fought off an attacking boar by thrusting a volume of Aristotle down its throat! It seems thoroughly appropriate that Rowan Atkinson once studied here. To look

round the college, you must join a tour from the TIC.

University College

University College (☎ 276602) in High St has acquired new fame as the college where Bill Clinton didn't indulge in noxious substances. Despite claims that King Alfred founded it in the 9th century, the college was actually founded in 1249. There's a romantic memorial to the poet Shelley, who was sent down (meaning expelled) for publishing *The Necessity of Atheism* in 1811. The college is closed to visitors.

All Souls College

All Souls College (☎ 279379) in High St was founded in 1438, the souls in question being those of the soldiers who died in the Hundred Years' War. The 100 years theme is repeated in the tradition of 'All Souls Mallard', which will be re-enacted on 14 January 2000. The Warden leads a procession in search of a mythical mallard duck that appeared when the college foundations were being dug. No undergraduates are admitted to All Souls, a small college of just 70 fellows. Open on weekdays from 2 to 4.30 pm, the college chapel is particularly worth seeing.

Church of St Mary the Virgin

At the junction of High and Catte Sts the Church of St Mary the Virgin has a 14th-century tower offering splendid views (£1.40/70p). It's open daily 9 am to 6pm (5 pm from October to April).

Radcliffe Camera

The Radcliffe Camera is a round library ('camera' means room) built in 1748 in the Palladian style. It's not open to the public.

Brasenose College

Brasenose College (☎ 277830) is entered from Radcliffe Square and takes its name from an 11th-century snout-like door knocker which now graces the dining room. The college dates from the 16th century. It's open daily from 10 to 11.30 am and 2 to 5 pm.

New College

To reach New College (☎ 279555) turn down New College Lane under the **Bridge of Sighs**, a 1914 copy of the famous bridge in Venice. New College's 14th-century buildings are fine examples of the Perpendicular style. Don't miss the chapel, which has superb stained glass, much of it from the 14th century. The west window is a design by Sir Joshua Reynolds, and Epstein's disturbing statue of Lazarus is also here. The gardens contain a section of Oxford's medieval wall.

New College was founded in 1379 by William of Wykeham, Bishop of Winchester. A former college warden was William Spooner, whose habit of transposing the consonants of words in a phrase made his name part of the English language. He is said to have once reprimanded a student with the words, 'You have deliberately tasted two worms and can leave Oxford by the town drain'. The college is open from 11 am to 5 pm daily over Easter and between June and October; entry is £1. It may also be open winter weekend afternoons.

Sheldonian Theatre

In Broad St stands **Sheldonian Theatre**, the university's main public building. Commissioned by Gilbert Sheldon, Archbishop of Canterbury, it was Christopher Wren's first major work, and was built in 1667 when he was Professor of Astronomy. It's open from Monday to Saturday, 10 am to 12.45 pm and 2 to 4.45 pm (3.30 pm in winter). Admission costs £1/50p.

Bodleian Library

The Bodleian Library, Britain's second most important copyright library, is off the Jacobean-period **Old Schools Quadrangle**. Tours of the library (☎ 277000) take place at 10.30 am, 11.30 am, 2 pm and 3 pm daily (mornings only on Saturday) and show off Duke Humfrey's library (1488). They're popular, book up fast and cost £3 (no children under 14). Also here, and not to be missed, is the **Divinity School**, with its remarkable 15th-century architecture and

superb vaulted ceiling. Renowned as a masterpiece of the English Gothic style, it's open on weekdays from 9 am to 5 pm and on Saturday until 12.30 pm.

On the north side of Broad St, the Bodleian's new section provides a handy sun trap for lunching students.

Trinity College

Trinity College (☎ 279900) in Broad St was founded in 1555, but the existing buildings mostly date from the 17th century. It's open daily 2 to 5 pm.

Balliol College

Balliol College (☎ 277777) in Broad St was founded in 1263, but most of the buildings date from the 19th century. Look for the wooden doors between the inner and outer quadrangles that still bear scorch marks from when Protestant martyrs were burnt at the stake in the mid-16th century. It's open daily from 2 to 5 pm.

The Oxford Story

Across Broad St from Balliol is The Oxford Story (☎ 790055), a much-publicised 'ride through the university's history' in carriages designed to look like old college desks. Those who know nothing about the city will probably find it entertaining. It's open April to October, 9.30 am to 5 pm (9 am to 6 pm in July and August), 10 am to 4.30 pm for the rest of the year. Tickets cost £4.50/3.50.

Ashmolean Museum

Established in 1683, the Ashmolean is the country's oldest museum, based on the collections of the Tradescants and Dr Elias Ashmole, who presented his possessions to the university.

The present building is one of Britain's best examples of Neo-Grecian architecture, and dates from 1845. It houses extensive displays of European art (including works by Raphael and Michelangelo) and Middle Eastern antiquities (finds from Crete and Egypt). Other exhibits include a unique Saxon enamel portrait of Alfred the Great and Guy Fawkes' lantern.

SOUTHERN MIDLANDS

The museum (☎ 278000), on Beaumont St, is open Tuesday to Saturday, 10 am to 4 pm, Sunday afternoon, and on bank holiday Mondays. There's no entry charge, but a £2 donation is requested.

University Museum & Pitt Rivers Museum

Housed in a superb Victorian Gothic building on Parks Rd, the **University Museum** collection is devoted to natural science. The dinosaur skeletons are perfectly suited to the surroundings, the patterns of their bones echoed in the delicate ironwork and glass above. The dodo relics are particularly popular; they're along the wall to the left as you enter the museum.

You reach the **Pitt Rivers Museum** (☎ 270949) through the University Museum. The Pitt Rivers is a wonderful antidote to modern museum design. Instead of state-of-the-art displays that leave nothing to the imagination, the glass cases are crammed to overflowing with everything from a sailing boat to a gory collection of shrunken South American heads. There are said to be over one million items, and some (mainly musical instruments) have had to be shipped out to an annexe, the Balfour Building, on Banbury Rd.

Both museums are open Monday to Saturday, the University from noon to 5 pm, the Pitt Rivers from 1 to 4.30 pm. They're free but a £2 donation is requested.

Punting

There's no better way of letting Oxford's atmosphere seep in than by taking to the river in a punt. The secret to propelling these flat-bottomed boats is to take things very slowly, push gently on the pole to get the punt moving and then use it as a rudder to keep on course.

Punts are available from Easter to September and hold five people, including one punting. Both the Thames and the Cherwell are shallow enough for punts, but the best advice is to bring a picnic and head upstream along the Cherwell. You can rent a punt from C Howard & Sons (☎ 61586, £7 per hour,

£20 deposit) by Magdalen Bridge, or from the Cherwell Boat House (☎ 515978, £6 per hour, £30 deposit, £8 and £40 at weekends) further upstream at the end of Bardwell Rd.

Alternatively, follow the Cherwell downstream from Magdalen Bridge for views of the colleges across the Botanic Gardens and Christ Church Meadow.

Organised Tours

Guide Friday (☎ 790522) runs a hop-on, hop-off city bus tour every 10 minutes from 9.30 am to 6 pm in summer, less frequently in winter. It leaves from the railway station and tickets cost £7/2.

Spires & Shires (☎ 513998) runs guided bus tours to several places around Oxford, including Blenheim Palace (twice daily, £14/13 including entry), Bath and the Cotswolds (Tuesday, Friday, Sunday, £25/22.50).

Places to Stay

Finding a place to stay in summer can be difficult; arrange things in advance or join the queues in the TIC and pay £2.75 for their help.

Hostels The most convenient hostel is *Oxford Backpackers* (☎ 721761) at 9A Hythe Bridge Rd, less than five minutes walk from the railway station. There are 80 beds, mostly in dorms, and good cooking facilities. From April to September you need to book a week in advance and leave a deposit. Beds in dorms cost £9 each.

Oxford Youth Hostel (☎ 62997), 32 Jack Straw's Lane, gets booked up very quickly in summer although it's hardly centrally located. Catch bus No 14 or 14A outside the post office just down the hill from the TIC. It's open all year and the nightly charge is £9.10/6.15.

Camping *Oxford Camping International* (☎ 246551), 426 Abingdon Rd, is conveniently located by the Park & Ride car park 1½ miles south of the centre. Charges are £2.50 for a small tent, plus £1.50 per person and £2.50 for a car.

B&Bs & Hotels – Central In peak season you're looking at around £20 per person for B&B. The main areas are on Abingdon Rd to the south, Cowley/Iffley Rds to the east, and Banbury Rd to the north. All are on bus routes, but Cowley Rd has the best selection of places to eat.

The fairly basic *Becket Guest House* (☎ 724675), 5 Becket St, is just a short walk from the railway station and has singles/doubles from £20/36. West of the station, the small *River Hotel* (☎ 243475), 17 Botley Rd, by Osney Bridge, is a popular business hotel with singles/doubles from £39/52. The *Westgate Hotel* (☎ 726721), nearby at 1 Botley Rd, charges £28/38 or £39/56 with bath attached.

St Michael's Guest House (☎ 242101), 26 St Michael's St, just off Cornmarket St, couldn't be more central. Rooms with common bath are £25/42, but you need to book weeks in advance. The closest B&B to the bus station is the basic *Walton Guest House* (☎ 52137), 169 Walton St, with bathless rooms for £18 per person.

Oxford's choicest accommodation is also centrally located. Forte's *Randolph Hotel* (☎ 247481), opposite the Ashmolean Museum on Beaumont St, was built in 1864 in neo-Gothic style; rooms cost from £105/118 but there are reductions at weekends. The delightful *Old Parsonage Hotel* (☎ 310210) has well equipped rooms for £105/140 at 1 Banbury Rd. It has an excellent reputation for its food and the bar is open to the public.

Bath Place Hotel (☎ 791812), 4 & 5 Bath Place, is a luxurious 10-room retreat in which all the rooms are very different, and some have four-poster beds. Rooms cost from £50/75 with continental breakfast. There's an excellent restaurant.

B&Bs & Hotels – East East of the centre there are several B&Bs in the student area on Cowley Rd and numerous B&Bs along Iffley Rd to the south. There's another cluster to the north, along Headington Rd.

In summer, St Edmund Hall at 45-53 Iffley Rd turns into the *Isis Guest House*

(☎ 248894), offering student digs as superior B&B accommodation. There are 37 rooms for £25/42 with bathroom attached, £19/38 without.

Further out, the *Bravalla Guest House* (☎ 241326), at 242 Iffley Rd, charges from £18 per person. Some rooms have attached bath. *Brenal Guest House* (☎ 721561), at 307 Iffley Rd, has rooms from £18 to £20 per person. On Cowley Rd, the *Athena Guest House* (☎ 243124), at No 253, is within walking distance of shops and restaurants and has rooms for £18/36. A bit further out, the *Earlmont* (☎ 240236), at No 322, is large and comfortable, with rooms with bathrooms for £36/48.

B&Bs & Hotels – North There are several B&Bs along Banbury Rd, north of the centre. *Cotswold House* (☎ 310558), at No 363, is very comfortable; all the rooms have bathroom attached and cost around £35/54. *Burren Guest House* (☎ 513513), at No 374, is more basic and offers B&B from £18 a head.

B&Bs & Hotels – South Closest to the city centre is *Whitehouse View* (☎ 721626), 9 Whitehouse Rd, on a side road west off Abingdon Rd. Considering its location, this place is good value, with rooms from £18/34.

There are numerous places along Abingdon Rd. *Newton House* (☎ 240561), at No 82, is quite large, with doubles from £34. The *Sportsview Guest House* (☎ 01865-244268), 106 Abingdon Rd has rooms from £18/30.

Places to Eat

Many Oxford eateries are attuned to the wallets of wealthy parents and tourists. To eat cheaply you need to track down the places popular with students.

Self-caterers should visit the *Covered Market*, on the north side of High St at the Carfax end, for snacks, fruit and vegetables. Among the stalls, *Palm's Delicatessen* offers a good range of patés and cheeses. There are also several small cafés and the popular if not especially cheap *Beaton's Sandwich Deli and American Diner*.

The *Alternative Tuck Shop*, Holywell St, is the place to go for filled rolls and sandwiches at lunchtime, but the queues of students can be long. At *Parmentier's* in High St you can start the day with a bacon bap for £1.20.

A popular place for snacky meals is *St Giles' Café* in St Giles where fry-ups cost around £3.75, toasted sandwiches from £1.50. *George & Davis' Ice Cream Café*, Little Clarendon St, serves light meals as well as delicious home-made ice cream. It's open until midnight and very popular with students. If you can't get in there (very likely), there's more space at *Café Rouge* just along the road; a large bowl of soup with bread will cost about £4.

Browns Restaurant & Bar (☎ 511995), 5 Woodstock Rd, is a popular, stylish brasserie that looks more expensive than it is. Starters include toasted olive bread with sun-dried tomatoes (£1.85); main dishes range from vegetarian peasant's pot (£6.75) to Brown's lamb steak (£10.45).

The non-smoking *Nosebag Restaurant* (☎ 721033) has main dishes for around £4.50 and a fine selection of cakes.

If you're at the TIC around lunchtime the adjoining *Old School* pub does snack meals like filled baguettes at reasonable prices. Alternatively you can get a light lunch, tea or coffee in the *Convocation Coffee House* attached to St Mary the Virgin; soup and a roll costs £2.55, a bowl of chilli £4.85.

Among Oxford's many Indian restaurants, the *Taj Mahal* (☎ 243783), 16 Turl St, is particularly good, and is open daily until 11.30 pm.

Munchy Munchy (☎ 245710), near the railway station on Park End St, is a reasonably priced Indonesian place. Around the corner on Hythe Bridge St is the *Bangkok House* (☎ 200705), a Thai restaurant where a good meal costs around £15.

The city boasts several topnotch restaurants. Non-smoking *Whites* (☎ 793396), 16 Turl St, does a set lunch for £11.50; main dishes for dinner include roast venison (£17.95). The *Bath Place Hotel* (☎ 791812), 4 & 5 Bath Place, does two-course set lunches for £12; for dinner try the roast wood pigeon with game sauce and wild mushrooms (£12.75). The *Old Parsonage* (☎ 310210) also serves excellent meals in its bar. Main courses range from £5 to £17.

Entertainment

Oxford has some excellent city centre pubs and others within walking distance along the Thames.

The *Head of the River*, ideally situated by Folly Bridge, is very popular, particularly with summer visitors. Less prominent is the tiny *Turf Tavern* in Bath Place, hidden down an alley in the city centre with seating inside and out. The Turf featured in Hardy's *Jude the Obscure* but is perhaps better known for its role in the *Inspector Morse* TV series based on Colin Dexter's books.

Academics loosen up in the 17th-century *Eagle & Child* on St Giles where JRR Tolkein and CS Lewis used to meet in the 1940s for readings from *The Hobbit* and *The Chronicles of Narnia*.

The *Kings Arms* is a crowded student pub in the heart of the city, opposite the Sheldonian Theatre. In summer you can sit outside on the pavement. The *Bullingdon Arms*, 162 Cowley Rd, is a lively Irish local, also popular with students. Irish bands play most weekends and there's live jazz/blues on Wednesday evening.

The *Isis Tavern*, a 1½-mile walk along the towpath from Folly Bridge, is the perfect place to go on a sunny day, but unfortunately everyone knows that so it can be crowded in summer. The *Perch* is a traditional thatched pub by the river in Binsey, a 25-minute walk from the city centre; from Walton St, take Walton Well Rd and cross Port Meadow. There's a barbecue in the garden over summer weekends. After a few drinks here, you too may see the grey spectre that supposedly haunts the river bank.

Getting There & Away

See the fares tables in the Getting Around chapter. Oxford is 57 miles from London, 74 from Bristol and 33 from Cheltenham. The M40 provides fast access from London if you're driving. Oxford has a serious traffic problem and finding somewhere to park in the centre can be difficult. It's best to use the Park & Ride system; follow the signs as you approach the city to the four car parks. Parking is free but the buses to the city centre cost £1 return. They leave every 10 minutes throughout the day, Monday to Saturday.

Bus Several bus lines compete for business on the route to London. The Oxford Tube (☎ 772250) goes to Victoria Coach Station but also stops at Marble Arch, Notting Hill Gate and Shepherd's Bush; a 24-hour return to Victoria is £6.50; the journey takes around 1½ hours and the service operates 24 hours a day. The Oxford Tube also stops on St Clements St, which is near Cowley Rd.

National Express (☎ 0990-808080) has numerous buses to central London and Heathrow airport. There are three buses a day to Cambridge (three hours, £14), two or three services to/from Bath (two hours, £9.75) and Bristol (2¼ hours, £12.50), and two to/from Gloucester (1½ hours, £18.25) and Cheltenham (one hour, £7.75).

Oxford Citylink (☎ 711312) is the third major operator with frequent departures to London, Heathrow, Gatwick, Birmingham and Stratford-upon-Avon.

Train Oxford has a snazzy modern station with frequent services to London Paddington (1½ hours, £15.10 single).

There are regular trains north to Coventry and Birmingham, the main hub for transport further north, and north-west to Worcester and Hereford via Moreton-in-Marsh (for the Cotswolds).

To connect with trains to the south-west you have to change at Didcot Parkway (15 minutes). There are plenty of connections to Bath (1½ hours). Change at Swindon for another line running into the Cotswolds (Kemble, Stroud and Gloucester).

Getting Around

Bus Oxford was among the world's first cities to introduce electric buses. They run from the railway station into the city centre,

Monday to Saturday, 8 am to 6.30 pm, every 12 minutes for a flat fare of 30p.

The city has fallen victim to the worst excesses of bus deregulation, with so many competing buses plying Cornmarket St that it can be difficult to cross the road. The biggest companies are Thames Transit (☎ 772250) and Citylink (☎ 711312). Citylink bus No 4A serves the Iffley Rd and 11A and 52 the Cowley Rd. The information office in the bus station has full details.

Car For car hire, Budget (☎ 724884) is near the station on Hythe Bridge St.

Taxi There are taxis outside the railway station and near the bus station. Phone Radio Taxis (☎ 249743) or Paradise Cars (☎ 200560). A taxi to Blenheim Palace will cost around £13.

Bicycle Students have always espoused pedal power and there are cycle lanes along several streets. The *Cycle into Oxford* map (25p) shows all the local cycle routes.

Pennyfarthing (☎ 249368), 5 George St, near the bus station, offers three-speeds for £5 a day or £9 a week, and mountain bikes for £10/25.

Boat Salter Bros (☎ 243421) offers several interesting boat trips from Folly Bridge between May and September, including a two-hour trip to Abingdon (£5.70/8.85 for a single/return). See under Punting earlier in this section.

WOODSTOCK & BLENHEIM PALACE

The nearby village of Woodstock owes its fame and prosperity to glove-making and to the Churchill family. Although people usually come here en route to Blenheim Palace, there's also a fine collection of 17th and 18th-century houses, particularly the Bear Hotel and the Town Hall, built at the Duke of Marlborough's expense in 1766. The church has an 18th-century tower but a medieval interior. Opposite the church Fletcher's House contains the Oxfordshire County Museum (closed on Monday).

The TIC (☎ 01993-811038) is on Hensington Rd.

Blenheim Palace

One of Europe's largest palaces, Blenheim was a gift to John Churchill from Queen Anne and Parliament as a reward for his role in defeating Louis XIV. A vast Baroque fantasy, it was built by Vanbrugh and Hawksmoor between 1704 and 1722, and was the birthplace of Winston Churchill. It's now a World Heritage site.

You enter the house through the great hall where, 67 feet above, the ceiling is decorated with a painting by Sir James Thornhill showing the Duke of Marlborough presenting Britannia with his plan for the Battle of Blenheim. West of the great hall, apartments once used by the domestic chaplain now house the Churchill Exhibition; his slippers and a lock of his hair are preserved in the room where he was born.

Through the windows of the sumptuous state dining room you can see the tower of Bladon Church where Churchill and his parents are buried. Between the saloon and library are three state rooms, hung with tapestries commemorating Marlborough's campaigns.

You can also visit the chapel and grounds which cover over 2000 acres, some of it parkland landscaped by Capability Brown. Blenheim Park railway leads to the herb garden, the butterfly house, a large maze and bouncy castles, putting greens etc. A separate ticket lets you look round the current Duke and Duchess's private apartments.

Blenheim Palace (☎ 811325) is open from mid-March to October and entry is £7.30/5.30. The park is open every day, all year.

Places to Stay & Eat

B&Bs are pricey: *Mrs McCabe's* (☎ 812051), 14 Hensington Rd, charges £16 a head, or there's *Plane Tree House* (☎ 813075), 15 High St, at £35 a double. The best place in town is the *Feathers Hotel* (☎ 812291) on Market St, with luxurious rooms for £78/99. There are numerous tearooms and pubs. Bar food at the popular

Black Prince includes Mexican dishes and pizzas.

Getting There & Away

To get to Woodstock from Oxford, catch a Thames Transit Minibus (No 20/A/B/C from Oxford bus station, 30 minutes, £2.40 return). From Charlbury, Worths Motor Services (☎ 01608-677322) runs a frequent service to Woodstock (30 minutes, £1.45), Monday to Saturday.

OXFORDSHIRE COTSWOLDS

Although most of the Cotswolds lie in Gloucestershire, about a fifth falls within Oxfordshire.

Burford

• ☎ 01993

One of the loveliest Cotswold villages, Burford has one long street of handsome stone houses and attracts crowds of tourists in summer. Once an important coaching town, it boasts fine 14th to 16th-century houses and a medieval bridge over the River Windrush. The TIC (☎ 823558) is by the Lamb Inn on Sheep St.

The 16th-century Tolsey (Toll House), in the High St, houses a small summer-only museum (40p). From May to September one-hour guided walks leave from outside on Sundays at 2.30 pm; the cost is £1.

Just outside Burford is the **Cotswold Wildlife Park** (☎ 823006), a long-established outdoor zoo in the grounds of a Gothic mansion. It's open from 10 am to 6 pm (or dusk) daily and admission costs £4.90/3.20.

Places to Stay & Eat At *Chevrons* (☎ 823416), near the corner of Swan Lane and the High St, a room with attached bathroom is £24/32. *Byways* (☎ 823609), in Witney St, has a double with attached bathroom for £40, a room without for £20/30.

Burford's oldest pub, the 15th-century *Lamb Inn* (☎ 823155), in Sheep St, is now a very comfortable, if snooty, place to stay, with beamed ceilings and creaking stairs. Doubles with bathroom attached are £90 during the week, £100 at weekends.

Burford has several other good pubs. On the High St, the *Mermaid* does bar snacks and full meals. In Witney St, the *Angel* is popular not only for its real ale but also for imaginative dishes like buckwheat blinis with salmon, sour cream and red caviar. The High St has innumerable tea rooms; at *Huffkins* a Cotswold breakfast with kippers costs £3.20.

Getting There & Away From Oxford, Swanbrook Transport (☎ 01242-574444) runs four buses a day (only two on Sunday) to Burford via Witney (40 minutes, £2).

WITNEY
• *pop 19,000* • ☎ *01993*

Ten miles west of Oxford, Witney is one gateway to the Cotswolds. Since 1669, the town has specialised in the production of blankets. Sheep on the Cotswolds and the local downs provided the wool, whilst the River Windrush provided the water. High-quality blankets continue to be made and the Queen still orders hers from Early's of Witney.

Although the town has grown to absorb the demands of Oxford commuters and light industry, the centre retains some character. On the High St, blankets were formerly weighed and measured in the 18th-century Baroque-style Blanket Hall. In the market-place stands the 17th-century Buttercross, originally a covered market.

The TIC (☎ 775802) is in the 18th-century Town Hall on Market Square.

There are numerous daily buses from Oxford.

Cogges Manor Farm Museum
Clearly signposted in the suburbs of Witney is Cogges Museum (☎ 772602) where domestic farm animals roam around the grounds of a 13th-century manor house, drastically altered in the 17th and 18th centuries. Here you can sample cakes and scones freshly baked on the old range. It's open from late March to late October, Tuesday to Friday from 10.30 am to 5.30 pm (from noon at weekends). Admission is £3/1.50. The

Witney Weaver bus from Oxford to Witney drops you within walking distance.

Broughton Castle
Three miles south-west of ugly Banbury is Broughton Castle, a splendid, moated Elizabethan mansion, though the fortifications are mainly decorative. William Fiennes, who lived here during the Civil War, was a Parliamentarian, and Broughton was captured by the royalists after the Battle of Edgehill. There are arms and armour from the Civil War in the hall, a bedroom used by Queen Anne, and attractive plasterwork and panelling.

Broughton Castle (☎ 01295-262624) is open from mid-May to mid-September on Wednesday and Sunday, from 2 to 5 pm; and also on Thursday in July and August. Entry is £3.20/1.50.

SOUTH OF OXFORD
Dorchester-on-Thames
A street of coaching inns and a magnificent medieval church are more or less all there is of Dorchester-on-Thames although in Saxon times there was a cathedral here. In the 12th century an abbey was founded on the site. Following the Reformation it became the parish church and it's worth stepping inside to see the rare Norman lead font with figures of the apostles; a wonderful Jesse window with carved figures and stained glass tracing Christ's ancestry; and a 13th-century monument of a knight. There's a small museum and café in the Abbey Guest House which also dates back to the Middle Ages.

Thames Transit bus No 390 from Witney to Henley passes through Dorchester.

Abingdon
• *pop 30,000* • ☎ *522711*

Pretty Abingdon is a market town six miles south of Oxford. The impressive County Hall building, now a local museum, dates from 1678 and was designed by Christopher Kempster, who worked on St Paul's Cathedral in London. St Helen's Church, wider than it is long, is a fine example of Perpendicular

SOUTHERN MIDLANDS

architecture. The TIC (☎ 522711) is in Abbey Close, near the river.

On St Helens Wharf, overlooking the Thames, is the *Old Anchor*, a friendly pub that also serves meals.

The nicest way to reach Abingdon from Oxford is by boat (see Oxford). Alternatively, buses run here several times an hour.

Wantage
• *pop 9700*   • ☎ *01235*

Wantage lies at the foot of the Downs, 15 miles south of Oxford. Alfred the Great was born here in 849, and his statue dominates the main square. The Ridgeway is less than three miles to the south, and six miles west, along the Vale of the White Horse, is the famous equine chalk figure.

The **Vale & Downland Museum Centre** (☎ 771447), in a converted 16th-century cloth merchant's house in Church St, has info about King Alfred and life around the Ridgeway. It's open, free, from Tuesday to Saturday, 10.30 am to 4.30 pm (2.30 to 5 pm on Sunday). The TIC (☎ 760176) in the museum keeps the same hours.

Places to Stay & Eat Two miles south of Wantage, the *Ridgeway Youth Hostel* (☎ 760253), Court Hill, is a modern non-smoking hostel with great views. It's open daily in July and August, but not on Sunday from mid-February to May and September to mid-December. The nightly charge is £5/7.45.

The Chalet (☎ 769262), 21 Challow Rd, has beds from £15. The *Bell Inn* (☎ 763718), on the market square, is pricier at £45 a double. You can get bar meals in the *Lamb*, on Mill St, off the market square. The *Flying Teapot* beside the church does snacks like jacket potatoes for £2.30.

Getting There & Away Thames Transit (☎ 772250) has daily buses every 30 minutes from Wantage to Abingdon (30 minutes) and Oxford (50 minutes). On summer Sundays the Ridgeway Explorer ticket permits travel throughout the area for £4.

The White Horse
Cut into the hillside beside the Ridgeway, six miles west of Wantage, is probably the most famous chalk figure in Europe – the stylised image of a horse apparently galloping uphill. The mysterious figure (374 feet long and 160 feet wide) was carved into the turf about 2000 years ago, for reasons that are unknown. How the artist managed to get the lines and perspective so perfect when the whole horse can only be seen from a distance is also a mystery.

Above the chalk figure are the grass-covered earthworks of Uffington Castle. From the Ridgeway Youth Hostel, near Wantage, it's a wonderful five-mile walk along the Ridgeway to the White Horse.

Thomas Hughes, author of *Tom Brown's Schooldays*, was born in Uffington village. His house is now a museum. *The Craven* (☎ 01367-820449) is a thatched farmhouse offering B&B for around £20.

HENLEY-ON-THAMES
• *pop 11,000*   • ☎ *01491*

Henley is world-famous for its rowing regatta, one of those awfully English occasions of boaters and blazers, strawberries and cream, which these days thrives on its appeal to corporate 'entertainment'.

The town is dominated by St Mary's Church, which dates back to the 13th century. Henley Bridge was built in 1786. Above the arches are sculptures of Isis and Father Thames, and at one end of the bridge are two coaching inns, the Red Lion and the Angel. Both date back to well before their 18th-century heyday, and have played host to many eminent people, from the Duke of Wellington to James Boswell.

The TIC (☎ 578034) is in the basement of the Town Hall on Market Place.

Henley Royal Regatta
In 1829, the first Oxford and Cambridge boat race took place between Hambledon Lock and Henley Bridge. Ten years later a regatta was planned to increase Henley's growing reputation.

Each year, from Wednesday to Sunday at

the end of June, the regatta still plays host to the beau monde. Despite its peculiar mix of pomposity and eccentricity, it's a serious event which attracts rowers of the highest calibre.

There are two main areas for spectators – the stewards' enclosure and the public enclosure – although most people appear to take little interest in what's happening on the water. Epicurean picnics are consumed, large quantities of Pimm's (an alcoholic fruit cup) or champagne are drunk, and it's still a vital fixture in the social calendar. Those with contacts in the rowing or corporate worlds can get tickets to the stewards' enclosure; others pay £5 for a day ticket to the public enclosure on Wednesday, Thursday or Friday, £6 at weekends. For more information, phone the regatta office (☎ 572153).

Places to Stay & Eat

If you want to stay anywhere near Henley during the regatta, you need to book weeks in advance.

At other times, try *Mrs Lambert's* (☎ 573099), Alfrudis, 8 Norman Ave, a friendly B&B about five minutes walk from the centre. Doubles cost from £35 to £40 with bath. *Mrs Willis'* (☎ 577829), Avalon, 36 Queen St, charges £18 per person.

Mrs Williams' (☎ 573468), 3 Western Rd, has three double rooms at £35, or £20 for single occupancy. You can enjoy Australian hospitality at *Mrs Bridekirk's* (☎ 572982), The Laurels, 107 St Marks Rd, where rooms are £38 for a double with attached bath.

Several pubs offer reasonably priced food. Near the TIC, at 5 Market Place, the *Three Tuns* (☎ 573260) does good bar meals, including Sunday lunch for £5.25. Alternatively, there's a branch of *Café Rouge* (☎ 411733) in the High St.

Getting There & Away

Henley is 21 miles south-east of Oxford on the A423 and 40 miles west of London. Thames Transit (☎ 772250) runs about six buses daily between Henley and Oxford (50 minutes, £3.55), and between Henley and London (1½ hours, £4.50).

There's no direct rail link between Henley and Oxford; all journeys require a change in Twyford or Reading. Henley to London Paddington takes about one hour and costs £6.70.

A more pleasant way to approach would be by boat from Reading. Boats leave Salter's Wharf near Caversham Bridge at 1.30 pm for the two-hour trip; a single fare is £7.20.

AROUND HENLEY-ON-THAMES
Stonor Park

Stonor Park (☎ 01491-638587) has been occupied by the Stonor family, an unrepentant Catholic family that has suffered much indignity since the Reformation, for over 800 years. The house has a fine collection of paintings, including work by Tintoretto and Caracci.

Stonor Park is five miles north of Henley. You need your own transport to get here. It's open on Sunday in April, Wednesday and Sunday from May to September, plus Thursday in July and August, and Saturday in August. Opening hours are 2 to 5 pm; entry is £4.

Gloucestershire

Straddling the River Severn to the west, Gloucestershire is the source of the traditional picture of rustic, rosy-cheeked England typified by the Cotswolds, the limestone escarpment overlooking the Severn Vale between Bath and Chipping Campden; it is a region of stunningly pretty, gilded stone villages and remarkable views. Some of the villages are extremely popular and it can be difficult to escape the commercialism unless you have your own transport or are walking.

Accommodation can be pricey; there are few youth hostels, and not many places to camp.

The Severn Vale nurtures Cheltenham (Britain's best preserved Regency town), Tewkesbury (with a beautiful abbey) and Gloucester (the capital, with a historic cathedral) as well as Berkeley Castle and Slimbridge Wildfowl Trust. To the west, and geographically part of Wales, is the Forest of Dean, and, bordering Wales, the beautiful Wye Valley (see Wales).

In 1996 a new county of South Gloucestershire was created out of part of the old Avon. However, most places of interest to visitors are in the original Gloucestershire.

WALKS & CYCLE ROUTES

Gloucestershire and the Cotswolds are good for walking and cycling, with plenty of quiet roads, mild but rewarding gradients and fine pubs.

The 100-mile Cotswold Way (see the Activities chapter at the start of the book) runs from Bath to Chipping Campden. TICs stock walking guides and a useful pack of *Cycle Touring Routes in Gloucestershire*. Stephen Hill's *Cycling in the Cotswolds* (Sigma, £6.95) gives more details. The Cotswold Cycling Company (☎ 01242-250642) organises mountain-bike tours of the region, starting from Cheltenham.

Several companies offer guided or unguided walking tours; try Cotswold Walking Holidays (☎ 01242-254353), 10 Royal Parade, Bayshill Rd, Cheltenham.

GETTING AROUND

To get the best out of the limited public transport, pick up a copy of the *Public Transport County Map* and *Connections*, both free from TICs. There's also an invaluable Gloucestershire public transport inquiry line (☎ 01452-425543).

The Cotswolds bus system is more comprehensive than the rail network, which skims past the northern and southern borders.

NORTH COTSWOLDS

The northern Cotswolds are characterised by charming villages of soft, mellow stone built in folds between the rolling wolds. They owe their being to the medieval wool industry, but some now make their living out of tourism. Only a handful have been overwhelmed, but even these deserve a look.

Northleach

• *pop 1000*   • ☎ *01451*

Just off the A40 from Oxford, Northleach is built around a market square. The village is a marvellous mixture of architectural styles and evocative names, and is home to perhaps the finest of the wool churches, a masterpiece of the Cotswold Perpendicular style, with an unrivalled collection of medieval memorial brasses. Near the square is Oak House, a 17th-century wool house which contains Keith Harding's World of Mechanical Music (☎ 860181), a collection of clocks and musical boxes. More interesting is the Cotswold Countryside Collection in the old Northleach House of Correction on the Fosse Way, once a model 19th-century prison. It's open April to October, Monday to Saturday from 10 am to 5 pm (Sunday from 2 pm) for £1.50/75p. The TIC (☎ 860715) is housed in the prison.

Market House (☎ 860557), on the square, offers B&B for £18 per person. *Bank Villas Guest House* (☎ 860464) at West End has beds from £17. *Wickens* (☎ 860421), by the market square, is an upmarket restaurant that specialises in traditional English dishes. Three courses will cost about £21; it's open from Tuesday to Saturday. The cluster of pubs around the main square provide cheaper sustenance.

Northleach is nine miles from Burford (Oxfordshire) and 13 miles from Cheltenham. Swanbrook (☎ 01242-574444) runs several buses a day between Cheltenham and Oxford via Northleach.

Bibury

• *pop 500*   • ☎ *01285*

Described by William Morris as 'the most beautiful village in England', Bibury is a delightful place that manages to retain some dignity despite the hordes of visitors.

The Coln flows alongside the road and is filled with trout which you can pay to fatten at the local trout farm. There are some lovely houses, most notably Arlington Row, a line of NT-owned weaver's cottages. Opposite is Rack Isle, where cloth was once dried after weaving and fulling in the 17th-century

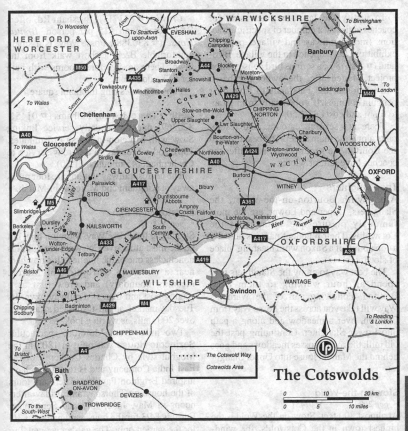

The Cotswold Way
Cotswolds Area

The Cotswolds

0   10   20 km
0   5   10 miles

Arlington Mill, now a folk museum
(☎ 740368). The Mill is open from Easter to
October from 10.30 am to 6 pm; admission
costs £1.80/1.

Jenny Wren's Tearoom offers afternoon
tea so filling you won't be able to manage
dinner. For a splash-out, book into *Bibury
Court* (☎ 740337) where a twin room costs
from £70.

Chedworth
You need your own transport to get to
Chedworth Roman Villa (☎ 01242-
890256; NT). Built around 120 AD for a

wealthy landowner, it contains some wonderful mosaics illustrating the seasons. It's
open from March to October, Tuesday to
Sunday, 10 am to 5 pm; phone for other
opening times; entry is £3.

Bourton-on-the-Water
- *pop 2600*   •   ☎ *01451*

Bourton is certainly attractive, with the River
Windrush passing beneath a series of low
bridges in the village centre and an array of
handsome houses in Cotswold stone, but
quite why it's become such a honeypot is a
mystery.

To justify the large area set aside for coaches and cars, a number of specific attractions (model railway and village, perfume exhibition) have opened in the village. Birdland (☎ 820480), a serious bird conservation project, started after the owner purchased two islands in the Falklands to save their penguin colonies. It's open daily from 10 am to 6 pm and costs £3/1.50.

There are several tearooms and restaurants along the main street. The best times to see Bourton are summer evenings after the coaches have left, or winter.

The Slaughters

Along with Bourton-on-the-Water, the Slaughters, Upper and Lower, are the most famously picturesque villages of the Cotswolds. Their repellent name is actually a corruption of a Saxon word meaning 'place of sloe trees'.

The best way to enjoy the Slaughters is to spend an hour walking to them from Bourton. Following part of the Warden's Way will take you across the Fosse Way from Bourton, over a meadow and along a path into Lower Slaughter. Continuing past the old mill, the route crosses meadows and goes behind the Manor House into Upper Slaughter.

Stow-on-the-Wold

• *pop 2000*   • ☎ *01451*

At almost 800 feet, Stow-on-the-Wold is the highest town in the Cotswolds, the windswept meeting point of eight routes and the site of the last Civil War battle. The pretty main square resembles an Italian piazza. The Royalist Hotel claims to be England's oldest inn; some of its timbers have been carbon-dated to the 10th century.

The TIC (☎ 831082), Hollis House, is on the square.

Places to Stay & Eat *Stow-on-the-Wold Youth Hostel* (☎ 830497) is on the east side of the market square. It's £7.45/5 per night, and open daily from March to October, except Sunday from March to May, and September and October.

Croyde (☎ 831711), Evesham Rd, offers B&B for around £15 per person. *Bretton House* (☎ 830388), Fosse Way, is a small, comfortable B&B a short walk from the town. There are just three rooms with bath for £42 a double.

Pubs and cafés ring the main square.

Getting There & Away Pulhams (☎ 01451-820369) operates a daily service linking Stow with Moreton-in-Marsh (15 minutes, 75p), and a Monday to Saturday service to Cheltenham (45 minutes, £1.20).

The nearest railway stations are four miles away at Kingham and Moreton-in-Marsh.

Moreton-in-Marsh

• *pop 2600*   • ☎ *01608*

Straddling the Fosse Way, Moreton may not be the most attractive Cotswold town, but is nonetheless one of the liveliest. It's nowhere near a marsh (a corruption of March, meaning boundary) and grew first as a staging post and then as a railway town. Its Tuesday market, an old-fashioned affair with over 200 stalls, is worth a look.

Two miles from Moreton, spectacular **Sezincote House** was built in 1805 in the Moghul style by Charles Cockerell of the East India Company and is thought to have inspired Brighton Pavilion. There are tours of the house on Thursday and Friday afternoons in May, June, July and September. Entry is £4/3 for the house and garden, £3/1 for the garden only. The garden is open 2 to 6 pm on the same days from January to November.

Places to Stay & Eat The nearest youth hostel is in Stow-on-the-Wold, four miles south. B&Bs in Moreton include *Treetops* (☎ 651036), London Rd, which has rooms at £30/40, all with bathroom attached. *Rest Harrow* (☎ 650653) is about a mile from the centre on Evenlode Rd, and does B&B from £15. *Moreton House* (☎ 650747), on the High St, has a restaurant and a range of rooms from £21/34. *Manor House Hotel* (☎ 650501), also on the High St, has luxurious rooms from £55/85.

Pubs include the atmospheric *White Hart Royal*, and the *Black Bear*, known for its excellent hot beef sandwiches.

Getting There & Away Pulhams Coaches (☎ 01451-820369) operates a daily service (limited on Sunday) between Moreton and Cheltenham (one hour, £1.25) via Stow-on-the-Wold (15 minutes, 75p) and Bourton-on-the-Water (90p). Many surrounding villages put on market-day buses.

There are trains roughly every two hours to Moreton from Oxford (35 minutes, £6.30), Charlbury (20 minutes, £3.30), Worcester (30 minutes, £7.10) and Hereford (one hour, £11.40).

Chipping Campden
• *pop 2000* • ☎ *01386*

In an area filled with exquisite villages and towns, Chipping Campden is one of the prettiest, not least because it's virtually unspoilt. In fact, it's little more than one long main street flanked by a succession of golden-hued terraced cottages, each subtly different from the next.

The TIC (☎ 841206) was in the Town Hall at the time of writing but may relocate. Nearby, the gabled Market Hall dates back to 1627. At the west end is St James, one of the finest Cotswold wool churches with some splendid 17th-century monuments. Nearby are the Jacobean lodges and gateways of the vanished manor house, and opposite is a remarkable row of almshouses.

Above the town **Dover's Hill** is named after Robert Dover who instigated the 17th-century Cotswold Olimpick Games, recently restarted. The games take place on Spring Bank Holiday and include sports such as slippery pole climbing and welly wanging, culminating in a torch-lit procession and dancing in the square. Transport is available from Campden square.

Four miles north-east of Chipping Campden, in secluded Hidcote Bartrim, are **Hidcote Manor Gardens** (☎ 438333; NT), a series of six lovely gardens, each of which

William Grevel's House, Chipping Campden

Cotswold Wool

Cotswold wool fleeces have been exported since at least the 8th century. By the Middle Ages, Cotswold wool was renowned throughout Europe and was being exported in vast quantities to satisfy the demands of Flemish weavers. The Cotswold breed of sheep, the Cotswold Lion, was said to be descended from Roman longwool sheep. They did well on the limestone grasses of the Cotswold escarpment and were the largest sheep in Britain, growing a long, heavy, yet glossy fleece. In the Middle Ages, loyal knights were rewarded with estates on the Cotswolds, which were quickly filled with Cotswold Lions. The great monasteries also stocked up on sheep to increase revenue, and it's thought that at the time of the *Domesday Book*, there were four times as many sheep as people in the Cotswolds.

At this time, wool accounted for about half of the nation's wealth, symbolised by the fact that, in Parliament, the chancellor sat on a sack of Cotswold wool, known as the Woolsack. But it was the chancellor's taxes which ultimately led to the decline of the wool trade and the rise of the cloth-making industry. In the end, the Industrial Revolution, which introduced new production methods, was the beginning of the end of the Cotswold wool industry.

As time passed, individuals who were not necessarily high born began to make fortunes as wool merchants. Some of them became very influential, and at the height of the industry, in the 15th century, immortalised their achievements in the form of endowments to churches. Their money rebuilt the Perpendicular churches of Chipping Campden, Northleach and Cirencester, and provided the glorious series of stained-glass windows at Fairford. The memorial brasses in these churches tell us something of the details of their lives.

Today, a couple of the mills in Stroud continue to turn out material for highly specialised use (tennis balls and regimental dress uniforms) and wool clothing is produced using traditional methods at Filkins. The Cotswolds are still used for sheep grazing, although the Merino has entirely replaced the Cotswold Lion. The latter is now a protected species, and can be seen at the Cotswold Farm Park at Guiting Power. ■

complements the next. The gardens are open daily except Tuesday and Friday, from April to September, 11 am to 7 pm, for £5.20/2.60.

Places to Stay & Eat There are numerous B&Bs but none are cheap. *Haydon House* (☎ 840275), a converted dairy in Church St, has three comfortable rooms with bath for £23/45. *Sparlings* (☎ 840505), Leysbourne, has two rooms with bath for £26.50/43.50.

The *Eight Bells* (☎ 840371) in Church St does delicious dishes like king prawns in garlic for £7.50. *Badger Bistro* (☎ 840520) in The Square does Sunday lunch for £5.25, while *Joel's Restaurant* (☎ 840598) in the High St has pasta from £4.95 and main dishes for £6 to £13. You can get tea and delicious cakes at the *French Coffee Shop*.

Getting There & Away Getting to Chipping Campden without a car is tricky. From Moreton a taxi will cost about £7. On Tuesday the market bus runs from Moreton. Midland Red South (☎ 01905-763888) has a

four-times-daily Monday to Saturday service from Stratford-upon-Avon

Getting Around You can hire a bike from Cotswold Country Cycles (☎ 438706) at Longlands Farm Cottage for £10 a day or £60 a week.

Broadway
- *pop 2000* • ☎ *01386*

Just over the border in Hereford & Worcester, this well-known and much-visited village is strung out along two sides of a broad street, just beneath the crest of an escarpment. Undeniably handsome, and largely unspoilt despite its fame, it has inspired artists and writers from JM Barrie to Edward Elgar. The most striking house is the Lygon Arms, now an internationally known hotel.

The unspoilt medieval **Church of St Eadburgha** is signposted from the town, a half-hour's walk away. For a longer walk, take the footpath opposite the church which leads up to **Broadway Tower** (☎ 852390), a crenellated 18th-century folly that stands above the town. On a clear day you can see 12 counties from the top and there's a small William Morris exhibition on one floor. Entry is £2.95/1.95.

The TIC (☎ 852937) is at 1 Cotswold Court, alongside some interesting shops.

Places to Stay & Eat Although Broadway is very touristy, you'll escape the coaches if you stay the night. *Cinnibar Cottage* (☎ 858623), 45 Bury End, is an excellent place about half a mile from the centre and charging £33 a double. *The Olive Branch Guest House* (☎ 853440), 78 High St, has rooms from £16.50/45.

The best place to stay is the *Lygon Arms* (☎ 852255) – if your gold card will stretch to £103/155. Food in its *Goblets Wine Bar* is cheaper than you might fear – minced lamb pie and veg for £5.45. For lighter meals try the *Farmer's Café* or *Roberto's Coffee House*, one of the few places open on Sunday.

Getting There & Away Broadway is six miles from Evesham (see Hereford & Worcester) and nine miles from Moreton-in-Marsh. Castleways (☎ 01242-602949) runs buses to Cheltenham via Hailes and Winchcombe (one hour, £1.45) and Evesham (25 minutes, £1.05).

Snowshill

Three miles south-west of Broadway, **Snowshill Manor** (☎ 01386-852410; NT) is furnished with an extraordinarily eclectic collection of items from Japanese armour to Victorian perambulators built up by the eccentric Charles Paget Wade. Even museum-haters will enjoy this place. The gardens are particularly delightful and the restaurant has wonderful views. It's open daily except Tuesday from April to October, from 1 to 5 pm (6 pm from May to September); entry is £5.20/2.60. You need your own transport to get here.

Hailes

Three miles north of Winchcombe along the Cotswold Way, this former Cistercian abbey, now a romantic ruin, was once an important place of pilgrimage; people came from all over Europe to see the phial of Christ's blood kept here. After the dissolution of the monasteries, the blood was revealed as a mixture of honey and saffron. Hailes Abbey (☎ 01242-602398; EH) is open daily from Easter to October, Wednesday to Sunday for the rest of the year; entry is £2/1.

The small neighbouring church, with medieval stained glass and murals, and heraldic tiles, is delightful. A short walk away is the organic Hayles Fruit Farm (good cider) and Orchard Tea Room.

Winchcombe

- ☎ 01242

In Saxon times, Winchcombe was the capital of its own county and the seat of Mercian royalty. Its Benedictine abbey was one of the country's main pilgrimage centres. Only splendid **St Peter's Church**, with its fine gargoyles, remains.

Winchcombe's main attraction is **Sudeley Castle** (☎ 604357) where the chapel houses the tomb of Catherine Parr, Henry VIII's last wife. Parts of the original building have been left in ruins but the rest was restored in the 19th century. It's open daily from 11 am to 5.30 pm, from Easter to October for £5.40/3.

An excellent 2½-mile hike along the Cotswold Way leads to **Belas Knap**, a fine false-entrance burial chamber built about 5000 years ago. The TIC (☎ 602925) in the High St has information about other local walks.

Places to Stay & Eat *Courtyard House* (☎ 602441) at 18 High St has two double rooms for £35 each. Further out *Blair House* (☎ 603626), 41 Gretton Rd, has rooms for £16/32. *Sudeley Hill Farm* (☎ 602344), overlooking the castle, about a mile from the centre, charges £25/40.

Pilgrims Bistro (☎ 603544), round the corner from the TIC at 6 North St, has main dishes from £6 to £13. *Petticoat Tails*

(☎ 603578) at 7 Hailes St does soup with tasty rosemary and raisin bread for £2.20 and a set tea for £3.95.

The *Old White Lion* in North St is an inviting 15th-century pub. The *Plaisterer's Arms*, near the church, does good meals and real ales.

Getting There & Away Castleways Coaches (☎ 602949) runs buses almost hourly, Monday to Saturday, from Winchcombe to Cheltenham (30 minutes, £1.35) and Broadway (30 minutes, £1.20).

Guiting Power & Temple Guiting

The Guitings lie about four miles east of Winchcombe. Gathered around a green, Guiting Power is particularly attractive, with a shop, post office, and two pubs. It even has its own music festival, held each June, and a remarkable Norman doorway to the church.
The Cotswold Farm Park (☎ 01451-850307) preserves endangered species of farm animal like the Gloucester Old Spot pig. It's open daily from April to October from 10 am to 5 pm (6 pm on Sunday) and costs £3.50/1.50.

CHELTENHAM

• *pop 88,000* • ☎ *01242*

Although Cheltenham is essentially an elegant Regency town, the planners have not been as kind to it as they have to Bath and the town's handsome squares, colourful public gardens and elegant early 19th-century architecture are interspersed with dreary shopping areas; High St, in particular, could be anywhere in the UK.

With plentiful restaurants and accommodation, Cheltenham makes an ideal base for exploring the western Cotswolds. It's also the scene of four important festivals: the National Hunt Meeting in March, during which the Cheltenham Gold Cup is run; the Music and Cricket Festivals in July; and the Literature Festival in October. At these times, it can be difficult finding anywhere to stay.

History

As a village midway between Gloucester and Tewkesbury, and on the road to Winchcombe and Oxford, Cheltenham received its market charter in 1226 when it was little more than a row of houses each side of the current High St. It remained important after the Civil War when the area between the south Cotswolds became associated, briefly, with tobacco production but really started to flourish after 1788, when King George visited to take the waters.

In 1716, pigeons pecking at a field under what is now the Ladies College turned out to be eating salt crystals from a spring. Following fashion, the owner's son-in-law built a substantial pump room and opened it to the public. The King's visit sealed the spa's future and several new wells were built, as well as houses to accommodate the hordes of visitors, amongst them Handel and Jane Austen. Not everyone succumbed to Cheltenham's charm though: William Cobbett, author of *Rural Rides*, derided the town as 'a nasty ill-looking place', filled with 'East India plunderers, West Indian floggers, English tax-gorgers, together with gluttons, drunkards and debauchees of all descriptions, female as well as male'.

For modern visitors, the buildings are more interesting than the waters. The classical, elegant Regency style shows itself off all around town in beautifully proportioned terraces, mostly creamy white and decorated with wonderful wrought-iron balconies and railings.

Orientation & Information

Cheltenham railway station is out on a limb to the west; bus F or G will run you to the centre for 60p. The coach station is more conveniently positioned immediately behind the Promenade in the town centre.

Central Cheltenham is eminently walkable. The High St runs roughly east-west and south from it is the Promenade, the most elegant shopping area ('the Bond St of the West'). The Promenade extends into Montpellier, a 19th-century shopping precinct, beyond which lie Suffolk Square and

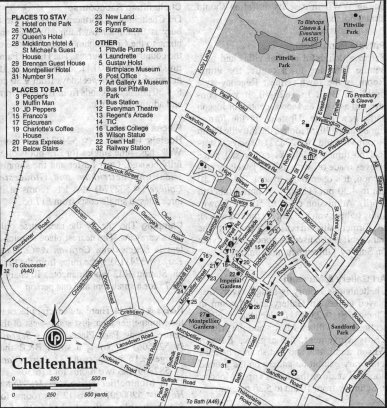

PLACES TO STAY
2 Hotel on the Park
26 YMCA
27 Queen's Hotel
28 Micklinton Hotel &
   St Michael's Guest
   House
29 Brennan Guest House
30 Montpellier Hotel
31 Number 91

PLACES TO EAT
3 Pepper's
9 Muffin Man
10 JD Peppers
15 Franco's
17 Epicurean
19 Charlotte's Coffee
   House
20 Pizza Express
21 Below Stairs

23 New Land
24 Flynn's
25 Pizza Piazza

OTHER
1 Pittville Pump Room
4 Laundrette
5 Gustav Holst
   Birthplace Museum
6 Post Office
7 Art Gallery & Museum
8 Bus for Pittville
   Park
11 Bus Station
12 Everyman Theatre
13 Regent's Arcade
14 TIC
16 Ladies College
18 Wilson Statue
22 Town Hall
32 Railway Station

Cheltenham

Lansdown Crescent. Pittville Park and the old Pump Room are one mile east of the High St.

The helpful TIC (☎ 522878) on the Promenade sells a Cheltenham access guide for disabled visitors (30p) and a set of cycling route maps for £2, as well as *The Romantic Road*, a guide to a 30-mile circular driving tour of the south Cotswolds (£1.50).

The Promenade
The Promenade is the heart of Cheltenham and looks lovely in summer with its hanging baskets full of flowers. The **Municipal**

Offices, built as private residences in 1825, are one of the best features of what has been described as Britain's most beautiful thoroughfare. In front of them stands a **statue of Edward Wilson** (1872-1912), a Cheltenham man who went on Scott's ill-fated expedition to the South Pole in 1911 and died in Antarctica.

Following the Promenade towards Montpellier, you come to the **Imperial Gardens** which were originally built to service the Imperial Spa, but were covered by the Winter Gardens in 1902. The iron and glass structure of the Winter Gardens was dismantled during WWII in case its reflection should attract bombs.

Pittville Pump Room

Set in a delightful area of villas and park ¾ mile from the town centre, the Pump Room is the town's finest Regency-style building. Built in 1825-30, it was constructed as a spa and social centre for Joseph Pitt's new estate. Upstairs, in the former library and billiard rooms, the Pittville Pump Room Museum (☎ 523852) displays historical costumes but looks rather sad since thieves made off with its fine jewellery collection. It's open daily except Tuesday, 10 am to 4.30 pm (11 am to 4 pm October to April). Admission costs £1.50/50p. Downstairs (where you can still try the spa water), the former ballroom is used for concerts. The park itself is also used for concerts ('Pittville on Sunday') throughout the summer.

Art Gallery & Museum

Cheltenham's history is imaginatively displayed at the Art Gallery and Museum in Clarence St (☎ 237431), which has excellent sections on William Morris and the Arts & Crafts Movement, the explorer Edward Wilson, and Dutch and British art. There's a temporary exhibition gallery on the ground floor and a café on the first. It's open Monday to Saturday from 10 am to 5.20 pm; entry is free.

Gustav Holst Birthplace Museum

The house at 4 Clarence Rd where the composer of *The Planets*, Gustav Holst, was born displays Holst memorabilia, while also showing what the interior of a house would have looked liked during the Regency and Edwardian periods. It's open Tuesday to Saturday, from 10 am to 4.20 pm (☎ 524846); entrance is £1.50/50p.

Cleeve Hill

Four miles north of Cheltenham, Cleeve Hill, at 1083 feet, is the highest point of the Cotswolds and of lowland England, and offers fine views over Cheltenham.

Cheltenham Racecourse

On Cheltenham's northern outskirts, Prestbury is Britain's most haunted village and home to the Cheltenham racecourse, one of the country's top courses. The Hall of Fame museum (☎ 513014), dedicated to its history, is open on weekdays from 9.30 am to 4.30 pm, at weekends from 10 am to 2 pm, and admission is free.

Places to Stay

Hostels The *YMCA* (☎ 524024), 6 Vittoria Walk, has some singles for £13 but is often fully booked. Over Easter and the summer vacation *Cheltenham and Gloucester College* (☎ 532774) also lets rooms at its three sites; a single costs from £17.65.

Camping The site by the racecourse only takes caravans. The nearest place to pitch a tent is *Longwillows Caravan & Camping Park* (☎ 674113), three miles from the town on Station Rd, Woodmancote. It charges £2.75 for a small tent and one person.

B&Bs & Hotels There are several places in the Montpellier area, just south-west of the centre. Along Park Place, there's *Segrave* (☎ 523606) at No 7, a small B&B that charges £16 per person. *32 Park Place* (☎ 582889) has two rooms for £16/30.

On Montpellier Drive, the *Micklinton Hotel* (☎ 520000) at No 12 has rooms for £38 a double with attached bath, £34 without. Nearby is *Lonsdale House* (☎ 232379) with beds from £18. At No 4, *St Michael's Guest House* (☎ 513587) is smaller and charges £22/35. *Number 91* (☎ 579441), Montpellier Terrace, where Edward Wilson was born, has rooms for £20/40. At *Lypiatt House* (☎ 224994) in Lypiatt Rd rooms cost from £48/55.

Also centrally located, the friendly *Brennan Guest House* (☎ 525904), 21 St Lukes Rd, has six rooms for £18/34, mostly with common bathroom.

There are a couple of good places on Shurdington Rd, south of the centre. The smart *Hallery House Hotel* (☎ 578450), at No 48, has rooms with bath from £45/65, from £21/42 without. At No 56 *Beaumont House Hotel* (☎ 245986) has rooms from £25/40.

The gracious Victorian *Queen's* hotel (☎ 514724) stands at the top of the Promenade, with rooms from £54/104. Edward VII, Edward Elgar and Arthur Conan Doyle all stayed here.

Between the town centre and Pittville Park, the luxurious Regency *Hotel on the Park* (☎ 518898) is at 38 Evesham Rd with a good restaurant attached. Well-appointed rooms (half overlooking the park) cost from £76/99.

Places to Eat

Cheap cafés litter the streets around the bus station; try *Muffin Man* at 3 Crescent Terrace or *Le Café* at 1 Royal Well Rd. For a good, reasonably-priced lunch in a central position try *Café Museum* in the Clarence St Art Gallery; soup, a roll and a pudding will cost less than £4. *Pepper's* (☎ 234232), 317 High St, is an inviting vegetarian restaurant where a nut roast and salad costs less than £5.

Below Stairs (☎ 234599), at 103 The Promenade, is a popular bistro specialising in seafood; main courses are between £8 and £18. At 119 The Promenade, the *New Land* (☎ 525346) is a good Vietnamese restaurant. *Flynn's* (☎ 252752), 16/17 Courtyard, Montpellier, is a convenient and moderately priced brasserie.

The excellent *Indus* (☎ 516676) at 226 Bath Rd is possibly the best of the town's Indian restaurants.

Franco's (☎ 224880), 49 Rodney Rd, is a traditional Italian restaurant where dinner for two will cost from about £35. It's closed on Sunday. *Pizza Express* (☎ 253896) in Belgrave House, Imperial Square has live jazz on Wednesday evenings. There's more live music in the evenings at *J. D. Pepper's* (☎ 528133) in Regent St where a bistro serves continental-style meals in trendy surroundings.

One of Cheltenham's top restaurants, the *Epicurean* (☎ 222466) at 81 The Promenade, also has a bistro and wine bar; bistro starters cost from £3.25, main courses from

£8. In the restaurant, a set three-course dinner is £32.50.

Entertainment

The *Everyman* theatre (☎ 572573) in Regent St stages everything from comedy to panto to Restoration comedy. *Pittville Pump Room* often hosts classical music concerts, while the *Town Hall* in Imperial Square goes for the more popular stuff; phone ☎ 227979 for bookings.

Getting There & Away

Cheltenham is 100 miles from London, 43 from Oxford, 40 from Bristol and nine from Gloucester.

Bus National Express (☎ 0990-808080) runs buses between Cheltenham and London (2¾ hours, £11.25), Oxford (1¼ hours, £7.50) and all other places on the National Express network. Swanbrook Coaches (☎ 574444) also has buses to Oxford (1½ hours, £4).

Stagecoach (☎ 522021) runs buses every 10 minutes to Gloucester (30 minutes, £1.15). Monday to Saturday it has buses every two hours to Cirencester (30 minutes, £1.45).

Pulhams Coaches (☎ 01451-820369) runs daily buses to Moreton (one hour, £1.20) via Bourton and Stow. Castleways Coaches (☎ 602949) operates about seven buses a day, Monday to Saturday, between Cheltenham and Broadway (45 minutes, £1.45) via Winchcombe. Monday to Saturday they also operate one bus a day to Warwick Castle.

Train Cheltenham is on the Bristol to Birmingham line, with hourly trains to London (2½ hours, £23.50), Bristol (345 minutes, £6.40) and Bath (30 minutes, £10.10), and frequent departures for Gloucester (10 minutes, £2.20).

Getting Around

Bicycle Crabtrees (515291), 50 Winchcombe St, rents mountain bikes for £8/35 a day/week (£50 deposit required).

SOUTHERN MIDLANDS

SOUTH COTSWOLDS

The southern Cotswolds are quite different in character to the northern area: the stone is more soberly coloured, the valleys are steeper and the area is less reliant on tourism. If you want to get away from the Cotswold honeypots, it's worth exploring some of these villages.

Painswick
- *pop 2800*   • ☎ *01452*

Sometimes called 'the Queen of the Cotswolds', Painswick is attractive and lively. **St Mary's Church**, with its ethereal spire, is particularly interesting, its grave-yard bristling with the table-top tombs of rich wool merchants who made the town prosperous from the 17th century. The yew trees are said to be uncountable but certainly number no more than 99; if a 100th should grow, superstition has it that the Devil would shrivel it. The church tower still displays Civil War cannonball scars, while rare iron spectacle stocks stand in the street just south of the church.

The streets behind the church are lined with handsome merchants' houses. Bisley St, with several 14th-century houses, was Painswick's original thoroughfare; New St was a medieval addition. Behind the Falcon Hotel is England's oldest bowling green.

Painswick Rococo Garden This garden (☎ 813204), half a mile north of the town in the grounds of Painswick House, is open from mid-January to November, Wednesday to Sunday, 11 am to 5 pm. It's best visited in February/March for its spectacular snow-drop displays.

Places to Stay & Eat In Edge Rd *Hambutt's Mynd* (☎ 812352) is a pleasant place catering especially for Cotswold Way walkers for £21/39. Inquire at Rudge House about camping beside Edge Rd at *Hambutt's Field* (☎ 812495) for £2.

Brookhouse Mill Cottage (☎ 812854), Tibbiwell Lane, a 17th-century cottage straddling a trout stream, offers B&B for around £19 per person. Sixteenth-century

Thorne (☎ 812476), Friday St, is one of the town's oldest buildings, with two doubles for £36. *Painswick Hotel* (☎ 812160) is the best hotel, with luxurious rooms for £70/98, many with views over the valley.

The *Royal Oak* (☎ 813129) in St Mary's St is a popular local. The *Country Elephant* (☎ 813564), on New St, has main dishes from £6.50 to £16.

Getting There & Away Frequent buses from Stroud to Gloucester and Cheltenham pass through Painswick.

Stroud
- *pop 37,800*   • ☎ *01453*

Stroud is the heart of the southern Cotswolds. The narrow, steep-sided Stroud Valley stands out from the rest of the area and was the scene of the Cotswold wool industry's final fling.

Stroud is built around a spur above the River Frome. Very little cloth is produced today but not long ago Stroudwater scarlet was famous throughout the world. Many of the old mill buildings remain, though most are now used for different purposes. A walk around the hilly streets of Stroud should take in the old Shambles meat market, the Tudor Town Hall, and, if it has reopened, the Stroud Museum. The Stroud Subscription Rooms on George St house the TIC (☎ 765768).

Places to Stay & Eat The *Imperial Hotel* (☎ 764077), opposite the railway station, does B&B from £25 a head. *Cairngall* (☎ 764595), 65 Bisley Old Rd, charges £14/30 for singles/doubles, as does *1 White-hall* (☎ 750766), a pleasant place with views over the valley.

The *Pelican*, Union St, is a pub with an entertaining atmosphere. There are several cafés for light lunches and teas in the pedestrianised streets behind the TIC. Try *Mother Nature Café* or *Mr Christopher's Tea and Coffee House*.

Getting There & Away There are nation-wide National Express connections. Stagecoach Stroud Valleys (☎ 763421) is the main local operator; No 46 runs every two hours to Painswick (10 minutes, 96p) and Cheltenham (40 minutes, £1.50). No 93 operates hourly to Gloucester (45 minutes, £1.40).

Slimbridge

Eleven miles south-west of Gloucester, the **Slimbridge Wildfowl & Wetlands Trust** (☎ 01453-890065) was established in 1946 by the late Sir Peter Scott. It's a breeding ground for many species of wildfowl, notably geese and swans. Open daily from 9.30 am to 5 pm, the centre is as interesting in winter (closes 4 pm), when Arctic visitors arrive, as it is in summer. Entry is £4.70/2.35. You get discounted entry if you stay the night before at *Slimbridge Youth Hostel* (☎ 01453-890275), half a mile to the south. The hostel is closed in December and on winter Sundays. The nightly charge is £9.10/6.15.

Badgerline's (☎ 0117-955 3231) No 308 service links Bristol with Gloucester and passes by the Slimbridge crossroads, a mile from the centre. There's a bus every two hours from Slimbridge to Gloucester (20 minutes, £2.05), Berkeley (10 minutes, £1.30) and Bristol (1½ hours, £2.70).

Berkeley

Best known as the place where Edward II met his grisly end, **Berkeley Castle** (☎ 01453-810332) has been home to the same family for 800 years. The unfortunate king's last days must have been as awful as his death (he was supposedly impaled on a red hot poker); the ventilation shaft in the murder room was connected to a pit in which the rotting carcasses of dead animals were kept.

The beautiful medieval castle is set in terraced Elizabethan gardens surrounded by lawns. It's open from May to September, Tuesday to Saturday, from 11 am to 5 pm (afternoon only on Sunday). Entry is £4.50/2.25.

Also in the village is the **Jenner Museum** (☎ 01453-810631), where Edward Jenner performed the first smallpox vaccination on 14 May 1796, leading to the eventual eradication of the disease. Opening hours are the same as the castle's. Entry is £1.50/50p.

Berkeley is six miles south-west of Slimbridge. Badgerline No 308 bus from Bristol to Gloucester passes this way.

Tetbury

• *pop 4500*   • ☎ *01666*

East of Wotton, on the A433, Tetbury has an interesting 18th-century Gothic church with a graceful spire and a wonderful interior. The 17th-century Market House was used for wool trading. The TIC (☎ 503552) is at Old Court House in Long St.

Westonbirt (☎ 880220), a huge arboretum with a magnificent selection of temperate trees, is 2½ miles south-west of Tetbury. The walks through the trees are particularly stunning in spring and autumn. It's open from 10 am to 8 pm (or sunset) daily. Admission costs £2.80/1.

The *Snooty Fox* (☎ 502436), in the Market Place, offers good bar food.

Lechlade

• ☎ *01367*

At the highest navigable point of the Thames, Lechlade is graced by the spire of St Lawrence's Church, celebrated by Shelley in 1815 as an 'aerial pile' in his poem *A Summer Evening Churchyard, Lechlade, Gloucestershire*. A wool church, it was rededicated to the Spanish saint by Catherine of Aragon, who held the manor in the 16th century.

Three miles east of Lechlade, **Kelmscott Manor** (☎ 252486) was home to William Morris, the poet, artist and founder of the Arts & Crafts Movement. The house is open from April to September on Wednesday; entry is £5/2.50. The Memorial Cottages boast a beautiful carving of Morris seated under a tree.

Fairford

Fairford's claim to fame is St Mary's Church, which houses Britain's only complete set of medieval stained-glass windows. The gift of wealthy wool merchant John Tame, who also

SOUTHERN MIDLANDS

rebuilt the church, the windows are thought to be by Barnard Flower, master glass painter to Henry VII. Tiddles, the church cat, is buried in the churchyard. The High St largely consists of 18th-century houses which sprouted as Fairford became an important staging post.

CIRENCESTER
• *pop 13,500* • ☎ *01285*
Cirencester is about 12 miles south of Cheltenham. Founded as a military base at the junction of the Roman Akeman St, Fosse Way and Ermin Way, it started life as Corinium, the second-largest Roman town after London. Eventually it was one of the principal towns of north-west Europe. The 2nd-century amphitheatre, on Cotswold Ave, is mostly grassed over, but was one of the largest in the country. The Saxons destroyed the town and built smaller settlements outside the walls, renaming it Cirencester. It only really regained its status in the Middle Ages when it became the most important Cotswold wool town.

These days it's an affluent medium-sized town with several worthwhile things to see. Weekly markets still take place every Monday and Friday.

Much of Cirencester remains within the confines of the Roman walls (now all but vanished), although the centre clusters round the parish church on the market square, where you will also find the TIC (☎ 654180), in the Corn Hall. West of the market square is Cirencester Park.

Church of St John the Baptist
One of England's largest churches, St John's seems more like a cathedral. It has a magnificent Perpendicular-style tower, built with the reward given by Henry IV to a group of earls who foiled a rebellion. The highlight of the exterior, however, is the three-storey south porch, which faces the square. Built by the abbots in the late 15th century as an office for the abbey (now vanished), it subsequently became the medieval Town Hall.

Inside the church several memorial brasses record the matrimonial histories of

important wool merchants. There's a 15th-century painted stone pulpit complete with hourglass and the east window contains fine medieval stained glass. A wall safe displays the Boleyn Cup, made for Anne Boleyn, wife of Henry VIII, in 1535, and bearing the family crest. The church is also notable for the oldest 12-bell peal in the country and continues to observe the ringing of the 'pancake bell' on Shrove Tuesday and the celebration of the Restoration on 29 May.

Corinium Museum
The museum (☎ 655611) in Park St shows local Roman finds in tableaux complete with impressive mosaics. It's open daily from Monday to Saturday, 10 am to 5 pm, 2 to 5 pm only on Sunday; closed on Monday in winter. Entry is £1.50/75p.

Cirencester Park
On the western edge of town, the park features magnificent geometrical landscaping, designed with the help of the poet Alexander Pope. The Broad Ride makes for an excellent short walk.

The house built by the First Earl Bathurst in 1714-18 hides behind one of the world's highest yew hedges. It's not open to the public.

Places to Stay
Camping If you're prepared to swap lack of facilities for a cheap stay, there's camping space for £2 at *Abbey Home Farm* (☎ 652808), an organic farm one mile north of Cirencester. The people who run the farm also own Cargo, the shop selling ethnic artefacts in the marketplace.

Hostel *Duntisbourne Abbots Youth Hostel* (☎ 821682) is five miles north-west of Cirencester in a Victorian vicarage. It's open daily except Sunday, March to October; and on Friday and Saturday most of winter. The nightly charge is £7.45/5, and the hostel is renowned for its food. You need your own transport to get here.

B&Bs & Hotels Victoria Rd is the place for B&Bs and guesthouses. *Clonsilla Guest*

House (☎ 652621), at No 7, has rooms for £18/30. *Apsley Villa Guest House* (☎ 653489), at No 16, has five rooms from £17/27. *26 Victoria Rd* (☎ 656440) has just three rooms, for £15/25. At No 91, non-smoking *Wimborne House* (☎ 653890) has rooms with bath from £20/30, including parking.

La Ronde Hotel (☎ 654611), 52 Ashcroft Rd, is a small, private hotel with bar and restaurant and rooms with bath for £35/50. The *White Lion Inn* (☎ 654053), 8 Gloucester St, is a 17th-century coaching inn, a five-minute walk from the town centre. Rooms with bath are £35/45.

The comfortable *Kings Head Hotel* (☎ 653322) is in the marketplace, opposite the church, so it couldn't be more central. Rooms cost £63/80 but prices drop for breaks of two days or more.

Places to Eat

Cirencester has several good places to eat, especially in Castle St where *Pizza Provencale* (☎ 650092) does good pizzas, the *Rajdoot Tandoori* (☎ 652651) has Sunday eat-as-much-as-you-want lunches for £6.95 (£4.95 vegetarian) and *Tatyans* (☎ 653529) does the sort of Chinese that makes the good food pages. *Harry Hare's* (☎ 652375), 3 Gosditch St, is similarly good, with a menu that features cassoulet for £9.50 and venison for £11.95.

For lighter lunches try *The Café-Bistro* in Brewers Courtyard, off Cricklade St; a range of filled baguettes and ciabatta rolls start at £2.10. There's another café inside the Brewery Arts Centre opposite but both are closed on Sunday.

Keith's Coffee Shop in Blackjack St has a handy espresso bar, while the *Swan Yard Café* at 6 Swan Yard does mouth-watering cakes. Coffees and teas are also served at *The Mad Hatter Wine Bar* in Castle St.

For putting together a picnic hamper you could hardly better *Gastromania*, beside the church in the marketplace. Here they claim to 'build' sandwiches rather than make them. The filled pastries are pretty scrummy too.

Cirencester has several decent pubs including the *Slug & Lettuce* near the marketplace. There's real ale at the otherwise dingy *Courtyard Bar* down the alley under the Kings Head and good pub food at the *Golden Cross* in Blackjack St where something like turkey in coconut cream sauce with rice costs around £3.20.

Getting There & Away

National Express buses run from Cirencester to London (2¼ hours, £18.50).

Thamesdown Transport (☎ 01793-428280) runs two buses a day to Gloucester. Stagecoach (☎ 01242-522021) runs to Cheltenham every two hours (30 minutes, £1.45).

Getting Around

Pedal Power (☎ 640505), 5 Ashcroft Rd, rents mountain bikes for £12/45 for a day/week.

GLOUCESTER

- *pop 106,600* • ☎ *01452*

The county capital (pronounced gloster) is on the vale beneath the Cotswold escarpment, beside the River Severn. The city has suffered much from fire, WWII bombing and unsympathetic urban planning but is still worth visiting, particularly for its wonderful Gothic cathedral and the cluster of museums recently created in the restored docks. It also has some of the cheapest accommodation around, which might make it a good base for exploring the surrounding area.

History

To the Romans, Gloucester was Glevum, an important military stronghold against the Welsh tribesmen. It remained important to the Saxons as a garrison town at the junction of the kingdoms of Mercia and Wessex and grew to become a major monastic centre.

When Ethelred, Alfred the Great's brother, was buried in the Saxon royal palace near the cathedral, Gloucester equalled Winchester in importance and it remained important to the Normans.

In 1216, Henry III's coronation took place in St Peter's Abbey. After the murdered King Edward II was buried here, Gloucester became an important place of pilgrimage,

---

Surfing the Severn Bore

A 'bore' is a tidal phenomenon that occurs when flood-tides pour into the wide mouth of an estuary in greater volume than can easily flow along the normal channel of the river. The incoming tide than sweeps over the slower river flow and pushes upstream, flooding the riverbanks as it goes.

In Britain the most striking bore occurs on the River Severn, the country's longest river. At its deepest point the Severn Bore can be 9 ft deep, although in October 1966 a bore measuring 9 ft 3 in and travelling at 13 miles an hour was recorded.

In recent years a new sport of Bore-surfing has developed, with surfers, body-boarders and canoeists lining up to catch the wave. If they time it right they can ride for a mile and a half upriver, much to the irritation of traditionallists who think they're spoiling a great natural phenomenon.

The best places to see the Severn Bore are between Awre, where the estuary narrows, and Gloucester. Gloucester TIC will be able to tell you the dates to go bore-watching. Wear wellies...the water floods the surrounding roads. ∎

---

which helped develop its commercial importance.

During the Civil War, it was a Puritan stronghold and withstood a 26-day siege. In the 18th century Gloucester flourished on the back of the iron, coal and timber industries of the Forest of Dean. Throughout the 20th century the city has been an industrial centre, producing at various times railway rolling stock, aircraft and motorcycles.

Orientation & Information

The centre of the city is based around Northgate, Southgate, Eastgate and Westgate streets which all converge on the Cross. The TIC (☎ 421188) is in St Michael's Tower at The Cross. On Sunday, information is available from the tourist information point in the National Waterways Museum (see below).

Gloucester Cathedral

The city's focal point is still the gorgeous Gothic cathedral, one of the earliest examples of the English Perpendicular style. Built as part of St Peter's Abbey, the cathedral's foundation stone was laid in 1089. When the abbey was dissolved in 1541, the church became the centre of the new Gloucester diocese. The nave has some wonderful Norman arcading, with the last two bays at the western end rebuilt in Perpendicular style in 1420. Note how the south wall of the south aisle leans out of true because of the defensive ditch of the Roman town beneath.

The magnificent 225-foot-high tower was constructed from 1450 to replace the 13th-century spire.

The east window, made in 1349 to commemorate local participation in the Battle of Crecy, is the largest in England, while the wooden choir stalls date from 1350. The late 15th-century Lady Chapel represents the final flowering of the Perpendicular style. The narrow 17th-century communion rails were designed to prevent dogs from entering the sanctuary.

In the south ambulatory is the effigy of Robert, William the Conqueror's eldest son. King Edward II's magnificent tomb, surmounted by an alabaster effigy, is in the north ambulatory.

The north transept, containing a 13th-century reliquary, leads into the treasury and also gives access to the tribune gallery with an exhibition on the cathedral's history. In the north aisle are memorials to John Stafford Smith, a Gloucester composer, who wrote the tune for the USA national anthem.

The Great Cloister has the country's oldest fan vaulting, dating from the 14th century.

The cathedral (☎ 528095) is open daily from 8 am to 6 pm. Donations of £3 are requested.

Every third year Gloucester Cathedral hosts the Three Choirs Festival. It will be Gloucester's turn next in 1998.

PLACES TO STAY
8 Twenty Three
10 New Inn
14 New County Hotel
26 The Warehouse

PLACES TO EAT
5 Comfy Pew Restaurant
7 Seasons Restaurant
18 The Place on the Lock
19 Steamboat Willies
20 Carwardine's Coffee
House & Pizza Piazza

OTHER
1 St Oswald's Priory
2 Bishop Hooper's Monument
3 Folk Museum
4 Cathedral
6 House of the
Tailor of Gloucester
9 Railway Station
11 Guildhall Arts Centre
12 TIC
13 Robert Raikes' House
15 Blackfriars
16 St Mary de Crypt
17 Regiments of
Gloucestershire Museum
21 Queen Boadicea II
Boat Trips
22 Museum of Advertising
& Packaging
23 Glass Heritage
24 Mariners Church
25 National Waterways
Museum
27 Greyfriars
28 City Museum & Art Gallery
29 City Library
30 Kings Theatre
31 Multiplex Cinema

SOUTHERN MIDLANDS

Quay & Docks

The present quay first recorded in 1390. Direct trade with foreign ports started in 1580 and by 1780 some 600 ships a year were docking at Gloucester, although large ships generally got only as far as Bristol. The 15 warehouses in the dock area were built for the 19th-century corn trade. Now redundant, they have been refurbished and most house museums, offices and restaurants.

Llanthony, the largest warehouse, houses the excellent **National Waterways Museum** (☎ 318054), which has a varied collection of

historic vessels and imaginative displays. In summer it's open daily, 10 am to 6 pm; in winter, 10 am to 5 pm; entry is £4.25/3.25.

The Albert Warehouse, part of the Victoria Dock which specialised in salt transhipment, houses **The Museum of Advertising and Packaging** (☎ 302309), Robert Opie's nostalgia-provoking collection of packaging ephemera. In summer it's open daily, 10 am to 6 pm; in winter, Tuesday to Sunday, 10 am to 5 pm. Entry is £2.95/95p. **Glass Heritage** (☎ 503803) in Reynolds Warehouse opposite is as much an opportunity to shop and have tea as to view some fine locally-made stained glass. It's open free Tuesday to Sunday, 10 am to 5 pm.

In the old Custom House, the **Regiments of Gloucestershire Museum** (☎ 522682) is more interesting than most military museums. It's open from 10 am to 5 pm Tuesday to Sunday, and also on summer Mondays; entry is £2.75/1.50.

On Hempsted Lane, across Llanthony Bridge from the dock area, are the remains of **Llanthony Priory**, one of the richest Augustinian houses in England when it was dissolved in 1538.

Other Things to See

The **Gloucester Folk Museum** (☎ 526467), at No 99 Westgate, is in a 16th-century former clothier's house. Displays include a dairy, an ironmonger's shop and a Victorian schoolroom. It's open daily in summer, but closed on winter Sundays; entry is free. St Nicholas House, next door, was the family home of the Whittingtons of pantomime fame, and one of those places where Elizabeth I slept. Nearby are the remains of St Oswald's Priory, and Gloucester's oldest church, St Mary de Lode.

At 5 Southgate, an Edwardian shop boasts a curious mechanical clock, with figures to represent the four countries making up the United Kingdom. **Blackfriars**, Ladybellegate, is Britain's finest surviving example of a Dominican Friary. Entry is free and it's open daily.

Along Eastgate are 15th-century St Michael's Tower; Eastgate Market (pop inside to inspect the Beatrix Potter clock); the remains of the East Gate itself; and the **City Museum & Art Gallery** (☎ 524131), on Brunswick Rd, open Monday to Saturday, 10 am to 5 pm.

Fans of the books will want to visit the **Beatrix Potter Gift Shop** (☎ 422856), in the house which inspired the story of *The Tailor of Gloucester*.

Places to Stay

Gloucester has a six-bed independent youth hostel, *Twenty Three* (☎ 418152) at 23 Alvin St

where beds cost £7.50 each. If that's full *The Bunk House* (☎ 302351) in The Warehouse climbing centre in Parliament St has beds in very basic bunkrooms for £3.50; there's a common room and café too. Phone ahead in case a climbing group has booked all the beds.

Many people prefer to day-trip from nearby Cheltenham but *Westville* (☎ 301228) at 255 Stroud Rd does B&B for £15. Along London Rd are more B&Bs, including *Glenmore Guest House* (☎ 528840), less than a mile from the centre at No 73, which charges £14.

Rotherfield House Hotel (☎ 410500), 5 Horton Rd, has doubles for £42. The impressively galleried *New Inn* (☎ 522177), on Northgate, is very central and is also a good place to drink; rooms with baths are £35/40.

The *New County Hotel* (☎ 307000), on Southgate, is a four-minute walk from the centre and has rooms with showers or baths for £35/45.

Places to Eat

The cathedral *Undercroft*, in part of the former monastery great hall, is a good place for lunches and teas. For fish & chips, go to *Ye Olde Fish Shoppe* on Hare Lane, which is attached to a restaurant just east of the cathedral. Also near the cathedral is the quaint *Comfy Pew Restaurant* (☎ 415648) which does teas, coffees and lunches. Opposite the Beatrix Potter shop the *Seasons Restaurant* (☎ 307060) does dishes like vegetable lasagne for £3.50.

Gloucester Docks has several good places to eat. *The Place on the Lock* (☎ 0330253), on the 1st floor of the Gloucester Docks Antiques Centre, is cheaper than you might fear (tea and scones for £2). The Kimberley Warehouse houses *Steamboat Willies* (☎ 300990) with Tex Mex dishes and pasta from £5.25. *Pizza Piazza* (☎ 311951), overlooking the water in Merchants Quay Shopping Centre, does pizzas from £3.95.

Getting There & Away

Gloucester is 105 miles from London, 49 from Oxford, 45 from Bath and 16 from Cirencester.

National Express has all the usual connections, and buses every two hours to London (3½ hours, £16.50). Cheltenham District runs buses every 15 minutes to Cheltenham (30 minutes, £1.10). Ebley Coach Services (☎ 01453-753333) operates the route to Painswick (30 minutes, £1.10), Monday to Saturday.

The quickest way to get to Cheltenham is by train (10 minutes, £2.20).

TEWKESBURY

- *pop 9500* • ☎ *01684*

Ten miles north of Gloucester, Tewkesbury is an attractive historic town of timber-framed buildings at the confluence of the Severn and Avon rivers. Its river location ensured that the town was already a borough by the time of the Domesday survey. The large Norman church is very impressive, and it's worth exploring the surrounding streets and alleys; Church St is particularly attractive. During the summer, daily Avon cruises (☎ 294088) depart from Riverside Walk.

The TIC (☎ 295027) is in the museum on Barton St.

Tewkesbury Abbey

The town's focal point is the church of the former Benedictine abbey, the last of the monasteries to be dissolved by Henry VIII. Stone to build it was brought by sea and river from Normandy in the 12th century. Tewkesbury's fortunes depended on the wool industry because the abbey owned land and sheep all over the Cotswolds. When the abbey was dissolved, the church survived because the townspeople bought it for £453.

One of Britain's largest churches, with a 132-foot-high tower, it has some fine Norman work in the nave, 14th-century stained glass above the choir and an organ dating from 1620. Look out for the tombs of Edward, Baron Le Despenser, who fought at Poitiers in 1356 and of John Wakeman, the last abbot, who is shown as a vermin-ridden skeleton.

By 1997 a new Visitors Centre with refectory should have opened. Visitors are asked to donate £1.50 a head.

Places to Stay

Several small places around Barton Rd, east of the TIC, charge around £15 per person. The *Bali Hai* (☎ 292049), at 5 Barton Rd, charges £20/28; there's also 2 *Wynyards Close* (☎ 292652) and 8 *Wynyards Close* (☎ 292904).

Church St overlooking the abbey has several attractive, if pricier, options. The *Crescent Guest House* (☎ 293395) at No 30 charges £25/34 with bath. The *Abbey Hotel* (☎ 294247) at No 67 charges £44/52 for rooms with bath. Nearby, at No 52, the *Bell Hotel* (☎ 293293) has rooms with bath for £85 a double. The inviting *Jessop House Hotel* (☎ 292017) at No 65 charges £55/75.

Places to Eat

My Great Grandfather's (☎ 292687), 85 Church St, between the abbey and the cross, is a homely restaurant and tearoom. Cream teas are £2.50, soup £1.95 and they do roast beef, pork or lamb for weekday lunches from £4.20. There's also the *Abbey Tea Rooms* (☎ 292215) at No 59.

Le Bistrot André (☎ 290357), 78 Church St, is a reasonably priced French restaurant. Starters are around £3; main dishes range from £8 to £13.

The *Royal Hop Pole*, mentioned in Dickens' *Pickwick Papers*, is a pub, restaurant and hotel on Church St. The *Olde Black Bear* in the High St or the *Berkeley Arms* in Church St are good places to drink.

Getting There & Away

Stagecoach connects Tewkesbury with Gloucester (25 minutes, every two hours), Cheltenham (25 minutes, hourly) and Worcester (one hour, every two hours), Monday to Saturday.

THE FOREST OF DEAN

Formerly a royal hunting ground, the Forest of Dean occupies a triangular plateau between Gloucester, Ross and Chepstow, and comprises an area of 42 sq miles (including 28 sq miles of woodland) subject to ancient forest law.

Few tourists make it to the Forest even

SOUTHERN MIDLANDS

though it's an excellent area for walking or cycling with some specific sights as well. The main TIC (☎ 01594-836307) in Coleford High St stocks walking and cycling guides. Impressive moated *St Briavels Castle Youth Hostel* (☎ 530272), Lydney, was once a hunting lodge used by King John. It's west of the forest above the Wye Valley and charges £8.25/5.55.

The **Clearwell Caves** (☎ 832535), near Coleford, have been mined for iron since the Iron Age, and you can wander through the dank, spooky caves and inspect the paraphernalia of the mine workings alongside pools and rock formations. Every Halloween something akin to an underground rave takes place in Barbecue Churn, the largest cave; you need to book well in advance to get in. The Caves are open daily from March to October from 10 am to 5 pm. Admission costs £3/2. The *Tudor Farmhouse* (☎ 833046) in Clearwell village has excellent double rooms with bath for £50.

Less than three miles away is the pretty village of **Newland**, dominated by All Saints, the so-called 'Cathedral of the Forest'. In the Greyndour Chantry look for the brass depicting a freeminer with a *nelly*, or tallow candle, in his mouth, a pick in his hand and a *billy*, or backpack, on his back. *Scatterford Farm* (☎ 836562) and *Cherry Orchard Farm* (☎ 832212) have reasonably-priced rooms.

At the Beechenhurst Enclosure near Cinderford (parking £1.50) you can follow the easy Forest of Dean **sculpture trail**.

The **Dean Heritage Centre** (☎ 822170), at Soudley, near Cinderford, recounts the history of the Forest and the freeminers. It's open daily from February to October, 10 am to 6 pm (weekends only in winter). Admission costs £2.75/1.60. The *Dean Heritage Kitchen* does lunches and teas.

Getting There & Away
There are buses from Gloucester and Monmouth to Coleford and on to the smaller villages. Trains also run to Lydney Junction. In summer you can take the Dean Forest

The Free Miners of the Forest of Dean
From before Roman times the Forest of Dean was an important source of timber, iron and stone. A coal seam covering thousands of acres also runs under the Forest. By a curious anomaly, for the past 700 years a select band of Foresters from St Briavels have retained the right to mine this coal, a right won by their forefathers as a reward for their skill in tunnelling under castle fortifications. Although many men could still lay theoretical claim to this right after working for a year and a day in a mine, only two full-time 'free mines' are still in operation and they are one-man operations. ■

Railway on to Norchard. For details ☎ 01594-845840.

NEWENT
The small town of Newent has some attractive architecture and **The Shambles** museum (☎ 822144) of Victorian-style shopfronts. It's open Tuesday to Sunday from Easter to December, from 10 am to 5 pm. Admission is £3.25/1.95. The TIC (01531-822145) is in the library in the High St.

At the **National Birds of Prey Centre** (☎ 820286), on the outskirts of Newent, you can watch hawks and owls in free flight during daily displays. It's open daily from February to November, 10.30 am to 5.30 pm; entry costs £4.50/2.50.

Hereford & Worcester

Herefordshire and Worcestershire were once separate counties. Herefordshire, bounded by the Malverns in the east and Wales to the west, is a sleepy place of fields and hedgerows, virtually untainted by tourism, while Worcestershire comprises the flattish plains of the Severn Vale and the Vale of Evesham, and is surrounded by hills, with the Malverns to the west and the Cotswolds to the south. The principal rivers are the Wye, the Severn and the Avon, and the county has many attractive market towns.

WALKS
Two long-distance paths pass through the county. Offa's Dyke Path runs along the western border with Wales; the 107-mile Wye Valley Walk begins in Chepstow (Wales) and follows the river's course upstream into England through Hereford & Worcester and back into Wales to Rhayader.

GETTING AROUND
Midland Red West (☎ 01905-763888) is the region's biggest bus company. Its Day Rover pass costs £3.50 and allows travel anywhere on its system. For general bus information, phone ☎ 0345-125436. There are rail links to Hereford and Worcester.

HEREFORD
- *pop 48,400*   •   ☎ *01432*

Hereford is a quiet market town rather than a bustling city, a place that rewards quiet rambling along the streets around the cathedral.

It owes its importance to its position on the River Wye on the border of Wales, where it became a garrison protecting the Saxons from the Welsh tribes. Capital of the Saxon kingdom of Mercia, and a cathedral city since the beginning of the 8th century, Hereford has always been favoured as a market centre. The main industry is cider production.

Orientation & Information
The High Town shopping centre is the heart of the city on the north bank of the Wye, with the cathedral a few blocks south along Church St. The bus and railway stations both lie to the north-east along Commercial Rd.

The TIC (☎ 268430) is at 1 King St, near the cathedral. There are guided walking tours June to September, Monday to Saturday, at 10.30 am, and on Sunday at 2.30 pm (£1/50p).

Hereford Cathedral
The purply-red cathedral (☎ 359880) is less aesthetically satisfying than many of the great English cathedrals, mainly because of the reconstruction necessitated after the west tower collapsed into the nave in the late 18th century.

Although parts of the cathedral date back to the 11th century and the 165-foot-high central sandstone tower was built in the 14th century, the west front is less than 100 years old. Inside the cathedral, much of the Norman nave, with its arches, remains. In the choir is the 14th-century Bishop's throne and King Stephen's chair, said to have been used by the king himself. In the north transept is the shrine of St Thomas Cantilupe, a 13th-century Hereford bishop whose tomb became an object of veneration and pilgrimage. The south transept contains three fine tapestries showing the Tree of Life designed by John Piper in 1976.

The cathedral is best known for two ancient treasures: the Mappa Mundi and the chained library of 1400 volumes, some of them dating back to the 8th century. To house them, a new edifice, described as a 'high tech medieval building', has been erected to the south-west side of the cathedral. This exhibition is open Monday to Saturday, 10 am to 4.15 pm and Sunday from noon to 4 pm. Admission costs £4/3.

The cathedral will host the Three Choirs Festival in 1997.

The Old House
Stranded in pedestrianised High Town, the Old House (☎ 364598) is a marvellous black and white three-storey wooden house built in 1621 and refitted with 17th-century wooden furnishings. Note the murals of the Muses on the first floor. It's open May to September, Tuesday to Saturday 10 am to 1 pm and 2 to 5.30 pm, and Monday morning (closed winter Mondays). Admission is £1/40p; £1.60/75p for a joint ticket with the Churchill House Museum.

Other Things to See
Near the cathedral, the **Bishop's Palace** contains one of England's oldest timber halls. East of the cathedral is the ancient Cathedral School and Castle Green, site of a

castle that was pulled down in 1652. Narrow streets and alleys lead from Cathedral Close to the shopping area.

The **City Museum & Art Gallery** (☎ 364691), above the Broad St library, contains Roman antiquities, English watercolours and traditional farming implements. It's closed Mondays. In the High St, **All Saints' Church** has a slightly bent 212-foot-high tower surmounted by England's largest weather-cock.

The **Churchill House Museum** (☎ 267409), in the outskirts of town, beyond the railway station, contains rooms designed in 18th and 19th-century style and collections of costumes and paintings. It's open Tuesday to Saturday 2 to 5 pm (summer Sunday afternoons too). Joint tickets for the Old House and Churchill House are available (see Old House above).

Cider Factory Tours
Just off the A438 to Brecon, the **Cider Museum & King Offa Distillery** (☎ 354207) is in Pomona Place in a former cider works. In 1984 production of cider brandy recommenced after a 250-year gap. The museum and distillery are open daily April to October 10 am to 4.45 pm, Monday to Saturday afternoons only in winter; entry is £2/1.50.

Bulmers Cider Mill (☎ 352000) offers two-hour factory tours (£2.95/1.95) starting from its visitor centre near the cider museum, Monday to Friday. You must book in advance and need transport to get between the visitor centre and the factory.

Places to Stay
Tenby Guest House (☎ 274783), 8 St Nicholas St (just north of the Wye Bridge), has a good range of rooms from £18 to £20 per person. The small *Lindencroft Guest House* (☎ 273965) at 1 Folly Lane charges from £16.50 a head.

At the centrally positioned, non-smoking *Collins House* (☎ 272416) at 19 St Owens St, rooms with continental breakfast cost from £27.50/35.

Merton Hotel (☎ 265925), convenient for the station in Union St, charges £30/40 at

weekends, £40/50 during the week. Just off the main street, across from the railway station, the comfortable *Aylestone Court Hotel* (☎ 341891), on Aylestone Hill, has rooms with attached bathroom from £28/48.

Castle Pool Hotel (☎ 356321), close to the cathedral in Castle St, was once the bishop's residence and has large well-equipped rooms with baths for £50/80, or smaller ones for £35/55. Unmissable on Broad St is *The Green Dragon* (☎ 272506) where you'll pay £68.50/77 a single/double for the usual city-centre comforts.

Places to Eat
For a good cup of coffee, try the *Coffee Bean Co* on St Owen St which does light lunches (toasties, jacket potatoes etc) and is open Monday to Saturday, until 8 pm in peak season. Tiny *Nutters* (☎ 277447), Capuchin Yard, Church St, is a good vegetarian restaurant with set specials like nut roast and two salads for £3.50. Nearby in Church St is *Moka*, an inviting non-smoking coffee shop which also does hot and cold lunches. If these smaller places are full, the vast *Marches* in Union St is bound to have a table.

Cherries at 2 Bridge St offers a wide selection of breakfasts starting at £1.50. *Saxtys Wine Bar* (☎ 357872), 33 Widemarsh St, is a reasonably priced wine bar/pub, with good-value lunches for around £5. The *Firenze* (☎ 270183), at 21 Commercial Rd, offers pizzas from £4.50, other main courses from £8.50.

Entertainment
Hereford's most prominent nightclub is *The Crystal Rooms* (☎ 267378) in Bridge St where you're advised to dress to kill. Of town centre pubs, you could try the *Spread Eagle* or *The Orange Tree* in King St. Both do food for when the cider gets too much.

Getting There & Away
Hereford is 140 miles from London, 25 from Worcester and 38 from Brecon in Wales.

Bus National Express (☎ 0990-808080) operates three services a day to London (four hours, £16) via Heathrow, Cirencester, Cheltenham, Gloucester, Newent and Ross-on-Wye. A special £12.50 day return fare is available if you start your journey from Hereford.

Midland Red West (☎ 01905-763888) connects Hereford and Worcester (1¼ hours, £2.60); and Hereford and Ludlow (£2.60). Red & White (☎ 01635-266336) operates to Brecon via Hay-on-Wye, Monday to Saturday, five times a day. For the Kilvert Connection, see the Brecon section later in this book.

Train Hereford is linked by rail to London (three hours, £28.50) via Newport or Worcester; although there's an hourly service, not many trains are direct. From Hereford, there are also rail services to Worcester (one hour, £4.40), Leominster (15 minutes, £2.90) and Ledbury (15 minutes, £3.20).

Getting Around
You can rent bikes from Coombes Cycles (☎ 354373), 94 Widemarsh St, for £5.75 a day for standard bikes or £10.35 for mountain bikes.

LEDBURY
* *pop 5000*   • ☎ *01531*

Birthplace of the poet John Masefield, Ledbury is a pretty market town known particularly for Church Lane, a narrow cobbled thoroughfare lined with ancient timbered houses. Among them are the old **Grammar School**, housing a heritage centre, and **Butcher Row House**, with a small folk museum. The Council Offices contain a **Painted Room** where 16th-century designs and writing on a wall were uncovered in the 1980s. It can be seen on weekdays between 11 am and 2 pm for £1.

Church Lane leads to the large, partly 11th-century **parish church**, with detached tower and lofty spire. In the High St the black-and-white **Old Market House** of 1633 is built on wooden pillars. Opposite it are the **St Katherine's Hospital** almshouses, built in 1822 on the site of the Bishop of Hereford's former palace.

The TIC (☎ 636147) is at 3 The Homend. Guided walking tours of the town (£2/1) depart on Tuesday, Thursday and Friday from May to September at 10.30 am and noon; call ☎ 634229 for details.

Places to Stay & Eat
B&Bs for around £16 a head include *Mrs Watkins Bevan* (☎ 634110), 34A The Homend, and *Foley House* (☎ 632471) at 39 Bye St.

There's good pub grub at the *Olde Talbot Hotel* (☎ 632963), 14 New St, a 16th-century inn said to be haunted by a poltergeist. Despite this, it's a good place to stay with rooms for £34/50 with bath, £29/50 without.

The comfortable *Feathers Hotel* (☎ 635266), a handsome timbered building in the High St, is Ledbury's best, with 11 rooms at £78.50 a double.

In Church Lane you can sample faggots and chips for £2.20 at the *Prince of Wales* pub. Alternatively the *Horseshoe Inn* in The Homend does chilli for £3.50.

Getting There & Away
Ledbury is 15 miles east of Hereford, on the Worcester-Hereford railway line and served by buses from Malvern, Gloucester and Hereford.

AROUND LEDBURY
Eastnor Castle
Built in 1812, Eastnor Castle (☎ 01531-633160), 2½ miles east of Ledbury, is a whimsical curiosity designed by Pugin, a leading architect in the Gothic revival, best known for the London Houses of Parliament. Set in a 300-acre deer park, the fortified exterior looks Norman, while inside, the library is Italian Renaissance and the drawing room a wonderfully over-the-top Gothic fantasy in red and gold.

It's open Sunday, noon to 5 pm from Easter to September, and from Sunday to Friday in July and August. Entry is £4/2.

ROSS-ON-WYE
- *pop 8300*   • ☎ *01989*

Winding through a landscape of woods and meadows, past Ross-on-Wye, Symonds Yat and then along the border with Wales, the River Wye empties into the Bristol Channel beneath the Severn Bridge. Built on a red-sandstone bluff, Ross makes a good base for exploring the **Wye Valley**, the most scenic part of the river.

There are fine views of the valley and ruined Wilton Castle from the **Prospect**, a clifftop public garden, designed by 17th-century town planner, John Kyrle, the 'Man of Ross', who also laid out some of the streets. His philanthropic works were much praised by Alexander Pope in *Of the Use of Riches*. Kyrle is buried in the parish church where the Plague Cross records the burial of 315 victims of the 1637 plague.

The **Lost St Museum** (☎ 562752) is at 27 Brookend St, in a courtyard behind the main street. Usually open daily, it recreates a street of shops and a pub as they would have been between 1885 and 1935.

The TIC (☎ 562768) is in Edde Cross St. Bikes can be rented from Revolutions (☎ 562639), 48 Broad St, from £10 a day.

Places to Stay
The nearest youth hostel is six miles south of Ross at Welsh Bicknor (see Goodrich below).

In Ross, *Vaga House* (☎ 563024), five minutes walk from the town centre in Wye St, does B&B from £18 per person. The excellent *Edde Cross House* (☎ 565088), Edde Cross St, charges from £21 to £23 per person. Some rooms have bathrooms.

Rosswyn Hotel (☎ 562733), at 17 High St, has rooms with bath attached for £30 to £70. The comfortable *King's Head Hotel* (☎ 763174), 8 High St, charges £25 to £35 per person.

Places to Eat
Oat Cuisine (☎ 566271), 47 Broad St, serves organic cider in its restaurant. The *Obilash Restaurant* (☎ 567860), on Gloucester Rd, is an Indian restaurant and takeaway open daily

until midnight. For a night out, *Pheasants Restaurant* (☎ 565751), 32 Edde Cross St, does fine English cuisine. It's open Tuesday to Saturday and main courses cost around £12. Alternatively head for *Meaders* (☎ 562803) where a Hungarian meal for two, with wine, costs £22.

Getting There & Away
Ross is 14 miles from Hereford and 16 from Gloucester, with bus links to London (via Cheltenham and Cirencester). Stagecoach Red & White (☎ 485118) operates a daily bus service between Hereford and Gloucester via Ross, and a Monday to Saturday Ross-Monmouth bus (for Goodrich and Symonds Yat).

AROUND ROSS-ON-WYE
Goodrich
Goodrich Castle (☎ 01600-890538; EH) is a red sandstone castle dating back to the 12th century. A royalist stronghold during the Civil War, it fell to the Roundheads after a siege lasting 4½ months and was destroyed by Cromwell. Admission costs £2/1.

Just under two miles from Goodrich is *Welsh Bicknor Youth Hostel* (☎ 01594-860300), a Victorian rectory standing in 25-acre grounds by the river. Beds cost £8.25/5.55. It's open daily in July and August; phone for other times.

Symonds Yat
Symonds Yat, 2½ miles south of Goodrich, is a popular beauty spot overlooking the Wye. It's crowded in the summer but worth visiting at quieter times. There are good views from Yat Rock, and rare peregrine falcons nest in the rockface. Telescopes enable you to watch them from April to August. Parking costs £1.50.

MALVERN
- *pop 30,000*   • ☎ *01684*

Malvern consists of several towns in the Malvern Hills, which rise suddenly from the vale in a long, humpy line. Famous for mineral water, a summer music festival (late May), a public school, Morgan motor cars

✠✠✠✠✠✠✠✠✠✠✠✠✠✠✠✠✠✠

On the Elgar Trail

Sir Edward Elgar, composer of Britain's almost-national anthem *Land of Hope and Glory*, was born in Broadheath, three miles west of Worcester, in 1857 and died in Worcester in 1934. He lived in Hereford for eight years and drew much of the inspiration for music like the *Pomp and Circumstance* marches and the *Enigma Variations* from the nearby Malvern Hills. The Hereford, Worcester and Malvern TICs stock a leaflet detailing a signposted 'Elgar Route' which takes you through places associated with his life.

The Elgar Birthplace Museum (☎01905-66224) in Lower Broadheath is open daily except Wednesday from mid-February to mid-January. He is buried in St Wulstan's church in Little Malvern, just south of Great Malvern. ■

✠✠✠✠✠✠✠✠✠✠✠✠✠✠✠✠✠✠

and fine scenery, Malvern is a pretty area with a gentle character.

The Malvern Hills provided the composer Sir Edward Elgar with the inspiration for the *Enigma Variations* and the *Pomp & Circumstance* marches. He was born in Upper Broadheath, three miles west of Worcester, and is buried in St Wulstan's Church in Little Malvern, just south of Great Malvern.

Walks in the Malvern Hills

In Great Malvern, cut up St Ann's Rd for a short, steep walk to the summit of Worcestershire Beacon (1395 feet), offering tremendous views. Herefordshire Beacon (1114 feet), south of Great Malvern, is the site of the British Camp, an Iron-Age fort. There's a superb walk along the path that meanders across the summits of the Malverns.

The TIC stocks *Malvern Map Sets* (£3), three maps covering the chain of hills.

Great Malvern

Great Malvern looks a bit like one of the Mid Welsh spa towns with a mini version of Gloucester Cathedral thrown in. Turner was inspired to paint it...before the grand Victorian piles started to straddle the hills, of course!

At the time of writing the TIC (☎ 892289) was in the Winter Gardens Complex in Grange Rd, together with the Malvern Festival Theatre (☎ 892277 for programme details). However, it was expected to move location shortly.

Great Malvern Priory The Priory Church, with Norman pillars lining the nave, is famous for its stained glass and tiles. Of particular note are the 15th-century west window, the clerestory windows of the choir, and the window in the Jesus Chapel in the north transept which shows the Coronation of Mary. The choir is decorated with 1200 medieval tiles, the oldest and finest such collection in the country.

Places to Stay Accommodation in this upmarket area can be pricey but there are some very pleasant places to stay. *Malvern Hills Youth Hostel* (☎ 569131), 18 Peachfield Rd, is in Malvern Wells, 1½ miles south of Great Malvern. It's open from mid-February to October for £7.45/5.

Goodrich Cottage (☎ 573237), on the hill a mile outside Great Malvern, offers bargain B&B for £15 a head. *Spa Guest House* (☎ 561178), at 16 Manby Rd, charges £35 a double.

Great Malvern Hotel (☎ 563411), 7 Graham Rd, is very central with rooms with baths for £45/60. A wonderful place is *Cottage in the Wood* (☎ 575859), in Holywell Rd, three miles away near Malvern Wells. Rooms cost from £68/89. Dinner in its excellent restaurant costs around £25.

Places to Eat The *Anupam Restaurant* (☎ 573814), at 85 Church St, above Boots, is an Indian restaurant and takeaway. *Russo's* (☎ 563063), Belle Vue Terrace, does English and Italian food; lasagne for £4.30.

Lady Foley's Tearoom (☎ 893033) is in the Victorian railway station in Imperial Rd. On Thursday, Friday and Saturday nights it becomes the *Brief Encounter* vegetarian restaurant, serving delicacies like Schezuan black beans and beancurd in a fiery sauce for £6.75.

SOUTHERN MIDLANDS

Getting There & Away Great Malvern is eight miles from Worcester and 23 miles from Cheltenham. It's linked by rail to London, Birmingham and Worcester. National Express has a daily bus between Great Malvern and London (four hours, £18.50) via Worcester and Pershore.

WORCESTER

• *pop 75,500* • ☎ *01905*

World-famous for its bone china, Worcester (pronounced wooster) also has an interesting cathedral where King John of Magna Carta fame is buried. Some streets boast the sort of black and white half-timbered buildings more usually associated with Stratford-upon-Avon.

Orientation & Information

The main part of the city lies on the east bank of the River Severn, with the cathedral rising above it. The High St, just to the north, runs through a bewildering number of name changes as it heads north: The Cross, The Foregate, Foregate and The Tything.

The TIC (☎ 726311) is in the Guildhall, in the High St. Walking tours (£2) leave from this point at 11 am and 2.30 pm on summer Wednesdays.

Worcester Cathedral

The present cathedral was begun in 1084 by Bishop Wulstan and the crypt, one of Europe's finest, is of this period. The choir and lady chapel were built in 13th-century Early English style, while the Norman nave was reconstructed in the 14th century in Decorated style.

Wicked King John, whose treachery towards his brother Richard left the country in turmoil at his death, is buried in the choir. Knowing he stood only a slim chance of making it past the Pearly Gates, the dying king is said to have asked to be buried disguised as a monk. When the tomb was opened in 1797, shreds of a monk's cowl were found over his skull.

There's also an ornate memorial to Prince Arthur, Henry VIII's elder brother, who is buried here. You should also see the impressive, mainly Norman chapter house, off the cloisters, its ribbed vault supported by a single central pillar.

The cathedral (☎ 28854) is open daily from 7.30 am to 6 pm. A £2 donation is requested. The cathedral choir sings evensong at 5.30 pm daily except Thursday, and at 4 pm on Sunday.

Commandery Civil War Centre

Housed in a splendid Tudor building along Sidbury, south-east of the Cathedral, the Centre (☎ 355071) is England's only museum dedicated to the Civil War. The building was used as King Charles II's headquarters during the Battle of Worcester which brought the War to an end in 1651. It's open Monday to Saturday, 10 am to 5 pm, Sunday 1.30 to 5.30 pm. Entry is £3.15/2.15.

Royal Worcester Porcelain

Worcester is most famous for the ornate bone china that has been manufactured there since 1751, the longest continuous production of any British porcelain company. Since 1789, the company has been granted a royal warrant, and Worcester remains the Queen's preferred crockery.

The **Royal Worcester Porcelain Works** (☎ 01905-23221) was moved to the current site on Severn St in 1840. Conducted tours lasting 45 minutes run from Monday to Friday. They cost £3.50/2.50 and should be booked in advance. In the gift shop, you can purchase a 25-piece dinner service for £1396, or single seconds for just a few pounds.

The **Dyson Perrins Museum**, also here, tells the factory's story and houses the world's largest collection of Worcester porcelain, including some of the first pieces. It's open Monday to Saturday, 9.30 am to 5 pm (from 10 am on Saturday). Entry is £1.50/1. ∎

Other Things to See

The splendid **Guildhall**, in the High St, is a Queen Anne building of 1721, designed by a pupil of Sir Christopher Wren.

Trinity House (on The Trinity, just off The Cross) is a half-timbered building which once belonged to the Guild of the Holy Trinity. Charles II is supposed to have hidden after the Battle of Worcester in **King Charles' House**, at 29 New St, now a restaurant.

Friar St is lined with fine Tudor and Elizabethan buildings. Built in 1480, **The Greyfriars** (☎ 23571; NT) has been painstakingly restored and is full of textiles and furnishings. It's open Wednesday, Thursday and Bank Holiday Mondays, 2 to 5 pm, Easter to October. Entry is £2.20. The **Museum of Local Life** (☎ 722349) evokes Worcester's past with reconstructed Victorian shops, displays of toys and costumes, and details of daily life during WWII. It's open daily except Thursday and Sunday for £1.50/75p.

Worcester City Museum and Art Gallery (☎ 25371) in Foregate St has exhibits about the River Severn and is open daily, except Thursday and Sunday, from 9.30 am to 6 pm (5 pm on Saturday). Entry is free.

Places to Stay

The nearest youth hostel is in Malvern, eight miles away. In summer, you can camp at *Worcester Racecourse* (☎ 23936); charges are £4.25 per person. Three miles north of Worcester is the *Mill House Caravan & Camping Site* (☎ 451283), which charges from £4.50.

Barbourne Rd, north of the centre, has several B&Bs. The *Shrubbery Guest House* (☎ 24871), at No 38, charges from £16 per person and has some rooms with private bath. The *Barbourne* (☎ 27507), at No 42, is similarly priced. There's another cluster of B&Bs at the north end of The Tything.

Park House Hotel (☎ 21816), 12 Droitwich Rd, has rooms with bath for £38/42. *Loch Ryan Hotel* (☎ 351143), near the cathedral at 119 Sidbury, has rooms from £35/45.

Fownes Resort Hotel (☎ 613151), in a converted warehouse on City Walls Rd, is a popular business hotel. The weekday per person price of £83 drops to £38 at weekends.

Places to Eat

You could do worse than lunch in the Guildhall's elaborate *Assembly Room* which is open to the public Monday to Saturday from 8.30 am to 5 pm. Otherwise head for New St and its extension into Friar St for the best choice of eateries.

At 29 New St, the 16th-century *King Charles Restaurant* (☎ 22449) offers set three-course lunches for £9.50. Next door is the picturesquely named, reasonably priced *Swan with Two Nicks*. At No 15, *Saffrons Bistro* (☎ 610505) offers everything from Thai to Mexican, while nearby *Chesters Café-Restaurant* (☎ 611638) at No 51 concentrates on Mexican but has jacket potatoes from £1.50 too.

Bottles Wine Bar (☎ 21958), at 5 Friar St, is open for food from Monday to Saturday, with live music some nights. The *Lemon Tree* (☎ 27770) offers modern British cooking in attractive surroundings; things like haddock and spinach cakes for £5.95. The menu at *Heroes Restaurant* (☎ 25451), at No 26, includes chilli, chicken and burgers.

Il Pescatore (☎ 21444), at 34 Sidbury near the Cathedral, is a popular Italian restaurant, offering light lunches for £7.50. Handy for the porcelain works and cathedral at 7 Severn St, the *Shepherd's Purse* does soup and a sandwich for £2.75.

Entertainment

The popular *Farrier's Arms*, in Fish St near the Cathedral, has some outdoor seating and tasty, cheap bar meals. Worcester's oldest pub, the *Cardinal's Hat* in Friar St, has open fires in winter.

Every third year Worcester hosts the Three Choirs choral festival (☎ 616211) at which music by Elgar is always played. It will be Worcester's turn in 1999.

SOUTHERN MIDLANDS

Getting There & Away

Worcester is 113 miles from London, 57 from Oxford, 26 from Stratford-upon-Avon and 25 from Hereford.

Bus National Express (☎ 0990-808080) runs at least one coach a day between Worcester, Heathrow and London (3½ hours, £16.50). Another service links Aberdare and Great Yarmouth via Worcester, Great Malvern and Hereford. Worcester to Great Malvern takes just 20 minutes.

Midland Red West (☎ 763888) operates services to Hereford, Tewkesbury and Evesham. A Day Rover ticket costs £3.80/2.35.

Train Worcester Foregate station (for trains to Birmingham and Hereford) is more central than Worcester Shrub Hill which offers regular trains to London (Paddington, 2¼ hours). Shrub Hill is a 15-minute poorly signposted walk to the centre. Bus 30 passes nearby or a taxi is about £1.75.

Getting Around

The Worcester Steamer Company (☎ 354991) operates cruises along the river. Alternatively, if you have £110 to spare, consider taking to the skies with Worcester Balloons (☎ 01684-594747). Peddlers (☎ 24238), 46 Barbourne Rd, hires out ordinary bikes for £8/30 for a day/week, and mountain bikes for £15.60.

AROUND WORCESTER
Elgar's Birthplace Museum

Three miles west of Worcester is Broadheath, birthplace of Sir Edward Elgar (1857-1934). The cottage (☎ 333224) is now a museum of Elgar memorabilia, open May to September, Thursday to Tuesday, 10.30 am to 6 pm; 1.30 to 4.30 pm in winter. Entry is £3/50p.

Severn Valley Railway

The Severn Valley Railway offers a scenic steam-powered journey between Kidderminster and Bridgnorth (Shropshire),

via the pretty village of Bewdley. For more information see Bridgnorth, Shropshire.

VALE OF EVESHAM

Worcestershire's south-eastern corner is a splendid sight in spring when its myriad fruit trees are in blossom. The Vale's two principal towns are Evesham itself and Pershore.

Evesham

- *pop 15,000* • ☎ *01386*

A quiet market town on the River Avon, Evesham was the scene of the battle where Prince Edward, son of Henry III, defeated Simon de Montfort in 1265. The TIC (☎ 446944), in the picturesque Almonry Centre on the south side of town, houses a small museum of battle-related exhibits; admission costs £1.25/50p.

The river flows close to the 16th-century bell tower of the lost Benedictine abbey, which makes a fine grouping with the twin medieval churches of All Saints and St Lawrence. Look out for the beautiful fan-vaulting of the Lichfield Chantry in All Saints.

Places to Stay & Eat *Berryfield House* (☎ 48214), 172 Pershore Rd, Hampton, does B&B from £16 for non-smokers only. *Park View Hotel* (☎ 442639), Waterside, has rooms from £18.50/35. The *Croft* (☎ 446035), 54 Green Hill, is a Georgian guesthouse 200 yards from the railway station with rooms for £30/38.

Comfortable *Evesham Hotel* (☎ 765566) in Cooper's Lane has rooms for £62/86.

Teashops abound around the Abbey site. Try *Naughty But...* with calorie-counted cakes for £1.60 and salads for £3.50, or the *Gateway Cake Shop* which does soup and a roll for £1.20.

At 16 Vine St the *Vine Wine Bar* (☎ 446799) offers delicacies like sea bass for £9.45.

Getting There & Away Midland Red West (☎ 01788-535555) has an hourly service to Pershore (25 minutes, £2.10) and Worcester (one hour, £2.60), Monday to Saturday. It also operates an hourly bus to Stratford-upon-Avon (one hour, £2.10), Monday to Saturday.

There are frequent trains to Worcester (20 minutes), and to London (two hours) via Oxford (one hour).

Pershore
• *pop 6900* • ☎ *01386*

A backwater town of graceful Georgian houses, Pershore is chiefly noted for its abbey which was founded in 689. The TIC (☎ 554262) is inside a travel agency at 19 High St.

Pershore Abbey When Henry VIII's henchmen moved in to dissolve Pershore Abbey the townsfolk bought the choir to serve as their parish church. All that now remains is this glorious choir, built in austere Early English style, and the earlier south transept, parts of which may predate the Norman Conquest.

Eight miles from Worcester, and seven miles from Evesham, Pershore is best reached by bus from either place; the railway station is 1½ miles north of the town.

Warwickshire & Coventry

Warwickshire is home to two of England's biggest tourist attractions: Stratford-upon-Avon, with its Shakespearian connections, and Warwick, with its popular castle. Although not a patch on either town, Coventry has a rich industrial history, and the county has plenty of museums, castles, market towns, canals and pleasant countryside. In the 1996 reorganisation of British counties, Coventry became a unitary authority administered separately from Warwickshire.

COVENTRY
• *pop 318,800* • ☎ *01203*

Coventry deserves full marks for trying.

Everywhere you turn in the town centre a plaque helpfully relays the history of the building it's attached to. But in the end you can't make silk out of a sow's ear, and away from the area immediately around the cathedral a combination of damage inflicted by German bombs during WWII and by British architects and town planners in the 1950s and 60s make for a dismal cityscape of car parks, ring roads and windswept shopping precincts.

History
Medieval Coventry was a thriving wool and cloth manufacturing centre; by the 14th century it was one of the four largest towns in England outside London. Then decline set in and Coventry was still essentially a medieval town when it caught the wave of the Industrial Revolution in the 19th century.

Coventry was one of the most inventive of the Victorian industrial centres and claims to be the birthplace of the modern bicycle. The first car made in Britain was a Daimler built in Coventry in 1896, and in the early years of the 20th century Coventry was Britain's motor manufacturing capital as well as a major aircraft manufacturing centre. But steady industrial growth switched to headlong decline in the 1970s and 80s as Sunbeam, Hillman, Singer, Humber and Triumph cars and Triumph motorcycles all disappeared. Now Jaguar cars are the only home-grown survivors, although French Peugeots are also assembled in Coventry.

SOUTHERN MIDLANDS

'Sent to Coventry'
At the end of Spon St stands 15th-century **St John's church**. During the Civil War Royalist troops imprisoned here were pointedly ignored by the local population – hence the expression 'sent to Coventry' to describe someone who is being cold-shouldered.

Others believe the expression arose when Royalist prisoners detained in Birmingham were moved to Parliament-sympathising Coventry and suffered the same fate. ■

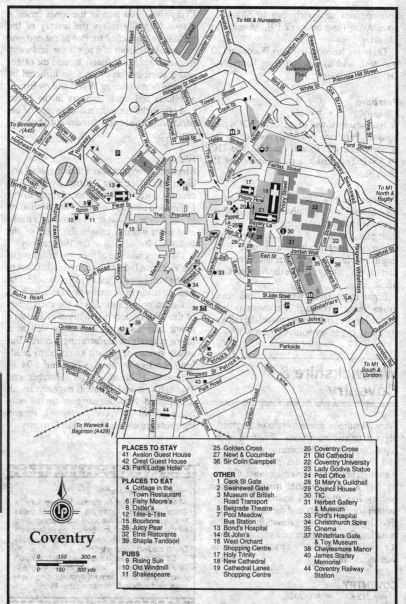

SOUTHERN MIDLANDS

Coventry

0   150   300 m
0   150   300 yds

PLACES TO STAY
41 Avalon Guest House
42 Crest Guest House
43 Park Lodge Hotel

PLACES TO EAT
4 Cottage in the
   Town Restaurant
6 Fishy Moore's
8 Ostler's
12 Tête-à-Tête
15 Bourbons
26 Juicy Pear
32 Etna Ristorante
39 Shapla Tandoori

PUBS
9 Rising Sun
10 Old Windmill
11 Shakespeare

25 Golden Cross
27 Newt & Cucumber
36 Sir Colin Campbell

OTHER
1 Cook St Gate
2 Swanswell Gate
3 Museum of British
   Road Transport
5 Belgrade Theatre
7 Pool Meadow
   Bus Station
13 Bond's Hospital
14 St John's
16 West Orchard
   Shopping Centre
17 Holy Trinity
18 New Cathedral
19 Cathedral Lanes
   Shopping Centre

20 Coventry Cross
21 Old Cathedral
22 Coventry University
23 Lady Godiva Statue
24 Post Office
28 St Mary's Guildhall
29 Council House
30 TIC
31 Herbert Gallery
   & Museum
33 Ford's Hospital
34 Christchurch Spire
35 Cinema
37 Whitefriars Gate
   & Toy Museum
38 Cheylesmore Manor
40 James Starley
   Memorial
44 Coventry Railway
   Station

Orientation & Information

Central Coventry is encircled by a ring road with most points of interest tucked inside. Much of the centre is dominated by the bleak Precinct, one of the first pedestrian-only shopping centres to rise from WWII destruction. Medieval Spon St features several half-timbered buildings relocated from elsewhere in the city.

The TIC (☎ 832303), in Bayley Lane immediately east of the old cathedral, sells an informative *Coventry City Centre Trail* (£1).

The city famed for the exploits of Lady Godiva was also home to George Eliot, female author of *The Mill on the Floss*, *Middlemarch* and *Daniel Deronda* in the mid-19th century. The TIC has details of guided tours of George Eliot Country costing £6.50/5.

Cathedrals Old & New

Founded in the 12th century and rebuilt from 1373, St Michael's was one of England's largest parish churches when it became a cathedral in 1918, its spire topped only by those of Salisbury and Norwich cathedrals. Then on 14 November 1940, a Luftwaffe raid gutted the cathedral, leaving only the outer walls and the spire standing amidst the smoking ruins.

After the war, it was decided that the ruins should be allowed to stand as a reminder. The new St Michael's Cathedral (☎ 227597) was built beside it and linked to it. Designed by Sir Basil Spence and built between 1955 and 1962, the cathedral is one of the few examples of post-war British architecture to inspire popular affection. It's noted for its soaring etched glass screen wall at the west end, for the superb Graham Sutherland tapestry above the altar and for Sir Jacob Epstein's sculpture of St Michael subduing the devil beside the entrance steps.

Between Easter and October the Visitors Centre screens an audio-visual presentation on the destruction of the old cathedral and the birth of its replacement. Visitors to the new cathedral are asked for a £2/1 donation. The old cathedral's spire still looks down on the ruins and the 180 steps up lead to magnificent views; entry is £1/50p.

Museum of British Road Transport

The museum (☎ 832425) has a huge collection of bicycles, motorcycles, racing cars, rally cars and even Thrust 2, the fastest wheeled 'thing' ever to hurtle across a salt flat, alongside plain, ordinary British family cars. The museum, in Hales St, is open daily, 10 am to 5 pm. Entry is £3.30/2.30.

Lady Godiva Statue

The statue of Lady Godiva at the edge of The Precinct is a Coventry meeting spot handily overlooked by the Coventry Clock. A figure of the naked lady parades from the clock each hour, while Peeping Tom peers out from above.

Herbert Art Gallery & Museum

The Herbert Gallery (☎ 832381) provides a quick run through Coventry's history. The upstairs art gallery has paintings of the Lady Godiva legend and the original sketches for Graham Sutherland's cathedral tapestry. It's open free Monday to Saturday, 10 am to 5.30 pm, and 2 to 5 pm on Sunday.

Places to Stay

Many visitors just want to check out the cathedral and the museums and then head on again. If you do want to stay the TIC makes bookings free (☎ 0800-243748), although many places are uncomfortably close to the noisy ring road.

There's no hostel but during university vacations the *Priory Halls of Residence* (☎ 838445) at Coventry University, Priory St, offer accommodation for £18 per person.

Friars Rd is a reasonably quiet residential enclave within easy walking distance of the centre. *Avalon Guest House* (☎ 251839), at No 28, has beds from £15 to £18 per person. Across the road, the *Crest Guest House* (☎ 227822), at No 39, charges £15 to £26 a head.

Places to Eat

Immediately opposite the bus station *Fishy*

Godiva City

The story of Lady Godiva is almost too well known to need retelling. Godiva, the Saxon wife of Earl Leofric of Mercia, pleaded with her husband to repeal onerous taxes on local people. Leofric agreed to do so if she would ride naked through the town centre, whereupon Godiva stripped off, let down her hair to hide her nakedness and took him up on his bet. Only one man, Peeping Tom, had the audacity to watch her.

Although Godiva was a real woman, Godgifu, who died in 1067, the story of her exploits first emerged a century later in the writing of Roger of Wendover. Peeping Tom was an even later addition; a 16th-century painting showing Godiva's ride has her husband's face at a window which may have given rise to the idea of the voyeur.

From 1218 Coventry held an annual Great Fair, a colourful event with music and dancing. In the 17th century a 'Godiva Procession' was incorporated into it, with a boy 'Godiva' riding through the city alongside the mayor and other dignitaries. By the 19th century the procession had degenerated until female 'Godivas' were riding almost as naked as their namesakes. The puritanical Victorians soon stepped in to ensure there would be no more 'Godivas' so drunk they fell off their horses.

The legend of Godiva dies hard. In 1996 a woman stripped off in the modern cathedral to protest against the admission of a car to the nave during celebrations for the centenary of Coventry's car industry. ∎

Moore's at 10-12 Fairfax St, serves decent fish & chips. Both the Museum of British Road Transport and the Herbert Museum have cafés. Near the cathedral at 10A Hay Lane the *Juicy Pear* bistro (☎ 633759) has a varied menu of English and Mexican dishes.

Olde-worlde Spon St has several eateries including *Ostler's* (☎ 226603), at No 166, which serves steaks and vegetarian dishes and *Tête-à-Tête* , which scoops the afternoon tea market. Nearby, at 1-3 Ryley St, off Hill St, the excellent *Cottage in the Town* (☎ 223642) has a bistro downstairs and a restaurant above. It's closed Sunday evening.

The *Shapla Tandoori*, by Greyfriars Green, south of the centre, occupies a former school building attended by author George Eliot in the 19th century.

With a car, you could drive five miles to Ryton-on-Dunsmore to eat healthily at the *Ryton Organic Gardens* restaurant (☎ 303517).

Entertainment

With two universities, Coventry has a thriving student life. The *Golden Cross Inn*, in the shadow of the cathedrals in Hay Lane, is a popular student hang-out and one of Coventry's oldest pubs (though much restored). Next to it is the equally popular, though centuries newer, *Newt & Cucumber*. At the corner of Gosford and Whitefriars Sts, the *Sir Colin Campbell* has entertainment every night during term.

Spon St offers the pleasantly quiet *Old Windmill*, the popular *Rising Sun* and the *Shakespeare*.

The University of Warwick, four miles south of the city, has the largest Arts Centre (☎ 524524) outside London, with a regular programme of events and a popular cinema. The Belgrade Theatre (☎ 553055) is on Corporation St.

Getting There & Away

Birmingham International Airport (☎ 767 5511) is actually closer to Coventry than Birmingham.

The railway station is just across the ring road, south of the centre. Coventry is on the main rail route to London (£21.90, less than 1½ hours). Birmingham is £2.60 by rail.

Pool Meadow bus station is in Fairfax St. Services in the West Midlands are coordinated by Centro (☎ 559559). One-way National Express tickets cost £12.75 to London, £8.50 to Oxford and £14.25 to Bath. Coachlinks (☎ 20077) offers services to Birmingham, Northampton and Peterborough.

Stagecoach (☎ 01788-535555) is the main local operator. Its Explorer tickets, costing £4.25/2.25, allow a day's bus travel to Birmingham, Evesham, Kenilworth, Leamington, Northampton, Oxford, Stratford and Warwick.

Getting Around
Phone ☎ 559559 for local bus service information; a £3.70 Daytripper ticket gives you a day's use of local bus and train services.

WARWICK
• *pop 22,000* • ☎ 01926
Warwickshire's pleasantly quiet county town is home to Warwick Castle, one of England's major tourist attractions. It's also a handy base for visits to Stratford-upon-Avon.

Orientation & Information
Warwick is a simple town to navigate; the A429 runs right through the centre with Westgate at one end and Eastgate at the other. The old town centre lies just north of this axis, the castle just south. The TIC (☎ 492212) is in Jury St, near the junction with Castle St.

Warwick Castle
Warwick Castle (☎ 408000) is one of England's finest medieval castles. Madame Tussaud's now looks after it, but a visit is still fun.

Warwick was first fortified in Saxon times, but the first real castle was constructed on the banks of the River Avon in 1068, soon after the Norman conquest. The castle's external appearance principally dates from the 14th and 15th centuries, but the interiors are from the late 17th to late 19th centuries, when the castle changed from a military stronghold to a grand residence. Capability Brown landscaped the magnificent grounds in 1753.

You enter the castle through a gatehouse beside the armoury and the dungeon and torture chamber. Just inside a sign points to the 'Kingmaker' exhibition. The most powerful of all the castle's powerful owners was Warwick the Kingmaker, Richard Neville,

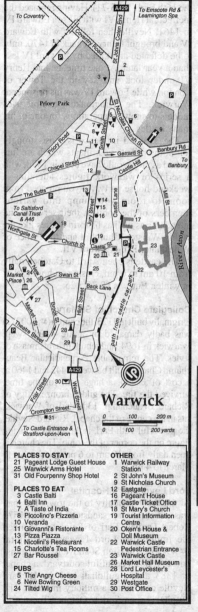

Warwick

PLACES TO STAY
21 Pageant Lodge Guest House
25 Warwick Arms Hotel
31 Old Fourpenny Shop Hotel

PLACES TO EAT
3 Castle Balti
4 Balti Inn
7 A Taste of India
8 Piccolino's Pizzeria
10 Veranda
11 Giovanni's Ristorante
13 Pizza Piazza
14 Nicolini's Restaurant
15 Charlotte's Tea Rooms
27 Bar Roussel

PUBS
5 The Angry Cheese
6 New Bowling Green
24 Tilted Wig

OTHER
1 Warwick Railway Station
2 St John's Museum
9 St Nicholas Church
12 Eastgate
16 Pageant House
17 Castle Ticket Office
18 St Mary's Church
19 Tourist Information Centre
20 Oken's House & Doll Museum
22 Warwick Castle Pedestrian Entrance
23 Warwick Castle
26 Market Hall Museum
28 Lord Leycester's Hospital
29 Westgate
30 Post Office

the 16th Earl (1428-71). Having replaced the ineffectual Henry VI with his son Edward IV in 1461, Neville then fell out with Edward IV and brought Henry VI back in 1470, only to be defeated and killed by Edward IV less than a year later. At one time, he had Henry VI under lock and key in the Tower of London while Edward IV was his prisoner at Warwick. The 'Kingmaker' exhibit uses models to shows preparations for one of his many battles.

The Tussaud influence is most strongly felt in the private apartments which are furnished as they would have been in 1898, with a series of waxwork figures attending a weekend house party. As you proceed from room to room you bump into various members of the nobility, their servants and attendants as well as historic figures like the young Winston Churchill and the Prince of Wales, later King Edward VII.

The castle is open April to October, daily from 10 am to 6 pm, closing an hour earlier in winter. Entry is £8.75/5.25.

Collegiate Church of St Mary
Originally built in 1123, the church (☎ 400771) was badly damaged by a fire which swept Warwick in 1694, and rebuilt in a mishmash of styles. The remarkable Perpendicular Beauchamp Chapel, built between 1442 and 1460 at a cost of £2400, a huge sum for the time, survived the fire. The gilded bronze effigy of Richard Beauchamp, 13th Earl of Warwick, sits in the centre of the chapel. Richard Neville, the powerful 16th Earl, is the sinister-looking figure on the corner of the tomb. The church is open daily from 10 am to 6 pm (November to March to 4 pm)

Lord Leycester's Hospital
At the Westgate entry to the town, the road was cut through a sandstone cliff. In 1571 Robert Dudley, Earl of Leicester, founded the impressive Lord Leycester Hospital (☎ 491422), in High St above it, as an almshouse. It has a beautiful courtyard, a chapel of 1383 and a guildhall built by Richard Neville containing a military museum. The hospital is open April to October, Tuesday to

Sunday, 10 am to 5 pm, in winter to 4 pm. Entry is £2.50/1.25.

Museums
The **Market Hall Museum** (☎ 412500) in the 1670 market building has displays on natural history and archaeology. It's open Monday to Saturday, 10 am to 5.30 pm; from May to September it's also open Sunday, 2.30 to 5 pm. Entry is free.

In Castle St, the **Doll Museum** (☎ 412500) is in half-timbered medieval Oken's House. **St John's House** (☎ 412132), in a 1620 mansion on St John's, has exhibits on the county's social history.

Places to Stay
The nearest youth hostel is in Stratford-upon-Avon.

Emscote Rd, the east end of the main road through Warwick, and its extension into Leamington Spa, has several budget-priced B&Bs. The *Avon Guest House* (☎ 491367) at No 7 has rooms from £15 per person.

Alternatively, *Pageant Lodge Guest House* (☎ 491244) at 2 Castle Lane is terrifically located, right in the town centre and overlooking the castle. Singles with bath are £25 to £35, doubles £40 to £45.

At 17 High St, the staid *Warwick Arms Hotel* (☎ 492759) has rooms with bath from £30/45. The *Old Fourpenny Shop Hotel* (☎ 491360) at 27-29 Crompton St charges from £35/40 to £54/60 a single/double.

Places to Eat
Pizza Piazza (☎ 491641) at 33-35 Jury St does reasonable pizzas at £5 to £7. Further east, *Piccolino's Pizzeria* (☎ 491020), 31 Smith St, is popular locally. Try also *Giovanni's Ristorante* (☎ 494904) at 15 Smith St.

For something Indian, try the *Castle Balti* (☎ 493007), on St John's, or, along Smith St, the *Veranda* (☎ 491736) at No 24 or *A Taste of India* (☎ 492151) at No 35.

There are a few alternatives to pasta or curry. The *Angry Cheese* (☎ 400411), on St Nicholas Church St, is a wine bar-cum-bistro specialising in Mexican food. At 11 Market

Place, the *Tilted Wig* (☎ 410466) does a ploughman's lunch for £3.75. *Charlotte's Tea Rooms* on Jury St, has lunch specials for about £6 and is open in the evening too.

Getting There & Away

Trains operate to Birmingham, Stratford-upon-Avon and London but there are more connections from nearby Leamington Spa. Midland Red buses (☎ 01788-535555) stop in Market Place, while National Express buses operate from Old Square.

AROUND WARWICK

Warwick is easy day-tripping distance from Stratford-upon-Avon. **Leamington Spa** (population 57,000) and **Kenilworth** (population 21,000) are virtually contiguous with Warwick. Leamington has some Regency architecture, classy shops and spa baths but is really rather dull. The industrial town of **Rugby** (population 60,000) is famous only for the public school, founded in 1567, which provided the setting for *Tom Brown's Schooldays*. It was here that a pupil picked up a football and ran with it, thereby inventing the sport of rugby!

Kenilworth Castle

Between Warwick and Coventry stand the imposing ruins of Kenilworth Castle (☎ 01926-52078; EH), founded around 1120 and enlarged in the 14th and 16th centuries. Edward II was briefly imprisoned here before being transferred to Berkeley Castle where he was subsequently murdered. In 1563, Elizabeth I granted the castle to her favourite, Robert Dudley, Earl of Leicester. Between 1565 and 1575 she visited him at Kenilworth on four occasions and the theatrical pageants he arranged for her in 1575 were immortalised in Sir Walter Scott's 1821 work *Kenilworth*. The castle was deliberately ruined in 1648, after the Civil War. Admission costs £2/1.

STRATFORD-UPON-AVON
• *pop 22,000* • ☎ *01789*

An otherwise ordinary Midlands market town, Stratford chanced to be William Shakespeare's home and shrewd management of the cult of Bill has made it one of the busiest tourist attractions outside London. Just beyond the northern edge of the Cotswolds, Stratford makes a handy stopover on your way to or from the north.

Orientation & Information

Stratford is easy to explore on foot. The main street changes names several times as it extends from the river to the railway station.

The TIC (☎ 293127) on Bridgefoot, close to the river, has plenty of information and will make bookings for the numerous B&Bs and hotels. It's open Monday to Saturday, 9 am to 6 pm, and Sunday, 11 am to 5 pm; from November to March it closes an hour earlier and all day on Sunday.

The Shakespeare Properties

The Shakespeare Birthplace Trust (☎ 204016) looks after five buildings associated with Shakespeare. In summer the crowds can be horrendous and none of the houses was designed to accommodate such a squash; visit out of season if you possibly can. Note that wheelchair access to the properties is very restricted.

Three of the houses are centrally located, one is a walk away, one a drive or bike ride out. A £9/4 ticket lets you into all five properties, or you can pay £6/2.75 for the three town houses. To pay for each place individually would cost more. From late March to mid-October, the properties are open Monday to Saturday, 9 or 9.30 am to 5 or 5.30 pm, and Sunday from 9.30 or 10 am. In winter, they open Monday to Saturday, 9.30 or 10 am to 4 pm, and Sunday from either 10 or 10.30 am.

Shakespeare's Birthplace The number one Shakespeare attraction, in Henley St, probably bears little relation to what his home actually looked like because it's been extensively rebuilt over the centuries. However it's been a tourist attraction for three centuries; famous 19th-century visitors scratched their names on one of the windows. Shakespeare's father lived here from 1550

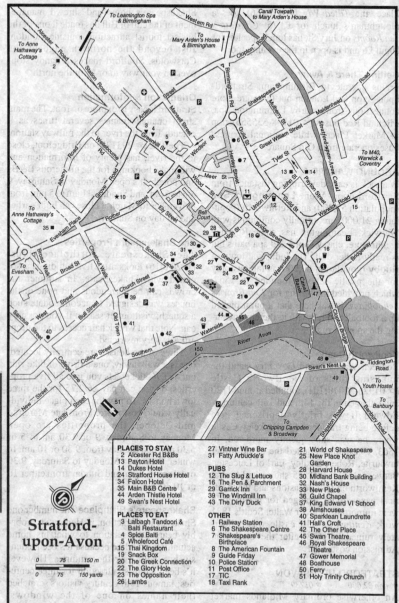

Stratford-upon-Avon

```
0    75    150 m
0    75    150 yards
```

SOUTHERN MIDLANDS

PLACES TO STAY
2 Alcester Rd B&Bs
13 Payton Hotel
14 Dukes Hotel
24 Stratford House Hotel
34 Falcon Hotel
35 Main B&B Centre
44 Arden Thistle Hotel
46 Swan's Nest Hotel

PLACES TO EAT
3 Lalbagh Tandoori &
  Balti Restaurant
4 Spice Balti
5 Wholefood Café
8 Thai Kingdom
19 Snack Box
20 The Greek Connection
22 The Glory Hole
23 The Opposition
26 Lambs

27 Vintner Wine Bar
31 Fatty Arbuckle's

PUBS
12 The Slug & Lettuce
16 The Pen & Parchment
29 Garrick Inn
39 The Windmill Inn
43 The Dirty Duck

OTHER
1 Railway Station
6 The Shakespeare Centre
7 Shakespeare's
  Birthplace
8 The American Fountain
9 Guide Friday
10 Police Station
11 Post Office
17 TIC
18 Taxi Rank

21 World of Shakespeare
25 New Place Knot
  Garden
28 Harvard House
30 Midland Bank Building
32 Nash's House
33 New Place
36 Guild Chapel
37 King Edward VI School
38 Almshouses
40 Sparklean Laundrette
41 Hall's Croft
42 The Other Place
45 Swan Theatre
46 Royal Shakespeare
  Theatre
47 Gower Memorial
48 Boathouse
50 Ferry
51 Holy Trinity Church

William Shakespeare

The greatest dramatist of all time was born in Stratford-upon-Avon in 1564, the son of a local tradesman. At the age of 18 he married Anne Hathaway, eight years his senior, and their daughter Susanna was born about six months later. Boy and girl twins, Hamnet and Judith, followed two years later, but the son died at the age of 11.

Around the time of the twins' birth, Shakespeare moved to London and began to write for the Lord Chamberlain's Company. This successful company enjoyed the finest theatre (the Globe) and the best actors. It was not until the 1590s that Shakespeare's name appeared on the plays he wrote. Prior to that time, the company's name was felt to be more important than that of its dramatist.

Shakespeare's plays made novel and inventive use of the English language but they also had superb plot structures and deep insights into human nature – characteristics which have ensured not only their survival over the centuries but also their popularity in other languages. His earliest writings included comedies like *Comedy of Errors*, historical accounts like *Henry VI* and *Richard III* and the tragedy *Romeo & Juliet*. The new century saw his great tragedies, first *Hamlet* and then *Othello*, *King Lear* and *Macbeth*.

Around 1610 he retired, moved back to Stratford-upon-Avon, and lived in comfortable circumstances until his death in 1616. He was buried in the parish church; and his wife outlived him by seven years.

Remarkably little is known about Shakespeare's life. Despite his prodigious output of plays, no letters or other personal writing have survived and the little that is known about him and his family is pieced together from birth, death and marriage files and other official records (including his will in which he left his wife his 'second-best bed'!). Partly because of this paucity of information, some intriguing theories have developed suggesting that Shakespeare did not actually write the plays that bear his name. None of them have survived in manuscript form so there is no evidence from his handwriting that they are his. Theorists also speculate that Shakespeare's comparatively humble origins and education would not have given him the background, experience and knowledge to write his plays. Various people have been suggested as the real author of Shakespeare's plays, including either the Earl of Derby or the Earl of Oxford who, it is speculated, may have wished to remain anonymous. ■

William Shakespeare's House

and William Shakespeare was born here in 1564. A ticket costing £3/1.50 includes admission to the adjacent Shakespeare Centre.

New Place & Nash's House In retirement, the wealthy Shakespeare bought a fine home at New Place on the corner of Chapel St and Chapel Lane, but the house was demolished in 1759 and only the site and grounds remain. An Elizabethan knot garden has been laid out on part of the New Place grounds. The adjacent Nash's House, where his granddaughter lived, tells the town's history and contains an interesting picture of what the house looked like in 1876 and after a complete facelift in 1911. Entry is £2/1.

Hall's Croft Shakespeare's daughter Susanna married Dr John Hall, and their fine Elizabethan town house stands on Old Town. Displays describe medical practice in Shakespeare's lifetime. Entry is £2/1.

Anne Hathaway's Cottage Before their marriage, Shakespeare's wife lived in Shottery, about a mile west of Stratford, in a pretty thatched farmhouse with garden and orchard. A footpath (no bikes allowed) leads to Shottery from Evesham Place. Entry is £2.40/1.20.

Mary Arden's House Probably the most interesting of the Shakespeare properties was once the home of William's mother. It now houses the Shakespeare Countryside Museum with exhibits tracing local country life over the last four centuries. The turn-of-the-century Glebe Farmhouse is also here. Entry is £3.30/1.50. Mary Arden's House is at Wilmcote, 3½ miles west of Stratford. If you cycle there via Anne Hathaway's Cottage, follow the Stratford-upon-Avon Canal towpath to Wilmcote rather than retracing your route or riding back along the busy A3400.

Holy Trinity Church
The Holy Trinity Church (☎ 266316) transepts date from the mid-13th century when it was greatly enlarged, and there have been frequent later additions; the spire dates from 1763. In the chancel, there are photocopies of Shakespeare's baptism and burial records, his grave and that of his wife, and a bust which was erected seven years after Shakespeare's death but prior to his wife's and thus assumed to be a good likeness. To see these mementos a donation of 50p is requested, and there's an offputting barrier across the choir to collect it. In summer, the church is open Monday to Saturday, 8.30 am to 6 pm, and Sunday from 2 to 5 pm.

Other Things to See
Harvard House on High St was home to the mother of John Harvard, founder of Harvard University in the USA. Next door is the **Garrick Inn**, while across the road the **Midland Bank Building** has reliefs illustrating scenes from Shakespeare's plays. In 1887 an American journalist presented the **American Fountain**, at the junction of Wood and Rother Sts, to the town.

Erected in 1881, the **Gower Memorial** features a statue of Shakespeare surrounded by four of his characters – Falstaff, Hamlet, Lady Macbeth and Prince Hal. It overlooks the canal basin, where the Stratford-upon-Avon Canal meets the Avon River, a popular place to watch narrowboats 'working the lock'.

The **Guild Chapel**, at the junction of Chapel Lane and Church St, dates from 1269, although it was rebuilt in the 15th century. Next door is **King Edward VI School** which Shakespeare probably attended; it was originally the Guild Hall.

The **Royal Shakespeare Theatre** (☎ 205301) dates from 1932 and exhibits the RSC Collection of props, costumes and theatrical paraphernalia. It's open Monday to Saturday, 9.30 am to 5 pm and Sunday, noon to 4.30 pm (3.30 pm on winter Sundays). Theatre tours operate Monday to Friday, 1.30 and 5.30 pm (except matinee days), Sunday at 12.30, 1.45, 2.45 and 3.45 pm. The tour costs £4/3, including entry to the RSC Collection.

The **World of Shakespeare** (☎ 269190), in the Waterside Studio Theatre, offers a

25-minute audiovisual introduction to Elizabethan England. It's open daily from 9.30 am to 5.30 pm (9.30 pm in summer). Admission costs £4/3.

Places to Stay

Hostel The *Youth Hostel* (☎ 297093), Hemmingford House, Alveston, is 1½ miles from the town centre. From the railway station, walk right through town, past the TIC, across the river and to the left (northeast) along Tiddington Rd (B4086). Bus No 18 runs to Alveston from Bridge St. The hostel is open from early January to mid-December and charges £12.60/9.40.

B&Bs Prices for B&Bs can be ridiculously expensive during summer. The prime hunting ground for cheaper places is Evesham Place, Grove Rd and Broad Walk, only a couple of minutes walk from the town centre. The TIC offers a free booking service.

Possibilities in Evesham Place include the cheerful *Grosvenor Villa* (☎ 266192) at No 9; the *Dylan Guest House* (☎ 204819) at No 10; the good-value, non-smoking *Clomendy* (☎ 266957) at No 157; and the *Arrandale* (☎ 267112) at No 208. Others along Grove Rd include *Woodstock Guest House* (☎ 299881) at No 30, or the *Ambleside Guest House* (☎ 295239) at No 41.

More expensive Evesham Place B&Bs include the frilly *Virginia Lodge* (☎ 292157) at No 12, where all rooms have bathrooms; *Twelfth Night* (☎ 414595) at No 13; and *Aberfoyle* (☎ 295703) at No 3. Some rooms at the *Carlton Guest House* (☎ 293548), at No 22, have private bathrooms.

There are several places on Alcester Rd, near the railway station. *Hunter's Moon Guest House* (☎ 292888) at No 150 has rooms from £18 to £25 a head. The *Moonlight Guest House* (☎ 298213) at No 144 has beds from £14 to £16.50 per person. Rooms with baths at *Moonraker House* (☎ 299346), at No 40, cost from around £40.

Hotels Numerous more expensive hotels cater to international package tours. Theatre-goers could hardly do better than stay at the *Arden Thistle Hotel* (☎ 294949), immediately across the road from the theatre, but prices start at £45 per head. The *Falcon Hotel* (☎ 279953) on Chapel St is a historic building which costs from £40 per person. *Dukes Hotel* (☎ 269300) on Payton St backs on to the canal and has rooms with bath from £35 per person.

Cheaper hotels include the *Payton Hotel* (☎ 266442), across the road at 6 John St, a small hotel charging from £26 per person, and the *Stratford House Hotel* (☎ 268288) at 18 Sheep St which charges from £20 a head.

Places to Eat

Sheep St has the best selection of dining possibilities. The *Greek Connection* (☎ 292214) at the river end serves Greek dishes for £8 to £10. The *Glory Hole* (☎ 293546), at No 21, offers steaks for £6.25. The *Opposition* (☎ 269980), at No 13, has slightly pricey pasta and steak. *Lambs* (☎ 292554) has pre or post-theatre pasta, salad and a glass of wine for £5.95. The *Vintner Wine Bar* (☎ 297259), at No 5, is a restaurant and wine bar.

Fatty Arbuckle's (☎ 267069), at 9 Chapel St, is stylish, if not especially cheap, with a very comprehensive menu.

Asian restaurants include *Lalbagh Balti Restaurant* (☎ 293563), at 3 Greenhill St, and the *Spice Balti* (☎ 267067) at No 7. Nearby, the *Wholefood Café* is good for lunch provided you get there early.

The *Boathouse* by Clopton Bridge has a pleasant café and bar.

Entertainment

A pint at the *Dirty Duck* (AKA the Black Swan), close to the river in Waterside, is an essential Stratford experience because of its theatrical connections. The very popular *Slug & Lettuce*, at 38 Guild St, also does food. The *Windmill Inn*, in Church St, is reputed to be the oldest pub in town, although the *Falcon Hotel*, in Chapel St, has been licensed for the longest continuous period.

Seeing a Royal Shakespeare Company production (☎ 205301) is a must. Performances take place in the main *Royal Shakespeare Theatre*, the adjacent *Swan Theatre* or the nearby *Other Place*. Tickets typically cost from £11 to £26 and are sometimes available on the day of performance. Get in early; the box office opens at 9 am. Stand-by tickets are available immediately before performances (£10.50 or £14.50) and standing room tickets are usually available up to the last moment for £4.50 or £5.

Getting There & Away

See the fares tables in the Getting Around chapter. Stratford is 93 miles from London, 40 miles from Oxford and eight miles from Warwick.

Bus National Express (☎ 0990-808080) buses link Birmingham, Stratford, Warwick, Oxford, Heathrow and London several times a day. Singles from Stratford include Birmingham £4.65 and Heathrow/Victoria £11.50. The National Express stop is on Bridge St, opposite McDonald's.

Midland Red West (☎ 535555) operates to Warwick (20 minutes, £1.75) and Coventry (one hour, £2.20), to Birmingham (one hour, £2.60) and to Oxford (1½ hours, £3.50). Walkers heading south for the Cotswold Way can also catch a bus to Chipping Campden.

Train Stratford station is on Station Rd a few minutes walk north-west of the centre. There are several daily services direct from London Paddington (2½ hours, £14.50).

Coming from the north, it's sometimes easier to transfer at Leamington Spa, sometimes at Birmingham. Services from Birmingham depart from Moor St station (£3.20, 50 minutes).

Getting Around

Call the Busline (☎ 535555) for local bus information. Bus No 18 operates via the Alveston Youth Hostel to Warwick and Leamington Spa, Monday to Saturday, hourly.

Guide Friday (☎ 299866), 14 Rother St,

operates open-top buses round the five Shakespeare properties every 15 minutes during peak summer months for £7/2.

Stratford is small enough to explore on foot but a bicycle is good for getting out to the surrounding country or the rural Shakespeare properties. The canal towpath offers a fine route to Wilmcote. Punts, canoes and rowing boats are available from the Boathouse by Clopton Bridge for £4 an hour.

Although there are lots of car parks, there's also lots of competition for the space.

AROUND STRATFORD-UPON-AVON

Stratford-upon-Avon is ringed by pretty villages, atmospheric pubs and stately homes. The popular Cotswold villages of Chipping Campden and Broadway are only a short distance south, and Warwick, Coventry and Birmingham are within day-tripping distance. You could even walk or cycle to Birmingham along the Stratford-upon-Avon Canal towpath.

Charlecote Park

Sir Thomas Lucy is said to have caught the young Shakespeare poaching deer in the grounds of Charlecote Park (☎ 01789-470277; NT), five miles east of Stratford-upon-Avon. The park, which was landscaped by Capability Brown, still has deer. The house was built in the 1550s and rebuilt in the 1830s. It's open April to October, Friday to Tuesday, 11 am to 5 pm. Entry is £4/2.

Ragley Hall

Ragley Hall (☎ 01789-762090) is a Palladian house a couple of miles south-west of Alcester. The house was built in 1679-83 but the over-the-top plaster ceilings and huge portico were added later. The intriguing South Staircase Hall with its murals and ceiling painting was painted between 1968 and 1982. The house is open April to September, daily except Monday and Friday, 1 to 5 pm, with guided tours at 11 am and noon. Entry is £4.50/3.

Birmingham

• *pop 1,014,000* • ☎ *0121*

Birmingham is the second largest city in Britain. Despite the collapse of many traditional industries it remains a major manufacturing centre and a city of fierce pride and boundless vitality. Although there are no essential sights and the city centre is submerged and disconnected by ring roads, Birmingham still has some interesting corners, particularly around the old canal system which runs through the heart of the city.

The city was one of the great pioneers of the Industrial Revolution with important inventors like steam pioneers James Watt (1736-1819) and Matthew Boulton (1728-1809), gas lighting inventor William Murdock (1754-1839), printer John Baskerville (1706-75) and chemist Joseph Priestley (1733-1804). In the mid-19th century, the city that was by then known as the 'workshop of the world' exemplified everything that was bad about industrial development but under mayors like Joseph Chamberlain (1869-1940), father of the unfortunate Neville Chamberlain, it also became a pioneer in civic development. Air raids shattered the city in WWII and the post-war ring roads and motorways virtually obliterated the old city centre.

The Birmingham accent consistently tops the ratings for England's most unattractive regional dialect. Locally, the city is known as *Brum*, the inhabitants are *Brummies* and the dialect is known as *Brummie*.

Orientation

Birmingham is initially a very confusing city to find your way around, particularly if you're driving. Even when you abandon your car in one of the many car parks it's not much simpler: ring roads and roundabouts continually divert you or cut you off from your intended destination.

Birmingham centres around a pedestrian precinct in front of the huge Council House.

Continue west from here to Centenary Square, the Convention Centre and Symphony Hall and the Gas St Basin on the canal.

Information

The most useful TIC is the Birmingham Convention and Visitor Bureau (☎ 693 6300) at 130 Colmore Row, on Victoria Sq. It's open every day, year round: Monday to Saturday, 9.30 am to 6 pm, and on Sunday from 10 am to 4 pm. The other four TICs are at 2 City Arcade (☎ 643 2514), in the Central Library entrance foyer, in Birmingham airport, in the National Exhibition Centre and in the International Convention Centre. The National Exhibition Centre is actually about midway between Birmingham and Coventry, adjacent to Birmingham airport.

What's On (free at the TIC, otherwise 80p) is a fortnightly listings guide to entertainment in Birmingham and the Midlands.

Town Centre

The central pedestrian precinct of Victoria and Chamberlain Squares features a statue of Queen Victoria, a fountain, a memorial to Joseph Chamberlain and some of Birmingham's most eye-catching architecture. The imposing Council House forms the north-east front for the precinct and includes the Art Gallery & Museum, connected by a bridge to another building topped by the clocktower known as Big Brum. The north-west corner of the precinct is formed by the modernistic Central Library, an inverted zigurrat sitting atop the Paradise Forum restaurant centre. Finally, there's the Town Hall, completed in 1834 and designed by Joseph Hansom (who also created the Hansom Cab) to look like the Temple of Castor & Pollux in Rome.

South-west of the precinct, Centenary Square is another pedestrian square closed off at the end by the International Convention Centre and the Symphony Hall, and overlooked by the Repertory Theatre. In the centre of the square is the Hall of Memory War Memorial and the curious modern statue depicting the diversity of Brummies.

SOUTHERN MIDLANDS

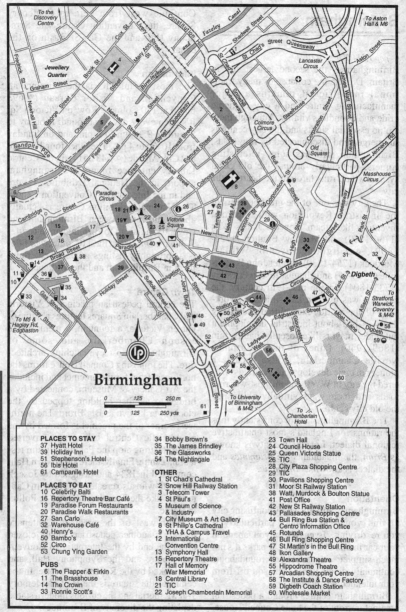

Birmingham

PLACES TO STAY
37 Hyatt Hotel
39 Holiday Inn
51 Stephenson's Hotel
56 Ibis Hotel
61 Campanile Hotel

PLACES TO EAT
10 Celebrity Balti
16 Repertory Theatre Bar Café
19 Paradise Forum Restaurants
20 Paradise Walk Restaurants
27 San Carlo
32 Warehouse Café
40 Henry's
50 Bambo's
52 Circo
53 Chung Ying Garden

PUBS
6 The Flapper & Firkin
11 The Brasshouse
14 The Crown
33 Ronnie Scott's

34 Bobby Brown's
35 The James Brindley
36 The Glassworks
54 The Nightingale

OTHER
1 St Chad's Cathedral
2 Snow Hill Railway Station
3 Telecom Tower
4 St Paul's
5 Museum of Science
   & Industry
7 City Museum & Art Gallery
8 St Philip's Cathedral
9 YHA & Campus Travel
12 International
   Convention Centre
13 Symphony Hall
15 Repertory Theatre
17 Hall of Memory
   War Memorial
18 Central Library
21 TIC
22 Joseph Chamberlain Memorial

23 Town Hall
24 Council House
25 Queen Victoria Statue
26 TIC
28 City Plaza Shopping Centre
29 TIC
30 Pavilions Shopping Centre
31 Moor St Railway Station
38 Watt, Murdock & Boulton Statue
41 Post Office
42 New St Railway Station
43 Pallasades Shopping Centre
44 Bull Ring Bus Station &
   Centro Information Office
45 Rotunda
46 Bull Ring Shopping Centre
47 St Martin's in the Bull Ring
48 Ikon Gallery
49 Alexandra Theatre
55 Hippodrome Theatre
57 Arcadian Shopping Centre
58 The Institute & Dance Factory
59 Digbeth Coach Station
60 Wholesale Market

The opposite direction from the Council House takes you into the shopping heart of Birmingham, along pedestrianised New St to the modern City Plaza, Pallasades, Pavilions and Bull Ring shopping centres and the landmark Rotunda office block.

Canal System

Birmingham has a canal system more extensive than Venice's, and restorations have begun to make the canals a tourist attraction rather than an eyesore. The Gas St Basin is the centre of the city's canal network and visiting narrowboats can moor right in the heart of the city. It's a pleasant ¾-mile stroll from the Gas St Basin, overlooked by the Hyatt Regency Hotel and flanked by trendy pubs and restaurants, along the canal banks to the Museum of Science & Industry. Along the way, the walk passes the International Convention Centre and the Symphony Hall. Other much longer walks can be made along the canal towpaths.

St Philip's Cathedral

The superb stained-glass windows by 19th-century Birmingham artist Edward Burne-Jones make this the most interesting church in Birmingham. In the centre of the city, on Colmore Row, it was built between 1709 and 1715 and became a cathedral in 1905.

Museum & Art Gallery

Right in the centre of the city, the museum (☎ 235 2834) has displays on archaeology, local history and natural history, but pride of place goes to the art collection, particularly the pre-Raphaelite paintings. The centre is open Monday to Saturday, 10 am to 5 pm and on Sunday to 5.30 pm. Entry is free.

Museum of Science & Industry

Right beside the canal, the Museum of Science & Industry (☎ 235 1661) recounts the city's dazzling industrial heritage with features that include a working 1779 steam engine made by Watt and Boulton, the huge City of Birmingham railway locomotive, WWII Spitfire and Hurricane fighter planes and the Railton Mobil Special land speed record car of 1947. The museum is open Monday to Saturday, 10 am to 5 pm and on Sunday afternoon. There's no entry charge.

Jewellery Quarter

Birmingham continues to be a major jewellery manufacturing centre and the jewellery quarter is packed with manufacturers and showrooms. The Jewellery Quarter Magazine has an interesting walking tour map taking you past the 1903 Chamberlain Clock and various other sights.

The Discovery Centre (☎ 554 3598), at

SOUTHERN MIDLANDS

The Pre-Raphaelites and the Arts & Crafts Movement

The Pre-Raphaelite Brotherhood was formed in 1848 by three young British artists: Dante Gabriel Rossetti, William Holman Hunt and John Everett Millais. Four other artists soon joined them in their rejection of contemporary English art and reverence for the directness of art prior to the High Renaissance, especially the work of Raphael (1483-1520).

Often unashamedly romantic in its view of the past, their work was characterised by almost photographic attention to detail, a combination of hyper-realism and brilliant colours that ensured the movement's popularity to this day.

Birmingham Museum & Art Gallery has one of the best collections of works by the 19th-century artists called the Pre-Raphaelites. If you get the bug, there are more fine paintings in the Lady Lever Art Gallery at Port Sunlight near Liverpool.

The Arts & Crafts Movement followed Pre-Raphaelitism in its rejection of contemporary standards and its yearning for an earlier, purer and more naturalistic style. The socialist William Morris, the movement's leading light, had worked with Rossetti and projected the same ideals into tapestries, jewellery, stained glass and textile prints. Cheltenham Art Gallery & Museum has a fine display of Arts & Crafts furniture, as does Arlington Mill in Bibury in Gloucestershire. ■

77-79 Vyse St, shows you the Smith & Pepper jewellery factory, exactly as it was on the day it closed in 1981 after 80 years' operation. The centre is open Monday to Friday, 10 am to 4 pm and Saturday, 11 am to 5 pm. Entry is £2/1.50. The jewellery quarter is north of the city centre; walk there in 15 to 20 minutes.

Aston Hall

Built between 1618 and 1635, this Jacobean mansion (☎ 327 0062) is in Aston Park on Trinity Rd, Aston, about 1½ miles north of the ring road. It's open from April to October, daily from 2 to 5 pm and entry is free.

Other Galleries & Museums

The small collection at the **Barber Institute of Fine Arts** (☎ 472 0962) is principally old masters. It's at the University of Birmingham, 2½ miles south of the city centre. The **Ikon Gallery** (☎ 643 0708) at 58-72 John Bright St is very close to the centre and features changing exhibitions of modern art.

At Bickenhill, near the airport and midway between Birmingham and Coventry, the **National Motorcycle Museum** (☎ 01675-443311) has hundreds of British motorcycles – BSAs used to be made in Birmingham, Triumphs in Coventry. The **Birmingham Railway Museum** (☎ 707 4696), just south-east of the centre at 670 Warwick Rd, Tyseley, has 12 steam locomotives.

The **Black Country Museum** (☎ 557 9463), a 26-acre re-creation of a turn-of-the-century Black Country village, is west of the centre at Tipton, Dudley.

Cadbury World

Chocolate freaks should make a beeline to Cadbury World to find the full story of chocolate and visit the chocolate packaging plant. Entry is £5/3.45 but this is a very popular visit on weekends and school holidays when it may be advisable to book a place by phoning ☎ 451 4159. Opening hours are daily, 10 am to 5.30 pm, but the site is closed a number of odd days so phone to check. Cadbury World is at Bournville near the A38.

Trains run to Bournville station from Birmingham New St station.

Organised Tours

Guide Friday operates seven daily 90-minute bus tours during the summer months at a cost of £6.50/1.50. Guided walking tours of the city centre depart from the Central Library in summer on Wednesday and Saturday at 10.30 am and 1.30 pm.

There are a variety of canal trips from the Gas St Basin or from the Convention Centre quay (☎ 236 7057). Typical costs are around £3, and there are longer trips to Selly Oak.

Places to Stay

Centrally located accommodation is principally aimed at business visitors. Since a day is quite sufficient to see the city's main attractions and as the B&Bs are some distance from the centre, it's quite easy to stay further out and day-trip into Birmingham. Stratford-upon-Avon is a short train ride away.

There are often deals to be found on weekends or during the summer months at business-oriented hotels. Rooms are sometimes available at £25 to £30 per person in the flashiest places in town. The TIC will make suggestions.

You need to take a bus or train to an adjoining suburb to find an economic B&B. Popular areas include Edgbaston (just southwest) and Acocks Green (south-east). The friendly *Ashdale House Hotel* (☎ 706 3598), 39 Broad Rd, Acocks Green, is a good place. There are six singles from £20, and three doubles from £30; some rooms have bathroom attached. Breakfasts are traditional or vegetarian.

The centrally located, modern *Ibis Hotel* (☎ 622 6010), at Ladywell Walk in the Arcadian Centre, has double rooms at £44 plus £5.25 for breakfast. The huge, old but renovated *Chamberlain Hotel* (☎ 606 9000) on Alcester St is a little beyond the Ibis but in a very dreary area. Rooms with attached bathroom are £35/40 including breakfast.

Just outside the ring road, the *Campanile Hotel* (☎ 622 4925), at 55 Irving St, offers motel-style accommodation. Doubles with attached bath are £36.50 (£29.95 on Friday and Saturday); breakfast is £4.50 per person.

Places to Eat

Restaurants Birmingham's own contribution to world cuisine is the Balti, a uniquely Midlands version of Indian food. Balti houses are spreading all over the country but Birmingham is their heartland and *The Essential Street Balti Guide* is the essential introduction to the best of them. The most down-to-earth Baltis are in the suburbs, but they are also found in the city centre. The *Celebrity Balti* (☎ 632 6074), at 44 Broad St, is much glossier than average, but the food is delicious. Baltis range from £6.50 to £9.50. For cheaper local Baltis, the Sparkbrook and Sparkhill areas, two miles south of the centre, are good hunting grounds. Take a bus No 4, 5 or 6 from Corporation St.

Circo (☎ 643 1400), 6 Holloway Circus, is an excellent and very popular new tapas bar. There's a £5 lunchtime special of a kilo of mussels, french fries, salad and mayonnaise. As well as a good range of tapas (with vegetarian options) Circo boasts 24 varieties of vodka.

Bambos (☎ 643 5261), at 61 Station St, features Greek food and live music. There's excellent Cantonese cuisine at *Chung Ying Garden* (☎ 666 6622), 17 Thorpe St, open daily from noon to midnight (11 pm on Sunday).

Centrally located restaurants in Fletcher's Walk, Paradise Place, immediately south of the Paradise Forum, include the Italian *Ciao Bella* (☎ 233 2484) at No 4, and the Spanish *Casa Paco* (☎ 233 1533) at No 7. *Henry's Café Bar* (☎ 631 3827), on Hill St, is a big, busy place serving a range of food including burgers and pizzas.

Pubs There are a number of pleasant pubs by the canal, all serving food, including the *James Brindley* (☎ 643 1230), right on the Gas St Basin, which is named after the canal pioneer. The trendy *Glassworks* (☎ 643 1234) also overlooks the Gas St Basin. On Broad St, on opposite sides of the canal, are the *Brasshouse* (☎ 633 3383) and the *Crown* (☎ 643 0444), while the *Flapper & Firkin* (☎ 236 2421), a little further along at Cambrian Wharf, is decorated in canal style.

Fast Food & Cafés In the same building as Friends of the Earth, at 54 Allison St, Digbeth, the *Warehouse Café* (☎ 633 0261) is a vegan food specialist open Monday to Saturday until 9 pm.

Paradise Forum, underneath the central library, has a variety of fast-food and restaurant outlets. There's also a choice of eating places at the *Arcadian Centre* on Hurst St, Birmingham's Chinatown.

The *Edwardian Tea Room* in the Museum & Art Gallery is a stylish place for a light meal or snack. In summer, the open-air section of the *Repertory Theatre Café Bar* (☎ 233 4118) is a popular gathering place.

Entertainment

See the pubs section under Places to Eat for good drinking spots. Birmingham has great jazz, including *Ronnie Scott's* famous jazz club (☎ 643 4525) on Broad St, which charges £8 to £12 entry depending on the night.

The *Institute/Dance Factory* (☎ 643 7788), Digbeth High St, is a large nightclub which often has live music. *Steering Wheel* (☎ 622 3385), Wrottesley St, Chinatown, is a busy club with three dancefloors. The *Nightingale* (☎ 622 1718), 40 Thorp St, is a popular gay club.

There's a ticket shop (☎ 643 2514) in the City Arcade office of the TIC. From 11 am daily you can get half-price theatre tickets here. The City of Birmingham Symphony Orchestra plays in the ultramodern *Symphony Hall* (212 3333). Big rock acts appear at the *National Exhibition Centre* (☎ 780 4133). Theatres include the *Hippodrome* (☎ 622 7486), home of the Birmingham Royal Ballet; the *Alexandra Theatre* (☎ 633 3325), home of the D'Oyly Carte Opera Company; and the *Repertory Theatre* (☎ 236 4455).

The *Triangle Cinema* (☎ 359 3979), at

SOUTHERN MIDLANDS

Aston University's triangular campus, is just 15 minutes walk from New St station and has an interesting arthouse programme.

Getting There & Away

See the fares tables in the Getting Around chapter. Birmingham also boasts an increasingly busy international airport (☎ 767 7000) with flights to numerous European destinations and to New York.

Bus Birmingham is a major transport hub, particularly for buses. National Express (☎ 0990-808080) has links to most parts of Britain from the Digbeth coach station. Local buses operate from the Bull Ring bus station.

Train New St station is underneath the Pallasades Shopping Centre, which in turn is linked with the Bull Ring bus station and Bull Ring Shopping Centre. Local trains, including the service to Stratford-upon-Avon, operate from Moor St station, which is only a few minutes walk from the main station. There's also the Snow Hill station.

Getting Around

For rail and bus services in and around Birmingham, the Centro phone number is ☎ 0121-200 2700. A Daytripper ticket (£3.70) gives you all-day travel on buses and trains (after 9.30 am).

Northamptonshire

Northampton itself has just a handful of buildings of interest but the surrounding area has two of the finest Saxon churches in the country, an interesting canal museum and Britain's most important motor racing circuit.

NORTHAMPTON

• *pop 154,000* • ☎ *01604*

Thomas à Becket was tried for fraud in Northampton Castle in 1164 but nothing significant remains of it. A fire in 1675 left few

other reminders of medieval Northampton. The Industrial Revolution made the town a shoe-manufacturing centre and the **Central Museum & Art Gallery** (☎ 39415), Guildhall St, has a collection of shoes to make any foot fetishist salivate. That aside, there's little to linger in Northampton for, although the **Holy Sepulchre** church has curiosity value as one of only four round churches in the country. The TIC (☎ 22677) at 10 Giles Square, directly across from the Guildhall, has information about surrounding attractions.

AROUND NORTHAMPTON
Stoke Bruerne Canal Museum

On a pretty stretch of the Grand Union Canal at Stoke Bruerne, eight miles south of Northampton, the excellent Canal Museum (☎ 01604-862229) has displays on the development of English canals and models of pioneering examples of canal engineering. Entry to the museum is £2.60/1.60 – the £1 car park fee will be refunded with the ticket. It's open daily, from May to September, 10 am to 6 pm, and in winter, Tuesday to Sunday, 10 am to 4 pm.

Silverstone

The British Grand Prix motor race is held in July at Silverstone (☎ 01327-857271), just south of the A43. It's still one of the fastest racing circuits in Europe, with a lap record of more than 140 mph, despite the addition of extra corners to slow cars down.

All Saints, Brixworth

Eight miles north of Northampton, All Saints, England's largest relatively intact Saxon church, was founded around 680 and incorporates Roman tiles from an earlier building. The defensive tower and stair turret were added after it was sacked by Vikings in the 9th century; the spire was added around 1350.

All Saints, Earls Barton

Eight miles east of Northampton, the Saxon church at Earls Barton is notable for its solid, square fortress tower with patterns imitating

Saxon tower of Earls Barton church

wooden buildings, built during the reign of Edgar the Peaceful (959-95). The clock was added in 1650 but the door beneath it may have offered access to the tower if a Viking raid threatened. Around 1100, the Norman nave was added to the original tower; other features were added in subsequent centuries.

Eleanor Crosses

Edward I's wife, Eleanor of Castile, died in 1290 at Harby in Nottinghamshire, eight miles west of Lincoln. At each of the 12 places between Lincoln and Charing Cross where her funeral cortege stopped, an elegant Eleanor Cross was erected. Of the three survivors, two are in Northamptonshire, one dominating the pretty village of **Geddington** (off the A43 between Corby and Kettering), another south of Northampton, just before the A508 crosses the A45. (The third is at Waltham near London.)

Buckinghamshire

Buckinghamshire is uneventful commuter country, a pleasant mix of urban and rural landscapes. In the south the gentrified dormitory towns of Beaconsfield and High Wycombe are bypassed by the M40 motorway to Oxford and Birmingham. The county town of Aylesbury is centrally located, and in the north, beside the M1, is Milton Keynes, the country's most famous planned new town and home to more than a quarter of Buckinghamshire's population.

Amongst the many commuters drawn to the county were the influential Rothschilds, who constructed several impressive houses around Aylesbury. In 1852 they built Mentmore Towers (now the HQ of the Transcendental Meditation organisation), enlarged Ascott House and created an imitation French château at Waddesdon. Other well-known figures who have lived in Buckinghamshire include the poets John Milton (in Chalfont St Giles, where his cottage is now open to the public), T S Eliot (Marlow), Shelley (also Marlow), and Robert Frost (Beaconsfield).

Despite the urbanisation, there's still some attractive countryside. Stretching across the south of Buckinghamshire, the Chilterns are a range of chalk hills famous for their beech woods. The countryside is particularly attractive in autumn when the beeches turn golden brown.

WALKS

The 85-mile Ridgeway follows the Chilterns

SOUTHERN MIDLANDS

to Ivinghoe Beacon in the east of the county. There are forest trails in the Chilterns and along the Grand Union Canal, which runs from London to Birmingham across the county's north-eastern edge.

GETTING AROUND

For Buckinghamshire bus information, phone the week-day inquiry line (☎ 01296-382000).

AYLESBURY

- *pop 52,000*   •   ☎ *01296*

Affluent Aylesbury has been the county town since 1725. Apart from being a transport hub with frequent trains to London's Marylebone station (one hour, £8), Aylesbury has little to offer visitors. However, the TIC (☎ 330559) at 8 Boughton St can provide general Buckinghamshire information.

AROUND AYLESBURY
Waddesdon Manor

Designed by French architect Destailleur for Baron Ferdinand de Rothschild, Waddesdon Manor (☎ 01296-651282; NT) was completed in 1889 in Renaissance style to house the baron's art collection, Sèvres porcelain and French furniture.

Several million pounds has recently been spent on restoring the house. It's open late March to mid-October, Thursday to Saturday, from 12.30 to 4.45 pm; Sunday and bank holiday Monday from 11 am to 5.15 pm; and also on Wednesday afternoon in July and August. Entry is £6. The grounds are open from March to Christmas Eve, Wednesday to Sunday, 11 am to 6 pm; entry is £3/1.50.

The château is six miles north-west of Aylesbury. From Aylesbury bus station, take Aylesbury Bus (☎ 84919) No 16 (15 minutes, £1.45).

Claydon House

The decoration of Claydon's grand rooms is said to be England's finest example of the light, decorative rococo style which developed from the more ponderous Baroque in early 18th-century France. Florence Nightingale lived here for several years and a museum houses mementos of her Crimean stay.

Claydon House (☎ 01296-730349; NT) is open from April to October, Saturday to Wednesday, 1 to 4.30 pm; entry is £3.70/1.85. It's 13 miles north-west of Aylesbury and buses drop you in Middle Claydon, two miles from the house.

Stowe Landscape Gardens

Four miles north of Buckingham, the superb gardens of Stowe, a famous private school, are open to the public during school holidays. The greatest of British landscape gardeners, Charles Bridgeman, William Kent and Capability Brown, all worked on the grounds.

The gardens are known for the 32 temples, created in the 18th century by the wealthy owner Sir Richard Temple whose family motto was *Templa Quam Delecta*: 'How Delightful are your Temples'. Among them, the Temple of British Worthies displays busts of Shakespeare and others.

Phone ☎ 01280-822850 for exact opening days. Entry is £4. For another £2 you can also look round parts of the house.

CHILTERN HILLS

The nearest range of hills to London, the Chilterns stretch from the outskirts of Reading (Berkshire) 40 miles north-east across southern Buckinghamshire. There are good though undramatic views and this is a popular walking area.

Wendover

Wendover is an attractive small town on the Ridgeway, a base for several good walks. The TIC (☎ 01296-696759) is in the Clock Tower in the High St.

At 852 feet, **Coombe Hill**, 1½ miles west of Wendover, is the highest point in the Chilterns, with lovely views from its summit and a network of footpaths. Chequers, the country seat that comes with being British prime minister, is to the west near Kimble.

There are frequent trains to Wendover from London's Marylebone (45 minutes,

£6.90). Aylesbury Bus runs a regular daily service between Aylesbury and Wendover.

Ivinghoe Beacon

This bare hill, marking the end of the Ridgeway, can be crowded with walkers over summer weekends. If you've just finished the Ridgeway walk, you can step out again along the 105-mile Icknield Way which crosses Bedfordshire to join the Peddars Way at Knettishall Heath (Suffolk).

Standing 756 feet above sea level, Ivinghoe was the site of one of the many beacons set up to summon men to arms if the Spanish invaded. Half a mile to the south is Pitstone Windmill, the country's oldest windmill, built in 1627.

Places to Stay *Ivinghoe Youth Hostel* (☎ 01296-668251) is in a Georgian mansion half a mile from the windmill, and one mile from Ivinghoe Beacon. From April to August it's open daily except Sunday; in March, September and October it's closed on Sunday and Monday; in February, November and until mid-December it's only open on Friday and Saturday. Beds cost £7.45/5.

Getting There & Away The nearest railway station is Tring, 2½ miles to the south-west, on the line from London's Euston to Milton Keynes. From London, it's 40 minutes (£7.30) by rail. Aylesbury Bus (☎ 01296-84919) has buses from Aylesbury to Ivinghoe via Tring hourly from Monday to Saturday and every two hours on Sunday. On Sunday and public holidays, from mid-May to late September, the Chiltern Ramblers bus (☎ 01582-574191) runs to Ivinghoe and Tring from Hemel Hempstead (Hertfordshire).

Jordans

Two miles east of Beaconsfield, **Jordans Quaker Meeting House** was built in 1688, its simple style reflecting the tenets of the Christian sect founded in 1650. One of its best known followers was William Penn, founder of Pennsylvania, who is buried in the graveyard. Nearby is the **Mayflower Barn**, possibly constructed from the timbers of the ship that took the Pilgrim Fathers to America.

Half a mile away is *Jordans Youth Hostel* (☎ 01494-873135), open from April to August, daily except Thursday. Phone for other opening days. The nightly charge is £6.75/4.60.

The closest railway station and bus stop are at Seer Green, just under a mile from the hostel.

Bedfordshire

Bedfordshire is compact, peaceful and largely agricultural. The River Great Ouse winds across the fields of the north and through Bedford; the M1 motorway roars across the uninteresting semi-industrial south.

If Bedfordshire is known to tourists at all, it's for its associations with John Bunyan, the 17th-century Nonconformist preacher and author of *The Pilgrim's Progress*, who lived in the county town of Bedford. South-east of Bedford there's the much-publicised stately home, Woburn Abbey.

GETTING AROUND

For information on buses around the county, phone the inquiry line (☎ 01234-228337). Stagecoach (☎ 01604-20077), the main regional bus company, has an Explorer ticket allowing a day's travel anywhere on its routes for £4.80/3.35 for adults/children.

BEDFORD

- *pop 77,000*   •   ☎ *012343*

Most places with links to John Bunyan are in and around Bedford, a pleasant riverside town with an interesting art gallery.

Information

The TIC (☎ 215226) is just off the High St at 10 St Paul's Square. It stocks *John Bunyan's Bedford*, a free guide to places in the Bedford area with a Bunyan connection.

SOUTHERN MIDLANDS

The Bunyan Meeting

The **Bunyan Meeting** (☎ 358870) in Mill St is a church built in 1849 on the site of the barn where Bunyan preached from 1671 to 1678. Bronze doors inspired by Ghiberti's doors for the Baptistry in Florence show scenes from *The Pilgrim's Progress*. As a hostage in Beirut, envoy Terry Waite took comfort from a postcard of the stained-glass window showing Bunyan in jail. From April to October the church is open to visitors from Tuesday to Saturday, 10 am to 4 pm. The small museum of Bunyan memorabilia is open in the afternoons only at present, but plans exist to expand these hours so more people can see some of the 169 editions of *The Pilgrim's Progress* from around the world. Admission costs 50p/30p.

Cecil Higgins Art Gallery

The **Cecil Higgins Art Gallery** (☎ 211222), Castle Close, houses a splendid collection of watercolours and drawings including works by Dürer, Turner and Ben Nicholson. It's open from Tuesday to Saturday, 11 am to 5 pm, and 2 to 5 pm Sunday, and it's free. **Bedford Museum** next door is open the same hours.

Places to Stay & Eat

Bedford makes an easy day trip from London but if you want to stay there are several hotels and B&Bs along leafy De Pary's Ave which leads north from the High St to Bedford Park. At No 59, *Bedford Park House* (☎ 215100) has rooms for £18/30. *De Pary's Guest House* (☎ 261982) is at No 48, with nine singles and six doubles. Rooms cost from £18 a head.

The historic *Swan Hotel* (☎ 346565), right beside the river, does two-night weekend breaks including half-board for £39.50 per head.

In summer you can snack alfresco on filled potatoes or sandwiches in the Piazza immediately behind St Paul's church. Pub meals are available at the *Saracen's Head* in St Paul's Square or *The Hogshead* in High St. Alternatively *Polly's Tea Rooms*, upstairs in Polly Flinder's at 13 High St, does soup and a roll for £1.75 or more substantial lunches for around £4.

Getting There & Away

Bedford is 50 miles north of London and 30 miles west of Cambridge.

The best way to get here is by rail from London, with frequent departures from King's Cross Thameslink (one hour, £12.30 day return). Most trains stop at Midland station, which is a well-signposted 10-minute walk west of the High St.

National Express has direct links between Bedford and London, Cambridge and Cov-

---

John Bunyan & *Pilgrim's Progress*

The son of a tinker, John Bunyan was born in 1628 at Elstow, near Bedford. He joined a nonconformist church and became an accomplished preacher. In 1660, when the monarchy was restored, the government tried to restrain nonconformist sects by forbidding preaching. Bunyan was arrested and spent the next 12 years in jail.

The allegorical work he started in prison, *The Pilgrim's Progress from this world to that which is to come*, became one of the most widely read books ever written.

An immediate success when it was published in 1678, its popularity stems from the fact that it's a gripping adventure story as well as a religious text. The pilgrim Christian, with his knapsack full of sins, embarks on a journey to paradise, via the Slough of Despond and Hill of Difficulty. On the way he is tempted by Vanity Fair, and imprisoned in a giant's castle but triumphing over these difficulties, he finally reaches the Celestial City.

Pilgrim's Progress has since been translated into over 200 languages. The TIC produces a leaflet listing places associated with Bunyan in and around Bedford. ■

entry. The main local bus operator is Stage-coach (☎ 01604-20077). The bus station is half a mile west of High St.

WOBURN ABBEY & SAFARI PARK

Not an abbey but a grand stately home built on the site of a Cistercian abbey, **Woburn Abbey** (☎ 01525-290666) has been the seat of the dukes of Bedford for the last 350 years. The house dates mainly from the 18th century, when the building was enlarged and remodelled into a vast country mansion. In 1950, half of the building was demolished because of dry rot but it remains impressive.

Woburn Abbey is stuffed with furniture, porcelain and paintings. The 3000-acre deer park is home to the largest breeding herd of Pére David deer, extinct in their native China for a century (although a small herd was returned to Beijing in 1985).

It's open daily from late March to October, 11 am to 4 pm; weekends only from January to March. Entry is £6.85/2.50. It's easily accessible off the M1 motorway or by public transport, with buses from Milton Keynes and Leighton Buzzard daily except Sunday.

One mile from the house is **Woburn Safari Park** (☎ 01525-290246), the country's largest drive-through animal reserve. It's open from late March to October; weekends only in winter. Entry is £8.50/5.50. If you visit the Abbey first you qualify for 50% discount.

WHIPSNADE

Whipsnade Wild Animal Park (☎ 01582-872171) is an offshoot of London Zoo which was originally established to breed endangered species in captivity; it claims to release 50 animals into the wild for every one captured. The 2500 animals in the 600-acre site can be viewed by car, on the park's railway, or on foot. It's open daily all year from 10 am to 6 pm (4 pm November to March); entry is £7.50/5.50, plus £6.50 for a car if you want to drive round.

In summer you can get to Whipsnade by Green Line bus from near Victoria Coach Station (☎ 0181-668 7261) or from Luton or Dunstable (☎ 01582-415252).

Hertfordshire

Hertfordshire is a mixture of commuter-belt housing estates in the south and rolling farm-land in the north. The M25 London orbital motorway sweeps round the southern border of the county and the busy M1 and A1(M) whisk traffic north.

Lively, interesting St Albans dates back to Roman times and has an abbey dedicated to Britain's first Christian martyr. North of St Albans, the house where George Bernard Shaw died is preserved as Shaw's Corner. Six miles east of St Albans is Hatfield House, one of Britain's most important stately homes and Hertfordshire's top attraction.

GETTING AROUND

Bus and rail timetables are available from TICs; the *Central Area Travel Guide* is the most useful. Phone ☎ 01992-556765 for public transport information.

ST ALBANS

- *pop 77,000*   • ☎ *01727*

Just 25 minutes train ride to the north, the cathedral city of St Albans makes a pleasant day trip from London. To the Romans, St Albans was Verulamium, and their theatre and parts of the ancient wall can still be seen to the south-west of the city.

Orientation & Information

The town centre is St Peter's St, 10 minutes walk west of St Albans railway station. St Peter's becomes Chequer St and then Holywell Hill as it heads south. The cathedral lies to the west, off High St, with the ruins of Verulamium even further to the west.

The TIC (☎ 864511) in the grand Town Hall on Market Place sells the useful *Discover St Albans* town trail (95p).

St Albans Abbey & Cathedral

In 209, a Roman citizen named Alban was put to death for his Christian beliefs, becoming Britain's first Christian martyr. In the 8th century King Offa of Mercia founded an abbey on the site of his martyrdom. The Norman abbey church was built in 1077, incorporating parts of the Saxon building and many Roman bricks, conspicuously in the central tower. After the dissolution of the monasteries in 1538 the abbey church became the parish church. Considerable restoration took place in 1877 when it was redesignated a cathedral.

In the heart of the cathedral is St Alban's shrine, immediately behind the presbytery and overlooked by a wooden watcher's loft where monks would stand guard to ensure pilgrims didn't pilfer relics. Look out for a particularly fine 14th-century mural of St Wilfrid on a nearby column.

The Norman nave columns are decorated with 13th and 14th-century murals, mainly of crucifixion scenes.

In the south aisle you can watch an 18-minute audiovisual account of the cathedral's history. From Monday to Friday there are screenings from 10 am to 4 pm, with the last showing at 3.30 pm on Saturday (afternoons only on Sunday). The cost is £1.50/1.

Verulamium Museum

This interesting museum of everyday life in Roman Britain (☎ 819339) is in St Michael's St and is open daily from 10 am to 5.30 pm (afternoon only on Sunday); admission is free. In the surrounding streets and adjacent Verulamium Park you can also inspect remains of a basilica, theatre and bathhouse.

Museum of St Albans

This museum (☎ 819340) in Hatfield Rd gives a quick rundown of the city's history since Roman times, although the displays of tools on the ground floor are of fairly specialist interest. It's open from Monday to Saturday 10 am to 5 pm and Sunday 2 to 5 pm; admission is free.

Gardens of the Rose

The Gardens of the Rose (☎ 850461), three miles south-west of St Albans, are open in summer only. With about 30,000 specimens, these gardens contain the world's largest rose collection. They're open from June to mid-October for £4 (children free).

Places to Stay

B&Bs convenient to the railway station include *Mrs Jameson's* (☎ 865498), 7 Marlborough Gate (off Upper Lattimore Rd), which charges £14/28 with shared bathroom; and *Mrs Tilt's* (☎ 863680), 3 Upper Lattimore Rd, where rooms cost £20/30. *Care Inns* (☎ 867310), 29 Alma Rd, is very close to the station, and has rooms with bath for £25/39.

The *Black Lion Inn* (☎ 851786), 198 Fishpool St, is on the west side of town by Verulamium Park. Rooms are £39 on Friday and Saturday, £59 during the week.

Places to Eat

Affluent St Albans has no shortage of places to eat, and good food is available in the many pubs. In George St, west of the High St, the *Tudor Rooms Restaurant* (☎ 853233) is part of the lively *Tudor Tavern*; a three-course lunch costs £5.95. Further down George St, the *Bottom Drawer Tea Rooms* can do you a lighter, cheaper lunch.

Along the alley opposite the 15th-century clocktower, *Upstairs Downstairs* (☎ 854843) has a three-course set menu for £10.99 (£14.50 on Saturday). Village Arcade nurtures *Abigail's Tearooms* for tea and sandwiches. The *Pasta Bowl* in the High St does reliable Italian food; a two-course meal with coffee costs £4.99.

There's a branch of *Pierre Victoire* (☎ 830480) in Hatfield Rd. *Café des Amis* (☎ 853569), 31 Market Place, serves food right through from breakfast time in stylish surroundings.

The *Fighting Cocks* off George St, near the abbey, is one of the claimants to being England's oldest inn. There's interesting Mexican food and good beer at the *Garibaldi*, 61 Albert St, off Holywell Hill. Live jazz at Sunday lunchtime packs drinkers into the *Goat*, Sopwell Lane, off Holywell Hill, but it's popular throughout the week.

Getting There & Away

There are eight trains an hour from London's King's Cross Thameslink to St Albans (£5.40). For London's Victoria Coach Station, take a bus to Bricket Wood and change.

The main bus company serving this area is Sovereign Buses (☎ 854732). There are several buses an hour to Hatfield railway station forecourt (20 minutes, £1.45), for Hatfield House and at least one bus an hour for Wheathampstead (15 minutes, £1.35) and Shaw's Corner.

HATFIELD HOUSE

Only 25 minutes north of London by rail, Hatfield House is England's most impressive Jacobean house, a graceful red-brick and stone mansion full of treasures, built between 1607 and 1611 for Robert Cecil, first Earl of Salisbury and secretary of state to both Elizabeth I and James I. Of an earlier Tudor palace where Elizabeth I spent much of her childhood, only the restored great hall and one wing converted into stables survive.

Inside, the house is extremely grand with a wonderful Marble Hall. There are famous portraits of Queen Elizabeth and numerous English kings. The oak Grand Staircase is decorated with carved figures, including one of John Tradescant, the 17th-century botanist responsible for the gardens.

Five-course Elizabethan banquets, complete with minstrels and court jesters, are held in the great hall at 7.30 pm on Tuesday, Friday and Saturday, and also on Thursday from April to September. Phone ☎ 01707-262055 for tickets (£27 to £29.25 depending on the day) and information.

Hatfield House (☎ 01707-262823) is 21 miles from London and eight from St Albans. It's open Tuesday to Saturday from noon to 4.15 pm, Sunday from 1.30 pm; admission

is £5.20/3.30. The entrance is opposite Hatfield railway station, and there are numerous trains from London's King's Cross station (25 minutes, £5.40 day return).

KNEBWORTH HOUSE

The home of the Lytton family since 1490 is a Tudor house sheathed in Victorian Gothic stucco – a fantasy of battlements, towers and turrets. Most of the alterations were made by Edward Bulwer-Lytton, Victorian statesman and author. The Tudor great hall survives and the house contains 17th and 18th-century furniture and paintings, and an exhibition on the British Raj. The 250-acre grounds boast a herd of deer and an adventure playground. In summer when the grounds play host to huge rock concerts the house may be closed.

Knebworth House (☎ 01438-812661) is one mile south of Stevenage, where there's a railway station with frequent connections to London's King's Cross (30 minutes). In summer, it's open daily from 11 am to 5.30 pm (Monday noon to 5 pm), weekends only in spring and autumn; entry is £4.50/4.

SHAW'S CORNER

The Victorian villa in Ayot St Lawrence where the Anglo-Irish playwright George Bernard Shaw died in 1950 is preserved much as he left it. In the garden is the revolving summer house (revolving to catch the sun) where he wrote several works, including *Pygmalion*, the play on which *My Fair Lady* was based.

Shaw's Corner (☎ 01438-820307; NT) is open from April to October, Wednesday to Sunday and bank holiday Mondays, 2 to 5.30 pm; entry is £3.

Bus No 304 from St Albans drops you at Gustardwood, 1¼ miles from Ayot St Lawrence.

SOUTHERN MIDLANDS

Eastern England

HIGHLIGHTS

- Lavenham
- Boating on the Norfolk Broads
- Cambridge University
- Choral Evensong at King's College Chapel
- Punting on the River Cam
- Fitzwilliam Museum
- Ely & Peterborough Cathedrals

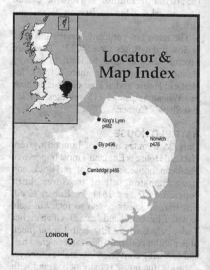

Locator & Map Index

King's Lynn p482
Norwich p476
Ely p496
Cambridge p485
LONDON

With the exception of Cambridge, most of the eastern counties – Essex, Suffolk, Norfolk and Cambridgeshire – have been overlooked by tourists. East Anglia, as the region is often known, has always been distinct, separated from the rest of England by the fens (reclaimed marshlands) and the Essex forests.

To the east of the fens, Norfolk and Suffolk have gentle, unspectacular scenery that can still be very beautiful. John Constable and Thomas Gainsborough painted in the area known as Dedham Vale, the valley of the River Stour. Villages like East Bergholt (Constable's birthplace), Thaxted and Cavendish are quintessentially English, with beautiful churches and thatched cottages.

The distinctive architectural character of the region was determined by the lack of suitable building stone. Stone was occasionally imported for important buildings, but for humble churches and houses three local materials were used: flint, clay bricks and oak. The most unusual of the three, flint, can be chipped into a usable shape, but a single stone is rarely larger than a fist. Often the flint is used in combination with dressed stone or bricks to form decorative patterns.

More than any other part of England, East Anglia has close links with northern Europe. In the 6th and 7th centuries it was overrun by the Norsemen. From the late Middle Ages, Suffolk and Norfolk grew rich trading wool and cloth with the Flemish; this wealth built

scores of churches and helped subsidise the development of Cambridge. The windmills, the long, straight drainage canals and even the architecture (especially in King's Lynn) call the Low Countries to mind.

ORIENTATION & INFORMATION

Norwich, Harwich, King's Lynn and Cambridge are all easily accessible from London by train and bus. Harwich is the main port for ferries to Germany, Holland, Denmark and Sweden.

There are youth hostels at Cambridge, Brandon, Blaxhall, King's Lynn, Hunstanton, Sheringham, Norwich, Great Yarmouth, Colchester, Castle Hedingham, Saffron Walden, Harlow and Epping Forest.

The East Anglia Tourist Board (☎ 01473-822922) can provide further information.

WALKS & CYCLE ROUTES

The Peddars Way and Norfolk Coast Path link to form a 94-mile walking track which

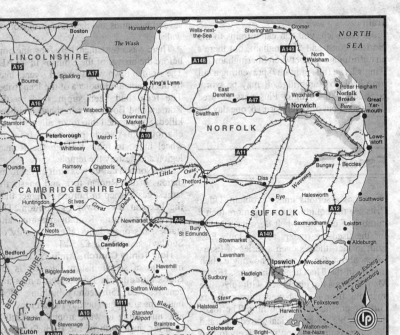

Eastern England

crosses the middle of Norfolk to Holme-next-the-Sea and follows the coastline south to Cromer. See the Activities chapter for more information.

This is ideal cycling country. Where there are hills, they're gentle. Bicycles can be hired very cheaply in Cambridge, and the TICs can suggest several interesting routes.

OTHER ACTIVITIES
Boating
The Norfolk Broads, a series of inland lakes (ancient, flooded peat diggings) to the east of Norwich, is a popular boating area.

Several companies rent boats of all types – narrow boats, cruisers, yachts and houseboats. See the Norfolk Broads section later in this chapter for information.

GETTING AROUND
Bus
Bus transport around the region is slow and disorganised. You can get timetables and information by phoning Essex ☎ 01245-492211; Cambridgeshire ☎ 01223-317740; Norfolk ☎ 01603-613613 (also freecall 0500-626116); and Suffolk ☎ 01473-265676.

Train

From Norwich, you can catch trains to the Norfolk coast and Sheringham, but there's an unfortunate gap between Sheringham and King's Lynn (bus or hitch?) preventing a rail loop back to Cambridge. It may be worth considering the Anglia Plus passes: three days travel out of seven for £16, one day for £7.

Essex

Essex has a serious image problem. Other Brits see the county as nothing more than a number of commuter-belt dormitory towns for the used-car traders of London's East End; in fact, there's even a series of Essex jokes about the people who made their money in the Thatcher boom years. 'Essex Man' drives a hot hatchback with furry dice swinging from the rear-view mirror; 'Essex Girl' preens herself beside him. The jokes don't rate highly on political correctness, and the image is unfair – you're as likely to find stereotypes such as these in any of the other counties surrounding London.

Despite being one of the largest counties in England, Essex has no vital sights. Each year, several million passengers transit the county through Stansted airport and the Harwich ferries. If you are passing through, you should certainly stop in Colchester, and the landscape along the border with Suffolk, which inspired the painter Constable, is also worth visiting.

GETTING AROUND

For information on buses in the county, phone ☎ 01245-492211; for rail information, phone ☎ 0345-484950.

COLCHESTER

- *pop 88,000* • ☎ *01206*

Britain's oldest recorded town, Colchester was the capital of Roman Britain when London was just a minor trading post. It's a surprisingly interesting place with a castle,

several museums and the remains of Roman walls.

There was a settlement here for some time before the arrival of the Romans in 43 AD. The Roman town was sacked 17 years later by the infamous Boudicca of the Iceni tribe. The Iceni had been suppressed by the Romans and Boudicca's husband had been killed. She stormed into town, allegedly in a chariot with swords protruding from its wheel hubs, to mow through the Roman legion and destroy the temple.

The Norman **castle** was built on the foundations of the Roman fort, and boasts the largest castle keep in Europe – bigger than the keep at the Tower of London. The museum contains Roman mosaics and statues. It's open daily (afternoon only on Sunday), and entry is £2.50/1.

Holy Trinity Church, Trinity St, is now a museum of social history. Nearby is the **Clock Museum**, in Tymperleys, a magnificent restored 15th-century building. Both museums are open Tuesday to Saturday. It's also interesting to walk around the **Dutch Quarter**, just north of the High St, established in the 16th century by Protestant refugee weavers from Holland.

Orientation & Information

There are two railway stations – most services stop at North station, about half a mile north of the town. The bus station is in the centre of town, near the TIC and the castle.

The TIC (☎ 282920) is at 1 Queen St. There are guided walking tours (£2/1.50p) of the town, June to September, daily at 2 pm (11 am on Sunday).

Places to Stay

Colchester Youth Hostel (☎ 867982), East Bay House, 18 East Bay, charges £7.45/5 for a bed. It's at the eastern end of town, on the river bank opposite Colchester Mill Hotel.

Scheregate Hotel (☎ 573034), Osborne St (near St John's St), offers reasonable B&B in the town centre. Rooms cost from £18.50/33 for singles/doubles, some with bath attached. The *Peveril Hotel* (☎ 574001), 51 North Hill, is also conveniently located on the road to the railway station. There are 17 rooms and they cost from £25/36.

The Old Manse (☎ 45154), 15 Roman Rd, offers comfortable accommodation for non-smokers. It's in a quiet square beside Castle Park, and part of the Roman wall is at the bottom of the garden. Rooms start at £25/35. If you have a car, *The Chase* (☎ 540587), 2 The Chase, is an excellent place to stay. It's two miles west of Colchester, near the A12; rooms are £25/36.

The *Rose & Crown Hotel* (☎ 866677), East St, is probably the best place to stay. There are 30 rooms, all doubles with bathroom attached, from £58 to £99.

Places to Eat

The *Rose & Crown Hotel* (see above) serves inexpensive meals in the large bar. The *Foresters Arms*, Castle St, is another good pub; there's live folk music on Tuesday.

Toto's (☎ 573235), 57 Museum St, is a café and takeaway that does pizzas and pasta. Main dishes are from around £5. For something more upmarket, try the *Warehouse Brasserie* (☎ 765656), 12 Chapel St North. There are set lunches from £7.95 and good vegetarian choices.

Getting There & Away

Colchester is 62 miles from London. There are daily National Express buses from London and frequent rail services between Colchester and London's Liverpool St station.

HARWICH
• *pop 15,000* • ☎ *01255*

Although the old harbour is interesting, the only real reason to come here is to catch a ferry to Holland, Scandinavia or Germany. Direct train services from London's Liverpool St station take around 70 minutes. See the Getting There & Away chapter at the start of the book.

The TIC (☎ 506139) is at Parkeston Quay. B&Bs near the ferry terminal and railway station include *Reids of Harwich* (☎ 506796), 3 West St, for £16 per person;

and *359 Main Rd* (☎ 502635), which costs around £14 per person.

DEDHAM VALE

In the Stour Valley, on the border with Suffolk, Dedham Vale was made famous by the paintings of John Constable, who was born here. It's now rapidly being overwhelmed by the number of tour buses that descend on the area. Flatford Mill (not the original) and Willy Lott's House, of *Haywain* fame, are now run by the Field Studies Council, which holds art courses here. Phone ☎ 01206-298283 for information.

Bridge Cottage (☎ 01206-298260; NT) also features in some Constable landscapes and now houses a display about the famous painter. It's open daily from June to September, 10 am to 5.30 pm, and for shorter hours (but not on Monday and Tuesday) the rest of the year. It's closed from December to February. Entry, with guided tour, is £1.50, children free.

Eastern Counties (☎ 01473-265676) and several other companies operate buses from Colchester to East Bergholt, three-quarters of a mile from Bridge Cottage. It's better to come by train (get off at Manningtree), since you then get a wonderful 1¾-mile walk along footpaths through Constable country.

THAXTED & SAFFRON WALDEN

These two attractive villages are in the north-western corner of the county. Thaxted dates from Saxon times and prospered in the 15th century through its links with the cutlery industry. The guildhall and some of the half-timbered, colour-washed houses are from this period. There's a small museum and a good view from the early 19th-century windmill, open at weekends from 2 to 6 pm.

Saffron Walden is named after the saffron crocus, which was cultivated in the surrounding fields. The church is one of the largest in Essex. The Sun Inn, nearby, is decorated with elaborate plasterwork. On the eastern side of the town, on the common, is an ancient earthen maze; a path circles for almost a mile, taking you to the centre if you follow the right route. *Saffron Walden Youth Hostel* (☎ 01799-523117), 1 Myddylton Place, is in a 15th-century building on the north-western side of the town; beds are £7.45/5. The TIC (☎ 01799-510444), 1 Market Place, has accommodation lists for the numerous other places to stay in both Saffron Walden and Thaxted.

Cambridge Coach Services (☎ 01223-236333) runs buses from London and Cambridge to Saffron Walden. The nearest railway station is Audley End, 2½ miles to the west.

AUDLEY END HOUSE

Once one of the largest houses in England, this Jacobean mansion was used as a royal palace by Charles II. Built in the early 17th century, it was described by James I as 'too large for a king'. Set in a fine park landscaped by Capability Brown, the house was originally built for Thomas Howard, Earl of Suffolk, and was remodelled by Robert Adam after two-thirds of the building had been demolished.

One mile west of Saffron Walden, Audley End House (☎ 01799-522399; EH) is open from April to September, Wednesday to Sunday, 12 noon to 6 pm (last entry 5 pm). Entry is £5.30/2.80. Audley End railway station is 1¼ miles from the house.

Suffolk

Once one of the richest parts of the country, Suffolk is now something of a backwater – and all the better for it as far as the visitor is concerned. Like most of East Anglia, the county is fairly flat, but the landscape has a serene beauty in parts.

Along the border with Essex is the Stour Valley, made famous by the painters Thomas Gainsborough and John Constable. Constable enthused about the county's 'gentle declivities, its luxuriant meadow flats sprinkled with flocks and herds, its well-cultivated uplands, its woods and rivers, with numerous scattered villages and churches, farms and picturesque cottages'. The description still holds true for much of the county today.

The region's economic boom as a wool trading centre lasted until the 16th century, and has left the county with its magnificently endowed 'wool' churches, many built to support much larger populations than live here now. Some of the villages have changed little since then, and Suffolk buildings are famous for their *pargeting* – decorative stucco plasterwork.

GETTING AROUND

Public transport around Suffolk is not great, particularly along the coast. For bus information, phone the county helpline (☎ 01473-265676). Numerous small bus companies operate in the area.

For train information, phone ☎ 0345-484950.

IPSWICH

• *pop 129,600* • ☎ 01473

In Saxon times, Ipswich was one of the principal towns in England. Less important now, it's still a major commercial and shopping centre, and Suffolk's county town. Ipswich is a transport hub for the region and, if you're passing through, you should stop to see the Ancient House and Christchurch Mansion.

The TIC (☎ 258070) is in St Stephen's Church, off St Stephen's Lane, near the bus station and the Ancient House. The railway station is a 15-minute walk along Princes St and across the roundabout.

Dickens used the *Great White Horse Hotel* (☎ 256558), Tavern St, in *Pickwick Papers*. The 'mouldy, ill-lighted rooms' he mentions have undergone something of a makeover and it's now a comfortable hotel that charges £42/54 (£5 reduction at weekends). The TIC can suggest cheaper options.

There are some good places to eat by the renovated Wet Dock.

Things to See

Combine browsing with sightseeing and visit the **Ancient House**, the town's best bookshop. It's faced with one of the finest examples of pargeting in the country, the overhanging upper storey decorated with white stucco.

Set in a large park to the north of the town, **Christchurch Mansion** (☎ 253246) is a fine Tudor house built in 1548 and now furnished as a country house. It has a good collection of works by Gainsborough and Constable, and is open from Tuesday to Saturday, 10 am to 5 pm, and on Sunday from 2.30 to 4.30 pm; entry is free.

At **Ipswich Museum**, on the High St, there's a replica of the Sutton Hoo ship burial found near Woodbridge, east of Ipswich, in 1939. It was the richest archaeological discovery in the country; the original artefacts are now in the British Museum.

Getting There & Away

National Express runs daily coaches to Ipswich. Eastern Counties (☎ 01603-622800) is the largest of the several local bus companies.

For rail information, phone ☎ 0345-484950. There are frequent trains from London's Liverpool St station (1¼ hours) and direct connections to Colchester, Bury St Edmunds, Norwich and Lowestoft.

STOUR VALLEY

Running along the border between Suffolk and Essex, the River Stour flows through a soft pastoral landscape that has inspired numerous painters, of which the most famous are Constable and Gainsborough. For Dedham Vale, the area known as Constable country, see the Essex section.

Long Melford
- *pop 2800*   • ☎ *01787*

Known for its long High St and timber-framed buildings, Long Melford has a magnificent church, with some fine stained-glass windows, two stately homes and the obligatory antique shops.

Melford Hall (☎ 880286; NT) is a turreted Tudor mansion in the centre of the village. There's an 18th-century drawing room, a Regency library, a Victorian bedroom and a display of paintings by Beatrix Potter, who used to stay here. It's open from May to September, Wednesday, Thursday, Saturday and Sunday from 2 to 5.30 pm; phone for other times; entry is £4.

On the edge of the village, down a tree-lined avenue, lies **Kentwell Hall** (☎ 310207), another red-brick Tudor mansion, but one that's privately-owned and makes much more of its Tudor origins. Between mid-June and mid-July, over 200 Tudor enthusiasts descend on Kentwell Hall to re-create and live out a certain year in the Tudor calendar. The house is surrounded by a moat, and there's a Tudor Rose brick-paved maze and a rare breeds farm. It's open daily from April to October, noon to 5 pm; entry is £4.75/2.75, more expensive during the historical re-enactment period.

There are buses to Long Melford from Sudbury and Bury St Edmunds.

Sudbury
- *pop 17,800*   • ☎ *01787*

Sudbury's prosperity was founded on the cloth industry and it continues to produce silk to this day, although on a much smaller scale than before. The TIC (☎ 881320) is in the town hall, open from April to October, Monday to Saturday.

Gainsborough (1727-88) was born in Sudbury and **Gainsborough's House** (☎ 372958), 46 Gainsborough St, is preserved as a shrine to the painter, with the largest collection of his work in the country. It's open from Tuesday to Saturday, 10 am to 5 pm, and on Sunday and bank holiday Mondays from 2 to 5 pm. Entry is £2.50/1.25.

Sudbury has a railway station with services to Colchester and London, and there are frequent buses to Cambridge and Norwich.

LAVENHAM
- *pop 1700*   • ☎ *01787*

A tourist honeypot, Lavenham can get crowded with bus tours but it's nevertheless worth seeing. The attraction is that this is a beautifully preserved example of a medieval

EASTERN ENGLA

wool town, with over 300 listed buildings. Some are timber-framed, others decorated with pargeting. There are cosy, pink, thatched cottages, crooked houses, antique shops and art galleries, quaint tearooms and ancient inns. When the wool industry moved to the west and north of England in the late 16th century, none of Lavenham's inhabitants could afford to build anything more modern and, as long as there are not too many tourists around, you can feel as if you're in a time warp walking through parts of the village.

The Market Place, off the High St, is dominated by the handsome **Guildhall** (☎ 247646; NT), a superb example of a close-studded, timber-frame building, dating back to the early 16th century. It's now a local history museum with displays on the wool trade, and is open daily from late March to October; entry is £2.60.

In Water St, **The Priory** has preserved its old-world charm and atmosphere. Once the home of Benedictine monks, then medieval cloth merchants, it is now privately owned, but can be visited from March to October, 10.30 am to 5.30 pm, daily; entry is £2.50/1. The herb garden, presided over by the statue of a Benedictine monk, is particularly attractive. Another private house worth seeing is **Little Hall**, which has soft ochre plastering and grey timber. It's open April to October, on Wednesday, Thursday and at weekends, 2.30 to 5.30 pm; entry is £1/50p.

At the southern end of the village, opposite the car park, is the **Church of St Peter & St Paul**. Its soaring steeple is visible for miles around. The church bears witness to Lavenham's past prosperity at the centre of the local wool trade.

The TIC (☎ 248207), Lady St, has lists of places to stay. Since most people come just for the day, there are numerous teashops offering light lunches.

Chambers runs buses from Bury St Edmunds; Ipswich Buses service No 757 runs from Colchester. There are no direct buses from Cambridge; you must go via Sudbury, seven miles to the south, also the ....tion of the nearest railway station.

BURY ST EDMUNDS
- *pop 30,500*   • ☎ *01284*

The most attractive large town in Suffolk, Bury is situated on the rivers Lask and Linnet amid gently rolling farmland. The town has a distinct Georgian flavour, with street upon street of handsome, 18th-century façades, harking back to a period of great prosperity. It's now a busy agricultural centre, and cattle, vegetable and fruit markets are held every Wednesday and Saturday. Greene King, the famous Suffolk brewer, is based here.

Centrally placed, Bury is a convenient point from which to explore west Suffolk. The ruined abbey is set in a beautiful garden and is worth seeing. There's also a fascinating clock museum, and recommended guided tours of the brewery.

History
Bury's motto 'Shrine of a King, Cradle of the Law' recalls the two most memorable events in its history. Edmund, a Christian prince from Saxony who was destined to be the last king of East Anglia, was decapitated by the Danes in 856 and his body brought to Bury for reburial in 903. The shrine to the saint became the focal point of the Benedictine monastery. The abbey, now in ruins, became one of the most famous pilgrimage centres in the country; for many years St Edmund was patron saint of England.

The second memorable episode in Bury's early history took place at the abbey. In 1214, at St Edmund's Altar, the English barons drew up the petition which formed the basis of the Magna Carta.

Orientation & Information
Bury is an easy place to find your way around because it has preserved Abbot Baldwin's 11th-century grid layout.

The TIC (☎ 764667), 6 Angel Hill, is open every day from June to September and daily except Sunday for the rest of the year. There are guided walking tours (£2/75p) from here, June to September, Monday to Saturday at 2.30 pm, and Sunday at 10.30 am.

There are tours around Greene King Brewery (☎ 763222), Crown St, from

Monday to Thursday at 2.30 pm. Tickets are £4; tours are popular, so you need to book ahead.

Walking Tour

Outside the TIC, there are many fine Georgian buildings on Angel Hill, such as the 18th-century Angel Hotel, which is covered in thick Virginia creeper.

The Abbey & Park Although the abbey is very much a ruin, it's a spectacular one, set in a beautiful garden. After the dissolution of the monasteries, the townspeople made off with much of the stone – even St Edmund's grave and bones have disappeared.

To reach the abbey, walk right along Angel Hill until you're opposite the second Abbey Gate, which is still as impressive in its austere regality as it was in Norman times. Cross over and walk round the green, which is home to Elizabeth Frink's statue of St Edmund (1976). From here, you can see the remains of part of the west front and Samson Tower, which have houses built into them.

The abbey is open daily until sunset and entry is free. There's a visitors centre, and an excellent 45-minute Walkman tour (£2.50) is available. Alternatively, you can guide yourself around the ruins using the information boards, which help to show how large a community this must have been with its chapels and priory, its chapter house and treasury, abbot's palace and garden. The huge church dominated everything in the vicinity. It was built in the shape of a cross, and contains a crypt and St Edmund's Altar, near which is the plaque commemorating the barons' pledge of 1214.

Walk down to the river, past the old dovecote, before turning back to head for the superb formal gardens. Leave by the Gothic Gate, and turn left to reach the cathedral.

St Edmundsbury Cathedral The cathedral dates from the 16th century, but the eastern end was added between 1945 and 1960 and the northern side was not completed until 1990. It was made a cathedral in 1914. The interior is light and lofty, and it has a painted hammerbeam roof. It's open daily from 8.30 am to 8 pm in summer, shorter hours in winter.

St Mary's Church From the cathedral, turn left out of the west door and walk past the Norman Tower to reach St Mary's. Built around 1430, it contains the tomb of Mary Tudor (Henry VIII's sister and one-time queen of France). A curfew bell is still rung, as it was in the Middle Ages.

Manor House Museum On Honey Hill, near St Mary's, is a magnificent museum of horology, art and costume, housed in a Georgian building. It's worth being here around noon, when all the clocks strike. Manor House (☎ 757072) is open daily from 10 am to 5 pm (afternoon only on Sunday); entry is £2.50/1.50.

Art Gallery & Moyse's Hall Retrace your steps along Honey Hill and Crown St, then turn left up Churchgate St, turning right at the end onto Guildhall St. Up the street, on the right, is Market Cross, remodelled in 1774 by Robert Adam and now the Art Gallery.

Turn right by the Corn Exchange and continue to the Buttermarket, where Moyse's Hall, dating back to the 12th century, is probably East Anglia's oldest domestic building. Now a local museum, its exhibits include archaeological remains and curios. Admission is free, and opening times are the same as for the Manor House Museum.

Places to Stay

On the A134 at Alpheton, nine miles from Bury and seven from Sudbury, there's cheap accommodation at *Alpheton Independent Hostel* (☎ 01284-828297) from £5.50 per person. The nearest youth hostel is even further away: 13 miles north in a detached house near Thetford Chase, the largest remaining forested area in England. *Brandon Youth Hostel* (☎ 01842-812075) is open every day from June to August, but with complex opening times outside this period –

phone for details. The nightly charge is £8.25/5.50.

In Bury, there's good-value B&B at *Hilltop* (☎ 767066), 22 Bronyon Close, off Flemyng Rd. It charges around £14 per person. Five miles north-west, by the Icknield Way trail, there's B&B for £13 per person at *The School House* (☎ 728792).

Ounce House (☎ 761779), in Bury, Northgate St, is very comfortable, centrally located and non-smoking. Charges range from £32 to £40 per person, and rooms have bathroom attached, some with garden views.

Charles Dickens stayed at the *Angel Hotel* (☎ 753926), in the centre of Bury, on Angel Hill. It's an upmarket place with upmarket prices, starting at £59/69 (breakfast extra). Weekend breaks are cheaper at £40 per person B&B or £55 including a four-course dinner.

Places to Eat
Cupola House (☎ 754093), 7 The Traverse, is an inn with a pavement café that does morning coffee, light lunches and afternoon tea. Dishes are priced from £2.95 to £4.95.

Holland & Barrett (☎ 706677) is a vegetarian restaurant and café at 6 Brentgovel St; most dishes are under £3. It's open from Monday to Saturday until 4.30 pm.

Mortimer's (☎ 760623), 31 Churchgate St, is a highly recommended seafood restaurant. Main dishes (brill, sea bream, monkfish etc) range from £7.50 to £15.

The best known pub in Bury is the *Nutshell*, which is the smallest pub in the country. It's off Abbeygate, on The Traverse.

Getting There & Away
Bury is 75 miles from London, 35 from Norwich and 28 from Cambridge.

From Cambridge, Stagecoach Cambus (☎ 01223-423554) runs buses to Bury (35 minutes, £3.95 for a day return) every two hours from Monday to Saturday; the last bus back to Cambridge leaves at 5 pm. Buses to Norwich are operated by Simonds Coaches (☎ 01263-513442); there's no Sunday service and you may need to change in Diss or Thetford. There's a daily National Express

bus to London, and frequent services to Lavenham and Colchester.

Bury is on the Ipswich to Ely line, so trains to London (1¾ hours) go via these towns. From Cambridge, it's a little quicker and cheaper to go by bus; there are trains every two hours to Bury (45 minutes, £5.10; £7.60 for a day return).

AROUND BURY ST EDMUNDS
Ickworth House & Park
Three miles south-west of Bury on the A143, Ickworth House is the eccentric creation of the Earl of Bristol. It's an amazing structure, with an immense oval rotunda, dating back to 1795. It contains a fine collection of furniture, silver and paintings (Titian, Gainsborough and Velasquez). Outside, there's an unusual Italian garden and a park designed by Capability Brown, with waymarked trails, a deer enclosure and a hide.

Ickworth House (☎ 735270; NT) is open from Easter to October, daily except Monday and Thursday, from 1 to 5 pm. The park is open daily all year from 7 am to 7 pm. Entry is £4.75/2 for the house and park, £1.75/50p for the park alone. To get here by bus, take Eastern Counties buses bound for Haverhill, leaving from outside Bury railway station.

SUFFOLK COAST
This is a coast of great contrasts that includes traditional seaside resorts like Lowestoft in the north, the busy port of Felixstowe (now freight only – passenger ferries all go from Harwich) in the south, and some of the least visited sections of coastline in Britain in-between. It's a coastline that's being gradually whittled away by the sea – the old section of the village of Dunwich now lies under water. One of the reasons that it's not well visited is that public transport along the coast is nonexistent in places.

Aldeburgh
• *pop 2800* • ☎ *01728*
The sea is closing in on Aldeburgh, where the beach is now only yards from the village. The place is best known for the Aldeburgh Festival, an annual programme of music and

the arts that was begun in 1948 by Benjamin Britten and Peter Pears. It takes place each June in venues around Aldeburgh and at Snape Maltings, three miles up the river. It's the most important festival in Eastern England. For information and bookings, phone the box office on ☎ 453543.

The TIC (☎ 453637), on the High St, is open from Easter to October. *Blaxhall Youth Hostel* (☎ 688206) is 4½ miles from Aldeburgh, near Snape Maltings; beds are £6.75/4.60. Eastern Counties buses run between Ipswich and Aldeburgh.

Orford

Few visitors get to this little village, six miles south of Snape, but there are several worthwhile attractions. The ruins of Orford Castle (EH) date from the 12th century; only the keep has survived.

The other draw is gastronomic. Two smokehouses do good business selling smoked fish, meat and fresh oysters. From Orford Quay, MV *Lady Florence* (☎ 0831-698298) takes diners on four-hour lunch or dinner cruises, year round. The smokehouses supply the food.

Norfolk

Noel Coward once famously remarked that Norfolk was very flat. It is, but he didn't just mean the landscape. Although the nightlife may have become a little more lively in Norwich since then, it's still not Monte Carlo. Once a busy wool-producing and trading area, making use of the ports of King's Lynn and Great Yarmouth, Norfolk is now much quieter and less populated than it was in the Middle Ages. It's a sleepy county, not yet overrun by tourists, with a superb, unspoilt coastline and several nature reserves that attract bird-watchers. Norwich, the county town, is a very pleasant place with an interesting castle and cathedral; the Norfolk Broads is a network of inland waterways that have long been popular for boating holidays; and King's Lynn is a historic port

on the River Ouse, with several very well-preserved buildings. The whole area is easily accessible from Cambridge.

WALKS & CYCLE ROUTES

Several waymarked walking trails cross the county, the best known being the Peddars Way (see the Activities chapter at the start of this book). The Weavers Way is a 57-mile walk from Cromer to Great Yarmouth via Blickling and Stalham. The Angles Way follows the valleys of the Waveney and the Little Ouse for 70 miles. The Around Norfolk Walk is a 220-mile trail linking the Peddars Way, the Norfolk Coast Path, the Weavers Way and the Angles Way. TICs have information leaflets on these walks and on cycle routes.

GETTING AROUND

The public transport county phone line (☎ 01603-613613, freephone 0500-626116) has information on bus routes; there are several operators, the largest being Eastern Counties First Bus (☎ 01603-622800).

Norwich, King's Lynn, Cromer and Great Yarmouth are accessible by rail. For rail information, phone ☎ 0345-484950.

NORWICH
- *pop 170,000* • ☎ *01603*

Norfolk's county town (pronounced norridge) was once larger than London. For several centuries, when its prosperity was based on trade with the Low Countries, it was the second-largest town in England.

The East Angles had a fortified centre at Norwich that was burnt down twice by marauding Danes. The Normans built the splendid castle keep, now the best preserved example in the country. Below the castle lies what has been described as the most complete medieval English city. Clustered round the castle and cathedral, there are more than 30 parish churches within the circle of river and city walls.

Norwich is a surprisingly lively city with a large student population; the University of East Anglia is on the western outskirts.

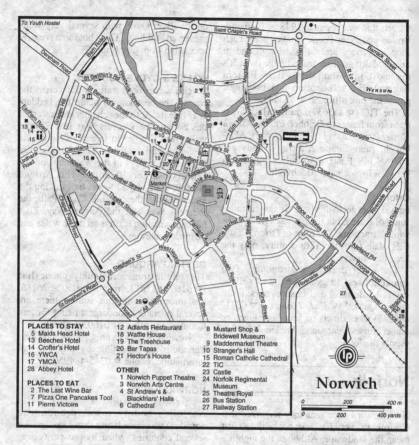

PLACES TO STAY
5 Maids Head Hotel
13 Beeches Hotel
14 Crofter's Hotel
16 YWCA
17 YMCA
28 Abbey Hotel

PLACES TO EAT
2 The Last Wine Bar
7 Pizza One Pancakes Too!
11 Pierre Victoire

12 Adlards Restaurant
18 Waffle House
19 The Treehouse
20 Bar Tapas
21 Hector's House

OTHER
1 Norwich Puppet Theatre
3 Norwich Arts Centre
4 St Andrew's & Blackfriars' Halls
6 Cathedral

8 Mustard Shop & Bridewell Museum
9 Maddermarket Theatre
10 Stranger's Hall
15 Roman Catholic Cathedral
22 TIC
23 Castle
24 Norfolk Regimental Museum
25 Theatre Royal
26 Bus Station
27 Railway Station

Norwich

Orientation & Information

The castle is in the centre of Norwich, the TIC two blocks west. There are two cathedrals – Roman Catholic to the west and Anglican to the east.

The TIC (☎ 666071) is in the guildhall, Gaol Hill. It's open Monday to Saturday, 10 am to 5 pm, and on Sunday morning in summer. Guided walking tours (1½ hours, £1.50) take place at various times, including the evening – phone the TIC for details.

Outside the TIC is the market, a patchwork of stall awnings known as tilts. This is one of the biggest and longest running

markets in the country. It was moved here 900 years ago from its original site in Tombland, by the cathedral.

Norwich Castle

Two blocks east of the market square is the massive Norman castle keep. It was built in about 1160, measuring 90 feet square by 70 feet high, a solid sentinel on the hill overlooking the medieval and modern cities. It's the best surviving example of Norman military architecture after the Tower of London, and has worn pretty well, although it was refaced in 1834.

The castle is now a museum, housing archaeological and natural history exhibits, as well as providing a gallery for the paintings of the Norwich School. Founded by John Crome in the early 19th century, this group, which included John Cotman, painted local landscapes and won acclaim throughout Europe. The museum (☎ 223624) is open from 10 am to 5 pm (afternoon only on Sunday); entry is £2.20/1.50. Beside the castle is the **Norfolk Regimental Museum**. It's open Monday to Saturday, 10 am to 5 pm; entry is £1.40/70p and also includes the Bridewell and Stranger's Hall museums (see below).

Other Museums

About 250 yards north of the castle, there are three museums in the same area. **The Mustard Shop**, 3 Bridewell Alley, has a small museum (entrance free, closed on Sunday) that tells the story of Colman's Mustard, a famous local product. Nearby is **Bridewell Museum**, Bridewell Alley, which has surprisingly interesting displays of local industries throughout the last 200 years. It's open Monday to Saturday, 10 am to 5 pm; entry is £1.40/70p.

Stranger's Hall is 300 yards west of here, along St Andrew's and Charing Cross Sts. It's a medieval town house, with rooms furnished in period styles. There's also a large collection of costumes and textiles, however, it was closed for renovations at the time of writing. Entry times and prices were the same as for the Bridewell Museum.

Elm Hill

Thanks to imaginative restoration, this street has retained its medieval charm and atmosphere, and is, appropriately enough, the centre of the local antique business. It's one of the most attractive parts of the city. Walk down Wensum St to Tombland, where the market was originally located. 'Tomb' is an old Norse word for 'empty' – hence space for a market.

Norwich Cathedral

The focal point of the city, the Anglican cathedral has retained the appearance and characteristics of a great Anglo-Norman abbey church more than any other English cathedral, apart from Durham.

The foundation stone was laid in 1096, and the building took 40 years to complete. In 1463 it was made fireproof by means of a magnificent stone lierne vault (a kind of inside roof), which, with its sculpted bosses, is one of the finest achievements of English medieval masonry.

As you enter the cathedral through the west door, the first thing that strikes you is the length of the nave. Its 14 bays are constructed in yellow-beige stone. Above, on the amazing vault, stories from the Old and New Testament are carved into the bosses. Beyond the tower, which is richly patterned, is probably the most beautiful part of the cathedral – the eastern section.

At the eastern end, outside the War Memorial Chapel, is the grave of Edith Cavell, a Norfolk nurse who was shot by the Germans in Belgium during WWI for helping POWs to escape. Her famous last words were, 'I realise patriotism is not enough. I must have no hatred or bitterness towards anyone'.

The Cathedral Close contains some handsome houses and the old chapel of the King Edward VI School – which was where Nelson was educated.

The cathedral (☎ 764385) is open daily from 7.30 am to 7 pm (6 pm in winter).

Sainsbury Centre for the Visual Arts

To the west of the city, on the university campus (a 20-minute bus trip from Castle Meadow), this gallery is remarkable both for the building itself and the art it contains. It was designed by Norman Foster and filled with an eclectic collection of works by Picasso, Moore, Bacon and Giacometti, displayed beside art from Africa, the Pacific and the Americas. It's open from Tuesday to Sunday, noon to 5 pm; entry is £1/50p.

Places to Stay

Hostels The *Norwich Youth Hostel* (☎ 627647), 112 Turner Rd, is open every day from April to August; phone for other opening times. The nightly charge is £8.25/5.50. It's two miles from the railway station, on the western edge of the city.

The *YMCA* (☎ 620269), 48 St Giles St, is in a better location. Singles cost £12.50 with breakfast; £8.50 in a dorm. In the same area, there's a friendly *YWCA* (☎ 625982), at 61 Bethel St, which has women-only singles for £10.71. You need to book in advance, especially in summer.

Camping One mile south of the centre is *Lakenham Camping* (☎ 620060), which charges £3.75 per person (plus £3 if you're not a C&C member), and is open from April to September.

B&Bs & Hotels Most of the B&Bs and cheaper hotels are outside the ring road, along Earlham and Unthank Rds to the west, and around the railway station.

The B&Bs along Earlham Rd become more expensive the closer they are to the centre. *Aberdale Lodge* (☎ 502100), at No 211, charges £15/30 with shared bath. *Barton Lodge* (☎ 454874), at No 148, is a 15-minute walk from the centre. There are two singles for £15 with shared bath, and two doubles for £38 with shower attached.

Edmar Lodge (☎ 615599) is a friendly place at 64 Earlham Rd, with singles from £21 and doubles from £33, some with attached bath. Still in Earlham Rd, in the shadow of the RC cathedral, *Crofter's Hotel* (☎ 613287), at No 2, has 15 rooms for £34.50/49.50, all with bathroom attached.

In the railway station area, the *Abbey Hotel* (☎ 612915), 16 Stracey Rd, charges £16/32 with shared bath. There are several other places in this area.

In the centre is the comfortable and historic *Maid's Head Hotel* (☎ 761111), a 700-year-old former coaching inn, on Tombland. Room charges are £69/90 (plus £8.75 for breakfast) during the week, £41/82 including breakfast at weekends.

Places to Eat

The *Treehouse* (☎ 763258), 14 Dove St (above the healthfood shop), is an excellent vegetarian restaurant serving such delicacies as nut and moonbeam paté. Main courses come in two sizes – £3.35 and £4.45.

Around the corner at No 7 Pottergate there's a branch of *Pierre Victoire* (☎ 766667), with the usual good-value lunches. Opposite is *Bagley's Bistro* (☎ 626763); main dishes are £4.25 to £8.95, cheaper upstairs in the bar. *Bar Tapas* (☎ 764077), 18 Exchange St, is another busy place: most tapas are £3.95.

The *Waffle House* (☎ 612790), 39 St Giles St, specialises in savoury and sweet Belgian waffles made with stoneground wholewheat or white flour. They range in price from £1.40 to £4.85 and there's a wide selection of fillings.

Hector's House (☎ 622836), 18 Bedford St, is a café/bar that serves coffee and light lunches. There's no food available in the evening – the place is so popular there wouldn't be room to serve it.

Pizza One Pancakes Too! (☎ 621583), 24 Tombland, is near the cathedral and does as its name says. Next door is *Boswells*, a wine bar with live jazz or blues most nights.

For a splurge, there's *Adlards Restaurant* (☎ 633522), 79 Upper St Giles St, offering classic French cuisine. It's open from Tuesday to Saturday for lunch and dinner; dinner costs £32 for four courses.

Entertainment

The *Theatre Royal* (☎ 630000), Theatre St, features programmes by touring drama and ballet companies.

Norwich Arts Centre (☎ 660352), Reeves Yard, St Benedicts St, features a wide-ranging programme of drama, concerts, dance, cabaret and jazz.

On St George's St, *St Andrew's & Blackfriars' Halls*, once home to Dominican Blackfriars, now serve as an impressive civic centre where concerts, antique and craft markets, the Music and Arts Festival and even the annual beer festival are held; there's also a restaurant in the crypt.

The *Norwich Puppet Theatre* (☎ 629921), St James, Whitefriars, is popular, particularly with children. Tickets are around £4.50/3.50.

Getting There & Away

Cambridge Coach Services (☎ 01223-236333) has four buses a day to Cambridge (two hours, £7), and National Express has a daily bus to Cambridge and London. Eastern Counties (☎ 01603-622800) runs buses to King's Lynn (1½ hours, £4.15), Peterborough and Cromer. There's no bus service to Ely, and for Bury St Edmunds you must change in Diss.

From the railway station (☎ 0345-484950) there are direct services to London, Cambridge, Ely, Cromer and Great Yarmouth.

AROUND NORWICH
Blickling Hall

Anne Boleyn, one of Henry VIII's unfortunate wives, lived in the original Blickling Hall. It's said that on the anniversary of her execution, a coach drives up to the house – drawn by headless horses, driven by headless coachmen and containing the queen with her head on her lap.

The house dates from the early 17th century and is filled with Georgian furniture, pictures and tapestries. There's an impressive Jacobean plaster ceiling in the long gallery. The house is surrounded by parkland offering good walks.

Blickling Hall (☎ 01263-733084; NT) is 15 miles north of Norwich, and open from Easter to October, daily except Monday and Thursday, 1 to 5 pm; entry is £5.50/3.

Eastern Counties runs buses here from Norwich in summer. Aylsham is the nearest railway station, 1¾ miles away.

NORFOLK BROADS

The Norfolk Broads is an area of rivers, lakes, marshland, nature reserves and bird sanctuaries on the Norfolk/Suffolk border. The area, measuring some 117 sq miles, has 'national protected status', which is equivalent to it being a national park.

A broad is a large piece of water formed by the widening of a river. The main river is the Bure, which enters the Broads at Wroxham and is then joined by several other rivers, including the Ant and the Thurne. The Waveney joins the Yare to meet the Bure at Great Yarmouth, where this large network of rivers flows into the sea. What makes this area special is that all these lakes, rivers and their tributaries are navigable. In all, there are 125 miles of lock-free waterways.

There's little variety of scenery, but the ecology of the area means that it's a wonderful place for nature lovers, and for people who like being on or near the water. The habitat includes freshwater lakes, slow-moving rivers, water meadows, fens, bogs and saltwater marshes, and the many kinds

---

The Origin of the Broads

For many years the origin of the Norfolk Broads was unclear. The rivers were undoubtedly natural and many thought the lakes were too – it's hard to believe they're not when you see them – but no-one could explain how they could have been formed.

The mystery was solved when records were discovered in the remains of St Benet's Abbey (on the River Bure). They showed that, from the 12th century, certain parts of land in Hoveton Parish were used for peat digging. The area had little woodland and the only source of fuel was peat. Since East Anglia was well populated and prosperous, peat digging became a major industry.

Over a period of about 200 years, approximately 2600 acres were dug up. However, water gradually seeped through causing marshes, and later lakes, to develop. The first broad to be mentioned in records is Ranworth Broad (in 1275). Eventually, the amount of water made it extremely difficult for the diggers, and the peat-cutting industry died out. In no other area of Britain has human effort changed the natural landscape so dramatically. ∎

of birds, butterflies and water-loving plants that inhabit them.

How Hill, a mere 40 feet above sea level, is the highest place in the Broads. Since there's nothing to impede the path of sea breezes, this is a good area for wind power. Many wind pumps (which look like windmills) were built to drain the marshland and to return the water to the rivers.

Orientation

The Broads form a triangle, with Norwich at the apex, the Norwich-Cromer road as the northern side, the Norwich-Lowestoft road as the southern side and the coastline as the base.

Wroxham, on the A1151 from Norwich, and Potter Heigham, on the A1062 from Wroxham, are the main centres. Along the way, there are plenty of waterside pubs, villages and market towns where you can stock up on provisions, and stretches of river where you can feel you are the only person around.

Information

The Broads Authority (☎ 01603-610734), Thomas Harvey House, 18 Colegate, Norwich NR3 1BQ, can supply information about the conservation centres and RSPB bird-watching hides at Berney Marshes, Ranworth, Bure Marshes, Cockshoot Broad, Hickling Broad, Horsey Mere, How Hill, Strumpshaw Fen and Surlingham Church Marsh.

You can also get information about the Broads from the Norwich TIC (☎ 01603-666071).

Getting Around

Two companies that operate boating holidays are Blakes (☎ 01603-782911) and Hoseasons (☎ 01502-501010). Costs depend on the boat size, the facilities on the boat, the time of year and the length of the holiday. A boat for two to four people is £350 to £450 for a week – fuel is extra, though you're unlikely to use much. Short breaks (three to four days) during the off season are much cheaper.

Many boat yards (particularly in the Wroxham and Potter Heigham areas) have a variety of boats for hire by the hour, half-day or full day. Charges still vary according to the season and the size of the boat, but they start from £9 for one hour, £24 for four hours and £40 for a day.

No previous experience is necessary, but remember to stay on the right side of the river, that the rivers are tidal, and to stick to the speed limit – you can get prosecuted for speeding. If you don't feel like piloting your own boat, Broads Tours runs pleasure trips from April to September, with a commentary, from £4.95/3.95 per person. Broads Tours has two bases: The Bridge, Wroxham (☎ 01603-788207), and Herbert Woods, Potter Heigham (☎ 01692-670711).

NORFOLK COAST
Great Yarmouth

- *pop 54,800*   -   ☎ *01493*

This is one of Britain's most popular seaside resorts, complete with all the tacky trimmings such as amusement arcades and greasy-spoon cafés, but it's also an important port for the North Sea oil and gas industries.

As well as a wide, sandy beach, other attractions include a number of interesting buildings in the old town. The **Elizabethan House Museum**, South Quay, was a merchant's house and now contains a display of 19th-century domestic life. The **Old Merchant's House**, Row 111, South Quay, is a group of typical 17th-century town houses. The **Tolhouse Museum**, Tolhouse St, was once the town's courthouse and jail; prison cells can be seen and there's a display covering the town's history. There's also a maritime museum. The TIC (☎ 846345) is in the town hall. There's another TIC (☎ 842195) on Marine Parade.

There are numerous B&Bs, and *Great Yarmouth Youth Hostel* (☎ 843991), 2 Sandown Rd, is near the beach, three-quarters of a mile from the railway station.

Tunstall Camping Barn (☎ 700279), Manor Farm, Tunstall, Halvergate, is an independent hostel offering 20 sleeping platforms in a barn for £3.50 per person. It's

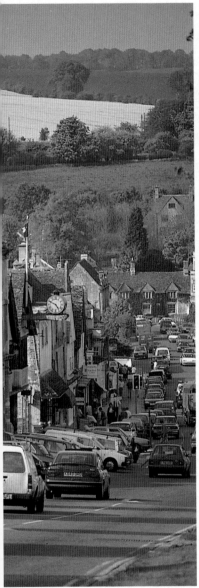

Left: Burford, Oxfordshire
Top Right: Bicycle parking, Cambridge
Bottom Right: Punting on the River Cam, Cambridge

SEAN SHEEHAN

TONY WHEELER

RICHARD EVERIST

BRYN THOMAS

Top: Brighton Pier, Brighton, East Sussex
Middle: Everything you need at the beach, Weymouth, Dorset
Bottom Left: Donkey rides on the beach, St Andrews, Fife
Bottom Right: Beach at St Ives, Cornwall

about six miles from Great Yarmouth, on the Norwich road.

Great Yarmouth is on main bus and rail routes to Norwich. Eastern Counties runs an hourly service between Norwich and Great Yarmouth (40 minutes, £2.45).

Cromer

In the late Victorian and Edwardian eras, Cromer was transformed into the most fashionable resort on the coast. It's now somewhat run down, but with its elevated seafront, long, sandy beach and scenic coastal walks, it's still worth visiting. Cromer has long been famous for its crabs, and they're still caught and sold here. The TIC (☎ 01263-512497) is by the bus station, and this is one of the few coastal resorts with a railway station linked to Norwich.

Two miles south-west of Cromer, **Felbrigg Hall** (☎ 01263-837444; NT) is one of the finest 17th-century houses in Norfolk. It contains a collection of 18th-century furniture; outside is a walled garden, orangery and landscaped park. It's open from Easter to October, daily except Tuesday and Friday, from 1 to 5 pm; entry is £5/2.50.

Cley Marshes

Between Cromer and Wells, Cley Marshes (☎ 01263-740380) is one of the top birdwatching places in Britain, with over 300 species recorded. There's a visitors centre built on high ground to give good views over the area.

Wells-Next-The-Sea

- *pop 2400*   •   ☎ *01328*

Set back from the sea, Wells is both a holiday town and a fishing port. It's a pleasant place, with streets of attractive Georgian houses, flint cottages and interesting shops. The TIC (☎ 710885) is in Staithe St, and is open daily in summer.

Holkham Hall (☎ 710227) is a most impressive Palladian mansion situated in a 3000-acre deer park two miles from Wells. The grounds were designed by Capability Brown. The house is open daily, except Friday and Saturday, from June to September; entry is £6/3 and includes the Bygones Museum and the park.

A narrow-gauge steam railway runs five miles to **Little Walsingham**, where there's a Catholic shrine that has been an object of pilgrimage for almost 1000 years.

KING'S LYNN

- *pop 37,500*   •   ☎ *01553*

Situated three miles from the sea, on the River Great Ouse, Lynn (as the locals call it) was one of England's chief ports in the Middle Ages. It was also a natural base for fishing fleets and their crews, and home to a number of religious foundations. The old town is a fascinating mixture of these three elements and Lynn is still a port today, though much less busy than it once was.

Orientation & Information

The old town lies along the eastern bank of the river. The railway station is on the eastern side of the town. Modern Lynn and the bus station are between them.

The TIC (☎ 763044) is in the Old Gaol House, Saturday Market Place, but may soon be moving to the Custom House. There are three market days each week – Tuesday, Friday and Saturday. In July, there's the popular King's Lynn Festival of Music and the Arts.

Walking Tour

This walk takes around 2½ hours. Start in the Saturday Market Place at **St Margaret's** parish church, founded in 1100 with a Benedictine priory. Little remains of the original buildings, but the church is impressive for its size (235 feet long) and contains two Flemish brasses which are among the best examples in the country. By the west door there are flood-level marks – 1976 was the highest, but the 1953 flood claimed more lives.

Walk south down Nelson St to see a fine collection of domestic and industrial buildings. Their frontages are 17th and 18th century, but their interiors are much older. On the corner of St Margaret's Lane, and dating back to the 15th century, is a restored

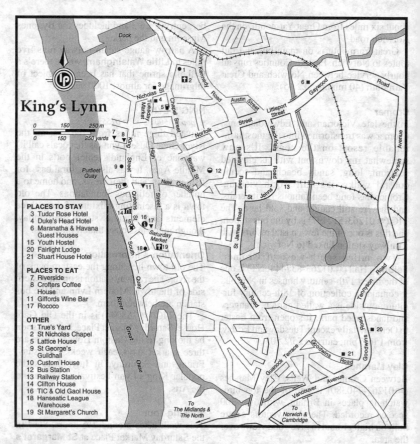

King's Lynn

0 150 250 m
0 150 250 yards

PLACES TO STAY
3 Tudor Rose Hotel
4 Duke's Head Hotel
6 Maranatha & Havana
   Guest Houses
15 Youth Hostel
20 Fairlight Lodge
21 Stuart House Hotel

PLACES TO EAT
7 Riverside
8 Crofters Coffee
   House
11 Giffords Wine Bar
17 Rococo

OTHER
1 True's Yard
2 St Nicholas Chapel
5 Lattice House
9 St George's
   Guildhall
10 Custom House
12 Bus Station
13 Railway Station
14 Clifton House
16 TIC & Old Gaol House
18 Hanseatic League
   Warehouse
19 St Margaret's Church

To
The Midlands &
The North

To
Norwich &
Cambridge

building that was once the warehouse or 'steelyard' of the Hanseatic League (the Northern European merchants' group).

Continue west along Margaret Plain to College Lane and the former Thoresby College, which was founded in 1508 to house priests and is now the youth hostel. Across Queen St is the town hall, dating back to 1421. Next to it is the building which houses the town museum and heritage centre. The **Old Gaol House** has been converted into a tourist attraction with self-guided Walkman tours. Lynn's priceless civic treasures, including the 650-year-old

King John Cup, can be seen in the basement. It's open daily from Easter to October (Friday to Tuesday for the rest of the year), 10 am to 5 pm; entry is £2/1.50.

Continuing down Queen St, you pass Clifton House, with its quirky barley-sugar columns and its waterfront tower, which was used by merchants scanning the river for returning ships. Walk down the lane to the river, past the sturdy, red floodgates. The stately Bank House is on your right. Opposite the square is **Purfleet Quay**, in its heyday the principal harbour. The quaint little building with the lantern tower is the

Customs House (the TIC may be moving here soon), which dates back to 1683.

Turn into King St, where the second medieval town begins. It was planned in the latter half of the 12th century, and had its own church, guildhall, market and friary. There are many interesting buildings in King St, especially on the left-hand side, where the wealthier merchants built their homes and warehouses on reclaimed land. **St George's Guildhall** is the largest surviving 15th-century guildhall in England. It has served as warehouse, theatre, courthouse and armoury (during the Civil War), and now contains art galleries, a theatre, restaurant and coffee-house. This is the focal point of the annual King's Lynn festival.

At the end of King St is the spacious **Tuesday Market Place**, which fulfils its original role once a week. It's bordered with old buildings, including the Corn Hall (1854) and the Duke's Head Hotel (1689).

Walk diagonally across the Tuesday Market Place and turn right into St Nicholas St to reach the **Tudor Rose Hotel**, a late 15th-century house with some very interesting features, including the original main door. North of here, on the corner of St Ann's St, is **True's Yard**, where the two remaining cottages of the fishing community that used to be here have been restored.

Return to Chapel St, and on the corner of Market Lane is an attractive building known as **Lattice House** – originally 15th century, it was restored in 1982 and is now a pub, and a good place to stop.

Places to Stay

Excellently located, the *King's Lynn Youth Hostel* (☎ 772461), Thoresby College, College Lane, is open fully from 1 July to 31 August and haphazardly outside that time. A bed costs £7.45/5.

In the north of the town, on Gaywood Rd, there are two B&Bs next door to each other. At No 115, *Maranatha Guest House* (☎ 774596) has six rooms from £14 per person. There are two singles and one room has a bathroom attached. *Havana Guest House* (☎ 772331) is at No 117, also with six

rooms, four with bath attached. It charges from £14 to £18 per person. Both these places are open year-round.

Fairlight Lodge (☎ 762234), 79 Goodwins Rd, is a comfortable guesthouse with seven rooms, four with attached bathroom, which charges £16 to £25 per person.

The *Tudor Rose Hotel* (☎ 762824), St Nicholas St, is a 15th-century house with B&B from £35/50 for a single/double. The town's top hotel is the *Duke's Head Hotel*, a fine classical building overlooking Tuesday Market. Charges are from £39 per person; there are also special break deals.

Places to Eat

For teas or light meals there's *Crofters Coffee House*, King St, in the guildhall undercroft at the Arts Centre. It's open from Monday to Saturday, 9.30 am to 5 pm.

Giffords Wine Bar (☎ 769177), Purfleet St (off King St), is open daily (closed on Sunday evening). It's a pleasant, friendly place; many dishes are between £4 and £5. There's a good range of fresh ground coffees.

At the *Lattice House*, on the corner of Chapel St and Market Lane, as well as a popular pub there's a restaurant serving good-value Thai food.

For something more upmarket there are two very good options. The *Riverside* (☎ 773134) is right by the river, near the undercroft. Main courses range from £4.95 (fisherman's pie) to £16.95. Opposite St Margaret's is the excellent *Rococo* (☎ 771483), 11 Saturday Market Place. A two-course lunch costs £9.50, and three-course dinners range from £20.50 to £29.50.

Getting There & Away

King's Lynn is 43 miles north of Cambridge on the A10.

There are hourly trains from Cambridge (50 minutes, £8.50). Buses are less convenient, with just one National Express service each day, and this must be booked in advance. Eastern Counties (☎ 01603-622800) runs a daily bus service to Norwich (1½ hours, £4.15).

AROUND KING'S LYNN
Castle Rising Castle
The amazingly well-preserved 12th-century keep of this castle is set in the middle of a massive earthwork. It was once the home of Queen Isabella, who arranged the murder of her husband Edward II. Open daily from 10 am to 6 pm, entry is £1.30/60p (☎ 01553-631330; EH). Eastern Counties bus Nos 410/411 run here from King's Lynn, five miles to the south.

Sandringham
The Queen's country pile is set in 60 acres of landscaped gardens and lakes, and it's open to the hoi polloi when the court is not in residence. The house was bought by Queen Victoria in 1862 and the royal family still spends three weeks here from mid-July to early August. The museum contains a collection of vintage cars and other royal trinkets.

Sandringham (☎ 01553-772675) is open from April to September (except when the royal family is here), daily from 11 am to 4.45 pm. Entry is £4/2, less if you only want to see the grounds and museum. There are buses from King's Lynn, which is 10 miles south-west.

Houghton Hall
Built for Sir Robert Walpole in 1730, Houghton Hall (☎ 01485-528569) is an example of the Palladian style, and is worth seeing for the ornate state rooms alone. It's open from April to September on Thursday and Sunday afternoons; entry is £5.50/3.

Cambridgeshire

The county of Cambridgeshire is best known for its beautiful university town. Cambridge is situated in the southern part of the county, on the edge of the fens – the flat, fertile region, previously under water, that covers the rest of the county. Cambridge has the advantage of being smaller and more compact than Oxford, and does not have heavy industry. Its position on the River Cam

gives it a rural flavour – cattle and horses graze within half a mile of the city centre.

The lack of hills makes this excellent cycling country. A towpath winds all the way from Cambridge to Ely (15 miles), where the superb cathedral, on ground slightly higher than the surrounding plain, is known as the 'ship of the fens'. In the north of the county there's another fine cathedral at Peterborough.

GETTING AROUND
Public transport centres on Cambridge. For timetable information, phone the helpline (☎ 317740). The main bus companies operating in the area are Stagecoach Cambus (☎ 423554) between Cambridge, Ely and Bury St Edmunds; Cambridge Coach Services (☎ 236333) from Cambridge to Norwich; and Stagecoach United Counties (☎ 01480-453159) from Cambridge to Huntingdon and Peterborough.

Cambridge is only 55 minutes by rail from London. This line continues north through Ely to terminate at King's Lynn in Norfolk. From Ely, a branch line runs east through Thetford and Norwich, and south-east into Suffolk. For rail information, phone ☎ 0345-484950.

CAMBRIDGE
• *pop 88,000* • ☎ *01223*
Cambridge is unquestionably one of the great universities of the world. With over 60 Nobel prizewinners, it is at the top of the research league in British universities; it owns a prestigious publishing firm and a world-renowned examination syndicate; it is the leading centre for astronomy in Britain; its Fitzwilliam Museum contains an outstanding art collection; and its library is used by scholars from around the world.

The university was founded in the 13th century, about a century later than Oxford. There is a fierce rivalry between the two cities and the two universities, and a futile debate over which is best and most beautiful. If you have the time, visit both. Oxford draws many more tourists than Cambridge. Partly because of this, if you only have time

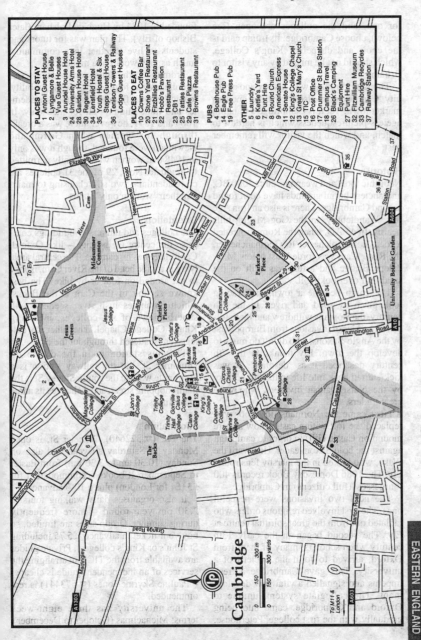

PLACES TO STAY
1 Antoni Guest House
2 Lyngamore & Belle Vue Guest Houses
24 Arundel House Hotel
28 Garden House Hotel
30 Regent Hotel
34 Lensfield Hotel
35 Youth Hostel & Six Steps Guest House
36 Tenison Towers & Railway Lodge Guest Houses

PLACES TO EAT
10 Clowns Coffee Bar
20 Stone Yard Restaurant
21 Fitzbillies Restaurant
22 Robb's Pavilion Restaurant
23 CB1
25 Tatties Restaurant
29 Cafe Piazza
31 Browns Restaurant

PUBS
4 Boathouse Pub
14 Eagle Pub
19 Free Press Pub

OTHER
5 Laundry
6 Kettle's Yard
7 Punt Hire
8 Round Church
9 American Express
11 Senate House
12 King's College Chapel
13 Great St Mary's Church
15 TIC
16 Post Office
17 Drummer St Bus Station
18 Campus Travel
26 Black's Camping Equipment
27 Punt Hire
32 Fitzwilliam Museum
33 Cambridge Recycles
37 Railway Station

Cambridge

0   150   300 m
0   150   300 yards

To M11 & London

EASTERN ENGLAND

for one, and the colleges are open (see below), choose Cambridge. Its trump card is the choir and chapel of King's College, which should not be missed by any visitor to Britain.

Though brimming with history and antiquity, Cambridge is also a bustling, modern market town. Yet it is Cambridge's tranquil, ageless picturesqueness which is hardest to match, and which the visitor will remember best.

History

Neolithic tools and weapons, circa 3000 BC, and ancient burial grounds have been found around Cambridge. There is also an Iron Age fort, Wandlebury, in the Gog Magog hills nearby. In 43 AD, when the Romans needed a road from Colchester to Godmanchester, the River Cam was forded just below Magdalene Bridge and a fort was built on the small hill overlooking it.

The camp became a town, and trading took place by road and river. In the 5th century, the Romans withdrew and there followed a series of invasions from Europe, first by the Anglo-Saxons, who didn't do much to develop the town: Ely monks in the 7th century described it as 'desolate'. It was kick-started back into life in the 9th century by the Norse/Danish invaders, who were great traders.

Next came the Normans, in 1066, who replaced the fort with a castle (now a mere mound on Castle Hill) in order to campaign against the bold Saxon leader, Hereward the Wake, who lurked in the marshy fens round Ely. The 1086 Domesday Book records 400 'burgesses' (full citizens) in Cambridge.

The next two invasions were peaceful ones. The first involved religious orders who radiated out from the great spiritual centre at Ely. The second began in the early 13th century when scholars, many of them from Oxford, arrived to form the nucleus of a university. This gave Cambridge a fresh impetus and signalled a vital new development. The collegiate system, unique to Oxford and Cambridge, came into being gradually with the first college, Peterhouse,

founded in 1284 by Hugh de Balsham (later Bishop of Ely). The plan was for tutors and students to live together in a community, much as they would in a monastery.

From the 14th century onwards, a series of colleges was founded by royalty, nobility, leading church figures, statesmen, academics and trade guilds – all for men only. In 1869 and 1871, however, there was a breakthrough for women when Girton and Newnham were founded, though it was only in 1948 that women were actually permitted to graduate. Now, 29 of the 31 colleges are co-residential – two still choosing to maintain their 'women only' status.

Orientation

The colleges and university buildings comprise the centre of the city – like Oxford, Cambridge has no campus. The central area, lying in a wide bend of the River Cam, is easy to get around on foot or by bike. The best known section of the Cam is the Backs, which combines lush river scenery with superb views of six colleges, including King's College Chapel. The other 25 colleges are scattered throughout the city.

The bus station is in the centre on Drummer St, but the railway station is a 20-minute walk to the south. Sidney St is the main shopping street, and it changes its name many times.

Information

The TIC (☎ 322640), Wheeler St, is open Monday to Saturday all year, and also on Sunday (10.30 am to 3.30 pm) from Easter to September. It books accommodation for £3 (£4 for London) plus a 10% advance.

It also organises daily walking tours at 2.30 pm year-round – more frequently during summer. Group sizes are limited, so buy your ticket in advance (£5.75 including St John's or King's colleges). Private guides are available from the TIC, but arranging the services of an independent guide is cheaper – Pauline Skyrme-Jones (☎ 573441) is recommended.

The university has three eight-week terms: Michaelmas (October to December),

Lent (mid-January to mid-March) and Easter (mid-April to mid-June). Exams are held from mid-May to mid-June. There's general mayhem for the 168 hours following exams – the so-called May Week. Most colleges are closed to visitors for the Easter term, and all are closed for exams. Precise details of opening hours vary from college to college and year to year, so contact the TIC for up-to-date information. A few colleges have started charging admission to tourists (£1 to £2).

There's an American Express office (☎ 351636) at 25 Sidney St, and a laundrette at 12 Victoria Ave, just north of the bridge and near Chesterton Rd.

Walking Tour 1

This three-hour walk visits King's College Chapel and the most central colleges, and includes a stretch along the river.

From the TIC, walk one block west to King's Parade, turn right and continue north to **Great St Mary's Church**. This 15th-century university church, built in the Perpendicular style, has a feeling of space and light inside, thanks to its clerestory, wide arch and wood carving. The traditional termly university sermons are preached here. To get your bearings, climb the tower (£1) for a good view of the city. The building across King's Parade, on the right-hand side of the square, is the **Senate House**, designed in 1720 by Gibbs. It's the most beautiful example of pure classical architecture in the city; graduations are held here.

Gonville & Caius Now walk into Trinity St, head north, and turn left into the first gateway to reach this fascinating old college. It was founded twice, first by a priest called Gonville, in 1347, and then again by Dr Caius (pronounced keys), a brilliant physician and scholar, in 1551. Of special interest here are the three gates: Virtue, Humility and Honour. They symbolise the progress of the good student, since the third gate (a fascinating confection with a quirky dome and sundials) leads to the Senate House and thus graduation. Walk through 'Porta Honoris',

turn right, then left, to reach King's College Chapel.

King's College Chapel All the college chapels are individually remarkable but King's College Chapel is supreme in its grandeur. It's one of the finest examples of Gothic architecture in England, and comparable with Chartres.

Conceived as an act of piety by the young Henry VI and dedicated to the Virgin Mary, the foundation stone was laid by the king in 1446 and the building completed around 1516. Henry VI's successors, notably Henry VIII, glorified the interior (and themselves in so doing). Services are led by its choir, originally choristers from Eton College, another of Henry VI's foundations. The choir's Festival of the Nine Lessons and Carols on Christmas Eve is heard throughout the world.

Enter through the south porch. Despite the original stained-glass windows, the atmosphere inside is light. Cromwell's soldiers destroyed many church windows in East Anglia but it is believed that, having been a Cambridge student, their leader saved King's.

The stunning interior of 12 bays is about 12 yards wide, 24 yards high and 88 yards long. This vast expanse is the largest in the world canopied by fan vaulting. It's the work of John Wastell, and is a miracle of beauty and skill.

The elaborate carvings, both in wood and stone, include royal coats of arms, intertwined initials, and the royal beasts of heraldry and flowers that were the emblems of Tudor monarchs and related families. Among the Yorkist roses on the western wall, there is the figure of a woman within a rose. Some claim she is Elizabeth of York, but it's more likely that she's the Virgin Mary.

The ante-chapel and the choir are divided by the superbly carved **wooden screen**, another gift of Henry VIII. The screen bears Henry's initials entwined with those of Anne Boleyn. The work is attributed to Peter the Carver. The one angry human face, almost concealed by the mythical beasts and symbolic flowers, is perhaps his jest for posterity.

Originally constructed between 1686 and 1688, the magnificent organ has been rebuilt and developed over the years, and now its pipes top the screen on which they rest.

The **choir stalls** were made by the same craftsman who worked on the screen, but the canopies are Carolingian. Despite the dark wood, the impression is still of lightness as one approaches the **high altar**, which is framed by Rubens' *Adoration of the Magi* and the magnificent east window.

The excellent **Chapel Exhibition** is in the northern side chapels, to the left of the altar. Here, you can see the stages and methods of building set against the historical panorama from inception to completion. On display are costumes, paintings, illuminated manuscripts and books, plans, tools and scale models, including a full-size model showing how the fan vaulting was constructed.

Entry costs £2.50/1.50. The vergers are helpful with information, but their guided tours take place only at the weekend. Tours during the week can be arranged at the TIC. King's College Chapel comes alive when the choir sings; even the most pagan heavy-metal fan will find **Choral Evensong** an extraordinary experience. There are services from mid-January to mid-March, mid-April to mid-June, mid-July to late July, early October to early December, and on 24 and 25 December. Evensong is sung at 5.30 pm, Tuesday to Saturday (men's voices only on Wednesday), and at 3.30 pm on Sunday.

Trinity College From King's College Chapel, return to King's Parade and follow it north into Trinity St; the entrance to the college is opposite Heffers bookshop. Henry VIII founded Trinity in 1546, but it was left to Dr Nevile, Master of Trinity (1593-1615) in Elizabeth's reign, to fulfil his wishes.

Walk through the impressive brick gateway, which dates back to 1535, and start reaching for superlatives. The Great Court is the largest of its kind in the world. The Gothic ante-chapel is full of huge statues of famous Trinity men, like Newton and Tennyson. The vast hall has a hammerbeam roof and lantern. Beyond the hall are the cloisters of Nevile's Court and the dignified Wren Library. The library is open to visitors from noon till 2 pm and is certainly worth visiting, though you may have to queue.

There are some amusing details in Trinity, although much of the college is larger than life (like its founder). On the great gateway, Henry VIII's statue dominates from the top niche, although in one hand he's holding a chair leg instead of the regal sceptre. Students kept removing the sceptre, so the porters thought up this substitute. Newton is reputed to have discovered the Law of Gravity by observing a falling apple; the tree at the entrance is said to be the progeny of this apple. Entry is £1.50.

Along the Backs Walk out of the cloisters and turn right to look at St John's New Court on the western bank. It's a 19th-century residence block, connected with the rest of **St John's College** by two bridges: Kitchen Bridge and the **Bridge of Sighs** (a replica of the original in Venice). Cross Trinity Bridge and turn left, following the footpath until you come to Garret Hostel Bridge. Pause on top to watch the punts below and look upstream to the bridge at **Clare**. It's ornamented with decorative balls and is the oldest, most interesting bridge on the Backs. Walk on, then turn right into Trinity Hall.

Trinity Hall This is a delightfully small college, wedged among the great and the famous. Despite the name, it has nothing to do with Trinity College. You enter through the newest court, which overlooks the river on one side and has a lovely Fellows' garden on another. Walking into the next court, you pass the quaint 16th-century library.

Old Schools As you walk out of the first court, you'll see a tall, historic gate. It receives little attention. It's the entry to Old Schools, the administrative centre of the university. The lower part dates back to 1441, though the upper section was added in the

1860s. You are now back in the heart of the university.

Walking Tour 2

This walk visits Christ's College, Jesus College, the Round Church and Magdalene. This must be a morning tour if you wish to go inside Christ's, which is only open from 9.30 am to noon. The walk should take about two hours and you could continue afterwards to see the Kettle's Yard art gallery. Start outside Christ's, on the corner of St Andrew's and Hobson Sts.

Christ's College Christ's was founded in 1505 by that pious and generous benefactress, Lady Margaret Beaufort, who also founded St John's. It has an impressive entrance gate, emblazoned with heraldic carving. The figure of the founder stands in a niche, hovering over all like a guiding spirit. Note the stout oak door leading into **First Court**, which has an unusual circular lawn, magnolias and wisteria creepers. The court is a mixture of original buildings and 18th-century facings and windows. The hall was rebuilt in neo-Gothic style last century, and the chapel's early sections include an oriel window which enabled the founder to join in services from her 1st-floor room.

The **Second Court** has an interesting Fellows' building, dating back to 1643. Its gate leads into a Fellows' garden, which contains a mulberry tree, under which Milton reputedly wrote *Lycidas*. Continuing through Iris Court, you're confronted by the stark, grey, modern students' block, which seems totally out of place. Look at the little theatre tucked into the right-hand corner, then walk out past New Christ's into Hobson St, turn right, then left and right into Jesus Lane. You'll pass Westcott, another theological college (not part of the university), then All Saints Church – affectionately dubbed St Op's (St Opposite) by Jesus students.

Jesus College The approach to Jesus via the long 'chimney' is impressive, as is the main gate, which is under a rebus of the founder, Bishop Alcock. A rebus is a heraldic device suggesting the name of its owner: the bishop's consists of several cockerels. The spacious First Court, with its red-brick ranges, is open on the western side – an unusual feature.

The best parts of Jesus are the tiny, intimate cloister court, to your right, and the chapel, which dates back to the St Radegund nunnery. The bishop closed the nunnery, expelled the nuns for misbehaving and founded the new college in its place.

The chapel is inspiring, reflecting Jesus' development over the centuries. It has a Norman arched gallery from the nunnery building, a 13th-century chancel and beautiful restoration work and Art Nouveau by Pugin, Morris (ceilings), Burne-Jones (stained glass) and Madox Brown.

The other buildings in Jesus are rather an anticlimax, but the extensive grounds, which include a cricket pitch, are pleasant to walk through.

Round Church Turn right out of Jesus College, go up Jesus Lane, turn right into Park St and left into Round Church St. At the top of this street is the amazing Round Church, or Church of the Holy Sepulchre. It was built in 1130 to commemorate its namesake in Jerusalem, and is one of only four in England. It is strikingly unusual, with chunky, round Norman pillars which encircle the small nave. The rest of the church was added later in a different style; the conical roof dates from only the 19th century. No longer a parish church, it's now a brass-rubbing centre.

Magdalene College Turn right down Bridge St. It was around Magdalene Bridge that the Romans built the bridge that marked the origins of Cambridge. Boats laden with cargo tied up and unloaded where the block of flats now stands on the river bank. Facing you across the river is Magdalene (pronounced mawdlin), which you enter from Magdalene St.

Originally a Benedictine hostel, the college was refounded in 1542 by Lord Audley. Its river setting gives it a certain appeal, but its greatest asset is the Pepys Library, housing the magnificent collection of books the famous diarist bequeathed to his old college – he was a student here in 1650-3.

Walking Tour 3

Taking in the colleges just to the south of the centre, this walk takes about two to three hours.

Corpus Christi From King's Parade, turn into St Benet's St to see the oldest structure in Cambridge – the 11th-century Saxon tower of the Franciscan parish church. The rest of the church is newer, but full of interesting features. The church served as chapel to Corpus Christi, next door, until the 16th century. There's an entrance to the college leading into Old Court, which has been retained in its medieval form and still exudes a monastic atmosphere. Christopher Marlowe was a Corpus man, as a plaque, next to a fascinating sundial, bears out. New Court, beyond, is a 19th-century creation.

The college library has the finest collection of Anglo-Saxon manuscripts in the world which, with other valuable books, were preserved from destruction at the time of Henry VIII's dissolution of the monasteries.

Queens' College Queens', one of the Backs' colleges, was the first Cambridge college to charge admission – now £1. It was initiated to pay for soundproofing its vulnerable site on this busy street. It takes its name from the two queens who founded it – Margaret and Elizabeth, in 1448 and 1478 respectively – yet it was a conscientious rector of St Botolph's Church who was its real creator.

Its main entrance is off Queens' Lane. The red-brick gate tower and Old Court, which immediately capture your attention, are part of the medieval college. So is Cloister Court, the next court, with its impressive cloister and picturesque, half-timbered President's Lodge (President is the name for the Master). The famous Dutch scholar and reformer Erasmus lodged in the tower early in the 16th century. The Cam is outside Cloister Court,

and is crossed by a quaint wooden bridge which brings you into the 20th-century Cripps Court.

Peterhouse College Founded in 1284 by Hugh de Balsham, later Bishop of Ely, this is the oldest and smallest of the colleges. It stands on the left of Trumpington St, just beyond Little St Mary's Church (formerly St Peter's, which gave the college its name). A walk through Peterhouse gives you a clear picture of the 'community' structure of a Cambridge college, though, unusually, the Master's house is opposite the college, not within it.

First Court, the oldest, is small, neat and bright, with hanging baskets and window boxes. The 17th-century chapel is on the right, built in a mixture of styles which blend well. Inside, the 19th-century, luminous, stained-glass windows contrast with the older eastern window.

The Burrough range, on the right, is 18th century, and the hall, on the left, a restored late 13th-century gem. Beyond the hall are sweeping grounds extending to the Fitzwilliam Museum. Bearing right, you enter a court with an octagonal lawn, beyond which are the library, theatre and First Court.

Pembroke College Pembroke has several courts linked by lovely gardens and lawns. As usual, the oldest court is at the entrance. It still retains some medieval corner sections. The chapel, on the extreme right, is an early Wren creation (1666): it is interesting to compare this with his two other Cambridge buildings, the chapel at Emmanuel College and the library at Trinity College.

Crossing Old Court diagonally, walk past the handsome dining hall and into charming Ivy Court. Walk through and round the corner to see a sweeping lawn with an impressive statue of Pitt the Younger (prime minister in the 18th century) outside the ornate library clocktower.

Continue through the garden, past the green where students play croquet after exams in summer, and out, right, into Pembroke St.

Emmanuel College Emmanuel College, on St Andrews St, was founded in 1584. It's a medium-sized college comprising a community of some 600 people.

If you stand in Front Court, one of the architectural gems of Cambridge faces you – the Wren chapel, cloister and gallery, completed in 1677. To the left is the hall; inside, the refectory-type tables are set at right angles to the high table.

The next court, New Court, is round the corner. It has a quaint herb garden, reminiscent of the old Dominican priory which preceded the college. There are a few remnants of the priory in the *clunch* (chalk) core of the walls of the Old Library. Turn right to re-enter Front Court and go into the chapel. It has interesting windows, a high ceiling and an Annigoni painting. Near the side door, there's a plaque to a famous scholar, John Harvard (BA 1632), who was among 30 Emmanuel men who settled in New England. He left money to found the university that bears his name in the Massachusetts town of Cambridge.

Fitzwilliam Museum

Designed by Basevi in 1848, this massive neoclassical edifice, with its vast portico, was a bequest (along with his art treasures) to the university by Viscount Fitzwilliam. It was one of the first public art museums in Britain, and has been called the 'finest small museum in Europe'.

In the lower galleries are ancient Egyptian sarcophagi and Greek and Roman art, as well as Chinese ceramics, English glass and illuminated manuscripts. The upper galleries contain a wide range of paintings, including works by Titian, Rubens, the French Impressionists, Gainsborough, Stubbs and Constable, right up to Cezanne and Picasso. It also has fine antique furniture.

The Fitzwilliam (☎ 332900) is open from Tuesday to Saturday, 10 am to 5 pm, and on Sunday afternoon, when there are guided tours. Admission is free.

Kettle's Yard

Situated on the corner of Northampton and Castle Sts, this gallery was the home of Jim Ede, a former assistant keeper at the Tate Gallery in London. It contains his early 20th-century art collection (Gaudier-Brzeska and British). The atmosphere is intimate because the paintings and sculpture are placed amid ceramics, glass and furnishings. There's also an adjoining exhibition gallery.

Kettle's Yard (☎ 352124) was given to the university by the Edes in 1966. Admission is free, and it's open from Tuesday to Sunday, 2 to 4 pm.

Cambridge – a University Town

Students' lives are centred around their colleges, where they eat, sleep, study and relax – in theory only moving out to lectures and to write exams. Colleges are planned, in a monastic manner, as a series of courtyards (known as 'courts', not 'quads' as at Oxford) with study/bedrooms, dining hall, chapel and gardens.

In contrast to the colleges, the university's role is to hold lectures, conduct examinations, award degrees and promote research. It owns numerous buildings (lecture halls, laboratories, libraries, museums, administrative centres etc), yet it is not a place but a body of people, embracing the chancellor right the way down to the undergraduate.

Though town and university have clashed at times – for example, during the Civil War when the university supported the king and the town supported Cromwell – the atmosphere today is largely amicable. Although the university and colleges have continued to infiltrate the town, mainly through building and buying property, this is more integration than domination. The relationship is mutually beneficial, as demonstrated by the town's innovative business and science parks. ■

EASTERN ENGLAND

Punting

Taking a punt along the Backs is sublime, but it can also be a wet and hectic experience, especially on a busy weekend. Look before you leap. If you do wimp out, the Backs are also perfect for a walk or a picnic – cross the bridge and walk along the river to the right.

Scudamore's (☎ 359750), just south of Silver St, rents punts (for up to six people) at £8 per hour, but requires a £30-50 deposit. Punting the three miles up the river to the idyllic village of Grantchester makes a great day out.

Walks & Cycle Routes

The best outing in the area is to Grantchester (see the next section), three miles along the towpath. You can go on foot, by bike or in a punt. For longer walks, the TIC stocks a number of guides, including *Walks in South Cambridgeshire*.

If you're a lazy cyclist, the flat topography makes for ideal biking country, although the scenery can get a little monotonous. *Cycle Cambridge* (£3.99), by Barny Hill, is a useful guide with maps covering 12 circular routes in the area.

Organised Tours

Guide Friday (☎ 62444) runs hop-on hop-off tour buses round the city, calling at the railway station. Tours are daily, year-round; tickets cost £6.50/2 for adults/children, and £4.50 for students.

Places to Stay

Hostels The *Cambridge Youth Hostel* (☎ 354601), 97 Tenison Rd, has small dormitories and a restaurant. Near the train station, it's very popular – book ahead. For B&B, seniors/juniors are charged £12.80/9.60.

Camping *Highfield Farm Camping Park* (☎ 262308), Long Rd, Comberton, is four miles south-west of Cambridge. In summer it costs £7.75 for a two-person tent.

B&Bs & Hotels There are numerous B&Bs at all times, even more during university vacation from late June to late September. There are several on Tenison Rd, including the *Railway Lodge Guest House* (☎ 467688) at No 150 which is good value with rooms from £24/28 with attached bathroom. The *Tenison Towers Guest House* (☎ 566511) at No 148 charges from £14 per person in rooms with common bath. The *Six Steps Guest House* (☎ 353968) at No 93 costs from £17 per person.

The other B&B area is in the north of the city around Chesterton Rd. *Antoni Guest House* (☎ 357444), 4 Huntingdon Rd, is good, with four singles and four doubles at £18 and £30. A bit farther out, *Benson House* (☎ 311594), 24 Huntingdon Rd, has well-equipped doubles with attached showers for £36, and basic rooms from £15 per person.

Closer to the city centre, there's *Lyngamore House* (☎ 312369), 35-37 Chesterton Rd, with rooms from £14 to £18 per person. The *Belle Vue Guest House* (☎ 351859), 33 Chesterton Rd, has comfortable doubles for £34. *Arundel House Hotel* (☎ 67701), at No 53, is a pleasant place to stay. There are 42 single rooms ranging from £37.50 to £57, and 57 doubles from £53.50 to £77; almost all with bathrooms attached. *Ashley Hotel* (☎ 350059), at No 74, is cheaper and much smaller, with rooms for £27.50/49.50 with attached bath.

Further east along Chesterton Rd, there's *Acorn Guest House* (☎ 353888), at No 154, with rooms from £18/30 to £40/50, most with bathroom attached. There are several other places nearby, including *Kirkwood House* (☎ 313874), at No 172, which is similarly priced, and the *Hamilton Hotel* (☎ 365664), at No 156, which has singles/doubles from £20/40. There's a licensed bar here.

In the South, near the Fitzwilliam Museum, the *Lensfield Hotel* (☎ 355017), 53 Lensfield Rd, is well located but nothing special. It has 32 rooms and charges from £34/52 to £44/62.

The *Regent Hotel* (☎ 351470), at 41 Regent St, is in the centre by Parker's Piece. All rooms have bathroom attached and cost £59/79.

The posh *Garden House Hotel* (☎ 259988), Mill Lane, is by the river, in the centre, and has pastoral views from many rooms. There are 118 luxurious bedrooms with prices to match – £99/130 (not including breakfast), and weekend rates of £78 per person per night including dinner and breakfast. The *University Arms Hotel* (☎ 351241), on Regent St, overlooking Parker's Piece, is the other top place in town, charging £95/115.

Places to Eat

Cambridge has a good selection of reasonably priced restaurants. Some give student discounts.

Rainbow (☎ 321551), 9 King's Parade, is a busy vegetarian restaurant opposite King's College. It's open daily from 9 am to 9 pm. Main dishes are £4.75; soups are £1.75.

CB1 (☎ 576306), 32 Mill Rd, is an Internet café. Tea, coffee and light snacks are served. There are currently six terminals; for non-account customers they charge 10p per minute. CB1 is open daily from 10 am to 8 pm.

Clowns (☎ 460453), 54 King St, is popular with students, and serves light meals that are good value. *Hobb's Pavilion* (☎ 67480), Park Terrace, occupies the old cricket pavilion and has a house speciality of filled pancakes. It's open Tuesday to Saturday from noon to 2.15 pm and 7 to 10 pm.

There are quite a number of reasonably priced restaurants on Regent St. Now revamped, and with a liquor license, *Tatties* (☎ 358478), at No 26, has long been a budget favourite. Open 10 am to 10 pm daily, it specialises not only in baked potatoes stuffed with a variety of tempting fillings (from £1.75 to £4.95) but also in breakfasts, filled baguettes, salads and cakes. Their garlic horse mushrooms on granary toast (£3.95) are highly recommended.

During the day, the *Stone Yard Restaurant*, next door to St Andrew's Baptist Centre, serves very cheap cafeteria-style food. *Café Piazza* (☎ 356666), 83 Regent St, has pizzas from £3.95, with a resident DJ some nights.

Fitzbillies (☎ 352500), 52 Trumpington St, is a brilliant bakery/restaurant. The Chelsea buns are an outrageous experience, and so is the chocolate cake beloved by generations of students, but there are many other temptations in addition to the usual sandwiches and pies – stock up before you go punting.

Browns (☎ 461655), 23 Trumpington St, is part of the chain that has branches in several university towns. It's not as expensive as it looks.

Twenty-two (☎ 351880), 22 Chesterton Rd, may look like just another house among the hotels and B&Bs on this road, but inside it's a gourmet restaurant. A four-course dinner costs £19.95, plus £5 for fish dishes.

The city's best cuisine is served overlooking the river at *Midsummer House* (☎ 69299), on Midsummer Common. It's a smart, sophisticated place, said to have one of the most comprehensive wine lists outside Paris. There are set lunch menus from £17 to £30, and set dinners from £24 to £40. It's open for lunch from Tuesday to Friday and on Sunday; for dinner, from Tuesday to Saturday.

Entertainment

To find out what's on, get a copy of *Varsity* magazine. The *Corn Exchange* (☎ 357851), near the TIC, is the city's main centre for arts and entertainment, with recent shows as diverse as the English National Ballet and Sesame Street Live! The Arts Theatre, under restoration for years, should be re-opening soon. The King's College Choir (see above) is unique to Cambridge – don't miss it.

As you might expect in a city full of students, there are some excellent places for a pint. The *Anchor*, Silver St, is by the river; punts are available from here. The *Boathouse*, 14 Chesterton Rd, can be visited by punt and even has its own mooring place. Pub grub here is good value and includes some solid British puddings such as spotted dick. It can get very crowded.

The *Free Press*, Prospect Row, is a pub and boat club, hence the decorative theme. As well as being a good place to drink, it has some of the best bar food in Cambridge, including good vegetarian choices.

Nobel-prizewinning scientists Crick and Watson spent equal time in the laboratory and *The Eagle* in Benet St, so perhaps Greene King, the Suffolk brewers, played a part in the discovery of the structure of DNA. This 16th-century pub was also popular with American airmen in WWII; they left their signatures on the ceiling.

Getting There & Away

Cambridge can easily be visited as a day trip from London (although it's worth staying at least a night) or en route north. It's well served by rail, not so well by bus. See the fares tables in the Getting Around chapter.

Bus For bus information, phone ☎ 317740. National Express (☎ 0990-808080) has hourly buses to London, and four buses a day to/from Bristol (two stop at Bath). Unfortunately, connections to the north aren't straightforward. To get to Lincoln or York, you'll have to change at Peterborough or Nottingham respectively. King's Lynn is also only accessible via Peterborough – it's easier to take a train.

Cambridge Coach Services (☎ 236333) runs the Inter-Varsity Link via Stansted Airport to Oxford (three hours, six per day, £7/10 for a single/return). It also runs buses to Heathrow (£13) and Gatwick (£15) airports.

Train There are trains every half-hour from London's King's Cross and Liverpool St stations (one hour). Network South-East cards are valid. If you catch the train at King's Cross you travel via Hatfield (see Hatfield House in the Southern Midlands section) and Stevenage. There are also regular train connections to Bury St Edmunds, Ely (£2.70) and King's Lynn (£8.50). There are connections at Peterborough with the main northbound trains to Lincoln, York and Edinburgh. If you want to head west to Oxford or Bath, you'll have to return to London first. For more information, phone ☎ 0345-484950.

Getting Around

Parking is difficult in Cambridge – leave your car on a double yellow line and you risk a tow-away charge of £125. It's best to use the well-signposted Park & Ride car parks.

Bus Cambus (☎ 423554) runs numerous buses around town from Drummer St, including Bus No 1 from the railway station to the town centre (70p).

Taxi For a taxi, phone A1 Taxis (☎ 359123) or United Taxis (☎ 352222). Unless you have a lot of luggage, it's not really worth taking one from the railway station to the centre. It costs £3 and takes about 15 minutes; you can walk it in 20 minutes.

Bicycle It's easy enough to get around Cambridge on foot, but if you're staying out of the centre, or plan to explore the fens, a bicycle can be useful. You don't need a flash mountain bike because there are few hills; most places rent three-speeds. Geoff's Bike Hire (☎ 365629), 65 Devonshire Rd, near

---

The Fens

The fens were strange marshlands that stretched from Cambridge, north to The Wash and beyond into Lincolnshire. They were home to people who led an isolated existence amongst a maze of waterways; fishing, hunting and farming scraps of arable land. In the 17th century, however, the Duke of Bedford and a group of speculators brought in Dutch engineer Cornelius Vermuyden to drain the fens, and the flat, open plains, with their rich black soil, were created. The region is the setting for Graham Swift's excellent novel *Waterland*.

As the world's weather pattern changes and the sea level rises, the fens are beginning to disappear underwater again. It's estimated that by the year 2030 up to 400,000 hectares could be lost. ∎

the youth hostel, charges £6 per day and £15 per week, but gives a 10% discount to YHA members. Cambridge Recycles (☎ 506035), 61 Newnham Rd, charges £5 to £8 per day.

AROUND CAMBRIDGE
Grantchester
Three miles from Cambridge, Grantchester is a delightful village of thatched cottages and flower-filled meadows beside the Granta River (as the Cam is known here). Its quint-essential Englishness was recognised by the poet Rupert Brooke, who was a student at King's before WWI, in the immortal lines: 'Stands the church clock still at 10 to three, And is there honey still for tea?' When the clock stopped, it was left at this time, but it was recently reported that Casio has offered to get it going again – a clever bit of publicity, and one that finds favour with more than a few villagers.

Grantchester's most famous resident is the novelist Jeffrey Archer, who lives in the Old Vicarage.

There are teashops, some attractive pubs and the *Orchard Tea-garden*, where cream teas are served under apple trees. The best of the pubs is the *Red Lion*, near the river, which has a very pleasant garden.

Get here via the towpath or hire a punt.

American War Cemetery
Four miles west of Cambridge, at Madingley, this is a very moving cemetery with neat rows of white marble crosses stretching down the sloping site to commem-orate the Americans killed in WWII while based in Britain.

Duxford Aircraft Museum
Right by the motorway, nine miles south of Cambridge, this airfield played a significant role in WWII, especially during the Battle of Britain.

Today, it is home to Europe's biggest collection of historic aircraft, ranging from WWI biplanes to jets, including Concorde. Air shows are frequently held here, and bat-tlefield scenes are displayed in the land-warfare hall.

Buses leave regularly for Duxford from Drummer St in Cambridge. Entry is £6.20/3.10.

Wimpole Hall
Until recently, this was the home of Rudyard Kipling's daughter, but Wimpole Hall is now a NT property. It consists of a large, gracious, 18th-century mansion set in 350 acres of beautiful parkland. Wimpole Home Farm, next to it, was established in 1794 as a model farm; today, it preserves and shows rare breeds.

Wimpole Hall (☎ 01223-207257; NT) is eight miles south of Cambridge on the A603. Entry is £5, or £6.50, including the Home Farm; children half-price. There's no charge to just walk in the park. It's open from Easter to October, daily except Monday and Friday, 10.30 am to 5.30 pm.

Whippet service No 175 passes this way from Cambridge. Alternatively, you could try walking the Wimpole Way, a 13-mile waymarked trail from Cambridge. A leaflet is available from the TIC.

ELY
• *pop 9000*   • ☎ *01353*

Ely (pronounced eelee) is an unspoilt market town with neat Georgian houses, a river port and one of the country's great cathedrals. It stands in the centre of the fens – swamps that extended for miles because the sea level was once higher than the land. Ely used to be an island and derived its name from the eels that frequented the surrounding waters.

Ely is an easy day trip from Cambridge. The TIC (☎ 662062) is in Oliver Cromwell's House. In summer, it's open daily from 10 am to 6 pm.

Ely Cathedral
The cathedral's origins stem from a remark-able queen of Northumbria called Etheldreda. She had been married twice, but was determined to pursue her vocation to become a nun. She founded an abbey in 673 and, for her good works, was canonised after her death. The abbey soon became a pilgrim-age centre.

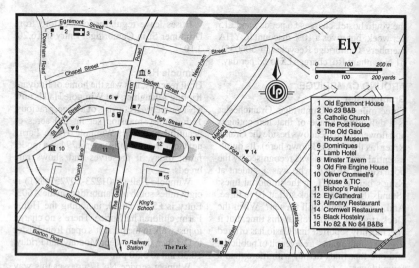

Ely

1 Old Egremont House
2 No 23 B&B
3 Catholic Church
4 The Post House
5 The Old Gaol
   House Museum
6 Dominiques
7 Lamb Hotel
8 Minster Tavern
9 Old Fire Engine House
10 Oliver Cromwell's
   House & TIC
11 Bishop's Palace
12 Ely Cathedral
13 Almonry Restaurant
14 Cromwell Restaurant
15 Black Hostelry
16 No 82 & No 84 B&Bs

It was a Norman bishop, Simeon, who began the task of building the cathedral. It was completed in 1189 and remains a splendid example of the Norman Romanesque style. In 1322, after the collapse of the central tower, the octagon and lantern, for which the cathedral is famous, were built. They have fan vaulting and intricate detail.

Other features of special interest include the Lady Chapel, the largest of its kind in England, which was added in the 14th century. The niches were rifled by iconoclasts, but the delicate tracery and carving remain intact. There's an amazing view from just inside the west door, right down the nave, through the choir stalls and on to the glorious east window – no clutter, just a sublime sense of space, light and spirituality.

Ely was the first cathedral in the country to make an admission charge (£3) and, with funds gathered since 1986, it has managed to restore the octagon and lantern tower. There are free guided tours of the cathedral and also an octagon and roof tour. There's also a stained glass museum (£1.80) in the triforium. The cathedral (☎ 667735) is open daily from 7 am to 7 pm (5 pm in winter). Sunday services are at 10.30 am and 3.45 pm.

Other Things to See
The area round the cathedral is historically and architecturally interesting. There's the Bishop's Palace, now a nursing home, and King's School, which supplies the cathedral with choristers.

Oliver Cromwell's House (☎ 662062) stands on the left, across St Mary's Green. Cromwell lived with his family in this attractive, half-timbered, 14th-century house from 1636-46, when he was the tithe collector of Ely. The TIC, which occupies the front room in the house, offers an audiovisual presentation and an interesting tour of the rooms (£2.30).

The **Old Gaol House** is a new museum that should be opening soon, incorporating the old museum in the High St.

It's worth walking down to the river – follow the signs. There is an interesting antiques centre near the river. The Old Maltings, which stages exhibitions and has a café, is nearby. The **River Great Ouse** is a busy thoroughfare – swans and ducks compete with boats for river space. The towpath winds up and downstream: for a quiet walk, turn left; turn right for the pub and tea garden. If you continue along this path, you'll see the fens stretching to the horizon.

Places to Stay

Now that the youth hostel has closed there are few budget options in Ely. On Broad St, *No 82* (☎ 667609) and *No 84* (☎ 666862) have a room each at £15/26.

There are several B&Bs on Egremont St. At No 31, *Old Egremont House* (☎ 663118), offers comfortable B&B for £27.50/40 in an attractive house with a large garden. At *No 23* (☎ 664557) B&B costs £21/36. *The Post House* (☎ 667184), at 12A, is unmissable with the Union Jack raised outside. They charge £17 per person.

The *Black Hostelry* (☎ 662612), right by the cathedral on Firmary Lane, is a medieval house offering upmarket B&B in very comfortable surroundings. There are two doubles (no singles) at £49.

Places to Eat

Eels are a local delicacy served in several of the restaurants. The *Lamb Hotel* offers oak-smoked eel on lettuce for £5.50.

The cathedral operates a *Refectory* and there is an attractive garden restaurant, the *Almonry* (☎ 666360), to the left of the Lady Chapel.

Dominiques (☎ 665011), on St Mary's St, serves cream teas, as well as lunches and set dinners (£16.50). It's closed on Monday and Tuesday. Totally non-smoking, it has good vegetarian choices (eg wild mushroom risotto with parmesan and salad).

The *Old Fire Engine House* (☎ 662582), on St Mary's St, seems more like the comfortable house of a friend than a restaurant. The food is, however, excellent. Main dishes are all about £11.50. It's open daily except Sunday.

Getting There & Away

Ely is on the A10, 15 miles from Cambridge. Following the Fen Rivers Way (map from TICs, £2) it's a 17-mile walk.

There are frequent trains from Cambridge (15 minutes, £2.70) and buses from Cambridge's Drummer St bus station; they stop on Market St.

PETERBOROUGH
- *pop 113,500*   •   ☎ *01733*

Peterborough may call itself the capital city of shopping, but it is the wonderful cathedral that is the only point of interest in this city. It's an easy day trip from Cambridge.

The cathedral precinct is an extension of the busy Cowgate, Bridge St and Queensgate. The TIC (☎ 01733-317336), 45 Bridge St, is nearby, and the bus and railway stations are within walking distance.

Peterborough Cathedral

In Anglo-Saxon times, when the region was part of the kingdom of Mercia, King Peada, a recent convert to Christianity, founded a monastic church here in 655. This was sacked and gutted by the Danes in 870. In 1118, the Benedictine abbot, John de Sais, founded the present cathedral as the monastic church of the Benedictine abbey. It was finally consecrated in 1237.

As you enter the precinct from Cathedral Square, you get a breathtaking view of the early 13th-century western front, one of the most impressive of any cathedral in Britain.

On entering you're struck by the height of the nave and the lightness, which derives not only from the mellow Barnack stone (quarried close by and transported via the River Nene), but also from the clerestory windows. The nave, with its three storeys, is an impressive example of Norman architecture. Its unique timber ceiling is one of the earliest of its kind in England (possibly in Europe) and its original painted decoration has been preserved.

The Gothic tower replaced the original Norman one, but had to be taken down and carefully reconstructed after it began to crack in the late 19th century.

In the north choir aisle is the tombstone of Henry VIII's first wife, the tragic Catherine of Aragon, buried here in 1536. Her divorce, engineered by the king, led to the Reformation in England. Directly opposite, in the south aisle, two standards mark what was the grave of Mary Queen of Scots. On the accession of her son, James, to the throne, her body was moved to Westminster Abbey.

The eastern end of the cathedral, known as the New Building, was added in the 15th century. It has superb fan vaulting, probably the work of master mason, John Wastell, who worked on King's College Chapel.

The cathedral (☎ 897337) is open from 8.30 am to 6.15 pm (7.30 pm in summer); admission is free (donations are encouraged).

Getting There & Away

Peterborough is 37 miles north of Cambridge. Stagecoach United Counties (☎ 01480-453159) and National Express run buses from Cambridge; some services require a change in Huntingdon. There are hourly trains from Cambridge (55 minutes, £9.40).

Northern Midlands

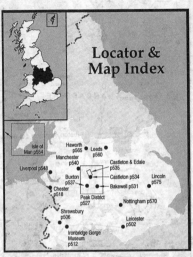

Locator & Map Index

The northern Midlands are often dismissed as England's industrial backyard. The dense motorway network gives forewarning of the claustrophobic development and the continuing economic importance of the region, despite the decline of some traditional industries.

In a very real sense this is England's working-class heartland. There is a wide gap between these northern cities and those south of Birmingham. Since the Industrial Revolution created them, life for their inhabitants has often been an uncompromising struggle. The horrific excesses of 19th-century capitalism gave birth to a bitter and protracted class struggle that continues today. This is the home of British trade unionism, the Labour Party and football.

ORIENTATION

The main industrial corridor runs from Merseyside (Liverpool) to the River Humber. All the major cities – Manchester, Liverpool, Bradford, Leeds, Doncaster, Sheffield, Nottingham, Derby and Leicester – sprawl into the countryside, burying it under motorways, grim suburbs, power lines, factories and mines.

There are, nonetheless, some important exceptions: Lincoln, one of the great cathedral cities; walled Chester, a starting point for North Wales; and attractive Shrewsbury. On the eastern and western extremes in Shropshire and Lincolnshire (especially the Wolds) there is beautiful, little-visited countryside. In the centre there's the Peak District National Park, and in the north some of the dramatic Yorkshire Dales.

PLACES TO STAY

Many towns in the northern Midlands are important business destinations. At the weekends, business hotels are likely to be half-empty and willing to drop their rates to attract non-business guests. You can sometimes find a room at a three or four-star hotel at a price that's only a little more than a cheaper B&B.

GETTING AROUND

See the regional sections of this chapter for public transport information. For train inquiries, ring ☎ 0345-484950.

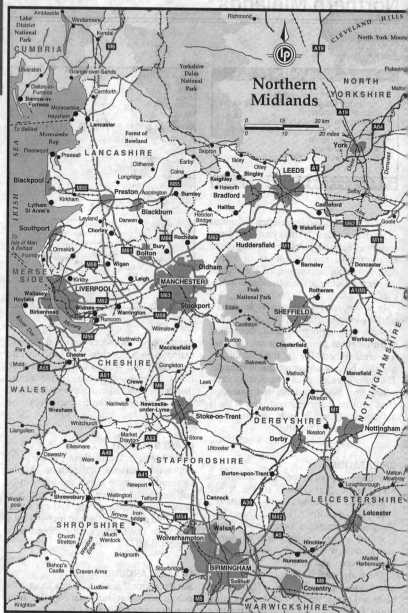

Note: See Britain Counties map on p.20 for more detail on Unitary Authorities in Manchester and Liverpool area

Leicestershire

Leicestershire, at first glance another grey Midlands county, has several interesting towns and historic sites.

LEICESTER
• *pop 320,000* • ☎ *0116*

Leicester (pronounced lester) is another Midlands town which has suffered the triple disasters of wartime damage, uninspired post-war development and recent industrial decline. There are Roman ruins as well as more recent sites, but what makes the city interesting to the non-Asian traveller is the large and vibrant Asian community. The main religions of the Indian subcontinent are represented with temples: Hindu, Moslem, Jain, Sikh. There are some of the best Indian, Bangladeshi and Pakistani restaurants in the country; and many of the city's most interesting events are staged around Asian festivals such as Holi, Diwali, and Eid-ul-Fitr.

The city's history dates back to Roman times; it was later one of the five Danelaw towns and was the traditional home of Shakespeare's tragic King Lear and his daughters. In 1239 Simon de Montfort, Earl of Leicester, captured the castle. Leicester became a centre for manufacturing stockings in the medieval era but it was still a small town until the rapid industrial growth of the 19th century. The word Luddite came from Leicester, after apprentice Nedd Ludd smashed stocking frames in a protest against modern production methods. The Luddite riots took place from 1811 to 1816.

Orientation & Information
Leicester is initially difficult to navigate as there are few landmarks and, for those on wheels, it's plagued by the usual maze of one-way streets and forbidden turns.

The TIC (☎ 265 0555) is at 7-9 Every St, Town Hall Square. In summer it's open Monday to Friday, 9 am to 5.30 pm, Saturday to 5 pm, and until 4 pm on Sunday. There's

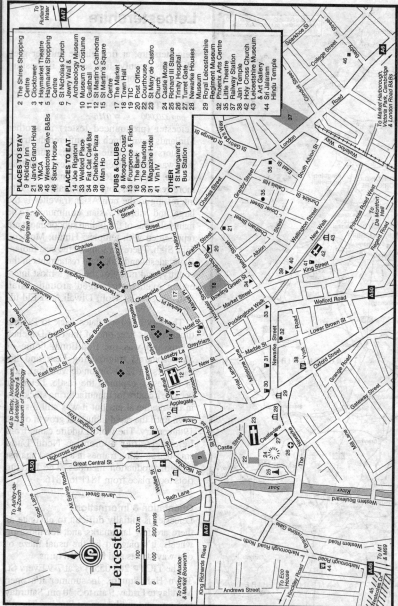

Leicester

PLACES TO STAY
9   Holiday Inn
21 Jarvis Grand Hotel
36 YMCA
45 Westcotes Drive B&Bs
46 Saxby House

PLACES TO EAT
14 Joe Rigatoni
33 Welford Place
34 Fat Cat Café Bar
39 Cheikhos Plaza
40 Man Ho

PUBS & CLUBS
8   Mosquito Coast
13 Fourpence & Firkin
16 The Bank
30 The Charlotte
31 Magazine Hotel
41 Vin IV

OTHER
1   St Margaret's
    Bus Station

2   The Shires Shopping
    Centre
3   Clocktower
4   Haymarket Theatre
5   Haymarket Shopping
    Centre
6   St Nicholas Church
7   Jewry Wall &
    Archaeology Museum
10 Museum of Costume
11 Guildhall
12 St Martin's Cathedral
15 St Martin's Square
    Centre
17 The Market
18 Town Hall
19 TIC
20 Post Office
22 Courthouse
23 St Mary de Castro
    Church
24 Castle Motte
25 Richard III Statue
26 Trinity Hospital
27 Turret Gate
28 Newarke Houses
    Museum
29 Royal Leicestershire
    Regiment Museum
32 Phoenix Arts Centre
35 Little Theatre
38 Railway Station
42 Jain Temple
43 Holy Cross Church
44 Leicestshire Museum
    & Art Gallery
44 Sri Jalaram
    Hindu Temple

Thomas Cook & Modern Tourism

Leicester can lay claim to being the birthplace of modern mass tourism as a result of Thomas Cook's excursion to Loughborough in 1841. The world's first package tour provided transport (by steam train), refreshments (a cup of tea and a ham roll) and musical accompaniment (a brass band), all for the princely sum of one shilling. That first trip proved so successful that tours followed to other locations in Leicestershire, then to other locations in England and then all over the world. Today Thomas Cook is a major name in international tourism.

Thomas Cook was born in 1808 in Melbourne in nearby Derbyshire and was a dedicated promoter of temperance. In Gallowtree Gate, near the clocktower, the 1894 offices of T Cook & Sons can still be seen. Cook lived at 'Cook's Rooms', 26-28 Granby St, from 1845 to 1854. His Temperance Hotel formerly occupied 121 Granby St and after his death in 1892 he was buried in Welford Rd Cemetery. ■

another office (☎ 251 1301) in St Margaret's bus station in the summer.

Belgrave Rd – the Golden Mile – is the centre of the Asian community. It's about a mile north-east of the centre.

Jewry Wall & Museums

All Leicester's museums are open Monday to Saturday, 10 am to 5.30 pm, and on Sunday from 2 to 5.30 pm; there's no entry charge.

On St Nicholas Circle, by the Holiday Inn, the **Museum of Leicestershire Archaeology** (☎ 247 3021) is adjacent to the excavated site of a Roman baths. The name of the Roman wall has nothing to do with the Jewish faith and the wall is the largest Roman civil structure in Britain. The museum has some wonderful Roman mosaics and wall paintings.

The **Leicestershire Museum & Art Gallery** (☎ 255 4100) on New Walk has exhibits of British paintings. The **Newarke Houses Museum** (☎ 247 3222) displays the social history of the county since medieval times in buildings dating from the early 16th and early 17th centuries.

Churches

Adjacent to the Jewry Wall excavation, **St Nicholas Church** is the oldest church in the city. Material from Roman buildings can be seen in the walls and tower, the nave is Saxon and the restored tower originally dated from the 11th and 12th centuries. **St Martin's Cathedral** started as a Norman church but

was rebuilt in Early-English style, and then in a Victorian interpretation of Early-English style, before becoming a cathedral in 1927. Adjacent to the cathedral is the fine **Guildhall**, dating from the 14th to 16th centuries.

St Mary de Castro Church dates back to 1107 but has also had a variety of reconstructions and rebuilds from Norman times through to the 14th century. Apart from services it's only open on Saturday in summer from 2 to 5 pm.

Temples

The **Jain Temple** (☎ 254 3091), on the corner of Oxford St and York Rd, is a fascinating place to visit. Materials were shipped in from India to convert this disused church into the first Jain temple outside the subcontinent. The building is faced with marble and inside there's a forest of beautifully carved pillars. Jainism evolved in India at around the same time as Buddhism. The temple is open to visitors Monday to Friday, 2 to 5 pm.

There are several Hindu temples in the Belgrave Rd area. On Narborough Rd, the **Shree Jalaram Temple** (☎ 254 0117) opened in 1995. Dedicated to the Hindu saint Pujya Bapa, there are marble carvings depicting his life and colourful murals of various Vedic scriptures.

Close to the Jewry Wall is the **Guru Nanak Gurdwara** (☎ 262 8606), at 9 Holybones. As well as this Sikh temple there's a small museum, with an impressive model of the Golden Temple in Amritsar. It's open on Thursday only, 1 to 4 pm.

Great Central Railway

The Great Central Railway (☎ 01509-230726) operates steam locomotives between Leicester North and Loughborough Central. The eight-mile trip runs every weekend and daily from May to August. The round trip costs £6.50/4.50.

Places to Stay

The *Copt Oak Youth Hostel* (☎ 01530-242661) is on Whitwick Rd, Copt Oak, eight miles north-west of the centre, near junction 22 on the M1. The nightly cost is £6.10/4.15. From April to October it's open daily except Tuesday.

Richard's International Hostel (☎ 267 3107) is three miles north of the centre, just off the A6 at 157 Wanlip Lane. Book ahead. The nightly cost is £8, £3 for tent space or (if you have a sleeping bag) in the chalet.

The *YMCA* (☎ 255 6507) at 7 East St, just across from the railway station, has a few single rooms at £11. There are some cheap places on Saxby St, off London Rd just south of the railway station. *Saxby House* (☎ 254 0504) at No 24 is just £11 per person.

The TIC makes free accommodation bookings but apart from expensive hotels there's little accommodation in the centre. Try Westcotes Drive for B&Bs; it's off Narborough Rd. The *Scotia Hotel* (☎ 254 9200) at No 10 has singles from £21 to £27, doubles from £38 to £42, some with attached bath. The *Cumbria Guest House* (☎ 254 8459) at No 16 and the *Beaumaris* (☎ 254 0621) at No 18 are slightly cheaper with rooms from £15/26.

The centrally located *Jarvis Grand Hotel* (☎ 255 5599), Granby St, has rooms from £50/60 during the week, £32.50/50 at weekends. Rooms at the *Holiday Inn* (☎ 253 1161) at St Nicholas Circle drop from £89 during the week to £54 at weekends.

Places to Eat

The Belgrave Rd area, to the north of the centre, is noted for its fine Indian cuisine and excellent vegetarian food. The award-winning but budget-priced *Friends Tandoori* (☎ 266 8809) is at 41-43 Belgrave Rd and serves North Indian food. Others include *Sharmilee* (☎ 261 0503) at No 71/73, for Gujarati and Punjabi vegetarian cuisine, *Bobby's* (☎ 266 0106) at No 154 and *Sayonara Thali* (☎ 266 5888) at No 49, both with South Indian vegetarian dishes such as masala dosa.

In the centre of town, the *Fat Cat Café Bar* (☎ 255 3610), 41 Belvoir St, is a stylish place that's very popular. It's good value, with full breakfasts (veg or non-veg) for £3.65, main dishes from £4.25 (eg chilli con carne) and steaks from £9.95.

Welford Place (☎ 247 0758), at 9 Welford Place, has a club-like atmosphere and is open for breakfast, lunch and dinner. Although not cheap, it's not as expensive as its appearance might indicate.

Getting There & Away

Leicester is 105 miles from London, 40 from Birmingham, and 25 from Coventry and Nottingham.

Bus St Margaret's bus station is on Gravel St, north of the centre, and National Express (☎ 0990-808080) operates from there. There are hourly bus services to London. The Busline (☎ 251 1411) offers general bus information.

Train The mainline railway station is on London Rd, south-east of the centre. A statue of Thomas Cook waits outside the station. Trains from London's St Pancras operate every half-hour and the fastest InterCity express takes just over one hour. There are hourly services between Birmingham and Cambridge or Norwich via Leicester.

BOSWORTH BATTLEFIELD

It was south-west of Leicester at Sutton Cheny, two miles from Market Bosworth, where Richard III was defeated by the future Henry VII in 1485, ending the Wars of the Roses. 'A horse ... a horse ... my kingdom for a horse' was his famous cry. The Visitor Centre (☎ 01455-290429) is open April to October, daily 1 to 5 pm; £2.30/1.50, plus 50p parking charge.

ASHBY-DE-LA-ZOUCH

Travelling from Leicester to Derby it's easy to divert via this pleasant little town with its **castle** (☎ 01530-413343; EH). Built in Norman times, and owned by the Zouch family until 1399, it was extended in the 14th and 15th centuries then reduced to its present picturesque ruined state in 1648 after the Civil War. Bring a torch (flashlight) to explore the underground passageway which connects the tower with the kitchen. Admission costs £1.50/80p.

DONINGTON PARK

The Donington Park motor racing circuit at Castle Donington, 20 miles north-west of Leicester, hosts the annual British Motorcycle Grand Prix and also features the **Donington Collection** (☎ 01332-810048) of racing cars and motorcycles. This is probably the world's best collection of Formula 1 racing cars but, unfortunately, it's displayed with a stunning lack of imagination. The collection is open daily, 10 am to 4 pm; £5/2.50.

BELVOIR CASTLE

In the north-east corner of the county is Belvoir (pronounced beever) Castle (☎ 01476-870262), near Grantham, off the A607 and A52. This Baroque and Gothic fantasy was built between 1654-68. It's open April to September, on Tuesday, Wednesday, Thursday and Saturday, from 11 am to 5 pm, and Sunday from 11 am to 6 pm. In October it opens only on Sunday; £4.25/2.75.

Shropshire

Many counties claim to be beautiful, peaceful and uncrowded, but for Shropshire this is actually true. Covering the rolling hills between Birmingham and the Welsh border, it's a large county with a relatively small population that is centred on the attractive regional capital of Shrewsbury and the new town of Telford. Just outside Telford is Ironbridge, where a series of remarkable museums commemorate the place where the Industrial Revolution began.

Shropshire is bisected by the River Severn, which flows west to east through Shrewsbury. To the north the countryside is largely flat and uninteresting, but to the south lie the Shropshire Hills, the 'blue remembered hills' of local poet AE Housman. They're a series of ridges of which the best known are Wenlock Edge, the Long Mynd and the Stiperstones. Mostly below 1700 feet, this is excellent open walking country that sees relatively few hikers compared to many other parts of Britain.

CYCLE ROUTE

Starting from Shrewsbury, there's a good five or six-day cycle route that takes you round the most interesting and scenic parts of Shropshire. The route is under 100 miles long which allows time to explore the sights. You can rent bikes in Church Stretton and Ludlow but not in Shrewsbury or Ironbridge.

The route goes from Shrewsbury via Wroxeter to Ironbridge (14 miles), Ironbridge to Much Wenlock (only five miles but there's a lot to see in Ironbridge), Much Wenlock to Ludlow (20 miles), Ludlow to Clun (an easy 17-mile ride), Clun to Church Stretton (15 miles), and Church Stretton to Shrewsbury (16 miles, along side roads parallel to the busy A49).

GETTING AROUND

Public transport is not bad between the main towns in Shropshire, with railway lines and most bus routes radiating from Shrewsbury. Getting to country areas without a car is less easy but the county council has a useful phoneline (☎ 0345-056785) for bus and rail information. They also publish the invaluable *Shropshire Bus & Train Map*, available free from TICs, showing all bus routes around the county.

SHREWSBURY

- *pop 60,000* • ☎ *01743*

When Charles Dickens was staying at the Lion Hotel in Shrewsbury, he wrote, 'I am lodged in the strangest little rooms, the ceilings of which I can touch with my hands. From the windows I can look all downhill and slantwise at the crookedest black and white houses, all of many shapes except straight shapes'.

The county's capital can still claim to be the finest Tudor town in Britain, famous for its half-timbered buildings and winding medieval streets. There are no vitally important sights, and because of this, Shrewsbury has been saved from inundation by tourists, which makes it a good base for exploring Shropshire and a convenient stop on the way to Wales.

History

Strategically sited within a defensible loop of the River Severn, Shrewsbury has been important since the 5th century; the Saxon town of Scrobbesbryrig was established on the two hills here. After the Norman Conquest in 1066, the town came under the control of the Norman earl, Roger de Montgomery, who built the castle. The Benedictine abbey, of which only the church remains, was founded in 1083.

For many centuries Shrewsbury played an important part in the control of the Welsh,

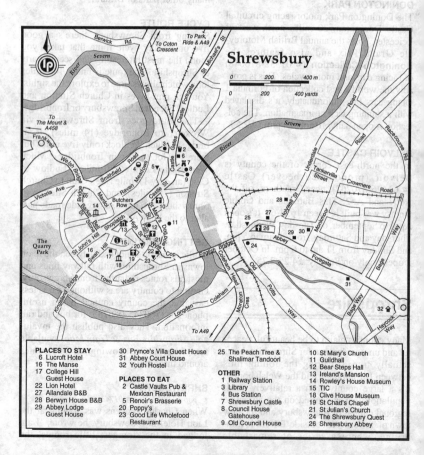

Shrewsbury

PLACES TO STAY			
6	Lucroft Hotel	30	Prynce's Villa Guest House
16	The Manse	31	Abbey Court House
17	College Hill Guest House	32	Youth Hostel
22	Lion Hotel		**PLACES TO EAT**
27	Allandale B&B	2	Castle Vaults Pub & Mexican Restaurant
28	Berwyn House B&B	5	Renoir's Brasserie
29	Abbey Lodge Guest House	20	Poppy's
		23	Good Life Wholefood Restaurant

25 The Peach Tree & Shalimar Tandoori

OTHER
1 Railway Station
3 Library
4 Bus Station
7 Shrewsbury Castle
8 Council House Gatehouse
9 Old Council House
10 St Mary's Church
11 Guildhall
12 Bear Steps Hall
13 Ireland's Mansion
14 Rowley's House Museum
15 TIC
18 Clive House Museum
19 St Chad's Chapel
21 St Julian's Church
24 The Shrewsbury Quest
26 Shrewsbury Abbey

and in 1283 David III of Wales was executed here. Despite problems with its unruly neighbours, the town prospered from the wool trade with the Welsh hill farmers. Many of the beautiful Tudor buildings were built by wealthy wool merchants.

By the 18th century Shrewsbury was a fashionable county town on the main stagecoach route. Robert Clive, who laid the foundations for the British control of India, was mayor of Shrewsbury in 1762.

The most famous former resident is Charles Darwin, born here in 1809 and educated at Shrewsbury's famous public school. There's a statue of him outside the library near the railway station. The town has also done Darwin the questionable honour of naming the shopping mall after him.

Orientation & Information

The railway station lies across the narrow land bridge formed by the loop of the Severn, a five-minute walk north of the centre of town. The bus station is central and the whole town is well signposted. Many of the old winding streets still have names that reflect the occupations of their former inhabitants – Butcher Row, Fish St, Milk St.

There's an efficient TIC (☎ 350761), The Square, with theatre-booking facilities (including for the Royal Shakespeare Company at Stratford). From Easter to September, it's open Monday to Saturday, 9.30 am to 5 pm, and on Sunday until 4 pm.

From May to October there are daily walking tours (£2/1) from the TIC at 2.30 pm. They're highly recommended. In mid-July there's usually an open-air Shakespeare play in the castle grounds.

Early closing in Shrewsbury is on Thursday.

Walking Tour

Start from the TIC, which is in the old **Music Hall**, built in 1839. Opposite, in the square, is the **Market Hall**, an open-sided building erected in 1595. Until the mid-19th century trade was carried on in this square and, on the insides of the pillars at the

northern end of the Market Hall, you can still see holes for the markers that were used to record the numbers of fleeces sold.

Walk across the square into the High St and turn left. On your left is the 16th-century **Ireland's Mansion**, the most impressive of the town's timber-frame buildings.

Retrace your steps along the High St and turn left into narrow Grope Lane with its overhanging buildings. Cross Fish St and go up the steps into St Alkmund's Place. This was the original town square. The only remaining medieval part of **St Alkmund's Church** is the tower; the rest of the building was remodelled at the end of the 18th century. The 14th-century **Bear Steps Hall** has been completely restored and is well worth a look. Nearby St Julian's Church is now a craft centre that's worth a visit. There are several black and white houses along **Butcher Row**, including the Abbot's House, built in 1450.

St Mary's Church, no longer used for worship, is famous for its stained glass, in particular the great Jesse Window of rare English glass dating from the mid-14th century. The spire collapsed in 1894 – because the townsfolk were planning a memorial to Charles Darwin, according to the vicar.

Opposite the north side of the church, by the 17th-century **St Mary's Cottages**, is a narrow alley known as **St Mary's Shut**. A *shut* is a partially covered passage. Follow this and you emerge into Castle St.

At the far end of the street is **Shrewsbury Castle** where the **Shropshire Regimental Museum** reopened recently. Entry to the castle and museum costs £2/1, the grounds are free. The entrance gate is Norman but much of the castle was remodelled by Edward I. Thomas Telford added Laura's Tower in 1787.

Down the alley by the former church, near the entrance to the castle, is the **Council House Gatehouse** in Jacobean style dating from 1620, and beyond it, the **Old Council House** which was where the Council of the Welsh Marches, responsible for the control of this region, met.

Back on Castle St, on the opposite side to the castle, is the library and **statue of Charles Darwin**. Retrace your steps to St Mary's St and follow it down Dogpole. Opposite the timber-frame **Cromwell Hotel** is the **Guildhall**, built in 1696.

At the end of Dogpole turn right onto Wyle Cop. The name means 'hilltop' in Welsh. The **Lion Hotel** was where Dickens stayed on his visit to Shrewsbury; a 200-year-old gilded lion marks its entrance. Henry VII is said to have stayed in the **Henry Tudor House**, on the other side of Barracks Passage, before the battle of Bosworth.

Follow Barracks Passage and Belmont Bank to **St Chad's Chapel**, the remains of the medieval church. Continue to the **Clive House Museum** (☎ 354811), College Hill. Robert Clive lived here when he was mayor in 1762 and although there's not much about Clive, the house contains interesting displays of social and domestic life in 18th and 19th-century Shrewsbury. There's also a fine collection of Coalport and Caughley porcelain. The museum is open Tuesday to Saturday, 10 am to 4 pm, and on Sunday in summer; £1/50p. It's a short walk back to the TIC.

Rowley's House Museum

Shrewsbury's main museum (☎ 361196), on Barker St, is housed in a restored 16th-century timber-frame building and an adjoining 17th-century mansion built by a wealthy merchant.

The museum has displays outlining Shropshire's prehistoric and Roman past, including some of the finds from the nearby Roman town of Wroxeter. One gallery is devoted to the town's medieval history. It's open from Tuesday to Saturday, 10 am to 5 pm, and on Sunday in summer until 4 pm; £2/1.

Shrewsbury Abbey

This church is all that remains of the Benedictine monastery that was founded by Roger de Montgomery in 1083. Inside, the great west window is of particular interest. There's also a memorial to Wilfred Owen, one of the best known of the WWI poets, killed only a week before the end of the war. It's open every day and there are services on Sunday.

The Shrewsbury Quest

Across the street from the abbey is the Shrewsbury Quest (☎ 243324), opened in the summer of 1994 on the site of some of the old abbey buildings. Inspired by the Brother Cadfael books, the theme is one of medieval mystery with clues to find amongst the displays of 12th-century monastery life. Fans of the Ellis Peters books will love it. It's open daily from 10 am to 5 pm (4 pm in winter); £3.75/2.

Brother Cadfael

Shrewsbury provides the setting for the Brother Cadfael Chronicles, a link much touted by the local TIC. Brother Cadfael is a fictional medieval sleuth, the subject of 19 books by Ellis Peters.

Cadfael was not always a monk, having learnt of the ways of the world as soldier, sailor and Crusader before becoming a herbalist and part-time detective at the Benedictine abbey. The turbulent 12th-century backdrop provides at least one corpse per book around which the brother can employ his sleuthing skills.

Although the television series was filmed in Hungary, it brought a flood of fans to Shrewsbury when first shown in 1994. One critic wrote that the British public were learning more about the medieval period from Brother Cadfael than from any other source. Cashing in on the free publicity, a new attraction, the Shrewsbury Quest, was opened and a range of leaflets, including Brother Cadfael walks and Brother Cadfael car tours, was published by the TIC. Shropshire Tourist Board even has plans for Brother Cadfael fly-drive packages! ■

The Quarry Park

There are pleasant walks in this riverside park. The sunken flower garden was left by Percy Thrower, the famous gardening expert who was Shrewsbury's parks' superintendent for 28 years. The annual flower show, held in August, is the second biggest in Britain.

Places to Stay

Hostel The *Shrewsbury Youth Hostel* (☎ 360179), Abbey Foregate, is one mile from the train and bus stations, just off the roundabout by Lord Hill's Column. Open daily from July to August, daily except Sunday from March to June and in September and October, and with limited opening days for the rest of the year. It's a great place to stay; the nightly charge is £8.25/5.55.

Camping At the riverside site of *Severn House* (☎ 850229), at Montford Bridge, four miles north of Shrewsbury on the B4380, you can camp for around £2.50 per person.

B&Bs & Hotels While most hotels are in the historic central area (some of them in appropriately historic timber-frame buildings), B&Bs are further afield. There are three B&B areas: in and around Abbey Foregate, to the north up Coton Hill, and to the west along the A458 and A488.

In the Abbey Foregate area, overlooking the Abbey on Park Terrace, there are several well-located but small B&Bs, with rooms from around £15 per person. Try *Allandale* (☎ 240173), or *Glynndene* (☎ 352488). Nearby at 14 Holywell St is *Berwyn House* (☎ 354858), a comfortable family house with B&B from £13 per person.

There are several B&Bs along Monkmoor Rd, also off Abbey Foregate. The black and white *Prynce's Villa Guest House* (☎ 356217), at No 15, has accommodation from £13 per person.

Back on Abbey Foregate, at No 134, the *Abbey Court House B&B* (☎ 364416) is a comfortable place to stay. Rooms with attached bathroom cost from £16.50 per person.

North of the town centre, in the Coton Hill area, is another group of B&Bs and hotels. It's about a 10-minute walk to the railway station. On Coton Crescent, there's *Mrs Colley's* (☎ 354712) at No 3, *Bancroft Guest House* (☎ 231746) at No 17, and *The Stiperstones Guest House* (☎ 246720) at No 18. All offer B&B from around £15 per person.

The central *Lucroft Hotel* (☎ 362421), Castlegates, on the way into town from the train station, is clean, comfortable and central. Rooms are £18/34 for singles/doubles.

At 16 Swan Hill, *The Manse* (☎ 242659) is a beautiful Georgian town house that offers superior B&B from £17 per person. It's an excellent place to stay but there are only two rooms. *College Hill Guest House* (☎ 365744), 11 College Hill, has six rooms and is similarly priced.

Dating from 1460, *Tudor House* (☎ 351735), 2 Fish St, is centrally located on this quiet medieval street. They charge around £20 per person; some rooms have attached bathroom.

The Lion Hotel (☎ 353107), Wyle Cop, is a Forte Heritage hotel with well-appointed rooms for £59/69 during the week, £50/67.50 for a double at weekends. They also offer cheaper leisure breaks including dinner, bed and breakfast. Rooms at the luxurious *Prince Rupert Hotel* (☎ 499955), on Butcher Row, cost £65.

Places to Eat

Shrewsbury has a good range of places to eat. For a quick bite, between Castle St and Shoplatch there are several cheap cafés and fast-food joints. Opposite the railway station is the Italian-run *Al Piccolino Pizza* (☎ 358133), which does excellent pizzas to take away.

Tearooms abound. Right next to the TIC, *Oscar's Café & Bistro* (☎ 358057) is open every day for lunches and teas. *Poppy's* (☎ 232307), 8 Milk St, is popular, open until 5 pm in summer.

Renoir's Brasserie (☎ 350006) is a small place down an alley off Castle St. Home-made soup and bread is £1.75. Main dishes in the evening are from £6.95 to £11.95.

Owens Café Bar (☎ 352007), on Butcher Row, is an excellent place for a drink or a meal. They have a good range of wines, bottled and draught beers, and interesting dishes. Opposite is *Henry's Restaurant & Bar* (☎ 353117), a 14th-century timber-frame building; main dishes cost from £5.50 to £11.95, less in the bar.

There's a branch of *Pierre Victoire* (☎ 344744) at 15 St Mary's St, offering set lunches for £4.90 and more expensive dinners. Nearby at 11 Dogpole, *Cromwell's Hotel* (☎ 361440) has a popular restaurant with main dishes from £7.95; there's also excellent bar food.

Barracks Passage is a little restaurant-lined alley off Wyle Cop. The *Good Life Wholefood Restaurant* (☎ 350455) does light lunches (quiches, baked potatoes and excellent salads) and teas that are also good value, but it closes at 4.30 pm and isn't open on Sunday. Opposite is the *Old Lion Tap* (☎ 363633), a pub/restaurant in a restored timber-frame building.

There are several restaurants around the Abbey, on Abbey Foregate. *The Peach Tree* (☎ 355055), at No 21, specialises in British cuisine, and does it well. It's closed on Monday. Two doors down is *Shalimar Tandoori* (☎ 344440).

Entertainment

Many of Shrewsbury's pubs are worth visiting for their Tudor architecture alone. There's the *Castle Vaults* (☎ 358807), on Castle St, which also has a good Mexican restaurant; the *Lion & Pheasant* (☎ 236288), 50 Wyle Cop; and the *Three Fishes* (☎ 344793) on Fish St, which is a non-smoking pub.

In the same building as the TIC, the Cinema in the Square shows recent releases, classics and foreign films to small audiences. Visiting groups perform at the theatre.

Getting There & Away

See the fares tables in the Getting Around chapter. Shrewsbury is 150 miles from

London, 68 from Manchester, 43 from Chester and 27 from Ludlow.

Bus National Express (☎ 0990-808080) has three buses a day to and from London (five hours) via Telford and Birmingham. Change at Birmingham for Oxford and Stratford-upon-Avon.

For information on transport in Shropshire, contact the county help line (☎ 0345-056785). Williamsons (☎ 231010) runs an interesting service, the X96 Wrekin Rambler, between Birmingham and Shrewsbury via Ironbridge. There are daily departures in both directions. Midland Red West (☎ 01905-763888) has regular buses to and from Ludlow (service No 435).

Train Two fascinating small railways terminate at Shrewsbury, in addition to plenty of main-line connections. It's possible to do a brilliant, highly-recommended rail loop from Shrewsbury around north Wales. Timetabling is a challenge – phone ☎ 0345-484950 for information. The journey is possible in a day as long as you don't miss any of the connections, but it's much better to allow at least a couple of days as there are plenty of interesting places to visit along the way. The North & Mid-Wales Flexi Rover ticket is the most economical way of covering this route. It costs £23/15.20 and allows travel on three days out of seven.

From Shrewsbury you head due west across Wales to Dovey Junction (1¾ hours), where you connect with the famous Cambrian Coast Line, which hugs the beautiful coast on its way north to Porthmadog (1½ hours).

At Porthmadog you can pick up the Ffestiniog Railway, a superbly restored narrow-gauge steam train that winds up into Snowdonia National Park to the slate-mining town of Blaenau Ffestiniog (1¼ hours). From Blaenau another small railway carves its way through the mountains and down the beautiful, tourist-infested Conwy Valley to Llandudno (1¼ hours) and Conwy. From there it's a short trip to Chester.

Another famous line, promoted as the

Heart of Wales Line, runs south-west to Swansea (four hours), connecting with the main line from Cardiff to Fishguard (six hours, £22.70).

There are numerous trains to and from London's Euston station (three hours), and regular links to Chester (one hour, £5.50). There are also regular trains from Cardiff to Manchester via Bristol, Ludlow and Shrewsbury.

AROUND SHREWSBURY
Attingham Park
This elegant neoclassical house is four miles south-east of Shrewsbury on the B4380. Set in a 230-acre deer park, it's the grandest of Shropshire's stately homes. Built in the late 18th century, there are magnificent state rooms with decorated ceilings, a 300-piece collection of Regency silver, and a picture gallery designed by John Nash. There's a bee house in the walled garden and good walking trails in the park.

Attingham Park (☎ 01743-709203; NT) is open from late March to September, Saturday to Wednesday, 1.30 to 5 pm (from 11 am on Monday); and at weekends in October. Entry to the house and park is £3.50/1.75.

Hawkstone Park
This restored 100-acre park is an 18th-century fantasyland of follies, woodland, caves and cliffs, most of them artificially created. A 2½-hour walking tour takes you up the White Tower (from which a dozen counties are said to be visible), over the Swiss Bridge, into the Hermit's Cave and rhododendron jungle, and through a rocky chasm. It's a bizarre place but fans of Disneyland may find it a little tame.

Hawkstone Park (☎ 01939-200300) is about 10 miles north of Shrewsbury, and you need your own transport to get here. It's open daily from April to October; £4/2.

IRONBRIDGE GORGE
The World Heritage Site at Ironbridge, on the southern edge of Telford, is a monument to the Industrial Revolution. It was here, almost 300 years ago, that Abraham Darby pion-

eered the technique of smelting iron ore with coke leading to the production of the first iron wheels, the first iron rails, the first steam locomotive and the first iron bridge. Ironbridge can rightly claim to be the Silicon Valley of the 18th century, the place where the modern industrial world began. What made it all possible was the fact that deposits of iron ore and coal were both available in the same location, and there was easy transportation on the Severn.

The Ironbridge Gorge Museum is Britain's best museum of industrial archaeology and an interesting place to visit even if you're not an industrial archaeology nut. The gorge (more a valley) is attractive and the seven museums and several smaller sites are spread over six square miles, centred on the beautiful old iron bridge.

Orientation & Information
It's best to see the museums on the west side of Ironbridge first; the video at the Museum of the River gives a good introduction.

There's a TIC (☎ 01952-432166) near the bridge and this is the only place in Ironbridge where you can change money.

There are boat trips (45 minutes, £3/2) along the river and under the bridge from the car park near the Museum of the River.

If you don't have your own transport there's a lot of walking involved – it's three miles from Blists Hill to the Museum of Iron.

Ironbridge Gorge Museum
The Ironbridge Gorge Museum (☎ 01952-433522) is open daily from 10 am to 5 pm (6 pm in summer). A passport ticket (valid for a year) allowing entrance to all the museums costs £8.95/5.30 for adults/students. Separate tickets to each of the museums are also available for around £3.

Museum of the River Visitor Centre This is the best place to start, although it's run by the local water company which makes sure you know what a good job it's doing. There's an interesting video and a model of the gorge as it was in 1796.

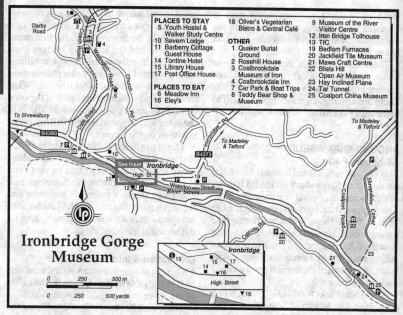

Ironbridge Gorge Museum

Coalbrookdale Museum of Iron It was here that it all began, and the furnace in which Abraham Darby first succeeded in smelting iron ore with coke is lovingly preserved.

Rosehill House About 100 yards up the hill from the Museum of Iron, this 18th-century house is maintained as it was when lived in by an ironmaster in the early 19th century. It was built by the Darbys who were Quakers; there's a Quaker burial ground near the house.

Iron Bridge & Tollhouse As well as providing a crossing of the river, the world's first iron bridge was constructed to draw attention to the new iron-based technology and the ironworks of this area. It was begun in 1777 and officially opened in 1781. It was used by vehicles of all kinds up until 1930; it's now only open for pedestrians. There's a small display in the tollhouse.

Blists Hill Open Air Museum This museum covers 50 acres and re-creates a working community from the 1890s. Visitors are invited to stop first at the bank where their pounds and pence are exchanged for old money at the rate of £1 for 2½d. The money can be spent in the village pub and shops. Blists Hill is designed as an open museum, staffed by craftspeople in period costume who demonstrate the old skills. You can visit the butcher's, sweetshop, doctor's surgery, church, candlemaker's, foundry and carpenter's. On certain days they fire up the wrought ironworks, now the only one still operating in the Western world.

Coalport China Museum By the early 19th century, the revolutionary iron-making skills had spread to other parts of the world and Ironbridge was declining. The development of porcelain and decorative tile industries around Coalport and Jackfield halted this decline, however. Fine Coalport china was

TONY WHEELER

RICHARD EVERIST

TONY WHEELER

TONY WHEELER

Top Left: Grey and green Castleton, Peak District, Derbyshire
Top Right: Albert Dock, Liverpool
Bottom Left: Two by two, rowing boats on the River Dee, Chester, Cheshire
Bottom Right: Winnatts Pass, Peak District, Derbyshire

TONY WHEELER

TONY WHEELER   RICHARD EVERIST   TONY WHEELER

TONY WHEELER

A	
B	C	D
E	

A: Pub In old Portsmouth, Hampshire
B: Typical pub sign, England
C: On the ferry from Ullapool to Stornoway

D: Pub on the Royal Mile, Edinburgh
E: Having a few beers, Westminster, London

made at the factory until its move to Staffordshire in 1926.

Jackfield Tile Museum You can cross the river on the footbridge to this museum where there are large displays of the decorative tiles produced until the 1960s.

Other Things to See By the Blists Hill site is the **Hay Inclined Plane**, designed to transport boats between the River Severn and the Shropshire canal. Nearby is the **Tar Tunnel**, a natural source of bitumen discovered in 1785.

Places to Stay
The excellent *Ironbridge Gorge Youth Hostel* (☎ 433281) is fully open from February to October. They get a lot of school groups during term time but tend to be less busy in the holidays. The nightly charge is £9.10/6.15. There's camping at *Severn Gorge Caravan Park* (☎ 684789), Bridgnorth Rd, Tweedale, which is three-quarters of a mile north of Blists Hill. They charge £5 for two people and a tent.

Other accommodation in Ironbridge comprises upmarket B&Bs and hotels. *Post Office House* (☎ 433201), 6 The Square, overlooks the famous bridge. There are just three rooms, one with bathroom attached, at £17.50 per person. The *Tontine Hotel* (☎ 432127), also on the square, has rooms for £20/35 without bathroom attached, £30/45 with bathroom.

Across the river is *Barberry Cottage Guest House* (☎ 882110), 71 Bower Yard, a comfortable and friendly place. Singles/doubles are £20/34.

The two top places to stay are the Library House and Severn Lodge. The *Library House* (☎ 432299), 11 Severn Bank, is right in the centre of Ironbridge. It's very well run and a single/double is £36/48. A short walk above the river is the delightful *Severn Lodge* (☎ 432148), an attractive Georgian house with a secluded garden. There are two doubles and a twin room, all with attached bath, for £48.

Places to Eat
There are *cafés* at the Museum of Iron, Blists Hill (two cafés and a pub), and at Rosehill House. The other places to eat are all near the centre of Ironbridge. For a snack or a picnic, *Eley's* is a butcher's on the square that does an excellent, really porky, pork pie (80p) amongst other pies and pasties.

Oliver's Vegetarian Bistro (☎ 433086), 33 High St, is open for lunch and dinner from Tuesday to Saturday. Upstairs is *The Coracle Restaurant* (☎ 433913), which is more expensive: main dishes are from £8.50.

Nearby, the *Central Café* serves everything with chips; it's cheap and cheerful. The *Tontine Hotel* has some seating outside and serves cheap bar meals. There are several teashops that also do light meals.

The best place to drink is the *Coalbrookdale Inn* (☎ 433953), which has real ale and serves pub grub daily except Sunday. It's near the youth hostel. The *Meadow Inn* (☎ 433193), Buildwas Rd, has been recommended for its food.

Getting There & Away
Ironbridge is 14 miles from Shrewsbury. If you're driving from the other direction it's well signposted off the M54. See the Shrewsbury Getting There & Away section for buses. The nearest railway station is at Telford and there are regular buses to Ironbridge from there.

WENLOCK EDGE
There are great walks along this steep escarpment that stretches 15 miles between Much Wenlock and Craven Arms, with superb views across to the Long Mynd to the west. It's geologically famous, in particular for its ancient coral reef exposures. Wenlock limestone was formed 400 million years ago when this area was under the sea.

Wilderhope Manor is a large limestone house on the southern slopes of Wenlock Edge, seven miles south-west of Much Wenlock. It's unfurnished but can be visited on Wednesday and Saturday afternoon; it costs £1. Part of the building is leased to the YHA. *Wilderhope Manor Youth Hostel*

(☎ 01694-771363) is open March to October, Monday to Saturday. The nightly charge is £8.25/ 5.55. There are several trails, including one west along the top of Wenlock Edge. Buses are rare in this area; you really need your own transport.

THE LONG MYND & CHURCH STRETTON

The Long Mynd is probably the best known of Shropshire's hills – an excellent area for walking. Mynd is an abbreviation of the Welsh *mynydd* (mountain) but since these hills are below 1800 feet, they cannot be defined as mountains. Nevertheless, there are superb views from the top of the ridges. **The Portway** is an ancient track that runs the full length of the Long Mynd.

The village of Church Stretton is a good base for walks on the Long Mynd. The Victorians called the area Little Switzerland, bottled the local spring water and started to promote Church Stretton as a health resort.

You can get walking information and leaflets from the Shropshire Hills Information Centre (☎ 01694-723133), in the library in Church St. It's open from Easter to September, Monday to Saturday. Bikes can be rented from Longmynd Cycles (☎ 01694-722367), Sandford Ave, for £14 per day or £60 per week. It's open Monday to Saturday and its staff can also advise about routes. Cyclists must keep to bridleways or special cycle paths.

Walks

The **Carding Mill Valley** trail is a popular walk from Church Stretton, and from the 1695-foot-high summit of the Long Mynd there are views of the Stiperstones, the range to the east. You can drive part of the way and there's a National Trust information centre and teashop in the valley. On the other side of the A49, the walk up **Caer Caradoc**, where there's an ancient fort, is less busy. It's a five-mile trip taking about 2½ hours. There are numerous other walks in the area.

Places to Stay

The *Bridges Long Mynd Youth Hostel* (☎ 01588-650656) is five miles from Church Stretton at Ratlinghope. It's in the old village school in the valley between the Long Mynd and the Stiperstones. Open from March to November, the nightly charge is £6.75/4.60. The nearest railway station is at Church Stretton and the walk takes a couple of hours.

At *Woodbank House* (☎ 01694-723454), Watling St South, there's B&B from £15 per person. *Brookfields Guest House* (☎ 01694-722314), Watling St North, charges £28 per person for very comfortable rooms with bathroom attached.

The 16th-century *Jinlye Guest House* (☎ 01694-723243) is on Castle Hill, just outside All Stretton, which is two miles north of Church Stretton. Located on the Long Mynd, it's highly recommended; rooms have showers attached, and cost around £22 per person.

The *Longmynd Hotel* (☎ 01694-722244), Cunnery Rd, stands above Church Stretton. There's a heated swimming pool, sauna and solarium. Rooms are from £38 per person.

Getting There & Away

Church Stretton is on the main bus and rail routes between Shrewsbury and Ludlow. Midland Red West bus No 435 takes 45 minutes from Shrewsbury, 35 minutes from Ludlow. The train is more than twice as fast.

BISHOP'S CASTLE

In the south-west corner of the county, the main reason for visiting is not for the castle (which no longer exists) but for a pint. The *Three Tuns* (☎ 01588-638797), on Salop St, is a pub that still brews its own beer.

The TIC (☎ 01588-638467) is in Old Time, a shop on the High St. There are good walks around Bishop's Castle. Eight miles to the north are the **Stiperstones**, an inhospitable landscape of ridges topped with rough rocks. When the mist comes down and Satan settles into The Devil's Chair, it can be a sinister place.

CLUN

About six miles south of Bishop's Castle is the village of Clun, with its wonderful ruin of a castle. There's more good walking country here, and Clun is just a few miles east of Offa's Dyke. Despite the lack of large numbers of trees, this area is known as Clun Forest, since it was once a royal hunting ground.

Clun Mill Youth Hostel (☎ 01588-640582) occupies an old water mill on the outskirts of the village. It costs £6.75/4.60 and is open April to August daily except Wednesday. *Clun Farm* (☎ 01588-640432), on the High St, does B&B for £14 per person.

Midland Red West service No 742/5 runs this way from Ludlow.

LUDLOW
• *pop 7500* • ☎ 01584

Ludlow is a beautiful town of black and white buildings, and a rambling ruined castle rising above the River Teme. There are nearly 500 listed buildings and it's certainly one of the most attractive towns in England.

Ludlow developed around its castle, built in the 11th century. Involved in the medieval wool trade, it prospered from the sale of fleeces and the manufacture of woollen cloth. The town was also an important administrative centre and until 1689 the Council of the Marches, which governed Wales, was based here.

The TIC (☎ 875053), Castle St, is open Monday to Saturday from 10 am to 5 pm, and also on Sunday in summer. There are guided tours of the town at 2.30 pm on summer weekends, from the castle entrance. Early closing in Ludlow is on Thursday.

Mountain bikes can be rented from Pearce Engineering (☎ 876016), Fishmore Rd, a ¾ mile north-east of the town centre.

Ludlow Castle
Built around 1090 by Roger de Lacy, to control the Welsh, much of this impressive castle still stands. It's a huge fortification with a large outer courtyard where the townspeople could shelter if attacked, and has solid keep of generous proportions. In the 14th century the castle was turned into a palace by Roger Mortimer, whose mistress was Queen Isabella, wife of Edward II.

In late June and early July the castle forms a perfect open-air theatre for the Shakespeare plays held during the Ludlow Festival.

The castle (☎ 873355) is open daily from February to November, closing at 5 pm in summer; £2/1.50.

Other Things to See
Lined with many of Ludlow's most attractive buildings, **Broad St** has been described as one of the handsomest streets in England. One street to the east, the timber-frame **Feathers Hotel**, on Bull Ring, is possibly the finest Jacobean building in the country. For an introduction to the town's history visit the small **museum** on Castle Square.

The large **Church of St Laurence** is worth visiting, and in the graveyard the poet AE Housman, who wrote *A Shropshire Lad*, is commemorated. His love of the Shropshire landscape has provided the county's tourist offices with a rich source of quotes for its brochures.

Places to Stay & Eat
Ludlow Youth Hostel (☎ 872472), Ludford Lodge, faces the town across Ludford Bridge, just south of the town. It costs £6.75/4.60 and is open March to August daily except Sunday, and September and October daily except Sunday and Monday.

B&Bs in Ludlow can be expensive. *Cecil Guest House* (☎ 872442), Sheet Rd, has 10 rooms and charges from £18.50 per person. It's about a mile from the centre. If you can possibly afford it, you should stay at the *Feathers Hotel* (☎ 875261), Bull Ring. Some of the rooms have four-poster beds and staying in this beautiful building is a delightful experience. Luxury costs from £65/88.

The *Unicorn* (☎ 873555), Lower Corve St, is a pub with good food; they also do B&B from £20 per person.

You can get light lunches and teas at *Aragons* (☎ 873282), 5 Church St. It's open in the evening on Friday and Saturday.

Getting There & Away
Ludlow is 29 miles from Shrewsbury, and 24 miles from Hereford. There are bus services

which take you to Hereford, Birmingham and Shrewsbury.

From Ludlow railway station there are direct services to Shrewsbury (30 minutes), Church Stretton (15 minutes), Hereford (25 minutes), Cardiff, Liverpool and Manchester.

Staffordshire

Most visitors simply pass through Staffordshire, which stretches from the northern edge of Birmingham nearly to the southern fringes of Manchester. It's worth a pause to see Lichfield with its wonderful cathedral, to sample the beer in Burton upon Trent or to scare yourself silly at Alton Towers. To the north-east the Staffordshire moorlands blend into the Peak District National Park.

LICHFIELD
• *pop 25,000* • ☎ *01543*

With its triple spires, **Lichfield Cathedral** started as a Saxon church in 700 and was rebuilt as a Norman cathedral around 1100 and again as a Gothic cathedral from around 1200. St Chad, the first Bishop of Lichfield, was laid to rest in each of the buildings in turn. His gold-leafed skull was once kept in St Chad's Head Chapel, just to the west of the south transept where busts of Samuel Johnson and David Garrick can be seen.

The beautiful vaulting of the mid-13th century Chapter House is one of the cathedral's prime attractions and the Lichfield Gospels, a superb illuminated manuscript from 730, is displayed here.

Samuel Johnson was born in Lichfield in 1709, and although his pioneering dictionary established his name as one of the great scholars, critics and wits of the English language, this larger than life character was, like a modern superstar, more famous for who he was than what he did. His close friend James Boswell's *The Life of Samuel Johnson* is still looked upon as one of the great biographies, and statues of Johnson and Boswell stand in the Market Square. The **Birthplace of Samuel Johnson Museum** is on the square and is open daily from 10 am to 5 pm; £1/60p. The town's **Heritage & Treasury Exhibition**, also on the square, is open the same hours.

The TIC (☎ 252109) is on Market Square.

BURTON UPON TRENT
Burton upon Trent has been a brewing centre for centuries and the **Bass Museum & Visitor Centre** (☎ 01283-531111) tells the full story. Founded in 1777, Bass is now Britain's biggest brewer. The centre is open daily, 10.30 am to 4 pm, and the £3.45 entry fee includes an end-of-visit Bass beer if you're of drinking age.

ALTON TOWERS
With over 100 rides and a single entrance fee of £16, Alton Towers (☎ 01538-702200) is the most popular theme park in Britain; it's between Stoke-on-Trent and Ashbourne.

Cheshire

You can scan the stars with the gigantic radio telescope at Jodrell Bank, investigate canal travel at the wonderful waterways museum at Ellesmere Port, and if your Roller is playing up you can return it to its birthplace at Crewe, but when it comes right down to it Cheshire is all about Chester.

CHESTER
• *pop 80,000* • ☎ *01244*

Despite steady streams of tourists Chester remains a beautiful town, ringed by an almost continuous red sandstone wall that dates back to the Romans and is the best preserved in Britain. The impression that this is really a medieval theme park is reinforced by the fact that many of the 'medieval'-looking buildings are actually only Victorian!

Roman Chester was the fortress city of Deva, a bulwark against the fierce Welsh tribes. The city was not totally abandoned when the Romans withdrew from England in the 5th century, but the border of Wales is only a stone's throw west of Chester and the Welsh remained a threat long after the Romans had departed. Not until the 14th century did the danger subside, and the regulations which banned the Welsh from the town after dark and stipulated that they could not bear arms, hold meetings or enter pubs, were withdrawn.

In the early 10th century Chester came under the control of Aethelflaeda, daughter of Alfred the Great.

Medieval Chester became the largest port in the north-west but in the Civil War the city took the Royalist side and was besieged for 18 months (1645-6) by Cromwell's forces. It was not until the next century that the walls were finally repaired and took on a new role as a tourist attraction. The first guidebook to Chester was published in 1781!

Orientation

Built in a bow formed by the River Dee, the walled centre is now surrounded by suburbs. Most of the places of interest are within the walls where the Roman street pattern is relatively intact. From the High Cross, the stone pillar which marks the town centre, four roads fan out to the four principal gates. A ring road, which actually cuts through the city walls, also encircles the central area.

Information

The TIC (☎ 318356) is in the Town Hall opposite the cathedral. From May to October it's open Monday to Saturday, 9 am to 7.30 pm and Sunday, 10 am to 4 pm. The rest of the year it's open Monday to Saturday, 9 am to 5.30 pm. The Chester Visitors Centre (☎ 351609) is in Vicar's Lane. It's open April to October, daily from 9 am to 6 pm. November to March it opens daily, 9 am to 5 pm. There's also a small TIC at the railway station.

City walks depart daily from the Town Hall at 10.45 am and cost £2.25/1.75; in summer there's even a wall walk led by a Roman legionary! Walks also depart from the Chester Visitors Centre and, on summer

The Rows
Chester's unique two-level shopping streets are a mystery which may date back to the city's Roman past. The Romans had been gone for nearly 1000 years when Chester began to develop as a medieval town. The Roman walls had crumbled into rubble and it's surmised that traders built their shops against the rubble banks while later arrivals built theirs on top of the banks. Whatever the origins, the Rows make a convenient sheltered shopping promenade along the four ancient streets fanning out from the Cross. Today the Rows also lead into modern shopping centres like the Forum and Grosvenor Precinct. The Forum also encompasses the old covered market. ■

weekends, there's a night-time Ghost Hunter Trail (£2.25/1.75).

There's a laundrette at St Anne St, north of the centre.

City Walls

The Chester city walls were originally built around 70 AD to protect the Roman fort of Deva. Between 90 and 120 AD they were rebuilt in stone by the Roman 20th Legion. Over the following centuries the walls were often altered but their present position was established around 1200. During the Civil War the city took the Royalist side and an 18-month siege caused great damage which was not repaired until 1702-1714, when the walls were rebuilt to become a fashionable promenade.

The two-mile circuit of the city walls is an excellent introduction to Chester and will take about 1½ to two hours. **Eastgate**, with the prominent **Eastgate Clock**, is the starting point from where this walk proceeds clockwise. The clock was built for Queen Victoria's Diamond Jubilee in 1897 and stands atop the 1769 gate. In Roman times this was the entrance from their city of York.

The **Thimbleby Tower**, also known as the Wolf Tower, was destroyed during the Civil War and never rebuilt. From here you can look down to the foundations of the southeast angle tower of the old Roman fort. Just

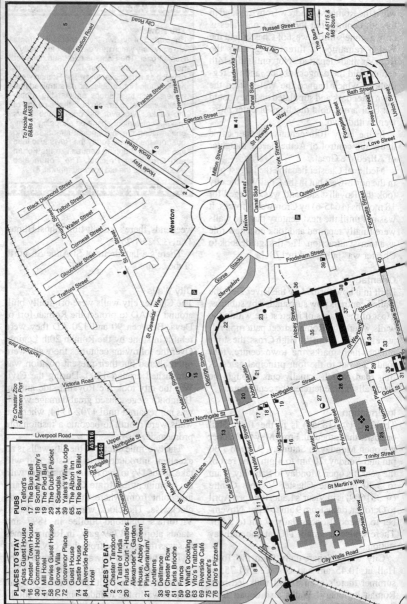

PLACES TO STAY
4   Aplas Guest House
16 Chester Town Hotel
30 Commercial Hotel
41 Mill Hotel
58 Davies Guest House
70 Grove Villa
72 Grosvenor Place
    Guest House
74 Castle House
84 Riverside Recorder
    Hotel

PLACES TO EAT
2   Chester Tandoori
3   A Taste of India
20 Rufus Court - Hattie's
    Alexander's, Garden
    House, Abbey Green
21 Pink Geranium
33 Jonliems
46 Delifrance
51 Chester Row
59 Paris Brioche
60 Francs
63 Whist Cooking
69 Vito's Trattoria
75 Riverside Café
75 Vincent's
76 Dino's Pizzeria

PUBS
8   Telford's
17 The Blue Bell
18 Scruffy Murphy's
19 The Pied Bull
29 The Dublin Packet
34 Scandals
39 Yates's Wine Lodge
65 The Albion Inn
81 The Bear & Billet

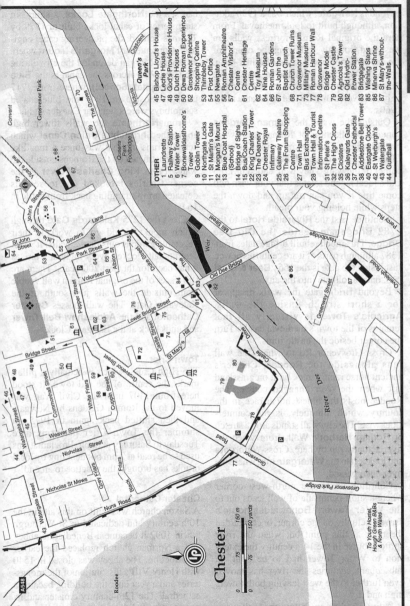

Chester

OTHER
1 Laundrette
5 Railway Station
6 Water Tower
7 Bonewaldesthorne's Tower
9 Goblin Tower
10 Northgate Locks
11 St Martin's Gate
12 Morgan's Mount
13 Blue Coat Hospital (School)
14 Bridge of Sighs
15 Bus/Coach Station
22 King Charles Tower
23 The Deanery
24 Chester Royal Infirmary
25 Gateway Theatre
26 The Forum Shopping Centre
27 Town Hall
28 Town Hall & Tourist Information Centre
31 St Peter's
32 The High Cross
35 Cloisters
36 Kaleyards Gate
37 Chester Cathedral
38 Addlestone Bell Tower
40 Eastgate Clock
42 St Werburgh's
43 Watergate
44 Guildhall
45 Bishop Lloyd's House
47 Leche House
48 God's Providence House
49 Dutch Houses
50 Dewa Roman Experience
52 Grosvenor Precinct Shopping Centre
53 Thimbleby Tower
54 Post Office
55 Newgate
56 Roman Amphitheatre
57 Chester Visitor's Centre
61 Chester Heritage Centre
62 Toy Museum
64 Nine Houses
66 Roman Gardens
67 St John the Baptist Church
68 Church Tower Ruins
71 Grosvenor Museum
73 Military Museum
77 Roman Harbour Wall
78 Grosvenor
79 Bridge Model
79 Chester Castle
80 Agricola's Tower
82 Old Hydro-Power Station
83 Bridgegate
85 Wishing Steps
86 Minerva Shrine
87 St Mary's-without-the-Walls

beyond is **Newgate**, which was a 1938 addition, although built to look medieval. From here the original Roman fortress walls ran westward, roughly following the course of the modern ring road to St Martin's Gate. From Newgate the remains of part of the **Roman Amphitheatre** can be seen. It was only discovered in 1928 and excavated in the 1960s.

Outside the walls the **Roman Gardens** contain a collection of Roman stonework brought here from excavations around Chester. Descend the **wishing steps** at the corner of the wall. They were added in 1785 and a local legend relates that your wish will come true if you can run up and down the steps while holding your breath.

Continue past the **Riverside Hotel** to the 1782 **Bridgegate** beside the **Old Dee Bridge**. This much rebuilt bridge dates from 1387 although parts of it are centuries newer. Just inside the gate is the 1664 **Bear & Billet** pub, once a tollgate into the city.

Beyond Bridgegate the walls disappear for a short stretch. Inside the walls, **Agricola's Tower** is virtually all that remains of the town's medieval castle. Turn the corner beside the castle ruins.

Cross Grosvenor Rd to where the wall runs alongside the **Roodee**, Chester's ancient horse racing track built on grassland left when the river changed course. The Roodee hosts the oldest horse race in the country which, uniquely, is run counterclockwise. The city wall stands atop a stretch of **Roman Harbour Wall**, from when the river actually ran by here. Cross **Watergate** and look left to the **Watergate Inn**, where the river once passed.

Continue on to the north-west corner where a short peninsula of wall leads out to the **Water Tower**. **Bonewaldesthorne's Tower**, actually on the corner, once guarded the river at this point but when the river shifted course in the 14th century the extension to Water Tower had to be built. In subsequent centuries the river has moved even further to the west leaving both towers high and dry.

A little further on, below the walls, you can see the **Northgate Locks**, a short but steep series of canal locks built in 1779 by Thomas Telford, the pioneering canal engineer. Continue past **Morgan's Mount** where a Captain Morgan defended the city during the Civil War. Across the canal is the **Blue Coat Hospital (School)**, where from 1717 until its closure in 1949 the blue-coated schoolboys were a familiar Chester sight.

From **Northgate** the walls tower high above the **Shropshire Union Canal** which actually runs in what was once a moatlike ditch constructed by the Romans outside the walls. From **King Charles' Tower** at the corner Charles I looked out to see his defeated army straggling back from battle in 1645.

Cross the 1275 **Kaleyards Gate** through which monks would go to work in their vegetable gardens outside the walls. It's still ceremonially locked every night at 9 pm, as it has been for the past 700 years. There are still traces of the original Roman wall visible from outside the walls just south of the Kaleyards Gate. The walk passes **Chester Cathedral** and the **Addleshaw Bell Tower** and ends back at the Eastgate Clock.

Town Crier

The High Cross, which is actually a pillar, marks the centre of the old town. It stood here from 1407 until the Civil War, was moved to the Roman Gardens by Newgate and then shifted back again in 1975. In summer the Town Crier performs here Tuesday to Saturday at noon. Proclamations used to be read at 2 pm but heckling by local drunks has brought the practice to an end!

Chester Cathedral

A Saxon church was built on this site in the 10th century and dedicated to St Werburgh but in 1092 it became a Benedictine abbey and a Norman church replaced the earlier construction. The abbey was closed in 1540 with Henry VIII's dissolution of the monasteries and a year later the building became a cathedral. The 12th-century cloister and its surrounding buildings are essentially unaltered and retain much of the early monastic structure.

The present cathedral (☎ 32476) was built between 1250 and 1540 but there were later alterations including a great deal of Victorian reconstruction. It's open daily from 7 am to 6.30 pm; but you can't walk round if there's a service in progress. A donation of £2 is suggested for visitors; and there's a useful free leaflet that explains the main points of interest.

Dewa Roman Experience

This new attraction aims to show what life was like in Roman times. The experience begins in a reconstructed galley. You're then moved into a Roman street and, having taken in the rather unconvincing sights and sounds, there's an entertaining audiovisual presentation. You can then wander at your own pace past the Roman foundations of the castle and medieval rubbish pits, and through the interesting museum and finds room. The Dewa Roman Experience (☎ 343407), Pierpoint Lane (off Bridge St), is open daily from 9 am to 5 pm; entry is £3.80/1.90.

Museums

The **Grosvenor Museum** (☎ 321616) has the usual hodgepodge of paintings and silver but the displays on the Roman era in Chester and particularly the Roman tombstones are very good. The Stuart, mid-Georgian and Victorian period rooms are definitely worth seeing. The museum is on Grosvenor St and is open Monday to Saturday, 10.30 am to 5 pm, and Sunday from 2 to 5 pm; free.

Chester Heritage Centre (☎ 321616) is in an old church building on the corner of Pepper and Bridge Sts. It has interesting displays and audiovisuals on the town's architecture, the churches, the development of the Rows and the events of the Civil War. It's open Monday to Saturday, 11 am to 5 pm, and Sunday from noon to 5 pm; it costs £1/50p.

The **Chester Toy Museum** (☎ 346297) at 13A Lower Bridge St displays Dinky and Matchbox Toys. There's a **Military Museum** in the Castle. **On the Air** (☎ 348464), 42

Bridge St, is a museum of the history of broadcasting.

Along the River

Cross the Old Dee Bridge and turn right into Edgar's Field to find a small sandstone ridge with the **Minerva Shrine**, a small and time-worn Roman monument to the goddess.

The **Groves** is the popular riverside promenade and park just outside the city walls. Rowing boats (£3 to £4 an hour) and pedal boats (£3 to £4 a half-hour) can be hired here and there are a variety of short cruises available. Typical costs are around £2/1 to £3/2.50 for a half-hour trip.

Zoo

Chester has the largest zoo (☎ 380280) in England, noted for its gardens and natural setting. The zoo is on the A41 just three miles north of the city centre. There are direct buses from the railway station in summer (£1.55). The zoo is open daily from 10 am; £7.50/5.

Places to Stay

Chester has numerous places to stay although unbooked late arrivals on a summer evening may have to do a little searching. There are more places outside the city walls than inside – many of them are within easy walking distance of the centre and car parking is likely to be easier. The TIC does not charge for making bookings.

Hostel The *Youth Hostel* (☎ 680056), 40 Hough Green, is a mile from the city centre across Grosvenor Park Bridge. The nightly cost is £9.10/6.15.

The Chester Backpackers Hostel (☎ 400118), The Old Mill, Steam Mill St, should be opening soon. In a converted mill, 400m from the railway station, dormitory accommodation costs from £8 to £10.

B&Bs & Hotels – outside the walls There are numerous good-value B&Bs from around £15 per person, particularly along Brook St near the railway station. The *Aplas Guest House* (☎ 312401) at No 106 is very comfortable, only a five-minute walk from the railway station, and costs from £12.50 to £15 per person.

Hoole Rd, beyond the railway lines, is still within walking distance from the centre. It's the road to or from the M53/M56 and is lined with numerous low-price to medium-price B&Bs. The *Pear Tree Guest House* (☎ 323260) at 69 Hoole Rd costs from £15 per person. Nearby are the similar *Ba Ba Guest House* (☎ 315047) at No 65 and *Glen-Garth Guest House* (☎ 310260) at No 59. The *Glann Hotel* (☎ 344800) at 2 Stone Place off the Hoole Rd is an attractive small hotel costing from £21 per person.

Grove Villa (☎ 349713) is at 18 The Groves, right on the River Dee, and has rooms (all with attached bathroom) from £15 to £17 per person. The *Mill* (☎ 350035) is on Milton St right beside the canal. It's a larger place with good facilities from £45/50. There's an interesting restaurant court, and canal cruises are available.

B&Bs & Hotels – inside the walls

Grosvenor Place Guest House (☎ 324455) at 24 Grosvenor Place is centrally situated and has rooms at £20/25 or £30/40 with attached bathroom. Nearby is *Castle House* (☎ 350354) at 23 Castle St. The building dates back to the 16th century and rooms (some with attached bathroom) cost from £21 per person.

Davies Guest House (☎ 340452) at 22 Cuppin St is a basic but centrally located B&B with rooms from £14. *Commercial Hotel* (☎ 320749), is hidden away in St Peter's Church Yard, but it could be a bit noisy as this is also a pub. Rooms cost from £20 per person.

The *Riverside Recorder Hotel* (☎ 326580) at 22 City Walls is just off Lower Bridge St, near Bridgegate. This small hotel has a car park and costs from £25 per person for rooms with attached bathroom. The *Chester Town House* (☎ 350021) at 23 King St dates from 1680 and is on a quiet, pleasantly old-world street. All rooms have attached bathroom and cost £35/48.

Places to Eat

Restaurants The deservedly popular *Francs* (☎ 317952) at 14 Cuppin St turns out traditional French food every day. Nearby at 14-16 Grosvenor St on the corner of Cuppin St, *What's Cooking* (☎ 346512) offers burgers and other American-style food. *Vito's Trattoria* (☎ 317330) at 25 Lower Bridge St is a standard pizza and pasta specialist. A little further down at No 51, *Dino's Pizzeria* (☎ 325091) has similar fare while *Vincent's* (☎ 310854) at No 58-60 has Caribbean cuisine. *Chester Row* (☎ 316003) at 24 Watergate Row turns out traditional English food.

Rufus Court, already mentioned as a teahouse, also has the *Abbey Green Restaurant* (☎ 313251) and *Garden House* (☎ 320004) both of which serve English food; the Garden House has some vegetarian choices. Just outside the court at 2 Abbey Green is the *Pink Geranium/Jomtiens* (☎ 313522) which serves Thai dishes in the evening.

There are plenty of Chinese and Indian restaurants around town. Brook St, between the centre and the railway station, has the *Chester Tandoori* (☎ 347410) at No 39-41 and *A Taste of India* (☎ 311585) at No 54.

Cafés & Pubs Chester has the usual selection of international fast-food outlets, plus plenty of bakeries and sandwich bars and some centrally located fish & chip places, particularly down Lower Bridge St. *Paris Brioche* and *DeliFrance* both turn out good sandwiches and baguettes either to take away or eat there.

Hattie's is a genteel teahouse at Rufus Court, right by the Northgate. The *Riverside Café* is nicely situated by the Queens Park Footbridge.

Chester pubs are worth checking out: many of them are old and have interesting histories. They also have good, basic food at reasonable prices. There are several of them on Northgate St: The *Blue Bell* (☎ 317758) is at No 65, while *Scruffy Murphy's* (☎ 321750) at No 59 and the *Pied Bull* (☎ 325829) are side by side. The *Albion Inn* (☎ 340345) is a fine old Edwardian pub on

Park St, just inside the city walls. Good English food is served – with no chips or fry-ups. *Scandals* (☎ 317830) at 2-6 Music Hall Passage near the cathedral is a busy pub-cum-wine bar. The *Watergate* on Watergate St is also popular.

Entertainment

Alexander's Jazz Theatre (☎ 340005), Rufus Court, right by Northgate, is a combination of wine bar, coffee bar and even tapas bar. Entry at night is sometimes free before 10 pm, otherwise it's £2 to £7.50 depending on the act.

Pubs which have live music include *Yates's Wine Lodge* on Frodsham St which attracts a noisy, young crowd at night, *Scruffy Murphy's* (see Cafés and Pubs), and *Telford's Warehouse* (☎ 390090) at Tower Wharf.

The *Gateway Theatre* (☎ 40392) is at Hamilton Place beside the Forum Centre.

Getting There & Away

Chester is 188 miles from London, 85 from Birmingham, 40 from Manchester and 18 from Liverpool. It has excellent transport connections, especially to and from North Wales.

Bus The National Express bus station is just north of the city walls and just inside the ring road. National Express (☎ 0990-808080) has numerous services: one a day to Glasgow (six hours, £23); three a day to Manchester (1¼ hours, £4.35) and Bristol (four hours, £17.50); two a day to Llandudno (1¾ hours, £5.25); four a day to Liverpool (one hour, £4.65); five a day to Birmingham (2½ hours, £8.25) and London (5½ hours, £19.50).

For information on local bus services, which are quite well organised, ring the Cheshire Bus Line (☎ 602666). Local buses leave from Market Square behind the town hall. On Sunday and bank holidays a Sunday Adventurer ticket gives you unlimited bus travel in Cheshire for £3 or £6 for a family ticket.

Train The railway station is a 15-minute walk from the city centre via City Rd or Brook St. Any bus stopping at the station goes into the city for 30/15p.

There are numerous trains to: Shrewsbury (one hour, £5.30); Manchester (one hour, £6.80) and Liverpool (£3.10); Holyhead (2¼ hours, £11) via the North Wales coast, for Ireland; London's Euston (three hours, £34).

Getting Around

The compact walled city is easy to get around on foot and most places of interest are close to the wall walk.

City buses depart from the Town Hall Bus Exchange. Call Chester City Transport (☎ 347452) for details. Guide Friday offers its regular open-top double-decker tours of the city; an all-day ticket costs £5/3.50. Chester Bus & Boat Company (☎ 307410) runs similar buses and also includes a half-hour river cruise. Tickets are £6/4.

Davies Cycles (☎ 319204), 6-12 Cuppin St, has a few mountain bikes for hire at £10 per day. You could also try South Cheshire Cycle Hire (☎ 01829-271242) at Farndon, eight miles south of Chester.

ELLESMERE PORT

The superb Boat Museum (☎ 0151-355 5017) on the Shropshire Union Canal has a large collection of canal boats and a series of indoor exhibits. The museum is eight miles north of Chester, a 10-minute walk from the Ellesmere Port railway station and near junction 9 on the M53. It's open April to October, daily from 10 am to 5 pm. The rest of the year it opens Saturday to Wednesday, 11 am to 4 pm; £4.70/3.

Derbyshire

Derbyshire has the industrial centre of Derby and some wonderful stately homes but its major attraction is the Peak District, most of which falls within the county boundaries (see the Peak District section later in this chapter).

DERBY

- *pop 220,000*   •   ☎ *01332*

Derby (pronounced darby) has a Roman and medieval history but it was the Industrial Revolution which transformed the city, first into a pioneer in silk production, then into a major railway centre, and in this century into the home of Rolls-Royce aircraft engines. It's a pleasant enough place but there are no major tourist attractions.

Derby Cathedral boasts a 212 ft tower, one of the highest in England.

A short walk from the cathedral, on Silk Mill Lane, **Derby Industrial Museum** (☎ 255308) recounts Derby's industrial history with pride of place going, of course, to Rolls-Royce aircraft engines. There are examples of engines from WWI right through to today's huge RB211 engines. Other museums include the **Derby Museum & Art Gallery** (☎ 255586) on the Strand, and **Pickford's House Museum** (☎ 255363), 41 Friar Gate, which is a museum of Georgian life. All these museums are free and open daily (afternoons only on Sunday).

For information on tours of the **Royal Crown Derby** china factory, 194 Osmaston Rd, phone ☎ 712800.

The TIC (☎ 01332-255802) is in the Assembly Rooms at the Market Place off Full St.

Places to Stay & Eat

The TIC makes free accommodation bookings. Crompton St is central and has a number of standard B&Bs like the *Wayfarer* (☎ 348350) at No 27 and *Chuckles* (☎ 367193) at No 48. The per-person cost in these places is £13 to £17 and parking on the street is usually OK.

The *Hotel International* (☎ 369321), is just south of the centre at 288 Burton Rd. It's a large modern place charging £32.50 to £49.50 per person.

Arkwright's is a popular café-bar on the square by the TIC. They serve a wide range of meals and drinks. For good Indian food head south down Normanton Rd, where there's a large Asian community.

Getting There & Away

Derby is 130 miles from London, 60 from Manchester, 40 from Birmingham and 30 from Leicester.

The bus station is close to the centre; contact Busline (☎ 292200) for bus information. The TransPeak TP service operates from Manchester through the Peak District

---

Rolls-Royce

The name Rolls-Royce is so firmly linked with expensive cars that it's easy to forget that the small-scale production of very old-fashioned cars in Crewe, Cheshire, is dwarfed by the large-scale production of very high-tech aircraft engines in Derby, Derbyshire.

The company started with Henry Royce's development of an experimental car in 1903. Royce, the engineer, was introduced to Rolls, the salesman, in 1904 and their names linked to live to this day although Rolls died in 1910, only 33 years of age. Their cars quickly established a name for matchless quality and reliability, and WWI pushed Henry Royce into the production of aircraft engines. In 1918 Rolls-Royce Eagle engines powered the first aircraft to fly nonstop across the Atlantic and the development of piston engines continued through to the Merlin, over 150,000 of which were produced through WWII and powered numerous aircraft including the famous Spitfire.

Rolls-Royce was a pioneer in the development of jet engines and had produced several hundred by the end of WWII. The Gloster Meteor was the only Allied jet aircraft to see service in the war. Post-war, Rolls-Royce continued with the world's first turboprop engine, the Dart, launched in 1948 and still in service in a multitude of aircraft. Numerous aircraft, including the latest Boeing 747-400s, use the powerful Rolls-Royce RB211 fan jet and the company is the largest employer in Derby.

Rolls-Royce aircraft engines and Rolls-Royce cars are now two totally separate companies, related only by their historic name. ■

to Derby and on to Nottingham. Other Derby-Nottingham services include the R5, R5B and R5C but the express TP only takes 30 minutes. Phone ☎ 0115-924 0000 for timetable information on these Rainbow Route services.

InterCity trains link Derby with London in just under two hours.

AROUND DERBY
Kedleston Hall
Construction of this superb neo-classical mansion (☎ 01332-842191; NT) with its Palladian front was started in 1758 by a trio of architects. The Curzon family has lived at Kedleston since the 12th century and Sir Nathaniel Curzon tore down an earlier house in order to construct this stunning master-piece. He also moved Kedleston village a mile down the road so it would not interfere with the landscaping! Only the medieval village church beside the house remains.

The entrance into the Marble Hall with its statues of Greek and Roman gods and goddesses is breathtaking. Remarkably, the 20 alabaster columns were originally plain but in 1776-7 it was decided that the room was too austere and fluting was chiselled into the columns *in situ*. The circular saloon with its domed roof was modelled on the Pantheon in Rome.

The whole house is lavishly decorated and includes an Indian Museum displaying Lord Curzon's oriental collection. From 1898-1905 he was the viceroy of India – a century earlier, Government House in Calcutta (now Raj Bhavan) was modelled on Kedleston Hall. The adjacent church houses a collection of family memorials, their increasing magnificence indicating the Curzons' escalating fortunes.

Kedleston Hall is five miles north-west of Derby. It is open April to October, Saturday to Wednesday, 1 to 5.30 pm; £4.50/2.20.

Melbourne
Melbourne was the birthplace of package-travel pioneer Thomas Cook and home of Victorian prime ministers Lord Palmerston and Lord Melbourne, after whom Mel-bourne, Australia, was named. Melbourne Hall (☎ 01332-862502) was the abode of both lords. It's only open in August, Tuesday to Sunday, 2 to 5 pm; £2/75p.

Calke Abbey
Built in the period from 1701-3 and frozen in time since the last baronet died in 1924, Calke Abbey (☎ 01332-863822; NT) has a varied collection ranging from natural history to a caricature room. Entry is by a timed ticket and at busy periods it's wise to phone ahead and check the situation. The house is open April to October, Saturday to Wednesday, 1 to 5.30 pm; £4.70/2.30. The house is in Ticknall, near Melbourne and 15 miles south of Derby.

CHESTERFIELD
• *pop 70,000*   • *☎ 01246*
Located on the eastern edge of the Peak District, Chesterfield is famous for **St Mary's & All Saints Church** with its twisted spire. The 228-foot-high spire leans nearly 10 feet to one side and performs a painful-looking twist, the result of heavy lead tiles over a poorly seasoned timber frame. Construction of the church was started in the early 1200s and finished in 1360. It's also been famous for its market since 1165. The market is held here on Monday, Friday and Saturday. The TIC (☎ 207777) is on Low Pavement.

AROUND CHESTERFIELD
Hardwick Hall
Hardwick Hall (☎ 01246-850430; NT), 'more glass than wall', was Bess of Hardwick's crowning achievement and the ES initials on the walls loudly trumpet her ownership as Elizabeth, Countess of Shrewsbury. Separated from her fourth husband, the Earl of Shrewsbury, Bess moved to Hardwick after buying it from her bankrupt brother in 1583. Since she did not have the means to build a home commensu-rate with her own high opinion of herself she settled for rebuilding Hardwick Old Hall but as soon as her husband died in 1590, and she

Bess of Hardwick

If Maggie Thatcher had a previous incarnation it may well have been Bess of Hardwick. This was one tough lady, definitely not interested in turning anywhere at all, and her name crops up regularly in Derbyshire. Elizabeth Hardwick (1527-1608) was born a minor member of the aristocracy. She used that position as a launching pad and via four husbands, each of them an advance on his predecessor and all of whom she outlived, she progressed to considerable wealth and even greater power.

Her houses, particularly Chatsworth and Hardwick, pay ample tribute to her wealth and ego but her magnificently pretentious memorial in Derby Cathedral sums it all up, in her own words of course. The Latin inscription quickly runs through the four husbands, then lists her six children (three sons at length, three daughters in less detail), then reels off the houses, their contents and their magnificence and concludes with the belief that she was confidently 'expecting a glorious resurrection'. ■

got her hands on his fortune, work started on Hardwick Hall.

The house features the very best of late 16th-century design including vast amounts of glass, a considerable status symbol at the time. It's notable for the many late 16th to early 17th-century tapestries on the walls and for a remarkably thorough inventory taken in 1601. Many items from that inventory, taken nearly 400 years ago, are still there. Over the centuries the house managed to escape both modernisation and neglect so it retains a wonderfully ancient feel. Despite the airy appearance it's a grim and rather stern place.

The house is open April to October, Wednesday to Thursday and Saturday to Sunday, 12.30 to 5 pm (or sunset if earlier); £5.50/2.70. The adjacent ruins of Hardwick Old Hall are watched over by EH and are open the same hours; £1.60/75p. Hardwick Hall is about 10 miles south-east of Chesterfield, just off the M1 between junctions 28 and 29.

Peak District

Although the Peak District is principally in Derbyshire it also spills into five other counties. It's a remarkable region – smack in the middle of one of the most densely populated, and at times greyest and dullest, parts of England is one of the country's best loved national parks. Dotted with pretty villages,

historic sites and fascinating limestone caves, the Peak District also encompasses some of the most beautiful and wildest scenery in England.

ORIENTATION

Although it's squeezed between Manchester and Sheffield with the industrial towns of Yorkshire to the north and the southern Midlands to the south, there are no towns of any size actually in the Peak District.

There is no actual *peak* in the peak district; the name comes from the ancient people who once inhabited the region. The 555 square miles of the Peak National Park is divided into two areas: the harsher, wilder Dark Peak to the north, and the more pastoral and 'prettier' White Peak to the south. Both areas are on limestone but the higher Dark Peak moorlands are on coarse gritstone, while the green fields of the White Peak are patterned with dry-stone walls, much like Ireland, and divided by deep-cut dales.

INFORMATION

There are TICs in Bakewell, Castleton, Edale and other locations, generally shared with National Park offices. The Ordnance Survey (OS) *Peak District* map (1:63,360), £4.25, covers the whole park adequately for most casual users. Pick up a copy of the *Peakland Post*, the park's annual free guide, from TICs.

WALKS & CYCLE ROUTES

The Pennine Way has its southern end at Edale in the Peak District. See the Activities

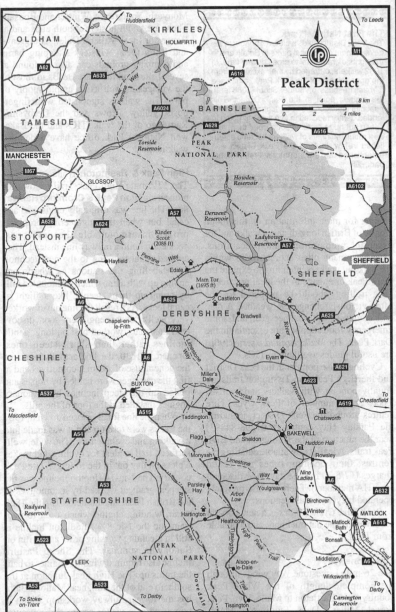

✦✦✦✦✦✦✦✦✦✦✦✦✦✦✦✦✦✦✦✦✦✦

The First National Park
The Peak District holds a place of honour in the development of national parks in Britain and in the rights of 'ramblers' to cross private land. In 1932 walkers, outraged by their exclusion from the open country of the Dark Peak, organised a 'mass trespass' on Kinder Scout (2088 feet), the highest point in the Peak District. This peaceful attack on the entrenched rights of the landed gentry resulted in five walkers going to prison but huge protests soon freed them and as a result the rights of walkers became established in law. In 1951 the Peak District was established as the country's first national park. ■

✦✦✦✦✦✦✦✦✦✦✦✦✦✦✦✦✦✦✦✦✦✦

chapter for more information on this tough classic of British long-distance walks and for essential preparations and precautions. There are many other shorter walks within the park but walkers intending to explore the Dark Peak or engage in the local practice of 'bog trotting' should be prepared for the often viciously changeable weather. A map and compass, wet weather gear and some emergency food supplies are essential in the Dark Peak. The *Walks Around...* series (90p) are useful guides available in TICs.

Cycling is also popular in the Peak District and the High Peak and Tissington trails are equally popular with walkers and cyclists. There are a number of Peak Cycle Hire centres around the Peak District, including the Parsley Hay centre (☎ 01298-84493) near the junction of the Tissington and High Peak trails. A leaflet is available detailing the centres, their opening times and rental charges (£7/5.30 for one day, 10% discount for YHA members). There are also privately operated bicycle rental locations.

Peak Park Cycle Routes is a new booklet produced by the national park and available from TICs.

Limestone Way
The 26-mile Limestone Way winds through the complete length of the White Peak country from Castleton to Matlock via Peak Forest, Miller's Dale, Taddington, Flagg,

Monyash, Youlgreave, Winster and Bonsall. There are youth hostels at both ends and at Ravenstor (near Miller's Dale), Youlgreave and Elton (near Winster). Camping barns and camping grounds can also be found at several sites and there are B&Bs in most of the villages as well as an ample supply of pubs. The walk is signposted with finger-posts, yellow arrows and the Derbyshire Ram logo of the walk. TICs and the Bake-well National Park office have a detailed walk leaflet.

High Peak & Tissington Trails
The 17½-mile High Peak Trail follows the pioneering **High Peak & Cromford Railway line**. The line was originally envisaged as a canal but when the engineering problems proved insurmountable the developers decided to build a railway line instead. They applied canal thinking to the new technology, labelling the stations as wharfs and ending up with a line which surmounted hills by going up them steeply, like a flight of canal locks. As a result the line never worked very well; railway engineers soon discovered that trains worked best on long, gentle inclines rather than short, steep ones. Opened in 1830, the line actually predated the general use of steam locomotives and at first the carriages were hauled by horses and pulled up the steep inclines by stationary engines installed at the tops of the hills.

When the line finally closed down in 1967 the tracks were torn up and it was made into a walking and cycling track. The wide, well-surfaced trail is ideal for cycling and makes a pleasant day out in the rolling White Peak country. The 1-in-14 Hopton Incline was the steepest gradient worked by locomotives in the British Isles. At Middleton Top the 1829 steam winding engine which used to haul trains up the 1-in-8¾ Middleton Incline is still in gleaming working order and is run on Sunday in summer. The Sheep Pasture Incline also required winding engines to haul the trains up. The High Peak Junction at the southern end of the trail, near Matlock Bath, has the former railway workshop which is now used as a visitor centre and museum.

Goods were transferred to boats on the Cromford Canal at this point. In later years it took trains up to seven hours to cover the distance a cyclist can now comfortably ride in just a couple!

The 13-mile Tissington Trail was a much later line, opened in 1899, but it never proved economically feasible and like the High Peak Trail was finally completely closed in 1967. The two trails meet just south of Parsley Hay and continue further north, although not all the way to Buxton.

Bicycles can be hired on the trails at Parsley Hay (☎ 01298-84493), at Middleton Top, towards the southern end of the High Peak Trail, or at Mapleton Lane, at the southern end of the Tissington Trail. If you've got time it's a pleasant day's ride from Parsley Hay down the High Peak Trail and up the Tissington Trail, linking the two trails by the B5053 from Matlock Bath to Ashbourne. This makes about a 40-mile round trip and the B5053 section undulates a lot so make sure you allow plenty of time.

Monsal Trail

Like the High Peak and Tissington trails, the Monsal Trail follows a disused railway line. This trail along the deep valley of the River Wye is used by walkers more than cyclists (unlike the other two) because there are three long tunnels which have been closed because they would require substantial rebuilding and permanent lighting before they could be used by walkers or cyclists. As a result deviations have to be made around the tunnels. The railway tunnels along the other trails are short affairs.

The 8½-mile trail actually starts from the Coombs Rd Viaduct just east of Bakewell but there is no view of the viaduct from the trail. You can also walk from Rowsley on the A6 to the beginning of the trail. The old railway station at Hassop near Bakewell has been converted into the Country Bookstore. At Monsal Head there's a pub and a superb view of the **Monsal Viaduct**, a man-made wonder of the Peak District and a subject of considerable controversy when it was first built. **Cressbrook Mill** opened as a water-powered

cotton mill in 1783 and continued in operation, powered by steam, from 1890 until 1965. **Litton Mill** opened in 1782 and was infamous for its owner's callous exploitation of young child labourers. Walking west, the final tunnel requires a detour which can be very muddy, slippery and wet. The trail ends at Blackwell Mill Junction, a short walk from the A6, three miles east of Buxton.

Other Walks

The Peak District is crisscrossed with other good walks and much printed information is available. Castleton and Bakewell in the White Peak are particularly good centres for short walks. From Edale you can walk in either direction, north to the Dark Peak and nearby Kinder Scout or south towards Castleton. Hayfield, from where the first 'mass trespass' onto Kinder Scout was conducted, is another good starting point for walks into the Dark Peak.

OTHER ACTIVITIES

The limestone of the Peak District is riddled with caves including 'showcaves' open to the public in Castleton, Buxton and Matlock Bath. For information on caving trips and courses contact Pennine National Caving (☎ 01831-44919). *The Caves of Derbyshire* by TD Ford (Dalesman Publishing) has extensive information on the county's caves.

The Peak District has been a training ground for some of Britain's best known mountaineers, and cliff faces like High Tor, overlooking Matlock Bath, are popular to this day. Jumping off those cliff faces is becoming equally popular with hang-gliders. That patron saint of fishing, Izaak Walton, made regular pilgrimages to the Dove River but on most rivers in the Peak District the fishing is private.

See under the upcoming Walks & Cycle Routes section for information on these activities in the Peak District.

PLACES TO STAY

There are plenty of accommodation possibilities in the Peak District including numerous youth hostels.

Walkers may appreciate the camping barn system (☎ 01629-816316) which offers a roof over your head for a nightly cost of £3 per person. A leaflet is available showing the locations of the barns and explaining how to book a place. Another brochure details camping grounds in and around the Peak District. Farmhouse accommodation is particularly popular in the area, either B&B or self catering. Regular B&B accommodation is widely available.

GETTING THERE & AWAY

There are train services from Derby to Matlock, at the southern edge of the Peak District, or from Sheffield across the northern part of the district through Edale to New Mills and on to Manchester. There's also a Manchester-New Mills-Buxton service. The very convenient TransPeak TP bus service operates right across the Peak District, running Nottingham-Derby-Matlock-Bakewell-Buxton-New Mills-Manchester. It takes about 3½ hours from Nottingham all the way to Manchester. Matlock to Buxton takes about an hour. Yorkshire Traction has services from Barnsley into the district from the north and down to Castleton and Buxton.

A Derbyshire Wayfarer ticket costs £6.80 (including one child or dog) and gives you one day's unlimited travel on most train and bus services into and around the Peak District. There's also an Explorer ticket which gives you all-day travel on Trent and Barton buses including the TransPeak TP service. It costs £4.95 and includes one child free. The Busline information service can be contacted at Buxton (☎ 01298-23098), Chesterfield (☎ 01246-250450) and Derby (☎ 01332-292200).

GETTING AROUND

Within the Peak District there are extensive bus services and the region is compact enough to make cycling a good option.

BAKEWELL

• *pop 3900*   • *01629*

This pretty village is actually the largest population centre within the Peak National Park boundaries. The village has earned its place in cookbooks due to the accidental invention of the Bakewell pudding.

Information

The TIC (☎ 813227) is in the 17th-century Market Hall on Bridge St and has an informative display about the national park. It's open daily, 9.30 am to 5.30 pm (later on summer weekends and in August, earlier in winter). The market operates on Monday. There's a laundrette on Water St, off Rutland St by the Red Lion.

Things to See

The **All Saints Church** has Norman features and there's a Saxon cross from around 800 in the graveyard. The **Old House Museum** in Cunningham Place near the church has a local collection housed in a 1534 building.

The pretty **bridge** over the River Wye has five arches and dates from medieval times. The popular **Monsal Trail** walking and cycling track starts just outside Bakewell but there are many other good walking routes around the village including trails to Magpie Mine, Haddon Hall and Chatsworth House.

Places to Stay

Hostel The *Youth Hostel* (☎ 812313) is on Fly Hill and costs £6.75/4.60 a night. It's open daily except Sunday from April to October; only on Friday and Saturday for the rest of the year.

B&Bs & Hotels *Riverdene* (☎ 813490), near the river, costs £17 to £19 per person. *Erica Cottage* (☎ 813241) on Butts Rd charges £15 per person.

The accidentally gastronomically pioneering (see Which Bakewell Pudding?) *Rutland Arms Hotel* (☎ 812812) is a fine establishment right on the main square in town and has singles/doubles for £45/64. Front rooms can be a bit noisy. The *Milford House Hotel* (☎ 812130) on Mill St has rooms at £38/64.

Places to Eat

There are cafés, like the *Green Apple* (☎ 814404) in Diamond Court off Water St or the vaguely Australian *Outback Diner* (!) – also a bar, takeaways (fish & chips and Chinese) and pubs, but for a place as small as Bakewell there are some surprisingly adventurous restaurants too. *Aitch's Wine Bar* (☎ 813895) on Rutland St and *Scotties Bistro* (☎ 814336) on Bridge St by the river both have interesting menus.

There are plenty of pubs, including the *Red Lion*, the *Queen's Arms* and the *Rutland Tavern*.

Getting There & Away

The TransPeak TP bus services the Buxton-Bakewell-Matlock route.

Getting Around

Bicycles can be rented from Noton Cycle Centre (☎ 814195) at Noton Barn Farm, Over Haddon, just south of Bakewell. Mountain bikes cost £8.50/6 a day.

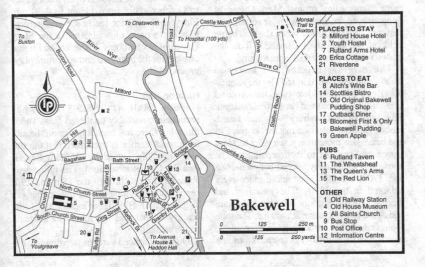

PLACES TO STAY
2 Milford House Hotel
3 Youth Hostel
7 Rutland Arms Hotel
20 Erica Cottage
21 Riverdene

PLACES TO EAT
8 Aitch's Wine Bar
14 Scotties Bistro
16 Old Original Bakewell Pudding Shop
17 Outback Diner
18 Bloomers First & Only Bakewell Pudding
19 Green Apple

PUBS
6 Rutland Tavern
11 The Wheatsheaf
13 The Queen's Arms
15 The Red Lion

OTHER
1 Old Railway Station
4 Old House Museum
5 All Saints Church
9 Bus Stop
10 Post Office
12 Information Centre

Bakewell

Well Dressing

Well dressing is the practice of decorating wells or springs, a thanksgiving for a local supply of water. The practice may have started in pre-Christian times although it's known that Tissington began its well dressing after the village miraculously escaped from the Black Death in 1350, as a result of the purity of its water supply. After a spell of Christian suppression, well dressing became a popular annual event, with Peak District villages now competing to produce the finest designs. The well dressing pictures are produced by spreading a thin layer of clay over a wooden frame and then outlining a design with bark and filling in the colours with flower petals, leaves, stones, sand and other entirely natural materials. Well dressing takes place in Peak District villages from May to mid-September with June and July the peak months. TICs will have a list of when village well dressings will be displayed. Wirksworth, Eyam and Youlgreave are three villages particularly renowned for their well dressings. ■

Well dressing, Chesterfield

AROUND BAKEWELL

Chatsworth

More than two-thirds of this sumptuous house (☎ 01246-582204) is still occupied by the Duke of Devonshire's family. Only 26 of the 175 rooms are included in the general admission price; there's an extra fee for the eight 'Scots suite' rooms. Mary Queen of Scots stayed in these rooms several times between 1570 and 1581 when she was being held, at the behest of Elizabeth I, in the custody of the 6th Earl of Shrewsbury.

The original Elizabethan house at Chatsworth was started in 1551 by the inimitable Bess of Hardwick (see the Around Chesterfield section) and her second husband. The Earl of Shrewsbury was her fourth husband and her suspicion that the 'knave, fool and beast' was more than just a jailer to Mary Queen of Scots led to their separation. The house was extensively altered between 1686 and 1707 and then even more extensively enlarged in the 1820s. The amazing, and recently restored, Baroque ceiling paintings are one of the house's prime attractions. The state room ceilings are particularly fine but all the rooms are a treasure trove of splendid furniture and magnificent artworks.

The house is surrounded by 100 acres of gardens with a superb cascade, ponds and fountains. Beyond these stretch another 1000 acres of parkland forming one of Capability Brown's best landscape works.

Chatsworth is about three miles north-east of Bakewell. The house is open from Easter to October, daily from 11 am to 4.30 pm. Entry is £5.75/3 for the house and garden, plus £1 to park, plus £1/50p for the Mary Queen of Scots rooms. There are additional charges for the farmyard and adventure playground.

Haddon Hall

Haddon Hall (☎ 01629-812855) has remained remarkably unaltered from Tudor times but there has been a house on the site from much earlier. It's recorded that the site was originally owned by William Peveril (see the Castleton section). The house was abandoned right through the 18th and 19th centuries, accounting for the minor changes in that period. Highlights include the 14th-century chapel and the medieval kitchens and great hall.

Outside, terraced gardens step down to the River Wye near an old stone packhorse bridge. The house is only 1½ miles from Bakewell on the A6 and is open April to September, Tuesday to Sunday, 11 am to 5.15 pm. In July and August it closes on Sunday; £4.50/2.80.

Dovedale

The steep-sided valley of the **River Dove** is one of the most famous and most beautiful of the Derbyshire Dales. The river flows beneath natural features like Thorpe Cloud, Dovedale Castle, Lovers' Leap, the Twelve Apostles, Tissington Spires, Reynard's Kitchen and Ilam Rock. **Beresford Dale**, upstream from Dovedale, was a favourite haunt of Izaak Walton, author of *The Compleat Angler*, and the 1674 Fishing Temple is a memorial to him.

EYAM

- *pop 900*   • ☎ *01433*

The small village of Eyam (pronounced ee-em) is famous as the plague settlement. In 1665 a consignment of cloth from London delivered to a local tailor brought with it the plague, the Black Death. As the dreaded disease spread through Eyam, the village rector, William Mompesson, convinced the villagers that rather than carry it to other villages Eyam should quarantine itself. By the time the plague finally burnt itself out in late 1666, more than 250 of the 350-strong population of the village were dead, including the rector's wife.

The **Church of St Lawrence** has an *Eyam History Trail* map showing historical sites, particularly those associated with the plague. The church dates from Saxon times and has many reminders of the events of 1665-6, including a cupboard said to have been made from the wooden box which carried the infected cloth to Eyam. The plague register records the names of those who died during the outbreak. The church also has a leaflet describing some of the intriguing monuments and headstones in the churchyard, which has an 8th-century **Celtic cross**, one of the finest in the country. Many of the plague victims were buried in the churchyard but apart from that of Catherine Mompesson,

the rector's wife, only one other headstone relating to the plague has survived. Other victims were buried around the village – at the Riley graves, Mrs Hancock buried all seven members of her family one by one.

Next to Eyam's church are the **plague cottages** where the tailor lived and where the disease first broke out. A walk up Water Lane from the village square, or a drive towards Grindleford from Hawkhill Rd, will bring you to **Mompesson's Well**. Food and other supplies for the villagers were left here by friends outside Eyam. Back in the village the 17th-century **Eyam Hall** (☎ 631976) is open Easter to late October, Wednesday, Thursday and Sunday, 11 am to 4.30 pm; £3.25/2.25.

Places to Stay & Eat

The *Youth Hostel* (☎ 630335) on Hawkhill Rd charges £7.45/5 a night. The *Miner's Arms* pub on the square, which dates from 1630, turns out good sandwiches. *Delf View House* (☎ 631533), Church St, offers comfortable B&B in a Georgian house from £19 per person.

CASTLETON

- *pop 900*   • ☎ *01433*

Overlooked by 1695-foot-high Mam Tor, the village features caves and a castle and is the northern terminus of the Limestone Way. Mam Tor marks the boundary between the limestone of the southern White Peak and the gritstone of the northern Dark Peak.

Orientation & Information

Castleton nestles at the western end of the Hope Valley. Mam Tor's unstable condition undermined the A625 road through Castleton and is now bypassed by the spectacular Winnats Pass road which goes through a steep-sided dale. Castleton is a small place with a car park on the north side, while on the south side Castle St is home to the church, pubs, B&Bs, the youth hostel and the National Park Information Centre (☎ 620679).

The information centre is open Easter to October, daily from 10 am to 1 pm and 2 to

5.30 pm. The rest of the year it is open only on weekends, closing at 5 pm.

Peveril Castle

Castleton is overlooked by the ruins of Peveril Castle (☎ 620613; EH), built by William Peveril, son of William the Conqueror. The keep, which is about all that remains, was added by Henry II in 1176. The castle actually sits more or less on top of Peak Cavern. From the castle there are superb views north to Mam Tor and the Dark Peak and south over pretty Cave Dale, directly behind the castle. Entry costs £1.50/80p.

Walks

Start the 26-mile Limestone Way by taking the narrow, rocky entrance into beautiful Cave Dale behind the castle. There are many other excellent walks in and around Castleton. A fine day walk (see the Castleton & Edale map) of about seven miles can be

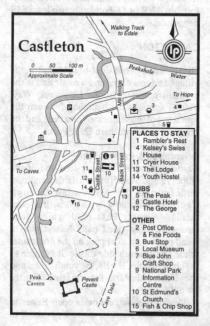

Castleton

PLACES TO STAY
1 Rambler's Rest
4 Kelsey's Swiss House
11 Cryer House
13 The Lodge
14 Youth Hostel

PUBS
5 The Peak
8 Castle Hotel
12 The George

OTHER
2 Post Office & Fine Foods
3 Bus Stop
6 Local Museum
7 Blue John Craft Shop
9 National Park Information Centre
10 St Edmund's Church
15 Fish & Chip Shop

taken by going south along the Cave Dale track to a road where you turn right and right again to pass by Rowter Farm and meet the Buxton Rd just beyond Winnats Pass. The route then climbs up to Mam Tor where ditches marking a pre-Roman fort can be distinguished on the top. The trail follows the ridge to Back Tor, but just before reaching that high point there's a path down from the ridge directly into Castleton along Hollowford Lane and Mill Bridge. Another pleasant day walk makes a seven-mile round-trip walk via Edale, starting point of the Pennine Way.

Caves

The area around Castleton is riddled with caves, four of which are commercially operated and open to the public. Although most of the caves are natural, the area has also been extensively mined for Blue John, a reddish-pink local form of fluorspar, as well as lead, silver and other minerals. Miners often broke into natural chambers during the course of their excavations.

The **Peak Cavern** (☎ 01433-620285) (popularly known as the Devil's Arse!) is a natural cave reached by a pretty streamside walk from the village centre. Unfortunately the ugly wall, erected to stop you sneaking a free peek into the yawning 60 by 100-foot chasm, rather detracts from the natural beauty. Ropemakers' houses used to stand just inside the cave entrance; rope was made here until 1974. Entry is £3/2.

Treak Cliff Cavern (☎ 01433-620571) (£4.20/2) is a small, rather pretty cave with stalactites and stalagmites. The unique selling point of **Speedwell Cavern** (☎ 01433-620512) is the long flooded tunnel along which you travel by an electric boat to the 'bottomless' pit at the end. The tunnel has been artificially flooded and prior to electrification the boatman would propel the boat along the tunnel by 'walking' it with his feet on the tunnel roof; entry is £5/3. On the other side of the closed section of road by Mam Tor is the impressive **Blue John Cavern** (☎ 01433-620638); £4.50/2.50. It's thought that Blue John may have been mined here in

Roman times. One of the cave's chambers has a collection of 19th-century mining equipment.

Experienced potholers have many other caves to explore, including the **Odin Mine** below Mam Tor, and the **Suicide Cave** and **Old Tor Mine** on Winnats Pass. The remains of prehistoric animals have been found in **Windy Knoll Cave**. Castleton is a good place to be introduced to caving.

Places to Stay

The large *Youth Hostel* (☎ 620235) is on Castle St, across from the church, and costs £8.25/5.55 a night. There are lots of B&Bs in Castleton. *Cryer House* (☎ 620244), also on Castle St by the youth hostel, costs from £15.50. *Rambler's Rest* (☎ 620125), on Mill Bridge, charges from £17.50. *The Lodge* (☎ 620526), on Back St just south of the main road and near the church, costs from £18.

Kelseys Swiss House Hotel (☎ 621098), on the main road on the Hope side of the village, is a slightly pricier place offering pleasant rooms with attached bathroom at £29.50/40.

Places to Eat

For picnic provisions you can't do better than *Fine Foods* (☎ 620547), a deli which has a range of delicious sandwiches from £1. It's by the post office. There's also a *fish & chip shop* round the corner from the hostel.

Cafés and pubs are the predominant eating possibilities. The *Castle Hotel* has a restaurant serving very traditional but nicely done food. Also on Castle St is the very popular *George* pub. The *Peak* is another popular pub for a meal or a pint.

Getting There & Away

There's a railway station at Hope, two miles east of Castleton. Trent and South Yorkshire PTE buses run to Castleton. Mainline buses run to Sheffield.

EDALE
- *pop 350*   • ☎ 01433

Tiny Edale is the southern terminus of the 250-mile Pennine Way and marks the southern

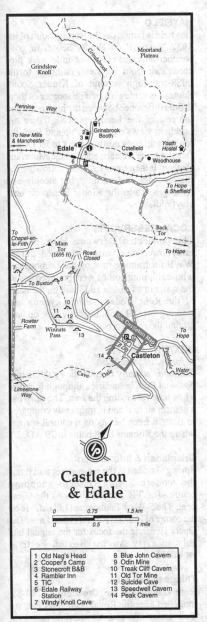

Castleton & Edale

| 0 | | 0.75 | | 1.5 km |
| 0 | 0.5 | | 1 mile | |

1 Old Nag's Head	8 Blue John Cavern
2 Cooper's Camp	9 Odin Mine
3 Stonecroft B&B	10 Treak Cliff Cavern
4 Rambler Inn	11 Old Tor Mine
5 TIC	12 Suicide Cave
6 Edale Railway	13 Speedwell Cavern
Station	14 Peak Cavern
7 Windy Knoll Cave	

fringe of the Dark Peak. It's a good starting point for short walks, whether it's north on to Kinder Scout or south to Mam Tor, the ridge overlooking Castleton.

Edale is strung out from the main road and railway station up to the Old Nag's Head pub. The National Park Information Centre (☎ 670207) is open daily from 9 am to 5.30 pm (5 pm in winter). The mountain rescue service is based here.

Walks
You can make pleasant short walks from Edale up to the ridge between Mam Tor and Back Tor, overlooking Castleton. Alternatively you can walk north on to the Kinder Plateau; Jacob's Ladder is the easiest route onto Kinder. If the weather is cooperative, a fine six-mile walk takes you from the information office, past the youth hostel, and then climbs up onto the moors along the southern edge of Kinder before dropping back down to Edale.

Places to Stay & Eat
The large *Youth Hostel* (☎ 670302) is at Rowland Cote, Nether Booth, about two miles east of the village; there's a shortcut walking path. The nightly cost is £9.10/6.15.

The small *Fieldhead Campsite* (☎ 670386) charges £2.85 per person and is right by the information centre. Showers are 50p. In the north of the village, *Cooper's Camp* (☎ 670372) charges £2.25 per person.

The *Rambler Inn* (☎ 670268) is right by the railway station and has B&B at £22 per person. Continuing past the information centre and church you reach *Stonecroft B&B* (☎ 670262) from £23 per person.

The *Old Nag's Head* (the pub which is the official starting point of the Pennine Way) and the *Rambler Inn* both have reasonable pub grub. There's a small shop at Cooper's Camp for provisions.

Getting There & Away
Trains operate across the Peak District from Sheffield to Manchester via the Edale station.

HAYFIELD
Hayfield is famous as the starting point of the 1932 'trespass' on Kinder Scout. In good weather an excellent seven-mile walk proceeds east from Hayfield, climbing to the 2088-foot-high summit of Kinder Scout. Summit is somewhat of a misnomer as there is little difference between the high point and the rest of the Kinder plateau. There are excellent views on the way up and from the top the trail runs north to the Kinder Downfall along the western edge of the Moorland Plateau. It then turns east, still following the plateau edge, before dropping steeply and turning south to the Kinder Reservoir near Hayfield.

LOCAL RESERVOIRS
The connected Derwent, Howden and Ladybower reservoirs were used during WWII for training runs by the Dambusters, whose skipping bombs were bounced across the water in a famous 1943 raid on the dams of the Ruhr. Today, sailing, cycling and walking are all popular activities on and around the reservoirs.

BUXTON
• *pop 19,500*   • *01298*
Buxton is actually outside the Peak District National Park boundaries although it makes a fine base for visiting the area. The town has a genteel air to it and is frequently compared to Bath; it even has its own natural springs where the Romans built baths in 79 AD.

Orientation & Information
Spring Gardens is the main street and it has the modern Spring Gardens shopping centre. The TIC (☎ 25106) is on the Crescent. The 5-Ways Laundrette (and café) is on the corner of London Rd and Green Lane. The Opera House is the focus for the annual late July to early August Buxton Festival (☎ 60395).

Things to See & Do
Renovations of the **Crescent** (1784-8), modelled after the Royal Bath Crescent, are well underway and it's starting to regain

some of its former elegance. Across from it is the **Pump Room** which dispensed Buxton's spring water for nearly a century from 1894 to 1981. Until recently it housed a display of insects but this has now closed and there are plans to return the building to its original purpose. Fill your water bottle with delicious warm mineral water from **St Ann's Well**, next to the Pump Room.

Across the road, the TIC is housed in the old **Natural Baths** building where you can still see the spa water source. On the corner of the Square and the Crescent is the **Old Hall**

Hotel. Mary Queen of Scots stayed here; the hotel was rebuilt a century later in 1670. Buxton's fine **Opera House** opened in 1903 and stands in a corner of Pavilion Gardens. Behind it is the glassy **Pavilion** of 1871 and the **Pavilion Gardens Concert Hall** of 1876. The **Museum** is on Terrace Rd, round the corner from the Town Hall. It's open Tuesday to Friday, 9.30 am to 5.30 pm, and on Saturday until 5 pm; £1/50p.

The **Poole's Cavern** (☎ 26978), located less than a mile from the centre, is a natural cave known since Neolithic times. It's amply

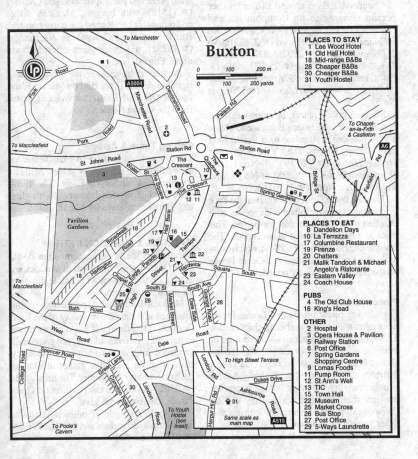

Buxton

0   100   200 m
0   100   200 yards

PLACES TO STAY
1 Lee Wood Hotel
14 Old Hall Hotel
18 Mid-range B&Bs
28 Cheaper B&Bs
30 Cheaper B&Bs
31 Youth Hostel

PLACES TO EAT
8 Dandelion Days
10 La Terrazza
17 Columbine Restaurant
19 Firenze
20 Chatters
21 Malik Tandoori & Michael Angelo's Ristorante
23 Eastern Valley
24 Coach House

PUBS
4 The Old Club House
16 King's Head

OTHER
2 Hospital
3 Opera House & Pavilion
5 Railway Station
6 Post Office
7 Spring Gardens Shopping Centre
9 Lomas Foods
11 Pump Room
12 St Ann's Well
13 TIC
15 Town Hall
22 Museum
25 Market Cross
26 Bus Stop
27 Post Office
29 5-Ways Laundrette

supplied with stalactites and stalagmites and is open May to September, daily from 10 am to 5 pm, and April, May and October, Thursday to Tuesday; £3.60/1.80. A 20-minute walk from the cave through Grin Low Wood leads to **Solomon's Temple** (Grin Low Tower), an 1896 folly with fine views over the town.

Places to Stay

The *Youth Hostel* (☎ 22287) is south of the centre at Sherbrook Lodge, Harpur Hill Rd, and costs £6.75/4.60 a night.

Cheaper B&Bs at around £16 or less per person congregate on Compton Rd and Grange Rd. Places to try on Compton Rd include the *Griff Guest House* (☎ 23628) at No 2, *Compton House* (☎ 26926) at No 4, and the *Templeton Guest House* (☎ 25275) at No 13. On Grange Rd there's *Arnemetia House* (☎ 26125) at No 14 and *Lynstone* (☎ 77043) at No 3.

Medium-priced places, at around £20 per person, can be found along Broadwalk. This is a very pleasant, traffic-free road overlooking the Pavilion Gardens. There's the *Grosvenor House Hotel* (☎ 72439) at No 1, the *Hartington Hotel* (☎ 22638) at No 18, and the *Roseleigh Hotel* (☎ 24904) at No 19.

The *Lee Wood Hotel* (☎ 23002) on the Park is a more expensive place with rooms with attached bathroom from £39 per person. This price is often discounted at weekends. The historic *Old Hall Hotel* (☎ 22841), which overlooks the Pavilion Gardens and Opera House on the Square, is similarly priced.

Places to Eat

For non-veg picnic provisions, Lomas Foods does takeaway whole barbecue chickens for £2.99, or local lamb henries – a shoulder of lamb in mint sauce for £2.50. Vegetarians should head for *Dandelion Days* (☎ 22843), 5 Bridge St. This excellent healthfood store is under new management but the restaurant upstairs should reopen soon. They still do takeaways: pilafs, vegetarian curries and other vegetarian lunches.

La Terrazza (☎ 72364) is a pleasant café

upstairs in Cavendish Arcade on the Crescent. Market Place, in front of the Town Hall, is the dining centre of Buxton. Among the many possibilities here are *Malik Tandoori* (☎ 72392) and *Michael Angelo's Ristorante* (☎ 26640), which share the same building. *Eastern Valley* (☎ 25700) is another Indian restaurant, just off the square at 7-9 Concert Place. On this same side of the square is the *Coach House*, a popular local fish & chippery.

On the other side of Market Place, Eagle Parade has *Firenze* (☎ 72203), a straightforward pizza and pasta specialist, and *Chatters* (☎ 71516), with burgers, Mexican dishes and a popular bar. Round the corner on Hall Bank is the *Columbine Restaurant* (☎ 78752), a fancier place offering traditional English fare.

Popular pubs include the *King's Head*, right beside the Town Hall on Market Place, and the *Old Club House*, on Water St, across from the Opera House.

Getting There & Away

Trains run from Buxton to Manchester via New Mills. You can change at New Mills for the Sheffield service via Edale. The Trans-Peak TP bus service between Nottingham and Manchester stops by Market Place.

MATLOCK & MATLOCK BATH

Located on the south-eastern edge of the Peak District, the twin towns of Matlock and Matlock Bath are another possible jumping-off point to the region.

Matlock Bath has a spectacular setting, squeezed into the narrow valley of the River Derwent. Despite this it has a rather down-at-heel air; it feels like a geographically displaced British seaside resort. Motorcyclists from far and wide gather in Matlock Bath on Sundays in summer. The helpful TIC (☎ 01629-55082), in the pavilion on Grand Parade, can suggest B&Bs.

Matlock, a couple of miles beyond, has more shops, restaurants and the *Youth Hostel* (☎ 01629-582983).

Manchester

• *pop 460,000* • ☎ *0161*

Probably best known around the world for its football team, the city that produced Oasis, Take That and Simply Red is a grim monument to the industrial history of Britain. In the 19th century, Friedrich Engels (co-author of the *Communist Manifesto)* used the city to illustrate the evils of capitalism, and after more than a decade of painful decline it would again make a fascinating study.

Following its successful bid as the venue for the Commonwealth Games in 2002, the city will, no doubt, be given a makeover. As yet, the streets are dominated by empty warehouses and factories, the fantastical grandeur of Victorian Gothic buildings, rusting train tracks, and motorway overpasses.

To love the place requires a massive act of selective vision – but plenty of proud Mancunians manage it. The question for the traveller is: Why try? To those looking for picture-book packages the answer is don't. However, to city lovers who are interested in one of the principal battlefields of the Industrial Revolution and English culture, the answer is do. Underneath the unprepossessing skin, burrowed away to withstand the weather, there's plenty of life. The less time you have, the lower your chances of finding it, but it's there, especially at night in the clubs and pubs.

History

Manchester has been important since Roman times. In the 14th century, Flemish weavers (who worked primarily in wool and linen) settled the area. They found the humid climate ideal for their industry. When cotton from the American colonies became available in the 18th century the city, with its weaving tradition, accessible supplies of coal and water and links to surrounding towns by a system of canals, became the hub of the new industry and, in effect, of the Industrial Revolution.

As the city grew, demands increased for reform of the parliamentary system and for free trade; the artificial protection of corn prices by the Corn Law tariffs was particularly unpopular. In 1819 there was a mass meeting of 50,000 people on St Peter's Field, a site now occupied by the Free Trade Hall. The authorities ordered mounted troops to arrest the speakers. In the ensuing melee 11 people were killed and 400 injured. The affair came to be known as Peterloo – the poor man's Waterloo – and it provided a rallying point in the battle for reform. Two years after Peterloo, the *Manchester Guardian* was founded to foster parliamentary reform and free trade; today's *Guardian* is a direct descendent.

The first half of the 19th century was the era of railways. The world's first passenger railway opened between Stockton and Darlington in 1825. By 1838 there was a rail link from Manchester to London.

The 1870s ushered in more than two decades of economic depression. Textile exports suffered from growing competition from the USA and Europe, but rather than re-equip themselves with modern machines the mill owners exploited the captive markets of the Empire, a process that was to continue into the 20th century and lead to the industry's final decline.

In an attempt to reduce the loss of its industry to Liverpool and to reduce its reliance on cotton, the Ship Canal was built to the Mersey. It was opened in 1894 and made Manchester Britain's third-largest port until the post-WWII decline.

Manchester was badly damaged by bombing during WWII, and, in 1996, by an IRA bomb. It has been further battered by the decline in manufacturing industries since then. However, it remains one of the most important commercial and financial centres in Britain, and a thriving cultural tradition has also survived.

Orientation

The centre of Manchester is easy to get around on foot and with the help of the excellent Metrolink tramway. The University of

Manchester lies to the south of the city centre (on Oxford St/Rd). Continue south on Oxford and you reach Rusholme, a thriving centre for cheap Indian restaurants. To the east of the university is Moss Side, a ghetto with very high unemployment and a thriving drug trade controlled by violent gangs. Further east again, near the Bridgewater Canal, is Old Trafford, the home of Manchester United, the most famous football team in England, and the Lancashire County Cricket Club's oval.

Information

The TIC/Manchester Visitor Information Centre (☎ 234 3157) is in the town hall extension, off St Peter Sq. It's open from Monday to Saturday, 10 am to 5.30 pm, and 11 am to 4 pm on Sunday. There's a 24-hour interactive tourist information touch screen outside. There are also two information desks at the airport.

The TIC sells tickets for excellent guided walks around the city. These operate most weekends of the year and almost daily from June to September. They follow themes like 'Canals Under the City Streets' and 'King Cotton'. Most last between one and two hours; £2.50/1.

City Life (£1.40) is an invaluable what's on magazine.

Castlefield Urban Heritage Park

Castlefield (☎ 834 4026) has twice been at the heart of Manchester's fortunes, and hopes to become so again. The first time was in 79 AD when a Roman fort was built here and the second was from 1761 when the Bridgewater Canal opened and ushered in an era when Castlefield was at the hub of a revolutionary transport network. In 1830 the world's first passenger railway station was opened on Liverpool Rd (on a site now occupied by the museum).

The legacy is an extraordinary industrial landscape littered with enormous relics that have been tumbled together like giant pieces of Lego – canals, viaducts and bridges, weather-stained brick and rusting cast-iron,

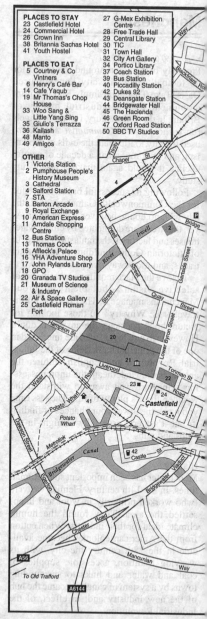

PLACES TO STAY
23 Castlefield Hotel
24 Commercial Hotel
26 Crown Inn
38 Britannia Sachas Hotel
41 Youth Hostel

PLACES TO EAT
5 Courtney & Co Vintners
6 Henry's Café Bar
14 Cafe Yaqub
19 Mr Thomas's Chop House
33 Woo Sang & Little Yang Sing
35 Giulio's Terrazza
36 Kailash
48 Manto
49 Amigos

OTHER
1 Victoria Station
2 Pumphouse People's History Museum
3 Cathedral
4 Salford Station
7 STA
8 Barton Arcade
9 Royal Exchange
10 American Express
11 Arndale Shopping Centre
12 Bus Station
13 Thomas Cook
15 Affleck's Palace
16 YHA Adventure Shop
17 John Rylands Library
18 GPO
20 Granada TV Studios
21 Museum of Science & Industry
22 Air & Space Gallery
25 Castlefield Roman Fort
27 G-Mex Exhibition Centre
28 Free Trade Hall
29 Central Library
30 TIC
31 Town Hall
32 City Art Gallery
34 Portico Library
37 Coach Station
39 Bus Station
40 Piccadilly Station
42 Dukes 92
43 Deansgate Station
44 Bridgewater Hall
45 The Hacienda
46 Green Room
47 Oxford Road Station
50 BBC TV Studios

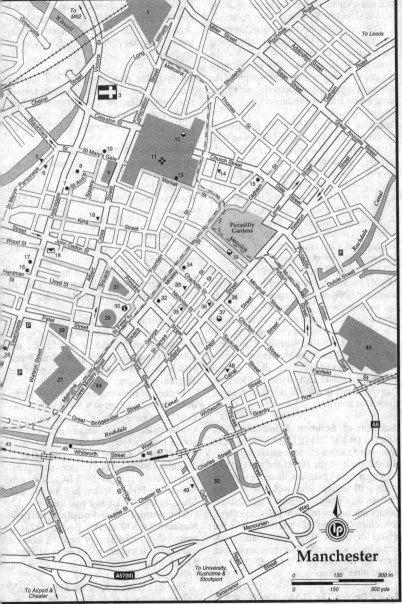

Manchester

To M62

R Irwell

Greengate

To Leeds

Miller Street

Rochdale Road

Addington Street

Swan Street

Oldham Road

Great Ancoats Street

Victoria Station

Long Millgate

Shudehill

Thomas St

Chapel Street

Blackfriars St

Corporation Street

Cateaton St

St Mary's Gate

Deansgate

St Ann's Square

Cross Street

Market St

Church Street

Oldham Street

Dale Street

Lever Street

Newton Street

Piccadilly Gardens

Metrolink

Rochdale Canal

St Mary's Parsonage

King Street

Wood St

John Dalton St

Hardman St

Lloyd St

Albert Square

Princess Street

Fountain St

Mosley Street

Charlotte St

Nicholas St

George Street

St James Street

Portland Street

Minshull Street

Aytoun Street

Chorlton Street

Sackville Street

Major Street

Canal Street

Whitworth Street

Granby Row

Oxford Street

Dulcie Street

London Road

Piccadilly

Fairfield St

Deansgate

Peter Street

Watson Street

St Peter's Square

Lower Mosley Street

Great Bridgewater Street

Rochdale Canal

Whitworth Street West

Cambridge Street

Lower Byrom Street

Chester St

Chester St

Hulme Street

Charles Street

Oxford Road

Mancunian Way

Medlock Street

Grosvenor Street

To University, Rusholme & Stockport

To Airport & Chester

A57(M)

A6

1 3 5 6 7 8 9 10 11 12 13 14 15 16 17 18 19 26 27 28 29 30 31 32 33 34 35 36 37 38 39 40 43 44 45 46 47 48 49 50

0   150   300 m
0   150   300 yds

warehouses and market buildings – all in various stages of decay and renovation.

Unpromising as this may sound, the result is fascinating, and the region is now being imaginatively developed. It includes the Granada Studios Tour, the Museum of Science & Industry, a reconstruction of the Roman fort, as well as footpaths, boat trips, pubs, hotels and a youth hostel.

Granada Studios Granada Studios is responsible for many of the best-loved television series to come out of Britain, including *Brideshead Revisited*, *The Adventures of Sherlock Holmes* and last, but not least, *Coronation Street*. *Coronation Street* is the archetypal soapie where fact has become so confused with fiction it is scarcely possible to draw a distinction. It deals with the lives of the residents of Coronation Street in the fictional Lancashire town of Weatherfield and has run continuously since 1960.

The Granada Studios Tour is based roughly on the idea pioneered by Universal Studios in Hollywood. The material Granada has to work with lacks something of the latter's panache, but the end result is a similar mix of sets, live shows and cinemas. The studios (☎ 833 0880), Water St, Castlefield (on the same block as the Museum of Science & Technology), are open daily except Monday from 9.45 am to 4 pm; £12.99/8.99. There are restaurants and shops on the site; allow four hours.

Museum of Science & Industry The museum (☎ 832 2244), Liverpool Rd, is an impressive monument to the Industrial Revolution. Built on the site of the world's first passenger railway station, there are working steam mill engines (that look like intricate modern sculptures), steam locomotives, factory machinery from the mills, an exhibition telling the story of Manchester from the sewers up, and an Air & Space Gallery featuring historic aircraft. The museum is open every day from 10 am to 5 pm; £5/3. Allow at least three hours.

G-Mex Centre The G-Mex Centre (☎ 834 2700) hosts exhibitions, concerts and indoor sporting events. It has been cleverly converted from the derelict Central railway station, originally built in 1876. Pity about the name.

Bridgewater Hall Opposite the G-Mex Centre is the enormous and impressive Bridgewater Hall (☎ 834 3697), new home of the world famous Hallé Orchestra. It was completed in 1996 at a cost of £42 million.

Getting There & Away Castlefield is served by Deansgate station with rail links to Piccadilly, Oxford Rd and Salford Crescent station. Metrolink has a number of stops in the city; Castlefield is served by the G-Mex stop.

City Centre

Dominating Albert Square is the **Town Hall**, an enormous Victorian Gothic building completed in 1876. The 280-foot-high tower is a feature of the skyline. It's worth checking the interior, rich in sculpture and Baroque decoration.

The distinctive circular building on St Peter's Square is the **Central Library**, one of the largest in England; it also houses the Library Theatre. On Peter St, the **Free Trade Hall** is the third to be built on the site of the Peterloo massacre.

Further to the west on Deansgate is the **John Rylands Library** (☎ 834 5343), a particularly fine example of the Victorian Gothic style, built in memory of a wealthy cotton manufacturer. It is has a fine collection of early printed books (including a Gutenberg Bible, several Caxtons and manuscripts dating back to 2000 BC). It's open Monday to Friday, 10 am to 5.30 pm, and Saturday from 10 am to 1 pm; free.

The **Pumphouse People's History Museum** (☎ 839 6061), Bridge St, is a museum of social history and the Labour movement. It's open daily except Monday, 11 am to 4.30 pm; entry is £1 (free on Friday).

The area around King St and St Ann's Square is known as the **West End**. It's the most attractive part of the city centre and the pedestrianised streets are lined with up-market shops.

On the east side of St Ann's Square is the imposing **Royal Exchange**, originally at the hub of the city's commerce. Trading boards still show the exact price of raw cotton around the world the day the building closed. It is now home to a café/bar and a 'space-age' theatre in the round that's currently being restored following IRA bomb damage in 1996.

Further up Deansgate is the **Cathedral**, which was at the centre of medieval Manchester. Most of it is in Perpendicular style dating from the 15th century, but it was substantially restored after bomb damage in WWII.

Across Fennel St from the Cathedral is **Chetham's Hospital School & Library**, a medieval manor house, now a national school for young musicians.

To the east lies the **Arndale Centre**, covering 26 acres and claimed to be one of the largest covered shopping areas in Europe (it includes a large local bus station). Damaged by the IRA bomb in 1996, it's currently being rebuilt.

Piccadilly Square is another important commercial focal point served by many buses and the Metrolink. To the north along Oldham St is **Affleck's Palace**, a run-down building at the centre of Manchester's energetic youth culture. There are stalls, shops, hairdressers and cafés selling clubbing gear from young designers, second-hand clothes, crystals, leather gear, records – you name it. It's a thriving, buzzy place with a great atmosphere. It's open Monday to Saturday, 10 am to 5.30 pm; don't miss it.

The **City Art Gallery** on the corner of Princess and Mosley Sts was designed by Sir Charles Barry (the architect for the Houses of Parliament) in 1824. It has an impressive collection from early Italian, Dutch and Flemish painters to Gainsborough, Blake, Constable and the Pre-Raphaelites. It's open Monday to Saturday, 10 am to 5.45 pm, and Sunday, 2 to 5.45 pm; admission is free.

Oxford Street/Oxford Road

The **University of Manchester** does not enjoy an attractive campus, but it is nonetheless one of the largest and best universities in the country.

Further south, the **Whitworth Art Gallery** (☎ 273 4865) has an important collection of English watercolours (including 53 Turners and various Blakes), contemporary paintings and a large collection of textiles and wallpapers. It's open Monday to Saturday, 10 am to 5 pm, Thursday until 9 pm; free. There's also an excellent gallery bistro with an outside terrace open in summer.

Further south again, you reach the suburb of Rusholme with its many Indian/Pakistani restaurants.

Old Trafford

Manchester United Manchester United's Old Trafford stadium is regarded by many as holy ground – almost every week supporters demonstrate this literally by requesting to have their ashes scattered on the pitch (and they are – behind the goals, where it doesn't matter if the ash damages the grass).

There are tours (☎ 877 4002) every hour from 10 am to 2 pm (daily except Monday and pre-match and match days). There's also a museum, open daily, except Monday, from 9.30 am to 4 pm. Admission to the museum and the tour is £4.95/2.95, to the museum only £2.95/1.95. Seats for matches cost around £15.

Lancashire County Cricket Club The Lancashire Club (or Old Trafford as it is commonly known) Warwick Rd, hosts county matches throughout the summer, and international test matches. Phone ☎ 872 0261 for information. Admission to county games is £6 to £8.

Places to Stay

There's a reasonable range of places to stay, but most cheap options are some distance from the city centre. The big central hotels tend to cater to businesspeople during the week so many offer excellent weekend rates. The TIC has a free booking service which is recommended and they will also know of any special offers.

Hostels The stunning new *Youth Hostel* (☎ 839 9960) is across the road from the Museum of Science & Industry in the Castlefield area, and has comfortable four-bedded rooms for £11.60/8.20 per person. From late June to late September, the University of Manchester lets students' rooms to visitors from around £9 per person. Contact *Montgomery House* (☎ 226 3434), *Loxford Tower* (☎ 247 1334) and *Woolaton Hall* (☎ 224 7244).

Three miles south of the centre at 10 Hornby Rd, off Warwick Rd, Stretford, is *International Backpackers' Hostel/Joan's Place* (☎ 872 3499). There's dorm accommodation from £9 and rooms from £13/22.

Hotels & B&Bs – central The *Commercial Hotel* (☎ 834 3504), 125 Liverpool Rd, Castlefield, is a traditional pub close to the museum. Rooms are £20/34. The *Crown Inn* (☎ 834 1930), 321 Deansgate, is nearby and has similar prices.

Opposite Piccadilly railway station, the renovated *Hotel International* (☎ 236 7484), 34 London Rd, is well-placed. Singles/doubles are from £31/51 (less on the weekend).

The *Britannia Sachas Hotel* (☎ 228 1234), Portland St, was a famous 1851 cotton warehouse that has been converted into a luxurious four-star hotel. Rooms are from £31 to £45 for a single, £51 to £65 for a double.

Hotels & B&Bs – suburbs Didsbury is an attractive suburb to the south of the university. There are some good local pubs and the bus links into the city are frequent. There's quite a strip of hotels in converted Victorian houses along Wilmslow and, particularly, Palatine Rds.

The *Baron Hotel* (☎ 434 0941), 116 Palatine Rd, West Didsbury, is about half a mile from the M63 amongst a batch of similar-standard hotels. It's a nice place with rooms

with private bathroom from £16/21 to £30/35.

The *Elm Grange Hotel* (☎ 445 3336), 561 Wilmslow Rd, is a comfortable hotel with rooms from £16/36 to £30/50.

The *Crescent Gate Hotel* (☎ 224 0672), Park Crescent, has a particularly good location within walking distance of the Indian restaurants in Rusholme and well served by numerous buses into the city centre. Most of the comfortable rooms have bathroom; rooms are £35/48.

The *Fernbank Guest House* (☎ 01625-523729) 188 Wilmslow Rd, is 12 miles from the centre but only 10 minutes from the airport. It's a comfortable place; rates range from £16/36 to £30/50.

The suburb of Chorlton is another good area for B&Bs. It's reasonably convenient for Old Trafford to the south-west of the city centre.

Places to Eat
The most distinctive restaurant zones are Chinatown in the city centre and Rusholme in the south. Chinatown is bounded by Charlotte, Portland, Oxford and Mosley Sts, and it has a number of restaurants – not all Chinese, and most not particularly cheap. Rusholme is to the south of the university on Wilmslow Rd, the extension of Oxford St/Rd, and has numerous popular, cheap and very good Indian/Pakistani places. If you're shopping in Affleck's Palace, there are several good cafés there.

There are some excellent vegetarian restaurants. The *Fallen Angels* (☎ 273 4327), 263 Upper Brook St, is near the Manchester Royal Infirmary. It's open only in the evenings and you can BYOB. For lunch try *On the Eighth Day* (☎ 273 4878), 111 Oxford Rd, next to the Metropolitan University. In Rusholme, there's the *Greenhouse* (☎ 224 0730), 331 Great Western St,.

The cheapest place to eat in Manchester, possibly in Britain, is the *Cafe Yaqub* (☎ 834 8067), Union St. It's a bit tricky to find, the decor is spartan, but the food is very good value. It's open Monday to Friday, 10 am to 5.30 pm, and on Sunday from 10 am to 3 pm.

Homesick Americans could try *Amigos* (☎ 236 8438), 14 Oxford Rd (opposite the BBC studios), one of the oldest Mexican restaurants in the UK. It's good value with main meals around £4.50. The nearby *Lass O'Gowrie* pub, Charles St off Oxford St, is another student hang-out, and has an excellent small brewery on the premises and good-value bar meals.

Homesick Vietnamese, Thais and Australians should check out the *Hong Pat Restaurant* (☎ 228 2485), 78 Portland St, Manchester's only Vietnamese restaurant, with set menus from £20 for two.

The most acclaimed Chinese restaurant in town is the *Little Yang Sing* (☎ 237 9257), 17 George St. It also specialises in Cantonese cuisine, but has many vegetarian choices. Their set menus start at £15, but you could easily end up paying a fair bit more if you venture further into the menu and wine list.

Café bars have taken off in a big way in Manchester. The first, *Dry 201* (☎ 236 5920), 28 Oldham St, and *Manto* (☎ 236 2667), 46 Canal St, are both still among the best.

Entertainment

Manchester comes into its own at night, offering a remarkable range of high-quality entertainment. *City Life* gives a full listing.

Theatre The *Green Room* (☎ 236 1677), 54 Whitworth St West, is the premiere fringe venue and also has a good bar/café. And there's nearly always something interesting on in the *Royal Exchange* (☎ 833 9833), St Ann's Square.

Music & Clubs Music runs the full gamut of possibilities – from high to low. Manchester is home to two world-famous symphony orchestras, the Hallé and the BBC Philharmonic.

The famous scene that spawned The Smiths, Joy Division, New Order, the Stone Roses, Simply Red and James and the Happy Mondays (amongst others) continues, although in more subdued form than at its peak. One of the best venues for live music

Gay & Lesbian Manchester

Manchester is the gay capital of the north. *City Life* lists numerous gay bars, clubs, galleries and groups, including the Gay Centre (☎274 3814) on Sydney St. The Gay Switchboard (☎274 3999) operates from 4 to 10 pm, daily.

The centre of Manchester's enormous gay nightlife scene is Canal St (local wags drop the first letters of these two words!). There are said to be over 30 bars and clubs in the so-called 'Gay Village'. The groundbreaker here was the *Manto Bar* (☎236 2667), 46 Canal St, which has been copied around the world. Across the canal is *Metz* (☎237 9852), another café bar, and currently more fashionable than Manto. There are several more traditional pubs nearby, including the *New Union*. On Friday there's a women-only night at the upstairs bar at the *Rembrandt Hotel* (☎236 1311), Sackville St.

The club scene changes so quickly it's difficult to make recommendations. The *Paradise Factory* (see Music & Clubs) is currently very popular. *Cruz* (☎237 1554), nearby at 101 Princess St, is the largest gay nightclub in the city.

Britain's biggest gay and lesbian arts festival, It's Queer Up North (IQUP), takes place every two years – next in spring 1998. ∎

is *Band on the Wall* (832 6625), Swan St, which has an eclectic variety of acts from jazz, blues and folk to pop.

Paradise Factory (☎ 228 2966), 116 Princess St, is a club that's currently at the cutting edge, with gay nights at the weekend. The *Hacienda* (☎ 236 5051), Whitworth St West, once the undisputed centre of Manchester's nightlife, survives and still has the occasional live band.

PJ Bells (☎ 834 4266), 85 Oldham St, concentrates on jazz and blues. *Manchester Board Walk* (☎ 228 3555), Little Peter St, The *Venue* (☎ 236 0026), 17 Whitworth St, and the *Academy* (☎ 275 2930), Oxford Rd – part of the university student union – are other venues.

Getting There & Away

See the fares tables in the Getting Around chapter. Manchester is about 200 miles (three hours) from London, 3½ hours from Glasgow, two hours from York and 35 miles (half an hour) from Liverpool by road. STA Travel (☎ 834 0668) has an office at 75 Deansgate.

Air Manchester airport (☎ 489 3000) serves 35 countries and over 11 million passengers a year, so it's the largest outside London. It's worth considering if you're heading to/from the north or to the Lake District. The excellent TIC at the airport can recommend nearby B&Bs, some of which will organise to pick you up and drop you off.

Bus There are numerous coach links with the rest of the country. National Express (☎ 0990-808080) serves 1000 destinations! Chorlton St station is in the centre of the city.

Train Piccadilly is the main station for trains to and from the rest of the country, although Victoria station serves Halifax and Bradford. The two stations are linked by Metrolink.

Getting Around
For general inquiries about local transport, including night buses, phone ☎ 228 7811 (open daily, 8 am to 8 pm).

Bus Buses from the city centre to West Didsbury cost around £1; to the university it's 70p.

Metrolink Metrolink is a new system of light-rail vehicles (trams) that operate on a combination of disused rail tracks and tracks laid along the city-centre streets. In the centre there are frequent links between Victoria and Piccadilly train stations and G-Mex (for Castlefield). Buy tickets from the machines on the platforms.

Merseyside

In the 1996 local government reforms, the county of Merseyside was broken up into a number of separate authorities, the most important of which is the city of Liverpool.

The area is, however, still referred to as Merseyside.

LIVERPOOL
- *pop 510,000* • *☎ 0151*

Liverpool greets a visitor with a distinctly gap-toothed smile. The holes testify to wartime bombing and economic collapse, and although there are still many wonderful Victorian and Edwardian buildings, they tend to startle with their incongruity, like gold teeth.

Nonetheless, Liverpool is deeply fascinating, and it retains an irrepressible sense of place. It has a dramatic site, rising on a series of steps above the broad Mersey estuary – with its shifting light, its fogs, its gulls and its mournful emptiness. The combination of grandeur and decay, of decrepit streets, boarded windows, massive cathedrals and imperious buildings, creates some of the most arresting sights in Britain.

Liverpool's economic collapse has been even more dramatic than Manchester's and this gives the whole city an edge. When people party, it seems they do it with a touch of desperation, certainly with plenty of abandonment. On weekend nights the city centre vibrates to music in countless pubs and clubs.

There aren't many large cities of note in the UK; most are undistinguished and can be safely avoided. Liverpool, however, is one that is definitely worth visiting. The Albert Dock, the Western Approaches Museum, the looming cathedrals, the brilliant architecture and the city streets themselves give vivid testimony to the city's rugged history and the perverse exhilaration of its present-day decline.

History
For over 100 years, slavery played an important role in the triangular commerce that created Liverpool's wealth. From 1700 ships carried cotton goods and hardware from Liverpool to West Africa, slaves from West Africa to the West Indies and Virginia, then sugar, rum, tobacco and raw cotton back to Liverpool.

As a great port, it was natural the city should become home to a cosmopolitan mixture of people. It attracted thousands of immigrants from Ireland and Scotland and it still has strong Celtic influences.

Between 1830 and 1930 nine million emigrants – mainly English, Scots and Irish, but including many Swedes, Norwegians and Russian Jews – sailed for the New World from Liverpool.

WWII led to a resurgence in Liverpool's importance. Over one million GIs disembarked on the Mersey docks prior to D-day and the port was, once again, enormously important as the western gateway for supplies from across the Atlantic. The city was also the site for the Combined Headquarters of the Western Approaches, which co-ordinated the transatlantic convoys and the battle against German U-boats.

Liverpool has long had a reputation for left-wing radicalism. The outrageous excesses of 19th-century capitalism led to bitter and violent confrontations with increasingly well-organised labour organisations. In modern times, unemployment and housing problems have dogged the city. In the early '80s racial tensions added to these problems and led to large-scale rioting in the suburb of Toxteth to the south of the city centre.

When left-wing politicians finally did take control of the city's government they were dogged by financial crises, vicious political infighting, and serious allegations of corruption. Sometimes it seemed that arcane doctrinal disputes and the battle for personal power left them little time to do anything constructive. In any event, economic realities and a Conservative government at Westminster gave them little chance and things have calmed down considerably since the late 1980's.

Orientation

Liverpool stretches north-south along the Mersey estuary for more than 13 miles. The main visitor attraction is Albert Dock (which is well signposted) to the south of the city centre. The centre, including the two cathe-drals to the east, is quite compact – about 1½ miles by one mile.

Lime St, the main railway station, is just to the east of the city centre. The National Express coach station is on the corner of Norton and Islington Sts in the north of the city. The bus station is in the centre on Paradise St.

Information

The main TIC (☎ 709 3631), also known as the Merseyside Welcome Centre, is in the Clayton Square Shopping Centre. It's open from Monday to Saturday 9.30 am to 5.30 pm. There's also a branch at Albert Dock (☎ 708 8854) which is open daily from 10 am to 5.30 pm. Both have accommodation-booking services.

Look for the excellent booklet *Liverpool Heritage Walk* (£3.95), an illustrated guide to the city's historical landmarks (which are identified by numbered metal markers set into the footpath).

Both TICs sell tickets to two highly recommended bus tours of the city. There's a one-hour city tour (£4.50) leaving at least hourly from near the TIC and Albert Dock in summer (only one in winter), and a 2¼-hour Beatles tour (see following section).

A little caution is justified in Liverpool. Although the main hazard is likely to be over-friendly drunks, one should avoid dark side streets.

Albert Dock

Built between 1841 and 1848, the Albert Dock is one of the earliest enclosed docks in the world. Seven acres of water is surrounded by a colonnade of enormous cast-iron columns and impressive five-storey warehouses.

In the 1980s they were restored and they now house a number of outstanding modern museums, numerous shops and restaurants, offices, studios for Granada TV, a branch of the TIC and several tacky tourist attractions. Even if you're only vaguely interested the site could easily absorb four hours.

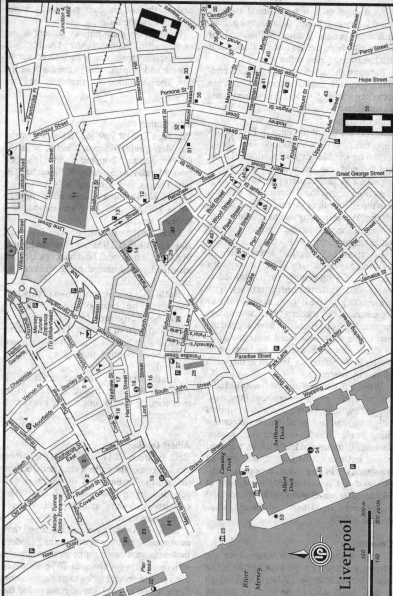

Liverpool

PLACES TO STAY		39	Philharmonic Hotel	20	Royal Liver Building
1	Atlantic Tower	42	Ye Cracke	21	Isle of Man Ferries
12	Britannia Adelphi Hotel	49	Baa Bar	22	Mersey Ferries
26	Liverpool Moat House	51	Pumphouse Hotel	23	Cunard Building
31	YMCA			24	Port of Liverpool
32	Aachen Hotel &	**OTHER**			Building
	Belvedere	2	Western Approaches	25	Museum of Liverpool
33	The Feathers Hotel	3	Town Hall		Life
35	University of Liverpool,	4	Moorfields Railway	27	Bus Station & Parking
	Mulberry Court		Station	28	Bluecoat Arts Centre
38	YWCA	7	Post Office	29	Post Office
		8	Liverpool Museum &	30	Central Railway Station
PLACES TO EAT			Walker Art Gallery	34	Metropolitan Cathedral
5	Casa Bella	9	National Express	40	Philharmonic Hall
6	Casa Italia & Risorante		Coach Station	41	Unity Theatre
	del Secolor	10	St George's Hall	43	Institute for Performing
36	Everyman Theatre &	11	Lime Street Railway		Arts
	Bistro		Station	45	Blue Angel
37	El Macho	14	TIC (Merseyside	48	Heebiejeebies
44	Far East		Welcome Centre)	50	Merseyside Academy
46	Café Tabac	15	American Express	52	Merseyside Maritime
47	St Petersburg Russian	16	Thomas Cook		Museum
	Restaurant	17	Cavern Club	53	Tate Gallery Liverpool
		18	No 16 Cook St	54	TIC (Albert Dock)
PUBS		19	James Street Railway	55	The Beatles Story
13	American Bar		Station	56	Anglican Cathedral

Merseyside Maritime Museum This museum has a large and growing range of exhibits that have been imaginatively developed. It is divided into three: the Main Museum and the HM Customs & Excise National Museum in the warehouse on the northern side of the dock, and ships on the quays further to the north across the Canning Dock.

The major displays include Emigrants to a New World, the WWII Battle of the Atlantic, the World of Models, and Builders of Great Ships.

The museum (☎ 207 0001) is open daily from 10.30 am to 5.30 pm. Admission is £3/1.50, and the ticket also gives entry to the excellent Museum of Liverpool Life.

Museum of Liverpool Life This museum follows three main themes: Mersey Culture, especially entertainers; Making a Living, showing regional trades; and Demanding a Voice, about the growth of unionism and democracy. It's open daily and entry is on the same ticket as for the Maritime Museum.

Tate Gallery Liverpool This is an extension of the Tate Gallery in London; a Liverpool connection is appropriate since the original benefactor of the London gallery was Henry Tate, who co-founded the famous Tate & Lyle sugar business in Liverpool. The Albert Dock gallery is well designed and has high-quality changing exhibitions. The gallery (☎ 709 0507) is open Tuesday to Sunday, 10 am to 6 pm; free.

The Beatles Story The name says it all. Unfortunately this attraction fails to capitalise on the potential of its subject – fanatics won't discover anything they don't already know, and aside from some old TV clips there's nothing to kindle excitement for later generations (or those who preferred the Rolling Stones anyway). It's open daily from 10 am to 6 pm, but is questionable value at £5.45/3.95.

City Centre
The area to the north of Albert Dock is known as **Pier Head**, after a stone pier built in the 1760s. This is still the departure point for ferries across the Mersey to Birkenhead (see Getting Around), and it was for millions

of migrants their final contact with European soil.

Today it is dominated by a trio of self-important buildings dating from the time when Liverpool's star was still in the ascendant. The southernmost, with the dome mimicking St Paul's Cathedral, is the **Port of Liverpool Building**, completed in 1907. Next, in the style of an Italian palazzo, comes the **Cunard Building**, once the headquarters of the Cunard Steamship Line. Finally, there's the **Royal Liver Building**, opened in 1911 as the headquarters for the Royal Liver Friendly Society, crowned by the famous Liver (pronounced liever) Birds. The copper birds represent the symbol of Liverpool and stand 18 feet high. The original seal of Liverpool featured an eagle, but over time artists' representations came to show a bird closer to a seagull or cormorant!

At the end of Castle St, considered to be the centre of the city, is the **Town Hall**, designed by John Wood the Elder of Bath and completed in 1754. Both the dome and the impressive portico and balcony (where the Beatles were received by the Lord Mayor in 1964) were added later. **Water St** presents another fine Victorian/Edwardian streetscape. The entry to the Western Approaches wartime bunker is on Rumford St (see that section following).

No 16 Cook St, built in 1866, is regarded as an architectural landmark, foreshadowing modern architecture with its daring use of plate glass; the building's design was so thoroughly damned by contemporary critics that the architect, Peter Ellis, never received another commission.

A Victorian warehouse in Mathew St was home to a music venue called the **Cavern Club**. Between March 1961 and August 1963 the Beatles played here a staggering 275 times. Other bands who helped define 'beat' music and the 'Mersey sound', like Gerry & the Pacemakers, were also regulars. Cilla Black was in charge of the cloakroom! The original building was demolished for an underground railway that was never built, but in 1984 the **Cavern Walks** was opened with a faithful reproduction of the Cavern in its basement.

Clayton Square is now a modern shopping centre that includes the main TIC. **Bold St**, to the south of Central railway station, was a ropewalk used in the manufacture of ropes for the sailing ships in port. In the 19th century it became a fashionable shopping street; in addition to shops it now has a number of nightclubs and restaurants.

The **Britannia Adelphi Hotel** was completed in 1912 to serve wealthy passengers overnighting before or after the Atlantic crossing, and was considered one of the most luxurious hotels in the world.

Further north along Lime St is the superb Edwardian pub **Vines**, with its luxurious interior (built in 1906), the **American Bar**, favoured by the US forces during WWII, and the Art-Nouveau **Crown Hotel**, built in 1905. In the 19th century Lime St was famous for prostitution, and was immortalised in the song *Maggie May*.

Across the road from Lime St station is a group of Liverpool's most impressive buildings, although traffic funneling into the city and the entrance of the Queensway Mersey Tunnel can make it difficult to enjoy them. **St George's Hall** was built as a concert hall and is considered one of the greatest neoclassical buildings in the world – the exterior is Greek, the interior Roman. It was completed in 1854.

The **Liverpool Museum & William Brown Library**, opened in 1860, is a traditional museum with largely static displays. It does, however, sometimes have interesting temporary exhibitions, so it is worth finding out if anything is on. It's open Monday to Saturday from 10 am to 5 pm, Sunday from noon to 5 pm; free. The **Walker Art Gallery** has an important collection of Italian and Flemish paintings and some interesting Impressionists and post-Impressionists, including a Degas, Cezanne and Matisse. It has the same hours as the museum and is also free.

Heading up Mount Pleasant, which runs south-east of the Britannia Adelphi Hotel, you can begin an interesting loop that takes in the two cathedrals. At the top of the hill is the striking, modern Roman Catholic cathedral, the Metropolitan Cathedral (see following section), and beyond it the university.

On Hope St, the **Everyman Theatre**, one of the most famous repertory theatres in Britain, has featured the works of local playwright Alan Bleasdale, amongst many others. It also has the best value food in town (see Places to Eat). Located on the corner of Hope and Hardman Sts, the **Philharmonic Hotel**, built in 1900, is one of the most extraordinary hotels in Britain. The interior decoration (especially in the toilets!) is an overwhelming confection of etched glass, stained glass, wrought iron, mosaics and ceramic tiling.

Ye Cracke, on Rice St, has long been favoured by students from the nearby College of Art – John Lennon and Cynthia Powell were regular customers. The massive Anglican Cathedral (see following section), completed in 1978 and only exceeded in size by St Peter's and the Milan and Seville cathedrals, has a superb site overlooking the city.

Western Approaches The Combined Headquarters of the Western Approaches (☎ 227 2008), the secret command centre for the Battle of the Atlantic, was buried under yards of concrete beneath an undistinguished building behind the town hall in Rumford Square. At the end of the war the bunker was abandoned, with virtually everything left intact. It's open daily except Friday and Sunday. Tickets for adults/students are £3.99/2.50

Metropolitan Cathedral Originally Sir Edwin Lutyens, the creator of New Delhi, designed an enormous Roman Catholic cathedral which would actually have been larger than St Peter's! Unfortunately, the war and Liverpool's catastrophic decline interrupted and the priests were forced to temper their ambitions. The present church-in-the-round design (referred to as 'Paddy's Wigwam' by non-Catholics), incorporates Lutyen's crypt and was completed in 1967. The exterior is strikingly successful, soaring upwards almost like hands in prayer, and the interior space is impressive. Unfortunately,

the detailing is shoddy, the roof leaks badly and the modern decorations are less than successful. It's open 8 am to 6 pm. For information on services phone ☎ 709 9222.

Anglican Cathedral The Anglican Cathedral, the largest in Britain, was the life work of Sir Giles Gilbert Scott. Construction started in 1902 and Scott worked on the building until his death in 1960. The cathedral was built of red sandstone in neo-Gothic style; its scale is overwhelming and the best view in Liverpool is from the top of the 331-foot-high tower. The cathedral is open daily from 9 am to 6 pm; £1 suggested. The tower is open daily from 11 am to 4 pm; £2/1. There's an excellent, attractive refectory open from 11 am to 4 pm.

Beatles Tour
There are numerous sites around Liverpool associated with the Beatles, all of whom grew up here. Both TICs sell tickets to the Magical Mystery Tour, a 2¼-hour bus trip taking in homes, schools, venues, Penny Lane, Strawberry Fields and many other landmarks. It departs daily from inside the Albert Dock TIC at 2.20 pm and from the Merseyside Welcome Centre at 2.30 pm. Tickets are £7.95.

A re-creation of the original Cavern Club (☎ 236 9091) in Mathew St still attracts a big crowd. Phone for opening times.

Places to Stay
Hostels There's no official YHA hostel in Liverpool, but several other options. The *YMCA* (☎ 709 9516), 56 Mount Pleasant, offers a passable alternative for men and women, though it's definitely spartan. Singles/doubles are £12.50/22.60, including a full English breakfast. There's a good YWCA (☎ 709 7791) at 1 Rodney St (off Mount Pleasant); women only. Rooms are £11/20.

The *Embassie Youth Hostel* (☎ 707 1089), 1 Falkner Square, to the west of the Anglican Cathedral, but still within walking distance of the centre, has dorm beds from £9.50, and facilities including a laundry.

The *University of Liverpool* (☎ 794 6440) has single rooms at Mulberry Court, Oxford St, near the Metropolitan Cathedral, and self-catering apartments from March to April and July to September from £13.

B&Bs & Hotels There are a number of well-positioned hotels on Mount Pleasant, between the city centre and the Metropolitan Cathedral. The *Feathers Hotel* (☎ 709 9655), 119 Mount Pleasant, is a particularly good mid-range hotel. There are 80 rooms with a variety of facilities. Singles/doubles start at £25/35.

The *Aachen Hotel* (☎ 709 3477), 89 Mount Pleasant, has well-equipped rooms (most have showers) costing £22/34. The *Belvedere* (☎ 709 2356), 83 Mount Pleasant, is more basic, but cheaper from £16.50 per person.

The *Atlantic Tower* (☎ 227 4444), Chapel St, virtually beside the Royal Liver Building, is a modern, four-star, multistorey hotel with good views over the Mersey. Rooms are from £85/99, but there are good-value weekend breaks.

The weekend rate at the *Britannia Adelphi Hotel* (☎ 709 7200), Ranelagh Place, makes Liverpool's top hotel a worthwhile splurge. When it was completed in 1912 it was considered one of the most luxurious hotels in the world. Singles/doubles are £30/60 at weekends, £49/87 during the week. Breakfast (£8.95) is extra.

Places to Eat
There are lots of places to eat down Bold St in the city centre. At the eastern end of this street is *Café Tabac* (☎ 709 3735), No 124, a relaxed wine bar that attracts a young crowd. *St Petersburg Russian Restaurant* (☎ 708 9440), 114 Bold St, is authentic. There's live music in the evenings and good Russian fare such as blinis (from £2.50). Main dishes range from £6.50 to £10.95.

Everyman Bistro (☎ 708 9545), at 5 Hope St, underneath the famous Everyman Theatre, is highly recommended. It's a cafeteria-style set-up, but the food is cheap and good (main dishes under £4.50). Also on

Hope St, *El Macho* (☎ 708 6644), at No 23, has a cheerful atmosphere and enormous servings of spicy Mexican food (they're not afraid to use chilli). It's worth booking on the weekend. Most main dishes are around £6.95 but there are student specials and three-course set lunches for £5.95.

The *refectory* at the Anglican Cathedral serves excellent lunches that are great value. Dish of the day is £3.95.

Liverpool's Chinatown has declined since its glory days, but there are still a number of Chinese restaurants around Berry St. One of the best and most popular is *Far East* (☎ 709 3141), 27 Berry St, in the best tradition, above a Chinese supermarket. Set menus start at £13.50, but you could eat for less – there are plenty of dishes for around £6. Dim sum is popular on Sunday.

At 40 Stanley St, in the centre of town, are two Italian places, one above the other. Downstairs is *Casa Italia* (☎ 227 5774), a popular pizzeria. They're open Monday to Saturday; pizzas cost from £5. Upstairs is the posh *Ristorante del Secolo* (☎ 236 4004) with pasta from £7, meat dishes for around £12.

Entertainment
On a long summer evening, it's hard to imagine a more perfect programme than starting with a pint in the Philharmonic Hotel, eating at the Everyman and seeing a show, wandering into town to listen to some music, and finally, collapsing in comfort at the Adelphi. If possible, get hold of the free *In Touch* or *L: Scene* (£1), both monthly entertainment guides.

Theatre The *Everyman Theatre* (☎ 709 4776) is one of the best repertory theatres in the country. The *Bluecoat Arts Centre* (☎ 708 9050), School Lane, and the *Unity Theatre* (☎ 709 4988) both host innovative, small-scale companies.

Music The Royal Liverpool Philharmonic Orchestra (☎ 709 3789) has an excellent reputation. It's in the *Philharmonic Hall* on Hope St. For indie rock try the *Picket* on Hardman St

(☎ 709 3995), or try *Heebiejeebies* on Seel St (☎ 709 4776) for jazz/blues. The *Irish Centre* (☎ 709 4120) often has live bands.

Pubs & Clubs Liverpool has a thriving nightlife, but as always recommendations are difficult to make. Wander around Mathew St and south-east to Bold, Seel and Slater Sts and you'll stumble over an amazing array of clubs and pubs catering to every style you can imagine. Follow your ears – music seems to waft out of the side streets. The following gives just a brief idea of the myriad options.

A visit to the *Cavern* (☎ 236 9091), 10 Mathew St, the replica of the club where the Beatles made their name, is a must, but these days a disco is more likely than live music, so you probably won't hang around. It's also often closed for private parties. Opposite is the *Cavern Pub* (☎ 236 1957), full of memorabilia.

The *Blue Angel* (☎ 428 1213), 108 Seel St, is a club that's popular with students. The *Baa Bar*, Fleet St, attracts a more varied crowd. The *Casablanca* on Hope St is also very popular; check the downstairs bar. *Hardy's* (☎ 708 7958), Hardman St, has a variety of different nights.

Getting There & Away
See the fares tables in the Getting Around chapter. Liverpool is 210 miles (four hours) from London, 100 miles from Birmingham, 75 miles from Leeds and 35 miles (half an hour) from Manchester.

Air Liverpool airport (☎ 486 8877), eight miles to the south of the city centre, has flights to Belfast, Dublin and the Isle of Man.

Bus There are National Express (☎ 0990-808080) services linking Liverpool to most major towns. They leave from the new depot in the north of the city.

Rail Numerous InterCity services run to Lime St station.

Boat The Isle of Man Steam Packet Company (☎ 01624-661661) operates a service between Douglas and Liverpool (Pier Head) every Saturday throughout the year and more frequently during summer. The journey time is four hours. Adult singles/returns start at £23/37. Bicycles are transported free, but a car will cost from £36 each way.

At Douglas you can connect with a ferry in summer to Belfast, but close reading of the timetable is required. Travel times and prices for the Douglas-Belfast trip are basically the same as for the Liverpool-Douglas trip.

Getting Around
Public transport in the region is coordinated by Merseytravel (☎ 236 7676), which has a branch in the TIC at Clayton Square. There are various zone tickets, such as the £3.10 ticket for bus, train and ferry (except cruises). These are also sold at post offices.

Bus There are a number of bus companies. Smart Bus 1 runs from Albert Dock through the city centre to the university, and vice versa, every 20 minutes.

Taxi Try Davy Liver (☎ 709 4646) or Merseycabs (☎ 708 0505).

Ferry The ferry across the Mersey (85p), started 800 years ago by Benedictine monks but made famous by Gerry & the Pacemakers, still offers one of the best views of Liverpool. Boats depart from Pier Head Ferry Terminal, to the north of Albert Dock and next to the Liver Building, going to Woodside and Seacombe. Special one-hour commentary cruises run all year round, departing hourly from 10 am to 3 pm on weekdays and until 6 pm on weekends (£3.10/2.15). Phone ☎ 630 1030 for more information.

Isle of Man

• *pop 70,000*   • ☎ *01624*

The Isle of Man is all opposites. The number one industry is tax avoidance: this island is a place where wealthy Brits can shelter their wealth without having to move to Monte

Carlo or the Cayman Islands. But as well as a bolthole for the rich it's also motorcyclists' Mecca; each year's May-June TT races add 45,000 to the island's small population. Douglas, the capital, is a run-down relic of Victorian tourism with fading B&Bs and a chilly seaside but the island also has beautiful countryside and a proud heritage as the site of the world's oldest continuous parliament. The Isle of Man enjoys special status in Britain, and its annual parliamentary ceremony honours the 1000-year history of the Parliament of the Isle of Man, or Tynwald (a Scandinavian word meaning 'meeting field'). The Isle of Man is home to some unique creatures including the tailless Manx cat and the four-horned Manx loghtan sheep.

ORIENTATION & INFORMATION

Situated in the Irish Sea, equidistant from Liverpool, Dublin and Belfast, the Isle of Man is about 30 miles long by 10 miles wide.

Ferries arrive at Douglas, the port and main town on the south-east coast. Flights come in to Ronaldsway airport, 10 miles south of Douglas. Most of the interesting sites around the island are operated by Manx National Heritage (☎ 675522), which offers free entrance to NT or EH members. Unless otherwise indicated, standard Manx Heritage opening hours are Easter to September, daily, 10 am to 5 pm.

DOUGLAS

- *pop 20,000* • ☎ *01624*

Looking across the Irish Sea towards Blackpool, a not dissimilar Victorian seaside town, Douglas is not an endearing place. Half of the once fine, old Victorian seafront terraces are due for demolition, renovation, or at the very least a good coat of paint. What has been built recently has obviously involved some of Britain's most uninspired architects on their off days.

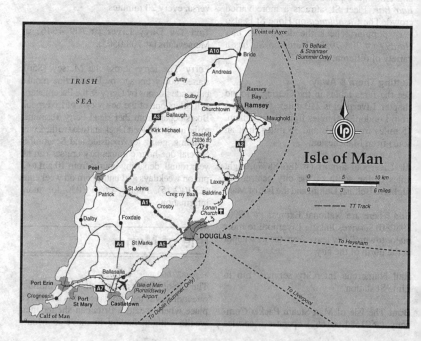

The Manx Museum (☎ 675522) gives a surprisingly thorough introduction to the island from prehistoric times down to TT race winners. The museum is open Monday to Saturday, 10 am to 5 pm; free.

The TIC (☎ 686766) is in the Sea Terminal Building and is open daily but for longer hours in summer.

Places to Stay

The TIC makes free accommodation bookings. Its camping grounds information sheet lists sites all around the island. Everything is booked out for TT week, often for years ahead.

There's B&B from £12 per person at *Matlock House* (☎ 676714), 16 Castle Mona Ave. There are several other budget-oriented places in this area.

The seafront promenade is shoulder-to-shoulder B&Bs from £20 per person or less. Two reasonable places, amongst the many along Loch Promenade, are the *Seabank Hotel* (☎ 674815) at No 21 and, more expensive, the *Modwena Hotel* (☎ 675728) at No 39-40.

The *Sefton Hotel* (☎ 626011) on Harris Promenade is a fine old upper crust establishment with comfortable rooms at £45/56.

Places to Eat

Douglas is not going to provide many culinary highlights. Even the big fast fooderies have not appeared so it's fish & chips, dismal-looking Chinese takeaways and a handful of restaurants.

Scott's Bistro (☎ 623764) on John St is pleasant and moderately priced. *Blazer's* (☎ 673222), on the corner of North Quay and Bank Hill, is a wine bar with pub-style food. It's located underneath the pricey *Waterfront* (same number).

L'Expérience (☎ 623103), at the bottom of Summerhill, is a smart French restaurant that serves queenies (local scallops). There are set menus from £14.95.

AROUND THE ISLE OF MAN

Petrol-heads are likely to start their island circuit with motorcycling's Mountain Circuit. At 50 mph some of the long sweeping bends are a delight; at 150 mph they must be bloody terrifying. Fortunately for the unconverted the island has other attractions, including the 90-mile *Raad ny Foillan*, or Road of the Gull, a coastal walking path which makes a complete circuit of the island.

Castletown & Cregneash

At Castletown, **Castle Rushen** (☎ 823326) dates from the 13th century; it's open daily and entry is £3/1.50. There's also a small **Nautical Museum** here.

On the southern tip of the island, the **Cregneash Village Folk Museum** recalls traditional Manx rural life. The **Calf of Man**, the small island just off Cregneash, is a bird sanctuary. Calf Island Cruises (☎ 832339) go to the island regularly during the summer for £6/3 from Port Erin.

Located between Castletown and Cregneash, the Iron Age hillfort at **Chapel Hill** encloses a Viking ship burial site.

Peel

Peel Castle, with its long curtain wall, is stunningly sited atop St Patrick's Island, joined to Peel by a causeway. Just before Peel is the **Tynwald Hill** at St John's where the annual parliamentary ceremony takes place on 5 July.

Peel has B&Bs. *Kilgallon's Bistro* (☎ 844366) is the best place to eat; there's also the popular *Creek Inn*.

Ramsey to Douglas

You can follow the TT course up and over the mountain or wind around the coast. The mountain route takes you close to the summit of **Snaefell** (2036 feet), the highest point on the island. It's an easy walk up to the summit or you can take the electric tram which climbs up from Laxey on the coast. The tram stops by the road where **Murray's Motorcycle Museum** displays motorcycles and TT memorabilia.

On the edge of Ramsey is the **Grove Rural Life Museum**, open standard Manx hours; entry is £2/1. At the small village of **Maughold**, the village church is on the site of an ancient monastery and a small shelter houses a collection of stone crosses and ancient inscriptions.

The **Laxey Wheel**, built in 1854 to pump water from a mine, is a truly stunning sight. Describing this monster (24 yards in diameter) as the 'great' wheel is no exaggeration. This Manx Heritage site is open standard hours; £2/1. At **Lonan Old Church** the wheel-headed cross is the most impressive early Christian cross on the island.

GETTING THERE & AWAY
Air
Manx Airlines (☎ 0345-256256) has frequent connections with Liverpool and Manchester. Jersey European (☎ 0345-676676) connects most frequently with Belfast and Blackpool. There are other smaller operators. Typically you're looking at around £100 return for a 'short break' Manchester connection.

Boat
The Isle of Man Steam Packet (☎ 661661) operates to Douglas from Dublin, Belfast, Heysham, Fleetwood, Liverpool and Ardrossan with regular car ferries and high-speed SeaCat catamarans. Short-break return fares can be as low as £37 for an adult, and £64 for a car. The crossing from Liverpool takes 2½ hours by SeaCat or four to 4½ hours by regular ferry.

GETTING AROUND
A taxi from the airport into Douglas will cost about £11. The airport bus costs £1.30. There are several car rental operators at the airport and others in Douglas and other centres. In Douglas, bicycles can be hired at Eurocycles (☎ 624909), 8a Victoria Rd.

There are a number of interesting rail services on the island, most operating Easter to September: the Douglas-Laxey-Ramsey electric tramway (☎ 861226), a steam train operating Douglas-Castletown-Port Erin (☎ 673623), the Snaefell Mountain Railway (☎ 861225), and the narrow-gauge Groudle Glen Railway (☎ 622138). A variety of unlimited-travel tickets are available: a ticket covering rides on these trains for three days in seven costs £13.70/6.85.

Lancashire

Traditionally, Lancashire was bound by the Mersey in the south, the sea in the west, the Pennines in the east and the Lake District mountains in the north. Today, Manchester, the region's natural capital, and Liverpool, the region's great port, are administered separately.

Business and commerce have seemingly gravitated to southern Lancashire – coal and cotton made it the hub of the Industrial Revolution – but today the depressed industrial towns of Preston, Blackburn, Accrington and Burnley have little appeal. Ribblesdale, with the ancient town of Clitheroe, is attractive.

Of the traditional seaside resorts serving Manchester and Liverpool, Blackpool lives splendidly (or tackily) on, but Morecambe is in sad decline.

LANCASTER
The historic city of Lancaster is certainly worth a visit if you're in the area. Standing on the banks of the River Lune, it dates back to Roman times but has a wealth of Georgian architecture.

The **castle**, part of which is still a prison, was built in the 11th century. There are regular tours which include the courtroom, Hadrian's Tower with its display of instruments of torture (including a cat o'nine tails last used 80 years ago), and the dungeons. It's open daily from April to September. The **Maritime Museum** on St George's Quay recalls the times when the city was a flourishing port at the centre of the slave trade.

The TIC (☎ 01524-32878), 28 Castle Hill, is open April to September from 10 am to 5 pm.

On the main west-coast railway line, Lancaster also has National Express bus links with many towns in the area.

BLACKPOOL

- *pop 147,000* • ☎ *01253*

Blackpool flourished thanks to the Industrial Revolution. Trade unions gradually secured holiday rights for workers. Eventually there were hundreds of thousands of northerners with time (albeit limited) on their hands, and money (albeit a pittance) in their pockets.

After a year cooped up in a factory and a depressing suburb, the broad Blackpool sands, the crowds, the flags and the lights must have been a fine sight. There were rowdy music hall shows, cheap B&Bs, funfairs, sideshows, freaks, puppet shows, donkey rides and, perhaps most important of all, enormous dances that provided one of the few opportunities for the sexes to mix. Things have changed surprisingly little.

In 1933, JB Priestley observed of Blackpool, 'To begin with, it is entitled to some respect because it has amply and triumphantly succeeded in doing what it set out to do. Nature presented it with very bracing air and a quantity of flat firm sand; and nothing else. Its citizens must have realised at once that charm and exclusiveness were not for them and their town.' There are those who visit because they have always done so, those who visit to reminisce and recapture the golden days of their youth, those who visit to get pissed and get laid and, as always, those who visit because limited time and money allow them no better option.

If you don't fit into one of these categories – and eight million people a year do – give the place a miss. On the other hand, if you have a morbid fascination with one of the most bizarre manifestations of English culture, or you're travelling with a group of uninhibited friends, you could have a good time.

Blackpool is famous for its **Illuminations**, a ploy to extend the brief summer holiday season that has been outstandingly successful. From early September to early November, five miles of the Promenade are illuminated with thousands of electric and neon lights.

Orientation

Blackpool is a surprisingly big city, but it can be easily managed without a car. If you do have wheels, the M55 and Yeadon Way bring you right into the heart of town, and there are a number of enormous car parks a short distance from the Promenade. The Promenade runs seven miles along the coast, but is served along its length by trams.

There's an unbroken stretch of 'amusement' centres with slot machines and bingo games from South Pier to Central and North piers – the so-called Golden Mile. South Pier, the least impressive, is alongside Pleasure Beach, the largest funfair, and Sandcastle, an enormous indoor pool complex. The town centre, and Tower World, are between Central and North piers.

Information

The TIC (☎ 21623), 1 Clifton St, is open Monday to Saturday from 9 am to 5 pm, Sunday from 10 am to 3.45 pm. It makes free bookings for local accommodation, but not for places further afield. There's also a branch at Pleasure Beach (☎ 403223).

Tower World

Built in 1894, the tower is Blackpool's best known symbol. Just the second metal tower in Europe, it's over 500 feet high, which probably did impress 19th-century mill workers. The entertainment complex underneath it has all the usual crap and a few more interesting offerings, including a laser show and an indoor circus.

The highlight, however – and it's the highlight of a trip to Blackpool – is the magnificent **ballroom**, a vast room with extraordinary rococo decoration, sculptured and gilded plasterwork, murals and chandeliers. There's a huge Wurlitzer organ and couples still glide across the floor to its melodramatic tones from 2 to 11 pm every day. It's as if *Saturday Night Fever* never happened.

Entry prices (☎ 22242) vary depending on time and season; tickets start at £16.85/5.95/4.95 for family/adults/children. Add £2 at peak times.

Pleasure Beach

Pleasure Beach is a 40-acre funfair with lots and lots of rides; the promo blurb says 550,000 burgers and three million portions of chips are sold each year, but doesn't tell you how many are eaten and subsequently regurgitated. The most interesting rides are the historic wooden rollercoasters – particularly the brilliant Grand National – and a steel rollercoaster, the Pepsi Max Big One.

Admission to the park, located near South Pier, is free. Rides are divided into categories and tickets can be bought for individual categories or for a mixture of them all.

Places to Stay

There are hundreds of B&Bs and small hotels – providing more visitor beds than in the whole of Portugal – but, if possible, take advantage of the TIC's free booking service.

At the top end the *Imperial* (☎ 23971), North Promenade, is an elegant hotel with all the luxuries. Singles/doubles start at £49 per person.

Right in the centre of town, close to the Tower and many pubs and discos, the *Boltonia Hotel* (☎ 20248) at 124 Albert Rd (off Central Drive) has comfortable rooms, most with private facilities, from £18 per person. The *Buxton Manor Hotel* (☎ 01253-23667), 41 Albert Rd, has TV in every room and some rooms have private bathroom. B&B is from £18.

Gynn Ave is about half a mile north of North Pier. It's a quiet location and the street is lined with B&Bs. Most are decent places with rates starting at about £18 per person. You could try the *Bramleigh Hotel* (☎ 351568) at No 13, the *Haldene Private Hotel* (☎ 353763) at No 4, or *The Austen* (☎ 351784) at No 6, amongst a number of others.

Places to Eat

Starving is an unlikely possibility in Blackpool, although getting decent food could be a problem. The place abounds in takeaway places of the worst kind – featuring hot dogs, burgers, doughnuts and chips. Most people eat at their hotels (often the evening meal will only be around £3), but the range of choice will almost certainly be limited to roast and three vegetables.

There are a few restaurants around Talbot Square (near the TIC) on Queen St, Talbot Rd and Clifton St. The most interesting possibility is on Queen St – the *Lagoonda* (☎ 293837), 37 Queen St, is an Afro-Caribbean restaurant. Starters average £3, main meals £9. *Giannini* (☎ 28926), 2 Queen St, is a good-value Italian place with pizza and pasta for around £4.

Entertainment

Blackpool is just full of people desperate to have a good time. A large number of venues have dress restrictions and these are policed by very big, very stupid bouncers. Essentially the restrictions mean no jeans, T-shirts or trainers. What this achieves is uncertain, other than to encourage sales of patent leather and see-through synthetic materials. Big groups of girls wearing revealing dresses and boys wearing shirts open to the fourth button (this in an Arctic climate) parade up and down the streets ogling each other's goosebumps before plunging into the loud and sweaty pubs and clubs.

Near the North Pier, *Yates Wine Lodge*, opposite the TIC on the corner of Clifton St and Talbot Rd, and *Counting House*, on the corner of Talbot Rd and the Promenade, are two civilised drinking places. A walk along the Promenade and the streets immediately parallel to it will reveal many less savoury possibilities.

Getting There & Away

Both Liverpool and Manchester are about 50 miles away and London is 250 miles distant.

Bus One interesting possibility is Primrose Coaches' (☎ 0191-232 5567) daily service to/from Newcastle via Kirkby Stephen, Raby Castle, Barnard Castle and Durham (X69).

National Express has services to most major towns in Britain. The central coach station is on Talbot Rd, near the town centre.

Train All intercity connections with Blackpool have to change at Preston (1½ hours). The journey from London takes about four hours.

Getting Around

For most visitors, the most useful public transport is provided by the vintage trams that run up and down the Promenade. From North Pier to South Pier the fare is 80p. Buses also run up and down the Promenade; they're a few pence cheaper but not as much fun.

Leeds & Bradford

For over 1000 years this area was known as West Riding of Yorkshire. In the 1974 local government reforms, bureaucrats created a new county, West Yorkshire, comprising Leeds, Bradford, Huddersfield, Wakefield and Halifax. Further meddling with local authority boundaries in 1996 removed West Yorkshire from the maps and replaced it with five separate unitary authorities.

The prosperity of the area depended on wool and cloth manufacturing for hundreds of years. The industry flourished through the Middle Ages, but with the advent of the improved machinery of the Industrial Revolution the West Riding boomed. The cottage industry that employed the women spinning downstairs and the men weaving upstairs was overtaken by factories.

By the beginning of the 20th century the West Riding, and particularly Leeds and Bradford, dominated the woollen industry. Sadly, as with cotton, the industry has almost completely disappeared since WWII.

Large parts of the landscape are still dominated by reminders of the industry. The long rows of weavers' cottages (with the windows in the second storey to provide light for the loom) and rows of workers' houses, built along the ridges, overlook multistorey mills with towering chimneys in the valleys below. Particularly in the north and west, the industrial

towns and valleys are still separated by wild stretches of the moors that have been so vividly captured by the Brontë sisters (who lived at Haworth).

The Leeds/Bradford conurbation is one of the busiest and most significant in the country and the surrounding area (including Halifax, Huddersfield, Wakefield etc) is a large and mostly unappealing series of suburbs.

GETTING AROUND

The Metro public transport network, based in Leeds, covers the area with integrated bus and rail services. The area is particularly well served by rail, with the towns in this section accessed by frequent trains. For any extensive travel, consider the extremely good-value bus and train Metro Dayrover tickets.

There's a Metro Travel Centre at the Leeds Central bus station (☎ 0113-245 7676) that answers phone inquiries on all public transport; it's open office hours from Monday to Saturday. It also publishes a number of very useful maps and timetables, most widely available in the TICs. If you plan to spend more than a week in the county, it is worth finding out about the Weekly Countrywide Train & Bus Metrocard.

For rail information, phone ☎ 0345-484950. The main bus operators are Yorkshire Rider (☎ 01422-365985), Harrogate & District (☎ 01423-527984), and Keighley & District (☎ 01535-603284).

LEEDS
• *pop 455,000* • ☎ 0113

Leeds is a substantial city, but not an immediately inspiring one. It has all the trappings one would expect – shops, museums, galleries, parks, sport and entertainment facilities – but none are outstanding (with the possible exception of those galleries associated with Henry Moore).

Function has almost inevitably triumphed over form, so although there are some Victorian architectural gems, most of the buildings are ordinary and the automobile seems to have been the principal beneficiary of 20th-century development. It's a livable city however, and since there's a very large student population there's a thriving nightlife.

Orientation & Information

The city lies on the north bank of the River Aire and the Leeds-Liverpool Canal. The railway, coach and bus stations are centrally located, but most affordable hotels are a bus ride away. The centre is a nightmare for motorists – there's a ring road with a series of complicated interchanges, the city streets are invariably one-way and some are pedestrianised or closed to private vehicles.

The Headingley Cricket Ground (for Test cricket fans) is to the north of the city in a pleasant suburb of the same name, along with a large population of students, plenty of pubs and restaurants.

There's an excellent TIC (☎ 242 5242), in the railway station; it's open Monday to Saturday from 9.30 am to 6 pm, and Sunday from 10 am to 4 pm. Apart from a good supply of information on Yorkshire and an accommodation service, it also sells

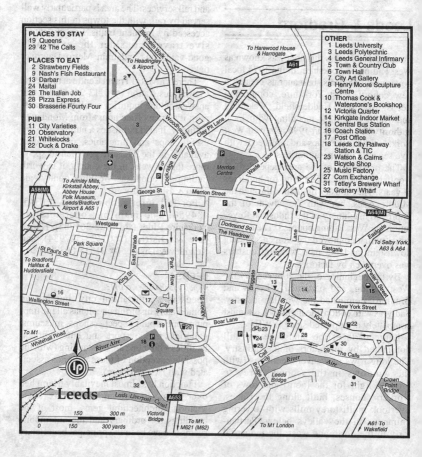

PLACES TO STAY
19 Queens
29 42 The Calls

PLACES TO EAT
2 Strawberry Fields
9 Nash's Fish Restaurant
13 Darbar
24 Maitai
26 The Italian Job
28 Pizza Express
30 Brasserie Fourty Four

PUB
11 City Varieties
20 Observatory
21 Whitelocks
22 Duck & Drake

OTHER
1 Leeds University
3 Leeds Polytechnic
4 Leeds General Infirmary
5 Town & Country Club
6 Town Hall
7 City Art Gallery
8 Henry Moore Sculpture Centre
10 Thomas Cook & Waterstone's Bookshop
12 Victoria Quarter
14 Kirkgate Indoor Market
15 Central Bus Station
16 Coach Station
17 Post Office
18 Leeds City Railway Station & TIC
23 Watson & Cairns Bicycle Shop
25 Music Factory
27 Corn Exchange
31 Tetley's Brewery Wharf
32 Granary Wharf

Leeds

National Express tickets. American Express (☎ 424433) has an office on the 1st floor of Prince William House, 19 Queen St.

City Centre

The **City Art Gallery** (☎ 247 8248) is not particularly inspiring, but its Henry Moore Collection, to the right inside the front entrance, is. Henry Moore (1898-1986) attended the Leeds School of Art and is considered one of the greatest sculptors of the 20th century.

One of the highlights of a visit to Leeds is the magnificent **Victoria Quarter** arcades – a broad street roofed with a stained-glass canopy, paved with mosaics and decorated with marble. The shops are suitably upmarket and intimidating.

Almost more magnificent and full of life is the **Kirkgate Indoor Market**, once home of Marks, who later joined Spencer. There are enormous arcades decorated with superb wrought iron and ceramic tiles. The place is full of excellent fresh produce and cheap bakeries – ideal for stocking up for a picnic. The market is open from Monday to Saturday, closing at 1 pm on Wednesday. The adjoining open-air markets function on Tuesday, Friday and Saturday.

Leeds has woken up to the value of its river and canal frontage. **Granary Wharf** is behind the railway station and is reached through the Dark Arches. It's a cobbled area under vaulted arches at the meeting point of the canal and the river, with art and craft shops, free entertainment and markets selling local, hand-made goods on Friday, Saturday and Sunday. There's a good café with snacks around £2.

By contrast, **Tetley's** (☎ 243 1888) is Leeds' answer to Disneyland, a flashy £6 million development off Bowman Lane which features a brewery tour for adults only, brewery horses, restaurants and various displays that show pub culture through the ages, with actors milling around in costume. It's expensive at £6.95/3.95 and the brewery tour is £2 extra, so plan to endure a whole day there to get your money's worth. Phone ahead for tour times.

Headingley

For many, Leeds means Headingley and Headingley means cricket. The first cricket match was played at Headingley in 1890, and it is still a venue for Test matches and the home ground for the Yorkshire County Cricket Club.

To get to the Headingley Cricket Ground, take bus Nos 73, 74 or 75 from opposite the town hall or consider catching a train from Leeds City station to Burley Park station, a short walk from the ground. For bookings for matches (from £17 for a Test match) phone ☎ 278 7394.

Places to Stay

Hostels There are no youth hostels in Leeds; the nearest are in Haworth and York. The alternative is one of two YWCAs, which do accept both sexes aged 16 to 30. The most central *YWCA* (☎ 245 7840) is at 22 Lovell Park Hill; £9.45.

Camping The most convenient camping ground is the *Roundhay Caravan Site* (☎ 265 2354), Elmete Lane, Roundhay, which from April to December has pitches for tents and vans from £3 per person.

B&Bs & Hotels There's a group of reasonably priced B&Bs behind Leeds University on Woodsley Rd, but you pay for the convenience. The *Avalon Guest House* (☎ 243 2545), at 132 Woodsley Rd, actually has reasonable decor, and it's also well run and comfortable. Most rooms have private bathroom and singles/doubles are from £20/32. The *Moorlea Hotel* (☎ 243 2653), 146 Woodsley Rd, is also good, though a bit expensive at £28/40. The *Glengarth Hotel* (☎ 245 7940), 162 Woodsley Rd, and the *Manxdene Hotel* (☎ 243 2586) at No 154 are also worth considering.

There's another batch of B&Bs on Cardigan Rd, Headingley; once again, rates are around £22/32. Possibilities include the *Ashfield Hotel* (☎ 275 8847), 44 Cardigan Rd, with singles/doubles from £24/35; the Highfield Hotel (☎ 275 2193), 79 Cardigan Rd; the *Manor Hotel* (☎ 275 7991), 34 Cardigan

Rd; and the curiously named *Trafford & Budapest Hotel* (☎ 275 2034), 16 Cardigan Rd.

Perhaps the best hotel in town is *42 The Calls* (☎ 244 0099), 42 The Calls, a converted grain mill overlooking the river. It also has an excellent restaurant. Rooms start at £77/102; booking is advised.

Places to Eat

Strawberry Fields (☎ 243 1515), 159 Woodhouse Lane, opposite the BBC, caters to a university crowd with a wine bar and a range of cheap vegetarian dishes; you should walk away with plenty of change from £10.

Brasserie Forty Four (☎ 234 3232), 44 The Calls, is part of the hotel next door, housed in restored warehouses overlooking the River Aire. It's not cheap, but is regarded as one of the best restaurants in Leeds. There's an early dinner menu (leaving your table by 8.15 pm) at £18.95.

Facing the Corn Exchange in the surviving gatehouse of the White Cloth Hall, a branch of the reliable *Pizza Express* chain produces good-value pizza and pasta. The *Italian Job* (☎ 242 0185), 9 Bridge End, is a fairly basic place with a good range of Italian food, plus burgers; most pastas are around £5.

Bryans is a classic northern fish & chip restaurant/takeaway on Weetwood Lane, up the hill through Headingley, with takeaways from £2. *Nash's Fish Restaurant* (☎ 2457194), off Briggate, has good £5 specials.

You enter through a modest doorway but *Darbar* (☎ 246 0381), 16 Kirkgate, is a very large, very grand restaurant serving Indian and Tandoori specialities. The food is excellent and most curries are from £5.50. *Maitai* (☎ 431989, at the bottom of Briggate, serves Thai dishes for around £6 each.

Entertainment

There are lots of entertainment sheets; collect *Alive* and *Leeds Nights* from the TIC. Albion St and Boar Lane are inevitably at the centre of the action, especially from Thursday to Saturday, with lots of young people wandering from pub to pub to bar.

The *City Varieties* (☎ 243 0808) in Swan St is one of the last old music halls in Britain, and the *West Yorkshire Playhouse* at Quarry Mount (☎ 244 2111) has a good reputation.

In the centre of the fray, the *Observatory*, 40 Boar Lane, is a trendy, popular bar in a grand building. The *Adelphi Hotel*, Leeds Bridge, is an ornate Edwardian pub with wood panelling, tiles and engraved glass and attracts a wide range of customers.

On Kirkgate, the *Duck & Drake* has an enormous range of real ales, and free bands. Perhaps the most famous Leeds pub is *Whitelocks*, Turk's Head Yard, off Briggate, another classic Edwardian pub with outside tables and good traditional pub food.

Two popular clubs are The *Warehouse* (☎ 246 1033), 19 Somers St, and the gay *Primos 2* (☎ 244 6300).

For indie rock bands check out the *Town & Country Club* (☎ 280 0100), Cookridge St, and the *Duchess of York* (☎ 245 3929), Vicar Lane, which also has comedy and folk acts.

Getting There & Away

See under Getting Around at the start of the West Yorkshire section for information on West Yorkshire's Metro system. There's a Metro Travel Centre at the Central bus station (☎ 245 7676), open office hours from Monday to Saturday, which answers phone inquiries on all public transport.

Air The Leeds-Bradford airport has both domestic and international flights (including to Amsterdam, Paris and Dublin).

Bus The coach station is in Wellington St, not far from the TIC. National Express has services to most main centres in Britain. There are nine coaches daily to/from London (3¾ hours).

Local buses and those serving the countywide Metro area use the Central bus station; the main operator is Yorkshire Rider (☎ 242 9614).

Yorkshire Coastliner (☎ 244 8976) has a

useful service that links Leeds, York, Castle Howard, Goathland and Whitby (Nos 840 and 842). It also has services that link Leeds, York and Scarborough.

Train Leeds City station, once at the centre of the Midlands Railway, is large and busy. There are nine lines that are part of the area's Metro system, numerous national services, and the famous Leeds-Settle-Carlisle Line (see the Northern England chapter). There are hourly services to London's King's Cross that take as little as two hours.

Getting Around
Airport The Leeds-Bradford airport is eight miles north of the city via the A65. Bus No 37 operates hourly between the airport and Leeds City Square (next to the railway station). A taxi will cost around £15.

Bus City buses are based at the Central bus station; the service is extensive.

Taxi Taxi firms include Telecabs (☎ 263 0404) and Streamline (☎ 244 3322); £3 gets you to most places within a three-mile radius from the centre.

Bicycle Watson & Cairns (☎ 245 8081), 157 Lower Briggate, hires mountain bikes for a minimum two days (£20) – it's best to book in advance.

HAREWOOD HOUSE
Harewood is one of the most beautiful houses in Britain, but it is also very much on the stately homes circuit, and very popular. The building is great, the interiors are over the top and the surrounding park is glorious, but it's so perfect and so commercial that it's rather 'cold'.

Harewood has been the house of the Lascelles family since it was built between 1759 and 1772. No expense has been spared – Capability Brown was responsible for the grounds, Thomas Chippendale was responsible for the furniture, and Italy was raided to create an appropriate art collection

(including works by El Greco, Tintoretto, Titian, Bellini and many others).

In addition to the house, there's the Stables Gallery, the Bird Garden and a children's adventure playground. There's also a pleasant café in the stables with meals for around £5 and cheaper snacks. There are a number of pleasant walks, including along Harewood Lake and to Harewood Church. **Harewood Church** is no longer in use (the original village it served was moved when the house was constructed!), but it dates from the 15th century and has some fascinating tombs and monuments.

The property (☎ 0113-288 6331) is open from April to October, daily from 11 am to 4.30 pm; £6/4. It's seven miles north of Leeds on the A61 to Harrogate.

BRADFORD
• *pop 296,000* • ☎ *01274*
The centre of Bradford is nine miles to the west of Leeds, but the two cities are virtually continuous. Until WWII Bradford was the uncontested capital of the world's wool trade. Sadly, however, the industry collapsed and the city has had a grim struggle to survive. Since the 1960s over 60,000 Indians and Pakistanis have settled in the area and they have also helped restore life.

The TIC (☎ 753678) is in the excellent **National Museum of Photography, Film & Television**. Situated in the centre of town, with plenty of parking, the museum is interactive and, consequently, very entertaining. You can play with lots of the new video and graphics technology, become a TV news reader, or a cameraperson. The history of photography is covered in detail.

The museum includes one of only two IMAX cinema screens in Britain – a massive 64 feet wide and 52 feet high – with up to six screenings a day, but booking (☎ 727488) is advised. The museum is open Tuesday to Sunday from 10.30 am to 6 pm; free.

Other worthwhile sights include the **Colour Museum** (☎ 390955), 82 Grattan Rd, the home of the Society of Dyers and Colourists, which is much more interesting than you would expect; the **Industrial**

Museum (☎ 631756), Moorside Rd; and the **Undercliffe Cemetery**, between Undercliffe Lane and Otley Rd, which has the best collection of Victorian funerary art in Britain.

In a town that markets 'curry tours', the *Kashmir* (☎ 726513), 27 Morley St, is a long-standing favourite restaurant, with excellent curries for under £4. The *Mumtaz Paan House* (☎ 571861), 386 Great Horton Rd, is another classic Indian café.

There are frequent trains from Leeds to the centre of town. Yorkshire Rider (☎ 734833) has a regular Monday to Saturday bus service to/from Harrogate (1½ hours).

HAWORTH

• *pop 5000*   • ☎ *01535*

Haworth rivals Stratford-upon-Avon as the most important literary shrine in England – it's the small town that was home to the Brontë family. The surrounding countryside seems haunted both by the Brontë sisters and by their literary creations. Even without this connection, the old section of the village would still manage to draw tourists; the cobblestoned Main St running steeply down to Bridgehouse Beck (stream) from the parish church provides a quintessential Yorkshire view.

Patrick Brontë and his family moved to the Parsonage in 1820. His wife Maria died of cancer at 38; Maria and Elizabeth died as children; Branwell, Emily and Anne died of between the ages of 29 and 31; and Charlotte died at 38. Only Patrick survived to old age, dying in the Parsonage at the age of 84. The Parsonage Museum gives a fascinating, sometimes eerie, insight into their lives.

Orientation & Information

The development of Haworth parallels the development of the textile industry. The old village – with its cottage-based weavers and spinners – grew up along the ridge above the valley. In the 19th century the outworkers were replaced by factories.

The TIC (☎ 642329), 2-4 West Lane, is open daily from 9.30 am to 5.30 pm. It has an excellent supply of information about the Brontës and on a number of interesting possible walks.

Brontë Parsonage

The Parsonage, now housing a fascinating museum, is in a Georgian house overlooking the town cemetery. The original core of the house can be seen furnished and decorated as it would have been when the Brontës lived there. Quite a few of the furnishings are original and there are many personal possessions on display. In the museum section there's a considerable amount of material, including the fascinating miniature books the children wrote.

The Parsonage (☎ 642323) is open daily from April to September, 10 am to 5 pm (and other times); £3.80/2.80.

Keighley & Worth Valley Railway

The K&WV Railway (☎ 645214 for timetable information) is a favourite with film crews, as much for the six restored stations as for the classic steam engines.

Especially on summer weekends when traffic can get hectic in Haworth, it's worth parking at Keighley, catching the train to Haworth station, and then the connecting bus to the old village. Bus No 812 links the Brontë Parsonage with Haworth every half-hour between 11.15 am and 5.30 pm.

Trains operate on weekends throughout the year pretty much hourly, except in winter when they run in the afternoon only. They only run Monday to Friday from mid-June to August, and again there are only four afternoon trains. An all-day Rover is £6/3 and a full-line return is £4.80/2.40.

Walks

The TIC has information on a number of interesting walks in the surrounding area that take in sights associated with the Brontë family. These include possibilities that can be worked in around the K&WV Railway, the Brontë Way, which links Haworth with Bradford and Colne, and two routes to Hebden Bridge (see that section). Haworth is just to the east of the Pennine Way.

There's an excellent pack of information

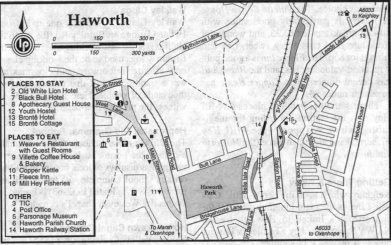

Haworth

```
0        150        300 m
0        150        300 yards
```

PLACES TO STAY
2 Old White Lion Hotel
7 Black Bull Hotel
8 Apothecary Guest House
12 Youth Hostel
13 Brontë Hotel
15 Brontë Cottage

PLACES TO EAT
1 Weaver's Restaurant
   with Guest Rooms
9 Villette Coffee House
   & Bakery
10 Copper Kettle
11 Fleece Inn
16 Mill Hey Fisheries

OTHER
3 TIC
4 Post Office
5 Parsonage Museum
6 Haworth Parish Church
14 Haworth Railway Station

---

describing the Brontë Way. One particularly interesting section is a fairly strenuous nine-mile walk from the Parsonage to Colne/Laneshawbridge via Top Withens (Wuthering Heights), Ponden Hall (Thrushcross Grange) and Wycoller Hall (Ferndean Manor). From Laneshawbridge you can catch a bus to Keighley, and from Keighley you can complete the loop by catching the K&WV Railway back to Haworth.

Places to Stay

Hostel The *Haworth Youth Hostel* (☎ 642234), Longlands Drive, Leeds Lane, is open from April to September daily, and more restricted times outside these months; £8.25/5.55.

B&Bs & Hotels There are a reasonable number of accommodation options; despite the fact that most visitors don't stay overnight it is worth booking ahead in summer.

Top billing goes to two places on West Lane, both of which also have restaurants that have been recommended. *Weavers Restaurant With Guest Rooms* (☎ 643822), and

the *Old White Lion Hotel* (☎ 642313), in an old coaching inn, both have very comfortable accommodation with B&B starting at around £34 per person.

The Brontë Hotel (☎ 644112), Leeds Lane, is not in the centre of Haworth, but it has a range of rooms from £20/36 for singles/doubles without bathroom to £28/42 with bathroom.

There are quite a number of interesting places to stay on Main St, which is the most atmospheric part of town. The *Black Bull Hotel* (☎ 642249) is famous for being Branwell Brontë's local. It has two doubles, with private bathroom, from £20 per person. Opposite the Black Bull, the *Apothecary Guest House* (☎ 643642), 86 Main St, is quite a large place with a range of rooms, most with bathroom, from £19.

There are also a number of simpler, but still decent places, including the *Brontë Cottage* (☎ 647012), 4 Park Top Row, Main St, with rooms from £17.50 per person.

Places to Eat

There are over a dozen places to eat along Main St and West Lane, so take a stroll and take your choice. The *Villette Coffee House & Bakery* is particularly good value with all-day breakfasts for £2.25, and wonderful Yorkshire curd tarts (very sweet, rich and filling) for 85p. The *Fleece Inn* is a good pub, with good-value lunches, and the *Black Bull* has decent dinners. The *Copper Kettle* has meals for under £3.

There's another batch of places on Mill Hey near the station, including the inevitable fish & chippery (the *Mill Hey Fisheries)* and an Indian place (the *Haworth Tandoori)*.

Getting There & Away

Keighley, which is on the Leeds-Settle-Car-lisle Line, is the main jumping-off point for Haworth; it's linked to Haworth by the K&WV Railway and by Keighley & District buses (☎ 603284). In summer, bus No 500 offers a service four times a day between Todmorden, Hebden Bridge, Haworth and Keighley (Wednesday and Sunday in winter).

HEBDEN BRIDGE

- *pop 4000*   • ☎ *01422*

The history of the immediate area actually begins at Heptonstall, half a mile to the north-east on the moorland ridge above the 'new' town. Heptonstall consists of typical stone weavers' cottages. When steam power arrived, mills were set up in the valley along the River Calder, and the Rochdale Canal was built to provide transport.

The mills have now closed and the town seems to huddle in the valley; you can feel the wild moors looming over your shoulder. Ted Hughes grew up near Hebden Bridge (Sylvia Plath is buried at Heptonstall) and has written many poems about the region.

Orientation & Information

There's a small one-way system in the centre of town; it's easy to get around on foot. The TIC (☎ 843831), 1 Bridge Gate, is open daily but hours vary. Information is available about walking across Hardcastle Crages, a nearby 400-acre area of woodland.

Walkley Clogs

Walkley Clogs (☎ 842061), one mile from Hebden Bridge on Burnley Rd (the A646 to Halifax), is the last working clog factory in Britain. Clogs used to be the working class' only affordable footware, and clog-making was a traditional craft that once employed thousands of people. Here it is possible to witness the process first-hand.

Heptonstall Old Grammar School

The Old Grammar School (☎ 843738), half a mile to the north-east in an old weavers' village, has displays of local history in a 17th-century school, complete with the old school furniture. Sylvia Plath (1932-63) is buried in the nearby Wesleyan chapel's cemetery.

Horse-drawn Canal Cruises

Calder Valley Cruising (☎ 845557), The Marina, New Rd, has a number of horse-drawn cruises along the Rochdale Canal, including a daily trip to Walkley Clogs for £5.95/3 return.

Places to Stay

Hostel The *Mankinholes Youth Hostel* (☎ 01706-812340), Todmorden, is four miles to the south-west of Hebden Bridge, to the south of the A646 to/from Rochdale, and half a mile from the Pennine Way. It's an ancient manor house in a typical Yorkshire village. Opening times are complicated; the nightly rate is £6.75/4.60. Todmorden is served by the regular train between Leeds and Manchester; the station is two miles from the hostel.

Camping There's the *Pennine Camp Site* at High Greenwood House (☎ 842287), Hepton-stall, which has 50 pitches suitable for tents or vans at £5, and *Jack Bridge Camp Site* (☎ 842795) at Colden, which is basically only suitable for hiking tents (£2 per person).

B&Bs & Hotels The *Hebden Lodge Hotel* (☎ 845272), New Rd, is a comfortable place with rooms for £37/47. *Redacre Mill* (☎ 885563), Redacre, Mytholmroyd, has two twins and three doubles with private bathroom in a canalside mill surrounded by gardens for £35.50.

The *Robin Hood Inn* (☎ 842593), Pecket Well, Keighley Rd, has four beautifully decorated rooms with nice views (from £18.50 per person), and the downstairs pub also serves good meals.

Royd Nell (☎ 845304), 35 Royd Terrace, is a friendly place three minutes from town; the bathroom is shared but the rate is only £13 per person. A similar place is *1 Primrose Terrace* (☎ 844747).

Places to Eat

There are a couple of options in the centre of town, including *Hebden's Bistro* (☎ 843745), Hanginroyd Lane, which has good pizzas for around £5. The local pubs are probably your best bet for good value – the *Robin Hood Inn* is a traditional country pub worth trying. The *Hebden Lodge Hotel*, New Rd, is open to nonresidents and serves high-quality food – a three-course meal is £18.

Getting There & Away

Hebden Bridge is within the Leeds Metro area. The rail service runs from Leeds and Bradford to Halifax, Hebden Bridge and Todmorden (for the youth hostel), then continues to Manchester's Victoria. Some services extend from York to Liverpool. There's also a regular rail service linking Halifax, Hebden Bridge and Blackpool. There are also buses, but these are less frequent than trains.

In summer, Keighley & District's bus No 500 offers a service four times a day between Todmorden, Hebden Bridge, Haworth and Keighley.

Sheffield & Around

Before the 1996 local government reforms, Sheffield was part of West Yorkshire, a county that has now ceased to exist. In its place are four separate authorities – Sheffield, Barnsley, Doncaster and Rotherham. This area takes in the eastern fringe of the Peak District but it's essentially one big city:

Sheffield and its satellites: Barnsley, Rotherham and Doncaster.

Conisbrough Castle, Monk Bretton Priory and Roche Abbey are three EH sites in the area, all in ruins.

SHEFFIELD
* pop 475,000 • ☎ 0114

Five hundred years ago Sheffield was already renowned for its cutlery production and the name Sheffield steel still has a familiar ring to it. Although the industry employs far fewer people than in the past, they're now turning out more knives and forks than ever before.

In the Victorian era, Sheffield was synonymous with industrial exploitation at its worst. Many buildings were damaged in WWII and postwar rebuilding added little to be admired. Despite this it's a lively place, in part due to its large student population, and is the fourth-largest city in England. Sheffield makes a convenient jumping-off point for the Peak District National Park.

Orientation & Information

The main TIC (☎ 273 4671) is in Union St, about 400 yards west of the city centre. There's a second office (☎ 279 5901) at the Sheaf St railway station, which is just east of the centre. Both offices are open Monday to Friday, 9.30 am to 5.15 pm, Saturday to 4.15 pm. The Pond St bus station is a couple of hundred yards north of the railway station.

Industrial Heritage

The **City Museum** (☎ 276 8588), one mile west of the centre in Weston Park, has a large local archaeology collection and lots of cutlery. It's closed on Monday; entry is free. One mile north of the centre on Kelham Island, the **Sheffield Industrial Museum** (☎ 272 2106) covers not just cutlery but the city's wider industrial heritage. Entry is £2.50/1.25; it's closed Friday and Saturday.

Abbeydale Industrial Hamlet (☎ 236 7731), four miles south-west on the A621, features a steel furnace and a water-powered forge. It's closed on Monday; entry is £2.50/1.25.

Art Galleries

Sheffield's most interesting gallery is the **Ruskin Gallery** (☎ 273 5299) at 101 Norfolk St, which houses a collection established by the Victorian critic and Gothic-revivalist John Ruskin in an attempt to meld art and industry. There's also an exhibition of crafts. It's open Monday to Saturday, 10 am to 5 pm; entry is free.

The nearby **Graves Art Gallery** (☎ 273 5158) displays contemporary British art atop the City Library on Surrey St. It's open the same hours as the Ruskin Gallery and is also free. The **Mappin Art Gallery** (☎ 272 6281) concentrates on Victorian art and is next to the university in Weston Park. It's closed on Monday; entry is free.

Places to Stay & Eat

The big and slightly spartan *YMCA* (☎ 268 4807) at 20 Victoria Rd caters to both sexes with B&B at £14/23. It's a fair walk to the west of the centre. B&Bs are also concentrated on this side of town: the TICs have lists.

Eccleshall Rd and Division St are good places to search for food, including the inevitable selection of Indian restaurants. *Blue Moon Café* (☎ 276 3443), Norfolk Row, is a nice little vegetarian place. *Le Neptune* (☎ 279 6677), 141 West St, is an excellent French restaurant; main courses range from £7 to £16. The *Fat Cat*, near the Industrial Museum, is a good pub that brews its own beer. Popular music venues include the *Capital* (☎ 276 3523), 14 Matilda St, and the *Leadmill* (☎ 275 4500) at 6-7 Leadmill Rd.

Getting There & Away

Sheffield is 160 miles from London, just off the M1. There are frequent InterCity trains from London's St Pancras via Leicester and Nottingham or Derby. National Express (☎ 0990-808080) has services linking Sheffield to London as well as to other major centres in the north.

Located on the east side of the Peak District, Sheffield is a jumping-off point for this region. The railway line which cuts through the northern part of the Peak District via Edale runs between Sheffield in the east and New Mills and Manchester in the west. The X23 bus service links Sheffield with Bakewell in the centre of the Peak District and Buxton on its western periphery.

Nottinghamshire

There's not much left of Sherwood Forest although Robin Hood, his merry men and the Sheriff of Nottingham have been roped into a variety of amusement parks. Nevertheless, the city of Nottingham itself is a surprisingly livable Midlands city and there are several other interesting attractions in the county.

NOTTINGHAM

- *pop 275,000* • ☎ *0115*

At first glance Nottingham might be another of those Midlands disaster areas, a confusing tangle of ring roads around a drab city centre with memories of Robin Hood long forgotten. Surprisingly, it can be a bright, active and interesting place, once you delve beneath the surface.

The city developed in Saxon times with the less than charming name of Snotingham but its modern peak came with the Victorian lace industry, which transformed the central city and still leaves its mark today. Nottingham was a centre for the Luddite riots of 1811-6. Lace-making went into decline during the 1890s and was finally killed by WWI, although some small-scale lace production continues. The city remains an industrial centre and is the home of Raleigh bicycles.

Orientation & Information

Like other Midlands cities, Nottingham is chopped about and confused by an inner ring road. The railway station is south of the canal on the southern edge of the city centre. There are two bus stations: the Victoria bus station is hidden away behind the Victoria Shopping Centre, just north of the city centre, while the Broad Marsh bus station is behind the Broad Marsh Shopping Centre to the south.

The TIC (☎ 947 0661) is in the Council House; it makes free accommodation bookings. It's open Monday to Friday, 8.30 am to 5 pm, on Saturday, 9 am to 5 pm, and in summer, Sunday from 10 am to 4 pm. Brights Laundrette is at 150 Mansfield Rd, near the Huntingdon St junction.

Nottingham is noted for its peculiar Midlands dialect. If someone greets you with a hearty 'ayupmeduck', a suitable response is 'hello'.

Nottingham Castle
Nottingham Castle was demolished after the Civil War and replaced with a mansion in 1674, which in turn was converted into a museum in 1875. The **Castle Museum** (☎ 948 3504) features the interesting story of Nottingham and includes an art gallery. The alabaster carvings for which Nottingham was noted between 1350 and 1550 are of particular interest. It's open daily, 10 am to 5 pm; £1/50p. Outside the castle is a statue of Robin Hood.

Wollaton Hall & Industrial Museum
Built in 1588 by Sir Francis Willoughby, land and coal mine owner, Wollaton Hall (☎ 928 1333) is a fine example of Tudor architecture at its most extravagant. Robert Smythson, its architect, had earlier built the equally avant-garde Longleat. Wollaton Hall now houses the **Nottingham Natural History Museum**.

The Industrial Museum (☎ 928 4602), adjacent to Wollaton Hall, has lace-making equipment, Raleigh bicycles, a gigantic 1858 beam engine, and oddities like a locally invented 1963 video recorder which never got off the ground. Opening hours for both museums are April to September, Monday to Saturday, 10 am to 7 pm, and Sunday, 1 to 5 pm. Winter hours are shorter. Combined entry is £1/50p. Wollaton Hall is on the western edge of the city, 2½ miles from the centre; get there on a No 11B bus.

Other Things to See
The **Brewhouse Yard Museum** (☎ 948 3504) is virtually below the castle, housed in five 17th-century cottages on Castle Boulevard. The museum re-creates everyday life in Nottingham over recent centuries with particularly good displays of traditional shops. Entry to the Castle Museum includes this museum. An underground passageway known as Mortimer's Hole leads from the castle to the Brewhouse Yard and the adjacent Trip to Jerusalem pub. It's said that Roger Mortimer, who arranged the murder of Edward II at Berkeley Castle, was captured by Edward III's supporters who entered via this passage.

The **Museum of Costume & Textiles** (☎ 948 3504), on Castle Gate, is more interesting than it sounds. There are displays of costumes from 1790 to the mid-20th century arranged in period rooms, as well as tapestries and lace. Across from the castle is the small **Lace Centre** (☎ 941 3539) in Severn's Building on Castle Rd.

In the impressive Shire Hall building on High Pavement, the **Galleries of Justice** (☎ 952 0555) has restored the Victorian courts and opened a new interactive attraction, Condemned. Visitors are issued with a criminal identity, tried and given a sentence – flogging, transportation or hanging. It's open daily, 10 am to 5 pm; entry is £3.95/2.95. Next door, there's more lace at the **Lace Hall**.

The **Canal Museum** (☎ 959 8835) on Canal St is open Wednesday to Sunday, 10 am to noon and 1 to 5 pm; admission is free. Kids might be amused by **Tales of Robin Hood** (☎ 948 3284) at 30-38 Maid Marian Way. East of the centre at 14 Notintone Place, Sneinton, the **William Booth Memorial Complex** (☎ 950 3927) is dedicated to the founder of the Salvation Army. Sneinton also has **Green's Mill** (☎ 950 3635), a fully functioning 19th-century windmill on Windmill Lane.

Places to Stay
The cheapest accommodation is at the *Igloo Tourist Hostel* (☎ 947 5250) at 110 Mansfield Rd, a short walk north from the Victoria bus station. A bunk bed in a dorm is £8;

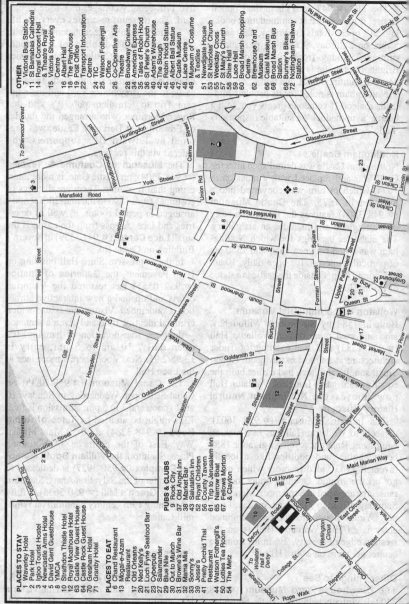

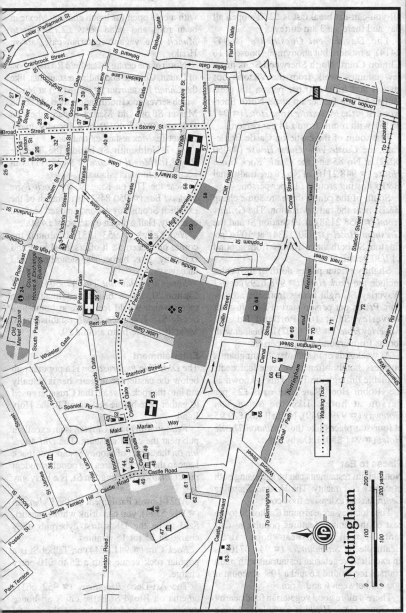

Nottingham

200 m
200 yards
0   100   200
0   100   200

Walking Tour

all-you-can-eat breakfast is £2. It's open all day and there's a 3 am curfew.

The *David Gent Guesthouse* (☎ 947 2414), a modern but anonymous house at 16 Clinton Court, North Sherwood St, is just a few minutes' walk from the Victoria bus station and from £10 per person it's great value. A little further up at 68 North Sherwood St is the *Newcastle Arms Hotel* (☎ 947 4616), with rooms from £14 per person.

Just south of the castle on Castle Boulevard, the *Castle View Guest House* (☎ 950 0022) at No 85 and the *Castle Rock Guest House* (☎ 948 2116) at No 79 are traditional B&Bs costing around £15 per person.

South of the centre there are some cheap B&Bs near the railway station. The *Granby Hotel* (☎ 958 2158) at 19 Station St and the *Gresham Hotel* (☎ 950 1234) at 109 Carrington St both have rooms from around £17/30 per night.

Slightly pricier places north of the centre include the *Park Hotel* (☎ 978 6299) at 5-7 Waverley St, right across from the arboretum. Prices per person start at £25. Just off Waverley St at 107 Portland Rd, the *Waverley Hotel* (☎ 978 6707) is cheaper with rooms from around £20 per person.

At weekends or in summer, Nottingham's business hotels often have excellent deals available through the TIC. This is known as the 'Robin Hood Rate' and costs £25 per person at hotels like the *Nottingham Gateway* (☎ 979 4949), Nuthall Rd; £29.95 at four-star places like the *Strathdon Thistle Hotel* (☎ 941 8501), Derby Rd.

Places to Eat

Nottingham restaurants can be surprising both in variety and quality. The *Victoria Shopping Centre* has an extensive food court.

The Hockley area, around Carlton St to the east of the centre, features popular restaurants as well as off-beat shops. At 23 Heathcote St, *Salamander* (☎ 941 0710) is an excellent vegetarian restaurant with main courses for around £6 and a 10% discount if you eat between 6 and 7 pm.

There's more good vegetarian food nearby on Goose Gate. *Hiziki* is a wholefood store with a café open for lunch and tea. Mexican bean rolls and salad costs £2.75. *Out to Munch* is a vegan/vegetarian café, above Hiziki.

North of the centre, Mansfield Rd has a host of Italian, Chinese and Indian restaurants, like the *Chand Restaurant* (☎ 947 4103) at No 26 which serves good north Indian food. At 26-28 Market St off Old Market Square, the *Old Orleans* (☎ 947 4012) is a friendly mass-market TexMex restaurant and bar.

At 7 Goldsmith St beside the Theatre Royal, the *Mogal-e-Azam* (☎ 947 2911) is an acclaimed Indian restaurant.

Near the TIC on King St, the *Loch Fyne Seafood Bar* (☎ 950 8481) is a branch of the excellent Scottish oyster and smoked seafood company. Half a dozen oysters cost £4.90.

Ned Kelly's (☎ 953 1531) is around the corner on Queen St. It offers good beer and company, plus barbecues, steamboats and takeaways.

Sonny's Restaurant (☎ 947 3041) at 3 Carlton St, has a bright and imaginative menu which would feel quite at home in a trendy San Francisco or LA establishment. Main dishes are from around £9.

Entertainment

The *Olde Trip to Jerusalem* is a popular pub below the castle; the upstairs bar is actually cut into the rock. It's said that Crusaders used to gather here before setting off to the Holy Land.

Fellows Morton & Clayton is an excellent pub near the canal museum. The *Old Angel Inn* on the corner of Stoney St and Woolpack Lane in the Hockley area is a popular student pub. *Gatsby's*, Huntingdon St, is a busy gay bar.

At 21 Lower Parliament St, the *Cyberpub* (☎ 947 5394), you can drink while you surf. Said to be the UK's first cyberpub, they charge £1.25 for 15 minutes.

Rock City (☎ 941 2544) on Talbot St is a popular rock venue with a £5 to £10 entry charge.

The Art-Deco *Broadway* (☎ 952 6611) cinema on Broad St is the city's art-house movie centre and the site for the annual

'Shots in the Dark' thriller movie festival. Theatrical venues include the *Nottingham Playhouse* (☎ 941 9419) on Wellington Circus and the adjacent *Albert Hall*, or the *Co-operative Arts Theatre* (☎ 947 6096) on George St. The *Royal Concert Hall* and *Theatre Royal* share a booking office (☎ 948 2626) and an imposing building close to the centre.

Getting There & Away
Nottingham is 135 miles from London, around 75 from Manchester and Leeds, and 50 from Birmingham.

Bus Sherwood Forester buses (☎ 924 0000) operate to tourist attractions all over Nottinghamshire in the summer. An unlimited travel Ranger Ticket costs £3 (£6 for a family) and gives reduced-price access to some attractions. National Express buses operate from the Victoria bus station.

Rainbow Route services by Trent & Barton Buses (☎ 01773-712265) operate to Derby and continue through the Peak District to Manchester (TransPeak). They operate from the Victoria bus station and their one-day Explorer Ticket costs £5.35; one child goes free.

Train Nottingham is not on the main direct railway routes through the Midlands but there are regular services to London's St Pancras taking 1¾ hours.

Getting Around
The Transport Information Centre (☎ 950 3665) on King St, just north of Old Market Square, has information on local bus services. A Day Rider ticket gives you unlimited travel for one day for £2. Bunney's Bikes (☎ 947 2713) at 97 Carrington St near the railway station has bicycles from £5 to £8.50 per day.

AROUND NOTTINGHAM
Newstead Abbey
Converted into a home after the dissolution of the monasteries in 1539, Newstead Abbey (☎ 01623-793557) is chiefly notable for being the residence of Lord Byron (1788-1824) but the Byronic connections are sparse.

The façade of the ruined priory church is adjacent to the house, which was pretty ruined itself in Byron's day. It was already in bad shape when Byron inherited the house from his great-uncle and the continuing decline of the family fortune forced him to sell it in 1817. The poet used to hold shooting sessions indoors and a friend commented that a visit was so pleasant it 'made one forget that one was domiciled in the wing of an extensive ruin'.

The house is open April to September, daily, noon to 6 pm; the garden is open year-round. Entry to house and garden is £3.50/1. The house is 11 miles north of Nottingham, off the A60. The Sherwood Forester bus runs right there in summer; otherwise take bus No 63 and walk one mile from the abbey gates.

DH Lawrence Birthplace Museum
The birthplace (☎ 01773-763312) of Nottingham's controversially famous author DH Lawrence (1885-1930) is in Eastwood, about 10 miles north-west of the city. The house at 8A Victoria St where he was born is now a museum, open April to October, daily, 10 am to 5 pm, and the rest of the year to 4 pm; £1.50/75p.

Sherwood Forest
Only tiny fragments of Robin Hood's mighty forest remain. Nearly 300 years ago, Daniel Defoe commented that if Robin Hood was still around there was scarcely enough forest left to conceal him for a week. Today a pack of school children would have him tracked down in half an hour.

A quarter of a million visitors go to the 450-acre Sherwood Forest Country Park every year; it's one of the few bits of forest left. At least the hokey Sherwood Forest Visitor Centre (☎ 01623-824490) keeps some of the crowds out of the real woods where the rather propped up Major Oak was probably just a Minor Acorn when Robin was around.

The park is 20 miles north of Nottingham, just north of the village of Edinstowe. Sherwood Forester buses run to the park from Nottingham.

WORKSOP
- *pop 37,000* • ☎ *01909*

The TIC (☎ 501148) is in the Public Library on Memorial Ave. It has leaflets on cycle tours in the **Dukeries**, the parklands surrounding this industrial town.

The **Worksop Museum** (☎ 501148) on Memorial Ave recounts the history of the Pilgrim Fathers who came from this part of Nottinghamshire and sailed the *Mayflower* to the New World.

Mr Straw's House (☎ 482380) at 7 Blyth Grove is a very unusual NT property. When their parents died in the 1930s the Straw brothers, William and Walter, simply kept everything in the house exactly as it was. Nothing changed for the next half-century. The house is open April to October, Tuesday to Saturday, 1 to 5.30 pm, but you must phone to book; £2.70/1.30.

Lincolnshire

Sneering southerners who've never visited tend to think of Lincolnshire as flat and boring. The fact that it has few hills of any significance means that it's certainly easy cycling and walking country, but it has other attractions that make a visit worthwhile. Lincoln Cathedral is one of the most spectacular in Britain and the county has a wealth of beautiful parish churches, built on the proceeds of the flourishing wool trade.

The unspoiled nature of some of the Lincolnshire towns – cobbled streets, solid stone-built houses with red-tiled roofs – attracts film companies as well as tourists. Stamford was the setting for BBC TV's dramatisation of George Eliot's *Middlemarch*.

The Lincolnshire Wolds, to the north and east of Lincoln, are comprised of low rolling hills and small market towns. In the south-east of the county are the Lincolnshire Fens, fertile agricultural land reclaimed from the sea.

GETTING AROUND
Regional transport is poor but the main routes are well enough served. Phone ☎ 01522-553135 for information on buses and trains.

The Viking Way is a 140-mile waymarked trail that runs from the Humber Bridge, through the Lincolnshire Wolds, to Oakham in Leicestershire.

Renting a bike in Lincoln, or bringing one with you, is an excellent idea. TICs stock sets of *Lincolnshire Cycle Trails* (£3.90).

LINCOLN
- *pop 81,500* • ☎ *01522*

Since it's not on a direct tourist route, many people bypass Lincoln, missing a magnificent 900-year-old cathedral (the third-largest in Britain) and an interesting city with a compact medieval centre of narrow winding streets. The suburbs, however, are unattractive and depressed, but perhaps because Lincoln escapes the hordes of visitors that places like York attract, the people are particularly friendly.

History
For the last 2000 years, most of Britain's invaders have recognised the potential of this site and made their mark. Lincoln's hill was of immense strategic importance, giving views for miles across the surrounding plain. Communications were found to be excellent – below it is the River Witham, navigable to the sea.

The Romans established a garrison and a town they called Lindum. In 96 AD it was given the status of a colonia, a chartered town – Lindum Colonia, hence Lincoln. Gracious public buildings were constructed and it became a popular place for old soldiers past their prime to spend their twilight years.

In the 5th century, when the Romans sensibly gave up on Britain as both colony and retirement home, Lincoln fell first to raiding bands of Anglo-Saxons, then to the Vikings. Next came the Normans, starting work on the castle in 1068 and the cathedral in 1072.

In the 12th century the wool trade developed and wealthy merchants established themselves. The city was famous for the cloth known as Lincoln green, said to have been worn by Robin Hood. Many of the wealthiest merchants were Jews, but following the murder of a nine-year-old boy in 1255 for which one of their number was accused, they were mercilessly persecuted and many were driven out.

During the Civil War the city passed from Royalist to Parliamentarian and back again, but it began to prosper as an agricultural centre in the 18th century. In the following century, after the arrival of the railway, Lincoln's engineering industry was established. Heavy machinery produced here included the world's first tank, which saw action in WWI.

Orientation & Information

The cathedral sits on top of the hill in the centre of the old part of the city, with the

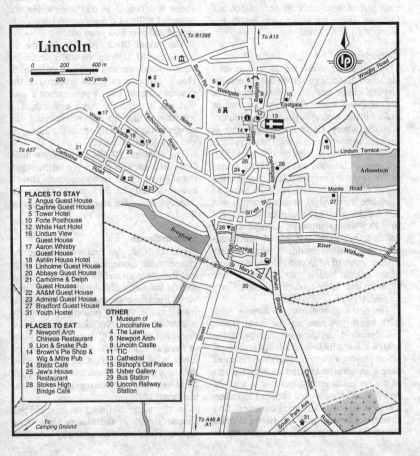

Lincoln

PLACES TO STAY
2 Angus Guest House
3 Carline Guest House
5 Tower Hotel
10 Forte Posthouse
12 White Hart Hotel
16 Lindum View
    Guest House
17 Aaron Whisby
    Guest House
18 Ashlin House Hotel
19 Linholme Guest House
20 Abbaye Guest House
21 Carholme & Delph
    Guest Houses
22 AA&M Guest House
23 Admiral Guest House
27 Bradford Guest House
31 Youth Hostel

PLACES TO EAT
7 Newport Arch
   Chinese Restaurant
9 Lion & Snake Pub
14 Brown's Pie Shop &
   Wig & Mitre Pub
24 Stadz Café
25 Jew's House
   Restaurant
28 Stokes High
   Bridge Café

OTHER
1 Museum of
   Lincolnshire Life
4 The Lawn
6 Newport Arch
8 Lincoln Castle
11 TIC
13 Cathedral
15 Bishop's Old Palace
26 Usher Gallery
29 Bus Station
30 Lincoln Railway
   Station

castle and most of the other things to see conveniently nearby. A 15-minute walk down from the cathedral lies the new town, and the bus and railway stations. These two parts of Lincoln are connected by the appropriately named Steep Hill. This road, and the High St, are pedestrianised.

The TIC (☎ 529828) is in the old black and white building at 9 Castle Hill. It's open Monday to Thursday daily from 9 am to 5.30 pm, and until 5 pm on Friday and at weekends.

Guided walking tours (£2/1) from the TIC take place daily in summer at 11 am and 2 pm, and at weekends in September and October. There are also Guide Friday bus tours (☎ 01789-294466).

Cathedral

This superb cathedral is the county's greatest attraction. Its three great towers dominate the city and can be seen from miles around. The central tower stands 271 feet high, which makes it the second-highest in the country after Salisbury Cathedral. While this is impressive enough, imagine it twice as high, which it was until toppled by a storm in 1547.

Lincoln Cathedral was built on the orders of William the Conqueror, and construction began in 1072. It took only 20 years to complete the original building, which was 325 feet long with two western towers, but in 1185 an earthquake caused severe damage. Only the west front of the old cathedral survived. Rebuilding began under Bishop Hugh of Avalon (St Hugh) and most of the current building dates from the late 12th to late 13th centuries, in the Early English style.

The entrance is below the famous mid-12th century frieze on the **west front**. Unfortunately, the frieze is currently hidden behind the scaffolding of a long-term restoration project. Emerging into the **nave** most people are surprised to find a substantial part of the cathedral empty, but this is actually how it would have looked back in 1250 when it was completed. Medieval cathedrals and churches, like mosques and Hindu temples today, did not have pews. This open area is now used for concerts and plays; services take place in St Hugh's choir. The stained glass in the nave is mostly Victorian, but the **Belgian marble font** dates back to the 11th century.

There are interesting stained-glass windows at each end of the transepts. The **Dean's Eye** contains glass that has been here since the 13th century; the glass in the **Bishop's Eye** dates from the 14th century. High above in the central tower, Great Tom is a 600-lb bell that still sounds the hours.

St Hugh's Choir was the first section of the original church to be rebuilt. The vaulting above is arranged at odd angles, but the canopied stalls of the choir are beautifully carved and over 600 years old.

The **Angel Choir**, named after the 28 angels carved high up the walls under the highest windows, was built as a shrine to St Hugh. Modern pilgrims search for the famous **Lincoln Imp**, a stonemason's joke that has become the city's emblem. The legend goes that this malevolent being was caught trying to chat up one of the 28 angels and was turned to stone.

The cathedral (☎ 544544) is open daily from 7.15 am to 6 pm (5 pm on Sunday); donation of £2.50 recommended. There's evensong daily at 5.15 pm (3.45 pm on Sunday), and sung matins at 11.15 am on Sunday.

Lincoln Castle

Begun in 1068, just four years before the cathedral, the castle was built over the original Roman town and incorporates some of the old Roman walls. As well as the usual views from the battlements that one expects from a castle, the old prison is particularly interesting. Public executions used to draw crowds of up to 20,000 people, taking place in front of Cobb Hall, a horseshoe-shaped tower in the north-east corner that served as the city's prison for centuries. The red-brick building on the east side replaced it and was used until 1878.

In the same building as the chapel, Lincoln's copy of the Magna Carta is on display. This document, signed by King John in 1215 to establish the rights of his people, is the basis for the laws and freedoms not only of this country but of many others, including the USA. Clauses 39 and 40 state that no free person will be imprisoned or punished without judgment by the law of the land, and that justice may not be sold, denied or delayed.

Lincoln Castle (☎ 511068) is open daily until 5.30 pm in summer, and until 4 pm in winter; £2/1.20.

Walking Tour

After looking round the cathedral and the castle, leave by the castle's west exit. Across the road is **The Lawn**, a former lunatic asylum that now houses a concert hall and several exhibition areas. The **Sir Joseph Banks Conservatory**, in this complex, is a tropical glasshouse containing descendants of some of the plants brought back by this Lincoln explorer who accompanied Captain Cook to Australia. The **National Cycle Museum** (☎ 545091), also here, has over 100 pushbikes, which makes it the largest collection in the country. There's everything from 1820s boneshakers to mountain bikes.

A short walk up Burton Rd is the **Museum of Lincolnshire Life** (☎ 528448). It's a fairly interesting museum of local social history – everything from an Edwardian nursery display to a WWI tank built here. It's open daily from 10 am to 5.30 pm; £1.20/ 60p.

Return to Westgate and continue east to Bailgate. Turn left to see the **Newport Arch**. Built by the Romans, this is the oldest arch in Britain that still has traffic passing through it. Walk back along Bailgate and continue past the TIC down **Steep Hill**. There are several shops to tempt the tourist, including second-hand bookshops, teashops and even a hand-made chocolate shop. As well as the black and white Tudor buildings on Steep Hill, **Jew's House** is of particular interest, being one of the best examples of 12th-century domestic architecture in Britain. It's now an upmarket restaurant (see Places to Eat).

Located one block east of Jew's House is **Usher Gallery**, the city's art gallery. There's a large watch collection, watercolours by Peter de Wint and temporary exhibitions. It's open daily (afternoon only on Sunday); 80p/40p.

Places to Stay

Hostel *Lincoln Youth Hostel* (☎ 522076), 77 South Park Ave, provides excellent budget accommodation at £8.25/5.55. It's open daily in July and August; daily except Sunday in April and June; daily except Sunday and Monday in September, October and March; and at weekends in November.

Camping *Hartsholme Country Park* (☎ 686264), Skellingthorpe Rd, is about two miles south-west of the railway station. They charge £2.50 for a small tent and two people.

B&Bs & Hotels About 10 to 15 minutes' walk from the cathedral, there are two B&B areas – around West Parade and Carholme Rd leading west to the A57, and in the north-west around the intersection of Yarborough Rd and Carline Rd. In the south on South Park Ave and Newark Rd there's another collection of B&Bs, but it's a long walk to the cathedral.

On Yarborough Rd there's *Alisa Guest House* (☎ 534961) at No 161 with B&B from £14. More upmarket is *Carline* (☎ 530422), 1 Carline Rd. Most of the rooms have attached bath and the cost is from £20/32 for a single/double. They're vehemently non-smoking and promise eggs from their own hens for breakfast.

There's a good group of B&Bs on West Parade, west of the modern centre of Lincoln. *Linholme Guest House* (☎ 522930), at No 116, is also small with two twins and a double at £16 per person. It's a pleasant place to stay and most rooms have private bathroom.

Parallel to and just south of West Parade is Carholme Rd, with numerous B&Bs. *Carholme Guest House* (☎ 531059) at No 175, and *Delph Guest House* (☎ 529578) at No 177 are large B&Bs charging £14 or £15 per person. The best value place is probably the *Admiral Guest House* (☎ 544467), just off

Carholme Rd on Nelson St. There are nine rooms from £14 per person.

Right in the centre at 28 Burton Rd, the *Old Bakery* (☎ 576057) has a few rooms from £19/35. Conveniently located east of the cathedral at 3 Upper Lindum St, *Lindum View Guest House* (☎ 548894) has rooms, most with attached bathroom, at £25/38. South, at 67 Monks Rd, *Bradford Guest House* (☎ 523947) is good value at £16/28. Some rooms have showers attached.

Most hotels in the very centre of the old town are expensive. There's the *Tower Hotel* (☎ 529999), at 38 Westgate, and a *Forte Posthouse* (☎ 520341) right by the cathedral on Eastgate. Lincoln's top hotel is the *White Hart* (☎ 526222), on Bailgate and also by the cathedral. It's a luxurious place with prices to match – £80/100.

Places to Eat

As one might expect in a city of this size, there's a reasonable range of places to eat, some of them particularly good value. There's a good *bakery* on the corner of Westgate and Bailgate. At the cathedral there's a *coffee shop* just off the cloisters.

The *Lion & Snake Hotel* (☎ 523770) was founded in 1640, which makes it Lincoln's oldest pub. Situated on the Bailgate, it's probably better known for its real ale and good-value home-made bar food. *Newport Arch Chinese Restaurant* is north along Bailgate, beside the old Roman arch.

Brown's Pie Shop (☎ 527330), 33 Steep Hill, is close to the cathedral and popular with tourists. It's nonetheless worth eating here since pies, pork pies in particular, are a Lincolnshire speciality. A two-course meal of soup and a pork pie will cost £5. They have a great range of other pies – turkey and smoked bacon is good – but offer alternatives; grilled trout, for example.

The *Wig & Mitre* (☎ 535190), 29 Steep Hill, is near Brown's Pie Shop. It's a pub with a restaurant, open daily.

Stadz Café (☎ 512323) dominates the north end of the High St, and it's probably the coolest place to hang out in Lincoln. They also serve pub food; main dishes are around £3.95. There's live music occasionally, sometimes on Tuesday and Thursday.

Stokes High Bridge Café (☎ 513825), 207 High St, is popular with tourists since it's in a 16th-century timbered building right on the bridge over the River Witham. You can get lunches and teas. It's open Monday to Saturday from 9 am to 5 pm.

Lincoln's top restaurant is the *Jew's House* (☎ 524851), occupying a 12th-century building that's an attraction in its own right. A three-course set dinner costs £19.95; set lunches are £11.95.

Getting There & Away

See the fares tables in the Getting Around chapter. Lincoln is 132 miles from London, 85 from Cambridge and 75 from York. For Lincolnshire bus and rail information phone ☎ 553135.

Bus National Express (☎ 0990-808080) operates a daily direct service between Lincoln and London (five hours), via Stamford. There are also direct services to Birmingham, Bristol and Glasgow. For Cambridge you must change at Peterborough.

The main local bus company is Lincolnshire Roadcar (☎ 522255). It runs hourly buses between Lincoln and Grantham (1¼ hours, £2.23), Monday to Saturday. Only National Express serves Stamford – and you need to book in advance. From Lincoln to Boston there are buses only on Wednesday and Saturday, run by Enterprise (☎ 722705).

Train There's no direct rail service between Lincoln and London; you must change at Newark or Peterborough on the main London to Edinburgh line. You don't, however, usually have to wait long for a connection. London to Newark takes 1¼ hours, Newark to Lincoln takes half an hour, and there are frequent departures. For York or Edinburgh, a further change is usually necessary at Doncaster. For Cambridge change at Peterborough.

Getting Around
Bus The city bus service is efficient. From the bus and railway stations bus No 51 runs past the youth hostel, and Nos 7 and 8 link the cathedral area with the lower town. Fares are around 60p.

Taxi Newland Taxis (☎ 520400) operates a 24-hour service.

Bicycle You can rent everything from a three-speed to an £800 mountain bike from F&J Cycles (☎ 545311), 41 Hungate, but 21 speeds are hardly an essential requirement for cycling in this flat county. Rent a three-speed from £6 per day or £15 per week.

GRANTHAM
- *pop 31,000* • ☎ *01476*

This pleasant red-brick town has an interesting parish church, **St Wulfram's**, with a 282-foot-high spire, the sixth-highest in England. It dates from the late 13th century. Sir Isaac Newton lived in Grantham, and there's a **monument** to him in front of the Guildhall. The town's **museum**, St Peter's Hill, has sections devoted both to him and to Margaret Thatcher who was born in Grantham. Her father's famous corner shop was at 2 North Parade.

Three miles north-east of Grantham on the A607 is **Belton House** (☎ 66116; NT), one of the finest examples of Restoration country house architecture. Built in 1688 for Sir John Brownlow, the house is known for its ornate plasterwork ceilings and wood carvings attributed to Grinling Gibbons. Set in a 1000-acre park, it's open April to October, Wednesday to Sunday, 1 to 5.30 pm; £4.50/2.20. Bus Nos 601 and 609 pass this way.

The TIC (☎ 66444) is by the Guildhall on Avenue Rd. It's open Monday to Saturday, 9.30 am to 5 pm.

Places to Stay & Eat
Grantham was formerly a main stop on the stagecoach route north from London and many pubs and inns still offer cheap accommodation. Try the *Nag's Head* (☎ 63157) on Wharf Rd, or the *Black Dog* (☎ 66041) on Watergate. Both do B&B from around £13 per person.

The *Beehive* (☎ 67794) on Castlegate is best known for its pub sign – a real beehive full of live bees! The bees have been here since 1830, which makes them one of the oldest populations of bees in the world. Good, cheap pub grub is available, and the bees stay away from the customers.

Getting There & Away
Grantham is 25 miles south of Lincoln. Lincolnshire Roadcar runs buses every hour between these two towns, Monday to Saturday. Travelling by train you'll need to change at Newark.

STAMFORD
- *pop 16,000* • ☎ *01780*

This beautiful town of stone buildings and cobbled streets was made a conservation area in 1967, and is one of the finest stone towns in the country. The BBC TV serialisation of George Eliot's *Middlemarch* was filmed here and the tourists still come to see Dr Lydgate's house and sample the Middlemarch fudge.

The TIC (☎ 55611) is in the arts centre on St Mary's St.

It's best just to simply wander round the town's winding streets of medieval and Georgian houses, but **Stamford Museum** (☎ 66317), Broad St, is certainly worth the 50p entry charge (free on Friday). As well as displays charting the history of the town, there's a model of local heavyweight Daniel Lambert, who tipped the scales at 735 lbs before his death in 1809. In summer it's open daily (afternoon only on Sunday).

Places to Stay & Eat
Finding somewhere reasonably cheap to stay that's also central is difficult in Stamford. *Walsoken House* (☎ 64195), St Peter's St, charges £14 to £16 per person. At *Mrs Ward's* (☎ 51559), 5 Barn Hill, there's B&B for £20 per person.

There are a number of historic pubs that also offer accommodation. The *Bull & Swan* (☎ 63558), on the High St, does good meals and has rooms with bathroom attached for £35/45. Across the street, the *George* (☎ 55171) is the top place to stay. It's a wonderful old coaching inn, parts of the building dating back to the last millennium. There's excellent upmarket pub fare, a cobbled courtyard and luxurious rooms for £72/105.

Getting There & Away
Stamford is 46 miles from Lincoln and 21 miles south of Grantham.

National Express serves Stamford from London (2½ hours, £13.50) and Lincoln (1¾ hours, £6 return). Lincolnshire Roadcar (☎ 01522-522255) operates buses between Stamford and Grantham (1½ hours, £2.15), Monday to Saturday.

Stamford is on the main rail line between London, York and Edinburgh; services are frequent.

AROUND STAMFORD
Burghley House
Just one mile outside Stamford, this immensely grand Tudor mansion is the home of the Cecil family. It was built between 1565 and 1587 by William Cecil, Queen Elizabeth's adviser.

It's an impressive place with 18 magnificent state rooms. The Heaven Room was painted by Antonio Verrio in the 17th century and features floor-to-ceiling gods and goddesses disporting amongst the columns. There are over 300 paintings, including works by Gainsborough and Brueghel, state bedchambers, including the four-poster Queen Victoria slept in, and cavernous Tudor kitchens.

The house (☎ 01780-52451) is open from April to early October, daily from 11 am to 4.30 pm. Entry is £5.50 for an adult and there's no additional charge for one accompanying child. It's a pleasant 15-minute walk through the park from Stamford railway station.

BOSTON
- *pop 34,000* • ☎ *01205*

A major port in the Middle Ages, Boston lies near the mouth of the River Witham, on the bay known as The Wash. It was from Boston that the Pilgrim Fathers made their first break for the freedom of the New World in 1607. They were imprisoned in the **Guildhall**, where the cells that held them are now a tourist attraction.

Visible for miles around, the 288-foot-high tower of **St Botolph's Church** is known as the Boston Stump. You can climb the 365 steps for a wonderful view of the fens, and it's open Monday to Saturday, 9 am to 4.30 pm, and also on Sunday between services.

The TIC (☎ 01205-356656) is under the Assembly Rooms on Market Place.

Places to Stay & Eat
A five-minute walk from the marketplace, at 85 Norfolk St, *Park Lea* (☎ 356309) has singles/doubles from £17/30, or £20/32 with attached bath. The *White Hart* (☎ 364877), Bridge Foot, does good pub food and also has some rooms with bathroom attached at £39.95/49.50.

Getting There & Away
From Lincoln it's easier to get to Boston by train than by bus, but even that involves a change at Sleaford.

SKEGNESS
'Skeggy' is a classic English seaside resort, the Blackpool of the east coast. There are rows of jolly B&Bs, bingo every evening and donkeys on the beach. Danny La Rue and Bobby Davro appear at the Embassy Centre and the whole place twinkles with 25,000 light bulbs every night from July to October during the Skegness Illuminations. It's the kind of place the English middle and upper classes wouldn't dream of being seen dead in.

The TIC (☎ 01754-764821), in the Embassy Centre on Grand Parade, has all the information on B&Bs. They can be cheap, from £11 per person. There are direct rail and bus connections to Boston and Lincoln.

East Riding of Yorkshire

Formerly known as Humberside, East Riding of Yorkshire regained its old name in the 1996 local government reforms. The word Riding comes from the Danish *treding* and dates back to the 9th century when the conquering Danes divided Yorkshire into administrative regions.

The county is mostly flat, although the Wolds extend northwards in a narrow spine from Lincolnshire and they are rolling, attractive hills. The Wolds end at Flamborough Head and are the northernmost of the chalk downs originating in Wiltshire. The rest of the county was once largely marshland, which has been drained and is now intensively (and rather unattractively) farmed.

Hull, or Kingston-upon-Hull as it is officially known, is a large port and university town, with ferries to Zeebrugge (Belgium) and Rotterdam (Netherlands). It's not a particularly attractive place, partly because it was heavily bombed in WWII.

However, 10 miles to the north, on the edge of the Wolds, there is the small, unspoilt market town of Beverley. Usually overlooked by tourists, it has two superb churches. Many believe Beverley Minster is one of the most beautiful in Europe.

GETTING AROUND

The county council has a 24-hour travel line (☎ 01482-884900), or you can contact them on ☎ 01482-884358. The principal bus operators are East Yorkshire (☎ 01482-327146), York Pullman (☎ 01904-608854) and Yorkshire Coastliner (☎ 01653-692556). National Express also has a good range of bus services to Hull.

The only relevant railway line runs from Hull to Beverley, Bridlington, Filey and Scarborough. Hull is easily reached by rail.

KINGSTON-UPON-HULL

Hull was hard hit during WWII and modern developments are mostly less than inspiring.

The town has historically been a major port, and remains one today.

The main TIC (☎ 01482-223344) is in the Central Library, Albion St, but there is also a branch at the ferry dock (to the east of the city centre off Hedon Rd). Paragon railway station is just to the west of Queen Victoria Square, in the centre of town.

The most important museum is **Wilberforce House,** the birthplace in 1759 of the anti-slavery crusader William Wilberforce. Wilberforce House was built in 1639 and the museum, which covers the history of slavery and the campaign against it, overflows into several attractive Georgian houses.

Hull is on a branch line off the main line between London's King's Cross and Edinburgh; it therefore has good rail links north and south, but also west to York and the Northern Midlands. North Sea Ferries (☎ 01482-377177) has daily services to Zeebrugge and Rotterdam.

BEVERLEY

- *pop 20,000* • ☎ *01482*

Beverley developed at the centre of a rich agricultural region and became the capital of Yorkshire's East Riding. It's dominated by beautiful Beverley Minster, once a monastic church, and still the equal of many cathedrals in size and magnificence. The town itself is not spectacular, but the absence of tourists, the interesting mix of vernacular architecture (especially the handsome 18th-century brick houses), the market square and the thriving shops along the cobblestoned streets make it a charming escape from the tourist traps of North Yorkshire.

Orientation & Information

The Beverley TIC (☎ 867430), The Guildhall, Register Sq, has a good supply of information and an accommodation service. It's open Monday to Friday from 9.30 am to 5.30 pm, Saturday from 10 am to 5 pm, and Sunday from 10 am to 2 pm (the accommodation service closes 30 minutes early).

A general market is held on Saturday, and the Wednesday Market takes place between

9 am and 4.30 pm. A 400-year-old cattle and pig market is held just to the north of the town centre every Tuesday and Wednesday (Wednesday is the big day; selling starts at 10.30 am and finishes by 1 pm).

Beverley Minster

The first church on the site was built in the 7th century; the present building dates from 1220 but construction continued for two centuries spanning Early English, Decorated and Perpendicular styles. The best known aspect of the building is the magnificent west front (1420) in Perpendicular style, with its twin towers and wonderful sculpture.

The sculpture throughout the building is outstanding, and includes the 10th-century Frith Stool, or sanctuary chair, the canopy of the Percy Tomb (to the north of the altar), the 68 misericords (support ledges for choristers), not forgetting the extraordinary medieval faces and demons that peer from every possible vantage point.

The Minster is open Monday to Saturday from 9 am to 5 pm (later in summer) and Sunday from 2.30 to 5 pm.

Places to Stay

Hostel The *Friary Youth Hostel* (☎ 881751), Friar's Lane, is in a beautiful, restored 14th-century Dominican friary. It's open daily from April to October except Sunday; £6.75/4.60.

B&Bs & Hotels There's a good range of places to stay, although most of the cheap B&Bs are a bit of a walk south of the minster.

At the top of the heap, the *Beverley Arms Hotel* (☎ 869241), North Bar Within, has singles/doubles from £55/90. The *Kings Head Hotel* (☎ 868103), Saturday Market Place, is in a refurbished Georgian building right in the centre of town. Rooms are £39.50/49.50, but they also have special weekend rates.

The *Eastgate Guest House* (☎ 868464), 7 Eastgate, has singles/doubles with bathroom at £26/38, and without bathroom at £18/30.

For a standard B&B you could try *Mrs P Collman* (☎ 01482-868617), 4 Ellerker Rd, who has a single and a twin at £14 per person.

Getting There & Away

Beverley is on the railway line that runs between Hull and Scarborough. The railway station is to the east of the town centre and the bus station is to the north on Sow Hill.

Bus There are reasonably regular buses between York (railway station) and Hull via Beverley. These services also connect with Leeds and are operated by East Yorkshire Motor Services, Yorkshire Coastliner and York Pullman.

Train There are trains between Hull and York (1¼ hours) and trains between Hull and Beverley (15 minutes), which are frequent from Monday to Saturday, but there are only four on Sunday afternoon. Trains do continue on to Filey and Scarborough from Beverley from Monday to Saturday, but only every couple of hours and there are none on Sunday.

Northern England

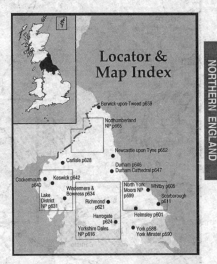

Northern England is quite different from the rest of the country, although it is misleading to think of it as a single entity. The three major sections are North Yorkshire to the south; Durham and Northumberland in the north-east; and Cumbria in the north-west. The last two areas border on Scotland.

As a rule, the countryside here is harder and more rugged than in the south, and it is as if history reflects this, because every inch has been fought over. The central conflict has been the long struggle between north and south, with the battle lines shifting over the centuries.

In the years before Roman invasion, the entire area from the Humber River to the Firth of Forth was ruled by a confederation of Celtic tribes known as the Brigantes. The Romans were the first to attempt to delineate a border with Hadrian's Wall, but the struggle did not end until the 18th century.

In the 9th century the Danes made York their capital and ruled the Danelaw – all of England north and east of a line between Chester and London. Later their Norman cousin William the Conqueror found the north rebellious and difficult, and he responded with brutal thoroughness. After 500 knights were massacred at Durham, he burnt York and Durham and devastated the surrounding countryside. Seventeen years later, when the royal commissioners arrived

to record the tax capacity of Yorkshire (for the *Domesday Book*), they recorded the simple, but frighteningly eloquent, 'waste' beside many, many parish names. It took the north generations to recover.

Later, the Normans left a legacy of spectacular fortresses and the marvellous Durham Cathedral. The region prospered on the medieval wool trade, and this sponsored the great cathedral at York, and enormous monastic communities, the remains of which can be seen at the Rievaulx and Fountains abbeys.

The countryside is a grand backdrop to this human drama, containing four of England's best national parks and some spectacular coastline. The Lake District and the Yorkshire Dales are best known and arguably the most beautiful of the parks, but the North York Moors has a great variety of landscapes, and includes a superb coastline. All three parks can be very crowded in summer, and while it is easier to escape the

583

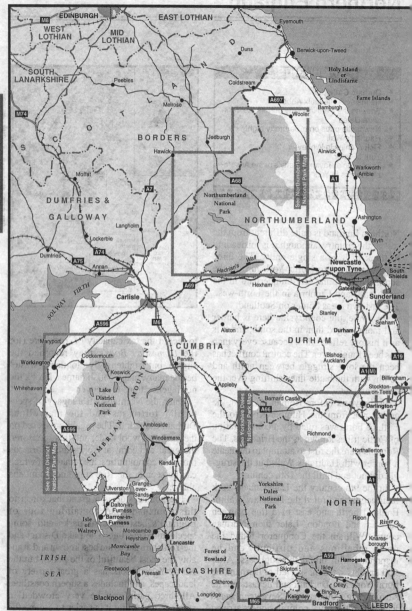

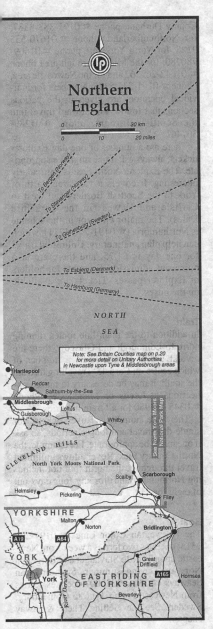

masses in the North York Moors park, visitors seeking seclusion should opt instead for the Northumberland park.

The Danish heritage survives today, especially in the language, but also, some would argue, in the independent spirit of the people. Place names ending in *thorp*, *kirk* and *by* all have a Danish origin.

ORIENTATION & INFORMATION

The dominating geological feature is the Pennine Hills, which form a north-south spine dividing the region into eastern and western halves and provide the source for numerous major rivers (the Mersey, Ribble, Aire, Tees and Tyne, among others).

The major transport routes basically run either side of this spine: from York to Newcastle upon Tyne and Edinburgh along the eastern side; from Manchester to Carlisle and Glasgow along the western. East-west transport, except between Carlisle and Newcastle upon Tyne and between Manchester and York is slow. Newcastle upon Tyne is an important ferry port for Scandinavia.

There are youth hostels at York and Newcastle upon Tyne and, even more importantly, dozens scattered about the national parks. Make sure you book in summer.

WALKS

There are more great hikes in this region than in any other in England. The most famous is the Pennine Way, which stretches 250 miles from Edale in the Peak District to end at Kirk Yethom in Scotland. Unfortunately, its popularity means that long sections turn into unpleasant bogs, so it is worth considering quieter alternatives.

For example, it is possible to walk sections of Hadrian's Wall, or to tackle sections of the difficult 190-mile Coast to Coast Walk which crosses the Lake District, Yorkshire Dales and North York Moors. Alfred Wainwright describes the walk in his inimitable fashion in *A Coast to Coast Walk*.

The Lake District is hikers' Mecca, crisscrossed with countless walks, ranging from easy half-hour strolls to demanding multiday hikes. A visit to any decent bookshop in London, the Lake District TICs or the huge outdoor-equipment shops in the Lake District towns will turn up dozens of guidebooks and maps. See the Activities chapter for details on the Cumbria Way, which runs 70 miles north-south across the LakeDistrict.

The Yorkshire Dales and the North York Moors also have numerous walks. See the Activities chapter for information on the beautiful Cleveland Way. In the Dales, consider the relatively easy, but still interesting, Dales Way, which runs 81 miles from Ilkley to Windermere, linking two national parks.

CYCLE ROUTES

Cycling is a great way to see this part of England; the only disadvantages are the weather, the hills and the fact that, on the weekends, even some of the minor B-roads can be very crowded. On the whole, however, all you need is a good map and some imagination, and you'll have a great time.

There are two official, circular cycleways in the region that are worth considering. The Cumbria Cycle Way (see the Cumbria section) loops around the Lake District, avoiding the car-packed national park; it's 259 miles long and could be done in five days, although a week would be better. The Dales Way (see the Yorkshire Dales National Park section) mostly follows the rivers, but there are still some steep climbs; it's 130 miles long.

There is also a new 88-mile Sea to Sea cycle route from Whitehaven on the west coast to Sunderland or Newcastle on the east coast. A good map and accommodation guide is available from Sustrans (☎ 0117-926 8893), 35 King St, Bristol BS1 4DZ.

GETTING THERE & AROUND
Bus

Bus transport around the region can be difficult, particularly around the national parks. For timetables and information covering Cumbria, phone ☎ 01228-812812; for County Durham, phone ☎ 0191-383 3337; for Northumberland, phone ☎ 01670-533 3128; for North Yorkshire phone ☎ 01609-780780; for the Middlesbrough area phone ☎ 01642-262262 and for the Newcastle area, phone ☎ 0191-232 5325. Numbers for individual operators are given in the various sections that follow. For onward travel into the Scottish Borders, phone ☎ 01289-307461.

There are a number of one-day Explorer tickets; always ask if one might be appropriate. The Explorer North East is particularly interesting. It covers a vast area north of York to the Scottish Borders and west to Carlisle and Hawes (in the Yorkshire Dales). The major operator in the scheme is Northumbria (☎ 0191-232 4211), which can help plan an itinerary. Unlimited travel for one day is £4.75, and there are also numerous admission discounts for holders of Explorer passes. Tickets are available on the buses.

Train

In addition to the main-line routes running north to Edinburgh and Glasgow, there are several useful branch lines, a number of which centre on Carlisle. Travelling to/from the south, it may be necessary to make connections at Leeds or Manchester. Phone ☎ 0345 484950 for all train inquiries.

There are numerous Rover tickets, for single-day travel and longer periods, so ask if one might be appropriate. For example, the North Country Flexi Rover allows unlimited travel throughout the north (but not including Northumberland) for any four days out of eight for £49.

Boat

The Norwegian Color Line (☎ 0191-296 1313) operates two ferries a week from Newcastle upon Tyne to Stavanger and Bergen in Norway. During summer, Scandinavian Seaways (☎ 0990-333000) operates ferries from Newcastle upon Tyne to Gothenburg, Sweden. See the Getting There & Away chapter.

North Yorkshire

North Yorkshire is one the largest counties, containing some of the finest monuments, most beautiful countryside and most spectacular coastline in the country. It includes two national parks (the Yorkshire Dales and North York Moors), the medieval city of York, the great monastic ruins of Rievaulx and Fountains, the classical beauty of Castle Howard, and the grim castles of Richmond and Bolton.

Most of North Yorkshire was untouched by the Industrial Revolution and, to a large extent, the accompanying agricultural revolution. The winter climate is harsh and much of the countryside lends itself to sheep grazing, an activity that has continued largely unchanged from medieval times. Great fortunes – private and monastic – were founded on wool.

In the west the Pennines, including the peaks of Ingleborough and Pen-y-ghent, dominate the beautiful dales, whose flanks are defined by snaking stone walls and overlooked by wild, heather-clad plateaus. In the east, stone villages shelter at the foot of bleak and beautiful moors. These run to the high cliffs of the east coast, with its fishing villages and the holiday resort of Scarborough.

GETTING AROUND

North Yorkshire has a transport inquiry line (☎ 01609-780780). Explorer tickets are available on Dalesbus, Harrogate & District and Keighley & District. Ask about day ticket deals. Yorkshire Coastliner (☎ 01653-692556), which has some interesting services around the North York Moors, York, Whitby and Scarborough, has a day Freedom ticket for £7.50. North East Buses/Tees & District (☎ 01325-355415) has services around Whitby.

YORK

- *pop 123,000*   • ☎ *01904*

For nearly 2000 years York has been the capital of the north. It's city walls, built during the 13th century, are among the most impressive surviving medieval fortifications in Europe. They encompass a thriving, fascinating centre with medieval streets, grand Georgian town houses, riverside pubs and modern shops. The crowning glory is the Minster, England's largest Gothic cathedral, but there is a bewildering array of things to see and do.

York attracts millions of visitors, and the July and August crowds can get you down; try and visit out of season if you can.

History

The Brigantes probably had a settlement at the meeting point of the rivers Foss and Ouse before the Romans arrived to set up a walled garrison called Eboracum in 71 AD.

Eboracum was strategically important, hence the visits of several emperors: Hadrian used it as a base in 121; Septimius Severus used it to hold Imperial Court in 211; and in 306 Constantius Chlorus died here and was succeeded by his son, Constantine, the first Christian emperor and founder of Constantinople (now Istanbul), was probably proclaimed emperor on the site of the cathedral.

The Anglo-Saxons founded the cathedral city of Eoforwic on the Roman ruins. Eoforwic was the capital of the independent kingdom of Northumbria which, like that of the Brigantes, stretched from the Humber to the Firth of Forth.

In 625 Christianity was brought by Paulinus, a Roman priest who had joined Augustine's mission in Canterbury. Somehow he succeeded in converting the Saxon king of Northumbria, King Edwin, and his nobles. The first wooden church was built in 627 and became a centre of learning that attracted students from around Europe.

The Danish Vikings captured and burnt the city in 867, but then made it their capital, Jorvik, for nearly 100 years. Under their rule it became an important trading port. Not until 954 did the kings of Wessex succeed in reuniting the Danelaw with the south, but their control remained tenuous. King Harold was forced to tackle a Norwegian

NORTHERN ENGLAND

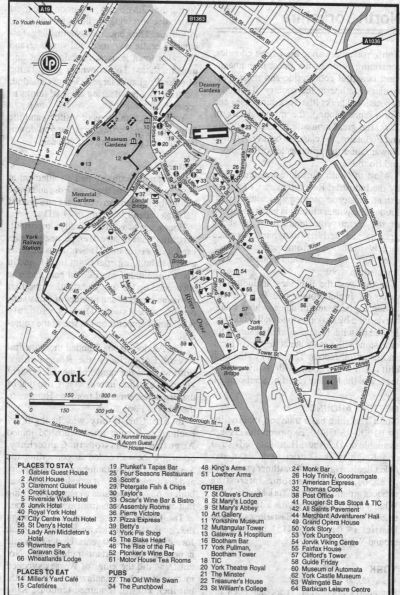

York

invasion-cum-uprising at Stamford Bridge, east of York, immediately before the Battle of Hastings.

William the Conqueror was also faced with rebellion. After the north's second uprising in 1070, he burnt York and Durham and laid waste the countryside...the 'harrying of the North'. Afterwards the Normans rebuilt the walls and erected two castles and a new cathedral. York once again became an important port, and the centre of the profitable new trade in wool.

In the 15th century the city declined, losing influence and power to London. During the Civil War, York twice came under siege from the Parliamentarian army. The first siege was lifted after two months by the arrival of an army under the command of King Charles' nephew Prince Rupert. In the bloodiest battle of the war, Prince Rupert chased the retreating Parliamentarians to Marston Moor, where they turned on him and cut his army to pieces, killing 4000 men. The siege was resumed, and the city finally fell in July 1642. Fortunately the commander of the Parliamentarian forces was Sir Thomas Fairfax, a local man, who prevented the troops pillaging the Minster.

The coming of the railway in 1839 once again placed York at the hub of the north-east.

Orientation

Although the centre is relatively small, York's streets are a confusing medieval tangle. Bear in mind that in York, *gate* means street, and *bar* means gate.

The city is circled by a ring road. There are five major landmarks in the centre: the wall that encloses the city centre; the Minster at the northern corner; Clifford's Tower, a 13th-century castle and mound at the southern end; the River Ouse that cuts the centre in two; and the enormous railway station just outside the western corner.

The main bus dropping off point is on Rougier St (off Station Rd, inside the city walls on the western side of Lendal Bridge), but some local buses leave from the railway station.

Information

There's a small TIC at the railway station, and another in Rougier St where the long-distance buses stop, but the main centre is across the river near Bootham Bar (621756), De Grey Rooms, Exhibition Square. It's open Monday to Saturday from 9 am to 5 pm (to 7 pm during August) and on Sunday from 9.30 am to 2 pm.

The TICs sell a York Visitor Card which costs £1 but gives discounts to all the major sights and a York Discount Card (£2.95) which offers two people various discounts on attractions, tours and meals for four days. It also sells a *Disabled Person's Guide to York* for £2.25.

York Minster

York Minster (☎ 624426), or the Cathedral & Metropolitan Church of St Peter, is Europe's largest medieval cathedral and one of the world's most inspiring buildings. The word 'minster' suggests that one of the previous buildings was once connected with a monastery. The minster is the seat of the Archbishop of York, who holds the title of Primate of England, and is second only in importance to the Archbishop of Canterbury, the Primate of *All* England!

The cathedral is a time capsule incorporating the remains of seven buildings but is most famous for its extensive medieval stained glass, particularly in the enormous Great East Window.

The first church on the site was a wooden chapel built for Paulinus's baptism of King Edwin on Easter Day 627; its site is marked in the crypt. This church, however, was built near the site of a Roman basilica, a vast assembly hall at the heart of Roman military headquarters; parts can be seen in the foundations. A stone church was started, but fell into disrepair after Edwin's death. St Wilfred built the next church, but this was destroyed as part of William's brutal response to a northern rebellion. The first Norman church was built in stages between 1060 and 1080; surviving fragments can be seen in the foundations and the crypt.

The present building was mainly built

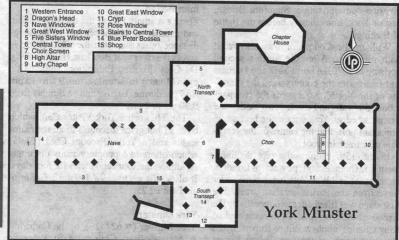

1 Western Entrance	10 Great East Window
2 Dragon's Head	11 Crypt
3 Nave Windows	12 Rose Window
4 Great West Window	13 Stairs to Central Tower
5 Five Sisters Window	14 Blue Peter Bosses
6 Central Tower	15 Shop
7 Choir Screen	
8 High Altar	
9 Lady Chapel	

York Minster

between 1220 and 1480, and incorporates several architectural styles. The north transept was built in Early English style between 1241 and 1260; the nave, choir and octagonal Chapter House were built in Decorated style between 1260 and 1405; and the central, or lantern, tower was the last addition, built in Perpendicular style between 1460 and 1480.

Enter from the western end. The nave is unusually tall and wide and, although the aisles (to the side) are roofed in stone, the central roof is wood painted to look like stone. On both sides of the nave are the shields of nobles who met Edward II at a parliament in York. Also note the **dragon's head** projecting from the gallery – it's a crane believed to have been used to lift a font cover. There are several fine **windows** dating from the early 14th century, but the most dominating is the **Great West Window** from 1338, with beautiful stone tracery.

The transepts are the oldest part of the building above ground, and the **Five Sisters Window**, with five lancets over 50 feet high, is the cathedral's oldest complete window; most of it is from around 1260. In 1984 the south transept was destroyed in a fire. Six of

the **bosses** in the new roof were designed by children who won a competition sponsored by the popular TV programme, *Blue Peter*.

The Chapter House is a magnificent example of the Decorated style. Superb stonework decorated with tiny individual stone heads surrounds a wonderful space uninterrupted by a central column.

The heart of the church is dominated by the awesome **central tower**. The 15th-century **choir screen** depicts the 15 kings from William I to Henry VI.

The **Lady Chapel** behind the **high altar** is dominated by the **Great East Window**, believed to be the largest intact medieval window in the world. It was created between 1405 and 1408 and illustrates the beginning and end of the world as described in Genesis and the Book of Revelation.

Entered from the south choir aisle, the **crypt** contains fragments from the Norman cathedral. The font shows King Edwin's baptism and marks the site of Paulinus' original wooden chapel.

In the south transept, the **Rose Window** commemorates the union of the royal houses of Lancaster and York through the marriage of Henry VII and Elizabeth of York, which ended the Wars of the Roses and began the Tudor dynasty. The entry to the stairs up to the tower and down to the Foundations & Treasury is also in the south transept. The reward for a steep and claustrophobic climb (275 steps) to the top of the tower is an excellent view over York and the surrounding countryside.

The **Foundations & Treasury** shouldn't be missed. In 1967 the foundations were excavated when the central tower threatened to collapse; while engineers worked frantically to save the building, archaeologists uncovered Roman and Norman ruins which now illustrate the site's ancient history – one of the most extraordinary survivals is a Roman culvert, still carrying water to the River Ouse. The Treasury houses artefacts from the 11th century, including relics from the graves of medieval archbishops.

To see everything could easily absorb the best part of a day. The cathedral itself is free, but a donation of £1.50 is requested. To visit the Chapter House costs 70p/30p; to see the Foundations & Treasury £1.80/70p; to see the crypt 60p/30p; and to climb the tower £2/1.

The cathedral is open daily in summer from 7 am to 8.30 pm and in winter from 7 am to 6 pm. The Foundations, Treasury, Chapter House and central tower are open all day from Monday to Saturday and on Sunday afternoons.

Around the Cathedral

Owned by the cathedral since the 15th century, **St William's College** (☎ 637134), College St, is an attractive half-timbered building housing an excellent restaurant (see Places to Eat).

The **Treasurer's House** (☎ 624247; NT), Minster Yard, was home to the minster's medieval treasurers. Substantially rebuilt in the 17th and 18th centuries, it now houses a fine collection of 18th-century furniture. It's open April to October, daily from 10.30 am to 5 pm; £3/1.50.

City Walls

You can get onto the walls via steps by the

Bootham Bar (on the site of a Roman gate) and follow them as far as Monk Bar walk which offers particularly beautiful views of the Minster.

Monk Bar is the best preserved medieval gate, with a small **Richard III Museum** (☎ 424953) upstairs. The museum sets out the case of the murdered 'Princes in the Tower' and invites visitors to decide whether their uncle, Richard III, killed them. It's open daily from March to October from 9 am to 5 pm (4 pm in winter); admission is £1/50p.

Walmgate Bar is England's only city gate with an intact barbican – an extended gateway designed to make life difficult for uninvited guests.

Museum Gardens

The Museum Gardens (open daily to dusk) make a peaceful city-centre oasis. Assorted picturesque ruins and buildings include the **Museum Gardens Lodge** (Victorian Gothic Revival, 1874) and an **Observatory**. The **Multangular Tower** was the western tower of the Roman garrison's defensive wall. The small Roman stones at the bottom have been built up with 13th-century additions.

The **Yorkshire Museum** (☎ 629745), in a classical building completed in 1829, has some interesting Roman, Anglo-Saxon, Viking and medieval exhibits and is particularly worth visiting if there's a good temporary exhibition. It's open daily from 10 am to 5 pm; £3/2.

The **Gatehall** was the main entry to **St Mary's Abbey**, a Benedictine monastery founded in 1080 with a later Early English-style church. The ruined 15th-century gateway provided access from the abbey to the river. The adjacent **Hospitium** dates from the 14th century, although the timber-framed upper storey is a much-restored survivor from the 15th century; it was used as the abbey guesthouse. **St Mary's Lodge** was built around 1470 to provide VIP accommodation.

St Olave's Church dates from the 15th century, but there has been a church dedicated to the patron saint of Norway on this site since at least 1050.

> **Medieval Guilds**
>
> In medieval and Tudor times, craftsmen and tradesmen formed themselves into guilds, which were basically a form of trade union or professional association. Crafts and trades were restricted to the members of an appropriate guild except at markets (which were usually weekly) or fairs (which were usually annual).
>
> The guilds checked workmanship, investigated complaints and regulated prices. Competition was only allowed in terms of quality and service. Admission was restricted to apprentices who had served a seven-year apprenticeship and paid a fee. An apprentice was completely bound to his master and received little more than food and board. He could not do anything without explicit permission – this included having any relations with the opposite sex. ■

Merchant Adventurers' Hall

The Merchant Adventurers' Hall (☎ 654818), Fossgate, was built in the mid-14th century and testifies to the power of the medieval guilds who controlled all foreign trade into and out of York – a handy little monopoly. The Great Hall with its massive oak timbers is outstanding.

The hall is open daily from 9 am to 5 pm (closed on Sunday in winter) for £1.80/60p.

Jorvik Viking Centre

Between 1976 and 1981 excavations in Coppergate uncovered Jorvik, the 9th-century Viking settlement that preceded modern York. The Jorvik Viking Centre (☎ 643211), Coppergate Centre, is one of York's most popular attractions. You travel back in time in a 'time car', winding up in a smells-and-all recreation of what the Viking town probably looked like, complete with fibreglass figures speaking a language derived from modern Icelandic. At the end of the ride there's a chance to inspect finds from the site.

It's open from April to October, daily from 9 am to 7 pm, and November to March daily from 9 am to 5.30 pm; £4.95/3.25.

The Jorvik people also run the **ARC** (Archaeological Research Centre;

☎ 643212) in St Saviourgate, which allows hands-on exploration of archaeology for £3/2.

Clifford's Tower

After wasting the north as punishment for its rebellion, William the Conqueror built two mottes (mounds) crowned with wooden castles. The original building on this site was destroyed by fire during anti-Jewish riots in 1190; 150 Jews who were sheltering in the castle took their own lives. There's not much to see in the building (☎ 605515; EH), but the views over the city are excellent. Admission costs £1.50/80p.

York Castle Museum

The York Castle Museum (☎ 653611) is a museum of everyday life with complete Victorian and Edwardian streets, and fascinating reconstructions of domestic interiors. An extraordinary collection of everyday objects from the past 400 years includes old TVs, radios, washing machines, vacuum cleaners and gadgets guaranteed to bring childhood memories flooding back.

One of Britain's best museums, it's open Monday to Saturday from 9.30 am to 5.30 pm, Sunday from 10 am to 5.30 pm; £4.20/2.90. Allow at least two hours for a visit.

Museum of Automata

Despite a name which suggests a lot of boring engines, the splendid Museum of Automata (☎ 655550) in Tower St is an Aladdin's Cave of magical machines with buttons to press and levels to pull, guaranteed to bring out the child in all of us. It's open daily from 9.30 am to 5.30 pm for £3.50/2.

National Railway Museum

The National Railway Museum (☎ 621261), Leeman Rd, is one of the world's biggest railway museums. The history of railways is traced via an impressive collection of carriages (including Queen Victoria's saloon) and locomotives (including the record-breaking *Mallard*). Allow two hours to do it justice.

It's open Monday to Saturday from 10 am to 5 pm and Sunday from 11 am to 5 pm; £4.20/2.10.

Medieval Churches

Of York's 41 pre-16th-century churches, 20 still survive, often with their stained-glass intact. Finest is **All Saints, North St** which John Betjeman dubbed 'the best reconstruction of a medieval interior', with wonderful glass and all sorts of bits and bobs. It's easily spotted by the octagon rising above its tower.

Just as atmospheric, if more homely, is **Holy Trinity, Goodramgate**, tucked away in a churchyard popular with lunching shopworkers off Goodramgate. Inside, box pews surround an 18th-century two-tier pulpit and there's never a straight line in view.

Other Things to See

Fairfax House (☎ 655543), Castlegate, is a fine Georgian house with a renowned collection of 18th-century furniture and clocks. It's open March to December, Monday to Saturday (not Friday except in August and September) from 11 am to 5 pm, Sunday from 1.30 to 5 pm; £3/1.50.

The **Barley Hall** (☎ 652398), off Stonegate, is a restored 15th-century timber-framed merchant's house. It's open July and August, Monday to Saturday, 10 am to 5 pm.

The **York Story** (☎ 628632) in St Mary's Church in the Coppergate Centre relates York's history through models, audiovisuals etc. It's open daily 10 am to 5 pm (1 to 5 pm on Sunday) and costs £1.60/1.10 (50p discount with combined Castle Museum ticket).

York Dungeon (☎ 632599) at 12 Clifford St is what you'd expect...a series of gruesome historical reconstructions, intended to scare those who find the Chamber of Horrors tame. It's open daily from 10 am to 5.30 pm (4.30 pm October to March) and costs £3.50/2.25.

Friargate Museum and Black Cave (☎ 658775) in Lower Friargate is one of Britain's last remaining waxwork museums. Alongside the predictable historical figures on show, look out for more ordinary mortals, many of them failed first attempts at the famous. The Black Cave is a kind of haunted house which the more squeamish can avoid by turning left rather than right at the bottom of the stairs on the way out. It's open daily from Easter to October (closed on Friday in winter) from 10 am to 4 pm. Admission costs £3/2.

Beneath the Roman Bath pub in St Helen's Square are the remains of a **Roman bath** which used to be inside the fortress of Eboracum. They're open daily 10 am to 9 pm for £1.

Opposite the TIC in St Leonard's Place, York's **Art Gallery** has a range of paintings, including works by Lely, Reynolds and Lowry. It's open from Monday to Saturday 10 am to 5 pm, Sunday 2.30 to 5 pm. Admission is free.

In the heart of York, the quaintly cobbled **Shambles** hints at what a medieval street might have looked like. It takes its curious name from the Saxon word *shamel*, meaning slaughterhouse, although these days the old butchers' shops mainly sell tacky tourist souvenirs.

Organised Tours

Yorkwalk (☎ 622303) offers a series of two-hour themed walks on Roman York, medieval York, the snickelways (alleys) of York, and saints and sinners of York. Each walk costs £4 (children under 16 free) and walkers get a £1 discount off Guide Friday tours. Walks depart from Museum Gardens Gate. Pick up details from the TIC.

Christian Heritage Walks leave St Michael Le Belfry church at 2.30 pm each Sunday from March to November. They cost £4.

It's worth considering the innovative and excellent Yorspeed Walkman Guided Tour (☎ 762622), available from the TIC. For £4 you get an informative tape with atmospheric sound effects and a walkman, and you can wander around at your own speed.

For a good overall introduction, York Pullman (☎ 622992) runs guided double-decker bus tours which circle the city calling at the main sites; you can get on and off where you please (buses run every 20 minutes) and tickets are valid all day. The main starting point is Exhibition Square opposite the TIC and its office is in Bootham Tower. Tickets are £4.50/1.50. Guide Friday (☎ 640896), 8 Tower St, operates similar tours for £6.50/1.50.

York now has so many companies offering ghost walks that ghost wars have broken out on the streets, with stories of moved signs and other nefarious activities. The following are the bare bones details: the Original Ghost Walk of York (☎ 373090) leaves the Kings Arms at 8 pm daily and costs £3/2; the Ghost Trail of York (☎ 633276) leaves the front entrance of the Minster at 7.30 pm daily and costs £3/2; and the Victorian Ghost Walk (☎ 6440031) leaves James Tea Rooms in Low Petergate at 8.30 pm daily and costs £3.50/2.50.

See the Getting Around section for information on bicycle and boat tours.

Places to Stay

Despite the existence of hundreds of hotels and B&Bs, it can be difficult to find a bed in midsummer or when the races are on. Prices also jump significantly, say from an average of £16 per person to £23 per person, in the high season. The TIC can help with accommodation and at the heart of summer it may be worth paying its £2.75 fee to avoid wasting time.

Hostels The *Youth Hostel* (☎ 653147), Water End, Clifton, is open all year. Once the home of the Rowntree family, this is a large, modern hostel, with four beds in most rooms. It's popular, so make sure you book ahead in summer. The nightly rate of £13.50/10.00 includes breakfast. It's about one mile from the TIC: turn left into Bootham, which becomes Clifton (the A19), then left into Water End. Alternatively, there's a riverside footpath from the station.

The *City Centre Youth Hotel* (☎ 625904), 11 Bishophill Senior, is equally popular, particularly with school and student parties. There's a range of rooms, from 20-bed dorms (£9) to twin bunk rooms (£12 per person). If

you don't have a sleeping sheet, sheet hire is an additional £1. Bikes are available for £4.50 a day.

The University of York offers accommodation in its halls of residence in holiday times. *Fairfax House* (☎ 432095), 99 Heslington Rd, is a 15-minute walk southeast of the city. The single rooms have washbasins and the nightly rate is £16.

Camping There are a dozen camping grounds and/or caravan parks around York, but most are at least four miles from the centre. *Riverside Caravan & Camp Site* (☎ 704442) is three miles south in Ferry Lane, Bishopthorpe. *Rowntree Park Caravan Site* (☎ 4658997), just over Skeldergate Bridge, charges £3 a night for a van plus £3.20 an adult. There's no grass on the sites, so although tents are allowed, camping wouldn't be pleasant without something soft to sleep on.

B&Bs & Hotels There are lots of B&Bs and hotels in the streets north and south of Bootham (the A19 to Thirsk) to the northwest of the city. There are also quite a few to the south-west in the streets between Bishopthorpe Rd (over Skeldergate Bridge) and the A1036 to Leeds.

B&Bs & Hotels – north-west Leaving Bootham Bar along Bootham, the first main intersection is Gillygate to the right. Turn right and then second left for Claremont Tce and several reasonably priced guesthouses. The *Claremont* (☎ 625158), at No 18, has rooms with bath from £28 to £30.

Continue along Bootham and the first street you come to is Marygate, which follows the Museum Gardens down to the river. The *Jorvik Hotel* (☎ 653511), at No 50, has a walled garden and 23 comfortable rooms with bath. Doubles cost from £40 to £60 and there's one single from £26. Continue down to the river, where there are a couple of places right on the bank. The *Abbey Guest House* (☎ 627782), 14 Earlsborough Tce, is a standard B&B with rooms from £16/26. The comfortable *Riverside*

Walk Hotel (☎ 646279), 9 Earlsborough Tce, has rooms with bath from £17.50 a head.

Back on Bootham, *Hudson's Hotel* (☎ 621267), at No 60, has 30 rooms with all mod cons in a well-designed, modern annexe and a restaurant and bar in a Georgian town house. Doubles with bath cost from £80.

The next street on the left, St Mary's, has two very pleasant mid-range places: *Crook Lodge* (☎ 655614) at No 26 does B&B from £20; and *23 St Mary's* has fully equipped rooms from £30/44.

Running along the railway line, Bootham Tce (south of Bootham) and Grosvenor Tce (north of Bootham) are virtually lined with B&Bs. Most are pretty standard, but the position is good. Pleasant *Brontë House* (☎ 621066), 22 Grosvenor Tce, has rooms with private bath from £16 per person depending on the season.

Inviting places on Sycamore Place, off Bootham Tce, include *Elliots* (☎ 623333), with good rooms and private facilities for £29 per person, and *Alcuin Lodge* (☎ 632222), at No 15, which has some rooms with private bath, others with shared facilities, from £17 per person.

There are several cheapish places on Bootham Crescent. Most have private bathroom and charge around £16 per person.

Several large detached Victorian mansions in St Peter's Grove offer something quiet but reasonably grand. *Holme Lea Manor Guest House* (☎ 623529), 18 St Peter's Grove, Bootham, is particularly nice and has four doubles from £44.

B&Bs & Hotels – south-west There are more places clustered around Scarcroft Rd, Southlands Rd and Bishopthorpe Rd, the continuation of Bishopgate, which takes off from the southern corner of the wall after Skeldergate Bridge.

On Bishopthorpe Rd itself, *Nunmill House* (☎ 634047), at No 85, is a good place with rooms from £20 per person. Just in from the corner of Bishopthorpe and Southlands Rds, the *Acorn Guest House* (☎ 620081), 1 Southlands Rd, is a decent two-star guesthouse with TV in all rooms and singles/doubles from £17/33. Right next door, the *Staymor* (☎ 626935) has beds from £11, while *Bishopgarth* (☎ 635220) charges £13.

Wheatlands Lodge (☎ 654318), 75 Scarcroft Rd, takes up a whole row of attractive listed Victorian villas. Most rooms are sunny and rates start at around £25 per person in a double with bath. In the Victorian *Dairy Guesthouse* (☎ 639367), at 3 Scarcroft Rd, vegetarian food is served. Singles/doubles start at £25/32.

Next door to the railway station, *Royal York Hotel* (☎ 653681) is a huge Victorian edifice with wonderful grounds and views. Rooms here cost £95/115 for a single/double without breakfast.

Also worth trying, to the east of the city, is the *City Centre Guesthouse* (☎ 624048), 52 Walmgate, a Georgian town house which has B&B for £14.

Places to Eat

Restaurants There are several decent restaurants along Goodramgate from Monk Bar. *Caesar's Pizzeria & Ristorante* has pasta and pizzas for around £5 and the *Palace of India* (☎ 639886) has thalis for under £8. *La Piazza* (☎ 642641) does standard pizzas and pasta in a fine half-timbered hall.

Further up the hill, along Micklegate, are some of York's best places. The most acclaimed vegetarian café is through the back of the *The Blake Head Bookshop* (☎ 623767) at 104 Micklegate. Soup and a roll costs £2.25, a main-course salad £4.25, a set three-course lunch £6.50. It's open daily from 10 am to 5 pm. Along the road *The Rise of the Raj* (☎ 622975) offers a standard range of Indian dishes like chicken tikka masala for £6.15.

Back toward the town centre, *St William's College Restaurant* in the College, off College St, is a great spot to relax after exploring the cathedral. It's open from 10 am to 5 pm and does soups from £1.50 and various casseroles and vegetarian dishes for around £3. In good weather, the city has few more pleasant spots than its beautiful cobbled courtyard.

Atmospheric *Oscar's Wine Bar & Bistro* in Little Stonegate has an outdoor area and a wide range of interesting dishes (including vegetarian). Most main meals (for example, smoked-haddock pasta, or chicken tikka masala) are around £5. Across the road *The Rubicon* (☎ 676076), Little Stonegate, is a BYO (bring your own bottle of wine) vegetarian restaurant offering two-course lunches for £6 and three-course meals for £12.50.

Near Bootham Bar, *Plunket's* (☎ 637722) at 9 High Petergate has a particularly international menu. Paella is £4.15, Thai chicken £3.85 and Mexican beef £3.95.

Petergate has two other places that habitually send queues curling down the street. The first is *Petergate Fish & Chips*, with excellent fish to eat in or take away. The second is *Scott's*, the pork butcher's, where you can buy pork pies to make the taste buds weep from £1.80.

Millers Yard Café, in Millers Yard, off Gillygate, is an excellent vegetarian place with a small outdoor eating area. Hot dishes are £2.50 to £3.50, quiches and pizzas £1.75, and mugs of tea 80p. At the entrance to the yard *Cafetiéres* does lasagne for £3.50.

Opposite the Art Gallery in St Leonard's Place, the mainly Tudor *King's Manor* has a student refectory with filling food like gammon and pineapple for £3 to £4.

The *Pizza Express* (☎ 672904) at 17 Museum St serves the usual range of good pizzas in the elegant surroundings of what was once a York gentlemen's club overlooking the Ouse.

Pubs The *King's Arms* on King's Staithe is a pub with tables overlooking the river on the south-eastern side of the Ouse Bridge (the middle of the three main bridges). Nearby, the *Lowther Arms*, on the corner of King's Staithe and Cumberland St, has bar meals for less than £4 and a restaurant where you pay about £2 more per dish.

Cafés All your sightseeing is likely to make you thirsty. *Betty's* is an extremely popular,

extremely elegant bakery and tearoom in the centre of town; depending on your mood you can choose to relax in the spacious, airy upstairs or the wood-panelled no-smoking downstairs. A pot of tea for one is £1.60, sandwiches are £3.50 to £4.50 and hot dishes are around £6. Betty's is open until 9 pm. The same menu is also on offer upstairs in *Taylor's*, 46 Stonegate, where queues are as likely as at Betty's. A traditional Yorkshire high tea here costs £8.30 and would set you up for a week.

You can take tea in even more genteel surroundings in the *Grand Assembly Rooms* (☎ 632754) round the corner in Blake St. The Assembly Rooms are in a basilica-like building lined with paired Corinthian columns and hung with chandeliers. A cream tea here costs £2.35, soup and a roll £1.85 and creamy fish pie £4.95.

Entertainment
There are several pubs on the south-eastern side of the Ouse Bridge, and some outdoor tables by the river if you want somewhere central to start exploring York's nightlife.

Places worth checking out include *The Punchbowl*, in Stonegate, which nearly always has live folk music. There can be jazz at *Oscar's Wine Bar*. The *Old White Swan* on Goodramgate also has bands.

It's worth seeing what's on at the *York Theatre Royal* (☎ 623568), near the TIC; it can have excellent productions. Despite its name, the *Grand Opera House* (☎ 671818) in Cumberland St puts on a wide range of productions; ask at the TIC for details.

For big-name concerts head for *York Barbican Centre* (☎ 656688), in an interesting, partly pyramidal modern building in Barbican Rd.

Getting There & Away
Train York has reasonable transport connections. As the ex-headquarters of the York & North Midland Railway, it's well served by rail. There are numerous trains from London's King's Cross (two hours, £47) which continue to Edinburgh (a further 2¾ hours, £26).

North-south trains also connect with Peterborough (1½ hours, £20.50) for Cambridge and East Anglia (three hours, £26.50). There are good connections with south-west England, via Bristol (4½ hours, £37), Cheltenham, Birmingham and Sheffield. There's also a service to Oxford (4½ hours, £26.50), via Birmingham.

Local trains to Scarborough take 45 minutes and cost £7.60. For Whitby it's necessary to change at Middlesbrough. Trains to/from the west and north-west go via Leeds.

Bus By road it's about 200 miles to London and Edinburgh, 25 miles to Leeds and Helmsley and 90 miles to Nottingham. See the fares tables in the Getting Around chapter.

National Express (☎ 0990-808080) buses leave from Rougier St. There are at least three services a day to London (4½ hours), two a day to Birmingham (4½ hours) and one to Edinburgh (six hours).

For information on local buses (to Castle Howard, Helmsley, Scarborough, Whitby etc), contact York Rider Buses (☎ 624161) adjoining the TIC at the Rougier St bus terminal (open Monday to Friday from 8 am to 5 pm and Saturday from 9 am to 4.30 pm).

Yorkshire Coastliner (☎ 01653-692556) has buses to Leeds, Malton and Scarborough. A one-day Freedom ticket costs £7.50/5.

The best deal if you're heading north or east is the Explorer North East ticket (£4.50), which is valid on most bus services and gives unlimited travel for one day – United Auto (☎ 01325-465252) has a bus north to Ripon where you can link into the network.

Cumberland's (☎ 63222) runs between York and Keswick via Harrogate (Yorkshire Dales), Skipton, Kendal and Ambleside (Lake District) on Monday, Wednesday, Friday and Saturday. On Saturday the service extends to Grasmere and Keswick.

Car The TIC has a full list of car rental possibilities. One good-value option is Prac-

tical Car & Van Rental (☎ 01904-624848), 10 Fetter Lane.

Getting Around

York gets as congested as most British cities in summer and car parking in the centre can be expensive (up to £7 for a day). There's a Saturday Park & Ride scheme; for details ring ☎ 431388.

Taxi Try ABC Blue Circle (☎ 638787) or Ace Taxis (☎ 638888).

Bicycle You can hire bikes for £9.50 a day from Bob Trotter by Monk Bar (☎ 622868).

Tours – bus Public transport to some of the nearby surrounding attractions can be difficult, so it's worth considering a tour. York Pullman (☎ 622992), Bootham Tower, Exhibition Square, has a range of good-value day tours into the surrounding countryside. These include Castle Howard for £4.75, North York Railway & Whitby for £13.50, and Yorkshire Dales & Herriot Country for £13.50. Prices don't include admission charges. Children under 16 travel free.

From April to October Yorktour (☎ 645151), 8 Tower St, has daily afternoon tours to Castle Howard (£6) as well as a number of other trips into the countryside. Tickets are also available from the TIC.

Tours – boat The White Rose Line (☎ 628324), Lendal Bridge, operates cruises along the River Ouse. Hour-long round trips depart from King's Staithe (behind the fire station) and Lendal Bridge (next to the Guildhall, under Lendal Bridge). From February to November trips operate every 30 minutes from 11 am; the rest of the year there are three trips a day; £3.80/1.50.

CASTLE HOWARD

There are few buildings in the world that are so perfect that their visual impact is almost a physical blow – Castle Howard, of *Brideshead Revisited* fame, is one. It has a picturesque setting in the rolling Howardian Hills and is surrounded by superb terraces and landscaped grounds dotted with monumental follies.

Castle Howard is, not surprisingly, a major tourist attraction, and it draws enormous crowds. Outside weekends, however, it's surprisingly easy to find the space to appreciate this extraordinary marriage of art, architecture, landscaping and natural beauty. Wandering about the grounds, views open up over the hills, the Temple of the Four Winds and the Mausoleum, but the great Baroque house with its magnificent central cupola is an irresistible visual magnet.

In 1699 the Earl of Carlisle made an audacious choice when he picked a successful playwright and army captain, Sir John Vanbrugh, as architect. Vanbrugh in turn chose Nicholas Hawksmoor, who had worked for Christopher Wren, as his clerk of works. This successful collaboration was subsequently repeated at Blenheim Palace.

The house is full of treasures, and the grounds include a superb walled rose garden.

Castle Howard (☎ 01653-648333) is 15 miles north of York off the A64. It's open mid-March to October, daily from 10 am (grounds) or 11 am (house) to 4.30 pm. Entry to the house and garden is £6.50/3.50, to the garden only £4/2. All in all, it could absorb the best part of a day; take a picnic.

Getting There & Away

The castle can be reached by several tours and occasional buses from York. Check with the York TIC for up-to-date schedules; they cost around £5. Yorkshire Coastliner (☎ 01653-692556) has a useful service that links Leeds, York, Castle Howard, Pickering, Goathland and Whitby (Nos 840 and 842). A day return ticket from York costs £3.30.

North York Moors National Park

Only Exmoor and the Lake District rival the North York Moors National Park for natural beauty, but the North York Moors are less crowded than the Lake District and more expansive than Exmoor. The coast is superb, with high cliffs backing onto unspoilt countryside. From the ridge-top roads and open moors there are wonderful views, and the dales shelter abbeys, castles and small stone villages.

One of the principal glories of the moors is the vast expanse of heather – the largest in the UK. There are a number of different species, and they flower spectacularly, in an explosion of purple, from July to early September. Even outside the flowering season, their browns-tending-to-purple on the hills, in vivid contrast to the green of the dales, give the park its characteristic appearance.

ORIENTATION

The western boundary of the park is a steep escarpment formed by the Hambleton and Cleveland hills; the moors run east-west to the coast between Scarborough and Staithes. Rainwater escapes from the moors down deep, parallel dales – to the Rye and Derwent rivers in the south and the Esk in the north. After the open space of the moors, the dales form a gentler, greener landscape, sometimes wooded, often with a beautiful stone village or two.

Heather

The North York Moors have the largest expanse of heather moorland in England. Three types can be seen: ling is the most widespread, has a pinkish-purple flower, and is most spectacular in late summer; bell heather is deep purple; and cross-leaved heather (or bog heather) prefers wet ground, unlike the first two, and tends to flower earlier. Wet and boggy areas also feature cotton grass, sphagnum moss and insect-eating sundew plants.

The moors have traditionally been managed to provide an ideal habitat for the red grouse – a famous game bird. The shooting season lasts from the 'Glorious Twelfth' of August to 10 December. The heather is periodically burned, giving managed moorland a patchwork effect – the grouse nests in mature growth, but feeds on the tender shoots of new growth. ∎

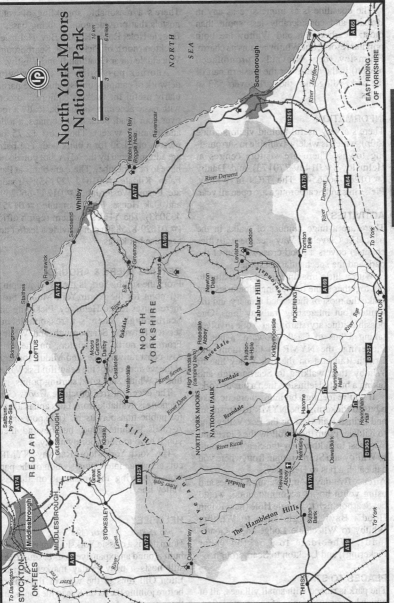

North York Moors
National Park

NORTH SEA

NORTHERN ENGLAND

The coastline is as impressive as any in Britain, and considerably less spoilt than most; Scarborough and Whitby are both popular resorts, but Whitby retains its charm. Helmsley (near Rievaulx, pronounced reevoh) is the centre for the western part of the park. Altogether, the park covers 553 sq miles.

INFORMATION

There's a very useful tabloid visitors guide (50p), which is widely available in surrounding towns. There are visitors centres at Helmsley (☎ 01439-770173) and Danby (☎ 01287-660654). The TICs in Whitby, Pickering and Scarborough are open all year.

ACTIVITIES

There are a huge number of walks in the park. The Cleveland Way (see the Activities chapter) covers a good cross-section of the park and the spectacular coastline.

With a little imagination, it's possible to put together some interesting itineraries that make the most of the varied scenery and the limited, but interesting, railway lines. One possible itinerary starting at York involves taking a bus to Castle Howard, a bus to Pickering, the NYMR to Grosmont and British Rail east on the Esk Valley line to Whitby, then walking to Scarborough and taking a bus to Helmsley, then a bus to York.

If you're feeling a bit more energetic, take a bus to Pickering, the NYMR to Grosmont and British Rail west on the Esk Valley line to Kildale. From there, follow the Cleveland Way east to Saltburn-by-the-Sea, then south to Whitby and Scarborough, from where you can catch a bus to Helmsley.

An easy five-day loop, covering 52 miles and using youth hostel accommodation, would be: Scarborough to Boggle Hole (near Robin Hood's Bay); Boggle Hole to Whitby; Whitby to Wheeldale Lodge (near Goathland); Wheeldale to Lockton (near Pickering); and Lockton to Scarborough.

PLACES TO STAY

The park is ringed with small villages, all of which have a good range of accommodation.

There's a reasonable sprinkling of youth hostels that provide good walking bases at Boggle Hole, Robin Hood's Bay, Helmsley, Lockton (north of Pickering), Scarborough, Wheeldale (near Goathland) and Whitby.

Another possibility is the growing network of camping barns, which are particularly useful for walkers equipped to cope with basic accommodation (basically a roof over your head, bunk beds perhaps, a toilet and running water). They cost £2.75 per person, or £4.50 for a bunk bed. The barns are administered by the YHA, but you do not have to be a member. There are barns at Park Farm, Kildale (☎ 01642-722135); Broadgate Farm, Westerdale (☎ 01287-660259); and Oak House, High Farndale (☎ 01751-433053). The YHA's northern region office (☎ 01629-825850) can provide a leaflet and organise bookings.

GETTING THERE & AROUND

From the south, York is the usual jumping-off point for the North York Moors. From there, buses run to Helmsley, Pickering and Scarborough. There's a reasonable bus service between Scarborough and Whitby. From the north, Darlington, on the main east-coast railway line, and Middlesbrough, at the western end of the beautiful Esk Valley line to Whitby, are good starting points.

The excellent free brochure *Moors Connections* is available from TICs and is a must for public-transport users. Transport on the A-roads is quite good, but beyond them you'll have to find your own way.

The North York Moors Railway (NYMR) cuts across an interesting section of the park from Pickering to Grosmont on the Esk Valley line.

HELMSLEY
- *pop 1500*   • ☎ 01439

Helmsley is a classic Yorkshire market town, built around an expansive market square that still hosts a busy Friday market. Narrow Etton Gill runs to the west of the square, before joining the River Rye in the south, and there are some fascinating cottages along its banks – many built traditionally in grey-yellow limestone with red pantile roofs.

Almost all the elements of the moors' history and architecture come together in and around Helmsley: the ruins of a 12th-century Norman castle stand to the south-west of Market Square; the superb 12th-century ruins of the Cistercians' Rievaulx Abbey shelter in Ryedale 3½ miles to the west; a 16th-century manor house, Nunnington Hall, is 4½ miles to the south-east; a grand 18th-century country house, Duncombe Park, lies beyond the castle; and there is the vernacular architecture of the town itself.

Helmsley makes an ideal base for exploring the North York Moors. There are numerous short walks in the surrounding countryside that take in the aforementioned sights, and, for the more ambitious, Helmsley is the starting point for the Cleveland Way.

Orientation & Information

Everything radiates out from the central Market Square – the parish church is to the north-west, and the castle and Duncombe Park are to the south-west.

The TIC (☎ 770173) is open April to October, daily from 9.30 am to 6 pm, and November to March, weekends from 10 am to 6 pm. It has a particularly good range of information on the North York Moors National Park, the Cleveland Way and local cycling routes.

Helmsley Castle

The castle (☎ 770442; EH) is most famous for its extensive surrounding earthworks – huge earthen banks and ditches – but parts of the curtain wall, the keep and a 16th-century residential wing survive. Begun in the early 12th century, various additions were made through to the Civil War, when, after a three-month siege in 1644, it surrendered.

A retired London banker bought Helmsley in 1689, however, and later built neighbouring Duncombe Park; once the castle was no longer used as a residence it fell into disrepair, but it still makes a picturesque sight; admission is £2/1.

Duncombe Park

Duncombe Park dates from 1713 and was built for retired London banker, Thomas

NORTHERN ENGLAND

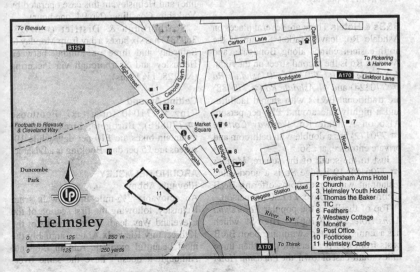

To Rievaulx

B1257

Carlton Lane

To Pickering & Harome

A170 Linkfoot Lane

High Street

Canons Garth Lane

Church St

Bondgate

Ashdale Road

Footpath to Rievaulx & Cleveland Way

Market Square

Pottergate

Castlegate

Bridge Street

Duncombe Park

Helmsley

Ryegate Station Road

River Rye

A170   To Thirsk

0   125   250 m
0   125   250 yards

1 Feversham Arms Hotel
2 Church
3 Helmsley Youth Hostel
4 Thomas the Baker
5 TIC
6 Feathers
7 Westway Cottage
8 Monet's
9 Post Office
10 Footloose
11 Helmsley Castle

Duncombe, by William Wakefield, a friend of Vanbrugh. The building is neo-classical and is beautifully located in 600 acres of landscaped parkland. There are enormous lawns and terraces with views across the moors and surrounding countryside (see Rievaulx Terrace & Temples section); the park has a number of walks.

The entrance to the house (☎ 770213) is signposted from the A170 to/from Thirsk. It's open from 5 April to 3 November daily from 11 am to 6 pm; tickets for the house and grounds are £4.95/3.95; entry to the grounds only is £2.95/1.50.

Places to Stay
Hostel The *Helmsley Youth Hostel* (☎ 770433), Carlton Lane, is a purpose-built hostel a quarter of a mile east of Market Square. To get there, take Bondgate from the north-eastern corner of the square and turn left at Carlton Rd. Opening times vary, so phone ahead. The nightly rate is £7.45/5.

Camping Two miles to the south-east of town, *Foxholme Caravan Park* (☎ 770416), Harome, has 60 individual pitches amongst trees from £6 per day.

B&Bs & Hotels There are several places on Ashdale Rd; leave Market Square at the north-eastern corner along Bondgate, and Ashdale Rd is the second street on the right. *4 Ashdale Rd* (☎ 770375), *20 Ashdale Rd* (☎ 770324) and *41 Ashdale Rd* (☎ 770488) are traditional B&Bs with shared facilities and a nightly rate around £14 per person. Also on Ashdale Rd, *Westway Cottage* (☎ 770172) has a double with bathroom and private entrance, at £36.

Just to the south of the square, *Monet's* (☎ 770618), 19 Bridge St, is a good-value restaurant with three rooms offering B&B accommodation above; £17.50 per person.

Top of the list is the popular *Feversham Arms Hotel* (☎ 770766), 1 High St, which has a tennis court and swimming pool; B&B costs from £35 per person. Less than three miles south-east of town, the *Pheasant Hotel*

(☎ 771241) in Harome is in much the same league; B&B is from £51 per person.

Places to Eat
Thomas the Baker, on Market Square, is very good and cheap – an ideal place to stock up for a picnic.

Monet's (☎ 770618), 19 Bridge St, to the south of Market Square, serves morning and afternoon teas, lunches for around £5 and a more expensive evening meal.

Check the pubs around the square, but you may well find yourself drawn to the popular *Feathers* (☎ 770275), an interesting old inn with excellent bar food (most mains from £5). The *Feversham Arms* also has excellent bar meals.

Getting There & Away
Helmsley is 25 miles from York, 16 miles from Malton and 14 miles from Pickering and Thirsk.

Bus There are two Stephenson's buses (☎ 01347-838990) a day between York and Helmsley (No 57, 1¼ hours). There are also three very slow buses a day between Malton railway station (on the York-Scarborough line) and Helmsley, in this case operated by Yorkshire Coastliner (No 94, one hour).

Scarborough & District (☎ 01723-369331) has six buses a day from Monday to Saturday and three on Sunday between Helmsley and Scarborough via Pickering (No 128, 1¾ hours).

Getting Around
Ring ☎ 771040 for a taxi. Footloose (☎ 770886), Borogate, hires bicycles; mountain bikes are £10 per day, while 10-speeds are £5 per day. Booking is advisable.

AROUND HELMSLEY
Rievaulx Abbey
An enjoyable 3½-mile uphill walk from Helmsley, following the first section of the Cleveland Way, leads to the remains of the 13th-century Rievaulx Abbey, arguably the most beautiful monastic ruin in England. Although it doesn't have the same over-

whelming grandeur as Fountains, the site is incomparable. It lies in a secluded, wooded valley beside a small village and the River Rye.

At the time when the site was granted to a group of 12 Cistercians in 1132, Ryedale was a complete wilderness, but the monks proved to have extraordinary energy and skills. The enormous profits from the 'agrobusiness' they developed (which included fishing, sheep and textiles) allowed them to build quickly and on an impressive scale.

By 1170 there were 150 monks, more than 250 lay brothers and 250 hired workmen, and by the end of the century most of the building was completed (the nave is Norman, the transepts are Transitional and the choir is Early English). By the dissolution in 1539, however, there were only about 20 monks. Many of the surrounding buildings, including much of pretty Rievaulx village, were constructed from stone pillaged from the ruins.

Rievaulx Abbey (☎ 776228; EH), on the B1257 to Stokesley, is open daily from 10 am to 6 pm (4 pm in winter); £2.50/1.90.

Rievaulx Terrace & Temples
In the 1750s Duncombe Park was landscaped to create a romantic series of views overlooking Rievaulx Abbey, Ryedale and the Hambleton Hills. Rievaulx Terrace & Temples (☎ 798340, NT) consists of a half-mile-long grass-covered terrace with carefully planned openings in the surrounding woods. There is no access to the Abbey from the Terrace. The Terrace is open April to October, daily from 10.30 am to 6 pm (or dusk if earlier); last admissions are at 5 pm; £2.50/1.

Nunnington Hall
Nunnington Hall (☎ 748283, NT) is an attractive manor house set on the banks of the River Rye, about 4½ miles south-east of Helmsley. It includes sections from the 16th century, but most of the building dates from the 17th. There's a tearoom and an attractive garden. It's open from April to October, Tuesday to Saturday (not Wednesday) from

2 to 6 pm and Sunday from noon to 6 pm; £3.50/1.50.

THIRSK
Thirsk is a small market town just beyond the western edge of the national park, below the Hambleton Hills in the Vale of Mowbray. It is the fictional 'Darrowby' of James Herriot's stories of life as a Yorkshire vet, but it remains a very normal, untouristy place (unlike some of the villages made famous by the TV series *All Creatures Great & Small*).

The TIC (☎ 01845-522755), 14 Kirkgate, is a helpful place open March to October, Monday to Saturday from 9.30 am to 5 pm, and Sunday from 2 to 4 pm.

The *Three Tuns Hotel*, (☎ 01845-523124) on Market Square, has bar meals from £4, and a restaurant with a four-course dinner for £10; it also has rooms with bathroom from £25. The *Golden Fleece* (☎ 01845-523108) is a bit swisher with a good variety of bar meals around £6; it also has rooms.

There are infrequent bus services between Thirsk and Helmsley operated by Stephenson's (☎ 01347-838990). There are also bus links between Market Place and Thirsk railway station, which is one mile to the west on the A61 to Ripon. Thirsk is on the main east-coast line between London's King's Cross and Edinburgh.

AROUND THIRSK
Sutton Bank
On the A170 between Thirsk and Helmsley, Sutton Bank is the western escarpment of the Hambleton Hills, with magnificent views across the Vale of Mowbray to the Pennines and Yorkshire Dales. From the car park on the top there are walks to Lake Gormire and the Kilburn White Horse, and along part of the Cleveland Way. There's also a National Park Visitors Centre (☎ 01845-597426) with a tearoom, open Easter to November, daily from 10 am to 5 pm, and November to March, weekends only from 11 am to 4 pm.

The Thirsk TIC's accommodation guide quotes James Herriot on Sutton Bank: 'I must have stopped at this very spot thousands of times because there is no better place for a short stroll along the green path which winds around the hill's edge with the wind swirling and that incredible panorama beneath. I know I keep saying these things about Yorkshire BUT this is the finest view in England'.

DANBY

Danby (sometimes referred to as Danby-in-Cleveland) is at the head of Eskdale, and the surrounding countryside is particularly beautiful. Fourteenth-century Danby Castle can be seen from the road; Danby Beacon, two miles to the northeast, has great views; and Duck Bridge, downstream from the village, is a 14th-century packhorse bridge.

Danby is home to the Moors Centre (☎ 01287-660654), the main headquarters for the national park, and half a mile from the village proper. There are displays, information, an accommodation-booking service and tearooms in an 18th-century manor house. The centre is open April to October, daily from 10 am to 5 pm, and November to March, weekends only from 11 am to 4 pm. There are five short circular walks from the centre.

Places to Stay & Eat

A number of local farms have good-value B&B, costing around £14; these include *Crag Farm* (☎ 01287-660279) and *Danby Castle Farm* (☎ 01287-660164).

Danby Watermill (☎ 01287-660330), near the railway station, is the last working mill on the River Esk; it's an interesting place with a coffee shop and a number of bedrooms (including a single) from £15 per person. The *Duke of Wellington* pub (☎ 01287-660351) has good bar meals, and rooms for around £22 per person.

Getting There & Away

There are only four trains a day on the Esk Valley line from Monday to Saturday, and it's easy to imagine that economic rationalists will want to close it completely. Ring British Rail to confirm the times.

STAITHES

Tucked underneath high cliffs and running back along the steep banks of a small river, the old fishing village of Staithes is one of the most picturesque on the English coast. In many ways, it seems untouched by the 20th century, focusing still on its centuries-old battle with the sea. James Cook served as an apprentice grocer in a shop that has since been reclaimed by the sea; legend says that fishermen's tales of the high seas and bad treatment by his master led him to steal a shilling from the till and run away to Whitby. There are a couple of pubs and guesthouses.

WHITBY

- *pop 15,000* · ☎ *01947*

Somehow Whitby transcends the coaches and fish & chip shops – the imposing ruins of an abbey loom over red-brick houses that spill down a headland to a beautiful estuary harbour. This small town has had a disproportionate impact on world history, both as the site for the Synod of Whitby, which determined the nature of the medieval English church, and as the starting point for the maritime career of one of the world's greatest explorers – Captain James Cook.

Whitby is one of the most interesting and attractive towns on the British coast and among the highlights of a trip to the north. It's the perfect base from which to explore the cliffs, coves, fishing villages and beaches to the east and west, which are amongst the most spectacular on this island. If only there was regular surf and it was 10 degrees warmer...

The town itself combines the colour of a working harbour on the estuary of the River Esk, a muddle of medieval streets with a range of restaurants and pubs, the silhouette of the abbey which seems to float over the town, and the paraphernalia of a seaside resort. It attracts a diverse group of people – not just retirees and young families.

The past is powerfully evoked, particularly when mists roll up the valley of the Esk, but also when it is at its sunniest and loveliest. You cannot easily forget the grand bishops and the monks and nuns debating the

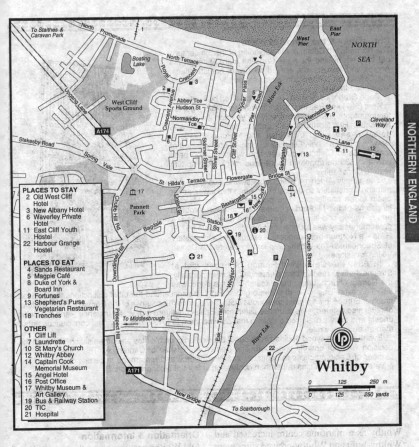

PLACES TO STAY
2 Old West Cliff
   Hotel
3 New Albany Hotel
6 Waverley Private
   Hotel
11 East Cliff Youth
   Hostel
22 Harbour Grange
   Hostel

PLACES TO EAT
4 Sands Restaurant
5 Magpie Café
8 Duke of York &
   Board Inn
9 Fortunes
13 Shepherd's Purse
   Vegetarian Restaurant
18 Trenches

OTHER
1 Cliff Lift
7 Laundrette
10 St Mary's Church
12 Whitby Abbey
14 Captain Cook
   Memorial Museum
15 Angel Hotel
16 Post Office
17 Whitby Museum &
   Art Gallery
19 Bus & Railway Station
20 TIC
21 Hospital

Whitby

NORTHERN ENGLAND

future of the English church on their windy headland, or the generations of Whitby traders, whalers, fishermen and explorers in their Whitby-built ships.

History

The Romans had a signal station on the high cliffs to the east of town. Over 200 years later Celtic Christianity was firmly established in the kingdom of Northumbria by St Aidan, who in 635 founded the great Lindisfarne monastery (see the Holy Island section). In 657 St Hilda – a Northumbrian princess – established a monastery at Streoneshalh (as

Whitby was known before the Danish Viking invasions). In 664 the Celtic and Roman churches met at the abbey to resolve their differences. Eventually the synod (or council) decided in favour of the Roman church and its organisation based at Canterbury.

The Danish destroyed the abbey in 867, but they recognised Whitby's potential as a port. The abbey was refounded by Benedictines in 1078 and flourished until the Dissolution in 1539 – the Benedictine ruins survive today.

From the Middle Ages, the importance of

Christianity & the Synod of Whitby

The Romans left Britain at the beginning of the 5th century, but they left behind them the Christian faith. Although the Angles and Saxons who arrived next were not Christians, the Celts kept the religion alive, especially in Cornwall, Wales and Ireland.

Pope Gregory's missions to the Angles, led by Augustine in Kent (597) and Paulinus in Northumberland (627), gained tenuous footholds, but lasted only six years in the case of Paulinus. His Northumbrian patron, King Edwin, was defeated and killed by Welsh and Mercian invaders. However, Edwin's heir, Oswald, was exiled on the island of Iona, a Celtic Christian outpost, and when he won back power in 635 he appealed to the Iona monks to help him restore Christianity.

The saintly Aidan met this request and succeeded in planting Christianity so deeply in the north that it was never again to be challenged. The conversion of the Mercian kingdoms of the Midlands commenced, and the forgotten arts of writing and keeping records were re-established. A great monastery was founded on Lindisfarne, and in 657 St Hilda – a Northumbrian princess – established a monastery at Streoneshalh (as Whitby was known before the Danish Viking invasions).

In 664, the Celtic and Roman churches met at Streoneshalh to resolve their differences. Most importantly, the Roman church, under the leadership of the pope, was intent on establishing a centralised organisation that transcended the tribal distinctions that had left much of Europe in an almost continuous state of war since the collapse of the Roman Empire. Matters of ritual also differed – the churches celebrated Easter on different days, for instance – and the Celtic priests and monks preferred a system that allowed them to follow their individual consciences rather than an autocratic rule.

Eventually, the synod decided in favour of the Roman church's rites and organisation, although the decision was not entirely one-sided. The Roman Archbishop of Canterbury, Theodore, allowed a number of Celtic practices to continue, including divorce and remarriage in certain cases, and the private confession of sins rather than confession in front of a congregation. ■

Whitby as a maritime centre increased and Whitby-built and Whitby-crewed ships were used in trading and whaling. In 1746, the 18-year-old James Cook arrived in Whitby as an apprentice to a local shipowner. For nine years Cook worked on Whitby cats, unique Whitby-built colliers that carried coal south from the Durham coalfields to London. These sturdy flat-bottomed vessels were specially designed to allow them to be beached for loading and off-loading.

In 1755 Cook joined the Navy, and in 1768 he began the first of three voyages of discovery. On all three voyages the ships he chose to use, including the *Endeavour*, were Whitby cats.

Orientation & Information

Old Whitby grew up along the steep sides of the Esk estuary. Until the 18th century, the eastern bank was the most important but in the 19th century a new town, catering to the new seaside tourist industry with terraced crescents, grew up on the western side, and this is also where most 20th-century development has occurred.

The TIC (☎ 602674), Langborne Rd, is just across the road from the bus and railway stations. It's open May to September, daily from 9.30 am to 6 pm, and from October to April, daily from 10 am to 4.30 pm. It has information on a number of interesting self-catering possibilities in the North York Moors National Park and along the coast.

Interesting evening ghost walks depart from the Arts Centre, Market Square on Church St, on summer evenings at 8 pm (£2).

There's a laundry at the top of Skinner St.

Whitby Abbey & St Mary's Church

Nothing survives of the Saxon abbey founded by St Hilda; it lay a little to the north of the existing ruins. A Benedictine abbey was re-established on the site in 1078, and the remains visible today are of the Benedictine church built in the 13th and 14th centuries (mainly in the Early English style).

In many ways, the nearby St Mary's Church is more interesting than the abbey ruins. It is a lovely medieval church with a low Norman tower and an atmospheric and extraordinary interior full of skewwhiff Georgian galleries and box pews.

The abbey (☎ 603568; EH) is open daily from 10 am to 6 pm; £1.60/1.20. The church is open daily; admission is free. Those with vehicles pay £1.50 for parking.

Captain Cook Memorial Museum

The museum is in the harbourside house below the abbey once owned by John Walker, the Quaker captain to whom Cook was apprenticed. Cook sometimes lodged in the attic. It's well worth a visit for the house itself and for the interesting displays on Cook's life and voyages.

The museum is open April to October, daily from 9.45 am to 5 pm, and weekends only in March. Admission is £2/1.20.

Whitby Museum

Whitby Museum (☎ 602908), Pannett Park, was founded in 1823 and is a traditional place full of dusty glass cabinets that just happen to be full of the most fascinating stuff. It's surrounded by a beautiful, steep garden with views that give you a completely new perspective on the town.

The museum is open May to September, Monday to Saturday from 9.30 am to 5.30 pm and Sunday from 2 to 5 pm; telephone

for the irregular hours between October and April; £1.50/1.

Walks

Consider attempting the 5½-mile clifftop walk to Robin Hood's Bay; the last Tees & District bus returns to Whitby around 4 pm. There are also some beautiful small fishing villages, like Staithes, to the north.

Other Things to See & Do

Apparently the **Dracula Experience** is the most popular tourist attraction in Whitby. The connection is actually fairly tenuous, although Bram Stoker did write the story while staying in a local B&B, and Dracula was a brief visitor when, in the shape of a dog, he leapt off the wreck of the *Demeter*.

There are several companies along the eastern bank of the estuary that offer boat and fishing trips.

Jet (black fossilised wood) is found around Whitby; in Victorian times over 200 workshops produced jet jewellery; only a few still do so today.

Places to Stay

There are plenty of places to stay, but beware the Whitby Festival (8 to 23 June) and Whitby Regatta (August), when the place can be booked out.

Hostels The *East Cliff Youth Hostel* (☎ 602878) is at the top of 199 steps, beside the ruined abbey, with great views over the town. It's open daily between 20 May and 7 September but for other times ring ahead; £6.75/4.60.

The alternative is the well-designed, new *Harbour Grange Hostel* (☎ 600817), Spital Bridge, on the eastern side, opposite the marina (£7, £1.40 for linen). It's open all year.

Camping The *Sandfield House Farm Caravan Park* (☎ 602660) is just a mile west of town on Sandsend Rd (the A174). It has half a dozen tent sites and about 50 touring pitches from £3 per night.

B&Bs & Hotels Right in the centre of the medieval town, on the eastern side of the river, there are some pleasant rooms above the *Shepherd's Purse Vegetarian Restaurant* (☎ 820228), 95 Church St. B&B (including a vegetarian breakfast) in a room with five beds is £14 per person while doubles are from £32.

Most places, however, are on the western side, the part of town that developed in Victorian times. A walk along Royal Crescent, Crescent Ave, Hudson St/Abbey Tce and East Tce will turn up many decent possibilities. (To confuse matters, one street sometimes has two names; for example, the southern side of one street is Hudson St, while the northern side is Abbey Tce.)

The *New Albany Hotel* (☎ 603711), 3 Royal Crescent, has rooms with sea views for £21 per person.

The *Ashford Guest House* (☎ 602138), 8 Royal Crescent, is an unspoilt place, with sea views and a range of rooms, around £19 per person.

The *Waverley Private Hotel* (☎ 604389), 17 Crescent Ave, has doubles from £19.50 per person. In a nice old Victorian building, the *Old West Cliff Hotel* (☎ 603292), 42 Crescent Ave, has six doubles with bathroom for £23 per person.

Possibilities on Hudson St/Abbey Tce include *Lansbury Guest House* (☎ 604821), 29 Hudson St, with basic singles and doubles from £15 per person; *Grantley House* (☎ 600895), 26 Hudson St, £18; and *Rosslyn Guest House* (☎ 604086), 11 Abbey Tce, which also has singles and doubles from £13.50.

The Old Hall Hotel (☎ 602801), Ruswarp, is in a Jacobean house built in 1603, and overlooks the Esk Valley. There's quite a range of rooms, some with bathroom, from £19 to £25 per person.

Places to Eat

There are plenty of reasonable eating places in Whitby, with a predictable emphasis on seafood.

One of the most famous contributors to English cuisine is *Fortunes*, Henrietta St, a small family company that has produced kippers since 1872. Kippers are fish (traditionally herring) that have been salted and smoked.

It has been claimed that the *Magpie Cafe* (☎ 602058), 14 Pier Rd, does the best fish & chips in the world, but unfortunately most of the world knows, so there are often long queues. Staff will fry, grill or poach the fish of your choice (from £5.50 to £9); there are also set menus from £9 to £13.50. It is open from 11.30 am to 9 pm. *Trenchers* (☎ 603212) near the railway station is also very highly regarded for its fish.

There are numerous other fish & chips places in the town, costing a good £2 less – just take your pick.

Overlooking the sea, *Sands Restaurant*, on the cutting that links the western cliffs and the old town, is a spic-and-span, efficient operation with vegetarian meals for £5.95 and cod & chips for £5.25.

On the eastern side of the river, the *Shepherd's Purse Vegetarian Restaurant* (☎ 820228), 95 Church St, is through the wholefood shop opposite the market building. It has starters like stilton and onion soup for £1.95 and mains like leek and sunflower quiche for £4.95. Takeaways are available and it also has an outside courtyard – and pleasant rooms (see Places to Stay).

At the end of Church St and overlooking the harbour, there are two pubs that offer good-value bar meals. The *Duke of York* is more atmospheric than the *Board Inn*. At one time or other when you're in Whitby you will be duty bound to try some crab, either in a salad or sandwich; salads are £5.50 at the Duke of York. You can get fish & chips for under £5.

Entertainment

There are several quite lively pubs; if the inclination for music and Tetleys (beer) strikes, go for a wander. The *Angel Hotel*, New Quay, has live music, and the *Tap & Spile*, opposite the railway station, also pulls a crowd.

Getting There & Away

Whitby is 20 miles from Scarborough, 230 miles from London and 45 miles from York.

Bus Tees & District (☎ 602146) has a number of services in the Whitby area. There are regular buses to/from Scarborough (Nos 93, 93A and 93C, one hour) via Robin Hood's Bay. Yorkshire Coastliner (☎ 01653-692556) has an interesting service (No 840/842/843) between Whitby and Leeds via Goathland, Pickering (the latter two on the NYMR) and York.

Train Although it is not, in some ways, particularly efficient, you can get to Whitby by train, and the Esk Valley line from Middlesbrough is one of the most attractive in the country – more interesting scenically than the much-promoted NYMR (see that section).

En route, it is possible to connect with the northern terminal of the NYMR at Grosmont (to visit Danby) and Kildale (a possible starting or finishing point for the Cleveland Way). There are only four trains a day, Monday to Saturday. Ring British Rail to check the times.

Alternatively, you could catch a train to Scarborough from York, then a bus from Scarborough.

Getting Around

Taxi The main taxi rank is beside the TIC, opposite the railway and bus station, or phone Geoff Harrison Taxis (☎ 600606). The standard charge is 73p per mile, with a minimum fare of £1.30.

COOK COUNTRY

Explorer and navigator Captain James Cook was born and raised in the north of this area, and there are a number of museums and monuments commemorating his life. The Cook Country Walk, a 40-mile hike, links the most important sites of Cook's early years. The first half basically follows the northern flanks of the Cleveland Hills east from Marton (near Middlesbrough), then the superb coast south from Staithes to Whitby. It's designed to be broken into three easy days.

A booklet describing the route, *The Cook Country Walk* (£1.70), is available from local

TICs and the North York Moors National Park Information Service (☎ 01439-770657), The Old Vicarage, Bondgate, Helmsley YO6 5BP.

The **Captain Cook Birthplace Museum** (☎ 01642-311211), Stewart Park, Marton, Middlesborough, is an excellent museum open April to October, daily from 10 am to 5.30 pm, and November to March, daily from 9 am to 4 pm.

There are railway links to Saltburn-by-the-Sea and Whitby, on the Cleveland Way, and to Marton (Esk Valley line) for the start of the Cook Country Walk. There are also regular connections to Darlington for the main north-south line.

ROBIN HOOD'S BAY

Bay, as the locals call it, probably has a lot more to do with smugglers than it has to do with the Sherwood Forest hero, but it's a picturesque haven. A steep, cobbled road drops from the coastal plateau, down to the sea. There's compulsory parking at the top – don't even think about cheating and driving down, because there's hardly even room to turn at the bottom.

The village is a honeycomb of cobbled alleys and impossibly small houses that seem to hide in secret passages. There are a few gift shops and a trail of pubs (start from the bottom and work your way up), but really this is a place to just sit and watch the world go by, preferably out of season.

Unless you book, or are prepared for a one-mile walk (along the beach at low tide, or the cliff at high) to the popular *Boggle Hole Youth Hostel* (☎ 01947-880352), don't plan on staying. *The Laurel*, halfway down Main St, serves excellent real ales from a bar carved of solid rock. *The Dolphin* in King St has huge bar meals for about £5 and sea views.

There's an hourly Tees & District (☎ 01947-602146) service between Whitby and Scarborough which stops at the Bay. In the summer the Coast to Coast Packhorse (☎ 017683-71680) service runs from St Bees on the west coast to the Bay, delivering backpacks and/or bodies along the route of Alfred

NORTHERN ENGLAND

Wainwright's Coast to Coast Walk (see Kirkby Stephen).

SCARBOROUGH
- *pop 39,000*   • ☎ *01723*

Scarborough is a large, often kitsch, seaside resort. Unlike Blackpool (and many other places of that ilk), however, it has a long history and, most importantly, a spectacular site. These, combined with the traditional trappings of an English seaside holiday resort, make it an appealing and enjoyable place.

Although some parts are a bit run-down and you do not get a good impression as you arrive, it has, for the most part, survived the 20th century and the impact of cheap package holidays to the Mediterranean. It has remained a classic resort, with two beautiful bays separated by a castle-crowned headland, but has added sufficient mod cons and amusements to remain attractive to young families and the elderly from all round the north. Unfortunately, there don't seem to be many visitors between the ages of 18 and 25.

History
The headland that separates the North and South bays has an impressive defensive position and has been occupied since Celtic times. A fishing village was, according to tradition, established by Vikings in the 9th century around what is now known as the Old Harbour. The Normans built their castle from around 1130, and it survived until 1648, when it was slighted by the Parliamentarians. It was also bombarded by a German battleship in 1914.

The medieval fishing and market town grew up around the old harbour. Mineral springs were discovered in 1620 and it was transformed into a fashionable spa town. It became one of the first places in Britain where sea bathing was popular, and from the mid-18th century it has been a successful seaside resort. It therefore has a legacy of fine Georgian, Victorian and Edwardian architecture.

Orientation
Modern suburbs sprawl to the west of the town centre, which is above the old town and the South Bay. The town is on a plateau above the beaches; three cliff lifts, steep streets and footpaths provide the link. The Victorian development to the south is separated from the town centre by a steep valley, which has been landscaped and is crossed by high bridges.

The railway and coach stations are conveniently central.

Information
The busy TIC (☎ 373333), Valley Bridge Rd, is open May to September, daily from 9.30 am to 6 pm, and October to April, daily from 10 am to 4.30 pm.

Things to See & Do
Well it's a beach resort, innit? So there are all the things the British do at beaches, plus some bonuses. **Scarborough Castle** (☎ 372451; EH), which is approached via a 13th-century barbican, survives, as do the curtain walls dating from around 1130 and the shell of a keep built around 1160. There are excellent views; £1.80/1.40.

Below the castle is **St Mary's Church** from 1180, rebuilt in the 15th and 17th centuries, with some interesting 14th-century chapels. Anne Brontë is buried in the churchyard. The old town lies between the church and castle and the Old Harbour.

The **Stephen Joseph Theatre** (☎ 370541), by the railway station, hosts the world premieres of plays by local playwright Alan Ayckbourn.

Places to Stay
Hostel The *White House Youth Hostel* (☎ 361176), Burniston Rd (the A166 to Whitby; catch a No 3 or 10 minibus from the centre), is two miles north of town in a converted water mill. It has a complex set of opening times, so ring ahead and check what's going on. In 1996, it was open daily between 21 July and 8 September but closed for parts of the weekend at other times; admission is £6.75/4.60.

NORTHERN ENGLAND

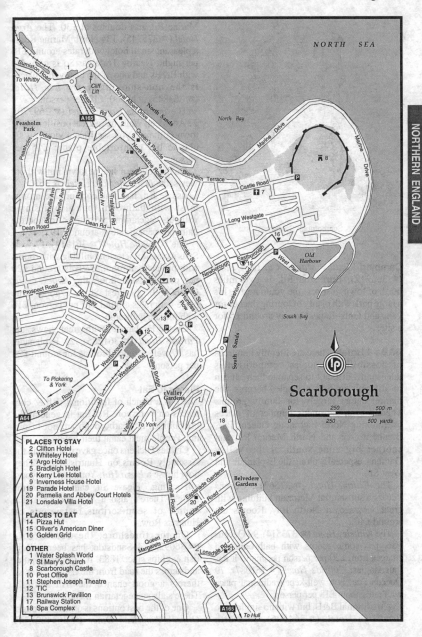

North York Moors National Park

NORTH SEA

North Bay

Burniston Road

To Whitby

Cliff Lift

Royal Albert Drive

North Sands

Peasholm Park

A165

Peasholm Drive

Tennyson Ave

Ravine

Beechville Ave

Ashville Ave

Columbus

Dean Road

Dean Rd

Prospect Road

Northway

Castle Road

Trafalgar Rd

Trafalgar Square

North Marine Road

Queen's Parade

Blenheim Terrace

Castle Road

Long Westgate

St Thomas St

Aberdeen Walk

Newborough

Barr St

Huntriss Row

Victoria Road

Westborough

Westwood Rd

Westwood

Valley Road

Valley Bridge

Valley Gardens

To Pickering & York

Falsgrave Road

A64

To York

Ramshill Road

Queen Margarets Road

Esplanade Gardens

Avenue Victoria

Esplanade Road

Belvedere Gardens

Lonsdale Rd

Filey Road

A165

To Hull

North Bay

Marine Drive

Marine Drive

Castle Road

Eastborough

Foreshore Road

West Pier

Old Harbour

South Bay

South Sands

Esplanade

Scarborough

| 0 | 250 | 500 m |
| 0 | 250 | 500 yards |

PLACES TO STAY
2 Clifton Hotel
3 Whiteley Hotel
4 Argo Hotel
5 Bradleigh Hotel
6 Kerry Lee Hotel
9 Inverness House Hotel
19 Parade Hotel
20 Parmelia and Abbey Court Hotels
21 Lonsdale Villa Hotel

PLACES TO EAT
14 Pizza Hut
15 Oliver's American Diner
16 Golden Grid

OTHER
1 Water Splash World
7 St Mary's Church
8 Scarborough Castle
10 Post Office
11 Stephen Joseph Theatre
12 TIC
13 Brunswick Pavillion
17 Railway Station
18 Spa Complex

NORTHERN ENGLAND

Scarborough Castle

Camping *Scalby Manor Caravan Park* (☎ 366212), Burniston Rd, is two miles north of town, just past the youth hostel. It's a large park with plenty of touring pitches for vans and tents. Expect to pay around £5 for a site.

B&Bs & Hotels There are literally hundreds of possibilities and, as competition is intense, it's difficult to separate them. It can be difficult to find a single, because the market caters largely for family groups. There are an enormous number of places overlooking North Bay along Queens Pde, Blenheim Tce and North Marine Rd, and another big zone south of the Valley Gardens, especially along the Esplanade and West St.

The *Clifton Hotel* (☎ 375691), Queens Pde, is a substantial Victorian building with great views over North Bay. Rooms are around £40.

The *Whiteley Hotel* (☎ 373514), 99 Queens Pde, has some rooms with bathroom and charges from £20 per person per night. It has four singles. *Cliffside Hotel* (☎ 361087), 79 Queens Pde, is a well-kept traditional place with rates about £18 per person.

A traditional B&B, but with no singles, the *Bradleigh Hotel* (☎ 364596), 35 North

Marine Rd, has doubles at £30. The *Argo Hotel* (☎ 375745), 134 North Marine Rd, is a pleasant small hotel with rates around £16 per night. Nearby Trafalgar Sq is crowded with B&Bs and one of the best value places is the non-smoking *Kerry Lee Hotel* (☎ 363845) at No 60; £12 per person.

The *Inverness House Hotel* (☎ 369770), 22 Aberdeen Walk, has a great position in the town (although you sacrifice a view). It's a classic but comfortable place; £15 per person.

On the southern side of town, but without views, the *Lonsdale Villa Hotel* (☎ 363383), Lonsdale Rd, has nine comfortable rooms, most with bathroom, but also a single without. Vegetarians are catered for and the daily per-person rate is around £19.

The *Parmelia Hotel* (☎ 361914), 17 West St, is a classic Victorian building with rooms with private bathroom. B&B is around £20 per person. Next door, the *Abbey Court* (☎ 360659), 19 West St, is a good-value place with rates around £17 per person, £16 with private bathroom.

On the Esplanade, with great views, the *Parade Hotel* (☎ 361285), 29 Esplanade, has 17 well-equipped rooms for around £23 per person.

Places to Eat

There is a bunch of traditional fish & chip places on Foreshore Rd, but in general the possibilities in Scarborough are not inspiring. People must eat at their hotels.

Charles Dickens once gave readings in the Assembly Rooms on Huntriss Row. They now house a *Pizza Hut*. You may find yourself saying, 'Please Sir, can I have some more?' There's also a *McDonald's* and a couple of semi-serious restaurants on Huntriss Row.

On the foreshore, the *Golden Grid* (☎ 360922), 4 Sandside, has been selling fish & chips since 1883. It's bright, popular and across the road from the fishing fleet, so there's a good chance the fish is fresh. There's also a vegetarian menu.

One of the best options is on Eastborough. *Oliver's American Diner* (☎ 364422), 49

Eastborough, is the real thing. The food, from £3.50 to £10, has a Mexican bias and the 40 oz burger is free – if you manage to eat it all!

Getting There & Away

See the fares tables in the Getting Around chapter. Scarborough is 230 miles from London, 70 miles from Leeds, 16 miles from Pickering and 22 miles from Whitby.

Bus There are reasonably frequent buses travelling west along the A170 to Pickering and Helmsley (No 128, 1½ hours); contact Scarborough & District (☎ 375463). They leave from Westborough.

Tees & District (☎ 01947-602146) has regular buses to/from Whitby (Nos 93, 93A and 93C; one hour) via Robin Hood's Bay. Yorkshire Coastliner (☎ 01653-692556) has a frequent service between Leeds and Scarborough (No 843) via York.

Train Scarborough is a good transport hub, connected by rail with Leeds via Harrogate, Knaresborough and York, and Kingston-upon-Hull via Filey and Beverley. The journey from Leeds shows a good cross section of Yorkshire, with potential stop-overs in attractive Knaresborough and majestic York worth considering.

Getting Around

Bus Local buses leave from the western end of Westborough pedestrian mall and outside the railway station.

Taxi There are a number of local operators. Nippy's is a 24-hour service (☎ 370888 or 377377), or try Z Cars (☎ 377177); £3 should get you most places.

PICKERING

Once you get away from the traffic along the A170, Pickering is a surprisingly attractive little town. As the main starting point for trips on the NYMR, it also draws an enormous number of tourists.

The award-winning TIC (☎ 01751-473791), Eastgate car park, is open April to October, daily from 9.30 am to 6 pm, and November to March, from 10 am to 4.30 pm. It has loads of information on the NYMR, walks and mountain biking on the moors.

Pickering Castle (☎ 01751-474989, EH) was founded by William the Conqueror, but the remaining ruins date from a later period. Some of the curtain walls with towers, and part of the keep on a 40-foot-high motte, survive. It's a beautiful site, with good views over the town; £2/1.50.

The nearest youth hostel is the *Old School Youth Hostel* (☎ 01751-460376) at Lockton, about four miles to the north on the A169 between Pickering and Whitby. It's about two miles from the NYMR station at Levisham, and is passed by Yorkshire Coastliner's No 840 bus between Leeds/York and Whitby. The hostel makes a good walking base. It's open April to September, except Sunday; the nightly rate is £5.35/3.75.

The *Black Swan* (☎ 472286), 18 Birdgate, is a popular pub so don't expect to sleep before closing time. B&B starts at £23.50 per person; allow a couple more pounds if you want a bathroom.

The cheapest option for food is the excellent *Thomas of Pickering* bakery on Market Place – stock up for picnics, train rides and walks. The *Rose* pub, on Bridge St near the NYMR station, has a nice beer garden beside the river and cheap food.

For excellent fish & chips (£2.15), eat in or takeaway, try the *Little Scarboro Restaurant*, Hungate, to the west of the roundabout on the A170.

There are reasonably frequent buses along the A170 between Scarborough and Helmsley, as well as the Yorkshire Coastliner's service mentioned above.

NORTH YORKSHIRE MOORS RAILWAY

Aside from appealing to railway enthusiasts with some magnificent restored engines and carriages, the NYMR cuts across an interesting section of the moors and opens up some excellent day walks. And it can still fulfil its original function of providing a link to Whitby.

History

The line from Pickering to Whitby was the third passenger line to be opened in Yorkshire, coming 10 years after the Stockton-Darlington Railway.

For the first 10 years of its life, carriages on the Pickering-Whitby line were pulled by horses, except at Beck Hole, where the 1:15 incline was conquered by a balancing system of water-filled tanks, and on downhill stretches where the horses were put in a carriage and the train freewheeled! The first steam locomotive was used in 1847.

In the 1950s the increasing domination of private cars led to the first closures, and after 1965 only the Esk Valley line remained in operation. Thousands of locals opposed the 'rationalisation', however, and in 1967 a volunteer preservation society was formed to restore and operate the Grosmont-Pickering line. Today the NYMR carries 300,000 passengers a year.

Orientation & Information

The NYMR runs north-south and links Grosmont (on British Rail's Esk Valley line between Whitby and Middlesbrough) with Pickering. It's 18 miles long and the full journey takes an hour and costs an adult £6.90.

The main station is at Pickering (☎ 01751-472508). At all the stations there is information about waymarked walks, designed as family strolls lasting between one and four hours. The railway, Pickering and the surrounding countryside can easily absorb a day. Look for the *Walks from the Train* booklet (70p).

On Friday and Saturday from 3 May to 27 September a special train leaves Grosmont station at 7.20 pm; dinner is served and it returns at 9.45 pm (don't forget the long summer evenings). The train and meal price is £28. Most Sundays from April to October there's also a train on which lunch, for around £18, is served.

The timetable is too complicated to be repeated here, but there is a recorded timetable (☎ 01751-473535). Roughly speaking,

there are up to eight trains a day between Easter and 3 November.

The Journey

Most passengers begin and end their journey at Pickering.

From Pickering the line follows Pickering Beck. The first stop is **Levisham station**, 1½ miles west of beautiful **Levisham** village, which in turn faces **Lockton** across a steep valley. Lockton, just off the A169 between Whitby and Pickering, has *The Old School Youth Hostel* (see the Pickering section).

Goathland is a picturesque village 500 feet above sea level amongst the heather-clad moors. There are a number of good walks from the station.

Wheeldale Lodge Youth Hostel (☎ 01947-896350) is three miles south-west of Goathland station. It's open Friday to Tuesday from April to June, and in September; and daily except Wednesday in July and August; £5.50/3.75. There are also camping grounds at *Abbott's Farm* (☎ 01947-896270) for £4.50, and at *Brow House Farm* (☎ 01947-896274).

The *Mallyan Spout* (☎ 896486) pub has good bar food, and bedrooms from £30 per person.

Grosmont (pronounced growmont) is a sleepy little village with accommodation at *Hazelwood House* (☎ 01947-895292), one pub, and that's about it.

Getting There & Away

It is possible to connect with British Rail's Esk Valley line at Grosmont, but considerable waits might be involved. The Esk Valley line does not operate on Sunday; Whitby and Middlesbrough-bound trains stop at Grosmont.

Tees & District (☎ 01947-602146) has two buses Monday to Friday from Whitby to Goathland. Yorkshire Coastliner (☎ 01653-692556) has an interesting service (No 840/842) between Whitby and Leeds via Goathland, Pickering and York.

Yorkshire Dales National Park

Austere stone villages with simple, functional architecture; streams and rivers cutting through the hills; wide, empty moors and endless stone walls snaking over the slopes – this is the region that was made famous by James Herriot and the TV series *All Creatures Great & Small*.

The landscape of the Dales is completely different from that of the Lake District – the overwhelming impression is of space and openness. The high tops of the limestone hills are exposed moorland, and the sheltered dales between them range from Swaledale, which is narrow and sinuous, and Wensleydale and Wharfedale, which are broad and open, to Littondale and Ribblesdale, which are more rugged.

The Yorkshire Dales are very beautiful, but in summer, like the Lake District, they are extremely crowded. Avoid weekends and the peak summer period, or try to get off the beaten track. The famous Pennine Way runs to the area and can be unbelievably busy while other local footpaths are deserted.

ORIENTATION

The Dales can be broken into northern and southern halves: in the north, the two main dales run parallel and east-west. Swaledale, the northernmost, is particularly beautiful. If you have private transport, the B6270 from Kirkby Stephen to Richmond is highly recommended. Parallel and to the south is broad Wensleydale.

In the southern half, north-south Ribblesdale is the route taken by the Leeds-Settle-Carlisle (LSC) railway line (see separate section), which provides access to a number of attractive towns. Wharfedale is parallel and to the east.

Skipton is the most important transport hub for the region, although apart from its castle it is not very interesting. Richmond is a particularly beautiful town and is handy for the north. For those without transport, the best bet will be those places accessible on the LSC line; Kirkby Stephen, Dent and Settle all have nearby youth hostels.

INFORMATION

The main National Park Visitors Centre (☎ 01756-752774) is at Grassington, six miles north of Skipton; it's open daily, except Monday to Friday from November to April. It publishes the useful *Visitor* newspaper.

WALKS

There is a huge range of walks in the national park, ranging from easy strolls to extremely challenging hikes; the TICs are good places to start if you're looking for information on day walks.

The Pennine Way crosses the park; it's a demanding and deservedly popular walk to the rugged western half. Another possibility is the Dales Way which begins in Ilkley, follows the rivers Wharfe and Dee to the heart of the Dales, and finishes at Bowness-on-Windermere in the Lake District. If you started at Grassington (see above), it would be an easy five-day, 60-mile walk.

CYCLE ROUTES

Outside of busy summer weekends, the Dales provide ideal cycling country. Most of the roads follow the rivers along the bottom of the dales, so, although there are still some steep climbs, there's also plenty on the flat.

The CTC (see the Activities chapter) and the National Park Centre at Grassington have information about the 131-mile Yorkshire Dales Cycle Way that loops around through some of the lesser known dales, following small B-roads.

The first 24-mile stage is from Skipton to Malham: start by heading east to Bolton Abbey, then head north to Appletreewick, then north-west to Grassington and Malham.

The second 22-mile stage starts by heading north to Malham Tarn, then continues west to Settle, Clapham and Ingleton.

The third 23-mile stage heads north to Dent along Kingsdale, then east along Dentdale and on to Hawes.

The fourth 20-mile stage runs east along

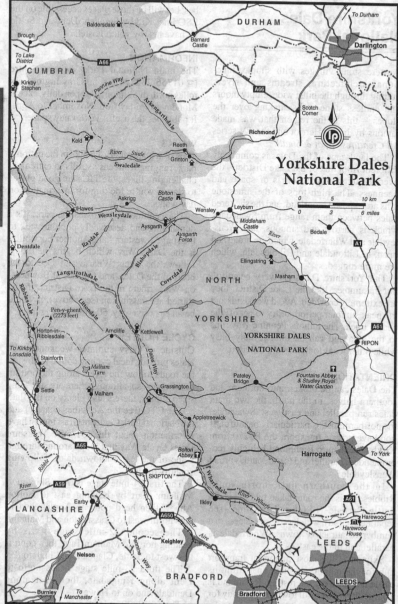

NORTHERN ENGLAND

Yorkshire Dales
National Park

0		5		10 km
0		3		6 miles

Wensleydale to Askrigg, where it turns north over the moors to Swaledale, then east to Grinton.

The fifth 22-mile stage turns south to Bolton Castle, east to Wensley, then south-west down Coverdale to Kettlewell.

The final 20-mile stage back to Skipton follows Wharfedale south to Grassington, then retraces the route through Appletreewick and Bolton Abbey.

GETTING THERE & AROUND

For public-transport users from the south, the Dales are best accessed from Leeds using the LSC line to Skipton, which also gives good access to the west. This line also makes Carlisle a jumping-off point in the north-west. Life is more difficult in the north-east and east, although buses run from Darlington to Richmond and Barnard Castle, and Harrogate and Ripon are also accessible.

As a rule, however, public transport is grim. Bus users need a copy of the *Dales Connections* timetable, available from TICs. Cycling is an excellent way to get around; see the following Cycle Routes section.

LEEDS-SETTLE-CARLISLE LINE

The Leeds-Settle-Carlisle (LSC) line is one of the greatest engineering achievements of the Victorian era, and it takes passengers across some of the best countryside in England. It services a number of attractive market towns (several with nearby youth hostels) and gives excellent access to the western dales.

Orientation & Information

The LSC line runs between Leeds and Carlisle, from Leeds along the Aire Valley, then to Ribblesdale, Dentdale and the western edge of the Dales. There are good walks from a number of the small stations along the way and free guided walks each Saturday and some Sundays and Wednesdays.

For up-to-date information, contact British Rail. There are trains roughly every two hours from Monday to Saturday all year, and three on Sunday from April to October.

The entire journey takes three hours one way and costs £15.50 for a day return.

The Journey

The first section of the journey is along the Aire Valley from **Leeds** (see the separate section).

Keighley (see the separate section) is the starting point for the Keighley & Worth Valley steam railway to Haworth (of Brontë fame: see section on West Yorkshire in the Northern Midlands chapter).

Skipton is considered the gateway to the southern dales. After Skipton the railway crosses the moors to Ribblesdale and the attractive market town of **Settle** (near which is a youth hostel; see the Settle section).

Next is the spectacular Ribbleshead Viaduct and Blea Moor Tunnel, linking Ribblesdale to Dentdale. The *Dentdale Youth Hostel* (☎ 015396-25251), an old shooting lodge beside the River Dee, is two miles south of the station. The attractive and popular village is four miles to the west. The hostel is open daily except Thursday from April to August, and from Friday to Tuesday in September and October; £7.45/5.

After Garsdale, the train reaches its highest point (1169 feet) at Ais Gill. Before **Kirkby Stephen** (which has a youth hostel; see the separate section) are the ruins of Pendragon Castle, built in the 12th century and reputed to be the home of King Arthur's father.

Appleby is the home of a famous Gipsy Horse Fair, held on the second Wednesday of June. After Appleby and to the east is Cross Fell, at 2930 feet, the highest point on the Pennines. **Langwathby** is just to the north-west of Penrith, a jumping-off point for the Lakes, connected by bus to Keswick and Newcastle upon Tyne (see the following Getting There & Away section). Armathwaite Viaduct is above the village and castle of **Combe Eden**, after which you reach **Carlisle** (which has a youth hostel; see the separate section).

Getting There & Away

For information about connecting services,

see the Leeds and Carlisle sections. Another interesting possibility is the summer-only trans-Pennine bus service between Newcastle upon Tyne and Keswick, which connects with the LSC line at Langwathby railway station. The service is operated by Wright Brothers (☎ 01434-381200). There are three services from Monday to Saturday and one on Sunday going across country from Newcastle upon Tyne to Keswick, via Langwathby, on the LSC line, and Hexham and Corbridge, on Hadrian's Wall.

SKIPTON

Skipton is a popular gateway to the Dales and a market town, so it can get very busy on summer weekends. The TIC (☎ 01756-792809), 9 Sheep St, is open Monday to Saturday from 10 am to 5 pm, and Sunday in summer from 2 to 5 pm.

Skipton Castle is considered to be one of the best preserved medieval castles in Britain. It's open every day from 10 am to 6 pm (2 pm on Sunday); £3.20/1.50.

Pennine Boat Trips (☎ 01756-790829), Coach St, runs hour-long trips along the canal almost every day between Easter and October at noon and 1.30 and 3 pm, and at 7 pm in July and August; £3.40/1.70.

The *Unicorn Hotel* (☎ 01756-794146), Keighley Rd, has rooms with bathroom for around £20 per person. Similarly priced are *Craven House* (☎ 794657), 56 Keighley Rd and the *Highfield Hotel* (☎ 793182) at No 58.

South of town on Keighley Rd beside the bridge over the canal, *Eastwood's Fish Restaurant & Takeaway* is a large restaurant with an extensive menu of fish dishes as well as traditional fish & chips. *Bizzie Lizzies* (☎ 793189), 36 Swadford St, is much more spartan, but it is locally famous for the quality of its fish & chips.

There are National Express buses direct from London. During summer, Cumberland's X9 (☎ 01946-63222) service runs between York and Ambleside (Lake District) via Kirkby Lonsdale, Settle, Skipton and Harrogate (Yorkshire Dales) on Monday, Wednesday, Friday and Saturday.

Skipton is on the famous LSC line, and is only three stops north of Keighley (for the Keighley & Worth Valley Railway to Haworth).

GRASSINGTON

Grassington is an attractive village that makes an excellent base for exploring the Dales, especially Upper Wharfedale.

There is a useful National Park Visitors Centre (☎ 01756-752774) south of town, with a large car park. It has an accommodation-booking service and lots of information on the park and walks and cycle routes within it.

The *Linton Youth Hostel* (☎ 01756-752400), Linton, is just three-quarters of a mile south of Grassington, in the adjoining hamlet of Linton. It's open daily, except Sunday, from April to September but telephone for its complicated opening schedule the rest of the year; £8.25/5.55.

Raines Close (☎ 01756-752678), 13 Station Rd, has comfortable doubles and twins from £18 to £25 per person. *Farfield* (☎ 752435), Wharfeside Ave, Threshfield, is a little less expensive.

From Skipton railway station, Keighley & District buses (☎ 01535-603284) depart irregularly Monday to Saturday. There's a Sunday service from April to September.

Bikes are available from *Grassington Hardware Shop* (☎ 01756-752592), 5 Chapel St.

SETTLE

Settle is a pleasant market town in Ribblesdale, on the edge of the geological fault that delineates the limestone to the north and the gritstone to the south.

The TIC (☎ 01729-825192) is in the town hall; it's open daily in summer from 10 am to 5 pm, and in winter from 10 am to noon. There are a couple of excellent bakeries on Church St, north-west of Market Place.

The *Stainforth Youth Hostel* (☎ 01729-823577), Stainforth, is 2½ miles north of Settle on the B6479 to Horton-in-Ribblesdale. It's open daily from April to September (except Sunday in April and September) and on Friday and Saturday the rest of the year; £7.45/5. *Knight Stainforth Hall* (☎ 01729-822200), Stackhouse Lane, opposite the high school, is about three miles from town and has tent sites from £6.50.

The *Royal Oak* (☎ 01729-822561), Market Place, is a good pub with bar meals starting around £5, including plenty of vegetarian dishes and salads; it also has rooms for £33/54.

Penmar Court (☎ 01729-823258), Duke St (the main street to the east of Market Place), has a number of rooms from £16 per person.

For Cumberland's X9 service, see under Skipton.

AROUND SETTLE
Three Peaks
The countryside to the north is dominated by the well-known Three Peaks, which are part of a challenging 26-mile circuit involving 5000 feet of ascent. Beginning at Horton-in-Ribblesdale, you follow the Pennine Way to **Pen-y-ghent** (2273 feet), with a distinctive sphinx-like shape.

Next is **Whernside** (2414 feet), actually the northernmost peak, then, finally, **Ingleborough** (2373 feet), which has a distinctive flat top of gritstone and was the site for a Celtic settlement – hut circles and parts of a defensive wall can still be seen. Cumberland's X9 service stops at Ingleton for the Peaks, with a bus on Wednesday, Friday and Saturday during the summer only.

KIRKBY LONSDALE
• *pop 1800*   • ☎ 015242
Kirkby Lonsdale is a beautiful, unspoilt market town with an excellent position midway between the Lakes and the Dales. In common with quite a few of the Lake District towns, it is rather artfully unspoilt, a bit cutesy and a bit unreal.

Orientation & Information
Kirkby Lonsdale is actually a part of Cumbria. It is outside the park borders, but

for visitors it is essentially a Dales town, both in appearance and as a useful touring centre.

The excellent TIC (☎ 71437), 24 Main St, is open from Easter to October daily from 9 am to 1 pm and 2 to 5 pm, and in winter from Thursday to Sunday.

Places to Stay & Eat
The *Sun Hotel* (☎ 71965), Market St, is a very old inn, dating to the 17th century, with interesting meals in its *Mad Carews* restaurant. Peking duck pancakes are £4.50, tagliatelle carbonara £5.95. The *Snooty Fox* (☎ 71308), Main St, is well known for good food, with an imaginative menu ranging from £5 to £8; it also has rooms from around £22 per person.

The *Copper Kettle Restaurant* (☎ 71714) has a large traditional English menu (with plenty of roasts), with dishes from £4 to £8. There are also four comfortable rooms from £15 per person.

Getting There & Away
Kirkby Lonsdale is 17 miles from Settle and 15 miles from Windermere; the nearest railway connection is at Oxenholme (12 miles).

For Cumberland's X9 service, see under Skipton.

Getting Around
Taxi Ring Mainline Taxis on ☎ 0374-642752.

KIRKBY STEPHEN
• *pop 1600*   • ☎ 017683
Kirkby Stephen is a classic market town with stone Georgian-style houses flanking an attractive High St. There's nothing very remarkable about the place, but in some ways that adds to its appeal – it is not inundated with visitors.

Orientation & Information
Kirkby Stephen is actually part of Cumbria. It is outside the park borders, but for visitors it is a useful touring centre for the Dales and the surrounding Eden Valley.

The excellent TIC (☎ 71199), Market Square, is open Easter to October, daily from

9.30 am to 5 pm, and in winter with shorter hours from Monday to Saturday.

Walks & Cycle Routes

Following Wainwright's Coast to Coast Walk to the east, it's 13 miles from Kirkby Stephen to Keld, which also has a youth hostel (see Hawes, Walks & Cycle Routes). Following the Coast to Coast Walk west, the next stops are Orton, Shap, Patterdale and Grasmere.

Places to Stay

Hostel The *Kirkby Stephen Youth Hostel* (☎ 71793), Fletcher Hill, is in a converted chapel in the centre of town, just south of Market Square. It's open April to June except Monday, daily from June to August, and September and October except Monday and Tuesday; £7.45/5.

B&Bs The *Old Court House* (☎ 71061), High St, has excellent accommodation, and yes, it is in the Old Court House. There are rooms from £15 per person. The *Jolly Farmers House* (☎ 71063), 63 High St, has a number of rooms from £15 per person.

Places to Eat

There are several excellent bakeries and good-value tearooms. The *Pennine Hotel*, Market St, is a straightforward pub with straightforward bar meals from £4. The *Old Forge Bistro* (☎ 71832), 39 North Rd, serves excellent vegetarian dishes for around £3 at lunch, tzatzini with pitta for example, and £6 in the evening. B&B is also available at £15 per person.

Getting There & Away

Kirkby Lonsdale is 25 miles away, Hawes is 16 miles away and Carlisle is 50 miles away.

Bus Primrose Coaches (☎ 0191-232 5567) has a daily X69 service between Newcastle upon Tyne and Blackpool via Durham, Barnard Castle, Raby Castle and Kirkby Stephen.

Coast to Coast Packhorse Kirkby Stephen is home to the innovative Coast to Coast Packhorse (☎ 71680), a daily minibus that runs from St Bees on the west coast to Robin Hood's Bay on the east from Easter to October.

It has several services including to some of the villages and towns along the route of Alfred Wainwright's 190-mile Coast to Coast Walk. These towns include Penrith, Keswick, Cockermouth, Whitehaven, St Bees and back through Ennerdale, Rosthwaite, Keswick, Grasmere, Patterdale and Shap to Kirkby Stephen. Another route is Kirkby Stephen through Keld, Richmond, Blakey and Grosmont to Robin Hood's Bay.

The minibus will take bodies or backpacks or both. Backpacks (and bodies where appropriate) are delivered to a pick-up point at the next stop on the walk. Packs cost £3 per stop if booked, 50p more if unbooked; it's £51 (booked) all the way from St Bees to Robin Hood's Bay.

Getting Around

Bicycle Mortlake Mountain Bikes (☎ 71666), 32 Market St opposite the tourist office, is a very well organised operation. Apart from hire, it organises tours and can suggest routes. Mountain bikes are £15 per day; panniers an additional £2.

RICHMOND
* *pop 8000* * ☎ 01748

Richmond is one of the most beautiful towns in England – and, even better, surprisingly few people know. A ruined castle perches high on a rocky outcrop overlooking a rushing stream, and looms over a steeply sloping Market Square surrounded by Georgian buildings. Cobbled streets, closely lined with stone cottages, radiate from the square and run down to the river, providing exhilarating glimpses of the surrounding hills and moors.

Orientation & Information

Richmond is actually outside and to the east of the national park, but it makes an excellent touring base for the park and it is definitely in the Yorkshire Dales.

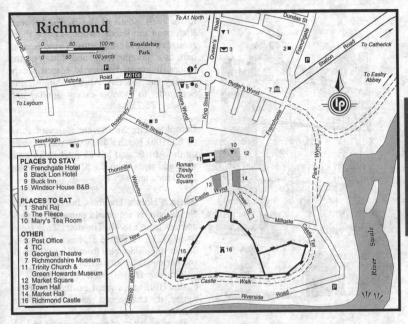

Richmond

0   50   100 m
0   50   100 yards

Ronaldshay Park

To A1 North
Dundas St
Queen's Road
Frenchgate
Station Road
To Catherick

To Easby Abbey

To Leyburn

Victoria Road A6108

Rosemary Lane
Friars Wynd
King Street
Finkle Street
Newbiggin

Ryder's Wynd

Thornhills
Waterloo
Road

New Road

Bridge Street

Roman Trinity Church Square

Castle   Wynd
Tower St
Millgate
Castle Ter

Park – Wynd

River Swale

Castle — — — Walk —

Riverside   Road

PLACES TO STAY
2 Frenchgate Hotel
8 Black Lion Hotel
9 Buck Inn
15 Windsor House B&B

PLACES TO EAT
1 Shahi Raj
5 The Fleece
10 Mary's Tea Room

OTHER
3 Post Office
4 TIC
6 Georgian Theatre
7 Richmondshire Museum
11 Trinity Church &
    Green Howards Museum
12 Market Square
13 Town Hall
14 Market Hall
16 Richmond Castle

NORTHERN ENGLAND

Finkle St, off Market Square, has some interesting shops including Gordon Sargent, for outdoor gear, and the excellent Richmond Bakery.

The TIC (☎ 850252), Friary Gardens, Victoria Rd, is open April to October, daily from 9.30 am to 5.30 pm, and November to March, Monday to Saturday from 9.30 am to 4.30 pm. It has good brochures showing walks around the town and surrounding countryside (including to Easby Abbey, which is recommended).

Richmond Castle

Begun in 1071, Richmond Castle (☎ 822493; EH) has surviving 11th-century curtain walls, a gatehouse, a chapel and what is believed to be the oldest surviving Norman great hall (Scollard's Hall). The impressive keep (1171), beside the gatehouse, is in remarkably good condition. It has been refloored and reroofed to give an idea of what it was like in medieval times. Entry to the castle is £1.80/1.40.

It is a dramatic ruin so it is not surprising that legends (however unlikely) cling to it like moss: some say an underground tunnel links it to Easby Abbey, and that King Arthur and his knights are in a magical sleep here and will wake when the country needs them.

Museums

There are three small but interesting museums in Richmond. The **Georgian Theatre** (☎ 823710), Victoria Rd, was built in 1788 and is the oldest theatre in the UK surviving in its original form. It's open for guided tours from April to October, Monday to Saturday from 11 am to 4.45 pm and Sunday from 2.30 to 4.45 pm; £1/70p. **Richmondshire Museum** (☎ 825611), Ryder's Wynd, is an interesting local museum open from Good Friday to late October daily from 11 am to 5 pm; £1/80p. The **Green Howards Museum** (☎ 822133), Trinity Church Square, shows the history of

Richmond Castle

the Green Howards, a famous Yorkshire regiment; open from 8.45 am to 4.15 pm; £2/1.

Cycle Routes

Cycling on the narrow Dales roads would be no fun on a busy summer weekend; that point aside, this is great cycling country.

One cycle route to consider is a 20-mile trip to Barnard Castle along the edge of the Cleveland Plain. Take the B6271 to Gilling West, then the B-roads to the south of the A66 through Whashton, Kirby Hill, Gayles, Dalton, Newsham, Barningham and Greta Bridge, then turn right onto the A66 for a short section, then left for Barnard Castle (a steep climb).

Another possibility is the 33-mile trip to Kirkby Stephen along beautiful Swaledale.

Places to Stay

Hostel The nearest youth hostel is 10 miles to the west, south of the B2670 between Richmond and Reeth. *Grinton Lodge Youth Hostel* (☎ 01748-884206), Grinton, was built as a shooting lodge and is high on the moors. It's open January to March except Sunday and Monday, April to August, and September to October except Sunday and Monday; £6.75/4.60.

Camping The *Swaleview Caravan Park* (☎ 823106), Reeth Rd, is to the west of town on the A6108, and has 25 pitches for both vans and tents from £2.20 per person plus £1.30 for a tent.

B&Bs & Hotels The *Buck Inn* (☎ 822259), Newbiggin, is a nice old pub with singles/doubles from £18/48. The *Black Lion Hotel* (☎ 823121), 12 Finkle St, has a number of decent singles/doubles from £19 per person, and bar meals for around £4.

Windsor House B&B (☎ 823285), 9 Castle Hill, has a great position near the square; the charge is a reasonable £15 per person.

There's a batch of pleasant places in 17th and 18th-century town houses on cobbled Frenchgate. At the top end, the *Frenchgate Hotel* (☎ 822087), No 59, has a number of comfortable rooms with singles/doubles between £28 and £37 per person. Amongst a number of other possibilities, *Mrs Fifoot* (☎ 823227), No 58, has one double for £36; and *Willance House* (☎ 824467), No 24, has doubles with bathroom and a twin for £17 per person.

Places to Eat

Mary's Tea Room has delicious baked goods, including Yorkshire curd tarts and home-made game pies. There's also an upstairs café with afternoon tea for £3.95 and hot lunches for around £3.50.

The *Shahi Raj* (☎ 826070), 8 Queen St, has vegetable thalis for £6.95 or a curried T-bone steak for £7.95. A takeaway service is also available.

The pubs are also worth trying; the *Black Lion Hotel* on Finkle St has good bar meals from around £4. *The Fleece* pub, close to the tourist office, has three-course meals for £6 or main dishes for £3.65.

Getting There & Away
Richmond is 230 miles from London, 50 miles from Leeds and 45 miles from Newcastle upon Tyne.

Bus United (☎ 01325-468771) has regular services (Nos 27 and 28) to Darlington, which has a railway station. Stagecoach (☎ 01325-384573) also has an express bus (X90) to Darlington, which continues to Newcastle on Saturday.

Train The nearest station is Darlington, 12 miles to the north-east, which is on the main east-coast line from London's King's Cross to Edinburgh.

Getting Around
Bicycle Arthur Caygill (☎ 825469), Gallowfields, may have bikes for hire. Also worth trying is the youth hostel.

FOUNTAINS ABBEY & STUDLEY ROYAL WATER GARDEN
Sheltered in a secluded valley, with a number of monumental buildings surrounded by extensive parkland and gardens, this 800-acre complex in the narrow valley of the River Skell has been designated a World Heritage Site.

It includes the magnificent ruins of a 12th-century Cistercian abbey (Fountains Abbey), a five-storey Jacobean mansion built in 1610 (Fountains Hall), a sumptuous Victorian church built in the 1870s (St Mary's Church), and a number of 18th-century follies – all set within a beautiful 18th-century landscaped park built around a number of artificial lakes and designed to feature the abbey ruins.

History
Fountains Abbey began as a small breakaway group of 13 monks from the Benedictine abbey of St Mary's in York. In 1132, the Archbishop of York granted them land in what was virtual wilderness. Lacking any assistance from an established abbey or order, they turned to the Cistercian order for help.

The Cistercians were often called the White Monks because they wore a habit of undyed wool, reflecting the austerity and simplicity of their order. They were committed to long periods of silence and eight daily services. Clearly, this did not leave a lot of time for practical matters, so the Cistercians ordained lay brothers who lived within the monastery but pursued the abbey's ever-growing business interests – wool, lead mining, quarrying, animal breeding and so on.

Sadly, idealism and purity did not last long, and after economic collapse in the 14th century, the monks rented their lands to tenant farmers and replaced lay brothers with servants. By the beginning of the 16th century the vast abbey had a population of only 30 monks.

After the dissolution the estate was sold into private hands and between 1598 and 1611, Fountains Hall was built with stone from the abbey ruins. The hall passed through several families until it and the ruins were united with the Studley Royal Estate in 1768.

The main house of Studley Royal burnt down in 1946, but the superb landscaping survives virtually unchanged from the 18th century. Studley Royal was owned by John Aislabie, who spent 20 years creating an extensive park. Major engineering works were required to create the lakes and to control the flow of the river.

Orientation & Information
Fountains lies four miles to the west of Ripon off the B6255. There are two entrances, one leaving the B-road 1½ miles from Ripon, for the Canal Gates entrance, and one at three miles for the impressive new Visitors Centre (☎ 01765-608888;NT).

The abbey and garden are open all year, daily except Friday in January, November and December. The deer park is open daily until dusk. Fountains Hall is open April to September, daily from 11 am to 6 pm, and

January to March and October to December daily from 11 am to 4 pm. St Mary's Church is open from May to September daily from 1 to 5 pm. The Visitors Centre is open April to September daily from 10 am to 5 pm, and October to March daily from 10 am to 5 pm.

Admission to the abbey, hall and garden is £4/2; the deer park and St Mary's Church are free.

There are free one-hour guided tours from April to October at 2.30 pm, and at 11 am and 3.30 pm between 20 May and 23 September.

There's a pleasant restaurant in the Visitors Centre; hot dishes cost around £5.

HARROGATE
- *pop 65,500* • ☎ *01423*

After the grimy cities of the Midlands and parts of Yorkshire, Harrogate is reminiscent of the more prosperous south. Primarily built in the 19th century as a fashionable spa town, it has managed to remain affluent although its original excuse for existence – the health-giving effect of mineral spring water – is no longer very convincing.

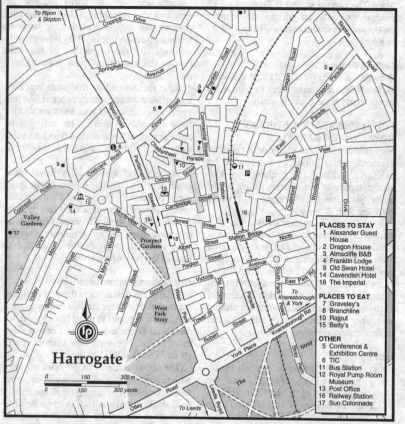

Harrogate

PLACES TO STAY
1 Alexander Guest House
2 Dragon House
3 Almscliffe B&B
4 Franklin Lodge
9 Old Swan Hotel
14 Cavendish Hotel
18 The Imperial

PLACES TO EAT
7 Graveley's
8 Branchline
10 Rajput
15 Betty's

OTHER
5 Conference & Exhibition Centre
6 TIC
11 Bus Station
12 Royal Pump Room Museum
13 Post Office
16 Railway Station
17 Sun Colonnade

The town is famous for its spring/summer floral displays, but the extensive gardens flanked by stately Victorian terraces are beautiful at any time of the year. There are a large number of high-quality hotels and B&Bs (we're definitely not talking nylon sheets in Harrogate) and, even more remarkable, a wide range of interesting restaurants.

Orientation & Information

Harrogate is actually outside and to the south-east of the national park, but it makes an excellent touring base. The town is almost surrounded by gardens, in the south by the 200-acre Stray.

The TIC (☎ 525666) is in the Royal Baths Assembly Rooms, Crescent Rd. It has an accommodation-booking service and also has details of free guided walking tours (from April to September, Monday to Thursday and Sunday). The Harrogate Flower Show is held in April.

Things to See & Do

There are no particularly important sights in Harrogate, but the town is, nonetheless, an attractive place. Strolling in the gardens and taking tea seem to be the principal activities. A wander should start at the **Royal Pump Room Museum**, built in 1842 over the most famous of the sulphur springs. It gives quite a curious insight into the phenomenon. It's open April to October on Monday from 10 am to 5 pm, all year Tuesday to Saturday from 10 am to 5 pm and on Sunday from 2 to 5 pm; £1.50/75p.

The **Valley Gardens**, the site for the town's flower show, are attractive. They're flanked by a 600-foot-long glass-covered walk. At the top of Montpellier Hill, **Betty's** is a classic Edwardian tearoom that has been in business since 1919 (see Places to Eat).

Places to Stay

The nearest youth hostel is in York. Two miles north of town, *Bilton Park* (☎ 863121), Village Farm, Bilton, has sites for tents for £7; open April to October.

Starting from the top, *The Imperial* (☎ 565071), Prospect Place, is a very grand

hotel in the centre of town; rooms cost from £80/95. The *Old Swan Hotel* (☎ 500055), Swan Rd, is an ivy-clad 18th-century coaching house. This is where Agatha Christie chose to hide from the world when she went missing in 1926; rooms cost from £75/85.

There are a number of comfortable, medium-priced hotels overlooking the beautiful Valley Gardens; most have private bathroom. Amongst others, the *Cavendish Hotel* (☎ 509637), 3 Valley Drive, is from £28/50; *Ashbrooke House*, at No 140, is from £21/45.

There are two good-value places in Dragon Parade: *Dragon House* (☎ 569888) at No 6 and *Daryl House Hotel* (☎ 502775) at No 42. Rooms are without bathroom; from £15 per person.

One of the best streets for the cheaper options is Franklin Rd, which is lined with B&Bs. *Almscliffe* (☎ 507027), located at 5, is fairly basic, as is *Franklin Lodge* (☎ 563599), at No 6. Both charge about £15. The comfortable *Alexander Guest House* (☎ 503348), 88 Franklin Rd, is £20.

Places to Eat

Betty's (☎ 502746), 1 Parliament St, is a classic Yorkshire tearoom, open from 9 am (for breakfast) to 9 pm. It has a large variety of teas, coffees and teacakes and reasonably priced soups, sandwiches and main meals. A pianist plays from 6 pm.

There's a wide range of possible eating places. Walk up Cheltenham Parade for Spanish food at *Fino's Tapas Bar* (☎ 565806) or Indian at *Rajput* (☎ 562113). Both charge under £5 for dishes. A few doors up is *The Blue Piano* (☎ 530448) where dishes from around the world – Cajun, Chinese, Japanese, Mediterranean – are mixed and matched. Each dish is under £4. Across the road *Graveley's* (☎ 507093) serves a good-value and tasty fish & chips meal with tea and bread for £4.25. A left turn into Commercial St leads to *Branchlines* for wholefood dishes and light snacks, but closing at 4 pm, and *Le Rendezvous* (☎ 506174) where a set meal of meat or fish is £15.

Getting There & Away

Harrogate is roughly between Leeds (15 miles) and York (22 miles), 75 miles from Newcastle upon Tyne and 210 miles from London.

Bus Harrogate & District (☎ 566061) is the most important local operator. There are frequent buses to Knaresborough (Nos 1 and 22, 20 minutes), Leeds (No 36, 40 minutes) and Ripon. The X50 runs daily between Scarborough and Skipton via Harrogate and York.

For Cumberland's X9 service, see under Skipton.

Train Harrogate is on the Harrogate line from Leeds (half an hour); this runs on to York hourly.

Cumbria

Much of Cumbria is a scenic feast, with the Lake District National Park at its heart. The mountains, valleys and lakes are beautiful, although since they were popularised by the Romantics of the early 19th century they have been the centre of a major tourism industry. Nonetheless, if you avoid summer weekends and the main roads, and do some walking, it is still possible, like Wordsworth, to wander 'lonely as a cloud'.

The M6 and west-coast railway line cut the county into an eastern third, which runs into the Yorkshire Dales and Pennine Hills, and a western two-thirds that includes the Lake District National Park and England's highest mountains. Not surprisingly, the western two-thirds draws the largest crowds, although parts to the east, particularly the Eden Valley, are also very beautiful.

The Celtic people of the Lakes, like the Welsh, called themselves Cymry, from which the modern name of Cumbria is derived. Names beginning with Pen, like Penrith, are Celtic. The Roman legions left traces at a fort below spectacular Hardknott Pass, and the extraordinary ruins of

Hadrian's Wall (see separate section) that runs eastwards from the Solway coast. The next serious settlers were Norwegian Vikings. Many Lakeland words have Norse origins: dales from *dalr*, fells from *fjall*, becks from *bekr*, tarns from *tjorns* and force from *foss*. The ending 'thwaite' means a clearing in the forest.

WALKS

Cumbria includes some of the best walks in Britain. See the Activities chapter for information on the Cumbria Way, and the following Lake District National Park section.

CYCLE ROUTES

There's plenty of good cycling in this region, but keen cyclists should consider the Cumbria Cycle Way. This 259-mile circular route could be done in five full days, but a full week would be better.

The way is waymarked, and there is a good range of information available (the TIC at Carlisle is a good place to start). There's also a guidebook, *The Cumbria Cycle Way* by Roy Walker and Ron Jarvis, published by Cicerone, for £5.99.

GETTING AROUND

Cumbria Travel Link (☎ 01228-812812) gives information and advice on all bus and railway services to and within Cumbria; it's open Monday to Friday from 9 am to 5 pm.

Bus The main operator is Cumberland (☎ 01946-63222). It has an Explorer ticket giving unlimited travel on all Cumberland services, including the No 685 to Newcastle upon Tyne.

Train The county includes three of Britain's most scenic railway journeys. British Rail's Cumbrian Coast line runs all the way round the west coast from Carlisle to Ulverston and Lancaster (on the main line to Carlisle and Glasgow); see the separate Cumbrian Coast line section. There's a branch line from Oxenholme (also on the main line) to Windermere. And, finally, the LSC line (see that section), which starts in South Yorkshire, enters Cumbria south of Kirkby Stephen on its journey through to Carlisle.

CARLISLE
• *pop 72,000* • ☎ *01228*

For 1600 years, Carlisle defended the north of England, or south of Scotland, depending on who was winning.

The city's character was spoilt to some degree by industrialisation in the 19th century; however, it's a 'real' and interesting place and its strategic location can be exploited by visitors to Northumberland, Hadrian's Wall, Dumfries and Galloway and the Borders (the beautiful Scottish border counties) and the Lake District. It is also the hub for five excellent railway journeys.

History
The story of Carlisle's first 1700 years is one of almost constant warfare; it seems almost miraculous that it could be peaceful today. The Romans under Agricola built a military station here, probably on the site of a Celtic camp or *caer* (preserved in the modern name *Car*lisle).

Later, Hadrian's Wall was built a little to the north, and Carlisle became the Roman administrative centre for the north-west. Even the mighty Roman Empire was hard-pressed to maintain control, however, and the Picts sacked the town in 181 and 367.

The town survived into Saxon times, but was under constant pressure from the Scots and was sacked by Danish Vikings in 875. The Normans seized the town from the Scots in 1092 and William Rufus began construction of the castle and town walls, although the Scots once again regained control between 1136 and 1157. Forty years later the city withstood a siege by the Scottish King William, and 60 years later it did so again against William Wallace during the Scottish War of Independence.

The Borders, or the Debateable Lands as they were known, were virtually ungoverned and ungovernable from the late 13th century to the middle of the 16th century. The great families with their complex blood feuds fought and robbed the English, the Scots and each other. The city's walls and the great gates that slammed shut every night served a very real purpose.

During the Civil War, Carlisle was Royalist, and was eventually taken by the Scottish army after a nine-month siege in 1644-5. It also surrendered to Bonnie Prince Charlie in 1745, who proclaimed his father king at the market cross.

After the Restoration, peace came at last to Carlisle – and so did industry, cotton mills and railways.

Orientation & Information
The city is well signposted. The railway station is to the south of the city centre, a 10-minute walk to Town Hall Square (the market square) and the TIC. The bus station is on Lowther St, just one block east of the square.

The TIC & Visitors' Centre (☎ 512444) is particularly informative and has an enormous amount of literature. It's open June to September, Monday to Saturday from 9.30 am to 6 pm (6.30 pm in August), and Sunday from 11 am to 4 pm; and the rest of the year from Monday to Saturday from 9.30 am to 5 pm.

From May to September there are daily guided walks (except Saturday in July and August) at 1.30 pm; £2 and £5 on Sunday, including lunch. The TIC has a foreign exchange counter (3% commission), and there is a nearby Thomas Cook office on the Town Hall Square, open Monday to Saturday from 9 am to 5.30 pm. Outdoor equipment is available from Famous Army Stores, Scotch St, just around the corner from the TIC. Early-closing day is Thursday.

Carlisle Castle
Carlisle Castle (☎ 591922; EH), probably built on the site of British and Roman fortresses, is a dour and evocative fortress, well worth exploring. It was first built in 1092 by William Rufus and there is a fine Norman keep, but this was definitely a working castle, so there were many alterations and additions. There is a maze of

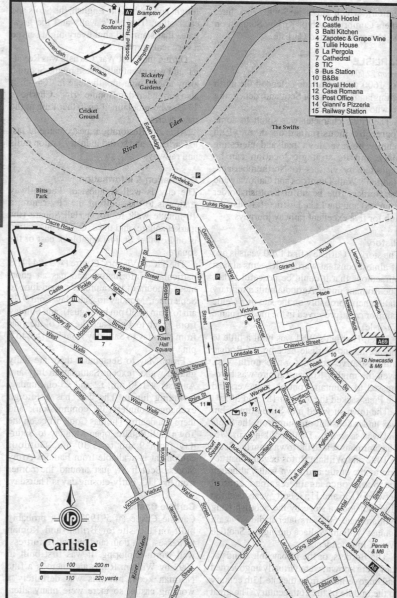

1   Youth Hostel
2   Castle
3   Balti Kitchen
4   Zapotec & Grape Vine
5   Tullie House
6   La Pergola
7   Cathedral
8   TIC
9   Bus Station
10 B&Bs
11 Royal Hotel
12 Casa Romana
13 Post Office
14 Gianni's Pizzeria
15 Railway Station

NORTHERN ENGLAND

Carlisle

0   100   200 m
0   110   220 yards

passages and chambers and great views from the top; £2.50/1.90.

Carlisle Cathedral

The cathedral was originally constructed as a priory church in 1123, but it became a cathedral in 1133. It's a small building in north Cumbria's distinctive red sandstone. Life in Carlisle was dangerous and difficult, however, and this is reflected in the fabric of the building.

The most serious indignity it suffered was during the 1644-5 siege, when two-thirds of the nave was torn down to provide stone for repairing the city wall and castle. Serious restoration did not begin until 1853, but a surprising amount survives – including the east window and part of the original Norman nave.

The cathedral is open all year from 7.30 am to 6.30 pm.

Tullie House Museum

The museum is one of the best in Britain, drawing on the fascinating history of the region and presenting it imaginatively (but without descending to vulgarity). It's particularly strong on Roman Britain, of which it has some remarkable relics, and the Border reivers. Allow at least two hours. The museum (☎ 34781) is open all year, Monday to Saturday from 10 am to 5 pm and Sunday from noon to 5 pm; £3.50/2. There's a good restaurant.

Places to Stay

Hostel The *Carlisle Youth Hostel* (☎ 23934) is for sale and may not be open in 1997 (not that it's a great hostel, but there are no alternatives). It's open February to June except Sunday and Monday, and July and August, and September and October except Sunday and Monday; the nightly rate is £6.10/4.15.

Camping The *Dalston Hall Caravan Park* (☎ 710165), just off the B5299 to the south of the city, has van and tent sites from £5.50.

B&Bs & Hotels There are plenty of comfortable B&Bs within walking distance of the centre, and you shouldn't need to pay more than £15.

There are plenty of reasonable options on Warwick Rd. From the station, cross Botchergate, walk around the crescent and take Warwick Rd on your right. *Cornerways Guest House* (☎ 21733), No 107, is large and convenient with B&B for £13 per person. *East View Guesthouse* (☎ 22112), No 110, has rooms with bathroom and colour TV from £18/32. *Calreena Guest House* (☎ 25020), No 123, charges from £13 to £15.

There's also a good range of more upmarket places. North of town, *Forte Posthouse* (☎ 31201), Parkhouse Rd, is a modern business hotel with rooms for £56. Right in town, two minutes from the railway station, the *Royal Hotel* (☎ 22103), 9 Lowther St, has a range of singles/doubles from £21/35.

Places to Eat

Gianni's Pizzeria (☎ 21093), Cecil St, is a popular spot with the usual pastas and pizzas from around £5. Around the corner at 44 Warwick St *Casa Romana* (☎ 591969) is a smarter and tastier place and only a little more expensive. *La Pergolo*, 28 Castle St, also does pastas and pizzas and has a happy hour between 5.30 pm and 7 pm with dishes for £3.30.

Zapotec (☎ 512209), 18 Fisher St, has good-quality Spanish and Mexican dishes around £10. *Balti Kitchen* (☎ 599992), 21 West Tower St, serves Bangladeshi dishes and much more from its vast menu. Takeaway dishes are around £5, a couple of pounds more in the restaurant.

The *Grape Vine* (☎ 46617), 22 Fisher St, in the YMCA building, is an excellent café, open during the day (not Sunday) for imaginative light meals; most choices around £3.

Getting There & Away

See the fares tables in the Getting Around chapter. Carlisle is 295 miles from London, 95 miles from Glasgow, 98 miles from Edinburgh, 115 miles from York and Manchester, 58 miles from Newcastle upon Tyne, 107 miles from Stranraer, 25 miles from Cockermouth and nine miles from Brampton.

Bus There are numerous National Express connections which can be booked at the TIC. There are four buses to/from London (5½ hours) and many to Glasgow (two hours). One service a day comes all the way through from Cambridge (eight hours) and Bristol (eight hours); and from York (five hours).

OK Travel (☎ 01388-45000) has a daily service between Darlington and Carlisle via Appleby, Kirkby Stephen, Barnard Castle and Penrith (X74).

There is a Rail Link coach service that runs from the railway station to Hawick, Selkirk and Galashiels in the Scottish Borders.

Cumberland's Lakeslink service (the X5) links Carlisle to Penrith, Keswick, Cockermouth and Whitehaven.

See the Hadrian's Wall section for services to Newcastle upon Tyne.

Train There are 15 trains a day to Carlisle from London's Euston station (four hours).

Carlisle is the terminus for five famous scenic railways; contact British Rail for detailed information. Most of the following lines have day Ranger tickets that allow you unlimited travel – inquire for details.

Leeds-Settle-Carlisle line (see that section) cuts south-east across the Yorkshire Dales through beautiful, unspoilt countryside.

Lake District line branches off the main north-south line between Preston and Carlisle at Oxenholme, just outside Kendal, for Windermere; there are plenty of trains seven days a week.

Tyne Valley line follows Hadrian's Wall to/from Newcastle upon Tyne. There are some fine views, and it is useful for visitors to the wall; see the Newcastle upon Tyne and Hadrian's Wall sections.

Cumbrian Coast line (see that section) follows the coast in a great arc around to Lancaster, with views over the Irish Sea, and back to the Lake District.

Glasgow-Carlisle line is the main route north to Glasgow, and it gives you a taste of the grand scale of Scottish landscapes. Most trains make few stops (1½ hours).

Getting Around

Taxi Try Radio Taxi (☎ 27575) or County Cabs (☎ 596789).

Bicycle The nearest mountain-bike hire is from Talkin Tarn (☎ 016977-3129), near Brampton.

Lake District National Park

I wandered lonely as a cloud
That floats on high o'er dales and hills
When all at once I saw a crowd...

The Lake District is the most beautiful corner of England: a combination of green dales, which are so perfect they could almost be parks, rocky mountains that seem to heave themselves up into the sky, and lakes that multiply the scenery with their reflections. The Cumbrian Mountains are not particularly high – none reach 1000 metres – but they are much more dramatic than their height would suggest.

Unfortunately, there are over 10 million visitors a year, and they ain't all daffodils. The crowds are so intense it is questionable whether it is worth visiting on any weekend between May and October, or any time at all from mid-July to the end of August. It is particularly bizarre and horrible to be stuck in a traffic jam in such idyllic surroundings. It is also common. Scenery and weather are best, and crowds smallest, on weekdays in May and June, followed by weekdays in September and October.

Fortunately, the countryside is being carefully managed – the National Trust owns a quarter of its total area, including all the central fell area, and six of the main lakes. This is partly thanks to Beatrix Potter, especially around Coniston. She sold the NT half of her large estate at cost and bequeathed the rest.

ORIENTATION

The two main bases for the Lakes are

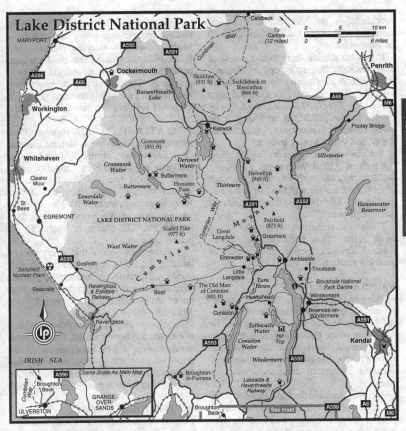

Lake District National Park

NORTHERN ENGLAND

Keswick in the north (particularly for walkers) and Windermere and Bowness in the south (two contiguous tourist traps). Coniston and Cockermouth are less hectic alternatives. All these towns have youth hostels, plus numerous B&Bs and places to eat.

Ullswater, Grasmere, Windermere, Coniston Water and Derwent Water are often considered to be the most beautiful lakes, but they also teem with boats. Wast Water, Crummock Water and Buttermere are equally spectacular and are much less crowded.

In general, the mob stays on the A-roads, and the crowds are much thinner west of a line drawn from Keswick to Coniston.

INFORMATION

Hundreds of guidebooks and brochures have been produced on this region, and a frightening quantity are available from TICs. The Windermere and Keswick TICs are good places to start exploring the Lake District; both have an excellent range of information (and free local booking services). The national park has nine TICs in the area, and a visitors' centre (☎ 015394-46601) at

Brockhole, on the A591 between Windermere and Ambleside, but there are about 30 dotted around.

If you are staying more than a couple of days, consider buying a copy of *National Park Walks in the Countryside*, which has 40 walks of all grades, even for kids, and costs only £1.99. *The Good Guide to the Lakes* by Hunter Davies (£4.95) is an idiosyncratic guide covering background, practicalities, walks, and where to stay and eat.

The classic walking guides are the seven volumes of Alfred Wainwright's *Pictorial Guide to the Lakeland Fells*. Each is a work of art – handwritten and hand-drawn – and they are still useful despite their age and cost (about £10 each).

There are numerous walking/climbing shops in the region, particularly in Ambleside and Keswick; they are good sources of local information.

WALKS & CYCLE ROUTES

Walking or cycling are the two best ways to get around, but bear in mind that conditions can be treacherous, and the going can be very, very steep. Off-road mountain biking is very popular, but there are also some good touring routes. See the Getting Around sections for listings of companies that hire bikes.

Everyone walks in the Lake District; there are countless possibilities. A number of outdoor shops and centres hire boots, tents and hiking equipment. There is a useful weather service phone line if you plan to stay a while (☎ 017687-75757). See the following information sections.

See the Activities chapter for details on the Cumbria Way; also see the Cumbria section for information on the Cumbrian Cycle Way.

PLACES TO STAY & EAT

There are over 30 youth hostels in the region, many of which are within walking distance of each other. They are very popular so it is worth booking well in advance in summer.

The Lake District National Park (☎ 017687-72803) administers a small, but growing, network of camping barns. These traditional barns, no longer required by modern farmers, are kitted out with basic facilities (wooden sleeping platform, tap, toilet, table, benches). You need camping equipment (except a tent) and the cost is £3 per person. They are all in picturesque locations and they are highly recommended. The TICs and park centres have more information.

The NT (☎ 015395-31273) operates three excellent camping grounds for tents and vans (not caravans): at the head of Great Langdale, eight miles from Ambleside on the B5343; at the head of Wasdale, on the western shore of Wast Water; and at Low Wray, three miles south of Ambleside on the western shore of Windermere (access from the B5286). The charge is around £3 per person per night.

It sometimes seems that every second building is a B&B, but despite this, in midsummer, especially on weekends, you are advised to book and be prepared for high prices. At peak times prices jump 25% to 50%.

In general, food is reasonably priced and of a reasonably high standard. The best place to start looking is in the local pubs, where the prices are keen, the servings are hearty and the menus are often surprisingly imaginative (almost always having vegetarian choices).

GETTING THERE & AWAY

There is a direct railway link with Manchester airport to Barrow-in-Furness (2½ hours) and Windermere (2¼ hours). Carlisle (see that section), a major transport hub, has a number of bus services to Keswick, which is the centre of the northern lakes.

Windermere (see that section) has a railway station and good road links, and is the main centre for the southern lakes.

To both Windermere and Carlisle, coaches from London take about 6½ hours, trains 3½ hours.

GETTING AROUND

The distance in miles between most points is actually quite small (for example, Ambleside is five miles from Windermere), so it is also worth considering taxis; expect to pay around £1.50 per mile, with a minimum total charge of £2.

Bus
The innovative Coast to Coast Packhorse (☎ 017683-71680) has a daily minibus service from St Bees on the west coast to Robin Hood's Bay on the east from Easter to October. See the Kirkby Stephen section.

Cumberland (☎ 01946-63222) has some excellent bus services in the area, including the No 555 Lakeslink between the main towns and on to Carlisle; the No 505/506 Coniston Rambler minibuses on the Beatrix Potter Trail – hourly links between Bowness, Windermere, Ambleside, Hilltop, Hawkeshead and Coniston; and the No 517 Kirkstone Rambler over Kirkstone Pass. The free paper *Explorer* has full details.

Train
Aside from British Rail's Cumbrian Coast line (see that section) and the branch line from Oxenholme to Windermere, there are a number of steam railways; the TICs have brochures.

Boat
Windermere, Coniston Water and Derwent Water are all plied by ferries. Some of these can provide useful links with walks. See the Windermere & Bowness, Coniston and Keswick sections for details.

CUMBRIAN COAST LINE
The Cumbrian Coast railway line serves the industrial towns and ports of the Cumbrian coast. For most of the way it skirts the coast and although parts are beautiful – especially between Ravenglass and Barrow-in-Furness – there are also some depressing industrial towns in a state of terminal decline.

Although most of it lies outside the park boundary, the line provides some useful starting points for the western lakes. It is also a potential return link for walkers on the Cumbria Way who have left their vehicles at Carlisle, and walkers on the Coast to Coast Walk who have left their cars at St Bees.

Orientation & Information
The Cumbrian Coast line loops around the Cumbrian coast 120 miles from Carlisle to Lancaster; both cities are on the main line between London's Euston and Glasgow.

Telephone British Rail's national inquiry number for detailed information. Basically, however, there are five services a day from Monday to Saturday, but none on Sunday.

WINDERMERE & BOWNESS
• *pop 8300*   • ☎ *015394*

Thanks to the railway, the Windermere and Bowness conglomerate is the largest tourist town in the Lake District. At times it feels like a seaside resort, thanks to the crowds and the tourist tat.

It's the most important centre in the Lake District, and although there are plenty of places to stay and eat, there are better options.

Orientation
The word Windermere used alone really refers to the lake, the largest in England. Windermere the town is a reasonably modern development that followed on the heels of the railway (which arrived in 1847). Adjoining Bowness-on-Windermere, as it is correctly known, is on the lakeside, about 1½ miles downhill from Windermere railway station.

Information
The Windermere TIC (☎ 46499), Victoria St, is excellent; visitors can send and receive faxes at reasonable cost. It's open daily from 9 am to 6 pm. The Brockhole National Park Visitor Centre (☎ 46601) is three miles north of Windermere on the A591. There is also a TIC down in Bowness by the lake, on Glebe Rd south of the Promenade.

Coaches and long-distance buses leave from the railway station. There is a laundrette opposite the Royalty cinema on Crag Brow, Bowness.

Lakeland Leisure (☎ 44786), Lake Rd, runs paragliding courses and guided cycling tours.

NORTHERN ENGLAND

NORTHERN ENGLAND

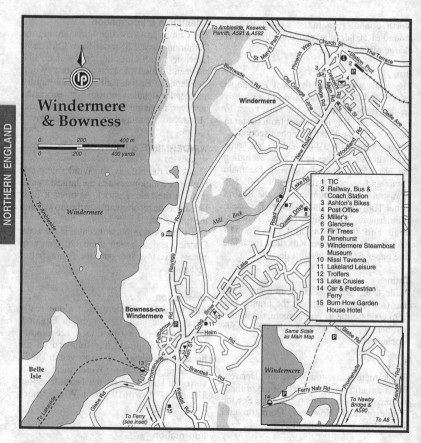

Windermere & Bowness

0   200   400 m
0   200   400 yards

To Ambleside, Keswick,
Penrith, A591 & A592

Windermere

Windermere

Bowness-on-
Windermere

Belle
Isle

To Lakeside

To Ambleside

Mill Beck

To Ferry
(see inset)

Same Scale
as Main Map

Windermere

Ferry Nab Rd

To Newby
Bridge &
A590

To A6

1 TIC
2 Railway, Bus &
   Coach Station
3 Ashton's Bikes
4 Post Office
5 Miller's
6 Glencree
7 Fir Trees
8 Denehurst
9 Windermere Steamboat
   Museum
10 Nissi Taverna
11 Lakeland Leisure
12 Troffers
13 Lake Crusies
14 Car & Pedestrian
   Ferry
15 Burn How Garden
   House Hotel

Windermere Steamboat Museum

The museum (☎ 45565), Rayrigg Rd, to the
north of Bowness on the lakeside, has a
fascinating collection of steam and motor
boats, including the oldest mechanically
powered boat in the world. It also has trips
on a small steam launch, the SL *Osprey*. It's
open daily from Easter to October.

Cruises

A number of companies run cruises around
Windermere (the lake) from Bowness Promenade. Their prices are competitive and their
routes are very similar, so the most important

variables are their timetables and the aesthetic appeal of the boats they operate. Most
operators ply Windermere from Ambleside
in the north to Lakeside in the south, via
Bowness. Cruises to Ambleside take about
half an hour and to Lakeside about 40
minutes.

The Windermere Iron Steamboat
Company (☎ 31188) has three beautiful old
cruisers. Single/return tickets from Bowness
to Lakeside and Ambleside start from £3.30;
a full circuit of the lake from £8.50. It also
has combined tickets and timetables that tie
in with the Lakeside to Haverthwaite Steam

Railway (☎ 31594). The railway operates over Easter and from May to October and its round trip takes 40 minutes.

Rowing boats are hired at £2 per person, per hour.

Walks & Cycle Routes

One of the classic Lakeland views, from Orrest Head, is a short walk and steep climb from Windermere railway station. Across the main road from the station, Orrest Head is about half a mile away along a signposted route.

Beatrix Potter's cottage at Hill Top and the village of Hawkshead are easily accessible to walkers. Catch the ferry across Windermere, and it's a two-mile walk to Hill Top. Follow the road around to the western side of Esthwaite Water (turn left at Near Sawrey) for another two miles and you reach Hawkshead Youth Hostel (☎ 015394-36293). From the hostel it's one mile to Hawkshead and from Hawkshead it's five miles to Coniston (see the separate section).

Places to Stay

Hostel The *Windermere Youth Hostel* (☎ 43543), High Cross, Bridge Lane, Troutbeck, is a large hostel, but it's quite a distance (two miles) from the station. Leave Windermere on the A591 to Ambleside; turn right up Bridge Lane at Troutbeck Bridge, one mile north of Windermere. Numerous buses run past Troutbeck Bridge. Beds cost £7.45/5

Camping *Park Cliffe* (☎ 31344) on Birks Rd is a camping and caravan estate with all mod cons and 250 pitches on grass with great views; £8 per two-person tent.

B&Bs & Hotels – bottom end & mid-range

In Windermere, *Brendan Chase* (☎ 45638), at 1 and 3 College Rd, is good value with eight rooms ranging from £11.50 to £22; further along, *Applegarth* (☎ 43206) has 16 rooms ranging from £19.50 to £40. *Denehurst* (☎ 44710), at 40 Queens Drive, has rooms from £15 to £20 and great breakfasts.

There is a small place worth trying on High St: *Lingmoor* (☎ 44947), No 7, is a non-smoking place with rooms from £17 to £27.

Cambridge House (☎ 43846), 9 Oak St, is quiet but central and offers vegetarian breakfasts; £14.50 to £18 per person. *Westbeck* (☎ 44763), 11 Oak St, is similarly priced.

Lake Rd, which runs down to Bowness, is the main run for small hotels. Most have rooms around £20 a night, but many show their prices at the front, so it's good to stroll down and investigate; look for cheaper places in the side streets.

Coming down from Windermere, two places with good reputations are *Fir Trees* (☎ 42272), a non-smoking hotel with eight rooms with private bathroom from £19.50 to £26, and across the road, *Glencree* (☎ 45822), with rooms from £18.50 to £30.

B&Bs & Hotels – top end In the heart of Bowness overlooking the lake, the elegant old Georgian country mansion *The Old England* (☎ 42444), Church St, has an open-air heated pool beside the lake; singles/doubles from £63.75/75.

Holbeck Ghyll (☎ 32375), Holbeck Lane, is an acclaimed hotel in a 19th-century hunting lodge overlooking the lake. Prices range from £50 to £85 per person.

A two-minute walk from the lake, with a mixture of motel-style chalets and rooms and a restaurant in a large Victorian house, *Burn How Garden House Hotel* (☎ 46226), Back Belsfield Rd, has rooms from £36 to £69 per person.

Places to Eat

There is a stack of restaurants in Bowness and Windermere. They range from some of the best in England to some of the worst. The *Burn How* and *Holbeck Ghyll* hotels are recommended for their top-class, expensive cuisine, or you could enjoy a coffee with a plate of biscuits in the lakeside serenity of the *Old England* for under £2. *Millers* in Windermere and *Gibby's* a few doors down both offer tourist menus of standard dishes.

Probably the best bet, and one way to avoid queuing for a seat and the usual overcooked fare, is to buy a roll and pastries from one of the many bakeries in Bowness (try *Troffers* in Ash St), then hire a rowing boat and picnic on an island in the lake. Opposite Troffers, the *Porthole* is a wine buff's heaven and offers expensive but good Italian and French dishes for around £13.

For a snack or cream tea in Bowness go to the *Hedgerow Teashop* on Crag Brow, opposite the car park. It has light lunches for around £3 and closes at 5.30 pm.

Just up the road on Crag Brow is the *Nissi Taverna* (☎ 45055), the locals' favourite Greek restaurant, with mains, such as kebabs from £7, and lobster soup for £3.

Getting There & Away

See the fares tables in the Getting Around chapter. Windermere is 265 miles from London, 55 miles from Blackpool, 45 miles from Carlisle and five miles from Ambleside.

Bus There are two National Express buses a day from Manchester via Preston (three hours) and on to Keswick. There's also a service from London via Birmingham (seven hours) and on to Keswick.

Stagecoach Cumberland (☎ 01946-63222) has a number of important services. One of the most important is the No 555 Lakeslink, which links Lancaster with Keswick, via Kendal, Windermere (railway station, Troutbeck Bridge and Brockhole), Ambleside and Grasmere. No 518 runs between Windermere and Barrow-in-Furness, on the Cumbrian Coast line. No 505/506, the Coniston Rambler, runs from Kendal to Coniston via the Steamboat Museum, Brockhole and Ambleside. The No 599 service, using open-topped double-deckers, runs between Grasmere, Ambleside, Brockhole, Bowness, Windermere railway station and Kendal.

A Stagecoach Round Robin Ticket allows five breaks of journey between Bowness and Grasmere for £4.20.

Train Windermere is at the end of a spur line off the main line between London's Euston station and Glasgow. Windermere trains leave the main line at Oxenholme. There are 10 trains a day from London's Euston station (four hours, £46).

Boat See the earlier Cruises section.

Getting Around

Taxi Services include Alistairs (☎ 46535) and Cooper (☎ 45282); expect to pay around £1.20 per mile and a minimum of £2.

Bicycle Ashton's Windermere Cycles (☎ 47779), 12 Main Rd, Windermere, hires mountain bikes. So too does Lakeland Leisure (☎ 44786) on Lake Rd.

AMBLESIDE

Ambleside has an attractive position half a mile north of the lake. It's smaller, easier to manage and more laid-back than Windermere, but there are still a few decent places to eat, and a myriad B&Bs. It's one of the major centres for climbers and walkers and is a good base for the southern lakes – there are so many possible walks that this writer literally doesn't know where to begin. Pester the helpful people in the TIC (☎ 015394-32582), Church St; open Easter to October, daily from 9 am to 5 pm, and November to March, Friday and Saturday from 9 am to 5 pm.

Stewart R Cunningham Outdoor Centre (☎ 015394-32636), 1 Rydal Rd, hires bikes and boots. The Climber's Shop (☎ 015394-32297), Compston Rd, is a very large shop, also hiring camping gear, boots and waterproofs.

One mile south of the village is the *Ambleside Youth Hostel* (☎ 015394-32304), Windermere Rd (the A591). It's open all year except 7 January to 8 February; £9.10/6.15. *Low Wray* (☎ 015394-32810), a NT camping site, is three miles south of Ambleside on the western shore of Windermere (access from the B5286). The charge is around £2.50 per person per night plus £2 for a car.

There are plenty of B&Bs in the centre of town. On Church St, consider *3 Cambridge Villas* (☎ 015394-32307), a classic B&B with singles and doubles from £13.50 to £18.50 per person. On Compston Rd, the comfortable *Compston House Hotel* (☎ 015394-32305) has views and comfortable rooms with bathroom from £17.50 to £27.50 per person.

For food, a quick wander around town will fill you in on the options. *Pippins* on Lake Rd is a decent place for breakfast and snacks, open until 11 pm. *Ginger & Pickles*, 3 Kelsick Rd, is good for rolls and sandwiches. *Zeffirelli's Wholefood Pizzeria*, Compston Rd, is part of a cinema and shopping complex.

AROUND AMBLESIDE

The country around Ambleside is Wordsworth country, although numerous other writers visited or stayed in the area (including Coleridge, Keats, Charlotte Brontë and George Eliot).

There's a deservedly popular 2½-mile walk between Rydal Mount, Dove Cottage and Grasmere.

Rydal Mount

Even while he lived, as many as 100 fans a day would visit Rydal Mount in the hope of catching a glimpse of their hero, William Wordsworth. Rydal Mount is a 16th-century farmhouse with 18th-century additions set in beautiful grounds (originally landscaped by Wordsworth) with great views. It contains a considerable amount of his furniture and some manuscripts and possessions.

The house (☎ 33002) is still owned by one of Wordsworth's descendants. It's open from March to October daily from 9.30 am to 5 pm, and November to February daily from 10 am to 4 pm; £3/1. It's just off the A591 (to the east) between Ambleside and Grasmere.

Dove Cottage & Wordsworth Museum

Dove Cottage is the main Wordsworth shrine, embodying Wordsworth's philosophy of 'plain living and high thinking'. While at Dove Cottage, he wrote his greatest poems. The cottage has been lovingly restored to the way it would have been in Wordsworth's day and the entertaining guided tours are recommended.

The nearby Wordsworth Museum houses an enormous collection of manuscripts along with many personal possessions. Finally there are two rooms devoted to local history.

The complex (☎ 35544), just off the A591 at Town End, is open daily, except mid-January to mid-February, from 9.30 am to 5.30 pm; £4.10/2.05. Joint tickets with Rydal Mount are available.

Grasmere

Grasmere is a picturesque village, closely associated with the Wordsworths, and consequently overrun with tourists. Most of the village buildings date from the 19th and 20th centuries, but the village is ancient. St Oswald's Church dates from the 13th century and the Wordsworth family's graves are in the churchyard.

There are two youth hostels in Grasmere, one close to the village, the other a mile away in an old farmhouse. *Butterlip How Youth Hostel* (☎ 35316) is just north of the village; follow the road to Easedale for 150 yards, then turn right; it's open daily most of the

NORTHERN ENGLAND

year except some Mondays. *Thorney How Youth Hostel* (☎ 35591) is further out on Easedale Rd, and is open April to August (and other times). Both charge £8.25/5.55.

The *Travellers' Rest Inn* (☎ 35604), half a mile north of Grasmere on the road to Keswick, is a popular pub with good meals. It has rooms from £15 to £27.

Grasmere is on the main transport link between Windermere and Keswick; see those sections.

Elterwater

Elterwater has a superb location at the end of a small lake, tucked in under the Langdales. It's on the Cumbria Way and there are a number of good walks around and about. There's a wondrous view from Loughrigg Terrace at the southern end of Grasmere, looking north over the lake and the village (follow the road to High Close Youth Hostel and continue to the east, taking a footpath to the right off the road. It is approximately three miles return to Elterwater). It has a shop (which closes at 5 pm), a good pub and a handful of B&Bs.

There's a nice slate hostel in town, over the bridge. The *Elterwater Youth Hostel* (☎ 37245) is open most of the year but closing nights vary; £7.45/5. Up on the hills to the east, one mile from the village, *High Close Youth Hostel* (☎ 37313) is a rambling Victorian mansion surrounded by extensive gardens – there are great views. It's open April to August, and September and October except Sunday (also other times); £8.25/5.55.

Barnhowe (☎ 37346), 100 yards from the village centre, has two doubles and a single from £15 per person. The *Britannia Inn* (☎ 37210) has a pleasant patio overlooking the 'main' street. The food is good, and good value. Main meals featuring various pies and sausages are around £5. It also has rooms for around £30 per person.

Elterwater is 3½ miles from Ambleside and five miles from Coniston.

Hill Top

Beatrix Potter wrote many of her famous children's stories in this 17th-century house

at Near Sawrey (☎ 36269;NT) which is packed with visitors in summer. It's open from April to October, Saturday to Wednesday, from 11 am to 5 pm. It's two miles south of Hawkstead. See Walks & Cycle Routes in the Windermere section for details of how to get there.

CONISTON

• *pop 1800*   • ☎ *015394*

Coniston has the manicured look of a classic Lake District tourist town, but magnificent craggy hills glower over it, and there are refreshingly few 'tourist' shops. It's still a tourist town, but it's decidedly smaller and less busy than Keswick or Windermere and Bowness, and the lake is beautiful.

Information

The TIC (☎ 41533) is open April to October from 10 am to 5 pm. Summitreks (☎ 41212), 14 Yewdale Rd, next to the TIC, has walking and climbing gear, and is also the base for Coniston Mountain Bikes.

Boat Trips

The steam yacht *Gondola* was launched for use on Coniston Water in 1859. She was described by the *Illustrated London News* as 'a perfect combination of the Venetian gondola and the English steam yacht' – she's a beautiful craft. By 1977 little remained intact, but the National Trust painstakingly restored her. Aside from her beautiful lines, the luxurious saloons and silent progress makes her unique.

The *Gondola* (☎ 41288) operates every day from April to October and services Brantwood and Park-a-Moor on the eastern side of Coniston. A round trip is £4.30/2.50; there are no reductions for NT members.

The motor launch *Coniston Launch* (☎ 36216) also links Coniston with Brantwood House for £3.80 return.

Brantwood

Brantwood, the house created by John Ruskin, has a beautiful site overlooking Coniston Water with the Old Man of Coniston behind.

It's open all year, daily from mid-March to mid-November from 11 am to 5.30 pm. The best way to get there is by the SY *Gondola* or ML *Coniston Launch*. Entry is £3.50; children free. There is a good teashop.

Places to Stay

Hostels There are two excellent youth hostels near the town. *Holly How Youth Hostel* (☎ 41323) is a few minutes' walk from the town centre, just off Ambleside Rd (the A593). It's open in April and from 5 July to 21 September and weekends at other times; £7.45/5.

Coppermines Youth Hostel (☎ 41261) has a spectacular mountain setting, but it's only just over a mile from the village. Take the minor road between the Black Bull Hotel and the Co-op. Ring ahead because it closes on different days at roughly monthly intervals; £6.75/4.60.

Camping *Coniston Hall Camp Site* (☎ 41223) is a large camping ground on the lake with plenty of tent sites (£5.40 per night). Turn left opposite the Catholic church and keep left down to the lake.

B&Bs & Hotels There's a reasonable range of places to stay. On Yewdale Rd, there's the *Beech Tree* (☎ 41717), formerly the Old Vicarage, with vegetarian cooking and half a dozen rooms, some with bathroom, from £16 to £22 per person. Also on Yewdale, there's *Oaklands* (☎ 41245), a small, non-smoking place with rates from £16 to £17 per person; and *Orchard Cottage* (☎ 41373), with rooms with private bathroom from £16.50 to £19 per person.

Tiberthwaite Ave to the east of town has *Lakeland House* (☎ 41303), with mostly doubles from £15 to £20 per person; and *Shepherds Villa* (☎ 41337), with rooms with private bathroom from £15.50 to £20 per person.

The highly regarded *Coniston Lodge Hotel* (☎ 41201) has six rooms with private bathroom from £26 to £35 per person.

Places to Eat

The *Sun Hotel* (☎ 41248) is a little tricky to find, but it's worth looking for (walk out of town towards Ulverston, cross the bridge and turn right up the hill). There are good blackboard specials with choices like vegetable peanut roast for £5.25, and home-made pies from £4.95. It also has rooms from £35 per person.

Getting There & Away

Bus Cumberland's No 505/506 Coniston Rambler service runs from Bowness Pier to Brockhole, Ambleside, Skelwith Bridge and Coniston. There are half a dozen services a day during the week, but only three on Sunday.

Getting Around

Bicycle Summitreks at 14 Yewdale Rd (☎ 41487), and Lake Rd (☎ 41212) has bikes for £13 a day. Climbing gear is also available.

ULVERSTON

Ulverston is still a real town – not dandified as most Lake District towns are. The cobbled streets and alleyways are not yet lined with teashops and tourist tat. The town is the starting point for the Cumbria Way and is on the Cumbrian Coast line.

The TIC (☎ 01229-57120), Coronation Hall, County Square, open April to October, is particularly helpful in making bookings for accommodation along the Cumbria Way.

The *Empress Hotel* (☎ 01229-582532), a long way down North Lonsdale Rd, is a pub with three large rooms from £14 to £16. *Rock House* (☎ 01229-586879), 1 Alexander Rd, has three large family rooms and a single for £16 per person. *Church Walk House* (☎ 01229-582211), Church Walk, is opposite Stables furniture shop and has rooms with bathroom for £19 per person.

The *Rose & Crown* in the centre of town is a classic pub with excellent food, enormous servings and very reasonable prices.

See the earlier Cumbrian Coast line section for details of that service, and the

Windermere & Bowness section for bus connections.

COCKERMOUTH
• *pop 7000*   • *☎ 01900*

Cockermouth officially lies outside the national park, but it's an attractive and fascinating little town well positioned for exploring the less populous north-west (especially beautiful Crummock Water and Buttermere). In fact, being outside the park seems to have saved it from the worst excesses of Lakes tourism, although this situation is changing. It has definitely been discovered, but it has not yet been spoilt.

Information
The TIC (☎ 822634), Town Hall, is open January to March and November and December, Monday to Saturday from noon to 4 pm, April to June and October, Monday to Saturday from 10.30 am to 4.30 pm, and July to September, Monday to Saturday from 9.30 am to 5.15 pm and Sunday from 2 to 5 pm. Early-closing day is Thursday and market day is Monday. Fellside Sports has outdoor gear.

Wordsworth House
This Georgian country house (☎ 824805; NT), built in 1745, was the birthplace and childhood home of William Wordsworth. The house is furnished in 18th-century style and there are some of Wordsworth's personal effects. It's open April to October, weekdays from 11 am to 5 pm; £2.50/1.25.

Jenning's Brewery
If you spend some time in Cumbria and appreciate decent beer, you'll very quickly find yourself enjoying Mr Jenning's traditionally brewed products; the Dark Mild and Bitter are particularly popular. The brewery (☎ 823214) is alongside the River Cocker and there are one-hour tours (£2.70/1.50) from April to September, Monday to Friday from 10.30 am to 2 pm. Children under 12 are not admitted.

Places to Stay
Hostel The *Cockermouth Youth Hostel* (☎ 822561), Double Mills, is in a 17th-century water mill on the south edge of town. From Main St follow Station St, then Station Rd. Keep left after the war memorial then left

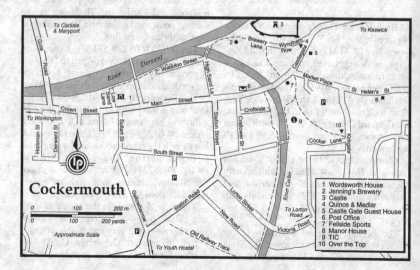

Cockermouth

1	Wordsworth House
2	Jenning's Brewery
3	Castle
4	Quince & Medlar
5	Castle Gate Guest House
6	Post Office
7	Fellside Sports
8	Manor House
9	TIC
10	Over the Top

0 100 200 m
0 100 200 yards
Approximate Scale

RICHARD EVERIST

GLENN BEANLAND

RICHARD EVERIST

Top: Watching the tide come in, Robin Hood's Bay, North Yorkshire Moors
National Park
Middle: Colour pencils scenery, Keswick, Lake District, Cumbria
Bottom: A prospect of Whitby, North Yorkshire Moors National Park

Top: Castle Howard, near York, North Yorkshire
Middle Left: Churchyard of St Just-in-Roseland, Cornwall
Middle Right: Parnham House, Dorset
Bottom: Grounds of Stourhead, Wiltshire

into Fern Bank Rd. Take the track at the end of Fern Bank. The hostel is open April to June and September to October daily except Tuesday and Wednesday, July and August daily except Wednesday; £6.75/4.60.

B&Bs Opposite the Quince & Medlar restaurant, the *Castlegate Guest House* (☎ 826749), 6 Castlegate, is a listed Georgian town house; B&B is from £16 to £19 per person.

Two more old town houses are recommended: *Manor House* (☎ 822416), St Helen's St, is a nice, central B&B with two family rooms and one single from £15 per person; and *Rose Cottage* (☎ 822189), in Lorton Rd (a continuation of Victoria Rd), from £17 to £21.

Places to Eat
There are a number of excellent restaurants, and the food in the pubs is good value. *Over the Top* (☎ 827016), Kirkgate, is a tiny restaurant/café open Tuesday to Saturday from 10 am to 4 pm and on Tuesday, Wednesday and Saturday evenings.

The *Quince & Medlar* (☎ 823579) is considered one of the best vegetarian restaurants in the country and booking is advisable. The menu features dishes like aubergine and red pepper gateau (£7.50) and roasted hazelnuts, buckwheat and leek parcels (£7.70).

The *Trout* pub (☎ 823591), Main St, next to William Wordsworth's birthplace, and the *Bush*, also on Main St, both have good-value traditional bar meals for under £5.

Getting There & Away
Cockermouth is 300 miles from London, 12 miles from Keswick and 25 miles from Carlisle.

Bus Cumberland has two or three services a day, Monday to Saturday, to/from Carlisle (No 600, two hours). The more frequent X5 service between Whitehaven, Keswick and Carlisle also stops at Cockermouth; there are even three buses on Sunday between Cockermouth and Keswick.

Getting Around
Taxi Phone ☎ 822795 or 826649. You should be able to get around town for £3.

Bicycle Track & Trail (☎ 827243), has mountain bikes at £12 delivered to your accommodation.

KESWICK
* *pop 5000*   • ☎ *017687*
Keswick is the northern centre for the Lakes and is very busy indeed. It is an important walking centre, and although the town centre lacks the green charm of Windermere, the lake is particularly beautiful. Controversy rages as to whether Derwent Water, Ullswater or Crummock Water is the most beautiful lake, but Derwent Water is the most accessible of these three if you don't have private transport.

Keswick lies between the great rounded peak of Skiddaw and the lake, although the town is cut off from the lake shore. The town is an old market centre, but it became the centre of a mining industry in the 16th century. It's been on the tourist map for over 100 years, and most buildings are Victorian. It's on the Cumbria Way.

Information
The busy, but helpful, TIC (☎ 72645), Moot Hall, Market Square, has complicated opening hours but is open daily all year from 10 am to 4 pm; most of summer it's open 9.30 am to 5.30 pm, and at peak times to 7 pm. Early-closing day is Wednesday, while market day is Saturday.

George Fisher (☎ 72178), 2 Borrowdale Rd, is an enormous outdoor equipment shop with gear for hire. Various outdoor activities and courses, like canoeing, abseiling and cycling, are organised by the Climbing Wall & Activity Centre (☎ 72000), situated behind the pencil museum. This costs about £10 a day as part of a group.

Cruises
Derwent Water does not have vintage boat trips, but it does have an excellent lake transport service (what price progress?). From

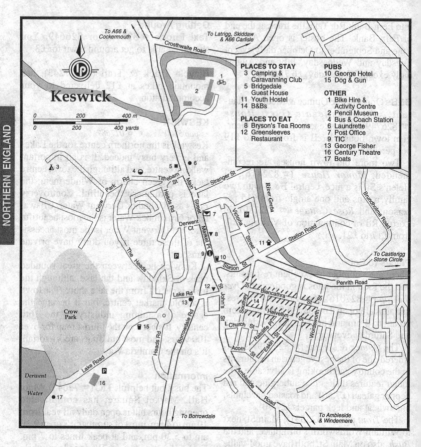

Keswick

PLACES TO STAY	PUBS
3 Camping & Caravanning Club	10 George Hotel
5 Bridgedale Guest House	15 Dog & Gun
11 Youth Hostel	**OTHER**
14 B&Bs	1 Bike Hire & Activity Centre
PLACES TO EAT	2 Pencil Museum
8 Bryson's Tea Rooms	4 Bus & Coach Station
12 Greensleeves Restaurant	6 Laundrette
	7 Post Office
	9 TIC
	13 George Fisher
	16 Century Theatre
	17 Boats

March to November (and on a reduced time-table from December to February) there's a frequent service calling at seven landing stages around the lake: Ashness Bridge, Lodore Falls, High Brandlehow, Low Brandlehow, Hawse End, Nichol End and back to Keswick.

The Keswick on Derwent Water Launch Company (☎ 72263) boats leave every half-hour, one going clockwise, the next going anticlockwise; the round trip takes 50 minutes (£4.50); each stage is about 10 minutes (70p). Tickets can be bought at the TIC. The company also has rowing boats for hire.

The launches give access to some excellent walks, and also provide a useful exhaustion-saving option for those walking the Cumbria Way (the long walk from Elterwater or Dungeon Ghyll). The walk around the western side of the lake is not particularly interesting, but Borrowdale is beautiful.

Castlerigg Stone Circle
The egg-shaped stone circle is set on a hilltop in an open field between Skiddaw and Helvellyn, and has brilliant views. It's a Neolithic and Bronze Age sacred meeting place,

The standing stones at Castlerigg

and one of the most beautiful circles in Britain, with none of the horrible tourist infrastructure of other circles. It's 1½ miles east of Keswick, an EH site open 'any reasonable time'. But entry is over a fence.

Pencil Museum

For those who ever lusted after a full set of Derwent Watercolour pencils... This is their home, and the museum tells the story of pencils from the discovery of graphite to the present day. The museum and the world's largest pencil shop (☎ 73626) are open daily from 9.30 am to 4 pm; £2/1.

Walks & Cycle Routes

The possibilities are endless, and many interesting walks or rides can be built around the network of youth hostels. Walkers could consider climbing Skiddaw and continuing on to *Skiddaw House Youth Hostel* and/or Caldbeck along the Cumbria Way, or catching the launch to the southern end of the lake and walking up Borrowdale. (See the earlier Keswick Cruises section for information about the launches.)

Cyclists could make a challenging 30-mile circuit: head south along the western bank of Derwent Water, along Borrowdale (the B5289), passing a hostel at Borrowdale,

then climb the brutally steep Honister Pass, passing another hostel, then run down to beautiful Buttermere (past another hostel) and Crummock Water. From Buttermere you could finish the loop by returning below Knott Rigg along the Keskadale Beck past Stair. Alternatively, you could continue on to Cockermouth and return via the B5292.

Places to Stay

Hostel *Keswick Youth Hostel* (☎ 72484) is a short walk down Station Rd from the TIC (turn left on the walkway by the river). It's open April to October (also other times); £9.10/6.15.

Camping There are camping grounds at the *Braithwaite Camping Site* (☎ 78343), just off the A66 on the B5292, from £5. The *Camping & Caravanning Club Site* (☎ 72392), on the lake shore a few minutes' walk from town, has van sites and camping grounds from £3 per person.

B&Bs & Hotels One of the best value B&Bs in the Lake District, the *Bridgedale Guest House* (☎ 017687-73914), 101 Main St, has a range of rooms with TV, some with private showers, for a bargain £13 per person. Without breakfast this drops to £11, which is only slightly more expensive than the youth hostel.

There's a major cluster of B&Bs just to the east of the town centre along Southey, Blencathra, Helvellyn and Eskin Sts. Prices are very competitive and standards are high. Unless otherwise noted, rooms have private bathroom and the price is per person per night.

On Eskin St, *Allerdale House* (☎ 73891), No 1, has excellent rooms from £18 per person; *Charnwood* (☎ 74111), No 6, has comfortable family rooms from £17.50 to £21; *Clarence House* (☎ 73186), No 14, includes several singles from £18 to £23; and *Braemar* (☎ 73743), No 21, includes three singles for £15.

On Southey St, *Bluestones* (☎ 74237), No 7, has rooms from £13 to £17; *Glendene* (☎ 73548) from £13.50; *Avondale*

(☎ 72735), No 20, from £14.50 to £18.50; and *Edwardene* (☎ 73586) at No 26 which has a range of rooms, from £21.

On Blencathra St, *The Derwentdale* (☎ 74187), No 8, has a good range of rooms including singles from £18; and *The Blencathra* (☎ 71435), No 48, is a small place with two family rooms for £14 per person.

Places to Eat

Don't miss *Bryson's Tea Room* (☎ 72257), 38 Main St, an excellent bakery also serving light meals during the day. *Abraham's Tearoom* (☎ 72178), 2 Borrowdale Rd, is at the top of the enormous George Fisher outdoor-equipment shop, and has great views and good light meals.

In the evening, pubs are probably your best bet. The *Dog & Gun* (☎ 73463), Lake Rd, is good value. The *George Hotel* (☎ 72076), 3 St John's St, is also popular.

Greensleeves Restaurant (☎ 72932), St John's St, is a large 'tourist' restaurant, but it has a good-value menu with pasta from around £7, vegetarian dishes around £5 and meat dishes like chicken korma for £6.

Getting There & Away

Keswick is 285 miles from London, 12 miles from Cockermouth, 31 miles from Carlisle and 15 miles from Penrith.

Bus See the Windermere & Bowness section for information on National Express and Cumberland buses and connections to Keswick.

In summer, Keswick can also be reached from Penrith railway station (three services Monday to Saturday, one on Sunday) with Wright Brothers' (☎ 01434-381200) No 888 service. This service continues across the country to Langwathby, on the LSC line, to Hexham and Corbridge, on Hadrian's Wall, and finally to Newcastle upon Tyne.

Cumberland's Lakeslink (No 555) runs from Carlisle to Lancaster via Keswick, Ambleside, Windermere and Kendal. There are frequent services between Keswick and Kendal. Three a day go on to Carlisle from

Monday to Saturday, but only one on Sunday.

Getting Around

Taxi Try Davies (☎ 72676) or Keswick (☎ 72206).

Bicycle Keswick Mountain Bikes (☎ 75202), situated behind the pencil museum, has bikes for hire from £12.50.

Boat See the Keswick Cruises section for information.

AROUND KESWICK
Places to Stay

There's an excellent network of youth hostels around Keswick, most linked by mountain paths.

Derwent Water Youth Hostel is on the eastern side of the lake, two miles from Keswick, five miles from Longthwaite and Thirlmere and 11 miles from Grasmere. (☎ 77246)

Longthwaite Youth Hostel is at the head of beautiful Borrowdale, two miles from Honister, five miles from Derwent Water and seven miles from Buttermere. Price: £9.10/6.15 (☎ 77257)

Thirlmere Youth Hostel is at the head of Thirlmere on the A591 to Ambleside, five miles from Keswick, six miles from Longthwaite, seven miles from Grasmere and nine miles from Skiddaw House. Price: £7.45/5 (☎ 73224)

Honister House Youth Hostel is at the summit of Honister Pass, three miles from Black Sail, two miles from Longthwaite, four miles from Buttermere, and 13 miles from Cockermouth. Price £5.50/3.75 (☎ 77267)

Buttermere Youth Hostel overlooks Buttermere and is four miles from Honister, seven miles from Longthwaite, nine miles from Keswick and 10 miles from Cockermouth. Price £6.75/4.60 (☎ 70245)

Black Sail, Ennerdale, Cleator, Cumbria CA3 3AY (book by post) is in a remote location at the head of Ennerdale, three miles from Honister and Buttermere, and can only be reached on foot. Price: £6.10/4.15.

Skiddaw House Youth Hostel, Bassenthwaite, Keswick CA12 4QZ (book by post) is in a remote location behind Skiddaw, six miles from Keswick and eight miles from Carrock Fell, and can only be reached on foot. Price: £5.50/3.75.

Durham & Around

The Durham area includes some of the most beautiful parts of the northern Pennines, one of the greatest Christian buildings in the world, and an ancient mining heritage that has left a legacy of uninspiring half-towns.

Although its history is not as turbulent as that of neighbouring Northumberland (which actually formed Durham's defensive buffer), Durham has known its fair share of bloodshed. In the Middle Ages it was still sufficiently wild to warrant the Prince Bishops of Durham having virtually limitless power. They combined lay and religious responsibilities as the rulers of a palatinate (a kingdom within a kingdom). The Prince Bishop (AKA the Count Palatine) had the right to have his own army, nobility, coinage and courts. His great cathedral and castle was once described by Sir Walter Scott as, 'Half church of God, half castle 'gainst the Scot'.

The Prince Bishops did bring peace to Durham, and this allowed the county to develop long before Northumberland, a fact reflected in the higher population density and the neat hedges and stone-walled fields. The western half of the county is dominated by the heather-covered hills of the northern Pennines, while the eastern half has, since the 18th century, been the centre for a major coal mining industry (which has now largely disappeared).

GETTING AROUND
The Durham County Council inquiry line (☎ 0191-383 3337) is open from 8.30 am to 5 pm (4.30 pm on Friday). The Explorer North East ticket (see the Northern England Getting Around section) is valid on many services in the county.

DURHAM
• *pop 83,000*   •   ☎ *0191*
Durham is the most dramatic cathedral city in Britain, with a massive Norman cathedral dominating a wooded promontory high above a bend in the River Wear. Other cathedrals are more refined but none have more impact – it's an extraordinary structure built to survive to the end of time, with utter confidence in the enduring qualities of faith and stone.

The story of Durham begins with the monks of Holy Island fleeing from Viking raiders with their most precious treasures, St Cuthbert's body and the illuminated Lindisfarne Gospels. The Lindisfarne monastery had thrived for 240 years, but in 875 the monks began a search for a safer site. Finally, in 995, they found a perfect, easily defended position above the River Wear. The current cathedral is the third church to be built on the site; its foundation stone was laid on 12 August 1093.

The Prince Bishops reached the peak of their power in the 14th century, and although they survived with great pomp and ceremony into the 19th century, their real influence ebbed away. In 1836 the last privileges were returned to the Crown and the last Count Palatine gave the castle to the newly founded Durham University, the third-oldest university in England (founded in 1832). Durham is still the centre for local government.

Orientation
The Market Place (and TIC), castle and cathedral are all located on the teardrop-shaped peninsula surrounded by the River Wear. The railway station is situated above and to the north-west of the cathedral on the other side of the river. The bus station is also positioned on the western side. Using the cathedral as your landmark, you can't really go wrong.

Durham is surprisingly small. The centre of town is limited by the space available on the peninsula, and although the city, and especially the university, has now overflowed to some extent, everything is within easy walking distance.

Information
The TIC (☎ 384 3720), Market Place, is just a short walk to the north of the castle and cathedral. There's also a Thomas Cook office on Market Place.

NORTHERN ENGLAND

NORTHERN ENGLAND

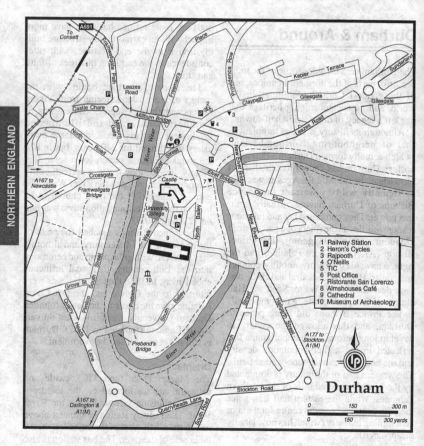

1 Railway Station
2 Heron's Cycles
3 Rajpooth
4 O'Neills
5 TIC
6 Post Office
7 Ristorante San Lorenzo
8 Almshouses Café
9 Cathedral
10 Museum of Archaeology

Durham

0   150   300 m
0   150   300 yards

Durham Cathedral

Built as the shrine for St Cuthbert, Durham Cathedral dates almost entirely from the 12th century and is the most complete and spectacular example of Norman architecture. The Romanesque style as developed by the Normans had a monumental simplicity, characterised by great scale, round arches, enormous columns and zigzag chevron ornament – all shown at their best in Durham. The cathedral's vast interior is like a cave that is only partly artificial, its exterior like timeworn cliffs.

History The choir, transepts and nave of the cathedral were built between 1093 and 1133 and still survive in uncompromised Romanesque form. There have been four major additions, all successful: the beautiful Galilee Chapel, with its slim pillars of Purbeck marble at the western end, built between 1170 and 1175; the western towers, built from 1217 to 1226; the Chapel of Nine Altars, with the pointed arches and carved capitals of the Early English style, built between 1242 and 1280; and the central tower, which was rebuilt between 1465 and 1490.

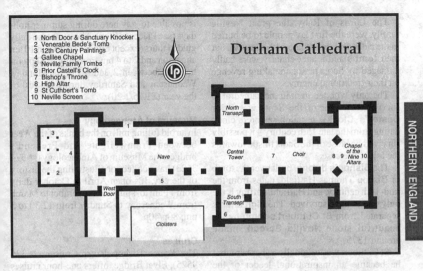

1 North Door & Sanctuary Knocker
2 Venerable Bede's Tomb
3 12th Century Paintings
4 Galilee Chapel
5 Neville Family Tombs
6 Prior Castell's Clock
7 Bishop's Throne
8 High Altar
9 St Cuthbert's Tomb
10 Neville Screen

Durham Cathedral

North Transept

Nave · Central Tower · Choir · Chapel of the Nine Altars

West Door

South Transept

Cloisters

Information The cathedral (☎ 386 2367) is open daily, May to August from 7.15 am to 8 pm, and September to April from 7.15 am to 6 pm; a donation is requested. There are tours from 27 May to 6 September, weekdays at 10.30 am. Evensong is at 5.15 pm weekdays (not Monday) and at 3.30 pm on Sunday. The Treasury Museum is definitely worth visiting as it includes relics of St Cuthbert from the 7th century and a collection of illuminated manuscripts and cathedral 'paraphernalia'. It's open Monday to Saturday from 10 am to 4.30 pm and Sunday from 2 to 4 pm; £1/20p. There's also a restaurant open daily.

There are a number of walks that give good views of the exterior; perhaps the two most famous are from Framwellgate Bridge and Prebend's Bridge, although the approach across Castle Green is also very impressive.

Inside the Cathedral The main entry is through the **north door**. Note the great bronze knocker. This was a sanctuary knocker and was used by people escaping from the rough justice of the Middle Ages and seeking the protection of the church. They would bang the knocker to attract the attention of two watchmen who slept in a room above the door and were then allowed to choose between trial and voluntary exile.

The nave is dominated by massive carved piers; every second one is round and carved in geometric designs; the round piers have an equal height and circumference of 22 feet. Durham was the first European cathedral to be roofed with stone-ribbed vaulting and has the earliest pointed transverse arches in England.

The **Galilee Chapel** is one of the most beautiful parts of the cathedral. The **paintings** on the northern side are among the few surviving examples of 12th-century wall painting and probably feature St Cuthbert and St Oswald. The chapel also contains the **tomb of the Venerable Bede**, the author of the *Ecclesiastical History of the English People*. Bede was an 8th-century Northumbrian monk, a great historian and polymath whose work held a pre-eminent role in Latin literature for four centuries and is still the prime source of information on the development of early Christian society and institutions in Britain. Amongst other things, he began the practice of dating years from the birth of Jesus.

The Lords of Raby, the great Neville family, were the first lay people to be buried in the cathedral (in the late 14th century), but their **tombs** and a later chantry were badly damaged by Scots prisoners taking revenge on their traditional enemy.

The only wooden item in the cathedral to survive the anger of the Scots was **Prior Castell's Clock**, a much-restored clock dating from the late 15th century – it possibly survived because of the Scots thistle towards the top of the case.

The **Bishop's throne**, built over the tomb of Bishop Thomas Hatfield, dates from the mid-14th century, and Hatfield's effigy is the only one to have survived. The **high altar** is separated from **St Cuthbert's tomb** by the beautiful stone **Neville Screen**, made around 1375.

St Cuthbert was originally a shepherd, but he became an inspirational leader of the northern church. At times he would meditate for days without food, but he was also widely loved by the northern peasants. It is said that eider ducks would nestle in his clothing. He died in 687, and when the Viking raids made Lindisfarne untenable, the monks carried his miraculously preserved body with them. His reputation attracted vast numbers of pilgrims to Durham.

The Chapel of the Nine Altars actually did once have nine altars – in order to facilitate giving Mass to all the monks!

Cloisters The monastic buildings are centred on the cloisters. They were heavily rebuilt in 1828. The west door to the cloisters is particularly famous for its 12th-century ironwork. On the western side is a monastic dormitory, now a library, and an undercroft which now houses the Treasury and restaurant.

Durham Castle

The castle was begun in 1072 and served as the home for Durham's Prince Bishops. It has been substantially rebuilt over the years, but still preserves the fundamental layout of a Norman motte-and-bailey castle. It is now a residential college for the university, and it

is possible to stay here during summer holidays (see Places to Stay). There are also daily guided tours (except Sunday) between 10 am and noon and 2 to 4 pm from July to September, and between 2 and 4 pm on Monday, Wednesday and Saturday during the rest of the year (£1.75/1.20).

Museum of Archaeology

In an old fulling mill on the banks of the Wear between Framwellgate and Prebend's bridges, the Museum of Archaeology (☎ 374 3623) has a collection illustrating the history of the city. It's open April to October daily from 11 am to 4 pm, and November to March from Wednesday to Sunday from 12.30 to 3 pm; 80p/40p.

Cruises

The Prince Bishop River Cruiser (☎ 386 9525), Elvet Bridge, offers one-hour cruises along the river. Trips run from June to September at 12.30, 2 and 3 pm; £3/1.50.

Rowing boats can be hired for £2 per person per hour from Browns Boathouse (☎ 386 3779), below Elvet Bridge.

Walks

There are superb views back to the cathedral and castle from the outer bank of the river; walk around the bend between Elvet and Framwellgate bridges, or hire a boat at Elvet Bridge.

Places to Stay

The TIC makes local bookings free, which is useful since convenient B&Bs are not numerous; the situation is particularly grim during graduation week in late June. The youth hostel has closed but it may be worth checking with the TIC in case a new venue has been found.

Camping *Grange Camping & Caravan Site* (☎ 384 4778), Meadow Lane, is two miles from the city centre. A car, two people and a tent costs from £8.10.

B&Bs & Hotels Several colleges rent their rooms during the university vacations (particularly July to September). The most exciting possibility is *University College*, in the old Durham Castle (☎ 374 3863), which has B&B singles/doubles from £18.50 per person. *Van Mildert College* (☎ 374 3900) has singles/doubles from £16.50/33.

There are a number of B&Bs starting around £15 per person on Claypath and Gilesgate. Leave the market square from its northern end and cross over the freeway onto Claypath, where you'll find *Country View Guest House* (☎ 386 1436) with rooms from £20/34.

Claypath becomes Gilesgate, where *Mrs Koltai* (☎ 386 2026), No 10, has three rooms at £15/25; *The Pink House* (☎ 386 7039), No 16, has two family rooms from £15 per person; and *Green Groves* (☎ 384 4361) at No 99 charges from £17/32.

In the centre of town, the *Three Tuns* (☎ 386 4326), New Elvet, is a historic hotel with luxury facilities and singles/doubles from £89/109.

Places to Eat
Most of the eating possibilities are within a short walk of the market square. The *Ristorante San Lorenzo* (☎ 384 0096), just over the old Elvet Bridge, is good value with pizzas and pastas from £5; it has a cheap special menu from 11.30 am to 2.30 pm and from 5.30 to 7 pm. On the other side of the peninsula, *Pizzaland* and *Bella Pasta*, on the eastern side of Framwellgate Bridge, have good views over the river; most pizzas are around £5 and pastas are from £5.

The *Almhouses Café*, Palace Green, serves some simple but very good food. It's open from 9 am to 5 pm and from June to September it closes at 8 pm. Recent choices included chestnut, orange and ginger pate with French bread and salad (£3.20) and parsnip and apple soup (£2).

Rajpooth (☎ 3861496), 80 Claypath, has a good reputation for Indian food; £8 for set meals and £5 for vindaloo curries.

Entertainment
It's worth checking what is going on; a half-hour walk will give you an idea. There are a

couple of pubs on Gilesgate, including the pleasant *Travellers Rest*. There are a couple of rowdy possibilities on the western side of Framwellgate. The *Swan & Three Cygnets*, Old Elvet Bridge, is a bright riverside pub with tables overlooking the river and good bar food. *O'Neills*, on Claypath, is an Irish theme pub.

Getting There & Away
See the fares tables in the Getting Around chapter. Durham is 260 miles from London, 75 miles from Leeds and 15 miles from Newcastle upon Tyne.

Bus There are five National Express (☎ 261 6077) buses a day to London (4½ hours), three to Edinburgh (five hours), and numerous buses to/from Birmingham (5¾ hours) and Newcastle upon Tyne (half an hour). There's one bus a day (No 370) between Durham and Edinburgh via Jedburgh and Melrose in the Scottish Borders.

Primrose Coaches (☎ 413 2257) has a daily service between Newcastle upon Tyne and Blackpool via Durham, Barnard Castle, Raby Castle and Kirkby Stephen (X69). It leaves Durham from the Durham Sutton bus shelter (under the railway viaduct).

There are regular buses from Durham to Newcastle upon Tyne from the Durham bus station (50 minutes).

Train There are numerous trains to York (one hour), a good number of which head on to London (three hours) via Peterborough (for Cambridge). Frequent trains from London continue through to Edinburgh (three hours).

Getting Around
Taxi Pratt's Taxis (☎ 386 0700) charges a minimum of about £2.

Bicycle Ring Heron's on ☎ 384 0319.

BEAMISH OPEN AIR MUSEUM
Beamish has been founded on the ruins of Durham's coal industry; overheard from a grizzled ex-miner sitting in the sun at the entrance waiting for his grandchildren to

return, 'Spent half my life down a pit. No way am I going to pay seven quid to go down one again!'

Visitors can go underground, and explore mine heads, a working farm, cottages, a school, a pub and shops.

Beamish (☎ 01207-231811) is open April to October, daily from 10 am to 5 pm (until 6 pm from 20 July to August and 4 pm in winter). Allow a minimum of two hours to do the place full justice. Ticket prices range from £2.99/1.99 in winter to £7.99/4.99 in August.

Beamish is about eight miles north-west of Durham; it's signposted from the A1 (take the A691 to the west). From late July to early September, a special service runs between Durham railway station and Beamish (X79, half an hour). There's a regular service from Newcastle upon Tyne (No 709).

BARNARD CASTLE

Barnard Castle is not as self-contained and picturesque as Richmond, but it is still an attractive market town, and it makes a good base for exploring Teesdale and the northern Pennines.

The TIC (☎ 01833-690909), 43 Galgate, is open all year.

The ruins of **Barnard Castle** (☎ 638212, EH) cover almost six acres and testify to its importance; it was founded by Guy de Bailleul and rebuilt by his nephew around 1150; £2/1.50.

Housed in a wholly unexpected 19th-century French château 1½ miles west of town, the **Bowes Museum** (☎ 690606) contains a magnificent collection of artworks, including paintings by El Greco and Goya. A prime exhibit is the 18th-century mechanical silver swan in the hall; ask when you can see it in operation. The museum is open daily from 10 am to 5.30 pm (Sunday from 2 to 5.30 pm). Admission is £3/2.

Accommodation can be hard to find in summer, so the TIC's accommodation-booking service can be particularly useful. The *Old Well* pub (☎ 01833-690130), 21 The Bank (downhill from the Market Cross), which also has interesting food, has doubles with bathroom for £47. *Mrs Wilkinson* (☎ 01833-631383), 2 Wesley Terrace, has a single and double from £14.50 per person.

One of the best-value restaurants in Northern England is *Prior's Vegetarian Restaurant* (☎ 01833-638141), 7 The Bank (downhill from the Market Cross). Most mains are £3 and include interesting dishes like chickpea fritters with a sweet and sour sauce for £2.95. Unfortunately, it's only open during the day: Monday to Friday from 10 am to 5 pm, Saturday from 10 am to 5.30 pm, and Sunday from noon to 5.30 pm.

Primrose Coaches (☎ 0191-232 5567) has a daily service between Newcastle upon Tyne and Blackpool via Durham, Barnard Castle, Raby Castle and Kirkby Stephen (X79/71). United (☎ 0191-384 3323) has four services Monday to Saturday to/from Durham (via Bishop Auckland and Raby Castle).

AROUND BARNARD CASTLE

One mile south of Barnard Castle, the ruins of Egglestone Abbey are on a lovely bend of the Tees. The countryside around Barnard Castle is extremely beautiful, especially **Teesdale** to the north-west. In particular, **High Force** waterfall, where the Tees jumps

---

The Rising of the North

Barnard Castle played its most important role in 1569 during the reign of Elizabeth I. The Percys (Earls of Northumberland) and the Nevilles (Earls of Westmorland) plotted at Raby Castle to release Mary Queen of Scots from Bolton Castle in Wensleydale, where she was imprisoned, place her on the throne and restore Roman Catholicism.

Sir George Bowes remained loyal to Elizabeth, however, and he and other loyalists held Barnard Castle. On 2 December, 5000 rebels besieged Barnard. On 8 December, the walls were breached and Bowes retreated to the Inner Ward. On 12 December, Bowes was finally forced to surrender, but the delay had allowed the Earl of Sussex to assemble his forces at York and the rebels were defeated. ■

50 feet, is considered to be one of the best in Britain. There are a number of popular walks, including several sections of the Pennine Way.

Raby Castle

Raby Castle (☎ 01833-660202) is a romantic-looking 14th-century castle, a stronghold of the Neville family until the Rising of the North. Most of the interior has been substantially altered, but the exterior remains true to the original design, built around a courtyard and surrounded by a moat. The castle and its beautiful grounds are open May and June, Wednesday and Sunday afternoon from 1 to 5 pm, and July to September, Monday to Saturday from 1 to 5 pm; £3.50/1.50. It's six miles north-east of Barnard Castle off the A688 (see Barnard Castle for bus transport).

Newcastle upon Tyne

• *pop 210,000* • *☎ 0191*

Newcastle is the largest city in the north-east. It grew famous as a coal-exporting port, and in the 19th century it became an important steel, shipbuilding and engineering centre – all industries that went into serious decline after WWII. It has had a dour struggle to survive, but has retained some 19th-century grandeur, and the famous six bridges across the Tyne are an arresting sight.

There are no major tourist attractions, although both St Nicholas' Cathedral and Castle Garth are worth visiting. Shopaholics might be tempted by the Metro Centre at Gateshead, an enormous shopping centre – the largest in Europe – with 350 shops, 50 places to eat (mostly fast food), fairground rides... The Eldon Square development in the centre of town is another enormous modern shrine to consumerism. Needless to say, old Grainger Market is *much* more interesting.

Orientation

Although Newcastle is dauntingly large, the city centre is easy to get around on foot, and the Metro (convenient for the youth hostel and B&Bs) is cheap, efficient and pleasant to use.

The central railway station is just to the south of the city centre. The coach station is on Gallowgate. Local buses leave from Eldon Square, buses for the north leave from Haymarket, and buses for Beamish leave from Worswick St.

Driving in and around Newcastle is not much fun thanks to the web of roads and motorways, the bridges and the one-way streets in the centre – avoid peak hours.

Information

The railway station TIC (☎ 230 0030) is open October to May, Monday to Saturday from 10 am to 5 pm, and June to September, Monday to Friday to 8 pm, Saturday to 6 pm and Sunday to 4 pm. There is also a main office in the Central Library (☎ 261 0610); both have a free map, guide and accommodation list and a free booking service.

American Express (☎ 221 2244) has an office at 51 Grey St. Thomas Cook has an office on the corner of Pilgrim St and New Bridge. Blacks, the outdoor equipment chain, has a shop on Grainger St and The Map Centre in Grey St has a good supply of maps and guides.

Castle Garth

Castle Garth is the new castle from which the city gets its name. The original was built in wood, but the current construction dates from 1168. It is a fine example of a square keep, with good views and some interesting displays on the history of the city. Open Tuesday to Sunday from 9.30 am to 5.30 pm; £1/30p.

Tyne Bridges & River Tours

The most famous view in Newcastle is of the six bridges over the Tyne, and the most famous of the bridges is the **Tyne Bridge**, built in 1925-8, about the same time as, and reminiscent of, the Sydney Harbour Bridge. Perhaps the most interesting is the **Swing Bridge**, which pivots in the middle. The **High Level Bridge**, designed by Robert

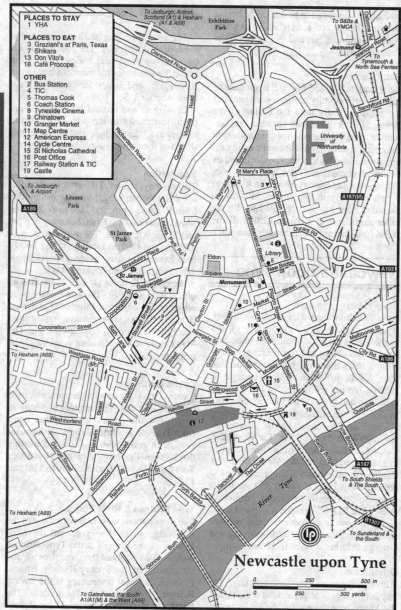

PLACES TO STAY
1 YHA

PLACES TO EAT
3 Graziani's at Paris, Texas
7 Shikara
13 Don Vito's
18 Café Procope

OTHER
2 Bus Station
4 TIC
5 Thomas Cook
6 Coach Station
8 Tyneside Cinema
9 Chinatown
10 Granger Market
11 Map Centre
12 American Express
14 Cycle Centre
15 St Nicholas Cathedral
16 Post Office
17 Railway Station & TIC
19 Castle

Newcastle upon Tyne

0   250   500 m
0   250   500 yards

Stephenson, was the world's first road and railway bridge and was opened in 1849.

Sightseeing cruises run from Newcastle Quayside on Sunday afternoons in the summer. They depart at 2 pm and last for three hours; £6/3.

Markets

Grainger Market is in a magnificent building on Grainger St. When it opened in the 1830s it was Europe's largest undercover shopping centre, a position now proudly claimed by the Metro Centre. It mainly sells fruit and vegetables, but there are other interesting stalls, including the Marks & Spencer Original Penny Bazaar. **Bigg Market** is held in the street of the same name on Tuesday, Thursday and Saturday. The **Quayside Market** is held beneath the Tyne Bridge on Sunday between 9 am and 2.30 pm and is a popular flea market.

Jarrow

The eastern suburb of Jarrow is embedded in labour history for the 'Jarrow Crusade' in 1936, when 200 men set out to walk all the way to London to protest against the appalling conditions brought about by unemployment.

Today's visitors to this grim district might think little has changed. However, Jarrow is also famous as the home of the Venerable Bede (author of the *History of the English People*, and parts of St Paul's Church date back to the seventh century. Together with a museum and Jarrow Hall, it forms part of the **Bede's World** park (☎ 489 2106) with many reconstructed medieval buildings. It's open April to October, Tuesday to Saturday from 10 am to 5 pm, Sunday 2 to 5 pm, and November to March Tuesday to Saturday from 11 am to 4.30 pm, Sunday 2.30 to 5.30 pm. Admission is £2.50/1.25. You can reach Jarrow on the Metro to Bede station.

Places to Stay

Hostel The *Newcastle Youth Hostel* (☎ 281 2570), 107 Jesmond Rd, not far from the city centre, is open from March to October (and other times); £6.75/5.

The *North East YMCA* (☎ 281 1233), Jesmond House, Clayton Rd, accepts male and female guests at £16.50 per person. Turn left on Osborne Rd from Jesmond station and take the second street on the right.

Camping The nearest sites are in South Shields: *Lizard Lane* (☎ 454 4982) and *Sandhaven* (☎ 454 5594; it's around £6 for a two-person tent.

B&Bs & Hotels A lot of places have cheaper rates at weekends. There are quite a number of B&Bs along Osborne Rd. To get there, catch the Metro to Jesmond station, or catch bus No 33/33B from the central railway station, Grainger St or the corner of New Bridge and Pilgrim St.

Right beside the station, the impressive *Royal Station Hotel* (☎ 232 0781), Neville St, has rooms from £52/65, as well as cheaper weekend deals.

Herrons Hotel (☎ 281 4191), 40 Jesmond Rd, is in a Georgian building, on a cul-de-sac, with a private car park; rooms cost £22/36.

Osborne Rd has the greatest concentration of B&Bs. At the top end, the *Cairn Hotel* (☎ 281 1358), No 97, is a large four-star hotel with rooms from £52/66, dropping by £20 on weekends.

Mere mortals hunting on Osborne Rd should consider the *Gresham Hotel* (☎ 281 4341), No 92, a medium-sized, comfortable hotel from £22/32, although at that price in Newcastle you still share a bathroom. The *Minerva Hotel* (☎ 281 0190), No 105, is a small place with decent prices; £18/31.

Fern Ave is the fifth street on the right if you head down Osborne Rd from Jesmond station. *Fern Guest House* (☎ 281 3363), No 32, is an attractive terraced house with a number of rooms at £20/34. The *Gowan Hotel* (☎ 0191-281 3129), No 88, is similar.

Places to Eat

Newcastle has a most un-English attitude to food. Geordies believe in going out to eat and they believe the food should be cheap. As a result, Newcastle has a remarkable number of good restaurants.

Restaurants are fairly widely scattered. There are some at the northern end of town (handy for the university and the youth hostel), and Chinatown is on Stowell St to the west of Eldon Square. Perhaps the most interesting zone to explore, however, is south of the city centre. Walk south down Grey St (lined with beautiful Georgian and Victorian offices), which becomes Dean St and takes you down to the River Tyne and Quayside.

On Grey St itself, *Don Vito's* (☎ 232 8923) is extraordinarily good value, with pizzas and pastas starting at a bargain £2.75. The *Café Procope* (☎ 232 3848), 35 The Side, has an imaginative modern menu, with plenty of vegetarian dishes, with prices around £8.

There are a number of interesting pubs at the bottom of the hill. *Flynns Waterfront Bar* right on Quayside has a beer garden and cheap food and drink, but check out the *Pumphouse*, *Bob Trollop* and *Redhouse*; the latter two have pub meals for about £3.

At the other end of town, *Graziani's at Paris, Texas* (☎ 261 5084), St Mary's Place, is a lively rock café with pizzas and pastas under £5 and even better specials before 7.30 pm.

One of the most acclaimed restaurants in town is *Shikara* (☎ 233 0005), 52 St Andrew's St, serving excellent Indian food; it's cheap for lunch, most mains in the evening costing between £7 and £10. More Indian restaurants can be found in Dean St.

Entertainment

Newcastle caters to most tastes, with high culture and low. The Royal Shakespeare Company is a regular visitor to the superb Theatre Royal (☎ 232 2061) in Grey St, but there are also fringe companies like the Live Theatre Company (☎ 232 1232), 27 Broad Chare, Quayside. The Tyneside Cinema is always worth checking out. There are a number of guides to what's on to look for: *Paint it Red* and *the crack* (free), and the *Evening Chronicle* on Wednesday.

Geordies take going out, drinking beer

and dancing seriously (though not necessarily in that order). The Bigg Market area is notorious around the country for the enormous crowds of young people it attracts – especially on Friday nights when groups of scantily clad young women and increasingly drunken young men circulate around the street ogling each other. Be prepared for infuriating dress codes and queues; trainers will be out, and some places insist on a collar and tie.

The pubs and clubs around Quayside tend to be more relaxed. The *Cooperage* (☎ 232 8286), 32 The Close, Quayside, is a popular dance club with a wide-ranging clientele; £3.50 admission. *Rockshots* (☎ 232 9648) is free and *Powerhouse* (☎ 261 4507) in Waterloo St is a gay place.

Getting There & Away

Newcastle is 275 miles from London (about five hours by car), 105 miles from Edinburgh (about 2½ hours), 57 miles from Carlisle, 35 miles from Alnwick and 15 miles from Durham. It's a major transport hub, so travellers have many options, including air and sea links.

Air Newcastle international airport (☎ 286 0966) is seven miles north of the city, linked by the Metro and about 20 minutes away by car. There are direct scheduled services to Aberdeen, London, Dublin, Belfast, Oslo, Amsterdam, Paris and Brussels.

Bus There are numerous National Express connections with virtually every major city in the country. There are buses every two hours to London (5¼ hours) and Edinburgh (3¼ hours), and a number of buses each day from York (2¼ hours).

For local buses around the north-east, don't forget the excellent-value Explorer North East ticket, valid on most services. The central inquiry bureau (☎ 232 4211) has details on services to Berwick-upon-Tweed and along Hadrian's Wall (see the appropriate sections).

In summer, Keswick can be reached with

Wright Brothers' (☎ 01670-533128) daily No 888 service.

Train Newcastle is on the main London-Edinburgh line so there are numerous trains; Edinburgh (1¾ hours), London's King's Cross (four hours), York (1¼ hours). Berwick-upon-Tweed and Alnmouth (for Alnwick) are north on this line.

There is also an interesting, scenic line known as the Tyne Valley line west to Carlisle. See the Hadrian's Wall section.

Boat See the Getting There & Away chapters for details of ferry links to Stavanger and Bergen in Norway, Gothenburg (Sweden) and Hamburg (Germany).

Getting Around

There's an excellent, cheap Metro with fares from 40p. A day ticket is £2.50 or you can get a day Rover, covering all modes of transport, for £3. For advice and information ring the travel line (☎ 232 5325).

The Airport The airport is linked to town by the excellent Metro system. There are frequent services seven days a week, and the cost is £1.10.

The Ferry Terminal Bus No 327 links the ferry (at Tyne Commission Quay), the central railway station and Jesmond Rd (for the youth hostel and B&Bs). It leaves the railway station 2½ and 1¼ hours before each sailing; £2.50/1.25.

There's a taxi rank at the terminal; £8.60.

Taxi Taxis can be hard to come by on weekend nights; try NODA (☎ 222 1888 or 232 7777).

Bicycle The Newcastle Cycle Centre (☎ 222 1695), 165 Westgate Rd, has mountain bikes for hire at £10 per day or £35 per week.

Northumberland

Taking its name from the Anglo-Saxon kingdom of Northumbria (north of the River Humber), Northumberland is one of the wildest and least spoilt of England's counties. There are probably more castles and battlefield sites here than anywhere else in England, testifying to the long and bloody struggle with the Scots.

The Romans were the first to attempt to draw a line separating north from south: Hadrian's Wall, stretching 73 miles from Newcastle upon Tyne to Bowness-on-Solway near Carlisle, was the northern frontier of the empire for almost 300 years. It was abandoned around 410, but enough remains to bring the past dramatically alive.

After the arrival of the Normans, large numbers of castles and fortified houses, or *peles*, were built. Many of them changed hands several times as the Scottish border was pushed back and forth for the next 700 years. Most have now lapsed into peaceful ruin, but others, like Bamburgh and Alnwick, were converted into great houses, which can be visited today.

The Northumberland National Park lies north of Hadrian's Wall, incorporating the open, sparsely populated Cheviot Hills. The walks cross some of the loneliest parts of England and can be challenging. The most interesting part of Hadrian's Wall is also included (along the southern boundary) – see the Hadrian's Wall section.

GETTING AROUND

The county council produces the excellent *Northumberland Public Transport Guide*, available for £1.25 from local TICs or for £1.75 from the Public Transport Officer (☎ 01670-533000), Northumberland County Council, County Hall, Morpeth NE61 2EF. Transport options tend to be sparse, with the exception of the link between Carlisle and Newcastle upon Tyne and along the east coast to Berwick-upon-Tweed. The principal operators are

Northumbria (☎ 0191-232 4211) and OK (☎ 01388-604581).

WARKWORTH

Warkworth is a picturesque small village beneath the formidable remains of a 14th-century castle and set in a loop of the River Cocquet. Of interest are the impressive ruins of **Warkworth Castle** (☎ 01665-711423; EH); £2/1.50.

There are a number of B&Bs in the village, including a couple of places on Waterhaugh Rd: *Elmwood* (☎ 711357), with a single, double and family room from £18 per person and *Aulden* (☎ 711583), with two doubles from £15 per person.

Warkworth is served by Northumbria's X18 bus service that links Newcastle upon Tyne, Warkworth, Alnmouth and Alnwick. There's a railway station on the main east-coast line, about 1½ miles to the west of town.

ALNWICK

- *pop 7000*   • ☎ *01665*

Alnwick (pronounced annick) is a charming market town that has grown up in the shadow of magnificent Alnwick castle. The attractive old town still has a medieval feel with narrow, cobbled streets and a market square.

The castle is on the northern side of town, overlooking the River Aln. The TIC (☎ 510665) is at The Shambles, the traditional location for butchers' stalls, adjacent to the market.

Alnwick Castle

Outwardly the castle has not changed much since the 14th century, but the interior has been substantially altered, most recently in the 19th century. If you enjoy castles, don't miss this one.

The six rooms open to the public – state rooms, dining room, guard chamber and library – have an incredible display of Italian paintings, including 11 Canalettos and Titian's *Ecce Homo*. There are also some fascinating curiosities, including Oliver Cromwell's camp pillow and night cap, and

a hairnet used by Mary Queen of Scots which is actually made from her hair.

The castle (☎ 510777) is open from Easter to mid-October from 11 am to 4.30 pm; £4. For a great view back to the castle, looking up the River Aln, take the B1340 towards the coast.

Places to Stay & Eat

Aln House (☎ 602265), South Rd, is an Edwardian house with rooms for £19 per person. Similarly priced is *Bondgate House Hotel* (☎ 602025), 20 Bondgate Without, a small hotel near the town's medieval gateway.

The pubs present the best options for a meal; have a wander around town before you make a choice. The *Market Tavern*, Fenkle St, near the market square, is a bit tatty, but it's friendly and the food is good and generous. The *King's Place*, 2 Market Place, is a spotlessly clean coffee house and restaurant with a wide range of meals around £5.

Getting There & Away

Alnwick has reasonable transport links since it's on the A1 between Newcastle upon Tyne and Edinburgh. Northumbria (☎ 0191-232 4211) has a number of services linking Newcastle upon Tyne and Berwick-upon-Tweed. There are also services to the attractive towns of Warkworth and Alnmouth (also stopping at the railway station).

The nearest railway station is about three miles away on the eastern side of Alnmouth.

FARNE ISLANDS

The Farne Islands lie three to four miles offshore from Seahouses, and despite being basically bare rock, they provide a home for 18 species of nesting sea birds. These include the extraordinary puffins, kittiwakes, Arctic terns, eider ducks, cormorants and gulls. There are also colonies of grey seals. There are few places in the world where you can get so close to nesting sea birds – so close you can almost touch them. It's an extraordinary experience.

St Cuthbert, of Lindisfarne fame, died on the islands in 687, and there is a tiny chapel to him on Inner Farne, where it is possible to land. The best time to go is in the breeding season (roughly May to July), when you can see the chicks being fed by their parents.

Crossings can be rough – and may not be possible at all in bad weather. The tours take between two and three hours; inexplicably, none of the boats have proper cabins, so make sure you've got warm, waterproof clothing if there's a chance of rain.

There are various tours and tour operators to choose from. There's really nothing to separate the operators, but it is definitely worth landing on one of the islands – preferably Inner Farne. From April to August, tours start at 10 am. A three-hour tour around the islands and a landing on Inner Farne will cost £5/4; there is an additional £3.60/1.80 fee payable to the NT (if you're not a member). The islands are owned and managed by the NT.

Tickets are available from booths beside the pier in Seahouses, a couple of miles along the coast from Bamburgh. Operators include John Mackay (☎ 01665-721144), Billy Shiel (☎ 01665-720308) and Hanveys (☎ 01665-720388).

BAMBURGH

Bamburgh is an unspoilt hamlet just inland from miles of magnificent sandy beaches, and dominated by the romantic profile of an enormous castle.

Bamburgh Castle

This impressive fortress, situated on a basalt crag rising from the sea, dominates the coast for miles. It's impressive by day but even more impressive by night. The site has been occupied since prehistoric times, but the current castle is largely a 19th-century construction and is not particularly interesting inside.

The castle (☎ 016684 208) is open daily, Easter to October from 1 pm; closing times vary; £3/1.50.

Places to Stay

Waren Caravan Site (☎ 01668 214366) has grass pitches and all mod cons, including a pool and laundrette. The price of a pitch for four varies according to the season from £7.50 to £10. Otherwise, *Burton Hall* is open all year and costs £20 to £25.

Getting There & Away

Northumbria's No 501 bus service runs from Alnwick to Berwick-upon-Tweed via Seahouses and Bamburgh; Monday to Saturday there are three services a day.

HOLY ISLAND (LINDISFARNE)

The most exciting part of Holy Island (or Lindisfarne as it was once known) is the drive from the mainland over a causeway that crosses three miles of fascinating muddy flats. Even in the off season, the windswept two-mile square island is jammed with tourists and seems to have very few facilities for them.

St Aidan founded a monastery here in 635, and it became a major centre of Christianity and learning. The exquisitely illustrated *Lindisfarne Gospels*, which originated here, can be seen in the British Library. Saint Cuthbert lived on Lindisfarne for a while, but even he didn't like it and went back to the Farne Islands after a couple of years.

Lindisfarne Priory (☎ 01289-89200; EH) consists of the remains of the priory's church and the later 13th-century St Mary the Virgin Church. There's a museum next to these which shows the remains of the first monastery and how monks used to live. It's open April to October from 10 am to 6 pm, closing at 4 pm during the winter; £2.50/1.90.

Lindisfarne Castle (☎ 01289-389244; NT) was built in 1550, and restored and converted by Sir Edward Lutyens in 1903. Note that it is half a mile from the village, and there's no toilet. It's open April to October from 1 to 5 pm; £3.70.

It is possible to stay on the island, but try to book. Probably the best bet (of a small selection) is the rather tacky *Crown & Anchor* pub (☎ 01289-389215), which has reasonable pub meals and B&B from £18 per person. There are not many other places to eat.

NORTHERN ENGLAND

Lindisfarne can be reached by the No 477 bus from Berwick-upon-Tweed and is 14 miles from Berwick-upon-Tweed railway station. Tide times are printed in local papers, and the island is cut off for about five hours each day.

BERWICK-UPON-TWEED
• *pop 13,000* • ☎ *01289*

Berwick is the northernmost town in England, at the mouth of the River Tweed. The stony town has a dramatic site flanking the river estuary, which is often graced with flotillas of swans. The river is crossed by a low stone bridge (built in 1634), the soaring arches of the railway bridge (1850) and a concrete span for road traffic (1928).

Between the 12th and 15th centuries, Berwick changed hands between the Scots and the English 13 times. This merry-go-round ceased prior to the construction of massive Elizabethan ramparts that still enclose the town centre – although, reflecting geographical realities, the football team still plays in the Scottish League!

There are a number of small museums, but nothing, apart from the walls, that must be seen. Berwick is, nonetheless, a great place to explore on foot.

Orientation & Information
The fortified town of Berwick proper is on the northern side of the Tweed; the three bridges link with the suburbs of Tweedmouth, Spittal and Eastcliffe. The centre of town is quite compact and easy to get around on foot, but some of the B&Bs are quite far-flung.

The TIC (☎ 330733), Castlegate car park, is open daily in summer from 10 am to 7 pm, and from November to Easter, Monday to Saturday, from 10 am to 1 pm and 2 to 4 pm.

The Walls
Berwick has had two sets of walls: the first were built during the reign of Edward II, and little remains of them; the ones that still guard the town today were begun in 1558 and are still intact. They represented the most advanced military technology of the day and were designed both to house the increasingly effective artillery (in arrow-head shaped bastions) and to withstand it (the walls are low and massively thick).

It's possible to walk virtually the entire length of the walls, and this is a must for visitors. There are some wonderful views and the entire circuit takes about 1½ hours. The TIC has a brochure describing the main sights, and in summer there are recommended guided tours, Monday to Friday, at 10.30 am and 2 pm (£2.50/free).

Places to Stay
The cheapest B&Bs tend to be south of the river in Tweedmouth, Spittal and Eastcliffe; fortunately there are frequent buses. The B1 runs from the main bus station on Marygate (High St) across the bridge to Tweedmouth, before turning off and heading to Spittal.

Mrs May Law (☎ 304454), 4 The Crescent, Spittal, is the last house to the south, but it's a great B&B with views out to sea and a warm welcome; from £15 per person.

There's also a group of places on North Rd: *Dervaig* (☎ 307378), No 1, has two double rooms with bathroom from £18 per person; *Drousha* (☎ 306659), No 29, is similar.

It would be preferable to stay in the centre of town, but it can be hard to find a room. The *Alletsa Guest House* (☎ 308199), 66 Ravensdowne, has nine rooms; from £15. Similarly priced is the *Wallace Guest House* (☎ 306539), 1 Wallace Green.

The *Berwick Walls Hotel* (☎ 330770), 34 Ravensdowne, is a four-star hotel with well-equipped rooms from £20 per person.

Places to Eat
The most unusual is *Humble Pie* (☎ 303223) in a lane that runs off Marygate. It's open to 8 pm on weekdays and to 10 pm on weekends, and the menu features cheap and simple vegetarian meals – on weekends it has live blues.

Union Jacks (☎ 306673), Wallace Green, has a large variety of pub-type meals around £5. Last orders are taken at 8 pm. The *Magna Tandoori* (☎ 302736), 39 Bridge St, has

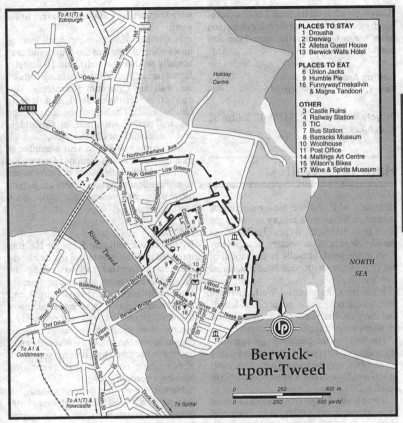

PLACES TO STAY
1 Drousha
2 Dervaig
12 Alletsa Guest House
13 Berwick Walls Hotel

PLACES TO EAT
6 Union Jacks
9 Humble Pie
16 Funnywayt'mekalivin
& Magna Tandoori

OTHER
3 Castle Ruins
4 Railway Station
5 TIC
7 Bus Station
8 Barracks Museum
10 Woolhouse
11 Post Office
14 Maltings Art Centre
15 Wilson's Bikes
17 Wine & Spirits Museum

Berwick-upon-Tweed

good-quality tandoori dishes: most main dishes are around £5, so with a side dish or two and a beer you should be able to eat for around £10.

Funnywayt'mekalivin (☎ 308827), 41 Bridge St, is the best restaurant in town, offering five-course gourmet dinners for £22.50 (booking is recommended). Vegetarians are well cared for.

Getting There & Away

Berwick is quite a transport hub; it's on the main east-coast railway line and road, and also has good links into the Scottish Borders.

Bus Northumbria (☎ 0191-232 4211) has several services linking Newcastle upon Tyne and Berwick. The No 501 service runs to Alnwick via Seahouses and Bamburgh.

Berwick is a good starting point if you wish to explore the Scottish Borders. There are buses on to Edinburgh around the coast via Dunbar and west to Coldstream, Kelso and Galashiels; see those sections. Lowland (☎ 307461) is the main Scottish operator; look out for its Waverley Wanderer ticket (£9.50), which will take you as far as Peebles and Edinburgh, and the Reiver Rover (£6.50), which will take you through the Borders, nearly as far as Carlisle.

Train Berwick is on the main London-Edinburgh east-coast line, and there are numerous trains south to Newcastle upon Tyne and north to Edinburgh.

Getting Around
Taxi Try Blue Star (☎ 305660).

Bicycle Wilson's (☎ 331476), 17 Bridge St, hires bikes.

Hadrian's Wall

Hadrian's Wall was the most monumental attempt in the island's history to divide the north from the south – it cuts 73 miles across the narrow neck of the country, from Solway Firth in the west, virtually to the mouth of the Tyne in the east, through beautiful, varied countryside.

It has been designated a World Heritage Site, and although it is mainly foundations that survive, the ruins and their beautiful locations are extraordinarily evocative.

The wall was the greatest single engineering project undertaken by the Roman Empire – it involved moving two million cubic yards of soil and took over six years (from 122) to build.

It was built of stone from Newcastle upon Tyne to the River Irthing, then from turf blocks to the Solway – roughly 10 feet thick and 15 feet high. A 10-foot-deep, 30-foot-wide ditch and mound was excavated immediately in front (except where there were natural defences). Every Roman mile (1620 yards) there was a gateway guarded by a small fort (milecastle) and between each milecastle were two observation turrets. Milecastles are numbered right across the country, starting with Milecastle 0 at Wallsend and ending with Milecastle 80 at Bowness-on-Solway. The intermediate turrets are tagged A and B, so Milecastle 37 (quite a good one) will be followed by Turret 37A, Turret 37B and then Milecastle 38. A second ditch (the vallum) and a military road

were built between 200 and 500 feet to the south.

A number of forts were developed as bases some distance to the south (and may actually predate the wall), and 16 actually lay astride it. The prime remaining forts on the wall are Cilurnum (Chesters), Vercovicium (Housestead) and Banna (Birdoswald). The best of the forts behind the wall are Corstopitum, at Corbridge, and Vindolanda, at Chesterholm.

Today it is possible to visit a number of picturesque surviving sections of the wall, a number of milecastles, forts and turrets, and some excellent museums. There are several attractive small towns that make good touring bases.

HISTORY
By building a wall, the Emperor Hadrian intended to establish control over a clearly delineated frontier and to reduce the demand on manpower at the same time. He came to Britain in 122 to see it started, and the actual building was undertaken by Roman legions. The wall was primarily a means of controlling the movement of people across the frontier – it could easily have been breached by a determined attack at any single point – and of preventing low-level border raiding.

No-one knows when the troops finally left their posts; it's most likely that around 400 Britain was simply set adrift as the empire fragmented. When pay stopped arriving those soldiers left on the wall would simply have disappeared for greener pastures.

ORIENTATION
Hadrian's Wall crosses beautiful, varied country. Starting in the lowlands of the Solway coast, it crosses the lush hills east of Carlisle to the ridge of basalt rock known as Whin Sill (which is bleak and windy, still) overlooking the Northumberland National Park, and ends in the urban sprawl of Newcastle upon Tyne. The most spectacular section is between Brampton and Corbridge.

Both Carlisle, in the west, and Newcastle

upon Tyne, in the east, make good starting points, but Brampton, Haltwhistle, Hexham and Corbridge all make good bases.

The B6318 basically follows the course of the wall from the outskirts of Newcastle upon Tyne to Birdoswald; from Birdoswald to Carlisle it pays to have a detailed map. The main A69 road and the railway line follow three or four miles to the south.

INFORMATION

Both the Carlisle and Newcastle upon Tyne TICs make good starting points for information, but there are also TICs in Hexham and Haltwhistle open all year, and in Corbridge and Brampton open seasonally. There's a National Park Information Centre (☎ 01434-344396) off the B6318 at Once Brewed. It is open daily from mid-March to October from 9.30 am to 5 pm.

See the Hadrian's Wall section in the Activities chapter for information on walking the wall.

PLACES TO STAY & EAT

See the Newcastle upon Tyne and Carlisle sections. Brampton and Corbridge are the most attractive small towns close to the wall, but Haltwhistle is also convenient, and bustling Hexham is another good possibility. All have plentiful B&Bs. There are also three usefully placed youth hostels (book in summer): Greenhead, Once Brewed and Acomb. See the following sections for details.

GETTING THERE & AROUND
Bus

West of Hexham the wall runs parallel to the A69, between Carlisle and Newcastle upon Tyne. Northumbria's (☎ 0191-232 4211) No 685 runs between those cities on the A69 hourly on weekdays and two-hourly on Sunday. It passes relatively near the youth hostels and two to three miles south of the main sites.

From mid-July to early September a special hail-and-ride bus runs between Hexham and Haltwhistle railway stations, connecting with trains. The No 890 service

follows the B6318, which runs very close to the wall, calling at the main sites, and the National Park Visitor Centre and youth hostel at Once Brewed. This puts the youth hostels at Acomb and Greenhead within easy reach. Earlier and later in the season, the No 682 operates along a similar route. For further information contact the Hexham TIC (☎ 01434-605225).

Explorer tickets on all theses services cost £4.50/3.50.

The easy option is to take a tour from Carlisle where the TIC (☎ 01228-512444) organises coach tours.

Train

The railway line between Newcastle upon Tyne and Carlisle has stations at Corbridge, Hexham, Haydon Bridge, Bardon Mill, Haltwhistle and Brampton. This service runs seven days a week, but all trains do not stop at all stations. Contact British Rail for further details.

Taxi

Hadrian's Wall Taxi Service (☎ 01434-344272) operates a service from Bardon Mill to most sites in the area – Bardon Mill to Housesteads is £6 each way. Sproul's (☎ 01434-321064) in Haltwhistle has a similar service.

CORBRIDGE

Corbridge vies with Brampton as the most attractive town near the wall. It is on the banks of a beautiful stretch of the River Tyne, 16 miles west of Newcastle upon Tyne, and has attractive stone houses (some very old) lining tree-shaded cobbled streets. It has an ancient history beginning with the Romans. An Anglo-Saxon monastery followed and the town thrived despite being burnt three times in border clashes.

St Andrew's Church, mostly rebuilt in the 13th century but with some Anglo-Saxon features, also has a fascinating 14th-century pele tower (a fortified vicarage) in its grounds.

The TIC (☎ 01434-632815), Hill St, is open April to September, Monday to Saturday from 10 am to 1 pm and 2 to 6 pm, and Sunday from 1 to 5 pm.

There are a number of attractive hotels, most with rooms and bar meals. The *Angel Inn* (☎ 01434-632119) is a 17th-century inn with very good, quite adventurous food and comfortable rooms with bathroom for £39/54. *Holmlea* (☎ 01434-632486), Station Rd, near the station, is a terraced house with a comfortable double and family room from £16 per person. *Town Barns* (☎ 01434-633345) offers a single, a double and a family room for £15 per person. The pubs are probably your best bet for food, or you could try the *Corbridge Tandoori* on the central square.

The No 685 bus between Newcastle upon Tyne and Carlisle comes through Corbridge, and the town is also on the railway line.

CORBRIDGE TO HEXHAM
Corbridge Roman Site & Museum
Corbridge (or Corstopitum to the Romans) was a garrison town; there were a succession of forts and supply depots, and a surrounding civil settlement. It lies south of the wall on what was the main road from York to Scotland.

The site (☎ 01434 632349, EH) is half a mile west of Corbridge on a minor road (just over one mile from the Corbridge railway station); £2.50/1.90.

HEXHAM
• *pop 9500* • ☎ *01434*
Hexham is quite an interesting town, but it is rather marred by the fact that it is such a busy shopping centre. Hexham Abbey, surrounded by a park, is considered a fine example of Early English architecture. The crypt survives from St Wilfrid's Church, which was built in 674, and inscribed stones from Corstopitum can be seen in its walls.

The TIC (☎ 605225), Hallgate, is open mid-May to September, Monday to Saturday from 9 am to 6 pm and Sunday from 10 am to 5 pm, and the rest of the year Monday to Saturday from 9 am to 5 pm.

Hexham's size means it is the best endowed place near the wall for accommo-

dation and places to eat. *West Close House* (☎ 603307), Hextol Terrace, off Allendale Rd (the B6305), has a range of comfortable rooms from £17.50 per person. The *Beaumont Hotel* (☎ 602331), Beaumont St, overlooks the abbey and has high-quality accommodation from £45 per person.

There are a number of decent restaurants on the quaintly named Priestpopple, near the bus station – possibilities include the *Restaurant Fortini*, with pizza and pasta from £4; the *Diwan-E-Am Tandoori*; and the *Coach & Horses*, a nice pub with a beer garden and bar meals from £4.

The No 685 bus between Newcastle upon Tyne and Carlisle comes through Hexham, and the town is also on the railway line. Bikes are available for hire from Fewsters (☎ 607040), Priestpopple, from £10 per day.

HEXHAM TO HALTWHISTLE
Chesters Roman Fort & Museum
Chesters (☎ 01434-681379; EH) is even more extensive and well preserved than Housesteads, but although the surroundings are attractive, they are not as dramatic as the latter's. The remains are of a Roman cavalry fort and include part of a bridge across the River North Tyne (very complex and beautifully constructed), an extraordinary bathhouse and a well-preserved under-floor heating system. The museum has an extensive collection of Roman sculpture and stone inscriptions; £2.50/1.90.

Chesters is half a mile west of Chollerford on the B6318 and 5½ miles from Hexham.

The *Brunton Water Mill B&B* (☎ 01434-681002) at Low Brunton is just a stone's throw from the Chollerford bridge and costs £20 per person. The much pricier but very pleasant *George Hotel* (☎ 01434-681611) is right by the bridge and costs £90/110. The Chesters fort site has an excellent café and the George Hotel has bar meals and a restaurant.

Housesteads Fort & Museum
Perched high on a ridge overlooking the

moors of the Northumberland National Park, Housesteads (☎ 01434-344363; EH) is one of the best known, best preserved and most dramatic of the sites on the wall. The fort covers five acres and the remains of many buildings, including granaries, barracks, latrines and a hospital, can be seen. This is the starting point for some excellent walks and the one to Steel Rigg is considered the most spectacular section of the entire wall.

Housesteads is 2½ miles north of Bardon Mill on the B6318, and about three miles from Once Brewed. It's popular, so try to visit outside summer weekends; £2.50/1.90.

Vindolanda Fort & Museum

Vindolanda (☎ 01434-344277) is an extensively excavated fort with accompanying civil buildings. There are reconstructions of the stone wall with a turret, a length of turf wall and a timber milecastle gate. The museum has some extraordinary relics, including a leather shoe and a fragment of a letter on a wooden writing tablet that talks of socks and underclothes being sent to a soldier on the wall. Nothing has changed: in this climate you can never have too many.

The site is 1½ miles north of Bardon Mill between the A69 and B6318, one mile from Once Brewed. It's managed by the Vindolanda Trust and is open April to October, daily, 10 am to 6 pm, and the rest of the year daily from 10 am to 4 pm. Entry is £3/1.75 or £4.50/2.75 with a joint ticket for the Roman Army Museum.

Hostels

Once Brewed Youth Hostel (☎ 01434-344360) is a modern, well-equipped hostel central for both Housesteads Fort (three miles) and Vindolanda (one mile). The Northumbria No 685 bus (which you can catch at Hexham or Haltwhistle railway stations) will drop you at Henshaw, two miles south, or you could leave the train at Bardon Mill 2½ miles to the south-east. It's open April to October (and other times); £8.25/5.55.

The *Acomb Youth Hostel* (☎ 01434-602864) is on the edge of a small village about 2½ miles north of Hexham and two miles south of the wall. Hexham can be reached by bus or train. It's open March to mid-July, September and October, daily except Monday, every day between mid-July to August; £5.50/3.75.

HALTWHISTLE
• *pop 4000*   • ☎ *01434*

Haltwhistle is a small market town that straggles some distance along Main St. It's a pleasant enough place, just to the north of the A69, but it doesn't have quite the charm of either Brampton or Corbridge.

The TIC (☎ 322002), Main St, is open mid-May to September. Opening hours vary, but are essentially Monday to Saturday from 10 am to 1 pm and 2 to 5 pm, and Sunday from 1 to 5 pm.

Ashcroft (☎ 320213) is an attractive B&B with rooms from £16 per person. *Hall Meadows* (☎ 321021), Main St, in the centre of town, charges a pound less. The *Manor House Hotel* (☎ 322588), Main St, is centrally located, very friendly and has good pub food; B&B starts at £12.50 per person.

The No 685 bus between Newcastle upon Tyne and Carlisle comes through Haltwhistle, and the town is also on the railway line. Local taxi services include Bainbridge's (☎ 320515) and Sproul's (☎ 321064). See the Greenhead Youth Hostel section for information on the nearest bicycle hire.

HALTWHISTLE TO BRAMPTON
Roman Army Museum

One mile north-east of Greenhead near Walltown, the museum (☎ 016977-47485) has models and reconstructions featuring the Roman army and the troops that garrisoned the wall. It's open 10 am to 4, 5, 5.30 or 6 pm depending on the time of year, but is closed from mid-November to mid-February. Entry is £2.50/1.50, or £4.50/2.75 if you have a joint ticket with Vindolanda.

Places to Stay

Greenhead and nearby Gilsland have a number of pubs and B&Bs. *Greenhead Youth Hostel* (☎ 016977-47401) is in a converted

Methodist chapel three miles west of Haltwhistle railway station. It is also served by Northumbria's No 685 bus service, which runs between Newcastle upon Tyne and Carlisle (see the main Hadrian's Wall Getting There & Around section for this and other transport possibilities). It's open April to June daily except Sunday, July and August daily, September to mid-December daily except Wednesday and Thursday (also other times); £6.75/4.60.

Birdoswald Roman Fort

Birdoswald (☎ 016977-47602; EH) is one of the most interesting of the ruins along the wall, with a well-preserved fort on an escarpment overlooking the beautiful Irthing Gorge. The Willowford bridge abutment, across the river, is worth seeing. There's also a good stretch of wall. It's on a minor road off the B6318 about three miles west of Greenhead. It's open daily from April to October from 10 am to 5.30 pm; £1.95/1.

Brampton

Brampton is a charming market town built in the red Cumbrian sandstone and surrounded by beautiful countryside. The town is particularly interesting on market day (Wednesday). It would make a great base for exploring Hadrian's Wall, and it's on the Cumbrian Cycle Way.

The TIC (☎ 016977-3433) is open Easter to October, Monday to Saturday from 10 am to 5 pm, and June to August, also on Sunday from 11 am to 4 pm.

The *White Lion Hotel* (☎ 016977-2338), High Cross St, is one of a number of pubs that serve good bar meals for around £5. It also has comfortable rooms with bathroom from £15 to £20 per person. *Halidon* (☎ 016977-2106), is a traditional B&B with a couple of rooms at £15 per person.

The No 685 bus between Newcastle upon Tyne and Carlisle comes through Brampton, and the town is also on the railway line. Mountain bikes are available from Talkin Tarn Country Park (☎ 016977-3129), a couple of miles south of town.

Northumberland National Park

The Northumberland National Park covers 398 sq miles of some of emptiest country in the British Isles. The landscape is characterised by windswept grassy hills, cut by streams, and is almost empty of human habitation.

After the Romans left, the region remained a contested zone between Scotland and England, and home to warring clans and families. Few buildings constructed prior to the 18th century survive, partly because few were built. The cattle-farming families lived in simple structures of turf that could be built quickly and cheaply, and be equally quickly abandoned. Peace came in the 18th century, but coincided with new farming practices, so the tenant farmers were dispossessed, leaving large estates. Unlike the rest of England, this area has no scattering of villages, no stone walls and few small farms. Scenically, it has a bleak grandeur, with wide horizons and vast skies.

ORIENTATION & INFORMATION

The park runs from Hadrian's Wall in the south, takes in the Simonside Hills and runs into the Cheviot Hills along the Scottish border. There are few roads.

For more information, contact the National Park Officer (☎ 01434-605555), Eastburn, South Park, Hexham, Northumberland NE46 1BS. There are information centres in Ingram and Rothbury (open Easter to October). There's also a centre at Once Brewed, plus, in partnership with the National Trust, at Housesteads on Hadrian's Wall; see section under Housesteads Port & Museum. All handle accommodation bookings.

WALKS & CYCLE ROUTES

Walkers are attracted to the Pennine Way, which enters the park at its south-eastern corner on Hadrian's Wall, continues to Bellingham, crosses The Cheviot (2670 feet

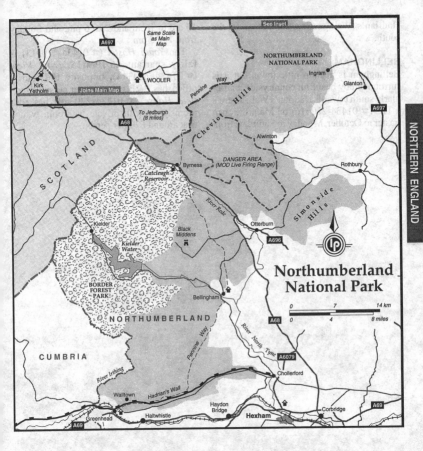

Northumberland National Park

high), and leaves the park near Kirk Yetholm. This is a demanding walk and should be undertaken only by those who are properly equipped to deal with tough conditions.

Cycling in the park would be a pleasure; the roads are good and the traffic is light.

PLACES TO STAY

There are plenty of accommodation options in the south around Hadrian's Wall, but the possibilities further north are extremely limited. There are a small number of B&Bs in Bellingham and Otterburn, and hostels in Bellingham and Byrness (on the Pennine

Way). The *Byrness Youth Hostel* (☎ 01830-520425) is open April to mid-July and September daily except Tuesday, mid-July to August; £6.10/4.15.

GETTING THERE & AROUND

Aside from buses on the A68, the public-transport options are extremely limited. The No 808 operates four times a day between Otterburn and Newcastle upon Tyne, and National Express has three services a day that run between Newcastle upon Tyne and Edinburgh via Otterburn, Byrness, Jedburgh, Melrose and Galashiels. See the

Hadrian's Wall section for access to the south.

BELLINGHAM

Bellingham is a plain little town, but it is surrounded by beautiful countryside, particularly south towards Hadrian's Wall. There's a TIC (☎ 01434-220616) on Main St, open Easter to October, Monday to Saturday, from 10 am to 1 pm and 2 to 6 pm, and Sunday from 1 to 5 pm.

The *Youth Hostel* (☎ 01434-220313) is fairly spartan; £6.10/4.15. *Lynn View* (☎ 01434-220344), opposite the tourist office, has B&B from £16 per person. *Westfield House* (☎ 01434-220340) has four rooms, two with private bathroom, which cost around £20 per person.

Facts about Scotland

No visitor to Britain should miss the chance to visit Scotland. Despite its official union with England in 1707, it has managed to maintain an independent national identity that extends much further than the occasional display of kilts and bagpipes.

Virtually without exception, it is also very beautiful. The wild and untamed Highlands, in particular, are extraordinary. There's a combination of exhilarating open space and a rain-washed quality to the light that illuminates a wonderful range of colours – subtle purples, browns and blues, interspersed with vivid greens and gold.

The climate is harsh, but bad weather, with scudding clouds and water spilling from storm-wrapped hills and mountains, can be spectacular. It's not an easy country, and

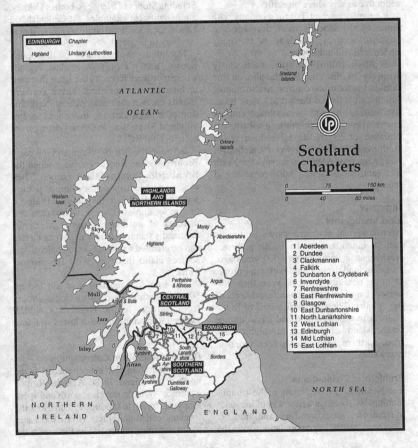

EDINBURGH   Chapter

Highland   Unitary Authorities

ATLANTIC
OCEAN

Shetland
Islands

Orkney
Islands

Scotland Chapters

| 0 | | 75 | | 150 km |
| 0 | 40 | | 80 miles | |

Western
Isles

Skye

HIGHLANDS
AND
NORTHERN ISLANDS

Moray

Aberdeenshire

Highland

Perthshire
& Kinross

Angus

Mull

Argyll & Bute

CENTRAL
SCOTLAND

Stirling

Fife

Jura

EDINBURGH

Islay

North
Ayrshire

East
Ayr-
shire

South
Lanark-
shire

SOUTHERN
SCOTLAND

Borders

Arran

South
Ayrshire

Dumfries &
Galloway

NORTH SEA

1 Aberdeen
2 Dundee
3 Clackmannan
4 Falkirk
5 Dunbarton & Clydebank
6 Inverclyde
7 Renfrewshire
8 East Renfrewshire
9 Glasgow
10 East Dunbartonshire
11 North Lanarkshire
12 West Lothian
13 Edinburgh
14 Mid Lothian
15 East Lothian

NORTHERN
IRELAND

ENGLAND

even Scottish engineers and 20th-century technology have failed to tame it completely. When the winds howl, a human being can still feel extremely vulnerable. At times, it's hard to imagine how human settlement has survived here for so many thousands of years – let alone why anyone would have fought to stay.

But then the clouds will break, and shafts of sunlight will play across the landscape, highlighting snow-capped mountains and heather-covered hills, vast lochs and fast-running streams. And then come the balmy, sunny days, when the countryside is as seductive as anywhere on earth.

It's hardly a secret, but for a country with some of the world's most dramatic and unspoilt scenery, Scotland is curiously underrated and unknown.

Scottish culture survives particularly strongly in the countryside and on the islands, but the urban centres are also unique: Edinburgh is one of the world's most beautiful cities; Glasgow is a vibrant cultural centre, vigorously reinventing itself after the collapse of its traditional industries; St Andrews is Scotland's answer to Cambridge; and prosperous Aberdeen surveys the North Sea (and its oilfields) with proprietorial interest.

HISTORY
First Immigrants
Archaeological evidence shows Scotland's earliest inhabitants to be hunter-gatherers who began arriving about 6000 years ago, from England, Ireland and northern Europe. Over the next few thousand years these colonisers came in waves to different parts of the country. There are indications of Baltic cultures in east Scotland and Irish cultures on the islands of the west. Mesolithic flints from northern France have been found at many sites.

Prehistoric Civilisations
The Neolithic era, beginning in the 4th millennium BC, brought a new way of life, with agriculture, stockbreeding and trading. Unprecedentedly large populations were the result and more complex patterns of social organisation evolved to control them. With organised groups of workers, more ambitious construction projects were now possible.

Scotland is rich in Neolithic sites; in fact, some of the most impressive in Europe are in Orkney, Shetland and the Western Isles. The chiefs who led these growing populations required elaborate tombs like the great passage grave at Maes Howe, Orkney, constructed from carefully dressed boulders. Stone circles date from the late Neolithic and Bronze Age; the Ring of Brodgar and the Standing Stones of Stenness, both in Orkney, are magnificent examples. At Callanish, on Lewis, there's a stone circle similar to that at Avebury in England.

Neolithic people usually built wooden houses, and it's only in treeless regions where they were forced to use stone that their architecture has survived. These northern islands contain rare examples of Neolithic domestic architecture; there's an entire village at Skara Brae in Orkney dating from around 3100 BC.

Between the late Neolithic and the early Bronze Age the Beaker People reached the British Isles from mainland Europe. They were so named because they burned pottery with their dead but they also introduced bronze for knives, daggers, arrowheads and articles of gold and copper. Many of Scotland's standing stones and stone circles can be credited to the Beaker People. Some sources claim that they were the original Celts.

The Iron Age reached Scotland around 500 BC, with the arrival of Celtic settlers from Europe. In the Highlands, which escaped Roman influence, it lasted well into the Christian era.

Roman Attempts at Colonisation
The Romans didn't have much success in the north of the island. In 80 AD, the Roman governor Agricola marched north and spent four years trying to subdue the wild tribes the Romans called the Picts (from the Latin pictus, meaning painted). The Picts were the

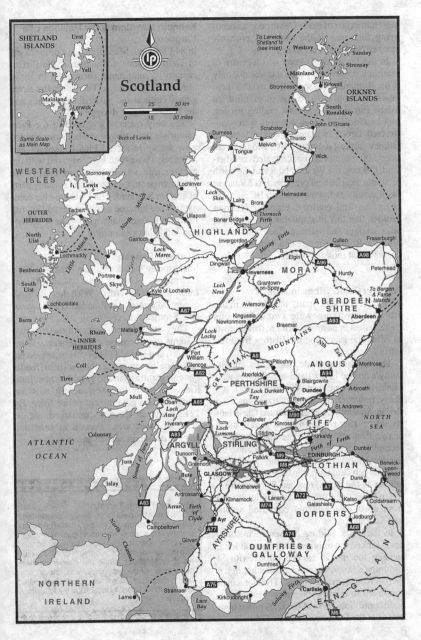

most numerous of many Celtic peoples occupying this area at the time and probably reached Scotland via Orkney.

In the far north, Orkney was a centre of maritime power and posed a threat not only to the Romans (who sent a fleet against them in 84 BC) but also to the other northern tribes. For defence against raiding parties, *brochs* (fortified stone towers) were constructed. Broch architecture was perfected in Orkney in the 1st century BC, and there are over 500 examples, concentrated in Shetland, Orkney, the Western Isles and the north of Scotland. The best preserved, at Mousa in Shetland, dates from around 50 BC.

By the 2nd century, Emperor Hadrian decided that this inhospitable land of mists, bogs, midges and warring tribes had little to offer the Roman Empire and began work on the wall that took his name.

Feuding Celtic Tribes in Alba

When the Romans finally left Britain in the 4th century, there were two indigenous Celtic tribes in northern Britain, then known as Alba: the Picts, and the Britons from the south.

The historian, Bede, attributes Christianity's arrival in Scotland to St Ninian who established a centre in Whithorn in 397. It's likely, however, that some of the Romanised Britons in south Scotland adopted Christianity after the religion was given state recognition in 313. St Columba founded a second important early Christian centre on the tiny island of Iona, off Mull, in 563.

In the 6th century a third Celtic tribe, later known as the Scots, reached Scotland from Ireland. In the 7th century Anglo-Saxons from north-east England colonised south-east Scotland.

In the 790s, raiding Norsemen in long-boats sacked the religious settlement at Iona, causing the monks to flee inland with St Columba's bones to found a cathedral in the Pictish Kingdom at Dunkeld. The Norsemen continued to control the entire western seaboard until Somerled of the Isles broke their power at the Battle of Largs in 1263.

Kenneth MacAlpin & the Makings of a Kingdom

In 843 Kenneth MacAlpin, king of the Scots of Dalriada, took advantage of the Pictish custom of matrilineal succession to make himself king of Alba. Thereafter the Scots gained cultural and political ascendancy and the Pictish culture disappeared.

The only material evidence of the Picts comprises their unique symbol stones which were set up to record Pictish lineages and alliances. These boulders, engraved with the mysterious symbols of an otherwise unknown people, can be found in many parts of eastern Scotland. The Picts are also commemorated in place names prefixed 'Pit' (eg Pitlochry). Their language may have been of non Indo-European origin.

Canmore Dynasty

Shakespeare's Malcolm was Malcolm III, a Canmore, who killed Macbeth at Lumphanan in 1057. With his English queen, Margaret, he founded a dynasty of able Scottish rulers.

They introduced new Anglo-Norman systems of government and religious foundations, and David I (1124-53) increased his influence by adopting the Norman feudal system, granting land to great Norman families in return for their acting as what amounted to a government police force. By 1212 Walter of Coventry remarked that the Scottish court was 'French in race and manner of life, in speech and in culture'.

Finding a King: Tanistry
Unlike the matrilineal Picts, the Scots preferred tanistry – selection of a suitable male heir from anyone in the family who could claim a king as great grandfather. Shakespeare described the dire consequences for Scottish history to great effect in *Macbeth*. While the play is neither historically nor geographically accurate, it certainly manages to evoke the dark deeds, bloodshed and warring factions of the following centuries.

BRYN THOMAS

RICHARD EVERIST

BRYN THOMAS

TONY WHEELER

RICHARD EVERIST

A: Awaiting the piper's lament,
    Ayrshire coast
B: Pillarbox on Arran, Ayrshire
C: Old Waverley Hotel, Edinburgh
D: Balmoral Hotel, Edinburgh
E: Edinburgh skyline

TONY WHEELER

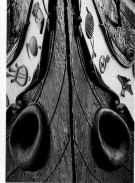
TONY WHEELER

TONY WHEELER

BRYN THOMAS

TONY WHEELER

A	B	C
D	E	

A: Bow of HMS *Victory*, Portsmouth
B: Bow of HMS *Great Britain*, Bristol
C: Detail of HMS *Victory*, Portsmouth
D: HMS *Discovery*, Dundee

E: Lighthouse at the Needles, Isle of Wight

Clans & Feudalism

The old society was based on ties of kinship between everyone in the tribe, or clan, and its head. Unlike a feudal lord, a chief might still command the loyalty of his clan whether he was a landowner or not.

Vestiges of this tribalism remain, in references to the separate law of the Scot and the Briton. The Normans, Bruces, Frasers, Grants and Stewarts, for example, were settled from Strathclyde, up through Perth and Angus and eventually into Aberdeen and Moray, assisting the crown to establish new forms of government along the Highland fringes. Although the initial reception was bloody, the feudal system was eventually grafted onto the old system, creating families and clans who were enormously powerful in terms of land ownership and loyal fighting men.

Highlands & Lowlands

Inaccessible in their glens, the Highland clans remained a law unto themselves for another 600 years. A cultural and linguistic divide grew up between Gaelic-speaking Highlanders, and the Lowland Scots who spoke an English dialect known as Lallans.

In the Lowlands, small commercial centres like Berwick, Roxburgh, Stirling, Edinburgh and Forfar grew up through the trading activities of Angles, Scandinavians and Flemings. These centres later became independent, self-governing burghs, trading wool from the monasteries of the Borders for Flemish cloth or wine from Burgundy. Most of the population, however, eked out a subsistence from the land. Until quite recently, the rural Scots' diet consisted of oatmeal, barley, milk, cheese, herrings or occasionally meat, and kail (cabbage).

Wars of Independence (1286-1390)

Two centuries of the Canmore dynasty effectively ended when Alexander III fell to his death in the River Forth in 1286. Edward I of England then began the attempted conquest of Scotland that earned him the title

The Taking of the Stone of Destiny

Alleged to have accompanied the Scots in all their mythical journeyings, the original Stone of Destiny (the Fatal Stone) was a carved block of sandstone on which the Scottish monarchs placed their feet during the coronation.

Stolen by Edward I in 1296, this venerable talisman was incorporated into the Coronation Chair, used by all English (and later British) monarchs, in London's Westminster Abbey. Apart from being taken to Gloucester during the air raids in WWII, the Stone lay undisturbed for centuries.

On Christmas Eve 1950, however, a plucky band of Scottish students drove down from Glasgow, jemmied the door of Westminster Abbey and made off with the Stone. English officialdom was outraged. The border roads had roadblocks on them for the first time in 400 years, but as Scots living in London jeered the English police as they searched the Serpentine Lake and the River Thames, the Stone was being smuggled back to Scotland.

King George VI was 'sorely troubled about the loss', but the students issued a petition affirming their loyalty to him, stating that they would give back the Stone as long as it could remain on Scottish soil. The authorities refused to negotiate and, three months after it had been stolen, the Stone turned up on the altar of the ruined Abbey of Arbroath. It was here, in 1320, that the Arbroath Declaration had been signed, reaffirming the right of Scots to self-rule and independence from England. Before the public were aware that the Stone had even been found, it was back in London. No charges were brought and Ian Hamilton, the student who led this jolly caper, published his story in *The Taking of the Stone of Destiny*.

Many Scots, however, hold that the original Stone is safely hidden somewhere in Scotland, and that Edward I was fobbed off with a shoddy imitation. This is very likely to be true, for descriptions of the original state that it was decorated with carvings, not that it was a plain block of sandstone. Given that Scottish nationalist feelings are currently running higher than at any time this century, this powerful symbol of Scotland would surely have been brought out by now if it hadn't been quite so safely hidden. ■

Hammer of the Scots, and there followed 100 years of struggle for independence from English domination.

Edward took full advantage of the Scottish monarchy's weakness, as did later English kings; in 1290 there were no less than 13 'tanists' or contestants for the throne. In 1291 Edward travelled the country forcing the clan leaders to sign a declaration of allegiance to him. In a final blow to Scottish pride he removed the Stone of Destiny, the coronation stone on which the kings of Scotland had been invested for centuries, and sent it from Scone to London. (In 1996 the government decided that the Stone should be returned to Scotland.)

Resistance broke out throughout the country, some of it, like the efforts of William Wallace, more serious than others. In 1297, Wallace's forces succeeded in defeating the English at the Battle of Stirling Bridge. After further skirmishes he was captured and subjected to barbaric execution, being hanged, drawn, emasculated, burnt and quartered. He is still remembered as the epitome of patriotism and a great hero of the resistance movement, as portrayed by Mel Gibson in the recent film, *Braveheart*.

After 30 years of virtual civil war, Robert the Bruce murdered his rival Red Comyn, had himself crowned king of Scotland and went on to defeat the English at the Battle of Bannockburn in 1314, a turning point in Scotland's fight for independence from England.

According to myth he was later in hiding on Rathlin Island, off the coast of Ireland, when he was inspired by a spider's persistence in spinning its web to renew his own efforts. After his death, the country was ravaged by endless warfare and plague epidemics. The Wars of Independence strengthened links with France and Europe; the Auld Alliance first agreed with France in 1295 was constantly renewed up to 1492.

The Stewarts & the Barons

Bruce's son, who became David II of Scotland, was so friendly with Edward III that he appointed Edward's son as his heir. But when David died in 1371, the Scots were quick to crown Robert Stewart (Robert the Bruce's grandson).

The early Stewart kings were ruthless in their attempts to break the power of the magnates. These were not peaceful years. Time and again the king met with an untimely death and clans like the Douglases and the Donalds (Lords of the Isles after the Norsemen were driven from the Hebrides in 1266) grew to wield almost regal power.

James IV & the Renaissance

James IV married the daughter of Henry VII of England, thus linking the Stewarts with the Tudors. This did not, however, prevent the French from persuading James to go to war with his in-laws. He was killed at the battle of Flodden Hill in 1513, along with 10,000 of his subjects.

Renaissance ideas flourished in Scotland during James's reign. Much graceful Scottish architecture dates from this time, and examples of the Renaissance style can be seen in alterations made to the palaces at Holyrood, Stirling, Linlithgow and Falkland.

The building of collegiate churches and universities brought opportunity for education at home, along French lines. St Andrews University was founded in 1410, Glasgow in 1451 and Aberdeen in 1495.

Mary Queen of Scots & the Reformation

In 1542, James V died – broken-hearted, it is said, after his defeat by the English at Solway Moss. His baby daughter, Mary, became Queen of Scots.

At first the country was ruled by regents, who rejected Henry VIII's plan that Mary should marry his son, and sent her to France where she eventually married the dauphin. Henry was furious at the snub, and his armies ravaged the Borders and sacked Edinburgh – the Rough Wooing, as it was called.

While Mary, a devout Catholic, was in France, the Reformation of the Scottish church was underway. The wealthy Catholic church was riddled with corruption and the preachings of John Knox, pupil of the Swiss

Mary Queen of Scots

reformer, Calvin, found sympathetic ears. In 1560 the Scottish Parliament created a Protestant church that was independent of Rome and the monarchy. The Latin mass was abolished and the pope's authority denied.

Following her husband's death, Mary returned to Scotland. Still only 18 and a stunning beauty, she was a headstrong Catholic and her conduct did nothing to endear her to the Protestants. She was implicated in the murder of her second husband, Lord Darnley, and confused everyone by marrying her abductor, the Earl of Bothwell.

Forced to abdicate in favour of her son, James VI, Mary was imprisoned in the castle in the middle of Loch Leven. Aided by a besotted young admirer, she escaped to England and her cousin, the Protestant Elizabeth I. Since Mary had claims to the English throne, and Elizabeth had no heir, she was seen as a security risk and Elizabeth kept her under lock and key. It took her 19 years to agree to sign the warrant for Mary's execution. When Elizabeth died in 1603, James VI of Scotland united the crowns by also becoming James I of England.

Religious Wars of the 17th Century
Religious differences led to civil war in Scotland and England. The fortunes of the Stuarts (spelt the French way following Mary's Gallic association) were thereafter bound up with the church's struggle to establish independence from Rome. To complicate

matters, religious reform in Scotland was divided between Presbyterians, who shunned all ritual and hierarchy, and less extreme Protestants who were more like the Anglicans south of the border. The question of episcopacy (rule of the bishops) was particularly divisive.

Earning himself the nickname of the Wisest Fool in Christendom, James VI/I pursued a moderate policy despite the reformers' fervour. But he also insisted that his authority came directly from God and was therefore incontestable (the Divine Right of Kings), and encouraged the paranoia which led to witch hunts, with many innocent people, set up as scapegoats, suffering appalling deaths by torture and burning.

In 1625 James was succeeded by his son, Charles I, a devout Anglican who attempted to impose a High Anglican form of worship on the church in Scotland.

The Covenanters
In 1637 the Dean of St Giles Cathedral in Edinburgh was reading the liturgy when he was floored by a stool thrown by Jennie Geddes, an Edinburgh greengrocer. The common people wanted a common religion and riots ensued which ended with the creation of a document known as the National Covenant. The Covenanters sought freedom from Rome and from royal interference in church government, the abolition of bishops and a simpler ritual.

The dispute developed into civil war between moderate royalists and radical Covenanters. The Marquis of Montrose is still remembered as a dashing hero who, though originally a Covenanter, eventually held out for the king. He was betrayed to the English Republicans while hiding at Ardvreck Castle in Loch Assynt and executed as a traitor.

Civil war raged in England. Charles I was defeated by Oliver Cromwell and beheaded in 1649. His exiled son, Charles, was offered the crown in Scotland as long as he signed the Covenant. He was crowned in 1650 but soon forced into exile by Oliver Cromwell.

After Charles II's restoration in 1660, episcopacy was reinstated. Many of the clergy rejected the bishops' authority and started holding outdoor services, or Conventicles. In 1690, however, episcopacy was abolished in Scotland.

Union with England in 1707

The wars had left the country and economy ruined. During the 1690s, famine killed up to a third of the population in some areas.

Anti-English feeling ran high. Graham of Claverhouse (Bonnie Dundee) raised a band of Highlanders and routed the English troops at Killiecrankie, near Pitlochry. The situation was exacerbated by the failure of an investment venture in Panama set up by the Bank of England to boost the economy, which resulted in widespread bankruptcy in Scotland.

In 1692, people were horrified by the treacherous massacre, on English government orders, of Macdonalds by Campbells in Glencoe. In this atmosphere, the lure of trade concessions to boost the economy and the preservation of the Scottish church and legal system offered by the Act of Union of 1707 persuaded the Scots to let their parliament be disbanded and absorbed into the English one.

The Jacobites (1715-45)

The Jacobite rebellions, most notably of 1715 and 1745, were attempts to replace the Hanoverian kings of England with Catholic Stuarts. Despite Scottish disenchantment with the Act of Union, however, there was never much support for the Jacobite cause outside the Highlands, owing to the fear of inviting Catholicism back into Scotland.

James Edward Stuart, known as the Old Pretender, was the son of the exiled James VII. With support from the Highland clans he made several attempts to regain the throne but fled to France after the unsuccessful 1715 rebellion. In an effort to impose control on the Highlanders, General Wade and the English military (the Redcoats) were sent to construct roads into the previously inaccessible glens.

In 1745, James's son, Charles Edward Stuart (Bonnie Prince Charlie) landed in Scotland to claim the crown for his father. He

was at first successful, getting as far south into England as Derby. Back in Scotland, the Young Pretender and his Highland supporters suffered catastrophic defeat at Culloden in 1746. Dressed as a woman, the prince escaped via the Western Isles assisted by Flora MacDonald.

After 'the '45' (as it became known), the government banned private armies, the wearing of the kilt and the playing of the pipes. Many Jacobites were transported or executed, or died in prison; others forfeited their lands. Those who still raise their glasses in a toast to The King over the Water are expressing a nostalgia for a way of life, the inevitable disappearance of which was accelerated by these events.

Beginnings of the Industrial Revolution

From the second half of the 18th century, Lowland factories began to draw workers out of the glens. The tobacco trade with America boomed before the War of Independence and then gave way to the textile industry. People came to work in the cotton and linen mills in Glasgow and Lanarkshire. Established in 1759, the Carron ironworks became the largest ironworks in Britain. The jute trade developed in Dundee and shipyards opened on the Clyde in the early 19th century.

Scottish Enlightenment

In the flowering of intellectual life known as the Scottish Enlightenment of the 18th century, the philosophers David Hume and Adam Smith emerged as influential thinkers nourished on generations of theological debate.

After the bloodshed and fervent religious debate of the Reformation, people applied themselves with the same energy and piety to the making of money and the enjoyment of leisure. There was a revival of interest in vernacular literature, reflected in Robert Fergusson's satires and Alexander MacDonald's Gaelic poetry. The poetry of Robert Burns, a man of the people, achieved lasting popularity. Sir Walter Scott, the prolific poet and novelist, was an ardent patriot.

Highland Clearances & the 19th Century

With the banning of private armies, the relationship of chief to clansman in the late 18th and early 19th centuries became one of economic, not military, consideration. The kelp industry (the production of soda ash from seaweed) was developed and Highland populations continued to grow.

By the mid-19th century, overpopulation, the collapse of the kelp industry and the potato famine of the 1840s led to the Clearances. People were forced off the land and shipped or tricked into emigrating to Canada and America. Those who remained were moved to smallholdings, known as *crofts*. Rents were extortionate and life for the crofters was extremely precarious. Common grazing ground was confiscated for sheep or deer runs. In 1886, however, the Crofters Commission was set up to ensure security of tenure and to fix fair rent for smallholders.

In the 19th century, it became fashionable for wealthy southerners to holiday in the Highlands to shoot deer and grouse. Queen Victoria had Balmoral built in 1848 and spent a great deal of time there, disguising herself as a simple Scotswoman and promenading in the company of her servant, John Brown.

Elsewhere, the new urban society saw a growing bourgeoisie take precedence in politics over the still powerful landed aristocracy. Political life was more closely integrated with England, and the (Scottish) Liberal, Gladstone, was popular.

There was much constitutional and parliamentary reform throughout the Victorian era. Legislation to improve the education system was connected with reform and dissension in the church. Desire for betterment might send a farmer's child, barefoot and with a sack of oatmeal on its back, to the university. The education system remains distinct from that of England.

In the great industrial cities, conditions among the working classes were hard. In the notorious Glasgow Gorbals, where typhoid epidemics were rife, people lived in overcrowded tenements on barely subsistence wages. Despite prosperity from the thriving shipyards, coal mines, steel works and textile mills, Glasgow and Clydeside still harboured many unemployed, unskilled immigrants from Ireland and the Highlands.

The Economy in the 20th Century

Industry continued to thrive through WWI, with Clydeside a munitions centre. The postwar slump didn't make itself felt in Scotland until the 1920s; but the Great Depression of the 1930s hit so hard that heavy industry never recovered. In fact, the seeds of Scotland's 20th-century economic failure could be said to lie in the success of the preceding industrial era.

The discovery of oil and gas in the North Sea in the 1970s brought prosperity to Aberdeen and the surrounding area, and to the Shetland Islands. However, most of the oil revenue has been siphoned off to England.

Light engineering and high-tech electronics companies have replaced the defunct coal mines and steel works of the Central Lowlands, but many are foreign owned. The fishing industry, profitable until Britain joined the European Union (EU), is now in decline, crippled by fishing quotas imposed from Brussels.

Depopulation of the rural areas continues although grant schemes subsidise new business initiatives away from agriculture and fishing.

GEOGRAPHY

Scotland is about half the size of England, and covers 30,414 sq miles. Roughly two-thirds of the country is mountain and moorland. Geographically, it can be divided into three areas: the Southern Uplands, the Central Lowlands, and the northern Highlands and Islands.

South of Edinburgh and Glasgow are the Southern Uplands, with fertile coastal plains and ranges of hills bordering England. The Central Lowlands comprise a triangular slice from Edinburgh and Dundee in the east to Glasgow in the west, and contain the industrial belt and most of the population. A coastal plain runs all the way up the east coast.

The Highland Line, a geographical division, runs north-east from Helensburgh (just west of Glasgow) to Stonehaven (just south of Aberdeen) on the east coast; to the north of it are the Highlands and Islands. The area includes mountain ranges of sandstone, granite and metamorphic rock, with severe glaciation in the north-west. Mountains over 3000 feet – there are almost 300 of them in Scotland – are known as Munros, after the man who first listed them. Some rise directly from the steep sea fjords, or lochs, of the west coast. Ben Nevis, in the western Grampians, is Britain's highest mountain, at 4406 feet.

The main Highlands watershed is near the west coast, giving long river valleys running east, many containing freshwater lochs and some arable areas. The Great Glen is a fault line running from Fort William to Inverness, containing a chain of freshwater lochs (including Loch Ness) connected by the Caledonian Canal.

Of Scotland's 790 islands, 130 are inhabited. The Western Isles comprise the Inner Hebrides and the Outer Hebrides. To the north are two other island groups, Orkney and Shetland, the northernmost reaches of the British Isles.

Edinburgh is the capital and financial centre, Glasgow the industrial centre and Aberdeen and Dundee the two largest regional centres.

What's in a Name?

England dominates the rest of the UK in all things to such an extent that not only the English but most of the world tend to say 'England' when referring to the UK as a whole. The island of Britain (England, Scotland and Wales) together with Northern Ireland make up the country whose official name is the United Kingdom of Great Britain and Northern Ireland.

It may seem an obvious point but it's important to get the name of the country right. The Scots, the Welsh and the people of Northern Ireland will find it deeply insulting if you tell them how much you like being 'here in England' when you're in their part of the UK. ■

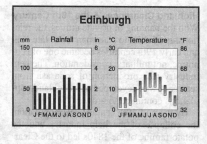

CLIMATE

'Varied' may be a vague way to describe a country's climate but it perfectly describes Scotland's many moods. Whenever you visit, you're likely to see both sun and rain. One good thing about the climate is that it changes quickly – a rainy day is often followed by a sunny one. There are also wide variations in climate over small distances; while one glen broods under a cloud, the next may be basking in sunshine.

Considering how far north the country lies (Edinburgh is on the same line of latitude as Moscow), you might expect a colder climate, but the winds that blow in from the Atlantic are warmed by the Gulf Stream. The west and east coasts have relatively mild climates, but the Highlands can have extreme weather at any time. The ski resorts aside, many facilities (including B&Bs and TICs) close from the end of September to the end of March.

The east coast tends to be cool and dry – rainfall averages around 650 mm, and winter temperatures rarely drop below 0°C, although winds off the North Sea can rattle your teeth. The west coast is milder and wetter, with over 1500 mm of rain and average summer highs of 19°C.

May and June are generally the driest months, but expect rain at any time.

ECOLOGY & ENVIRONMENT

Scotland's wild, open countryside may look as if no harm could possibly befall it. However, what may look natural can sometimes turn out to conceal an environmental threat. In many areas you'll notice thick evergreen plantations. Over the last few decades government grants and tax concessions to landowners have encouraged the planting of these fast-growing trees, despite serious ecological drawbacks. As well as destroying wildlife habitat, conifers increase the acidity of the soil and may even have a detrimental effect on weather patterns. In the far north, bogland has been destroyed.

Tourism can also have damaging effects on the landscape. The Cairngorms Chairlift Company would like to replace their ageing chairlift which can't operate in high winds with an all-weather year-round funicular railway. However, plans were put on hold after Scottish Natural Heritage argued that the flora and fauna of the delicate Arctic plateau couldn't cope with the inevitable increase in visitor numbers.

Scotland is home to many animals and birds that are rare elsewhere in the UK (see Flora & Fauna section), but they too are constantly threatened by the changing environment. The habitat of the once common corncrake, for example, has been all but destroyed by modern farming methods; farmers can now claim a subsidy for mowing

in corncrake-friendly fashion. Other threats don't even have an economic justification; the osprey nest at Boat of Garten has to be watched round the clock to prevent egg collectors whipping the eggs.

FLORA & FAUNA

Although much of the country was once covered by the Caledonian forest – a mix of Scots pine, oak, silver birch, willow, alder and rowan, with heather underfoot – deforestation has reduced this mighty forest to a few small pockets of indigenous trees.

Almost three-quarters of the country is uncultivated bog, rock and heather. In mountainous areas like the Cairngorms, alpine plants thrive; in the far north there are lichens and mosses found nowhere else in Britain. Acidic peat covers almost 2,000,000 acres, most notably in the Flow Country of Caithness and Sutherland, now a conservation area.

Scotland's national flower is actually the harebell or bluebell, although the thistle is more commonly associated with the country. Yellow flag, wild thyme and yarrow abound in the summer.

The Monarch of the Glen
The red deer, the Monarch of the Glen, is rapidly becoming a serious ecological problem in Scotland. Unlike many species, the red deer is not hurtling towards extinction but rather multiplying way out of control. There are now over 300,000 of them and huge areas of vegetation are being damaged.

Fencing off woodland is not the answer to the problem as it reduces the territory of the deer and leads to even heavier grazing of these areas. In some parts of Scotland, no new trees have been able to grow since deer populations started to increase 300 years ago.

The balance of nature was upset when the natural predator of the red deer, the wolf, was eradicated in the 17th century. In recent years, too few deer have been culled by farmers and estate managers, and, with milder winters, fewer deer have died from lack of food. If nothing is done to reduce deer numbers, the last few areas of indigenous forest in the country may be destroyed. ∎

Red deer are found in Scotland in large numbers. The reindeer, beaver and auroch (wild ox) are all now extinct, and the last wolf was shot near Scone in the 17th century. Once nearly extinct, wild boars have been reintroduced in the south-west. There are still some wildcats but, like wild goats, they're rarely seen.

Sheep graze the grass-covered hills, and much of the Lowlands is given over to agriculture. Hairy Highland cattle were bred here to survive the cold. Take care in approaching these diminutive bovines – they look cuddly but have foul tempers.

Throughout the country, foxes and red squirrels are to be found, with pine martens in the forests. Otters are rare, though less so than in England; and minks, escaped from fur farms, are multiplying fast.

Large numbers of grouse graze the heather on the moors, and gamekeepers burn vast areas to encourage the new shoots that attract this small game bird. In heavily forested areas you may be lucky enough to see a capercaillie, a black, turkey-like bird, the largest member of the grouse family. Birds of prey like the eagle, osprey, peregrine and hen harrier are protected. Millions of greylag geese winter on the Lowland stubble fields.

Since 80% of Britain's coastline is in Scotland, it's not surprising to find millions of sea birds here. Whale-watching trips follow more substantial photographic prey, and seals are frequently seen. The major rivers attract anglers from all over the world to fish for the famed Scottish salmon.

GOVERNMENT & POLITICS

Scotland is essentially ruled from London. The Secretary of State for Scotland, a member of the British Cabinet, is responsible for Scotland's administration in the form of five departments – education and health; development; planning; agriculture and fisheries; and the judicial system. There are 72 Scottish members in the Houses of Parliament and all Scottish peers have a seat in the House of Lords.

Following the 1996 local government reforms, there are now 32 administrative

---

Radical Politics – the Birth of the Labour Party & the SNP

The radical Scottish tradition that produced John Knox and other church reformers also generated some influential political thinkers.

The trade unions produced James Keir Hardie, who helped form the Scottish Labour Party in 1888 and the Independent Labour Party for Great Britain in 1893. The economic distress of the 1930s pushed Scottish political opinion further to the left. Several major players in the Communist Party of Great Britain were Scots.

The formation in 1934 of the Scottish National Party (SNP) was initiated by several distinguished men of letters – Hugh MacDiarmid, Eric Linklater, Sir Compton Mackenzie, Neil Gunn and Lewis Grassic Gibbon. It's only quite recently, however, that this party has achieved any political success, most Scots being traditional Labour supporters. ■

---

regions in Scotland, roughly corresponding to the old counties (eg Argyll, Perthshire etc) which existed prior to the 1974 reforms.

Some laws in the British Houses of Parliament are passed exclusively for Scotland. The country appears to be the testing ground for more controversial policies – Scotland had the poll tax first, for example.

Self-Rule for Scotland?

Since 1979, the Scots have been ruled by a government they didn't elect – the Conservatives now hold only nine of the 72 Scottish seats in the House of Commons. While there have been grumbles about the imbalance of the relationship with England ever since the union in 1707, nationalist feelings are stronger now than they have been for many decades.

In 1967 the Scottish National Party (SNP) won their first seat, and support for it has grown ever since. Both the Labour Party and the Conservatives have toyed with offering Scotland devolution, or a degree of self-government. In 1979 Scots voted in a referendum over whether to set up a directly elected Scottish Assembly in Edinburgh to decide some Scottish affairs. Although more people voted for devolution than against it (33% to 31%), a vote of at least 40% was required for the motion to be carried so nothing happened.

Few visitors will be aware of anti-English feelings but these are growing, fanned by organisations like Scottish Watch and Settler Watch who try to dissuade the English from buying holiday homes in the Highlands.

Scotland will probably gain some measure of self-rule soon. The Labour Party is committed to holding a new referendum over the creation of a Scottish Parliament if it wins the 1997 election. Scotland already participates in the EU as a distinct cultural entity; the community's very different needs and concerns are reflected in increasingly different voting patterns from the rest of Britain. Given the emergence of several new small nations in Europe in the 1990s, the prospect of a totally independent Scotland doesn't seem as unlikely as it might have done a decade ago.

ECONOMY

All is far from well with Scotland's economy. The last coal mines and steel works have closed, and although oil and gas are still extracted from the North Sea platforms, the oil-boom days in Shetland, Invergordon and Inverness are over.

The country is struggling to replace the old heavy industries with high-tech engineering projects (Scotland has its Silicon Glen), and finance and service industries. Tourism is very much a growth industry, and Edinburgh is an important international finance centre.

Some traditional industries survive. Woollens, tweeds and tartans from Harris and the Borders are world-renowned, as are the whisky distilleries. Some sheep and cattle farming continues in the Highlands, although the grouse moors, deer forests and salmon rivers are a better bet economically. The fertile lowland plains produce barley, oats, wheat, potatoes, turnips, cattle and sheep. European Union policy, however, currently requires farmers to put upwards of 15% of arable land out of production. EU

fishing quotas also continue to harm the fishing industry.

POPULATION

Scotland has just over five million people, around 9% of the UK's total population.

Glasgow is the largest city with 680,000 people, followed by Edinburgh with 420,000, Aberdeen with 214,000, and Dundee with 175,000. The Highland region is Britain's most sparsely populated administrative area, with an average of 20 people per sq mile – 30 times fewer than the national average.

PEOPLE

The Scots of popular imagination can be kilted life-and-soul-of-the-party types, apparently friendly but dangerous football hooligans with flick knives, or dour misanthropes threatening hellfire and brimstone from the pulpit. All of these caricatures have some origin in fact.

Early history describes a belligerent people of mixed origin. Invading Romans, raiding Vikings, avaricious English kings and clan warfare never gave them a chance to settle down. Centuries-old disagreements between clans are remembered, and even today a Colquhoun will not sit down with a MacGregor because of the massacre of Colquhouns by Rob Roy and a band of MacGregors almost 300 years ago. Religious differences also play a part as is clear whenever Catholic Celtic plays Protestant Rangers on the Glasgow football pitches.

Influences from different parts of Europe have created a country of people who are far from homogenous. The 'hurdy-gurdy' accent of Shetlanders and Orcadians betrays their Scandinavian roots. Gaelic is still spoken in parts of the Highlands and Islands, and Highland society is very different to the anglicised Lowlands.

Generally speaking, however, you'll probably find the Scots more welcoming to foreign visitors than the English. While most Scots love to party and partake of *uisge-bha* (the water of life: whisky), after a few drams some will begin to exhibit symptoms of what is known as the Celtic Twilight, a fanciful streak of melancholia stemming as much from their turbulent history and current economic problems as from their uncertain weather.

EDUCATION

Until recently, Scotland's education system was one of the best in the world, the Scottish love of learning and pride in education being a by-product of the church reformation. Now, however, more young people leave school without qualifications than in almost any other European country. Academic Scots are well catered for, with good sixth-form colleges and universities with high standards, but they're the favoured few.

Education was long controlled by the church and the great universities were set up to provide a source of educated churchmen. By the 17th century there was a school in every parish and standards continued to rise until the Industrial Revolution, when the use of child labour increased. Basic education became compulsory in 1872.

The 1962 Education Act introduced a uniform system preserving the broader-based Scottish system from erosion by anglicisation. Schools today are run by the Scottish Education Department and still follow a curriculum and examination system different from England's. There are a few independent fee-paying schools along English lines.

ARTS & SCIENCE

Between them, Edinburgh and Glasgow dominate the arts in Scotland. Both have an energetic cultural scene, partly reflected by their respective festivals, which showcase an extraordinary range of performers and artists. Historically, however, although the Scots have had a disproportionate impact on science, technology, medicine and philosophy, they are under-represented in the worlds of art, music and literature.

Scottish scientists include John Napier, the inventor of logarithms; Lord Kelvin, who described the second law of thermodynamics; and James Clerk Maxwell, who described the laws of electrodynamics.

The technologists include James Watt, who revolutionised steam power; John Dunlop, who invented the pneumatic wheel; John MacAdam, who invented the road surface that bears his name; Charles Mackintosh, who invented waterproof material; Alexander Graham Bell, who invented the telephone; John Logie Baird, who invented television; and Sir Robert Watson Watt, who invented radar.

The doctors include John and William Hunter, who pioneered anatomy; Sir Joseph Lister, who pioneered the use of antiseptics; and Alexander Fleming, who discovered penicillin.

The philosophers and thinkers include David Hume and Adam Smith.

Many reasons have been given for this

Scottish Inventions & Discoveries

The inventiveness of the Scots is remarkable, given the size of the country. Perhaps it was the weather that caused thinking Scots to remain indoors pondering life, the universe and all that is within it – it was the Scots that gave the world the mackintosh. The long list of things they either discovered or invented includes:

anaesthetics	insulin	shrapnel
breech-loading rifles	lawnmowers	speedometers
bicycles	logarithms	steam engines
carbon dioxide	mackintosh	steel ships
colour photography	marmalade	tarmacadam roads
decimal fraction point	morphine	telephones
electric light	penicillin	telescopes
fire alarms	pneumatic tyres	television
gas-masks	postage stamp (adhesive)	thermos flasks
grand pianos	radar	ultrasound
golf	refrigeration	water softeners

extraordinary roll-call, but one of the most obvious is the long tradition of high-quality education that can be traced back as far as the earliest monastic institutions.

However, the arts never seem to have caught the Scottish popular imagination – or at least not in a form recognised by modern culture vultures. Perhaps the need for creative expression took different, less elitist paths – in the *ceilidh* (see under Culture), in folk music and dance, oral poetry and folk stories. In a way, the great Scottish writers – Robert Burns, Sir Walter Scott and even Robert Louis Stevenson – could be seen as direct inheritors and popularisers of this folk tradition.

There are few internationally known figures in the visual arts, although the National Gallery in Edinburgh and the galleries in Glasgow, Aberdeen, Perth and Dundee have important Scottish collections. Since the 19th century, Glasgow has dominated the Scottish scene, partly thanks to the Glasgow School of Art, which has produced several outstanding artists.

ARCHITECTURE

Scottish architecture can be divided into six periods: Celtic (up to the 11th century), Anglo-Norman (up to the 16th century), post-Reformation or Renaissance (up to the

17th century), Georgian (18th century), Victorian Baronial (19th century), and 20th century (which so far evades simple characterisation).

Interesting buildings can be seen throughout Scotland, but Edinburgh has a particularly remarkable heritage of superb architecture from the 12th century to the present day.

Celtic

Few Celtic buildings survive, although the islands have some of the best surviving examples in Europe. The best known are the stone villages of Skara Brae (from 3100 BC) in Orkney, Jarlshof (from 1500 BC) in Shetland, and the characteristic stone towers (*brochs*), probably built by chieftains, that can be seen in a number of places.

The crofters' blackhouses of the Highlands and Islands were probably little changed from Celtic times through to the 19th century, but only a few remain. Originally they were circular, but at some point they came to be long, low rectangular buildings. They had thick dry-stone walls, and thatched roofs, sometimes augmented with skins and canvas, tied down with ropes and nets. There were no chimneys; smoke from a central peat fire simply leaked through the thatch. The kitchen and communal area was in the centre; the family slept to one side, the animals to the other.

Anglo-Norman

The Normans were great builders, and their Romanesque style – with its characteristic round arches – can still be seen in David I's church at Dunfermline (1128) and the church at Leuchars (12th century).

Military architecture was also influenced by the Normans in castles like Caerlaverock (1290) and, later, at Stirling (1496). Most feudal lords, however, built more modest tower, or peel, houses, like Threave and Smailholm (14th century). These had a single small entrance, massively thick stone walls and a single room at each of about five levels.

As the Gothic style developed in England and Europe, it was brought to Scotland and adapted by the religious orders. The characteristic pointed arches and stone vaulting can be seen in Glasgow Cathedral (13th century) and the ruins of great border abbeys like Jedburgh (12th century).

Post-Reformation

After the Reformation most churches were modified to suit the new religion, which frowned on ceremony and ornament. In some areas, tower houses and castles became less relevant because of the increasing effectiveness of artillery. The gentry therefore had the luxury of expanding their houses and at the same time making them more decorative. Features like turrets, conical roofs, garrets and gables became popular in buildings like Castle Fraser (1636) and Thirlestane Castle.

Georgian

The greatest exponents of the austere, symmetrical Georgian style in Scotland were the Adam family, in particular Robert Adam. Amongst other buildings, he designed Hopetoun, Mellerstain and Culzean Castle in the mid-18th century.

Victorian Baronial

As the Scottish identity was reaffirmed by writers like Burns and Scott, architects turned to the towers and turrets of the past for inspiration. Fanciful buildings like Balmoral, Scone Palace and Abbotsford were created, and the fashion is also exhibited in many civic buildings.

20th Century

Scotland's most famous 20th-century architect and designer is Charles Rennie Mackintosh of Glasgow, one of the most influential exponents of Art Nouveau. The best known example of his work is Glasgow School of Art, which still looks modern almost 90 years after it was built.

In general, the quality of modern building has not been high, although there are notable exceptions like the impressive gallery housing the Burrell Collection in Glasgow. On the whole, however, the larger towns and cities have suffered badly under the onslaught of the motor car and the unsympathetic impact of large-scale, shoddy council housing. The vernacular architecture of the countryside has not so much been modernised as wiped out.

CULTURE
Bagpipes

One of the oldest musical instruments still used today is the bagpipe. Although no piece of film footage on Scotland is complete without the drone of the pipes, their origin probably lies outside the country. The Romans used bagpipes in their armies, and modern versions can be heard as far away from the Highland glens as India and Russia.

The Highland bagpipe is the type most commonly played in Scotland. It comprises a leather bag inflated by the blowpipe and held under the arm; the piper controls the flow of air through the pipes by squeezing the bag. Three of the pipes, appropriately known as the drones, play all the time without being touched by the piper. The fourth pipe, the chanter, is the one on which tunes can be played.

Queen Victoria did much to repopularise the bagpipe, with her patronage of all things Scottish. When staying at Balmoral she liked to be wakened by a piper playing outside her window.

Ceilidh
The Gaelic word 'ceilidh' means 'visit' since a ceilidh was originally a social gathering in the house after the day's work was over. A local bard (poet) presided over the telling of folk stories and legends, and there was also music and song. These days, a ceilidh (pronounced 'kaylee') means an evening of entertainment including music, song and dance.

Clans
A clan is a group of people who claim descent from a common ancestor. In the Highlands and Islands, where the Scottish clan system evolved between the 11th and 16th centuries, many unrelated families would have joined clans to be under the protection of the clan chief. Although they may share the same name, not all clan members are actually related by blood.

Clan members united in raiding parties into the more prosperous Lowlands or into neighbouring glens to steal other clans' cattle. After the Jacobite rebellions the suppression of Highland culture brought the forced breakdown of the clan system but the spirit of clan loyalty remains strong, especially among the 25 million Scots living outside the country. Each clan still has its own chief, like the Queen merely a figurehead, and its own tartan (see under Tartans later in this section).

Crofting
In the Highlands and Islands, a few acres of land supporting some sheep or cows, or a small market garden, are known as a croft.

Crofting has always been a precarious way of life. In the 19th century crofters were regularly forced off the land by landlords demanding extortionately high rents. In the 20th century, unrealistic demands upon the land by agricultural economists almost killed off the crofting tradition.

Today, however, there is increased interest in crofting, and some communities now support more people than they have done since the mid-19th century.

Highland Games
Highland Games take place throughout the summer, and not just in the Highlands. Assorted sporting events with piping and dancing competitions attract locals and tourists alike.

The original games were organised by clan chiefs and kings who would recruit the strongest competitors for their armies and as bodyguards. Even now the Queen never fails to attend the Braemar Gathering, the best known, and most crowded, of all Highland Games in September.

Some events are peculiarly Scottish, particularly those that involve the Heavies in bouts of strength testing. The apparatus used can be pretty primitive – tossing the caber involves heaving a tree trunk into the air. Other popular events in which the Heavies take part are throwing the hammer and putting the stone.

(For other sports, see Spectactor Sports in Regional Facts for the Visitor at the front of the book.)

Tartans
The oldest surviving piece of tartan, a patterned woollen material now made into everything from kilts to key-fobs, dates back to the Roman period. Tartan is now popular the world over, and beyond – astronaut Al Bean took his MacBean tartan to the moon and back.

Particular *setts* (patterns) didn't come to be associated with certain clans until the 17th century, although today every clan, indeed every football team, has a distinctive tartan.

The wearing of Highland dress was banned after the Jacobite rebellions but revived under royal patronage in the following century. For their visit in 1822, George IV and his English courtiers donned kilts. Sir Walter Scott, novelist, poet and dedicated patriot, did much to rekindle interest in Scottish ways. By then, however, many of the old setts had been forgotten – some tartans are actually Victorian creations.

RELIGION

It's probably true to say that religion has played a more influential part in the history of Scotland than it has in any other part of Britain. This remains true today; while barely 2% of people in England and Wales regularly attend church services, the figure for Scotland is 10%.

Christianity reached Scotland in the 4th century although in some places vestiges of older worship survived. As recently as the 18th century, Hebridean fishing communities conducted superstitious rites to ensure a good catch. With the Reformation the Scottish Church rejected the pope's authority. Later a schism developed amongst Scottish Protestants, the Presbyterians favouring a simplified church hierarchy without bishops, unlike the Episcopalians.

Two-thirds of Scots belong to the Presbyterian Church (or Kirk) of Scotland. There are also two Presbyterian minorities: the Free Church of Scotland (known as the Wee Frees) and the United Free Presbyterians, found mainly in the Highlands and Islands. Their strict adherence to the scriptures means that ferries are not always allowed to operate on Sunday.

The Episcopal (Anglican) Church of Scotland, once widespread North of the Tay, now has only about 35,000 members, many of them from the landed gentry.

There are about 800,000 Catholics, mainly in the Glasgow area and many of them descended from 19th-century Irish immigrants. Some islands, like Barra, and areas of Aberdeenshire and Lochaber, were converted to Roman Catholicism as a result of secret missionary activity after the Reformation. Although not remotely on the scale of Northern Ireland, sectarian tensions can be felt in Glasgow, especially when the Protestant Rangers and Catholic Celtic football teams play.

LANGUAGE

An English dialect with French and Scandinavian influences known as Lallans has been spoken in the Lowlands for centuries. Until the 12th or 13th centuries, however, Gaelic was spoken in all of Scotland. Now only about 66,000 people speak it, mainly in the Hebridean islands and north-west Scotland. Efforts are being made to halt its decline; typical of the renewed interest is the Mod, a cultural event held in different locations each October.

Aye, but the Scottish accent can make English almost impenetrable to the *Sassenach* (an English person or a lowland Scot) and other foreigners, and there are numerous Gaelic and Scots words that linger in everyday speech. Ye ken? See the glossary at the back of this book for some terms you might encounter.

Facts for the Visitor

PLANNING

When to Go

The best time to visit Scotland is between May and September – April and October are acceptable weather risks, although many things are closed in October. The Highlands are pretty much off limits during winter, but Edinburgh and Glasgow are still worth visiting. Edinburgh becomes impossibly crowded during the festival in August; book a long way ahead if you plan to visit during this time.

The further north you go in summer, the longer the days become; the midsummer sun sets at 10.30 pm in the Shetland Islands, but even in Edinburgh there are seemingly endless evenings.

See also the Climate section in the Facts about Scotland chapter.

What Kind of Trip?

Fifty per cent of visitors restrict themselves to an Edinburgh city break, but the rest of Scotland is too beautiful to be given such a cursory look. However, getting around the remoter parts of the country is time-consuming because of the twisty, single-track roads; you need time to do it justice, especially if you want to take in some of the islands too.

With limited time your best bet might be to take one of the hop-on, hop-off bus transport only tours operated by Go Blue Banana or Haggis Backpackers (see Getting Around). The same companies also offer more formal three and six day tours of the main highlights. These are specifically designed for backpackers, aged roughly 18 to 30.

Maps

If you're driving up from England you'll probably already have a road atlas showing Scotland in adequate detail for touring. Alternatively, TICs have free maps at a scale of at least one inch to 10 miles.

You'll need an Ordnance Survey map for greater detail. Their Landranger maps at 1¼ inches to one mile are adequate for walkers, but if you want even more detail they also publish Pathfinder/Tourist maps at 2½ inches to one mile. TICs usually stock a selection.

For general touring the clear *Leisure Map – Touring Scotland* (£3.25) shows most tourist attractions. Munro-baggers should look out for the Bartholomew map of the Munros (£3.99).

What to Bring

Don't forget to bring some form of waterproof clothing or an umbrella. If you're going to be walking, it's worth treating your boots with a waterproofing agent as some trails cross boggy ground. In the summer you'll need insect repellent to ward off the midges (see Dangers & Annoyances later in this chapter).

See also the Regional Facts for the Visitor chapter at the beginning of this book.

TOURIST OFFICES

Outside Britain, contact the British Tourist Authority for information.

Local Tourist Offices

The Scottish Tourist Board (STB) (☎ 0131-332 2433) has its headquarters at 23 Ravelston Terrace, Edinburgh EH4 3EU.

In London, contact the STB (☎ 0171-930 8661) at 19 Cockspur St, London SW1 5BL, just off Trafalgar Square, for routes, detailed information and all kinds of reservations.

Most towns have TICs that are open weekdays from 9 am to 5 pm, often opening at weekends in summer. In small places, particularly in the Highlands, TICs only open from Easter to September.

VISAS & DOCUMENTS

No visas are required if you arrive from England or Northern Ireland. If you arrive from the Republic of Ireland or any other country, normal British customs and immigration regulations apply (see the Regional Facts for the Visitor chapter at the beginning of this book). There are several diplomatic missions in Edinburgh.

MONEY
Costs
Because backpacker accommodation is more readily available in Scotland than England, you'll be able to keep sleeping costs right down. Edinburgh is more expensive than most other mainland towns but prices also rise quite steeply in remote parts of the Highlands and in the islands where supplies depend on ferries. Petrol can cost 10p a litre more on the islands than in the central lowlands.

Currency
The pound sterling is valid on both sides of the border. However, the Clydesdale Bank, Royal Bank of Scotland and Bank of Scotland still issue their own banknotes, including pound notes. You may have difficulty trying to change one of these pounds in a bureau de change in Greece, but they don't usually present a problem in Britain. If they do, any bank will exchange them.

Cards
If you have a MasterCard/Access card, you can use cash machines belonging to the Royal Bank of Scotland and Clydesdale Bank; if you have a Visa card you can use Bank of Scotland, Royal Bank of Scotland, Clydesdale Bank and TSB; if you have an American Express card you can use the Bank of Scotland.

If you have a UK bank account with one of the banks south of the border, then you can use a National Westminster or Midland cash card at Clydesdale, and a Lloyds or Barclays cash card at Royal Bank of Scotland or Bank of Scotland.

BOOKS
Scotland's literary heritage is so rich that most parts of the country have a piece of writing that perfectly captures its spirit.

Guidebooks
There are numerous local guidebooks, the most useful mentioned in the text. See also the Books & Maps section in the Regional Facts for the Visitor chapter at the beginning of this book.

Travel
One of the greatest Scottish travelogues is *The Journal of a Tour to the Hebrides with Samuel Johnson*, by James Boswell. This famous lexicographer and his Scottish biographer visited Skye, Coll and Mull in 1773, and met Flora MacDonald (who had helped Bonnie Prince Charlie escape after the battle of Culloden).

More recently *Native Stranger*, by Alistair Scott (1995), recounts the efforts of a Scot who knew 'more about the Sandinistas' to get to grips with the realities of modern Scotland by travelling the length and breadth of the land.

History & Politics
Michael Lynch's *Scotland – A New History* provides a good historical background and is reasonably up to date. Tom Steel's *Scotland's Story* is readable and well illustrated but stops in the early 1980s. *A Concise History of Scotland*, by Fitzroy Maclean, is also recommended.

If you want to find out more about the Highland Clearances, the massacre in Glen Coe or the battle of Culloden, John Prebble has written passionate accounts of all these subjects. To flesh out some of the great figures of Scottish history, there are many well-written biographies, including Antonia Fraser's *Mary Queen of Scots* and Fitzroy Maclean's *Bonnie Prince Charlie*.

General
Sir Walter Scott's prodigious output did much to romanticise Scotland and its historical figures. *Rob Roy* portrays the cattle rustler/blackmailer rather rosily; the descriptions of the Trossachs, in which the MacGregor family operated, are more accurate.

Several Robert Louis Stevenson novels

have Scottish settings; *Kidnapped*, set on the island of Mull, Edinburgh and Rannoch Moor, captures the country most vividly.

Sir Compton Mackenzie's *Whisky Galore* is required reading for long Hebridean ferry rides; it's the witty tale of what happens when a cargo of whisky runs aground on one of the islands during WWII, something that really happened. Derek Cooper's more serious *Hebridean Connection* is also recommended.

Gavin Maxwell wrote several books about his life amongst otters and other wildlife in the Highlands; *Ring of Bright Water* is probably best known.

If you're visiting Orkney, you should try to read at least one of George Mackay Brown's novels. *Greenvoe* is a wonderfully poetic description of an Orkney community. His short story collection *A Calendar of Love* is delightful.

The Silver Darlings, Neil Gunn's story of the north-east's great fishing communities in the days before EU quotas, is worth seeking out. In *A Scot's Quair*, Lewis Grassic Gibbon evocatively recaptures early 20th-century village life in Aberdeenshire.

Muriel Spark's shrewd portrait of 1930s Edinburgh, *The Prime of Miss Jean Brodie*, was made into an excellent film. In sharp contrast, Irvine Welsh's *Trainspotting* takes the reader on a guided tour of the modern city's underworld of drugs, drink and despair.

The grim realities of contemporary Glasgow are vividly conjured up in James Kelman's short story collection, *Not Not While the Giro*. Kelman won the 1994 Booker Prize with *How Late It Was, How Late*, but the language it was written in provoked controversy. Alasdair Gray's acclaimed *Lanark* is also set in a run-down city based on modern Glasgow. Duncan McLean's *Bucket of Tongues* is an equally disturbing short story collection set in assorted depressed urban locations.

Collections of ballads and poems by the national bard Robert Burns are widely available. Scotland's finest modern poet is Hugh MacDiarmid. Perhaps the worst is William MacGonagall, who is celebrated for the sheer awfulness of his rhymes. His *Poetic Gems* offers a taster.

ONLINE SERVICES

For services covering Britain as a whole, see Facts for The Visitor at the front of this book. Edinburgh Fringe Festival-goers can access their own web page on http://www.presence.co.uk/fringe – edifringe.

NEWSPAPERS & MAGAZINES

The Scots have been publishing newspapers since the middle of the 17th century but most papers sold elsewhere in Britain are also available north of the border. Scotland's home-grown dailies include the right-wing *Scotsman* and the *Glasgow Herald*, and the tabloid *Daily Record*. The *Sunday Post* is the country's best-selling Sunday paper, with a circulation of over 2½ million – over half the population.

If you're in Glasgow or Edinburgh, look out for *The List*, a fortnightly listings magazine similar to London's *Time Out*.

RADIO & TV

Radio and TV stations are linked to the national network, although there are considerable variations to provide an appropriately regional slant.

USEFUL ORGANISATIONS
Scottish Youth Hostel Association

The SYHA has its headquarters (☎ 01786-451181) at 7 Glebe Crescent, Stirling FK8 2JA. It markets an Explore Scotland ticket – including a seven-day Citylink bus pass, six overnight accommodation vouchers, a bus timetable, a Scotpass Discount Card, free YHA membership and an SYHA handbook, and a Historic Scotland Pass – for £130, a very worthwhile saving, especially if you're not a student. It also offers a Scottish Wayfarer ticket, a similar package but including travel by rail and ferry – eight days for £170, 15 days for £270.

Historic Scotland

Historic Scotland (HS) (☎ 0131-668 8800),

✝✝

Scotland on Film

When *Braveheart*, the Mel Gibson spin on the William Wallace saga, won an Oscar in 1996 the Scottish Tourist Board was up there cheering with the luvvies, anticipating a boom in tourists lured not so much by the violence meted out to Wallace but by the glorious scenery in the background.

Time was when the film most closely associated with Scotland was probably *Local Hero*, Bill Forsyth's gentle story of an oil magnate turned conservationist for love of the scenery. But 1996 was certainly the year of the Scottish film, with *Loch Ness*, a romantic comedy focussing on the monster myth, following fast on the success of *Trainspotting*, the grim film rendition of Irvine Welsh's novel set in Edinburgh. All this, when memories of *Rob Roy*, the 1995 rendition of the outlaws' tale, starring Liam Neeson and Jessica Lange with wonky Scottish accents, were only just fading.

What the STB wasn't shouting about, however, was the fact that most of *Braveheart* was actually filmed in Ireland which has been assiduously wooing Hollywood film-makers with tax breaks. ■

✝✝

Longmore House, Salisbury Place, Edinburgh EH9 1SH, manages more than 330 historic sites, including top attractions like Edinburgh and Stirling castles. A year's membership costs £17/11 for an adult/child, giving free entry to HS sites and half-price entry to English Heritage properties in England, and Cadw properties in Wales. It also offers short-term 'Explorer' membership – seven/14 days for £12/17.

There are standard HS opening times. In summer (1 April to 30 September) properties open Monday to Saturday from 9.30 am to 6.30 pm, and on Sunday from 2 pm to 6.30 pm. In winter (1 October to 31 March) they close two hours earlier. Last entry is 30 minutes before closing time.

In this book, the initials HS are used to indicate a Historic Scotland property – and, unless indicated otherwise, standard opening times will apply.

National Trust for Scotland

The National Trust for Scotland (NTS) (☎ 0131-226 5922), 5 Charlotte Square, Edinburgh EH2 4DU, is a separate organisation from the National Trust (England, Wales & Northern Ireland), although there are reciprocal membership agreements. The NTS has over 100 properties and 100,000 acres of countryside in its care.

A year's membership of the NTS costing £24 (£10 if you're aged under 24) offers free access to all NTS & NT properties. Short-term membership (touring ticket) costs

£12/22 for one/two weeks. YHA members and student-card holders get half-price entry to NTS properties.

In this book, the letters NTS are used to indicate a National Trust for Scotland property.

DANGERS & ANNOYANCES

Edinburgh and Glasgow have all the usual big-city problems, so normal caution is advised.

Highland hikers should be properly equipped and cautious: the weather can become vicious at any time of the year. But the most infuriatingly painful problem facing visitors to the west coast and Highlands is midges. These tiny blood-sucking flies are related to mosquitoes. From late May to mid-September, and especially from mid-June to mid-August, they can be prolific – it's at least partly thanks to them that much of Scotland remains a wilderness. They're at their worst in the evening or in cloudy or shady conditions.

There are several possible defences. Cover up, particularly in the evening; wear light-coloured clothing (midges are attracted to dark colours); and, most importantly, buy a reliable insect repellent containing DEET or DMP.

BUSINESS HOURS

Minimum banking hours are weekdays from 9.30 am to 3.30 pm; a few places close between 12.30 and 1.30 pm, but the tendency is to longer hours. Post offices and shops are open from 9 am to 5.30 pm on weekdays; post offices close at 1 pm on Saturday and shops in small towns sometimes have an early-closing day mid-week.

PUBLIC HOLIDAYS

Although bank holidays are general public holidays in England, in Scotland, they only apply to banks and some other commercial offices. Christmas and New Year's Day are usually general holidays, and Scottish towns normally have a spring and autumn holiday. Dates vary not only from year to year but also from town to town.

In 1997, Scottish banks will be closed on 1 and 2 January, 28 March, 5 and 26 May, 4 August and 25 to 26 December.

ACTIVITIES

See the Activities chapter at the beginning of this book for details.

ACCOMMODATION
Hostels

The SYHA (see under Useful Organisations) is a separate organisation from the YHA. Its hostels are generally cheaper and often better than those south of the border. The SYHA produces its own handbook (£1.50), which gives details on around 80 hostels, including transport links. In big cities, costs are £10.45/9 for seniors/juniors; the rest range from £4.10/3.40 to £7.80/6.40.

There's also a growing number of independent hostels/bunkhouses, most with prices around £8. Look out for *Independent Hostel Guide – Budget Accommodation* (20p) which lists 50 hostels in Scotland and is available from some TICs. Alternatively send a stamped, addressed envelope to Independent Backpackers Hostels of Scotland (☎ 01478-640254), Croft Bunkhouse, 7 Portnalong, Isle of Skye IV47 8SL.

In university towns, cheap accommodation is usually available in student hostels during college vacations. Local TICs have details.

Camping

You can camp free on all public land (unless it's specifically protected). Commercial camping grounds are geared to vans and vary widely in quality. A tent site will cost around £6. If you plan to use a tent regularly, invest in *Scotland: Camping & Caravan Parks* (£3.99), available from most TICs. Camping and caravanning parks are graded by the STB from one to five ticks, reflecting the level and quality of facilities.

B&Bs, Guesthouses & Hotels

B&Bs and guesthouses tend to be cheaper than their English counterparts; budget travellers are unlikely to have to pay more than £15 per person.

At the other end of the scale, however, there are some wonderfully luxurious places to stay, including country-house hotels in superb settings, and castles complete with crenellated battlements, grand staircases and the obligatory rows of stags' heads. You can pay anything from around £50 to well over £100 per person to stay in places like these.

The TICs have local booking services (usually £1) and a Book-A-Bed-Ahead scheme (£2.75). A refundable deposit is also required for most bookings. The service is worth using in July and August, but isn't necessary otherwise, unless you plan to arrive in a town after business hours when the local TIC will be closed. If you arrive late, it may still be worth going to the TIC, since some leave a list in the window showing which B&Bs had rooms free when they closed.

Short-Term Rental

There's plenty of self-catering accommodation but, in the summer at least, the minimum stay is usually one week. Details are listed in the accommodation guides available from TICs. Alternatively, buy a copy of the STB's *Scotland: Self-Catering Accommodation* (£5.50).

FOOD

Scotland's chefs have an enviable range of fresh ingredients at their disposal – meat,

✝✝

Haggis – Scotland's National Dish
A popular rhyme, penned by an English poet, goes:

> For the land of Burns
> The only snag is
> The haggis

Scotland's national dish is frequently ridiculed by the foreigner, on account of its recipe. The ingredients of a haggis are unlikely to get your mouth watering, but once you've got over any delicate sensibilities you may have towards tucking in to chopped lungs, heart and liver mixed with oatmeal and boiled in a sheep's stomach, with the accompanying glass of whisky it can all taste surprisingly good.

Haggis should be served with tatties and neeps (mashed potatoes and turnips, with a generous dollop of butter and a good sprinkling of black pepper).

Although the dish is eaten at any time of the year, it's central to the celebrations on 25 January in honour of Scotland's national poet, Robert Burns. Scots unite all round the world on Burns Night to revel in their Scottishness. A piper announces the arrival of the haggis and Burns' poem *Address to a Haggis* (otherwise known as the Selkirk Grace) is recited to this 'Great chieftan o' the puddin-race', before the bulging stomach is lanced with a dagger known as a *dirk* to reveal the steaming offal within.

Vegetarians (and quite a few carnivores, no doubt) will be relieved to know that veggie haggis is now available in some restaurants in Scotland. ■

✝✝

seafood and vegetables – yet it's only recently that restaurant standards have begun to rise. Unfortunately, the country still has a long way to go before it shakes off a culinary reputation as dismal as England's.

The fact that the Scots now boast Europe's highest rate of heart disease is fair warning. This is partly due to their high consumption of alcohol and cigarettes but also the result of eating a less healthy diet (high on fried foods, refined sugar and white bread) than previous generations.

The quality of cooking at hotel restaurants and B&Bs that provide evening meals is variable. In small villages the alternatives will usually be bleak, although village bakeries have a good range of pies, cakes and snacks. In towns there are Indian and Chinese alternatives, as well as branches of international fast food chains and the classier Pierre Victoire and Littlejohn's.

Lunch is served between 12.30 and 2 pm, and dinner from 7 pm until around 9 pm. As an alternative to dinner there's high tea (from about 4.30 to 6.30 pm), when a main dish is served along with tea and cakes.

Some of the best places to eat are members of the Taste of Scotland scheme. The STB's annual *Taste of Scotland Guide* (£4.95) is worth buying to track down these restaurants and hotels.

A surprising number of restaurants cater for vegetarians; look for *The Vegetarian Guide to the Scottish Highlands & Islands* (£2.85), which lists B&Bs, hotels and restaurants.

Scottish Breakfast
A Scottish breakfast begins with porridge, often a meal in itself. This can be followed by kippers (smoked herrings) or a fry-up similar to an English breakfast (bacon, eggs etc) but also including such exotica as black pudding (a type of sausage made from dried blood). As well as toast, there may be oatcakes (oatmeal biscuits) to spread your marmalade upon. In the Aberdeen area there may also be butteries – delicious butter-rich bread rolls.

Snacks
As well as ordinary scones (similar to American biscuits), Scottish bakeries usually offer milk scones, potato scones and girdle scones. Bannocks are a cross between scones and pancakes. Savoury pies include the *bridie* (a pie filled with meat, potatoes and sometimes other vegetables) and the Scotch pie (minced

meat in a plain round pastry casing – best eaten hot).

Dundee cake, a rich fruit cake topped with almonds, is highly recommended. Black bun is another type of fruit cake, eaten over Hogmanay (New Year's Eve).

Soups

Scotch broth, made with barley, lentils and mutton stock, is highly nutritious and very good. Cock-a-leekie is a substantial soup made from a cock, or chicken, and leeks.

You may not be drawn to *powsowdie* (sheep's-head broth) but it's actually very tasty. Rather more popular is *cullen skink*, a fish soup containing smoked haddock.

Meat & Game

Steak eaters will want to get their teeth into a thick fillet of world-famous Aberdeen Angus beef. Venison, from the red deer, is leaner and appears on many menus. Both are often served with creamy whisky sauce.

Gamebirds like pheasant and the more expensive grouse, traditionally roasted and served with game chips and fried bread-crumbs, are also available. They're definitely worth trying, but watch your teeth on the shot, which is not always removed before cooking.

Then, of course, there's haggis, Scotland's much-maligned national dish...

Fish & Seafood

Scottish salmon is well known but there's a big difference between farmed salmon and the leaner, but more expensive, wild version. Both are available either smoked (served with brown bread and butter) or poached. Smoked trout is cheaper, and also good.

As an alternative to kippers (see Scottish Breakfast earlier in this section) you may be offered Arbroath smokies (lightly smoked fresh haddock), traditionally eaten cold.

Herrings in oatmeal are good if you don't mind the bones. *Krappin heit* is cod's head stuffed with fish livers and oatmeal.

Prawns, crab, lobster, oysters, mussels and scallops are all available in coastal towns and around the lochs, although much is exported.

Cheeses

The once declining Scottish cheese industry is now growing again. Cheddar is its main output but there are a number of specialty cheese-makers whose products are worth sampling. Many are based on the islands. Brodick Blue is a ewes' milk blue cheese made on Arran. Lanark Blue is rather like Roquefort. There are several varieties of cream cheese (Caboc, St Finan, Howgate) which are usually rolled in oatmeal.

Scottish oatcakes make the perfect accompaniment for cheese.

Puddings

Traditional Scottish puddings are irresistibly creamy, calorie-enriched concoctions. *Cranachan* is made with toasted oatmeal, raspberries, or some other fresh fruit, and whisky, all mixed into thick cream. *Atholl brose* is similar but without the fruit – rather like English syllabub.

Clootie dumpling is delicious, a rich steamed pudding filled with currants and raisins.

DRINKS
Nonalcoholic Drinks

On quantity drunk, tea probably qualifies as Scotland's national drink, but coffee is widely available.

Definitely an acquired taste is the virulent orange-coloured fizzy drink, Irn-Bru. 'Made in Scotland from Girders', goes the advertising slogan, but those girders were 100% sugar plus some pretty weird flavouring.

Alcoholic Drinks

Whisky Whisky (always spelt without an 'e' if it's Scottish) is Scotland's best-known product and biggest export. The spirit was first distilled in Scotland in the 15th century; over 2000 brands are now produced.

There are two kinds of whisky: single malt, made from malted barley, and blended whisky, which is distilled from unmalted grain (maize) and blended with selected malts. Single malts are rarer (there are only about 100 brands) and more expensive than blended whiskies. Although there are

The Malt Whisky Trail

Roughly 45 Scottish whisky distilleries are open to the public and you should certainly try to visit one while you're in Scotland.

In some, showing tourists around has become a slick marketing operation, complete with promotional videos, free drams, gift shops that rival the distillery in size and an entry charge of around £2. Eight Speyside distillers – Glenfiddich, Cardhu, Glenfarclas, Glen Grant, The Glenlivet, Strathisla, Tamdhu and Tamnavulin – promote themselves in the Malt Whisky Trail, a pleasant drive around the Spey Valley, although visiting all eight might be overkill. You can also create your own malt whisky trail – on the island of Islay, seven distilleries can be visited.

The process of making malt whisky begins with malting. Barley is soaked in water and allowed to germinate so that enzymes are produced to convert the starch in the barley to fermentable sugar. The barley is then dried in a malt kiln over the peat fire that gives malt whisky its distinctive taste. Since most distilleries now buy in their malted barley, tourists rarely see this part of the process.

The malt is milled, mixed with hot water and left in a large tank, the mash tun. The starch is converted into sugar and this liquid, or 'wort', is drawn off into another large tank, the washback, for fermentation.

This weak alcoholic solution, or wash, is distilled twice in large copper-pot stills. The process is controlled by the stillman, who collects only the middle portion of the second distillation to mature in oak barrels. The spirit remains in the barrels for at least three years, often much longer. During bottling, water is added to reduce its strength.

Some recommended distillery tours include: Glenfiddich, The Glenlivet and Strathisla on Speyside; any of the Islay distilleries; and Highland Park on Orkney, one of the few distilleries where you can still see the barley malting process. ■

distilleries all over the country, there are concentrations around the Spey Valley and on the isle of Islay.

As well as blends and single malts, there are also several whisky-based liqueurs like Drambuie. If you must mix your whisky with anything other than water try a whisky-mac (whisky with ginger wine). After a long walk in the rain there's nothing better to warm you up.

When out drinking, Scots may order a dram (measure) of whisky as a chaser to a pint of beer. Only tourists say 'Scotch' – what else would you be served in Scotland?

Beer Most popular is what the Scots call 'heavy', a dark beer similar to English bitter. Most Scottish brews are graded in shillings so you can tell their strength, the usual range being 60 to 80 shillings (written 80/-). The greater the number of shillings, the stronger the beer.

As in England, the market is dominated by the big brewers; here they're Youngers, McEwans and Tennants. Look out for beer from local breweries, some of it very strong – the aptly-named Skullsplitter from Orkney is a good example. Caledonian 80/-, Maclays 80/- and Bellhaven 80/- are others worth trying.

Long before hops arrived in Scotland, beer was brewed from heather. Reintroduced recently, heather ale is surprisingly good and now available in some pubs.

ENTERTAINMENT

As in England and Wales, the local pub is the place to go and you'll get a warm reception at most watering holes. The Scots take their drinking seriously, spending an average 9% of their weekly income on booze and cigarettes, the highest consumption in Britain. Ask at your B&B or hotel for recommended places. Some pubs in the more depressed areas of the big towns have a reputation for late-night brawls and should be avoided by non-pugnacious visitors.

Many tourist centres stage a ceilidh or Highland show featuring Scottish song and dance, most nights during the summer. Some local restaurants also combine a floor show with dinner.

If you fancy trying an eightsome reel, ceilidhs with dancing you can join in usually take place on Friday or Saturday. Ask at the local TIC for details. It's not as difficult as it looks and there's often a 'caller' to lead everyone through their paces.

THINGS TO BUY

Making things to sell to tourists is big business in Scotland, and almost every visitor attraction seems to have been redesigned to funnel you out through the gift shop. Amongst the tourist kitsch, some high-quality goods offer very good value.

If you're interested in visiting mills, factories and craftshops, pick up a copy of the STB publication *See Scotland at Work*.

Tartan, Tweed & Other Textiles

Scottish textiles, particularly tartans, are popular and tartan travelling rugs or scarves are often worth buying. There are said to be over 2000 designs, some of them officially recognised as clan tartans. Many shops have a list and will be able to tell you if your family belongs to a clan, but these days if you can pay for the cloth you can wear the tartan. There are also some universal tartans, like the Flower of Scotland, that are not connected with a clan.

For about £200 to £400, you can have a kilt made up in your clan tartan, but this shouldn't be worn without a *sporran* (purse), which can cost anything from £25 for a plain version up to £1000 for an ornate silver-dress sporran. Full kilts are traditionally worn only by men, while women wear kilted or tartan skirts.

There are mill shops in many parts of the country, but the best-known textile manufacturing areas are the Borders and Central regions, particularly around Stirling and Perth. Scotland is also renowned for a rough woollen cloth known as tweed – Harris Tweed is, of course, world-famous. There are various places on this Hebridean island where you can watch your cloth being woven.

Knitwear

Scottish knitwear can be great value and is sold in shops throughout Scotland. Shetland is the place most closely associated with high-quality wool, and at knitwear factory shops you can buy genuine Shetland sweaters for as little as £14. The most sought-after sweaters bear the intricate Fair Isle pattern – the genuine article from this remote island will cost at least £40.

Jewellery

Queen Victoria is said to have started the fashion for Scottish jewellery. Silver brooches set with cairngorms (yellow or wine-coloured gems from the mountains of the same name) are popular. Jewellery decorated with Celtic designs featuring mythical creatures and intricate patterns is particularly attractive, although some pieces are actually made in Cornwall.

Food & Drink

Sweet, butter-rich Scottish shortbread makes a good gift if you can resist breaking into the packet before you get home. The biggest manufacturer, Walkers, bakes such prodigious quantities of the stuff that the Spey Valley town of Aberlour smells of nothing else. Dark, fruity Dundee cake lasts well and is available in a tin, but is heavy to take home by air.

If you've not got far to go, smoked salmon or any of the other smoked products (venison, mussels etc) are worth buying, but some countries don't allow you to import meat and fish.

As for souvenir bottles of Scotch, you're better off buying it duty-free at the airport than in high street shops, unless it's a particularly rare brand. If you go on a distillery tour, you may be given a pound or so discount to buy a bottle there. Miniatures are available and make good presents.

Getting There & Away

AIR

There are direct air services from London and other European cities to Edinburgh, Glasgow, Dundee, Aberdeen, Inverness or Kirkwall, and from North America to Glasgow or Edinburgh. The fare from New York to Glasgow is around US$600 (£390). Travelling from Europe you'll often be best off flying to London and then taking the train or bus north. The cheapest standard flights from London to Glasgow or Edinburgh are around £95. No frills one-way tickets can, however, be as low as £29. See the Getting Around chapter at the start of the book.

Within the UK, British Airways (☎ 0345-222111) has flights from London's Heathrow, Gatwick and Stansted, and from Birmingham, Manchester and Belfast; Air UK (☎ 0345-666777) flies from Stansted; and British Airways Express/Loganair (☎ 0345-222111) flies from Manchester. Easyjet (☎ 01582-445566) flies from London's Luton airport.

Flying time from London to Edinburgh is about one hour, but once you add the time taken to get between the airports and the city centres, and boarding time, the four-hour centre-to-centre rail trip takes only about an hour more in actual travelling time.

LAND

Bus

Long-distance buses (coaches) are usually the cheapest method of getting to Scotland. The main operator is Scottish Citylink (☎ 0990-505050), part of the nationwide National Express group, with numerous regular services from London and other departure points in England (see the Edinburgh chapter, and also the Glasgow section in the Southern Scotland chapter).

Fares on the main routes are now very competitive, with new operators undercutting National Express. From London, single tickets cost from £20.50, and returns from £25.50.

The budget bus company Slow Coach, which operates between youth hostels in England, also ventures into Scotland – but only to Edinburgh. There are similar Scotland-only operators (see under Bus in Scotland's Getting Around chapter).

For more information, see this book's introductory Getting Around chapter.

Train

British Rail InterCity services can take you from London's King's Cross (☎ 0345-484905) to Edinburgh in as little as four hours, or to Glasgow in five hours (see those sections).

The cheapest adult return ticket between London and Edinburgh or Glasgow is the SuperApex, which costs only £34. Numerous restrictions apply to these tickets, which must be purchased 14 days in advance and are particularly difficult to get hold of in summer. Apex tickets (£46 return) must be bought seven days in advance and are more readily available. See the Getting Around chapter at the beginning of this book for more information.

Car & Motorcycle

The main roads are busy and quick. Edinburgh is 373 miles from London, and Glasgow is 392 miles from London. Allow eight hours for the trip. It makes more sense to break the journey en route, perhaps in York or Chester, or in the Lake District.

Hitching

It's easy enough, if not necessarily very wise, to hitch to Scotland along the A68 (to Edinburgh) or the A74 (to Glasgow). The coastal routes are slow.

See also Hitching in the Getting Around chapter at the start of this book.

SEA

Scotland has ferry links to Larne, near Belfast in Northern Ireland, from Cairnryan

(P&O, ☎ 01574-274321) and Stranraer (Stena Line, ☎ 0990-455455), both located south-west of Glasgow. There's also a high-speed catamaran between Stranraer and Belfast. For details of the ferries and the catamaran, see the Getting There & Away chapter at the start of this book.

From early June to late August, P&O also operates one ferry a week between Bergen (Norway), Lerwick (Shetland Islands) and Aberdeen. Bergen to Lerwick, leaving at 2 am on Sunday morning, costs from £55. There's also a twice-weekly Stradfaraskip Landsins ferry between the Faroe Islands and Aberdeen (leaving Aberdeen on Thurs-

day and Sunday), with the cheapest tickets ranging from £60 to £105. To make a fascinating northern sea route, you could link these two ferries with the Smyril Line's Denmark-Norway-Iceland-Faroes service, also summer only. The sailing order is Denmark (Saturday) to the Faroes (Monday), to Norway (Tuesday), to the Faroes (Wednesday), to Iceland (Thursday), to the Faroes (Friday), to Denmark (Saturday) and so on. During the high season, the one-way couchette fare from Norway to the Faroes is £61. P&O (☎ 01224-572615) is the agent for Smyril and Stradfaraskip Landsins and can book this complete route.

Getting Around

PASSES

If you're not a student, it's worth considering the Freedom of Scotland Travelpass – see the passes table in this chapter for details. For more information contact ScotRail (☎ 0345-484950), which administers the scheme. Tickets are available from the Scottish Travel Centre, at London's Victoria and King's Cross railway stations, and from the stations in Glasgow and Edinburgh.

The Scottish Youth Hostels Association (SYHA; ☎ 01786-451181) markets an Explore Scotland ticket that includes a seven-day Citylink bus pass and six nights' SYHA accommodation, a bus timetable, a Scotpass discount card, free SYHA membership and a handbook and a Historic Scotland pass for £130. The Scottish Wayfarer ticket gives a similar package but includes travel by rail and on Caledonian MacBrayne's west-coast ferries. It costs £170/270 for eight/15 days' travel.

AIR

Several carriers, including British Airways Express/Loganair (☎ 0345-222111), British Airways (☎ 0345-222111) and Air UK (☎ 0345-666777), connect the main towns, the Western Isles, Orkney and Shetland.

It might be worth flying to Barra to experience landing on a beach. Otherwise, flying is a pricey way to get round relatively short distances. It's worth checking whether any passes are available.

BUS

Privatisation, takeovers and buyouts have reduced Scotland's internal bus network to one major player, Scottish Citylink (☎ 0990-505050), part of the nationwide National Express group, and numerous smaller regional companies which come and go with astonishing rapidity.

From June to September, Haggis Backpackers (☎ 0131-557 9393), 11 Blackfriars St, Edinburgh, runs a daily service on a circuit between the hostels in Edinburgh, Perth, Pitlochry, Aviemore, Inverness, Loch Ness, Isle of Skye, Fort William, Glencoe, Oban, Inverary, Loch Lomond and Glasgow (although there's no obligation to stay in the hostels). You can hop on and off the minibus wherever and whenever you like, booking up to 24 hours in advance. There is no fixed time for completing the circuit but you can only cover each section of the route once. At other times of year there are still five or six departures a week. See the passes table in this chapter for more information.

Go Blue Banana (☎ 0131-220 6868), Suite 8, 28 North Bridge, Edinburgh, also runs a jump-on, jump-off service on the same circuit; see the passes table for more details.

Both companies also offer excellent-value three-day Highlands tours for £65. They start in Edinburgh but are based in Inverness.

The National Express Tourist Trail Pass (see the Getting Around chapter at the start of this book) can be used on all Scottish Citylink services. Citylink also honours all European under-26 cards, including the Young Scot card, which costs £7 and provides discounts all over Scotland and Europe.

If they don't have one of these cards, full-time students and people aged under 26 have to buy the ironically titled Smart Card (more bureaucratic insanity, and you can't even blame the government) which is equivalent to the National Express Discount Coach Card (see the Getting Around chapter at the start of the book). On presentation of proof of age, or student status (an NUS or ISIC card), a passport photo and a £7 fee, you get the Smart Card to add to your collection. It entitles you to a 30% discount, so chances are you'll be ahead after buying your first ticket.

There are lots of Royal Mail postbuses, which can be particularly useful for walkers. For information and timetables, contact Royal Mail Communications (☎ 0131-228 7407), 102 West Port, Edinburgh EH3 9HS.

Citylink buses don't carry bicycles, but most local buses will.

TRAIN

Scotland has some stunning train routes but they're limited and expensive, so you'll probably have to use other modes of transport too. The West Highland line through Fort William to Mallaig, and the routes from Stirling to Inverness, Inverness to Thurso,

SCOTTISH TRANSPORT PASSES

Pass Name	Cost (Prices for adults/ discount card holders)	Bus/train/ferry services offered
Freedom of Scotland Travelpass	£99 for 8 days consecutive travel £110 for 8 days out of 15 £139 for 15 days consecutive travel	33% discount on postbuses and most important regional bus lines. All trains. Most Caledonian MacBrayne to West Coast Islands ferries; 33% discount on P&O Orkney to Scrabsterferry; 20% discount on P&O Aberdeen to Shetland, Aberdeen to Orkney Orkney to Shetland; 20% discount and Stena Line services to Northern Ireland.
National Express Tourist Trail Pass	As for Britain – see Getting Around chapter	All National Express and Scottish Citylink buses.
National Express Discount Coach Card (full time students; under 26; over 60.)	£7	30 % off adult fares on all Scottish Citylink buses.
National Express Britexpress Card	£12	As for Britain.
Explore Scotland	£130	Seven day Citylink bus pass, with six nights' SYHA accommodation and a Historic Scotland pass, plus other benefits.
Scottish Wayfarer	£170 for 8 days £270 for 15 days	Similar to Explore Scotland, but also includes rail travel and CalMac west-coast ferries.
ScotRail Rover	£60 for 4 out of 8 consecutive days; £88 for 8 consecutive days; £115 for 12 out of 15 consecutive days.	All ScotRail network.
Young Person's or Senior's Railcard	£16 per annum	34% off rail throughout Britain.
Go Blue Banana Haggis Backpackers	Both £65	Jump on, jump off circuit route.
Flexipass	As for Britain	

and Inverness to Kyle of Lochalsh are some of the best in the world. You can make ScotRail bookings by credit card on ☎ 0345-550033.

The BritRail pass, which includes travel in Scotland, must be bought outside Britain. ScotRail's Freedom of Scotland Travelpass (see under Passes earlier in this chapter) and Regional Rover tickets can be bought in Britain, including from most railway stations in Scotland.

Regional Rover tickets cover the North Highlands (£39 for four out of eight consecutive days); West Highlands (£39 for four out of eight consecutive days); and the central area (Festival Cities, £24 for three out of seven consecutive days).

The ScotRail Rover covers all of the ScotRail network and costs £60 for four out of eight consecutive days, £88 for eight consecutive days, or £115 for 12 out of 15 consecutive days. Holders of either the Young Person's or Senior Citizen's Railcard get a 30% discount.

Reservations for bicycles (£3) are compulsory on many services.

CAR & MOTORCYCLE

Scotland's roads are generally good and far less busy than those in England, so driving is more enjoyable. The fast A9, which runs up the centre, is the busiest road. In the Highlands and Islands the main hazards are suicidal sheep...and the distracting beauty of the landscape!

In some areas, roads are only single track, with passing places indicated by a pole. It's illegal to park in these places. In the same areas petrol stations are few and far between and sometimes closed on Sunday. Petrol prices also tend to rise as you get further from main population centres.

HITCHING

Hitching is reasonably good in Scotland, although the north-west is difficult because there's so little traffic; you could easily be stuck for a day or two, and public transport won't necessarily rescue you. Again in the north and west, the Sunday Sabbath is still widely observed, and traffic is even sparser than usual.

See also Hitching in the Getting Around chapter at the start of this book.

BOAT

Caledonian MacBrayne (CalMac) (☎ 01475-650100) is the most important ferry operator on the west coast, with services from Ullapool to the Outer Hebrides, and from Mallaig to Skye and on to the Outer Hebrides. Its main west-coast port, however, is Oban, with ferries to virtually all the west-coast islands except Harris and Lewis.

As an example, a single passenger fare from Oban to Lochboisdale, South Uist (Hebrides), is £15.95. However, it pays to plan your complete trip in advance since CalMac's Island Hopscotch tickets are usually the best deal, with ferry combinations over 23 set routes. CalMac also has Rover tickets, offering unlimited travel for eight and 15 days (£36/51).

P&O (☎ 01224-589111) has ferries from Aberdeen and Scrabster to Orkney, and from Aberdeen to Shetland. From June through August, the cheapest one-way tickets to Stromness (Orkney) cost £14 from Scrabster and £38 from Aberdeen. Between Aberdeen and Shetland, fares start at £52. There's a 10% student discount.

Taking a car on the ferries is expensive. You can save some money by hiring once you get onto the islands.

Edinburgh

Locator & Map Index

Central Edinburgh p710
Royal Mile p704

Greater Edinburgh p724

EDINBURGH

- *pop 425,000* • ☎ *0131*

Sometimes called the 'Athens of the North', Edinburgh has an incomparable location, studded with volcanic hills on the edge of an enormous loch. The superb architecture ranges from extraordinary 16th-century tenements to monumental Georgian and Victorian masterpieces – all dominated by a castle on a precipitous crag in the city's heart. Sixteen thousand buildings are listed as architecturally or historically important, in a city which is now a World Heritage Site.

The geology and architecture combine to create an extraordinary symphony in stone. The Old Town, with its crowded tenements and bloody past, stands in contrast to the orderly grid of the New Town with its disciplined Georgian buildings. There are vistas from every street – sudden views of the Firth of Forth, the castle, the Pentland Hills, Calton Hill with its memorials, and rugged Arthur's Seat.

Since it became a royal capital in the 11th century, all the great dramas of Scottish history have played at least one act in Edinburgh. Even after the union of 1707 it remained the centre for government administration (now the Scottish Office), the separate Scottish legal system and the Presbyterian Church of Scotland.

In some ways, however, it's the least

Scottish of Scotland's cities – partly because of the impact of tourism, partly because of its closeness to England, partly because of its multicultural, sophisticated population.

Edinburgh has a reputation for being civilised and reserved, especially in comparison with intense, gregarious Glasgow. On the other hand, there's a vibrant pub scene, and the dynamism unleashed every August creates the world's greatest arts festival.

No one should forget the behind-the-scenes reality of life in the surrounding council estates. The flipside to the gloss is a thriving drugs scene and distressing AIDS problem, aspects of Edinburgh life portrayed in sordid detail in *Trainspotting*, the highly successful 1996 film based on Irvine Welsh's book of the same name.

HISTORY

Edinburgh is dominated by Castle Rock, a volcanic crag with three vertical sides. This natural defensive position was probably what first attracted settlers; the earliest signs of habitation date back to 850 BC.

The Northumbrian Angles captured Lothian in the 6th century, rebuilding a fortress, known as Dun Eadain, on Castle Rock. This served as the Scots' southern outpost until 1018 when Malcolm I established a frontier at the River Tweed. Nonetheless, the English have sacked the city no less than seven times.

Edinburgh really began to grow in the 11th century when markets developed at the foot of the fortress, and from 1124 when David I held court at the castle and founded the abbey at Holyrood.

The first effective town wall was constructed around 1450 and circled the Old Town and the area around Grassmarket. This restricted, defensible zone became a medieval Manhattan, forcing its densely packed inhabitants to build tenements that soared to 12 storeys.

A golden era that saw the foundation of the College of Surgeons and the introduction of printing ended with the death of James IV at the Battle of Flodden in 1513. England's Henry VIII attempted to force a marriage between Mary (James V's daughter) and his son, but the Scots sent the infant Mary to France to marry the dauphin. The city was sacked by the English, and the Scots turned to the French for support.

The Scots were increasingly sympathetic to the ideas of the Reformation, and when John Knox returned from exile in 1555 he found fertile ground for his Calvinist message.

When James VI/I succeeded to the Scottish and English crowns, he moved the court to London, and for the most part, the Stuarts ignored Edinburgh. When Charles I tried to introduce episcopacy (the rule of the bishops) in 1633 he provoked the National Covenant and more religious turmoil which finally ended in triumph for Presbyterianism.

The Act of Union in 1707 further reduced Edinburgh's importance, but cultural and intellectual life flourished. In the second half of the 18th century a new city was created across the ravine to the north. The population

was expanding, defence was no longer vital and the thinkers of the Scottish Enlightenment planned to distance themselves from Edinburgh's Jacobite past.

The population exploded in the 19th century – Edinburgh quadrupled in size to 400,000, not much less than it is today – and the old city's tenements were taken over by refugees from the Irish famines. A new ring of crescents and circuses was built to the south of the New Town, and grey Victorian terraces sprung up.

In the 20th century the slum dwellers were moved into new housing estates which now foster massive social problems.

ORIENTATION

The most important landmark is Arthur's Seat, the 800-foot-high rocky peak to the south-west of the city. The old and new towns are separated by Princes St Gardens, with the castle dominating both of them.

The main shopping street, Princes St, runs along the north side of the gardens. Buildings are restricted to its north side, which has the usual High St shops. At the east end, Calton Hill is crowned by several monuments. The Royal Mile (Lawnmarket, High St and Canongate) is the parallel equivalent in the Old Town.

The TIC is between Waverley railway station and Princes St, above the Waverley Market Shopping Centre. The bus station in the New Town is a bit trickier to find, just off the north-east corner of St Andrew Square to the north of Princes St.

INFORMATION

Edinburgh and Glasgow's answer to *Time Out* is *The List* (£1.80), a fortnightly guide to films, theatre, cabaret, music – the works.

Tourist Information Centres

The busy main TIC (☎ 557 1700) is at Waverley Market, Princes St, EH2 2QP. There's also a branch at Edinburgh airport (☎ 333 2167; credit card bookings possible). They have information about all of Scotland, and sell an *Essential Guide to Edinburgh* for 25p. Their accommodation service charges a

The Flodden Wall

In 1513 the Scots were defeated by the English at the Battle of Flodden, and King James IV and 10,000 of his followers were killed. The citizens of Edinburgh were thrown into such despair by this episode that they decided to separate their city from the outside world altogether. To that end they built the Flodden Wall across High St between what are now the World's End and Royal Archer pubs. Part of the wall can still be seen in the basement of the World's End. ■

steep £3 fee. What's more they will only book one night ahead...hopeless during busy periods when forward planning is essential. Instead get their free accommodation brochure and ring round yourself.

The TIC is open November to March, Monday to Saturday from 9 am to 6 pm; April and October, Monday to Saturday from 9 am to 6 pm, and Sunday from 11 am to 6 pm; May, June and September, Monday to Saturday from 9 am to 7 pm, and Sunday from 11 am to 7 pm; July and August, Monday to Saturday from 9 am to 8 pm, and Sunday from 11 am to 8 pm.

Three branches of Thomas Cook will also make hotel reservations for you. The Edinburgh airport office (☎ 333 5119) charges a flat £3; the office in Waverley Steps (☎ 557 0905) charges a flat £4; and the office on Platform One of Waverley Station (☎ 557 0034) charges 10% of the booking fee up to a maximum £4...but with no charge for bookings under £20.

At 11 Blackfriars St you can get information about hostels and tours, and book tickets for National Express, Stena Line, P&O and many other services at the Backpackers Centre (☎ 557 9393) beside Haggis Backpackers.

Consulates & High Commissions

Scotland's capital houses several consulates and high commissions:

Australia
    Hobart House, 25 Bernard St, EH6 6PW(☎ 555 4263)

Belgium
    19 Ainslie Place, EH3 6AJ (☎ 226 6881)
Denmark
    4 Royal Terrace, EH7 5AB (☎ 556 4263)
France
    11 Randolph Crescent, EH3 7TT (☎ 225 7954)
Germany
    16 Eglinton Crescent, EH12 5DG (☎ 337 2323)
Italy
    32 Melville St, EH3 7HA (☎ 226 3631)
Japan
    2 Melville Crescent, EH3, 7HW (☎ 225 4777)
Netherlands
    53 George St, EH2 2HT (☎ 220 3226)
Spain
    63 North Castle St, EH2 3LJ (☎ 220 1843)
Sweden
    6 Johns Place, Leith, EH6 7EL (☎ 554 6631)
Switzerland
    66 Hanover St, EH2 1EL (☎ 226 5660)
USA
    3 Regent Terrace, EH7 5BW (☎ 556 8315)

Money

The tourist office bureau de change is open long hours, including 10 am to 6 pm on Sunday; it charges 2.75% commission with a minimum of £2.50. American Express (☎ 225 7881) has an office at 139 Princes St, open business hours Monday to Friday, from 9 am to noon Saturday. Thomas Cook, 79 Princes St (☎ 220 4039) is open all day Saturday.

Post

The main post office is inconveniently tucked away inside the sprawling St James' Shopping Centre, off Leith St. It's open Monday from 9 am to 5.30 pm, Tuesday to Friday from 8.30 am to 5.30 pm and Saturday from 8.30 am to 6 pm. Items addressed to Poste Restante will automatically be sent here.

Bookshops

The HMSO bookshop (☎ 228 4181) at 71 Lothian Rd has an excellent selection of books and maps on Scotland.

Left Luggage

Depending on the security situation, left-luggage facilities may be available at Waverley railway station (from £2 all day), and at St Andrew bus station (from £1 all day).

Camping & Outdoor Gear
Tiso's (☎ 225 9486), 121 Rose St, is a well-stocked outdoor equipment shop.

ROYAL MILE
Following a ridge that runs from Edinburgh Castle to Holyrood Palace, the Royal Mile is one of the world's most fascinating streets. From the west end you can look past craggy Arthur's Seat and over the waters of the Firth of Forth, with tantalising glimpses of the Old and New Towns through the *closes* (entrances) and *wynds* (alleyways) on either side. Although there are tourists and shops stuffed with tacky Scottish souvenirs aplenty, the street still feels a real part of a thriving city. It's lined with extraordinary buildings, including multistoreyed *lands* dating from the 15th century.

To see all the numerous sites would take several days, but even with limited time, it's worth ducking through a *pend* (arched gateway) or close to explore the narrow wynds and courts beyond.

Edinburgh Castle
Edinburgh Castle dominates the city. It sits astride the core of an extinct volcano, its three sides scoured almost vertical by glacial action. Archaeological research has proved there was a settlement here as early as 850 BC, although the first historical references date to the 6th century when the Northumbrian king Edwin rebuilt a fortress here as a defence against the Picts.

Although it was a favoured royal residence from the 11th to the 16th centuries, Edinburgh only became Scotland's capital at the end of the Middle Ages. The oldest surviving part of the castle is St Margaret's Chapel, a simple stone edifice, probably built by David I in memory of his mother sometime around 1130.

Although it looks impregnable, the castle often changed hands between the Scots and English, and the last time it saw action was just 250 years ago. During the Wars of Independence (1174 to 1356), the English captured it several times. In 1313 it was actually demolished by the Scots as part of Robert the Bruce's scorched earth policies and wasn't rebuilt (by David II) until 1371.

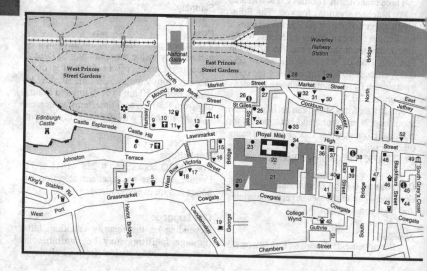

Little of this work survives, however, because the castle was strengthened and renovated in the 16th, 17th and 18th centuries. From the 16th century the royal family

built more comfortable domestic accommodation at places like Holyrood, and the castle developed as a seat of government and military power. However, in 1566 Mary Queen

PLACES TO STAY
35 Royal Mile Backpackers
42 Central Youth Hostel
46 High St Hostel
48 Scandic Crown Hotel

PLACES TO EAT
2 Mamma's Pizzas & Pierre Victoire
4 Gennaro
11 Singapore Sling
16 Pierre Victoire
17 Beppe Vittorio
19 Elephant House
24 Patisserie Florentin
30 Viva Mexico
31 Doric Wine Bar & Bistro
37 Elephant's Sufficiency
44 Black Bo's
52 Dubh Prais
58 Clarinda's Tea Room

PUBS
1 Fiddler's Arms
3 White Hart Inn
5 Last Drop

12 Jolly Judge
18 Bow Bar
32 Malt Shovel Inn
39 Ceilidh House
40 City Café
41 Green Tree
43 Bannermans
51 World's End
54 The Royal Archer

OTHER
6 Scotch Whisky Heritage Centre
7 Tolbooth Kirk
8 Ramsay Gardens
9 Camera Obscura
10 Church of Scotland General Assembly Hall
13 Gladstone's Land
14 Lady Stair's House
15 Brodie's Close
20 National Library
21 Parliament House
22 St Giles Cathedral
23 Heart of Midlothian

25 Traveline
26 Bank of Scotland
27 Edinburgh Festival Box Office
28 LRT Travel Shop
29 Fruitmarket Gallery
33 Edinburgh City Chambers
34 Mercat Cross
36 Fringe Festival Box Office
38 Tron Kirk
45 Haggis Backpackers
47 The Vaults
49 Museum of Childhood
50 Scottish Experience
53 John Knox's House
55 The People's Story
56 Canongate Kirk
57 Huntly House
59 Queen Mary's Bath House
60 Abbey Lairds
61 Parking for Radical Rd Walk

EDINBURGH

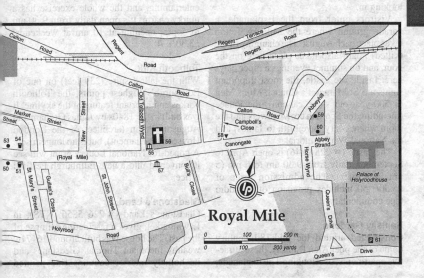

Royal Mile

of Scots underlined its continuing symbolic importance when she chose to give birth to her son in the castle. In 1573 much of it was destroyed when loyalists attempted to hold it for Mary; the oldest substantial work – including the Half Moon Battery and Portcullis Gate – survives from the subsequent rebuilding. The castle was then taken in turn by the Covenanters (in 1640), Cromwell (in 1650) and King William and Queen Mary (the last true siege, in 1689). In 1715 and 1745 the Stuarts tried unsuccessfully to recapture it. In the gaps between sieges more defences were added, and by the mid-18th-century the castle looked much as it does today.

Partly thanks to Sir Walter Scott, in the 19th century the castle began to be recover its importance as a Scottish symbol, and efforts were made to improve its appearance and to restore important buildings, including St Margaret's Chapel, then in use as a powder magazine. In the 1920s the massive Scottish National War Memorial was added to the complex.

The castle crawls with tourists, and although the views are great, you may decide it's more impressive from the outside looking in.

Visitors enter from the Esplanade, a parade ground where the Military Tattoo takes place each August. The changing of the (kilted) guard also takes place here on the hour, and on summer evenings a piper plays here. Inside the castle, the most important sights are St Margaret's Chapel, Mons Meg (a 500-year-old siege cannon), the Palace (including the Scottish crown jewels and the room where Mary gave birth to James) and the National War Memorial.

The castle (☎ 225 9846) is open April to September, daily from 9.30 am to 6 pm (5 pm in winter). The admission price of £5.50/1.50 includes provision of an audio tape commentary.

Ramsay Gardens

Constructed around the mid-18th-century home of the poet Alan Ramsay, these attractive apartments, overlooking The Esplanade, were designed in the 1890s by an early town planner called Patrick Geddes in an attempt to revitalise the Old Town. They are now very expensive, very wonderful private apartments.

Scotch Whisky Heritage Centre

If you'd like to know how whisky is manufactured the Scotch Whisky Heritage Centre (☎ 220 0441) in Castle Hill offers a tour with several audiovisual presentations followed by a ride in a barrel past a tableau explaining the history of the 'water of life'. If you're pushed for time you can take the ride only (15 minutes) for £3/1. The shop sells hundreds of different brands of whisky. The centre is open daily from 10 am to 5.30 pm; the full experience costs £4.20/2.

Camera Obscura

Just beyond Ramsay Lane, the Camera Obscura (☎ 226 3709) offers great views over the city. The 'camera' itself is a curious device (originally dating from the 1850s, although improved in 1945) a bit like a periscope, which uses lenses and mirrors to throw a 'live' image onto a large interior bowl. The accompanying 'guided tour' is entertaining, and the whole exercise has a quirky charm. It's open daily from 9.30 am to 5 pm, opening at 10 am at weekends; £3.30/1.70.

Tolbooth Kirk

With the tallest spire (239 feet) on one of Edinburgh's highest points, the Tolbooth Kirk is an important feature of the skyline. It was built in the 1840s by James Graham and Augustus Pugin (architect of the London Houses of Parliament), but is no longer used. A hoped-for National Lottery grant will see it converted into a new Edinburgh Festival office.

Gladstone's Land

Gladstone's Land (☎ 226 5856; NTS), in Lawnmarket, gives a fascinating glimpse of the past. The house was built around 1617 by wealthy merchant Thomas Gledstanes and its homely interior contains fine painted walls and beams and some splendid furniture. It's open April to late October, Monday to Saturday from 10 am to 5 pm, Sunday from 2 to 5 pm; £2.60/1.70.

Lady Stair's House

Lady Stair's House was built in 1622 but has been altered to house the Writers' Museum (☎ 529 4901) of manuscripts and memorabilia belonging to Robert Burns, Sir Walter Scott and Robert Louis Stevenson. The static displays will only entertain enthusiasts of these writers but it's open Monday to Saturday from 10 am to 5 pm and, during the Edinburgh Festival, on Sunday from 2 to 5 pm; free.

Brodie's Close

Brodie's Close is named after the father of the notorious William Brodie, a deacon and respected citizen by day, a burglar by night. Brodie was the inspiration for Robert Louis Stevenson's *Dr Jekyll & Mr Hyde* and, some would say, a dramatic reflection of Edinburgh's schizophrenic undercurrents. He met his end on the gallows in 1788.

Parliament Square

Lawnmarket ends at the crossroads of Bank St and George IV Bridge; at the south-east corner, brass strips set in the road mark the site of the scaffold where public hangings took place until 1864. From here the Mile continues as High St.

Parliament Square, largely filled by St Giles, the High Kirk of Edinburgh, is on the south side. This was the heart of Edinburgh until the 18th century, and a cobblestone **Heart of Midlothian** is marked on the ground. Passers-by traditionally spit on it for luck. This was the site of the entrance to the Tolbooth, originally built to collect tolls, but subsequently a meeting place for parliament, the town council and the General Assembly of the Reformed Kirk, then law courts and, finally, a prison and place of execution.

The 19th-century **Mercat Cross** takes the place of the original 1365 cross and marks the spot where merchants and traders met to transact business and Royal Proclamations were read.

The square's southern side is flanked by **Parliament House**, the meeting place of the Scottish Parliament from 1639; its neoclassical façade was added in the early 19th century. After the Act of Union in 1707 the building became the centre for the Scottish legal system – the Court of Session and High Court – which retains its independence to this day. The most interesting feature is **Parliament Hall**, where the parliament actually met, which is now used by lawyers and their clients as a meeting place.

St Giles' Cathedral

There has been a church on this site since the 9th century. A Norman-style church was built in 1126, but this was burnt by the English in 1385; the only substantial remains are the central piers that support the tower. The present church was then built in stages, with the crown spire completed in 1495.

Near the entrance is a life-size statue of John Knox who was minister from 1559 to 1572; from here he preached his uncompromising Calvinist message and launched the Scottish Reformation. The new austerity this ushered in led to changes in the building's interior – decorations, stained glass, altars and the relics of St Giles were thrown into the Nor Loch.

The High Kirk of Edinburgh has been at the heart of Edinburgh's struggle against episcopacy (the rule of the church by bishops). In 1637 when Charles I attempted to re-establish episcopacy and made the kirk a cathedral, he provoked a possibly apocryphal outburst by Jenny Geddes which, according to popular belief, led to the signing of the National Covenant at Greyfriars the following year. Jenny hurled a stool at a preacher who was using the English prayer book (a symbol of episcopacy); a tablet marks the spot and a copy of the National Covenant is displayed on the wall.

One of the most interesting corners of the kirk is the Thistle Chapel built for the Knights of the Most Ancient and Most Noble Order of the Thistle between 1909 and 1911.

EDINBURGH

The carved Gothic-style stalls have canopies topped with the helms and arms of the 16 knights.

Entry to the Kirk is free but a donation of £1 is requested.

Edinburgh City Chambers
The City Chambers were originally built by John Adam (brother of Robert) in 1761 to replace the Mercat Cross and serve as a Royal Exchange, but the merchants continued to prefer the street, and the building has been used by the town council since 1811.

Tron Kirk
At the south-western corner of the intersection with South Bridge, Tron Kirk owes its name to a salt *tron* or public weighbridge that stood on the site. It was built in 1637 on top of Marlin's Wynd which has now been excavated to reveal a cobbled street with cellars and shops on either side. The church acts as a visitor centre for the Old Town. It's open from April to May and October, Thursday to Monday from 10 am to 5 pm, and June to September daily from 10 am to 7 pm.

John Knox's House
Perhaps the most extraordinary building on the Royal Mile, John Knox's House (☎ 556 9579) dates from around 1490. The outside staircase, overhanging upper floors and crow-stepped gables are all typical of a 15th-century town house. John Knox is thought to have occupied the 2nd floor from 1561 to 1572, and the labyrinthine interior now has an interesting display on his life including a recording of his interview with Mary Queen of Scots, whose mother was a target of his diatribe *First Blast of the Trumpet Against the Monstrous Regiment of Women*. It's open Monday to Saturday from 10 am to 4.30 pm; £1.75/75p.

Museum of Childhood
The Museum of Childhood attempts to cover the serious issues related to childhood – health, education, upbringing and so on – but more enjoyable is the enormous collection of toys, dolls, games and books which fascinate children and, for adults, brings childhood memories back. The museum (☎ 529 4142) is open Monday to Saturday from 10 am to 5 pm, and, during the Edinburgh Festival only, on Sunday from 2 to 5 pm; free.

Netherbow Port
The High St ends at the intersection with St Mary's and Jeffrey Sts. The city's eastern gate, Netherbow Port, no longer exists, although it's commemorated by brass strips set in the road. The next stretch of the Mile, Canongate, takes its name from the canons (priests) of Holyrood Abbey. From the 16th century, it was home to aristocrats attracted to Holyrood Palace. Originally governed by the canons, it remained an independent burgh until 1856.

The People's Story
Canongate Tolbooth, with its picturesque turrets and projecting clock, is an interesting example of 16th-century architecture. Built in 1591, it served successively as a collection point for tolls (taxes), a council house, a courtroom and a jail. It now houses a fascinating museum (☎ 331 5545) telling the story of the life, work and pastimes of ordinary Edinburgh folk from the 18th century to the present day. It's open Monday to Saturday from 10 am to 5 pm, and, during the Edinburgh Festival only, on Sunday from 2 to 5 pm; free.

Huntly House
Built in 1570, Huntly House is a good example of the luxurious accommodation the aristocrats built themselves along Canongate; the projecting upper floors of plastered timber are typical of the time. It now houses a local history museum (☎ 529 4143) with some interesting displays, including a copy of the National Covenant of 1638 which was signed in protest against Charles I's attempt to re-establish episcopacy and the English prayer book. It's open Monday to Saturday from 10 am to 5 pm, and, during the Edinburgh Festival only, on Sunday from 2 to 5 pm; free.

Canongate Kirk

Attractive Canongate Kirk was built in 1688. In 1745 Prince Charles Stuart (the Young Pretender) used it to hold prisoners taken at the Battle of Prestonpans. A number of famous people are buried in the churchyard, including the economist Adam Smith, author of *The Wealth of Nations*, who lived nearby in Panmure Close.

Abbey Lairds

On the left-hand side of Abbey Strand, flanking the entrance to Holyrood Palace, the Abbey Lairds provided sanctuary for aristocratic debtors from 1128 to 1880. They could avoid prison as long as they remained within the palace and Holyrood Park, although they were allowed out on Sunday.

Queen Mary's Bath House

Legend has it that Queen Mary used to bathe in white wine and goat's milk in this small, 16th-century turreted lodge – but only twice a year! It's more likely to have been a summer house or dovecot.

Palace of Holyroodhouse & Holyrood Abbey

The Palace of Holyroodhouse developed from a guesthouse attached to medieval Holyrood Abbey. It was a royal residence at various times from the 16th century, and is still the Queen's official residence in Scotland, so access is very restricted. If you brave the queue, a few apartments can be visited on brief guided tours. The grounds are private, although you can visit the abbey ruins.

The abbey was founded by David I in 1128, and was probably named after a fragment of the Cross (*rood* is an old word for cross) said to have belonged to his mother St Margaret. As it lay outside the city walls it was particularly vulnerable to English attacks, but the church was always rebuilt and survived as Canongate parish church until it collapsed in 1768. Most of the surviving ruins date from the 12th and 13th centuries, although a doorway in the far south-eastern corner survives from the original Norman church.

King James IV extended the abbey guesthouse in 1501 to create more comfortable living quarters than were possible in bleak and windy Edinburgh Castle; the oldest surviving section of the building, the north-west tower, was built in 1529 as a royal apartment. Mary Queen of Scots spent 16 eventful years living in the tower. During this time she married Darnley (in the abbey) and Bothwell (in what is now the Picture Gallery), and this is where she debated with John Knox and witnessed the murder of her secretary Rizzio.

Although Holyrood was never again a permanent royal residence after Mary's son James VI/I departed for London, it was further extended during Charles II's reign.

Tours are perfunctory and crowded, although there's a certain fascination to following in Mary's footsteps and seeing the room where Rizzio was cut down. Standard opening hours are from April to October, Monday to Saturday from 9.30 am to 5.15 pm, and Sunday from 9.30 am to 4.30 pm; November to March, Monday to Saturday from 9.30 am to 3.45 pm. Entry is £5/2.50.

The complex is sometimes closed for state functions or when the Queen is in residence, usually in mid-May, and from mid-June to around 7 July; phone ☎ 556 1096 to check.

Holyrood Park & Arthur's Seat

Edinburgh is blessed in having a real wilderness on its doorstep. Holyrood Park covers 650 acres of varied landscape, including mountains, moorland, lochs and fields. The highest point is the 822-foot-high extinct volcano, Arthur's Seat.

The park can be circumnavigated by car or bike, and there are several excellent walks. Opposite the palace's southern gate, the Radical Rd runs along the base of the Salisbury Crags to Jeanie Dean's Cottage. A fairly easy half-hour walk leads from Dunsapie Loch to the summit of Arthur's Seat, with magnificent views. Duddingstone Loch, the one natural lake, is now a bird sanctuary.

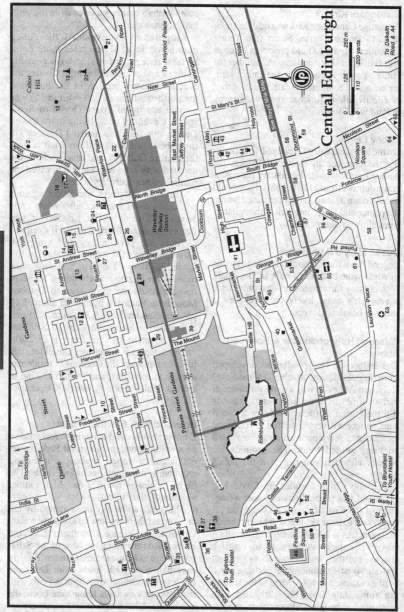

Central Edinburgh

EDINBURGH

PLACES TO STAY		PUBS		22	Venue
24	Princes St Hostel	15	Café Royal Bar	23	Register House
25	Old Waverley Hotel	35	Whigham's Wine	26	TIC
36	Caledonian Hotel		Cellars	28	Sir Walter Scott of
40	Thistle Inn Hotel	44	Bannermans		Scotland Monument
42	High St Hostel	53	Bertie's	29	Royal Scottish
49	Sheraton Grand Hotel	54	Greyfriars Bobby		Academy
				30	Thomas Cook
PLACES TO EAT		OTHER		31	Tiso's
1	Giuliano's	2	Playhouse Theatre	34	American Express
5	Gringo Bill's	3	St Andrew Bus Station	37	St John's Church
6	Henderson's	4	Scottish National	38	St Cuthbert's Church &
7	Chez Jules		Portrait Gallery &		Watchtower
10	Café Rogue		Museum of	39	National Gallery
11	Bar Napoli		Antiquities	41	St Giles' Cathedral
27	Tiles Bar-Bistro	8	Georgian House	43	Museum of Childhood
32	Next Café	9	West Register House	45	Byzantium Market
33	Bewley's	12	St Andrew's & St	46	Usher Hall
51	Dario's Restaurant		George's Church	47	Royal Lyceum Theatre
52	Loon Fung	13	Melville Monument	48	HMSO Bookshop
56	Negociant's	14	Dundas House	50	Filmhouse
59	Khushi's	16	St James's Shopping	55	Greyfriars Kirk
60	Kebab Mahal		Centre	57	Royal Museum of
64	Seeds	17	Main Post Office		Scotland
65	Pierre Lapin & Pear	18	City Observatory	58	Edinburgh University
	Tree Pub	19	National Monument	61	Campus Travel
		20	Nelson Monument	62	Central Cycle Hire
		21	Royal High School	63	Royal Infirmary

SOUTH OF THE ROYAL MILE

The area to the south of the Royal Mile includes some of the oldest, most crowded and atmospheric parts of the Old City at the foot of Castle Rock and the Mile. Around the university and the beautiful Meadows it opens up to run into sturdy Victorian suburbs like Bruntsfield, Marchmont and Grange.

One of the city's main traffic arteries (carrying traffic to/from the A68 and A7), with many shops, restaurants and guesthouses, runs down the eastern side – beginning as North Bridge and becoming successively South Bridge, Nicolson St, Clerk St, Newington Rd, Minto St, Mayfield Gardens and Craigmillar Park.

Grassmarket

The Grassmarket is Edinburgh's nightlife centre, with numerous restaurants and pubs, including the White Hart Inn which was patronised by Robert Burns. An open area hedged by tall tenements and dominated by the looming castle, it can be approached from George IV Bridge, via Victoria St, an unusual two-tiered street clinging to the ridge below the Royal Mile, with some excellent shops.

The site of a market from at least 1477 to the start of this century, Grassmarket has always offered a focal point for the Old City. This was the main place for executions and over 100 hanged Covenanters are commemorated with a cross at the east end. The notorious murderers Burke and Hare operated from a now vanished close off the west end. In around 1827 they enticed at least 18 victims here, suffocated them and sold the bodies to Edinburgh's medical schools.

Leading off the south-east corner, Candlemaker Row climbs back up to George IV Bridge and Greyfriars Kirk.

Greyfriars Kirk & Kirkyard

At the bottom of a stone canyon made up of tenements, churches, volcanic cliffs and the castle, Greyfriars Kirkyard is one of Edinburgh's most evocative spots – a peaceful oasis dotted with memorials and surrounded by Edinburgh's dramatic skyline.

EDINBURGH

The Kirk was built in 1612 on the site of a Franciscan friary. It was here that the National Covenant was signed in 1638, rejecting Charles I's attempts to reintroduce episcopacy and a new English prayer book, and affirming the independence of the Scottish church. Many of those who signed were later executed in the Grassmarket and, in 1679, 1200 Covenanters were held prisoner in terrible conditions in an enclosure in the yard.

Tour groups, however, come to pay homage to a tiny statue of Greyfriars Bobby, a Skye terrier who maintained a vigil over the grave of his master from 1858 to 1872, a story immortalised as a novel by Eleanor Atkinson in 1912 and later turned into a film. Inside the Kirk you can buy *Greyfriars Bobby – The Real Story at Last* (£3.50), Forbes Macgregor's debunking of some of the myths.

Cowgate
Cowgate, which runs off the eastern end of Grassmarket parallel to the Royal Mile, is less a canyon than a bleak tunnel, thanks to the bridges that were built above it. Once a fashionable place to live, it now has a couple of Fringe Festival venues and several excellent pubs.

Edinburgh University
The University of Edinburgh is one of Britain's oldest and biggest: founded in 1583, it now has around 17,000 undergraduates. The students make a major contribution to the lively atmosphere of Grassmarket, Cowgate, and the nearby restaurants and pubs. The university sprawls for some distance, but the centre is the Old College, at the junction of South Bridge and Chambers St, a Robert Adam masterpiece designed in 1789.

Royal Museum of Scotland
The Royal Museum of Scotland houses a comprehensive collection covering geology and fossils, Egyptology, Chinese, Islamic and European decorative art, and even technology, with one section featuring the world's oldest steam locomotive. It's open Monday to Saturday from 10 am to 5 pm, Sunday from 2 to 5 pm; free.

The new Museum of Scotland being developed beside it should open in 1998. It will house the collection of the old Museum of Antiquities.

CALTON HILL
Calton Hill, at the east end of Princes St, is another distinctive component of Edinburgh's skyline, 330 feet high and scattered with grandiose memorials mostly dating from the first half of the 19th century. This is where you get one of the best views of Edinburgh, taking in the entire panorama – the castle, Holyrood, Arthur's Seat, the Firth of Forth, the New Town and Princes St.

Approaching from Waterloo Place, you pass the imposing **Royal High School**, dating from 1825 and modelled on the Temple of Theseus in Athens. Former pupils include Robert Adam, Alexander Graham Bell and Sir Walter Scott. In the 1970s it was refurbished to be home to the Scottish Assembly. Since the failed referendum it has been in limbo, although Scottish Nationalists still view it as a potential parliament. A small but dedicated band of separatists has been conducting a vigil beside it since the 1992 election.

The largest structure is the **National Monument**, an over-ambitious attempt to replicate the Parthenon, in honour of Scotland's dead in the Napoleonic Wars. Construction began in 1822, but funds ran dry when only 12 columns were complete.

The **City Observatory** now houses the **Edinburgh Experience** (☎ 556 4365), a 20-minute 3-D portrayal of Edinburgh's history. It's open April to October from 10 am to 5 pm (2 to 5 pm Monday to Friday from April to June and from mid-September to October). Admission is £2/1.

Looking a bit like an upturned telescope, the **Nelson Monument** was built after Nelson's death at Trafalgar. It's theoretically open (for great views) April to September, Monday from 1 to 6 pm, Tuesday to Saturday from 10 am to 6 pm; October to March, Monday to Saturday from 10 am to 3 pm; £1.

There are also two historic observatories, and a small circular temple commemorating Dugald Stewart (1753-1828), an obscure professor of philosophy.

NEW TOWN

The 200-year-old New Town lies to the north of the Old Town, separated from it by the Princes St Gardens and occupying a ridge that runs below, but parallel to, the Royal Mile. It's in complete contrast to the chaotic tangle of streets and buildings that evolved in the Old Town, and typifies the values of the Scottish Enlightenment.

Despite being confined behind city walls, the Old Town was still periodically sacked by the English or torn by civil wars and disputes. The overcrowding and non-existent sanitation gave it its nickname, Auld Reekie, so when the Act of Union in 1707 brought the prospect of long-term stability, aristocrats were keen to find healthier, more spacious surroundings. Cowgate was bridged to open up the south, the Nor Loch at the northern foot of Castle Rock was drained and the North Bridge was constructed.

In 1767 23-year-old James Craig won a competition to design a New Town. His plan was brilliant in its simplicity. George St followed the line of the ridge between Charlotte and St Andrew Squares. Building was restricted to one side of Princes St and Queen St only, so the town opened onto the Firth of Forth to the north, and to the castle and Old Town to the south.

The New Town continued to sprout squares, circuses, parks and terraces, and some of its finest neoclassical architecture was designed by Robert Adam. Today, the New Town is the world's most complete and unspoilt example of Georgian town planning and architecture.

Princes St

Princes St was originally envisaged as the back of the New Town, as it was literally and figuratively turning away from its Jacobite past, but the transport links and stunning outlook soon led to its development as Edinburgh's principal thoroughfare.

The main railway station at the east end is now overshadowed by the uninspiring **Waverley Centre**, with the entrance to the main TIC via the street level piazza.

The street's north side is lined with a standard selection of High St shops, and few 18th-century buildings survive. One exception is the beautiful **Register House**, designed by Robert Adam to hold Scotland's official records, opposite North Bridge. About halfway along, the massive Gothic spire of the **Sir Walter Scott Monument**, built by public subscription after his death in 1832, testifies to a popularity largely inspired by his role in rebuilding pride in Scottish identity. You can climb the 281 steps to the top Monday to Saturday from 9 am to 6 pm (3 pm from October to March) for £1.50.

The Princes St Gardens are cut by **The Mound**, a mound of earth dumped during the construction of the New Town which provides a road link between the Old and New Towns. The Royal Scottish Academy and the National Gallery of Scotland are also here (see separate sections following).

St John's Church, at the west end of Princes St, stands above some interesting shops and the *Cornerstone Coffee House*. **St Cuthbert's Church**, round the corner, has a watch tower in the graveyard – a reminder of the Burke and Hare days when graves had to be guarded against robbers.

Royal Scottish Academy

Built in Grecian style in 1826, the Academy (☎ 225 6671) hosts temporary exhibitions throughout the year. It's open Monday to Saturday from 10 am to 5 pm, Sunday from 2 to 5 pm; free (although there may be charges for some exhibitions).

National Gallery of Scotland

The National Gallery is an imposing classical building dating from the 1850s. It houses an important collection of European art dating from the 15th-century Renaissance to

19th-century post-Impressionism. There are paintings by Tintoretto, Titian, Holbein, Rubens, El Greco, Poussin, Rembrandt, Gainsborough, Turner, Constable, Monet, Pissaro, Gauguin and Cezanne, but perhaps the most interesting section shows specifically Scottish art in the basement. Look out, too, for Canova's statue of the Three Graces, owned jointly with London's Victoria & Albert Museum. More than £7 million was raised to purchase this single sculpture. The gallery (☎ 556 8921) is open Monday to Saturday from 10 am to 5 pm, Sunday from 2 to 5 pm; free.

George St & St Andrew Square
George St was originally envisaged as the main thoroughfare of the residential New Town. It's now Scotland's Wall St, home to highly successful Scottish financial institutions which control billions of pounds and came through the 1980s relatively un-scathed. **St Andrew's and St George's Church**, built in 1784, boasts a wonderful oval plaster ceiling.

Dominated by the Melville Monument, St Andrew Square is not particularly architecturally distinguished (partly thanks to the bus station at the north-east corner), but the Royal Bank of Scotland is based in the impressive **Dundas House** which has a spectacular dome.

Charlotte Square & the Georgian House
At the western end of George St, Charlotte Square was designed in 1791 by Robert Adam and is regarded as the jewel of the New Town. The Church of St George is now **West Register House**, an annexe to Register House in Princes St and home to Scottish records and occasional exhibitions.

The north side is one of Robert Adam's masterpieces. Number 7, the **Georgian House** (☎ 225 2160; NTS), has been beautifully restored and refurnished to show how Edinburgh's wealthy elite lived at the start of the 19th century. Videos lasting 35 minutes bring it to life rather well. It's open from April to October, Monday to Saturday from

10 am to 5 pm, Sunday from 2 to 5 pm; £3.60/2.40.

Scottish National Portrait Gallery
The gallery is housed in a large Italian-Gothic building dating from 1882 (at the junction of St Andrew and Queen Sts). The hall is decorated with a frieze showing all the main players in Scottish history and the balcony with frescos of important moments in Scottish history painted by William Hole in 1897.

The National Portrait Gallery (☎ 556 8921) records Scottish history through the portraits of its most important players. The subjects are probably the main source of interest, but some portraits are also fine paintings. It's open Monday to Saturday from 10 am to 5 pm, Sunday from 2 to 5 pm; free. The *Queen Street Café* in the gallery serves delicious home cooking from 10 am to 4.30 pm.

WEST END
The last part to be built, the West End is an extension of the New Town. Huge **St Mary's Episcopal Cathedral**, built in the 1870s in Palmerston Place, was Sir Gilbert Scott's last major work.

Alongside the Water of Leith, **Dean Village** is an odd corner of Edinburgh – once a milling community, it's being taken over by yuppies. A pleasant walk begins on the left bank of the Water of Leith at Belford Bridge. The footpath takes you up onto the Dean Path, then onto Dean Bridge, from where you can look down on the village. You continue on the right bank of the Leith, through Stockbridge, and can then detour to the Botanical Gardens.

National Gallery of Modern Art
Beyond the West End and Dean Village, the Gallery of Modern Art (☎ 556 8921), Belford Rd, is difficult to get to without your own transport, but certainly repays the effort. It's housed in an impressive classical building (an ex-school) and surrounded by a sculpture park. The collection concentrates on 20th-century art, with work by Matisse,

Picasso, Kirchner, Magritte, Miro, Mondrian and Giacometti. It's small enough not to overwhelm and is open Monday to Saturday from 10 am to 5 pm, Sunday from 2 to 5 pm; free.

NORTH OF THE NEW TOWN

The New Town's Georgian architecture extends north to Stockbridge and the Water of Leith, a rewarding area to explore since it's well off the tourist trail. **Stockbridge** is a trendy area with its own distinct identity, some interesting shops (particularly in St Stephen St), and a good choice of pubs and restaurants.

Royal Botanic Gardens

The lovely gardens (☎ 552 7171) in Inverleith Row are worth visiting for the strange new perspective you get on the Edinburgh skyline from the terrace café. They're open November to February, daily from 10 am to 4 pm; March, April, September and October, daily from 10 am to 6 pm; May to August from 10 am to 8 pm; free. Bus Nos 8, 19, 23, 27 and 37 will get you there.

SOUTHERN SUBURBS
Edinburgh Zoo

Parents of young children will be relieved to know there's a zoo (☎ 334 9171) to provide relief from all the museums. It's open daily, April to September, 9 am to 6 pm, October to March 9 am to 4.30 pm (opens Sunday at 9.30 am). Admission costs £5.80/3. Bus Nos 2, 26, 31, 69, 85 and 86 pass by.

BUS TOURS

Open-topped buses leave from Waverley Bridge outside the main railway station and offer hop-on, hop-off tours of the main sights. Guide Friday charges £6.50 and the Edinburgh Classic Tour £5. They're a good way of getting your bearings – although with a bus map and a one-day ridacard you could do the same thing, without a commentary, for £2.

SPECIAL EVENTS

For more than 50 years the **Edinburgh Inter-** **national Festival** has been growing into one of the world's largest and most important arts festivals, with the best performers playing to capacity audiences.

The **Fringe Festival** has grown up in tandem to showcase would-be future stars. It claims to be the largest such event in the world, with over 500 amateur and professional groups presenting every possible kind of avant-garde performance. Just to make sure that every B&B for 40 miles around is full, the **Military Tattoo** is held at the same time.

Those who don't see themselves as culture-vultures might find the prospect of all the performances, performers, hangers-on and tourists daunting, but it's actually a great time to be in Edinburgh. The city is at its best, and the Fringe is not at all elitist. In most cases the performers and front of house people are friendly and relaxed – they're grateful to have an audience – so there's no need to feel intimidated. Just be prepared to take the bad with the good...

The International and Fringe festivals run from mid-August to early September. The last week is a good time to go, because the Tattoo finishes at the end of August, reducing the number of visitors. If you want to attend the International Festival, it's best to book ahead; the programme is published in April and is available from the Edinburgh Festival Office (☎ 225 5756; fax 226 7669), 21 Market St, EH1 1BW. Prices are generally reasonable, and any tickets that remain unsold are sold half-price on the day of performance (1-5 pm) from the Festival Box Office in Market St or from the venue one hour before each performance.

The Fringe is less formal, and many performances have empty seats left at the last moment. It's still worth booking for well-known names, or if the production has good reviews. Programmes are available, from June, from the Fringe Office (☎ 226 5257; fax 220 4205), 180 High St, EH1 1QS.

To book for the Military Tattoo, an extravaganza of regimental posturing and swirling bagpipes, contact the Tattoo Office (☎ 225 1188), 33-34 Market St, EH1 1QS.

EDINBURGH

In recent years **Hogmanay**, the Scottish celebration of the New Year, has grown into another major fixture in Edinburgh's festival calendar. Plans are already afoot for the street party to end all parties to celebrate the year 2000. For details call the Hogmanay Information Line on ☎ 0891-881996.

For all these festivals, booking accommodation months ahead is strongly advised.

PLACES TO STAY

Edinburgh has masses of accommodation, but the city can still fill up quickly over the New Year, at Easter and between mid-May and mid-September, particularly while the festivals are in full swing. Book in advance if possible, or use an accommodation booking service (see the introductory Information section for possibilities).

Hostels & Colleges

There are several independent backpackers' hostels. The long-established, well-equipped *High St Hostel* (☎ 557 3984) at 8 Blackfriars St is a popular choice although some have found it noisy. Beds cost £8.90 per night in a 10-bed dorm, plus £1.20 for breakfast. It's opposite the Haggis Backpackers tour-booking office.

Not far away is *Royal Mile Backpackers* (☎ 557 6120) at 105 Royal Mile which charges £9.50 for beds in dorms of up to 10 beds. It's right beside Custos Café.

Princes St Hostel (☎ 556 6894), 5 West Register St, is also well positioned, just behind Princes St and close to the bus station, although you do have to negotiate 77 exhausting steps to reach it. Dorm beds cost £8.50 or there are a couple of doubles for £22. Breakfast costs from £1 to £2.

The *Belford Youth Hostel* (☎ 225 6209), 6 Douglas Gardens, is in a converted church and although some people have complained of noise, it's well-run and cheerful with good facilities. Dorm beds cost £8.50, and there are a couple of doubles for £27.50.

There are also three good SYHA hostels. *Eglinton Youth Hostel* (☎ 337 1120), 18 Eglinton Crescent, is about one mile west of the city near Haymarket railway station;

beds cost £10.45/9. Walk down Princes St and continue on Shandwick Place which becomes West Maitland St; veer right at the Haymarket along Haymarket Terrace, then turn right into Coates Gardens which runs into Eglinton Crescent. It's closed in December.

Bruntsfield Youth Hostel (☎ 447 2994), 7 Bruntsfield Crescent, is trickier to get to; it has an attractive location overlooking Bruntsfield Links about 2½ miles from Waverley railway station. Catch bus No 11 or 16 from the garden side of Princes St and alight at Forbes Rd just after the gardens on the left. It's closed in January and rates are £7.80/6.40.

The *Central Youth Hostel* (☎ 229 8660), Robertson Lane, Cowgate, has a great position in a college residence with single bedrooms; it's open July to early September and advance bookings are required. Rates are £8.80/7.40.

Women and married couples are welcome at the *Kinnaird Christian Hostel* (☎ 225 3608), 14 Coates Crescent, where beds in a Georgian house cost from £11.

During university holidays the *Pollock Halls of Residence* (☎ 667 0662), 18 Holyrood Park Rd, has modern (often noisy) single rooms from £23.50 per person including breakfast. *Cowgate Tourist Hostel* (☎ 226 2153), 112 Cowgate, has singles and doubles with self-catering facilities from £9.80 per person.

Camping

The *Mortonhall Caravan Park* (☎ 664 1533), Frogston Rd, East Edinburgh, is 15 minutes from the centre. Sites are £7.75; it's open from March to October.

B&Bs & Guesthouses

On a tight budget the best bet will be a private house; get the TIC's free accommodation guide and phone around. Outside Festival time you should get something for around £16, although it will probably be a bus ride away in the suburbs. Places in the centre are not always good value if you have a car, since parking in the New Town is severely restricted.

Guesthouses are generally two or three pounds more expensive, and to get a private bathroom you'll have to pay around £22. The main concentrations are around Pilrig St, Pilrig; Minto St (a southern continuation of North Bridge), Newington; and Leamington Terrace, Bruntsfield.

Averon Guest House (☎ 229 9932), 44 Gilmore Place, is within walking distance of Princes St, and has beds from £15.

There are a couple of places in Eyre Place, north of the New Town near Stockbridge and the Water of Leith, one mile from the centre. *Ardenlee Guest House* (☎ 556 2838), at No 9, has beds from £16 to £26 per person (£2 more for a private bath). *Blairhaven Guest House* (☎ 556 3025), at No 5, does B&B from £15.

Pilrig St, left off Leith Walk (veer left at the east end of Princes St), has lots of guesthouses. *Balmoral Guest House* (☎ 554 1857), at No 32, is within easy reach of the centre, with beds from £17 to £19. The *Barrosa* (☎ 554 3700), at No 21, has similarly priced rooms with bath. At No 94, the attractive two-crown *Balquhidder Guest House* (☎ 554 3377) has rooms with bath from £17 to £24 a head.

There are lots of guesthouses in Newington, which is south of the city centre and university on either side of the continuation of North/South Bridge, with plenty of buses to the centre. This is the main traffic artery from the south and carries traffic from the A7 and A68 (both routes are signposted). The best places are in the streets to either side of the main road.

Salisbury Guest House (☎ 667 1264), 45 Salisbury Rd, just east of Newington and 10 minutes from the centre by bus, is quiet and comfortable. Rooms with private bath cost from £22 to £26 per person.

The welcoming *Avondale Guest House* (☎ 667 6779), 10 South Gray St, just west of Minto St, is a comfortable, traditional B&B with beds from £14 a head.

Hamilton House Guest House (☎ 667 2540), 12 Moston Terrace, just east of May-field Gardens, is a pleasant Victorian villa catering for vegetarians. The range of rooms includes a single from £18.

Millfield Guest House (☎ 667 4428), at 12 Marchhall Rd, just east of Dalkeith Rd past Pollock Halls of Residence, is a pleasant Victorian house with beds from £16.

Using the same bus stop as for Bruntsfield Youth Hostel, you can get to the *Lugtons Guest House* (☎ 229 7033), 29 Leamington Terrace, which has singles/doubles from £20 to £28 per person. Virtually next door is the similar *Menzies Guest House* (☎ 229 4629).

There are a couple of quiet guesthouses in Hartington Gardens, off Viewforth, itself off Bruntsfield Place. *Aaron's Guest House* (☎ 229 6459) is handy for drivers since it has a private car park. Beds go for £25 each in comfortable en-suite rooms.

Casa Buzzo (☎ 667 8998) is quite a way out at 8 Kilmaurs Rd, also just east of Dalkeith Rd. It has two doubles for £13 per person.

Hotels

Not surprisingly, the international hotels right in the centre are extremely expensive, although there can be good deals outside summer, especially at weekends.

There's a handy batch of mid-range places on Coates Gardens, off Haymarket Terrace near Haymarket railway station. Comfortable *Boisdale Hotel* (☎ 337 1134), at No 9, has rooms with private bath from £25 to £35 per person. Other possibilities include the *Argus Hotel* (☎ 337 6159) at No 14 and the *Beresford Hotel* (☎ 337 0850) at No 32.

The *Rothesay Hotel* (☎ 225 4125), at 8 Rothesay Place, a quiet, central street in the West End, has pleasantly spacious rooms, mostly with bathroom, from around £30 per person.

Royal Terrace has a great position on the north side of Calton Hill. *Ailsa Craig Hotel* (☎ 556 1022), is a refurbished Georgian building at No 24. Rooms, often with bath, cost from £25 per person. The *Claymore Hotel* (☎ 556 2693), at No 6, the *Halcyon* (☎ 556 1032) at No 8, the *Greenside* (☎ 557 0022), at No 9, and the *Adria Hotel* (☎ 556

7875), at No 11, are similar. Also in Royal Terrace is the thoroughly swish *Royal Terrace Hotel* (☎ 557 3222) with singles for £110 and doubles for £150.

The *Thistle Inn Hotel* (☎ 220 2299), at 94 Grassmarket, right in the heart of the Old Town, is one of the city's nightlife centres. Singles/doubles with private bath and TV cost from £32/54. Every floor is accessible by lift. (Don't confuse it with the bigger, more expensive King James Thistle Hotel beside the shopping centre, off Leith St.)

The *Old Waverley Hotel* (☎ 556 4648), 43 Princes St, has a prime site opposite Waverley station, and many rooms have castle views. Rooms with private bath cost from £65.50 a head.

The *Scandic Crown Hotel* (☎ 557 9797), 80 High St, is a purpose-built hotel whose exterior mimics the Royal Mile's 16th-century architecture. The interior is, nonetheless, as modern as you could hope for. Rates vary from £48 to £115 per person.

The *Sheraton Grand Hotel* (☎ 229 9131), 1 Festival Square, is opposite the Royal Lyceum Theatre, off Lothian Rd, east of the castle. You pay for, and get, luxury. Rates vary from £83.75 to £169 per person.

More personal than these chain hotels is *Sibbet House* (☎ 556 1078) at 26 Northumberland St, where prices of £56 to £70 might include an impromptu bagpipe recital by your host.

PLACES TO EAT

There are good-value restaurants scattered all round the city. For cheap eats, the best areas are Leith Walk, near the Playhouse theatre; around Grassmarket, just south of the castle; and near the university around Nicolson St, the extension of North/South Bridge. Most restaurants offer cheap set menus at lunchtime. Many close on Sunday evening, so ring ahead to make sure.

Royal Mile

Despite being a tourist Mecca, the Royal Mile has lots of good-value, enjoyable eating oases.

Restaurants The excellent, small *Singapore Sling* (☎ 226 2826), 503 Lawnmarket, is not particularly cheap by Edinburgh standards, but satays are a speciality and good-value five-course banquets cost £13.90 per person.

Viva Mexico (☎ 226 5145), Cockburn St, is a cheerful, atmospheric restaurant. Some tables have views across to the New Town, and the food is good quality. Two courses cost around £10.

The *Doric Wine Bar & Bistro* (☎ 225 1084), 15 Market St, has a good-value bar menu (meals from £2 to £3) from noon to 6.30 pm. The small upstairs bistro offers classic Scottish dishes like haggis, neeps and tatties for £8.55.

Pleasant *Black Bo's* (☎ 557 6136), 57 Blackfriars St, offers an imaginative vegetarian menu. Main courses like stuffed leeks in puff pastry and cassis sauce cost around £7.50.

Across the road from John Knox's house you can sample Scottish cooking at *Flora's Parlour* (☎ 557 9350); soups include cullen skink (smoked fish) or cock a leekie (clear chicken & leek) for £1.65; potatoes, beef and onions costs £2.65. *Dubh Prais* (☎ 557 5732), 123 High St, is considered one of the best places to try Scottish cuisine and is popular with locals and tourists. The menu features dishes like seafood broth for £4.30, grilled salmon for £12.50 and saddle of hare for £13.50.

Cafés *Patisserie Florentin*, St Giles St, attracts a rather self-consciously Bohemian crowd, but has excellent light meals and pastries, and good coffee for £1. It stays open till the early hours during the festival.

Lower Aisle Café, beneath St Giles' Cathedral, is peaceful outside peak lunchtimes. Soup and a roll costs 95p.

Elephant's Sufficiency (☎ 220 0666), 170 High St, is a bustling lunch spot. Try the Orkney burger for £3.15 or the elephant burger for £4.15.

At 21 George IV Bridge the enormously popular *Elephant House* (☎ 220 5355) is a café with gooey cakes, newspapers, a good noticeboard...and lots of elephants in all shapes and sizes.

The new *Custos Café* (☎ 558 3083), 105 High St, does delicious gourmet sandwiches from £1.70 and filled focaccia sandwiches from £2.50. The *Netherbow Theatre Café*, just downhill from John Knox's House, serves cheap breakfasts in an outdoor courtyard up to noon, then lunches (big portions), salads and quiche for around £3.

Clarinda's Tea Room, 69 Canongate, lurks at the rather inhospitable Holyrood end of the Mile. There are a variety of teas from 48p and delicious cakes from 78p. *Brambles Tearoom*, opposite the People's Story, does soup and a roll for £1.10.

New Town
The New Town is neither particularly well endowed with eating places nor a particularly interesting part of town at night, but there are a few reasonable options, especially in Hanover St.

Chez Jules (☎ 225 7893), 61 Frederick St, is a spin-off from the Pierre Victoire success story (see the Leith St section), offering similar simple, cheap, but good-quality French food. Soup is 80p, pigeon is £3 and a three-course lunch is £5. In the same French vein there's a branch of the popular *Café Rouge* chain nearby.

In Hanover St, *Henderson's* (☎ 225 2131), at No 94, is an Edinburgh institution which has been churning out vegetarian food for more than 30 years. Hot dishes start at £3 but it's worth checking if there's a lunch or dinner special offering several courses and a drink thrown in. At No 110 *Gringo Bill's* (☎ 220 1205) does a meal and a drink at lunchtime for £5 all in. *Bar Napoli* (☎ 225 2600), at No 75, is a cheerful Italian restaurant, open until 3 am, with pasta and pizza for around £4 a dish.

Stockbridge
Villagey Stockbridge is popular with the young and affluent and has some enjoyable pubs.

Ross Coffee House, at the junction of Dean

St and Raeburn Place, has some outside tables and is often packed with shoppers.

The *Patisserie Florentin* (☎ 220 0225), 5 North West Circus Place, has excellent quiche, pastries and coffee like its sister shop off the Royal Mile.

Leith St
Leith St has several places pitching for Playhouse Theatre-goers.

The *Ferris Restaurant* (☎ 556 5592), does pasta or pizza for under £5, or there's a branch of *Pierre Victoire* (☎ 557 8451), at 8 Union St, with a relaxed style and main courses for around £8. Pick of the bunch, however, is friendly, informal *Giuliano's* (☎ 556 6590), 18 Union Place, opposite the Theatre. It's open to 2 am, and serves pastas and pizzas for around £5.

Princes St
Midway along Princes St are two pleasant cafés. The *Next Café*, at No 119, has bow windows, a sunny atmosphere and flowers on the tables. Cappuccinos are £1.20, tea and a cake is £2.45, and there are usually lunchtime specials.

Nearby, at 4 South Charlotte St, is a branch of *Bewley's* (☎ 220 1969), the Irish coffee shop which also serves lunch and breakfast.

Dalry Rd (West End)
A few places on Dalry Rd are convenient for those staying in the West End.

The branch of *Howie's Bistro* (☎ 313 3334) at No 63 is so popular that advance booking is wise. House specialities are venison and banoffi pie. A two-course lunch is a bargain at £6.50; the set evening menu is £14.95.

At the north end of Dalry Rd, the *New Star of Bengal* (☎ 346 0204), at No 13, has tasty food, with a three-course set vegetarian dinner for £8.95 and single dishes for much less.

Lothian Rd
A few places around the south end of Lothian Rd cater for the Royal Lyceum Theatre's clientele. Big, jolly *Dario's Pizza & Spaghetti*

EDINBURGH

House (☎ 229 9625), at No 85, is open until 4 am Sunday to Thursday; until 6 am on Friday and Saturday. Set lunches cost £3.75 and, in the evening, pasta and pizzas start from around £5.

Behind the theatre, *Loon Fung* (☎ 229 5757), 32 Grindlay St, has excellent Cantonese cooking, especially seafood. You'll be able to eat well for around £10, a bit less if you're careful. A weekday three-course lunch costs £6, but rice and noodle dishes are £6 to £8.

Bruntsfield

There's a batch of moderately-priced restaurants on Leven St (which becomes Bruntsfield Place), but the more interesting places are further out, past the youth hostel.

Efes (☎ 229 7833), 42 Leven St, has various kebabs and pizzas. They're cheaper to take away but if you eat in, a doner kebab will cost between £5.40 and £7, a garlicky pizza from £3.60 to £5.

Parrots (☎ 229 3252), 3 Viewforth, off Bruntsfield Place, is a deservedly popular non-smoking restaurant that sells excellent-value meals in pleasant parrot-themed surroundings. The extensive menu offers everything from Baltis for £5.75, to mushroom and nut fettuccine for £3.45. One pudding consists of chocolate muffin with chocolate ice cream, cream, bits of chocolate and a chocolate liqueur for £3.25. It's even possible to eat alone here without feeling like a leper.

Montpeliers (☎ 229 3115), 159 Bruntfield Place, serves cappuccinos and cakes all day, and excellent Scottish breakfasts. The interesting dinner menu has things like lamb in poppyseed crust for £6.90, and mushroom and spinach strudel in blue cheese sauce for £5.60.

At 208 Bruntsfield Place there's a branch of *Howie's Bistro* (☎ 221 1777) in an old bank (see the earlier Dalry Rd section for details).

Lauriston

If you're staying in Minto St or Mayfield Gardens there are several good choices on either side of the main road back towards the centre.

Pierre Lapin (☎ 668 4332), 113 Buccleuch St, offers a French vegetarian version of the popular Pierre Victoire menu – the four-course set menu is a bargain at £9.60. There is always a fish dish on offer as well.

There's also another branch of *Howie's Bistro* (☎ 668 2917) at 75 St Leonards.

Grassmarket

The lively pubs and restaurants on the north side of Grassmarket cater to a young crowd – it's a good starting point for a night out.

Gennaro (☎ 226 3706) at No 64 has standard Italian fare, with minestrone at £1.60, cannelloni at £5.20 and pizzas from £4 to £7. Popular *Mamma's Pizzas* (☎ 225 6464) at No 28, does excellent pizzas with imaginative toppings.

Pierre Victoire (☎ 226 2442), 38 Grassmarket, is part of the chain that serves good-value French food (see the earlier Leith St section for details). There's also a branch at 10 Victoria St, which curves up to George IV Bridge from the north-east corner of Grassmarket.

Also part of Pierre's empire, *Beppe Vittorio* (☎ 226 7267), 7 Victoria St, follows the same formula – authentic, good-value food – although in this case it's Italian. Minestrone is £1.40, and you can mix and match sauces and pastas from £4.90.

University

There are lots of places near the university. Many student favourites are between Nicolson St and Bristo Place at the end of George IV Bridge.

Kebab Mahal (☎ 667 5214), in Nicolson Square, is a legendary source of cheap sustenance with excellent kebabs from £2.50, and curries from £3.25. You sit at a counter bathed in fluorescent light.

Vegetarians should look for *Susie's Diner* (☎ 667 8729), in West Nicolson St (west off Nicolson St), which has good, inexpensive food – a main meal will set you back less than £4.

Negociant's (☎ 225 6313), 45 Lothian St, is a very hip café and music venue with good-value food – main courses from £3 for a filled roti to £7.20 for a steak. The basement bar is open until 3 am.

Kalpna (☎ 667 9890), 2 St Patrick's Square, is a highly acclaimed, reasonably priced Gujarati (Indian) restaurant. On Wednesday nights it lays on a gourmet buffet of 20 dishes from one region of India – the region varies each week.

Spartan, atmospheric *Khushi's* (☎ 556 8996), 16 Drummond St, is the original Edinburgh curry house and not much has changed since it opened in 1947. You can bring your pint in from the pub next door. A set lunch is £5.45 but the lamb bhuna at £4.60 is said to be the local favourite.

Chinese Home Cooking (☎ 668 4946), 34 West Preston St, is a real bargain BYO restaurant with spartan décor but filling, tasty food. A starter and main course will cost around £7.

ENTERTAINMENT
For full coverage of all the options, from film to theatre, every kind of music and clubs, buy *The List* (£1.80) Edinburgh's and Glasgow's fortnightly events guide.

Theatre & Cinema
Probably because of the frantic festival activity, Edinburgh has more than its fair share of theatres. The *Festival Theatre* (☎ 529 6000), 13-29 Nicolson St, stages everything from ballet to pantos. The *Royal Lyceum Theatre* (☎ 229 9697) opposite Festival Square hosts concerts...Tony Bennett through to Mark Knopfler. Nearby *Usher Hall* (☎ 228 1155) puts on classical concerts. Across the road at 88 Lothian Rd the *Filmhouse* (☎ 228 2688) shows less mainstream films.

Pubs
Edinburgh has over 700 pubs and bars which are as varied as the population...everything from Victorian palaces to rough and ready drinking holes.

Royal Mile The pubs on the Royal Mile are not very inspiring, although there are some classics along the side streets. The *Jolly Judge*, 495 Lawnmarket, retains its distinctive 17th-century character, and there's a cheering fire in winter. The *Malt Shovel Inn*, 13 Cockburn St, has a good range of beers and jazz on Tuesday nights.

One of Edinburgh's most entertaining pubs is *The Ceilidh House* below the Tron Tavern. It's the atmospheric home to the Edinburgh Folk Club. Most nights, there are informal, but high-quality, jam sessions. There's more live music, on Saturday nights and Sunday afternoons, at the *Hebrides*, 17 Market St.

Grassmarket & Around The *Bow Bar* is a popular pub. Despite its picturesque name, *The Last Drop* actually commemorates the executions that used to take place nearby.

Greyfriars Bobby in Candlemaker Row and the *Pear Tree* in West Nicolson St are popular student hang-outs with reasonable food. The Pear Tree has a large outdoor courtyard – pleasant on sunny afternoons and warm evenings.

There are also several cheerful, friendly places on Cowgate, which runs off the southeast corner of Grassmarket. The *Green Tree* at No 182 has a beer garden. *Bannermans*, at No 212 on the corner of Blackfriars St, attracts students, locals and backpackers, and there's often live music.

New Town Rose St may have lots of pubs, but they're not all worth frequenting. Two exceptions are the *Abbotsford* at No 3, which has Victorian décor, and the *Rose St Brewery* at No 55, which has a good range of beers, most brewed on the premises. The *Phoenix* in trendy Broughton St stays open late; the *Globe Café* two doors away opens early to feed breakfast to all-nighters.

It's worth sticking your nose through the door of *Café Royal Bar*, 17 West Register St, to see its amazing Victorian interior. Not far away in Andrew St the *Tiles Bar-Bistro* is similarly lavish.

At the west end, in Hope St between

Princes St and Charlotte Square , *Whigham's Wine Cellars* is an old (and pricey) wine bar in atmospheric cellars.

Bruntsfield *Bennets Bar*, 8 Leven St, is an olde worlde pub with marvellous stained glass and tiled walls. The *Golf Tavern*, 30 Wright's Houses, parallel to Bruntsfield Place and overlooking Bruntsfield Links, is decorated with golfing memorabilia; there's a good selection of whiskies.

Clubs

There are some interesting music/club venues in old vaults under the George IV and South Bridges. *The Vaults*, 15 Niddry St under South Bridge, has a café as well as a variety of reliable club nights.

It's a bit hard to know where to slot the *City Café* (☎ 220 0125), 19 Blair St. It's a seriously cool bar, but there are also meals, snacks and all-day breakfasts. Downstairs, there's a dance floor, *City 2*, with different music depending on the night.

The *Venue*, 17 Calton Rd, is well worth checking out; at the time of writing its Saturday night *Pure* club was a favourite night spot.

Scottish Evenings

The Scottish Experience (☎ 557 9350) at 12 High St (Royal Mile) offers an evening of eating, singing and dancing for £29.95, or £35 with whisky and wine. The action kicks off at 7.30 pm and ends around 10.15 pm, depending on how much the audience gets into the swing of things.

GETTING THERE & AWAY

Edinburgh is 378 miles from London, 46 from Glasgow, 105 from Newcastle upon Tyne, and 194 from York. See the introductory Scotland and Britain Getting Around chapters.

Air

Edinburgh airport (☎ 333 1000), six miles west of the city, has domestic services and a limited number of international services. Air

UK, British Airways and British Midland all have regular services.

Bus

Buses from London are very competitive and you may be able to get cheap promotional tickets. See the Glasgow section in the Southern Scotland chapter; prices are the same and the journey takes half an hour less.

There are numerous links with cities in England, including Newcastle (2¾ hours, £7.50) and York (5½ hours, £26).

Buses and coaches leave from the St Andrew Square bus station where Scottish Citylink has an inquiry and ticket counter. Scottish Citylink (☎ 0990-505050) has buses to virtually every major town in Scotland. Most west-coast towns are reached via Glasgow. There are numerous buses to Glasgow, with off-peak singles/returns for £4.50/6.50, and to St Andrew, Aberdeen and Inverness.

Train

The main railway station is Waverley in the heart of the city, although most trains also stop at Haymarket Station, which is convenient for the West End.

There are 20 trains a day from London's King's Cross; apart from Apex fares which must be booked in advance they're expensive, but they're also quicker and more comfortable than buses.

ScotRail has two northern lines from Edinburgh: one that cuts across the Grampians to Inverness (3½ hours) and on to Thurso, and another that follows the coast around to Aberdeen (three hours) and on to Inverness. All services are non-smoking.

There are numerous trains to Glasgow (50 minutes, £6.70).

For all rail enquiries, phone ☎ 0345-484950.

GETTING AROUND
The Airport

Frequent buses run from Waverley railway station to the airport, taking 35 minutes and cost £3.20. A taxi costs around £12.

Bus

Bus services are frequent and cheap, but two main companies compete with each other and their tickets are not interchangeable. You can buy tickets when you board buses, but on maroon Lothian Regional Transport buses you must have exact change. For short trips, fares are 40p to 55p. A ridacard, available from newsagents for £2, covers a whole day's travel. After midnight there are special night buses. The TIC has a free map showing the most important services, or during weekdays contact Traveline (☎ 225 3858) at 24 St Giles St.

Train

Frequent trains link Waverley railway station and Haymarket, but it's cheaper to catch a bus down Princes St.

Taxi

There are numerous central taxi ranks and costs are reasonable; £5 will get you almost anywhere. Local companies include Capital (☎ 228 2555), Central (☎ 229 2468), City (☎ 228 1211) and Radiocabs (☎ 225 9000).

Car Rental

In addition to the big national operators, the TIC has details of reputable local car rental companies. Melville's (☎ 337 5333), 9 Clifton Terrace, has Ford Escorts with unlimited mileage from £110 per week. Century (☎ 455 7314), at 1 Murrayburn Rd, sometimes offers small Fiats with unlimited mileage from £99 a week.

Bicycle

Although there are plenty of steep hills to negotiate, Edinburgh is ideal for cycling – nothing is more than half an hour away and the traffic is fairly tolerable.

Edinburgh Cycle Hire (☎ 556 5560), 29 Blackfriars St, hires mountain and hybrid bikes for £10 to £15 a day, or £50 a week. David's Bicycle Store (☎ 229 8528), 39 Argyle Place, hires out bikes for £8 a day (mountain bikes £12 a day); lower prices for longer rentals. He also has used bikes from £30 and will buy them back from people

staying less than six months, the price depending on the state they come back in.

Around Edinburgh

Craigmillar Castle

Massive Craigmillar Castle is still impressive, although Edinburgh's suburbs are snapping at its ankles. Dating from the 15th century, the tower house rises above two sets of walls that enclose an area of 1½ acres. Close your eyes and imagine the days when Mary Queen of Scots took refuge here after the murder of Rizzio; it was here too that plans to murder her husband Darnley were laid. Look for the prison cell complete with built-in sanitation, something some British prisons only finally managed in 1996. Recently the castle provided the set for a BBC production of Walter Scott's *Ivanhoe*.

The castle (☎ 244 3101; HS) is just off the A68 to Dalkeith, about two miles south of the city centre. Entry costs £1.50/75p. Bus Nos 14, 21, C3 and C33 pass by.

Leith

Leith is and was Edinburgh's port, although it remained an independent burgh until the 1920s. It's still among Britain's busiest ports, but in the 60s and 70s it fell into a sad state, abandoned to council housing, a prey to drug dealers, blighted by AIDS.

Since the 1980s a revival has taken place and there are now many interesting pubs and restaurants. Parts are still distinctly rough – as are sections of Leith Walk, the main approach – but it's a distinctive corner of Edinburgh. The most interesting parts are bounded by Great Junction St, Commercial St and Constitution St, but the prettiest area is around The Shore, where the Water of Leith path to Balerno starts.

Places to eat include *The Shore* (☎ 553 5080) with three-course lunches for £6.95 and live traditional music on Wednesday and Saturday at 9 pm, and *Fishers Bar-Bistro* (☎ 554 5666) in a 17th-century signal tower. You can brunch on a boat moored in the dock

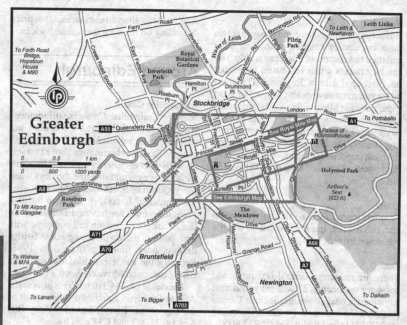

on Saturday and Sunday from 11 am to 5 pm. Pub food is available in two historic pubs, the *King's Wark* and the *Malt and Hops*. There's a vegetarian café in the *Malmaison Hotel* (☎ 555 6868) in a 19th-century sailor's home. This is a wonderfully stylish hotel, with doubles for £80.

Newhaven

Immediately to the west of Leith is Newhaven, once a small, distinctive fishing community, now absorbed into the Edinburgh conurbation. Recently the old Fishmarket building acquired a *Harry Ramsden's* fish shop (☎ 551 5566) and a **Heritage Centre** which is well worth a visit. A 15-minute video reveals the astonishingly tribal lifestyle that survived here until the 1950s when overfishing put paid to the traditional source of income. In a matriarchal society, women in distinctive dress dominated the fish market and life in the home. On Gala Days they dressed up in fine striped skirts and aprons; to see the real thing you'd need to look out for a performance of the Newhaven Fisherlassies' Choir which has been going strong since 1896. The Centre is open daily from noon to 5 pm; admission free.

Lauriston Castle

Three miles north-west of the centre, Lauriston Castle (☎ 336 2060) started life in the 16th-century but was 'modernised' in 19th-century baronial style. There are 40-minute guided tours daily except Friday from April to October, and on weekend afternoons in winter. Admission costs £3.50/2.50. Bus Nos 40 and 41 pass by.

South Queensferry & the Forth Bridges

South Queensferry lies on the south bank of the Firth of Forth, at its narrowest point. From early times it was a ferry port, but it's now overshadowed by two magnificent bridges.

The magnificent Forth Rail Bridge is one of the finest Victorian engineering achievements. Completed in 1890 after seven years work and the deaths of 57 men, it's over a mile long and the 50,000 tons of girders take three years to paint. The Forth Road Bridge was not completed until 1964 and is a graceful suspension bridge.

In the pretty High St there are plenty of places to eat and a small **museum** (☎ 331 5545) containing some interesting background info on the bridges. The prize exhibit is a model of the Furry Man; on the first Friday of August, some hapless male still has to spend nine hours roaming the streets covered from head to toe in burrs and clutching two floral staves in memory of a medieval tradition. It's open Monday and Thursday to Saturday from 10 am to 1 pm and 2.15 to 5 pm, Sunday 2 to 5 pm, free.

The *Maid of Forth* (☎ 331 4857) leaves from Hawes Pier and cruises under the bridges to Inchcolm Island (see following section) and Deep Sea World, the huge aquarium in North Queensferry (☎ 01383-411411). There are daily sailings from July to early September (weekends only from April to June). In summer, evening cruises with jazz or folk music cost £7.95 a head.

Inchcolm Island & Abbey
Inchcolm Island has one of Scotland's best preserved medieval abbeys which was founded for Augustinian priors in 1123. In well-tended grounds stand remains of a 13th-century church and a remarkably well-preserved octagonal chapter house with stone roof.

It's half an hour to Inchcolm, and you're allowed 1½ hours ashore. Admission to the abbey is £2/1, included in the £6.75/3.50 ferry cost (HS members should show their cards for reduction); non-landing tickets cost £4.75/2.50 and will allow you to see the island's grey seals, puffins and other seabirds.

You can reach South Queensferry by frequent train to Dalmeny station (15 minutes).

Hopetoun House
Two miles west of South Queensferry, Hopetoun House, one of Scotland's finest stately homes, has a superb location in lovely grounds beside the Firth of Forth. There are two parts, the older built to Sir William Bruce's plans between 1699 and 1702 and dominated by a splendid stairwell, the newer designed between 1720 and 1750 by three members of the Adam family, William and sons Robert and John. The rooms have splendid furnishings and staff are on hand to make sure you don't miss details like the revolving oyster stand for two people to share. The Hope family supplied a Viceroy of India and a Governor-General of Australia so the upstairs museum displays interesting reminders of the colonial life of the ruling class. Even further up there's a viewing point on the roof, ideal for photos.

Hopetoun House (☎ 331 2451) can be approached from Queensferry, or from Edinburgh – turn off the A90 onto the A904 just before the Forth Bridge Toll and follow the signs. It's open April to September from 10 am to 4.30 pm; £4.20/2.10 (less for the grounds only).

EDINBURGH

Southern Scotland

✠✠✠✠✠✠✠✠✠✠✠✠✠✠✠✠✠✠✠✠✠✠✠✠

Locator & Map Index

EDINBURGH

Glasgow p738

Kelso p731

Arran p756

Stranraer p768

Southern Scotland is a large and beautiful region, although in many ways it is something of a 'no man's land'. Historically, it was the buffer between the rambunctious and imperialist English and the equally unruly Scots.

Although the inhabitants of today are proudly and indisputably Scottish they are, in fact, truly unique – like but unlike the Scots further to the north, like but unlike the northern English to the south. This duality is perhaps not incompatible with the fact that this region was home to the two men – Robert Burns and Sir Walter Scott – who, in the late 18th and early 19th centuries, did most to reinvent and popularise Scottishness.

The Romans attempted to draw a clean line across the map with Hadrian's Wall, leaving the Celtic Picts to their own devices. The great Anglo-Saxon kingdoms of Bernicia and Northumbria, however, dominated the east and the south-west and succeeded in driving many Celts further to the north. Another wave of Anglo-Saxons arrived from northern England after 1066, bringing with them a language which evolved into Lowlands Scots – like but unlike English, as Robert Burns so vividly illustrated.

The Norman invasion of England led inexorably to war with the Scots, although in times of peace, especially in the south, the aristocracy intermarried, leading to complicated land holdings on both sides of the border. The wars of Scottish independence fought at the end of the 12th century and the beginning of the 13th took a terrible toll on southern Scotland. And although the Scots succeeded in consolidating their independence, and great monastic estates were established, the south was still periodically trampled on by opposing armies.

Worse than that, large parts of today's Borders and Dumfries & Galloway regions were basically allowed to go to hell – neither the English nor the Scottish had any real interest in bringing stability to their enemy's border. Although there were periods of relative calm when great monasteries were constructed (and reconstructed), the Debateable Lands, as they were known, were virtually ungoverned and ungovernable from the late 13th to the mid-17th century. The great families with their complex blood

726

feuds fought and robbed the English, the Scots and each other. This amounted to a continuous state of guerrilla warfare, and some have argued that the effect on the region and its people was indelible.

After the union of the two countries, peace allowed a new surge of development. The Borders, partly thanks to the abbeys, had traditionally been an important wool growing and processing region, and during the 19th century the knitting and weaving industries that survive today were created.

The countryside varies from gentle open fields in the east, to beautiful hilly countryside flanking the River Tweed, to the high Glenken and Galloway hills in the west. The region is certainly not undiscovered by tourists – it's too obvious a stopover point for those heading to/from Glasgow and Edinburgh. However, it's easy to escape the crowds, particularly in the south-west. Outside the main roads, there's very little traffic, which makes for particularly good cycling country.

ORIENTATION

Southern Scotland can effectively be divided into four quarters. The southern uplands divide the region into northern and southern halves. In the north-west, the former region of Strathclyde has been divided into North & South Lanarkshire, and North, South & East Ayrshire, plus smaller unitary authorities around Glasgow. Lothian is in the north-east (linked with Edinburgh). The Borders, in the south-east, also look to Edinburgh, and there are good bus links with that city. With the exception of the main routes to Stranraer (for Northern Ireland ferries), Dumfries & Galloway, in the south-west, is one of the most isolated regions in Britain.

Ayrshire was the birthplace of Scotland's national poet, Robert Burns, though it's the least spectacular part of the region. In Dumfries & Galloway the coast and mountains approach the grandeur of the north. The Borders have beautiful countryside, particularly around the Tweed, and pleasant towns built around monastic ruins. Lothian, most of which is easily accessible on day trips

from Edinburgh, has some wild, bleak hills and Craigmillar Castle.

INFORMATION

Tourism is an increasingly important industry, so every small town has an excellent TIC with free accommodation booking services (BABA for £2.75) and an excellent range of brochures. Southwaite TIC (☎ 016974-73445), on the M6 south of Carlisle, has a lot of info on southern Scotland; it's open April to September, daily from 10 am to 6 pm; October to March, Monday to Friday from 10 am to 5 pm, and Saturday from 10 am to 2 pm. There's another useful TIC, the Gretna Gateway to Scotland (☎ 01461-338500), on the A74.

The TICs have information on a number of car touring routes, including the Burns Trail, from near Ayr where he was born to Dumfries where he died; the Solway Coast Heritage Trail, from Gretna Green around the beautiful coast to Ayr; and the Scottish Borders Woollen Trail, taking in the mills and mill shops.

Youth hostels are scarce and, in general, not very accessible unless you have a car. The exceptions to the rule are at Melrose, Minnigaff (near Newton Stewart) and Ayr. There are also hostels at Kendoon, Wanlockhead, Snoot, Broadmeadows, Kirk Yetholm, Abbe St Bathans and Coldingham.

WALKS

Especially in the valley of the Tweed, there are numerous circular walks that can be made around the small towns; the TICs have information.

The most famous walk is the Southern Upland Way, Britain's first official coast-to-coast footpath. It runs 212 miles from Portpatrick on the south-west coast (near Stranraer) to Cockburnspath on the east coast.

The route includes some very long and extremely demanding stretches, so walkers tackling the entire length must be both fit and experienced. Parts of the route are sparsely populated, with shelter and transport virtually nonexistent. Proper equipment is essential; in summer you can expect to experience

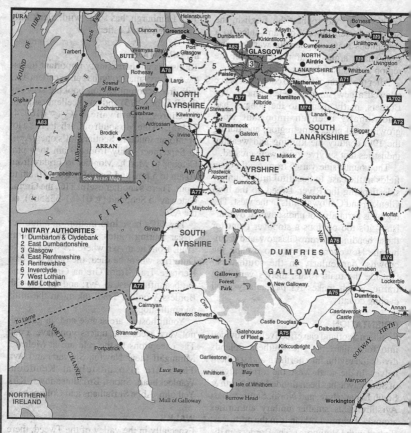

SOUTHERN SCOTLAND

UNITARY AUTHORITIES
1 Dumbarton & Clydebank
2 East Dumbartonshire
3 Glasgow
4 East Renfrewshire
5 Renfrewshire
6 Inverclyde
7 West Lothian
8 Mid Lothian

everything from snow to a heat wave. Although the entire route is waymarked, it is a necessity that walkers are able to navigate with map and compass when the visibility is bad.

Walkers are advised to walk from west to east and the walk could take anything between 10 and 20 days, although 14 is a fair guess. The way incorporates clifftop paths, old Roman roads, hill ridges and droving trails. It passes over high hilltops and wide moors, through valleys, forests, farms and villages.

The excellent official guide to the walk, *Southern Upland Way* (£17.50), is published by HMSO and comes complete with two 1:50,000 OS route maps. It's available from bookshops, TICs and the HMSO bookshops in London and Edinburgh.

Accommodation is quite difficult to find in parts, and many walkers use tents. Book accommodation in advance, especially in the busy summer months. Local TICs can help, and supply a free accommodation leaflet.

Shorter, less demanding sections of the walk can be undertaken. Two that have been suggested are Portpatrick to New Luce (23 miles) and Yair Bridge to Melrose (7½ miles).

Southern Scotland

CYCLE ROUTES

With the exception of the main north-south A-roads and the A75 to Stranraer, traffic is sparse, which along with the beauty of the countryside makes this ideal cycling country. Bear in mind the prevailing winds are from the south-west. Local TICs have information on a number of possible routes.

The Tweed Cycle Way is a waymarked route running 62 miles along the beautiful Tweed valley following minor roads from Biggar to Peebles (13 miles); to Melrose (16 miles); to Coldstream (19 miles); and to Berwick-upon-Tweed (14 miles). The Jed-

burgh TIC (☎ 01835-863435), Murrays Green, Jedburgh TD8 6BE, has information.

Another interesting route is outlined in the guide, the *Scottish Border Cycle Way*, although this is not a waymarked route. It runs 210 miles from Portpatrick to Berwick-upon-Tweed – coast to coast via Three Lochs, Talnotry, Castle Douglas, Dumfries, Ruthwell, Gretna Green, Newcastleton, Hawick, Jedburgh and Coldstream. Contact Jedburgh TIC for information.

There are numerous other possibilities that a decent map will reveal. The Tweed Valley is hard to ignore, but the Galloway Hills (north of Newton Stewart) and coastal routes to Whithorn (south of Newton Stewart) are also excellent.

GETTING AROUND
Bus
Bus transport is excellent around Glasgow and Ayrshire, in the Borders and Lothian, reasonable on the main north-south routes and the A75 to Stranraer, but limited elsewhere in Dumfries & Galloway. The relevant inquiry lines and the telephone numbers for the major operators are given in the following sections. Various explorer tickets are available. These can be bought from the bus drivers or from bus stations, and are nearly always the best value option if you are travelling reasonably extensively.

Train
Train services are limited. There are stations at Berwick-upon-Tweed (on the English side of the border in Northumberland, but the natural jumping-off point for the Tweed valley) on the main east-coast line; at Dumfries on the main west-coast line; and at Stranraer, which is linked to Glasgow.

Borders Region

There is a tendency to think that the real Scotland doesn't start until you are north of Perth, but the castles, forests and glens of the Borders have a romance and beauty of their own. The region survived centuries of war and plunder and was romantically portrayed by Robert Burns and Sir Walter Scott.

Although parts, especially to the west, are wild and empty, the fertile valley of the River Tweed has been a wealthy region for 1000 years. The population was largely concentrated in a small number of *burghs* (towns, from burh, meaning a defensive ring of forts), which also supported large and wealthy monastic communities. These provided an irresistible magnet during the border wars and they were destroyed and rebuilt numerous times.

The monasteries met their final fiery end in the mid-16th century, burnt by the English yet again, but this time English fire combined with the Scottish Reformation and they were never again rebuilt. The towns thrived once peace arrived and the traditional weavers provided the foundation for a major textile industry, which still survives.

Relatively few people pause in their rush to get to Edinburgh, but if you do stop, you'll find the lovely valley of the Tweed, rolling hills, castles, ruined abbeys and sheltered towns. This is excellent cycling and walking country. Two possibilities among many are the challenging coast-to-coast Southern Upland Way and the Tweed Cycle Way (see the Walks and Cycle Routes sections at the start of this chapter).

The Borders Region lies between the Cheviot Hills along the English border, and the Pentland, Moorfoot and Lammermuir Hills, which form the border with Lothian and overlook the Firth of Forth. The most interesting country surrounds the River Tweed and its tributaries.

Consider buying the Border Heritage Pass (available from TICs), which for £12.99 gives admission to as many as five of the following houses: Abbotsford, Bowhill, Floors, Manderston, Mellerstain, Paxton, Thirlestane and Traquair.

GETTING AROUND
Bus
There's a good network of local buses. For those coming from the south-west, there is a Rail Link coach service that runs between Carlisle in north-west Cumbria and Galashiels; there are six a day from Monday to Saturday, three on Sunday (£14).

Lowland (☎ 01289-307461) has numerous buses between Edinburgh and Galashiels, and frequent buses between Galashiels and Melrose. Regular Lowland buses run between Berwick-upon-Tweed and Galashiels via Melrose. Another useful and frequent Lowland service links Jedburgh, Melrose and Galashiels. Lowland's Waverley Wanderer ticket allows a day's unlimited travel around the Borders, and includes Edinburgh (£9.60).

National Express has one bus a day (No 383) between Chester and Edinburgh via Manchester, Leeds, Newcastle, Jedburgh and Melrose.

Train
The main lines north from Carlisle and Berwick-upon-Tweed skirt the region. Buses are the only option.

COLDSTREAM
Coldstream is a small, relatively uninspiring town, lying on the banks of the Tweed. It is best known as the birthplace of the Coldstream Guards, and the history of the regiment (from 1650, the oldest in continuous existence) is covered in the local **museum** (☎ 01890-882630).

The TIC (☎ 01890-882607), Town Hall, is open April through October, Monday to Saturday.

The *Coldstream Caravan & Camping Site* (☎ 01890-883376) has a beautiful grassy site beside the river; it's £2 for a cyclist and tent.

The *Crown Hotel* (☎ 01890-882558), Market Square, south of the main road towards the river, is a family-run hotel with good-value bar meals. Rooms cost £18/34 (£26/46 with attached bathroom).

There's a regular bus service between Kelso and Berwick-upon-Tweed via Coldstream – about half a dozen a day Monday to Saturday. The main operator is Swan (☎ 01289-306436).

KELSO
- *pop 5500*   • ☎ *01573*

Kelso is a prosperous market town, with a broad cobbled square, flanked by Georgian buildings, at the hub of narrow cobbled streets. There's an interesting mix of architecture and the town has a lovely site at the junction of the Tweed and Teviot rivers. It's busy during the day, but dies completely in the evening. It's a real town, however, not a tourist trap.

The Pennine Way, which starts its long journey at Edale in the Lake District, ends at Kirk Yetholm Youth Hostel, about six miles south-east on the B6352. Less ambitious walkers should leave the market square by Roxburgh St, and take the signposted alley to the Cobby Riverside Walk, which is a pleasant ramble along the river (past some very expensive fishing spots) to Floors Castle (although you have to rejoin Roxburgh St to gain entry).

Information
The TIC (☎ 223464), Town House, The Square, is open April through October, Monday to Saturday from 10 am to 5.30 pm, Sunday from 10 am to 1 pm (extended hours in July and August). Accommodation can be difficult to find during a number of local festivals and markets held between late June and mid-September; ring ahead to be sure.

Kelso Abbey
Kelso Abbey was built by Tironensians, an order founded at Tiron in Picardy, and brought to the Borders around 1113 by David I. Once one of the richest abbeys in southern Scotland, English raids in the 16th century reduced it to ruins. Today, there is little to see, although the abbey precincts are attractive and the nearby octagonal **Parish Church** (built in 1773) is intriguing. The abbey is open daily from April through December; admission is free.

Kelso Museum & the Turret Gallery
Turret House, one of Kelso's oldest and most interesting buildings, is run by the Scottish NT, and houses a museum and local art

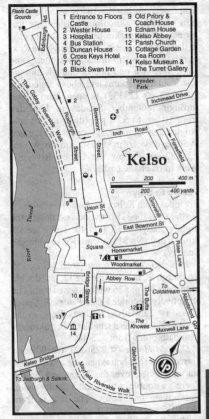

	1 Entrance to Floors Castle	9 Old Priory & Coach House
	2 Wester House	10 Ednam House
	3 Hospital	11 Kelso Abbey
	4 Bus Station	12 Parish Church
	5 Duncan House	13 Cottage Garden Tea Room
	6 Cross Keys Hotel	14 Kelso Museum & The Turret Gallery
	7 TIC	
	8 Black Swan Inn	

Kelso

gallery. The museum has interesting displays on education, the abbey and a reconstructed skinner's workshop (illustrating a once important local trade). The museum is open from Easter through October, Tuesday to Saturday from 10 am to noon and 1 to 5 pm, Sunday from 2 to 5 pm; entry is £1.25/75p.

Floors Castle
Floors Castle is an enormous mansion – Scotland's largest inhabited house – overlooking the Tweed about a mile west of Kelso. Built by William Adam in the 1720s, the original Georgian simplicity was

SOUTHERN SCOTLAND

'improved' during the 1840s with the addition of rather ridiculous battlements and turrets. Floors makes no bones about being in the tourist business, and although the Roxburgh family is still in residence, there is no sense this is a real house, and visitors are restricted to 10 rooms and a busy restaurant.

Floors (☎ 223333) is open from Easter through September, Sunday to Thursday from 10 am to 5.30 pm (daily in July and August); in October, it's open Sunday and Wednesday from 10.30 am to 4 pm; £3.90/2.20. Follow the Cobby Riverside Walk to reach the castle.

Places to Stay

Six miles from Kelso, the *Kirk Yetholm Youth Hostel* (☎ 420631) is the nearest hostel; the nightly charge is £5.40/4.40. There are six buses a day (No 81) to/from Kelso (three on Sunday).

In Kelso, *Wester House* (☎ 225479), 155 Roxburgh St, has a single at £12, and double rooms at £30, or £36 with attached bath. The attractively decorated *Old Priory & Coach House* (☎ 223030), 12 Abbey Row, in the heart of Kelso, has a small number of rooms with bathrooms from £25/40.

Duncan House (☎ 225682), Chalkheugh Terrace, is an old house near the town centre, but with a view over the Tweed and Teviot. There's a double, a twin and a family room, and private bathrooms. The rate is from £13.50 per person.

The top place to stay is the comfortable *Ednam House Hotel* (☎ 224168), Bridge St, a Georgian house with fine gardens overlooking the river. They have a range of rooms, including singles, all with bathrooms. B&B is from £48/66.

Places to Eat

The *Cottage Garden Tea Room*, 7 Abbey Court, is tucked away in a quiet corner near the museum and has some outdoor seating. They serve tea, coffee and light lunches for between £2.50 and £4.

The *Black Swan Inn* (☎ 224563), Horsemarket, has decent, generous bar meals from around £5; it doesn't look very prepossessing outside, but it's comfortable inside. They also have B&B from £19 per person.

Bar lunches at the *Ednam House Hotel* are affordable – from £4.50 – but dinners are quite expensive (£18.50).

Getting There & Away

Kelso is 340 miles from London, 44 from Edinburgh, 18 from Galashiels, 11 from Jedburgh, and nine from Coldstream.

Bus See the Coldstream section for details on the service to Berwick-upon-Tweed. Lowland (☎ 224141) has a good service (No 20) linking Kelso, Jedburgh and Hawick; there are half a dozen Monday to Friday, three on Sunday. They also have plenty of buses to/from Galashiels via Melrose, some of which also go via Smailholm village and Mellerstain.

AROUND KELSO
Smailholm Tower

Smailholm Tower is one of the most evocative sights in the Borders, and in Britain. Perched on a rocky knoll above a small lake, the narrow stone tower brings the bloody uncertainties of the Borders alive, and there is a panoramic view from the top.

The nearby farm, Sandyknowe, was owned by Walter Scott's grandfather. As Scott himself recognised, his imagination was fired by the ballads and stories he heard at Sandyknowe as a child, and by the ruined tower of his ancestors a stone's throw away.

The tower (☎ 01573-460365; HS) is six miles west of Kelso, a mile south of Smailholm village on the B6937. It's open April through September, Monday to Saturday from 9.30 am to 6.30 pm, Sunday from 2 to 6.30 pm; £1.50/75p.

Mellerstain House

Mellerstain House (☎ 01573-410225) is considered to be Scotland's finest Robert Adam designed mansion and, in particular, is famous for its ornate interiors. It was completed in 1778 and has a classically elegant style. It's open May through September,

Sunday to Friday from 12.30 to 5 pm; £4/1.50.

MELROSE
• *pop 2000* • ☎ *01896*

Melrose is the most charming of the border towns, lying at the foot of the three heather-covered Eildon Hills. It's a spic-and-span little town, with a classic market square, some attractive parks and rugby ovals (which are home to the famous Melrose Sevens competition), and one of the great abbey ruins. It's also the only border town with a convenient youth hostel.

There are many attractive walks in the surrounding countryside, and the coast-to-coast Southern Upland Way passes through.

Information
The TIC (☎ 822555), Abbey House, is open April through October, Monday to Saturday from 10 am to 5.30 pm, Sunday from 1.30 to 5.30 pm (extended hours in July and August).

Melrose Abbey
The abbey was founded by David I in 1136 for Cistercians from Rievaulx in Yorkshire. It was repeatedly destroyed by the English in the 14th century, but was rebuilt by Robert the Bruce, and it is here that his heart is buried. The ruins date from the 14th and 15th centuries and were repaired by Sir Walter Scott in the 19th. They are pure Gothic and are famous for their decorative stonework. The adjoining museum is not particularly interesting.

The abbey (☎ 822562; HS) is open April through October from Monday to Saturday, 9.30 am to 6.30 pm, Sunday from 2 to 6.30 pm, and October through March, Monday to Saturday from 9.30 am to 4.30 pm and Sunday from 2 to 4.30 pm; £2.50/1.

Next door to the abbey are the sheltered **Priorwood Gardens** (☎ 822965; NTS), which feature plants used for dried flower arrangements (NT; £1 donation requested).

Places to Stay
Hostel The large *Youth Hostel* (☎ 822521)

Melrose Abbey

is on the edge of town. From the market square, follow the signposting for the A68. It's open from Easter through September and the nightly charge is £6.95/5.85.

Camping The attractive *Gibson Park Caravan Club Park* (☎ 822969) is off High St, virtually in the centre of town. Charges are £7 for non-CC members, £4 for members.

B&Bs & Hotels Melrose B&Bs and hotels are not cheap by Scottish standards, but they are of a high standard; this would not be a bad place to treat yourself. There aren't all that many, so consider booking.

Orchard House (☎ 822005), High St, is a comfortable place with a double and twin for £15 per person; it's open from April to October.

Near the abbey, *Braidwood* (☎ 822488), Buccleuch St, is an excellent B&B with high-standard facilities and a warm welcome. There's a single, double and twin, and rates are around £17.

Burts Hotel (☎ 822285), Market Square, dates from the late 18th century and offers upmarket B&B for £42/75. The *Bon Accord Hotel* (☎ 822645), Market Square, is a small comfortable hotel. Rooms cost £40/68 with bathroom attached.

Places to Eat

There's excellent pub grub at *Burts Hotel*, from around £5. The acclaimed *Melrose Station Restaurant* (☎ 822546), Palma Place, is open for morning teas and lunches from Tuesday to Sunday, for evening meals from Wednesday to Saturday. Book for evening meals; four courses will cost £17.95. Lunches are much cheaper with baguettes from £1.95 and light meals around £5.

The *Bon Accord Hotel* (☎ 822645), Market Square, has good food; soup of the day is £1.70, vegetarian meals are around £5.50.

Getting There & Away

Melrose is 340 miles from London, 38 from Edinburgh, and 12 from Kelso and Jedburgh.

Bus Lowland has regular bus links to Galashiels, an important transport hub in the Borders. There are regular buses to Kelso, Jedburgh and Peebles. Some of the buses to Kelso travel via the village of Smailholm and Mellerstain House.

AROUND MELROSE
Dryburgh Abbey

The most beautiful and most complete of the border abbeys is Dryburgh, partly because the neighbouring town of Dryburgh no longer exists (another victim of the wars), and partly because it has a lovely site in a sheltered valley by the Tweed. The abbey belonged to the Premonstratensians, a religious order founded in France, and was built from about 1150.

The pink-stoned ruins were chosen as the burial place for Sir Walter Scott and later for Earl Haig, the allied commander during WWI. There are some beautiful picnic spots.

The abbey (☎ 01835-822381; HS) is five miles south-east of Melrose on the B6404, which passes famous Scott's View, which overlooks the valley. Alternatively, it's a five-mile walk from Melrose. It's open Monday to Saturday from 9.30 am to 6.30 pm, Sunday from 2 to 6.30 pm, closing 2½ hours earlier between October and March; £2/75p.

Abbotsford

The home of Sir Walter Scott is definitely not an architectural masterpiece – the best one can say is that it's disjointed and kitsch – but it has a beautiful site, and is quite fascinating. There's an extraordinary collection of the great man's possessions. It's well worth visiting.

The house (☎ 01896-752043) is about three miles west of Melrose between the Tweed and the B6360. Frequent buses run between Galashiels and Melrose; alight at the Tweedbank traffic island and walk 15 minutes. It's open mid-March through October, Monday to Saturday from 10 am to 5 pm and Sunday from 2 to 5 pm; £3/1.50.

Thirlestane Castle

Thirlestane is one of the most fascinating of Scotland's castles. The massive original keep was built in the 13th century, but was refashioned and extended in the 16th century – with fairytale turrets and towers, but without compromising the scale and integrity of the building. It's still very much a family home and as a visitor you feel almost as if you're prying.

The castle (☎ 01578-722430) is 10 miles north of Melrose, near Lauder, off the A68. It's open during Easter, May, June and September on Sunday, Monday, Wednesday and Thursday, and July and August daily except Saturday. The grounds are open from noon to 6 pm and the castle is open from 2 to 5 pm; £4.

GALASHIELS
• *pop 13,500* • ☎ 01896

Galashiels is a busy, unprepossessing mill town strung along the A6091 three miles east of Melrose. It's something of a transport hub, but there are few pressing reasons to stay.

The TIC (☎ 755551), 3 St John St, is open April through September, Monday to Saturday from 10 am to 5 pm, Sunday from 1 to 3 pm (extended hours in July and August); and in October, Monday to Saturday.

Lowland (☎ 758484) is the main operator. There are frequent buses to/from Edinburgh, Melrose, Hawick and Peebles.

Gala Cycles (☎ 757587), 58 High St, hires mountain bikes from £10 per day.

SELKIRK
- *pop 5500*   • ☎ 01750

Selkirk is an unusual little town that climbs a steep ridge above Yarrow Water, a tributary of the Tweed. Mills came to the area in the early 1800s, but it's now a quiet place (much quieter than Galashiels or the textile centre of Hawick).

The TIC (☎ 720054), Halliwell's House, is open April through October, Monday to Saturday from 10 am to 5 pm, Sunday from 2 to 4 pm (extended hours July and August). The adjoining local **museum** is interesting.

The *County Hotel* (☎ 721233), 35 High St, Market Square, has good bar meals and accommodation from £23 per person.

Selkirk is on Lowland's No 95 service that runs between Hawick, Selkirk, Galashiels and Edinburgh.

JEDBURGH
- *pop 4000*   • ☎ 01835

Jedburgh has a number of interesting sites, which it has capitalised on with efficiency. It's the most visited of the Borders towns and has a tendency to look like a film set. On the other hand, it's an attractive town, and many of the old buildings and wynds have been intelligently restored.

The TIC (☎ 863435), Murray's Green, is large, efficient and open daily from April through October, and Monday to Friday from November through March.

Early-closing day is Thursday.

Jedburgh Abbey

Jedburgh Abbey dominates the town; it was founded in 1138 by David I as a priory for Augustininan canons. It was the site for a royal wedding and a coronation, but it has suffered the usual cycle of sacking and rebuilding. In fact, the red sandstone ruins are roofless, but comparatively complete.

The abbey (☎ 863925; HS) is open April through September from Monday to Saturday, 9.30 am to 6.30 pm, Sunday from 2 to 6.30 pm, and October through March, Monday to Saturday from 9.30 am to 4.30 pm and Sunday from 2 to 4.30 pm; £2.50/1.

Mary Queen of Scots House

Mary stayed here in 1566 after her famous ride to visit the injured Earl of Bothwell, her future husband, at Hermitage Castle. Although it's a beautiful 16th-century tower house, and worth a visit, the displays are spiritless and uninteresting. The house (☎ 863331) is open from March to mid-November, daily from 10 am to 5 pm; £2/1.

Places to Stay

B&Bs & Hotels The *Craigowen* (☎ 862604), 30 High St, has some rooms overlooking the abbey from £15 per person.

The *Kenmore Bank* (☎ 862369), Oxnam Rd, overlooks the abbey and is good value. The twins, doubles and family rooms all have bathrooms and the cost is around £22 per person.

Glenfriar's Hotel (☎ 862000), Friarsgate, is a very comfortable place with two singles, two twins and two doubles all with bathrooms, for £35/64.

Camping The *Elliot Park Camping & Caravanning Club Park* (☎ 863393), Edinburgh Rd, is about a mile north of the city centre; sites are around £6.

Places to Eat

The *Castlegate Restaurant* (☎ 862552), 1 Abbey Close, has a standard menu, with dishes like steak and kidney pie. It's a good place for either a full meal or just a cup of tea.

The *Pheasant Lounge Bar* (☎ 862708), 61 High St, has a good range of bar meals under

£5, including some interesting offerings like braised pheasant wrapped in bacon with wine sauce.

Getting There & Away

Jedburgh is 330 miles from London, 45 from Edinburgh, 17 from Galashiels and Selkirk, and 11 from Kelso.

Bus Jedburgh has good bus connections around the Borders. Lowland (☎ 01896-752237) is the main operator. There are regular connections to/from Hawick, Galashiels and Kelso. The No 23 service runs to/from Berwick-upon-Tweed via Kelso and Coldstream. The No 29 Edinburgh-Jedburgh service runs six times a day in each direction.

PEEBLES
- *pop 6500*   • ☎ *01721*

Peebles is a prosperous little town set among rolling hills on the banks of the River Tweed. There's a broad, attractive High St, an interesting local **museum**, and although it's not particularly notable, Peebles is a pleasant place to stay. The TIC (☎ 720138), High St, is open from April through October, Monday to Saturday from 10 am to 5 pm, Sunday from 1 to 3 pm (extended hours in July and August).

Places to Stay & Eat

Rowanbrae (☎ 720630), Northgate, has only two rooms but it's very pleasant. B&B costs £15.50 per person.

The Green Tree Hotel (☎ 720582), 41 Eastgate, is a well-organised, tidy hotel. There are a range of rooms, including singles, most with bathrooms. The nightly rate is £27.50 per person.

The County Hotel (☎ 720595), 35 High St, is a good pub, often with live music in the evening. It has some rooms (£19 per person), decent bar meals from around £5 and a more expensive restaurant.

Two miles from Peebles on the A703, *Cringletie House* (☎ 730233) is a comfortable country house hotel with an excellent restaurant. Rooms are from £54/65. There are set lunches for £15, set dinners for £26.

Getting There & Away

There are hourly Lowland buses to Edinburgh, Galashiels and Melrose.

Bicycle Scottish Border Trails (☎ 722934), Venlaw High Rd, organise bicycle tours – both on and off road. They also hire mountain bikes from £18 per day and tourers for £12. Prebooking is recommended, and if you're in a group of four or more there are discounts and bikes will be delivered to you free in the Peebles area.

AROUND PEEBLES
Neidpath Castle

Neidpath Castle is a tower house perched on a bluff above the River Tweed, one mile west of Peebles on the A72. It's a lovely spot, although there's not much to see inside. The castle (☎ 01721-720333) is open from Easter through September, Monday to Saturday from 11 am to 5 pm, Sunday from 1 to 5 pm; £2/1.

Traquair

Traquair (pronounced trarkweer) is one of Britain's great houses; there are many that are more aesthetically pleasing, but this one has a powerful, atmospheric beauty – and an exploration is like time travel.

Parts of the building are believed to have been constructed long before the first official record of its existence in 1107. The massive tower house was gradually expanded over the next 500 years, but has remained virtually unchanged since 1642.

Since the 15th century the house has belonged to various branches of the Stuart family and the family's unwavering Catholicism and loyalty to the Stuart cause is largely why development ceased when it did. The family's estate, wealth and influence was gradually whittled away after the Reformation, and there was neither the opportunity, nor, one suspects, the will, to make any changes.

One of the most fascinating rooms is the

concealed priest's room where priests secretly lived and gave mass – up to 1829 when the Catholic Emancipation Act was finally passed. Other beautiful time-worn rooms hold fascinating relics, including the cradle used by Mary for James VI of Scotland (who was also James I of England) and many letters written by the Stuart pretenders to their supporters.

In addition to the house, there's a maze, an art gallery, a small brewery producing Bear Ale, and an active craft community.

Traquair (☎ 01896-830323) is 1½ miles south of Innerleithen, about six miles east of Peebles. It's open July and August, daily from 10.30 am to 5.30 pm; April, May, June and September, daily from 12.30 to 5.30 pm; and in October, Friday to Sunday, 2 to 5 pm. Entry is £3.80/1.80.

HERMITAGE CASTLE

Hermitage Castle is a massive pile of stone with a heavy cubist beauty; it sits isolated beside a rushing stream surrounded by bleak and empty moorland. Dating from the 13th century, but substantially rebuilt in the 15th, it embodies the brutal history of the Borders; the stones themselves almost speak of the past. Sir Walter Scott considered it his favourite castle.

It is probably best known as the home of the Earl of Bothwell, and the spot where Mary Queen of Scots rode in 1566 to see him after he had been wounded in a border raid. It is also the spot where, in 1338, Sir William Douglas imprisoned his enemy Sir Alexander Ramsay and deliberately starved him to death. Ramsay survived for 17 days by eating grain that trickled into his pit (which can still be seen) from the granary above.

The castle (☎ 013873-76222; HS) is situated 5½ miles north-east of Newcastleton off the A7. It's open April through September from Monday to Saturday, 9.30 am to 6.30 pm, Sunday from 2 to 6.30 pm; and from October through March, Saturday from 9.30 am to 4.30 pm and Sunday from 2 to 4.30 pm; £1.20/75p.

Glasgow

• *pop 755,000* • *☎ 0141*

Glasgow is one of Britain's largest, liveliest and most interesting cities. It doesn't have the beauty of Edinburgh, although it does have a legacy of interesting Victorian architecture and some distinguished suburbs of terraced squares and crescents. What makes it appealing is its vibrancy and energy. 'Glasgow's Alive', say the billboards in the city, and it's true.

Twenty-five years ago, to outsiders the city's name stood for unemployment, economic depression and urban violence. It was known for the bloody confrontations that occurred between rival supporters of Protestant Rangers and Catholic Celtic football teams, and as the home of the Glasgow Kiss (a head butt). Yet by 1990 it had been elected European City of Culture. Between these years the city reinvented itself, rediscovering its rich cultural roots, proclaiming a new pride in itself through a well-orchestrated publicity campaign. In 1999 Glasgow will be the UK's City of Architecture & Design. Glasgow is now the third most popular destination in Britain for foreign tourists, after London and Edinburgh.

In the 80s and 90s there has been an incredible outburst of musical talent from Glasgow. This is the city that produced Simple Minds, Tears for Fears, Deacon Blue, Aztec Camera and Wet Wet Wet, as well as comedians like Billy Connolly and Stanley Baxter. Glasgow's Mayfest is now the UK's second-biggest arts festival after the Edinburgh Festival.

Although influenced by thousands of Irish immigrants, Glasgow is the most Scottish of cities – quite different to Edinburgh and completely different to anything south of the border. There's a unique blend of friendliness, urban chaos, black humour and energy. Glasgow has some excellent art galleries and museums (including the famous Burrell Collection) and all of them are free. There are numerous cheap restaurants, countless pubs

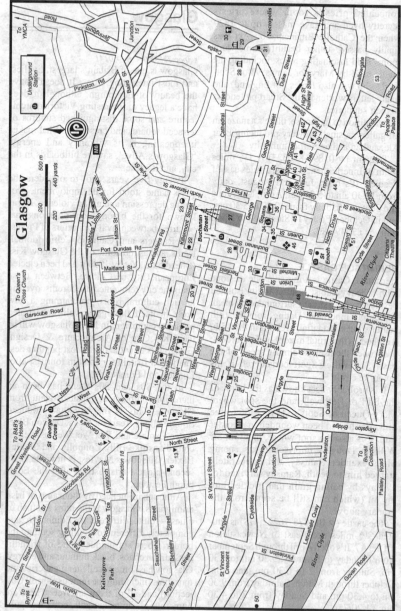

Glasgow

Underground Station

0   250   500 m
0   220   440 yards

and bars and, not just during Mayfest, a very lively arts scene. If the English cities are too bland for your taste, Glasgow should be the antidote.

History

Glasgow grew up around the cathedral founded by St Mungo in the 6th century. In 1451 the University of Glasgow was founded, and is the fourth-oldest university in Britain. Unfortunately, with the exception of the cathedral, virtually nothing of the medieval city remains. It was swept away by the energetic people of a new age – the age of capitalism, the Industrial Revolution, and the empire.

In the 18th century, much of Europe's tobacco trade with America came through Glasgow, and this was a great source of wealth for the city. Rum and sugar were also major imports from the New World. The city continued to prosper in the 19th century, when the tobacco trade was replaced by textile manufacture, shipbuilding, and the coal and steel industries.

The new industries created a huge demand for labour and peasants poured in from Ireland and the Highlands to crowd the city's tenements. In the mid-18th century the population was 17,500; by the end of the century it had risen to 100,000. Twenty years later it had doubled and by 1860, 400,000 people lived here. Working conditions in the factories were as dire as in other parts of the country, particularly for women and children. Life expectancy was a mere 30 years in the city in the second half of the 19th century, and there were four major outbreaks of cholera during this period.

While the workers suffered, the textile barons and shipping magnates prospered, and Glasgow could justifiably call itself the second city of the empire. Grand Victorian public buildings were constructed. Some of Glasgow's wealthy spent their fortunes on amassing the large collections of art which now form the basis of the city's excellent galleries.

In the first half of the 20th century Glasgow was the centre of Britain's munitions industry, supplying arms and ships for the two world wars. Glasgow's port and heavy industries then went into terminal decline. By the early 1970s the city looked doomed. Glasgow has always been predominantly working class (and proud of it) and,

SOUTHERN SCOTLAND

unlike middle-class Edinburgh with its numerous service industries, it had nothing to fall back on as the recession hit. Unemployment spiralled.

Certainly there is now renewed confidence in the city but behind all the hype and publicity, life in Glasgow is still tough for many people. Unemployment is high, housing often inadequate and the average standard of living low by UK standards. The city maintains its reputation as the heart attack capital of the world – according to a recent report women in Glasgow are seven times more likely to die from a heart attack than women in Spain or China. The record for men is not much better.

Orientation

Glasgow's sights are spread over a wide area. The city centre is built on a grid system on the north side of the River Clyde. The two railway stations (Central and Queen St), the bus station (Buchanan St) and the TIC are all within a couple of blocks of George Square, the main city square. Running along a ridge in the northern part of the city, Sauchiehall St (first syllable pronounced soch as in loch) has a pedestrian mall with numerous High St shops at its eastern end, and pubs and restaurants at the western end. Merchant City is the commercial district east of George Square.

The university and the youth hostel are north-west of the city centre around Kelvingrove Park, an area known as the West End. Pollok Country Park and the Burrell Collection are south-west of the centre, in South Side.

Motorways bore through the suburbs and the M8 sweeps round the western and northern edges of the centre. The airport is 10 miles to the west.

Information

Tourist Offices The main TIC (☎ 204 4400), 11 George Sq, has a free accommodation booking service and a bureau de change. It's open Monday to Saturday from 9 am to 6 pm with extended opening hours until 7 pm in June and September, and 8 pm in July and August. It's also open on Sunday from May through September, 10 am to 6 pm. There's also a branch at Glasgow airport.

Make sure you pick up a copy of the *Visitors Transport Guide Map* (free) which gives all the local transport options on a useful map. Travel information is also available from the St Enoch Sq Travel Centre (☎ 226 4826), St Enoch Square. It's open Monday to Saturday.

From the main TIC, there are guided walks (1½ hours, £2.50/1.50) of the city centre from May through September, Monday to Friday at 6 pm, and on Sunday at 10.30 am. There's also a cathedral walk at 2.15 pm on Wednesday and Sunday.

Cruises on the Clyde aboard the *Waverley*, the world's last ocean-going paddle steamer, leave from the Waverley Terminal. Operating in the summer only, there are cruises to numerous islands and coastal towns; phone ☎ 221 8152.

The List, available from newsagents (£1.80), is Glasgow's and Edinburgh's fortnightly guide to films, theatre, cabaret, music – the works. Invaluable.

Money American Express is at 115 Hope St (☎ 221 4366); it's open commercial hours from Monday to Friday, and to noon on Saturday.

Emergency As anywhere in the UK, dial ☎ 999 on any phone (free call).

George Square & City Chambers

The TIC is on George Square, a good starting point for exploring the city. The square is surrounded by imposing Victorian architecture, including the post office, the Bank of Scotland and the City Chambers. There are statues of Robert Burns, James Watt, Lord Clyde and, atop a 267-foot-high doric column, Sir Walter Scott.

The grand City Chambers (☎ 221 9600), the seat of local government, were built in the 1880s at the high point of the city's wealth. Their interior is even more extravagant than their exterior, and the chambers are sometimes used as a movie location to represent the Kremlin or the Vatican. There are free tours lasting 45 minutes from the main entrance, Monday to Friday, 10.30 am and 2.30 pm.

A Walk Through Merchant City

An interesting hour-long walk can be taken from George Square to Glasgow Cathedral through Merchant City, a planned 18th-century civic development. The Tobacco Lords were the entrepreneurs who opened up European trade with America, importing tobacco, rum and sugar in the 18th century. With their wealth they built the warehouses, offices and gracious houses here. The area has been redeveloped, with warehouses being converted into apartments for Glaswegian yuppies, and stylish shopping malls such as the Italian Centre to serve their retail needs.

Once you've seen the City Chambers, cross George Square and walk one block south down Queen St to **Stirling's Library**. This colonnaded building was once the Royal Exchange, where business transactions were negotiated. Built in 1827, it later became a library, and is now being converted into an art museum.

The library faces Ingram St, which you follow east for two blocks. To the right, down Garth St, is **Trades House**, designed by Robert Adam in 1791 to house the trades guild. This is the only surviving building in Glasgow by this famous Scottish architect. A further two blocks east along Ingram St brings you to **Hutchesons' Hall**. Built in 1805 to a design by David Hamilton, this elegant building is now maintained by the National Trust for Scotland. It's open on weekdays until 5 pm and on Saturday until 4 pm.

Retrace your steps one block and continue south down Glassford St past **The Warehouse**, a distinctive Art-Nouveau building that now houses designer clothes shops. Turn right into Wilson St and first left along Virginia St, lined with the old warehouses of the Tobacco Lords. The **Tobacco Exchange** became the Sugar Exchange in 1820 and many of the old warehouses here are now being converted into flats.

Back on Wilson St, the bulky **Sheriff Court House** fills a whole block. It was originally built as Glasgow's town hall. Continue east past **Ingram Square**, another warehouse development, to the **City Halls**, now used for concerts. The city's markets were once here. Turn right from Albion St into Blackfriars St. Emerging onto the High St, turn left and follow the street up to the cathedral.

Walks & Cycle Routes

There are numerous green spaces within the city. **Pollok Country Park** surrounds the Burrell Collection and there are many wooded trails here. Nearer the centre of the city, the Kelvin Walkway follows the River Kelvin through Kelvingrove Park, the Botanic Gardens and on to Dawsholm Park.

There are several long-distance pedestrian/cycle routes that originate in Glasgow and follow off-road routes for most of the distance. The TIC has a range of maps and leaflets detailing these routes, most of which start from Bell's Bridge (by the SECC).

The Glasgow-Loch Lomond Route follows the Clyde walkway on the north side of the river through residential and industrial areas, reaching Loch Lomond via the towpath by the River Leven. There's an extension to this route all the way to Killin, from Balloch via Aberfoyle, Loch Katrine and Callander to link with the Glen Ogle Trail.

The Glasgow-Greenock Route runs via Paisley, this first section mainly on roads. From Johnstone to Greenock the route follows a disused railway line. Sculpture from a local community arts project brightens parts of the way.

The Glasgow-Irvine/Ardrossan Cycle Way runs via Paisley, then off-road as far as Glengarnock. From here to Kilwinning minor roads are used. Ferries to the Isle of Arran, popular with cyclists, leave from Ardrossan.

The West Highland Way is a long-distance footpath that begins in Milngavie, seven miles north of Glasgow. (See the Activities chapter at the start of this book for more information.)

Glasgow Cathedral & Precincts

The oldest part of the city is centred on Glasgow Cathedral, to the east of the modern centre. The area was given a facelift with the opening of St Mungo's Museum of Religious Life & Art. The money for the restoration of the cathedral was sensibly spent on updating the heating system rather than on giving the blackened exterior a high-pressure hose-down. Nearby, Provand's Lordship, the city's oldest house, completes a trio of interesting sights.

The crumbling tombs of the city's rich and famous crowd the recently-renovated necropolis behind the cathedral.

It takes about 15 to 20 minutes to walk here direct from George Square but numerous buses pass this way. Nos 11, 12, 38 and 51 follow Cathedral St; Nos 1, 6, 6A, 8 and 41 run along George St.

Glasgow Cathedral As the only Scottish cathedral on the mainland to have survived the Reformation intact, Glasgow Cathedral (☎ 552 6891) is regarded as a perfect example of pre-Reformation Gothic architecture.

This has been hallowed ground for over 1500 years. The site was blessed for Christian burial in 397 by St Ninian. In the following century Kentigern, also known as St Mungo, accompanied the body of a holy man from Stirlingshire to be buried here. He stayed to found a monastic community, and built a simple church. The first stone building was consecrated in 1136, in the presence of King David I, but burnt down in 1197 and was rebuilt as the lower church. The current building dates from the early 13th century, and the tower with its spire is the only one still standing on a Scottish medieval church.

You enter through a side door into the **nave**, hung with regimental colours. To your left, Francis Spear's 'The Creation' fills the west window, dedicated in 1958; much of the

cathedral's stained glass is modern. Above the nave, the wooden roof has been restored many times since its original construction but some of the timber still dates from the 14th century.

The cathedral is divided by the late 15th-century quire screen, decorated with seven pairs of figures to represent the Seven Deadly Sins. Beyond is the **quire**. The four stained-glass panels of the east window, depicting the apostles and also by Francis Spear, are particularly effective. At the north-east corner is the entrance to the 15th-century **upper chapter house**. Glasgow University was founded here; it's now used as a sacristy.

The most interesting part of the cathedral, **the lower church**, is reached by a stairway. Its forest of pillars creates a powerful atmosphere around St Mungo's tomb, the focus of a famous medieval pilgrimage that was believed to be as meritorious as a visit to Rome. Edward I paid three visits to the shrine in 1301.

The cathedral is open to visitors Monday to Saturday from 9.30 am to 6 pm, and from 2 to 5 pm on Sunday. In winter it closes at 4 pm daily. Sunday services are at 11 am and 6.30 pm.

St Mungo's Museum of Religious Life & Art Standing near the cathedral, the award-winning St Mungo Museum (☎ 553 2557) was opened in 1993. From its inception, it was a highly controversial project, but it's understandably difficult to attempt to outline the world's main religions and choose works of art to represent each one. The result, however, is well worth visiting, and is small enough to give visitors time to take everything in.

The building that houses the collection may look like a renovated old building, but it's only a few years old, a £6.5 million reconstruction of the bishop's palace that once stood here. Inside it's best to watch the 10-minute video before looking round the museum. There are three galleries, representing religion as art, religious life and, on the top floor, religion in Scotland. In the main gallery Dali's *Christ of St John of the Cross* hangs beside statues of the Buddha and Hindu deities. Outside, there's Britain's only Zen garden.

There's a good restaurant downstairs serving vegetarian dishes and an occasional non-veg option. Soup and a roll is £1.25, main dishes £3.50. The fact that you won't find beef on the menu has nothing to do with the BSE scare; it would hardly be appropriate in a museum of this nature.

The museum is open daily from 10 am to 5 pm (from 11 am on Sunday); entry is free.

Provand's Lordship Across the road from the St Mungo Museum, Provand's Lordship (☎ 552 8819) is the oldest house in Glasgow. Built in 1471 as a manse for the chaplain of St Nicholas Hospital, it's said to have been visited by Mary Queen of Scots, James II and James IV. It's now a museum of various period displays connected with the house. These are as diverse as a 16th-century room of one of the chaplains who lived here, and a 20th-century sweet shop. Provand's Lordship is open daily until 5 pm; entry is free.

Burrell Collection
The Burrell Collection (☎ 649 7151), Glasgow's top attraction, was amassed by wealthy industrialist Sir William Burrell before it was given to the city and housed in a prize-winning museum in the Pollok Country Park, three miles south of the city. It's an idiosyncratic collection, including Chinese porcelain, medieval furniture, and paintings by Renoir and Cézanne. It is not so big as to be overwhelming, and the stamp of the individual collector creates an intriguing coherence.

The building was the result of a design competition in 1971. If it had not been run during a postal strike, necessitating an extension of the closing deadline, Barry Gasson's winning entry would not have been completed. The result is a building which from the outside seems something of a hybrid but from the inside is truly spectacular, an inspired setting for an exquisite collection of tapestries, oriental porcelain, paintings, and European stained glass. Floor-to-ceiling windows let the natural light flood in, and the trees and landscape outside blend with the exhibits to stunning effect.

Carpeted floors mean silence to contemplate the beautifully displayed treasures, which both enhance and are in turn enhanced by their environment. Carved-stone Romanesque doorways are incorporated into the structure so one actually walks through them. Some galleries are reconstructions of rooms from Hutton Castle, the Burrell residence. Even the seating provided for the public is of superb design and production quality.

The inexpensive café on the lower ground floor is light and airy with the same floor-to-ceiling windows, hung with heraldic glass medallions.

The Burrell Collection is open from 10 am to 5 pm, Monday to Saturday, and from 11 am on Sunday; entrance is free. There are occasional guided tours. Numerous buses pass the gates (including Nos 45, 48A and 57 from the centre), and there's a bus service between the gallery and the park gates (a pleasant 10-minute walk). Alternatively, catch a train to Pollokshaws West from Central station (one every half-hour; the second station on the light blue line to the south). Bring a picnic lunch if the weather allows.

Pollok House & Haggs Castle
Also in Pollok Country Park, and a 10-minute walk from the Burrell Collection, Pollok House (☎ 632 0274) contains a fine collection of Spanish paintings, including works by El Greco and Goya. The house is Georgian and parts have been redecorated with historically correct but bizarre-looking colour schemes. The whole place has a faintly institutionalised feel but is enlivened by the cheery and chattering staff. There's a tearoom in the old kitchens. Entrance is free and it's open daily until 5 pm.

Haggs Castle (☎ 427 2725), a 15-minute walk north from the Burrell Collection through the park, is a children's museum.

There are clear explanations of Scottish history and several hands-on exhibits. It's open daily.

Mackintosh Buildings

There are a number of superb Art-Nouveau buildings designed by the Scottish architect and designer, Charles Rennie Mackintosh (CRM). There are occasional day tours of several of these buildings, two or three times a month in summer. Contact the CRM Society (☎ 946 6600) for details.

Glasgow School of Art Widely recognised as Mackintosh's greatest building, the Glasgow School of Art (☎ 353 4526), 167 Renfrew St, still houses the educational institution. You can't fail to be impressed by the thoroughness of the design; the architect's pencil seems to have shaped everything inside and outside the building. The interior design is strikingly austere, with simple colour combinations (often just black and cream) and those uncomfortable-looking high-backed chairs for which he is famous. The library, designed as an addition in 1907, is a masterpiece of rectangular pillars, horizontal beams and Mackintosh's characteristic linear style.

There are guided tours of the building Monday to Friday at 11 am and 2 pm, and on Saturday at 10.30 am (£3.50/2), but parts of the school may be closed to visitors if they're in use. The building is closed on Saturday afternoon and on Sunday.

Willow Tearoom Located at 217 Sauchiehall St, the Willow Tearoom (☎ 332 0521) is more Mockintosh than Mackintosh – a reconstruction of the tearoom Mackintosh designed and furnished in 1904 for restaurateur Kate Cranston. The restaurant closed in 1926 and the premises were then occupied by a series of retail businesses. Reconstruction took two years and the Willow opened as a tearoom again in 1980. Sauchiehall means 'lane of willows', hence the choice of a stylised willow motif.

Charles Rennie Mackintosh

The quirky, linear and geometric designs of this famous Scottish architect and designer have had almost as much influence on the city as have Gaudi's on Barcelona. Many of the buildings Mackintosh designed in Glasgow are now open to the public, and you'll see his tall, thin, Art-Nouveau typeface repeatedly reproduced.

Born in 1868, he studied at the Glasgow School of Art. In 1895, when he was aged only 27, his design won a competition for the School of Art's new building. The first part was opened in 1899 and is considered to be the earliest example of Art-Nouveau in Britain, and Mackintosh's supreme architectural achievement. This building demonstrates his skill in combining function and style.

Mackintosh applied himself to every facet of design, from whole facades to the smallest window fastener. As a furniture designer and decorative artist, he designed the interiors for Kate Cranston's chain of Glasgow tearooms between 1897 and 1911. The Willow Tearoom, 217 Sauchiehall, has now been fully restored and reopened as a tearoom.

Although Mackintosh's genius was quickly recognised on the Continent (he contributed to a number of exhibitions in France, Germany and Austria), he did not receive the same encouragement in Scotland. His architectural career here lasted only until 1913 when he moved to London to concentrate on furniture design. He died in 1928. ∎

Queues for light meals and tea (see Places to Eat) often extend into the gift shop and jeweller's downstairs.

Queen's Cross Church Now the headquarters of the CRM Society, Queen's Cross Church (☎ 946 6600), 870 Garscube Rd, is the only one of Mackintosh's church designs to be built. The simplicity of the design is particularly inspiring.

There's an information centre, a small display and a gift shop. It's open to visitors on Tuesday, Thursday and Friday from noon to 5 pm, and on Sunday from 2.30 pm. Admission is free.

Other Mackintoshiana The principal rooms from CRM's house have been reconstructed as the **Mackintosh House** at the Hunterian Art Gallery. At the Kelvingrove Art Gallery & Museum there's a display of his paintings and decorative art.

Scotland Street School (☎ 429 1202), 225 Scotland St, is an impressive Mackintosh building dominated by two glass-stair towers. It's now a museum of education, which may sound dull but is actually fascinating. It's open Monday to Saturday, 10 am to 5 pm, and on Sunday from 2 pm. Admission is free.

Although designed in 1901 as an entry to a competition run by a German magazine, the **Art Lover's House**, Drumbreck Rd, Bellahouston Park, was built only in 1990. There are plans to open the house to the public in 1997. Contact the CRM Society (☎ 946 6600) for times.

Twenty-three miles north-west of Glasgow at Helensburgh is **Hill House** (☎ 01436-673900), Mackintosh's domestic masterpiece now in the hands of the National Trust for Scotland.

The Tenement House
For an extraordinary time-capsule experience, visit the small apartment in the Tenement House (☎ 333 0183), 145 Buccleuch St. It gives a vivid insight into middle-class city life at the turn of the century, with box-beds, original kitchen range and all the fixtures and fittings of the family who lived here for more than 50 years. It's an interesting place but very National Trust – surely the Toward family wouldn't have kept it quite so squeaky clean and orderly as the National Trust for Scotland manages to now.

Despite the additional exhibition area in the ground-floor flat, it can get crowded. The flat is open daily from 1.30 to 5 pm from March to October. For the rest of the year it's open at weekends only, from 2 to 4 pm. Entry is £2.60/1.70.

Hunterian Museum & Art Gallery
Part of the university, and now housed in two separate buildings on either side of University Ave, the Hunterian was opened in 1807 as Scotland's first public museum. It houses the collection of William Hunter (1718-83), famous physician, medical teacher and one time student of the university.

The Hunterian Museum (☎ 330 4221), in the university building, comprises a disparate collection of artefacts including a notable coin collection, fossils and minerals, dinosaur eggs, Romano-British stone slabs and carvings, a display detailing the archaeological history of Scotland, and some of Captain Cook's curios from his voyages to the South Seas.

The Hunterian Art Gallery (☎ 330 5431) is nearby at 82 Hillhead St. Behind a pair of imposing cast-aluminium doors by Edinburgh-born Paolozzi is the art collection, opened in its new home in 1980. The Scottish colourists – Peploe, JD Fergusson, Cadell – are well represented, including McTaggart's Impressionistic Scottish landscapes, and a gem by Thomas Millie Dow. There is a special collection of James McNeill Whistler's limpid prints, drawings and paintings. Some of his own furniture and household goods are also here, and it's interesting to compare them to the contents of the Mackintosh House, the final section in the gallery.

Set up as a reconstruction of architect Charles Rennie Mackintosh's Glasgow home which had to be demolished, the style of the Mackintosh House is quite startling even today. You ascend from the gallery's gloomy ground floor into the cool, white austere drawing room. There is something other-worldly about the very mannered style of the beaten silver panels, the long backed chairs, and the surface decorations echoing Celtic manuscript illuminations. The guest bedroom is impossibly elegant and dazzling, in blue and white stripes.

The Hunterian is open Monday to Saturday, from 9.30 am to 5 pm; the Mackintosh House is closed from 12.30 to 1.30 pm. Entrance is free. There's a coffee bar by the museum's entrance and next to the art gallery is the student refectory. Bus Nos 44 and 59 pass this way from the city centre.

Kelvingrove Art Gallery & Museum

Opened in 1902, this grand Victorian cathedral of culture (☎ 357 3929) should not be missed, particularly for its excellent collection of Scottish and European art.

The impressive central hall is dominated at one end by organ pipes; recitals are an integral part of the museum programme. An authentic museum smell emanates from the natural history of Scotland section that is popular with school tours. Also downstairs there's a rather dowdy presentation of some interesting artefacts, including archaeological finds of prehistoric Scotland, European arms and armour, and silver.

The art gallery upstairs houses the city's art collection of 19th and 20th-century works. Scottish painters of luminous landscapes and still lifes are comprehensively represented – Melville, McTaggart, Cadell, Crawhall; and, among the moderns, Paolozzi, Bruce McLean, Hockney and Jasper Johns. Other paintings include Rembrandt's wonderful *Man in Armour*, and works by Botticelli, Monet, Van Gogh and Picasso.

Grandly set back from the road in Kelvingrove Park, just west of Kelvin Way, the art gallery and museum are open daily from 10 am to 5 pm (from 11 am on Sunday); entrance is free. Any bus for Dumbarton Rd passes this way; Kelvin Hall is the nearest

underground station. There's an inexpensive café here but it does not beckon with style or atmosphere.

Other Things to See

Across the street from the Kelvingrove Art Gallery & Museum is a surprisingly interesting and very comprehensive **Museum of Transport** (☎ 357 3929). Exhibits include a reproduction of a 1938 Glasgow street scene that's very well done, a display of cars made in Scotland, plus assorted railway locos, trams, bikes and model ships. It's open daily from 10 am to 5 pm (from 11 am on Sunday); entrance is free.

On Glasgow Green, the city's oldest park, **The People's Palace** (☎ 554 0223) was built in the late 19th century as a cultural centre for Glasgow's East End. It's now a splendid museum of social history, telling the story of the city from 1175 to the present. The adjoining Winter Gardens are also worth seeing. It's open daily from 10 am (11 am on Sunday) until 5 pm.

The Barrows (pronounced barras), Glasgow's flea-market on Gallowgate, should not be missed. There are almost 1000 stalls and people come here just for a wander as much as for shopping, which gives the place a holiday air. It takes place only on Saturday and Sunday. Watch your wallet.

Special Events

Not to be outdone by Edinburgh, Glasgow has developed two major festivals of its own. Mayfest, in the first three weeks of May, has a strong mix of Scottish and international performers. There is an excellent international jazz festival early in July.

Other festivals include the international folk festival which takes place in late June, the Scottish Proms (classical music) in mid-June, and the World Pipe Band Championships in mid-August.

Places to Stay

Finding somewhere decent in July and August can be difficult – for a B&B, get into town reasonably early and use the TIC's free booking service. Unfortunately, Glasgow's

B&Bs are expensive by Scottish standards – you may have to pay up to £16. At weekends many of the expensive business hotels slash their prices by up to 50%, making them great value for tourists.

Hostels & Colleges The excellent *Youth Hostel* (☎ 332 3004), is at 7 Park Terrace. The building was once a hotel, so there are mainly four-bed rooms, many with *en suite* facilities, as well as a small number of doubles. In summer, it is advisable to make a booking. It's open all day and the nightly charge is £10.45/9. From Central station take bus No 44 or 59 and ask for the first stop on Woodlands Rd.

Berkeley Globetrotters (☎ 221 7880), 63 Berkeley St, has beds from £8 (£6.50 if you have your own bedding) in dorms, £9.50 in twin rooms. Phone ahead for bookings. Berkeley St is a western continuation of Bath St (one block south of Sauchiehall St). The hostel's just past the Mitchell Library.

Near the YHA hostel, the *Glasgow Backpackers Hostel* (☎ 332 5412), Kelvin Lodge, 8 Park Circus, is one of the university's halls of residence, and so is only open from July through September. Beds are from £8.90. This is an Independent Backpackers Hostel, and very popular. Nearby, at 4, 5 and 12A Woodlands Terrace, Woodlands Houses (☎ 644 5391) provide backpacker accommodation for £10. They're also only open in the summer.

The *University of Glasgow* (☎ 330 5385) has a range of B&B accommodation at £20.50/36, and self-catering at £11 from mid-March to mid-April, and July, August and September.

The *University of Strathclyde* (☎ 553 4148) also opens its halls of residence to tourists during the vacation period; charges are from £8.50. If you don't mind staying farther out of town, its cheapest B&B accommodation is at Jordanhill Campus, 76 Southbrae Drive. Comfortable rooms are £18/28, and bus No 44 from Central station goes to the college gates. The university's impressive Art-Deco Baird Hall offers some

B&B accommodation year round for £22/36. It's in a great location at 460 Sauchiehall St.

The *YMCA Glasgow Aparthotel* (☎ 558 6166), David Naismith Court, 33 Petershill Drive, is a characterless tower block north of the M8. With continental breakfast the nightly charge is £17/28.

Camping *Craigendmuir Caravan Park* (☎ 779 4159), Campsie View, Stepps, is the nearest, but it's still a 15-minute walk from Stepps station. It takes vans and tents for £5.50 (two people).

B&Bs & Hotels – city centre *McLay's Guest House* (☎ 332 4796) is labyrinthine, but brilliantly located at 264 Renfrew St, which is behind Sauchiehall St. Considering the location, you can't quibble at £17.50 for a single room without bathroom, or £19.50 with. There are doubles for £33, or £37 with bath.

If you can't get in there try *The Victorian House* (☎ 332 0129), 212 Renfrew St – just down from the School of Art. It's a large guesthouse; prices are £21/36 with shared bathroom, £27/40 attached. There are several other similarly priced places along this street, including the *Willow Hotel* (☎ 332 2332) at No 228 and *Hampton Court Hotel* (☎ 332 6623) at No 230.

Babbity Bowster (☎ 552 5055), 16 Blackfriars St, is a very lively pub/restaurant (see the Entertainment section) with six bedrooms. Singles/doubles with attached bathrooms cost £40/60. It's a great place to stay but forget it if you like to turn in early with a nice cup of cocoa.

The *Charing Cross Tower Hotel* (☎ 221 1000), in the newly-renovated tower above Charing Cross railway station, offers good-value accommodation at £38.50 for a double room with attached bath. Breakfast is £5 in the self-service restaurant.

The *Town House Hotel* (☎ 332 3320), West George St, is a very comfortable hotel right in the centre of the city, and near the TIC. It costs £90/100 during the week, £55/65 at the weekend. Breakfast is an extra £8.50.

B&Bs & Hotels – east There's a batch of reasonable-value B&Bs to the east of the Necropolis. *Brown's Guest House* (☎ 554 6797), 2 Onslow Drive, has rooms from £15/26. *Craigpark Guest House* (☎ 554 4160), 33 Circus Drive, charges from £16/28.

One of the best places to stay in Glasgow is the small *Cathedral House Hotel* (☎ 552 3519), 28 Cathedral Square. Housed in a Victorian baronial-style building complete with turrets, it's very close to the cathedral and easily accessible from the M8. There's a pleasant café-bar, and in Glasgow's only Icelandic restaurant here diners cook at the table on hot rocks. The well-appointed rooms cost from £50/65.

B&Bs & Hotels – West End Many of the places to stay in this area are on or around Great Western Rd. There are several B&Bs on Hillhead St (just south of Great Western Rd and near Byres Rd), including *Chez Nous Guest House* (☎ 334 2977) at No 33, with rooms from £18.50/37 to £25/50 and *Iona Guest House* (☎ 334 2346), at No 39, which is smaller and a little cheaper.

Kelvin View Guest House (☎ 339 8257), 411 North Woodside Rd, is just north of Great Western Rd and the M8. Rooms here are from £17/32, and they also have a few rooms with attached bathroom. There are several other similarly priced B&Bs on this road.

The *Kirklee Hotel* (☎ 334 5555), 11 Kensington Gate, is more upmarket, and like the plants in the window boxes here you'll be very carefully tended. This place is highly recommended. All rooms have attached shower/bath and they cost £44/59. A little further west along Great Western Rd, at 14 Belhaven Terrace, the *Terrace House Hotel* (☎ 337 3377) is a very comfortable place to stay. There are 17 rooms, with attached bathrooms. They charge £55/76 during the week and £40/60 at weekends. In the same area, *The Town House* (☎ 357 0862), 4 Hughenden Terrace, is similar to these last two places, very well run and an excellent choice. Rooms are from £48/59.

There are a number of places just south of Kelvingrove Park. The *Alamo Guest House* (☎ 339 2395), 46 Gray St, with rooms from £17/30, is good value. *Smith's Hotel* (☎ 339 6363) is at 963 Sauchiehall St. They charge £17/31 for their budget rooms.

Probably the best hotel in Glasgow is *One Devonshire Gardens* (☎ 339 2001), address the same, just off Great Western Rd. Sumptuously decorated, and occupying three classical terrace houses, the atmosphere is that of a luxurious country house. There are 27 rooms, each very well appointed, at £148/187. At the weekend, doubles are £120. As one might expect, there's an excellent restaurant here, too.

B&Bs & Hotels – south of the Clyde On and around Pollokshaws Rd, on the way to Pollok Country Park and the Burrell Collection, there are several places to stay in this quiet suburb. *Regent Guest House* (☎ 422 1199), 44 Regent Park Square, has B&B accommodation from £20 per person. Some rooms have attached bath. *Reidholm Guest House* (☎ 423 1855), further down the terrace at No 36, is a little cheaper.

On the other side of Pollokshaws Rd, just south of Queen's Park, *Boswell Hotel* (☎ 632 9812), 27 Mansionhouse Rd, off Langside Ave, can be an entertaining place to stay. The Boswell is better known as a watering hole, with its four bars and live folk music on Saturday, jazz on Sunday. Singles/doubles are £38.50/55 during the week, £30/45 at weekends; all with attached bath/showers.

North of Pollok Country Club, in the Bellahouston area just off the M8, there's another group of B&Bs, but most are small places. *Mrs Sinclair's* (☎ 427 1006), 23 Drumbreck Rd, costs from £18 per person and is open from January to September. *Mr Bristow's* (☎ 427 0129), down the same road at No 56, is similarly priced and open year-round. *Mrs Ross's* (☎ 427 0194), 3 Beech Ave, has rooms from £25/36 with shower.

Places to Eat
Twenty-five years ago, when the pubs in Scotland closed at 10 pm, Glaswegians went

to restaurants to take advantage of extended licensing hours, not for the food. Things are very different now and Glasgow not only has an excellent range of places to eat but many are also very moderately priced.

The West End probably has the greatest range of restaurants, everything from Glasgow's most famous place to eat, the upmarket Ubiquitous Chip, to cheap cafés where they really do serve chips with everything. In the city centre, however, and along Sauchiehall there's also no shortage of places to eat.

If you're on a budget, have your main meal at lunchtime – the set lunches offered by many restaurants are usually very good value at £3 to £5.

West End The main restaurant/pub area in the West End is about ¾ mile west of the YH, around Byres Rd. The nearest underground station is Hillhead. Just off Byres Rd, on the east side, Ashton Lane is packed with places to eat. Cheapest is the *Grosvenor Café* (☎ 339 1848), at No 35, where you can get soup and filled rolls during the day, and hot meals after 7 pm. Try the pizza with egg. This is a popular student hangout.

Some of Glasgow's top restaurants are also on Ashton Lane. *The Ubiquitous Chip* (☎ 334 5007), at No 12, has earned a solid reputation for its excellent Scottish cuisine, fresh seafood and game, and for the length of its wine list. A three-course dinner with coffee will set you back £26. Set amongst potted plants of arboreal proportions this is an excellent place for a night out. There's a cheaper restaurant here, *Upstairs at the Chip*, where a couple of courses at lunchtime will cost less than £9. *Mitchells* (☎ 339 2220), No 31, is an informal bistro with excellent Scottish dishes.

Back on Byres Rd, *The University Café* (☎ 339 5217) at No 87, is a university institution. It's very cheap; there's fish and chips, excellent pizza and superb home-made ice-cream.

On the west side of Byres Rd is Ruthven Lane where, amongst the whacky shops, are a number of interesting places to eat. At *Back Alley* (☎ 334 7165), 8 Ruthven Lane, the range of sauces and toppings make this very much more than just a burger joint. At No 11 is the *Puppet Theatre* (☎ 339 8444) a classy new place featuring Scottish cuisine. Dinner is £19.95 for three courses; lunch £9.95 for two courses. Down the lane at No 61 is *Di Maggio's* (☎ 334 8560), good for pizzas and pasta.

Those staying in the vicinity of Kelvingrove Park will find a scattering of restaurants along Gibson St and on and around Great Western Rd. *Shalimar* (☎ 339 6453), 25 Gibson St, is a large Indian restaurant which offers a five-course buffet dinner for £8.50.

Insomnia Café (☎ 332 5500), 38 Woodland Rd, has never closed since it first opened in October 1995. There are sandwiches from £1.75, a wide range of other light meals, herbal teas and coffees in Scotland's first 24-hour café.

Near the Kelvingrove Art Gallery, Dutch-run *Janssens* (☎ 334 9682), 1355 Argyle St, serves good lunches, everything from interesting sandwiches to full meals.

The vegetarian *Bay Tree Café* (☎ 334 5898), 403 Great Western Rd, is a workers' co-operative that's excellent value. Filling main dishes cost less than £4, salads are generous, and there's a good range of hot drinks. The Café is famous for its all-day Sunday brunch, served from 11 am to 8 pm, including vegetarian sausage, tattie scone, mushrooms and beans (£2.90). Open daily except Monday, it closes at 9 pm (8 pm on Sunday). If you're in a hurry, the café also serves takeaways.

City Centre There are a number of good choices on Sauchiehall St. *Ristoro Ciao Italia* (☎ 332 4565), at No 441, is an efficient Italian restaurant where you should be able to eat and drink for around £10. One block east, *Loon Fung* (☎ 332 1240), 417 Sauchiehall, is one of the best Chinese places in town. There are set dinners from £15; a three-course lunch is £5.95.

There's a pleasant café with sandwiches, salads and a small range of main courses (£4 to £6) at the *Centre for Contemporary Arts* (☎ 332 7521), 346 Sauchiehall St.

The main branch of Glasgow's best known bakery chain, *Bradford's*, is at No 245, and there's a good tearoom upstairs where they also do light meals.

The *Willow Tearoom* (☎ 332 0521), above a jewellery shop at 217 Sauchiehall St, was designed as a tearoom by Charles Rennie Mackintosh in 1903. Last orders are at 4.15 pm, and for lunch and tea the queues can be long. Avoid them by arriving when it opens at 9 am (11 am on Sunday) and splash out on a superior breakfast of smoked salmon, scrambled eggs and toast (£3.25).

Continuing east along Sauchiehall, there's a branch of the patisserie chain, *Delifrance* (☎ 353 2700), at No 119. Their filled baguettes (£1.70) are good.

Glasgow's first Balti restaurant, the *Balti Bar* (☎ 332 6289), is at 51 West Regent St. It's very good value and popular with students. Upstairs is the more expensive *Bombay Bistro* (☎ 331 1980).

At Princes Square, the stylish shopping centre on Buchanan St, one floor is given over to restaurants and foodstalls ranging from Caribbean to Chinese. Just off Buchanan St, at 11 Exchange Pl, is *Rogano* (☎ 248 4055), a stunning Art-Deco bar and restaurant modelled on the saloons of the *Queen Mary* (built in the shipyards of the Clyde). Famous for its seafood, it's an expensive place to eat; the *Café Rogano* downstairs is cheaper.

Near the St Enoch Centre is the *Granary* (☎ 226 3770), 82 Howard St. It's mainly vegetarian but also has a few non-veg choices.

In Merchant City, near the City Halls at 64 Albion St, is *Café Gandolfi* (☎ 552 6813). Once part of the old cheesemarket, it's now an excellent bistro and upmarket coffee shop – very much the place to be seen.

One of the best restaurants in the city is *The Buttery* (☎ 221 8188), 652 Argyle St, just west of the M8. The menu is Scottish, a three-course dinner will cost £20 to £25, and it's closed on Sunday. Downstairs is the cheaper bistro, the *Belfry* (☎ 221 0630). A

two-course theatre-dinner (served from 6 to 7.30 pm) costs £8.95.

At 157 North St, near the Mitchell Library, is *Mitchell's* (☎ 204 4312), an excellent bistro.

Entertainment

Some of the best nightlife in Scotland is to be found in the pubs and clubs of Glasgow. Most pubs also do food, although many stop serving around 8 pm. For the latest information, get a copy of *The List*. Also look out for the freebie leaflet, *The Live Scene*, a monthly listing of Glasgow's live music scene.

If it's a wee bit of Scottish dancing you're after, rather than a night in the pubs or clubs, go to the *Riverside* (☎ 248 3144), Fox St (off Clyde St) on Friday or Saturday evening for the ceilidh. Doors open at 8 pm and the band starts at 9 pm. It's good clean fun for a fiver.

Note that owing to an odd law currently in force in Glasgow you may not be allowed entrance to a club after 1 am. Check the clubs recommended in this section for the current regulations.

Pubs – West End The *Halt Bar*, 160 Woodlands Rd, is a popular university pub that hasn't yet been tarted up. There's live music (free) most nights, great atmosphere, and it's open until midnight on Friday and Saturday, 11 pm on other nights.

Further along Woodlands Rd, at No 246, there's the *Uisge Beatha* (Water of Life), which keeps the same hours. The name's Gaelic for whisky. It's a friendly place with eclectic décor and three bar areas.

Chimmy Chunga's (☎ 334 0884), 499 Great Western Rd, is a Mexican theme pub that offers a full range of meals. From noon to 7 pm you can get two main courses for £5.

There are numerous pubs on or around Byres Rd. *Curlers* (☎ 334 1284), at No 256, is very popular with students who come for the bargain three-course set lunch (£3.25) and stay on for the live jazz (midweek) – or to watch MTV here. Much smarter is *Cul de Sac* (☎ 334 4749), the place to be seen in Ashton Lane, at No 44; meals are cheap – £3

SOUTHERN SCOTLAND

to £4. The *Ubiquitous Chip* at No 12 also has a bar.

Pubs – city centre By the Union St exit of Central station is the basement *Underworld* (☎ 221 5020), opened in 1996. It's a wacky, stylish but not too pretentious place with a restaurant area serving Tex-Mex food.

Bar 10 (☎ 221 8353) is a stylish café bar at 10 Mitchell Lane, off Buchanan St. It was designed by Ben Kelly who was responsible for Manchester's famous Dry Bar and Hacienda.

The subterranean *Brunswick Cellars* (☎ 353 3667), 239 Sauchiehall St, is a popular bar that also does cheap food. Their lunches are excellent value, and between 3 pm and 7 pm they give student discounts on food.

The 13th Note (☎ 553 1638), 80 Glassford St, is a vegan café and pub that serves meals from noon to 7 pm, with main courses from less than £3. There's lasagne, pitta pizzas and even vegan ice-cream. It's also a good place to hear new bands (Tuesday and Thursday).

Just south of here is the *Scotia Bar* (☎ 552 8681), 112 Stockwell St, Glasgow's oldest pub with live folk music at 8.30 pm on Wednesday, 3.30 pm on Saturday. There's live blues on Sunday at 3.30 pm.

Babbity Bowster (☎ 552 5055), 16 Blackfriars St, is a popular upmarket Merchant City pub with a good range of real ales, excellent pub grub and live folk music on Sunday. There's also a hotel here, and a restaurant noted for its Scottish cuisine.

The Horse Shoe (☎ 221 3051), 17 Drury Lane, may have the longest bar in Europe, but its more important attraction is what's served over it – real ale and good food that's also good value. The pub's been here for over 100 years and is largely unchanged. It's well worth a visit and not far from Queen St station.

By Mitchell's on North St is the traditional *Bon Accord* (☎ 248 4427), with the city's best range of real ales and malt whiskies. There's also great pub grub – including the popular breakfast bun (£2.50) served on a Sunday until 5 pm.

Clubs Glasgow's club scene rivals that of London and Manchester, but it changes so quickly it's difficult to make recommendations. The following places, however, seem to remain popular. Check *The List* and ask around for the latest places.

Glaswegians don't start hitting the clubs until after the pubs have closed, so many clubs will offer discounted entry and cheaper drinks if you get there before 10 or 11 pm. Most also usually give discounts for students. Don't arrive in trainers or you'll be turned away from most places.

Off Jamaica St and under Central station, *Arches* (☎ 221 9736) is the place to go at weekends – Slam on Friday (£7, 10.30 pm to 3 am), various others (Cool Lemon, Cream, Boutique Love etc) on Saturday.

King Tut's Wah Wah Hut (☎ 221 5279), 272 St Vincent St, has live music most nights from local, national and, occasionally, international bands. The downstairs bar is open every day. Tickets for the bigger events need to be bought in advance.

The Tunnel (☎ 204 1000), 84 Mitchell St, is a stylish club in the West End. The gents' loos are famous for their designer waterworks. This is one Glasgow attraction women might have to miss out on!

The Volcano (☎ 337 1100), 15 Benalder St, is as hot and sweaty as the name suggests. Popular with students, it's at the south end of Byres Rd. Music played by DJs varies from night to night – mainstream dance one night, house another. Entry is around £5; £4 for students.

There are half a dozen gay pubs and clubs, including *Austins*, 183 Hope St; *The Squire's Lounge*, 106 West Campbell St; *GHQ*, 8 West George St; and the funkier *Del Monica's*, 68 Virginia St. *Bennet's* (☎ 552 5761), 80 Glassford St, and *Club Xchange* (☎ 204 4599), 25 Royal Exchange, are the main clubs.

And then? On Friday and Saturday head for *Change at Jamaica* (☎ 429 4422), 11 Clyde Place, where infamous breakfasts are served from midnight to 5 am. This café is just south of the river, under the railway bridge.

SOUTHERN SCOTLAND

Concerts, Theatre & Film For tickets phone the Ticket Centre (☎ 227 5511).

The *Theatre Royal* (☎ 332 9000), Hope St, is the home of Scottish Opera, and the Scottish Ballet often performs here. The Royal Scottish National Orchestra plays at the modern *Glasgow Royal Concert Hall* (☎ 227 5511), 2 Sauchiehall St.

Rock and pop bands on the international circuit usually play at the *SECC* – the Scottish Exhibition & Conference Centre (☎ 248 3000) – which is a modern aircraft hangar of a place by the river. Some bands choose the *Barrowland Ballroom* (☎ 552 4601), on Gallowgate, a vast dance hall in the East End that's far funkier.

The *Citizens' Theatre* (☎ 429 0022), Gorbals St, is one of the top theatres not just in Scotland but in the whole country and it's well worth trying to catch a performance here. The *Tron Theatre* (☎ 552 4267), 63 Trongate, stages contemporary Scottish and international performances. There's a good café here.

The *Centre for Contemporary Arts* (☎ 332 7521), 350 Sauchiehall St, is an interesting centre for the visual and performing arts – it also has a pleasant café. A couple of blocks east, the *Glasgow Film Theatre* (☎ 332 8128), 12 Rose St, off Sauchiehall St, screens new releases, classics and popular re-runs.

Getting There & Away
See the fares tables in the Getting Around chapter. Glasgow is 405 miles from London, 97 from Carlisle, 42 from Edinburgh and 166 from Inverness.

Air Glasgow airport (☎ 887 1111), 10 miles west of the city, handles domestic traffic, and international flights.

Bus Buses from London are very competitive. The London Liner (☎ 332 2283) is currently the best deal, at £16/18 for a single/return, and the journey takes 7¾ hours. The service is very popular so you'll need to book. Tickets are available from any branch of the travel agent AT Mays, and buses leave London from Transpak, 71 Pancras Rd (near King's Cross station).

Silver Choice (☎ 333 1400) costs £20/24 and leaves from Victoria Coach Station in London. National Express (☎ 0990-808080) also leaves from here and costs £20.50/25.50. The best option is to catch the 8.30 am bus, so that you arrive in good time to organise accommodation. There are direct links with Heathrow and Gatwick airports.

There are numerous links with other English cities. National Express services include: three buses per day from Birmingham (5¼ hours); one from Cambridge (nine hours); numerous from Carlisle (two hours); one from Newcastle (four hours); and one from York (6½ hours).

National Express/Scottish Citylink has buses to most major towns in Scotland. Most of the east-coast towns are reached via Edinburgh. There are numerous buses to Edinburgh with singles/returns from £4.50/6.50 (off peak), Stirling (one hour), Inverness (4¼ hours), three to Oban (2¾ hours), Aberdeen (four hours), Fort William (three hours) and Skye (5¼ hours). There's a summer service for Stranraer, connecting with the ferry to Larne in Northern Ireland (five hours).

Fife Scottish/Stagecoach Express (☎ 01592-261461) operates buses to St Andrews (2¼ hours, £5, hourly) and Dundee (2½ hours, £5, hourly) via Glenrothes.

Walkers should check out Midland Bluebird (☎ 01324-613777) , which runs hourly buses to Milngavie (30 minutes), the start of the West Highland Way.

Train As a general rule, Central station serves southern Scotland, England and Wales, and Queen St serves the north and east. There are frequent buses between the two (40p). There are 20 trains a day from London's Euston station; they're not cheap, but they are much quicker (4¾ hours) and more comfortable than the bus.

ScotRail has one major line heading north to Oban and Fort William (see those sections) and direct links to Dundee, Aberdeen and Inverness. There are numerous trains to Edinburgh (50 minutes, £6.70).

For all rail enquiries call ☎ 0345-484950.

Car There are numerous car rental companies; the big names have offices at the airport. Try Melvilles Motors (☎ 632 5757), 192 Battlefield Rd.

Cabervans (☎ 01475-638775), Caberfeidh, Cloch Rd, Gourock, have vans for rent from around £240 per week, and can deliver to Glasgow airport or railway stations.

Getting Around

The Roundabout Glasgow ticket (£3.20/1.60) covers all public transport in the city for a day; the Roundabout Glasgow Plus ticket (£5.80/2.90) also includes the Discovering Glasgow hop-on hop-off tourist buses that run along the main sightseeing routes.

The Airport There are buses every 20 minutes from the airport to Buchanan bus station; they take 20 minutes and cost £2.20. A taxi would cost about £12.

Bus Bus services are frequent and cheap. You can buy tickets when you board buses, but on some you have to have exact change. Routes are shown on the *Visitors Transport Guide Map* (see under Information earlier in this section). For short trips in the city, fares are 50p. After midnight there are special night buses.

Discovering Glasgow (☎ 204 0444) runs tourist buses every half-hour along the main sightseeing routes. You get on and off as you wish and fares are £5/3.50 for a day ticket. Guide Friday (☎ 556 2244) is similar with a slightly longer route.

Train There's an extensive suburban network; tickets should be bought before travel if the station is staffed, or from the conductor if it isn't.

There's also an underground line that serves 15 stations in the centre, west and south of the city (60p). An Underground Heritage Trail Pass (£2) gives unlimited travel on the system for a day.

Taxi There's no shortage. If you order a taxi from Glasgow Wide Taxis (☎ 332 6666) by phone you can pay by credit card.

Bicycle West End Cycles (☎ 357 1344), 16 Chancellor St, is at the southern end of Byres Rd and rents mountain bikes for £8 per day or £45 per week. They demand two IDs and a £50 deposit.

Around Glasgow

Glasgow is surrounded by a grim hinterland of post-industrial communities. Industrial archaeologists could have a field day here and some might see a perverse beauty in the endless suburbs of grey council house architecture. But it is here, possibly, that the Glasgow area's gritty black sense of humour is engendered.

PAISLEY
* *pop 85,000* * ☎ 0141

This is the town that gave its name to the well-known fabric design of swirling stylised teardrops or pinecones called the Paisley Pattern.

Now really a suburb west of Glasgow, Paisley grew up around the **abbey**, heavily 'restored' by the Victorians, which was founded here in the 12th century. By the 19th century the town was a major producer of printed cotton and woollen cloth. The famous design was, in fact, copied from shawls brought back from India. The history of the Paisley Pattern is outlined in an interesting exhibition at the **Museum & Art Galleries** (☎ 889 3151), on the High St, with a large display of Paisley shawls. It's open Monday to Saturday from 10 am to 5 pm; entry is free. At one time, Paisley was the largest producer of cotton thread in the world; the Coats family of threadmakers have enjoyed a long association with the town.

Trains leave Glasgow's Central station several times each hour for Paisley's Gilmour St station; and there are frequent

SOUTHERN SCOTLAND

buses. Walk down Gilmour St, turn left into Gauze St and the TIC (☎ 889 0711) is in the large town hall over the river. There's no need to stay here but, should you wish to, the TIC has the usual accommodation lists.

FIRTH OF CLYDE

The ghosts of once great shipyards still line the banks of the Clyde west of Glasgow. Ten miles downstream, the impressive Erskine Bridge links the north and south banks. The only place of any interest at all along the coast west of here is Greenock, although in the otherwise unprepossessing town of **Port Glasgow** you could stop to see the replica of the *Comet*, Europe's first commercial steamship.

GREENOCK

James Watt, who perfected the steam engine, was born in this large town. In the **Mclean Museum & Art Gallery** (☎ 01475-723741), 15 Kelly St, displays chart the history of steam power and Clyde shipping. The museum is closed on Sunday. The **Custom House Museum** (☎ 01475-726331), on the quay, traces the history of the Customs and Excise service. Robert Burns and Adam Smith were former employees. Worth a visit, it's open from Monday to Friday, 10 am to 12.30 pm and 1.30 to 4.30 pm; admission is free.

Greenock is 27 miles from Glasgow. There are three trains an hour from Glasgow Central, and hourly buses. The Glasgow to Greenock pedestrian/cycle route follows an old railway track for 10 miles (see the Glasgow section).

GOUROCK

• *pop 11,000*   •   ☎ *01475*

Three miles west of Greenock, CalMac ferries (☎ 650100) leave the run-down seaside resort of Gourock for Dunoon (30 minutes, £2.25) on Argyll's Cowal peninsula. There are frequent departures every day. Another service operates to Kilcreggan (10 minutes, 11 per day) and Helensburgh (30 minutes, four per day), Monday to Saturday. There's a seasonal TIC (☎ 639467) by the station.

Lanarkshire

East of Glasgow are the large, depressed satellite towns of Motherwell and Hamilton. Further upstream, the Clyde passes through Lanarkshire, once an important coal mining district and still important for its fruit farms. The area's potential for growing soft fruit was recognised by the Romans who introduced the tomatoes that are still produced here in large quantities.

BLANTYRE

This town's most famous son was David Livingstone, the epitome of the Victorian missionary-explorer, who opened up central Africa to Europe. Born in the one-roomed tenement that now forms part of the David Livingstone Centre, he worked by day in the local cotton mill from the age of 10, educated himself at night, and took a medical degree in 1840 before setting off for Africa.

The **David Livingstone Centre** (☎ 01698-823140) on Station Rd tells the story of his life as a missionary, his battle against slave traders, and his famous meeting with Stanley. It's down by the river and is open daily from 10 am to 5 pm (Sunday in the afternoon only); tickets cost £2.70/1.50. There's a café here.

It's a 20 to 30-minute walk down the river to **Bothwell Castle** (☎ 01698-816894; HS), regarded as the finest 13th-century castle in Scotland. Built of red sandstone, the substantial ruins include a massive circular keep standing above the river. Much fought over during the wars of independence, it's open April to September, daily except Thursday afternoon, Friday all day, and Sunday morning. For the rest of the year it's also closed on Monday and Tuesday. Entry is £1.50/75p.

It's best to come by train (20 minutes from Glasgow Central) since the David Livingstone Centre is a short walk from Blantyre station. The buses stop on Main St, a 15-minute walk away.

LANARK & NEW LANARK

Below the market town of Lanark, in an attractive gorge by the river, are the restored mill-buildings and warehouses of New Lanark. This was once the largest cotton spinning complex in Britain but it was better known for the pioneering social experiments of Robert Owen, who managed the mill from 1800. An enlightened capitalist, he provided his workers with housing, a co-operative store (that was the inspiration for the modern co-operative movement), a school and adult education classes, and a social centre he called The New Institute for the Formation of Character.

Orientation & Information

The TIC (☎ 01555-661661) is in Lanark, and the bus and railway stations are close by. It's a 20-minute walk down to New Lanark, worth walking for the views, and there's also a bus service (No 35; hourly) from the railway station. Returning to Lanark, the last bus leaves New Lanark at 5.03 pm.

Things to See

There's a **Visitor Centre** (☎ 01555-661345) in New Lanark, and £3.45/2.25 gets you entry to the one restored millhouse, the Annie McLeod Experience (a rather disappointing ride where the spirit of a 10-year-old mill girl recalls life here in 1820) and the village shop. It's open every day from 11 am to 5 pm. There are craft shops in the restored buildings and good-value woollens on sale.

Probably the best way to get the feel of this impressive place is to wander round the outside of the buildings and then walk up to the **Falls of Clyde** through the nature reserve. Visit the **Scottish Wildlife Trust Visitor Centre** by the river in New Lanark first. It's a couple of miles to the power station, then half a mile to the beautiful **Cora Linn** (waterfalls) and, beyond them, **Bonnington Linn**.

Places to Stay & Eat

The *New Lanark Youth Hostel* (☎ 01555-666710) on Wee Row, very pleasantly located near the river, was opened in 1994 and is currently the only accommodation available in the village. Nightly charges are £8.80/7.70 with continental breakfast, and it's open year-round.

There's no real reason to linger up in Lanark although the TIC has a free accommodation list for the area. There are numerous B&Bs, including *Mrs Gair's* (☎ 01555-664403) at 10 Park Place, who charges around £15 per person, and *Parkview Guest House* (☎ 01555-663313), 27 Hyndford Rd (near the TIC), with rooms with attached bath and satellite TV from £18 per person.

In the New Lanark Visitor Centre there's a *restaurant*, otherwise you must return to Lanark to eat. The *Wallace Cave* is a recommended local pub on Bloomgate, near St Nicholas Church. Self-caterers can stock up at the large supermarket conveniently situated by the TIC.

Getting There & Away

Lanark is 25 miles south-east of Glasgow. Trains run between Glasgow Central and Lanark only from Monday to Saturday; every hour. If you want to take a bus, Sunday is the only day on which there's a direct bus service; on other days you must change at Carluke.

Ayrshire

The rolling hills and farmland of Ayrshire are best known for being the birthplace and home of poet Robert Burns. These rich pastures were once also famous for the Ayrshire breed of dairy cattle, since largely replaced by Frisians. Parts of the coast comprise attractive sandy beaches and low cliffs overlooking the hilly island of Arran.

There are famous golf courses at Troon and Turnberry. It was at Prestwick Golf Club that the major golf tournament, the British Open Championship, was initiated in 1860.

NORTH AYRSHIRE
Great Cumbrae Island
Included here because it's reached from North Ayrshire, the island is administered as part of Argyll & Bute. There's actually nothing very great about it – it's only four miles long – but it's bigger than privately owned Little Cumbrae Island just to the south.

A 15-minute CalMac ferry ride links the town of Largs with Great Cumbrae. Buses meet the ferries for the 3½-mile journey to **Millport**, which boasts Europe's smallest cathedral, and a marine life museum. There's a seasonal TIC (☎ 01475-530753) by the pier and several bike hire places including Mapes (☎ 01475-530444), 3 Guildford St (£2.20 for two hours).

Ardrossan
The main reason for coming here is to catch a CalMac ferry to Arran. Trains leave Glasgow Central (one hour, £3.80) five times a day to connect with ferries (see Arran section).

In summer there are also ferries for the Isle of Man (8 hours, £30) on Saturday, returning the next day.

ISLE OF ARRAN
- *pop 4800* • ☎ *01770*

'Scotland in miniature' they call it, and parts of this island certainly are reminiscent of other areas of the country. There are challenging walks in the mountainous northern part of the island, often compared to the Highlands. The landscape in the south is gentler, similar to the rest of southern Scotland.

Since Arran is easily accessible from Glasgow and the south of the country, being only an hour's ferry ride from Ardrossan, it's very popular. Despite its popularity the 20-mile-long island seems to be big enough to absorb everyone. The bucket and spade brigade fills the resorts in the south, cyclists take to the island's circular road and hikers

tackle the hills, the highest (at 2866 feet) being Goat Fell. With seven golf courses, Arran is also popular with golfers.

Orientation & Information
The ferry from Ardrossan docks at Brodick, the island's main town. To the south, Lamlash is actually the capital, and, like nearby Whiting Bay, a popular seaside resort. From the village of Lochranza in the north there's a ferry link to the Kintyre peninsula.

On Brodick pier, the TIC (☎ 302140) is open June through September, daily from 9 am to 7.30 pm (5 pm on Sunday); and for shorter hours at other times of the year.

The week-long Arran Folk Festival takes place in early June. Phone ☎ 302341 for information.

Arran is known for its local cheeses, and Arran mustard is also worth buying. Watch out for the woollens, though. Real Aran (one 'r') sweaters come from the Irish island of Aran, not this one.

Things to See

The town of **Brodick** is not of great interest. Taking the road north you come to the small **Heritage Museum** (☎ 302636), open Monday to Saturday, 10 am to 5 pm (£1.50/75p). Continuing round Brodick Bay, look out for seals which are often seen on the rocks here. Two types live in these waters, the Atlantic grey and the common seal. They're actually quite easy to tell apart – the common seal has a face like a dog; the Atlantic grey seal has a Roman nose.

Brodick Castle (☎ 302202) and park is 2½ miles north of town. The ancient seat of the dukes of Hamilton is now in the hands of the NTS. It's an interesting stately home, with rather more of a lived-in feel than some NTS properties. The kitchens and scullery, complete with displays of peculiar kitchen devices, are well worth a look. The grounds are now a country park with various trails amongst the rhododendrons. The walled garden is particularly attractive. The house is open April to October from 11.30 to 4.30 pm; entry is £4.10/2. The park is open year-round, daily from 9.30 am to sunset.

The road follows the coast to the small village of **Corrie**, and one of the tracks up Goat Fell starts here. After **Sannox**, where there's a sandy beach, the road cuts inland.

Lochranza is a village in a small bay at the north of the island. In summer there's a ferry link to the Kintyre peninsula from here. There's also a youth hostel, camping ground and several B&Bs. On a promontory stand the ruins of the 13th-century **Lochranza Castle**, said to be the inspiration for the castle in *The Black Island*, Hergé's Tintin adventure. Also in Lochranza is Scotland's newest distillery, Isle of Arran Distillers (☎ 830264), opened in 1995. It can be visited daily from 10 am to 6 pm. Two miles beyond Lochranza, the whitewashed cottages of **Catacol** are known as the Twelve Apostles.

On the west side of the island, reached by the String Rd across the centre, are the **Machrie Moor standing stones**. It's an eerie place, and these are the most impressive of the six stone circles on the island. There's another group at nearby **Auchagallon**.

Blackwaterfoot is the largest village on the west coast, and it has a large resort hotel. From here, you can walk down to the **King's Cave**, Drumadoon – Arran is one of several islands that lays claim to a cave where Robert the Bruce had his famous arachnid encounter. This walk could be combined with a visit to the Machrie standing stones.

The landscape in the southern part of the island is much gentler; the road drops into little wooded valleys. **Kildonan** has a pleasant beach and a castle, which is ivy-clad and in ruins.

Lamlash is a sailing centre. Out in the bay is **Holy Island**, recently bought by the Samyé Ling Tibetan Centre (Dumfriesshire) for use as a retreat. If they're still allowing day visits to the island, the ferry runs from Lamlash (30 minutes, £5). No dogs, alcohol or fires are allowed on the island. There's a good walk to the top of the hill (1030 feet), a two to three-hour round trip.

Walks & Cycle Routes

The walk up **Goat Fell** takes five to six hours for the round trip and, if the weather is good, there are superb views from the 2866-foot-high summit. It can, however, be very cold and windy up here so come well prepared. There are paths from Claddach, Brodick Castle or Corrie. Another good walk is up to **Coire Fhionn Lochan** from Thundergay; it takes about 1½ hours to reach the loch.

More moderate walks include the trail through **Glen Sannox** from the village of Sannox up the burn, a 3½-hour return trip. From Whiting Bay Youth Hostel there's an easy 2½-hour walk through the forest to the **Glenashdale Falls** and back.

The 50-mile circuit on the coastal road is popular with cyclists and has few serious hills – more in the south than the north. Traffic is not too bad, except at the height of the season.

Places to Stay

Hostels Located in the north of the island, *Lochranza Youth Hostel* (☎ 830631) is an excellent place to stay. It's a self-catering hostel open from March through October.

SOUTHERN SCOTLAND

The nightly charge is £6.95/5.85. In the south there's *Whiting Bay Youth Hostel* (☎ 700339), £5.40/4.40, with the same opening times.

Camping Camping without the permission of the landowner is not allowed, but there are several camping grounds. When choosing a site note that midges can be a major pain in sheltered spots.

Three miles from Brodick, you can camp at *Glen Rosa Farm* (☎ 302380), £4 for a tent and two people. In Kildonan, *Breadalbane Lodge* (☎ 820210) charges campers £3 each; it's very pleasantly located and the breeze here keeps the midges away. *Lochranza Golf* (☎ 830273), in Lochranza, costs £6.50 for a tent and two people.

B&Bs & Hotels – Brodick It's best to get out of Brodick to some of the smaller villages, although there are numerous places to stay in this town.

Opposite the pier, the *Douglas Hotel* (☎ 302155) charges from £11 (room only) per person, and is convenient if you're catching an early ferry. There are also rooms with attached baths. Along Shore Rd, guesthouses include *Tignamara* (☎ 302538) which charges from £15 per person; and *Belvedere* (☎ 302397) on Alma Rd, where rooms are from £14/28. Half a mile from the centre of Brodick *Rosaburn Lodge* (☎ 302383) is a comfortable B&B with three rooms for £29/38, all with attached baths.

B&Bs & Hotels – Glen Coy The island's best hotel is also its oldest building. The *Kilmichael Country House Hotel* (☎ 302219), in Glen Coy, two miles outside Brodick, is a tastefully decorated hideaway. It's a small, elegant hotel with six rooms from £45 to £55 for a single, £69 to £99 for a double. There's an excellent restaurant here.

B&Bs & Hotels – Corrie *North High Corrie Croft* (☎ 302203), Arran Estate Trust, Douglas Park, has bunkhouse accommodation for £5.20 per person. The *Corrie Hotel*

(☎ 810273) has rooms from £20/40 with shared bathroom, £25/50 with bathroom attached. The seafront *Blackrock Guest House* (☎ 810282) is open from March to October and offers B&B from £19 per person in rooms with shared baths.

B&Bs & Hotels – Lochranza Lochranza is a great place to stay. Apart from the youth hostel here, there's *Benvaren* (☎ 830647), overlooking the bay and near the ferry slipway, with rooms for £15 per person. *Castlekirk* (☎ 830202), a converted church, has two rooms for £16.50 per person and an inhouse darkroom for photographers (phone for information on art courses run here). *Kincardine Lodge Guest House* (☎ 830267) charges £17 to £19 per person and some rooms have attached baths. The best place to stay here is *Apple Lodge* (☎ 830229), with three double/twin rooms at £46. You'll be well looked after in very comfortable surroundings.

B&Bs & Hotels – Kildonan Kildonan is a very peaceful spot. The *Breadalbane Hotel* (☎ 820284) has holiday flats with bedrooms, bathroom and kitchen, sleeping four to six people. They charge from £60 to £180 per week depending on the season, and, outside the high season, they may let a flat for less than a week. There's B&B at balconied *Drimla Lodge* (☎ 820296) with rooms with attached shower from around £20 per person.

B&Bs & Hotels – Kilmory & Lagg *Kilmory House* (☎ 870342) is a converted flax mill with three rooms from £14 per person. Nearby at Lagg, there's the upmarket *Lagg Hotel* (☎ 870255), a former coaching inn dating from 1791. The comfortable rooms all have attached bathrooms and range from £30/60 to £45/90 for a single/double. The hotel restaurant is recommended.

Places to Eat
The award-winning *Creelers Seafood Restaurant* (☎ 302810) is 1½ miles north of Brodick by the Arran Aromatics shopping

centre. It's a bistro-style place with some outside seating, open daily except Monday. The imaginative menu includes main dishes from around £6. There's also a shop here selling seafood and smoked foods; and you can stock up on local cheeses from the cheese shop opposite.

Back in Brodick, *Stalkers Eating House* (☎ 302579), along the waterfront, does good-value meals. Home-made steak pie is £4.95, jacket potatoes are from £1.30, and there are solid British puddings like fruit crumble and sherry trifle. *Duncan's Bar* on Shore Rd and the *Ormidale Hotel* (near the golf club) both have good pub grub and occasional live music.

Two miles from Lochranza, the bar at *Catacol Bay Hotel* (☎ 830231) does excellent bar food including the island's best pizzas. There's often live music. There's also a restaurant here and the Sunday buffet is recommended.

In Kildonan, the *Breadalbane Hotel* (☎ 820284) does great homemade bar food. *Carraig Mhor* (☎ 600453) is the best restaurant in Lamlash, recommended for its seafood.

Getting There & Away

CalMac (☎ 302140) runs a daily car ferry between Ardrossan and Brodick (four to six per day, 55 minutes, £3.65); summer services between Claonaig and Lochranza (10 per day, 30 minutes, £3.35); and summer services on Monday, Wednesday and Friday between Brodick and the Isle of Bute (one each way, 1½ hours, £4).

If you're going to visit several islands it's worth planning your route in advance. CalMac has a wide range of tickets including Island Hopscotch fares that work out cheaper than buying several single tickets.

Getting Around

The island's efficient bus service is operated by Stagecoach Western Scottish (☎ 302000). There are about four buses a day from Brodick Pier to Lochranza (40 minutes, £1.40). A Daycard costs £2.50. For a taxi phone ☎ 600725.

In Brodick there are several places to rent bikes, including Mini Golf Cycle Hire (☎ 302272) on Shore Rd with bikes from £4 to £10 per day. You can also rent 3-speeds from Mr Kerr (☎ 830676) near Lochranza Youth Hostel for £4 per day.

SOUTH AYRSHIRE

Ayr

- *pop 49,500*   - ☎ *01292*

Ayr's long sandy beach has made it a popular family seaside resort since Victorian times. It's also known for its racecourse, the top course in Scotland, with more racing days than any other in Britain. Ayr is the largest town on this coast and makes a convenient base for a tour of Burns territory.

Information The TIC (☎ 288688) is opposite the railway station on Burns Statue Square. It's open Monday to Friday from 9.15 am to 5 pm (7 pm in June, July and August); and from April to October also at weekends at the same times.

Things to See Things to see in Ayr are mainly Burns related. The bard was baptised in the **Auld Kirk** (old church) off the High St. Several of his poems are set here in Ayr. In his *Twa Brigs*, Ayr's old and new bridges argue with one another. The **Auld Brig** was built in 1491 and spans the river just down from the church. In Burns' poem *Tam o'Shanter*, Tam spends a boozy evening in the pub here that now bears his name.

Cycle Routes With not too many steep hills, the area is well suited to cyclists. See the Glasgow section for the cycle way from that city. The TIC has a useful leaflet.

From Ayr, you could cycle to Alloway and spend a couple of hours seeing the Burns sights before continuing via Maybole to Culzean. You could either camp here after seeing Culzean Castle, or cycle back along the coast road to Ayr, a round trip of about 22 miles.

In Ayr, AMG Cycles (☎ 287580), 55 Dalblair Rd, rents bikes for £7 per day.

SOUTHERN SCOTLAND

Places to Stay The *Ayr Youth Hostel* (☎ 262322), 5 Craigweil Rd, is housed in a magnificent turreted mansion by the beach and is less than a mile south of the railway and bus stations. It's open from March through October; the nightly charge is £6.95/5.85 for seniors/juniors.

There's a smart caravan park in town but they don't take campers. *Crofthead Caravan Park* (☎ 263516) is two miles east of Ayr near the A70. They charge £6 for a small tent and two people.

There are numerous B&Bs and hotels. *Eglinton Guest House* (☎ 264623), 23 Eglinton Terrace, is a short walk west of the bus station and has rooms for £15/28.

A five to 10-minute walk from the station brings you to a crescent of upmarket B&Bs and small hotels. On Park Circus, *Belmont Hotel* (☎ 265588) at No 15 and *Lochinver Hotel* (☎ 265086) at No 32 both charge £15.50/30 with shared bathroom, £17.50/35 with bathroom attached. The *Richmond Hotel* (☎ 265153), at No 38, is a small, friendly and efficient place with rooms from £26/37. Park Circus continues into Bellevue Crescent and there are also several places to stay along here.

Places to Eat The *Hunny Pot* (☎ 263239), 37 Beresford Terrace, a short walk from the TIC, is a bit twee but does good teas and light meals (£4 to £5) from 10 am to 10 pm. There's a branch of that reliable Edinburgh chain *Pierre Victoire* (☎ 282087) at 4 River Terrace. The set lunch in this French restaurant is excellent value at £4.90.

The best place in town is *Fouters Bistro Restaurant* (☎ 261391), 2A Academy St, opposite the town hall. They specialise in Ayrshire produce and local seafood. Main dishes are £11.50 to £15, and there's a cheaper bistro menu. It's closed on Monday.

Getting There & Away There are at least two trains an hour from Glasgow Central to Ayr (50 minutes, £4.50) and the service continues south to Stranraer (1¼ hours from Ayr, £13). The main bus operator in the area is Stagecoach Western (☎ 613500) – their 501 service from Glasgow costs £2.80 and departs hourly.

Alloway

Three miles south of Ayr, Alloway is where Robert Burns was born. Even if you're not a fan it's still worth a visit, since the Burns-related exhibitions also give a very good impression of life in Ayrshire in the late 18th century. All the sights are within easy walking distance of each other.

The **Burns Cottage & Museum** (☎ 01292-441215) stands by the main road from Ayr. Born in the little box bed in this cramped thatched cottage, the poet spent the first seven years of his life here. There's a good museum of Burnsiana by the cottage exhibiting everything from his writing compendium to a piece of wood from his coffin. Light meals are available in the tearoom. The museum is open from June to August daily, 9 am to 6 pm; in April, May, September and October daily from 10 am to 5 pm (Sunday in the afternoon only); and for the rest of the year, Monday to Saturday until 4 pm. Entry is £2.50/1.25; the ticket also permits entry to the Burns Monument & Gardens.

From here you can visit the ruins of **Alloway Auld Kirk** where Burns' father, William Burnes (his son dropped the 'e' from his name) is buried, and the setting for part of *Tam o' Shanter*.

The nearby **Tam o'Shanter Experience** (☎ 01292-443700) has audio-visual displays (£1.75/75p) and a bookshop/giftshop, open daily until 6 pm in summer. The tearoom here does excellent home-made soup. The **Burns Monument & Gardens** (opening hours as for the Burns Cottage) are nearby. The monument was built in 1823 and affords a view of the 13th-century **Brig o'Doon**. There are also statues of Burns' drinking cronies in the gardens.

The *Burns Monument Hotel* (☎ 01292-442466) has a reasonable restaurant but no food in the bar. Conveniently located, as its name suggests, rooms are £37/57. *Northpark House Hotel* (☎ 01292-442336) is off the road to Ayr. It's a small, luxurious hotel and prices are from £67.50/90.

✿✿

Robert Burns

Best remembered for penning the words of *Auld Lang Syne*, Robert Burns is Scotland's most famous poet, and a popular hero whose birthday (25 January) is celebrated as Burns Night by Scots around the world.

He was born in 1759 in Alloway. Although his mother was illiterate and his parents poor farmers, they sent him to the local school where he soon showed an aptitude for literature and a fondness for the folk song. He began to write his own songs and satires, some of which he distributed privately. When the problems of his arduous farming life were compounded by the threat of prosecution from the father of Jean Armour, with whom he'd had an affair, he decided to emigrate to Jamaica. He gave up his share of the family farm and published his poems to raise money for the journey.

The poems were so well reviewed in Edinburgh that Burns decided to remain in Scotland and devote himself to writing. He went to Edinburgh in 1787 to publish a second edition, but the financial rewards were not enough to live on and he had to take a job as a customs officer in Dumfriesshire. He contributed many songs to collections published by Johnson and Thomson in Edinburgh, and a third edition of his poems was published in 1793. Burns died in Dumfries in 1796, aged 37, after a heart attack.

While some dispute Burns' claim to true literary genius, he was certainly an accomplished poet and songwriter, and has been compared to Chaucer for his verse tale *Tam o'Shanter*. Burns wrote in Lallans, the Scottish Lowland dialect of English that is not very accessible to the Sassenach, or foreigner; perhaps this is part of his appeal. He was also very much a man of the people, satirising the upper classes and the church for their hypocrisy.

Many of the local landmarks mentioned in *Tam o'Shanter* can still be visited. Farmer Tam, riding home after a hard night's drinking in a pub in Ayr, sees witches dancing in Alloway churchyard. He calls out to the one pretty witch but is pursued by them all and has to reach the other side of the Doon river to be safe. He just manages to cross the Brig o'Doon, but his mare loses her tail to the witches.

The Burns connection in southern Scotland is milked for all it's worth and TICs have a *Burns Heritage Trail* leaflet leading you to every place that can claim some link with the bard. There's a Burns festival in early June. There was a major jamboree in 1996, the bicentenary of his death. ∎

There are few buses between Alloway and Ayr. Contact the TIC for details or rent a bike and cycle here.

Culzean Castle & Country Park

Well worth seeing, Culzean (pronounced cullane), 12 miles south of Ayr, is one of the most impressive of Scotland's great stately homes. Perched dramatically on the edge of the cliffs, this 18th-century mansion was designed by Robert Adam to replace the castle built here in the 16th century.

The original castle belonged to the Kennedy clan, who, after a feud in the 16th century, divided into the Kennedys of Culzean and Cassillis, and the Kennedys of Bargany. Because of the American connection (Eisenhower was a frequent visitor) most people wrongly assume that the Culzean Kennedys are closely related to JFK. Culzean Castle was given to the National Trust for Scotland (NTS) in 1945.

Robert Adam was the most influential architect of his time, renowned for his meticulous attention to detail and the elegant classical embellishments with which he decorated his ceilings and fireplaces. The beautiful oval staircase here is regarded as one of his finest achievements.

On the 1st floor, the opulence of the circular saloon contrasts splendidly with the views of the wild sea below. The other rooms on this floor are also particularly interesting and Lord Cassillis' bedroom is said to be haunted by a lady in green mourning for a lost baby. Even the bathrooms are palatial, the dressing room beside the state bedroom being equipped with a state-of-the-art shower that directs jets of water from almost every angle.

Set in a 560-acre park combining woodland, coast and gardens, there's much more to see than just the house. An interesting exhibition in the Gas House explains how gas was produced here for the house. There's also a visitor centre, swan pond and aviary.

Culzean Castle (☎ 01655-760269) is the NTS's most visited property and it can get quite crowded on summer weekends. It's open April to October, from 10.30 am to 5.30 pm. The park is open year-round from 9.30 am to sunset. Entry is £5.50/3 (£15 for a family ticket), or £3/1.50 if you want to visit only the park.

It's possible to stay in the castle but gracious living does not come cheap. A night for two in the Eisenhower suite costs £300 and the cheapest rooms are £150 for a double. If you're not in that league there's a Camping and Caravanning Club site (☎ 01655-760627) in the park. It costs £3.85 per person plus £3.50 for a tent.

Maybole is the nearest railway station but since it's four miles away it's best to come by bus from Ayr (six per day, 30 minutes, £1.95). The bus passes the park gates but it's still a 20-minute walk through the grounds to the castle.

Turnberry

To play the world-famous golf course here you must usually stay at the luxurious *Turnberry Hotel* (☎ 01655-331000). Rooms are a mere £231.50/323 including dinner in the award-winning restaurant.

Ailsa Craig

From much of South Ayrshire, curiously-shaped Ailsa Craig can be seen, looking like a giant bread roll floating out to sea. Rock quarried from here is used for curling stones. It's now a bird sanctuary and taking a cruise from Girvan is about as close as you'll get to the gannets that crowd this 1114-foot-high rocky outcrop.

Dumfries & Galloway

The tourist board bills this region as Scotland's surprising south-west, and it is surprising if you expect beautiful mountain and coastal scenery to be confined to the Highlands. Only the local architecture disappoints; otherwise, with mountains (which reach over 2000 feet), lochs and an interesting coastline, it is reminiscent in some ways of the Lake District. There are even stone walls running up hill and down dale. This is, however, one of the forgotten corners of Britain, and beyond the main transport routes to Stranraer, traffic and people are sparse.

Dumfries & Galloway covers the southern half of Scotland's southern elbow. Warmed by the Gulf Stream, this is the mildest corner of Scotland, a phenomenon that has allowed the development of a number of famous gardens. There are many notable historic and prehistoric attractions linked by the Solway Coast Heritage Trail (information from TICs). Caerlaverock Castle, Threave Castle and Whithorn Cathedral & Priory are just three of many. Kirkcudbright is a beautiful town, and would make a good base.

This is excellent cycling and walking country, and it is crossed by the coast-to-coast Southern Upland Way (see the Walks and Cycle Routes sections at the beginning of this chapter).

Dumfries & Galloway lies to the south of the Southern Uplands. Stranraer is the ferry port to Larne in Northern Ireland; it's the shortest link from Britain to Ireland. Youth hostels can only be found at Newton Stewart, Kendoon and Wanlockhead.

GETTING AROUND

The regional council has a travel information line (☎ 0345-090510), Monday to Friday from 9 am to 5 pm.

Bus

National Express (☎ 0990-505050) has long-distance coaches from London, Birmingham (via Manchester and Carlisle), and Glasgow/Edinburgh to Stranraer. These coaches service the main towns and villages along the A75 (including Dumfries, Kirkcudbright and Newton Stewart). Stagecoach Western (☎ 01387-253496) provides a variety of local bus services.

The Day Discoverer (£5) is a useful day

ticket valid on almost all buses in the region and also on Cumberland Motor Services buses from Carlisle.

Train

Two lines from Carlisle to Glasgow cross the region, via Dumfries and Moffat respectively. The line from Glasgow to Stranraer runs via Ayr.

DUMFRIES

• *pop 31,000* • ☎ *01387*

Dumfries is a large town with a strategic position that placed it smack in the path of a number of vengeful English armies. As a result, although it has existed since Roman times, the oldest standing building dates from the 17th century.

It has escaped modern mass tourism, although it was the home of Robert Burns from 1791 to his death in 1796, and there are several important Burns-related museums. The centre is rather run-down and uninspiring, but there are some pleasant 19th-century suburbs built in the area's characteristic red sandstone.

Information

The TIC (☎ 253862), by the river in the town centre, is open all year: October through April from 10 am to 4.30 pm (closed between 1 and 2 pm); May, June and September from 10 am to 5 pm; and July and August from 9.30 am to 6 pm. You can book National Express/Citylink buses here.

The main bus station is by the TIC; the railway station is a 10-minute walk to the north-east. Early-closing day is Thursday.

Burnsiana

On Burns St, **Burns House** (☎ 255297) is a place of pilgrimage for Burns enthusiasts; it is here the poet spent the last years of his life and there are some interesting relics, and original letters and manuscripts. It's open all year (except Sunday and Monday from October to March), Monday to Saturday from 10 am to 1 pm and 2 to 5 pm, Sunday from 2 to 5 pm; 80p/40p.

The **Robert Burns Centre** (☎ 264808),

Mill Rd, is an award-winning museum on the banks of the river in an old mill. It tells the story of Burns and Dumfries in the 1790s. There's also a café/gallery. It's open April to September, Monday to Saturday from 10 am to 8 pm, Sunday from 2 to 5 pm; October to March, Tuesday to Saturday from 10 am to 1 pm and 2 to 5 pm; free (80p/40p for the audio-visual presentation).

Burns' **mausoleum** is in the graveyard at St Michael's Kirk. At the top of the High St is a **statue** of the bard.

Places to Stay

There are a number of good-value B&Bs near the railway station, in a quiet and pleasant suburb; prices are around £15/25. *Cairndoon* (☎ 256991), 14 Newell Terrace, has large, comfortable rooms with TVs and a warm welcome. There are a number of places on Lovers Walk, including the *Fulwood Hotel* (☎ 252262) and the *Torbay Lodge Guest House* (☎ 253922).

The recently-renovated *Edenbank Hotel* (☎ 252759), Laurieknowe, is a short walk from the centre of town. It's a small, family-run hotel with a range of rooms including two singles, all with bathrooms, for £40/50.

Places to Eat

For vegetarian lunches try *Opus*, above the shop at 95 Queensbury Rd. *Olivers* on the pedestrianised High St has a range of good-value baked goods, sandwiches and baked potatoes.

The set lunch menu at *Pierre Victoire* (☎ 265888), 113 Queensbury Rd, is excellent value at £4.95. Dinner is more expensive but the usual high quality you can expect from this chain.

Bruno's (☎ 255757), on Balmoral St, is one of the best places to eat in Dumfries. Next to this Italian restaurant is a highly-recommended fish & chip shop, run by the same family.

The *Globe Inn*, 56 High St, is a traditional pub, said to be Burns' favourite watering hole.

Getting There & Away

Dumfries is 330 miles from London, 75 from Edinburgh, Glasgow and Stranraer and 35 from Carlisle.

Bus National Express' No 920 service runs thrice daily between London and Belfast, via Birmingham, Manchester, Carlisle, Dumfries, the towns along the A75, and Stranraer. There are also regular local buses to Kirkcudbright and the towns along the A75 to Stranraer (three hours, £6.20). Stagecoach Western has two buses a day (No 100) to/from Edinburgh.

Train Dumfries is on a line that leaves the main west-coast line at Gretna, and from Dumfries runs north-west along Nithsdale to join the Glasgow-Stranraer line at Kilmarnock. You can join the service at Carlisle or Glasgow; Monday to Saturday there are frequent trains between Carlisle and Dumfries (35 minutes), and half a dozen between Dumfries and Glasgow (1½ hours); there's a reduced service on Sunday.

Getting Around

Taxi Try Hastings Taxi (☎ 252664).

Bicycle Grierson & Graham (☎ 259483), 10 Academy St, and the Nithsdale Cycle Centre (☎ 254870), 46 Brooms Rd, both hire bikes.

AROUND DUMFRIES
Caerlaverock Castle

The ruins of Caerlaverock Castle (☎ 0131-668 8800; HS), on a beautiful stretch of the Solway coast, are among the loveliest in Britain. Surrounded by a moat, lawns and stands of trees, the unusual pink-stoned triangular castle looks impregnable. In fact it fell several times. The current castle dates from the late 13th century. Inside, there is an extraordinary Scottish Renaissance facade to apartments that were built in 1634.

It's open April to September, Monday to Saturday from 9.30 am to 6 pm, Sunday from 2 to 6 pm; October to March, Monday to Saturday from 9.30 am to 4 pm, Sunday from 2 to 4 pm; £1.95. Monday to Saturday the castle can be reached from Dumfries by half a dozen buses (No 371) operated by Stagecoach Western.

A visit to the castle can be combined with a visit to the **Caerlaverock Wildlife & Wetlands Centre** (open daily from 10 am to 5 pm; £2.95) a mile away, which protects 1400 acres of salt marsh and mud flat, the habitat for birds, including the barnacle goose. There are hides and observatories.

NEW GALLOWAY

New Galloway is a quaint little town, surrounded by beautiful countryside. There's nothing much to bring you here, however, unless you want to get away from it all.

On the High St, the *Kenmure Arms* (☎ 01644-420240) has rooms from £15/31; the *Leamington Hotel* (☎ 01644-420327), has rooms with bathrooms from £16/32.

There's some attractive countryside around New Galloway. To the south-west there's the Galloway Forest Park, with great whale-backed heather-covered mountains (although, sadly, the lower slopes have been devastated by the Forestry Commission). The countryside to the south-east, however, is particularly beautiful and unusual. You feel as if you're on a high plateau, surrounded by tumbling short-pitched hills. There's a sense of space unusual in Britain.

CASTLE DOUGLAS

- *pop 3500*   •   ☎ 01556

Castle Douglas is an open, attractive little town that was laid out in the 18th century by Sir William Douglas, who had made a fortune in the Americas. Beside the town is the small but beautiful Carlingwark Loch. At the Loch's western end is the National Trust of Scotland's **Threave Garden**, which is spectacular in spring. It's open daily all year; £3.60.

The TIC (☎ 502611), Markethill, is open from Easter through October from 10 am to 5 pm.

The *Lochside Caravan & Camping Site* (☎ 502949) is an attractive spot alongside Carlingwark Loch; there are sites for vans and tents from £6.50. *Craigvar House*

(☎ 503515), 60 St Andrew St, is a comfortable B&B, with rooms from £26/36. The *Douglas Arms Hotel* (☎ 502231), King St, has good food, and a range of comfortable rooms, most with bathrooms. Rates are from £26 per person.

The No 501 bus service between Dumfries and Kirkcudbright calls frequently (only two on Sunday, however). Ace Cycles (☎ 504542), 11 Church St, hires touring and mountain bikes from £10 per day.

AROUND CASTLE DOUGLAS
Threave Castle
Three miles west of Castle Douglas, off the A75, Threave Castle (HS) is an impressively grim tower on a small island in the middle of the lovely River Dee. It's basically only a shell, but it is a romantic ruin nonetheless. It was built in the late 14th century and became a principal stronghold for the Douglases.

It's a 10-minute walk from the car park, and visitors are ferried across to the island in a small boat. The castle's open April through September, Monday to Saturday from 9 am to 6 pm, Sunday from 2 to 6 pm; £1.50, including the ferry.

KIRKCUDBRIGHT
• *pop 3500*   • ☎ *01557*
Kirkcudbright (pronounced kirkcoobree), with its dignified streets of 17th and 18th-century merchants' houses and its interesting harbour, is the ideal base if you wish to explore the beautiful southern coast. The lovely surrounding countryside has distinctive choppy hills covered in gorse – it is almost as if they have been heaped up to make a golf course.

Orientation & Information
Everything in town is within easy walking distance. The TIC (☎ 330494), Harbour Square, is open April through October from 10 am to 5 pm. There are some useful brochures giving walks and car tours in the surrounding district.

Early-closing day is Thursday.

Things to See
All the sights are fairly modest, but they provide an excuse for exploring the town, and they do have charm. **McLellan's Castle**, near the harbour and TIC, is a large ruin, built in 1582. Nearby, the **Hornel Art Gallery** in 17th-century Broughton House is a reminder of the town's 19th-century artist's colony, featuring paintings by Australian-born EA Hornel and a beautiful Japanese garden. The **Tolbooth Arts Centre** caters to today's local artists, and the **Stewartry Museum** is a particularly interesting local museum.

Places to Stay & Eat
Silvercraigs Caravan & Camping Site (☎ 330123) overlooks the town and has great views. There are van sites from £6.

Parkview (☎ 330056), 22 Millburn St, is a small B&B charging around £14 per person. *Gladstone House* (☎ 331734), 48 High St, offers upmarket B&B to non-smokers from £25 per person in an attractively-decorated house.

The recently-renovated *Royal Hotel* (☎ 331213), St Cuthbert St, is a large, well-run place. Rooms with bathrooms are £19/38. They have good-value bar meals, including an all-you-can-eat buffet from noon to 2.30 pm for £4.95.

The *Selkirk Arms Hotel* (☎ 330402), High St, has good bar meals; there's also a more expensive dining room. There are a number of well-equipped rooms, all with bathrooms, for £47.50/75.

The best place to eat is the *Auld Alliance* (☎ 330569), 5 Castle St, open daily for dinner only. The alliance is local fresh Scots produce (such as small scallops known as queenies) and French wine. Main dishes range from £8.50 to £14; booking is advised.

Getting There & Away
Kirkcudbright is 25 miles from Dumfries, 50 from Stranraer.

There are regular bus services to Dumfries (£2.50) and Stranraer (£4.90).

SOUTHERN SCOTLAND

GATEHOUSE OF FLEET

- *pop 900*   • ☎ *01557*

Gatehouse of Fleet is an attractive little town, on the banks of the Water of Fleet and surrounded by hills – completely off the beaten track. The *Bank O' Fleet Hotel* (☎ 814302), 47 High St, has good bar meals, and rooms with bathroom from £21.50 per person. One mile to the south-west on the A75, **Cardoness Castle** is a classic 15th-century tower house with good views.

NEWTON STEWART

- *pop 2000*   • ☎ *01672*

Surrounded by beautiful countryside, and set on the banks of the River Cree, Newton Stewart is a centre for hikers and fishing folk. Walkers head for Galloway Hills in the Galloway Forest Park, 300 sq miles of lochs, mountains and forest. If you're interested in renting fishing gear, contact the Creebridge House Hotel (see below).

The TIC (☎ 402431), Dashwood Square, is open April through October, daily from 10 am to 4.30 pm (extended hours in July and August).

Places to Stay & Eat

The *Minnigaff Youth Hostel* (☎ 402211) is open April through September; the nightly rate is £5.40/4.40. The *Creebridge Caravan Park* (☎ 402324), 300 metres from the bridge, charges £3.80 for one person and a tent. They have bicycle hire from £7 per day.

The *Creebridge House Hotel* (☎ 402121) is a magnificent 18th-century mansion built for the Earl of Galloway. There's a good restaurant and huntin', shootin' and fishin'. The rooms are tastefully decorated and all have bathrooms; prices range from £25/40 to £40/70.

Right on the banks of the River Cree is the friendly *Flowerbank Guest House* (☎ 402629), Millcroft Rd, Minnigaff, five minutes from town. There are seven rooms and B&B starts from £16 per person (£17.50 in a room with bathroom attached).

Getting There & Away

Newton Stewart is served by all the buses that run between Stranraer and Dumfries, including the No 920 (National Express) and the No 500 (various operators, at least two a day). It is also a starting point for buses south to Wigtown and Whithorn.

WIGTOWN

- *pop 1000*   • ☎ *01988*

Overlooking Wigtown Bay and the Galloway Hills, Wigtown has expansive views and is surrounded by attractive rolling countryside. There's nothing here but a curious air of slightly decrepit charm. The *County Hotel* has bar meals. The *Craigmount Guest House* (☎ 402291) has a range of rooms including a single and a couple with private bathrooms. B&B is from £15 per person.

GARLIESTON

You can't get further off the beaten track in Britain. There's a neat little harbour with a ring of 18th-century cottages running onto a bowling green. The *Harbour Inn* (☎ 01988-600685) is a basic pub with great views and accommodation in five rooms from £15 per person.

WHITHORN

- *pop 1000*   • ☎ *01988*

Whithorn has a broad, attractive High St virtually closed at both ends – designed to enclose a medieval market. The last few years have been unkind to the town and there are virtually no facilities – a couple of shops, but not even one pub. It's worth visiting, however, because it has a fascinating history.

In 397, while the Romans were still in Britain, St Ninian established the first Christian mission beyond Hadrian's Wall (predating St Columba on Iona by 166 years) in Whithorn. The modest ruins of Whithorn Cathedral Priory, once the centrepoint of an important medieval pilgrimage, are now the centrepoint for the **Whithorn Dig** (☎ 500508). The substantial remains of the old monastic settlement are being excavated and there are exhibitions and videos. There's also a museum with some important finds and early Christian sculpture. It's open

Easter through October, daily from 10.30 am to 5 pm; £2.70/1.50.

Stagecoach Western has regular buses to/from Newton Stewart.

ISLE OF WHITHORN

The Isle of Whithorn, once an island but now part of a peninsula, is a curious, raggedy sort of place with an attractive harbour. **St Ninian's Chapel**, probably built for pilgrims who landed nearby, is on a windswept, evocative spot.

On the quayside, the *Steam Packet Hotel* (☎ 01988-500334) has popular bar meals that are excellent value – everything from soup of the day to fresh lobster. There's B&B in rooms with attached bathrooms from £22.50 per person. *Dunbar House* (☎ 01988-500336), Tonderghie Rd, has B&B from £13 per person. Stagecoach Western has regular buses to/from Newton Stewart.

PORTPATRICK

• *pop 600* • ☎ *01776*

Portpatrick is a charming port on a rugged stretch of coast. Until the mid-19th century it was the main port for Northern Ireland, so it is quite substantial. It's now a Coastguard station, a quiet resort, and the starting point for the Southern Upland Way. There are fishing trips on the *Cornubia* (☎ 810468) for £7.50 for half a day.

Formerly the customs house, the *Harbour House Hotel* (☎ 810456), 53 Main St, is a popular pub with a range of rooms, some with bathrooms; prices start at £18 per person.

The Knowe Guest House & Tea Room (☎ 810441), 1 North Crescent, is a charming place overlooking the harbour; B&B with private bathrooms is £16 per person. *Ard Choille Guest House* (☎ 810313), 1 Blair Terrace, has a number of doubles, including one with a private bathroom. Rates start at £15 per person.

There are regular Stagecoach Western buses (No 67), Monday to Saturday, to Stranraer.

It's possible to follow the Southern Upland Way virtually all the way to Stranraer (nine miles). It's a clifftop walk, followed by sections of farmland and heather moor. Start at the way's information shelter at the north end of the harbour. The walk is waymarked until a half-mile south of Stranraer, where you get the first good views of the town. The way continues south-eastwards. From Stranraer, walk westward along High St, turn left into Glebe St and follow the Portpatrick road. A waymarker points to the right shortly after reaching the top of the hill.

STRANRAER & CAIRNRYAN

• *pop 10,000* • ☎ *01776*

Stranraer is rather more pleasant than the average ferry port, but there's no pressing reason to stay, unless you're catching a ferry. Make for the south coast (maybe even nearby Portpatrick) or Glasgow.

Stena Line ferries and fast SeaCat catamarans depart for Northern Ireland from Stranraer. P&O ferries depart from Cairnryan, a couple of miles away on the other side of Loch Ryan.

Information

The TIC (☎ 702595), 1 Bridge St, is a bit of a walk from the Sealink and SeaCat terminals; it's open April through October from 10 am to 5 pm.

Early-closing day is Wednesday.

Places to Stay

The *Aird Donald Caravan Park* (☎ 702025), London Rd, is the nearest camping ground which takes vans and tents. Sites are around £6.

The *Harbour Guest House* (☎ 704626), Market St, is right on the harbour front near the town centre. Rooms cost from £15 per person (£13 without breakfast). There's a string of standard places along Agnew Crescent facing the harbour, including the friendly *Harbour Lights Guest House* (☎ 706261), at No 7, which has B&B from £14 per person.

The *Jan-Da-Mar Guest House* (☎ 706194), 1 Ivy Place, London Rd, is conveniently located, and has a range of rooms

SOUTHERN SCOTLAND

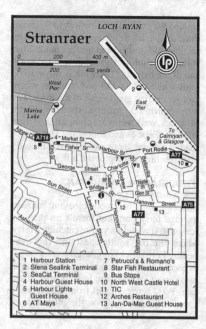

Stranraer

LOCH RYAN

1	Harbour Station
2	Stena Sealink Terminal
3	SeaCat Terminal
4	Harbour Guest House
5	Harbour Lights Guest House
6	AT Mays
7	Petrucci's & Romano's
8	Star Fish Restaurant
9	Bus Stops
10	North West Castle Hotel
11	TIC
12	Arches Restaurant
13	Jan-Da-Mar Guest House

(some with bathrooms). Singles are from £16, doubles from £28.

The most luxurious hotel in Stranraer is the *North West Castle Hotel* (☎ 704413), formerly the home of Arctic explorer Sir John Ross. It's expensive, but good, with singles from £50 and doubles from £70.

If you fancy a night in a lighthouse, *Corsewall Lighthouse Hotel* (☎ 853220) is an unusual place to stay, 10 miles north of Stranraer at Corsewall Point. Rooms are from £37.50/52, all with bathroom attached; one room is specially equipped for disabled travellers.

Places to Eat

There are reasonable pizzas and other fast food at two places in George St opposite St John's Tower – *Petrucci's* and *Romano's*. The *Star Fish Restaurant*, Pizza & Kebab House, 14 Charlotte St, is another option, and it's open until midnight.

The *Arches Restaurant*, near the TIC, is a

bright and popular café with main dishes from £4.50.

The best restaurant is at the *North West Castle Hotel* (☎ 704413). There's a set four-course dinner for £21, including a vegetarian choice.

Getting There & Away

Stranraer is 390 miles from London, 120 from Edinburgh, 80 from Glasgow and 75 from Dumfries.

Sea See the introductory Getting There & Away chapter for details on services to Northern Ireland. There are three alternatives: P&O (☎ 01581-200276) ferries from Cairnryan to Larne; Stena Line (☎ 01776-702262) ferries from Stranraer to Larne; and fast SeaCat (☎ 0345-523523) catamarans from Stranraer to Belfast.

The Cairnryan to Larne service is used mainly by motorists and hauliers, since Cairnryan is a couple of miles away from Stranraer on the north side of Loch Ryan, and there is no public transport connection. For a taxi (around £3) phone ☎ 704988 or ☎ 705555.

Stena Line ferries for Larne connect directly with rail and bus services. The railway station is on the ferry pier. The SeaCat terminal is just south of the ferry pier.

Bus A National Express service runs thrice daily between London and Belfast, via Birmingham, Manchester, Carlisle, Dumfries, the towns along the A75 and Stranraer. Stagecoach Western runs hourly buses to Glasgow (three hours, £6.20). There are also regular local buses to Kirkcudbright and the towns along the A75, like Newton Stewart (£1.95) and Dumfries.

Train There are regular services between Stranraer and Belfast via Larne (nine hours); and Stranraer and Glasgow (2½ hours).

AROUND STRANRAER
Castle Kennedy Gardens

Magnificent Castle Kennedy Gardens (☎ 01776-702024), several miles east of

Stanraer, are among the most famous in Scotland. They cover 67 acres and are set on a peninsula between two lochs and two castles (Castle Kennedy, burnt in 1716, and Lochinch Castle, built in 1864). The land-scaping was undertaken in 1730 by the Earl of Stair, who used unoccupied soldiers to do the work. The gardens are open from April through September, daily from 10 am to 5 pm (extended hours in summer); £2/1.

Central Scotland

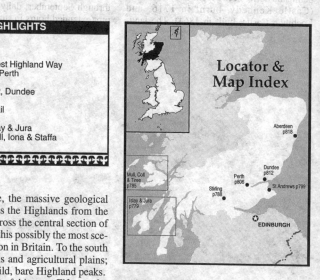

Locator & Map Index

Aberdeen p818

Dundee p812

Perth p806

St Andrews p799

Mull, Coll & Tiree p785

Stirling p788

Islay & Jura p779

EDINBURGH

The Highland line, the massive geological fault which divides the Highlands from the Lowlands, runs across the central section of Scotland, making this possibly the most scenically varied region in Britain. To the south are undulating hills and agricultural plains; to the north, the wild, bare Highland peaks.

In the south-east of this area, Fife was for centuries an independent kingdom. The attractive seaside town of St Andrews, its capital, was once the ecclesiastical centre of the country, but is now better known for its university and as the home of golf.

On the western side of central Scotland, less than 20 miles north of Glasgow, are the famous 'bonnie, bonnie banks' of Loch Lomond, straddling the Highland line. Tourists have been visiting this area and the Trossachs (the lochs and hills just east of Loch Lomond) and comparing them to England's Lake District for more than 150 years – Queen Victoria among them. Having set her heart on adding a Highland residence to her list of royal properties, she toured the area, eventually purchasing the Balmoral estate.

The town of Stirling, 26 miles north of Glasgow, has witnessed most of the great battles in the Scottish struggle against English domination. The spectacular castle, dramatically perched on a rock as is Edinburgh's castle, was for centuries of par-

amount strategic importance, controlling the main routes in the area.

To the west is Argyll and the western coastline, indented by long inlets and sea lochs forged by glaciers thousands of years ago. Off this coast are the popular islands of the Inner Hebrides. Accessible from the town of Oban, Mull sees the most tourists, but is large enough to absorb them. There are some wonderful mountain walks up Mull's challenging 3000-foot-high peaks. Off the furthest tip of Mull is the Isle of Iona, where St Columba, having sailed from Ireland, came to build his Christian foundation. To the west of Mull lie Coll and Tiree – long, low islands, seen from the ferry on a summer's day as a blue haze tinged with the silver of their sandy beaches. South-west of Oban are the isles of Colonsay, Islay and Jura. The latter's breast-shaped mountains are known as the Paps of Jura, and are visible from far away on a clear day. Islay is more agricultural and is famous for its whisky distilleries.

Perth is on the direct route from Edinburgh to Inverness. It was once the capital of Scotland, and is now an attractive town ringed by castles. Both Dunkeld and Pitlochry, to the north, are appealing (though touristy) villages, which are useful as walking bases. Frequent buses and trains service this route.

Following the coast to Aberdeen from Perth or St Andrews, you quickly reach Dundee, one of Scotland's largest cities. Despite its excellent location, it has not recovered from modern development and the loss of its jute and shipbuilding industries. It's worth pausing in Dundee to visit Captain Scott's Antarctic ship, *Discovery*, moored near the Tay Bridge.

The eastern Highlands is a great elbow of land that juts into the North Sea between Perth and the Firth of Tay in the south, and Inverness and Moray Firth in the north. There are excellent hill walks in the Grampians, and the Cairngorms are as bleak and demanding as any Scottish mountains. The coastline, especially from Stonehaven to Buckie, is particularly attractive. The valley of the Dee – the Royal Dee thanks to the Queen's residence at Balmoral – has sublime scenery. Braemar is surrounded by good walking country, and hosts Scotland's most important Highland Games, the Braemar Gathering, in September.

The largest city in the north east is prosperous Aberdeen, a lively and attractive place fattened on the proceeds of a long history of sea trade and currently through the North Sea oil industry, for which it is the onshore base.

The small fishing villages of the north coast are little-visited, but some are very pretty. Further west along this coast, experiments with alternative lifestyles continue at the Findhorn Foundation, an international spiritual community that welcomes outsiders with a range of eclectic courses. Further spiritual guidance is provided in neighbouring Speyside, where whisky distilleries welcome visitors with tours and free drams.

ORIENTATION & INFORMATION

This central section of the country comprises the administrative regions of Fife, Stirling, Perthshire & Kinross, Angus, Aberdeenshire, Moray, and Argyll & Bute.

The main mountain range is the Grampians, rising to over 3500 feet; the Cairngorms are over 4000 feet and border the Highland region. To the west the western coast, the islands of the Inner Hebrides – Islay, Jura, Colonsay, Mull, Iona, Coll and Tiree – are accessible from Oban.

There are TICs in all the main tourist centres, many open seven days a week in summer. Smaller TICs close completely from October to Easter. Some TICs make a charge for booking local accommodation, usually around £1; most will ask only for a 10% advance.

WALKS & CYCLE ROUTES

The West Highland Way, possibly the finest long-distance walk in Britain, cuts across the centre of this region from Milngavie (near Glasgow) to Fort William. See the Activities chapter at the start of this book for more information.

There is some superb hill walking in the Highland areas of central Scotland; Braemar is one of a number of good bases – there's a challenging walk from here through the Cairngorms to Aviemore. The isles of Mull and Jura have wild mountainous areas and are excellent places for walking holidays.

Aside from the busy A9, which roars up the middle of Scotland, the side roads are refreshingly free of traffic and excellent for cycling. There's an official cycle trail, the Glasgow, Loch Lomond & Killin Cycle Way, which follows forest trails, small roads and disused rail routes.

GETTING AROUND

Although the larger towns are easy to reach by bus and train, travel into the Grampians and other interesting walking areas is often difficult without your own transport. Furthermore, the division between the eastern and western Highlands reflects the transport realities – there are few coast-to-coast links across central Scotland. Cars can be hired in the larger towns.

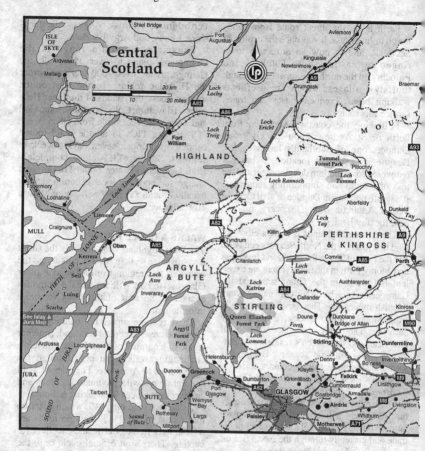

Bus

Scottish Citylink (☎ 0990-505050) links all the main towns in the area; Perth is a major hub for its services. Away from the population centres, there are few buses and, as has already been mentioned, travelling from the east to the west across central Scotland is difficult. Bus transport around the north-eastern coast, however, is fairly reasonable.

Midland Bluebird (☎ 01324-613777) and Bluebird Buses (☎ 01224-212266) are among the bigger operators of local services. There are some day passes, such as Midland Bluebird's Heart of Scotland Explorer ticket

(£6.60), which also gives you half-price travel on the buses of companies in neighbouring regions.

For information on local buses in Dundee phone ☎ 01382-201121; for Aberdeenshire and Moray buses phone ☎ 01224-664581; and for Fife, phone ☎ 01592-414141, extension 3103.

Train

The rail system in central Scotland has three lines running north to south, connected by a fourth running north-east from Glasgow through Stirling, Perth, Dundee and Aber-

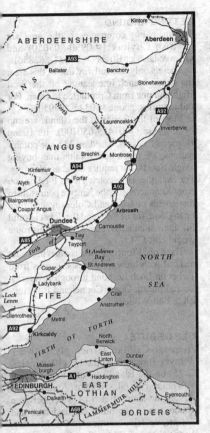

beautiful climb through the Cairngorms from Dunkeld to Aviemore.

ScotRail's regional Rover tickets cover parts of the system here. The West Highland Rover allows travel on this famous line for four days out of eight and costs £39. The North Highland Rover is the same price and runs north into the Highlands from Aberdeen.

For rail information phone ☎ 0345-484950.

Boat

From Aberdeen, P&O (☎ 01224-572615) has daily departures on Monday, Wednesday, Thursday and Friday leaving in the evening for Lerwick (Shetland). In summer, there are departures at noon on Tuesday and Saturday to Lerwick via Stromness (Orkney). See the Aberdeen section for more information.

Ferries to the Hebridean islands off the west coast are mostly run by Caledonian MacBrayne (CalMac) (☎ 01475-650100). Most of the routes depart from Oban, but there are also some services from Kennacraig, on the Kintyre peninsula. If you plan to island hop, you can save yourself a considerable amount by planning your trip in advance and buying one of CalMac's Island Hopscotch tickets covering set routes. There are also Island Rovers covering the whole system – £36 for eight days, £51 for 15 days. Taking a car can be expensive. Contact CalMac at the Ferry Terminal, Gourock PA19 1QP, for a free timetable and fare structure – also available from TICs.

deen. It's a reasonably efficient service, but has a major flaw – travel from the east to the west directly across central Scotland is impossible. You must return to Glasgow.

The West Highland line, possibly the most spectacular train journey in Britain, runs north across central Scotland from Glasgow to Fort William and Mallaig. A branch line from Crianlarich connects Oban to the system, and overnight trains run between London and Oban for ferries to the Hebridean islands.

Another scenic train journey in this area runs from Perth to Inverness and includes a

Argyll & Bute

Created in 1996 to replace the northern section of the large region of Strathclyde, Argyll & Bute stretches from the tip of the Kintyre peninsula (Paul McCartney's 'Mull of Kintyre') almost to Glen Coe, and east to Loch Lomond. It includes the Isle of Bute, parts of the Western Highlands, and the islands of the Inner Hebrides – Islay, Jura, Colonsay, Mull, Coll and Tiree.

This area is centred on the ancient kingdom of Dalriada, named by the Irish settlers (known as the Scots) who claimed it around the 5th century. From their headquarters at Dunadd, in the Moine Mhor (great bog) near Kilmartin, they gained ascendancy over the Picts and established the Kingdom of Alba, which eventually became Scotland.

Just 20 miles from Glasgow, Loch Lomond is a very popular destination. Its western bank, where most of the tourist activity takes place, lies in Argyll & Bute; the eastern bank in Stirling.

The Firth of Clyde, to the south, is a complex system of long, deep fjords, or sea lochs, such as Loch Long and Loch Fyne. This pattern of glacial valleys, drowned by the incoming sea, continues all the way up the western coast of Scotland, creating hundreds of miles of indented coastline. It's an area that records some of the highest rainfall in Britain.

Most people heading for the islands pass through the pleasant town of Oban, the only place of any size in the area, at least once. Ferries leave for the popular Isle of Mull (nothing to do with the Mull of Kintyre). It's a great place to hike, with peaks over 3000 feet. There are two interesting castles, Torosay and Duart, near the eastern port of Craignure, and a narrow-gauge railway. The pretty fishing port of Tobermory is in the north of the island.

A five-minute ferry trip to the west of Mull is the tiny Isle of Iona, which is where St Columba arrived from Ireland in the 6th century. Boat trips leave for the uninhabited Isle of Staffa, where the incredible fluted pillars of Fingal's Cave inspired Mendelsshon to compose the *Hebridean Symphony*.

Ferries continue from Tobermory to the islands of Coll and Tiree. South from Oban they link Colonsay and Islay. The latter is the most southerly island in the Hebrides, and is famous for its whisky distilleries, which produce wonderfully peaty single malts. Beside Islay is the wild Isle of Jura, where George Orwell wrote *1984*. There are ferry links from Islay to the Kintyre peninsula and the mainland.

GETTING AROUND

The main bus companies in the area are Scottish Citylink (☎ 0990-505050) and Oban & District Buses (☎ 01631-562856).

There's only one railway line in this area: the scenic branch line leading off the West Highland line from Crianlarich to Oban. For rail inquiries, phone ☎ 0345-484950.

Most of the ferries to the islands are run by CalMac (☎ 01475-650100). Its Island Hopscotch tickets, based on 23 route combinations, are much better value than buying single tickets, but require advance planning. For example, Hopscotch Ticket F takes you from Kennacraig on the Kintyre peninsula to the islands of Islay and Colonsay, and then on to Oban, for £15.40, and the ticket is valid for three months. To take a car on this route would cost £74.

The Argyll Tourist Route is a driving route marked with brown signposts. It runs from Tarbet on Loch Lomond through Inveraray, Lochgilphead, Oban, Connel and Balachulish to Fort William.

ISLE OF BUTE

Frequent CalMac ferries ply between Wemyss Bay and Rothesay (30 minutes, £2.75) on the island of Bute, long popular with holidaying Glaswegians. Another ferry crosses the short stretch of water between Rhubodach in the north of the island and Colintrave (five minutes). On Monday, Wednesday and Friday there's a ferry link with the Isle of Arran (1½ hours).

The resort of **Rothesay** is the island's only town, built around the substantial ruins of Rothesay Castle. Mock-Gothic **Mount Stuart**, the Marquess of Bute's house, opened to the public in 1995 and is well worth seeing. It's open from April to September from 11 am to 5 pm; entry is £5.50/ 2.50.

The TIC (☎ 01700-502151), 15 Victoria St, has long lists of B&Bs and hotels, but there's no youth hostel on the island. The main beach is in the south by Kilchattan Bay. In late July there's a popular folk festival on Bute.

LOCH LOMOND

After Loch Ness, this is perhaps the most famous of Scotland's lochs. Measuring 27½ square miles, it's the largest single inland waterway in Britain. Its proximity to Glasgow (it's only 20 miles north) means that parts of the loch can get quite crowded in summer. The main tourist focus, however, has always been on the western coast of the loch, along the A82, and at the southern end, around Balloch, which can be a nightmare of jet skis and motorboats. The eastern coast, which the West Highland Way follows, sees very few visitors.

The loch was formed 10,000 years ago by the action of glaciers, and it lay at the junction of the three ancient Scottish kingdoms of Strathclyde, Dalriada and Pictland. Some of the 37 islands in the loch made perfect retreats for early Christians. The missionary St Mirrin spent some time on Inchmurrin, the largest island, which is named after him.

The loch crosses the Highland line and its character changes quite obviously as you move from north to south, with the most dramatic scenery in the north. The highest mountain in the area is Ben Lomond (3194 feet) on the eastern coast.

Orientation & Information

The loch is 23 miles long and up to five miles wide. The A82 is a major route to the north and sticks to the western shore through Tarbet and on to Crianlarich. The main thoroughfare on the eastern coast is just a walking trail, the West Highland Way, although tiny roads touch this coast from Drymen and Loch Katrine.

There are TICs at Balloch (☎ 01389-753533), Balloch Rd, open March to October; Drymen (☎ 01360-660068), in the library on the square, open April to September; and Tarbet (☎ 01301-702260), on the main street.

Walks & Cycle Routes

The big walk here is the West Highland Way, but it's easy enough to access portions of the trail for shorter walks. See the Activities chapter at the start of this book.

From Rowardennan, you can tackle Ben Lomond (3194 feet), a very popular five to six-hour round trip. The route begins from the car park by the Rowardennan Hotel, and you can return via Ptarmigan (2398 feet) for good views of the loch.

The main cycle route in the area is the Glasgow to Killin Cycle Way, which reaches the loch at Balloch and Inversnaid. Most of the route is set back to the east of the loch, through the Queen Elizabeth Forest Park. Along the western coast, the A82 is very busy in summer, but there are sections of the old road beside it that are quieter.

Boat Trips

The main centre for boat trips is Balloch, where two outfits, Sweeney's Cruises (☎ 01389-752376) and Mullen's Cruises (☎ 01389-751481), offer a wide range of trips from £4/2 an hour for an adult/child. There's a 2½-hour cruise (£6) to the village of Luss, allowing 30 minutes ashore. If this twee village looks like a film set, that's because it is. The village is very popular with Scottish visitors hoping to catch a glimpse of the stars of the soap *Take the High Road*.

Cruise Loch Lomond (☎ 01301-702356) operates from Tarbet, and MacFarlane & Son (☎ 01360-870214) from Balmaha.

Places to Stay & Eat

Hostels One of the most impressive hostels in the country is *Loch Lomond Youth Hostel* (☎ 01389-850226). It's located in an imposing building set in beautiful grounds, two miles north of Balloch, near Arden. It's open from early March to the end of October, and over the New Year period. The nightly charge is £7.80/6.40 and you need to book in advance in summer. And yes, it is haunted.

Rowardennan Youth Hostel (☎ 01360-870259) is across the loch, halfway up the eastern coast and right by the water. It's also an activity centre, and is open from late February to the end of October. Beds are £6.95/5.85. It's the perfect base for climbing Ben Lomond.

Camping For campers, *Tullichewan Caravan Park* (☎ 01389-759475), Balloch, costs £6.50 per tent and two people; *Inverbeg Holiday Park* (☎ 01436-860267), Inverbeg, is similarly priced; the popular and well-located *Forestry Commission Cashel Campsite* (☎ 01360-870234), on the eastern shore, costs £3.95, and the *Ardlui Caravan Park* (☎ 01301-704243) costs £6 to pitch a tent – you can also rent boats here.

Also on the eastern side of the loch you can camp for free in the *bothies* (stone sheds) at Rowchoish (three miles north of Rowardennan) and Doune (4½ miles north of Inversnaid).

B&Bs & Hotels There are numerous B&Bs, centred on Balloch, Luss, Inverbeg and Tarbet.

There is, however, one pub in this area you shouldn't miss. The *Drover's Inn* (☎ 01301-704234), in Inverarnan at the northern end of the loch, has smoke-blackened walls, bare wooden floors, a grand hall filled with moth-eaten stuffed animals, and wee drams served by barmen in kilts. It's a great place for a serious drinking binge; and you can even stay here for £17 per person B&B.

Getting There & Away
There are several buses a day (Nos 915/16/35) from Glasgow to Balloch (40 minutes, £2.60); other services continue up the west coast to Luss (55 minutes), Tarbet (65 minutes), Ardlui (1¼ hours) and, north of the loch, Crianlarich.

There are two railway lines. From Glasgow, one serves Balloch (35 minutes, £2.80); the other touches the loch at Tarbet and Ardlui.

Getting Around
Ferry services run between Mid-Ross (one mile north of Arden) and Inchmurrin Island; Balmaha and the nature reserve on Inchcailloch Island; Inverglas and Inversnaid; and Inverbeg and Rowardennan.

INVERARAY
• *pop 450*   • ☎ *01499*
On the shores of Loch Fyne, Inveraray is a picturesque, small town with a number of interesting attractions. It's an early planned town, built by the Duke of Argyll when he revamped his nearby castle in the 18th century. The TIC (☎ 302063) is on the street that runs along the loch.

Inveraray Castle
On the edge of the town, Inveraray Castle has been the seat of the chiefs of Clan Campbell, the dukes of Argyll, since the 15th century. The current 18th-century building includes whimsical turrets and fake battlements. Inside is the impressive armoury hall, whose walls are patterned with an extensive collection of pole arms, dirks, muskets and Lochaber axes – more than 1000 of them. The dining and drawing rooms have ornate ceilings and there's a large collection of porcelain.

Near the castle, the Combined Operations Museum relates the part the town played in the training of Allied troops for the D-day landings.

The castle (☎ 302203) is open from early April to mid-October, daily except Friday (but open on Friday in July and August), 10 am to 12.30 pm and 2 to 5.45 pm (afternoon only on Sunday). Entry is £4/2; it's well worth visiting.

Inveraray Jail
The Georgian jail and courthouse, in the centre of the town, have been converted into an entertaining tourist attraction, where you sit in on a trial, try out a cell and discover the meaning of 'picking oakum'. Chatty warders and attendants in 19th-century costume accost visitors. The jail (☎ 302381) is open daily from 9.30 am to 6 pm (last entry 5 pm); tickets are £3.95/2.

Arctic Penguin
This three-masted schooner, built in 1911 and one of the world's last iron sailing ships, is now a 'unique maritime experience'. There are displays on the maritime history of the Clyde, archive videos, and activities for children. Open daily from 10 am to 6 pm (5 pm in winter), entry is £2.95.

Places to Stay & Eat

Inveraray Youth Hostel (☎ 302454) is a modern building on Dalmally Rd. Open from mid-March to September, the nightly charge is £5.40/4.40.

There are several B&Bs around the town. *Mrs Campbell's* (☎ 302258), Main St South, is open from April to October and charges £14.50 per person. The *Old Rectory* (☎ 302280) has nine rooms, around £18/33, and is open year-round.

The *Great Inn* (☎ 302466) looks out over the loch and offers pub meals; B&B costs £35 per person.

The best place to eat in the area is the *Loch Fyne Oyster Bar* (☎ 600236), six miles north of Inveraray. Half a dozen oysters are £4.90 and there's a good range of smoked fish and fresh seafood. Cheaper fish is sold in the attached shop.

Getting There & Away

There are six Citylink buses a day (four on Sunday) from Glasgow (1¾ hours, £4.90). There are also buses to Oban (1¼ hours).

KILMARTIN GLEN

This magical glen is at the centre of one of the most concentrated areas of prehistoric sites in Scotland. This is where the Irish invaders founded Dalriada and formed the kingdom of Alba, which eventually united a large part of the country, so this part of mid-Argyll is seen as the cradle of modern Scotland.

The oldest monuments date from 5000 years ago and comprise a linear cemetery of burial cairns, running south of Kilmartin village for 1½ miles. There are also ritual monuments, two stone circles at Temple Wood three-quarters of a mile south-west of Kilmartin. Three miles north of Lochgilphead, at Kilmichael Glassary, elaborate designs are cut into rock faces; their purpose is unknown.

The hill fort of Dunadd, four miles north of Lochgilphead, overlooks the boggy plain that is now the Moine Mhor Nature Reserve. It was chosen as the royal residence of the first kings of Dalriada, and this was probably where the Stone of Destiny, used in the investiture ceremony, was originally located. The faint rock carvings – an ogham inscription (an ancient script), a wild boar and two footprints – were probably used in some kind of inauguration ceremony.

There are some 10th-century Celtic crosses in Kilmartin churchyard. Beside the church, what promises to be a most interesting new museum will open in March 1997. **Kilmartin House** (☎ 01546-510278) will be a centre for archaeology and landscape interpretation with artefacts from the sites, interactive displays, guided walks and a tearoom. The project was partly funded by midges – the curator exposed himself in Temple Wood on a warm summer's evening and was sponsored per midge bite! Proposed opening is March to December, daily from 10.30 am to 6 pm, and there will be discounts for the environmentally-friendly traveller (ie those who don't arrive by car).

The nearest TIC is at Lochgilphead (☎ 01546-602344), eight miles south of Kilmartin.

Places to Stay & Eat

There's a good range of places to stay in and around Kilmartin. At *Cornaig* (☎ 01546-510224) there's B&B in an old manse from £14 to £18 per person. *Kilmartin Hotel* (☎ 01546-510250) charges £15 per person (£20 in a room with attached bath) and has a restaurant and bar; there's folk music here some weekends. The *Cairn Restaurant*, nearby, does good lunches and dinners.

At Ardfern, adjacent to Craobh Haven and in an idyllic, peaceful location overlooking the Sound of Jura, is *Lunga* (☎ 01852-500237), a grand 17th-century mansion. The hospitable laird offers B&B from £14 to £19 per person. There are also self-catering apartments on this 3000-acre estate. Lunga is about seven miles north of Kilmartin.

Getting There & Away

From Glasgow to Lochgilphead (2½ hours) there are three buses a day. For the eight miles to Kilmartin there's only one bus in summer, at 9.20 am. From Oban to Kilmartin (1 hour) there's a bus at 4 pm.

KINTYRE PENINSULA

Forty miles long and eight miles wide, the Kintyre peninsula is almost an island, with only a narrow strand to connect it to the wooded hills of Knapdale at Tarbert. Magnus Barefoot the Viking, who was allowed to claim as his own any island he had circumnavigated, made his men drag their longship across this strand to validate his claim.

Tarbert is the gateway to the peninsula. It's a busy fishing village that also attracts the yachting crowd. Above Tarbert is a small crumbling castle built by Robert the Bruce. The TIC (☎ 01880-820429) is by the harbour.

Apart from Scots who pack the B&Bs and camping grounds of Machrihanish, few other tourists venture down here, and public transport is very limited. There are CalMac ferry terminals at Kennacraig (☎ 01880-730253) for Islay, and at Claonaig (no phone) for Arran.

From Tayinloan, there are hourly ferries (20 minutes, £2) to the **Isle of Gigha** (pronounced ghee-a, with a soft 'g'), a flat island seven miles long by about a mile wide. It's known for the subtropical gardens of Achamore House, open daily from 9 am to dusk; entry is £2/1. Gigha cheese is sold in many parts of Argyll and is recommended, though not cheap. There are island walks and bikes can be rented from Gigha Stores. Several places do B&B: the *Post Office* (☎ 01583-505251) charges around £15 per person. The *Gigha Hotel* (☎ 01583-505254) has rooms for £35 per person, and a good restaurant and bar. You can rent bikes from the post office for £6 per day.

Campbeltown feels very much the end of the road. The town is linked by a daily Scottish Citylink bus to Glasgow. A narrow winding road leads to the **Mull of Kintyre**, popularised by the song – and the mist does indeed often roll in. A lighthouse marks the spot closest to Ireland – only 12 miles across the water. There's a TIC (☎ 01586-552056) by the quay in Campbelltown.

ISLE OF ISLAY

- *pop 4000*   • ☎ *01496*

The most southerly of the islands of the Inner Hebrides, Islay (pronounced eye-lah) is best known for its single malt whiskies, which have a highly distinctive smoky flavour. There are six distilleries, some of which welcome visitors with guided tours.

The island has a long history, which is related at the **Museum of Islay Life** in Port Charlotte. It was an early focus for Christianity. The 8th-century **Kildaton Cross**, at Kildaton Chapel, five miles north-east of Port Ellen, is one of the finest Celtic crosses ever found. Islay was also a seat of secular power for the Hebrides, and the meeting place of the Lords of the Isles during the 14th century. At **Finlaggan** are the ruins of the castle from which the powerful MacDonald Lords of the Isles used to administer their considerable island territories. At Bowmore, the **Round Church** was built in 1767 in this curious shape to ensure that the devil had no corners to hide in.

With a list of over 250 recorded species, Islay also attracts bird-watchers. It's an important wintering ground for white-fronted and barnacle geese. As well as the whisky and the wildfowl, there are miles of sandy beaches and good walks.

Since it's further from the coast than Arran or Mull, Islay receives far fewer visitors. It's definitely worth the trip.

Orientation & Information

Port Askaig is little more than a ferry terminal opposite Jura. Port Ellen is a larger place, with three distilleries nearby. Bowmore is the island's capital. It's 10 miles from both Port Askaig and Port Ellen, on the island's western coast. Around the bay, at the attractive village of Port Charlotte, is the youth hostel and museum.

The TIC (☎ 810254) is in Bowmore, and is open year-round. There's also a small TIC at Port Ellen, open when the ferry docks.

Places to Stay & Eat

There are several B&Bs and a hostel, the *Islay Youth Hostel* (☎ 850385), in Port Char-

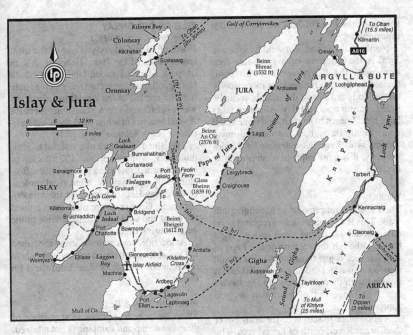

Islay & Jura

lotte. The hostel is open from March to October and has beds for £5.40/4.40. *Mrs Halsall's* (☎ 850431), Nerabus, has rooms with bath attached for £16.50 per person.

In Port Ellen, *Kintra Bunk Barns* (☎ 302051), Kintra Farm, Kintra Beach, has 30 beds for £5.50 (plus £2 if you need bedding). They also do farmhouse B&B from £15 per person. *Glenmachrie Farmhouse* (☎ 302560) has five rooms, all with attached bath, for £25 per person. Excellent meals are available. The *Trout Fly Guest House* (☎ 302204) has rooms from £16.50 per person; evening meals are £10.50.

In Bowmore, the *Harbour Inn* (☎ 810330) has a good restaurant that serves seafood; B&B is from £22 per person. *Tiree* (☎ 810633), Jamieson St, offers B&B from £14.

Getting There & Away

CalMac (☎ 302209) has a ferry from Kennacraig to Port Ellen (two hours, £5.90)

and another to Port Askaig (1¾ hours, £5.90). They operate daily except on Wednesday, when there's only a ferry to Port Askaig, and on Sunday, when there's only a ferry to Port Ellen. On Wednesday, there's a ferry between Colonsay and Port Askaig.

Getting Around

A very limited bus service operates between Port Ellen, Bowmore and Askaig.

ISLE OF JURA

- pop 195   • ☎ 01496

Jura is a magnificently wild and lonely island and one can quite understand why George Orwell chose it as a writer's retreat. He spent several months in Barnhill, a house in the north of the island. It's a wonderful place to walk – in fact there's really nothing else to do here, apart from visit the Craighouse distillery in the island's only village. The mountain scenery is superb and the distinctive shapes of the Paps of Jura are visible from miles around.

North of the island, between Scarba and Jura, is the epicentre of a great tide race known as the Corryvreckan whirlpool. Caused by the tide running out more slowly on the landward side of the islands, it can be heard roaring on a still day. Although stags have been known to swim it, and quite small boats to slip through, it has claimed many victims who have not calculated the tides properly. It is most impressive an hour after low tide.

Walks

The Paps of Jura provide a challenging hill walk. This is a tough walk that requires good navigational skills and takes around eight hours, although the record for the Paps of Jura fell race is just three hours! You should also look out for adders – the island is infested with them, but they are shy snakes that will move out of your way as you approach.

A good place to start is by the bridge over the Corran River, north of Lergybreck. The first pap you reach is Beinn a'Chaolais (2408 feet), the second is Beinn an Oir (2572 feet) and the third is Beinn Shiantaidh (2477 feet). Most people also climb Corra Bheinn (1866 feet), before joining the path that crosses the island to descend to the road.

Places to Stay & Eat

In Craighouse, there's B&B from £16 to £18 per person at *Gwen Boardman's* (☎ 820379), 7 Woodside. The *Jura Hotel* (☎ 820243) is a great place to stay and the place to drink on Jura. It charges from £28 per person; try to get the rooms at the front for the views. There's pub grub, and full set meals are £16.25.

Getting There & Away

You reach Jura via Islay. Western Ferries (☎ 840681) shuttles between Port Askaig and Feolin (five minutes, 80p) every half-hour from Monday to Saturday, and less often on Sunday. The ferry also takes cars.

ISLE OF COLONSAY
- *pop 105*   •   ☎ *01951*

North of Islay, Colonsay is one of the most remote isles of the Inner Hebrides. It's an unspoilt island of varied landscapes which has a good sunshine record and receives only half the rainfall of the Argyll mainland. As well as cliffs and a rocky coastline, there are several beaches of white sand, the most spectacular being Kiloran Bay.

The island is of particular interest to ornithologists, with more than 150 species of birds recorded, including golden eagles. Botanists will appreciate the subtropical gardens of Colonsay House, known for their rhododendrons. Grey seals are often seen around the coast and wild goats inhabit some of the neighbouring islets.

At low tide, you can walk across the strand to Oronsay, a small island to the south, where the ruins of the priory date from the 14th century.

Places to Stay & Eat

There are very few places to stay, none of them are cheap and camping is not allowed. For B&B, there's *Seaview* (☎ 200315), on the rugged western coast, charging £20 per person. The *Isle of Colonsay Hotel* (☎ 200316) is open from March to October and is the only hotel on the island. Most people stay on a B&B and dinner basis; rates are around £60 per person. Bicycle hire is included.

Getting There & Away

CalMac has ferries on Monday, Wednesday and Friday to Colonsay from Oban (2¼ hours, £8.20), and on Wednesday from Islay's Port Askaig (1¼ hours, £3) and from Kennacraig on the Kintyre peninsula (3¼ hours, £8.20).

OBAN
- *pop 7500*   •   ☎ *01631*

Oban can be inundated by visitors, but as the most important ferry port on the west coast, it manages to hold its own. By Highlands standards, it's quite a large town, but you can easily get around it on foot. There isn't a great deal to see or do, but it's on a beautiful bay, the harbour is interesting and there are some good coastal and hill walks in the vicinity.

Orientation

The bus, train and ferry terminals are all grouped conveniently together by the side of the harbour, on the southern edge of the bay. Argyll Square is one block east of the railway station, and George St leads north past the North Pier. From the pier, Corran Esplanade runs round the northern edge of the bay.

If you're driving from Inveraray, the A85 brings you into the northern end of town.

Information

Oban TIC (☎ 563122) is on Argyll Square, right next door to the site of the Tolerable Inn, where Johnson and Boswell stayed on 22 October 1773 on their travels through the Western Isles. The TIC is open in July and August, Monday to Saturday from 9 am to 9 pm, and on Sunday until 6 pm; May, June and September until 5.30 pm (5 pm on Sunday); and weekdays only for the rest of the year.

Things to See & Do

Crowning the hill above the town is **McCaig's Tower**, built at the end of the last century. It was intended to be an art gallery, but was not completed and now looks like an ugly version of Rome's colosseum. There are, however, good views over the bay from beside this peculiar structure. It's always open and there's no entry charge. There's an even better view from **Pulpit Hill**, to the south of the town.

For the last 200 years, **Oban Distillery** has been producing Oban single malt whisky in the centre of the town. There are tours (£2) from Monday to Friday, year-round, and also on Saturday from Easter to October. Even if you don't want the tour or the whisky, it's still worth visiting the distillery for the small exhibition in the foyer.

On the North Pier, **World in Miniature** is a bit twee but considerable skill must have been involved in the construction of these miniature houses and tableaux. Entry is £1.50/1, and it's open daily from 10 am to 6 pm.

Walks & Cycle Routes

It's a very pleasant 20-minute walk north from the youth hostel along the coast to **Dunollie Castle**, built by the MacDougall's of Lorne in the 15th century. It's open all the time and very much a ruin. You could continue along this road to the beach at Ganavan Sands, 2½ miles from Oban.

A TIC leaflet lists local bike rides. They include a seven-mile Gallanach circular tour, a 16-mile route to Seil Island and routes to Connel, Glenlonan and Kilmore.

Organised Tours

On Sunday, Oban & District (☎ 562856), the local bus company, operates a range of half-day tours to Loch Etive, Inveraray, Glencoe, Kilmartin and the Sea Life Centre (10 miles to the north).

Day trips from Oban to Mull and Iona leave from the northern side of the North Pier, which is where tickets are sold. MacDougall's Tours (☎ 562133) has a Mull and Iona tour for £14, Mull castles for £13 and a cruise to Tobermory for £10. There are also boat trips south to the Scottish Seafood & Salmon Centre, seven miles from Oban, where there's an excellent seafood restaurant.

Places to Stay

Hostels The popular *Oban Backpackers Lodge* (☎ 562107), Breadalbane St, charges £8 (including sheets). From the railway station and ferry terminal walk north right to the end of George St, past the cinema, and veer right into Breadalbane St. It's a very friendly place with a communal kitchen. Breakfast costs £1.40.

Oban Youth Hostel (☎ 562025) is on the Esplanade, north of town, on the other side of the bay to the terminals. Beds are £7.80/6.40, and it's open from late February to October.

Camping The nearest campsite is *Gallanachmore Farm Caravan & Camping*

Park (☎ 562425), two miles south of Oban on the road to Gallanach. It's by the sea and costs around £6.

B&Bs & Hotels The cheapest B&B in town is *Jeremy Inglis'* (☎ 565065), just across the square from the TIC, at 21 Airds Crescent. Jeremy Inglis (alias Mr McTavish's Kitchens) charges only around £7 per person, including continental breakfast, and so gets booked up quickly. There are some double and family rooms.

Convenient for the ferry terminal is *Maridon House* (☎ 562670), a large, blue house on Dunuaran Rd. There are 10 rooms and B&B ranges from £14 to £18.50 per person. Book in advance in summer.

The main area for B&Bs and guesthouses is at the northern end of George St, along Dunollie Terrace and Breadalbane St. *Sand Villa Guest House* (☎ 562803), Breadalbane St, is an efficient place with 15 rooms, charging from £14 to £18.50 per person. There are numerous other places in this area.

To the north of the town, Corran Esplanade is lined with more expensive guesthouses and small hotels, all facing seaward and most offering rooms with bathrooms attached. *Glenrigh Private Hotel* (☎ 562991) offers B&B at £26 per person. *Kilchrenan House* (☎ 562663), near the youth hostel, is an excellent place to stay, charging from £23 to £30 per person. At the far end of the Esplanade is *Barriemore Hotel* (☎ 566356), another recommended place, with B&B from £24 to £30 per person. They do an excellent dinner.

There are a number of B&Bs below McCaig's Tower. *Mrs Frost's* (☎ 566630), Laurgiemhor, Laurel Rd, is the white building that looks like a castle, nearest to the tower. There are superb views and great breakfasts, but only one single and a double. B&B is around £15 per person. In the same area is *Crathie Guest House* (☎ 562619), Duncraggan Rd, which has seven rooms priced from £14/28 for a single/double. On Ardconnel Terrace, there are good views from *Invercloy Guest House* (☎ 562058). It offers B&B from £14/28 to £18/38.

The *Palace Hotel* (☎ 562294) is right in the centre, on George St. B&B is from £16 to £25 per person and most rooms have bathroom attached.

Just north of the North Pier, on the Esplanade, the *Regent Hotel* (☎ 562341) is Oban's attempt at Art Deco. B&B in a room with bath attached costs £25 per person.

The top hotel is the *Manor House* (☎ 562087), south around the bay, on Gallanach Rd. Built in 1780, this house was originally part of the estate of the Duke of Argyll. It's worth eating in the hotel's restaurant if you're staying here. B&B and dinner ranges from £45 to £90 per person. Also highly recommended is *Heatherfield House* (see Places to Eat below), which has been described as a restaurant with rooms.

Places to Eat
There's no shortage of places to eat in Oban. Most are located along the bay between the railway station and the North Pier, and along George St.

You can't miss the highly publicised *McTavish's Kitchens* (☎ 563064), centrally located on George St. There's a self-service café, and a Scottish show in the restaurant each night (see Entertainment).

Opposite the Oban Distillery, the *China Restaurant* (☎ 563575) does a set lunch for £4.90, Monday to Friday.

The *Studio Restaurant* (☎ 562030), Craigard Rd, off George St, continues to deserve its good reputation. Local cuisine includes paté and oatcakes, roast Angus beef and Scottish cheeses. A three-course dinner costs £10.50 between 5 pm and 6.30 pm, £11.75 until 10 pm.

North of the North Pier, along Corran Esplanade, *Oban Sesame* is a healthfood store that sells snacks. Further along the Esplanade is *Coasters Wine Bar*, a popular place with cheap food such as fish & chips and spaghetti etc for under £5.

The *Waterfront Restaurant* (☎ 563110), by the railway quay, is an excellent place for seafood. Most courses are around £11 (eg Scallops Tobermory with prawns in cream sauce, £11.85), but there's also a cheaper bar menu.

The best place to eat in Oban is *Heatherfield House* (☎ 562681), Albert Rd. There's a set dinner in the non-smoking dining room for £16.50; they bake their own bread, cure their own hams and all seafood is locally-caught. There are also a few rooms here, from £44 to £51 per person including dinner, B&B.

Entertainment
The nightly Scottish show at *McTavish's Kitchens* (see Places to Eat) packs 'em in. It starts at 8.30 pm and there's dancing, a live band and a piper. It costs £1.50/75p for adults/children if you also eat here, £3/1.50 if you don't; there are also set meals from £7.95 including the show.

The *Gathering Restaurant & O'Donnells Bar* (☎ 564849), Breadalbane St, has live entertainment most nights. It's open from 5 pm to 1 am; steaks range from £11.90 to £17.90.

The best pub in Oban is the *Oban Inn*, overlooking the harbour by the North Pier. It's a lively place which dates from the 18th century. It has a good range of single malt whiskies and the bar food includes haggis (£3.95).

Getting There & Away
See the fares tables in the Getting Around chapter. Oban is 504 miles from London, 123 from Edinburgh, 115 from Inverness, 93 from Glasgow and 50 from Fort William.

Bus Scottish Citylink (☎ 0990-505050) runs three buses a day to Oban from Glasgow (three hours, £9.50). Oban to Inveraray is a 1¼-hour journey (£4.70). Another service follows the coast via the Sea Life Centre and Fort William (1½ hours; £5.50, £4.40 with a student card) to Inverness.

Train For rail inquiries, phone ☎ 0345-484950. Oban is at the end of a scenic branch line that leaves the West Highland line at Crianlarich. There's an overnight service leaving London's Euston station at 11.50 pm

and arriving in Oban at 11.12 am. At least three trains a day depart from Glasgow (three hours, £16). There's a free *Window Gazer's Guide* available on the train.

To get to other parts of Scotland from Oban, the train is not much use. To reach Fort William requires a trip via Crianlarich round three sides of a rectangle – take the bus.

Boat Numerous CalMac (☎ 562285) boats link Oban with the Inner and Outer Hebrides. There are services to Mull (seven a day), Colonsay (three times a week), Coll and Tiree (daily except Thursday and Sunday), Barra and South Uist (approximately five services a week). See the island entries for details.

There are also four services daily except Sunday to the nearby island of Lismore (five minutes, £1.95).

Getting Around
Bus Oban & District (☎ 562856) is the local bus company and it has services up to McCaig's Tower and to the beach at Ganavan Sands.

Bicycle The only place to rent bikes is Oban Cycles (☎ 566996), Craigard Rd.

ISLE OF MULL
• *pop 2700*
It's easy to see why Mull is so popular with tourists. As well as having superb mountain scenery, two castles and a narrow-gauge railway, and being on the route to the holy isle of Iona, it's also a charmingly endearing place. Where else would you find a police station that uses gerbils to shred important documents (really), or a stately home where notices actually encourage you to sit on the chairs? And there can be few places left in Britain where the locals don't bother to lock their doors at night. Despite the numbers of visitors who flock to the island, it seems to be large enough to absorb them all; and many of them stick to the well-worn route from Craignure to Iona, returning to Oban in the evening.

Orientation & Information

Two-thirds of Mull's population is centred on Tobermory, in the north. Craignure, on the eastern coast, is where most people arrive; it's a very small place.

There are TICs at Craignure (☎ 01680-812377), opposite the quay, and at Tobermory (☎ 01688-302182), Main St. In summer, they're both open daily until at least 5.30 pm.

Things to See

There's little at **Craignure** apart from the ferry quay and the TIC. The Mull & West Highland Railway (☎ 01680-812494) is a toy train that takes passengers 1½ miles south to Torosay Castle (10 minutes, £2/1.30). **Torosay Castle** (☎ 01680-812421) is a Victorian house in the Scottish Baronial style. 'Take your time but not our spoons', advises the sign, and you're left to wander at will. Set in a beautiful garden, the house is open from late April to mid-October, daily from 10.30 am to 5 pm; entry is £3.50/2.

A 20-minute walk beyond Torosay is **Duart Castle** (☎ 01680-812309), a formidable fortress dominating the Sound of Mull. The seat of the Maclean clan, this is one of the oldest inhabited castles in Scotland. The keep was built in 1360 and the castle was lost to the Campbells in 1745. In 1911, Sir Fitzroy Maclean bought and restored the castle. It comes complete with damp dungeons, vast halls and bathrooms equipped with ancient fittings. Lady Mac will take your £3.30 at the door (£1.60 for children) and in the excellent tearoom you can try to get her Aussie employees to reveal what goes into Lady Maclean's Chocolate Specials. The castle is open daily from May to September, 10.30 am to 6 pm.

In the north of the island is the beautiful little fishing port of **Tobermory**, Mull's capital. The brightly painted houses, reflected in the water, make this one of the most picturesque villages in Scotland. There are few things to see other than a small museum and the Tobermory distillery, open only during the week. You can't pass the doors of the chocolate factory without going in. Somewhere out in the bay is the wreck of one of the ships that was part of the Armada, sunk here in 1588. No one is quite sure if the ship was the *Florida*, the *San Juan* or the *Santa Maria*, but rumours of a cargo of gold have kept treasure-hunters looking since then.

Eight miles west of Tobermory, at Dervaig, is **Mull Little Theatre** (☎ 01688-400245). With only 43 seats, it's Britain's smallest. There are regular shows in summer and the place has a good reputation.

One mile north of Dervaig, at Torrbreac, Sea Life Surveys (☎ 01688-400223) operates the UK's only whale research centre and runs **whale-watching trips**. A four-hour family whale watch costs £26/21. There are also trips to the Treshnish Isles.

Walks

The highest peak on the island, Ben More (3170 feet), has spectacular views across to the surrounding islands when the weather is clear. If it's overcast or misty, wait until the next day because Mull's weather is notoriously changeable. A trail leads up the mountain from Loch na Keal, by the bridge on the A486 over the Abhainn na h-Uamha – the river 6½ miles south of Salen. Allow five to six hours for the round trip.

Places to Stay & Eat

Tobermory has the best choice of places to stay. *Tobermory Youth Hostel* (☎ 01688-302481), on the Main St, is open from mid-March to September. Beds are £4.10/3.40. Just under two miles from Tobermory is *Newdale Campsite* (☎ 01688-302306). They charge from £2 per person.

On Old Dervaig Rd, *The Cedars* (☎ 01688-302096) offers B&B for £16/28. *Tom-A-Mhuillin* (☎ 01688-302164), Salen Rd, charges £14 to £18 per person. *Failte Guest House* (☎ 01688-302495), Main St, is in a very central location and has singles/doubles from £25/40 to £40/50, all with attached bath.

The *Mishnish Hotel* (☎ 01688-302009), Main St, is the place to drink and the food's

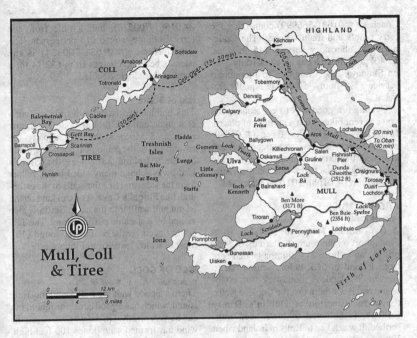

Mull, Coll & Tiree

good value. Main dishes at this pub range from £4.50 to £10. There's often live music and sometimes a disco.

Strongharb House (☎ 01688-302328), overlooking the bay in Tobermory, is an excellent place to stay. There are only four rooms, all with bathrooms attached, and they cost from £29.50 to £39 per person. The restaurant is highly recommended, particularly for seafood. One of the top hotels on Mull is the *Western Isles Hotel* (☎ 01688-302012), with superb views over the bay. It costs from £43 to £64 per person, and there's a good restaurant.

Mucmara Lodge (☎ 01688-400223), Torrbreac, Dervaig, has singles/doubles from £25/30. It's run by Sea Life Surveys who organise whale-watching excursions (see above). Also in the Dervaig area, beside the theatre, is the upmarket *Druimard Country Hotel & Restaurant* (☎ 01688-400345), which charges from £42.50 per person. A three-course set meal is £17.50.

In the Craignure area, *Fois-An-Iolaire* (☎ 01680-812423) is only 400 yards from the ferry; B&B costs around £15 per person.

Getting There & Away

There are seven ferries a day from Oban to Craignure; the trip takes 40 minutes and costs £3.05/18.85 for a passenger/small car. Smaller boats from Oban's North Pier ferry passengers out to Duart Castle; this is the cheapest way to reach Mull.

There's another ferry link between Fishnish and the mainland at Lochaline (20 minutes, £1.75), and boats run at least hourly every day. Ferries to Coll and Tiree leave from Tobermory, and they also hop across to Iona from Fionnphort. There are also ferries from Tobermory to Kilchoan (35 minutes, £2.90); from Monday to Saturday there are seven per day.

Getting Around

There's a basic bus service run by Essbee

Coaches (☎ 01631-566999) connecting the ferry points and main villages. The Craignure to Tobermory service (45 minutes, £2.40) goes thrice a day all week (only once on Sunday). The Craignure to Fionnphort service (1¼ hours, £3.20) is equally frequent.

Cycling is a good way to get around, and you can rent bikes from a number of places. In Salen, try On Yer Bike (☎ 01680-300501); they also have an outlet in the craft shop near the ferry terminal in Craignure. In Tobermory, contact Mrs MacLean at Tom-A-Mhuillin (☎ 01688-302164), Salen Rd.

AROUND MULL
Isle of Iona
A five-minute ferry ride (£1.25) from Fionnphort on the south-western tip of Mull brings you to Iona. St Columba landed here from Ireland in 563, before setting out to convert Scotland. A monastery was established and it was here that the Book of Kells, the prize attraction of Dublin's Trinity College, is believed to have been transcribed. It was taken to Kells in Ireland when Viking raids drove the monks from Iona.

The monks returned and the monastery prospered until its destruction in the Reformation. The ruins were given to the Church of Scotland in 1899, and in the early part of this century the abbey was reconstructed by a group of priests who established the Iona Community. It still appears to be a flourishing spiritual community and courses and retreats are regularly held.

Iona is indeed a very special place, but the stampeding hordes that daily pile off the tour buses make it difficult to appreciate. The best advice is to spend the night at one of the hotels or B&Bs here. After the crowds have gone, you can walk to the top of the hill, go to an evening service or look around the ancient graveyard where 48 of Scotland's early kings, including Macbeth, are buried. The grave of former Labour leader John Smith is also here, and a focus for tour groups.

For B&B try *Seaview* (☎ 01681-700373), opposite the ferry landing, or *Cruachan*

(☎ 01681-700523), half a mile from the ferry. Both are around £15 per person. The *Argyll Hotel* (☎ 01681-700334) is the island's best and charges from £32/74 for a comfortable single/double.

Isle of Staffa
This uninhabited island is a truly magnificent sight, and you'll quite understand how it inspired Mendelssohn. It's actually the eastern end of the geological phenomenon in Northern Ireland known as the Giant's Causeway – huge many-sided basalt pillars form the sides and line the walls of the cathedral-like **Fingal's Cave**. You can land on the island and walk into the cave. Staffa is also visited by a sizeable puffin colony. The TIC books tickets for the boat trips (around £10), most of which leave from Fionnphort.

ISLE OF COLL
• *pop 150*   • ☎ *01879*
There's a good walking trail round this little island, which has a good sunshine record but can be very windy. On the western coast, the wind has formed sand dunes 100 feet high. There's an RSPB reserve and two castles, both known as Breacachadh Castle and both built by the Macleans.

Near the castles, and 6½ miles from where the ferry docks at Arinagour, *Garden House* (☎ 230374), offers Castle Gardens, offers B&B from £15 per person, plus £10 for the evening meal. *Isle of Coll Hotel* (☎ 230334) is in Arinagour. It has singles/doubles for £30/50 and a good restaurant serving lobster (£15) and scallops, the local specialities. A set dinner is £21.

CalMac ferries run daily except Thursday and Sunday to Tiree (one hour, £2.40), Tobermory (1½ hours, £4.20) and Oban (3¾ hours, £9.85). Because the boat continues to Tiree and returns three hours later, it's possible to make a day trip from Oban or Tobermory.

ISLE OF TIREE
• *pop 820*   • ☎ *01879*
A low-lying island with some beautiful, sandy beaches, Tiree has one of the best

sunshine records in Britain, particularly during the early months of summer. It can also get fairly breezy, which makes it an excellent location for windsurfing – there are annual competitions in June.

If you want to camp, make sure you get the landowner's permission first. *Mrs Cameron's* (☎ 220503), The Shieling, Crossapol, Scarinish, does B&B for £16 per person. *Scarinish Hotel* (☎ 220308) is on the harbour and has rooms with bathroom attached for £22/40.

Tiree has an airport with links to Glasgow. CalMac ferries are as for Coll (see that section).

Stirling & Around

Stirling includes countryside on both sides of the Highland line: agricultural and industrial Lowlands to the south and the bare peaks of the Highlands to the north. Stirling was formerly known as Central region, a name appropriate not only for the region's location, but for the fact that this area has played a pivotal role in Scotland's history.

The administrative capital is also known as Stirling, and it has a superb castle placed on a high rock at the most strategically important spot in the country – at the head of the Firth of Forth and the route into the Highlands.

Loch Lomond lies on the western edge of the region (see the Argyll & Bute section). The Trossachs, Rob Roy country, is another busy tourist destination, currently receiving even more attention following the success of the movie about this Scots hero. The mountainous north of the region sees far fewer visitors; public transport here is patchy in parts, nonexistent in others.

GETTING AROUND
For local transport information in the Stirling administrative region, phone ☎ 01786-442707. Midland Bluebird (☎ 01324-613777) is the main operator. Its Heart of Scotland Explorer ticket (£6.60) gives you one day's travel on all its services in the Stirling region, West Lothian, and Kincardine, and half-price travel in Fife, Lothian and Strathclyde. Check to see if the service known as The Trossachs Trundler (☎ 01877-330969) has been reinstated. It was a useful summer bus service circling Aberfoyle, Callander and the pier on Loch Katrine. Some Day Rover tickets (eg from Glasgow) were valid on this bus.

Stirling city is the rail hub but the lines skirt around the edge of this region, so you'll be relying on buses if you don't have your own transport. For train inquiries, phone ☎ 0345-484950.

The West Highland Way cuts through the region from Glasgow to Fort William (see the Activities chapter at the start of this book). There are numerous other walks in the area. *Walk Loch Lomond & the Trossachs* is a useful guide published by Bartholomew and is available from TICs.

The Glasgow to Killin Cycle Way crosses the region from the centre of Glasgow via Balloch on the southern tip of Loch Lomond, Aberfoyle and Callander in the Trossachs, Loch Earn, Killin and Loch Tay. There are detours through Queen Elizabeth Forest Park and round Loch Katrine. It's a good route for walkers as well as cyclists because it follows forest trails, old railway routes and canal towpaths. A brochure showing the route is available from TICs.

STIRLING
* *pop 37,000* • ☎ *01786*
Stirling is such a strategic site that there's been a fortress here since prehistoric times. It was said that whoever held Stirling controlled the country, and Stirling has witnessed many of the struggles of the Scots against the English. The castle is perched high on a rock and dominates the town. It's one of the most interesting castles in the country to visit, better even than Edinburgh Castle.

Two miles north of Stirling, and visible for miles around, the Wallace Monument commemorates William Wallace. Mel Gibson's movie *Braveheart* recently revived interest in this hero of the wars of independence against England. You can climb this Victorian tower for a panoramic view of no less than seven battlegrounds – one of them at Stirling Bridge, where Wallace beat the English in 1297.

A more famous battlefield is two miles south of Stirling at Bannockburn, where, in 1314, Robert the Bruce and his small army of determined Scots (outnumbered four to one) put Edward II's English force to flight and reclaimed Stirling Castle. This victory turned the tide of fortune sufficiently to favour the Scots in the long struggle against the threat of English domination.

Although you can fit the main sights of Stirling into a day trip from Edinburgh or Glasgow, it's a very pleasant place to stay. There's an excellent youth hostel near the castle, and the town lays on enjoyable medieval markets and numerous other activities in the summer.

Orientation

The largely pedestrianised old town slopes up from the railway station and nearby bus

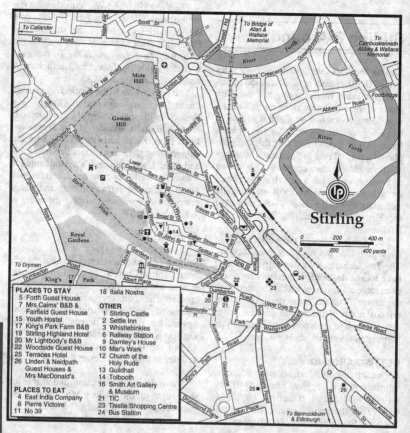

Stirling

200   400 m
200   400 yards

PLACES TO STAY
5 Forth Guest House
7 Mrs Cairns' B&B &
   Fairfield Guest House
15 Youth Hostel
17 King's Park Farm B&B
19 Stirling Highland Hotel
20 Mr Lightbody's B&B
22 Woodside Guest House
25 Terraces Hotel
26 Linden & Neidpath
   Guest Houses &
   Mrs MacDonald's

PLACES TO EAT
4 East India Company
8 Pierre Victoire
11 No 39

18 Italia Nostra

OTHER
1 Stirling Castle
2 Settle Inn
3 Whistlebinkies
6 Railway Station
9 Darnley's House
10 Mar's Wark
12 Church of the
   Holy Rude
13 Guildhall
14 Tolbooth
16 Smith Art Gallery
   & Museum
21 TIC
23 Thistle Shopping Centre
24 Bus Station

station to the castle, which sits 250 feet above the plain atop the plug of an extinct volcano. Stirling University's modern campus is to the north, by Bridge of Allan.

Information

The TIC (☎ 475019), 41 Dumbarton Rd, is open daily from June to October, from 9 am to 7.30 pm, and shorter hours, Monday to Saturday, for the rest of the year. As well as guided walks of the town, the TIC has details of the popular ghost walks (£5/3) that take place from Tuesday to Saturday.

The town puts on an entertaining programme of events in summer, including ceilidhs at the guildhall on Monday and Saturday evening, pipe bands on Tuesday and Saturday, and medieval markets. There are also 'living history' plays performed in and around the castle.

Stirling Castle

The location, architecture and historical significance of Stirling Castle combine to make it one of the grandest of all Scottish castles. It commands superb views across the surrounding plains.

There has been a fortress of some kind here for several thousand years, but the current building dates from the late 14th to the 16th centuries, when it was a residence of the Stuart monarchs. The Great Hall and Gatehouse were built by James IV. The spectacular palace was constructed in the reign of James V; French masons were responsible for the stonework. James VI remodelled the Chapel Royal and was the last king of Scotland to live here.

A £20-million programme of improvements at the castle is estimated to be still in progress until the end of the century, but enough of the castle is kept accessible to make a visit worthwhile. There's a visitor centre with audiovisual introduction to the history and architecture of the castle.

In the King's Old Building is the museum of the Argyll & Sutherland Highlanders, which traces the history of this famous regiment from 1794 to the present. The castle's kitchens are also very interesting.

Stirling Castle (☎ 450000; HS) is open daily from Easter to September, from 9.30 am to 5.15 pm (last entry); in winter, last entry is an hour earlier. Admission costs £3.50/1. There's a car park next to the castle (£2 for three hours).

Old Town

Below the castle is the old town, which grew from the time that Stirling became a royal burgh, around 1124. In the 15th and 16th centuries, when the Stuart monarchs held court in Stirling, rich merchants built their houses here.

Stirling has the best surviving town wall in Scotland and it can be followed on the **Back Walk**. It was built around 1547 when Henry VIII of England began what became known as 'Rough Wooing' – attacking the town in order to force Mary Queen of Scots to marry his son in order to unite the kingdoms. The walk follows the line of the wall from Dumbarton Rd (near the TIC) to the castle, continuing around Castle Rock and back to the old town. There are great views from the path, and you could make a short detour to Gowan Hill to see the **Beheading Stone**, now encased in iron bars to keep ritual axe murderers away.

Mar's Wark, on Castle Wynd at the head of the old town, is the ornate facade of what was once a Renaissance-style town house commissioned in 1569 by the wealthy Earl of Mar, Regent of Scotland during James VI's minority. During the Jacobite Rebellion in 1715, the Earl chose the losing side and his house became the town's barracks, eventually falling into ruin.

The **Church of the Holy Rude** is a little further down Castle Wynd, in St John St. It has been the town's parish church for 500 years. James VI was crowned here in 1567. The nave and tower date from 1456 and the church features one of the few surviving medieval, open-timber roofs. Behind the church is the **guildhall**, built by a rich merchant as an almshouse. It's now used for ceilidhs and concerts.

The **Mercat Cross**, in Broad St, is topped with a unicorn. This was once a bustling market. Nearby is the **Tolbooth**, built in 1705 as the town's administrative centre. A courthouse and jail were added in the following century. The **Old Town Jail** is Stirling's newest tourist attraction; it's open daily except in January, £2.50/1.75. There are displays on prison life, 'living history' performances, and a good view from the roof.

At the end of Broad St is **Darnley's House**, where Mary Queen of Scots' second husband, Lord Darnley, is said to have stayed.

Wallace Monument

Two miles north of Stirling is Scotland's Victorian monument to Sir William Wallace, who was hung, drawn and quartered by the English in 1305. It's surprising not only that it took the Scots so long to get around to honouring this famous patriot, but also that they couldn't have constructed something a little more attractive. Nevertheless, the view from the top is as breathtaking as the climb up to it, and the monument contains interesting displays including a parade of other Scottish heroes and Wallace's mighty two-handed sword. Clearly the man was no weakling.

The Wallace Monument (☎ 472140) is open daily from March to October, 10 am to 5 pm (9.30 am to 6.30 pm in July and August), and at weekends for the rest of the year; entry is £2.50/1.50. An open-top tour bus links the monument with Stirling Castle, but you could also walk (see Walks & Cycle Routes.

Bannockburn

On 24 June 1314, the greatest victory in the history of Scotland's struggle to remain independent took place at the Battle of Bannockburn. At the Bannockburn Heritage Centre (☎ 812664), owned by the NTS, the story is told with audiovisual displays. Outside is the Borestone site, said to have been Robert the Bruce's command post before the battle. There's also his grim-looking statue, dressed in full battle gear and mounted on a charger.

The site never closes but the heritage centre is open daily from April to October, 10 am to 5.30 pm; the last audiovisual show is at 5 pm. Entry is £2.10/1.40p.

Cambuskenneth Abbey

The only substantial remnant of this abbey, founded in 1147, is the belfry. In medieval times, Cambuskenneth became one of the richest abbeys in the country, and its high status is supported by the fact that Robert the Bruce held his parliament here in 1326, and James III and his queen are both buried here. The abbey is a mile from both Stirling Castle and the Wallace Monument. It's open April to September, Monday to Saturday from 9.30 am to 6.30 pm, and on Sunday afternoon; entry is free.

Walks & Cycle Routes

The best way to reach the Wallace Monument is on foot or by bike; it takes about 45 minutes to walk there. Cross the railway line on Seaforth Place, continue straight ahead into Forth Crescent and Abbey Rd. There's a footbridge over the River Forth to Cambuskenneth, where you should visit the ruins of the abbey. The Wallace Monument is located just one mile north of here; follow Adysneuk Rd and turn left at the junction with Alloa Rd.

Organised Tours

From May to early September, an open-top bus tour runs between the castle and the Wallace Monument daily from 10 am to 4 pm; there's one bus every hour. A day ticket costs £3.50/2.50.

Places to Stay

Hostels The facade of a 19th-century church conceals *Stirling Youth Hostel* (☎ 473442), which is in a perfect location in the old part of town in St John St. Open year-round, it's a superb modern hostel with 126 beds in small dorms; the nightly charge of £10.45/9 includes continental breakfast. The hostel has a less attractive annexe in Union St, open summer only.

Stirling Holiday Campus (☎ 467140), on

the edge of Bridge of Allan, three miles north of the town, lets student rooms in the summer for £17. There are only single rooms – 1030 of them – and there's also a pub, golf course and cinema on the landscaped campus.

Camping *Witches Craig Caravan Park* (☎ 474947) is on the edge of the Ochil Hills in Blairlogie, three miles east of Stirling by the A91. Tent pitches cost around £6.

B&Bs & Hotels There's a clutch of B&Bs on Linden Ave (just off Burghmuir Rd), which is fairly close to the bus station and less than half a mile from the railway station. *Linden Guest House* (☎ 448850), at No 22, charges around £16 per person. *Neidpath Guest House* (☎ 474840), at No 24, offers B&B for £16. *Mrs MacDonald's* (☎ 473418), at No 28, charges £15 per person.

Just across the road from the TIC, at 4 Back Walk, is *Woodside Guest House* (☎ 475470), where B&B costs from £17/34 in rooms with bathroom attached. Equally close to the TIC, at 1 Albert Place, *Mr Lightbody's* (☎ 451002) charges around £16; but has only three rooms.

Further out, but with superb views of the castle from across the plain, is *Kings Park Farm* (☎ 474142), on the A811/Dumbarton Rd, half a mile west of the TIC. B&B is £18 per person.

On the other side of town, a short walk north of the railway station, is the excellent *Forth Guest House* (☎ 471020), 23 Forth Place (just off Seaforth Rd). It's a small Georgian terrace house with a tiny rose-filled front garden and three comfortable rooms, all with bath attached. B&B costs from £20 per person and evening meals are available for £10.

Mrs Cairns' (☎ 479228), at 12 Princes St, is also conveniently located, and an easy walk from the railway station. B&B costs from £17 per person in a room with bath attached. At No 14 Princes St, *Fairfield Guest House* (☎ 472685) has six rooms, all with attached bathroom, for around £20/38.

The *Terraces Hotel* (☎ 472268), 4 Melville Terrace, is popular with businesspeople

during the week, when rooms are £59.50/69.50 for a single/double. If they're not busy at weekends you should be able to negotiate a lower rate. It's an efficient hotel run by a very jovial manager.

The smartest hotel in town is the *Stirling Highland Hotel* (☎ 475444), a sympathetic refurbishment of the old high school located on Spittal St. B&B and dinner costs £91/118 in summer. They do special B&B packages for over 60s, from £52 per person.

Places to Eat

There are good views from the restaurant at *Stirling Castle* but it's rather overpriced. Down the hill from the castle, at the end of Broad St, is *Darnley Coffee House* (☎ 474468), a conveniently-located pit stop as you walk around the old town.

The *Barnton Bar & Bistro*, 3½ Barnton St (opposite the GPO), is a very popular student hang-out serving excellent all-day breakfasts. Open daily and until 1 am at weekends, it's a great place to eat or drink. The *Causeway Head*, also on Barnton St, is an Italian café with espresso machines and good ice cream.

Italia Nostra (☎ 473208), 25 Baker St, is a busy Italian place that also does takeaways. If you haven't yet eaten at a branch of *Pierre Victoire* (☎ 448171), there's one here at 41 Friar St. Their £4.90 three-course set lunch really is unbeatable value.

The *East India Company* (☎ 471330), 7 Viewfield Place, is a very good Indian restaurant and takeaway. There's a cheaper Balti bar upstairs.

Very close to the castle is *No 39* (☎ 473929), 39 Broad St, an upmarket pub-restaurant that was formerly the town's bathhouse. It's open from Tuesday to Saturday. *Herman's* (☎ 450632) is round the corner at the Tolbooth, 32 St John's St. It's an excellent Scottish-Austrian restaurant

Melville's (☎ 472268), the restaurant at the Terraces Hotel, is popular with the locals. A steak with brandy and cream sauce is £12.50.

Entertainment

The *Portcullis* (☎ 472290), Castle Wynd, is

just below the castle, and serves pub meals all day.

There are two pubs further down St Mary's Wynd: the first is *Whistlebinkies* and the second is the very popular *Settle Inn* – the oldest pub in Stirling. The *Barton Bar & Bistro* (see Places to Eat) is another popular place for a drink.

Getting There & Away
Stirling is 26 miles north of Glasgow, 35 from Edinburgh and 420 from London.

Bus Scottish Citylink (☎ 0990-505050) has a number of routes, usually hourly, from Glasgow (45 minutes, £2.90). Some buses continue to Aberdeen via Perth and Dundee. Stirling to Aberdeen takes three hours and costs £11.90; you may need to change at Perth. Local services are operated by Midland Bluebird (☎ 446474).

Train ScotRail (☎ 0345-484950) runs services to Edinburgh (50 minutes, £4.20) twice an hour most of the day from Monday to Saturday, and hourly on Sunday. Not all services are direct. There are hourly trains from Glasgow (35 minutes, £3.70) and frequent services to Perth (35 minutes), Dundee (one hour) and Aberdeen (2¼ hours).

Car For car hire contact Arnold Clark (☎ 478686), Kerse Rd. Cheapest is a Fiat Cinquecento at £16 per day.

Getting Around
Bus It's easy enough to walk around the central part of the town. From the railway station to the castle is about three-quarters of a mile; there's a shuttle bus (50p/25p) if you want to save your feet on this uphill walk. It runs every 20 minutes from 9.30 am to 5 pm.

Taxi Woodside Taxis (☎ 450005) can organise sightseeing trips at around £12 per hour.

AROUND STIRLING
Dunblane
The name of Dunblane will for many years be associated only with the horrific massacre

that took place in the primary school in March 1996. Five miles north of Stirling, the main interest here is **Dunblane Cathedral**. Beloved of Ruskin, it is a simple, elegant, sandstone building, a superb example of the Gothic style. The lower parts of the walls date from Norman times, the rest is mainly 13th to 15th century. The roof of the nave collapsed in the 16th century, but the cathedral was saved from ruin by a major restoration project in the 1890s. It's open daily from Monday to Saturday, 9.30 am to 6.30 pm, and on Sunday afternoon.

The **cathedral museum** is situated on the square. It's a small museum relating the history of both cathedral and town, and it has a coffee shop attached. You can walk to Bridge of Allan from Dunblane along the Darn Rd, an ancient path used by the monks. Alternatively, there are frequent buses from Stirling.

There's a seasonal TIC (☎ 01786-824428) on Stirling Rd.

Doune
Nine miles north-west of Stirling, Doune is now a quiet rural town. It was once the capital of the ancient kingdom of Mentieth, and was later famous as a centre for the manufacture of pistols.

Doune Castle is one of the best preserved 14th-century castles in Scotland, having remained largely unchanged since it was built for the Duke of Albany. It was a favourite royal hunting lodge, but was also of great strategic importance because it controlled the route between the Lowlands and Highlands. Mary Queen of Scots stayed here, as did Bonnie Prince Charlie – the first as a guest, the second as prisoner. There are great views from the castle walls, and the lofty gatehouse is very impressive, rising nearly 100 feet. The castle is open standard HS hours (but in winter it's closed on Thursday afternoon and all day Friday); entry is £2/95p.

A mile from the castle is the **Doune Motor Museum** (☎ 01786-841203), the Earl of Moray's collection of 50 vehicles, including the second-oldest Rolls-Royce in the world and Scotland's only production model racing car, the JP Special. From April to September it's open daily from 10 am to 5 pm; entry is £3/2.

There are hourly buses to Doune from Stirling; less frequently on Sunday.

DOLLAR

About 14 miles east of Stirling, in the foothills of the Ochil Hills that run east into Perthshire, is the small town of Dollar. **Castle Campbell** is a 20-minute walk into the hills above the town. It's the spooky, old stronghold of the dukes of Argyll and stands between two ravines. It was occupied by them whenever they ventured down to the Lowlands. It is now ruined but you can clearly see why it was known as Castle Gloom. There's been a fortress of some kind on this site from the 11th century, but the present structure dates from the 15th century. Opening hours and charges are as for Doune Castle.

There are buses to Dollar from Stirling and Alloa. From Dunfermline, the R41 service runs Monday to Friday only.

THE TROSSACHS

Sometimes called the Scottish Lake District, the Trossachs is actually the name of the narrow valley between Loch Katrine and Loch Achray, though it's now used to describe the scenic area around the southern border of the Highlands.

As the tourist literature repeatedly informs you, this is Rob Roy country. Rob Roy Macgregor (1671-1734) was the wild leader of the wildest of Scotland's clans, Clan Gregor. Although he claimed direct descent from a 10th-century king of the Scots and rights to the lands the clan occupied, these Macgregor lands stood between powerful neighbours. Rob Roy became notorious for his daring raids into the Lowlands, to carry off cattle and sheep, but these escapades led to the outlawing of the clan – hence their sobriquet, 'Children of the Mist'. He also achieved a reputation as a champion of the poor. He lies buried in the churchyard at Balquhidder, by Loch Voil; there's a Clan Gregor centre nearby at Kingshouse.

Actor Liam Neeson was just the most recent of Rob Roy's popularists – Walter Scott's historical novel *Rob Roy* brought tourists to the region in the 19th century. Loch Katrine was the inspiration for Scott's *Lady of the Lake* and, since the turn of the century, the SS *Sir Walter Scott* has been taking visitors across Loch Katrine. The main centres in the area are Aberfoyle and Callander. During the summer months, a vintage bus, the Trossachs Trundler, links these two places with Loch Katrine.

Aberfoyle

Known as the southern gateway to the Trossachs, Aberfoyle is on the eastern edge of the Queen Elizabeth Forest Park, which stretches across to the hills beside Loch Lomond. The town makes a good base for walks and cycle rides in the area.

Three miles east is Scotland's only lake, Lake Menteith. The substantial ruins of the priory where Mary Queen of Scots was kept safe as a child, during Henry VIII's 'Rough Wooing', are on Inchmahome Island. A ferry takes visitors from the village to the priory. It's open April to September, Monday to Saturday from 9.30 am to 6.30 pm, and on Sunday afternoon; entry is £2/75p.

The TIC (☎ 01877-382352), Main St, is open from April to October. About half a mile north of Aberfoyle, on the A821, is the Queen Elizabeth Forest Park Visitors Centre (☎ 01877-382258), which has information about the numerous walks and cycle routes in and around the park.

Walks & Cycle Routes Waymarked trails start from the Visitors Centre on the hills above the town.

There's an excellent 20-mile circular cycle route that links with the ferry across Loch Katrine. From Aberfoyle, join the Glasgow-Killin Cycle Way on the forest trail, or take the A821 over Duke's Pass. Following the southern shore of Loch Achray, you reach the pier on Loch Katrine. The ferry should drop you at Stronachlachar,

CENTRAL SCOTLAND

on the western shore (note that it sometimes doesn't stop here). From Stronachlachar, follow the B829 via Loch Ard to Aberfoyle.

Places to Stay & Eat *Cobleland Campsite* (☎ 01877-382392), is off the A81, two miles south of Aberfoyle; tent pitches are from £3.95.

In Aberfoyle, *Mrs Sampson's* (☎ 01877-382597), Craig Rannoch, Main St, offers B&B from just £20 for a double room, or £35 for a double with attached bath. On Main St, in the middle of the village, the *Forth Inn* (☎ 01877-382372) does B&B for £21 per person in rooms with bath attached. Bar meals are available all day.

Getting There & Away Midland Bluebird (☎ 01324-613777) has four buses a day from Stirling. The Trossachs Trundler (☎ 01877-330969) has a day ticket that includes Callander and Stirling for £4.25.

Callander
• *pop 2300*   • ☎ *01877*
Fourteen miles north of Stirling, Callander is a large tourist town that bills itself as the eastern gateway to the Trossachs. It has been pulling in the tourists for over 150 years, and tartan shops now line the long main drag. The **Rob Roy & Trossachs Visitor Centre** (☎ 330342) is also the TIC. The audiovisual Rob Roy show grinds on daily from 9 am to at least 7 pm in July and August, 9.30 am to 6 pm in June and September and 10 am to 5 pm for the rest of the year (closed January and February); entry is £2.50/1.75.

Places to Stay & Eat There are numerous places to stay. *Ben A'an Guest House* (☎ 330317), 158 Main St, has five rooms and charges £15 per person. *Arden House Guest House* (☎ 330235) is just north of the town on Bracklinn Rd; B&B is £20 per person. It's an excellent place to stay and it was used as the setting for the TV series *Doctor Finlay's Casebook*. Evening meals are available. The *Roman Camp Hotel* (☎ 330003) is beautifully located by the river; it's an upmarket place dating from 1625 with a very good

restaurant. Rooms cost from £40 to £80 per person.

Getting There & Away Midland Bluebird (☎ 01324-613777) operates buses from Stirling (45 minutes, £2.60). The Trossachs Trundler calls here and reaches the pier on Loch Katrine 35 minutes later.

Loch Katrine
From April to September, the SS *Sir Walter Scott* sails across the loch, usually to Stronachlachar, from Trossachs Pier on the eastern tip of the loch. For bookings, phone ☎ 01877-376315; tickets are £3.50/2.10.

NORTH CENTRAL REGION
Crianlarich & Tyndrum
These villages are little more than service junctions on the main A82 road, although they are both in good hiking country and on the West Highland Way. At Crianlarich, there's a railway station and, nearby on Station Rd, is *Crianlarich Youth Hostel* (☎ 01838-300260). The hostel is open from late February to October. Beds are £7.55/6.45. Tyndrum has a useful TIC (☎ 01838-400246) in the car park of the Invervay Hotel.

Killin
In the north-eastern corner of the region, just west of Loch Tay, Killin is a popular destination for tour buses that bring people to see the pretty but undramatic Falls of Dochart, in the centre of the village. There's a TIC (☎ 01567-820254) in Main St.

Walks & Cycle Routes Killin is at the northern end of the cycle way from Glasgow (see Getting Around at the start of the Stirling section).

Five miles north-west of Killin, Ben Lawers (3984 feet) rises above Loch Tay. There's a Visitors' Centre here and trails lead to the summit (see West Perthshire in the Perthshire & Kinross section).

Places to Stay & Eat *Killin Youth Hostel* (☎ 01567-820546) is open from mid-March to the end of October. The nightly charge is £5.40/4.40.

There are numerous B&Bs and hotels. At the *Falls of Dochart Cottage* (☎ 01567-820363), in the middle of the village, there's B&B from £13 per person; dinner is £8. *Clachaig Hotel* (☎ 01567-820270) overlooks the falls; most rooms have attached bath and cost around £20 per person.

Getting There & Away Getting to Killin by bus is tricky. Midland Bluebird (☎ 01324-613777) operates a service on school days only from Stirling (1¾ hours, £4.45) via Callander. There's no bus from Pitlochry to Killin, but there is a daily postbus service between Aberfeldy and Killin (three hours).

Fife

This small region to the north of the Firth of Forth refers to itself as the Kingdom of Fife – it was home to Scottish kings for 500 years. Despite its integration with the rest of Scotland, it has managed to maintain an individual Lowland identity quite separate from the rest of the country. As they still say outside the region, 'It takes a long spoon to sup with a Fifer'.

To the west, the Lomond Hills rise to 1700 feet; the eastern section is much flatter. Apart from a number of small castles inland, the main attractions in Fife are mainly around the coast. As far as visitors are concerned, the focus of the region is undoubtedly St Andrews – an ancient university town and ecclesiastical centre that is also world-famous as the home of golf. To the south, along the indented coastline of East Neuk, are picturesque former fishing villages. This coast is pleasant walking country, and at Anstruther there's the interesting Scottish Fisheries Museum.

GETTING AROUND
If you're driving from the Forth Road Bridge to St Andrews, a slower but much more scenic route than the M90/A91 is along the signposted Fife Tourist Route, via the coast.

For information about buses in the region, phone ☎ 01592-414141 ext 3103. The council produces a useful map-guide, *Getting Around Fife*, available from TICs. Fife Scottish (☎ 01334-474238) is the main bus operator.

Trains are less useful in Fife than in some regions, as the rails no longer run as far as St Andrews; the service stops at Leuchars, eight miles from the town. For rail information, phone ☎ 0345-484950.

WEST FIFE
Culross
Around the 17th-century, Culross (pronounced cooross) was a busy little community, trading in salt and coal. Now it's the best preserved example of a Scottish burgh, and the National Trust for Scotland owns 20 of the buildings, including the palace, which it bought in 1932. It's a picturesque village with small red-tiled, white-washed buildings lining the cobbled streets.

Culross has a long history. As the birthplace of St Mungo, the patron saint of Glasgow, it was an important religious centre from the 6th century. The burgh developed as a trading centre under the businesslike laird George Bruce (a descendant of Robert the Bruce), whose mining techniques involved digging long tunnels under the sea to reach coal. A vigorous sea trade developed between Culross and the Forth ports and Holland. From the proceeds, Bruce built the palace, completed in 1611. When a storm flooded the tunnels and mining became impossible, the town switched to making linen and shoes.

The NTS Visitors Centre (☎ 01383-880359), in the lower part of the Town House, has an exhibition on the history of Culross. You can visit **Culross Palace**, more a large house than a palace, which features decorative, painted woodwork and an interior largely unchanged since the early 17th century. The **Town House** and the **Study**, also early 17th century, are open to the public, but the other NTS properties can only be viewed from the outside. Ruined **Culross Abbey**, founded by the Cistercians, is on the hill; the choir of the abbey church is now the parish church.

Culross is 12 miles west of the Forth Road Bridge, off the A985. It's open from May to September from 11 am to 5 pm (from 1.30 pm for the upper Town House and the Study); entry is £3.60/2.40. Bus No 14A runs hourly, daily, between Glasgow, Stirling, Culross and Dunfermline.

Dunfermline
• *pop 52,000*   • *☎ 01383*

Six Scottish kings, including Robert the Bruce, are buried at Dunfermline Abbey. Once the country's capital, Dunfermline is now a large regional centre surrounded by suburbs that are not particularly attractive, but the abbey's worth a visit.

David I founded the **abbey** on the hill here in the 12th century as a Benedictine monastery. It grew into a major religious centre, eventually eclipsing the island of Iona (off Mull) as the favourite royal burial ground. Most of the abbey, having fallen into ruins, has now been absorbed into the parish church, but the wonderful Norman nave, with its ornate columns, remains. Robert the Bruce is buried near the pulpit. Next to the abbey are the ruins of **Dunfermline Palace**, rebuilt from the abbey guesthouse in the 16th century for James VI. It was the birthplace of Charles I, the last Scottish king born on Scottish soil. Both buildings are open daily (closed on Thursday afternoon and Friday in winter), standard HS hours; entry is £1.50/75p.

Dunfermline's most famous former inhabitant was Andrew Carnegie, who was born in a weaver's cottage in 1836, now a museum. He emigrated to America in 1848 and by the late 19th century had accumulated enormous wealth, $350 million of which he gave away. Dunfermline benefited by his purchase of Pittencrieff Park, beside the palace. The **Andrew Carnegie Museum** (☎ 724302) is open daily from April to October, 11 am to 5 pm (afternoon only on Sunday), and afternoon only in winter; entry costs £1.50 for adults, children free.

The TIC (☎ 720999), Maygate, is open year-round. Dunfermline is a major transport hub, with frequent buses to Glasgow and Edinburgh. It's a half-hour train ride from Edinburgh, and there's one direct train an hour. The railway and bus stations are within walking distance of the abbey.

SOUTH COAST
Aberdour

It's worth pausing to see **Aberdour Castle** in this popular seaside town. It was built by the Douglas family in 1342 and the original tower was extended in the 16th and 17th centuries. By the 18th century, it was partly in ruins and abandoned by its owners. The east wing is still in use, however. One of the most impressive features of the castle is its attractive gardens, among the earliest of castle gardens. There's a fine circular dovecot (pronounced doocot in Scotland), shaped like a beehive, dating from the 16th century. St Fillan's Chapel, in the grounds, dates from the 12th century. The castle is open standard HS hours (but closed on Thursday afternoon and on Friday in winter); entry is £1.50/75p.

Bus Nos 57 and X57 run hourly to Edinburgh, daily; there are two buses an hour to Dunfermline.

Kirkcaldy
• *pop 50,000*   • *☎ 01592*

This is another town that's worth stopping in if you're passing through. It has an attractive promenade and an interesting museum and art gallery, but there's not much else to hold you here. Kirkcaldy (pronounced kirkoddy) sprawls along the edge of the sea for several miles. In the second half of the 19th century, it was the world's largest manufacturer of linoleum.

Kirkcaldy Museum & Art Gallery is a short walk from the railway and bus stations. As well as covering the town's history, there's an impressive collection of Scottish and English paintings from the 18th and 19th centuries and an exhibition on the political economist, Adam Smith, who was born here.

It's open every day (afternoon only on Sunday); entry is free.

After looking round the museum, you could walk along the Esplanade to ruined **Ravenscraig Castle**, in the park by the sea. Two miles north of Kirkcaldy, in Dysart, is the **McDouall Stuart Museum** (☎ 260732), the birthplace of the engineer and explorer who, in 1862, became the first person to cross Australia from the south coast to the north. It's open from June to August, 2 to 5 pm; entry is free. Bus No K7 from Kirkcaldy centre passes this way every hour.

The TIC (☎ 267775) is at 19 Whyte-causeway, and is open year-round. If you want to stay in Kirkcaldy, *Invertiel House* (☎ 264849), 21 Pratt St, is just south of the centre, by Beveridge Park. It's a comfortable place to stay with B&B from £17 per person.

A major transport hub, Kirkcaldy is on the main Edinburgh/Glasgow to Dundee/Aberdeen rail line. There are two trains an hour to Edinburgh (45 minutes). There are numerous buses from the bus station, two blocks back from the Esplanade.

CENTRAL FIFE
Falkland
Below the soft ridges of the Lomond Hills is Falkland, an attractive village surrounded by rich farmland in the centre of Fife. A very pleasant place to stay, it's known for its superb 16th-century **palace**, the country residence of the Stuart monarchs.

Mary Queen of Scots is said to have spent the happiest days of her life 'playing the country girl in the woods and parks' at Falkland. Built between 1501 and 1541 to replace a castle dating from the 12th century, French and Scottish craftspeople were employed to create a masterpiece of Scottish Gothic architecture. The chapel, which has a beautiful painted ceiling, and the king's bedchamber have both been restored; you can also look around the keeper's apartments in the gatehouse.

The wild boar that the royals hunted, and the Fife forest that was their hunting ground, have now disappeared. One feature of this royal leisure centre still exists: the oldest

royal tennis court in Britain, built in 1539 for James V, is in the grounds and still in use. Although the palace still belongs to the Queen, it's administered by the NTS.

Falkland Palace (☎ 01337-857397) is open from April to October, Monday to Saturday from 11 am to 5.30 pm, and on Sunday from 1.30 to 5.30 pm; entry is £4.10/2.10.

Places to Stay & Eat *Falkland Youth Hostel* (☎ 01337-857710), Back Wynd, is open from mid-March to September and on Saturday in winter. The nightly charge is £4.10/3.75. Opposite the palace, there's B&B at *Ladieburn Cottage* (☎ 01337-857016), High St. There are two rooms with bath attached costing £25/36 for single/double occupancy. Evening meals are also available.

Getting There & Away Falkland is 11 miles north of Kirkcaldy. There are a couple of buses a day to Kinross (see the Perthshire & Kinross section), and buses every two hours from Perth and Cupar. There's no railway station.

Cupar
• *pop 6700* • ☎ *01334*

Cupar is a pleasant market town and the capital of the region. There's no real reason to visit other than to see the Hill of Tarvit Mansion House nearby. There's a seasonal TIC (☎ 652874) on Coal Rd.

Hill of Tarvit Mansion House, two miles south of Cupar, was rebuilt for Frederick Sharp at the turn of the century by Scottish architect Robert Lorimer. Sharp was a wealthy Dundee jute manufacturer who bought the house as a showcase for his valuable collection of furniture, Dutch paintings, Flemish tapestries and Chinese porcelain. A 15-minute walk takes you to the top of the Hill of Tarvit, which has an excellent panoramic view. A NTS property, the house (☎ 653127) is open daily from May to September, 1.30 to 5.30 pm; and in October at weekends, 1.30 to 5.30 pm. Entry is £3.10/2.

Cupar is a busy transport centre with direct bus services to St Andrews, Dundee and Edinburgh. It's also on the rail line to Dundee.

ST ANDREWS
• *pop 10,600*   • ☎ *01334*

St Andrews is a beautiful, unusual seaside town – a concoction of medieval ruins, obsessive golfers, windy coastal scenery, tourist glitz and a schizophrenic university with wealthy English undergraduates rubbing shoulders with Scottish theology students.

Although St Andrews was once the ecclesiastical capital of Scotland, both its cathedral and castle are now in ruins. For most people, the town is the home of golf. It's the headquarters of the game's governing body, the Royal & Ancient Golf Club, and the location of the world's most famous golf course, the Old Course.

History
St Andrews is said to have been founded by the Greek monk, St Regulus, in the 4th century. He brought important relics from Greece, including some of the bones of St Andrew, who became Scotland's patron saint.

The town soon grew into a major pilgrimage centre for the shrine of the saint. The Church of St Regulus was built in 1130 (only the tower remains); the nearby cathedral was built in 1160. St Andrews developed into the ecclesiastical capital of the country and, around 1200, the castle was constructed (part fortress, part residence) for the bishop.

The university was founded in 1410, the first in Scotland. James I received part of his education here, as did James III. By the mid-16th century there were three colleges: St Salvator's, St Leonard's and St Mary's.

Although golf was being played here by the 15th century, the Old Course dates from the following century. The Royal & Ancient Golf Club was founded in 1754, and the imposing clubhouse was built a hundred years later. The British Open Championship, which was first held in 1860 in Prestwick, on the west coast near Glasgow, has taken place regularly at St Andrews since 1873.

Orientation
St Andrews preserves its medieval plan of parallel streets with small closes leading off them. The most important parts of the old town, lying to the east of the bus station, are easily explored on foot. The main streets for shops are Market and South Sts, running east-west. Like Cambridge and Oxford, St Andrews has no campus – the university buildings are integrated into the central part of the town. There's a small harbour near the cathedral and two sandy beaches: East Sands extends south from the harbour and the wider West Sands is north of the town.

Information
The TIC (☎ 472021), 70 Market St, is open all year. In June, July and August, opening hours are Monday to Saturday, 9.30 am to 8 pm, and on Sunday from 10 am to 6 pm; in May and September it closes at 6 pm; for the rest of the year it's closed on Sunday. It makes bookings for the theatre and the Edinburgh Tattoo, and sells NTS and Historic Scotland passes.

There are guided walks (£2.50) of the town, April to September, on Wednesday at 11 am, and at the same time also on Thursday and Sunday in July and August; contact the TIC for information and bookings.

Half-day closing is on Thursday, but in summer many shops stay open. Parking requires a voucher, which is on sale in many shops.

Walking Tour
The best place to start a walking tour is **St Andrews Museum** (☎ 477706), Double Dykes Rd, near the bus station. Displays chart the history of the town from its founding by St Regulus through its growth as an ecclesiastical, academic and sporting centre. Much more interesting than some local history museums, it's open April to September, daily from 10 am to 5 pm, and for the rest of the year for shorter hours; there's no entry charge.

Turn left out of the museum driveway and follow Double Dykes Rd back to the roundabout. Turn right, then left into South St. You

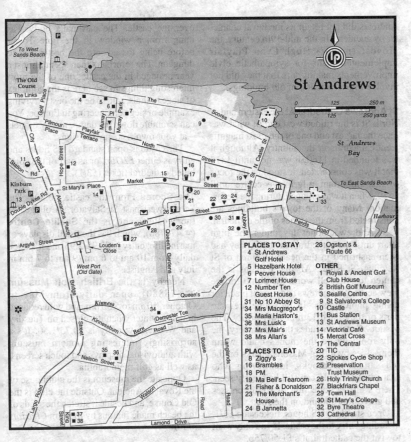

St Andrews

0   125   250 m
0   125   250 yards

To West
Sands Beach

The Old
Course

The Links

To East Sands Beach

St Andrews
Bay

Harbour

PLACES TO STAY	28 Ogston's &
4 St Andrews	Route 66
Golf Hotel	
5 Hazelbank Hotel	**OTHER**
6 Peover House	1 Royal & Ancient Golf
7 Lorimer House	Club House
12 Number Ten	2 British Golf Museum
Guest House	9 Sealife Centre
31 No 10 Abbey St	9 St Salvatore's College
34 Mrs Macgregor's	10 Castle
35 Maria Haston's	11 Bus Station
36 Mrs Lusk's	13 St Andrews Museum
37 Mrs Mair's	14 Victoria Café
38 Mrs Allan's	15 Mercat Cross
	17 The Central
PLACES TO EAT	20 TIC
8 Ziggy's	22 Spokes Cycle Shop
16 Brambles	25 Preservation
18 PM	Trust Museum
19 Ma Bell's Tearoom	26 Holy Trinity Church
21 Fisher & Donaldson	27 Blackfriars Chapel
23 The Merchant's	29 Town Hall
House	30 St Mary's College
24 B Jannetta	32 Byre Theatre
	33 Cathedral

pass through **West Port**, formerly Southgait
Port, the main entrance to the old city. It was
remodelled in 1589 on Netherbow Port in
Edinburgh. Walking down South St, you
pass **Louden's Close** on the right, a good
example of the closes built according to the
city's medieval street plan. Continuing along
South St, the apse of the 16th-century **Blackfriars Chapel**, stands in front of Madras
College.

Opposite the Victorian town hall is **Holy
Trinity**, the town's parish church, built in
1410. On the same side of the street as the
town hall is **St Mary's College**, founded in
1537; beside it is the university library. The
oak tree in the courtyard is over 250 years
old.

Cross over to cobbled Market St, one
street parallel to South St, via Church St.
Street markets are held around **Mercat
Cross**, although the cross is now a fountain.
The TIC is nearby, at No 70. Turn right out
of the TIC and follow Market St down to the
junction with South Castle St, turn left, and
then right into North St. On the right is **St
Andrews Preservation Trust Museum**, an
old merchant's house and a museum of local
social history. It's interesting to note that St

CENTRAL SCOTLAND

Andrews did not retain its medieval character by accident. In the mid-19th century, the provost (mayor) Hugh Lyon Playfair implemented plans for sympathetic civic improvements making sure that they did not involve the destruction of old buildings.

St Andrews Cathedral At the eastern end of North St is the ruined west end of what was once the largest and one of the most magnificent cathedrals in the country. Although it was founded in 1160, it was not until 1318 that it was consecrated. It stood as the focus of this important pilgrimage centre until 1559, when it was pillaged during the Reformation. Many of the town's buildings are constructed from the stones of the cathedral.

St Andrew's bones lay under the high altar; until the cathedral was built, they had been enshrined in the nearby Church of St Regulus (St Rule). All that remains is the church tower, well worth the climb for the view across St Andrews and a great place for taking photographs. In the same area are parts of the ruined 13th-century priory. The Visitors Centre includes the calefactory, the only room where the monks could warm themselves by a fire; Masons' marks on the red sandstone blocks, identifying who shaped each block, can still be clearly seen. There's also a collection of Celtic crosses and gravestones found on the site.

Open standard HS hours, tickets are £3/1, including entry to the castle. If you only want to visit the cathedral, it's £1.50/75p.

St Andrews Castle Around the corner from the cathedral, above the sea, the castle was founded around 1200 as the fortified home of the bishop. In the 1450s the young king James II often stayed here. A Visitors Centre gives a good audiovisual introduction and has a small collection of Pictish stones.

In the 16th century, much of the castle was pulled down to provide building materials for the harbour wall. Enough survives to give you an idea of what each of the chambers was used for. After the execution of Protestant reformers in 1545, other reformers retaliated by murdering Cardinal Beaton and taking over the castle. The cardinal's body was hung from a window in the Fore Tower before being tossed into the bottle-shaped dungeon. The reformers then spent almost a year besieged in the castle; one of the most interesting things to see here is the complex of siege tunnels, said to be the best surviving example of siege engineering in Europe. You can scramble down the damp, mossy tunnels – at your own risk, say the signs.

The castle is open standard HS hours and entry is either £2/75p, or as part of the combined cathedral ticket (£3/1).

The Scores From the castle, follow The Scores west past St Salvator's College. At the western end is the **Sealife Centre** (☎ 474786), which has the usual displays of marine life; entry is £3.95/2.95 and it's open daily from 10 am to 6 pm (9 am to 7 pm in July and August).

Nearby is the **British Golf Museum** (☎ 478880), open daily from May to October, 10 am to 5.30 pm, and with reduced hours in winter when it's closed on Tuesday and Wednesday; entry is £3.75/1.50. It's a surprisingly interesting modern museum with audiovisual displays and touch screens, as well as golf memorabilia.

Opposite the museum is the clubhouse of the Royal & Ancient. Outside the club is the Old Course, and beside it stretch the sands of the beach made famous by the film *Chariots of Fire*.

Walks & Cycle Routes

The TIC has a list of local walks and sells OS maps. You could walk from St Andrews to Crail along the coast, but it's about 15 miles and you'd have to take care not to get caught by the tide. There are some excellent shorter walks along the southern part of the East Neuk coast (see the upcoming East Neuk section).

Since there are no hills of any consequence in eastern Fife, cycling is no problem and there are some good rides along the quiet side roads. There are several castles within easy cycling distance, including Kellie and Hill of Tarvit. Following the coast road from

BRYN THOMAS

BRYN THOMAS

BRYN THOMAS

BRYN THOMAS

Top Left: Inveraray Castle, Inveraray, Central Scotland
Top Right: Post office on Mull, Central Scotland
Bottom Left: Boat trip to Staffa, Central Scotland
Bottom Right: Retired bus, Orkney

TONY WHEELER

BRYN THOMAS

RICHARD EVERIST

Top: St Paul's Cathedral, London
Left: St Magnus Cathedral, Kirkwall, Orkney
Right: Winchester Cathedral, Winchester, Hampshire

St Andrews to Crail and Anstruther would make another pleasant ride.

Places to Stay

There's no youth hostel, but there's a bunkhouse eight miles away near Anstruther (see below). Between June and September, however, you can stay for £10, room only, at the university's *Gannochy House* (☎ 464870) in North St. They have only single rooms, you must check in between 2 and 6 pm. Gannochy House is at the eastern end of North St, next to Younger Hall.

You can camp at the *Cairnsmill Caravan Park* (☎ 473604), one mile outside St Andrews on the A915, for £6.50 for a tent and two people.

The cheapest B&Bs in St Andrews are not central. There are two B&Bs on Nelson St that are excellent value at around £13 per person. *Maria Haston's* (☎ 473227) is at No 8, and *Mrs Lusk's* (☎ 472575) at No 2. To reach Nelson St from the bus station, walk south along City Rd into Alexandra Place and then into Bridge St. Nelson St is on the right, after about 500 yards.

Further south, on King St, there's *Mrs Allan's* (☎ 476326) at No 2, and *Mrs Mair's* (☎ 472709) at No 10, open year-round. Both charge around £15 per person.

Closer to the centre, at 8 Dempster Terrace (just over the burn (stream) from Kinnessburn Rd), *Mrs Macgregor's* (☎ 474282) has just one room with three single beds for £15 per person.

No 10 Abbey St (☎ 474094) is a bigger place with one single and four twin rooms. It's near the Byre Theatre, and charges £17.50/32.

Almost every house on Murray Park and Murray Place is a B&B. The area couldn't be more convenient but prices are on the high side – most places charge around £22 per person. Rooms tend to have bathrooms attached. During summer, you need to book in advance, but at other times it's probably best to knock on a few doors and pick what you like. *Lorimer House* (☎ 476599), 19 Murray Park, is open year-round and charges

from £20/44. *Peover House* (☎ 475787), 22 Murray Park, offers B&B from £22/44.

Number Ten Guest House (☎ 474601), 10 Hope St, is a good place to stay. There are 10 rooms, all with bathroom attached for £25 per person.

Facing the bay, more expensive hotels line The Scores. At No 28, *Hazelbank Hotel* (☎ 472466) has rooms from £34 to £62 per person. *St Andrews Golf Hotel* (☎ 472611), 40 The Scores, is an excellent upmarket hotel 200 yards from the Old Course. Prices range from £74/122 for a single/double. There are also cheaper two-night breaks. The hotel has a good restaurant and bar.

Just under two miles from the town centre, *Rufflets Country House Hotel* (☎ 472594), Strathkinness Low Rd, is a top-class hotel with a recommended restaurant. B&B and dinner ranges from £69 to £89, depending on the season.

If money's really no object, stay at the *St Andrews Old Course Hotel* (☎ 474371), the imposing building by the golf course, at the western end of town. Rooms at this luxurious establishment range from £185/225 to £485. There are resident golf pros and a team of therapists and beauticians providing massage for both body and ego. If you're planning to drop in out of the sky, note that you need prior permission to use the helipad.

Places to Eat

If you're on a very tight budget, *PM*, on the corner of Market and Union Sts, often does half-price baked potatoes. For more upmarket snacks, head for *Fisher & Donaldson*, which sells Selkirk bannocks (rich fruit bread), cream cakes and a wonderful range of pastries.

Ma Bell's Tearoom, 24 North St, is the place to go for coffee, cream tea or a light lunch. One of the busiest places at lunchtime is *Brambles*, College St, which has excellent salads and vegetarian dishes. It's not open in the evening. *The Merchant's House* (☎ 472595), 49 South St, is in a venerable building. It serves delicious home-made soup and is open from 10 am to 5.30 pm.

Ziggy's (☎ 473686), 6 Murray Place, is

popular with students, and has burgers from £3.60 and good vegetarian choices. *Ogston's* (☎ 473473), 116 South St, is a trendy bar and bistro. There's Italian cuisine at *Bar Italy* here from 6.30 pm. Next door at *Route 66* there are burgers and pizzas; at lunchtime nothing's over £4.

Apart from the pricey restaurant at *St Andrews Old Course Hotel* (see Places to Stay), you need a car to reach the top restaurants in the area. The recommended *Peat Inn* (☎ 840206), near Cupar on the A915, is open from Tuesday to Saturday for lunch and dinner. Set lunches are £18.50, set dinners, including excellent fresh seafood, cost around £30 per person, excluding wine. There's another top restaurant at Anstruther (see the upcoming Anstruther section).

Finally, don't leave town without sampling one of the 52 varieties of ice cream from *B Jannetta*, 31 South St. Don't confuse this main branch with the smaller shop at the other end of South St. This is a St Andrews institution. Most popular flavour? Vanilla. Weirdest? Irn Bru!

Entertainment
In July and August, the Royal Scottish Country Dance Society holds dances and will show novices the steps. Contact the TIC for information. There are also other country dances in summer.

The *Byre Theatre* (☎ 476288), Abbey St, started life as a cow shed. The new theatre was built in 1970 and the quality of performances, both touring and local, is often high.

St Andrews has a good supply of pubs, representing its varied population. The *Central*, on Market St, is all polished brass and polished accents, full of rich students from south of the border. The *Victoria Café*, South St, is popular with all types of students. There's a good bar at the *St Andrews Golf Hotel*.

Getting There & Away
St Andrews is 55 miles north of Edinburgh and 16 miles south of Dundee.

Bus Fife Scottish (☎ 474238) has six buses a day from St Andrew's Square, Edinburgh, to St Andrews (two hours, £4.50; £3 for students) and on to Dundee (¾ hour, £1.75).

Train The nearest station to St Andrews is Leuchars (one hour from Edinburgh, £6.80), eight miles away, on the Edinburgh-Dundee-Aberdeen-Inverness line. There are three direct trains to London each day. Bus Nos 94/95 leave every half-hour to St Andrews.

Playing the Old Course
Golf has been played at St Andrews since the 15th century, and by 1457 was apparently so popular that James II had to place a ban on it because it was interfering with his troops' archery practice. Everyone knows that St Andrews is the home of golf, but few people realise that anyone can play on the Old Course, the world's most famous golf course. Although it lies beside the exclusive, all-male Royal & Ancient Golf Club, the Old Course is a public course, and is not owned by the club.

Although open to the public, getting a tee-off time is something of a lottery. In fact, unless you book months in advance, the only chance you have of playing here is by entering a ballot before 2 pm on the day before you wish to play. Be warned that applications by ballot normally exceed available times by around 500%, and green fees are a mere £50. There's no play allowed on Sunday. You must present a handicap certificate or letter of introduction from your club to the St Andrews Links Management Committee (☎ 01334-475757). If you want to make a booking yourself, write a year in advance (for summer and autumn reservations) to The Secretary, St Andrews Links Management Committee, St Andrews, Fife KY16 9JA.

If your number doesn't come up, there are five other public courses in the area, none with quite the cachet of the Old Course but all of them significantly cheaper. Fees are as follows: New/Jubilee £25, Eden £10, Strathtyrum £14 and Balgrove £6. ∎

Car Ian Cowe Coachworks (☎ 472543), 76 Argyle St, rents Fiats from £24 per day.

Getting Around

Taxi Try Golf City Taxis (☎ 477788), 23 Argyle St. A taxi between the railway station at Leuchars and the town centre costs around £8.

Bicycle You can rent bikes at Spokes (☎ 477835), 77 South St; mountain bikes and hybrids cost from £8.50 per day.

AROUND ST ANDREWS

Earlshall Castle

Six miles north-west of St Andrews, solid Earlshall Castle was built by William Bruce in 1546 and restored by the renowned architect Robert Lorimer. Set in beautiful gardens, the castle (☎ 01334-839205) was open to the public but in late 1996 the only way to visit was to buy it. Phone to check the current viewing situation or make an offer.

Kellie Castle

Kellie is a magnificent example of Lowland Scottish domestic architecture and is well worth a visit. It's set in a beautiful garden, and many of the rooms contain superb plasterwork. The original part of the building dates from 1360; it was enlarged to its present dimensions around 1606. Robert Lorimer worked on the castle at the turn of the century, when it was not in good shape, and it was bought by the Lorimer family in 1948.

Kellie Castle (☎ 01333-720217) is three miles north of Anstruther. It's a NTS property, open daily from May to October, 1.30 to 5.30 pm, and in April at weekends, 1.30 to 5.30 pm. Entry is £3.10/2.

Secret Bunker

Three miles north of Anstruther is a fascinating attraction – what would have been one of Britain's underground command centres and a home for Scots leaders if nuclear war had broken out. Hidden down a 250-yard tunnel are the operation rooms, communication centre and dormitories. An audiovisual display explains how it would have been used.

The museum (☎ 01333-310301) is at Troy Wood, by the B940. It's open from Easter to October, 10 am to 6 pm daily; entry is £4.95/2.95. There are interesting guided tours at 11 am, 1 and 3 pm.

EAST NEUK

The section of the south Fife coast that stretches from Leven east to the point at Fife Ness is known as East Neuk. There are several picturesque fishing villages and some good coastal walks in the area.

Crail

• *pop 1000* • ☎ *01333*

One of the prettiest of the East Neuk villages, Crail has a much-photographed harbour surrounded by white cottages with red-tiled roofs. There are far fewer fishing boats in the harbour now than there once were, but you can still buy fresh lobster and shellfish here. The village's history and involvement with the fishing industry is outlined in the **Crail Museum**, Marketgait. There's a TIC (☎ 450869) at the museum, open from April to September. Crail is 10 miles from St Andrews.

Anstruther

• *pop 3000* • ☎ *01333*

A large former fishing village, nine miles south of St Andrews, Anstruther is worth visiting for the **Scottish Fisheries Museum** (☎ 310628), by the harbour. Displays include a cottage belonging to a fishing family, and the history of the herring and whaling industries that were once the mainstay of the local economy. It's open April to October, daily from 10 am to 5.30 pm (11 am to 5 pm on Sunday), and with shorter hours for the rest of the year. Entry is £3/2.

Other boats in the harbour will take you on sea angling trips or across to the **Isle of May**, a bird reserve. You can make reservations for both at the kiosk (☎ 310103) near the museum. A three-hour fishing trip costs £10. A three to five-hour excursion to the Isle of May is £10/4; the crossing is just under an hour. Between April and July, the cliffs are packed with breeding kittiwakes, razorbills, guillemots, shags and puffins. Inland is the remains of a 12th-century monastery.

The helpful TIC (☎ 311073) is by the Fisheries Museum. It's open April to September, daily from 9.30 am to 5.30 pm (noon to 5 pm on Sunday).

Places to Stay & Eat The *Bunkhouse* (☎ 310768), in West Pitkierie, is 1½ miles out of Anstruther. The nightly charge is £6, and it's best to book ahead in summer.

Behind the museum, at 15 East Green, *Mrs Dickson* (☎ 310377) charges around £15 for B&B. The *Spindrift* (☎ 310573), Pittenweem Rd, is a very comfortable guesthouse, a short walk from the village centre. All rooms have bathroom attached and cost from £27.50 per person.

As well as basic cafés, Anstruther boasts one of Scotland's top places to eat. *The Cellar Restaurant* (☎ 310378), 24 East Green, is famous for its seafood – crabs, lobster, scallops, langoustine, monkfish, turbot etc. Advance bookings are essential. There's a set dinner for £28.50.

Getting There & Away There are hourly buses, Monday to Saturday, between St Andrews, Anstruther, Elie and Earlsferry.

Pittenweem

This is now the main fishing port on the East Neuk coast, and there are lively fish sales in the early morning at the harbour. The village name means 'place of the cave', referring to the cave in Cove Wynd which was used as a chapel by the 7th-century missionary St Fillan. He was a saint who possessed miraculous powers – when he wrote his sermons in the dark cave, his arm would illuminate his work by emitting a luminous glow.

Perthshire & Kinross

This area includes most of the former region of Tayside – the area covered by the River Tay and its tributaries. It contains, in miniature, as many variations in terrain as

Scotland itself, from the bleak expanse of Rannoch Moor in the west, to the rich farmland of the Carse of Gowrie between Perth and Dundee.

More than any other part of Scotland, this area has had the closest association with Scotland's struggle to maintain its freedom from England. From 838, Scotland's monarchs were crowned at Scone. Robert the Bruce signed a declaration of independence from England at Arbroath Abbey in 1320. Mary Queen of Scots was imprisoned in Lochleven Castle, and at Killiecrankie, the Jacobites repelled the government forces.

The Highland line cuts across this region. In the north-west are the rounded, heathery Grampians, known as the Mounth. The county town of Perth, built on the Tay, has a medieval church and many fine Georgian buildings.

Running out of Loch Tay, in West Perthshire, the River Tay flows north-east through hills and woods towards Pitlochry. Queen Victoria, when looking for a place to buy, was quite taken by this area, particularly by the view over Loch Tummel. South of Pitlochry, the river turns south-east to Dunkeld, where the cathedral sits on its banks. Further north from Pitlochry, at Blair Atholl, is Blair Castle, ancestral seat of the dukes of Atholl.

GETTING AROUND

The A9, Scotland's busiest road, cuts across the centre of this region through Perth and Pitlochry. It's the fast route into the Highlands and to Inverness – watch out for speed traps. Buses and trains also follow this artery. Perth is a major transport hub.

The main bus operators in the area are: Scottish Citylink (☎ 0990-505050), Stagecoach (☎ 01738-629339), Strathtay Buses (☎ 01738-872772) and Fife Scottish (☎ 01334-474238). For rail information, phone ☎ 0345-484950.

LOCH LEVEN

In the extreme south of Perthshire is Loch Leven and, on an island in the loch, Lochleven Castle. The castle served as a fortress and prison from the 14th century. Its most famous captive was Mary Queen of Scots, who spent almost a year incarcerated here from 1567. Her infamous charms bewitched Willie Douglas, who managed to get hold of the cell keys to release her, then row her across to the shore. The castle is now ruined, but can be visited by ferry from Kinross. It's open standard HS hours and entry is £2.50/1, including the ferry trip.

If you want to stay in the area, there's basic B&B at the *Roxburghe Guest House* (☎ 01577-862498), 126 High St, Kinross, for around £16 per person. About two miles north of the town, on the outskirts of Milnathort, there's comfortable *Hattonburn Farmhouse* (☎ 01577-862362), Hattonburn, near the M90. It has one single and two doubles, each with their own bathroom next door; B&B costs around £15 per person and evening meals are available.

Scottish Citylink has an hourly service between Perth and Kinross (25 minutes, £2.50).

PERTH
• *pop 42,000* • ☎ *01738*

In *The Fair Maid of Perth*, Sir Walter Scott extolled the virtues of this county town. 'Perth, so eminent for the beauty of its situation, is a place of great antiquity,' he wrote. This is all still true and the town was recently voted the best place to live in Britain, for quality of life.

Perth's rise in importance derives from Scone (pronounced scoon), two miles north of the town. In 838, Kenneth MacAlpin became the first king of a united Scotland and brought the Stone of Destiny, on which all kings were ceremonially invested, to Scone. An important abbey grew up on the site. From this time on, all Scottish kings were invested here, even after Edward I of England carted the sacred talisman off to London's Westminster Abbey. In 1996 John Major persuaded the Queen to promise to return it to Scotland, but when it does come back it's likely to be to Edinburgh Castle rather than Scone.

Built on the banks of the River Tay, Perth grew into a major trading centre, known for weaving, dyeing and glove-making. It was originally called St John's Toun, hence the name of the local football team, St Johnstone. From the 12th century, Perth was Scotland's capital, and in 1437 James I was murdered here. There were four important monasteries in the area and the town was a target for the Reformation movement in Scotland.

Perth is now a busy market town and centre of service industries. It's the focal point for this agricultural region and there are world-famous cattle auctions of the valuable Aberdeen Angus breed. The bull sales in February draw international buyers.

The top attraction in the area is Scone Palace, but the town itself has a number of interesting things to see, including an excellent art gallery, housing the work of local artist JD Fergusson.

Orientation & Information
Most of the town lies on the western bank of the Tay; Scone Palace and some of the B&Bs are on the eastern bank. There are two large parks: North Inch, the scene of the infamous battle of the clans in 1396, and South Inch. The bus and railway stations are next to each other, near the north-eastern corner of South Inch.

The TIC (☎ 638353), 45 High St, is open daily from March to October, and from Monday to Saturday for the rest of the year. You can buy half-price tickets at the TIC for the hop-on, hop-off bus service (£2) that takes in Scone Palace.

Walking Tour
From the TIC, walk one block south to **St John's Kirk**. Founded in 1126, and surrounded by cobbled streets, this is still the centrepiece of the town. John Knox preached a powerful sermon here that was one of the sparks for the Reformation and the resulting destruction of the monasteries, including the one at Scone. The kirk was restored in the 1920s.

Four blocks south is the Round House, the old waterworks building on the edge of

South Inch that now houses the **JD Fergusson Gallery** (☎ 441944). This Perthshire artist, one of the group known as the Scottish Colourists, spent much of his time in Paris and the south of France in the early part of this century. The gallery is well worth seeing; it's open Monday to Saturday, 10 am to 5 pm; entrance is free.

Two blocks north of the High St is the **Art Gallery & Museum** (☎ 632488) which charts local history. There are displays of Perth art glass, an impressive silver collection and natural history displays. It's open the same hours as the Fergusson Gallery.

Nearby, on Curfew Row, is the **Fair Maid's House**, the house chosen by Sir Walter Scott as home for Catherine Glover, the novel's romantic heroine. The novel was set in the 14th century, but this house dates from the 16th, when it was a meeting hall for the town's glove manufacturers.

South-west of the Fair Maid's House,

Lower City Mills is a restored Victorian mill. In the north of the town, Balhousie Castle houses the **Black Watch Museum**, charting the campaigns (in almost every battle fought by Britain in the last 250 years) of Scotland's top regiment.

Scone Palace

Two miles north of Perth, Scone Palace, the home of the Earl and Countess of Mansfield, should not be missed. It was built in 1580 in the grounds of a former abbey; the abbey was destroyed in 1559 by a crowd inflamed by John Knox's sermon in St John's Kirk. With the destruction of the abbey buildings, the land passed to the Gowrie family and then to the Murrays.

In 1804, the palace was enlarged, and it now houses a superb collection of French furniture, including Marie Antoinette's writing table. Displays of 16th-century needle work include bed hangings worked

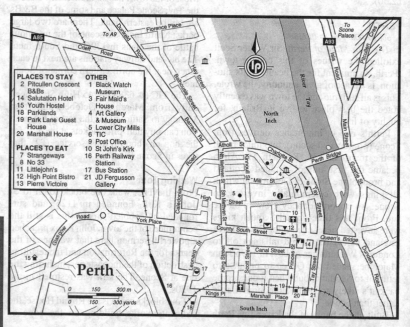

PLACES TO STAY
2 Pitcullen Crescent B&Bs
14 Salutation Hotel
15 Youth Hostel
18 Parklands
19 Park Lane Guest House
20 Marshall House

PLACES TO EAT
7 Strangeways
8 No 33
11 Littlejohn's
12 High Point Bistro
13 Pierre Victoire

OTHER
1 Black Watch Museum
3 Fair Maid's House
4 Art Gallery & Museum
5 Lower City Mills
6 TIC
9 Post Office
10 St John's Kirk
16 Perth Railway Station
17 Bus Station
21 JD Fergusson Gallery

Perth

by Mary Queen of Scots. In the library is a valuable collection of 18th and 19th-century porcelain. The palace is surrounded by parkland, including rare pine trees.

Scone Palace (☎ 552300) is open from April to mid-October, daily from 9.30 am to 5 pm. Entry is £4.70/2.35 for the house and grounds, half-price for the grounds only. The hop-on, hop-off bus (contact the TIC for tickets) goes this way, as do bus Nos 8 and 58.

Places to Stay

The excellent *Perth Youth Hostel* (☎ 623658), 107 Glasgow Rd, is open from late February to the end of October. The nightly charge is £6.95/5.85.

The main B&B areas are along Glasgow Rd, Dunkeld Rd, Dundee Rd and Pitcullen Crescent. *Iona Guest House* (☎ 627261), 2 Pitcullen Crescent, charges £17/34; some rooms have private showers. *Achnacarry Guest House* (☎ 621421), at No 3, is similarly-priced. Non-smokers should head for *Lochiel House* (☎ 633183), also on Pitcullen Crescent, which is a very friendly place that costs around £18 per person. At No 17, *Pitcullen Guest House* (☎ 626506) charges from £19 per person.

Closer to the centre, there are several places along Marshall Place, overlooking South Inch. *Marshall House* (☎ 442886), at No 6, has three rooms with private showers and charges £17.50 per person. The very comfortable *Park Lane Guest House* (☎ 637218), 17 Marshall Place, offers B&B at around £20 per person.

The *Salutation Hotel* (☎ 630066), 34 South St, boasts a ballroom haunted by the ghost of Bonnie Prince Charlie. Rooms cost up to £78 but if business is slack at weekends they sometimes offer B&B for as little as £25 per person.

Parklands (☎ 622451), St Leonards Bank, is one of the top places to stay. It's a small hotel and all rooms have bath attached, one with a spa. During the week, it costs from £47.50 per person; at weekends this drops to £37.50.

Places to Eat

If you're visiting *Scone Palace*, there's a good coffee shop and restaurant.

In the centre of Perth, *Littlejohn's* (☎ 639888), 24 St John's St, provides the same reliable menu it offers at other branches. Starters range from £1.30 to £5.95, main dishes from £4.10 to £12.35. Vegetarian choices include lasagne (£4.20), and vegetable fajitas (£7.15). There's also a branch of *Pierre Victoire* (☎ 444222), at 38 South St, with the usual excellent three-course lunch for £4.90. Over the road *High Port Bistro* (☎ 444049) undercuts Pierre's lunchtime menu by £1.40.

Strangeways (☎ 628866), 24 George St, is a bistro that's open every day. It's a good place to have a drink in the evening, but they stop serving food at 5 pm.

Number Thirty-three (☎ 633771), 33 George St, is one of the best places to eat in Perth. It's an oyster bar and restaurant specialising in seafood; popular items on the menu include creamy crab & prawn terrine, and salmon & thyme bake.

Getting There & Away

Scottish Citylink (☎ 0990-505050) has five services a day to London (9¼ hours, £36) including an overnight bus. There are also buses from Perth to Glasgow (1½ hours, £6.40), Edinburgh (1¼ hours, £4.30), Dundee (35 minutes, £2.80) and Aberdeen (2½ hours, £8.40).

There's an hourly train service from Glasgow Queen St (one hour, £10.50), two hourly on Sunday, and numerous trains from Edinburgh. See also the fares tables in the Getting Around chapter.

STRATHEARN

West of Perth, the wide *straths* (valleys) of the rivers Earn and Tay were once great forests, hunted in by medieval kings. The Earn, named after a Celtic goddess, runs from St Fillans (named after the mystic who lived on an island in Loch Earn), through Comrie and Crieff and eventually into the Tay near Bridge of Earn. The whole area is known as Strathearn, an attractive region of undulating farmland, hills and lochs. The Highlands begin in the western section of Strathearn and the so-called Highland line runs through Comrie and Crieff, and through Kirriemuir and Edzell to Stonehaven.

Crieff

- *pop 5000* • ☎ *01764*

Attractively located on the edge of the Highlands, Crieff has been a popular resort town since Victorian times. It was once the scene of a large cattle fair, since this was as far south as the Highlanders would drive their animals. Some vendors would come from as far away as Skye – swimming the cattle across to the mainland.

The main attraction now is the **Glenturret Distillery** (☎ 656565), about a mile from the centre of town. This whisky distillery and visitors centre is open daily from 9.30 am to 6 pm (afternoon only on Sunday); the last tour is at 4.30 pm. It's all fairly touristy but included in the price of £3.40 is a miniature bottle of 12-year-old single malt.

There's a TIC (☎ 652578) in the High St, open all year. *Braincroft Bunkhouse* (☎ 670140) has basic accommodation in small rooms for £8 per person. Braincroft is five miles from Crieff, two from Comrie, on the A85.

Auchterarder

- *pop 3000* • ☎ *01764*

In the south of Strathearn, this small town stands in the centre of a large farming community. Overlooking Auchterarder are the Ochil Hills, which run north-east into the Sidlaws. There's a TIC (☎ 663450), 90 High St, open all year.

The town is probably best known for the internationally famous hotel on its outskirts. *Gleneagles Hotel* (☎ 662231) has a championship golf course and room charges that range from £130 for a single to £1150 for the Royal Lochnagar Suite (antiques, silk-lined walls, hand-woven carpets and other little necessities). The hotel even has its own railway station, 1¼ hours (£8.30) from Glasgow, but if you can afford to stay here,

you can afford the limo from the airport (£125).

PERTH TO AVIEMORE

There are a number of major sights strung out along the A9, the main route north to Aviemore in the Highlands. There are frequent buses and trains along this route; most stop at the places described in this section.

Dunkeld & Birnam

Eleven miles from Perth, Dunkeld is an attractive town on the Highland line. There are some excellent walks in this wooded area. On High and Cathedral Sts is a collection of 20 artisans' houses restored by the NTS.

Dunkeld Cathedral must be among the most beautifully sited cathedrals in the country. Half of it is still in use as a church, the rest is in ruins. The oldest part of the original church is the choir, completed in 1350. The tower, also still standing, dates from the 15th century. The cathedral was damaged during the Reformation and burnt in the battle of Dunkeld in 1689.

Across the bridge is Birnam, made famous by *Macbeth*. There's not much left of Birnam Wood, but there are some good walks, including the Hermitage Woodland Walk from the car park, two miles west of Dunkeld. The well-marked trail follows the river to the Black Linn Falls, where the Duke of Atholl built a folly, the Hermitage, in 1758.

Dunkeld TIC (☎ 01350-727688) is at The Cross.

Pitlochry

- *pop 2200* • *01796*

Despite the rows of tartan shops and tripe for trippers, Pitlochry makes a useful base for exploring the area, and has good transport connections if you don't have your own wheels.

The TIC (☎ 472215), 22 Atholl Rd, is open daily (except Sunday in winter). From late May to mid-September, its opening hours are from 9 am to 8 pm.

The well-known **Pitlochry Festival**

Theatre (☎ 472680) stages a different play six nights out of seven during its season from May to October.

If you haven't yet been on a tour of a whisky distillery, Pitlochry has two. **Bell's Blair Athol Distillery** (☎ 472234) is at the southern end of the town. **The Edradour** (☎ 472095) is Scotland's smallest distillery, 2½ miles east of Pitlochry.

When the power station was built on the River Tummel, a **fish ladder** was constructed to allow the salmon to swim up to their spawning grounds. It's at the northeastern end of the town, and you can walk up from the Pitlochry Festival Theatre to watch the fish in the observation chamber – May and June are the best seasons.

Walks & Cycle Routes The TIC sells the useful publication *Walks – Pitlochry & District* (£1), which lists 16 walks in the area.

There's an 8½-mile hike round Loch Faskally, past the theatre and fish ladder, and up to the Pass of Killiecrankie (see following section). A seven-mile hike takes you to Blair Castle; you could catch the bus back, but check times with the TIC before you go. There's a steep three-mile round trip to Craigower, a viewpoint above Pitlochry. For a more spectacular view, tackle Ben y Vrackie (2755 feet), a steep six-mile walk from Moulin.

Places to Stay & Eat Pitlochry is packed with places to stay, but anything central tends to be pricey. *Pitlochry Youth Hostel* (☎ 472308) is above the town, in Knockard Rd, and has great views. It's open year-round and the nightly charge is £6.95/5.85.

The cheapest B&Bs are in Moulin, just over a mile to the north. At *Craig Dubh Cottage* (☎ 472058), Manse Rd, B&B costs around £13 per person; there's one double with bath attached for £28. Also on Manse Rd is *Lavalette* (☎ 472364), which is similarly priced.

There are plenty of places to stay along Atholl Rd, which runs through the centre of the town. *Craig Urrard Hotel* (☎ 472346), at No 10, charges around £25 per person. At

No 8, the luxurious *Acarsaid Hotel* (☎ 472389) has 18 rooms, all with attached bath, for £34 per person.

The top place in Pitlochry is the *Pitlochry Hydro Hotel* (☎ 472666), Knockard Rd, which has singles/doubles for £61/110.

The café at the *Festival Theatre* is recommended. The *Old Smithy* (☎ 472356) is a good restaurant on Atholl Rd; last orders are at 8 pm. There's tagliatelli with smoked ham and mushroom for £6.95, roast leg of lamb for £7.25, plus vegetarian choices.

Getting There & Away Scottish Citylink runs hourly buses between Inverness and Glasgow/Edinburgh. Journey times and prices to destinations from Pitlochry are: Inverness (two hours, £6.60), Aviemore (1¼ hours, £5.20), Perth (45 minutes, £3.80), Edinburgh (four hours, £5.90) and Glasgow (4¼ hours, £6.60).

Pitlochry is on the main rail line from Perth to Inverness. There are five trains a day from Perth (30 minutes, £7.10), fewer on Sunday.

Pass of Killiecrankie
The first skirmish of the Jacobite Rebellion took place in 1689 in this beautiful, rugged gorge, 3½ miles north of Pitlochry. A National Trust for Scotland Visitors Centre has a display on the battle. Highland soldiers led by Bonnie Dundee routed troops led by General Mackay. As they fled, one of the soldiers is said to have jumped across the gap now known as Soldier's Leap.

Blair Castle
One of the most popular tourist attractions in Scotland, Blair Castle is the seat of the Duke of Atholl. Outside this impressive white castle, set beneath forested slopes above the River Garry, a piper pipes in the crowds each day. In February 1996, the tenth duke died, leaving the castle and its 70,000 acres to a charitable trust and only the title to his heir, a distant cousin in South Africa. Since the new duke has refused to acknowledge his title and has no plans to move to Scotland it's unlikely that he will take his cousin's place

at the annual May parade of the Atholl Highlanders, the only private army in the country.

The original castle was built in 1269, but has undergone significant remodelling since then. In 1746, it was besieged by the Jacobites, the last castle in Britain to be subject to siege.

Thirty-two rooms are open to the public, and they are packed with paintings, arms and armour, china, lace and embroidery, presenting a wonderful picture of upper-class Highland life from the 1500s to the present. One of the most impressive rooms is the ballroom, which has a wooden roof and walls covered in antlers.

Blair Castle (☎ 01796-481207) is seven miles north of Pitlochry, and one mile from Blair Atholl village. It's open daily from April to October, 10 am to 6 pm (last entry 5 pm); tickets cost £5/4.

Other attractions in Blair Atholl village include a working water mill by the river. You can hire bikes from Atholl Activity Cycles (☎ 01796-481646). It has a leaflet listing cycle routes in the area, including a 16-mile ride along an estate road up Glen Tilt, a 12-mile ride around Bruar Falls and Old Struan, or a six-mile ride to Killiecrankie Pass and back. The *Atholl Arms* (☎ 01796-481205) is a pub near the station; B&B is £32.50 per person.

Elizabeth Yule Buses (☎ 01796-472290) runs a service every two hours between Pitlochry and Blair (20 minutes). There's a railway station in the village, but not all trains stop here. There's a free shuttle bus from the station to the castle.

For a continuation of this route, see the Aviemore section in the Highlands & Northern Islands chapter.

WEST PERTHSHIRE

The lochs and hills of this remote area are difficult to reach without your own transport.

From the A9, south of Pitlochry, the A827 heads west to Crianlarich and the western coast. At Aberfeldy, there's a TIC (☎ 01887-820276), The Square, open all year. One mile from the town, Castle Menzies is the seat of the Chief of the Clan Menzies; it's open

daily. West of Aberfeldy, the village of Fortingall is famous as the birthplace of Pontius Pilate.

The bulk of Ben Lawers (3984 feet) crouches like a lion over Loch Tay. It's in the care of the NTS which has a Visitors Centre in the shadow of the mountain. A trail leads to the summit from the visitors centre, but a more interesting seven-hour route is up Lawers Burn from Machuim Farm, just north of Lawers villages. You can walk around the ridges via Meall Garbh to the summit, but you should take a good map.

At the western end of Loch Tay is the village of Killin (see the Stirling section in this chapter).

Dundee & Angus

Formerly part of the region of Tayside, Dundee and Angus are now two separate unitary authorities.

Dundee was once a whaling port and the centre of the thriving jute industry. It's now a victim of 20th-century decline and chronic unemployment, but has several interesting attractions for visitors, including Captain Scott's ship *Discovery*.

The main draw in Angus is Glamis Castle of *Macbeth* fame. Angus is an attractive county of peaceful glens running down to the sea. The area was part of the Pictish kingdom in the 7th and 8th centuries, and there are interesting Pictish symbol stones at Meigle.

GETTING AROUND

For information on buses within the Dundee and Broughty Ferry area phone ☎ 01382-201121. For services outside this area contact Strathtay Buses (☎ 01382-228054).

The rail inquiry line is ☎ 0345-484950.

DUNDEE

• *pop 175,000* • ☎ *01382*

Poor Dundee. This grey city is an unfortunate example of the worst of 1960s and 70s town planning – ugly blocks of flats and office buildings joined by unsightly concrete

Pictish Symbol Stones

When the Romans left Britain in 410, virtually all of Scotland north of Edinburgh and Glasgow was occupied by the Picts, a warlike people about whom little is known. In the 9th century they suddenly disappeared, leaving very few archaeological remains and a scattering of Pictish place names beginning with Pit-, but literally hundreds of mysterious standing stones, decorated with intricate symbols. The capital of the ancient Southern Pictish kingdom is said to have been at Forteviot in Strathearn, and Pictish symbol stones are to be found throughout this area and all the way up the eastern coast of Scotland into Sutherland and Caithness.

It's believed that the stones were set up to record Pictish lineages and alliances, but no-one is yet quite sure exactly how the system worked. The stones fall into three groups. Class I, the earliest, are rough blocks of stone, carved with any combination from a basic set of 28 symbols. Class II are decorated with a Celtic cross as well as with symbols. Class III, dating from the end of the Pictish era (790-840), have only figures and a cross.

With your own transport, it's possible to follow a number of symbol-stone trails in the area. Starting at Dundee (visit the McManus Galleries first), drive north to Arbroath. On the outskirts is St Vigeans Museum which contains several interesting stones. Continue north along the A92 to Montrose, where there are more stones in the local museum. Along the A935, in Brechin Cathedral, is a good example of a Class III stone. Take the B9134 to Aberlemno, where there are excellent examples of all three classes. Along the A94, at Meigle, the museum holds one of the best collections of stones in the country.

For more information, it's worth getting a copy of *The Pictish Trail* (£3.95) by Anthony Jackson (Orkney Press), which lists 11 driving tours, or his more detailed *Symbol Stones of Scotland*, both available in TICs. ■

---

walkways. Once, there were more millionaires per head in Dundee than anywhere else in Britain. Today, it's Dole City, with the highest number of unemployed people in Scotland, second in the UK only to Liverpool.

In 1993, the city decided to stake all its tourist fortunes on one main attraction – Captain Scott's polar research ship *Discovery*, but the city's main asset is its people. Despite the feeling of desolation here, the vigour that remains in the city is in the hearts of the Dundonians, who are among the friendliest, most welcoming and most entertaining people you'll meet anywhere in the country.

It's worth staying here awhile. Dundee's hotels and restaurants are good value, there are some great drinking places and four miles east of the city is the seaside suburb of Broughty Ferry.

History

Dundee first began to grow in importance as a result of trade links with Flanders and the Baltic ports. It was awarded the first of its royal charters by King William in the late 12th century.

In its chequered history, Dundee was captured by Edward I, besieged by Henry VIII and destroyed by Cromwellian forces in the 17th century. It became the second most

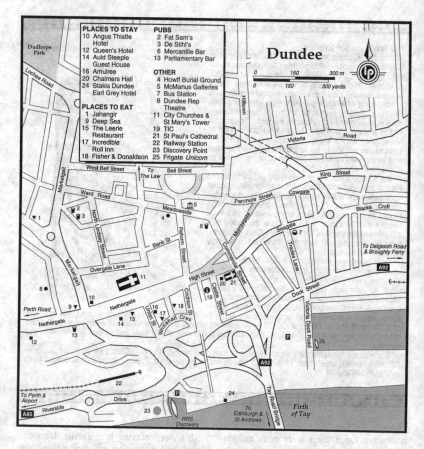

PLACES TO STAY
10 Angus Thistle Hotel
12 Queen's Hotel
14 Auld Steeple Guest House
16 Amulree
20 Chalmers Hall
24 Stakis Dundee Earl Grey Hotel

PLACES TO EAT
1 Jahangir
9 Deep Sea
15 The Leerie Restaurant
17 Incredible Roll Inn
18 Fisher & Donaldson

PUBS
2 Fat Sam's
3 De Stihl's
6 Mercantile Bar
13 Parliamentary Bar

OTHER
4 Howff Burial Ground
5 McManus Galleries
7 Bus Station
8 Dundee Rep Theatre
11 City Churches & St Mary's Tower
19 TIC
21 St Paul's Cathedral
22 Railway Station
23 Discovery Point
25 Frigate Unicorn

Dundee

important trading city in Scotland (after Edinburgh).

In the 19th century, Dundee was a major player in the shipbuilding and railway engineering industries. Linen and wool gave way to jute, and since whale oil was used in the production of jute, whaling developed alongside. At one time, there were as many as 43,000 people employed in the textile industry, but as the jute workers became redundant, light engineering, electronics and food processing provided employment.

Dundee is often called the city of the three 'Js' – jute, jam and journalism. No jute is produced here anymore, and when the famous Keiller jam factory was taken over in 1988, production was transferred to England. There is still journalism, and DC Thomson, best known for its comics (such as the *Beano)*, is the city's largest employer.

Orientation

Most people approach the city from the Tay Road Bridge or along the A85 from Perth; both routes take you right into the centre. The railway station and *Discovery* are near the bridge; the bus station is a short walk to the north, just off Seagate.

Four miles to the east of Dundee is Broughty Ferry, Dundee's seaside resort. It's connected by regular buses and is a very pleasant place to stay.

Information

The very helpful TIC (☎ 434664), 4 City Square, is open long hours. In July and August, it's open every day from 9 am to 8 pm (Sunday to 6 pm); in May, June and September, until 7 pm daily (Sunday to 6 pm); for the rest of the year, from 9 am to 6 pm on weekdays, and until 4 pm on Saturday (closed on Sunday). As well as the usual bed-booking facility, they sell Scottish Citylink tickets, and there's a bureau de change.

There are guided walks (£2) from the TIC – a heritage and industrial walk, and a maritime walk. Pick up a copy of *What's On*, free from the TIC.

Discovery Point

You won't be able to miss Dundee's much-publicised visitor attraction, centred on Captain Scott's famous polar expedition vessel, the research ship *Discovery*. The ship was constructed here in 1900, and was built with a hull at least two feet thick to survive the pack ice of the Antarctic. Scott sailed for the Antarctic in 1901 and, in a not uneventful voyage, spent two winters trapped in the ice.

After walking through the exhibitions and audiovisual displays in the main building, you go on board the ship to see the cabins used by Scott and his crew. The complex (☎ 201245) is on the bank of the Firth of Tay, near the Tay Road Bridge. It's open daily from 10 am to 5 pm (from 11 am on Sunday, and to 4 pm daily from November to March); entry is £4/2.90.

HM Frigate Unicorn

Unlike the *Discovery*, Dundee's other floating tourist sight is not tarted-up and retains the atmosphere of an old ship. Built as a warship in 1824, the *Unicorn* is the oldest British-built warship still afloat – perhaps because it never saw action. By the mid-19th century, sailing ships were outclassed by

steam and the *Unicorn* served as storage for gunpowder, then later as a training vessel. When it was proposed to break up the historic ship for scrap in the 1960s, a preservation society was formed.

Wandering around the four decks gives you an excellent impression of what it must have been like for the crew to live in such cramped conditions. The *Unicorn* (☎ 200900) is berthed in Victoria Dock, just east of the Tay Bridge. Open daily from 10 am to 5 pm, tickets are £2/1 and there are free guided tours.

Other Things to See

The **McManus Galleries** (☎ 432020), Albert Square, is a solid Victorian Gothic building, designed by Gilbert Scott, containing the city's art collection and museum. The exhibits are well displayed and interesting, and include the history of the city from the Iron Age. There's an impressive display of Scottish Victorian paintings, furniture and silver. Look out for the display on William McGonagall, Scotland's worst poet, whose lines about the Tay Rail Bridge disaster are memorably awful. The galleries are open Monday to Saturday from 10 am to 5 pm; entry is free.

Over the road is the **Howff Burial Ground**, a historic graveyard given to the people of Dundee by Mary Queen of Scots. The carved gravestones feature the signs and symbols of the old craft guilds and date back to the 16th century.

It's worth the hike up to **The Law**, at 571 feet the highest point in the city. It's the remains of an ancient volcanic plug and there are great views over the city and across to Fife. You also get a good view of the two bridges over the Tay. The 1½-mile road bridge was opened in 1966; the railway bridge is just over two miles long, the longest in Europe. It was built in 1887 to replace a bridge which blew down in a storm in 1879 while a train was crossing it – 75 people died.

Broughty Ferry

This pleasant suburb is four miles east of Dundee. There's a long, sandy beach (though not exactly spotless) and a number of good places to eat and drink.

Claypotts Castle was once in the country but has now been absorbed into suburbia. Looking like a house perched on top of a castle, it's actually one of the most complete Z-plan tower houses. It was built in the late 16th century. Currently closed it should be reopening in 1997. Contact the TIC for information.

Broughty Castle Museum (☎ 776121) is a reconstructed estuary fort on the point. It has an interesting display on the local whaling industry. Admission is free, but it's closed on Friday.

Places to Stay

Hostels There's no youth hostel yet; the nearest is in St Andrews. *Amulree* (☎ 223867), 20 Union St, is a basic guesthouse but you couldn't be more central. Many of the rooms are long-term lets, but overnight B&B costs around £13 per person. Just around the corner, and much more upmarket, is *Auld Steeple Guest House* (☎ 200302), 94 Nethergate. It charges £22/36 for a single/double with attached bath, £18/32 without.

If you're here in the university holidays, you can stay in the halls of residence at *Dundee University* (☎ 647171) in West Park, 1½ miles from the centre. There are single and twin rooms available from £20/30.

B&Bs & Hotels In the north of the city, a 10-minute walk from the bus station, is *Mrs Milne's* (☎ 225354), 8 Nelson Terrace, which has B&B for around £14. *Hillside Guest House* (☎ 223443), 43 Constitution St (off Constitution Rd), charges from £18 to £25 per person.

In the east, *Errolbank Guest House* (☎ 462118), 9 Dalgleish Rd charges £22/35 in a room with attached bath.

There's a good range of places to stay in Broughty Ferry. *Homelea* (☎ 774260), 56 Monifieth Rd, charges £16/30. It's a small, friendly place a five-minute walk from the beach. The *Fisherman's Tavern* (☎ 775941)

is an excellent pub that does B&B for around £20 per person.

On the western side of Dundee, just off the Perth Rd and about 1½ miles from the city centre, is the *Shaftesbury Hotel* (☎ 669216), 1 Hyndford St. It's a former jute baron's mansion, and an excellent place to stay; it's popular with businesspeople. During the week, it charges £49.50/68 for a single/double; at weekends it's £39.50/58. There's a good restaurant and the set dinner is £14.50.

The three main business hotels in the centre of the city are the *Angus Thistle Hotel* (☎ 226874), Marketgait, which is a modern block with B&B from £34 to £80; the *Queen's Hotel* (☎ 322515), 160 Nethergate, a grand Victorian hotel with similar prices; and the waterfront *Stakis Dundee Earl Grey Hotel* (☎ 229271), by the Tay Bridge, which charges from £36 to £95 per person. The lowest rates apply at the weekend.

Places to Eat

For one of the most depressed cities in the country there's a surprising number of interesting places to eat in Dundee, and prices are very competitive. For a snack, the *Incredible Roll Inn*, Whitehall Crescent, is a good sandwich shop with a wonderful range of hot and cold filled rolls. It's often packed with office workers picking up their lunch.

The *Het Theatre Café* (☎ 200813) is at the Dundee Rep Theatre on Tay Square. It's a European-style coffee-bar, a great place for coffee, a meal or a drink – the bar's open late all week.

The *Deep Sea*, 81 Nethergate, is the oldest fish & chip shop in Dundee, but it doesn't stay open late. Nearby, the *Leerie Restaurant*, Nethergate, is very cheap. Rather more upmarket, *Fisher & Donaldson* is an excellent bakery/patisserie with a café attached. For £1.95 you can have a cream tea.

It's worth going to *Jahangir* (☎ 202022), 1 Session St, for the decor alone. This Indian restaurant looks like a nightclub from the outside; inside, it's pure Moghul Hollywood, with an over-the-top tent and fountain. The food's good and they also do takeaways. Chicken curries start at £4.10. It's open until

1 am at the weekends, midnight during the week.

There are lots of interesting places to eat along Perth Rd, although some of them are a fair walk from the centre. The best restaurant in Dundee, *Raffles Restaurant* (☎ 201139), 18 Perth Rd, is not far, however, and main courses are good value at £6.50 to £8.

The most interesting restaurant here is the *Agacan* (☎ 644227), 113 Perth Rd, part Turkish restaurant, part art gallery, and a great place to spend the evening.

In Broughty Ferry, *Visocchi's*, Gray St, is an Italian ice-cream shop and café that's an institution. *Gulistan House* (☎ 738844) is an Indian restaurant and snooker club in an old church hall; in the early evening (5 to 7 pm, not Saturday) they have a set menu for £7.95.

Entertainment
The *Dundee Rep Theatre* (☎ 223530), Tay Square, hosts touring companies and also stages its own performances. The Dundee Jazz and Blues Festival (June) and the Folk Festival (July) are held here.

The *Parliamentary Bar* (☎ 202658), 134 Nethergate, is a large, stylish pub popular with students. There's live jazz some evenings. The *Mercantile Bar* (☎ 225500), 100 Commercial St, is a lively pub in the city centre.

In Broughty Ferry the beer is good at the *Fisherman's Tavern*, 12 Fort St. Another good place to drink is the *Ship Inn*, 121 Fisher St, which is also recommended for its pub grub.

Dundee has several nightclubs. *Fat Sam's*, South Ward Rd, is popular with students. Nearby, *De Stihl's* also gets busy.

Getting There & Away
See the fares tables in the Getting Around chapter. Dundee is 472 miles from London, 83 from Glasgow, 62 from Edinburgh, 67 from Aberdeen and 21 from Perth. If you're driving over the Tay Road Bridge from Fife, it's toll-free in that direction only.

Air The airport (☎ 643242) is very close to the centre, with flights to Aberdeen, Manchester and Denmark.

Bus National Express operates three services a day (two direct) to Dundee from London, including one night service. Scottish Citylink has hourly buses from Edinburgh (two hours, £5.90) and Glasgow (2¼ hours, £7.30). On some services, you may have to change in Perth. There are also hourly services to Perth (20 minutes, £2.80) and Aberdeen (1¾ hours, £6.10). To get to the western coast is a major pain – you must go via Glasgow to reach Fort William or Oban.

Train For rail information, phone ☎ 0345-484950. From Edinburgh/Glasgow (both 1¼ hours, £12.50) there are hourly trains Monday to Saturday; every two hours on Sunday. For Aberdeen (1¼ hours, £15.50), trains run via Arbroath and Stonehaven. There are two trains an hour, fewer on Sunday.

Car Rental companies include Arnold Clark (☎ 225382), Trades Lane, and Mitchell's Self Drive (☎ 223484), 90 Marketgait.

Getting Around
Bus Most city-centre buses pass along the High St, stopping by St Mary's Church.

It's possible to catch a train to Broughty Ferry, but the buses (15 minutes, 70p) are much more frequent.

Taxi Phone Tele Taxis (☎ 889333) if you need a cab.

GLAMIS CASTLE
Looking every bit a Scottish castle, with turrets and battlements, Glamis (pronounced glarms) was the legendary setting for Shakespeare's *Macbeth*. The Grampians and an extensive park provide a spectacular backdrop for this family home of the Earls of Strathmore and Kinghorne. A royal residence since 1372, the Queen Mother (née Elizabeth Bowes-Lyon) spent her childhood here and Princess Margaret (the Queen's sister) was born at Glamis.

The five-storey, L-shaped castle was given to the Lyon family in 1372, but was significantly altered in the 17th century. Inside, the most impressive room is the drawing room, with its arched plasterwork ceiling. There's a display of armour and weaponry in the crypt (haunted) and frescos in the chapel (also haunted). Duncan's Hall is where King Duncan was murdered in *Macbeth*. You can also look round the royal apartments, including the Queen Mother's bedroom.

Glamis Castle (☎ 01307-840242) is 12 miles north of Dundee. It's open daily from late March to October, 10.30 am to 5.30 pm (last entry 4.45 pm). You're escorted round in a guided tour which takes an hour and leaves every 15 minutes. Tickets are £4.70/2.50. There are two buses a day from Dundee (35 minutes, £1.80), operated by Strathtay Buses (☎ 01382-228054).

ARBROATH
• *pop 24,000*   • *☎ 01241*

Source of the famous Arbroath smokie (smoked haddock poached in milk), this fishing port was established in the 12th century. The settlement grew up around **Arbroath Abbey**, founded in 1178 by King William the Lion, who is buried here. It was at the abbey that Robert the Bruce signed Scotland's famous declaration of independence from England in 1320. Closed following the Dissolution, the fortified abbey fell into ruin, but enough survives to make this an impressive sight. There's a tall gable in the south transept, with a circular window that once held a shipping beacon. Parts of the nave and sacristy are intact. Open standard HS times, entry is £1.20/75p.

There's a TIC (☎ 872609) in the Market Place open all year. There are places to stay and eat around the harbour, including *Harbour House Guest House* (☎ 878047), charging from £13 to £16 per person. For fishing trips, call the skipper of the *Girl Katherine* (☎ 874510).

There are frequent buses from Edinburgh and Dundee, but it's best to go by train because it's a scenic trip along the coast from Dundee (20 minutes, £2.80, two trains an hour).

Aberdeenshire & Moray

Known from 1974 to 1996 as the Grampian region, the area is (not surprisingly) bound to the west and south by the Grampians. The largest place is prosperous Aberdeen, a tidy city of impressive granite architecture, still benefiting from the North Sea oil industry.

Aberdeenshire incorporates the valley of the grand River Dee, Royal Deeside – royal because Queen Victoria liked it so much that she bought Balmoral. The royal family still spends part of every summer here, appearing at the Braemar Gathering, the best known of the Highland Games.

Around the coast are the fertile plains, immortalised by Lewis Grassic Gibbon in his trilogy, the *Scots Quair*, which was based on the life of a farming community early in the 20th century. The east coasters, and particularly the Aberdonians, have always had a reputation for being hard-working and thrifty. Certainly anyone living near, or making a living from, the North Sea would have to be tough.

There is a vigorous culture in the northeast, quite separate from the rest of Scotland. Much of it is expressed in lively literary form (in dialect) in anecdote and poetry. The *bothy* ballads and bands which provided home entertainment among the workers on the big farms still get high billing on local radio and TV.

Along the northern coast of Banff and Moray are small fishing ports which have neat little streets looking out to sea, with nothing between them and Scandinavia to the north. This sandy coastline gets a lot of sun and not much rainfall, and the unspoilt, small towns have a brisk, no-nonsense feel.

There are many castles in the characteristic Scottish baronial style in this area. In the north-west, and across the border in the Highlands, the biggest industry is the distilling of whisky – many distilleries offer tours followed by free drams.

GETTING AROUND

For information on buses around Aberdeen phone ☎ 01224-650000. Bluebird Buses (☎ 01224-212266) is the main bus company in the area. Its Day Rover ticket (£8) covers all its services.

The only rail line runs from the south to Aberdeen and continues through Inverurie, Huntly and Elgin to Inverness. For rail information, phone ☎ 0345-484950.

There are some superb walks in the mountains in the south-western part of this region. TICs sell the very useful *Hillwalking in Grampian Highlands*.

ABERDEEN

- *pop 190,000* • *01224*

Aberdeen is an extraordinary symphony in grey. Almost everything is built of grey granite, including the roads, which are paved with crushed granite. In the sunlight, especially after a shower of rain, the stone turns silver and shines like a fairytale, but with low, grey clouds and rain scudding in off the North Sea, it can be a bit depressing.

Aberdeen was a prosperous North Sea trading and fishing port centuries before oil was considered a valuable commodity. After the townspeople supported Robert the Bruce against the English at the Battle of Bannockburn in 1314, the king rewarded the town with land for which he had previously received rent. The money was diverted into the Common Good Fund, to be spent on town amenities, as it still is today. It finances the regimented floral ranks that have won the city numerous awards, and helps keep the place spotless. As a result, the inhabitants have been inculcated with an almost overbearing civic pride.

The name Aberdeen is a combination of two Pictish-Gaelic words, 'aber' and 'devana', meaning the meeting of two waters. The area was known to the Romans, and was raided by the Vikings when it was an increasingly important port, with trade conducted in wool, fish, hides and fur. By the 18th century, paper and rope-making, whaling and textile manufacture were the main industries; in the following century it was a major herring port.

Since the 1970s, Aberdeen has become the main onshore service port for one of the largest oilfields in the world. Unemployment rates, once among the highest in the country, dropped dramatically, but have since fluctuated with the rise and fall of the price of oil.

Aberdeen is certainly worth a visit. It's a very lively city – there are more bars than would seem even remotely viable. Start with almost 200,000 Scots, add multinational oil workers and a large student population – the result: a thriving nightlife.

Orientation

Aberdeen is built on a ridge that runs east-west to the north of the railway and bus stations and the ferry quay. The bus and railway stations are next to each other, off Guild St. Old Aberdeen and the university are to the north of this area. To the east lies a couple of miles of clean, sandy beach; at the southern end is Footdee (pronounced fittee), a fishing community at the mouth of the River Dee.

Information

The TIC (☎ 632727) is in St Nicholas House, Broad St. It's open daily from June to September, 9 am to 5 pm. Between October and May, it's closed on Sunday. As well as the usual bed-booking facility, there's a bureau de change.

A free listings guide, *What's on in Aberdeen*, is available from the TIC. There's also the bi-monthly *Aberdeen Arts & Recreation Listings*.

The Harbour

The harbour has always been a busy place. From dawn until about 8 am, the fish market operates as it has for centuries; it's worth getting up early to see the auctions.

Maritime Museum Situated in Provost Ross's House, the oldest building in the city, the Maritime Museum (☎ 585788) explains Aberdeen's relationship (almost exclusively commercial) with the sea. There are some

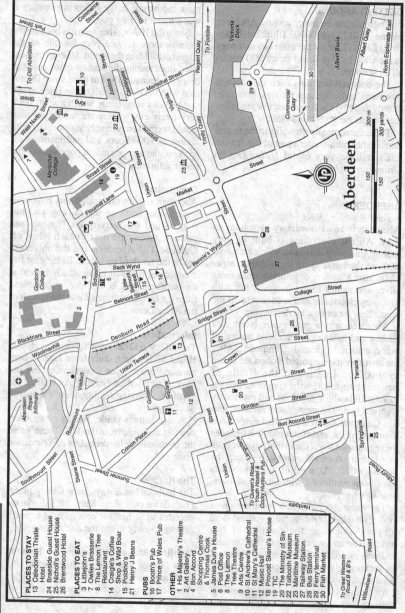

Aberdeen

PLACES TO STAY
13 Caledonian Thistle Hotel
24 Braeside Guest House
25 Nicholl's Guest House
26 Brentwood Hotel

PLACES TO EAT
3 Littlejohn's
7 Owlies Brasserie
8 The Lemon Tree Restaurant
14 Craigie's Coffee Shop & Wild Boar
15 Poldino's
21 Henry J Beans

PUBS
16 Booth's Pub
17 Prince of Wales Pub

OTHER
1 His Majesty's Theatre
2 Art Gallery
4 Bon Accord Shopping Centre
5 James Dun's House & Thomas Cook
6 Post Office
8 The Lemon Tree Theatre
9 Arts Centre
10 St Andrew's Cathedral
11 St Mary's Cathedral
12 Music Hall
18 Provost Skene's House
19 TIC
20 The Ministry of Sin
22 Tolbooth Museum
23 Maritime Museum
27 Railway Station
28 Bus Station
29 Ferry Terminal
30 Fish Market

interesting displays about shipbuilding and the whaling and fishing industries. Speedy Aberdeen clippers were a speciality of these shipyards in the 19th century, and attractive to British tea merchants in China for the transportation of exotic goods (opium, for instance). Closed for renovation until April 1997, opening hours are likely to be as before: Monday to Saturday, 10 am to 5 pm; admission free.

The City

Union St is the main thoroughfare in the city, lined with solid granite buildings, many of them Victorian. The oldest area is **Castlegate**, at the eastern end, where the castle stood. When it was taken from the English for Robert the Bruce, the password used by the townspeople was 'Bon Accord'. A street and shopping centre commemorate the password.

Provost Skene's House About 50 yards behind the TIC, surrounded by concrete and glass office blocks in what was once the worst slum in Aberdeen, is a late medieval, turreted town house occupied in the 17th century by the Provost (the Scots equivalent of a mayor) Lord Skene. It was commandeered by the Duke of Cumberland and his English redcoat soldiers, and later it became a dosshouse. It would have been demolished in the 1940s had it not been for the intervention of the present-day Queen Mother, who took an interest in it.

Typical of its kind, it has intimate, panelled rooms. The 1622 tempera-painted ceiling, with its Catholic symbolism, is unusual for having survived the depredations of the Reformation. It's a gem of its time, featuring earnest-looking angels, St Peter with cockerels crowing, and Cromwellian-looking soldiers. At the top of the house is an archaeology display and a gallery of local domestic artefacts.

Provost Skene's House (☎ 641086) is open Monday to Saturday, 10 am to 5 pm; there's no admission charge.

Marischal College Across the road from the TIC, this huge building houses the science section of the University of Aberdeen. It was founded in 1593 by the 5th Earl Marischal. The present building is late Victorian Gothic, made peculiar by the use of granite. It's the kind of building you either love or hate, but cannot avoid being impressed by.

The **museum** (☎ 273131) is straight ahead through the main quadrangle and up the stairs. In one room, there's a lively depiction of north-east Scotland through its famous people, customs, architecture, trade and myths. The displays are organised thematically, so visitors can get a good picture of the complex and rich local culture without having to make much of an effort.

The other gallery is set up as an anthropological overview of the world, incorporating objects from vastly different cultures. It's also arranged thematically (Polynesian wooden masks alongside gasmasks etc). There are the usual bizarre Victorian curios, an Indian kayak found in the local river estuary and some Eskimo objects collected by whalers.

The museum is well worth visiting. Open Monday to Friday, 10 am to 5 pm, and on Sunday afternoon; entry is free.

Tolbooth Museum Opened in 1995, this is a museum of social history, housed in the Tolbooth built in the early 17th century to accommodate prisoners awaiting trial.

There are displays in the cells, narrow winding staircases and tales of escape recounted by an animated model of prisoner William Baird.

The museum (☎ 621167), Castle St, is open from April to September daily except Monday and Sunday morning; entry is free.

Aberdeen Art Gallery Behind the grand facade of the art gallery is a cool, white space exhibiting the work of young contemporary painters, mostly of the Glasgow School, such as Gwen Hardie and Stephen Conroy. There is also a Francis Bacon and a brave selection of modern textiles, ceramics and jewellery. There's evidently a vigorous school of applied arts in Aberdeen. There are also several Joan Eardley landscapes; she lived in a cottage on the cliffs near Stonehaven in the 1950s and 60s, and painted tempestuous oils of the North Sea and poignant portraits of slum children.

Among the Pre-Raphaelites upstairs is a collection of 92 small portraits of artists, many of them self-portraits of now forgotten painters. The collection was begun around 1880 by George Macdonald, on the instigation of Millais.

Downstairs, a large, empty, white, circular room, with fish-scaled balustrades evoking the briny origins of Aberdeen's wealth, commemorates the 165 people who lost their lives in the Piper Alpha oil rig disaster in 1988.

The gallery (☎ 646333), Schoolhill, is open Monday to Saturday, 10 am to 5 pm, and on Sunday from 2 to 5 pm. Across the road, James Dun's House is a small, modern art gallery.

Old Aberdeen

One and a half miles north of the city centre is the separate suburb of Old Aberdeen. The name is somewhat misleading, since the area around the harbour is actually older; it's called Alton in Gaelic, meaning village by the pool, and this was anglicised to Old Town. The university buildings and St Machar's Cathedral are at the centre of this peaceful area.

It was here that Bishop Elphinstone established King's College, Aberdeen's first university, in 1495. Earl Marischal founded the college in the city centre in 1593 but it was not until the 19th century that the two colleges were united as the University of Aberdeen. **King's College Chapel** (closed at weekends) is easily recognisable by its crowned spire. The interior of the chapel is largely unchanged from the late 15th century and the stained-glass windows are impressive. **King's College Visitors Centre** houses a multimedia display on the university's history. It's open Monday to Saturday, 10 am to 5 pm, and on Sunday afternoon, year-round; there's no admission charge.

St Machar's Cathedral dates from the 14th century and, with its massive twin towers, is one of the few examples in the country of a fortified cathedral. According to legend, St Machar was ordered to establish a church where the river takes the shape of a bishop's crook, which it does just here. The cathedral is best known for its impressive heraldic ceiling, dating from 1520, which has 48 shields of kings, nobles, archbishops and bishops. It's open daily from 9 am to 5 pm; services on Sunday are at 11 am and 6 pm.

Places to Stay

Hostels *Aberdeen Youth Hostel* (☎ 646988), 8 Queen's Rd, is 1½ miles from the railway station. It's open all year except January; the nightly charge is £7.80/6.40 in small dormitories. Walk east along Union St and take the right fork along Albyn Place until you reach a roundabout; Queen's Rd continues on the eastern side.

During the university holidays, some colleges let rooms to visitors. The list of colleges offering accommodation changes from year to year – check with the TIC. *Robert Gordon University* (☎ 262140), Kepplestone Annexe, Queen's Rd, has a few single rooms for £10 per person and some self-catering flats. *Hunter & Mackie Halls* (☎ 480291), Craibstone Estate, Bucksburn, also has some budget accommodation.

Camping The nearest camping ground is *Hazelhead Caravan Park & Campsite* (☎ 321268), four miles west of the centre, with pitches for £3.55 in a woodland setting. Phone for directions.

B&Bs & Hotels There are clusters of B&Bs on Bon Accord St and Springbank Terrace (both close to the centre), and Great Western Rd (the A93, a 25-minute walk). They are more expensive than is usually the case in Scotland and, with all the oil industry workers here, single rooms are at a premium. Prices tend to be lower at the weekend.

The more expensive guesthouses are at the city end of Bon Accord St. At No 68, *Braeside Guest House* (☎ 581652) charges £20/30 for singles/doubles, but it's nothing special. *Crynoch Guest House* (☎ 582743),

164 Bon Accord St, has singles/doubles for £18/30. The two guesthouses next door are both similarly priced: *Denmore Guest House* (☎ 587751) at No 166, and *Dunrovin Guest House* (☎ 586081) at No 168.

In the same area, at 63 Springbank Terrace, *Nicoll's Guest House* (☎ 572867) is a recommended, friendly place with rooms at around £20/30 (£28/37 for rooms with bath attached). There are plenty of other alternatives on these two streets.

There are numerous places to stay along Great Western Rd. At No 189, *Penny Meadow Private Hotel* (☎ 588037) is a small, friendly place. Rooms with attached bath are from £35/44. *Abalone Guest House* (☎ 588739), at No 224, charges around £20/30.

Corner House Hotel (☎ 313063), at No 385, is a solid, turreted building with off-street parking, and evening meals if required. It charges from £35/46 for a single/double; all rooms have bathroom attached.

For non-smokers only, *Strathisla Guest House* (☎ 321026), at 408 Great Western Rd, is a comfortable place; all rooms have bath attached. Charges are around £25/40. *Aurora Guest House* (☎ 311602), 429 Great Western Rd, is another small, family-run B&B. There are five rooms, ranging from £19/30 to £20/34, all with shared bathroom.

Back in the centre of Aberdeen, *Brentwood Hotel* (☎ 595440), 101 Crown St, is very conveniently located and comfortable, but is often full during the week. Rooms cost from £65/75 for singles/doubles; about 50% less at weekends. The hotel has a bar and restaurant.

The *Atholl Hotel* (☎ 323505), Kings Gate, has an excellent reputation. It's an elegant, granite building on the western edge of the town. The luxurious rooms range from £44/52 at weekends to £74/84 during the week.

The top place to stay in the centre of town is the *Caledonian Thistle Hotel* (☎ 640233), Union Terrace. It has 80 rooms from £40/72 at weekends to £99/116 during the week.

Places to Eat

Aberdeen has an excellent range of places to eat, from branches of the big-name fast-food chains to expensive gourmet restaurants.

Check your e-mail over a cup of coffee at *Netropolis* (☎ 595223), 18 Bridge St. It's a 60s-vision-of-the-future style Internet café open daily from 8 am to midnight. You can surf on coin-operated PCs and there's a range of light meals.

For cheap Mexican food, burgers, dogs and cocktails, *Henry J Beans* is on Windmill Brae, below Bridge St.

The *Ashvale Fish Restaurant* (☎ 596981), 46 Great Western Rd, is a fish & chip shop that's well known outside the city, having won several awards. You should have your fish & chips (from £2.65 to take away) served with mushy peas – they don't taste as bad as they sound.

The café at the *Lemon Tree* (☎ 642230), the theatre at 5 West North St, does excellent coffee, meals and cakes. It's open daily from 10 am to 5 pm.

There are a number of good places to eat along Belmont St. *Craigies Coffee Shop* (☎ 621381) does snacks and baked potatoes at No 13. At No 19, the *Wild Boar* (☎ 625357) is a popular, stylish bistro. Boozy beef pie is £5.95, lamb steaks are £6.95, there are several vegetarian choices.

Poldino's (☎ 647777), 7 Little Belmont St, is an upmarket Italian restaurant. Pizza and pasta cost £6 to £7, and other main dishes cost up to £14. It's open from Monday to Saturday for lunch and dinner.

Despite its wimpy name, *Owlies Brasserie* (☎ 649267), in Littlejohn St, is highly recommended, good value and, consequently, very popular. It produces tasty food with unusual flavours – try the couscous Marocain (£5.90). It also has a good range of vegetarian food.

There's a branch of the reliable chain *Littlejohn's* (☎ 635666) on School Hill, with all the usual diversions, including the toy train. There are burgers from £4, other main dishes (eg char-grilled chicken) from around £8.

For a splurge, there are a number of choices. The *Silver Darling Restaurant* (☎ 576229) is at the southern end of the

Beach Esplanade on Pocra Quay, North Pier, Footdee. It's renowned for its seafood and superb location overlooking the entrance to the port. *Faradays Restaurant* (☎ 869666), 2 Kirk Brae, Cults, is four miles from the centre; it's another excellent place to eat. The cuisine is a combination of traditional Scottish and French, with lots of fresh, local ingredients. It's closed on Sunday.

Entertainment

You can book tickets for most plays and concerts on the Aberdeen Box Office line ☎ 641122.

The city's main theatre is *His Majesty's* (☎ 637788), Rosemount Viaduct, which hosts everything from ballet and opera to musicals and pantomimes. The *Music Hall*, Union St, is the main venue for pop and classical musical events. The *Arts Centre* (☎ 635208), King St, stages exhibitions at its gallery and drama in its theatre.

The *Lemon Tree* (☎ 642230), 5 West North St, usually has an interesting programme of dance, music or drama. It has an excellent restaurant and often has jazz and folk bands playing.

Aberdeen is a great city for a pub crawl – it's more of a question of knowing where to stop than where to start. Note that many pubs don't serve food in the evening. The *Prince of Wales* (☎ 640597), 7 St Nicholas Lane, is possibly the best known Aberdeen pub. Down an alley off Union St, it boasts the longest counter in the city, a great range of real ales and good-value pub grub at lunch. It can also get very crowded. Nearby, on Back Wynd, *Booth's* is a better place for a pub lunch. It has a good range of traditional pies.

Cocky Hunters (☎ 626720), 504 Union St, is a great place that often has live bands and ceilidh on Sunday. *Drummond's*, Belmont St, serves meals during the day, but is a wine bar/pub in the evening. Both these places are popular with students.

There are numerous nightclubs but they tend to cater to bored oilies with too much money. The *Ministry of Sin* (☎ 211661), Dee St, however, is a good place. It attracts the 20 to 35-year-olds and is based in a deconsecrated church. You won't get into any night club wearing trainers, and some will turn you away if you're wearing jeans.

Getting There & Away

See the fares tables in the Getting Around chapter. Aberdeen is 546 miles from London, 126 from Edinburgh and 106 from Inverness.

Air Aberdeen airport is seven miles northwest of the city centre. The presence of the oil industry ensures that there are flights to numerous cities in the UK, including Shetland and Stornoway (Hebrides), and international flights to the Netherlands and Scandinavia.

For airport information, phone ☎ 722331. Bus No 27 runs from the city centre to the airport, taking about 30 minutes.

Bus Scottish Citylink (☎ 0990-505050) has daily buses from London, but it's a tedious 12-hour trip (£41). There are direct services to Perth (2½ hours, £8.40), Dundee (1¾ hours, £6.10), Glasgow/Edinburgh (3¾ hours, £12.50) and Stirling (three hours, £12.10), plus other Scottish destinations.

Bluebird Buses (☎ 212266) is the major local bus operator.

Train For rail information, phone ☎ 0345-484950. There are numerous trains from London's King's Cross, taking an acceptable seven hours, although they're considerably more expensive than buses. Other destinations served from Aberdeen by rail include Edinburgh (2¾ hours), Glasgow (2¾ hours), Perth (1½ hours), Stirling (2¼ hours), Dundee (1¼ hours) and Inverness (2¼ hours).

Car Try Arnold Clark (☎ 248842), Girdleness Rd, or Morrison Brothers (☎ 826300), Broadfield Rd, Bridge of Don.

Boat The passenger terminal is a short walk east of the railway and bus stations. P&O (☎ 572615) has daily evening departures from Monday to Friday leaving for Lerwick (Shetland). The trip takes approximately 14 hours. A reclining seat costs £46/52 in the low/high season, one way.

In summer, there are departures on Tuesday and Saturday to Stromness (Orkney); 10 hours, £35/38.

Getting Around

Bus The *Aberdeen Map & Guide* is available from the TIC and gives full details of the bus services in Aberdeen. For local bus information phone ☎ 650000. The most useful services are Nos 18/19 and 24 from Union St to Great Western Rd, No 27 from the bus station to the youth hostel and No 20 for Old Aberdeen. If you're using the buses frequently, get a prepaid farecard (like a phonecard).

Taxi For a taxi, phone Mair's (☎ 724040). A trip to the airport costs around £10.

Bicycle Bikes can be rented from Alpine Bikes (☎ 211455), 70 Holburn St. It's open every day and charges £8 per day during the week and £24 for the weekend for a mountain bike.

DEESIDE

The region between Braemar and Huntly and east to the coast is castle country, and includes the Queen's residence at Balmoral. There are more fanciful examples of Scottish baronial architecture here than anywhere else in Scotland. The TICs have information on a Castle Trail, but you really need private transport to follow it.

The River Dee flows through the southern part of this area. Its source is in the mountainous area of the south-west, where the Grampian and Cairngorm ranges meet. This is the best walking country in the region.

Ballater

- *pop 1000*   • ☎ *01339*

This village supplies nearby Balmoral Castle with provisions, hence the shops sporting 'By Royal Appointment' crests. The place has been famous for its spring water since the 19th century. There are no great sights, but there are pleasant walks in the surrounding hills. The walk up Craigendarroch (1300 feet) takes just over an hour and is an easy ramble. Morven (2862 feet) is a more serious prospect, taking around six hours, but has good views from the top.

The TIC (☎ 755306), Station Square, is open from Easter to October. B&Bs include *Mrs Wright's* (☎ 755682), Prony, Glengairn, from £12.50 per person. The *Alexandra Hotel* (☎ 755376), 12 Bridge Sq, is a friendly hotel offering B&B for around £30 per person in comfortable rooms.

There are buses almost every hour from Aberdeen (1¾ hours, £4.60); every two hours on Sunday. The service continues to Braemar.

Balmoral Castle

Seven miles west of Ballater, Balmoral was built for Queen Victoria in 1855 as a private residence for the royal family. The grounds and an exhibition of paintings and other royal trinkets in the ballroom are open; the rest of the castle is closed to the prying eyes of the public. On the edge of the estate is Crathie Church, which the royals use when they're here.

Balmoral Castle (☎ 01339-742334) is open May to July, Monday to Saturday, 10 am to 5 pm, and attracts large numbers of visitors. Entry is £2.50 for adults (children free); it's by the A93 and can be reached on the Aberdeen-Braemar bus (see the next section).

Braemar

- *pop 400*   • ☎ *01339*

Braemar is an attractive, small town surrounded by mountains; it makes an excellent walking base. Above the town is Braemar Castle (☎ 741219), dating from 1628, which was a garrison post after the Jacobite Rebellion. It's open May to October from 10 am to 6 pm daily except Friday; entry is £2/1.

On the first Saturday in September, the town is invaded by 20,000 people, including the royal family, for the Braemar Gathering (Highland Games); bookings are essential.

There's a very helpful regional TIC (☎ 741600), The Mews, Mar Rd, open all year. It has lots of useful information on walks in the area.

Walks An easy walk from Braemar is up Creag Choinnich (1764 feet), a hill to the east of the town, above the A93. There are route markers and the walk takes about 1½ hours. For a longer walk (three hours) and superb views of the Cairngorms, climb Morrone (2819 feet), the mountain to the south of Braemar.

Places to Stay & Eat Budget accommodation includes the *Braemar Youth Hostel* (☎ 741659). It's open all year except November and December, and charges £6.95/5.85. The *Braemar Bunkhouse* (☎ 741242), 15 Mar Rd, has dorm accommodation from £7.

There are several B&Bs along Chapel Brae – *Birchwood* (☎ 741599) charges around £17 per person, while *Mayfield* (☎ 741238) charges a little less. *Callater Lodge Hotel* (☎ 741275), 9 Glenshee Rd, is a small hotel set in its own grounds; most rooms have bathroom attached and cost around £26 per person – evening meals are available. The top place to stay is the *Braemar Lodge* (☎ 741627), Glenshee Rd, which is a restored Victorian shooting lodge on the outskirts of the town. B&B costs around £34 per person.

The pubs are the best places for food and entertainment: *Fife Arms Hotel* has a daily carvery, and *Invercauld Arms Hotel* is a reasonable place for a pint.

Getting There & Away It's a beautiful drive between Perth and Braemar but public transport is limited. Check whether the summer bus service known as the Bluebird Heather Hopper (☎ 01738-629339) has been reinstated on this route. From Aberdeen to Braemar (2¼ hours, £4.75) there are several buses a day operated by Bluebird Buses (☎ 01224-212266), which travel along the beautiful valley of the River Dee.

Inverey
Five miles west of Braemar is the little settlement of Inverey. Numerous mountain walks start from here, including the adventurous Lairig Ghru walk – 21 miles over the pass to Aviemore. The Cairngorm peaks of Cairn Gorm and Ben Macdui (see the Aviemore section in the Highlands & Northern Islands chapter) are actually just this side of the regional border.

Inverey Youth Hostel (no telephone) is open from early June to early September. Beds are £4.10/3.40; there's an occasional postbus from Braemar, but you'll probably have to walk here.

Glenshee
Glenshee is Scotland's largest skiing area, on the border of Perthshire and Aberdeenshire. The A93 ploughs through the middle of the resort. Blairgowrie is the main accommodation centre for Glenshee, although there's a small settlement five miles south of the ski runs at Spittal of Glenshee. There's a TIC (☎ 01250-872960) at Blairgowrie, 26 Wellmeadow, which is open all year.

Places to Stay & Eat Apart from the accommodation centres of Braemar and Blairgowrie, places to stay are strung out along the A93 around Glenshee. At the Blairgowrie end, you could try the *Blackwater Inn* (☎ 01250-882234), Blackwater, where B&B costs around £16 per person. *Mrs Hardy's* (☎ 01250-882260), Blair View, Glenshee, is a non-smoking B&B charging from £13.50 per person.

The *Spittal of Glenshee Hotel* (☎ 01250-885215) is a large place offering B&B in rooms with attached bath from £20 to £24 per person. The *Dalmunzie House Hotel* (☎ 01250-885224), Glenshee, boasts the highest nine-hole golf course in Britain, and is set in a 6000-acre estate, 1½ miles off the main road. B&B costs from £54/83.

Getting There & Away Strathtay Buses (☎ 01382-228054) operates a service from Perth to Blairgowrie (50 minutes, £2.10), hourly from Monday to Saturday, and three times a day on Sunday. The only service from Blairgowrie to the Glenshee area is the postbus to Spittal of Glenshee.

INLAND ABERDEENSHIRE & MORAY

The direct, inland rail and road route from Aberdeen to Inverness cuts across rolling agricultural country that, thanks to a mild climate, produces everything from grain to flower bulbs. The grain is turned into that magical liquid known as malt whisky. You may be tempted by the **Malt Whisky Trail**, a 70-mile signposted tour which gives you an inside look and complimentary tastings at a number of famous distilleries (including Cardhu, Glenfiddich and The Glenlivet). TICs produce a leaflet covering the tour. See also the Food & Drink section in the Scotland Facts for the Visitor chapter.

This is also castle country, and there's a *Castle Trail* leaflet to guide you round. **Castle Fraser** (☎ 01330-833463), three miles south of Kemnay, looks rather like a French château, and dates from the 16th century. **Haddo House** (☎ 01651-851440), 19 miles north of Aberdeen, was designed by William Adam in 1731. It's best described as a classic English stately home transplanted in Scotland. **Fyvie Castle** (☎ 01651-891266), eight miles south of Turriff, is probably the grandest example of Scottish baronial architecture. There are numerous other castles, in various states of preservation.

Huntly

This small town, with an impressive ruined castle, is located in a strategically important position on a low-lying plain, along the main route from Aberdeen into the Strathspey and Moray regions.

On the northern edge of town, **Huntly Castle** (☎ 01466-793191), the former stronghold of the Gordons, is on the banks of the River Deveron. Over the main door is a superb carving that includes the royal arms and the figures of Christ and St Michael. It's open daily in summer (afternoon only on Sunday); entry is £2/75p.

The TIC (☎ 01466-792255), The Square,

is open daily from April to October. The Aberdeen to Inverness Bluebird bus (No 10) passes through Huntly, and the town is on the rail line that follows the same route.

Dufftown

Founded only in 1817 by James Duff, 4th Earl of Fife, Dufftown is 12 miles west of Huntly. It's a good place to start the Malt Whisky Trail.

To the north of the town is the **Glenfiddich Distillery Visitors Centre** (☎ 01340-820373), beside the ruins of Balvenie Castle. Visitors are guided through the process of distilling, and can also see whisky being bottled here – the only Highland distillery where this is done on the premises. It's open Easter to mid-October, Monday to Saturday from 9.30 am to 4.30 pm, and on Sunday from noon to 4.30 pm; there's no entry charge – your free dram really is free.

The TIC (☎ 01340-820501) is in the clocktower in the square. Buses link Dufftown to Elgin, among other places.

COAST

The Grampians meet the sea at Stonehaven, which is home to spectacular Dunnottar Castle. Continuing around the coast from Aberdeen, there are long stretches of sand and, on the north coast, some magical fishing villages – like Pennan, where the film *Local Hero* was shot.

Stonehaven

The only reason for stopping at this seaside resort town is to visit Dunnottar Castle, two miles to the south. If you want to stay, the TIC (☎ 01569-762806), 66 Allardice St, has a list of B&Bs. Stonehaven is on the main bus and rail routes between Dundee and Aberdeen.

The most pleasant way to reach **Dunnottar Castle** is on foot; the TIC has a walking leaflet. The castle ruins are spread out across a flat rock rising 150 feet above the sea – as dramatic a film set as any director could wish for. It was last used for Zeffirelli's *Hamlet*, starring Mel Gibson. The original fortress was built in the 9th century; the keep and gatehouse are the most substantial remains. The castle must have supported quite a large community, judging from the extent of the ruins.

The castle is open April to October, Monday to Saturday from 9 am to 6 pm, and on Sunday from 2 to 5 pm; November to March, Monday to Friday, 9 am to sundown and on Sunday from 2 pm to sundown (closed on Saturday). Entry is £1.50/90p and last admission is half an hour before closing.

Aberdeen to Fraserburgh
There are attractive beaches at Cruden Bay and Newburgh along this section of the coast, but little to hold the visitor. The remains of a once-great fishing industry is now based in Peterhead. Only a few years ago, the high-tech trawlers operating from here were so productive that they supported a local Ferrari-driving fishing community with a high disposable income.

At Fraserburgh, **Scotland's Lighthouse Museum** (☎ 01346-511022) is a new attraction with guided tours to the top of Kinnaird Head lighthouse. It's open year-round but closed on Sunday morning.

Banff & Macduff
A popular seaside resort, the twin towns of Banff and Macduff are separated by a long bridge. Banff is an attractive little town. Nearby Macduff is still a busy fishing port.

Duff House is by the golf course in Banff. It's an impressive Georgian Baroque mansion designed by William Adam, and completed in 1749. It's been a hotel, hospital and POW camp, and after recent refurbishment opened as an art gallery housing a collection of paintings from the National Gallery of Scotland. It's closed on Tuesday in summer, closed Monday to Wednesday in winter.

The TIC (☎ 01261-812419) is beside St Mary's car park in Banff. It's open daily in summer, and has a free Walkman tour to encourage you to look round the town.

Elgin
• *pop 18,800* • ☎ *01343*
At the heart of Moray, Elgin has been the provincial capital for the past eight centuries.

In medieval times, Elgin was of much greater importance than it is now. The great **cathedral**, known as the 'lantern of the north', was consecrated in 1224. In 1390, it was burnt down by the infamous Wolf of Badenach, the illegitimate son of Robert II, following a dispute with the bishop who had excommunicated him. It was rebuilt, but ruined once more in the Reformation. Open from April to September, Monday to Saturday from 9.30 am to 6 pm, and on Sunday from 2 to 6 pm; for the rest of the year, on Monday, Tuesday, Wednesday and Saturday from 9.30 am to 4 pm, and on Thursday from 9.30 am to noon. Entry is 1.20/75p.

The TIC (☎ 543388), 17 High St, is open from Easter to October.

Places to Stay & Eat A few minutes walk from the centre of the town, *Mrs McMillan's* (☎ 541515), 14 South College St, has singles/doubles from £18/32, with attached bath. *Southbank Guest House* (☎ 547132), 36 Academy St, has 11 rooms and charges from £14 to £17 per person. On the edge of the town, *Rosemount* (☎ 542907), 5 Mayne Rd, offers comfortable B&B in rooms with attached bath. It's a spacious house but there are only two rooms for guests; B&B is around £24 per person; evening meals are available.

Getting There & Away Bluebird Buses (☎ 01224-212266) runs buses along the coast to Banff and Macduff, south to Dufftown, west to Inverness, and also to Aberdeen. There are also frequent trains from Aberdeen to Inverness via Elgin.

Findhorn
Old and new hippies should check out the Findhorn Foundation (☎ 01309-673655), Forres IV36 0RD. The Foundation is an international spiritual community, founded in 1962. There are about 150 members and many more sympathetic souls who have

moved into the vicinity. With no formal creed, the community is dedicated to creating 'a deeper sense of the sacred in everyday life, and to dealing with work, relationships and our environment in new and more fulfilling ways'. In many ways it's very impressive, although it can become a bit outlandish. A recent course was entitled 'Devas, Fairies and Angels – A Practical Approach'.

There are daily tours at 2 pm in summer. The community is not particularly attractive itself – it started life in the Findhorn Bay Caravan Park and still occupies one end of the site. Far more attractive are the nearby fishing village of Findhorn (one mile) and the town of Forres (2½ miles). It's possible to stay in the *caravan park* (☎ 01309-690203), which has camping from £2. There are also week-long residential programmes from £235 to £335, including food and accommodation.

Findhorn is four miles north of Forres, which is on the main bus and rail route between Inverness and Elgin.

Highlands & Northern Islands

HIGHLIGHTS

- Callanish Standing Stones (Lewis)
- Plockton
- Cromarty's gabled cottages
- The Glen Shiel Valley
- Taking the train from Fort William to Mallaig
- Ullapool
- The boat ride to Cape Wrath
- Glen Coe
- Eilean Donan Castle (outside only)
- Walking around the Quiraing and the old Man of Storr on Skye
- The prehistoric sites of Orkney
- Wreck diving in Scapa Flow, Orkney
- Coast walks in Orkney – Hoy and Yesnaby
- Birdwatching in Shetland
- Sitting amongst the puffins in north Unst, the northernmost point in the UK

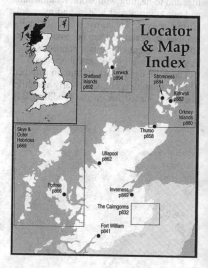

Locator & Map Index

Shetland Islands p892
Lerwick p894
Stromness p884
Kirkwall p882
Orkney Islands p880
Thurso p858
Skye & Outer Hebrides p669
Ullapool p862
Portree p866
Inverness p849
The Cairngorms p832
Fort William p841

Forget the castles, forget the towns and villages. The Highland and northern islands are all about mountains, sea, heather, moors, lakes – and wide, empty, exhilarating space. This is one of Europe's last great wildernesses, and it's more beautiful than you can imagine.

The Highlands is an imprecise term for the upland area which covers the northern half of mainland Scotland. This chapter covers the administrative region known as Highland, the Isle of Skye and the islands of the northern Inner Hebrides, the Outer Hebrides (Western Isles), Orkney and Shetland.

The east coast is dramatic, but it's the north and west, where the mountains and sea collide, that exhaust superlatives. South of mysterious Loch Ness are the Cairngorm Mountains and Ben Nevis (Britain's highest peak). The Orkney and Shetland islands are bleak and beautiful, and the Outer Hebrides are the last stronghold of Gaelic culture and the old crofting ways.

ORIENTATION & INFORMATION

The Great Glen, a series of deep, narrow lochs (including Loch Ness) which cuts across the country south-west to north-east, from Fort William to Inverness, neatly divides the southern Highlands from the north. In the south, Aviemore is the centre for the Cairngorms, and Ben Nevis dominates Fort William.

Most population centres in the rugged, wild Highlands are dotted around the coast, but several island groups are also reached from the Highlands. The Orkney Islands are just off the north-east corner, while even further north are the remote Shetland Islands. To the west are the Outer Hebrides, while closer in, between the Hebrides and the mainland coast, the beautiful Isle of Skye is just a stone's throw from the coast – and now connected to the mainland by a controversial bridge. For the Isle of Mull and other islands to the south, see the Central Scotland chapter.

There are TICs in all the major centres in the Highlands and islands but many smaller offices close during the low season; even those that open all year round usually have shorter winter opening hours.

Almost all the TICs charge £1 to £2 for accommodation bookings. The Highlands of Scotland Tourist Board (☎ 0990-143070) publishes free accommodation guides for the mainland area and Skye. The Western Isles Tourist Board (☎ 01851-703088) does the same for the Western Isles. There are also separate tourist boards for Orkney (☎ 01856-872856) and Shetland (☎ 01595-693434).

WALKS
The Highlands offer some of Scotland's finest walking country, whether it's round Loch Ness, along the coast, or to inland hills and peaks like Ben More Assynt, Ben Hope (Britain's most northerly 'Munro' – see below), Suilven (the Sugar Loaf) or Ben Klibreck, with its fabulous views of Ben Loyal (the Queen of Scottish Mountains).

The mountains can be treacherous and every year some walkers come unstuck. Mountaincall is a Highlands weather-report service – phone ☎ 01891-500441 for west Scotland or ☎ 01891-500442 for east Scotland. A handy leaflet, *Enjoy the Scottish Hills in Safety*, offers basic safety advice.

OTHER ACTIVITIES
Fishing is a popular Highlands activity but it's strictly regulated and some of the famous salmon fishing beats can be very expensive. Fishing for brown trout in the trout lochs is more affordable. Local tourist offices can advise on permits and equipment and suggest the best locations.

Thurso has some of Europe's best surf. Pony trekking, cycling and golf are other Highland activities.

GETTING AROUND
Aviemore, Inverness and Fort William are easily accessible by bus and train. Buses and trains also provide regular connections from Inverness up the east coast to Wick and Thurso, and from Inverness across the Highlands to Kyle of Lochalsh and Ullapool. However, making your way around the north and west coasts from Thurso to Ullapool and on to Kyle of Lochalsh by public transport can be difficult; consider hiring a car in Inverness or Fort William.

Bus
Wick, Thurso, Ullapool and Kyle of Lochalsh can all be reached by bus from Inverness, or from Edinburgh and Glasgow via Inverness or Fort William. See the Inverness and North & West Coast sections for more information.

There are several bus services specifically aimed at backpackers. Go Blue Banana (☎ 0131-228 2281) operates a hostel-to-hostel loop around Scotland with stops at Inverness, Kyleakin on the Isle of Skye and Fort William. Haggis Backpackers (☎ 0131-557 9393) has a similar service. See the introductory Scotland Getting Around section for details of both services. The Orkney Bus (☎ 01955-611353) operates an east-coast link from Inverness to Orkney via John O'Groats; for more details, see the Inverness section.

Train
The two Highland railway lines from Inverness – up the east coast to Wick and Thurso, and west to Kyle of Lochalsh – are justly famous.

The West Highland line also follows a spectacular route from Glasgow to Fort William and Mallaig (for Skye and the Inner Hebrides). The North Highland Rover ticket offers unlimited travel on the lines from Inverness to Wick and Thurso, Kyle of Lochalsh, Aberdeen and Aviemore for four days in eight for £35. The similar West Highland Rover ticket covers Glasgow, Fort William, Mallaig and Oban.

For rail information phone ☎ 0345-484950.

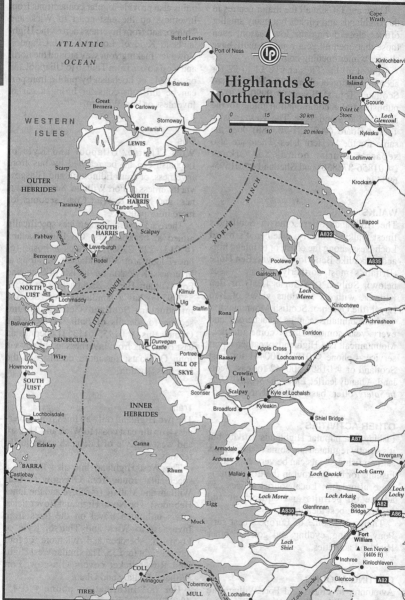

Highlands & Northern Islands

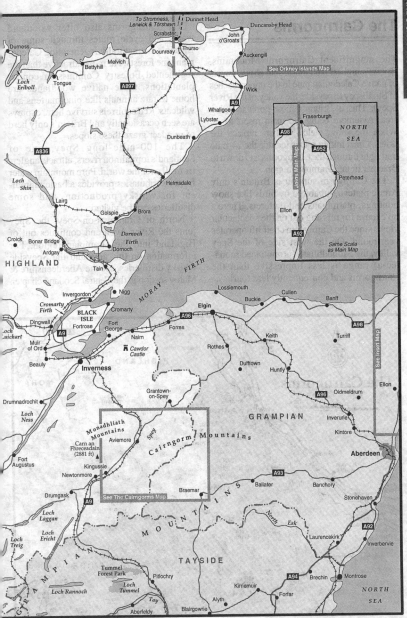

The Cairngorms

The magnificent Cairngorm Mountains, Britain's highest land mass, soar above forests of native Caledonian pine in the upper reaches of Strathspey (Speyside, the valley of the River Spey). This is Britain's most popular skiing area, Aviemore being the main resort town. When the snow melts, walkers replace the skiers. Great hiking routes include the 24-mile trail right through the Cairngorms and down to Braemar in the Grampian region.

The Cairngorm summit is Britain's only Arctic plateau, inhabited by birds like snow buntings, ptarmigans and dotterels. There's no excuse for missing out on the spectacular views since the Cairngorm chair lift operates year-round. On the west side of the Spey valley, the Monadhliath (pronounced mona-lee-a) range is less impressive than the Cairngorms and consequently less touristy.

The Cairngorms also offer woodland walks and cycle routes through some of Britain's last naturally regenerating Caledonian pine forests. Far more attractive than the regimented Forestry Commission conifer plantations, these native woodlands are home to rare animals like pine martens and wildcats. Red squirrels survive here, ospreys are seen occasionally and Britain's only herd of reindeer graze these slopes.

The 100-mile-long Spey, one of Scotland's top salmon rivers, attracts anglers from all over the world. Pure mountain water from its tributaries provides a basic ingredient for whisky production, and some distilleries can be visited.

North of Grantown-on-Spey, the Spey joins the River Avon and continues out of Highland into the Grampian region. For information on this area and the Speyside whisky distilleries, see the Aberdeenshire & Maroy section in the Central Scotland chapter.

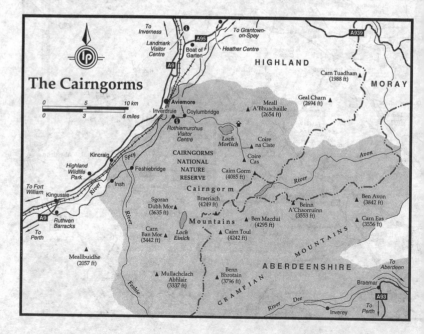

TONY WHEELER

TONY WHEELER

RICHARD EVERIST

Top: Ben Hope and Loch Hope, Highlands
Middle: Eilean Donan Castle, near Kyle of Lochalsh, Highlands
Bottom: Gloomy view of Loch Carron, Highlands

TONY WHEELER

TONY WHEELER

RICHARD EVERIST

RICHARD EVERIST

Left: Thatched cottage in Lyndhurst, New Forest, Hampshire
Top: Warehouse accomodation in London's Docklands
Middle: Tudor houses, Shrewsbury, Shropshire
Bottom: Author's backyard, Brixton, London

Munros & Munro Bagging
In 1891 Sir Hugh T Munro published his list of Scotland's 283 mountains higher than 3000 feet. The list has been argued about ever since – when is a summit the 'top' of a mountain as opposed to being a mountain in its own right. The current list of 'Munros' stands at 277. The practice of Munro Bagging, climbing the 3000-foot-plus peaks, must have started soon after the list was first published because by 1901 Reverend AE Robertson had climbed the lot. These days, Munro Bagging has become a national passion: speculate on a Munro record and it's probably been attempted, from 'first person to climb the lot with a mountain bike' to 'first woman to climb the lot in a single circuit'. The fastest circuit, occurring in 1988 and involving all 277 Munro peaks, took 66 days. Madness it may be, but Munros offer some wonderful walking and some great views; there's no reason why any reasonably fit visitor shouldn't bag a few during a Scottish visit. ■

AVIEMORE
• *pop 1500*   • ☎ *01479*
Less than forty years ago, Aviemore was a Highland village of 200 inhabitants. Today it looks more like a fringe resort in the Rockies that hasn't quite made it but keeps on trying. Swathed in snow it isn't too bad; in summer it's appalling. The new Santa Claus Land children's theme park (☎ 810624) just about says it all.

Orientation & Information
Aviemore is just off the A9 bypass. With almost everything located on tacky Grampian Rd you can hardly get lost. The railway station, bank and places to eat are all right in the centre.

Near the youth hostel, the busy TIC (☎ 810363) is 550 yards south of the centre, also on Grampian Rd. It's open year-round; in July and August, Monday to Saturday until 8 pm, and Sunday until 6 pm. There's a free accommodation guide but a £1 local booking charge is made. There's also a bureau de change and a good range of books and maps. The yellow Ordnance Survey Outdoor Leisure map *Aviemore & the Cairn-*

gorms (£5.40) covers the whole area, while Ernest Cross's *Walks in the Cairngorms* (£3.25) describes the main hikes.

Of the outdoor-equipment shops along Grampian Rd, try Ellis Brigham (☎ 810175) at No 9 which also organises skiing lessons.

The Cairngorm skiing/hiking area is eight miles east of Aviemore at the end of the Ski Rd which runs through two large forest estates: Rothiemurchus and Glenmore.

Rothiemurchus Estate
Extending from the Spey beside Aviemore to the tops of the Cairngorms, and taking in the villages of Inverdruie and Coylumbridge, this estate is owned by the Grants, the whisky family. As well as managing the extensive Caledonian pine forest, they also lay on many facilities for visitors. There's free access to 50 miles of footpaths and some particularly attractive trails through the forests and around Loch an Eilein. There are guided walks with rangers, Land Rover tours of the estate, and fishing for rainbow trout at the fish farm or salmon in the Spey. There's even a clay-pigeon shooting school.

The Rothiemurchus Estate Visitors Centre (☎ 810858), one mile from Aviemore along the Ski Road, is open daily from 9 am to 5.30 pm. A free *Visitor Guide and Footpath Map* is available.

Glenmore Forest Park
Beyond Rothiemurchus, the Ski Rd continues through Glenmore Forest Park, 5000 acres of pine and spruce set around Loch Morlich, seven miles from Aviemore centre. A popular **watersports centre** (☎ 861221) offers canoeing, windsurfing, sailing and fishing. There's a pleasant sandy beach, another youth hostel and a camping ground where you can swim in the loch.

A warden at the **Cairngorm Reindeer Centre** (☎ 861228) will take you to see and feed the reindeer. Walks leave daily at 11 am (and 2.30 pm from May to mid-October); the cost is £3.50/2.

The visitors centre (☎ 861220), near the loch, has a *Glenmore Forest Guide Map* (60p) detailing local walks.

Walks

To get straight to the area with the most spectacular views, take the chair lift (☎ 861261) to the Cairngorm plateau. It starts from the car park at the end of the Ski Rd and rises in two sections to the top (3600 feet), where there's a café – Britain's highest. It costs £4.60/3 return, and operates daily from 9.45 am to 4.45 pm. Plans to replace the lift with a more reliable funicular railway are currently on hold for fear that too many walkers could damage the plateau's delicate ecology.

From the top station, climb to the summit of Cairngorm (4084 feet). You can continue south to climb Ben Macdui (at 4296 feet, the second-highest peak in the country) but this can take six to eight hours, including the chair lift ride up.

The Lairig Ghru walk is a demanding 24-mile route from Aviemore over the Lairig Ghru Pass to Braemar. It can take up to eight hours and it's possible to link up with the Heather Hopper bus to return to Aviemore, although you'll probably have to spend a night in Braemar first. If you're not doing the full route, it's still worth walking up to the pass for the views; the round trip is a six-hour hike.

Hikers should always ensure they're properly prepared with food and drink, a map, a compass and a windproof jacket. The weather can change very quickly and snow even in mid-summer is not unknown. Take care – ill-equipped people have died.

Other Activities

Skiing Aviemore may not be Val d'Isere but with 28 runs it's Britain's biggest ski area, and if the pistes are good and the sun's shining, you can almost kid yourself you're in the Alps. The season runs from January until the snow runs out, which can be the end of April.

The ski area is about nine miles from Aviemore centre and lifts start from the main car park, connected to the car park at Coire na Ciste by shuttle bus. A day pass costs £17/11.30 for adults/under 18s and ski hire is around £12. The TIC stocks a free *Cairn-gorm Piste Map and Ride Guide* leaflet with advice for safe skiing and snowboarding.

During the season the TIC displays relevant avalanche warnings. Call the Ski Hotline (☎ 0891-654655) or tune into Ski FM on 96.6 for reports on snow conditions.

As well as downhill skiing, there are also several cross-country routes.

For more information on skiing see the Activities chapter at the start of this book.

Fishing Fishing is a major sport, both on the Spey and in most of the lochs. Salmon fishing permits, costing £22 to £28 per day depending on the beat, are available from local shops; rods can be hired for around £5 per day. Trout fishing permits cost £5 to £15 per day. The TIC's free booklet, *River & Loch Fishing Information* lists beats and places to buy permits.

Places to Stay

Hostels *Aviemore Youth Hostel* (☎ 810345), 25 Grampian Rd, offers upmarket hostelling in a newly refurbished building near the TIC and the start of the Ski Rd. The nightly charge is £7.80/6.40. It's open from late December to mid-November.

Seven miles from Aviemore, in Glenmore Forest Park, *Loch Morlich Youth Hostel* (☎ 861238) has a great location but you need to book ahead as it's very popular. Open from mid-November through to September, the nightly charge is £6.95/5.85. In the same area, the *Badaguish Centre* (☎ 861285) has dormitory accommodation from £5 to £8 per night.

Camping The nearest camping ground is *Campgrounds of Scotland* (☎ 810120) at Coylumbridge, 1½ miles along the Ski Rd. Charges are £3.50 per person. *Glenmore Camping & Caravan Park* (☎ 861271), five miles further along the road near Loch Morlich, charges £2.50 per person.

B&Bs & Hotels – centre Just off Grampian Rd, 400 yards north of the railway station, there's an enclave of B&Bs on Craig na Gower Ave. Most rooms have private baths and charges are around £16/30 for singles/doubles. Try *Mrs Sheffield's* (☎ 810698) at Dunroamin, and *Mrs Whelan's* (☎ 810031) at No 17. Friendly *Mrs Fraser's* (☎ 01479-811432), at Rafters, is a bit cheaper but lacks private baths. At *Mrs Campbell's* (☎ 810849), Karn, B&B is from £14 per person.

On Dalfaber Rd are two larger guesthouses. *Kinapol Guest House* (☎ 810513) charges from £14.50 a head; *Ardlogie Guest House* (☎ 810747) has rooms with bath for £16 a head.

Pleasant *Balavoulin Hotel* (☎ 810672), in Grampian Rd, has eight well-equipped double rooms with bath for £20 a head.

Right in the centre on Grampian Rd is the large *Cairngorm Hotel* (☎ 810233), otherwise known as the Cairn, which charges £21 a head for B&B or £36 with dinner.

One mile from Aviemore, on the Lynwilg road, is an excellent small country-house hotel, *Lynwilg House* (☎ 811685). B&B is £25 a head but the food is good and half-board costs £40.

B&Bs & Hotels – Ski Rd The first hotel along the Ski Rd is probably the most pleasant place to stay. The *Corrour House Hotel* (☎ 810220), 1½ miles from Aviemore, is open from December to October and rooms cost from £25/40 to £35/50 for singles/doubles with attached bath. There are splendid views of the mountains and Lairig Ghru Pass.

In Inverdruie, *Avondruie Guest House* (☎ 810267) charges from £18.50 a head in rooms with attached bathroom. *Mrs MacLean's* (☎ 810621), Bendruie, is cheaper, but with shared bathroom.

Just beyond Inverdruie, there are several B&Bs on Dell Mhor. *Mrs Mackenzie* (☎ 810235) can be found at No 1, and *Mrs Bruce* (☎ 01479- 810230) is at No 2; both offer B&B for £12.50 per person. *Mrs Harris* (☎ 810405), at No 5, charges £13.50 but has one double with private bath.

In Coylumbridge, the *Stakis Coylumbridge* (☎ 810661) is probably the best large resort hotel, and certainly the best located

The Highland bagpipe is the kind most commonly played in Scotland.

and closest to the ski slopes. Rates are from £40/44 a single/double.

Places to Eat

There's no shortage of places to eat, but few are particularly inviting. If you prefer to do things yourself there are three supermarkets right in the centre of Aviemore. For smoked trout, venison, pate and other delicacies visit the *Rothiemurchus Fish Farm* shop (☎ 810703), a short way along the Ski Rd.

Most places are along Grampian Rd. By the TIC, at No 43, the *Asha Indian Restaurant* (☎ 811118) also does takeaways. Closer to the station *Smiffy's Fish & Chip Restaurant* does a reasonable fry-up; prices are the same to eat in or take away. Nearby is *Sheffield's Café Bar* (☎ 811670), open daily from 9 am until 10 pm (late for these parts).

Further north along Grampian Rd, opposite the police station, a branch of *Littlejohn's* (☎ 811633) serves steaks, pizzas, burgers, ribs, potato skins, vegetable fajitas etc in slightly wacky surroundings. Main dishes are £6 to £8. Across the road at No 9, the *Ski-ing Doo* (☎ 810392) has a better range of steaks, including 16-oz T-bones (£11.99) and 10-oz sirloins (£10.99).

The *Winking Owl* (☎ 810646), on Grampian Rd, has a reasonable choice of pub food and great mountain views. You can sit outside if it's fine. Highly recommended is the *Old Bridge Inn* (☎ 811137), not far from the youth hostel, on Dalfaber Rd. Poached salmon with dill (£5.25) is a treat.

Along the Ski Rd, there's the pricey *Gallery Bistro & Coffee Shop* (☎ 810163) at Inverdruie, and a *café* in Glenmore Forest Park. The *Day Lodge* at the end of the Ski Rd has a restaurant and bar (open until 11 pm in July and August).

Entertainment

Every Tuesday at 7 pm in summer the *Old Bridge Inn* (☎ 811137) hosts a Highland Evening. For £16 a head you get a four-course Scottish meal (including soup, haggis, salmon and the delicious Scottish pudding, cranachan), a piper, Highland dancers and live music. Advance booking is advisable.

The *Aviemore Mountain Resort* (☎ 810624) is a large leisure complex, signposted from the centre, with ice rink, dry ski slope, cinema, bars and restaurants and a swimming pool.

Getting There & Away

Aviemore is 33 miles from Inverness, 62 from Fort William, 127 from Edinburgh and 505 from London.

Bus Buses stop on Grampian Rd; you can make bookings at the TIC.

Scottish Citylink connects Aviemore with Inverness (45 minutes) to the north; and to the south to Kincraig (10 minutes), Kingussie (15 minutes), Newtonmore (20 minutes), Dalwhinnie (40 minutes), Pitlochry (1¼ hours), Perth (two hours), Glasgow (3½ hours) and Edinburgh (3½ hours). You travel via Inverness to get to Aberdeen.

Highland Country Buses (☎ 01463-233371) has one early-morning service, Monday to Friday, from Newtonmore to Inverness via Aviemore and back. Aviemore to Inverness costs £3.60 and takes 40 minutes.

There's one direct daytime service to London's Victoria (11 hours, £39), another overnight service and an early-morning service requiring a change in Glasgow. There are also overnight services to Heathrow and Gatwick airports.

Train There are direct train services to London (eight hours, £70), Glasgow/Edinburgh (3 hours, £25.50) and Inverness (45 minutes, £8.20). For details phone ☎ 0345-484950.

Strathspey Steam Railway (☎ 810725) operates between Aviemore and Boat of Garten. At the time of writing work had started on an extension to Grantown. The station is across the tracks from the main railway station.

Car MacDonald's Self Drive (☎ 811444), 13 Muirton, hires out cars for £30 a day and will deliver/collect from your hotel. Highland Discovery Tours (☎ 811478), 27 Corrour Rd, hires out a 16-seat minibus and guide; phone for details of day trips to Loch Ness (£12) and Skye (£17).

Getting Around

The Cairngorm Chairlift Company (☎ 861261) runs an infrequent local bus service linking Aviemore with the towns along the Spey Valley (Grantown, Newtonmore, Kingussie, Kincraig) and provides the only service along the Ski Rd from Aviemore to Cairngorm (£1.80/90p).

Several places in central Aviemore hire out mountain bikes. You can also hire bikes in Rothiemurchus Estate and in Glenmore

Forest Park. Most places charge £9 to £14 per day.

Aviemore Mountain Bikes (☎ 811007), beside the dry ski slope, offers guided bike tours.

AROUND AVIEMORE
Kincraig
Kincraig, six miles south-west of Aviemore, is another good base for exploring the Cairngorms. An offshoot of Edinburgh Zoo, the **Highland Wildlife Park** (☎ 01540-651270), just outside the village features breeding stocks of local wildlife past and present. There's a drive-through safari park and then several woodland walks offering most people their best opportunity to come face to face with a dozy wildcat or furiously displaying male capercaillie. Admission costs £11.50 for a car with two people and £16 for a car with four. It's open April to October from 10 am to 4 pm (5 pm from June to August).

At Kincraig, the Spey widens into **Loch Insh**. The *Loch Insh Watersports Centre* (☎ 01540-651272) offers canoeing, windsurfing, sailing, bike hire and fishing trips. There's also some B&B accommodation from £14 a head in comfortable rooms with attached baths. Food here is good, especially after 6.30 pm when the café metamorphoses into a restaurant.

Glen Feshie extends east into the Cairngorms. About five miles from Kincraig, *Glen Feshie Hostel* (☎ 01540-651323) is a friendly, independent 15-bed hostel that's very popular with hikers. The nightly charge of £7 includes a steaming bowl of porridge to start the day.

Landmark Highland Heritage & Adventure Park
At Carrbridge, seven miles north-east of Aviemore, the Landmark Highland Heritage Centre (☎ (01479-841614) is set in a forest of Scots pine trees with a boardwalk running through it. Provided you don't suffer from vertigo, the raised Tree Top Trail makes it easier to look for red squirrels, crossbills and crested tits. The 20-minute slide presentation on the Highlands is mildly interesting if you're new to Scottish history. It's open daily from 9.30 am until 5 pm from November to March, 5.30 pm in September and October, 6 pm from April to mid-July and 8 pm from mid-July through August. Admission costs £4.50/3.

Boat of Garten
Six miles north-east of Aviemore, Boat of Garten is known as the Osprey Village, since these rare birds of prey nest at the RSPB reserve in Abernethy Forest. The hide is open to visitors from late April to August, daily, 10 am to 8 pm. The metal props holding the tree where the birds nest together is testimony to the determination of egg collectors and explains why RSPB volunteers guard the site throughout the nesting season.

The best way to get here is on the Strathspey Steam Railway (☎ 01479-810725) which runs from Aviemore – a ticket in 3rd class costs £4.40 return.

Dulnain Bridge
Nine miles north-east of Aviemore, the Heather Centre (☎ 01479-851359) is a garden centre-cum-visitor centre where you can find out about the innumerable uses to which heather has been put over the centuries. Afterwards you can sample one of 21 recipes for Scottish dumpling (actually rich fruit cake steamed in a *cloot* or linen cloth) in the adjacent *Clootie Dumpling Tearoom*; the Heather Centre Special comes with cream, ice cream, heather cream liqueur, chopped nuts and blackberry preserve for £2.85.

GRANTOWN-ON-SPEY
- *pop 2000*   • ☎ *01479*

This sedate Georgian town, 14 miles northeast of Aviemore, is in the heart of the Spey fishing area and catering for anglers is the town's main business. Most hotels can kit you up for a day by the river or put you in touch with someone who can. On the High St, the TIC (☎ 872773) is open daily from April to October.

Places to Stay & Eat

Grantown's accommodation reflects its clientele, with plenty of comfortable upmarket hotels notable for their food.

There are some budget places, however. At *Peter Cliff's* (☎ 872824), Ardenbeg, Grant Rd, dormitory accommodation costs £6; while the *Grantown-on-Spey Caravan Park* (☎ 872474), half a mile from the town centre, charges £6.50 for two campers, a car and a tent. In the High St, *Crann Tara Guest House* (☎ 872197) has beds from £15 with shared bath. The *Stonefield House Tearoom* (☎ 873325) in The Square does B&B for £14 and reasonably priced lunches and teas.

Ardconnel House (☎ 872104), Woodlands Terrace, is a Victorian villa highly commended for its food and atmosphere. Dinner, bed and breakfast costs from £39 per person, and all rooms have private baths. Elegant *Ravenscourt House Hotel* (☎ 872286), Seafield Ave, is a country-house hotel near the main square. At the time of writing it was undergoing refurbishment; expect to pay from £30 a head when it reopens.

Getting There & Away

Work is in progress to extend the Strathspey Steam Railway to Grantown.

In the meantime Highland Country Buses operates eight buses a day between Grantown and Aviemore (35 minutes), Monday to Saturday. The Heather Hopper bus runs this way on a route from Elgin via Rothes and Tomintoul to Aviemore. Contact Inverness bus station (☎ 01463-233371) for details.

KINGUSSIE

- *pop 1200*   • ☎ 01540

Twelve miles south-west of Aviemore, Kingussie (pronounced king-yewsie) is a small, peaceful town by the Spey.

The TIC (☎ 661297), just off the High St in King St, is open daily from late May to September.

Highland Folk Museum

At the Kingussie Highland Folk Museum (☎ 661307) in Duke St musical instruments, costumes and washing utensils are displayed in 18th-century Pitmain Lodge. In the grounds you can also examine a thatch-roofed Isle of Lewis blackhouse, a 19th-century corrugated-iron shed for smoking salmon, and assorted farm implements. In summer there are demonstrations of spinning, baking over a peat fire and wood carving. From April to October, the museum is open Monday to Saturday from 10 am to 6 pm, and on Sunday afternoon. In winter it's open from Monday to Friday, 10 am to 3 pm; £2.50/1.50.

Ruthven Barracks

Built on the site of an earlier 13th-century castle, Ruthven Barracks was one of four fortresses constructed after the first Jacobite uprising of 1715 as part of a Hanoverian scheme for controlling the Highlands. When you stand inside the ruins and look out at the views, the choice of site makes perfect sense. The Barracks were last occupied by Jacobite troops awaiting the return of Bonnie Prince Charlie after the Battle of Culloden. Learning of his defeat and subsequent flight, they destroyed the barracks before taking to the glens. There's free access to the ruins which are floodlit at night.

Walks

Far less popular than the more obvious Cairngorms, the Monadhliath range rises north-west of Kingussie and you can walk here for hours without seeing another hiker. During the stalking season (July to October), you should always check with the TIC before setting out.

The six-hour circular walk to the 2881-foot-high summit of Carn an Fhreceadain, above Kingussie, is recommended. You follow the road north out of the village to Pitmain Lodge and continue along the river, the Allt Mor, before climbing to the summit where there's a little stone shelter. You can then follow the ridge east to the twin summits of Beinn Bhreac before taking another track back to Kingussie.

Places to Stay & Eat

A new *Lairds Bothy Hostel* (☎ 661334) has

been built behind the Tipsy Laird pub in the High St. There are four family rooms and several eight-bedded dorms which cost £8 a head. Alternatively, you can camp at the *Caravan Park* (☎ 661600) by the golf course, which costs from £5 per tent.

Mrs Jarratt's (☎ 661430), St Helens, Ardbroilach Rd, has rooms with attached bath for £18 per person. On the western outskirts friendly *Homewood Lodge* (☎ 661507) does B&B for £15, with fine views just outside the front door.

The *Osprey Hotel* (☎ 661510), on the corner of Ruthven Rd, charges £24 for B&B in a comfortable Victorian house with good home cooking.

If you're feeling flush, *The Cross* (☎ 661166), at Tweed Mill Brae, Ardbroilach Rd, is one of the Highlands' top hotel-restaurants (closed Tuesday). Dinner, bed and breakfast costs from £85 a head.

Rather cheaper are pub meals at the *Tipsy Laird* in the High St. Of the High St cafés, the most promising is *La Cafetière*, with soup and a roll for £1.30 or toasties from £1.95.

Getting There & Away

Kingussie is 120 miles from Edinburgh, 75 from Perth and 40 from Inverness. It's on the main Edinburgh/Glasgow to Inverness route, so most trains and buses stop here. For rail information, phone ☎ 0345-484950.

KINGUSSIE TO FORT WILLIAM

Just north of Kingussie there's a choice of routes south. The A9 continues to Perth, leaving the Highland region via the bleak Pass of Drumochter. You can detour to visit **Dalwhinnie Distillery** (☎ 01528-522208) which claims to be Scotland's highest distillery. It's open Monday to Friday from 10 am to 4 pm (and summer Saturdays) and tours cost £2.

The A86 to Fort William leaves the A9 at Kingussie, continuing through Newtonmore to run along Loch Laggan and **Loch Moy**, a particularly fine stretch of water, with views of Ben Nevis.

The railway joins the road at Tulloch

station and follows Glen Spean to the Great Glen, through **Roybridge** and **Spean Bridge**. *Grey Corrie Lodge* (☎ 01397-712236), in Roybridge, is an independent hostel charging £7.50 per night. Two miles from Roybridge at Auchluachrach, another hostel, *Aite Cruinnichadh* (☎ 01397-712315), has beds for £7.

Six miles north of Fort William is the **Nevis Range** ski area (☎ 01397-705825), based around the slopes of Aonach Mor (4006 feet). The gondola cable car operates year-round (£5.75/3.90 for the return trip) and will carry you to the top station (2150 feet), with a restaurant and bar. There are excellent walks in this area. Bikes can be rented at the base station, and trails lead through nearby **Leanachan Forest**.

The Great Glen

The Great Glen is a natural fault line running across Scotland from Fort William to Inverness as a series of lochs – Linnhe, Lochy, Oich and Ness – linked by the Caledonian Canal. The Great Glen has always been a communication (and invasion) route. General George Wade built a military road along the south side of Loch Ness from 1724. The modern A82 road along the north side was completed in 1933.

CYCLE ROUTE

The 80-mile Great Glen Cycle Route from Fort William to Inverness via Fort Augustus follows canal towpaths and gravel tracks through forests to avoid the busy roads where possible. The *Cycling in the Forest* leaflet, available from TICs or the Forestry Commission, gives details.

GETTING AROUND

Bus

Inverness Traction (☎ 01463-239292) has a variety of day tours from Inverness to Loch Ness costing from £5 to £10. Citylink (☎ 01463-711000) has several daily services along the loch between Fort William and Inverness (two hours, £5).

FORT WILLIAM
- *pop 11,000*   • ☎ *01397*

Given its location on Loch Linnhe, amid some of the country's finest mountain scenery, you might expect Fort William to be an attractive little Highland town. Unfortunately insensitive civic planning has put paid to such hopes. Separated from its loch by a bypass, Fort William has been robbed of any charm it once had by modern development.

Despite this, it's a major tourist centre, easily reached by bus and train. Use it as a base for the mountains, but don't plan on hanging around.

Magical Glen Nevis begins near the north end of the town and extends west below the slopes of Ben Nevis. 'The Ben' – Britain's highest mountain at 4406 feet – and neighbouring mountains are a magnet for hikers and climbers. The glen is also popular with movie-makers – part of Mel Gibson's Oscar-winning *Braveheart* was filmed here.

Orientation & Information
The town meanders along the edge of Loch Linnhe for several miles. The bleak centre, with its small selection of shops, takeaways and pubs, is easy to get around on foot unless you're booked into a far-flung B&B.

The busy TIC (☎ 703781), in Cameron Square, has a good range of books and maps. For local walks, their series of *Great Walks* leaflets (30p), incorporating a map and basic information, are handy, but you'll need an OS map for more adventurous hikes, such as Ben Nevis. More information is available from the Glen Nevis Visitors Centre, near the youth hostel in the glen.

As you might expect, Fort William has well-stocked outdoor-equipment shops. Nevisport (☎ 704921), near the railway station, has a marvellous range of books and maps for mountaineers. West Coast Outdoor Leisure (☎ 705777) is at the other end of the High St.

Marco's An Aird Community Centre (☎ 700707), near the bus station, offers snooker, 10-pin bowling and other activities. Day membership (£2) lets you use the showers and store luggage.

West Highland Museum
Beside the TIC, this museum (☎ 702169) is packed with Highland memorabilia. Of particular interest is the secret portrait of Bonnie Prince Charlie. After the Jacobite rebellions, all things Highland were banned, including pictures of the exiled leader. This picture looks like nothing more than a smear of paint until placed next to a curved mirror, when it reflects a creditable likeness of the prince.

The museum is open from Monday to Saturday, until at least 5 pm, and in July and August on Sunday afternoon. At the time of writing it was closed for refurbishment. Expect prices to rise slightly from the old £1/40p.

Other Things to See
There's little left of the original **Fort William** from which the town takes its name, as it was pulled down in the 19th century to make way for the railway. It was originally built by General Monk in 1635 to control the Highlands, but the surviving ruins are of the fort built in the 1690s by General MacKay and named after the king, William III.

The local **Ben Nevis Distillery** (☎ 700200), at Lochy Bridge, has a visitors centre open weekdays all year round and weekends over Easter and in July and August. It offers free tours – and free drams at the end of them.

Walks & Cycle Routes
The most obvious local hike, up Ben Nevis, should not be undertaken lightly. You'll need warm clothes, food and something to drink, and a detailed map. The weather at the top is more often bad (thick mist) than good, so go prepared for the worst, even if it's sunny when you set off.

There are two main routes up. One path begins in Glen Nevis, either from the car park by Achintee Farm (on the north side of the river and reached by the road through Claggan), or from the youth hostel on the

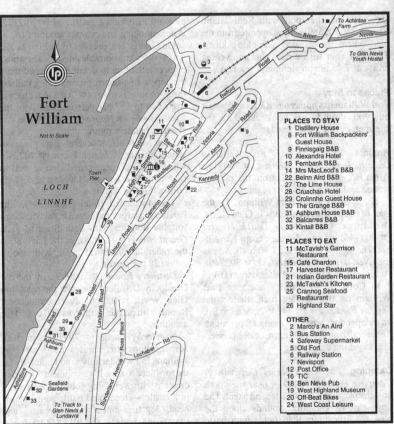

Fort William

Not to Scale

LOCH
LINNHE

Town
Pier

Seafield
Gardens

To Track to
Glen Nevis &
Lundavra

To Achintee
Farm

River   Nevis

To Glen Nevis
Youth Hostel

Ashburn
Lane

PLACES TO STAY
1 Distillery House
8 Fort William Backpackers'
  Guest House
9 Finnisgaig B&B
10 Alexandra Hotel
13 Fernbank B&B
14 Mrs MacLeod's B&B
22 Beinn Aird B&B
27 The Lime House
28 Cruachan Hotel
29 Crolinnhe Guest House
30 The Grange B&B
31 Ashburn House B&B
32 Balcarres B&B
33 Kintail B&B

PLACES TO EAT
11 McTavish's Garrison
   Restaurant
15 Café Chardon
17 Harvester Restaurant
21 Indian Garden Restaurant
23 McTavish's Kitchen
25 Crannog Seafood
   Restaurant
26 Highland Star

OTHER
2 Marco's An Aird
3 Bus Station
4 Safeway Supermarket
5 Old Fort
6 Railway Station
7 Nevisport
12 Post Office
16 TIC
18 Ben Nevis Pub
19 West Highland Museum
20 Off-Beat Bikes
24 West Coast Leisure

road up the glen. These two trails join after less than one mile, then follow the Red Burn before zigzagging up to the summit and the ruins of the old observatory.

The other path begins from the Ben Nevis distillery, follows the Allt a'Mhuilinn to the mountain rescue hut and eventually joins the other path for the zigzag approach to the summit. It can take three to five hours to reach the top and 2½ to four hours to get down again.

There are very pleasant (and far less strenuous) walks along Glen Nevis past waterfalls and through the gorge at the east end. You could also walk part of the West Highland Way from Fort William to Kinlochleven via Glen Nevis (14 miles) or even to Glencoe (21 miles to the junction with the A82).

The 80-mile Great Glen Cycle Route links Fort William and Inverness. The Forestry Commission's free leaflet gives details of this mainly off-road route.

Organised Tours
Outabout Lochaber runs half-day local tours (£5), leaving the railway station at 10 am and 2 pm, Monday to Friday. Book at the TIC.

There are also 1½-hour boat trips

(£5/2.50) on the loch with Seal Island Cruises (☎ 705589) – they operate from the pier, where there's also a booking kiosk. There are four trips a day, plus an evening cruise at 7.45 pm on summer weekdays.

Places to Stay

Fort William has numerous B&Bs and hotels but you should still book ahead in the summer, even for the hostels.

Hostels The popular *Fort William Backpackers' Guest House* (☎ 700711), Alma Rd, is a short walk from the railway station and charges £8.50 a night.

Three miles from Fort William, by the start of the path up Ben Nevis in Glen Nevis, the large *Glen Nevis Youth Hostel* (☎ 702336) is open all year except November. The nightly charge is £7.80/6.40. Across the river, *Ben Nevis Bunkhouse* (☎ 702240), Achintee Farm, is a good alternative (£6).

In Corpach, four miles north of Fort William on the Mallaig road, there's the *Smiddy Bunkhouse* (☎ 772467), Station Rd, an independent hostel charging £8 per night. There's also an activity centre (mountaineering, kayaking and sailing).

Camping The *Glen Nevis Caravan & Camping Park* (☎ 702191), near the youth hostel, charges £7.10 for a car and a tent. The few seasonal camping grounds along the glen are little more than fields with basic facilities.

B&Bs & Hotels The numerous B&Bs in and around Fassifern Rd are closest to the train and bus stations. *Mrs MacLeod* (☎ 702533), 2 Caberfeidh, Fassifern Rd, charges £14.50 per person.

Achintore Rd, which runs south along the loch, is almost solidly B&Bs and hotels, most of them large and characterless. More interesting is the B&B-cum-art gallery at *The Lime House* (☎ 701806) which has beds for £12. Comfortable *Ashburn House* (☎ 706000) has rooms with bath for around £32 per person.

Just off Achintore Rd, several B&Bs offer

pleasant loch views. *Balcarres* (☎ 702377) is non-smoking and charges around £16.

On Grange Rd, parallel to Achintore Rd, are two very comfortable guesthouses whose owners' attention to detail has earned them the top tourist-board rating. The excellent three-room *Grange* (☎ 705516) charges from £28 to £33 per person. Next door the *Crolinnhe Guest House* (☎ 702709) has one cheaper, bathless room.

Glen Nevis offers several more places to stay, including *Achintee Farm* (☎ 702240) which has B&B accommodation as well as the bunkhouse. A single/double without bath costs £18/30, a double with bath £36.

The *Alexandra Hotel* (☎ 702241), The Parade, is a large, traditional hotel with comfortable doubles with bath for £38. The *Grand Hotel* (☎ 702928), in the High St, is the other large, central hotel, with rooms from £28 per person.

Distillery House (☎ 702980), by the old Glenlochy Distillery opposite the road into Glen Nevis, is thoroughly recommended. Rooms with private baths cost £50 to £60 for a double.

Inverlochy Castle (☎ 702177), in 500-acre grounds three miles north of Fort William, is a wonderfully grand hotel, by far the top place to stay. It's an opulent Victorian creation with everything you'd expect to find in a castle – crenellated battlements, stags' heads, log fires and a wide staircase – and luxurious rooms for £128/240 for a single/double.

Places to Eat

With the honourable exception of the *Crannog Seafood Restaurant* (see below), Fort William is pretty much of a culinary desert. For those on a tight budget, the *Safeway Coffee Shop* is good value – chicken curry with a jacket potato is £2.85. It's open until 8 pm weekdays, 6 pm at weekends.

In the Alexandra Hotel, the *Great Food Shop* (☎ 702241) makes up with cheerful service for what it lacks in quality food. It stays open until 11 pm and serves vegetarian and children's meals, and pizzas from £2.99.

The *Nevisport Restaurant*, in the outdoor-equipment shop, does cheap meals but closes early – 7.30 pm in summer, 5 pm the rest of the year.

Most other places to eat line the High St. The *Harvester* (☎ 705224) is an inexpensive restaurant/takeaway. Nicer but only open during shop hours is *Café Chardon*, upstairs in P. Maclennan's store, with soup for £1.75 and filled ciabetta sandwiches for £2.50.

McTavish's Kitchen (☎ 702406), on the High St, has the same menu and floor show (see under Entertainment) as the Oban branch. There's a self-service café downstairs. Also in the High St, *McTavish's Garrison Restaurant* offers food only.

Indian Garden Restaurant (☎ 705011) is popular but not particularly cheap. They do takeaways and stay open late. You can also get takeaways from the town's only Chinese restaurant, the *Highland Star* (☎ 703905), which has a good reputation.

The best restaurant in town is also the best located. *Crannog Seafood Restaurant* (☎ 705589) is on the pier, giving diners an uninterrupted view over the loch. The food is excellent; half a dozen oysters for £7, main courses for between £6 and £10.

Entertainment

At *McTavish's Kitchen* (☎ 702406) they operate the pile 'em high, sell 'em cheap approach to Scottish cuisine and culture, but it's none the worse for that and quite fun as long as you enter into the spirit of things. There's a show every night from May to September at 8.30 pm, with dancing, a live band and a piper. It costs £1.50/1 if you also eat, £3/1.50 if you don't, and there are also set meals from £7.95 including the show. On Friday and Saturday night there's a disco (£3) from 10.30 pm.

On the opposite side of the High St, the Jacobite Bar in *Ben Nevis* is a popular music venue and a good place for a drink. The *Nevisport Bar*, in the Nevisport complex, beckons walkers and climbers.

Getting There & Away

Fort William is 597 miles from London, 146 from Edinburgh, 104 from Glasgow and 66 from Inverness. If you've got a spare week the best way to get here is on foot, along the 95-mile West Highland Way from just north of Glasgow (see the Activities chapter at the start of this book for more information).

Bus Scottish Citylink (☎ 0990-505050) has daily connections to London (12 hours, £42) with a change in Glasgow. Several other companies also run buses to Glasgow (three hours, £9), including the Citylink subsidiary Skye-Ways. There are three direct buses a day between Fort William and Kyle of Lochalsh (two hours).

Highland Country Buses (☎ 702373) has three buses a day, Monday to Saturday, between Fort William and Oban (1½ hours; £5). There's also a regular service along Loch Ness to Inverness (two hours, £5.80) and a daily bus to Mallaig. Another useful Monday to Saturday service runs to Glencoe (30 minutes, £1.40).

Train For rail inquiries, phone ☎ 0345-484950. The spectacular West Highland line runs from Glasgow via Fort William to Mallaig. There's a particularly wonderful wild section when the line crosses bleak Rannoch Moor. If you're travelling from Oban to Fort William, the Gaelic Bus service saves you from backtracking to Crianlarich.

There are three trains daily from Glasgow to Fort William (3¾ hours, £21.50), and four trains between Fort William and Mallaig (1½ hours, £6.80). The West Highland Rover ticket (£39) gives unlimited travel on four days in an eight-day period.

An overnight train connects Fort William and London (from £80 plus £25 for a sleeper) but you'll miss the views.

Car The TIC has a leaflet listing car hire places. Try MacRae & Dick (☎ 702500), Road to the Isles Filling Station, Lochy Bridge.

Getting Around

Bus Gaelic Bus No 17 runs from the bus station up Glen Nevis to the youth hostel (eight minutes), Monday to Saturday, but only four times a day. Buses to Corpach (15 minutes) are more numerous.

Bicycle Off-Beat Bikes (☎ 704008), 117 High St, has mountain bikes for £8/12 for a half/full day. They also run guided bike tours of the area for around £25, including bike hire. There's another branch at the Nevis Range base station.

FORT WILLIAM TO GLEN COE

South of Fort William, the A82 follows Loch Linnhe as far as **Inchree**. Accommodation includes *Inchree Bunkhouse* (☎ 01855-821287), with beds from £5.70 and a pub/restaurant on the site. It's easy to get here by bus as this is the main route between Fort William and Glasgow or Oban. For something more stylish, there's the *Lodge on the Loch* (☎ 01855-821237) in nearby **Onich**, with luxurious singles/doubles from £49.50/79 and a good restaurant.

At North Ballachulish you can either cross the bridge and continue along the A82 into Glencoe village or take the side road that runs up Loch Leven to Kinlochleven and back to Glencoe along the southern shore.

GLEN COE

Scotland's most famous glen was written into the history books 300 years ago when MacDonalds were murdered by Campbells in what became known as the Glen Coe Massacre. However, it's also one of the most beautiful glens, with steeply sloping sides and narrow-sided valleys that provided the cattle-rustling Highlanders with the perfect place to hide their stock. The glen is dominated by three massive, brooding spurs, known as the Three Sisters of Glencoe.

There are wonderful walks in this highly atmospheric glen, much of which is owned by the NTS, and some excellent accommodation.

Glencoe Village
- *pop 360*   • ☎ 01855

Standing by Loch Leven, at the entrance to the glen, the village is 16 miles from Fort William on the main Glasgow road. A small thatched **folk museum** aside, there's little to see in the village.

There's a NTS visitors centre (☎ 811307) 1½ miles from the village along the road into the glen. It's open daily from April to mid-October from 10 am to 5 pm, and 9.30 am to 6 pm in July and August. It's worth paying

---

The Glen Coe Massacre

The brutal murders that took place here in 1692 were particularly shameful, perpetrated as they were by one Highland clan on another (with whom they were lodging as guests).

In an attempt to quash remaining Jacobite loyalties amongst the Highland clans, the English king had ordered that all chiefs take an oath of loyalty to him by the end of the year (1691). Maclain, the elderly chief of the MacDonalds of Glen Coe, was late in setting out to fulfil the king's demand, and going first to Fort William rather than Inverary made him later still.

The Secretary of State for Scotland, Sir John Dalrymple, declared that the MacDonalds should be punished as an example to other Highland clans, some of whom had not bothered to even take the oath. A company of 120 soldiers, mainly of the Campbell clan, were sent to the glen. Since their leader was related by marriage to Maclain, the troops were billeted in MacDonald homes. It was a long-standing tradition for clans to provide hospitality to passing travellers.

After they'd been guests for 12 days, the order came for the soldiers to put to death all MacDonalds under the age of 70. Some Campbells alerted the MacDonalds to their intended fate, while others turned on their hosts at 5 am on 13 February, shooting Maclain and 37 other men, women and children. Some died before they knew what was happening, while others fled into the snow, only to die of exposure.

The ruthless brutality of the incident caused a public uproar and after an inquiry several years later, Dalrymple lost his job. There's a monument to Maclain in Glencoe village and members of the MacDonald clan still gather here on 13 February each year. ■

the 50p/30p entry fee to see the 14-minute video on the Glencoe Massacre.

Places to Stay & Eat You can camp at *Invercoe Caravans* (☎ 811210 where sites cost from £7.50 to £10 per night, or you can rent a caravan by the week.

Glencoe Youth Hostel (☎ 811219) is a 1½-mile walk from the village, on the north side of the river. It's very popular, particularly with climbers, so you'll need to book ahead. Open all year, the nightly charge is £6.95/5.85. Nearby, the *Leacantuim Farm Bunkhouse* (☎ 811256) has bunkhouse accommodation for £6.50, or £5.50 in the Alpine Barn where you pay extra for showers. They also run *Red Squirrel Campsite*, charging campers £3 each.

Less than a mile further along this track is *Clachaig Inn* (☎ 811252), which offers B&B in rooms with private bath from £19 a head. There's a pub, good food and live music on Friday and Saturday.

On the village outskirts, *Glencoe Guest House* (☎ 811244), Strathlachan, charges £14 to £18 per person.

Getting There & Away Highland Country Buses (☎ 01463-233371) runs buses from Fort William to Glencoe (30 minutes). Scottish Citylink buses run to Glasgow.

Glencoe Ski Centre

About 1½ miles from the Kingshouse Hotel, on the other side of the A82, is the car park and base station for this ski centre, where commercial skiing in Scotland first started in 1956. At the base station there's a **Museum of Scottish Skiing & Climbing**; among the relics is the ice axe Chris Bonington used to climb Everest.

The chair lift (☎ 01855-851226) operates all week in summer, from 10 am to 5 pm; £3.50/2.20 return. It's the easiest way to get to the 2400-foot-high viewpoint and several good walks.

Kingshouse Hotel

Scotland's oldest established inn, this isolated hotel (☎ 01855-851259) has been a landmark for so long that it now appears on maps, marked simply as 'Hotel'. It's on the West Highland Way at the east end of the glen, and hikers stop here to tuck into a plate of haggis, tatties and neeps and a refreshing drink in the bar. It's a good place to stay, with rooms from £22.50/44 plus £6.50 for breakfast.

Walks

This is serious walking country and you'll need maps, warm clothes, and food and water. The NTS visitors centre stocks lots of useful information.

A great six-hour hike leads through the Lost Valley to the top of Bidean nam Bian (3772 feet). Cross the footbridge below Alltna-Reigh and follow the gorge up into the Lost Valley, continuing up the rim, then along it, to the right, to the summit. You need to be very careful crossing to Stob Coire Nan Lochan as there are steep scree slopes. Descend the west side of this ridge and round into the Coire nan Lochan, where a path heads back to the road.

For something less strenuous, hike this route only as far as the **Lost Valley**, a hidden mountain sanctuary still haunted by the ghosts of murdered MacDonalds. Allow three hours for the return trip.

Aonach Eagach, the glen's northern wall, is said to be the best ridge walk on the Scottish mainland, but it's difficult in places and you need a good head for heights. Some parts could almost be graded a rock climb. It's best done from east to west, and there's a path up north of Allt-na-Reigh and down from Sgor nam Fiannaidh towards Loch Achtriochtan. The more direct gully that leads to Clachaig Inn is not a safe way down. It takes six to eight hours.

FORT WILLIAM TO FORT AUGUSTUS

It's 33 miles along the A82 from Fort William to Fort Augustus, but it's worth taking the slightly longer B8004 route at first to see **Neptune's Staircase**, a flight of eight locks which raises the water in the Caledonian Canal by 64 feet. Thomas Telford's canal was built from 1803-22 to connect the east and west coast of Scotland, from Inverness to Fort William. The lochs make up 38 miles of the canal's total 60 miles and there are 29 locks.

This side trip rejoins the A82 at the **Commando Memorial** to the WWII military force who trained here. The road then runs along the southern shore of **Loch Lochy** before crossing the canal by the Laggan Locks to run along the northern shore of narrow **Loch Oich**. At the start of Loch Oich, the **Well of the Heads** details the summary justice handed out to seven 16th-century murderers by their victims' aggrieved family.

FORT AUGUSTUS
• *pop 600* • ☎ *01320*

Fort Augustus is at the junction of four of General Wade's military roads and was the headquarters for his road-building operations from 1724.

The TIC (☎ 366367) in the car park is open Easter to October, and charges £2 for local bookings.

Fort Augustus Abbey
Between 1729 and 1742 General George Wade built a fort at the point where the River Tarff joined Loch Ness as part of his plan to pacify the Highlands. It was captured and later damaged by the retreating Jacobites but remained occupied until 1854. In 1876 Benedictine monks took over the building which became Fort Augustus Abbey (☎ 366232). Until 1994 there was a school here too but that has now closed and in its place has come a predictable Highlands Visitor Centre. With only 12 monks still living at the Abbey, it's future looks uncertain.

The Visitor Centre is open daily from 9 am to 5 pm; admission is £4/2.

Other Things to See & Do
The **five locks** which raise the water level of the Caledonian Canal by 40 feet at Fort Augustus are particularly impressive, but opening the swing bridge can cause long traffic jams on the busy A82.

Cruises on Loch Ness on the *Royal Scot*

(☎ 366221) operate all year round except in February. A one-hour trip costs £4.50/2.

There's a fine view over the loch from the promontory between the canal and the River Oich. On the loch edge, just outside Fort Augustus towards Inverness, is tiny **Cherry Island**, originally a *crannogh* or artificial island settlement.

Places to Stay & Eat
Abbey Backpackers (☎ 366233) offers beds in the Abbey gatehouse for £8 but is only open from April to October. Beside the canal, *Loch Ness Lodge Bunkhouse/Hostel* (☎ 366750) charges £6.50 for a dorm bed.

The *Old Pier House* (☎ 366418) is beautifully situated by the loch just north of the village and offers horse riding. Double rooms cost £45 in summer.

The *Coffee House* (☎ 366361) opposite the car park offers café-style food during the day but becomes a restaurant in the evening. Near the canal the *Jac-O-Bite* café deserves a visit for its name alone; pasta costs from £3.50. The *Bothy Bite* and *The Lock Inn* are alternative lunch spots with canal views. The *Abbot's Table* restaurant in the Abbey does everything from soup and a roll to main courses from £3.95.

LOCH NESS
It's 44 miles along the A82 on the north shore of Loch Ness from Fort Augustus, at the southern end, to Inverness, just beyond the northern end. The less busy but extremely picturesque B862 runs along the southern side. A complete circuit of the loch is about 70 miles – go anti-clockwise for the best views.

The long (23 miles), narrow (one mile), deep (700 feet), dark and bitterly cold waters of the loch have been extensively, and fruitlessly, explored for *Nessie*, the elusive Loch Ness monster. You're unlikely to spot her except in cardboard cutout form.

DRUMNADROCHIT
• *pop 600* • ☎ *01456*

Exploitation of poor Nessie reaches fever pitch at Drumnadrochit where two Monster

✝✝✝✝✝✝✝✝✝✝✝✝✝✝✝✝✝✝✝✝✝

Loch Ness Monster

Although tales have been dredged up of ancient Celtic legends about mysterious monsters, the craze has only really developed since 1933, when the A82 road was completed along the loch. The classic monster photograph of a dinosaur-like creature's long neck emerging from the water was taken in 1934, and the monster hunt was on. In recent years there have been sonar hunts, underwater cameras and computer studies, but unfortunately no monster has been turned up. The loch is very deep and very murky, so the Loch Ness Monster tourist business has to pedal very hard to make a go of it. Keep your camera handy – you could be the one to prove the monster does exist. ∎

✝✝✝✝✝✝✝✝✝✝✝✝✝✝✝✝✝✝✝✝✝

exhibitions vie for the tourist dollar. The villages of Milton, Lewiston and Strone are virtually contiguous with Drumnadrochit while Urquhart Castle is immediately south.

Monster Exploitation

The more prominent **Official Loch Ness Monster Exhibition Centre** (☎ 450573) features an audiovisual presentation plus exhibits of equipment used in the various monster hunts. It's open daily, 9.30 am to 4.30 pm for £4/2.50. Just down the road, the **Original Loch Ness Monster Centre** (☎ 450342) shows a poor quality 30-minute Loch Ness video for £3.50/2.75. If your English isn't wonderful, the video story comes with multilingual headsets; the audiovisual presentation doesn't. One-hour monster-hunting cruises on the loch in the *Nessie Hunter* (☎ 450395) operate from April to October, daily from 9.30 am to 6.30 pm and cost £7/4. There's even a Loch Ness Submarine (☎ 01285-760762) charging really avid Nessie hunters £69.50 for a dive in the lake.

Urquhart Castle

One of Scotland's best known castles, Urquhart (☎ 450551; HS) was taken and lost by Edward I, held by Robert the Bruce against Edward III and fought over by every-

one who passed this way. Not only was the castle repeatedly sacked, damaged and rebuilt over the centuries but the unfortunate inhabitants of the Great Glen were also regularly pillaged and robbed in the process.

Destruction and reconstruction followed so regularly that it's hard to trace the full story of the castle's development. By the 1600s it had become redundant, superseded by more palatial residences and more powerful fortresses at Fort William and Inverness. It was finally blown up in 1692 to prevent Jacobites using it and its remains perch dramatically on the edge of the loch, approached by a steep path from the roadside car park.

The castle was entered by a drawbridge which led into the gatehouse. The summit of the upper bailey at the southern end was probably used as a hillfort over 1000 years ago but by the 15th century the nether bailey at the northern end had become the focus of fortifications. At the site's extreme north end the five-storey tower house is the most impressive remaining fragment and offers wonderful loch views.

Admission costs £3/1. Highland Country Buses from Inverness pass by more or less hourly throughout the week.

Places to Stay & Eat

Loch Ness Backpackers (☎ 450807) is in East Lewiston, just south of Drumnadrochit and within walking distance of the monster centres and Urquhart Castle. They offer a daily pick-up service from Inverness station. The nightly cost in six-bed dorms is £8.50. *Loch Ness Youth Hostel* (☎ 01320-51274) is 13 miles down the loch at Glenmoriston and costs £5.40/4.40. There are numerous B&Bs in Drumnadrochit but single rooms are in short supply. With a car, try *Drumbuie Farm* (☎ 450634) on the right as you come into Drumnadrochit from Inverness. It's a welcoming place with good rooms from £28 a double.

The *Glen Café* (☎ 450282) and the more expensive *Fiddler's Restaurant & Pizza Bar* (☎ 450678) are both by the village green. *Polmaily House Hotel* (☎ 450343), beyond

Milton, has the award-winning *Urquhart Restaurant*.

Getting Around
You can hire a mountain bike from West End Garage (☎ 450228) in Milton for £10 a day.

INVERNESS
- *pop 41,800* • ☎ *01463*

Inverness is the capital of the Highlands, and the hub for transportation. The River Ness flowing through the middle more than makes up for the lack of world-class attractions; on a sunny day you can while away many a pleasant hour strolling along its banks and watching the birds it attracts. When that palls, you can take a boat out on the Moray Firth to look for bottlenose dolphins; perhaps 100 of them live in the Firth.

In summer Inverness overflows with visitors. Fortunately most are intrepid monster hunters and they don't hang around.

Orientation & Information
The River Ness flows through the town, linking Loch Ness to Moray Firth. The bus and train stations, the TIC and the hostels are all on the east side of the river, within 10 minutes walk of each other.

The TIC (☎ 234353) is on Bridge St, in the corner of the Museum building. There are smaller tourist offices on the entry roads to Inverness from the north and south.

Museum & Art Gallery
The small Museum & Art Gallery (☎ 237114) contains wildlife dioramas, period rooms, Pictish stones and other goodies, along with a variety of short-term events and displays. It's entered from Castle Wynd, off Bridge St, and is open Monday to Saturday, 9 am to 5 pm; free.

Inverness Castle
In the 11th century a timber castle probably stood to the east of the present site. In the 12th century it was replaced with a stone castle, which was then rebuilt in the 15th century. It was repaired in 1718 and expanded in 1725, only to be taken by the Jacobites in 1746 and blown up. The present dominating castle was constructed between 1837 and 1847.

Today it serves as the local Sheriff's Court and most of the young men hanging around outside are waiting for their cases to be heard. The Drum Tower now houses the **Castle Garrison Encounter** (☎ 243363), open from Easter to late November, daily from 10.30 am to 5.30 pm. In return for your £2.50/1.75 admission fee you meet actors representing various sections of the Hanoverian army of 1746. Good knowledge of English is required to get full benefit.

In front of the castle stands a statue of Highland heroine Flora McDonald, who helped Bonnie Prince Charlie escape.

Dolphin Watching
Moray Firth Cruises (☎ 717900) offers 1½ hour cruises to look for dolphins, seals and birdlife. Sightings can't be guaranteed but it's an enjoyable trip anyway, especially on fine days when there are distant glimpses of Ben Nevis. To find them, follow signs to Shore St harbour from the far end of Chapel St. Trips cost £10/5 and leave between 10.30 am and 4.30 pm (6 pm in July and August).

Other Things to See
Inverness's often violent history means that few buildings of real age or historical significance have survived, although **Abertaff House** in Church St dates back to 1593 and **Dunbar's Hospital**, also in Church St, to 1668. Much of the town dates from the completion of Telford's Caledonian Canal in 1822. Inverness's **Mercat Cross** stands in front of the very ornate **Town House**, the Gothic-style town hall.

Cross the river and walk south along the river bank to **St Andrew's Cathedral**, dating from 1866-69, and the **Eden Court Theatre**, where there are regular art exhibits. Continue to the pretty **Ness Islands**, connected to the riverbanks by footbridges.

Organised Tours
Over Easter and from mid-May to late September, Guide Friday (☎ 224000) operates

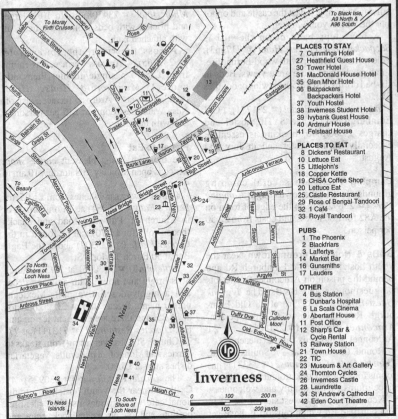

PLACES TO STAY
7 Cummings Hotel
27 Heathfield Guest House
30 Tower Hotel
31 MacDonald House Hotel
35 Glen Mhor Hotel
36 Bazpackers
    Backpackers Hotel
37 Youth Hostel
38 Inverness Student Hotel
39 Ivybank Guest House
40 Ardmuir House
41 Felstead House

PLACES TO EAT
8 Dickens' Restaurant
10 Lettuce Eat
15 Littlejohn's
18 Copper Kettle
19 CHSA Coffee Shop
20 Lettuce Eat
25 Castle Restaurant
29 Rose of Bengal Tandoori
32 1 Café
33 Royal Tandoori

PUBS
1 The Phoenix
2 Blackfriars
3 Laffertys
14 Market Bar
16 Gunsmiths
17 Lauders

OTHER
4 Bus Station
5 Dunbar's Hospital
6 La Scala Cinema
9 Abertarff House
11 Post Office
12 Sharp's Car &
   Cycle Rental
13 Railway Station
21 Town House
22 TIC
23 Museum & Art Gallery
24 Thornton Cycles
26 Inverness Castle
28 Laundrette
34 St Andrew's Cathedral
42 Eden Court Theatre

Inverness

regular hop-on hop-off bus tours of Inverness and the Culloden battlefield. An all-day ticket costs £6/2.

Guided walking tours of the town leave from the Flora MacDonald statue on summer Sundays at 10.30 am. Inverness Traction tours to Loch Ness leave from the TIC at 10.15 am daily and take in Fort Augustus Abbey and a cruise for £9.75/7.75.

From Tomnahurich Bridge, the *Jacobite Queen* (☎ 233999) operates daily cruises on Loch Ness. Costs vary from £9/7 to £11/8.50. A one-way trip to Urquhart Castle costs £8.50/7.

Places to Stay

In peak season, start looking for accommodation early. The TIC charges £2 for local bookings.

Hostels A backpackers' enclave is growing up on the hill above the castle where Old Edinburgh St meets Culduthel St. *Inverness Student Hotel* (☎ 236556), 8 Culduthel Rd, has the same owner as Edinburgh's High St Hostel – you can make phone bookings from there. It's friendly and homely with a great view and charges £8.50 per night in five to 10-bed dorms. It's a 10-minute walk from the railway station, just past the castle and opposite the SYHF youth hostel.

A few steps back down the hill is *Bazpackers Backpackers Hotel* (☎ 717663), a clean, new building with wood-burner fire, small garden and more great views. Beds in six-bed dorms cost £8.50; in twins or doubles £12.

Inverness Youth Hostel (☎ 231771), 1 Old Edinburgh Rd, is the SYHF hostel and charges £7.80/6.40; booking is essential, especially during Easter and in July and August.

Camping There are several camping grounds close to the town. *Bught Camping Park* (☎ 236920) is on the edge of town on the A82 for Loch Ness and costs from £2.50 per person.

B&Bs & Hotels – around town Near the youth hostel along Old Edinburgh Rd and behind the prison on Ardconnel St, are lots of guesthouses and B&Bs. The *Ivybank Guest House* (☎ 232796) at 28 Old Edinburgh Rd costs £16 to £22 per person. *Ardconnel House* (☎ 240455) at 21 Ardconnel St has beds from £16 each.

Round the corner at 27 Southside Rd, *Leinster Lodge Guest House* (☎ 233311) has rooms for £16/36. Look around at busy times since rooms vary in quality and welcome.

Kenneth St, on the west side of the river, and Fairfield Rd which runs off it, have yet more B&Bs.

In the centre, the *Cummings Hotel* (☎ 232531) in Church St has rooms (mostly with attached bath) from £39 to £45 per single and £60 to £70 per double.

B&Bs & Hotels – along the riverbanks For a few pounds more you can bag a river view in Ardross Terrace/Ness Walk, along the west side of the river, or Ness Bank, along the east side.

Ardmuir House (☎ 231151) at 16 Ness Bank has singles from £30.50, doubles from £49, all with private bath. *Felstead House* (☎ 231634) at No 18 has rooms with and without bath from £18 per person. *Glen Mhor Hotel* (☎ 234308) at No 10 is larger and pricier, with beds from £35 a head, all with attached bath.

Across the river, the *Tower Hotel* (☎ 232765), 4 Ardross Terrace, has rooms from £28/40 a single/double. Pleasantly genteel *MacDonald House Hotel* (☎ 232878) at 1 Ardross Terrace, just off Ness Walk, has rooms at £15 per person or £18 with bath.

Places to Eat
The museum has a pleasant *coffee shop*, which is open Monday to Saturday, 10 am to 4 pm.

For takeaway sandwiches from £1.95, try *Lettuce Eat* (☎ 715064) at 7 Lombard St or in Church St. Pub-style food and snacks (bacon rolls for £1.70) can be found in the *Copper Kettle* (☎ 233307) above the Eagle Bar at 50 Baron Taylor's St.

Littlejohn's (☎ 713005) at 28/30 Church St is bright and noisy, with amusing decor and a highly descriptive pasta-Mexican-burger menu. Pizzas start at £3.25, burritos at £6.25, and there are excellent ice creams too. *Dicken's Restaurant* (☎ 713111) at 77-79 Church St does everything from steaks to curries and Mongolian pork rolls. Vegetarian dishes start at £5.90.

The *Castle Restaurant* (☎ 230925), 41 Castle St, near the youth hostel, is a traditional café which prides itself on plentiful portions and low prices; haddock, chips and salad costs £3.90. A bit further up, newly opened *1 Café* (☎ 226200) is trying for something a bit classier; venison sausage costs £6.45 but there's plenty to choose from. Castle St also has the *Royal Tandoori* (☎ 712224), at No 99. Look for special deals pencilled up in the window.

Entertainment
Blackfriars and *The Phoenix* are popular pubs on Academy St near *Laffertys*, one of the new-style themed Irish pubs. The *Market Bar* upstairs in the *Old Market Inn* in the Market Hall off Church St has live music nightly. *Gunsmiths*, in Union St, also has less frequent live bands.

From June to September, Scottish Showtime at the *Cummings Hotel* (☎ 232531), Church St, costs £9/4. *Eden Court Theatre* (☎ 221718), Ness Walk, has regular theatre performances. *Riverside Screen*, at the same location, is Inverness's art-house cinema. *La Scala* in Strother's Lane shows mainstream films.

Getting There & Away

See the fares tables in the introductory Getting Around chapter. Inverness is 155 miles from Edinburgh, 110 from Aberdeen and 135 from Dundee.

Air Inverness airport (☎ 232471), at Dalcross, offers flights to Glasgow, Edinburgh and other centres.

Bus For Inverness bus station phone ☎ 233371. Citylink (☎ 0990-505050) has connections with lots of major centres in England, including London (12 hours, £40.50) via Perth and Glasgow. There are numerous buses to/from Glasgow (3½ hours, £10.30), Edinburgh via Perth (four hours, £11.20) and Aberdeen (three hours, £8.60).

In summer there are several buses daily to Ullapool (1½ hours, £6.30), connecting with the CalMac ferry to Stornoway on Lewis (not Sunday).

There are three or four daily Citylink services via Wick to Thurso and Scrabster (3¾ hours, £8.10) for the ferries to Orkney. In summer the Orkney Bus (☎ 01955-611353) operates a daily Inverness-John O'Groats bus, connecting straight through to Kirkwall. It costs £12 to John O'Groats, £22 to Orkney or £35 for a return permitting a stopover in John O'Groats.

Highland Country Buses (☎ 233371) has regular daily services along Loch Ness to Fort William (two hours, £5.80).

Highland Country Buses and Skye-Ways (☎ 710119) both operate two buses a day (one on Sunday) from Inverness to Kyle of Lochalsh and Portree, on Skye. The journey takes three hours and costs £8.

It's possible to head to the north-west

through Lairg. Inverness Traction (☎ 239292) has a Monday to Saturday service to Lairg (Sunday too in summer). In summer, buses also operate through to Durness. There's also a Monday to Saturday postbus service (☎ 256228), travelling Lairg-Tongue-Durness.

Train Phone ☎ 0345-484950 for Inverness rail inquiries. London to Inverness costs £59 most weekdays and takes nine to 10 hours. There are direct trains from Aberdeen (£15), Edinburgh (£26.50) and Glasgow (£26.50).

The line from Inverness to Kyle of Lochalsh offers one of the greatest scenic journeys in Britain. There are three trains a day on both routes (none on Sunday). The trip to Kyle of Lochalsh (£13.50) takes 2½ hours. The trip to Thurso (3¾ hours, £11.50) connects with the ferry to Orkney.

Car The TIC has a handy *Car Hire* leaflet. The big boys charge from around £36 per day or you could try Sharp's Reliable Wrecks (☎ 236694), 1st Floor, Highland Rail House, Station Square, for cheaper cars and vans.

Getting Around

Bus The airport is eight miles out and a bus service connects with most flights for £2.30. A taxi costs £8 to £9.

Inverness Traction (☎ 239292) and Highland Country Buses operate buses to places around Inverness including Nairn, Forres, the Culloden Battlefield, Beauly, Dingwall and Lairg. An Inverness Traction Day Rover Highland ticket costs £5/3, while a Highland Bus Day Rover ticket costs £6/3. The Highland Bus return fare to Culloden is £2; to Cawdor it's £3.55.

Bicycle There are some great cycling opportunities out of Inverness and numerous rental operators. Sharp's (see the preceding Car section) also has mountain bikes at £9 per day. Others are Thornton Cycles (☎ 222810) at 23 Castle St and Pedalway (☎ 233456) at 7 Lovat Rd.

AROUND INVERNESS
Beauly

In 1584, Mary Queen of Scots is said to have given this village (population 1100) its name when she exclaimed, in French, 'quel beau lieu' (what a beautiful place). **Beauly Priory** was founded in 1230 but is now a ruin. At the **Aigas Dam fish lift**, you can watch salmon taking advantage of a dam by-pass. It's open mid-June to early October, Monday to Friday, 10 am to 3 pm. Beauly has B&Bs, hotels and a couple of camping grounds.

Black Isle & Cromarty

Actually a peninsula rather than an island, Black Isle can be reached from Inverness by a short cut across the **Kessock Bridge**. At **Fortrose** the 14th-century south aisle and chapel are almost all that remains of medieval Fortrose Cathedral. In **Rosemarkie** the Groam House Museum (☎ 01381-620961) has a superb collection of Pictish stones incised with designs like those on Celtic Irish stones. It's open over Easter and from May to October, Monday to Saturday from 10 am to 5 pm, and Sunday from 2 to 4.30 pm (2 to 4 pm at weekends in winter); admission is £1.50/50p. A free leaflet describes a *Pictish Trail* of carved stones in nearby villages.

At the peninsula's eastern end the pretty village of Cromarty is full of gabled 18th-century stone houses, several now offering B&B from £13 a head; try *The Cobbles* (☎ 01381-600374) or *The Retreat* (☎ 01381-600400) in Church St. There's also a pleasant teashop *(Binnies)* in the High St, an inviting restaurant *(Thistles)* in Church St and a good pub *(The Cromarty Arms)* doing pub food.

Opposite the pub in Church St, Cromarty Courthouse (☎ 01381-600418) has a thoroughly interesting local-history museum, open April to October, daily from 10 am to 6 pm, shorter hours in winter; the £3/2 admission fee includes loan of headsets for a recorded tour of Cromarty's other historic buildings. Next to the Courthouse is author Hugh Miller's tiny thatched cottage (☎ 01381-600245; NTS). It's open Easter, and May to September, daily from 10 am to 1 pm and 2 to 5.30 pm; £1.60/1.

The Cromarty Firth is famous for the huge offshore oil rigs which are built here before being towed out to the North Sea, but Dolphin Ecosse (☎ 01381-600323) runs boat trips along it to see bottlenose dolphins and other wildlife.

From April to October a ferry (☎ 01862-871254) crosses between Cromarty and Nigg every half hour, cutting driving time to Invergordon. It costs £1.60 for passengers and £4.45 for car and driver, but there's only space for two cars. The church in Nigg village contains a fine Pictish carved stone. You can see it from Easter to October from 10 am to 4.30 pm, 5 pm on Sunday.

Cawdor

Cawdor Castle (☎ 01667-404615), the 14th-century home of the Thanes of Cawdor, was reputedly Macbeth's castle and the scene of Duncan's murder. The central tower dates from the 14th century but the wings were 17th-century additions. It's open May to October, daily from 10 am to 5 pm; £4.70/2.50.

Cawdor Tavern (☎ 01667-404777) in the village is worth a stop. Deciding what to drink can be difficult as they stock over 100 varieties of whisky. There's also good pub grub, with most specials under £6.

Culloden

Culloden is about six miles east of Inverness. The Battle of Culloden in 1746, the last fought on British soil, saw the defeat of Bonnie Prince Charlie and the slaughter of 1200 Highlanders in a 68-minute rout. The Duke of Cumberland won the label Butcher Cumberland for his brutal treatment of the defeated Scottish forces. The battle sounded the death knell of the old clan system, and the horrors of the clearances (see the Dunrobin Castle section) soon followed. The sombre 122-acre moor where the conflict took place has scarcely changed in the ensuing 250 years. The site, with its many markers and memorials, is always open.

The visitor centre (☎ 01463-790607; NTS) offers a 15-minute audiovisual presentation on the battle. It's open in summer, daily from 9 am to 6 pm, shorter hours in winter, closed completely in January. Admission is £2.60/1.70.

Clava Cairns
Clearly signposted 1½ miles east of Culloden, the Clava Cairns are a picturesque group of cairns and stone circles dating from the late Neolithic period (around 4000 to 2000 BC). There's a superb railway viaduct nearby.

Fort George
Covering much of the headland is a virtually unaltered, 18th-century artillery fortification, one of the best examples of its kind in Europe. It was completed in 1769 as a base for George II's army. The mile-plus walk around the ramparts offers fine views out to sea and back to the Great Glen. Given its size, you'll need several hours to look around. There's a visitors centre (☎ 01667-462777; HS). Admission costs £2.50/1.

Brodie Castle
Set in 175 acres of parkland, the castle (☎ 01309-641371; NTS) is eight miles east of the small seaside town of Nairn. Although the Brodies have been living here since 1160, the present structure dates from the 16th century. You can look round several rooms, some with wildly extravagant ceilings, but you may find the nannying of the NTS volunteer helpers offputting. Don't miss the huge Victorian kitchen beyond the small café.

The castle is open April to September from 11 am to 4.30 pm (1.30 to 4.30 pm on Sunday); £3.60/2.40. There are also woodland walks and an observation hide by the pond. Bluebird Bus No 10 takes ¾ hour to reach Brodie from Inverness via Culloden.

East Coast

The east coast starts to get interesting once you leave behind Invergordon's industrial development. Beyond this, great heather-covered hills heave themselves out of the wild North Sea, with touristy little towns moored precariously at their edge.

DINGWALL TO BONAR BRIDGE
Located at the head of Cromarty Firth, Dingwall (population 5000; ☎ 01349) was the legendary birthplace of Macbeth. Local military hero Sir Hector MacDonald features in the museum (☎ 65366) on High St (open May to September only) and in a monument overlooking the town.

Sir Hector Munro, another military hero, commemorated his most notable victory, the capture of the Indian town of Negapatam in 1781, by erecting the Fyrish Monument, a replica of the town's gateway, high above nearby **Evanton**. Turn towards Boath off the B9176; from the car park it's a 45-minute walk along the Jubilee Path.

Invergordon is the main centre for repairing North Sea oil rigs in the Cromarty Firth.

Tain was a centre for the management of the Clearances and has a curious 16th-century tolbooth in the town centre. St Duthac was born in Tain, died in Armagh (Ireland) in 1065, and is commemorated by the 11th to 12th-century ruins of St Duthac's Chapel, as well as by St Duthus Church, now part of a new **Tain Through Time** heritage centre (☎ 01862-894089), open daily from April to October from 10 am to 6 pm for £3/1.50.

The A9 goes right across Dornoch Firth. Alternatively, from Ardgay at the head of Dornoch Firth, a road leads 10 miles up Strathcarron to **Croick**, scene of notorious evictions during the 1845 Clearances. Refugee crofters from Glencalvie scratched their sad messages on the east windows of Croick Church.

Another detour from Ardgay leads to **Carbisdale Castle** (dating from 1914), which now houses Scotland's largest *Youth Hostel* (☎ 01549-421232). It's open from March to October and charges £9.65/8.25. The sweeping **Bonar Bridge** then crosses the head of the firth to rejoin the A9 just before Dornoch.

DORNOCH

• *pop 1000* • ☎ *01862*

On the coast, two miles off the A9, Dornoch is a pleasant seaside town clustered around **Dornoch Cathedral**. The original building was destroyed in 1570 during a clan feud. Despite some patching up, it wasn't completely rebuilt until 1835-37.

The TIC (☎ 810400) is in the main square.

Dornoch has several camping grounds and plenty of B&Bs. If you want to stay in grand *Dornoch Castle* (☎ 810216), the 16th-century former Bishop's Palace, the nightly, high-season cost is from £37/65 a single/double. *Sutherland House* (☎ 811023) just off the Square has cheap pub-style food (burgers from £4.50), or you can dine in style at Dornoch Castle for £19.

South of Dornoch, seals are often visible on the sand bars of **Dornoch Firth**.

North of Dornoch the A9 crosses the head of **Loch Fleet** on the Mound, an embankment built by Telford in 1815-6.

DUNROBIN CASTLE

Dunrobin Castle (☎ 01408-633177), the largest house in the Highlands (187 rooms), dates back to the 14th century. Additions were made in the mid-1600s and late 1700s, but most of what you see today was built in French style between 1845-50. One of the homes of the Earls and Dukes of Sutherland, it's richly furnished and offers an insight into their opulent lifestyle.

Judging by the numerous hunting trophies and animal skins, much family energy seems to have been gone into hunting. The house also displays innumerable gifts from farm tenants (probably grateful that they hadn't been asked to join in the Sutherlands' clearance activities). Behind the house formal gardens slope down to the sea and a summer house offers an eclectic museum of archaeological finds, natural-history exhibits and more big-game trophies.

One mile north of Golspie, the house is open at Easter and then May to mid-October, Monday to Saturday from 10.30 am to 5 pm, Sunday from 1 to 5 pm; in May and October last entry is 4 pm; £4.50/2.80.

BRORA & HEMSDALE

Between Dunrobin and Brora, the **Carn Liath Broch** is a well-preserved Iron-Age fort.

Brora, at the mouth of a river famed for its salmon, has a fine beach and plenty of B&Bs.

Helmsdale, with its pretty harbour and salmon river, is busy in summer and has a

Crofting & the Clearances

Many Highland settlements are described as crofting communities. The word croft comes from the Gaelic *coirtean*, meaning a small enclosed field. Until the early 19th century, Highland land was generally owned by clan chiefs, and their tenants farmed land on the 'run-rig' system. The land was divided into strips which were shared among the tenants. The strips were periodically shuffled around so no tenant was stuck with bad land or always enjoyed the good land. Unfortunately, it also meant they might end up with several widely scattered strips and with no incentive to improve them because they knew they would soon lose them. Accordingly, the system was changed and the land rented out to the tenants as small 'crofts', averaging about three acres. Each tenant then built their own house on their croft and the former tight cluster of homes became scattered. Crofters could also graze their animals on the common grazings, land which was jointly held by all the local crofters.

Crofting remained a precarious life. The small patch of land barely provided a living and each year the tenancy could be terminated and the crofter lose not only the croft but the house they had built on it. During the Highland Clearances, when many clan chiefs decided sheep farming was more profitable than collecting rent from poverty-stricken crofters, that was exactly what happened. The guidebook to Dunrobin Castle, seat of the Sutherland family, blithely notes that this family 'proceeded to make large-scale improvements to Sutherland's communications, land and townships which involved the clearance of some 5000 people from their ancestral dwellings'. Crofting tenancies still exist but complex regulations now protect the crofters. ■

well-stocked TIC (☎ 01431-821640) on the south side of town. The **Timespan Heritage Centre** (☎ 01431-821327) has details of a mid-19th-century Highlands gold rush and a model of Barbara Cartland (see below). It's open Easter to mid-October, Monday to Saturday from 10 am to 5 pm, Sunday from 2 to 5 pm; £2.75/1.65.

There are several B&Bs, or a bed at *Helmsdale Youth Hostel* (☎ 821577) costs £4.10/3.40. It's open from mid-May to September, but book well ahead for July or August.

Barbara Cartland, queen of romantic novelists, has been holidaying in Helmsdale for 62 years. You're unlikely to spot her, but Nancy Sinclair, proprietor of the *La Mirage* fish & chip shop in Dunrobin St (all-in fish supper £5.95), is a dead ringer for Cartland – they share the same hairdresser.

HELMSDALE TO DUNBEATH

North of Helmsdale, the road climbs to a fine viewpoint at the **Ord of Caithness**. About seven miles north of Helmsdale, it's a 15-minute walk along a footpath from the A9 to **Badbea**, where the ruins of crofts are perched on the clifftop. **Berriedale** has a llama farm and in early summer there are puffin colonies on the seashore. Just north of Dunbeath, the **Laidhay Croft Museum** (☎ 01593-731244) recreates crofting life from the mid-1800s to WWII. It's open Easter to October from 10 am to 6 pm; £1/20p.

CELTIC SITES

At the **Clann Gunn Centre** (☎ 015932-731370) in Latheron you learn that it was really a Scot, not Christopher Columbus, who discovered America. It's open June to September, Monday to Saturday from 11 am to 5 pm; Sunday in July and August from 2 to 5 pm; £1.20/75p.

There are several Celtic sites between Dunbeath and Wick. Turn north on the A895 at Latheron, and at Achavanich, wedged between Loch Rangag and Loch Stemster, double back on the road to Lybster to the 40 or so **Achavanich Standing Stones**. Continue on this road back to the main A9.

Just beyond Lybster, a turn-off leads to the **Grey Cairns of Camster**, five miles north of the A9. Dating from between 4000 and 2500 BC, the burial chambers are hidden in long, low mounds rising from an evocatively desolate stretch of moor. The Long Cairn is 200 feet by 70 feet. You can enter the main chamber but must crawl into the well-preserved Round Cairn. Afterwards you can continue seven miles north on this remote road to approach Wick on the A882.

The **Hill o'Many Stanes**, just beyond the Camster turn-off, is a curious, fan-shaped arrangement of 22 rows of small stones probably dating from around 2000 BC. Nearer to Wick at Whaligoe, the **Cairn of Get** is a quarter-mile off the A9, and then a long walk. Steps lead down to small, picturesque **Whaligoe** harbour, directly opposite the Cairn of Get.

WICK

- **pop 8000**   • ☎ 01955

Wick is a sad little town full of cut-price shops and boarded-up buildings, but the Heritage Centre definitely shouldn't be missed. Things were very different a century ago when Wick was the world's largest herring fishing port, its harbour crammed with fishing boats and larger ships to carry barrels of salted herring abroad, and thousands of seasonal workers streaming into town to pack the catch. After WWI, the herring began to disappear, and by WWII the town had died.

Wick's massive harbour was the work of the engineer and canal pioneer Thomas Telford, who also designed Pulteneytown, the model town commissioned by the engagingly named British Society for Extending the Fisheries & Improving the Sea Coasts of the Kingdom. A failed attempt to add a breakwater was the work of Thomas Stevenson, father of author Robert Louis Stevenson.

Information

The TIC (☎ 602596) is in Whitechapel Rd,

the road leading to the supermarket car park off High St.

Wick Heritage Centre

The town's award-winning local museum (☎ 605393) in Bank Row deserves all the praise heaped upon it. It tracks the rise and fall of the herring industry, and displays everything from fishing equipment to complete herring fishing boats.

The Johnston photographic collection is the museum's star exhibit. From 1863 to 1977, three generations of Johnstons photographed everything that happened around Wick, and the 70,000 photographs are an amazing portrait of the town's life. The museum even displays Johnston's photo studio; prints of superb early photos are for sale.

It's open May to mid-September, Monday to Saturday from 10 am to 5 pm; £2/50p.

Other Things to See

South of town, a path leads to the 12th-century ruins of **Old Wick Castle**, with the spectacular rock formations of the **Brough** and the **Brig**, or **Gote o'Trams**, just to the south. In good weather, it's a fine coastal walk to the castle.

Just past Wick airport, on the north side of town, you can watch the glass-blowing operations in **Caithness Glass Visitors Centre** (☎ 602286), Monday to Friday from 9 am to 4.30 pm. The shop stays open until 5 pm daily, opening at 11 am on Sunday.

Places to Stay

Riverside Caravan Club Site (☎ 605420), in Riverside Drive close to the centre, charges £4.50 for a car and a tent.

Wick's B&Bs tend to be rather anonymous. The *County Guest House* (☎ 602911) at 101 High St has rooms from £13 to £14 per person. At 41-43 High St, right behind the TIC, the *Wellington Guest House* (☎ 603287) has singles/doubles at £25/40. At 6 Rose St, close to the waterfront, the *Harbour Guest House* (☎ 603276) has singles/doubles from £15/26. At 7 Sinclair

Terrace, *Dunelm* (☎ 602120) has rooms from £15/28.

Places to Eat

There's a *Harbour Chip Shop* on Harbour Quay, and the *Lorne Restaurant* (☎ 602393) with a lasagne & chips-style menu near the Heritage Centre at 38 Bank Row, but most places are along High St and its continuation, The Shore. On The Shore, you'll find the *Spring Garden* Chinese takeaway, *Cabrelli's Café*, *Carter's*, with pub-style food, and the *Waterfront* (☎ 602550), a cavernous disco/nightclub with a pub-food menu.

Getting There & Away

Wick is 280 miles from Edinburgh and 125 from Inverness.

GillAir and British Airways Express fly to Wick from Aberdeen, Edinburgh and Orkney. There are regular bus and train services from Inverness to Wick and on to Thurso; see the Inverness section for details.

Getting Around

Richard's Garage (☎ 604123) on Francis St rents cars and bicycles.

JOHN O'GROATS

Sadly the coast at the country's north-east tip is not particularly dramatic, and modern John o'Groats is little more than a ramshackle tourist trap. Its name comes from Jan de Groot, one of three brothers commissioned by James IV to operate a ferry service to Orkney in 1496 for just four pence.

Two miles east of John o'Groats is **Duncansby Head**, home to many seabirds at the start of summer. A path leads to **Duncansby Stacks**, a spectacular natural rock formation soaring over 200 feet above the sea. There are a series of narrow inlets and deep coves on this wonderful stretch of coast.

The TIC (☎ 01955-611373) is open at Easter, and then May to September. There are also shops and a crafts complex.

Places to Stay & Eat

Three miles west of John o'Groats at Canisbay, the *John o'Groats Youth Hostel* (☎ 01955-611424) is open from April through October and costs £5.40/4.40. There are several B&Bs in John o'Groats and nearby Canisbay and a couple of camping grounds. The big *John o'Groats House Hotel* (☎ 01955-611203) has a reasonable restaurant, or there's the *Crofters Coffee Shop* for simple meals.

Getting There & Away

Highland Country Buses (☎ 01847-893123) runs regular buses to John o'Groats from Wick or Thurso for £2 from Monday to Saturday, and on Sunday from mid-May.

From May to September the MV *Pentland Venture* (☎ 01955-611353) shuttles across to Orkney; there's a free bus link from Thurso railway station. Day trips cost £27/13.50.

See the Inverness section for details of the Orkney Bus, which takes you straight to the islands from Inverness. See the Orkney section later in this chapter for ferry details.

DUNNET HEAD

Contrary to popular belief, John o'Groats is not the mainland's most northerly point, an honour which goes to Dunnet Head, a few miles to the west. The head is marked by a lighthouse that dates from 1832. The tricky Pentland Firth, the strait between Orkney and the mainland, stretches from Duncansby Head to Dunnet Head. *Dunnet Head Tearoom* (☎ 01847-851774) offers economically priced food, including meals for vegetarians, and B&B from £12 a head.

Just past Dunnet Head and a magnificent stretch of sandy beach, there's a turning to the tiny harbour at **Castlehill** where a heritage trail explains the evolution of the local flagstone industry.

North & West Coast

From just beyond Thurso, the coast round to Ullapool is mind-blowing. Everything is massive – vast, empty spaces, enormous lochs and snow-capped mountains. Ullapool

is the most northerly town of any significance and there's more brilliant coast round to Gairloch, along the incomparable Loch Maree and down to Kyle of Lochalsh (a short hop from Skye). From here you're back in the land of the tour bus; civilisation (and main roads) can be quite a shock after all the empty space.

Banks and petrol stations are few and far between in this corner of Scotland, so check your funds and fuel before setting out.

GETTING AROUND

Local tourist offices have excellent information leaflets about the coast route. Look for *Scotland's North Coast* (John o'Groats to Durness), *West Sutherland Coastal Route* (Durness to Elphin, just before Ullapool) and *Wester Ross Coastal Route* (Elphin to Kyle of Lochalsh).

Public transport in the north-west is very patchy. Getting to Thurso by bus or train is no problem, but then the problems start. Monday to Saturday there are services from Thurso to Bettyhill, but none further along the coast. Your only hope is one of the schoolbuses which only operate during term time, and only take passengers if the driver is willing.

The alternative is to come up from Inverness via Lairg. There are trains and Inverness Traction buses to Lairg, except on Sunday. In summer, the buses continue to Durness. Monday to Saturday postbus services (☎ 01463-234111) operate the Lairg-Tongue-Durness route and from Lairg to Lochinver; there are also services around the coast from Elphin to Scourie, from Drumbeg to Lochinver and from Shieldaig to Kishorn via Applecross, but always with gaps between towns. There are regular bus services between Inverness and Ullapool.

Renting a car or hitching are the other options.

THURSO & SCRABSTER

• *pop 9000*   • ☎ *01847*

The most northerly town on the mainland, Thurso is a fairly large, fairly bleak place looking across the Pentland Firth to Hoy, in

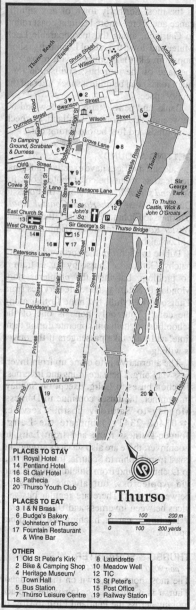

PLACES TO STAY
11 Royal Hotel
14 Pentland Hotel
16 St Clair Hotel
18 Pathecia
20 Thurso Youth Club

PLACES TO EAT
3 I & N Brass
6 Budge's Bakery
9 Johnston of Thurso
17 Fountain Restaurant
& Wine Bar

OTHER
1 Old St Peter's Kirk
2 Bike & Camping Shop
3 Heritage Museum/
Town Hall
5 Bus Station
7 Thurso Leisure Centre
8 Laundrette
10 Meadow Well
12 TIC
13 St Peter's
15 Post Office
19 Railway Station

Thurso

0   100   200 m
0   100   200 yards

Orkney. Medieval Thurso was Scotland's major port for trade with Scandinavia. Today, ferries cross from Scrabster, 2½ miles west of Thurso, to Orkney. The ferry aside, Scrabster is little more than a collection of BP oil storage containers.

Information
The TIC (☎ 892371), Riverside Rd, is open from Easter to October, daily in summer.

Things to See & Do
There's a **Heritage Museum** (☎ 892459) in Thurso Town Hall (open in summer). The ruins of **Old St Peter's Kirk** date mainly from the 15th and 16th centuries, but the original church on the site may have been centuries older. The small round building over the **Meadow Well** marks the site of a former well.

Thurso is an unlikely surfing centre, but the nearby coast has arguably the best and most regular surf in Britain. There's an excellent right-hand reef break on the east side of town, directly in front of Lord Caithness's castle, and another shallow reef break five miles west at Brimms Ness.

North of Scrabster harbour, there's a fine cliff walk along Holborn Head. Take care in windy weather.

Places to Stay
In July and August *Thurso Youth Club* (☎ 892964), Old Mill, Millbank, has basic dorm accommodation for £8; phone ahead to check though. *Thurso Camping Site* (☎ 893761) is by the coast, on the edge of Thurso towards Scrabster.

Thurso has many moderately priced B&Bs and the TIC charges £1 for local bookings. *Pathecia* (☎ 894751) at 3 Janet St costs from £13 to £15 per person, with another £1 to use the spa bath. Also centrally located on Sinclair St is the large *St Clair Hotel* (☎ 893730), with rooms from £25/42. The *Royal Hotel* (☎ 893191) on Traill St has singles from £20 to £32, and doubles from £35 to £52.

Places to Eat

Basic cafés include *Budge's Bakery* in the pedestrian mall and *Johnston of Thurso* at 10 Traill St. The *Fountain Restaurant & Wine Bar* (☎ 896351), at 2 Sinclair St by the square, has Indian, Chinese and European menus. It's not especially cheap but is the only place likely to be open after 7 pm. *I & N Brass* on Swanson St has good local ice cream.

Getting There & Away

Thurso is 290 miles from Edinburgh, 130 from Inverness and 21 from Wick. From Inverness, trains and Citylink buses operate via Wick to Thurso. There are four train services daily in summer, but space for bicycles is limited so book ahead. Highland Country Buses (☎ 893123) operate Wick-Thurso-Dounreay.

Getting Around

It's a two-mile walk from Thurso railway station to the ferry port at Scrabster, or there are buses for 70p. The Bike & Camping Shop (☎ 896124), The Arcade, 34 High St, rents mountain bikes from £6.50 a day. William Dunnet & Co (☎ 893101), Northern Motors (☎ 892777) and Practical Car Hire (☎ 894656) all rent cars.

THURSO TO DURNESS

It's 74 winding and often spectacular coastal miles from Thurso to Durness. Ten miles west of Thurso, on the coast at **Dounreay**, is an experimental nuclear power station. Just beyond Dounreay, **Reay** has fine beaches and an interesting little harbour. **Melvich** overlooks a fine beach and there are great views from **Strathy Point** – from the coast road, it's a two-mile drive, then a 15-minute walk.

Bettyhill is a crofting community named after Elizabeth, Countess of Sutherland, who kicked her tenants off their land at Strathnaver to make way for more profitable sheep, then resettled the tenants here. The **Strathnaver Museum** (☎ 01641-521418), in an old church in Bettyhill, tells the sad story. It's open Easter to September, Monday

to Saturday from 10 am to 1 pm and 2 to 5 pm; £1.50/40p. There's a Pictish cross in the graveyard behind the museum. From Bettyhill the B871 turns south for Helmsdale, through **Strathnaver**, where the Clearances took place.

The wonderful beach at **Coldbackie** is overlooked by the Watch Hill viewpoint. Only two miles further on is **Tongue**, overlooked by the 14th-century ruins of Castle Varrich. Down by the causeway, *Tongue Youth Hostel* (☎ 01847-611301) has a spectacular location looking up and down the Kyle of Tongue (a kyle is a narrow strait) for a nightly cost of £5.40/4.40.

From Tongue it's 30 miles to Durness – you can take the causeway across the **Kyle of Tongue** or the beautiful old road which climbs up to the head of the Kyle. A detour to **Melness** and **Port Vasgo** may be rewarded with the sight of seals on the beach. Continuing west, the road crosses a desolate moor past **Moine House** to the northern end of **Loch Hope**. A 10-mile detour up the loch leads to **Dun Dornaigil**, a well-preserved broch in the shadow of **Ben Hope** (3041 feet). If you'd like to bag this Munro it's a three to four-hour round trip along the route from the car park, which is two miles before the broch. Beyond Loch Hope, **Heilam** has stunning views out over **Loch Eriboll**, Britain's deepest sea inlet.

DURNESS

- *pop 300*   • ☎ *01971*

Durness trails from the **Smoo Cave**, a mile east of the village centre. The vast cave entry stands at the end of an inlet, or *geo*. A river cascades right through its roof and then flows out to sea. You can take a boat trip (£2/1) into the cave, although after heavy rain the waterfall can make it impossible to get past. Durness has several beautiful beaches, starting at Rispond to the east, and the sea offers some superb scuba-diving sites complete with wrecks, caves, seals and whales.

A disused radar station at **Balnakeil**, less than a mile beyond Durness, has been turned into a scruffy craft village. A walk along the beach to the north leads to **Faraid Head**, where puffin colonies can be seen in early summer.

Information

The TIC (☎ 511259) is open Easter to October, and has slide shows at the Village Hall and guided walks in summer.

Places to Stay & Eat

Durness Youth Hostel (☎ 511244) is at Smoo, on the east side of the village. It's open mid-May to September and costs £4.10/3.40 but is pretty basic. *Sango Sands Caravan Park* (☎ 511222) has camping grounds and the *Oasis Café*, one of the few places to eat in Durness. The pub food is unexceptional but there is a vegetarian selection. *Smoo Cave Hotel* (☎ 511227) does B&B from £15 a head and straightforward pub fare. Durness also has several private B&Bs, like *Morven* (☎ 511252) or *Puffin Cottage* (☎ 511208) from £14 per person.

DURNESS TO ULLAPOOL

It's 71 miles from Durness to Ullapool, with plenty of side trips and diversions to make along the way.

Cape Wrath

The cape is crowned by a lighthouse (dating from 1827) and stands close to the seabird colonies on Clo Mor Cliffs, the highest sea cliffs on the mainland. Getting to Cape Wrath involves a ferry ride (☎ 01971-511376) across the Kyle of Durness (£2 return) and a connecting minibus (☎ 01971-511287) for the 11 miles to the cape (£6 return). The services operate from May to September daily, and up to eight times a day in July and August.

South of Cape Wrath, **Sandwood Bay** boasts one of Britain's most isolated beaches. It's about two miles north from the end of the road running beyond Blairmore, but you should allow all day to walk from the cape south to the beach and on to Blairmore.

Handa Island & Scourie

Boats go out to Handa Island's important seabird sanctuary from Tarbet. You may see skuas and puffins, as well as seals. The **Old Man of Stoer** can be seen across Eddrachillis Bay. Scourie is a pretty crofting community with a well-known herd of highland cattle.

Kylesku & Loch Glencoul

Cruises on Loch Glencoul pass seal colonies and the 700-foot drop of **Eas-Coul-Aulin**, Britain's highest waterfall. In summer, Statesman Cruises (☎ 01571-844446) operate two-hour trips at 11 am and 2 pm from Kylesku Old Ferry Pier for £7.50/2.50. While you wait, you can have a pint and a snack or meal in *Kylesku Hotel* (☎ 01971-502231) overlooking the pier.

It's a fine three-hour, six-mile (round trip) walk to the top of the falls, starting from beside Loch na Gainmhich at the top of the climb out of Kylesku towards Ullapool. The OS Landranger 15 map shows the route.

The Old Man of Stoer

It's a roughly 30-mile detour off the main A894 to the Point of Stoer and the Rhu Stoer Lighthouse (1870) and back to the main road again. Along the coast road you need to be prepared for single-car-width roads, blind bends and summits...and sheep. The rewards are spectacular views, pretty villages and excellent beaches along the way. From the lighthouse, it's a good one-hour cliff walk to the Old Man of Stoer, a spectacular sea stack (a tower of rock rising from the sea). There are more good beaches between Stoer and Lochinver.

Lochinver

(population 300; ☎ 01571)
This popular little fishing port has a TIC (☎ 844330), open late March to October, a camping ground and the *Lochinver Youth Hostel* (☎ 844480) at Achmelvich, which costs £4.10/3.40. There are numerous B&Bs, and the sprawling waterfront *Culag Hotel* (☎ 844270), with beds from £20. The *Lochinver Larder & Riverside Bistro* (☎ 844356) has interesting local food, especially fish, to eat in or take away.

The hills of Assynt near Lochinver are

popular with walkers and include peaks like Suilven (2399 feet), Quinag (2651 feet), Ben More Assynt (3273 feet) and Canisp (2779 feet). The *Assynt Field Centre* (☎ 822218), in Inchnadamph on the Lochinver-Durness road, has 50 beds from £8.50. It's ideal for walkers and climbers.

The detour to the Old Man of Stoer and Lochinver returns to the main road at **Skiag Bridge**, by Loch Assynt.

Knockan & Inverpolly Forest

There's an information centre and geological and nature trails at Knockan, beside Inverpolly Forest, which has numerous glacial lochs and the three peaks of Cul Mor (2786 feet), Stac Polly (2010 feet) and Cul Beag (2523 feet). There are good views of Isle Martin from just before Ardmair and then of the Summer Isles, Loch Broom and Ullapool itself.

Reached by a circuitous route around Loch Lurgainn, Achiltibuie's **Hydroponicum** (☎ 01854-622202) grows tropical fruits and flowers. From April to September tours operate on the hour from 10 am to 5 pm, and cost £3.50/2. Boat trips also operate to the Summer Isles.

ULLAPOOL

• *pop 1000* • ☎ *01854*

Ullapool is a pretty fishing village from where ferries sail to Stornoway on the Isle of Lewis. Small though it is, Ullapool is the biggest settlement in Wester Ross. Although it's a long way around the coast in either direction, Ullapool is only 48 miles from Inverness via the A835 along beautiful Loch Broom. The small **Ullapool Museum**, in a church in West Argyle St, is open April to October, Monday to Saturday from 10 am to 6 pm; noon to 4 pm in winter; £2/free.

Information

The TIC (☎ 612987) at 6 Argyle St is open from April to November, daily from May to September. The only bank is the Royal Bank of Scotland in Ladysmith St. Ceilidh Place (see below) has an excellent bookshop, with lots of books on Scottish topics.

Places to Stay

The harbourside *Ullapool Youth Hostel* (☎ 612254) is open from mid-March to October. The nightly cost is £6.95/5.58; booking is advisable in Easter and summer. At the time of writing *West House* (☎ 612734) in West Argyle St was being converted into a bunkhouse where beds will probably cost about £8 a head. *Broomfield Holiday Park* (☎ 612664) has camping from £4 (hiker and tent) up to £8 or £9 (car and tent).

There are lots of B&Bs and guesthouses along Seaforth and Pulteney Rds, and on Argyle St near the Quay St junction. The *Arch Inn* (☎ 612454) at 11 West Shore St has rooms from £16 to £24 per person. Also right on the waterfront in Shore St, the *Brae Guest House* (☎ 612421) has rooms with and without bath from £15 per person.

The friendly *Eilean Donan Guest House* (☎ 612524) at 14 Market St has rooms from £15 per person. Nearby, *Ladysmith House* (☎ 612185) in Pulteney St charges from £18 per person. At the *Old Surgery Guest House* (☎ 612520) at 3 West Terrace, rooms with private bath cost £20 a head.

The *Ceilidh Place* (☎ 612103) at 14 West Argyle St has a hotel with rooms for £55 per person, or £50 for stays of three days or more; the much cheaper clubhouse section costs £10 to £14 per person. The big *Caledonian Hotel* (☎ 612306) in Quay St offers rooms with private bath from £30 to £47 a single, and £50 to £82 a double.

Places to Eat

Upstairs at the junction of Quay and Shore Sts, the *Quay Plaice Restaurant & Café* (☎ 612122) does good fish & chips. The *Arch Inn* (☎ 612454) and the *Ferry Boat Inn* (☎ 612366), both in Shore St, do pub food at lunch time and early evening. The *Scottish Larder* (☎ 612185) in Pulteney St does all sorts of pies from £4.25. For pricier restaurant meals the *Argyle Hotel* (☎ 612422) does full menus, with fish main courses from £5.25.

The *Ceilidh Place* (☎ 612103) has a daytime café (from 10 am) and a much

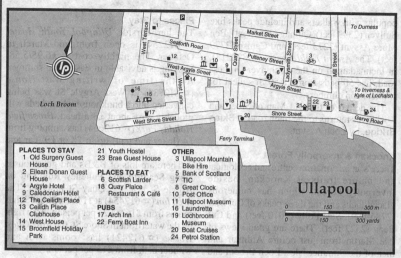

PLACES TO STAY
1 Old Surgery Guest House
2 Eilean Donan Guest House
4 Argyle Hotel
9 Caledonian Hotel
12 The Ceilidh Place
13 Ceilidh Place Clubhouse
14 West House
15 Broomfield Holiday Park

21 Youth Hostel
23 Brae Guest House

PLACES TO EAT
6 Scottish Larder
18 Quay Place Restaurant & Café

PUBS
17 Arch Inn
22 Ferry Boat Inn

OTHER
3 Ullapool Mountain Bike Hire
5 Bank of Scotland
7 TIC
8 Great Clock
10 Post Office
11 Ullapool Museum
16 Laundrette
19 Lochbroom Museum
20 Boat Cruises
24 Petrol Station

Ullapool

pricier evening restaurant, with dishes like filled crêpes from £8.95. It's also Ullapool's main entertainment centre, with live music most nights in summer.

Getting There & Away
Ullapool is 215 miles from Edinburgh and 60 from Inverness. See the Inverness section for information on bus and train links with the ferry to Stornoway on Lewis.

Getting Around
Bikes can be rented from Ullapool Mountain Bike Hire, 11 Pulteney St, for £10 a day.

Islander Cruises (☎ 612385) operates trips to the Summer Islands, landing on Bird Island, from 10.30 am in summer.

ULLAPOOL TO KYLE OF LOCHALSH
Although it's less than 50 miles as the crow flies from Ullapool to Kyle of Lochalsh, it's more like 150 miles along the circuitous coastal road, with fine views of beaches and bays backed by mountains all along the way.

Falls of Measach
The A832 doubles back to the coast from the A835, 12 miles from Ullapool. Just before

the junction, the Falls of Measach ('ugly' in Gaelic) spill 150 feet into the spectacularly deep and narrow Corrieshalloch Gorge.

Inverewe Gardens
At Poolewe on Loch Ewe, the subtropical Inverewe Gardens (☎ 01445-718229; NTS) are a testament to the warming influence of the Gulf Stream. The gardens were founded by Osgood Mackenzie in 1862 – a barren, windswept peninsula was gradually transformed into a luxuriant, colourful 64-acre garden. They're open all year, daily from 9.30 am to sunset; £3.60/2.40. Afterwards there's a bright new restaurant for soup and sandwich lunches.

Gairloch
This small town's **Heritage Museum** (☎ 01445-712287) tells of life in the west highlands, complete with a typical crofting cottage. It's open Easter to September, Monday to Saturday from 10 am to 5 pm; £1.50/50p. The TIC (☎ 712130) is across the car park.

For accommodation, there's a remote *Youth Hostel* (☎ 712219) at Carn Dearg, near Gairloch, which costs £5.40/4.40, and a *bunkhouse* (☎ 741291) at nearby Badachro with 13 beds for £7. There's plenty of B&B accommodation and bigger hotels like the *Myrtle Bank* (☎ 712004), which has rooms with attached bathroom from £28 to £36 per person.

Loch Maree & Victoria Falls
The A832 runs alongside craggy Loch Maree, sprinkled with islands and with a series of peaks along the north shore culminating in 3217-foot-high Ben Slioch. The Victoria Falls (commemorating Queen Victoria's 1877 visit) tumble down to the loch between Slattadale and Talladale. Look for the 'Hydro Power' signs to find it.

Kinlochewe to Torridon
Small Kinlochewe is a good base for outdoor activities. From here the road follows Glen Torridon, overlooked by the multiple peaks of Beinn Eighe (3309 feet) and Liathach (3456 feet). The road reaches the sea at Torridon, where a countryside centre offers information on walks in this rugged area. The Torridon *Youth Hostel* (☎ 01445-791284) charges £6.95/5.85.

Applecross & Loch Carron
A long side trip abandons the A896 to follow the coast road via the seaside village of Applecross. Turning inland from Applecross, the road climbs to the Bealachna Bo pass (2053 feet), then drops steeply to rejoin the A896. This winding, precipitous road can be closed in winter.

The road continues through the village of Lochcarron, then skirts Loch Carron itself.

PLOCKTON
• *pop 400* • ☎ 01599
From Stromeferry, there are two routes to Kyle of Lochalsh, from where ferries used to cross to Skye. The coastal route detours via idyllic Plockton, once a clearing centre for those displaced in the Clearances. If Scotland has a prettier village, it would be surprising. This is a delightful place to stay, its main street lined with palms and white-washed houses, each with a seagull perched on its chimneystack gazing out at the sea. Recently the steady throughput of visitors has been augmented with viewers of the popular TV series *Hamish McBeth*, coming in search of scenes from the stories.

From May to September there are seal-watching cruises (☎ 544306) for £3.50 a head with a money-back guarantee if no seals show.

Places to Stay & Eat
There are several pleasant places to stay in Harbour St; try *An Caladh* (☎ 544356) at No 25 with beds from £15 a head. Right by the sea *The Sheiling* (☎ 544282) charges about the same. The *Craig Highland Farm* (☎ 544205), 2½ miles north of Plockton, has beds from £13 a head in a delightful conservation centre. There are lots of animals around and if you don't want to stay you can still visit for £1.50/1.

Plockton Hotel (☎ 544274) in Harbour St isn't the village's prettiest building but its pub food is popular; fish dishes start at about £5. From mid-April to September more adventurous food is available at *Off The Rails* (☎ 544423) at Plockton Station; during the day you can get things like filled pitta bread for £2.25; in the evening lamb with all the trimmings costs £10.15. The best food of all is to be had at *The Haven Hotel* (☎ 544223) where four-course meals cost £22.

KYLE OF LOCHALSH
• *pop 800* • ☎ 01599
Until the Skye Bridge opened, Kyle of Lochalsh was the main jumping off point for trips to Skye. Now, however, its many B&B owners have to watch most of their trade whizzing past without stopping...and there really isn't anything to stop for. The TIC (☎ 534276) beside the main seafront car park is open from April to October and stocks information on Skye.

If you need a meal the *Seagreen Restaurant & Bookshop* (☎ 534388), on Plockton Rd, less than a mile from Kyle, has wonderful wholefood. Alternatively you could try the pricier *Seafood Restaurant* (☎ 534813) in Kyle Station.

Kyle can be reached by bus and train from Inverness (see Getting There & Away in that section), and by direct Citylink buses from Glasgow (five hours, £13.80), which continue across to Kyleakin and on to Portree (£15.50) and Uig (6½ hours, £16), for ferries to Tarbert on Harris and Lochmaddy on North Uist.

The 82-mile train ride between Inverness and Kyle of Lochalsh is one of Scotland's most scenic. It takes 2½ hours and costs £12. From May to September you can enjoy the view from the observation saloon, or the view and a meal from the dining car.

KYLE TO THE GREAT GLEN

It's 55 miles via the A87 from Kyle to Invergarry, which is between Fort William and Fort Augustus on Loch Oich.

Eilean Donan Castle

Photogenically sited at the entrance to Loch Duich, Eilean Donan Castle (☎ 01599-85202) may be Scotland's best looking castle, but there are only a couple of rooms and a history display panel inside for your £3/1.75. It was ruined in a Jacobite uprising in 1719 and not rebuilt until earlier this century. It's open Easter to September, daily from 10 am to 5.30 pm.

Citylink buses from Fort William and Inverness to Portree stop opposite the Castle.

Glen Shiel & Glenelg

From Eilean Donan Castle, the A87 follows Loch Duich into the spectacular Glen Shiel valley, with 3000-foot-high peaks soaring up on both sides of the road. Follow the road past Glenelg to see two fine ruined Iron Age **brochs**, Dun Telve and Dun Troddon. From Glenelg round to Arnisdale the scenery becomes even more spectacular.

ROAD TO THE ISLES

The scenic, 46-mile Road to the Isles runs from Fort William via Glenfinnan to Arisaig and Mallaig. Just outside Fort William, at Banavie, is **Neptune's Staircase**; see the earlier Fort William to Fort Augustus section for details.

At **Glenfinnan**, a visitors centre (☎ 01397-722250; NTS) recounts the story of Prince Charles Edward Stuart, or Bonnie Prince Charlie, whose 1745 rising started here and ended near here 14 months later when he fled to France. A lookout tower offers fine views over Loch Shiel. The centre is open April to September, daily from 10 am to 6 pm; £1/60p.

From **Arisaig**, the MV *Shearwater* (☎ 01687-450224) runs day trips to the islands of Rum, Eigg and Muck. From Arisaig, the road follows the coast past pretty bays, including the **Silver Sands of Morar**. The village of **Morar** is at the entrance to **Loch Morar**, Britain's deepest lake at a depth of 1000 feet and with its own monster named Morag.

MALLAIG
- *pop 900*   • ☎ 01687

Ferries run from Mallaig to Skye during the summer when the TIC (☎ 462170) by the harbour opens.

Marine World (☎ 462292) is an aquarium of mainly local species. In summer it's open daily from 9 am to as late as 9 pm; £2.50/1.50. There's also a Mallaig Heritage Centre, open Monday to Saturday from 11 am to 4 pm; £1.80/90p. Minch Charters (☎ 462304), at Harbour Slipways, runs whale and dolphin-watching cruises and trips to uninhabited St Kilda, a World Heritage Site.

There are several pleasant B&Bs here, and *Sheena's Backpacker's Lodge* (☎ 462764), at Harbour View, has beds for £8.50 and £11.

The beautiful West Highland railway line between Fort William and Mallaig operates four times daily (in summer) from Monday to Saturday, and once on Sunday, and costs £6.80. In July, one train each day is steam-operated. There are connections through to Oban and Glasgow.

Scottish Citylink operates one bus a day from Fort William to Mallaig from late April to late October. It costs £5.50 for a single.

Inland

It's easy to think of northern Scotland as a coast and forget the inland highlands, even though their presence is always so visible. Several roads, often single-track, run right across these highlands and give access to the bleak but inspiring high country.

From June to September, just south of **Lairg**, at the southern end of Loch Shin, salmon can be seen leaping the **Falls of Shin** on their way upstream. From Lairg, single-track roads run north to Tongue, Laxford Bridge (between Durness and Kylesku) and Ledmore (between Kylesku and Ullapool).

Inverness Traction buses (☎ 01463-239292) run from Inverness to Lairg via Tain on Monday to Saturday. From Lairg, there are postbus services to the coast; see the earlier North & West Coast section for details.

The A836 from Lairg to Tongue runs past Ben Klibreck (2366 feet) and Ben Loyal (2509 feet), while Ben Hope (3040 feet) is slightly to the west, at the head of Loch Hope.

Isle of Skye

• *pop 8200*   • ☎ *01478*

Skye is a rugged, convoluted island stretching about 50 miles from end to end. It's ringed by beautiful coastline and dominated by the Cuillins, immensely popular for the sport of Munro bagging. Tourism is a mainstay of the island economy, so until you get off the main roads, don't expect to escape the hordes. Come prepared for changeable weather; when it's nice it's very very nice, but often it isn't!

Portree and Broadford are the main population centres. Getting around the island midweek is fairly straightforward, with postbuses supplementing the normal bus services. But here as much as in the Highlands transport dwindles to nothing at weekends,

---

Over the Bridge to Skye

'Speed bonny boat like a bird on the wing...over the seas to Skye'. The words of the Skye Boat Song immortalised the flight of Bonnie Prince Charlie, disguised as Flora Macdonald's maid, after the Battle of Culloden and in doing so romanticised the idea of the boat trip to Skye.

The Caledonian MacBrayne ferry was hardly a rowing boat but did at least stick with the spirit of the song. Then in 1995 the new Skye Bridge from Kyle of Lochalsh to Kyleakin opened, a big concrete arch depriving Skye of its island identity.

That was bad enough, but when the tolls were announced (£4.30 rising to £5.20 in the peak season) there was outrage. Some people objected to the principle of having to pay for what was theoretically just another part of the British road network, while others pointed out that Skye was an area of high unemployment whose residents could ill afford the toll.

The toll soon turned into a mini version of the 1990s poll tax rebellion. SKAT (Skye and Kyle Against the Toll) encouraged people to refuse to pay, even if it meant going to court. Dingwall Sheriff's Court is now working its way through a backlog of 800-plus cases. ■

---

particularly in winter and even more dramatically (so it seems) when it rains.

Gaelic is still spoken by half of Skye's residents.

Despite the closing of the old Kyle of Lochalsh to Kyleakin ferry route when the Skye Bridge opened in 1995, there are still two ways to travel over the sea to Skye. In summer CalMac (☎ 01475-650000) operates from Mallaig to Armadale (30 minutes; cars from £13.50, passengers £2.30). There's also a six-car Glenelg to Kylerhea (☎ 01599-511302) service, April to October (not always on Sunday), taking 10 minutes and costing £5 for car and driver, 50p for passengers.

PORTREE

• ☎ *01478*

Portree is Port an Righ or the King's Harbour in Gaelic, named after a 1540 call paid by James V to pacify local clan chieftains. Portree is Skye's biggest settlement with

PLACES TO STAY
2   Isles Hotel
8   Craiglockhart
10 Tongadale Hotel
11 Portree Hotel
15 Rosedale Hotel
19 Tigh na Bruaich Hostel

PLACES TO EAT
4   Granary Bakery
5   Caledonian Hotel
6   Harbour View Restaurant
7   Ben Tianavaig Vegetarian Bistro

14 Gandhi Indian Restaurant
17 Lower Deck

OTHER
1   Caledonian MacBrayne (CalMac) Ferry Office
3   Clydesdale Bank
9   Post Office
12 Bus Stop
13 Island Cycles
16 Bank of Scotland
18 TIC
20 Pier Hotel
21 Hospital

Portree

most of the facilities like banks and petrol stations. The post office has foreign exchange facilities. The harbour itself is particularly pretty.

On the southern edge of Portree, the **Aros Skye Heritage Centre** (☎ 613649) offers a lively introduction to Skye life. It's open daily from 9 am to 6 pm (9 pm in summer). Admission is £3/2.

The TIC (☎ 612137) is on the brow of the hill overlooking the harbour.

Places to Stay

Tigh na Bruaich (☎ 613332) is a basic back-packer's hostel on waterfront Douglas Row with beds for £7.50. Alternatively, *Portree Backpackers Hostel* (☎ 613641) is on the Dunvegan Rd. Portree is packed with B&Bs; try friendly *Craiglockhart* (☎ 612233) over-looking the harbour with beds from £17, or the *Braeside*, *Benlee* or *Coolin View*, all in Bosville Terrace.

Portree hotels include the *Tongadale* (☎ 612115) in Wentworth St, with rooms from £20 to £28 per person. Right on the square, the *Isles Hotel* (☎ 612129) costs from £23 to £32 per person, while the *Portree Hotel* (☎ 612511) is slightly pricier. The *Rosedale Hotel* (☎ 613131), right on the waterfront, costs from £33 to £37 per person.

Places to Eat

The *Caledonian Hotel* has a café which is open from breakfast time onwards; baked beans on toast costs £1.50. The *Lower Deck* (☎ 613611) in the harbour sells fish & chips to take away but also offers a more pricey fish restaurant. The *Harbour View Seafood Restaurant* (☎ 612069) in Bosville Terrace is even better. There's pub food at the *Portree* or *Tongadale* hotels. You can even sample curry at the *Gandhi Indian Restaurant* (☎ 612681) on Bayfield Rd, or at the excellent *Ben Tianavaig Vegetarian Bistro* (☎ 612152) at 5 Bosville Terrace.

The *An Tuireann Art Centre Café* (☎ 613306) is out of town on the Struan road (B885) but does things like filled pitta bread for £2.50 between 10 am and 5 pm. Films are sometimes shown here and there's live music on Sunday from noon.

The *Pier Hotel* is a popular waterfront drinking spot.

Getting There & Away

Bus Somerled Square is the Portree bus stop. Citylink operates a Glasgow-Fort William-Kyle-Kyleakin-Portree-Uig route in conjunction with Skye-Ways Express (☎ 01599-534328). It operates three times daily in summer, takes three hours from Fort William to Portree and costs £11.20. There's a Highland Country Bus (☎ 612622) Inverness to Portree service twice daily Monday to Saturday, but only in school term time on Sunday. The three-hour trip costs £8.

Boat CalMac (☎ 612075) has an office just off Somerled Square in Portree.

Getting Around
Bikes can be hired at Island Cycles (☎ 613121) for £7 to £12 a day.

KYLEAKIN
• ☎ 01599
Even more than Kyle of Lochalsh, Kyleakin has had the carpet pulled from under its feet by the opening of the Skye Bridge. Still, it's a pleasant enough wee place with a couple of handy hostels. The SYHA *Youth Hostel* (☎ 534585) charges £7.80/6.40 a night and is just doors from friendly *Skye Backpackers* (☎ 534510) where beds cost £8.50. The *Pier Coffee House* on the waterfront is the place to go to mull over the rights and wrongs of the bridge over a light lunch.

Castle Moil Seal Cruises (☎ 544235) charges £4.50/2 for a cruise under the bridge to see a seal colony on Eilean Mhal.

KYLERHEA OTTER HAVEN
Shortly after leaving Kyleakin, there's a signpost to Kylerhea ferry. Before catching the private ferry across to Glenelg, you can follow a 1½-hour nature trail offering the chance to see otters from a shoreline hide. Even if the otters elude you, you should still see basking seals and assorted birds.

The ferry operates Monday to Saturday from April to mid-May from 9 am to 6 pm, daily from mid-May to August from 9 am to 8 pm (Sunday 10 am to 6 pm), and September and October daily from 9 am to 6 pm (Sunday first ferry at 10 am). A car and four passengers costs £5; a foot passenger 50p.

ARMADALE
It's still possible to arrive on Skye by boat from Mallaig. If you do that you'll wind up in remote Armadale. Here you can visit the **Clan Donald Centre** (☎ 01471-844305) in ruined Armadale Castle which tells you all you ever wanted to know about the MacDon-

ald clan. It's open Easter to late October, daily from 9 am to 5 pm; £3.40/2.20. There's a pleasant restaurant serving things like home-made soup for £1.50.

It's just 400 yards from the Armadale ferry terminal to the SYHA *Youth Hostel* (☎ 01471-844260), which is open from Easter to September and costs £5.40/4.40. Four miles along the road is the *Hairy Coo Backpackers Hotel* (☎ 01471-833231), a big, basic place with dorm beds for £7.50.

You can hire a bike from the Ferry Filling Station.

BROADFORD
There's nothing much to detain you in Broadford except the **Serpentarium** (☎ 01471-822209) where you can see and touch all sorts of snakes, most of them illegally imported, impounded by Customs and given refuge here. It's open Easter to October (£2/1), as is the TIC (☎ 01471-822361) in the main car park.

The *Youth Hostel* (☎ 01471-822442) is open from late February to November and charges £6.95/5.85. The *Fossil Bothy* (☎ 01471-822644) hostel, at nearby Lower Breakish, charges £6.50 a head.

You can hire a bike from Fairwinds Cycle Hire (☎ 01471-822270) or rent a car from Skye Car Rental (☎ 01471-822225).

THE CUILLINS & MINGINISH PENINSULA
The rocky Cuillins, west of Broadford, provide spectacular walking and climbing country. The complete ridge of the Black Cuillin requires two days and involves real climbing; make sure you're properly equipped. Sgurr Alasdair, at 3257 feet, is the highest point.

The camping ground at Sligachan is a popular jumping off-point for Cuillin climbers. There are two hostels in **Portnalong**: *Croft Bunkhouse* (☎ 01478-640254) is three miles from the **Talisker Distillery** and charges £5.50 (less for campers); the *Skye-walker Independent Hostel* (☎ 01478-640250) is at the Old School in Fiskavaig Rd and costs £6.

WATERNISH PENINSULA

On the west side of the Waternish Peninsula, magnificent **Dunvegan Castle** dates back to the 13th century although it was restored in romantic style in the mid-19th century. Inside you can visit several grand but not especially exciting dining rooms and lounges together with a decidedly alarming dungeon, right next door to a magnificent drawing room. The castle (☎ 01470-521206) is open late March to October, Monday to Saturday from 10 am to 5.30 pm, and Sunday from 1 to 5.30 pm; £4/2.20.

Monday to Saturday, you can get here by postbus from Portree, leaving at 10.15 am. The return is at 12.05 pm so you'll have to stay overnight. Of several possible places to stay, *Roskhill Guest House* (☎ 01470-521317) has beds from £15.50, and the *Tables Hotel* (☎ 01470-521404), one mile from the castle, has beds from £19.

TROTTERNISH PENINSULA

North of Portree, Skye's coastal scenery is at its finest in the Trotternish Peninsula. Look out in particular for the rocky column of the **Old Man of Storr**, the spectacular **Kilt Rock** and the ruins of **Duntulm Castle**. Inland the spectacular **Quiraing** also offers dramatic hill walking.

At the north end of the peninsula at Kilmuir, the **Skye Croft Museum** (☎ 01470-252213) recreates crofting life in a series of cottages overlooking marvellous scenery. It's open Monday to Saturday from 9.30 am to 5.30 pm; £1.50/50p.

The biggest settlement is tiny **Staffin** where you can stop for lunch or a drink at *The Oystercatcher* (☎ 01470-562384) except on Sunday.

Three miles north of Staffin in even tinier **Flodigarry** you can stay at the historic *Flodigarry Country House Hotel* (☎ 01470-552203), with singles from £25 to £36 and doubles from £40 to £90. The home of Highland heroine **Flora McDonald** is now part of the hotel, and her grave at Kilmuir indicates that she was a real victim of tourism – the 1955 memorial records that of the original

---

✿✿✿✿✿✿✿✿✿✿✿✿✿✿✿✿✿✿✿✿✿✿✿✿✿✿

Flora MacDonald – Queen of the Isles

You won't get far in the Highlands and Islands without coming across Flora MacDonald, the Highlands heroine famous for helping Bonnie Prince Charlie escape his defeat at the Battle of Culloden.

Flora was born in 1725 in South Uist, at a site now marked by a memorial cairn. After her mother's abduction by Hugh MacDonald of Skye, Flora was reared by her brother and educated in the home of the Clanranald chiefs.

In 1746 she helped Bonnie Prince Charlie escape from Benbecula to Skye disguised as her Irish servant. With a price on the Prince's head, their little boat was fired on, but they managed to land safely and Flora escorted the Prince to Portree where he gave her a gold locket containing his portrait before setting sail for Raasay.

Waylaid on the way home, the boatmen admitted everything. Flora was arrested and imprisoned in the Tower of London. She never saw or heard from the Prince again.

In 1747 she returned home, marrying Allan MacDonald of Skye and going on to have nine children. Dr Johnson stayed with her in 1773 during his journey round the Western Isles, but later poverty forced her family to emigrate to North Carolina. There her husband was captured by rebels. Flora returned to Kingsburgh on Skye where she died in 1790 and was buried in Kilmuir churchyard, wrapped in the sheet in which Bonnie Prince Charlie and Dr Johnson had slept. ■

✿✿✿✿✿✿✿✿✿✿✿✿✿✿✿✿✿✿✿✿✿✿✿✿✿✿

---

memorial, 'every fragment has been removed by tourists'.

The *Dun Flodigarry Hostel* (☎ 01470-552212) is much cheaper at £7 a head.

UIG

From tiny Uig, CalMac has services every day to Lochmaddy on North Uist (1¾ hours; cars from £30.50, passengers £7.35) and from Monday to Saturday to Tarbert on Harris (same times and prices). There's a TIC (☎ 01470-542404) beside the slipway.

Uig has a *Youth Hostel* (☎ 01470-542211), which is open from Easter to October and costs £5.05. There's a cluster of bungalow B&Bs with beds for around £15. The *Old Ferry Inn* (☎ 542242) is pricier at £25 a head, the *Uig Hotel* (☎ 542205) pricier

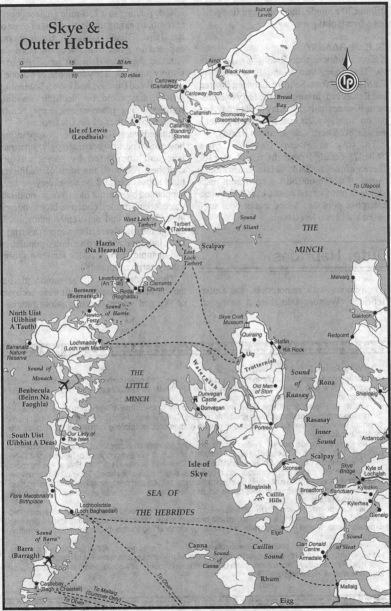

Skye & Outer Hebrides

0   15   30 km
0   10   20 miles

Butt of Lewis

Arnol

Black House

Carloway
(Carlabhagh)

Carloway Broch

Callanish

Broad
Bay

Callanish
Standing
Stones

Stornoway
(Steornabhagh)

Uig

Isle of Lewis
(Leodhais)

To Ullapool

West Loch
Tarbert

Tarbert
(Tairbeart)

Sound
of Sliant

THE

Harris
(Na Hearadh)

Scalpay

MINCH

East
Loch
Tarbert

Leverburgh
(An T-ob)

St Clements
Church

Rodal
(Roghadal)

Melvaig

Berneray
(Bearnaraigh)

North Uist
(Uibhist
A Tauth)

Newton
Ferry

Sound
of Harris

Gairloch

Redpoint

Lochmaddy
(Loch nam Madadh)

Skye Croft
Museum

Balranald
Nature
Reserve

Quiraing

Staffin

Kilt Rock

THE
LITTLE
MINCH

Uig

Trotternish

Waternish

Sound
of
Raasay

Rona

Sound
of
Monach

Benbecula
(Beinn Na
Faoghla)

Dunvegan
Castle

Dunvegan

Old Man
of Storr

Shieldaig

Our Lady of
The Isles

Portree

Rasasay
Inner
Sound

Ardarroch

South Uist
(Uibhist A Deas)

Scalpay

Sconser

Skye
Bridge

Kyle of
Lochalsh

Isle of
Skye

Minginish

Cuillin
Hills

Broadford

Otter
Sanctuary

Kyleakin

Flora Macdonald's
Birthplace

Lochboisdale
(Loch Baghasdail)

SEA OF

THE HEBRIDES

Kylerhea

Elgol

Glenelg

Sound
of Barra

Barra
(Barragh)

Canna

Sound
of
Canna

Cuillin
Sound

Clan Donald
Centre

Sound
of Sleat

Castlebay
(Bagh a Chaisteil)

To Mallaig
(Summer Only)

Armadale

To Oban

Rhum

Mallaig

To Oban

Eigg

still at £30 a single, but both have fine positions overlooking the bay.

ISLE OF RAASAY

If Skye is remote, then Raasay is even more so. This long, thin island is reached by CalMac ferry from Sconser, between Portree and Broadford. In summer, the ferry operates up to 10 times daily, Monday to Saturday, but not on Sunday. Cars cost £7.80 and passengers £1.80. There's no petrol on Raasay.

To stay at *Raasay Outdoor Centre* (☎ 01478-660266) costs from £14 to £16. There are bikes available for hire. *Raasay Youth Hostel* (☎ 01478-660240) is open from mid-May to September and costs £4.10/3.40. Forest Enterprise publishes a free leaflet with suggested walks and forest trails.

Outer Hebrides

Synonymous with remoteness, the Outer Hebrides (Western Isles) are a string of islands running in a 130-mile arc from north to south, shielding the north-western coast of Scotland. Bleak, isolated, treeless and exposed to gales that sweep in from the Atlantic, the Outer Hebrides are almost irresistibly romantic. They form one of Europe's most isolated frontiers and have a fascinating history, signposted by Neolithic standing stones, Viking place-names, empty crofts and folk memories of the Clearances.

Immediate reality can be disappointing, however. The towns are straggly, unattractive and dominated by stern, austere churches. Although the ruins of traditional blackhouses can still be seen, they've been supplanted by unattractive (though no doubt more comfortable) concrete-block bungalows. Rugged and apparently inhospitable though the islands are, they support a surprisingly large and widely distributed population and in summer the CalMac ferries disgorge a daily cargo of tourists.

The landscapes can be mournful, but they're also spectacular, with wide horizons of sky and water, dazzling white beaches,

---

The Wee Frees & Other Island Creeds

Religion plays a complex and important role in island life, and priests and ministers enjoy powerful positions in the community. The split between the Protestants to the north of Benbecula and the Catholics to the south creates, or perhaps reflects, a different communal atmosphere.

Hebridean Protestants have developed a distinctive fundamentalist approach, and Sunday is devoted to religious services, prayer and Bible reading. On Lewis and Harris, virtually everything closes down. In general, social life is restricted to private homes and, as drinking is frowned upon, pubs are mostly uninspiring.

The Protestants are further divided into three main sects, with convoluted, emotionally-charged histories. The Church of Scotland, the main Scottish church, is state-recognised or 'established'. The Free Presbyterian Church of Scotland and the Free Church of Scotland (or Wee Frees) are far more conservative and intolerant, permitting no ornaments, organ music or choirs. Their ministers deliver uncompromising sermons (usually in Gaelic) from central pulpits, and *precentors* lead the congregation in unaccompanied, but atmospheric, psalm singing. Visitors are welcome to attend services, but due respect is essential.

The most recent split occured in 1988 when Lord Mackay, a prominent Free Presbyterian, committed the awful crime of attending a friend's Catholic requiem mass. The church elders threatened him with expulsion, and he and his supporters responded by establishing the breakaway Associated Presbyterian Churches!

The Catholic Church south of Benbecula survived the Reformation. Although the priests were expelled early in the 17th century, and despite several missionary attempts, Protestantism failed to take hold. The Sunday Sabbath on South Uist and Barra is more easy-going, and the attitude towards the demon drink more relaxed. ∎

azure bays, wide peat moors, and countless lochs, mountains and stony hills. These are islands that reward an extended stay, especially if you travel on foot or by bike; a rushed tour will be less satisfying, and when driving you have to pay too much attention to the road (often single-tracked and sheep-ridden) to appreciate the views.

The local culture is not very accessible to outsiders, but it is distinctive. Of the 18,000 crofts registered in Scotland, 6000 are on the Outer Hebrides. Of the 66,000 Scottish Gaelic speakers, around 25,000 live on the islands. Religion still plays a central role in island life, especially in the Protestant north, where the Sunday Sabbath is strictly observed – even the swings in Stornoway's playground are padlocked.

These are deeply conservative parts where a Scot from Glasgow is as much an incomer as someone from London. But the EU is working to reduce the islands' isolation and many roads are being upgraded courtesy of loans from the European Regional Development Fund.

Life moves very slowly here, with supplies dependent on boats and planes. Often newspapers and bread are unavailable before 10 am. Bad weather can cause supplies to dry up altogether. Accommodation is in fairly short supply; book ahead in summer.

HISTORY

The first evidence of settlement dates back to around 4000 BC, when Stone Age farmers settled the islands. They constructed massive stone tombs and the mounds can still be seen (as at Barpa Langas, North Uist). Bronze Age Beaker People (named after their distinctive pottery) arrived around 1800 BC, and it's around this time that groups of standing stones were set up, most notably at Callanish on Lewis.

Around 1000 BC, the climate deteriorated and the peat that now blankets much of the islands (in places to depths of 20 feet) began to accumulate. Acidity increases when soil becomes permanently waterlogged, creating a sterile environment where bacterial activity slows, and where dead grass, sedge,

heather and moss build up in layers instead of rotting.

This spongy, nutrient-poor environment was no good for farming, and the population was forced onto the coastal fringe. When cut and dried, however, the peat provided the islanders with fuel. Every spring, families still cut it into bricks, which are wind-dried in neat piles before being stacked outside homes.

The Iron Age, Gaelic-speaking Celts arrived around 500 BC and several defensive brochs remain from this period, the most impressive at Carloway on Lewis.

Vikings settled in the islands by 850, and many island clans, including the Morrisons, Nicolsons, MacAulays and Macleods, are thought to have Norse backgrounds. The traditional island houses, the blackhouses that remained in common use into the 1930s, were essentially Viking longhouses. The Middle Ages saw a new influx of Gaelic-speaking Celts from Scotland and Ireland, and a weakening of the links to Norway, resulting in a Gaelic-speaking Celtic/Norse population.

LANGUAGE

Scottish Gaelic is basically the same as Irish Gaelic. About 75% of the islanders speak it (as opposed to just 1.5% of the total Scottish population), and efforts are being made to ensure its survival. Several Gaelic television and radio programmes are now produced.

All islanders speak English, and there's no reluctance to use it when speaking to outsiders. However, all road signs are in Gaelic which can cause confusion. When talking to outsiders, islanders use the anglicised version of a name, but this can bear little similarity to the Gaelic on the signs. CalMac ferry company and the airlines also use anglicised names. One of the first purchases a visitor should make is a bilingual road map showing both names; Estate Publication's red-covered *Official Tourist Map – Western Isles* (£3.75) is ideal.

This book uses English names where they are in common usage with the Gaelic name given in brackets at the first main reference.

ORIENTATION & INFORMATION

Lewis and Harris are actually one island with a border of high hills between them. The northern half of Lewis is low and flat with miles of peat moors; southern Lewis and Harris are rugged, with some impressive stony mountains and glorious beaches. Stornoway, on Lewis, is the largest town in the Outer Hebrides, with a reasonable range of facilities.

North Uist, Benbecula and South Uist are joined by bridge and causeway. These are low, flat, green islands half-drowned by sinuous lochs and open to the sea and sky. Benbecula has a large army and air force base.

There are several TICs – one in every ferry port, open late for ferry arrivals up to midnight from April to mid-October.

The main Western Isles Tourist Board (☎ 01851-703088), 26 Cromwell St, Stornoway PA87 2DD, produces a brochure showing all accommodation possibilities, from hotels to B&Bs and self-catering cottages. *The Outer Hebrides Handbook & Guide* (Kittiwake, £7.95), written by local experts, gives lots of data on the islands' history, culture, flora and fauna.

PLACES TO STAY & EAT

There are a few basic hostels in old crofts scattered around the islands, but most are difficult to get to without transport or a readiness to hike. Most are operated by the Gatliff Hebridean Hostels Trust, 71 Cromwell St, Stornoway, Lewis PA87 2DG, in association with the SYHA. Charges are the same as for SYHA grade 3 hostels. The hostels have bunk beds, blankets, cooking equipment, cold running water and open fires. Bring a sleeping bag and eating utensils. Local crofters look after them, but no advance bookings are accepted and they prefer people not to arrive or depart on a Sunday.

Camping grounds with facilities are scarce, but free camping is usually allowed, provided you get permission from the nearest house and remove all rubbish. Some landowners may ask a small fee.

The B&Bs provide an otherwise rare opportunity to meet the islanders, who are famous both for their hospitality and the size of their breakfasts. Few offer private bathrooms, but they are usually comfortable and clean and offer hearty dinners as well. Most B&B hosts, especially on Lewis and Harris, appreciate guests booking ahead if they are going to stay on Sunday night.

A few B&Bs are handy for the ferry ports, but most are scattered around the countryside. The ports themselves are generally uninspiring but always have at least one pub where meals are available. If you do stay in the countryside – which is recommended – check whether there's a convenient pub, or make arrangements to eat at your B&B.

Self-catering cottages are best booked in advance.

Options for eating out centre on the pubs, which are few and far between and not particularly cheap. The picture for vegetarians is improving; most hotels manage at least one suitable dish.

GETTING THERE & AWAY

Air

British Airways Express (☎ 0345-222111) fly to the islands, and there are airports at Stornoway, on Lewis, and on Benbecula and Barra. The main airport, just four miles east of Stornoway, is served by regular BA flights from Glasgow and Inverness (Monday to Saturday). British Airways Express also has flights to Benbecula and Barra from Glasgow from Monday to Saturday, with additional Sunday flights in peak summer months. At Barra the planes land on the beach, so the timetable depends on the tides. British Airways Express also links Barra and Benbecula with Stornoway.

Bus

Regular bus services to Ullapool, Uig and Oban connect with the ferries. The main operator to Ullapool and Oban is Scottish Citylink (☎ 0990-505050).

Skye-ways (☎ 01599-534328) operates from Glasgow and Inverness connecting with other routes to Uig on Skye.

Train

Spectacular train services run as far as Oban, Mallaig and Kyle from Glasgow and Edinburgh. To get to Ullapool, take the train to Inverness, then a bus to Ullapool. Phone ☎ 0345-484950 for rail details.

Boat

CalMac runs comfortable car and passenger ferries from Ullapool to Stornoway on Lewis (2½ hours; two or three times daily from Monday to Saturday); from Uig, on Skye, to Tarbert on Harris and Lochmaddy on North Uist (around 1¾ hours; once or twice daily, six or seven days a week); and from Mallaig and Oban to Lochboisdale on South Uist and Castlebay on Barra (3½ to seven hours; almost daily).

The timetables are complicated and, especially during summer, car space can fill up fast. Advance booking is essential, although foot and bicycle passengers should have no problems. Services often leave early in the morning or late in the evening.

There are over 20 different Island Hopscotch fares for set routes, offering worthwhile savings. Island Rover Passes give unlimited travel on most routes for 8 or 15 days; convenient certainly, but make sure you will use enough services to recoup the cost. For reservations and service details, contact Caledonian MacBrayne (☎ 01475-650000 for reservations, ☎ 01475-650100 for inquiries), The Ferry Terminal, Gourock PA19 1QP.

A one-way ticket from Stornoway to Ullapool is £11.05 for each passenger or driver, plus £47.50 for a car. From Otternish to Leverburgh (although you may have to take a circuitous Tarbert-Uig-Lochmaddy route) it's £4/19; from Lochboisdale to Castlebay £4.60/22.50; and from Lochboisdale or Castlebay to Oban £15.95/49.50. For a passenger this totals £35.60, for a car £138.50 – as against £32.50 and £125 for the equivalent hopscotch ticket. Allow at least a week to tackle this full north-south route. Bikes are carried free.

GETTING AROUND
Bus

Bus transport is extremely limited, although a bare-bones service allows crofters to get to the shops in the morning and return in the afternoon. The TICs have up-to-date timetables. Visitors without their own transport should anticipate a fair amount of hitching and walking.

Car

Most roads are single-track and the main hazard is posed by sheep wandering onto the roads. Petrol stations are far apart, expensive and frequently closed on Sunday.

Cars can be hired from around £20 per day from Arnol Motors (☎ 01851-710548), Arnol, Lewis; Mackinnon Self Drive (☎ 01851-702984), 18 Inaclete Rd, Stornoway; Harris Car Services (☎ 01859-502280), Scott Rd, Tarbert; Maclennan's Self Drive (☎ 01870-602191), Balivanich, Benbecula; Ask Car Hire (☎ 01870-602818), Liniclate Benbecula; and Laing Motors (☎ 01878-700267), Lochboisdale, South Uist.

Hitching

Hitching is feasible, although traffic is light and virtually stops on Sunday, especially on Harris and Lewis. The islanders are generally hospitable, and it's definitely safer than usual – a murderous psychopath has nowhere to run other than to a ferry and the waiting arms of the police.

See also the Hitching section in the Getting Around chapter at the start of this book.

Bicycle

Cycling from north to south is quite popular but allow at least a week for the trip. The main problems are difficult weather, strong winds (you hear stories of people cycling downhill and freewheeling uphill) and sheep that believe they have right of way.

Bikes can be hired from Alex Dan Cycle Centre (☎ 01851-704025), 67 Kenneth St, Stornoway, Lewis; DM Mackenzie (☎ 01859-502271), Pier Rd, Tarbert, Harris;

and Barra Cycle Hire (☎ 018714-284), 29 St Brendan Rd, Castlebay, Barra. Booking is advisable.

LEWIS (LEODHAIS)

The northern half of Lewis (population 21,500) is low and flat, and dominated by the vast Black Moor, a peat moor dotted with numerous small lochs. The coastal fringes have some arable land and are surprisingly densely populated, if not particularly attractive.

The old blackhouses (named after the soot left on the walls by the burning peat fire in the centre) may have gone, but most holdings are crofts that follow a traditional pattern dating back to medieval times. Most are narrow strips, designed to give everyone an equal share of good and bad land. Usually they run back from the foreshore (with its valuable seaweed), across the machair (the grassy sand dunes that were the best arable land), and back to the peaty grazing land.

Nowadays few crofts are economically viable, so most islanders supplement what they make from the land with other jobs. Many travel away to work on oil rigs or ships, and others work in the fishing industry (including a growing number in fish farming), service industries, or the traditional tweed weaving industry.

South of Stornoway and Barvas, the island is mountainous and beautiful, reminiscent of parts of the mainland's north-west coast. Three of the Outer Hebrides' most important sights – the Arnol Blackhouse, Dun Carloway Broch and Callanish Standing Stones – are also here.

Stornoway (Steornabhagh)

(population 8100; ☎ 01851)
The island's only sizeable town may lie on a beautiful natural harbour, but unfortunately that's the best you can say about it. Stornoway is a dismal, impoverished place with a drugs problem, perhaps because there's so little else to do. For tourists there are reasonable facilities and a small museum in Francis St (☎ 703773) but most people will want to escape as quickly as possible.

This is the Outer Hebrides' administrative and commercial centre, and the base for the Western Isles Council (Comhairle nan Eilan), a new hospital and the islands' Gaelic TV and radio stations. There's an airport and a ferry link with Ullapool (see the introductory transport sections).

Orientation & Information The ferry docks in the town centre, which is compact and easy to get around on foot. The bus station is on the foreshore to the east of the ferry terminal.

Some of the residential areas (and B&Bs) are a fair hike without a car, and many people commute in from communities around the island to work and shop, so there's more traffic than you might expect.

The main Western Isles Tourist Board (☎ 703088) is a short walk from the ferry pier. In theory you could use this office to book B&Bs around the islands, but in practice they simply phone other local TICs for them to do the chasing around. This can be time-consuming and silly – you end up with reservations for South Uist but not for Harris or North Uist – so take the free accommodation list and make the calls yourself.

For ferry information, phone CalMac (☎ 702361).

Places to Stay & Eat The *Laxdale Holiday Park* (☎ 703234), 6 Laxdale Lane, is 1½ miles north of town off the A857. The charge is £3 per tent and £2 to £2.50 per person.

Stornoway Backpackers Hostel (☎ 703628), 47 Keith St, is a five-minute walk from the ferry and bus station – walk east along pedestrianised Point St, which becomes Francis St, pass the post office, then turn left into Keith St. Rates are £8 per night in six-bed dorms and there's a self-catering kitchen.

B&Bs are widely scattered. *Hollsetr* (☎ 702796), 29 Urquart Gardens, is a long walk from the centre, but is immaculate and welcoming, with a single, twin and family room from £15 per person. There are a few pleasant places on Matheson Rd, within walking distance of the ferry: *Ravenswood*

(☎ 702673) at No 12, has a double and twin with bath from £18 a head, while *Englewood* (☎ 704180) at No 19, charges from £15.

Park Guest House (☎ 702485), with beds from £21, and *Tower Guest House* (☎ 703150), with beds from £16, are two comfortable guesthouses in Victorian homes in James St. To find them follow the waterfront to the east, then veer left at the signpost for the A866.

The old-fashioned *County Hotel* (☎ 703250), Francis St (continue east from the pedestrian mall), is the pick of the uninspiring hotels; expect to pay about £39.

Cheap breakfasts are available at the *Seaman's Mission* at 14 North Beach St. During the day *Merchants Coffee House* opposite the TIC does snacky meals in pleasant surroundings. After 6 pm you'll be struggling for anywhere to eat other than the pub-hotels. The *Crown Hotel* (☎ 703181), Castle St, has generous bar meals from £3.95. You can get a greasy and not especially cheap curry at *Ali's Tandoori* (☎ 706116) at 24 South Beach St.

Butt of Lewis (Rubha Robhanais)

Lewis's northern tip is windswept and rugged, with a lighthouse and large colonies of nesting fulmars. To get there, drive across the bleak expanse of Black Moor to **Barvas (Barabhas)**, then follow the densely populated west coast to the north-east. **St Moluag's Church** is an austere, barn-like structure believed to date from the 12th century but still used by the Episcopal Church. **Port of Ness (Port Nis)** is an attractive harbour with a popular sandy beach.

Arnol Blackhouse Museum

The most interesting and beautiful part of Lewis is south of Barvas and Stornoway. Situated just west of Barvas off the A858, the **Arnol Blackhouse Museum** (☎ 01851-710395; HS) is the only authentically maintained, traditional blackhouse – a combined byre, barn and home – left on the islands. Built in 1885, it was inhabited until 1964 and now offers a wonderful insight into the old crofting way of life. It's open April

to September, Monday to Saturday from 9.30 am to 6 pm, and October to March, Monday to Saturday from 9.30 am to 4 pm (closed 1 to 2 pm); £1.50/75.

At nearby **Bragar** a pair of whalebones form an arch by the road with the rusting harpoon that killed the whale dangling from the centre.

Carloway (Carlabagh)

Carloway looks across a beautiful loch to the southern mountains and has a post office and small store. At nearby **Garenin (Gearrannan)** some fascinating ruined blackhouses are quietly mouldering alongside new concrete cottages. Also here is the *Gearranan Crofters' Hostel*, itself a restored blackhouse. To get to the hostel from the war memorial by the church, cross the bridge and turn left. Don't take the road that passes under the bridge. Pass the shop, but don't turn left; continue straight on at the next junction. The hostel is half a mile further on at the end of the road. The warden, Mrs Pat Macgregor, lives at 3 Uraghag, one of the modern houses (with a large black and white cartwheel at its side) by the last road junction en route to the hostel.

Carloway Broch (Dun Charlabhaigh) is a well-preserved, 2000-year-old dry-stone defensive tower, in a beautiful position with panoramic views.

Callanish (Calanais)

The construction of the **Callanish Standing Stones** began around 4000 years ago, so they predate the Pyramids by 1000 years. Fifty-four large stones are arranged in the shape of a Celtic cross on a promontory overlooking Loch Roag, creating one of the most complete stone circles in Britain. Its great age, the mystery of its purpose, its impressive scale and its undeniable beauty have the dizzy effect of dislocating you from the present day.

The new **Calanais Visitor Centre** (☎ 01851-621422) is a *tour de force* of discreet design and provides a rare place to eat in the area. It's open (free) daily from April to September from 10 am to 7 pm (4 pm the rest of the year). There's an exhibition about the stones for £1.50/50p.

There are a couple of pleasant B&Bs nearby; try *Mrs Morrison* (☎ 621392) in the house right by the stones (from £17), or the attractive *Eschol Guest House* (☎ 621357), half a mile back towards Carloway (from £22). The *Doune Braes Hotel* (☎ 643252) in Carloway serves pub food until 9 pm, except on Sunday.

Mealista (Mealasta)

The road to Mealista (the B8011 south-west of Callanish, signposted to Uig) takes you through the most remote parts of Lewis. Follow the road right round towards Breanais for some truly spectacular white-sand beaches, although the surf can make swimming treacherous. The famous 12th-century walrus-ivory Lewis chess pieces were discovered in the sand dunes here in 1831; of the 78 pieces, 67 wound up in the British Museum in London.

HARRIS (NA HEARADH)

Harris has the islands' most dramatic scenery, combining mountains, magnificent beaches, expanses of machair (grass and wildflower-covered dunes) and weird rocky hills and coastline.

North Harris is actually the mountainous southern tip of Lewis, beyond the peat moors south of Stornoway – the Clisham is the highest point at 2600 feet. South Harris, across the land bridge at Tarbert, is also mountainous but has a fascinating variety of landscapes and great beaches.

Harris is famous for Harris Tweed, high-quality woollen cloth still handwoven in islanders' homes. The industry employs 750 independent weavers and 400 millworkers. Tarbert TIC can tell you about weavers and visitable workshops.

Tarbert (Tairbeart)
* *pop 500*   * ☎ 01859

Tarbert is a village port midway between North and South Harris with connections to Uig on Skye and Lochmaddy on North Uist. Not in itself particularly inspiring, it still has a spectacular location, overshadowed by mountains on the narrow land bridge between two lochs. Tarbert has basic facilities: a petrol station, Bank of Scotland and general store. The Harris Tweed Shop stocks a wide range of books on the islands.

The TIC (☎ 502011) is signposted up the hill and to the right from the ferry. For ferry information, phone CalMac on ☎ 502444. While you wait, the *Firstfruits* tearoom right beside the TIC does a few hot dishes as well as sandwiches and cakes. It's open from April to September.

Pick of the B&Bs is the cosy *Tigh na Mara* (☎ 502270), a five-minute walk from the ferry, with views of the east loch and beds from £13 to £15 per person.

Closer to the ferry terminal, *Waterstein House* (☎ 502358) has three rooms and charges £13 per person in an unpretty building.

Harris Hotel (☎ 502154) has a range of rooms, some with private bath, from around £30 a head. It also serves good-value pub meals (including something for vegetarians) from around £5 until 8.30 pm.

North Harris

North Harris is the most mountainous part of the Outer Hebrides. Roads are minimal, but there are many opportunities for climbing and walking.

The small village of **Rhenigidale (Reinigeadal)** has only recently become accessible by road. The *Reinigeadal Crofters' Hostel* can be reached on foot (three hours and six miles from Tarbert). It's an excellent walk, but take all necessary supplies. From Tarbert, take the road to Kyles Scalpay for two miles. Just beyond Laxdale Lochs, at a bend in the road, a signposted track, marked on OS maps, veers off to the left across the hills. The hostel is a white building standing above the road on the east side of the valley; the warden lives in the house closest to the shore. Beds cost £4.10/3.40.

South Harris

Beautiful South Harris is ringed by a tortuous 45-mile road. The beaches on the west coast, backed by rolling machair and mountains, with views across to North Harris and to offshore islands, are stunning.

The town of **Leverburgh (An T-ob)** is named after Lord Leverhulme (the founder of the conglomerate Unilever), who bought Lewis and Harris in 1918 and 1919. He had grand plans for the islands, particularly Obbe, as Leverburgh was then known, which was to be a major fishing port. It's now a sprawling, ordinary place but with a shop and a couple of pleasant B&Bs; try *Caberfeidh House* (☎ 520276) or *Garryknowe* (☎ 520246), both charging around £15.

There's a passenger ferry for Berneray and North Uist (in summer, Monday to Saturday, twice daily; in winter, three times weekly; £4). Tarbert TIC has information, or phone ☎ 01475-650100.

Three miles east at attractive **Rodel (Roghadal)** stands **St Clement's Church**, mainly built between the 1520s and 1550s, only to be abandoned in 1560 after the Reformation. Inside it contains the fascinating tomb of Alexander MacLeod, the man responsible for the rebuilding. Crude carvings show scenes of hunting, a castle, a galleon and various saints including St Clement clutching a skull.

The east, or Bays, coast is traversed by the Golden Road, derisively nicknamed by national newspapers that didn't think so much money should be spent on building it. This is a weird, rocky moonscape, still dotted with numerous crofts. It's difficult to imagine how anyone could have survived in such an inhospitable environment, but they did, and do. The SYHA operates the *Stockinish Youth Hostel* (☎ 01859-530373) in the small village of Caolas Stocinis. It's seven miles from Tarbert, costs £4.10/3.40, and you should bring all your supplies.

NORTH UIST (UIBHIST A TUATH)

North Uist is half-drowned by lochs, but has some magnificent beaches on the west side. There are also some great views north to the mountains of Harris. The landscape is a bit of an anticlimax after Harris but still has a sleepy, subtle appeal. For birdwatchers this is an earthly paradise, with huge populations of migrant waders – oystercatchers, lapwings, curlews and redshanks at every turn.

Lochmaddy (Loch nam Madadh)
* ☎ 01876

There isn't much to keep you in tiny Lochmaddy, but it has the ferry terminal for services to Uig on Skye and Tarbert on Harris, and there are a couple of stores, a Bank of Scotland, a petrol station, a post office and a pub. There's also a Museum and Arts Centre (☎ 500293) which is open March to December, Monday to Saturday from 10 am to 5 pm and has a café upstairs.

The TIC (☎ 500321) is open April to mid-October, Monday to Saturday from 9 am to 5 pm, and for late ferry arrivals. For ferry information, phone CalMac on ☎ 500337.

Lochmaddy's SYHA *Youth Hostel* (☎ 500368) is half a mile from the docks (signposted) and is open from mid-May to September for £5.40/4.40. An independent hostel at *Uist Outdoor Centre* (☎ 500480) has beds in four-bed rooms for £6.

The *Old Court House* (☎ 500358) is a comfortable B&B with two singles, a twin and a double, costing from £17 per person; the similarly-priced *Old Bank House* (☎ 500275) is also good. Extremely comfortable and well-presented is *Stag Lodge* (☎ 500364) in a pleasing whitewashed building; beds start at £18 and are well worth it. There's also a small restaurant here.

Lochmaddy Hotel (☎ 500331) is a traditional hotel with a range of rooms (some with private bath) from around £30 per person. Its restaurant serves excellent fish and seafood, or you can get bar meals until 8.30 pm. It's also a good place to stay if you're into fishing (and North Uist is famous for fishing); you can buy permits here.

Car ferries for Berneray, and passenger ferries for Berneray and Leverburgh, on South Harris, leave from **Newtonferry (Port nan Long)** – see the Leverburgh section under South Harris.

Balranald Nature Reserve

Eighteen miles west of Lochmaddy off the A865 is an RSPB nature reserve where you can watch migrant waders and listen for rare corncrakes. A very basic visitors centre provides refuge if it's raining from April to September.

Bharpa Langass & Pobull Fhinn

The chambered Neolithic burial tomb of Bharpa Langass stands on a hillside six miles south-west of Lochmaddy, just off the A867. It's believed to date back 5000 years. Take care as the path can be boggy.

Pobull Fhinn ('Finn's People) is a stone circle of similar age accessible from a path beside Langass Lodge Hotel. There are lovely views over the loch where seals can sometimes be seen.

BENBECULA (BEINN NA FAOGHLA)

Blink and you'll miss Benbecula, a low-lying island that's more water than land, linked by bridge and causeway to North and South Uist. Although the number of British soldiers based here is declining, they still hang on to a missile firing range. The troops and their families are quartered around hideous **Balivanich (Baile a Mhanaich)** where the big Naafi Family Store opens usual hours and on Sunday (until 1 pm). You can eat in the *Low Flyer* pub but it's pretty uninviting. There are flights Monday to Saturday to Glasgow.

SOUTH UIST (UIBHIST A DEAS)

South Uist is the second largest island in the Outer Hebrides. Once again, it lacks the drama of Harris, but although it's unassuming, there's an expansiveness that has its own magic. The west coast is low, with machair backing an almost continuous sandy beach. The east coast is quite hilly, with Beinn Mhor reaching 2030 feet, and cut by four large sea lochs. The island rewards those who explore beyond the main north-south road.

As you drive from Benbecula, watch for the granite statue of **Our Lady of the Isles** standing on the slopes of the Rueval hill.

Lochboisdale (Loch Baghasdail)

• ☎ *01878*

Lochboisdale is the most forgettable of the islands' ferry ports, but has links to Oban and Mallaig on the mainland and Castlebay on Barra.

The TIC (☎ 700286) is open April to mid-October, Monday to Saturday from 9 am to 5 pm, and for late ferry arrivals. For ferry information phone CalMac on ☎ 700288. There's a branch of Royal Bank of Scotland and petrol supplies.

Of the B&Bs, friendly *Lochside Cottage* (☎ 700472) has beds from £13, as does *Riverside* (☎ 700250). *Innis Ghorm* (☎ 700232) is a bit more expensive at £15. *Lochboisdale Hotel* (☎ 700332), above the ferry terminal, has a variety of rooms, most with private bath, for £30 to £40 a head. The pub has good, if not particularly cheap, food.

Howmore (Tobha Mor)

An attractive west coast village, Howmore has the *Tobha Mor Crofters' Hostel*. To get to it, take the turn-off from the A865 to Tobha Mor – the hostel is the white building with a porch by the church at road's end. The warden lives at Ben More House, at the junction with the main road.

The South

The southern tip of the island looks across to the islands of Eriskay and Barra. There's a car ferry to Eriskay and a passenger ferry (☎ 01878-720233) to Eoligarry on Barra's northern tip.

BARRA (BARRAIGH)

Barra is a tiny island, just 12 miles around and ideal for exploring on foot. With beautiful beaches, machair, hills, Neolithic remains and a strong sense of community, it could be said to encapsulate the Outer Hebridean experience.

The only sizeable village is **Castlebay (Bagh a Chaisteil)** where a castle was built by the MacNeil clan in the 12th century. It was sold in the 19th and restored in the 20th by American architect Robert MacNeil, who became clan chief. A standard flies above the castle when his son and heir is in residence.

The TIC (☎ 01871-810336) is open from April to mid-October. For ferry information, phone CalMac on ☎ 810306.

With only about 20 B&Bs scattered around the island and some ferries arriving late in the evening, it's best to book ahead. In Castlebay, try *Suidheachan* (☎ 890243), the former home of *Whisky Galore* author Sir Compton Mackenzie, with rates from £16, or *Faire Mhaoldonaich* (☎ 810441), where rooms with private bath cost from £16. *Craigard Hotel* (☎ 810200) has a range of rooms, some with private bath, from £29 to £32 per person.

Orkney Islands

Just six miles off the north coast of Scotland, this magical group of islands is known for its dramatic coastal scenery, ranging from 1000-foot-high cliffs to white, sandy beaches, for its abundant marine birdlife, and for a plethora of prehistoric sites, including an entire 4500-year-old village at Skara Brae.

Twenty of the 70 islands are inhabited. Kirkwall is the main town and Stromness is a major port – both are on the largest island, which is known as Mainland. The land is virtually treeless, but lush, level and cultivated rather than rugged. The climate, warmed by the Gulf Stream, is surprisingly moderate, with April and May being the driest months.

Over 1000 prehistoric sites have been identified on Orkney, the greatest concentration of any place in Europe. Since there has always been a lack of wood, everything was made from stone. This explains the survival of ancient domestic architecture that includes a 5000-year-old house, Europe's oldest, on Papa Westray. The most impressive ancient monuments – the village of Skara Brae, the tomb of Maes Howe and the Ring of Brodgar – are all on Mainland.

Orkney's Pictish rulers were replaced by Norse earls in the 9th century. The Norse ruled until the mid-13th century and built the magnificent St Magnus Cathedral in Kirkwall. Even today, there are hints of those distant Scandinavian connections in the lilting accent with which Orcadians speak English.

Orkney is popular with bird-watchers and the RSPB runs several reserves. From May to mid-July, vast numbers of seabirds come to nest on the cliffs. The clear waters around the islands attract divers, and Scapa Flow, south of Mainland, offers the most interesting wreck dive site in Europe.

If you're anywhere in the area around mid-June, don't miss the St Magnus Arts Festival. Sir Peter Maxwell Davies, one of the greatest living British composers, usually contributes to the festival – he lives on Hoy. The poet and writer George Mackay Brown also lives here. *Greenvoe*, or any of his other books set in Orkney, perfectly captures the special atmosphere of these islands.

GETTING THERE & AWAY
Air
There are flights to Kirkwall airport on British Airways/Loganair (☎ 0345-222111) daily except Sunday from Aberdeen, Edinburgh, Glasgow, Inverness and Shetland, with connections to London Heathrow, Manchester and Belfast. The cheapest return tickets (which must usually be bought 14 days in advance and require at least a Saturday night stay in Orkney) cost £193 from London and £104 from Inverness.

Bus & Boat
There are car ferries from Scrabster, near Thurso, to Stromness, operated by P&O (☎ 01856-850655). The crossing can be exhilaratingly rough. There's at least one departure a day all year, with single fares costing around £14. For Scrabster, Scottish Citylink (☎ 0990-505050) has daily coaches leaving Inverness at around 1 pm, and you can connect with this service on early morning departures from Glasgow or Edinburgh, or London on the overnight coach departing around 10 pm.

P&O also sails from Aberdeen (see that section in the Central Scotland chapter).

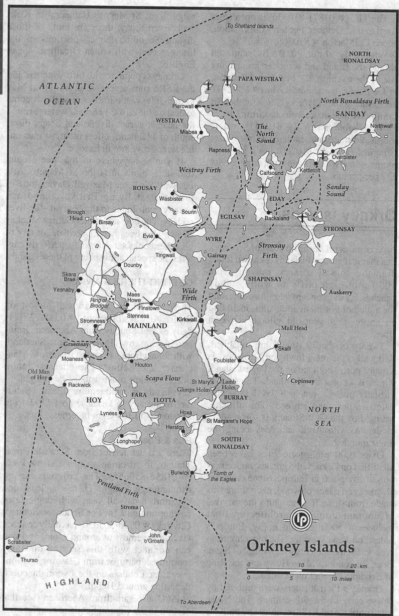

Orkney Islands

0   10   20 km
0   5   10 miles

John o'Groats Ferry (☎ 01955-611353) has a ferry (passengers and bicycles only) from John o'Groats to Burwick on South Ronaldsay from May to September (four per day). A one-way ticket is £13, but they also offer an excellent special deal: a return fare of £20 as long as you leave John o'Groats in the afternoon, and Orkney in the morning. A free bus meets the afternoon train from Inverness and a bus for Kirkwall (20 miles away) meets the ferry in Burwick. They also operate the Orkney Bus, a bus/ferry/bus through service between Inverness and Kirkwall via John o'Groats.

From Lerwick (Shetland), P&O sails to Stromness on Wednesday (summer only) and Friday (year-round). It's an eight-hour trip; the cheapest single ticket is £35.

KIRKWALL

• *pop 6000*   • ☎ *01856*

Orkney's capital is a bustling market town set back from the wide bay. Founded in the early 11th century by Earl Rognvald Brusson, the original part is one of the best examples of an ancient Norse town.

St Magnus Cathedral, one of Scotland's finest medieval cathedrals, is certainly worth a visit and there are a number of other things to see in the town; the whisky distillery tour is interesting.

Orientation & Information

Kirkwall is really just a big village and it's easy enough to get around on foot. The cathedral and most of the shops are set back from the harbour on Broad St, which changes its name several times along its length. Ferries leave from the harbour for the northern Orkney islands.

The TIC (☎ 872856), at 6 Broad St, by the cathedral, is open from April to September daily from 8.30 am to 8 pm, and for the rest of the year from Monday to Saturday from 9.30 am to 5 pm. It's a helpful place with a good range of publications on Orkney, and you can also change money. A recommended walking guide is *Walks in Orkney* by Mary Welsh (£5.95).

St Magnus Cathedral

Founded in 1137 and constructed from local red sandstone and yellow Eday stone, St Magnus Cathedral (☎ 874894) was built by masons who had worked on Durham Cathedral. The interior is particularly impressive and, although much smaller than the great cathedral at Durham, the same powerful atmosphere of a very ancient faith pervades the place.

Earl Rognvald Kolsson commissioned the cathedral in the name of his martyred uncle, Magnus Erlendsson, who was killed by Earl Hakon Paulsson on Egilsay in 1115. The building is the result of 300 years of construction and alteration, and includes Romanesque, Transitional and Gothic styles.

The bones of Magnus are interred in one of the pillars in the cathedral. Other memorials include a statue of John Rae, the Arctic explorer, and the bell from HMS *Royal Oak*, sunk in WWII with the loss of 833 crew.

The cathedral is open Monday to Saturday from 9 am to 6 pm. There's a Sunday service at 11.15 am.

Earl's Palace & Bishop's Palace

Near the cathedral, and on opposite sides of the street, these two ruined buildings are in the care of HS. They're open April to October, Monday to Saturday from 9.30 am to 6 pm, and in the afternoon only on Sunday. Entry is £1.20/75p or £6/2 for a ticket that also includes Maes Howe, Skara Brae and the Broch of Gurness.

The Bishop's Palace was built in the mid-12th century to provide comfortable lodgings for Bishop William the Old. There's a good view of the cathedral from the tower, and a plaque showing the different phases of the construction of the cathedral.

The Earl's Palace was once known as the finest example of French Renaissance architecture in Scotland. It was begun in 1600 by Earl Patrick Stewart, but he ran out of money and the palace was never completed.

Tankerness House Museum

This restored merchant's house (☎ 873191) contains an interesting museum of Orkney

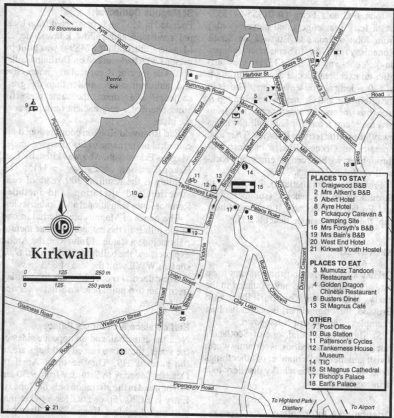

Kirkwall

PLACES TO STAY
1 Craigwood B&B
2 Mrs Aitken's B&B
5 Albert Hotel
8 Ayre Hotel
9 Pickaquoy Caravan &
  Camping Site
16 Mrs Forsyth's B&B
19 Mrs Bain's B&B
20 West End Hotel
21 Kirkwall Youth Hostel

PLACES TO EAT
3 Mumutaz Tandoori
  Restaurant
4 Golden Dragon
  Chinese Restaurant
6 Busters Diner
13 St Magnus Café

OTHER
7 Post Office
10 Bus Station
11 Patterson's Cycles
12 Tankerness House
   Museum
14 TIC
15 St Magnus Cathedral
17 Bishop's Palace
18 Earl's Palace

life over the last 5000 years. The house and garden are open daily until 5 pm (closed from 12.30 to 1.30 pm for lunch) and on Sunday afternoon in summer; £1.50/free.

Highland Park Distillery
Not only is Highland Park a very fine single-malt, but the tour of the world's most northern whisky distillery is also one of the best. You'll see the whole whisky-making process – this is one of the few distilleries that still does its own barley malting.

There are tours of the distillery (☎ 874619) every half-hour from noon to 4 pm, from April to October, Monday to Friday, and on Saturday from June to August. In winter there are tours from Monday to Friday at 2 pm and 3.30 pm (by appointment only in January and February). Your free dram's not free, though – tickets cost £2.

Organised Tours
Go Orkney (☎ 874260) has a selection of bus tours, including a morning visit to the monuments around Stenness for £6/3. Wildabout Orkney (book at the TIC) is a small tour company with tours for around £7/14 for half/full-day tours of various sights and

birdwatching areas. Also, Craigie's Taxis (☎ 872817) offers taxi tours for around £15 per hour for four people.

Places to Stay

Hostel The *Kirkwall Youth Hostel* (☎ 872243), Old Scapa Rd, is large and well equipped. It's a 20-minute walk from the harbour and costs £6.95/5.85 per night.

Camping The *Pickaquoy Caravan & Camping Site* (☎ 873535) is on the outskirts of town. It's OK but would be nicer if it were beside the sea. Charges are £2.35 for a small tent and one person.

B&Bs & Hotels There's a good range of cheap B&Bs, though most are very small and few have rooms with attached baths.

Mrs Aitken's (☎ 874193), Whiteclett, St Catherine's Place, is central, with three doubles for £14 per person. There are several places on nearby Cromwell Rd. Try *Craigwood* (☎ 872006), which charges £14/24.

Mrs Forsyth's (☎ 874020), at 21 Willowburn Rd, is a small, friendly place, and costs £14 per person. *Mrs Flett's* (☎ 872747), Briar Lea, 10 Dundas Crescent, is a comfortable B&B with two singles and two doubles for £16 per person. *Mrs Omand's* (☎ 872657), Elderwood, 4 Park Loan, has been recommended as an excellent B&B. There are just two rooms at £14 per person.

Mrs Bain's (☎ 872862), 6 Frasers Close, is down a quiet lane near the bus station. There are three rooms, one with attached bath, costing £14 per person.

The *West End Hotel* (☎ 872368), Main St, dates from 1824 and has singles/doubles for £32/52, all with attached baths. There's also a good restaurant.

The *Albert Hotel* (☎ 876000), Mounthoolie Lane, is central and has a couple of lively bars. Rooms are £45/75.

The harbourfront *Ayre Hotel* (☎ 873001) is the top place to stay. It's a very comfortable town house hotel, built 200 years ago. B&B costs £52/78; the most pleasant rooms are those with a sea view.

Places to Eat

St Magnus Café (☎ 873354), in the Kirkwall & St Ola Community Centre across the road from the cathedral, has good, cheap food – quiches, bacon rolls etc. It's open Monday to Saturday until 4 pm, and also in the evening on Monday and Thursday.

There are several places to eat around Bridge St, near the harbour. *Mumutaz Tandoori Restaurant* (☎ 873537), 7 Bridge St, has a wide range of main dishes from £6 to £10, and 10% discounts for takeaways. Opposite, *International Takeaway* dishes up fish & chips.

For Chinese food there are a couple restaurants that also do takeaways: the *Golden Dragon* (☎ 872933), 25A Bridge St, and the *Empire Chinese Restaurant* (☎ 872300), 51 Junction Rd.

Busters Diner (☎ 876717), 1 Mounthoolie Place, is an American/Mexican place serving pizzas, burgers and hotdogs. It's open daily until at least 10 pm, and also does takeaways.

The restaurant at the *Ayre Hotel* is recommended but expensive. At the *Albert Hotel* main dishes are around £13. For a really special occasion, go to the Creel Restaurant in St Margaret's Hope (see the upcoming section on South Ronaldsay).

Entertainment

The bar at the *Albert Hotel* is probably the liveliest place to drink, and you can also get meals. On Thursday, Friday and Saturday there's a disco – Matchmakers. The *West End Hotel* has a pleasant bar that does good pub grub.

Getting There & Away

The airport (☎ 872494) is 2½ miles from the town centre. For information on flying into Orkney, see the start of this section. For flights and ferries to the northern islands, see the following island sections.

From the bus station, JD Peace (☎ 872866) runs buses to Stromness (35 minutes, £2). There are 10 buses a day on weekdays, five on Saturday. For Houton (25 minutes, £1.20), they also have at least three buses a day from Monday to Saturday.

Causeway Coaches (☎ 831444) runs buses to St Margaret's Hope and Burwick, both on South Ronaldsay. And Rosie Coaches (☎ 751227) operates the service to Tingwall and Evie. Note that no buses run on Sunday in Orkney.

Getting Around

Car There are several rental places. Charges are from around £29 per day, or £160 per week. Try Scarth Hire (☎ 872125), Great Western Rd, or John G Shearer & Sons (☎ 872950).

Bicycle Patterson's (☎ 873097), Tankerness Lane, rents mountain bikes for £7/42 for a day/week.

WEST & NORTH MAINLAND
Stromness

- *pop 2100* • ☎ 01856

P&O ferries dock at this attractive little greystone village. As a place to stay, many visitors prefer Stromness to Kirkwall – it's smaller, it has more of the feeling of a working fishing village, and it's convenient for the island of Hoy. There are some excellent places to stay, including two hostels. The winding main street has a most civilised selection of shops that includes no less than three bookshops and even a place that does tarot readings.

Although Stromness was officially founded in 1620, it had been used as a port by the Vikings in the 12th century, as well as by earlier visitors. Its importance as a trading port grew in the 18th century and in the 19th century it was a busy centre for the herring industry. Until the beginning of this century, ships from the Hudson's Bay Company would stop to take on fresh water from Login's Well.

The TIC (☎ 850716) is in the ferry terminal and is open daily, staying open later when ferries dock.

Places to Stay *Ness Point Caravan & Camping Site* (☎ 873535) overlooks the bay at the south end of town, although it can be a little breezy. It costs £2.35 for a small tent.

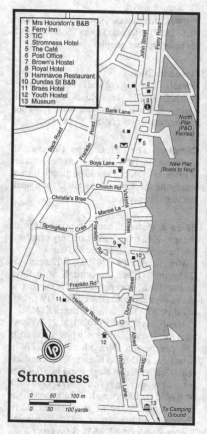

1 Mrs Hourston's B&B
2 Ferry Inn
3 TIC
4 Stromness Hotel
5 The Café
6 Post Office
7 Brown's Hostel
8 Royal Hotel
9 Hamnavoe Restaurant
10 Dundas St B&B
11 Braes Hotel
12 Youth Hostel
13 Museum

Stromness

Stromness Youth Hostel (☎ 850589), Hellihole Rd, is a 10-minute walk from the ferry terminal. The nightly charge is £5.40/4.40.

Brown's Hostel (☎ 850661), 45 Victoria St, is a very popular independent place. Open year-round, they have 20 beds (£7.50 each), and there's no curfew.

B&Bs include *Mrs Hourston's* (☎ 850642), 15 John St, from £16 per person; and *No 26 Dundas St* (☎ 850055), which charges around £14 per person and also organises diving excursions – from £195 for a week. Above the town on Back

Rd, *Beulah* (☎ 850860) has two rooms with attached bathrooms from £19 per person.

With views over Scapa Flow, the *Braes Hotel* (☎ 850495) has rooms from £20/36. They also have rooms with bath attached. Near the harbour, the *Ferry Inn* (☎ 850280) has rooms with attached baths from £21/38.

Places to Eat *The Café* (☎ 850368), 22 Victoria St, does pizzas, burgers and baked potatoes – to eat in or take away. There's also a fish & chip shop nearby.

There's a good bar at the *Ferry Inn* and a restaurant serving seafood. Main dishes are from around £6. For a pint try Orkney Dark Island, the local brew. The bar at the *Stromness Hotel* does cheaper meals. The most popular place to drink is the *Royal Hotel*, mainly because it stays open late.

The top place to eat is the *Hamnavoe Restaurant* (☎ 850606), 35 Graham Place. Main dishes at this excellent seafood restaurant are around £8.75. They're closed on Monday.

Getting There & Away For information on ferries to Scrabster, Lerwick and Aberdeen, see the start of the Orkney section. For boats to Hoy, see the upcoming Hoy section.

JD Peace (☎ 872866) runs buses to Kirkwall (35 minutes, £2), Monday to Saturday. Shalder Coaches (☎ 850809) has a bus to Birsay on Monday only.

Stenness

This village is little more than a petrol station and a shop which sells hats of the type you might wear to the races at Ascot. A mile east, however, are some of the most interesting prehistoric monuments on Orkney. Since the road between Stromness and Kirkwall passes through, you can travel by bus, every day except Sunday. Hitching is also easy.

Maes Howe Constructed about 5000 years ago, this is the finest chambered tomb in western Europe. A long stone passage leads into a chamber in the centre of an earth-covered mound which is over 22 feet high

and 115 feet across. The passage is aligned with sunset in midwinter.

Only a piece of a skull and some horse bones were found when the tomb was excavated in the 19th century. It's not known how many people were originally buried here or whether they were buried with any of their worldly goods. In the 12th century, however, Vikings returning from the Crusades broke into the tomb, searching for treasure. They found none, but left a wonderfully earthy collection of graffiti, carved in runes on the walls of the tomb. Some of it's pretty basic – 'Thorni bedded Helgi Carved', but 'Many a woman has walked stooping in here' is a little more subtle – you have to stoop to get through the passage.

Maes Howe is open April to September, from 9.30 am to 6.30 pm (afternoon only on Sunday), and for shorter hours in winter; £2/75p. There's also a combined ticket for £6/2, which includes Skara Brae, the Broch of Gurness and the Bishop's and Earl's Palaces. You buy your ticket in Tormiston Mill, on the other side of the road from Maes Howe. There's also a café and gift shop.

Standing Stones of Stenness Near Maes Howe stand only four of the original 12 mighty boulders that once formed a ring. They were erected around 2500 BC; one is over 16 feet high. There's no entrance charge.

Ring of Brodgar About a mile along the road from Stenness towards Skara Brae is a wide circle of standing stones, some over 16 feet tall. Twenty-seven of the original 60 stones are still standing amongst the heather. It's an impressive sight and a powerful place. These old stones, raised skyward 4500 years ago, still attract the forces of nature – on 5 June 1980, one was struck by lightning.

There's no entrance charge and the monument is always open.

Skara Brae

Eight miles north of Stromness, idyllically situated by a sandy bay, is northern Europe's best preserved prehistoric village. Even the stone furniture – beds, boxes and dressers – has survived the 5000 years since a community first occupied it. It was hidden under the sand until 1850, when a severe storm ripped the grass off the dunes.

Skara Brae is in the care of HS; entry times and prices are as for Maes Howe. It's worth buying the guidebook, which gives a guided tour involving eight viewpoints.

You need your own transport, except on Monday when there's a bus to Birsay. Alternatively, it's possible to walk along the coast from Stromness via Yesnaby.

Yesnaby Sea Stacks

Six miles north of Stromness are some spectacular coastal walks. A mile south of the car park is Yesnaby Castle, a sea stack similar to the Old Man of Hoy. Watch out during the nesting season in the early summer, as seabirds will dive-bomb you to scare you away from their nests.

Birsay

The small village of Birsay is five miles north of Skara Brae. The ruins of the **Earl's Palace** (always open; free) are in the centre of Birsay. The palace was built in the 16th century on an even grander scale than the palace in Kirkwall.

When the tide is down, you can walk out to the **Brough of Birsay**, ¾ of a mile from the Earl's Palace. It's a Norse settlement built around the 12th-century St Peter's Church, of which the foundations remain.

Birsay Hostel (☎ 01856-873535, ext 2404) was formerly the village school and has 26 beds for £5.40 per night each. It's open all year. There's B&B accommodation at *Primrose Cottage* (☎ 01856-721384), which overlooks Marwick Bay, for £13/26 or £34 for a double with bathroom attached.

Evie

About 1½ miles down a track from the tiny village of Evie, and past a sandy beach, is the **Broch of Gurness**. Although not nearly as impressive as Mousa Broch in Shetland, this is the best preserved example of a fortified stone tower in Orkney. Built around 100 BC,

it's surrounded by the remains of a large village. Standard HS hours and entry fees apply.

The *Eviedale Centre* (☎ 01856-751270), in the village, has a small bothy with four beds (£4 each), and a camping ground. A range of outdoor activities is offered at this centre, including canoeing and windsurfing. During the day, meals are available at the *Dale Kitchen Restaurant*.

EAST MAINLAND, BURRAY & SOUTH RONALDSAY

After a German U-boat sneaked into Scapa Flow and sank the battleship HMS *Royal Oak* in 1939, Churchill ordered better protection for the naval base. Using concrete blocks and old ships, the channels between some of the islands around Scapa Flow were blocked. The Churchill Barriers, as they are known, now link the islands of Lamb Holm, Glimps Holm, Burray and South Ronaldsay to Mainland. There are good sandy beaches by Barriers No 3 and 4.

East Mainland is mainly agricultural. There are large colonies of nesting seabirds at Mull Head and Gultak, and the shores of Deer Sound attract wildfowl.

On the island of Lamb Holm, the **Italian Chapel** is all that remains of a POW camp that housed the Italian prisoners who worked on the Churchill Barriers. They built the chapel in their spare time, using two Nissen huts, scrap metal and their considerable artistic and decorative skills. One of the artists returned in 1960 to restore the paintwork. It's definitely worth seeing.

On Burray, the road passes the **Orkney Fossil & Vintage Centre** (☎ 01856-731255), a quirky collection of local furniture and clothes, and 360 million-year-old fish fossils. Entry is £2/1 and the teashop is excellent.

The main village on South Ronaldsay is St Margaret's Hope, named after Margaret, the Maid of Norway, who was to have married Edward II of England but died here in 1290. The **Orkney Wireless Museum** (☎ 01856-874272) is a fascinating jumble of communications equipment. Entry is £1/50p.

Highly recommended is a visit to the **Tomb of the Eagles** (☎ 01856-831339). The 5000-year-old burial chamber was discovered by local farmers, the Simisons, who now run this privately owned visitors' attraction. It's as interesting for their entertaining and informative guided tour as for the tomb itself. After handling some of the skulls and eagles' claws found in the tomb, you walk across the fields, put on knee pads and crawl down the entrance passage. It's well worth the £2 ticket.

The summer-only ferry from John o'Groats docks in Burwick, on the south coast of South Ronaldsay. See the start of this section for details.

Places to Stay & Eat

Mrs Watt's (☎ 01856-731217), Ankersted, is an excellent B&B on Burray, with rooms with attached bath for £15/30. Diving can be organised here.

St Margaret's Hope on South Ronaldsay is a good place to stay. *The Anchorage* (☎ 01856-831456) charges £18/34 for rooms with bathrooms attached. The *Creel Restaurant* (☎ 01856-83311), Front Rd, is arguably the best place to eat in Orkney, and also has B&B accommodation for £35/50. Main dishes are £14.50; there's a three-course dinner for £22. Orcadian fish stew is excellent. It's closed on Monday.

Wheems Bothy (☎ 01856-831537), Eastside, is a very pleasant hostel offering basic bed and organic breakfast for £5. You can camp if the hostel is full.

Getting There & Away

Between Kirkwall and St Margaret's Hope, Causeway Coaches (☎ 01856-831444) run four buses a day on weekdays, two on Saturday. There's also a Kirkwall-Burwick service that connects with the ferries.

HOY

The highest hills in Orkney are on Hoy (the

Scapa Flow Wrecks

The wrecks that litter these clear waters make Scapa Flow the best diving location in Europe. Enclosed by Mainland, Hoy and South Ronaldsay, this is one of the world's largest natural harbours and has been used by vessels as diverse as King Hakon's Viking ships in the 13th century and the NATO fleet of today.

It was from Scapa Flow that the British Home Fleet sailed to meet the German High Seas Fleet at the Battle of Jutland on 31 May 1916. After the war, 74 German ships were interned in Scapa. Conditions for the German sailors were poor and there were several mutinies as the negotiations for the fate of the ships dragged on. When the terms of the armistice were agreed on 6 May 1919 with the announcement of a severely reduced German navy, Admiral von Reuter, who was in charge of the German fleet in Scapa Flow, decided to take matters into his own hands. On 21 June, a secret signal was passed from ship to ship and the British watched incredulously as every German ship began to sink.

Most of the ships were salvaged, but seven vessels remain to attract divers. There are three battleships – the *König*, the *Kronprinz Wilhelm* and the *Markgraf* – which are all over 25,000 tons. The first two were subject to blasting for scrap metal, but the *Markgraf* is undamaged and considered one of the best dives in the area. Four light cruisers (4400 to 5600 tons) – the *Karlsruhe*, *Dresden*, *Brummer* and *Köln* – are particularly interesting as they lie on their sides and are very accessible to divers. The *Karlsruhe*, though severely damaged, is only 30 feet below the surface. Its twisted superstructure has now become a huge metal reef encrusted with diverse sea life.

As well as the German wrecks, numerous other ships litter the Scapa Flow sea bed. HMS *Royal Oak*, which was sunk by a German U-boat in October 1939, with the loss of 833 crew, is now an official war grave.

If you're interested in diving Scapa Flow, contact the following: Dive Orkney (☎ 01856-874761), Polrudden, Pickaquoy Rd, Kirkwall; the Diving Cellar (☎ 01856-850055), 26 Dundas St, Stromness; or the Scapa Flow Diving Centre (☎ 01856-73225), Briarlea, Burray. ■

name means High Island), the second-largest island in the group. There's spectacular cliff scenery, including some of the highest vertical cliffs in Britain. St John's Head rises 1136 feet on the west coast. The island is probably best known for the **Old Man of Hoy**, a 450-foot-high rock stack that can be seen from the Scrabster-Stromness ferry.

The best scenery is in the northern part of the island, maintained as a nature reserve by the RSPB since 1983. There are some excellent walks, the most popular being to the edge of the cliffs opposite the Old Man of Hoy. You should allow about six hours for the return trip from Moaness Pier. There's basic accommodation in Rackwick, a two-hour walk from the pier through the beautiful **Rackwick Valley**. You pass the 5000-year-old **Dwarfie Stone**, the only example of a rock-cut tomb in Britain, and **Berriedale Wood**, the country's most northerly native forest.

Lyness, on the eastern side of Hoy, was an important naval base during both world wars, when the British Grand Fleet was based in Scapa Flow. With the dilapidated remains of buildings and an uninspiring outlook towards the Occidental Oil Terminal on Flotta Island, this is not a pretty place, but the **Scapa Flow Visitors Centre** (☎ 01856-791300) is well worth a visit. It's a fascinating naval museum and photographic display in an old pumphouse. It's open year round from Monday to Friday, 9 am to 4.30 pm, and in summer from 10.30 am to 3.30 pm on Saturday, and 9.30 am to 6.15 pm on Sunday; £1.50/80p.

Places to Stay & Eat
Hoy Outdoor Centre (☎ 01856-873535, ext 2404) is just over a mile from Moaness Pier. Beds cost £5.40 per person. BYO sleeping bag and supplies. Near the post office and the pier, the *Hoy Inn* (☎ 01856-791313) is a bar with a restaurant serving good seafood; the garlic clams are excellent. The RSPB has a small information centre here.

In Rackwick Valley, the *Rackwick Outdoor Centre* (☎ 01856-873535, ext 2404) has eight beds in two dorms; bring

your own sleeping bag. The nightly charge is £5.40 and the warden comes by to collect it each evening.

There are several B&Bs on the island, with accommodation at around £14 per person. At Lyness, *Mrs Budge's* (☎ 01856-791234) has two rooms. There's the *Anchor Bar* at Lyness, and also a *café* at the Scapa Flow Visitors Centre.

Getting There & Away
In summer, a passenger ferry (☎ 01856-850624) runs from Stromness to Moaness pier (30 minutes, £2.10), at 7.45 and 10.30 am and 4.30 pm on weekdays, and 9.30 am and 6 pm at weekends. In the other direction, the service runs half an hour later. The 7.45 am boat can call at Graemsay Island.

From Houton, on Mainland, two small car ferries (☎ 01856-872044) cross Scapa Flow to Lyness (45 minutes, £2.10) on Hoy and the island of Flotta, 20 minutes from Lyness. There are about seven sailings per day, plus a limited service on Sunday in summer. There's one service a day between Houton and Longhope.

NORTHERN ISLANDS
The group of windswept islands that lies north of Mainland provides a refuge for migrating birds and a nesting ground for seabirds; there are several RSPB reserves. This can be a hazardous area for shipping – the surrounding seas are littered with wrecks. Some of the islands are also rich in archaeological sites.

The TICs in Kirkwall and Stromness have leaflets with useful maps for each of these islands. Note that the pronunciation of the 'ay' ending of each island name is 'ee' (ie Shapinsay is pronounced shapinsee).

Orkney Islands Shipping Company (☎ 01856-872044) operates an efficient ferry service. From Kirkwall you can day-trip to many of the islands (except North Ronaldsay; see that section) on most days of the week, but it's really worth staying for at least a few nights.

Shapinsay

Just 30 minutes by ferry from Kirkwall, Shapinsay is a highly cultivated, low-lying island. **Balfour Castle**, built in 1850 in the Scottish Baronial style, is the most impressive sight and there are tours on Wednesday and Sunday afternoon. These must be arranged in advance at the TIC in Kirkwall.

There's B&B for £14/28 at *Mrs Wallace's* (☎ 01856-711256), Girnigoe. With home-made bread and jam, the breakfasts at this farmhouse are excellent, and they also do four-course dinners. It's also possible to stay at *Balfour Castle* (☎ 01856-711282), where dinner, bed and breakfast costs £68 per person. A private boat is available.

There are about six sailings every day (including Sunday in summer) between Kirkwall and Shapinsay (45 minutes).

Rousay

This hilly island, with a population of around 200 people, is known as 'the Egypt of the North' for its numerous archaeological sites. It also has an important RSPB reserve and three lochs for trout fishing.

West of the pier are four prehistoric **burial cairns** – the two-storeyed Taversoe Tuick, the stalled cairns of Yarso and Blackhammer and Midhowe Cairn. Containing the remains of 25 people and dating from the 3rd millennium BC, the Great Ship of Death, as Midhowe Cairn is called, is the longest chambered cairn in Orkney. Nearby, **Midhowe Broch** is the best example of a broch on these islands.

The TICs on Mainland have a useful leaflet, *Westness Walk*, describing the mile-long walk from Midhowe Cairn to Westness Farm. Bikes can be rented for £5 per day from Helga's (☎ 01856-821293), near the pier, and the island's one road makes a pleasant circuit of about 13 miles.

Places to Stay & Eat At *Trumland Farm* (☎ 01856-821252), half a mile from the ferry, there's dormitory accommodation for £5 (bring a sleeping bag) and tent sites for £2.50. You can get seafood at the *Pier Restaurant* by the pier.

Taversoe Hotel (☎ 01856-821325) has B&B accommodation at around £25 per person. There are superb views from the restaurant and a good selection of malt whiskies in the bar. It's closed on Monday.

Getting There & Away A small car ferry connects Tingwall (Mainland) with Rousay (30 minutes; £2.10 for a passenger, £6.30 for a car) and the other nearby islands of Egilsay and Wyre about six times every day. For bookings phone ☎ 01856-872044.

Egilsay & Wyre

These two small islands lie 1½ miles east of Rousay. On Egilsay, a cenotaph marks the spot where Earl Magnus was murdered in 1116. After his martyrdom, pilgrims flocked to the island and St Magnus Church, now roofless, was built.

Wyre is even smaller than Egilsay. In the mid-12th century it was the domain of the Viking baron Kolbein Hruga ('Cubbie Roo'). The ruins of his castle and church can be visited.

These two islands are reached on the Rousay-Kirkwall ferry, but you have to ask if you wish to land.

Stronsay

In the 18th century, the major industry on this island was the collection and burning of seaweed to make kelp, which was exported for use in the production of glass, iodine and soap. In the 19th century, it was replaced by herring-curing, and Whitehall harbour became one of Scotland's major herring ports.

A peaceful and attractive island, Stronsay now attracts seals, migratory birds and tourists. There are good coastal walks and, in the east, the Vat o' Kirbister is the best example of a gloup (natural arch) in Orkney.

Places to Stay & Eat The *Stronsay Hotel* (☎ 01857-616213) in Whitehall has rooms for £12 per person. In the bar you can get reasonable pub grub. At *Stronsay Bird Reserve* (☎ 01857-616363), on Mill Bay, there's B&B for £13 and you can also camp.

Getting There & Away BA Express (☎ 01856-872494) has two flights a day, Monday to Friday, from Kirkwall (£28/56 for a single/return).

A ferry service links Kirkwall with Stronsay (1½ hours, two per day, £4.20), and Stronsay with Eday (35 minutes, one per day, £2.10). There's a reduced service on Saturday, and on Sunday in summer.

Eday

Eday supplied some of the stone for St Magnus Cathedral in Kirkwall, and peat to most other northern islands. It has a hilly centre and cultivated fields around the coast. Occupied for at least the last 5000 years, Eday has numerous chambered cairns, and also one of Orkney's most impressively located standing stones, the **Stone of Setter**.

It's worth getting hold of the *Eday Heritage Walk* leaflet, which details an interesting four-hour ramble from the Community Enterprises shop up to the Cliffs of Red Head in the north of the island.

Places to Stay The basic *Eday Youth Hostel* (☎ 01857-622283) is operated by Eday Community Enterprises and is four miles from the ferry. There are 24 beds; £4.10 per night. There's B&B at *Mrs Cockram's* (☎ 01857-622271), Skaill, for around £23 per person including dinner, in a comfortable farmhouse.

Getting There & Away There are flights from Kirkwall (£28 per single) to London airport – that's London, Eday – on Wednesday only. The ferry service sails via Stronsay from Kirkwall (2½ hours). There's a twice-weekly link between Sanday and Eday.

Sanday

This island is aptly named, for the best beaches in Orkney are here – dazzling white sand of the sort you'd expect in the Caribbean. The island is 12 miles long and almost entirely flat, apart from the cliffs at Spurness.

There are several archaeological sites, the most impressive being the **Quoyness**

chambered tomb, similar to Maes Howe, and dating from the 3rd millennium.

The island is known for its knitwear, which is sold in Lady village, at the Wool Hall. Bikes and cars can be rented from Kettletoft Garage (☎ 01857-600321).

Places to Stay There's comfortable accommodation at the *Belsair Hotel* (☎ 01857-600206), which has six rooms, three with attached baths. Charges are from £15 per person. With permission, you can also camp on the island.

Getting There & Away Flights from Kirkwall (£28 single) operate to Sanday and Westray twice daily from Monday to Friday, and once on Saturday. There's at least one ferry a day between Kirkwall and Sanday (2½ hours) in summer.

Westray

This is the largest of the northern islands, with a population of around 700. It's quite a varied island, with prehistoric sites, some sandy beaches, impressive cliff scenery and the ruins of **Noltland Castle** (a fortified Z-plan house). It's also famous for the RSPB reserve at Noup Head Cliffs, which attracts vast numbers of breeding seabirds.

Pierowall is the main village and one of the best natural harbours in Orkney, once an important Viking base. Ferries also dock at Rapness, about seven miles to the south of Pierowall.

Places to Stay & Eat With permission, you can camp almost anywhere. Several places offer B&B from around £13/26. Try *Mrs Groat's* (☎ 01857-677374) at Sand o'Gill (where there are a couple of bikes for rent); she also has a six-berth van at around £80 per week. The *Pierowall Hotel* (☎ 01857-677208) is a popular pub with accommodation at £16/27.

The most comfortable place to stay is the *Cleaton House Hotel* (☎ 01857-677508), a refurbished Victorian manse. B&B costs from £22 to £25 per person. The bar and restaurant are open to nonresidents.

Getting There & Away For information on flights, see under Sanday. A ferry service links Kirkwall with Rapness and Pierowall on Westray, and Papa Westray. There's at least one service a day (1½ hours, £4.20) in each direction.

Papa Westray

This tiny island (four miles long and one mile wide) attracts superlatives – Europe's oldest domestic building is the Knap of Howar (built about 5500 years ago), the world's shortest scheduled flight is the two-minute hop over from Westray, and the largest colony of Arctic terns in Europe is at North Hill. The island was also the cradle of Christianity in Orkney – St Bonieface's Church was founded in the 8th century.

Places to Stay & Eat The excellent *Papa Westray Hostel* (☎ 01857-644267) is open all year. It's a couple of miles from the ferry. There are 16 beds and the nightly charge is £6.95. They also have three comfortable rooms with attached bathrooms on a B&B basis for £26/52. The community co-op runs a small shop here.

Getting There & Away Flying to Papa Westray or North Ronaldsay from Kirkwall is an amazing deal compared to other flights in Orkney – about twice the distance for half the price. To either island it's £12/24 for a single/return, and there are flights twice daily from Monday to Saturday.

There's one ferry between Westray and Papa Westray (40 minutes, £2.10), Tuesday to Friday, and on Sunday in summer. On Tuesday, Thursday and Sunday, there's a through service from Kirkwall (2¼ hours, £4.20).

North Ronaldsay

Pity the poor sheep on this remote, windswept island – they're kept off the rich farmland by a wall and forced to feed only on seaweed, which is said to give their meat a unique flavour.

North Ronaldsay is only three miles long and almost completely flat. About 50 people live here and the island is an important stopover point for migratory birds. The *Bird Observatory* (☎ 01857-633200) offers solar-powered accommodation and ornithological activities at £24 per person including dinner and packed lunch. *Rinarsay Guest House* (☎ 01857-633221) is similarly priced.

See Papa Westray for details of flights. There's also a weekly sailing from Kirkwall, not always on the same day of the week. Phone ☎ 01856-872044 for details.

Shetland Islands

Sixty miles north of Orkney, the Shetland Islands remained under Norse rule until 1469, when they were given to Scotland as part of a Danish princess's dowry. Even today these remote, windswept and treeless islands are almost as much a part of Scandinavia as of Britain – the nearest mainland town is Bergen, Norway.

Much bleaker than Orkney, Shetland is famous for its varied birdlife and teeming seabird colonies, a 4000-year-old archaeological heritage that includes the ancient settlement of Jarlshof, and for its rugged, indented coastline that offers superb clifftop walks.

Almost everything of interest is on the coast rather than inland, so you're much more aware of the presence of the sea than on Orkney's Mainland. In fact, in Shetland it's impossible to get further than three miles away from the sea. There are some impressively located places to stay, and budget accommodation includes four camping böds (barns).

Of the 100 islands, 15 are inhabited. Mainland is by far the largest; Lerwick is the capital. Shetland is the base for the North Sea oilfields, and pipelines feed Europe's biggest oil refinery at Sullom Voe, in north Mainland. Oil has brought a certain amount of prosperity to these islands. There are well-equipped leisure centres in many villages and the wide roads seem like motorways after Orkney's tiny, winding lanes.

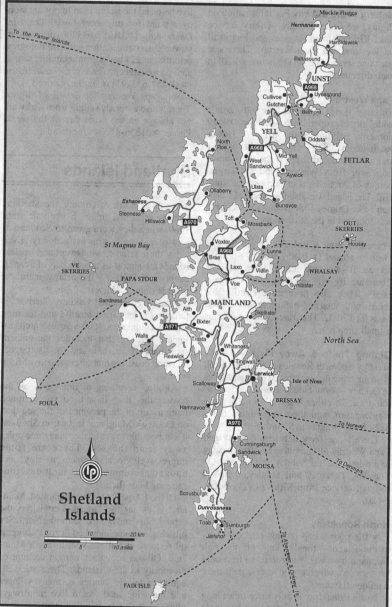

Shetland Islands

Birdwatching in the Shetlands

Lying on the north-south and east-west migration routes, this island group is internationally famous for its birdlife, and is one of Britain's top birdwatching locations. As well as being a stopover for migrating Arctic species, there are large seabird breeding colonies. Out of the 24 seabird species that nest in the British Isles, 21 can be found here; June is the height of the breeding season. The bird population vastly outnumbers the human population of 24,000 – there are said to be around 30,000 gannets, 140,000 guillemots, 250,000 puffins and 300,000 fulmars.

The RSPB maintains reserves on south Mainland at Loch of Spiggie, which attracts wildfowl in autumn and winter, Lumbister on Yell, a 4000-acre moorland reserve, and on the remote island of Fetlar, which supports the richest heathland bird community, known particularly for its snowy owls.

There are national nature reserves at Hermaness, where you cannot fail to be entertained by the clownish antics of the almost tame puffins – known here as the tammy norrie – and on the Isle of Noss, which can be reached from Lerwick. Fair Isle, owned by the NTS, supports large seabird populations and you can stay at the bird observatory.

Lerwick TIC has lots of ornithological leaflets. Take care when out birdwatching, as the cliff-edge sites can be dangerous. Also watch out for skuas ('bonxies') that will dive-bomb you if you go near their nests. Since they aim for the highest part of your body, it's wise to walk with a stick, pointing it above your head if they approach. And don't get too close to nesting fulmars or you'll be the target for their smelly, oily spittle! ■

GETTING THERE & AWAY

Unlike Orkney, Shetland is relatively expensive to get to from mainland Britain.

Air

The oil industry ensures that air connections are good. The main airport is at Sumburgh, 25 miles south of Lerwick. There are at least four flights daily between Sumburgh and Aberdeen, on British Airways (☎ 0345-222111) and Business Air (☎ 01382-566345). Fares are from around £100 return. You can also fly direct from Inverness, Glasgow, Edinburgh, Belfast and London.

BA operate low-flying ATPs daily between Orkney and Shetland (35 minutes, from £55 return).

Boat

P&O (☎ 01224-572615) runs car ferries between Lerwick, Aberdeen and Stromness (Orkney), see those sections for details. For details of the ferry link between Lerwick and Bergen (Norway) see Scotland's introductory Getting There & Away section.

LERWICK
- *pop 7500*   • ☎ *01595*

A pleasant town of grey-stone buildings built around a natural harbour, Lerwick is the only place of any size in Shetland.

Although the Shetland Islands have been occupied for several thousand years, Lerwick was established only in the 17th century. Dutch herring fleets began to shelter in the harbour, in preference to Scalloway, which was then the capital. A small community grew up to trade with them and by the late 19th century this was the largest herring town in north Europe.

The Folk Festival in April/May is well worth being here for, as is the Fiddle and Accordion festival in October.

Orientation & Information

The ferry terminal is a 20-minute walk north of the old harbour, which forms the focus of the town and is now used by visiting yachts and pleasure cruisers. Commercial St, one block back from the waterfront, is the main shopping street, dominated by the Victorian bulk of the Grand Hotel.

The TIC (☎ 693434), on Market Cross, is open April to September, Monday to Friday from 8 am to 6 pm, and until 5 pm at weekends. From October to March it's open weekdays only, from 9 am to 5 pm. There's a good range of books and maps, as well as brochures on everything from Shetland pony

HIGHLANDS & NTH ISLANDS

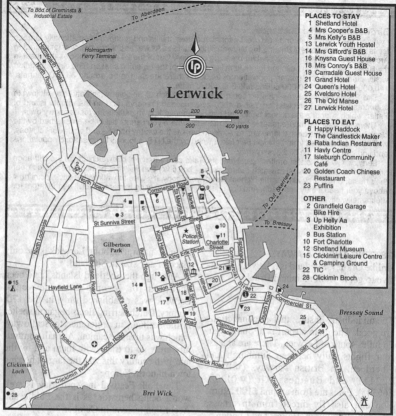

Lerwick

PLACES TO STAY
1 Shetland Hotel
4 Mrs Cooper's B&B
5 Mrs Kelly's B&B
13 Lerwick Youth Hostel
14 Mrs Gifford's B&B
16 Knysna Guest House
18 Mrs Conroy's B&B
19 Carradale Guest House
21 Grand Hotel
24 Queen's Hotel
25 Kveldsro Hotel
26 The Old Manse
27 Lerwick Hotel

PLACES TO EAT
6 Happy Haddock
7 The Candlestick Maker
8 Raba Indian Restaurant
11 Havly Centre
17 Isleburgh Community Café
20 Golden Coach Chinese Restaurant
23 Puffins

OTHER
2 Grandfield Garage Bike Hire
3 Up Helly Aa Exhibition
9 Bus Station
10 Fort Charlotte
12 Shetland Museum
15 Clickimin Leisure Centre & Camping Ground
22 TIC
28 Clickimin Broch

stud farms to lists of safe anchorages for yachts. *Inter-Shetland Transport Timetable* (70p) is an invaluable publication listing all local air, sea and bus services. *Walks on Shetland* by Mary Welsh (£6.50) is a good walking guide. There's also a bureau de change, and there's a seasonal TIC at the ferry terminal.

There are Danish, Dutch, Finnish, French, Icelandic, Norwegian, Swedish and German consulates in Shetland.

Best buys are the woollen jerseys, cardigans and sweaters for which Shetland is world-famous. There are numerous shops selling woollens, but for bargains you must go to the factories. Judane (☎ 693724), on the industrial estate north past the power station, sells plain sweaters for around £13, patterned ones for £26. Most sought-after are real Fair Isle sweaters, which cost from £45. To qualify as such, they must not only have the distinctive OXOXO pattern, but must also have been made on Fair Isle.

There's a laundrette on Market St.

Things to See

Above the town, there are good views from the battlements of **Fort Charlotte**, which was built in 1653 by troops from the Cromwellian fleet. There's not much to see in the fort itself, which housed the town prison in the 19th century and now provides the headquarters for the Territorial Army. It's open daily until 10 pm in summer; free.

The **Shetland Museum** (☎ 695057) is above the library and open Monday, Wednesday and Friday from 10 am to 7 pm, and until 5 pm on Tuesday, Thursday and Saturday; free. It's worth visiting for an introduction to the island's history. There are replicas of the St Ninian's Isle treasure, and displays detailing the fishing and knitting industries, including garments produced by local firm TM Adie & Sons and worn by Tenzing and Hilary on Mt Everest.

The **Up Helly Aa Exhibition** explains the Viking fire festival that still takes place on the last Tuesday in January, when locals dress up as Vikings and set fire to a ship built here. Opening hours are limited; contact the TIC for information.

Clickimin Broch is about one mile west of the town centre. This fortified site was occupied from the 7th century BC to the 6th century AD. It's always open; free.

The **Böd of Gremista**, about a mile north of the ferry terminal, was the birthplace of Arthur Anderson, one of the founders of P&O. It's been restored as an 18th-century fishing booth; there's also a small exhibition about Anderson. It's open Wednesday to Sunday; £1.50/1.

Places to Stay
Hostel The *Lerwick Youth Hostel* (☎ 692114), King Harald St, is a mile from the ferry terminal in the centre of town. It's open April to September; the nightly charge is £6.95/5.85.

Camping *Clickimin Caravan & Camp Site* (☎ 694555) is by the Clickimin Leisure Centre and the loch on the western edge of town. They charge around £4 for a small tent.

B&Bs & Hotels Most of Lerwick's B&Bs and guesthouses are small, homely affairs with only two or three rooms.

Mrs Cooper's (☎ 695976), 60 Burgh Rd, has two doubles and a twin at £17 per person. Further south along Burgh Rd, at No 12, there's *Mrs Gifford's* (☎ 693554), charging £18/32 for a single/double. At No 6 Burgh Rd, *Knysna Guest House* (☎ 694865) has rooms for £16/28. Beside it there's *Goudengarth Guest House* (☎ 696820), 2 South Rd, which is a bit more upmarket – some rooms have attached bathrooms. They charge from £18/32.

If you're sick of the wimpy, dribbling hosepipes that masquerade as showers in the bathrooms of most British B&Bs book into *Mrs Kelly's* (☎ 692330), 95 King Harald St. There's a wonderful shower, and comfortable rooms for £15 per person. Further south at No 36 King Harald St, there's *Carradale Guest House* (☎ 692251), and next door at No 34 is *Solheim Guest House* (☎ 695275). They're similarly priced at £18/32 for a single/double with shared bathroom.

At 43 Saint Olaf St, *Mrs Conroy's* (☎ 693687) is a pleasant place with just two twin rooms. She charges £18/32.

The *Old Manse* (☎ 696301), 9 Commercial St, is recommended, and one room has an attached bathroom. It's a comfortable B&B and charges are around £19 per person.

The *Queen's Hotel* (☎ 692826), Commercial St, is right by the harbour, and, if you can get a room with a view over the water, a very pleasant place to stay. Singles/doubles are £59/82. The top place to stay is the *Kveldsro House Hotel* (☎ 692195). Pronounced kelro, it's a very comfortable, small hotel, just off Greenfield Place, and overlooking the harbour. There are 17 rooms, and prices are £88.50/105.50 for a single/double. If they're not busy at the weekend you may be able to negotiate a special deal.

Places to Eat
Although there's good fresh fish, Shetland is no place for gastronomes. Restit is the best known local dish – lumps of mutton cured with salt and made into a soupy, salty stew traditionally eaten in the long winter months. It tastes quite as awful as it sounds and

consequently appears on menus only very rarely.

Fish & chips can be good – as they should be in the heart of a fishing community. There are several takeaways – try the *Happy Haddock*, north of the centre on Commercial Rd, or the *Fort Café* (☎ 693125), 2 Commercial Rd, which has a cheap restaurant as well as a takeaway.

The *Isleburgh Community Centre Café* (☎ 692114), near the youth hostel on King Harald St, is very cheap; it's open every day from 10 am to 5 pm and 6.30 to 9.30 pm (evening only on Sunday).

Highly recommended is the *Havly Centre*, 9 Charlotte St, a Norwegian Christian centre with an excellent café attached, and they don't quiz you on your religious beliefs. Their open sandwiches and gooey cakes are heavenly. *Puffins* (☎ 695065), Mounthooly St, has a small café open during the day.

The *Candlestick Maker* (☎ 696066), 33 Commercial Rd, is a small bistro where main dishes are around £7. They also do steaks and pizzas and are open daily (evening only on Sunday).

Raba Indian Restaurant, near the bus station, is the best curry house in Shetland. The *Golden Coach* (☎ 693848), Hillhead, is the only Chinese restaurant.

There's a good restaurant at the *Queen's Hotel*, but the *Kveldsro House Hotel* is the place to go for a special occasion.

Entertainment
The best place to drink is at *The Lounge*, near the TIC. There's live music some evenings and at lunchtime on Saturday. The Shetland Fiddlers play at a number of locations, and it's worth attending their sessions – inquire at the TIC for locations. The town's only nightclub is *Posers*, at the Grand Hotel.

Getting There & Away
See the start of this section for information on getting to Shetland. Ferries dock at the Holmsgarth terminal, a 20-minute walk from the town centre. From the main airport at Sumburgh, there are regular buses to meet flights.

Getting Around
Car It's cheaper to rent a car in Lerwick rather than at the airport. Try Star Rent A Car (☎ 692075), 22 Commercial Rd, or John Leask & Son (☎ 693162), The Esplanade.

Bicycle If it's fine, cycling on the islands' excellent roads can be an exhilarating way to experience the stark beauty of Shetland. It can, however, be very windy (windspeeds of up to 194 mph have been recorded!) and there are few places to shelter. For bike hire contact Eric Brown at Grandfield Garage (☎ 692709), North Rd.

AROUND LERWICK
Two islands lie across the water from Lerwick: Bressay, and beyond it the RSPB reserve of Noss, which is well worth visiting to see the seabirds nesting on its 600-foot-high cliffs. From the dock below Fort Charlotte in Lerwick, there are hourly ferries (☎ 01595-692024) every day to **Bressay** (five minutes, 75p). It's then a 2½-mile walk across the island; some people bring rented bikes with them from Lerwick. An inflatable dinghy shuttles across the water between Bressay and **Noss** (£2.50 return), daily except Monday and Thursday, from 10 am to 5 pm. Check with the TIC before leaving Lerwick as the Noss dinghy doesn't operate in bad weather, or after the end of August. There's accommodation on Bressay but you can't stay on Noss. There are also afternoon cruises from Lerwick around Noss.

Scalloway is the former capital of Shetland, just seven miles west of Lerwick, and connected by a daily bus service (20 minutes, £1). It's a busy fishing village with the ruins of **Scalloway Castle**, built in 1600, rising above the warehouses of the port. The small **museum** nearby is interesting for its displays on the 'Shetland Bus', the boats which the Norwegian resistance movement operated from Scalloway during WWII.

SOUTH MAINLAND
Sandwick
Opposite this little village, on the Isle of Mousa, stands the impressive double-walled

fortified tower, **Mousa Broch**, the best preserved broch in Britain. It was built between 100 BC and 100 AD. During the summer there are regular boat trips (15 minutes, £4.50 return), allowing 2½ hours on the island. You must phone (☎ 01950-431367) in advance for reservations. There are four buses a day, Monday to Saturday, between Lerwick and Sandwick (35 minutes, £1).

Sumburgh

At the southern tip of Mainland, this village is the location of the international airport and **Jarlshof** (☎ 01950-460112; HS), Shetland's most impressive archaeological attraction. This large prehistoric and Norse settlement was hidden under the sand until exposed by a gale at the turn of the century.

It's open from April to September, daily from 9.30 am to 6.30 pm (afternoon only on Sunday); £2/75p. You should buy the short guide which interprets the ruins from a number of vantage points. It's an interesting place, but the 20th century impinges with the airport being so close.

The *Sumburgh Hotel* (☎ 01950-460201) is a large, upmarket hotel with a bar and restaurant, right next to Jarlshof. Singles/doubles are £40/58. To get here from Lerwick take the airport bus (45 minutes, £1.80) and get off at the second-last stop.

NORTH MAINLAND

The basalt lava cliffs of **Eshaness**, in the north-west of Mainland, form some of the most impressive coastal scenery in Shetland, and this is good walking country. *Johnnie Notions Camping Böd* (£3 per night, book at Lerwick TIC) is at Hamnavoe.

Infrequent buses from Lerwick run only as far as **Hillswick**, seven miles from Eshaness, where the *Booth* (☎ 01806-503348) is Shetland's oldest pub. There's a vegetarian café, live music some nights and you can camp nearby. There's B&B accommodation here and at **Brae**, 11 miles along the road back to Lerwick. The *Busta House Hotel* (☎ 01806-522506), just outside Brae, is a luxurious country-house hotel with singles/doubles at £63/84. The restaurant is considered to be the best in Shetland; there are set four-course dinners for £22.50.

YELL & UNST

Yell and Unst are connected with Mainland by small car ferries between Toft and Ulsta, and Gutcher and Belmont. Prices are low (£2.60 for a car) but you must book in advance (☎ 01957-722259).

Yell is a desolate, heather-covered peat moor, but there are some good coastal walks. *Windhouse Lodge* (£3, book at Lerwick TIC) is a camping böd in the centre of the island below the haunted ruins of Windhouse.

Unst is the northernmost part of Britain. Fittingly, its northernmost point is a wonderfully wild and windy nature reserve, Hermaness, where you can sit on the cliffs, commune with the puffins and gaze across the sea into the Arctic Circle. Robert Louis Stevenson wrote *Treasure Island* while living on Unst – his father built Muckle Flugga lighthouse. There's B&B accommodation at *Barns* (☎ 01957-755249), Newgord, Westing and at *Mrs Firmin's* (☎ 01957-755234), Prestegaard, Uyeasound.

Haroldswick is 55 miles from Lerwick, and if you don't have a car you must spend the night on Unst as buses are infrequent. From Lerwick, if you catch the 8 am bus to South Yell you can make connections with ferries and other buses to reach Haroldswick before noon. It's then two miles to the Hermaness car park. Pause to mail a card from Britain's most northerly post office.

OTHER ISLANDS

Regular ferries connect Yell and Unst with **Fetlar**, where there's an RSPB reserve. West of Shetland is **Foula**, a windy island supporting a community of 50 people, 1500 sheep and 500,000 seabirds amidst dramatic cliff scenery. It's reached by twice-weekly ferries (☎ 01595-692024) from Walls and planes (£19 single) from Tingwall (☎ 01595-840246).

Fair Isle is Britain's most remote inhabited island. Known for its patterned knitwear, still produced in the island's co-operative, it's also a birdwatcher's paradise. Twenty-three miles from Sumburgh and only 3½ by 1½ miles in size, it was given to the National Trust for Scotland in 1954. Accommodation must be booked in advance and includes all meals. The *Fair Isle Lodge & Bird Observatory* (☎ 01595-760258) has full-board accommodation, charging £20 in the dorm and £34/56 for rooms. Locals also offer rooms with all meals, at around £25. Try *Mrs Stout's* (☎ 01595-760247).

From Tingwall (☎ 01595-840246) there are two flights a day and back (25 minutes, £34/68 for a single/return) on Monday, Wednesday, Friday and Saturday. A day return allows about six hours on the island, seven on Monday. The MV *Good Shepherd* (☎ 01595-760222) sails to/from Fair Isle (2¾ hours, £1.80) and Grutness (by Sumburgh) on Tuesday and Saturday in summer, and to/from Lerwick (four hours, £1.80) twice-monthly.

WALES

Facts about Wales

As soon as you cross the River Severn you know you're in a different country. Signs in Welsh bid you welcome with 'Croeso i Cymru'. All roadsigns are also in English – Wales has had the misfortune to be so close to England that it could not be allowed its independence, and far enough away to be conveniently forgotten. It is almost miraculous that anything Welsh should have survived the onslaught of its dominating neighbour, but the culture has proved to be remarkably enduring, and the language stubbornly refuses to die.

Wales' appeal lies in its countryside. In general, the towns and cities are not particularly inspiring. The best way to appreciate the Great Welsh Outdoors is by walking, cycling, canal boating, or using some other form of private transport. Simply catching buses or trains from one regional hub to another is not recommended. Instead, base yourself in a small town or farm B&B, and explore the surrounding countryside for a few days. Hay-on-Wye, Brecon, St David's, Dolgellau, Llanberis and Betws-y-Coed are possibilities that come to mind.

Although parts of the country are still breathtakingly beautiful, Wales can sometimes feel rather like England's unloved backyard – a suitable place for mines, pine plantations and nuclear power stations. Even the most enduring of its symbols – the grim mining towns and powerful castles – represent exploitation and colonialism.

Much of the most attractive countryside is now protected by the Pembrokeshire Coast National Park, the Brecon Beacons National Park and the Snowdonia National Park, but the Gower peninsula and the Llŷn peninsula are also outstanding. Outside the national parks, and particularly in the north, however, miles of coastline have been ruined by shoddy bungalows and ugly caravan parks.

Wales has an unsurpassed legacy of magnificent medieval castles. Edward I built a string of fortresses in the north-west –

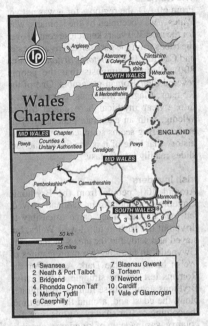

Caernarfon, Conwy, Beaumaris and Harlech are listed as World Heritage Sites and should not be missed.

HISTORY
Prehistory & the Celts

Wales is amongst the oldest countries in the world. Some of the rocks within its borders were formed over 3000 million years ago, and evidence of human habitation stretches back nearly 200,000 years. The stone frames of cromlechs (burial chambers) left by Neolithic people can still be seen in several parts of the country – Pentre Ifan in Pembrokeshire, for example.

The Celts arrived from Europe sometime after 600 BC. Little is known about them, although it is to their Celtic forebears that the modern Welsh attribute national characteristics like eloquence, warmth and imagination.

The Romans

From 60 AD, the region – for it was not yet Wales – was occupied by the Romans, who for the next 300 years kept close control over the tribes from the garrison towns at Chester and Caerlon. In his *Historia Britonum* (circa 800), Nennius suggests that the people revered their Roman governors. One of the Romans, Magnus Maximus, is transformed into a near mythical hero called Maxen Wledig, with an elaborate genealogy. This embroidering seems so much part of Welsh history that little of it is verifiable, and fact slides readily into fantasy.

Irish Invaders

Around 400, people from the Brythonic kingdom of Gododdin in Scotland arrived, led by Cunedda. They came ostensibly to drive out the Irish in north-west Wales, but stayed and settled in the area which became Gwynedd. In fact, the two main features of Welsh history in the Dark Ages after the Romans left are the struggle of the native Brythons against these raiding Irish pirates along the coast and, around the same time, the coming of Christianity. At this time, the country was made up of kingdoms, possibly remnants of administrative units set up under the Romans.

The Arrival of Christianity

The western sea routes were important for Wales. They brought the earliest settlers from the south and, later, traders from the Mediterranean. Christian missionaries came, probably from Ireland in the 5th century. Among them was a monk named Dewi, who sought converts in the south – in the Norman period, he became known as David, patron saint of Wales. A French connection is also to be found in the monastic character of the church, and in some of the inscriptions on early Christian stones.

Christianity was grafted on to the old Celtic belief system, with its sacred wells, holy men and hermit saints in the contemplative tradition, remembered in place names with the prefix *Llan* (enclosed place or church) and *Merthyr* (burial place of a saint). In 768, however, Christians became subject to the Church of Rome, which then dominated the Western world.

King Arthur & the Anglo-Saxons

From the 5th century to the 11th, the people in this region were under almost constant pressure from the Anglo-Saxon invaders of England. By the 8th century, the Brythons had been cut off by these invaders from their compatriots to the north in Cumbria, and it is around this time that they started to call themselves *Cymry* or fellow countrymen.

The legendary King Arthur is thought to have led the Brythons against the Anglo-Saxons at some time during this period. It seems that he was Christian and, as many of the Welsh were, Romanised. Scarcely a contemporary historical record of him survives and yet he has inspired a huge body of poetry and literature, not least by the Welsh in *The Mabinogion*. He is said to be buried on the 'Isle of Avalon' (Glastonbury) in England. The legends of his court at Camelot, with his knights of the Round Table, have sparked many a fruitless search into the annals for more than a tantalising scrap of evidence of his historical existence.

We do know that in the 8th century, Offa, the king of Mercia (one of the most powerful of the Anglo-Saxon kingdoms in southern Britain), constructed a dyke marking the boundary between the Welsh and the Mercians. Offa's Dyke can still be seen today – in fact you can walk its length (see the Activities chapter at the beginning of this book).

Early Unification of Wales

The 9th and 10th centuries were the time of savage attacks on the coasts by Danish and Norse pirates raiding into the south. It was also the time when the small kingdoms of Wales began unifying, through necessity, to repel the Vikings.

Rhodri Mawr (who died in 878) defeated a Viking force off Anglesey and began the

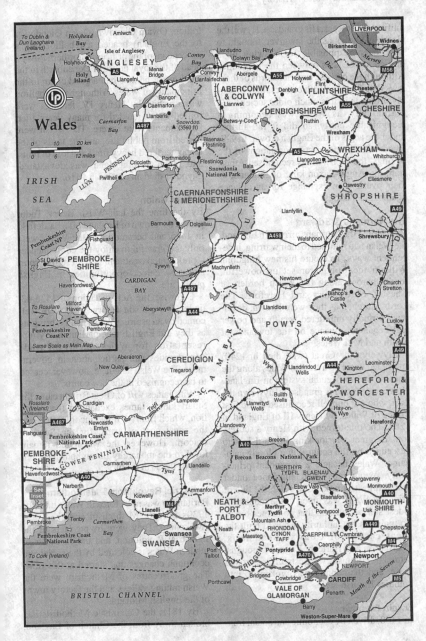

unification process. His grandson, Hywel the Good, is known as the lawgiver, thought to have been responsible for drawing up a unified set of laws between the kingdoms. Although the earliest written records of these laws date from the 13th century, they probably originate in this much older society.

Ironically, as Wales was becoming a recognisable entity, so did it fall further under the aegis of the English crown. In 927, faced with the destructive onslaught of the Vikings, the Welsh kings recognised Athelstan, the Anglo-Saxon king of England, as their overlord in exchange for an alliance against the Vikings.

The Normans & Edward I

By the time the Normans arrived in England, the Welsh had returned to their warring, independent ways. To secure his new kingdom, William the Conqueror set up powerful, feudal barons along the Welsh borders at Chester, Shrewsbury and Hereford. The Lords Marcher, as they were known, developed virtually unfettered wealth and power and began to advance on the lowlands of South and Mid Wales.

Llywelyn the Great (who died in 1240) attempted to set up a state in Wales along the lines of the new feudal system in England. However, it was his grandson, Llywelyn the Last, who got himself recognised as the first Prince of Wales, by Henry III of England in 1267. The tide turned with Henry's successor, the great warrior king Edward I, who descended on the country in a bloody campaign. Wales became a dependent principality, owing fealty and allegiance under feudal rules to England. In 1302, the title of Prince of Wales was given to the monarch's eldest son, a tradition that continues today. To maintain his authority, Edward built the great castles of Conwy, Beaumaris, Caernarfon and Harlech. English boroughs, settled by colonists, were established around these, and the country was broken up into counties English-style.

Owain Glyndŵr

In 1400, driven by economic and social frus-

tration, Owain Glyndŵr (Owen Glendower to the English) headed a rebellion. As a descendant of the princes of northern Powys, head of the royal house of Deheubarth in the south-west, he thus had a good claim to the principality of Wales. Although his rebellion was crushed by Henry IV, feelings were roused which rankled for many years after. Punishments were severe. The Welsh were barred from public life, and the lords of the manor suffered heavy fines and loss of rents, and much farming land was devastated. Glyndŵr died an outlaw in 1416.

Acts of Union

By the time the half-Welsh Henry Tudor picked the crown of England off a battlefield in 1485 and became king, the Welsh were only too grateful to enjoy the consequences – preferential treatment at the English court and new career opportunities in English public life.

Likewise, the Acts of Union of 1536-43, under Tudor's son Henry VIII, were welcomed by an aspiring Welsh gentry, bringing as they did English law, parliamentary representation for Wales, plenty of trade opportunities and participation in government. The Welsh language, however, ceased to be recognised in the law courts.

With James VI/I of Great Britain came the Stuart kings. James exchanged the Welsh lion, which Henry VII had incorporated into the royal coat of arms, for the Scottish unicorn. However, the Welsh did remain loyal to the monarchy throughout the Civil War of the 17th century.

Industrial Revolution & Methodism

Puritanism was not a force in Wales until the 1730s brought Methodism and the Great Awakening. They were by-products of the Industrial Revolution, and the character of modern Wales is coloured by the social and economic changes that started at this time. The great centres of Methodism were the Welsh mining valleys and the factory towns of the English Midlands.

By 1811, the Calvinistic Methodists had broken away from the Church of England,

and in 1851 nonconformists accounted for 76% of the church-going population. By this time, copper, iron and slate were being extracted and ironworks were in operation in the Merthyr Tydfil and Monmouth areas. The 1860s saw the Rhondda valleys opened up for coal mining, and Wales soon became a major exporter of coal. By 1875, most of the world's tin plate was produced in Wales.

Economic & Political Change

The population increased phenomenally with industrialisation. What had been almost exclusively a fragmented, rural population became concentrated in the south in mining and industrial communities, with a character and toughness of their own – vigorous, close-knit, self-reliant and nonconformist. Strikes and occasional violence broke out, as did protests against low wages and bad working conditions, but it was much later that a trade-union movement began to emerge.

Tension grew between the nonconformists and the anglicised 'squirearchy', who were the traditional ruling class. The church became a target for reform; the established church was seen as being unrepresentative and expensive to maintain. Nonconformism began to ally itself politically with liberalism, which favoured nationalism and the disestablishment of the church. It was not until 1920, while David Lloyd George, Welsh Liberal and champion for Home Rule in Wales, was prime minister of Britain, that the church was disestablished.

From around 1900, support began to grow for the Labour Party in South Wales. Keir Hardie was elected to Parliament from Merthyr Tydfil, and through the economic depression of the 1930s and after, this support increased. The severity of the Depression led to 242,000 people leaving the valleys.

Welsh Nationalism

In 1925, Plaid Cymru, the Welsh National Party, was formed by six men in a hotel room during the National Eisteddfod. Political independence through language and cultural differences was the goal of a small minority.

The Welsh Language Society, for instance, resorted to civil disobedience to press their point, with the result that in 1942 the Welsh language was made legally acceptable.

The colleges of Aberystwyth, Cardiff and Bangor had been united in 1893 as the University of Wales, and the eisteddfod had become a focus for the preservation of the language and culture. In 1955, Cardiff was made the official capital of Wales. In 1964, a Welsh minister of state was appointed with cabinet rank in the British government, and in 1966 a Welsh Nationalist was elected to Parliament. By 1978, a Labour-dominated Parliament passed an act to create an elected Welsh assembly with power over some Welsh domestic affairs, but a referendum in 1979 showed the enthusiasm of the 1960s had waned, and the subject was dropped. The country finally got a Welsh-language TV channel when S4C started in 1982.

Wales Today

The 20th century, especially the 1960s, 70s and 80s, saw the coal industry and the associated steel industry collapse. Large-scale unemployment persists as Wales attempts to move to more high-tech and service industries. Coal is king no more – Tower Colliery, Wales' last large coal mine, closed in 1994, although it was reopened a year later as a smaller, private concern. Tourism is now a major industry, accounting for 10% of all jobs in the principality. Wales is currently experiencing something of a tourist boom with record numbers of visitors.

The 1992 general election gave Plaid Cymru its best victory, with four seats in the House of Commons. Labour looks set to win the 1997 general election and their policies are more Welsh-friendly than those of the Conservatives. The likelihood, however, of Wales emerging as a nation independent of the rest of the UK is currently small – certainly smaller than Scotland's, with its independent judicial and education systems.

GEOGRAPHY

Covering an area of 8017 square miles, Wales is approximately 170 miles long and

60 miles wide. Surrounded by sea on three sides, its border to the east with England still runs roughly along Offa's Dyke, the giant earthwork constructed in the 8th century.

Wales has two major mountain systems: the Black Mountains and Brecon Beacons in the south, and the mountains of Snowdonia in the north-west. At 3650 feet, Snowdon is the highest peak in England and Wales, and more rugged than the rounded Brecon Beacons to the south. These glaciated mountain areas are deeply cut by narrow river valleys. Rolling moorlands between 600 and 2000 feet stretch from Denbigh in the north to the Glamorgan valleys in the south, ending on the west coast in spectacular cliffs and the plains of river estuaries.

The population is concentrated in the south-east, along the coast between Cardiff and Swansea and in the old mining valleys that run north into the Brecon Beacons.

CLIMATE

Although Welsh weather is as difficult to second-guess as anywhere else in Britain, it's probably fair to say that it suffers from an excess of rainfall; it would be unwise to arrive without rainproof clothing and mudproof footwear. Westerly and south-westerly winds can also make life pretty miserable, especially when it's raining as well. That said, the closeness of the mountains to the coast means that you can encounter very different climatic conditions within a relatively short geographical distance. It's also slightly warmer – but not so you'd notice – along the south coast.

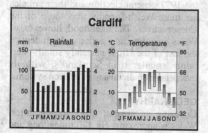

ECOLOGY & ENVIRONMENT

Anyone returning to South Wales who'd last seen the place in coal-mining days would scarcely recognise the valleys now. The mines have closed, many of the ugly slagheaps have been grassed over and the air is cleaner than it's been for centuries.

It's not been all good news for the environment over the past few years, though. In February 1996 Pembrokeshire hit the world news when the supertanker *Sea Empress* broke up off the Pembrokeshire Coast National Park, releasing 76,000 tonnes of light crude oil into the sea. More than 120 miles of coastline were covered with oil and an army of cleaners scrubbed at the rocks and sifted the sand in preparation for the tourist season. As a cosmetic exercise it was entirely successful and just two months later it was difficult to believe that some of the now spotless beaches had been under several inches of oil. The real damage to the environment, however, is always less obvious – a population of rare starfish was wiped out in West Angle Bay, for example – and it will be decades before the ecology completely recovers. As long as there's an oil refinery at Milford Haven, in the centre of the national park, there will always be a risk of further pollution.

One of the biggest tourist attractions in the country is the eco-friendly Centre for Alternative Technology, just outside Machynlleth in Mid Wales (see that section).

FLORA & FAUNA

Like Scotland, much of Wales was once covered by forest, mainly sessile oak, but very little remains and none of it is completely untouched. Most has long since been cleared for agriculture, or chopped down for shipbuilding, charcoal burning or construction – not least for pit props in the mines. Overgrazing also makes it hard for new oak saplings to take root; in Snowdonia the rampant spread of wild rhododendron bushes prevents them even seeding. Imported oaks, like the Turkey oak, actually seem to fare better. Pengelli Forest in

Pembrokeshire is as close as you'll get to untouched Welsh woodland nowadays.

Ash trees are also native to Wales and are common everywhere, especially along rivers and in woods and copses in the Gower peninsula and the Brecon Beacons. In their shade grow primroses, common dog violets and several species of orchid. Hornbeams were once restricted to south-east Wales but are now found elsewhere, too. You'll see plenty of wild cherry trees and field maples, and churchyards often harbour yew trees, as in England. Nor could anyone miss the massed stands of sitka spruce, popular with plantation-owners seeking a quick-growing source of timber, but far from ideal as habitats for native birds and mammals, the sturdy pine marten aside.

Wales' mountainous terrain has made it a perfect breeding ground for fragile alpine-Arctic plants, including the unique Snowdon lily, which brightens the slopes of Mt Snowdon between the end of May and the middle of June. Easier to spot are saxifrage plants and moss campion growing on the rocks. Amid the coastal sand dunes, you may find evening primroses, sea spurge, sea bindweed and marram grass, while the Gower peninsula is a good place for thrift, samphire and sea lavender. Around Tenby, you might even find the unique Tenby daffodil.

Like Scotland, Wales' lengthy coastline ensures it a sizeable seabird population. Indeed, Grassholm harbours one of the world's largest gannet colonies, with 30,000 breeding pairs. Wales also has 150,000 pairs of manx shearwaters, 30% of the world's population. The rockfaces of Skomer and Skokholm islands in particular are densely filled with colonies of guillemots, razorbills, storm petrels, kittiwakes and puffins. There are also a few pairs of rare choughs on Ramsey and Bardsey islands, and passing migrants include the occasional great northern diver.

In general, the Welsh inland bird population mirrors that of England, but with a few notable exceptions. It does have, for example, the only red kites left in Britain – 100 breeding pairs of them, mainly in the Elan Valley of Mid Wales. The mammal population is also similar to England's, although the greater horseshoe bat is now confined to Wales and corners of south-western England, and Skomer boasts a unique species of vole. Red squirrels are vanishing fast throughout Britain, but a few cling on around Lake Vyrnwy. Rare otters are also re-establishing themselves along the River Teifi and in the border area of Montgomeryshire. A colony of grey seals is breeding successfully on the west coast of Ramsey Island.

With so many fast-flowing rivers, it's hardly surprising that Wales has a wide variety of fish, including salmon (in the Usk and Wye), brown trout and char. Bala Lake also boasts a unique species, the white gwyniad, said to have been hanging around since the Ice Age. Cockles are still harvested at low tide in the Burry Inlet on the Gower peninsula and made into pies by the locals.

GOVERNMENT & POLITICS

Like Scotland, Wales is governed from London. Wales returns 38 MPs to Westminster. At the time of writing, 27 of them were from the Labour Party, six from the Conservatives, four from Plaid Cymru and one from the Liberal Democrats. The country is thus as resoundingly Labour in its attitudes as Scotland, no doubt because of its industrial history. Wales also returns four MEPs to the European Parliament.

In an attempt to recognise Wales as a distinct entity, all 38 Welsh MPs are entitled to meet as a Welsh Grand Committee to discuss bills which deal exclusively with Wales. However, a 1979 referendum saw proposals to set up a Welsh Assembly in Cardiff overwhelmingly rejected (of the 59% of the population who turned out to vote, only 20.3% voted in favour). By 1994, pressure for greater representation was again in the air, and the Labour Party at least was moving towards new proposals to give Wales more autonomy.

Wales is represented in the British government by a secretary of state for Wales who has overall responsibility for a wide range of functions including health, social services, education, local government, housing, tourism and the environment. The Welsh Office is based in Cardiff, with branches throughout the country.

The 1996 border commission has divided Wales into 22 so-called 'unitary authorities', in many cases bringing back the names of old counties such as Pembrokeshire (phased out in the 1974 reorganisation).

Wales is a principality and since 1302, when Edward I invested his son as Prince of Wales, the British sovereign's eldest son has been given the title. In 1969, Charles was formally invested as Prince of Wales at Caernarfon Castle. It goes without saying that few Welsh Nationalists are openly supportive of this state of affairs.

ECONOMY

Research carried out by the Wales Tourist Board (WTB) suggests that people who have never visited Wales imagine it a grim, grey country scarred by the ugly paraphernalia and detritus of heavy industry, primarily coal mining, steel manufacture and slate quarrying. In some ways nothing could be further from the truth; although the steel industry and slate quarrying linger on around Port Talbot and Blaenau Ffestiniog, coal mining has more or less vanished, turned into little more than an adjunct of the much cleaner heritage-tourism industry. The scale of the change is typified by the Rhondda Valley, where 50 pits once employed 40,000 men. There are now no large working pits left there.

Mass unemployment and the ensuing social disruption in parts of the South Wales valleys have led some commentators to draw not altogether ridiculous comparisons with the developing world. Probably the most successful modern industry – aside from agriculture and forestry – is tourism, but unfortunately that can rarely make up for the loss of well-paid manual jobs in the areas worst affected by the 1980s and 90s pit closures. Two-thirds of Welsh jobs are now in the service industries.

Luckily, Wales has had considerable success in attracting investment from overseas, particularly from Japanese companies, among them Sony, National Panasonic, Aiwa and Toyota. There has also been a mini-boom in new financial businesses opening or moving to Wales, a fact confirmed by a glimpse at the name-boards going up around Cardiff Bay.

In 1976, the Welsh Development Agency (WDA) was set up to help Wales make the awkward transition to new sources of employment. Its undoubted success in some areas was overshadowed in the 1990s by revelations of corruption in high places. The WDA has now made a fresh start, but for some years to come parts of Wales are likely to be blighted by the fallout from change.

POPULATION

Wales has a population of around 2.9 million, about 5% of the population of the UK. The largest centre of population is Cardiff, with 265,000 residents. Swansea and Newport, also in South Wales, are the other main population centres. Mid Wales is the least densely populated part of the country, although it's interesting to note that the population of Powys, the emptiest area, actually grew between 1981 and 1991, as people deserted the cities in favour of the countryside and an alternative lifestyle.

PEOPLE

The caricature Welshman of English imagination was a coal-miner who went to chapel on Sunday and spent his spare time singing or playing rugby. His wife wore long skirts with a pinafore and shawl, and a tall black top hat. The 1980s and 90s saw the mining part of this picture laid to rest, and the chapel-going, too, has died as much of a death in Wales as in England. The only places you're likely to see women in national costume nowadays are at the eisteddfodau or the Welsh Folk Museum. That said, the Welsh do remain a people apart, if only because of their accents and the fact that their language is still very much alive.

The long struggle of the Welsh to stay separate from England probably accounts for some of the continued sense of 'difference', not to mention the hostility some (but not many) visitors claim to experience in the Welsh-speaking enclaves of the north-west. As a foreign visitor, you're unlikely to experience any hostility, although the Welsh can sometimes be as reserved as the English when it comes to introducing themselves to strangers.

The indigenous Welsh are people of Celtic stock who seem to have arrived from the European mainland around 600 BC. During the Industrial Revolution, the population make-up was drastically altered as wealthy investors moved to Wales to take advantage of its mineral wealth, recruiting in their wake a large non-Welsh working force. It was at this time that the Welsh language began a decline which has only recently been halted.

Wales has a small ethnic, minority population, mainly concentrated in Cardiff, Newport and Swansea. But you'll probably be amazed at how many English people live in Wales and, in particular, how many of them make a living out of tourism: running B&Bs, craft centres, cafés and other attractions. In fact, if you're not careful, you could spend more time talking to English incomers than to native Welsh people.

EDUCATION

In most ways, the Welsh education system mirrors the English one. However, the recent revival of interest in the Welsh language makes for some inevitable differences. There are, for example, special Welsh-medium schools where the normal curriculum is taught in Welsh, and English is treated as a second language to be introduced at about age seven. Although there are plenty of Welsh-medium primary and junior schools, many parents chicken out when it comes to secondary education. In any case, there are currently too few Welsh-medium secondary schools to accommodate all the children coming up from the elementary schools. The status of Welsh in the national curriculum, introduced in 1990, seems, like so much else, to fluctuate from year to year.

There are universities at Cardiff, Aberystwyth, Bangor, Lampeter, Swansea and Treforest.

ARTS

For music and literature, Wales is seen as a country positively bursting at the seams with lusty male voice choirs, mysterious eisteddfodau and pretty female harpists. Everyone has heard of Dylan Thomas, even if they've never read Under Milk Wood or seen it performed, and Richard Burton and Anthony Hopkins have stamped Wales firmly into theatrical history.

The country hasn't been so blessed when it comes to the visual arts, with few Welsh artists other than Augustus and Gwen John achieving real fame. Graham Sutherland did, nevertheless, settle in Wales and do much of

---

Incomers
In the late 1980s, more people moved to Wales than moved out, and the subject of 'incomers' is a controversial one. Most Welsh accept their new neighbours readily enough, provided those neighbours make an effort to blend in. However, there's a hard core which sees the constant inflow of settlers from England as a threat to the Welshness of Wales. Not least, they point to the rise in house prices in areas attractive to settlers, and to the deadening effect weekend cottages, empty all the week, can have on small villages.

During the 1970s and 80s, British Coal's nationwide advertising campaign that carried the slogan 'Come Home to a Real Fire' came all too true for a few of the English owners of cottages in Wales. Their weekend retreats were torched by members of a Welsh protest group calling themselves Meibion Glyndŵr (Sons of Glendower). 'Come Home to a Real Fire', the joke went. 'Buy a Holiday Home in Wales'. ■

his work at Picton Castle. As if to make up for this dearth of indigenous talent, Gwendoline and Margaret Davies ploughed the money they inherited from their father (who created Barry Docks) into amassing a stunning collection of Impressionist paintings, including Monets, Manets, Sisleys and Pisarros, which are now on show at the National Museum of Wales in Cardiff.

ARCHITECTURE

On the architectural front, Wales is best known for the great medieval castles in various states of ruination which ring the coasts and Marches (border areas). Ironically, most of them were built by the English to ward off Welsh nationalists of the medieval kind. The finest of all are the ones Edward I had built in North Wales – Caernarfon, Harlech, Conwy and Beaumaris – but wherever you go in South or North Wales there'll be a ruined castle within reasonable reach. It's well worth making a special trip to see the following castles: Rhuddlan, Denbigh, Cricieth, Raglan, Pembroke, Kidwelly, Chepstow and Caerphilly. Most of them are cared for by Cadw, the Welsh Historic Monuments Agency (see the Wales Facts for the Visitor chapter).

The ruined castles aside, Wales is not noted for its wonderful architecture. Although the history of Christianity in Wales stretches back to the 5th century, medieval Wales never shared in the prosperity that led to the blossoming of splendid churches and cathedrals in England. Cadw cares for atmospheric ruined abbeys at Tintern, Neath, Strata Florida and Valle Crucis, and the cathedral at St David's is as splendid as many in England. There are also some pleasing towered churches in Pembrokeshire and Gwent, but the real boom in Welsh church-building came after the Industrial Revolution as people flooded into the newly industrialising areas.

This population growth coincided with the high point of interest in nonconformist religion. Wales is scattered from end to end with Methodist, Baptist and Congregationalist chapels, and since none of these sects believed in lavish church-building, their legacy is a landscape of small, plain chapels. What's more, none of these sects has gone to such lengths as the Anglican church to conserve its redundant premises, so wherever you go in Wales you'll see chapels boarded up, crumbling or converted for some wholly irreligious new function.

There are also a few fine houses, like Tredegar outside Newport, Williams Hall at Bodelwyddan, which now houses the National Portrait Gallery's Victorian collection, and Plas Newydd, the half-timbered house once occupied by the Ladies of Llangollen (see Llangollen section). Some of the finest houses are in the care of the National Trust for England and Wales. Cardiff also boasts two more unusual 'castles' – Cardiff Castle and Castell Coch – designed by the Victorian architect William Burges who specialised in love-it-or-hate-it repro Gothic.

Not surprisingly, Wales has an abundance of industrial architecture, and attitudes to this have changed enormously. The great colliery towers and winding gear once regarded as eyesores are now seen through the rose-tinted glasses of nostalgia, especially once they've been cleaned up and made presentable for their visitors. In South Wales it's well worth visiting Big Pit at Blaenafon or the Rhondda Heritage Centre, and in Mid Wales you can visit old slate-quarrying sites at Blaenau Ffestiniog.

CULTURE
Eisteddfodau

The eisteddfod is a thoroughly Welsh institution which tends to leave the non-Welsh mystified. Its precise origins are shrouded in legend, but the word means a gathering of bards, and the traditional eisteddfod was a contest involving poetry and music. The first recorded event seems to have taken place at Cardigan in 1176, but after the Act of Union in 1536, eisteddfodau seem to have become less frequent and less lively, a process accentuated in the 17th and 18th centuries as the dour nonconformist sects got their claws into Wales.

All this changed in the 1860s when the National Eisteddfod Society was established to revive the old traditions. There are now three major annual eisteddfodau: the International Eisteddfod in purpose-built premises at Llangollen every July; the Royal National Eisteddfod, which moves between North and South Wales each August; and the newer Urdd (Youth) Eisteddfod, which also alternates between sites in North and South Wales each May.

For details of the International Eisteddfod, phone ☎ 01978-860236. The Royal National Eisteddfod (☎ 01222-763777) will be at Bala in 1997 and Bridgend in 1998. The Urdd Eisteddfod (☎ 01970-623744) will take place at Crosskeys (Caephilly) in 1997 and at Pwllheli in 1998. Accommodation is likely to be in short supply around festival dates; book ahead.

If you'd like to see an eisteddfod but can't make any of the big competitions, it's still worth contacting the WTB for their events booklet, which also lists local contests.

Music

The Welsh male voice choir *(cor meibion)* is something of an institution, and most closely associated with the coal-mining communities of the South Wales valleys. Perhaps surprisingly, it was the nonconformist sects, particularly Methodism, that breathed life into these choirs, so their repertoires are stronger on hymns that might be anticipated. The collapse of the old coal-mining communities presents a threat to the survival of the choirs, but so far they're hanging in. The WTB booklet on events lists rehearsal nights for village choirs which are happy to host visitors. As a sign of the times, some of them now boast female voices, too.

Alternative Culture

In the 1980s, parts of Mid Wales in particular became popular refuges for people in search of an alternative lifestyle. At its most extreme, this has meant setting up tepee camps in remote valleys; at its most moderate, it has led to a rash of alternative bookshops and restaurants in small towns like Llanidloes and Machynlleth.

Near Machynlleth, the Centre for Alternative Technology (CAT) has brought together many of the characteristics of this craving for something different: organic farming, wind and water power, and the recycling of virtually everything, in a communal setting. CAT runs courses and welcomes volunteers; phone ☎ 01564-702400 for more details.

RELIGION

Christianity is believed to have been introduced to Wales in the 5th century, going its own way until the time of the Reformation, when the Welsh church was reorganised to become part of the regular Anglican Church. In 1588, Bishop Morgan translated the Bible into Welsh.

As the population grew in the 18th century, the new industrial working classes proved fertile recruiting ground for various Protestant nonconformist sects, particularly the Baptists, Methodists and Congregationalists. An 1851 survey discovered that almost 80% of the population was nonconformist, and in 1920 the Anglican Church actually ceased to be the established church of Wales. The nonconformist tradition brought a puritanical strain to Welsh life which might account for the rather dour image of its people. Until recently, it wasn't just shops that stayed shut on Sunday in Wales – pubs did too.

But all that has changed, and now it would be hard to argue that Wales is any more actively religious than England. The most recent survey found 108,400 people identifying themselves as members of the Anglican Church, 60,600 as Roman Catholics and 220,300 as Methodists, Baptists and assorted other nonconformists.

LANGUAGE

The one thing that marks Wales out so distinctly from the rest of Britain is the survival of Welsh as a living language. Despite its weird and seemingly unpronounceable double ls and consecutive consonants, Welsh is an Indo-European language, from a Celtic offshoot. Its closest linguistic cousins are Cornish and Breton.

During the Roman occupation, people in positions of authority probably spoke Latin, even if everyone else spoke Welsh. Gradually, a bilingual Latin/Welsh-speaking population emerged, and the influence of Latin on Welsh is clear, as is the influence of French (from the Norman period) and English. The language as it is spoken today seems to have been more or less fully developed by the 6th century, making it one of Europe's oldest languages.

Following the Act of Union in 1536, people were forbidden to hold high office unless they spoke English as well as Welsh. Bishop Morgan's translation of the Bible in 1588 is thought to have played an important part in keeping the language alive.

During the 17th and 18th centuries, the nonconformist sects that made such headway in Wales also supported the native language. However, the Industrial Revolution brought a whole new class of industrial landlords and employers, few of whom spoke Welsh. From then on, the number of native Welsh speakers went into steep decline. At the start of the 19th century, 80% of the population probably spoke Welsh, but by 1901 this had sunk to 50%. Now, only about 20% of the population speak Welsh. Welsh speakers are concentrated particularly in the north-western and western parts of the country where up to 75% of the population of a given locality may speak it. In contrast, only 2.4% of people living in Gwent know more than the odd word.

Reasons for the decline in the number of people speaking Welsh are not hard to find: television, better communications, emigration, mixed marriages and tourism are just some of those commonly cited. Perhaps what is more surprising is that so many people have continued to speak the language despite all these threats. Indeed, in the 1980s and 90s there was revived interest in the language, not least among incomers.

Since the 1960s the importance of Welsh has been officially recognised, and in 1967 the Welsh Language Act ensured that Welsh speakers could use their own language in court. Since then an increasing number of publications have been bilingual and it's rare nowadays to see a road sign in just one language. In 1982 Channel 4 set up S4C, which broadcasts daily Welsh television programmes and has even made the odd feature film. Radio Cymru also transmits in Welsh, and roughly 400 books a year are published in the language.

In 1988 a Welsh Language Board was set up to advise the secretary of state for Wales on everything to do with the language, while in 1994 a new Welsh Language Act gave equal validity to Welsh as a language for use in public-sector businesses – it's now illegal to discriminate against Welsh speakers in employment for example. Some shops and food producers are even developing bilingual signing and packaging.

If all this sounds almost too good to be true, there are those who would argue that that is, in fact, the case, and that the cause of the Welsh language has been espoused by middle-class incomers as a way of ensuring themselves grants and jobs. There are also English visitors who get very hot under the collar when they visit Welsh-speaking areas and find themselves unable to understand what is being said. It's a fascinating subject, but one on which it's probably not wise to express strong opinions without first getting a good grip on the facts.

For newcomers, Welsh is not the easiest language to master. Here is a brief guide to the pronunciation:

Vowels
The Welsh vowels are a, e, i, o, u, w and y. All except y have short and long versions.

long **a**	as in hard	*tad* (father)
short **a**	as in ham	*mam* (mother)
long **e**	as in sane	*hen* (old)
short **e**	as in ten	*pen* (head)
long **i**	as in geese	*mis* (month)
short **i**	as in tin	*prin* (scarce)
long **o**	as in more	*mor* (sea)
short **o**	as in fond	*offon* (walking stick)
long **w**	as in moon	*swn* (sound)

short **w**   as in look   *gwn* (gun)

y   has three possible pronunciations:
   as the 'ee' in geese   *dyn* (man)
   as in tin   *cyn* (before)
   as in run   *dynion* (men)

The accent usually falls on the second-last syllable in Welsh pronunciation.

Consonants

c	as in cat	*cath* (cat)
ch	as in loch	*chwaer* (sister)
dd	as 'th' in them	*yn dda* (good)
f	as in of	*y fam* (the mother)
ff	as in off	*ffenestr* (window)
g	as in garden	*gardd* (garden)
h	as in hat	*het* (hat)
ll	there is no equivalent sound in English. It's suggested that you put your tongue on the roof of your mouth, near the teeth, as if to pronounce 'l', and then blow the 'l'!	*llaw* (hand)
th	as in three	*byth* (ever)

Words & Phrases

If you're feeling brave, here are a few expressions you might try out in the Welsh-speaking parts of the country:

Good morning.	*Bore da.*
Good afternoon.	*Pryhnawn da.*
Good night.	*Nos da.*
How are you?	*Sut mae?*
What is your name?	*Beth ydy'ch enw chi?*
How much?	*Faint?*
Who is the victorious bard?	*Pwy ydy'r bardd buddugol?*
thanks	*diolch*
good	*da*
very good	*da iawn*
cheers	*hwyl*
women	*merched*
men	*dynion*

exit	*allan*
open	*ar agor*
hotel	*gwesty*
bus	*bws*
pub	*tafarn*

Numbers

1	*un*
2	*dau*
3	*tri*
4	*pedwar*
5	*pump*
6	*chwech*
7	*saith*
8	*wyth*
9	*naw*
10	*deg*
11	*un-deg-un*
12	*un-deg-dau*
13	*un-deg-tri*
20	*dau-ddeg*
21	*dau-ddeg-un*
30	*tri-deg*
40	*pedwar-deg*
50	*pum-deg*
60	*chwe-deg*
70	*saith-deg*
80	*wyth-deg*
90	*naw-deg*
100	*cant*
200	*dau cant*
500	*pum cant*
1000	*mil*

Wales is famous for having the longest place name in the world – Llanfairpwllgwyngllgogerychwyrndrobwlllantysiliogogogoch – which, translated, means 'St Mary's church in the hollow of the White Hazel near a rapid whirlpool and the church of St Tysilio near the Red cave'. Can be tricky to say after a pint of Brains.

See also the Glossary at the back of this book.

Facts for the Visitor

PLANNING

When to Go

Spring and autumn are probably the best times to visit Wales if you want to avoid the July and August crowds. The roads are least busy, and accommodation is emptiest in winter, but many of the attractions close in mid-October and don't open again until Easter. Some of the mountain passes can be snowbound in winter.

See also the Climate section in the Facts about Wales chapter.

What Kind of Trip?

Wales may be small but apart from the M4 across the south and the A55 Expressway along the north coast there are no fast roads. Trying to nip round ticking off the sights will only lead to frustration. The best idea is to base yourself in a small village or a farmhouse B&B near one of the national parks.

With two national trails and hundreds of miles of beautiful coastline Wales is an excellent place for walking. In fact it's popular for outdoor activities of all types. See the Activities section of this chapter.

Maps

The Wales Tourist Board's *Wales Tourist Map* (£2) is available at all TICs. It also includes town plans, suggested car tours and shows TICs. For walkers, large-scale OS maps relevant to the area are usually stocked by local TICs.

What to Bring

If you're walking, bring not only a waterproof jacket but also waterproof overtrousers since it may be windy as well as rainy. In summer a swimming costume is also useful; the sea can be surprisingly warm.

TOURIST OFFICES

Outside Britain, contact the BTA for information. The Wales Tourist Board (WTB) (☎ 01222-499909) has its headquarters on the 12th floor of Brunel House, 2 Fitzalan Rd, Cardiff CF2 1UY, and also operates a branch in the British Travel Centre (☎ 0171-409 0969), 12 Regent St, Piccadilly Circus, London SW1Y 4PQ.

Most major towns in Wales have TICs that are open weekdays from 9 am to 5 pm, with hours sometimes extending to weekends in summer. In small places, TICs only open from Easter to September.

VISAS & DOCUMENTS

No visas are required if you arrive from England. If you arrive from any other country, normal British regulations apply (see the Regional Facts for the Visitor chapter at the beginning of this book). There are several diplomatic missions in Cardiff, including a Thai embassy.

MONEY

Wales has the same currency as England and you will find the same banks and cash machines.

In surveys of value-for-money European destinations, Cardiff consistently comes out tops, with prices on average 5-10% less than in England.

BOOKS

Guidebooks

You'll come across a wide range of detailed guidebooks and books on Welsh life as you travel around Wales. Many are stocked by the larger TICs and by bookshops at visitor attractions like Cardiff Castle and the National Museum of Wales. See also the Books and Maps section in the Regional Facts for the Visitor chapter at the beginning of this book.

General

If you want to get to grips with Welsh mythology, the book to start with is *The Mabinogion*, a collection of tales that date back to the misty Celtic past, but which were not actually written down until the 14th century, or translated until the 19th.

Two other oldies you might want to dip into are *The Journey Through Wales* and *The Description of Wales*, medieval travel tales written by the 12th-century monk Giraldus Cambrensis (Gerald of Wales) as he journeyed round the country looking for recruits for the Third Crusade. If you find the originals heavy going, Cadw publishes *A Mirror of Medieval Wales*, which picks out the highlights of Gerald's prose. A more recent picture of Wales is given in *Wild Wales* by George Borrow, who walked around the country in 1854 and wrote an account some would regard as condescending.

For an impressionistic and entertaining description of Wales and its history, look for Jan Morris's *The Matter of Wales*, a modern travel writer's account of her home country. John Davies' *A History of Wales* fills in the more prosaic facts and figures.

Probably the best-known Welsh author remains Dylan Thomas, whose play *Under Milk Wood*, about life in a small Welsh seaside town, is required reading for anyone heading for his home in Laugharne. Your appetite once whetted, you could also try his *Collected Stories*, which includes 'Quite Early One Morning,' the story that grew up to become *Under Milk Wood*, and *Portrait of the Artist as a Young Dog*.

Only a little less well known is Richard Llewellyn, whose *How Green Was My Valley* is just the first of a set of four novels describing the life of a boy growing up in a South Wales mining community, which did much to create the mystique of the tough life it portrayed. Another excellent read is Bruce Chatwin's acclaimed novel *On The Black Hill*, which describes the life of twin farmers living and working on the English-Welsh border.

A quirky book to look out for if you're visiting Llangollen is Elizabeth Mavor's *The Ladies of Llangollen*, describing the equally quirky lesbian couple who eloped from Ireland to Wales and settled down in Plas Newydd, there to receive visits and gifts from many of the 18th century's great and good.

ONLINE SERVICES

For services covering Britain as a whole, see Facts for the Visitor at the start of the book. The Wales Tourist Board has an Internet site at http://www.tourism.wales.gov.uk.

NEWSPAPERS & MAGAZINES

You can buy all the standard London published daily and weekly newspapers in Wales, although you may want to sample local papers to find out what's going on in your area, or to pick up local gossip. The *Western Mail* is a reasonable Welsh national daily, with *Wales on Sunday* taking over at weekends.

In Cardiff, it's worth at least glancing at the *South Wales Echo*, while in Swansea you might want to pick up the *Swansea Evening Post*, not because it's a lively read (it isn't particularly) but because it's the paper on which Dylan Thomas cut his journalistic teeth.

RADIO & TV

Radio and TV stations are linked into the national network, although Wales does have its own alternative to Channel 4, Sianel Pedwar Cymru (S4C), which broadcasts Welsh-language (but not exclusively) programmes daily. BBC Radio Wales offers daily news and features on Wales, while BBC Radio Cymru transmits much the same in Welsh.

USEFUL ORGANISATIONS
Youth Hostels Association

Membership of the YHA (Hostelling International) for England covers Wales as well. For more details, see the Accommodation section in the Regional Facts for the Visitor chapter.

Cadw

Cadw (☎ 01222-500200), the Welsh Historic Monuments agency, looks after most of the ruined abbeys and castles in Wales, including the group of castles (Caernarfon, Harlech, Conwy and Beaumaris) in North Wales which has been designated a World Heritage Site by UNESCO.

Sianel Pedwar Cymru's Success

Currently receiving a subsidy of £58 million a year, making it the world's most heavily subsidised public television channel, Sianel Pedwar Cymru (SC4 – Channel 4 Wales) might not sound like a success story. The benefits of this Welsh-language TV service, on the air since the early 1980s, are only now becoming obvious to its critics, who thought the money could be better spent elsewhere.

SC4 came into being not through the beneficence of Whitehall, but after heavy campaigning by Cymdeithas yr Iaith Cymraeg (the Welsh Language Society), which included a hunger strike by Gwynfor Evans, the Welsh nationalist. Since then the channel has played an important part in rejuvenating the language, and it's now estimated that 32% of children in Wales can speak at least some Welsh. Accountants are no doubt pleased to see that the channel's benefits are not only cultural. SC4 has been successful in selling its programmes to other TV channels, and film-makers from abroad are starting to choose Welsh locations and use production companies based here.

The long-running Welsh soap *Pobol y Cwm* (People of the Valley) is now transmitted with subtitles to the rest of Britain on BBC2. Other acclaimed productions have included the children's cartoon *SuperTed*. SC4's greatest success to date, however, is *Hedd Wynn*, which won an Oscar in 1994 for Best Foreign Language Film. ■

A year's membership for an adult costs £18 and gives free admission to all Cadw sites. A young person (16-20) can join for £13, and a child for £11. Family membership, covering two parents and children aged under 21, is excellent value at £35. Cadw members are also eligible for half-price admission to EH and HS sites (free in the second year of Cadw membership). Three-day/seven-day Explorer Passes are also available, costing £9/14 per adult, £15/20 for two people, £20/25 for a family. Wheelchair-users and the visually-impaired, together with their assisting companion, are admitted free to all Cadw monuments.

Most Cadw sites have standard opening times. From late March to late October, properties are open daily from 9.30 am to 6.30 pm. In winter, they're open Monday to Saturday from 9.30 am to 4 pm, and Sunday from 2 to 4 pm. Last admissions are 30 minutes before closing time. Occasionally, opening times may vary, so before making a long trip to a remote site, it's as well to double check.

In this book, a Cadw-run property is indicated by the word Cadw, usually following a phone number.

National Trust

The NT covers England and Wales, so taking out membership in England will entitle you to free entry to Welsh properties too. For more details, see under Useful Organisations in the Regional Facts for the Visitor chapter. Bear in mind that in winter, some NT properties stay closed or have reduced opening times.

DANGERS & ANNOYANCES

Levels and types of crime in Wales are similar to those in the rest of Britain and it's wise to take the same precautions when hitching or walking in city centres at night. The Cardiff Bay area used to have an unenviable reputation for drunken violence, but nowadays is probably no worse than any other inner-city area.

Away from the towns, the annoyances you're most likely to experience relate to the weather. The general wetness aside, it's as well to treat the Brecon Beacons and Snowdonia national parks with the respect they deserve. Mists can come down with a startling suddenness, and you shouldn't venture to the heights without checking weather forecasts first. What's more, you should certainly make sure you're sensibly and warmly clad and shod, and that you have food, water and a compass for emergencies. Ideally, make sure someone knows where you're heading if it's off the beaten track or in dubious climatic conditions.

Some English visitors work themselves

into a quite unnecessary frenzy over the alleged 'unfriendliness' of Welsh-speaking natives. You might be unlucky and bump into a raving nationalist who wants to take issue with you if you mouth the wrong opinion in the wrong place. This is pretty unlikely, though. For the most part, the Welsh are as friendly and welcoming as most people, especially if you visit out of the high season, when the slower pace of life leaves more time for chatting.

BUSINESS HOURS & PUBLIC HOLIDAYS

Business hours and holidays are the same as in England. In the countryside, shops often close early on Wednesday. Pubs no longer close on Sunday.

ACTIVITIES

See the Activities chapter at the beginning of this book for full information on activities.

Wales has done much to promote itself as the country to come to for activity holidays and there are activity centres everywhere. You can trek, walk, climb, raft, ride, bird-watch, swim and otherwise indulge yourself all year round. TICs will have details of what's possible in their vicinity.

Wales has numerous popular **walks**; the most challenging are in the rocky Snowdonia National Park (around Llanberis and Betws-y-Coed) and the grassy Brecon Beacons National Park (around Brecon). There are seven long-distance walks; the most famous are the Pembrokeshire Coast Path and Offa's Dyke Path. Less well known and therefore slightly less busy are the 274-mile Cambrian Way, which runs across the Cambrian Mountains, and the 120-mile Glyndwr's Way, which cuts through Mid Wales.

The south-west coast of Wales has a number of good **surfing** spots. From east to west, try Porthcawl, Oxwich Bay, Rhossili, Manorbier, Freshwater West and Whitesands. You can get more details from the Welsh Surfing Federation (☎ 01639-886246), 71 Fairway, Port Talbot SA12

7HW. For surfing and weather reports phone ☎ 0839-505697 (premium-rate number).

Pony trekking centres are spreading like wildfire through the Welsh countryside, as EU subsidies to farmers are cut back and farm owners struggle to find alternative uses for their land. For more information, see the WTB free guide *Discover Wales on Horseback.*

There are plenty of rivers suitable for **canoeing** and **white-water rafting** in Snowdonia, and Llangollen on the River Dee has carved out quite a niche as a canoeing centre. There's a National Whitewater Centre on the River Tryweryn, near Bala.

ACCOMMODATION
Hostels

The YHA (England and Wales) publishes a single accommodation guide, available from YHA Adventure Shops and from many hostels. It lists 46 hostels in Wales, most of them in Snowdonia, the Brecon Beacons or along the coast. Generally speaking, these hostels are likely to offer the cheapest accommodation around, although some of it can be pretty basic. It's essential to book ahead for busy periods: May to September, Easter and Christmas/New Year. If you just want a list of the Welsh hostels, contact YHA Wales (☎ 01222-396766), 4th Floor, 1 Cathedral Rd, Cardiff CF1 9HA.

To book hostels in advance in the west Wales area phone the West Wales Booking Bureau (☎ 01437-720345). For information on the seven nights for the price of five deal in the Mid Wales area phone ☎ 01222-396766.

As well as the YHA/HI hostels, there are around 20 independent hostels in Wales. Many are mentioned in this book but see the *Independent Hostel Guide* (£3.95) for full details.

Camping

Camping grounds, too, are concentrated in the national parks and along the coast. The TICs have a free *Wales Touring Caravan and Camping* leaflet with sites graded for facilities and quality by the WTB. Expect to pay about £6 a night for a tent, although on some sites prices go much lower, especially out of high season. Most sites are only open from March or April to October, so phone before going out of your way at other times.

B&Bs, Guesthouses & Hotels

Wherever you go in Wales, you'll find reasonably priced, comfortable B&Bs, with prices from around £13. Outside Cardiff, Swansea and Newport, you're unlikely to have to pay more than £15 a head, even in high season. In national-park areas, many of the guesthouses are well used to walkers and climbers and serve breakfasts big enough to set them up for their day's activities; travel in winter and you'll find many of them stoked up with big, welcoming log fires to warm you up afterwards as well. Many (but not all) of these places are listed in the WTB publication *Wales Bed and Breakfast* (£2.95); establishments listed have been inspected and graded by the WTB, although the descriptions are provided by the hotel proprietors. As in England and Scotland, crowns (listed, one, two, three, four, five) are awarded for facilities, services and equipment; grades (Approved, Commended, Highly Commended and Deluxe) refer to quality.

You can phone any B&B or hotel and book it yourself; alternatively, TICs will be happy to do this for you. Local bookings cost nothing, although a deposit is required. This is a service you might want to make use of if you arrive in July and August without having booked in advance; at other times, it's probably not necessary.

Short-Term Rental

There's plenty of rental accommodation all round Wales, much of it of a high standard, but often you have to be prepared to book for periods of a week at a time. If you're after something out of the ordinary, there are even self-catering cottages at Portmeirion (☎ 01766-770228), Clough Williams-Ellis' Italianate fantasy estate near Porthmadog. TICs will have all the details and stock the WTB's *Wales Self-Catering* (£2.95).

FOOD

Outside Wales, it could hardly be claimed that Welsh cuisine has a high profile. Pressed, people might remember the lamb, the leeks and the rarebits, but that's about it. Taste of Wales was set up in 1988 to try and change all that, and TICs should be able to supply you with the *Taste of Wales Gazetteer*, listing 400 restaurants where you can eat good food with a Welsh tang. It also contains a list of delicatessens and markets where you'll be able to buy traditional Welsh produce.

Traditional Welsh dishes include cawl, a thick vegetable broth, often flavoured with meat; and laverbread, not a bread at all, but seaweed which is often served mixed up with oatmeal and bacon on toast – a surprisingly tasty combination. Welsh rarebit is a sophisticated variation of cheese on toast, with the cheese seasoned and flavoured with butter, milk and a little beer. Rarebit is a modern name – originally it was called Welsh rabbit.

Glamorgan sausages are made from cheese, breadcrumbs, herbs and chopped leek, making them good for vegetarians. Bara brith is spicy fruit loaf, made with tea and marmalade as well as the more conventional ingredients, while Welsh cakes are fruity griddle scones.

There's not much Caerphilly cheese being made in Caerphilly these days, but cheese-making generally has undergone a recent revival. If you're keen on cheese, it's worth combing the delis for Caws Ffermdy Cenarth, Llanboidy, Llangloffan, Skirrid, St Illytd or Y Fenni.

The big towns have the usual range of Pizza Huts, Burger Kings and McDonald's, as well as dingy cafés, majoring in greasy egg & chips. In popular tourist areas, choices will be better, with vegetarians increasingly catered for. In smaller, out-of-the-way places, don't hold your breath for gourmet delights, particularly if you arrive late in the day.

DRINKS

From the visitor's point of view, things are looking up on the alcohol front, inasmuch as the archaic licensing laws that had pubs closing on Sunday have finally been dropped. Don't leave Cardiff without downing a pint of Brains, the local brew.

ENTERTAINMENT

As everywhere in Britain, pubs tend to be the focal point of local social life and vary enormously in their décor and atmosphere. In country areas, you'll find cosy watering holes, with big fires, inviting menus and the TV tuned in to S4C. In the high season, so many tourists pass through that the locals keep pretty much to themselves; visit at other times of the year, however, and you may well find people happy to chat. In Cardiff and other big cities, you'll need to pick and choose carefully; some of the city-centre places are decidedly uninviting, especially for women travelling alone.

Whatever time of year you choose, there's bound to be a festival or special event taking place nearby; check with the local TIC for details. Particularly important ones to catch are the eisteddfodau (see Culture in the Facts about Wales chapter); the International Eisteddfod is held in Llangollen every July, while the Royal National Eisteddfod occupies a different site every August. At the end of May, it's worth trying to catch the St David's Cathedral Festival, with music recitals taking place in the glorious cathedral. Throughout the summer, the Mid Wales Festival of the Countryside spawns all manner of activities in the country's least visited region (phone ☎ 01686-625384 for more details).

THINGS TO BUY

The recent revival of craft industries in craft centres all over Wales has provided plentiful shopping fodder for visitors with a yen for pottery, knitwear and lovespoons. Indeed, there can be hardly a visitor attraction left which doesn't have its shop selling commemorative T-shirts, pencils, stationery, books and souvenir fudge. Even the industrial sites have got in on the act, hawking repro miner's lamps, coal sculptures and similar artefacts. Prices are often high, and quality variable, but amongst the furry red dragons there are some classy items to be had.

> **Lovespoons**
> All over Wales, craft shops are turning out wooden spoons with contorted handles in a variety of different designs, at a speed which would have left their original makers – village lads with their eyes on a lady – gawping in astonishment. The carving of these spoons seems to date back to the 17th century, when they were made by men to give to women to mark the start of courtship. If you want to see the carving in progress, the Welsh Folk Museum at St Fagans can usually oblige. Any number of shops will be happy to sell you the finished product. ■

Getting There & Away

AIR

The international airport (☎ 01446-711111) at Cardiff is mainly used for holiday charter flights, although there are some scheduled flights to Aberdeen, Amsterdam, Belfast, Brussels, the Channel Islands, Dublin, Edinburgh, Glasgow, the Isle of Man, Manchester and Paris.

LAND

Bus

Long-distance buses are the cheapest method of getting to Wales. National Express (☎ 0990-808080) has routes from London and Bristol along the south coast through Cardiff to Pembroke (for ferries to Ireland), from Birmingham through Shrewsbury to Aberystwyth, and from Chester and the Midlands along the north coast to Holyhead (for ferries to Ireland).

London to Cardiff should cost around £20 (£4.50 more if you travel on a Friday). As in England, return tickets usually cost only a fraction more than singles. London to Pembroke takes six hours and costs £25.

Train

Great Western InterCity services can take you from London's Paddington to Cardiff in as little as 1¾ hours, or to Fishguard (for the Ireland ferry) in four hours. A SuperSaver return ticket from Cardiff to London will cost £28 – about the same price as a single. There are also some Regional Railways services from London's Waterloo via Basingstoke to Cardiff.

Regional Railways trains link South Wales with Birmingham, York, Manchester, Liverpool and Newcastle. There are also services direct to the Southampton and Portsmouth ferry ports.

Fast trains from London's Euston operate to North Wales and Holyhead via Birmingham, Chester and Llandudno. About five trains a day connect Euston to Holyhead;

they take 4½ hours and a SuperSaver ticket costs £43.

The Channel Tunnel makes it possible to travel by rail direct from continental Europe to Cardiff via London's Waterloo station. In 1997, European Night Services (ENS) will start an overnight direct service between Swansea/Cardiff and Paris.

For all rail inquiries, phone ☎ 0345-484950.

Car & Motorcycle

Motorways bring you into Wales quickly and easily. The three-mile long Second Severn Crossing, Britain's longest bridge, opened in June 1996 downstream from the old Severn Bridge. The M4 travels west from London, across either bridge (both £3.80 toll, westbound traffic only) and deep into south Wales. London to Cardiff is 155 miles and takes about three hours.

The A55 coastal expressway whisks traffic along the north coast. Access to Mid Wales is trickiest and slowest, with no major roads to get you there quickly.

Hitching

Hitching along the M4 and A55 is relatively easy, although not necessarily wise for women. Heading into Mid Wales with your thumb sticking out, you should probably pack a good book.

See also Hitching in the Getting Around chapter at the start of this book.

SEA

There are ferry links with Ireland from four towns in Wales: Holyhead, in the north-west, to Dublin (Irish Ferries) and Dun Laoghaire, near Dublin (Stena Line); Pembroke, in the south-west, to Rosslare in south-east Ireland (Irish Ferries); Fishguard, in the south-west, to Rosslare (Stena Line); and, from March to early January, from Swansea to Cork (Swansea Cork Ferries).

Getting Around

Distances in Wales are small, but with the exception of links around the coast, public-transport users have to fall back on infrequent and complicated bus timetables. There are no internal flights in Wales.

BUS

The major operators serving Wales are Crosville Cymru (☎ 01492-596969), for the north and west, and South Wales Transport (SWT; ☎ 01792-580580), for the south. Rover tickets, which can be very good value, are available. For example, the Crosville Day Rover, covering all points north and west of Shrewsbury, costs £5.70 a day.

Crosville has two particularly useful daily Traws Cambria services, but there's only one bus a day each way. The No 701 (west coast) link runs between Cardiff, Swansea, Carmarthen, Aberystwyth, Porthmadog, Caernarfon and Bangor. Cardiff to Aberystwyth (four hours) costs £9.70; Aberystwyth to Porthmadog (two hours) costs £7.30. Service No 702 runs north from Cardiff along the border with England, via Brecon to Chester. SWT offers convenient shuttle services between Cardiff and Swansea (£5.25 return).

Bus Gwynedd (☎ 01286-679535) is a network of buses operating in the north-west corner of Wales – from Llandudno to Machynlleth, including all of Snowdonia.

WELSH TRANSPORT PASSES

Pass Name	Cost (Prices for adults/discount card holders)	Bus/train/ferry services offered
Freedom of Wales Rover	£54/35.65 for 7 days	Unlimited travel on all trains.
Regional Rover for example North and Mid-Wales	£36/23.75 for 7 days	All train travel north of Aberystwyth and Shrewsbury plus Blaenau Ffestiniog Railway plus most bus services in the area.
National Express Scottish Tourist Trail Pass	As for Britain and Scotland	Unlimited travel on all National Express and Scottish Citylink bus services.
National Express Discount Coach Card (full-time students; under 26; over 60)	£7	30% off adult fares on all National Express and Scottish Citylink bus services.
National Express Britexpress Card	£12	30% off a National Express journey nominated in a 30-day period.
Flexipass	As for Britain	
Young Person's or Senior's Railcard	£16 per annum	34% off rail throughout Britain.

Those using a Regional Railways North and Mid Wales Rover ticket can travel free on these buses as well. Bus Gwynedd public-transport guide-maps are available at TICs.

A more unusual way of getting round, especially in remote Mid Wales, is to make use of the Royal Mail postbuses that link up the villages. Local post offices should be able to help with details.

TRAIN

Wales has some fantastic train lines – both mainline (☎ 0345-484950) and private, narrow-gauge survivors. Apart from the main lines along the north and south coasts to the Irish ferry ports, there are some interesting lines that converge on Shrewsbury (see under Getting There & Away in the

Shrewsbury section of the Northern Midlands chapter). The lines along the Cambrian (west) coast and down the Conwy valley are exceptionally attractive.

There are several Rover tickets, including the Freedom of Wales Rover – see the passes table in this chapter for details. See also under Getting There & Away in the Shrewsbury section of the Northern Midlands chapter.

CAR & MOTORCYCLE

Getting round north and south Wales is made simple by the M4 and A55 respectively. Away from these highways, roads are still good but generally slower, especially in the mountainous areas and Mid Wales. Bear in mind that some of the highest roads may be

---

The Great Little Trains of Wales

Wales' narrow-gauge steam railways are survivors from its industrial heyday, when mine and quarry owners needed to move their produce more quickly than horses could manage in terrain that defied normal standard-gauge trains. In the 20th century, as these lines gradually lost their raison d'être, train enthusiasts took many of them over and now run steam-hauled services on them, particularly in summer. Most of these lines run through glorious scenery, primarily in north and mid Wales, so they're worth checking out even if you're not a rail buff.

Schedules vary depending on the time of year. Particular TICs usually have timetables for the routes nearest to them. Otherwise, contact any of these numbers for details: Bala Lake Railway (☎ 01678-540666); Brecon Mountain Railway (☎ 01685-722988); Ffestiniog Railway (☎ 01766-512340); Llanberis Lake Railway (☎ 01286-870549); Vale of Rheidol Railway (☎ 01970-625819); Talyllyn Railway (☎ 01654-710472); Welsh Highland Railway (☎ 01766-513402); and Welshpool & Llanfair Railway (☎ 01938-810441).

Wanderer tickets are available for all eight railways from 1 April to 31 October. A pass giving four days travel in any eight days costs £25/12.50 for adults/children; for eight days travel in any 15 days it's £32/16. Passes are sold at the main stations of the participating railways, or write to GLTW, The Railway Station, Llanfair Caerinion SY21 0SF. Holders of some mainline rail passes may be eligible for discounts. Some of the railways operate Santa Specials over the Christmas period. ∎

snowbound in winter. Even when the snow clears, ice can linger to make driving conditions treacherous, especially on windy, narrow mountain roads, which are often single-track affairs with passing places at intervals.

BICYCLE

Travelling around Wales by bike is increasingly popular, although the hilly terrain is really only suitable for experienced cyclists. Most towns have at least one shop where you can hire a bike for about £10 a day. If you're bringing your own, don't forget that you may need to book space to transport it on a train, and that you're rarely allowed to take bikes on trains during rush hours.

HITCHING

Hitching along the M4 and A55 and down to the ferry ports may be fairly quick and easy, but in the quieter, more remote areas you could be waiting a long time for lifts, especially on Sunday when traffic often fades away completely.

See also Hitching in the Getting Around chapter at the start of this book.

BOAT

You're most likely to use boats to get out to the islands off the Pembrokeshire coast (Skomer, Skokholm, Grassholm and Ramsey), or off the Llyn Peninsula (Bardsey). The *Dale Princess* plies back and forth between Skomer, Skokholm and Grassholm during the summer; details can be obtained from Dale Sailing Co (☎ 01646-601636), Brunel Quay, Neyland, Pembrokeshire, or from the Pembrokeshire/Dyfed Wildlife Trust (01437-765462). Ramsey Island Pleasure Cruises (☎ 01437-720285) operates boats to Ramsey. Sailings (and accommodation arrangements) for Bardsey are controlled by the Bardsey Island Trust; details can be obtained from Stabal Hen (☎ 01766-522239), Tyddyn Du, Cricieth, Caernarfonshire & Merionethshire LL52 0LY.

Barges can be hired to travel along the Llangollen Canal (☎ 01978-860702) and the Montgomery Canal (☎ 01938-552043).

South Wales

HIGHLIGHTS

- Cardiff Castle
- St Fagans & the Welsh Folk Museum
- Wye Valley and Tintern Abbey
- Chepstow Castle
- The Mumbles Mile – pub crawl in the suburb of Swansea
- Dylan Thomas Boathouse
- Pembrokeshire Coast National Park
- St David's
- Pwll Deri Youth Hostel
- Fishguard

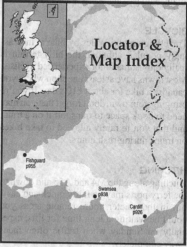

Locator & Map Index

Fishguard p955

Swansea p938

Cardiff p926

Stretching from the Wye Valley on the border with England, west to Pembrokeshire, this area includes the capital of Wales, Cardiff, the second-largest town in Wales, Swansea, and the 230-square-mile expanse of the Pembrokeshire Coast National Park.

The south coast from Newport to Swansea is heavily industrialised, but there are still stretches of beautiful coastline such as the Glamorgan Heritage Coast. This protected coastline stretches 14 miles from Aberthaw to Porthcawl.

The valleys running north into the Black Mountains and the Brecon Beacons National Park (see Mid Wales) are still struggling to come to grips with the loss of the coal-mining industry. Even so, the little villages that form a continuous chain along the valleys have their own stark beauty, more attractive now that the old slagheaps are being grassed over, and the people are particularly friendly.

The Pembrokeshire Coast National Park is the only largely coastal national park in Britain – it's also the smallest. Despite the many scenic attractions in the area, only the places on the milder southern part of the coastline have been developed into tourist resorts – the more exposed northern coast is still virtually unspoilt and offers some of the best walking in Britain.

South-Eastern Wales

This part of the country contains over half the population and most of Wales's factories. Hidden amongst the urban sprawl, however, are some interesting places. There's the Wye Valley and, between the traditional market town of Monmouth and the dramatically located castle at Chepstow, are the scenic ruins of Tintern Abbey.

To the west is Cardiff, a surprisingly lively city. The Welsh are proudly defensive of their capital, which has been rapidly transformed from a dull provincial backwater into a prosperous university city with an increasingly lively arts scene. Cardiff Castle is worth seeing for its striking Victorian interior. The National Museum of Wales packs in everything Welsh, but also includes one of the finest collections of Impressionist art in

Britain. The Welsh Folk Museum at St Fagans, five miles from Cardiff, is a popular open-air attraction with reconstructed buildings and craft demonstrations.

Swansea was where the poet and writer Dylan Thomas grew up. It's the gateway to the Gower, a sparsely populated peninsula with long, sandy beaches and attractive cliff scenery.

GETTING AROUND

Bus and train services are good in this part of Wales, although the country's mountainous geography means that direct journeys from South to North Wales are tricky and time-consuming. For information on buses in the Cardiff area, phone ☎ 01222-396521; in the Swansea area, phone ☎ 01792-580580.

Some bus companies sell day passes that are also valid on services run by other companies. SWT's Roverbus ticket costs £4.50 and is valid for a day's travel throughout South Wales on services run by SWT, Brewers, Rhondda, Red & White and Silverline Coaches. It's not valid on the Cardiff-Swansea Shuttle but you can use it on the slow X1 service between Cardiff and Swansea.

For rail information, phone ☎ 0345-484950. Valley Lines (☎ 01222-231978) has a one-day unlimited travel ticket for £5.25/2.65 allowing rail travel in the Cardiff area and the Valleys. On this ticket you could visit Cardiff Bay, Caerphilly Castle, the Rhondda Heritage Park and along the Taff and Rhymney rivers.

The Wye Valley Walk is a 107-mile waymarked trail, which runs alongside the river from Chepstow to Rhayader. There are youth hostels along the way at St Briavels, Monmouth and Welsh Bicknor. For more information visit the Chepstow TIC which also has a permanent exhibition on walks in the Wye Valley.

CARDIFF (CAERDYDD)

- *pop 265,000* • ☎ *01222*

At first sight, Cardiff, the Welsh capital, is not particularly attractive. Trains and buses deposit you on the edge of one of those faceless shopping centres which make you think the best thing to do would be to get on another bus (or train) and head straight out again. That would be a shame, because Cardiff has a striking city-centre castle, a world-class museum and art gallery, a cluster of small but interesting industrial heritage sites in the newly renovated docks area, and pockets of beautiful architecture.

Cardiff's heyday was in the 19th century, when the thriving coal industry of the valleys provided the Tiger Bay port with constant export material. The South Wales coal industry has virtually disappeared – the last mines seen off in the years since the catastrophic 1984 strike. These days, Cardiff is a bit-part player on the export/import scene. The Tiger Bay district was run-down, neglected and had a reputation for drunken violence, when plans to clean it up and turn it into a centre for tourism first hit the drawing boards in 1987. Now it has one of Britain's most imaginative visitors' centres, built in a hollow tube like the body of an aircraft overlooking the bay.

Redevelopment remains a controversial issue. A barrage is currently being built across the mouth of what is now called Cardiff Bay and this will allow a giant freshwater marina to be developed. Environmentalists complain that this will be at the price of losing the mud flats which have traditionally provided feeding grounds for thousands of wading birds.

Even if you don't want to linger in Cardiff, it's a good base for visiting a few sites in the surrounding area, including the Welsh Folk Museum at St Fagans, the castles at Caerphilly and Castell Coch, the Big Pit Mining Museum at Blaenavon and the Rhondda Heritage Park. Transport links are good, with the M4 linking Cardiff to Swansea and Bristol (via the Severn Bridge and the new Second Severn Crossing) and a new peripheral road being built across the bay.

History

The Romans first settled the area to the east of the River Taff, but once they pulled out of

SOUTH WALES

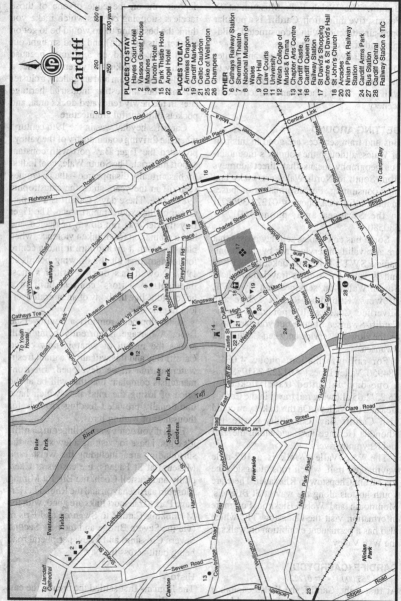

Cardiff

PLACES TO STAY
1 Hayes Court Hotel
2 Vassos Guest House
3 Maxines
4 Lincoln Hotel
15 Park Thistle Hotel
22 Angel Hotel

PLACES TO EAT
5 Armless Dragon
19 Cardiff Market
21 Celtic Cauldron
25 Duke of Wellington
26 Champers

OTHER
6 Cathays Railway Station
7 Sherman Theatre
8 National Museum of Wales
9 City Hall
10 Law Courts
11 University
12 Welsh College of Music & Drama
13 Chapter Arts Centre
14 Cardiff Castle
16 Cardiff Queen St Railway Station
17 St David's Shopping Centre & St David's Hall
18 St John's Church
20 Arcades
23 Ninian Park Railway Station
24 Cardiff Arms Park
27 Bus Station
28 Cardiff Central Railway Station & TIC

SOUTH WALES

Britain, the site seems to have been abandoned until after the Norman conquest. Robert Fitzhamon was responsible for the motte and bailey castle, remains of which still stand in the grounds of the later Cardiff Castle. Throughout the Middle Ages there was clearly a settlement at Cardiff (St John's Church in the city centre is a reminder of this period) but it was very small; even in 1801, the census figures suggest barely 1000 people lived here.

Cardiff really owes its development to the coal mining in the valleys to the north. In 1839, the Marquis of Bute had the first docks built in Cardiff, and the Bute family, who owned much of the land on which coal had been found, were able to insist all exported coal was traded through their ports. Cardiff boomed, and by the end of the 19th century there were probably about 170,000 people living here. However, hard times returned in the 20th century, especially during the slump of the 1930s. The city was also badly damaged by bombs during WWII, which explains some of the nastier modern development in the centre.

It was only in 1955 that Cardiff was designated the capital of Wales, a status which brought it renewed prosperity as government agencies concerned with Wales relocated their headquarters here. However, the docks could never recover their lost importance and it wasn't until the creation of the Cardiff Bay Development Corporation in 1987 that serious efforts were made to revive the area. Nor has Cardiff been immune from the fallout caused by the loss of mining and industrial jobs in surrounding areas, particularly the valleys. Some of the leafier suburbs exude continued prosperity, but walk around Butetown and you quickly form a very different impression.

Orientation

Cardiff originally grew up around Tiger Bay, but the city centre gradually migrated northwards as the port trade dried up. Consequently, Cardiff has two 'centres' as far as tourists are concerned.

Buses and trains arrive just south of the main thoroughfare of St Mary/High St, with the castle forming a useful landmark. Behind the castle stretches Bute Park, the city's main open space, with the River Taff running through it. Opposite the castle lies the main shopping area, where the most interesting places tend to be tucked away inside the network of 19th and early 20th-century arcades. The National Museum of Wales is grouped with the Law Courts, the Civic Hall and University College, east of the castle. Cardiff Bay and the docklands museums are a dreary half-hour's walk south. Take a bus.

Cardiff Central railway station is off Penarth Rd; the main bus terminal is right in front of it. Some local train services leave from Queen St station to the east. Bute St station is within walking distance of Cardiff Bay.

Information

The TIC (☎ 227281) is inside Cardiff Central station. It's open daily from 9 am to 6.30 pm (from 10 am on Tuesday, and from 10 am to 4 pm on Sunday). You can pick up free maps and accommodation lists here and there's a bureau de change.

The TIC stocks *The Buzz*, a free bimonthly magazine with information about events in all the city venues. It's also good on Cardiff's nightspots. If you're under 22 and planning to hang around, it may be worth buying a YouthCard (£7), which gives you discounts at many of the Cardiff venues; buy it at St David's Hall box office.

Thomas Cook (☎ 224886) is at 16 Queen St, and there's a branch of Campus Travel (☎ 220744) inside the YHA Adventure Shop at 13 Castle St.

The main Post Office is in St David's Shopping Centre.

Parking in the centre of Cardiff is usually subject to restriction. Many places require you to display vouchers which you need to buy in advance from local shops. A 50p voucher lasts one hour. You should scratch the time that you arrive onto the clock faces provided and leave the voucher(s) in the car window.

Cardiff Castle

It would be hard to miss the castle, which is ringed by a low wall with sculpted bears, lions and wolves crawling all over it. Although excavations on the site indicate it was first occupied by the Romans, the first substantial remains – a motte and bailey castle – date back to Norman times. The present Cardiff Castle is, however, much newer. It was designed for the third Lord Bute by the Victorian architect William Burges (1827-1881), who specialised in Victorian Gothic. The outrageous interior is now more Hollywood than medieval, but you'll only get to explore the Banqueting Hall, the Arab Room and the Fairytale Nursery on a guided tour.

The castle (☎ 878100) is open from 9.45 am to 6 pm, May to September, with tours at 20-minute intervals; in winter, the grounds are open from 10 am to 5 pm, but there are only four daily tours, the first at 10.30 am and the last at 3.15 pm. A visit and tour is £3.70/1.80; to explore only the grounds costs £2.30/1.20.

National Museum of Wales

In Cathays Park, the National Museum forms a pleasing turn-of-the-century grouping of grey-white buildings with the City Hall and the Law Courts. For anyone with children, this place is a must. There's a wonderful exhibition on the evolution of Wales, complete with mammoths that wave their trunks and waggle their ears.

The natural-history galleries are also excellent; in particular, look out for the rooms housing the skeleton of a young humpback whale washed up near Aberthaw in 1982 and the remains of a giant leatherback turtle found dead on the beach at Harlech in 1988.

On the fourth floor is a magnificent collection of paintings, including Gwendoline and Margaret Davies' bequest of Impressionist paintings, with some Monet *Waterlilies* and works by Sisley, Pisarro, Manet and Degas. There's also a version of Rodin's *The Kiss* and an even nicer model of *The Earth and the Moon*.

The museum (☎ 397951) is open Tuesday to Sunday from 10 am to 5 pm; entry is £3.25/2.

St John's Church

Jutting up incongruously from the tacky shopping precinct surrounding it is the graceful 15th-century tower of St John's Church. The church is a haven from the bustle outside and one of the few reminders of Cardiff's pre-Victorian past.

Cardiff Bay

The area once called Tiger Bay is now more prosaically named Cardiff Bay. On a sunny day, it's a pleasant place for a stroll, with works of sculpture dotted around the promenade, although while the barrage, peripheral distributor road and assorted insurance company buildings are constructed, there will inevitably be some noise and disruption.

The most striking edifice is the Pierhead Building, a huge, red-brick, Victorian masterpiece, not open to the public. A little away from the Bay itself, off James St, is Mount Stuart Square, which has some imposing Victorian architecture. It's a haven of restored grandeur amid the general drabness of Butetown.

Bus No 8 runs from the city centre to Cardiff Bay, or you can get a train to Bute St station and walk.

Welsh Industrial & Maritime Museum Not surprisingly, this museum (☎ 481919) contains exhibits relating to South Wales's industrial and maritime history. There are displays relating to the history of coal mining and you can have your own miner's badge made for you. In the railway gallery there are interesting displays on railway history to supplement the various engines and carriages dotted about outside.

One of the most interesting parts of the museum, containing old house and shop interiors, is housed separately at 126 Bute St. It's only open on the first Saturday of each month. The main museum is open from 10

BRYN THOMAS

BRYN THOMAS

BRYN THOMAS

BRYN THOMAS

Top: View of Aberystwyth, Mid Wales
Left: Old and new, Swansea, South Wales
Middle: On the summit of Mt Snowdon, North Wales
Bottom: Monmouth Bridge, Monmouth, South Wales

TONY WHEELER

TONY WHEELER

TONY WHEELER

TONY WHEELER

TONY WHEELER

TONY WHEELER

A	B
C	D
E	F

A: Pictish cross, Bettyhill, Highlands
B: Stone Circle, Avebury, Wiltshire
C: Roman mosaic, Littlecote, Wiltshire
D: Manx cross, Isle of Man

E: Stone cross, Eyam, Derbyshire
F: Stonehenge, Wiltshire

am to 5 pm, Tuesday to Saturday, and 2.30 to 5 pm Sunday; tickets cost £2/1.20.

Techniquest Techniquest (☎ 475475) is the UK's largest hands-on science exhibition, with everything from a machine that blows smoke rings to a wet area with exhibits pertaining to liquid. Just across from the Welsh Industrial and Maritime Museum, there's also a planetarium and science theatre.

It's open from 9.30 am to 4.30 pm, Monday to Friday, and 10.30 am to 5 pm at weekends; entry is £4.50/2.50 (75p extra for the planetarium).

Cardiff Visitors Centre Little more than a way of soft-soaping visitors into buying the Cardiff Bay Development Corporation's view of things, the visitors centre is at least housed in an imaginative building – a long, white tube that acts like a giant telescope overlooking the bay. Entry is free and it's open from 9.30 am to 4.30 pm, Monday to Friday, and from 10.30 am to 5 pm at weekends.

Llandaff Cathedral
If Cardiff sometimes seems too busy and brash for comfort, hop on bus No 21A, 25, 33 or 65X along Cathedral Rd to Llandaff, a peaceful, pretty northern suburb where Llandaff Cathedral (☎ 563848) sits in a dip in the landscape.

Dating from 1130, it was largely rebuilt in the 19th century, and extensively restored again after being damaged by a land mine in 1941. The west-end towers epitomise the cathedral's fragmented history; one was built in the 15th century, the other in the 19th. Nowadays, the most striking internal feature is the giant central arch carrying the organ and Jacob Epstein's striking *Majestas*. Fans of the Pre-Raphaelites will be interested in the Burne-Jones reredos in St Dyfrig's chapel and the stained glass by Rossetti and William Morris's company. Outside, the heads of the British monarchs are carved along the top of the south aisle wall; look out for the uncrowned head of Edward VIII, who abdicated before his coronation.

Organised Tours
During the summer, hop-on, hop-off open-top bus tours, run by Leisurelink (☎ 522202), circle 11 points around the city, from Llandaff in the north to Cardiff Bay in the south. If you stay on the bus for the whole tour, it takes one hour. Tickets cost £5.50/2 (£4 for students) and give you a 10% discount at the National Museum of Wales and the Welsh Industrial and Maritime Museum.

Places to Stay
Hostel The cheapest option is *Cardiff Youth Hostel* (☎ 462303), 2 Wedal Rd, Roath Park, where a bed costs £9.10/6.15. It's open daily from 2 January to 1 December. The hostel is two miles north of the city centre – bus Nos 78, 80 and 82 run this way from Cardiff Central railway station.

B&Bs & Hotels Cardiff has the usual range of B&Bs for around £15 a head; most of them can be found along Cathedral Rd, to the west, and Newport Rd, to the east. Both these roads are busy with traffic.

Vassos Guest House (☎ 664527), 152 Cathedral Rd, charges £15 per person. *Maxines* (☎ 220288), next door, does B&B for £18/35 for a single/double. On Newport Rd, good bets are *Tanes Hotel* (☎ 493898), at No 148, for £17/30, or the *Cardiff Hotel* (☎ 491964), at No 138, which costs from £17/28 for the most basic rooms. Out of season, many of the hotels along these two roads bring their prices down – look for offers in the windows. A quieter option is the guesthouse at *97 Allensbank Rd* (☎ 621230) in Heath, to the north, where rooms cost £15/28.

Middle-range hotels are also concentrated in Cathedral and Newport Rds. In Cathedral Rd, there's the *Hayes Court Hotel* (☎ 230420), at Nos 154-64, which has rooms for £35/42 with bath attached, and the *Lincoln Hotel* (☎ 395558), at No 118, charging £39.50/49.50. On Newport Rd, the *Marlborough House* (☎ 492385), at No 98, has rooms for £22/34 with shared bath and £38/48 with bathroom attached.

Hotels in the centre may look more

appealing but most are expensive. The *Angel Hotel* (☎ 232633), opposite the castle in Castle St, has grand public rooms and charges £78/92 for a single/double. Breakfast is an extra £9.25. At the weekend, however, they do B&B for £34 per person.

The newly-renovated *Park Thistle Hotel* (☎ 383471), in Park Place, off the Queen St shopping centre, is conveniently located and charges £95/105 for a single/double. It's also worth inquiring about their weekend breaks, which cost around £42 per person.

Places to Eat

If you're on a tight budget, head for Cardiff Market in The Hayes, where *Roche's Snack Bar* offers snack food at rock-bottom prices: sausage baps for 75p and cheese toasties for £1. The market is also the place to come if you're after cheese, cold meats, laverbread and rolls for a picnic.

Some of the nicest places to eat are tucked well out of sight in the maze of Victorian arcades behind the modern shopping-centre façade. A good place to start looking is Castle Arcade, immediately opposite the castle. Here you'll find the *Celtic Cauldron*, where you can sample traditional Welsh dishes like laverbread, cawl and oatmeal pancakes. It does good vegetarian meals, you can also get glasses of punch, and it's open Monday to Saturday until 6 pm.

In Duke St Arcade, *Garlands Coffeeshop* is a pleasant place for coffee, tea and light snacks. In Royal Arcade, *Swallows Coffee House* has jacket potatoes and quiche from £1.50. *Crumbs* in Morgan Arcade does good vegetarian food to eat in or take away. It's only open from 9.30 am to 3 pm, Monday to Friday, and 9.30 am to 4 pm on Saturday. City-centre pubs offer bargain bar lunches for £3 to £4.

Cardiff's strong Italian community guarantees plenty of pizza and pasta places to choose from. At 6 High St, there's a branch of *Bella Pasta*, which often has special deals. *Topo Gigio*, at 12 Church St, is not necessarily the cheapest, but it's pretty reliable.

More upmarket, although not in a very upmarket area, is the *Armless Dragon*

(382357) at 97 Wyeverne Rd. The à la carte menu is pretty pricey – dinner would set you back around £20 – but there are good-value set lunches (£7.95/9.95 for two/three courses and coffee).

At 60-61 St Mary St, there are three informal restaurants run by the same management – *La Brasserie* (☎ 372164), *Champers* (☎ 373363) and *Le Monde* (☎ 387376) – offering a range of Spanish, French and Welsh food, balanced with a good choice of seafood. Main courses range from £5 to £15 and the restaurants have been recently expanded and refurbished to seat 300 people.

The best French restaurant in Cardiff is *Le Cassoulet* (☎ 221905), 5 Romilly Crescent, off Llandaff Rd in the west of the city. Start your evening with one of the excellent cocktails. Set lunches range from £16 to £20, set dinners from £20 to £27. It's closed on Sunday and Monday; on Saturday it's open only for lunch.

In the Cardiff Bay area the recently-opened *Caribbean Restaurant* (☎ 252102), 14 West Bute St, Mount Stuart, does good-value food. Lamb curry is £4.20; steak, rice and veg costs £7. It's open daily from 11.30 am to 2 pm and 5 to 11 pm (until 2 am at weekends). It's a popular place.

Also in Cardiff Bay, the reconstructed Norwegian Church near the visitors centre has been turned into a cosy *teashop*, doing excellent cakes, waffles and sandwiches. Children's author Roald Dahl was christened here.

Entertainment

The local brew is Brains SA (Special Ale or Skull Attack depending on how many pints you have). There are numerous places to try it. The *Duke of Wellington* is a tidy pub centrally located on Caroline St. Popular with students is the recently refurbished *Gassey Jack's*, at 39 Salisbury Rd. It often has live music nights here. The *King's Cross* on Caroline St is a busy gay bar.

Cardiff's best-known entertainment is probably rugby, which takes place on Saturday afternoon at Cardiff Arms Park (☎ 390111).

★★★

Welsh Rugby

Although the Welsh play conventional football (soccer), it's really rugby union that marks Wales out from England. During the 1970s, the Welsh national team was immensely successful, winning six out of ten championships. Since then, however, things haven't gone quite so swingingly, and in 1991 Wales went down to ignominious defeat (63-6) at the hands of Australia. In 1994, however, Wales did win the Five Nations Championship, in which Wales, England, Scotland, Ireland and France compete against each other. This success has not yet been repeated.

If you'd like to see Wales play, their stadium is at Cardiff Arms Park in the centre of Cardiff. Tickets for normal fixtures should be easy to obtain at reasonable prices (£6 to £8 in the stands; phone ☎01222-390111 for details), although those for big events sell out months in advance of the match.

The most successful club sides are Cardiff, Swansea, Neath and Llanelli, and you can catch their matches between September and Easter. Most of the former mining valley towns also have their own sides. ■

★★★

If you're after something less frenetic in warmer surroundings, *St David's Hall* (☎ 878500), in The Hayes, offers a full range of theatrical events. There are also two smaller theatres, the *Sherman Theatre* (☎ 230451), in Senghennydd Rd, Cathays, and the *New Theatre* (☎ 878889), in Park Place, currently the home of the Welsh National Opera.

Most imaginative cinema programmes tend to be at the *Chapter Arts Centre* (☎ 399666) in Market Rd, Canton. It's popular with students; get there on bus Nos 12, 14 and 16-18.

There are regular classical music concerts in St David's Hall; less frequent ones in Llandaff Cathedral and St John's Church. The new *Cardiff International Arena* (☎ 224488) in Mary Ann St hosts large-scale pop concerts of the Barry Manilow type. The stately *Coal Exchange* in Mount Stuart Square takes the smaller gigs.

Getting There & Away

See the fares tables in the introductory Getting Around chapter. Cardiff is 155 miles from London, 50 from Bristol and 48 from Swansea.

Air Cardiff airport (☎ 01446-711111) is 12 miles south-west of the centre, connected to it by hourly bus services X91 and X92.

Bus National Express (☎ 0990-808080)

runs coaches between London (Victoria) and Cardiff (three hours, £20 to £25 single, every two hours). There are hourly services linking Cardiff and Bristol (£4.75). Via Birmingham, there are services between Cardiff and Llandudno (seven hours, £30, twice a day) and Cardiff and Rhyl (6¼ hours, £29.50, twice a day).

The SWT Shuttle (☎ 01792 580580) links Cardiff with Swansea (one hour, £5.25 return, almost hourly). The daily Cambrian Express connects Cardiff with Aberystwyth via Swansea, Carmarthen, Lampeter and Aberaeron. For more information, phone ☎ 396521.

Train Cardiff Central is on the main Inter-City London to Swansea route: London to Cardiff costs £36 one way (two hours, hourly services), and Cardiff to Swansea costs £7 (one hour).

Regional Railways' Alphaline also offers direct services between Cardiff and London's Waterloo, which are timed to connect with international services through the Channel Tunnel. In 1997 an overnight direct service to Paris will begin operating.

Direct train services connect Cardiff and Manchester, Liverpool, Birmingham, Nottingham and the ports at Portsmouth and Southampton. Trains to Chester continue to Holyhead (for Dun Laoghaire, £47.30). There are also trains connecting Cardiff and Pembroke Dock via Tenby (£12.90), Milford

Haven via Haverfordwest (£12.90), and Fishguard Harbour (for Rosslare, £12.90).

Valley Lines' services (from Cardiff Central or Queen St) link Cardiff with Merthyr Tydfil, Aberdare, Pontypridd, Treherbert, Rhymney and Coryton. The free bus map from Cardiff Bus Office includes a map of the valley rail routes.

Car & Motorcycle The M4 loops round Cardiff, linking it to Swansea, Bristol and London. The Peripheral Distributor Rd being built across Cardiff Bay will provide direct links to the M4, bypassing the city centre.

Boat In summer, you can get to Penarth, three miles from Cardiff, on the *Balmoral* or *Waverley* ships operating from Bristol.

Getting Around

Cardiff's sights are scattered around the city, so walking is really only feasible to get around the centre, parts of which are pedestrianised.

Bus Orange and white Cardiff Bus services provide quick, cheap access to most parts of town. Most buses (even the ones without notices saying so) want exact fares; the only way you'll get any change is to ask for a change ticket and either use it on another service or wait two days before cashing it in at the city bus office.

Capital Day Out tickets (£3; available from the driver) are available all day and can be used to get round the city centre, Penarth, Castell Coch, St Fagans, Llandaff and Cardiff Bay. If you're staying longer, there are weekly/monthly multiride tickets for £8.15/30.

Cardiff Bus Office (☎ 396521) is in St David's House, Wood St, right in front of the bus terminal. Their excellent free map shows not just the city bus routes but also the local railway lines as well.

Train There are local railway stations at Queen St, Cathays, Llandaff, Ninian Park and Bute Rd (for the bay).

Bicycle Cardiff is at the southern end of the Welsh National Cycle Route, Lôn Las Cymru, which runs the full length of Wales to end in Holyhead, Anglesey. From Cardiff the route follows the Taff Trail (see Brecon Beacons National Park). For cycle hire, take a City Line train north-west from Cardiff Central to Radyr station. Cross the river to Taff Trail Cycle Hire (☎ 59108) at Forest Farm Country Park, Whitchurch, where bike rental costs £7 per day. Bus Nos 33 and 133 also go to Radyr.

AROUND CARDIFF
Castell Coch

Rising up among the beech trees on a hill just north-west of the city, Castell Coch looks more like a Loire château than a standard Welsh castle. The summer retreat of the Bute family, it was designed by William Burges (like Cardiff Castle) in gaudy Victorian Gothic. Particularly interesting are the sitting room, with designs based on Aesop's Fables; the bedroom, which has a sink that swings up to empty out the water; and the kitchen, which has a fine Welsh dresser.

Castell Coch (☎ 01222-810101; Cadw) is open daily from 9.30 am to 6.30 pm; entry is £2.20/1.70. Cardiff Bus No 26 will take you to Tongwynlais: it's a 10-minute walk from there.

Caerphilly Castle

Nine miles north of Cardiff, Caerphilly is a fairy-tale, ruined, medieval castle complete with moat – although its setting is somewhat marred by the ugly development of Caerphilly itself, right on its doorstep.

The castle was built in stages between 1268 and 1277 by Gilbert de Clare, under constant threat of attack from Prince Llywelyn. It has a long external wall with a gatehouse opening onto a causeway over the moat. This leads to the keep, which stands on a platform. The castle was in a dismal state in the 19th century, when the Bute family offered funds to restore it to its present state.

Caerphilly Castle (☎ 01222-883143; Cadw) is open Easter to October, daily from 9.30 am to 6.30 pm, and from 9.30 am to 4 pm, Monday to Saturday, and 11 am to 4 pm on Sunday for the rest of the year; entry is £2.20/1.70. Caerphilly railway station is a quarter of a mile from the castle and there are frequent trains, or you can get there on Bus Nos 71/72.

St Fagans & the Welsh Folk Museum

Four miles west of Cardiff along the A4232, St Fagans is a small village with a vast tourist attraction. The 100-acre Welsh Folk Museum is a collection of 30 reconstructed buildings brought from all over the country. Among them are a tollhouse, a cockpit, a chapel and assorted houses, cottages, and a row of Victorian shops brought here from the valleys.

Craftspeople still work in many of the buildings, allowing visitors to see how clogs, barrels, cider and wooden artefacts were made. In the grounds, you can also see examples of peculiarly Welsh breeds of livestock and poultry. History is regularly brought to life here, especially on public holidays when the site can get horribly cluttered with families tucking into hot lamb sandwiches.

The folk museum (☎ 01222-569441) is open daily from 10 am to 6 pm (closed on Sunday in winter); tickets cost £5/2.50. Cardiff Bus Nos 32 and 32A run to St Fagans.

Penarth

A relatively demure seaside resort, Penarth has a Victorian pier from which you can take summer boat trips across to England – to Clevedon, Minehead, Ilfracombe and many other destinations. Some trips are on the last surviving operational paddle-steamer, SS *Waverley*. For details of boat departures, phone ☎ 01446-720656.

In Penarth, you can visit the **Turner House Gallery**, an offshoot of the National Museum of Wales, which displays objets d'art and touring exhibitions. You can get to Penarth on Cardiff Bus Nos L1, P2, P10 and P20 or by train.

Barry

- *pop 45,000*   •   ☎ *01222*

Eight miles west of Cardiff, Barry is an uninspiring dormitory town for commuters to the capital. If you've got children, however, Barry does boast a **Pleasure Beach** – a funfair on the Blackpool model, a **Rollerdome** and a **Quasar Centre**. Trains from Cardiff run directly to the fair (get off at Barry Island station) and Cardiff Bus offers hourly services (No 304) from Central station. In summer, boats link Barry with Bristol across the Bristol Channel.

Rhondda Valley & Heritage Park

If you're interested in the industrial history of the valleys, don't miss the Rhondda Heritage Park, 10 miles north-west of Cardiff, between Pontypridd and Porth. This was the centre of the late coal-mining industry in South Wales; the Heritage Park is built on the site of Lewis Merthyr colliery, which closed in 1983. Here, an exhibition brings the old colliery buildings back to life and tries to explain what life was like for those who worked here and their families. You can descend in a cage to the coalface, with a retired miner as your guide.

The park (☎ 01443-682036) is a half-hour train ride north from Cardiff Central station. The site is open daily from 10 am to 6 pm (except Monday from October to Easter); entry is £4.95/4.25 (students £3.50).

Newport

- *pop 116,000*   •   ☎ *01633*

Newport is a busy industrial and commercial centre, one of the biggest in Wales. The **town museum**, in the same building as the TIC, has interesting displays on the Roman fortress of Caerleon, and about the history of mining in the area. Also of interest is **Tredagar House**, a restored 17th-century mansion set in a park on the western outskirts of the town.

The fact that Newport is a major transport junction means that you may find yourself changing trains or buses here. The railway station is about 500 yards north of the bus station. The TIC (☎ 842962), John Frost Square, is across the road from the southern end of the bus station, in the same building as the museum and art gallery. The Newport

Centre (☎ 622622), at Kingsway, hosts big pop concerts. Trains link Cardiff and Newport daily until just before midnight.

Caerleon Roman Fortress

At Caerleon, four miles north of Newport, this is the most important Roman site in Wales. It was known as Isca in Roman times, after the River Usk which flows past the town.

There's an impressive amphitheatre dating from AD 90, fortress baths, and the only legionary barracks on display in Europe. There are excellent displays in the Roman Legionary Museum (☎ 01633-422518; Cadw). It's all very well presented and well worth a visit.

The amphitheatre is always open and free; joint entry to the baths and museum is £2.85/1.80.

WYE VALLEY

The River Wye flows 154 miles from its source at Plynlimon in Mid Wales to meet the River Severn at Chepstow. From the mossy spring where the water rises, it runs through the mountains to Rhayader, past Glasbury and Builth Wells, on through Hay-on-Wye (see the Brecon Beacons section in the Mid Wales chapter), Hereford and Ross-on-Wye (see the Hereford & Worcester section of the Southern Midlands chapter) and down through Monmouth, past the picturesque ruins of Tintern Abbey, to Chepstow. The Wye Valley Walk (see Getting Around at the start of this section) follows the river from Rhayader to Chepstow, and the section of the river from Monmouth to Chepstow is particularly attractive.

Monmouth

- *pop 7500*   • ☎ *01600*

Whilst Monmouth is a town of few distinctions, it's the attractive centre of an agricultural region. It has a beautiful and unique 13th-century bridge with a busy cattle market nearby. The town is on the Welsh side of the border with England.

The Normans built a castle on the town's easily defended site. It was the birthplace of Henry V, but was later destroyed and Great Castle House, still standing, was built from its stones. Occupied by both Royalists and Roundheads during the Civil War, Monmouth subsequently became the county town of Monmouthshire, prospering from livestock and country markets, and as the site of the regular Assize Court.

Monmouth's shape is governed by its position at the confluence of the Rivers Monnow, Wye and Trothy. The town is centred on Agincourt Square. From here, Monnow St, the principal thoroughfare, lined with shops, descends to the Monnow Bridge. Above the square, along a number of smaller lanes, are bookshops and pubs. The TIC (☎ 713899) is under the portico of the Shire Hall on Agincourt Square.

Things to See The symbol of the town is the **Monnow Bridge**, unique in Britain as the only complete example of a 13th-century stone-gated bridge. Built as part of the city defences, it was also a toll bridge.

The centre of the town is **Agincourt Square**, an irregularly shaped hub with the arcade of the Shire Hall, built in 1724, on one side. In front of it is the statue of Charles Rolls, Monmouth son and co-founder of the Rolls-Royce car and aero-engine company.

The **Nelson Museum & Local History Centre** (☎ 713519), on Priory St, houses an extraordinary collection of memorabilia relating to the great admiral, even though he had only the most tenuous of connections with the town. The collection includes letters to his mistress, Emma Hamilton. It's open all year, Monday to Saturday from 10 am to 1 pm, and from 2 to 5 pm, and on Sunday from 2 to 5 pm. Entry is £1/50p, and this gets you half-price entry to Chepstow and Abergavenny museums and Caldicot Castle.

Places to Stay *Monmouth Youth Hostel* (☎ 715116), Priory St School, is on Priory St, in the town centre. It's open from March to October and the nightly charge is £6.75/4.60. *Monmouth Bridge Caravan &*

Camping (☎ 714004) is beside the river and near the bridge. It charges £2.50 per tent.

There are many hotels in the surrounding area, but few in the town itself. The *Old Gaol Guest House* (☎ 712463), Hereford Rd, does B&B for £20/33 for a single/double. *Steeples* (☎ 712600), over the café on Church St, charges £25/40 – all rooms have bathroom attached.

The *Riverside Hotel* (☎ 715577), Cinderhill St, is the smartest place in town. It's just over the Monnow Bridge from the centre; rooms with attached bath are £48/68.

Places to Eat There are a number of places around or near Agincourt Square – the *Punch House* (☎ 713855) is an attractive pub. Alternatively, there are takeaways at *Pick-a-Pizza* (☎ 714998).

For a more expensive and sophisticated meal, try the *French Horn Brasserie* (☎ 772733), on St Mary St. *Higgins* (☎ 715549), 107 Monnow St does a set Sunday lunch for £7.50, and cheaper dishes (eg nut roast and veg, £4.95) during the week.

Getting There & Away There are regular buses to Chepstow (No R69), Lydney and Coleford.

There's no railway station but there are bus links, Monday to Saturday, to the nearest stations at Hereford and Newport, both 16 miles away.

Tintern Abbey

The tall walls and empty, arched windows of this 14th-century Cistercian abbey on the edge of the River Wye have been painted by Turner and lauded by Wordsworth. It's one of the most beautiful ruins in the country. As a result, the village of Tintern swarms with visitors in summer. The abbey ruins are indeed an awe-inspiring sight, though best visited towards the end of the day, after the crowds have dispersed.

This Cistercian house was founded in 1131 by Walter de Clare, but the present building dates largely from the 14th century. It lasted until the dissolution and, compared to other religious sites that were laid to waste at this time, a remarkable amount remains.

The abbey (☎ 01291-689251; Cadw) is

Tintern Abbey

open from late March to late October, daily from 9.30 am to 6.30 pm, November to March, Monday to Saturday, from 9.30 am to 4 pm, and from 11 am to 4 pm on Sunday. Entry is £2.20/1.70. The Walkman tours (£1/50p) are highly recommended.

The town follows the course of the River Wye with the abbey ruins located on the west bank. The TIC (☎ 01291-689566) is north of the town at the old station, a long walk from the abbey.

There's a regular Red & White bus service (No 69) between Chepstow and Monmouth from Monday to Saturday only.

Raglan Castle

Seven miles west of Monmouth on the road to Abergavenny, Raglan Castle is a very impressive and atmospheric ruin. Constructed in the 15th and 16th centuries, it was the last medieval castle to be built in the country. It's particularly interesting to see how castle design had evolved by this time to include flamboyant embellishments (such as the gargoyles and heraldic stonework on the gatehouse).

The castle is open standard Cadw times; entry is £2.20/1.70.

CHEPSTOW

• *pop 9000*   • ☎ *01291*

Just over the border from England, Chepstow is an attractive, small town near the confluence of the Wye and Severn rivers. It's noted for its superb castle, but is also well known for its racecourse. Although a day is certainly sufficient to explore the town, Chepstow is a good base from which to explore the area.

Essentially a Norman town, Chepstow (from Old English *chepe* and *stowe*, meaning marketplace) was developed as a base for the Norman conquest of south-east Wales. It later prospered as a port for the timber and wine trades but as river-borne commerce declined, so Chepstow's importance diminished to that of a typical market town.

Orientation & Information

The centre of Chepstow tapers upwards from the river in a wedge shape, with the castle on a bluff to the west and the A48 to the east. The main streets are Bridge St, High St and the pedestrianised St Mary St. The TIC (☎ 623772) is at the bottom of Bridge St, in the castle car park.

Things to See

The main attraction is **Chepstow Castle**, which is fairly well preserved in its dramatic location on a cliff overlooking the Wye – best seen as a whole from the English side of the river. Construction began in 1067, making it the first stone castle in Wales, perhaps in Britain – a sure sign of its importance. Its massive fortifications were added in the 12th century, followed by mostly domestic construction in the 13th century. Towards the end of the Civil War, it was used as a prison; by 1690, when the garrison was dispersed, it had become all but an irrelevance. Parts of the castle were later used for industrial purposes. The castle (☎ 624065; Cadw) is open daily from 9.30 am to 6.30 pm in summer, and until 4 pm in winter; entry is £3/2.

The well-preserved, 13th-century city wall – the **Port Wall**, or Customs Wall – was built more as a means of controlling entry than for defence. It can best be seen from the main car park off Welsh St or the vicinity of the railway station. The Town Gate, originally part of the Port Wall, was much restored in the 16th century.

Chepstow Museum (☎ 625981) is near the TIC in an 18th-century town house. Mostly devoted to the history of the port, it also has a collection of 18th and 19th-century prints and drawings of the Wye Valley. It's open from 10.30 am to 1 pm and 2 to 5.30 pm, Monday to Saturday, and 2 to 5.30 pm on Sunday (it opens half an hour later in winter); entry is £1/50p.

The handsome Wye River Bridge, made of iron, was built in 1816.

Places to Stay

Langcroft (☎ 625569), 71 St Kingsmark Ave, is a short walk from the centre, and has rooms at £15 per person. *Cobweb Cottage*

(☎ 626643), Belle Vue Place, Steep St, is similarly priced.

There are several B&Bs and hotels along Bridge St. The *Afon Gwy Hotel* (☎ 620158) has rooms overlooking the river, with bathroom attached, for £30/41. The restaurant is recommended. On Welsh St, the *Coach & Horses* (☎ 622626) is close to the castle and does B&B for around £20 per person. The *Castle View Hotel* (☎ 620349), on Bridge St, charges £37.50/49.95; breakfast is extra.

Next door to the city gate is the luxurious *George* (☎ 625363), which dates back to 1610. Rooms are £65/75. There's also a weekend B&B rate of £41 per person.

Places to Eat

St Mary's Tea Rooms, 5 St Mary St, does very good snacks and well-priced meals and cakes in the day, plus Italian food in the evening.

The *Three Tuns Inn* (☎ 623497), by the castle, does bar meals, whilst the *Castle View Hotel* (see Places to Stay) offers substantial and reasonably priced set dinners – two courses including steak for £13.95, for example.

The restaurant at the *Afon Gwy Hotel* (see Places to Stay) is an excellent place to eat, known for its Welsh cuisine. Its delicious 'Parcels from Wales' starter is three types of Welsh cheese cooked in pastry. Bar lunches cost £5 to £7, dinner £10 to £18.

Getting There & Away

Chepstow has good bus connections. Badgerline (☎ 0117-955 3231) runs at least five buses a day to Bristol (one hour, £2.30) from Chepstow bus station. Its X14 service goes to Monmouth via Tintern on Wednesday only. Stagecoach (☎ 01633-266336) operates services to Newport (45 minutes, every half-hour), Gloucester (1¼ hours) and Cardiff.

From the railway station, there are direct services to Cardiff (25 minutes, £4.60), Gloucester (30 minutes, £4.90) and Newport.

SWANSEA (ABERTAWE)
• *pop 175,000* • ☎ 01792

Swansea is the second-largest town in Wales, and the gateway to the superb coastal scenery of the Gower Peninsula. Dylan Thomas grew up in Swansea and later called it an 'ugly, lovely town'. It certainly is in a lovely location on the bay, but some of the concrete developments here are distinctly ugly. Amongst all this, though, are attractions that make it worth pausing in Swansea, including an excellent maritime museum beside the regenerated dockland, an interesting local art galley, a new literary centre and, around the bay at Mumbles, a mile of pubs that constitute one of the best pub-crawls in Britain.

The Vikings named this area Sveins Ey (Swein's Island), probably referring to the sandbank in the mouth of the river. The Normans built the castle, but Swansea's heyday didn't come until the Industrial Revolution, when it rapidly developed into a centre for the smelting of copper. Ore was imported first from Cornwall, easily accessible across the Bristol Channel by boat. By the 19th century, this was Copperopolis – the world centre for the nonferrous-metal's refining industry. Ore came from Chile, Cuba and the USA, while Welsh coal was sold in return.

By the 20th century, the heavy-industry base of the town had declined but the oil refinery and numerous factories were still judged a worthy target for the Luftwaffe, which devastated the centre of Swansea in 1941.

Orientation & Information

The railway and bus stations are about half a mile north of the town centre. Swansea University is to the west. About four miles further west around Swansea Bay is the seaside village of Oystermouth, also known as Mumbles. Its many pubs are as popular with today's students as they were with Dylan Thomas.

The TIC (☎ 468321) is on Singleton St, by the bus station. It's open Monday to Saturday from 9.30 am to 5.30 pm. There's also a seasonal TIC (☎ 361302) on the seafront in Mumbles.

SOUTH WALES

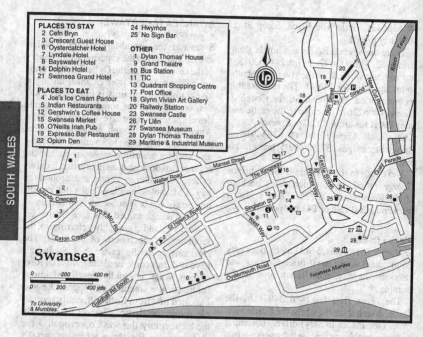

PLACES TO STAY	
2	Cefn Bryn
3	Crescent Guest House
6	Oystercatcher Hotel
7	Lyndale Hotel
8	Bayswater Hotel
14	Dolphin Hotel
21	Swansea Grand Hotel

PLACES TO EAT	
4	Joe's Ice Cream Parlour
5	Indian Restaurants
12	Gershwin's Coffee House
15	Swansea Market
16	O'Neills Irish Pub
19	Expresso Bar Restaurant
22	Opium Den

24	Hwymos
25	No Sign Bar

OTHER	
1	Dylan Thomas' House
9	Grand Theatre
10	Bus Station
11	TIC
13	Quadrant Shopping Centre
17	Post Office
18	Glynn Vivian Art Gallery
20	Railway Station
23	Swansea Castle
26	Ty Llên
27	Swansea Museum
28	Dylan Thomas Theatre
29	Maritime & Industrial Museum

Swansea

0   200   400 m
0   200   400 yds

To University & Mumbles

Swansea Castle

The castle, originally Norman, dates from the 14th century. The ruins are not substantial, but are quite picturesquely reflected in the mirrored glass of the surrounding tower blocks. Most of the castle was destroyed by Cromwell in 1647; what remained was converted into a prison in the 19th century. Swansea Castle (☎ 468321) is open year-round.

Glynn Vivian Art Gallery

This gallery (☎ 655006), located on Alexandra Rd, rightly claims to be 'one of Britain's liveliest provincial galleries'. There are works by Welsh artists, a display of Swansea china, European ceramics and clocks, and temporary exhibitions. The gallery is open from Tuesday to Sunday, 10 am to 5 pm; entry is free.

Maritime Quarter

The area around the old docks has recently been converted into a marina and tourist area, with dockside apartments, two museums, the Dylan Thomas Theatre and a rather odd-looking seated statue of the man.

On the north-east edge of the Maritime Quarter, **Swansea Museum** (☎ 653763), Victoria Rd, covers 200 centuries of local archaeology. It's open from Tuesday to Sunday, 10 am to 5 pm; entry is free.

Rather more interesting is the **Maritime & Industrial Museum** (☎ 650351), Museum Square. In the main hall is a Gilbern Invader, Wales's first contribution to the world's automotive industry. It's a sports car with a fibreglass body, powered by a Ford V6 engine. Even less successful, Clive Sinclair's C5, the plastic one-seater that he claimed would revolutionise personal transport in Britain, was built at the nearby vacuum-cleaner factory. Upstairs, there's a collection of boats, including the circular Welsh coracle, and machinery from the Neuth Abbey wool mill. Moored nearby are a lightship and a steam tug. In an annexe is the restored town tram that plied between Swansea and Mumbles on the world's first public passenger railway from 1804 to 1960. Opening hours are the same as the Swansea Museum.

Oystermouth Castle

Five miles west of Swansea centre, in Mumbles, Oystermouth Castle was the stronghold of the Norman Lords of Gower, who established a wooden fort here in the 1180s. They built a stone castle in the late 13th century; it's worth walking up to these ruins for the view over Swansea Bay. Open April to September from 11 am to 5 pm; entry is £1.

Walks & Cycle Routes

The Swansea Bike Path is a five-mile beachfront trail that runs out to Mumbles; it's also used by walkers. The Riverside Path is another cycle trail, running north along the River Tawe.

Other Things to See & Do

Dylan Thomas's house, 5 Cwmdonkin Drive, is not currently open to the public. You can walk past it but, apart from the plaque on the wall, there's nothing to distinguish it from the other houses on this street.

Ty Llên (☎ 463980), the National Literature Centre for Wales, was opened by Jimmy Carter in 1995. Open daily from 10.30 am to 5.30 pm, facilities include a theatre, exhibition galleries, bookshops, restaurant and bar.

The annual **Swansea Festival** lasts from late September to early November, and includes six weeks of drama, opera, film, ballet, jazz, classical music and dance competitions. For information, phone ☎ 475715.

If you're looking for a uniquely Welsh souvenir, one of the largest stockists of lovespoons in the country is the **Lovespoon Gallery**, 492 Mumbles Rd, Oystermouth; examples range from £2 to £200.

Places to Stay

Central Swansea There's no youth hostel in

Swansea; the nearest is at Port Eynon on the Gower.

Opposite the railway station, *Swansea Grand Hotel* (☎ 650541) is a bit shabby but good value at £15/20 for a single/double, but this doesn't include breakfast.

Oystermouth Rd, on the seafront, is lined with B&Bs and guesthouses. At No 322, the *Bayswater Hotel* (☎ 655301) has rooms from £17/28 for a single/double. At No 324, the *Lyndale Hotel* (☎ 653882) offers sea views from most rooms, which cost from £17/30, less for longer stays. The *Oystercatcher Hotel* (☎ 456574), at No 386, has 14 rooms, mostly with bathroom, and charges £16 per person. There's also a bar here.

In the rather more upmarket neighbourhood of Uplands, there's another clutch of B&Bs along Uplands Crescent and Eaton Crescent. *Cefn Bryn* (☎ 466687), 6 Uplands Crescent, charges £22/40 for comfortable rooms with bathroom. At 132 Eaton Crescent, the *Crescent Guest House* (☎ 466814) has six rooms, all with attached bath, for £25/40.

The *Dolphin Hotel* (☎ 650011), Whitewalls, is central and popular with businesspeople. It charges £59.50/69.50 for a single/double during the week, £35.50/45 at weekends.

Mumbles There are several guesthouses along Mumbles Rd, overlooking Swansea Bay. At No 708, the *Coast House* (☎ 368702) is run by a friendly family; B&B costs £16 per person in a room with attached bath. At No 734, *Beach House Hotel* (☎ 367650) has singles/doubles from £20/46, some with bathroom.

One of the most pleasant places to stay in South Wales is the *Hillcrest Hotel* (☎ 363700), 1 Higher Lane, Mumbles. It has a plain exterior but very comfortable bedrooms based on highly imaginative themes. The Safari room at the front is best, complete with four-poster bed, an imitation leopard-skin cover and African bush décor. The hotel also has an excellent restaurant. Rooms are £48/60 for a single/double with bathroom.

Places to Eat

Self-caterers should head for the Swansea Market, which has been operating at the same site since 1830. It's interesting to wander round even if you're not buying. Go to *Curds & Whey*, the stall with the best selection of Welsh cheeses. If EU regulations concerning how cockles should be washed and cooked haven't put the Pen-clawdd cockle pickers out of business, this is where they sell them, along with that other local delicacy, laverbread (seaweed). You'll find cockles with bacon and laverbread on the menus of many hotels and restaurants, and it's a delicious dish. The market is open Monday to Saturday from 8.30 am to 5.30 pm.

Opposite the railway station is the *Expresso Bar Restaurant*, with fish & chips for £2, lasagne, pork chops etc. Close to the TIC is *Gershwin's Coffee House*, Singleton St, which does breakfasts, lunches, cream teas and good coffee.

One block east of the No Sign Bar on Wind St, is *La Braseria* (☎ 469683), at No 26. It's a large place serving everything from Spanish dishes to jacket potatoes. Set price lunches at £6 are great value and very popular.

Hwyrnos (☎ 641437), Green Dragon Lane (off Wind St), puts on a Welsh night most evenings, with roast lamb in honey, cider and herbs eaten to the accompaniment of live harp music and folk songs, or Dylan Thomas readings.

The *Opium Den* (☎ 456161), 20 Castle St, is a recommended Cantonese restaurant. Bonnie Tyler and the Nolan sisters are past customers. The set menus (for two people) are good value and include a vegetarian menu.

On the western side of town is a line of Indian restaurants popular with students. The *Anarkali*, the *Moghul Brasserie* and the *Raj Balti House*, side by side on St Helen's Rd, battle out the curry wars trying to outdo each other with special offers. Their Sunday all-you-can-eat buffets (around £6.50) are very popular. Beside them, *Joe's Ice Cream Parlour* has been producing excellent, really creamy ice cream since 1922.

The *Hillcrest Hotel Restaurant* (☎ 363700), 1 Higher Lane, Mumbles, is an excellent place to eat. There's a set two-course dinner for £14.95 or £16.95 for three courses. Also in Mumbles, at 2 Woodville Rd, is *L'Amuse* (☎ 366006), a new French restaurant where the set lunches are £8.50, set dinners £16.50.

Entertainment

The *Dylan Thomas Theatre* (☎ 473238), Gloucester Place, is near his statue on Swansea Marina; his works are often performed here. The *Taliesin Arts Centre* (☎ 296883) stages a varied programme of music, theatre, dance and film at Swansea University, Singleton Park, on the west side of town. *Swansea Grand Theatre* (☎ 475715), Singleton St, is the town's main theatre, hosting everything from panto-mimes to ballet.

At weekends, the students head west to the many pubs that line Mumbles Rd in Oystermouth. This is certainly the most lively place to drink. To do the Mumbles Mile you have to have a drink in all 11 pubs, between Newton Rd and Bracelet Bay, in one night. Start with the *White Rose* and work your way via the new *Knab Rock* rock & roll pub to end at *Cinderella's* or *Neptune's*, the nightclubs. There are even T-shirts for those who finish. The Mumbles pub where Dylan Thomas used to drink is now called *Dylan's Tavern*, and is fairly touristy.

In the centre of Swansea, *O'Neill's* is an Irish pub opposite the post office on the Kingsway. The *No Sign Bar*, 56 Wind St, is a traditional pub with sawdust on the floor. It's a pleasant place for a pint, although its claim to be the 'best pub north of Salzburg' may be stretching things.

Getting There & Away

The Swansea-Cardiff Shuttle (☎ 475511) runs between these two cities (one hour, £5.25 return) hourly, Monday to Saturday; less often on Sunday.

Swansea is on the main line to London's Paddington via Cardiff and Bath. Swansea to Cardiff takes 50 minutes and costs £7. There are also direct trains to Fishguard for ferries to Ireland. An interesting cross-country line runs from Swansea, north-east through Llandrindod, Knighton and Craven Arms, to Shrewsbury (four hours).

There are daily ferries to Cork (Ireland) in summer, less frequent departures in winter, run by Swansea-Cork Ferries (☎ 456116). It charges from £20 to £29 per person. The terminal is on the opposite side of the river to the town centre. In mid-summer, there are ferries to Ilfracombe in Devon.

Getting Around
Bus There's an efficient local bus service, with colour-coded routes, run by SWT. A Swansea multiride ticket offers all-day bus travel in the Swansea and Mumbles area for £2.85. Bus Nos 2 and 2A run to Oystermouth and Mumbles.

Taxi For a taxi, phone Diamond Cabs (☎ 474747).

GOWER PENINSULA
Extending 15 miles east of Mumbles, the Gower Peninsula was the first part of Britain to be officially designated an Area of Out-standing Beauty, and it well deserves its title. A favourite haunt of Dylan Thomas, it has some superb sandy beaches and beautiful cliff scenery – good walking country. In summer, however, it can get very crowded.

Much of the Gower is owned by the NT. On the south coast is **Oxwich Bay**, the first sandy beach of any size you come to. Around Oxwich Point is **Port Eynon**, which has camping grounds and a youth hostel by the beach. The extreme western tip is known as **Worm's Head**, an apt name for this elongated, rocky headland. You can walk out across the causeway onto the Worm only during the two-hour period either side of low tide.

Rhossili is the village above Worm's Head. To the north stretch the three miles of the Gower's best and biggest beach, Rhossili Bay. Hang-gliders dive off the cliffs onto the wide expanse of sand. The **Rhossili Visitor**

Centre (☎ 01792-390707), at the start of the path to Worm's Head, is run by the NT.

In the 18th century, smugglers landed brandy and tobacco from France on these beaches and secret coves. The seas around this area are treacherous: over 250 boats have been lost off the Gower. On Rhossili Beach, the bows of the *Helvetica*, wrecked in 1880, stick out of the sand.

Walks
The OS's *Pembrokeshire & Gower Walks* (£6.95) has details of some of the excellent walks in this area. For a good five-hour ramble, start in the car park on the eastern side of Middleton, walk down to Worm's Head and back up to the visitors centre at Rhossili. Then climb up to the beacon on Rhossili Down, walk down to Hillend and then back to Rhossili and Middleton along the beach. Before you leave, if you phone the visitors centre to check the tide times for crossing to Worm's Head, you could stop either for lunch or tea at the Worm's Head Hotel.

Places to Stay & Eat
Hotels and guesthouses tend to be more expensive on the Gower Peninsula than in Swansea and Mumbles.

The *Port Eynon Youth Hostel* (☎ 01792-390706) is an old lifeboat house superbly situated right on the beach at Port Eynon, 15 miles from Swansea. It's open from April to September, except Sunday, but does open on Sunday on bank holiday weekends. Phone for other opening times. The nightly charge is £7.45/5. *Carreglwyd Camping Site* (☎ 01792-390795) is also at Port Eynon; £4 for an adult and a tent.

The *Worm's Head Hotel* (☎ 01792-390512) is in a splendid location overlooking Worm's Head and Rhossili Bay. B&B costs £30/45 for a room with bath. All the rooms, and the restaurant, have sea views. There's also a bar.

Getting There & Away
From Swansea bus station, SWT bus Nos 18, 18A and 18B run to South Gower, Port

Eynon, Rhossili and Horton, daily except Sunday. Bus No 17 runs to North Gower, Llanrhidian and Llangennith.

CARMARTHEN (CAERFYRDDIN)
• *pop 13,800*   • ☎ *01267*

It's difficult to believe that this unexciting place, Carmarthenshire's county town, was where Merlin the magician from the Arthurian legends was born. At least it's a little more Welsh than Swansea and Cardiff – you'll hear the language spoken here. There's no real reason to stop, but since it's an important transport hub, you may have to.

Carmarthen lies on the north side of the River Towy. The TIC (☎ 231557) is at 113 Lammas St, in the centre of the town; the bus station is to the south along Blue St. The railway station is across the bridge, on the southern bank.

Getting There & Away
From Swansea, bus Nos X11 and X30 run hourly to Carmarthen, and you can connect with bus No 222 to Laugharne for Dylan Thomas's Boathouse. Carmarthen is on the main railway line from London's Paddington, which goes through Cardiff and Swansea. West of Carmarthen, the line divides: one route continues to Pembroke Dock, another to Milford Haven and a third to Fishguard.

LAUGHARNE
• *pop 1000*   • ☎ *01994*

Pilgrims on the Dylan Thomas trail come to this little town on the west side of the Taff estuary to see the house where he lived, the pub where he perfected the drinking habit that finally killed him and the churchyard where he is buried. Even if you're not particularly a fan, it's an attractive place to visit.

The **Dylan Thomas Boathouse** is built into the hillside, a 15-minute walk down a steep lane from the town. He spent the last four years of his life here with his wife Caitlin, and the house is preserved as a shrine. There are photographs, manuscripts and recordings of the poet reading from his own works. Above the house, you can look

through the window in the old wooden shed – 'The Shack', he called it – where he wrote *Under Milk Wood*. Beside the house is a tearoom on the terrace, where you can look out across the 'heron priested shore' that inspired some of Thomas' best work. The Dylan Thomas Boathouse (☎ 427420) is open daily from Easter to October, 10 am to 5 pm, and in winter for shorter hours; entry is £2/1.

Laugharne is a pleasant town of Georgian houses and has the remains of a 12th-century castle. The poet's simple grave is in the churchyard of St Martin's Church. *Brown's Hotel* was where Thomas drank, and it's still a serious drinking place – no DT cocktails here for the visitors.

Getting There & Away
Bus No 222 runs hourly from Carmarthen, Monday to Saturday. You can get here from Swansea via Carmarthen for £4.50 using a Rover Bus ticket.

Pembrokeshire Coast National Park

Most of the coastline of the Pembrokeshire Coast National Park consists of rugged cliffs, broken up by stretches of superb sandy beaches – the best in Wales – and rocky coves. Pembrokeshire has some of the oldest rocks in the world, formed over 3000 million years ago.

The park is probably best known for the 186-mile Pembrokeshire Coast Path (see the Activities chapter at the start of this book), which runs from Amroth in the south to Poppit Sands in the north. But as well as excellent walks, there are numerous other outdoor activities – climbing, mountain biking, birdwatching, pony trekking, surfing, sea kayaking and canoeing.

The Preseli Hills are the only upland area in the park. Ancient trade routes run through them, and hill forts, standing stones and burial chambers are all evidence of the prehistoric people who once lived here.

The offshore islands of Skomer, Skokholm and Grassholm were given their names by Viking raiders. They're now inhabited by seabird colonies – puffins, guillemots, razorbills (the emblem of the park) and gannets. Ramsey and Skomer islands are breeding grounds for the grey seal. Caldey Island is owned and farmed by Cistercian monks. All of the islands can be visited.

Anyone who comes to Pembrokeshire should not miss St David's, where the superb cathedral, the most impressive in Wales, is a shrine to the country's patron saint.

ORIENTATION

The park covers about 230 square miles and includes 180 miles of rocky coastline. Within the park you're never more than 10 miles from the sea. In 1996, with the local government boundary reorganisation, the park acquired 5% more land and independence from the county council.

The park can be divided into four separate sections – the coastline east of Fishguard to Cardigan and inland to the Preseli Hills; the coastline west of Fishguard down to Milford Haven; the upper stretches of the Milford Haven waterway; and the coastline round the south of Pembroke peninsula. The industrial coastline around Pembroke and Milford Haven is not part of the park.

The highest point in the park is Foel Cwm Cerwyn in the Preseli Hills, which rises to 1760 feet. The hills are now acknowledged as being the source of the blue stones that form the inner circle of Stonehenge.

The southern part of Pembrokeshire is often known as 'Little England beyond Wales', because of the 50 castles built by the English invaders. The invasion continues today – resorts such as Tenby are very popular with English holiday-makers. Many of the B&Bs and guesthouses are run not by the Welsh but by incomers.

INFORMATION

The head office for the Pembrokeshire Coast National Park (☎ 01437-764636) is at Winch Lane, Haverfordwest.

There are several National Park Informa-

tion Centres in the park. They are open from Easter to September, and for the last week of October. Information Centres that are open seven days a week within this period include: Broad Haven (☎ 01437-781412), in the car park; St David's (☎ 01437-720392), The City Hall (which remains open throughout October); Saundersfoot (☎ 01834-811411), Harbour Car Park and Pembroke (☎ 01646-682148), 8A Castle Terrace.

The following information centres are open Monday to Saturday: Newport (☎ 01239-820912), Bank Cottages, Long St; and Haverfordwest (☎ 01437-760136), 40 High St.

It's also possible to get information from the TICs in Fishguard (☎ 01348-873484), Haverfordwest (☎ 01437-760110), Milford Haven (☎ 01646-690866), Tenby (☎ 01834-842402), Pembroke (☎ 01646-622388), Pembroke Dock (☎ 01646-622246), and Kilgetty (☎ 01834-813672).

The National Park organises a wide range of activities, including walks (along the coast and into the Preseli Hills), cycle and horse rides, island cruises, canoe trips and minibus tours. Details of all the organised activities are given in *Coast to Coast*, the useful freebie newspaper available from TICs and National Park Information Centres.

The area's warm, sunny climate makes it a place that you can visit all year round. In July and August, the main tourist areas can be very crowded. May and September are probably the best months for clear days and lack of crowds. A local weather-forecast service (☎ 01834-812516) operates during the main tourist season.

WALKS

The big walk here is the Pembrokeshire Coast Path (see the Activities chapter at the start of this book), and you should at least walk a section of this superb 186-mile-long trail.

Guides which cover the whole route include Dennis Kelsall's *Pembrokeshire Coastal Path* which follows the route from south to north, the recommended way to do it. CJ Wright's *A Guide to the Pembrokeshire*

Coast Path, and the National Trail Guide – Pembrokeshire Coast Path, both have more detailed mapping but cover the route in the opposite direction. TICs also sell local walking guides. The national park's excellent Six Circular Walks series cover St David's, Strumble Head, Newport, Broad Haven and Saundersfoot. The OS's Pembrokeshire and Gower Walks (£6.95) gives good coverage of some walks in the area.

National Park rangers lead guided walks. A half-day walk costs from £2 and a full-day from £3.50. They even have a 14-day guided walk of the complete Coast Path for £55. See the Coast to Coast leaflet for details.

CYCLE ROUTES

Although bikes are not allowed on the Pembrokeshire Coast Path, local lanes and bridleways offer excellent cycling. In the north of the country there are more difficult routes for mountain bikes. If you plan to cycle off the roads, it's best to check your route with the National Park (☎ 01437-764636).

There are several places in the area – St David's and Broad Haven among them (see those sections) – where you can hire both touring and mountain bikes. Cycle hire is not cheap at around £10 per day for a tourer and £15 per day for a mountain bike.

OTHER ACTIVITIES
Pony Trekking & Horse Riding

The fact that this is an ideal area for riding is reflected in the number of stables in the area. You can ride along the beaches, across open moorland, along wooded bridleways, or down quiet country lanes.

The riding stables at Hendre Eynon (☎ 01437-720474) are two miles north-east of St David's on the Llanrhian road. East Nolton Riding Stables (☎ 01437-710360) is three miles from both Broad Haven and Newgale. To ride here costs from £16 for 1½ hours.

Maesgwynne Riding Stables (☎ 01348-872659) is near Fishguard – turn off the A40 in Fishguard past Pendre pub and it's 200 yards down Maesgwynne lane on the left. Pembrokeshire Riding Centre (☎ 01646-682513), Pennybridge Farm, Hundleton, is 2½ miles south-west of Pembroke on the B4320.

The National Park also organises rides in the Preseli Hills. Contact the information centres or TICs for details.

Surfing & Windsurfing

The surf in this part of Britain is rarely as consistent as in Cornwall, but surfies are still drawn to the beaches at Whitesands, Newgale, Manorbier and Freshwater West.

Windsurfing is popular off many beaches and also on the sheltered waters of Milford Haven. Most of the villages near the coast have a place where you can hire equipment.

Haven Sports (☎ 01437-781354), Marine Rd, Broad Haven, rents windsurfers and runs courses; Newsurf (☎ 01437-721398), at the filling station at Newgale, rents boards and wetsuits.

Sea Kayaking & Canoeing

The Pembrokeshire coast is regarded as one of the best sea-kayaking areas in Britain, although you should be aware that rips and currents here can be powerful. For peaceful canoeing, head for the tranquil waters of the Dauggleddau estuary (the Milford Haven waterway).

Boating

Boat trips to see the wildlife on the island nature reserves are very popular and highly recommended. Boats to Ramsey Island, off St David's, depart from St Justinian or Whitesands Bay. Trips to Skomer, Skokholm and Grassholm islands are also possible from St Justinian, or from Martin's Haven. Boats to Caldey Island go from Tenby. As well as trips on small ex-fishing boats, there are also excursions on high-speed water-jet propelled inflatables.

Charges vary according to the length of the trip and the number of islands visited, but you should expect to pay £10 to £18 for a day trip.

SOUTH WALES

Fishing

To fish the rivers you must have a Environment Agency rod licence (£2 to £5) and the permission of the land/fishery owner. Clubs or associations may give day tickets. On small rivers, approach local farmers.

Sea fishing is also possible – Newgale is one of the best beaches in Wales to fish from. However, you'll need permission first if you want to fish off dock or harbour walls.

OTHER ATTRACTIONS

If you have children, the largest theme park in the area is Oakwood (☎ 891376), just off the A40 between Carmarthen and Haverfordwest, at Canaston Bridge. They recently opened an exhilarating £1.7 million wooden rollercoaster ride that tops 50 mph, has 11 crossovers and a maximum drop of 80 feet.

PLACES TO STAY & EAT

There's no shortage of accommodation and places to eat in this area, particularly in the more developed seaside resorts on the southern coast. At the cheaper end, there are camping grounds (from about £3 per tent) and plenty of youth hostels.

If you're booking two or more of the hostels in Pembrokeshire, you can use the West Wales Booking Bureau at *St David's Youth Hostel* (☎ 01437-720345). The service costs £2.50 and bookings must be made two weeks in advance. The other hostels in Pembrokeshire are: *Pentlepoir Youth Hostel* (☎ 01834-812333), near Saundersfoot; *Manorbier Youth Hostel* (☎ 01834-871803); *Marloes Sands* (☎ 01646-636667); *Broad Haven* (☎ 01437-781688); *Solva (Pen-y-Cwm)* (☎ 01437-720959); *Trevine (Trefin)* (☎ 01348-831414); *Pwll Deri* (☎ 01348-891233), at a wonderful location on cliffs 2¾ miles south of Strumble Head; *Poppit Sands* (☎ 01239-612936), St Dogmaels. Pentlepoir, Manorbier, Broad Haven and Solva offer a full meals service.

GETTING THERE & AWAY

There's a twice-daily National Express (☎ 0990-808080) bus from London to Haverfordwest.

From London's Paddington there's an hourly InterCity service as far as Swansea, where you may need to change to catch less frequent trains to Narberth, Kilgetty, Saundersfoot, Tenby, Penally, Manorbier, Lamphey and Pembroke. Some services from London continue beyond Swansea in summer.

Trains from Swansea also go to Haverfordwest and Fishguard. The service to Haverfordwest runs about seven times a day (less frequently on Sunday). The service to Fishguard goes twice a day. Trains from Swansea to Pembroke go approximately every two hours (1¾ hours, £7.40).

GETTING AROUND

Bus services around Pembrokeshire are reasonably good. Timetables are available from TICs.

The three main local operators are Richards Brothers (☎ 01239-613756), who run services from Haverfordwest to Newgale, St David's, Fishguard and Newport; South Wales Transport (SWT; ☎ 01437-763284) and Silcox Motor Coach Co (☎ 01646-683143), who offer services to Pembroke, Tenby and other places south of Haverfordwest. For transport information in the Carmarthen area phone ☎ 01267-231817.

Although the county names changed in 1996, there's still a Dyfed Day Rover ticket (£4/2) and Dyfed Weekly Rover ticket (£18/8), which allow unlimited travel on services in the former Dyfed area now split into Pembrokeshire, Carmarthenshire and Ceredigion. These tickets can be bought on the bus. Richards Brothers also has its own Day Explorer ticket (£3/2), only valid on those services.

Trains are less useful for getting round the area. There's no service to St David's in the west or connecting with the northern end of the coast path. You could, however, use the train to get from Tenby to Pembroke, and from Haverfordwest to Milford Haven or Fishguard. For rail inquiries, phone ☎ 0345-484950.

TENBY (DINBYCH Y PYSGOD)
- *pop 5500* • ☎ 01834

The Welsh name for this genteel seaside town, built around a beautiful bay, is as charming as Tenby itself. It means Little Fort of the Fishes.

The Normans built the castle on the promontory above the two sandy beaches. The town was fortified in the 13th century after several unsuccessful attempts by the Welsh to recapture it. It grew as a port and in the 19th century developed into a holiday resort. Unlike many other seaside resorts in Britain, Tenby has managed to avoid being overtaken by amusement arcades and fish & chip shops. Tenby gets crowded in summer but is nonetheless worth visiting, and the coast path runs right through the town.

Orientation & Information
The town extends east of the castle on the promontory, with the harbour and North Beach on one side and South Beach on the other. The railway station is on the western side, at the bottom of Warren St. The bus station is one block south of Warren St on Upper Park Rd.

There's a TIC (☎ 842402) in The Croft, open in July and August, daily from 10 am to 9 pm, and for shorter hours the rest of the year.

Tenby has an environmentally-friendly alternative to the hop-on hop-off tourist buses which crowd many of Britain's towns – horse-drawn carriage rides. They leave regularly from the Market Square and charges are £1.50/1.

Things to See
Tall, elegant Georgian houses, most of them now hotels, rise above the pretty harbour. The most interesting building to look round is the **Tudor Merchant's House** (☎ 842279; NT), Quay Hill, a late 15th-century house which shows how a merchant lived in this time. The remains of three frescos can be seen on the interior walls. The house is open from April to September, Monday to Friday from 10 am to 5 pm, and on Sunday from 1 to 5 pm; entry is £1.60/80p.

Other things to see in Tenby include the castle ruins (good for views over the bay) and the **Museum & Art Gallery** beside the castle. Some of the works of artist Graham Sutherland were moved to here from Picton Castle recently, on temporary loan until a new venue is found in St David's for the collection.

When the tide is down, you can walk across the sand to **St Catherine's Island**. The Victorian fortress here is not open to the public. A popular boat trip from Tenby harbour is across to Caldey Island (see Around Tenby).

Places to Stay
There are no youth hostels in Tenby, but there is one four miles east at Pentlepoir (see Saundersfoot), and another about six miles west at Skrinkle Haven (Manorbier).

There's a good choice of cheaper B&Bs along Harding and Warren Sts, near the railway and bus stations. The excellent *Ivy Bank Guest House* (☎ 842311), Harding St, has rooms with attached bath and continental breakfast for £16 per person, or £18 including a cooked breakfast. Even closer to the railway station is *Weybourne* (☎ 843641), 14 Warren St, which charges around £13 per person.

There's no shortage of places to stay along the Esplanade, above the South Beach, and on Victoria St, Picton Terrace and Sutton St, which lead off it. Prices range from £15 to £30 per person, depending on the size of the room and whether it has a sea view. On the Esplanade you will find the *Clarence House Hotel* (☎ 844371), *Bellini's Hotel* (☎ 843333) and also the *Panorama Hotel* (☎ 844976).

The *Atlantic Hotel* (☎ 842881), on The Esplanade, is an excellent place, with a heated pool, and a private garden leading onto the beach. B&B costs £48/70, and they have two-night dinner, bed & breakfast special breaks that are better value.

The *Fourcroft Hotel* (☎ 842886), The Croft, is a comfortable place that's been run by the same friendly family for the last 55 years. Rooms with attached bathroom range from £40.50/74 to £44.50/82. The hotel overlooks the bay and has a pool and private garden above the beach.

Places to Eat

In summer, Tenby has a glut of teashops and cafés serving overpriced snacks and lunches. *Candy Restaurant* near Tudor Square does set breakfasts for £3.95, and two-course lunches for £5.25; all with great views.

The *Bay Tree* on Tudor Square is good value, with main dishes from £7.50 to £10.95 and occasional live music. For excellent ice cream, head for *Adrianne Fecci's Ice Creamery*, Upper Frog St, which has over 50 varieties of the stuff and also does snacks. Upper Frog St is one block west of the High St.

Plantagenate Restaurant (☎ 842350), Quay Hill, is by the Tudor Merchant's House and claims to be the oldest house in town. As well as being an interesting building it's an excellent place to eat. Crab sandwiches cost £3.75; main dishes range from £4 to £14, and there are good vegetarian choices.

Most of the larger hotels have restaurants that are open to nonresidents. The restaurant at the *Fourcroft Hotel* (☎ 842886), The Croft, does a good set dinner for £15, and they can provide fresh lobster if given 24 hour's notice.

Getting There & Away

An hourly bus service, No 358/9, runs between Haverfordwest and Tenby (1½ hours, £2.45), from Monday to Saturday. There's also a direct train service from Swansea (1¾ hours, £6.90).

AROUND TENBY
Caldey Island

A twenty-minute boat trip from Tenby, Caldey Island is home to a small community of Cistercian monks, seals and seabirds. The monks make a variety of products for sale, including perfume, dairy products and chocolate – industries that now employ people from the mainland. There are guided tours of the monastery twice a day (men only), and great walks around the island, with good

views from the lighthouse. Make sure you visit the old priory and **St Illtyd's Church**, with its oddly-shaped steeple. Inside is a fascinating ogham stone, with inscriptions in this ancient Irish script.

There are regular services to the island (£4.95, including landing fee), generally from May to September, Monday to Friday (sometimes also on Saturday), depending on tide and demand. Tickets are sold from the kiosk in Castle Square, above the harbour.

Saundersfoot

• *pop 2200*   • ☎ 01834

Situated three miles north of Tenby, the attractive village of Saundersfoot was once a fishing port, which was also involved in the export of anthracite. It's now a busy seaside resort with a good beach. There's a National Park Information Centre (☎ 811411), open seven days a week, in the harbour carpark.

Pentlepoir Youth Hostel (812333), is 1½ miles inland from Saundersfoot, in the old schoolhouse in Pentlepoir village. It's open from Easter to October, daily except Wednesday and Thursday (every day in summer), and the nightly charge is £6.75/4.60. There are also numerous B&Bs and guesthouses in the area.

Buses run to Saundersfoot from Tenby (15 minutes, 95p). The railway station is one mile north of the town.

Manorbier

Above this village are the ruins of **Manorbier Castle**, with superb views over the sea. This 12th-century fortification was the birthplace of Giraldus Cambrensis, Gerald of Wales, one of the country's greatest scholars and tutor to both Richard the Lionheart and King John. 'In all the broad lands of Wales, Manorbier is the best place by far,' he wrote. In some of the castle's rooms you'll find waxworks in period costume – a job lot of rejects from Madame Tussaud's in London. Look for the two figures that were originally Prince Philip – in one room he's dressed in chain mail, and he pops up again in another, this time disguised as a 'Welsh Lady' beside a spinning wheel! The castle is open from

Easter to September, daily from 10.30 am to 5.30 pm; entry is £1.60/80p.

The impressive *Manorbier Youth Hostel* (☎ 01834-871803) is 200 yards from the sandy beach at Skrinkle Haven, on the east side of the village; you can also camp here. It's open daily in July and August, and daily except Sunday in April, May, June and September; phone for other opening days. The nightly charge is £9.10/6.15 and the hostel is 1½ miles south of Manorbier railway station. Bus service No 358/9 runs from Manorbier to Tenby (20 minutes, £1.30) and Pembroke (30 minutes, £1.40).

Carew Castle & Tidal Mill

Looming romantically over the River Carew, with its wide, empty windows reflected in the still water, Carew Castle is an impressive sight. These rambling ruins began as an early 12th-century castle, built by Gerald de Windsor, Henry I's constable of Pembroke. It was eventually converted into an Elizabethan country house. Abandoned in 1690, the castle is still home to a large number of bats, including the protected greater horseshoe bat. In summer a programme of events is held, which includes battle re-enactments and open-air theatre performances.

On the causeway nearby is the Elizabethan Tidal Mill. It was used to grind corn until WWI and is one of three working tidal mills in Britain; it was restored using its original machinery. The rising tide fills the millpond and, when the tide falls, a head of water is released through a sluice. This turns the main mill wheel, which in turn powers the machinery in the mill.

The castle and mill (☎ 01646-651782) are open from Easter to October, daily from 10 am to 5 pm. Entry to the castle only is £1.50/1; a combined ticket which includes the mill costs £2.20/1.40.

There's a fine **Celtic Cross**, dating from the 11th century, not far from the castle entrance. The nearby *Carew Inn* is a cosy pub, serving food from noon to 2 pm. Carew is four miles from Pembroke and five from Tenby. Bus No 361 runs between Tenby and

Pembroke via Carew Cross about four times a day.

PEMBROKE
- *pop 15,400*   • ☎ 01646

Founded over 900 years ago, Pembroke's medieval street plan has survived along with its castle, the oldest in west Wales. Although there are other castles in the country that have more atmosphere, this one is certainly worth a visit, but Pembrokeshire's county town need not delay you for much more than half a day.

The town is on the south bank of the Milford Haven waterway, and on either side of this wide, natural harbour is some ugly development, including oil refineries. Just over two miles to the west of Pembroke is Pembroke Dock, where ferries leave for Rosslare (Ireland).

Pembroke grew into an important trading centre after the castle was built in 1093. In 1154, local traders gained a monopoly in the area when an Act of Incorporation was passed, making it illegal to land goods in the Milford Haven waterway at anywhere other than Pembroke. The castle was home to the early Tudors, and the future King Henry VII was born here. During the Civil War, it was besieged by Cromwell for 48 days before it fell.

The Pembroke Visitors Centre and TIC (☎ 622388) is south of the castle on Commons Rd. It's open Easter to October, daily from 10 am to 5.30 pm; and on Tuesday, Thursday and Saturday in November, February and March. As well as the usual TIC services, there's also an interpretive display about the town. They stock a *Town Trail* walking guide. Beside the castle entrance is a National Park Information Centre (☎ 682148).

At Pembroke Dock, there's a TIC (☎ 622246) in the newly-restored Gun Tower, Front St.

Pembroke Castle

Pembroke's main attraction dominates the western end of town. Although a fort was established here in 1093 by Arnulph de

Montgomery, the current buildings mainly date from the 12th and 13th centuries. The fort was in use up until 1945, and was the home of the Earls of Pembroke for over 300 years.

The massive walls enclose a large area of grass and an ugly tarmac parade ground. Passages run from tower to tower, and a plaque in one marks the birthplace (in 1456) of Harry Tudor, who defeated Richard III to become Henry VII.

In the centre of the castle grounds stands a 75-foot-high tower. One hundred steps lead to the top and a glorious view, as long as you don't look in the direction of the Texaco oil refinery or the power station. If it's windy, the tower is closed.

The castle (☎ 681510) is open from April to September, daily from 9.30 am to 6 pm; in March and October, daily until 5 pm; and in November, daily until 4 pm. Entry is £2.50/1.70. In August a touring theatre group stages a Shakespeare play in the castle.

Museum of the Home

The Museum of the Home (☎ 681200), just across the road from the Castle at 7 Westgate Hill, is well worth visiting. It has a great collection of toys and games, including Roman die and the first snakes and ladders board, as well as cooking and eating implements and other objects of past eras, in a domestic setting. There are no labels – you're shown round by the enthusiastic owners. It's open May to September, Monday to Thursday from 11 am to 5 pm; entry is £1.20/90p.

Places to Stay & Eat

Wisteria-clad *Beech House* (☎ 683740), 78 Main St, does B&B from £12.50 per person in very comfortable surroundings. With rather more character, *Merton Place House* (☎ 684796), 3 East Back (by Main St), is a good place, with B&B from £15/28.

The *Kings Arms Hotel* (☎ 683611), also in Main St, does B&B from £32.50/45 and is an excellent example of an old county town hotel. There's a good restaurant and the bar

food is about the best in Pembroke. Faggots, peas and potatoes costs £3.75.

Henry's Gift & Coffee Shop (☎ 622293), is the unmissable pink building near the Kings Arms. It's a good place for lunches and teas and has an excellent range of cakes. It's open Monday to Saturday from 9 am to 5 pm. There are several other cafés near the castle.

The *Watermans Arms*, just over the bridge and by the river, has lovely views of the castle, and the terrace is a good place for a drink. More serious drinking is done in the *Old Cross Saws*, Main St.

Getting There & Away

Bus service No 359 operates hourly, Monday to Saturday, from Haverfordwest to Pembroke (50 minutes, £1.85). Service No 358 also goes to Pembroke but takes longer. Both services go to Pembroke Dock and stop near Pembroke centre. SWT (☎ 01437-763284) service No 333 runs from Swansea to Pembroke Dock via Carmarthen and Tenby, from Monday to Saturday. The No 361 goes to Saundersfoot and Kilgetty and is operated by Silcox Motors (☎ 683143).

Pembroke is connected to the branch railway line that runs through Tenby and terminates at Pembroke Dock.

Irish Ferries (☎ 684161) runs two ferries a day to Rosslare in Ireland, leaving in the early afternoon and halfway through the night for the 4¼-hour trip from Pembroke Dock.

HAVERFORDWEST (HWLFFORDD)
- *pop 13,700* • ☎ *01437*

Although this market town is not within the borders of the park, it's the commercial centre of the area and a focal point for public transport.

The town was founded beside the Western Cleddau River in about 1110, as a Flemish settlement. Overpopulation in Flanders had forced some of the inhabitants to seek other land, and the Flemings who reached Wales were granted land around this river. A castle was built at the time the town was founded. The port remained important until the arrival of the railway in the mid-19th century.

There's not much to see in Haverfordwest today – the castle ruins are fairly plain. The **Castle Museum & Art Gallery** (☎ 763708) is in the outer ward of the castle. The museum includes the rather dry Pembroke Yeomanry Historical Trust Collection. It's currently closed for renovation.

The TIC (☎ 763110) is near the bus station on Old Bridge St. The National Park Information Centre (☎ 760136) is at 40 High St.

Places to Stay & Eat

The TIC has an accommodation list and posts details of current vacancies after closing time.

Villa House (☎ 762977), on St Thomas Green, has B&B from £15 per person. There are several other places in this area.

The excellent *Penrhlwllan* (☎ 769049), Well Lane, Prendergast, is a short walk from the bus station. There are only two rooms, at £15/30.

The *Castle Hotel* (☎ 769322), on the corner of Castle Square and the High St, charges £37.50/50 for a single/double with attached bath. There's a good restaurant, and bar meals in the pub downstairs include boozy pie (£5.75).

The *Tuck Inn Restaurant* in Bridge St serves spaghetti bolognaise and other dishes from £2.95. The *Pembroke Yeoman*, 5 Goat St, serves breaded plaice and ploughman's lunches for under £3. The *Fishguard Arms* on Old Bridge St is a pleasant place for a drink.

Getting There & Away

Haverfordwest is 249 miles from London and about seven from Milford Haven.

There are buses from here to many parts of Pembrokeshire. Richards Brothers (☎ 01239-613756) runs buses from Haverfordwest via Fishguard to Cardigan (1¾ hours, £2.75), 11 times a day, Monday to Saturday. Other services link Haverfordwest with St David's and Pembroke.

There are about seven trains a day from Swansea (fewer on Sunday). The journey takes about 1½ hours and costs £7.80.

ST BRIDES BAY (BAE SAIN FFRAID)

St Brides Bay is at the western end of the 'landsker', the invisible boundary between the Welsh and Anglicised parts of Pembrokeshire. The best beaches in Wales line this wide bay, and they're big enough to absorb the crowds of holiday-makers they attract at the height of the summer season. There are numerous camping grounds, and most of the farmers will be happy to let you use one of their fields for a couple of pounds; you must ask permission first.

Skomer, Skokholm & Grassholm Islands

These islands, lying just off the coast on the south side of the bay, are nature reserves populated mainly by seabirds. The bird colonies are busiest between April and mid-August, so many escaped the oil slick that hit these islands in February 1996, when the *Sea Empress* ran aground off St Anne's Head. Although you won't see any evidence of oil, it has certainly entered the food chain and it will have an effect on the area for years to come.

It's possible to visit the islands and bookings can be made through any National Park Information Centre, or through Dale Sailing Company (☎ 01646-601636). Costs are from £11 to £22 per person, including landing fees.

Easiest to reach is Skomer, and from Martin's Haven there are departures daily except Monday, from 10 am. Boats return from about 3 pm, allowing several hours on the island. There's no shop or café so you need to bring a picnic.

Skokholm is famous for its Manx shearwaters and, with Skomer, provides shelter for 45% of the world's population of this bird. There are services to the island on Monday only, from early June to mid-August.

The largest gannetry in the northern hemisphere is on Grassholm, a small island 10 miles offshore. There are boat trips (£22) on Monday and Friday in summer.

Broad Haven

This is a lively seaside village with several

caravan parks and camping grounds, and a National Park Information Centre (☎ 01437-781412). Also here is the modern *Broad Haven Youth Hostel* (☎ 01437-781688), which is open daily from March to September; the nightly charge is £9.10/6.15 in July and August.

Haven Sports (☎ 01437-781354), Marine Rd, rents mountain bikes from £3 per hour, and £16 per day.

Newgale

This tiny village is beside the biggest beach in the area, popular with both swimmers and surfers. At very low tides, the fossil remains of a prehistoric forest can be seen. You can hire surf skis, boards, boogey boards and wet suits from Newsurf Hire Centre (☎ 01437-721398) at Newgale Filling Station. Body boards cost from £2 per hour, and full-size boards cost from £3.

Places to Stay & Eat There are several excellent camping grounds. *Newgale Camp Site* (☎ 01437-710253) is across the road from the beach; they charge from £2 per person. There's a café and a store nearby.

Solva Youth Hostel (☎ 01437-720959) is not at Solva but 1½ miles north of Newgale at Whitehouse. It's open from March to October and beds cost £7.45/5. There's also B&B at this hostel and they do excellent meals. There's more accommodation at Solva, Simpsons Cross and Nolton.

Getting There & Away Newgale is a stop on Richards Brothers hourly service No 411 (daily except Sunday) from Haverfordwest to St David's and Fishguard. The journey from Haverfordwest takes 25 minutes (£1.35) and it's 20 minutes from there to St David's.

ST DAVID'S (TY-DDEWI)
• *pop 1500*   • ☎ *01437*

There's something very special about St David's that even the crowds of holiday-makers in summer fail to extinguish. The magic must have worked for Dewi Sant (St David), who chose to found the first monas-

tic community here in the 6th century, only a short walk from where he was born. St David is dear to the hearts of the Welsh – he's their patron saint and his relics are kept in a casket in the cathedral.

Although St David's is no bigger than a village, with only one square and a few side roads leading off it, the cathedral's presence earns it the right to be called a city. As you approach the place you're unaware of the cathedral, which is just as its builders intended, for it was hidden in the depression below the square in the vain hope that passing Norse raiders might miss it. It's a magnificent sight, and if you visit only one cathedral in Wales, make it this one.

Information

The National Park Visitor Centre and TIC (☎ 720392) is in the Town Hall by the square; open daily.

The St David's Arts Festival, held in the first half of August, includes open-air Shakespeare plays in the Bishop's Palace that are well worth seeing. There's a music festival centred on the cathedral in late May.

St David's Bookshop, just off the square on the lane leading down to the cathedral, is very well stocked and also carries the full range of local walking guides.

St David's Cathedral

St David's Cathedral was built in the late 12th century, but there has been a church on this site since the 6th century. Norse pirates ransacked the site at least seven times, and various bishops added to the building between the 12th and 16th centuries. In the Middle Ages, two pilgrimages to the shrine of St David's were said to equal one to Rome – thus the cathedral has seen a constant stream of visitors.

Inside the cathedral, there's an atmosphere of great antiquity. The floor slopes three feet upwards and the pillars keel over drunkenly, the result of an earthquake in 1248. In the Norman nave is a superbly carved oak ceiling, installed in the 16th century. St David's shrine is by the north choir aisle. This cathedral is the only one in the UK in

SOUTH WALES

SOUTH WALES

which the reigning monarch has a permanently reserved stall.

Services are held at 7.30 and 8 am during the week, and on some days at 6 pm. On Sunday there are services throughout the morning, and a choral evensong at 6 pm. Some services are held in Welsh. Entry to the cathedral (☎ 720517) is free, although a donation of £1.50/60p is suggested; there are also photography charges.

Bishop's Palace
Beside the cathedral are the extensive ruins of the Bishop's Palace (☎ 720517; Cadw), largely built by Henry de Gower between 1328 and 1347. Until the 16th century, this was a grand residence. It now provides a spectacular setting for the open-air plays held in the summer. Most of the walls still stand – the ruins are substantial and impressive, and there are two small exhibitions on the site.

Entrance to the palace is £1.70/1.20; it's open daily from Easter to October, 9.30 am to 6.30 pm, and in winter from 9.30 am to 4 pm daily (afternoon only on Sunday).

St Non's Bay
St David is said to have been born three-quarters of a mile south of the cathedral, beside the bay that was later named after his mother. A small spring is said to have emerged on the site just as he emerged into the world. The shrine still attracts pilgrims, and the water is believed to have curative powers. Also here are the 13th-century ruins of St Non's Chapel, a modern chapel and a building used as a retreat.

Walks & Cycle Routes
Incorporating sections of the coast path, there are some excellent two to three-hour walks around St David's peninsula. *Six Circular Walks Around St David's*, available from the TIC and bookshops, is a handy guide.

From St David's, you could walk southwest to the coast at Porthclais, follow the coast path to Caerfai Bay and return to St David's – a walk that will probably take less than two hours.

A wonderful 4½-hour walk takes you from St David's to Porthclais, where you pick up the coast path. Continue right around the western tip of the peninsula (opposite Ramsey Island) to St Justinian's, where you follow the road back to St David's.

The quiet lanes that run parallel to the north coast of Pembrokeshire are perfect for cycling. Coastal Trader can give advice about routes.

Other Things to See & Do
Two sealife centres battle it out for the customers. There was originally just one but the partners fell out and started competing. The bigger of the two is the **Oceanarium** (☎ 720453), 42 New St.

Thousand Islands Expeditions (☎ 721686), Cross Square, offers several boat tours, from the Two Hour Spectacular on a water-jet boat (£16.50/10) to the Grand Island Voyage, an all-day trip (£30). Boats are booked here and depart from Whitesands Bay or St Justinian.

St David's Adventure Days (☎ 721611), is part of Twr-y-Felin Outdoor Centre and runs the *Viking Voyager*, an inflatable craft fitted with underwater video cameras, enabling you to see the sealife and wrecks on a trip to Ramsey Island (see the upcoming St David's to Fishguard section). Charges are £10/7 for adults/children; book at Coastal Trader, on the square.

Places to Stay
Hostel *St David's Youth Hostel* (☎ 720345) is 1½ miles north-west of St David's, near Whitesands Bay. It's open daily in July and August, and daily except Thursday between May and September; phone for winter opening times. The nightly charge is £7.45/5.

Camping Closest to St David's is *Caerfai Farm Camp Site* (☎ 720548), a 20-minute walk away. It's 400 yards from the beach and charges from £3.60.

The *Hendre Eynon Caravan & Camping Site* (☎ 720474) is two miles north-east of St

David's, situated between the Dowrog Common Nature Reserve and the coastal path, and is open from May to September. There's a riding school here, so pony trekking is possible. You can also camp at *Pencarnan Farm Caravan & Camping Site* (☎ 720324), at Porthsele, two miles from St David's, and at *Lleithyr Farm* (☎ 720245), near Whitesands Bay.

B&Bs & Hotels The *Alandale*, (☎ 720333) 43 Nun St, is a Victorian house offering B&B from £14.50 for a room with a shared bath, £16.50 with attached bath. *Ty Olaf* (☎ 720885), Mount Gardens, offers very comfortable B&B from £13.50 to £15.50 per person. It's an excellent place.

The *Old Cross Hotel* (☎ 720387) is in Cross Square, which is set back from the old market square. All rooms have an attached bathroom, and there's a restaurant and bar. B&B costs £41/72 (£33/62 outside the summer season); their two-night special breaks include dinner and are better value.

The excellent *Ramsey House* (☎ 720321), Lower Moor (half a mile from the cathedral) has seven rooms and is open all year. During the high season they do only dinner, bed & breakfast deals at £38 per person. Out of season, B&B costs from £23.

Places to Eat
There are several teashops to choose from, but the best is the *Gossip Column*, the Italian-run place above the Londis supermarket on the square. A large bowl of cawl (thick lamb soup with vegetables) is served with bread and cheese. It makes a filling meal for £2.99. They also do savoury crab pancakes, mussels in garlic butter and a range of sandwiches.

Cartref Restaurant (☎ 720422), Cross Square, is built round a 17th-century stone cottage. Main dishes range from £2.95 to £12. *Dyfed Café* (☎ 720250), also in the square, serves lunches and suppers and also has a fish & chip shop if you want takeaway.

For an upmarket meal, *Morgan's Brasserie* (☎ 720508), 20 Nun St, does excellent seafood and has an imaginative menu. Main dishes, including wild boar and sea trout, cost around £12.

The *Farmer's Arms*, Goat St, is the place to drink. They have excellent bar meals and there's a pleasant terrace.

For a high-calorie snack, you can't miss *Chapel Chocolates*, on the way down to the cathedral.

Getting There & Away
Bus service No 411 goes hourly from Haverfordwest, Monday to Saturday, and twice daily on Sunday in summer (45 minutes, £1.65), continuing to Fishguard.

Getting Around
Everything is within walking distance. Should you need a taxi, phone ☎ 720395.

Coastal Trader (☎ 721611), on the square, rents bikes at a price: £12 per day for tourers, and £15 for mountain bikes.

ST DAVID'S TO FISHGUARD
The coast from St David's to Fishguard is far less touristy than the southern part of Pembrokeshire. The coves and beaches, if they're accessible at all, are reached by tiny, winding lanes and footpaths. If you're only going to walk part of the Pembrokeshire Coast Path, this would be an excellent section to tackle.

Two miles north of St David's is **Whitesands Bay**, one of the finest beaches in Wales, and popular with surfers. It can get quite crowded but there's an excellent secluded beach at **Porthmelgan**, a 15-minute walk north.

Lying off St David's Head, **Ramsey Island** is an RSPB reserve with beautiful cliff scenery and varied birdlife, which includes a healthy population of choughs. It's reached by boat from St Justinian, three miles from St David's. Ramsey Island Pleasure Cruises (☎ 01437-720285) operates boats from April to September, departing daily at around 10 am and returning at 3.30 pm; tickets are £6/3, plus a £3/1 landing fee. Only 40 visitors are allowed onto the island each day. If you're there between late August and mid-November, you may see seal pups.

Porthgain is an interesting old coastal village, a former brickworks and slate centre. People now come here primarily to eat and drink. In an age of theme-pubs, the *Sloop Inn* is famous for its old-fashioned ordinariness. It's an excellent place for a pint and there are interesting photos showing what the village was like in its industrial heyday. There are reasonable pub meals from £3. Across the carpark there's the more upmarket *Harbour Lights Restaurant* (☎ 01348-831549); two-course dinners are £19.50, three courses for £22.50.

On the route between St David's and Fishguard are two well-located hostels, and numerous farmhouse B&Bs. *Trevine Youth Hostel* (☎ 01348-831414) is in the old school in the centre of **Trevine**, half a mile from the sea. It's 11 miles along the coast path from Whitesand's Bay. Also in the village is the *Old Court House* (☎ 01348-837095), a vegetarian guesthouse and walking holiday centre.

Eight miles further east from Trevine along the path is *Pwll Deri Youth Hostel* (☎ 01348-891233), in a spectacular location overlooking the bay.

FISHGUARD (ABERGWAUN)
• *pop 3200* • ☎ *01348*

Ferry ports tend to be ugly, depressing places, but Fishguard stands out as an exception to the rule. It's on a beautiful bay, and the old part of town – Lower Fishguard – was the location for the 1971 film version of *Under Milk Wood*, which starred Richard Burton and Elizabeth Taylor. The town has twice been the host for the National Eisteddfod.

Throughout 1997, the town will be commemorating the bicentenary of the last invasion of Britain. In February 1797, a band of French mercenaries and convicts landed at Carregwastad Point near Fishguard and conducted a series of undisciplined raids on houses in the Pen Caer area. During one particular raid, the invaders came upon large stocks of Portugese wine, which proved their undoing. With the invaders in a state of drunkenness, the local people were soon able

to round them up. Appropriately, the surrender was signed in the Royal Oak Inn. Local embroiderers have been busy for the last four years preparing a 100-foot tapestry telling the story of the invasion. Contact the TIC for information about bicentenary activities.

Orientation & Information
The railway station and harbour (for Stena Line ferries to Rosslare, Ireland) are at Goodwick, a 20-minute walk down the hill from Fishguard proper. To the east, the road winds round the picturesque harbour of Lower Fishguard.

The TIC (☎ 873484), 4 Hamilton St, is open seven days a week from Easter to October. If you're going to Ireland, they'll book you a guesthouse in Rosslare for a £5 booking fee.

A number of boats offer fishing trips and cruises from the harbour. Try *Anita Gee* (☎ 874539).

In late July, Fishguard stages a music festival, which includes classical and jazz musicians, some from abroad. For information, phone the festival office (☎ 873612).

Places to Stay
Hamilton Guest House & Backpackers Lodge (☎ 874797), 21 Hamilton St, is near the TIC in Fishguard. It's a very friendly place, open 24 hours, with 20 beds in small dormitories for around £9 per person. There's a kitchen for self-caterers, a TV lounge and laundry. The nearest HI hostel is at Pwll Deri, four miles west of Goodwick.

You can camp at *Fishguard Bay Caravan Park* (☎ 811415), six miles to the east, between Fishguard and Newport on the headland at Dinas Cross. It's well situated for the coastal path, and open from March to January; £3 for a tent and one person.

In Goodwick, *The Beach House* (☎ 872085) is just off Quay Rd above the railway line – it overlooks the bay and is a five-minute walk from the ferry. It's remarkably welcoming given the constant flow of visitors – B&B is from around £13 per person. There are several other B&Bs in this area, and also the large *Fishguard Bay Hotel*

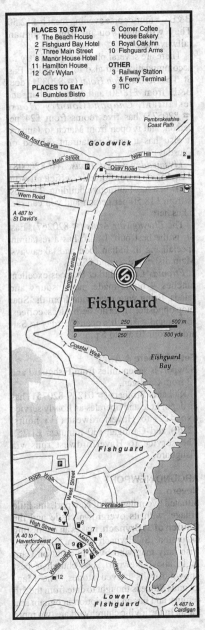

PLACES TO STAY
1 The Beach House
2 Fishguard Bay Hotel
7 Three Main Street
8 Manor House Hotel
11 Hamilton House
12 Cri'r Wylan

PLACES TO EAT
4 Bumbles Bistro

5 Corner Coffee
House Bakery
6 Royal Oak Inn
10 Fishguard Arms

OTHER
3 Railway Station
& Ferry Terminal
9 TIC

SOUTH WALES

(☎ 873571), formerly the Great Western Railways Hotel. Rooms with bath attached cost £40/60.

The excellent *Gifach Goch Farmhouse* (☎ 873871) is two miles north of Fishguard on the road to Cardigan – the Cardigan bus stops at its gate. The farmhouse has six rooms and a lovely garden and offers B&B from £20; it's open from March to November.

Back in Fishguard, there's comfortable B&B at *Cri'r Wylan* (☎ 873398), Penwallis, a short walk from the TIC. They charge from £14 to £16 per person, and it's a small place. On Main St, *Manor House Hotel* (☎ 873260) has sea views from the back rooms. B&B is from around £20 per person, £24 for a room with bathroom.

The nicest place to stay, however, is at nearby *Three Main Street* (☎ 874275), which has only three rooms, all with bath, from £25 per person. There's a superb restaurant here.

Places to Eat

Corner Coffee House Bakery & Restaurant, on the square, is cheap and cheerful. Nearby on West St is *Bumbles Bistro*, where you can get cream teas for £2.25, and light lunches.

The famous *Royal Oak Inn* (☎ 872514) is on the square, and full of invasion memorabilia, including an old musket taken off a drunken mercenary. There's a *fish & chip shop* opposite. The *Fishguard Arms*, Main St, is where the serious drinking is done.

Three Main Street (☎ 874275) is one of the best restaurants in South Wales – it's worth coming to Fishguard just to eat here. Main courses range from £9.50 to £13.95, and there are good vegetarian choices. You'll probably need to book.

Getting There & Away

Richards Brothers (☎ 01239-613756) operates an hourly service, Monday to Saturday, from Haverfordwest (45 minutes, £1.80). It also runs buses to St David's and Cardigan.

Fishguard is the northern terminus of a branch of the railway line that crosses South

Wales. Fishguard to London costs £40 (Super Saver single).

Stena Line (☎ 872881) runs a ferry and catamaran several times a day to Rosslare, Ireland.

Getting Around

Bus service No 410 runs on a regular circuit from Fishguard Square to Goodwick Square, Fishguard Harbour and back to Fishguard Square; it operates Monday to Saturday, every half hour.

NEWPORT (TREFDRAETH)

• *pop 1200*   • ☎ *01239*

This small town grew up around the castle, and the rocky outcrop **Carn Ingli**, which dominates the town and beach. The castle is Norman but there's evidence of much earlier settlements in the area. Newport makes a very pleasant base for walks along the wild coast or into the Preseli Hills to the south. It's also a pleasant walk up Carn Ingli, from where there are great views over the bay. There are several beaches – **Parrog**, close to the town, and the better **Newport Sands**, across the river and around the bay.

The National Park Visitors Centre (☎ 820912), Bank Cottages, Long St, is open Monday to Saturday. Bikes can be hired for £10 per day from Newport Mountain Bikes (☎ 820008) at Llysmeddyg Guest House, East St.

Places to Stay & Eat

Two miles from Newport, on the Cilgwyn road, is *Brithdir Mawr* (☎ 820164) where bunkhouse accommodation costs from £4. There's a camping ground west of Newport at Parrog Beach – *Morawelon Caravan & Camping Park* (☎ 820565) is open from April to September.

There's B&B from £14 at *2 Springhill* (☎ 820626), Parrog Rd, 400 yards from the coastal path, and with good sea views. It has six rooms and is open year-round.

On the outskirts of Newport, and 100 yards from the coast path, is the excellent *Grove Park Guesthouse* (☎ 820122), Pen-y-Bant. Charges are from £18 per person for

B&B – a four-course evening meal is £12.50. They will pick you up from Fishguard railway station.

There are several places you could try for accommodation and also for a meal in East St. The *Golden Lion Hotel* (☎ 820321) does B&B from £18/30 and it has a bar, and restaurant. *Cnapan Country House* (☎ 820575) has five rooms from £24 per person, and is open from March to January. It also has a good restaurant (closed on Tuesday).

Llysmeddyg Guest House (☎ 820008), East St, is a comfortable, efficiently-run B&B in a most attractive building. The cost is from £18.50 per person and you can rent bikes here.

The *Llwyngwair Arms* (☎ 820267), East St, is the best pub. It also has a restaurant specialising in Indian food and takeaways. Main dishes are around £5.75.

Ffronlas Café, Market St, does excellent lunches – home-made patés, soups and salads. Bring your own wine from the Spar shop opposite. There are herbal teas, coffees, scones and cakes. It's open Tuesday to Saturday from 10 am to 5 pm.

Getting There & Away

Newport is seven miles from Fishguard and 12 from Cardigan.

Richards Brothers (☎ 01239-820751) has its depot here and operates an hourly service (No 412) to Haverfordwest (1¼ hours, £2.20) and Cardigan (30 minutes, £1.75). The service to Haverfordwest runs via Fishguard.

AROUND NEWPORT
Nevern

Situated two miles east of Newport, this little village, with its overgrown castle and the **Church of St Brynach**, makes an interesting excursion. St Brynach was a 5th-century Irish holy man who lived in a hut on Carn Ingli, above Newport. The church is best known for its carved stones. The Maglocunus Stone is thought to date from the 5th century and has an inscription in ogham and Latin. In the idyllic churchyard are two more stones, one with another ogham inscription, and the other one of the most impressive Celtic crosses in Wales, dating from the 10th century. Some of the gravestones are interesting, and one of the yew trees is known as the 'bleeding yew', for the blood-like red sap that oozes from it.

Castell Henllys

Located two miles south-east of Nevern, this site was originally occupied 2500 years ago and has now been reborn as the **Castell Henllys Iron Age Settlement**. Some of the buildings – roundhouses, animal pens, a smithy and a grain store – have been partially reconstructed. It's open from March to October, daily from 10 am to 5 pm; tickets are £2.20/1.40.

To get there by bus, take the hourly service (No 412) from Newport towards Cardigan. Get off at the Melina Rd stop and it's a half-mile walk.

Pentre Ifan

Pentre Ifan is a 4500-year-old cromlech in a remote site, with views across to the sea – to the south stretch the Preseli Hills. It's said to be the best preserved Neolithic burial chamber in the country; the 16-foot-high capstone is supported by seven-foot-high boulders.

Situated two miles south of Nevern, Pentre Ifan is accessible by taking the bus to the same stop as for Castell Henllys, and then walking south down the side roads for about a mile.

Mid Wales

HIGHLIGHTS

- Pony trekking in the Brecon Beacons
- Brecon Jazz Festival
- Browsing for books in Hay-on-Wye
- Centre for Alternative Technology, Machynlleth
- Vale of Rheidol Steam Railway from Aberystwyth to Devil's Bridge

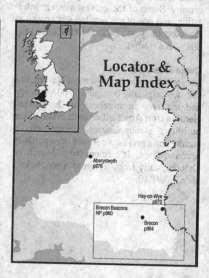

Locator & Map Index

The majority of visitors to this part of Wales head for the grass-capped mountains of the Brecon Beacons National Park, leaving the quiet valleys of Mid Wales to the Welsh.

This is unspoilt walking country – farming land interspersed with bare, rolling hills and small lakes. The 120-mile Glyndŵr's Way is a walking trail that visits sites associated with the Welsh hero between Knighton (on Offa's Dyke Path) and Welshpool via Machynlleth.

Aberystwyth, the only place of any size on the west coast, is a remarkably pleasant university town with good transport connections. Steam trains run through the Vale of Rheidol to Devil's Bridge, with spectacular views of the nearby waterfalls. Several of Wales' other Great Little Trains are found in Mid Wales.

Machynlleth is an attractive market town that makes a good base for exploring the region. On the outskirts of the town, the Centre for Alternative Technology experiments with green living in an interesting working community that welcomes visitors.

Brecon Beacons National Park

Formed in 1957, Parc Cenedlaethol Bannau Brycheiniog covers 522 sq miles of high,

grassy ridges, including the highest mountains in southern Britain, interspersed with wooded valleys. Most of the park is privately owned and the slopes provide grazing for thousands of sheep. Pen-y-Fan, at 2907 feet the highest point, and the 8000 acres surrounding it are in the hands of the NT.

Although they're referred to as mountains, the Brecon Beacons are hardly the Himalayas, and the countryside is less dramatic than Snowdonia to the north. Nevertheless, these bare escarpments are undeniably beautiful, rising in a series of great, green waves above the plains to the north and the former mining valleys to the south. From their crests, hikers are rewarded with spectacular views.

Two long-distance paths pass through the park: Offa's Dyke Path, along the eastern border, and the Taff Trail, south from Brecon. Most people come here to walk, but the region offers numerous other outdoor activities. Lôn Las Cymru, the Welsh

National Cycle Route, passes through the park on quiet minor roads and cyclepaths, from Cardiff to Brecon (77 miles), and on through Glasbury and Builth Wells.

This is perfect pony-trekking country, and you can also rent canoes or narrowboats on the Monmouthshire & Brecon Canal, go fishing, mountaineering or hang-gliding. To the south of the park, cavers are attracted to some of the deepest black holes in Britain.

On the northern edge, the eccentric town of Hay-on-Wye, where almost every other shop sells second-hand books, is well worth a visit. Just south of the park at Blaenavon is the Big Pit Mining Museum, and the guided tours which venture deep into this old coal mine are highly recommended. Just north of Merthyr Tydfil, vintage steam locos still operate on a short section of the Brecon Mountain Railway.

Since the park is only 25 miles from the Severn Bridge, it's easily accessible from London and the south of England. In spite of this, if you avoid the popular central Brecon Beacons area in summer, it can be far less crowded than Snowdonia.

ORIENTATION

The park is a mere 15 miles from north to south and 45 miles from west to east, yet it comprises four mountain ranges and a variety of terrain.

In the centre is the Brecon Beacons, the range that gives the park its name; the high ridges here form the focal point for hikers. To the west is Fforest Fawr, an area of hills, valleys and, to the south, waterfalls. Further west is the isolated Black Mountain. In the east are the confusingly named Black Mountains (plural), running north-south between Hay-on-Wye and Abergavenny.

The town of Brecon is the main urban centre within the park's boundaries, and it makes a good base, although the nearest railway stations are at Abergavenny and Merthyr Tydfil. The Monmouthshire & Brecon Canal follows the valley of the River Usk from Brecon through Abergavenny, which is a good base for the eastern area of

the park. Hay-on-Wye, on the northern edge, also has a wide range of accommodation.

INFORMATION

The National Park Visitors Centre (☎ 01874-623366) is sited in open countryside near Libanus, five miles south-west of Brecon off the A470. It's open daily, except Christmas Day, from 9.15 am, closing at 6 pm in July and August, 4.30 pm in winter and 5 pm at other times. There's also a gift shop and café here.

The other national park information centres at Brecon (☎ 01874-623156) and Abergavenny (☎ 01873-853254) may be more convenient. Although they're open only from April to September, they're in the same buildings as TICs, which are open year-round. The TICs also have information about the park.

There's also an information centre at Llandovery (☎ 01550-20693), open from April to September, and Pen-y-cae (☎ 01639-730395, Craig-y-nos Country Park), open in the summer.

A large range of publications and maps is on sale at these information centres and at TICs in the area. Most of the park is covered by Landranger maps Nos 160 and 161 or Pathfinder maps Nos 11-13. The park's walking booklets (£1 to £2.20) cover the main areas in enough detail for most people spending a few days here. The park even has a guide to the sites of *Aircraft Crashes in the National Park* (£1). Leaflets describing walks and other activities are listed below.

Check the weather forecast before setting out on a mountain hike. Take a sweater and waterproof clothing with you, even if it's a sunny day when you start, and be prepared to turn back if the mist comes down. Whatever the weather, it can be very windy on the exposed ridges. Bring something to eat with you, but resist the temptation to share it with the sheep or ponies, especially in unfenced areas, as they may become attracted to cars on the roads and cause accidents.

WALKS & CYCLE ROUTES

There's an almost infinite number of walks in the park, ranging from a strenuous mountain

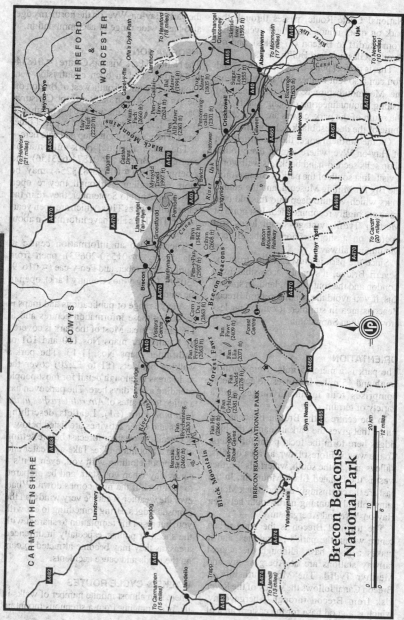

Brecon Beacons National Park

MID WALES

Top: Tintern Abbey, South Wales
Bottom: Under the slag heap, Blaenau Ffestiniog, North Wales

TONY WHEELER

RICHARD EVERIST

RICHARD EVERIST

Top: Lochinver, Highlands
Middle: Whitby, North Yorkshire Moors National Park
Bottom: Portpatrick, Southern Scotland

climb to a gentle stroll along the canal towpath.

In summer, traffic on the A-roads can make cycling hazardous, so stick to smaller roads. The Lôn Las Cymru/Taff Trail is the most interesting cycle route between Cardiff and Brecon.

Cycle hire is available in some towns (see the main sections below). Bicycle Beano (☎ 01982-560471) organises cycle camping holidays in this area, with vegetarian wholefood catering. Mountain Bike Guided Treks & Tours (☎ 01874-658242) offers half-day, day and weekend tours, and can arrange accommodation.

Brecon Beacons

The classic walk in the park is to the top of the highest of these ridges, Pen-y-Fan, but this area gets crowded in the summer and at weekends. The many routes up are covered in the leaflet *Walks in the Brecon Beacons Central Area* (£2.20).

The shortest trail is from the car park at Pont ar Daf or from the Storey Arms, a mile north (and no longer a pub). They're both on the bus route along the A470 between Brecon and Merthyr Tydfil. From here it's a 2½-hour hike to the top and back. If you're starting from the Llwyn-y-Celyn Youth Hostel, allow three hours for the return trip. Walking from Brecon it will take five to six hours; follow the side road out of town to the trailhead at Cwm Gwdi.

Directly below Pen-y-Fan, in the natural amphitheatre formed 10,000 years ago during the last Ice Age, there are less strenuous walks around the small lake with the tongue-twisting name of Llyn-cwm-Llwch (pronounced hlin-coom-hlooch).

Taff Trail & Lôn Las Cymru

Linking canal towpaths, disused railways and paths, the 77-mile trail between Cardiff and Brecon forms the first section of the Lôn Las Cymru, the Welsh National Cycle Route that runs across the country to Anglesey. From Cardiff the waymarked route follows the River Taff north via Castell Coch, the market town of Pontypridd, Merthyr Tydfil,

the Pontsticill Reservoir and Talybont-on-Usk to the canal at Pencelli, where there's a choice of routes into Brecon. You can either continue along the canal or follow the side road via Llanfrynach.

Usk Valley

The least demanding walks in the park are along the towpath of the Monmouthshire & Brecon Canal, which follows the valley of the River Usk. It's possible to walk the full 33-mile length of the canal between Brecon and Pontypool. Crickhowell, just north of the canal, would make an excellent overnight stop but there are numerous other villages along the route offering accommodation in B&Bs or pubs. Most walkers just hike the 20-mile Abergavenny to Brecon section.

Black Mountains

Some of the best views on the entire 168-mile length of Offa's Dyke Path are from the 17-mile section that runs through the Black Mountains from Pandy to Hay-on-Wye. Pandy is on the A465, on the bus route between Abergavenny and Hereford. The route is along a high, exposed grassy ridge that can be very windy.

It's definitely worth dropping down to visit the ruins of Llanthony Priory, where the remaining buildings now house a pub and a delightfully atmospheric hotel. Further north up this valley is the Capel-y-Ffin Youth Hostel. As a less strenuous alternative to walking along the ridge, you could follow the River Honddu from Llanfihangel, lower down in the valley. TICs stock the two leaflets that cover walks in the north and south parts of this area.

The highest point in the Black Mountains is Waun Fach (2660 feet). If you've got a car, it's best to drive via Patrishow (an interesting 13th-century church in an idyllic location) to the end of the track in the Mynydd Du Forest. Follow the old railway track up to Grwyne Fawr Reservoir, where a path runs up Waun Fach. Alternatively, the peak can be reached by climbing from Llanbedr up to the ridge that runs north via Pen-y-Gadair Fawr.

MID WALES

Around Abergavenny

There are rewarding walks up any of the three hills near Abergavenny, described in detail in *Thirty Walks in the South Black Mountains & the Abergavenny Area*, available from the TIC.

Three miles to the north is the cone-shaped Sugar Loaf (1955 feet). It's a steep climb to the top. A couple of miles south of the town is Blorenge (1833 feet), also popular as a launching pad for hang-gliders. Three miles north-east of Abergavenny is Skirrid-fawr, (1595 feet); from the top there are good views of Sugar Loaf, the Usk Valley and the Black Mountains.

Fforest Fawr & Waterfall Walks

There is a great variety of scenery in this area, which was once a Norman hunting ground. In the north there are mountain walks in terrain similar to that of the Brecon Beacons.

The youth hostel at Ystradfellte makes a good base, and along the rivers and streams to the south there are a number of attractive waterfalls in this wooded area. The most attractive is Sgwd-yr-eira (the spout of snow), where you can actually view the falls from behind the water. It's an easy two-mile walk south of Ystradfellte, on the River Hepste. There are other falls at Pontneddfechan and Coelbren. Look out for the leaflet on *Waterfall Walks* at the TICs.

Black Mountain

It's not surprising to find another Black Mountain in this range – when the weather is bad, any bare piece of high ground in the Brecon Beacons deserves the name. This western section of the park contains the wildest, least visited walking country. The highest point, Fan Brycheiniog (2630 feet), can be reached from the youth hostel at Llanddeusant or along a path that leads off the side road just north of the Dan-yr-ogof caves.

OTHER ACTIVITIES

The Talybont Venture Centre (☎ 01874-676458) in Talybont-on-Usk, five miles south-east of Brecon, offers a range of activities, including abseiling, caving, rock climbing, mountain biking and orienteering.

For **cavers**, there are several limestone cave systems in the south of the park, including some of the longest and deepest in Britain. Pick up a copy of the leaflet *Caving* (20p) from TICs and, unless you know what you're doing, contact one of the outdoor activity centres (see above). If a subterranean sound and light show with stalagmites illuminated in pretty colours is more your idea of going underground, the Dan-yr-ogof Show Caves are in the south-west area of the park.

Gliders are available for hire from the Black Mountains Gliding Club (☎ 01874-711463), near Talgarth, which offers introductory courses. The Welsh Hang Gliding Centre (☎ 01873-832100), Bryn Bach Park, Merthyr Rd, Tredegar, offers two-day courses in hang-gliding.

There are good **fishing** rivers in this area. Just to the north of the park, and flowing through Hay-on-Wye, the River Wye is reputed to be the finest salmon river south of the border with Scotland. In the park, the River Usk is among the best waters in Wales for brown-trout and salmon fishing. Many of the reservoirs, including the Usk and the Talybont, are stocked with trout and there's coarse fishing in the canal and Llangorse Lake. You'll need a permit from the owner of the fishing rights as well as a Water/Environment Agency licence.

Pony Trekking & Horse Riding

The open hillsides make this ideal pony-trekking country – no doubt the reason why the Wales Trekking & Riding Association (☎ 01873-858717) chose to base itself in Abergavenny.

A leaflet listing pony-trekking centres in the park is available from TICs for 20p. Charges are from £7 to £15 for a half-day, £12 to £25 for a full day, and many of the centres are on farms which also offer B&B accommodation. Places to try include the Grange Pony Trekking Centre (☎ 01873-890215) at Capel-y-Ffin, Llangorse Riding Centre (☎ 01874-658272) near Brecon and

Pegasus Trekking Centre (☎ 01873-890425) at Patrishow.

Serious riders interested in a superior mount should contact the aforementioned Llangorse Riding Centre, Trewysgoed Riding Centre (☎ 01550-740661) at Fforest near Abergavenny or Cwmfforest Riding Centre (☎ 01874-711398) at Talgarth. Cwmfforest offers a range of riding holidays, including the six-day Trans Wales Trail, with all food and accommodation, for £645.

Canal Cruising

The Monmouthshire & Brecon Canal links Brecon with Pontypool in Gwent. There are only six locks along its 33-mile length, and there's one lock-free section of 22 miles. Built for the iron industry in the early 19th century, it fell into disuse in the 1930s but has now been restored and opened to recreational traffic.

Traditional narrowboats can be hired by the hour, day or week from Cambrian Cruisers (☎ 01874-665315), Ty Newydd, Pencelli, near Brecon. Dragonfly Cruises (☎ 0831-685222), in Brecon, operates 2½-hour cruises, Wednesday to Sunday at noon and 3 pm, for £4/3. The 1½-hour cruises run by Water Folk (☎ 01874-665382), Old Storehouse, Llanfrynach, are more traditional, since the boats are horse-drawn.

PLACES TO STAY & EAT

There are five YHA youth hostels in the national park – Ty'n-y-Caeau (2½ miles from Brecon), Llwyn-y-Celyn (by the A470 Merthyr Tydfil to Brecon road), Capel-y-Ffin (eight miles south of Hay-on-Wye, and attached to a pony-trekking centre), Ystradfellte (in the waterfall and caving district) and isolated Llanddeusant below the Black Mountain.

Independent bunkhouses are opening in the area. Contact TICs or the Association of Barn Operators (☎ 01874-711120) for details of new bunkhouses. There are currently bunkhouses in Abergavenny, Llanbedr (near Crickhowell), Talgarth and Cantref (both near Brecon), and Erwood (near Builth Wells).

With the permission of the farmer or landowner, it's possible to camp almost anywhere in the park, but not on NT land. TICs have lists of camping grounds with full facilities.

There's a good range of B&Bs and hotels in and around the main centres of Brecon, Abergavenny and Hay-on-Wye, as well as in the villages along the Usk Valley. Some hotels offer all-inclusive activity holidays, including fishing or riding.

GETTING THERE & AWAY

It takes three to four hours to drive to the Brecon Beacons from London, via the M4 over the River Severn and along the A4024 from Newport.

Red & White (☎ 01633-266336) buses run between Cardiff, Merthyr Tydfil and Abergavenny; Brecon, Hay-on-Wye and Hereford; and Brecon, Abergavenny, Pontypool and Newport. Silverline (☎ 01685-382406) operates buses between Brecon and the railway stations at Merthyr Tydfil and Swansea. Crosville Cymru's service No 702 links Chester and Cardiff via Brecon.

There are rail services to Abergavenny (via Newport) and Merthyr Tydfil (via Cardiff) but not to Brecon. Phone ☎ 0345-484950 for information.

Between smaller villages, public transport is severely limited. Distances are not great, however, and if you're not prepared to walk it's worth considering a taxi.

BRECON (ABERHONDDU)
• *pop 7000*   • ☎ *01874*

The principal centre in the park is the attractive, historic market town of Brecon. It makes an excellent base for exploring the area, and has a good range of accommodation for all budgets, including a youth hostel just outside the town, and plenty of places to eat.

The nearby Celtic hill forts of Pen-y-Crug and Slwch attest to the fact that the area was occupied long before the Romans arrived in 75 AD. The remains of their camp at Y Gaer, three miles west of the town, can be visited. It was not until Norman times that Brecon

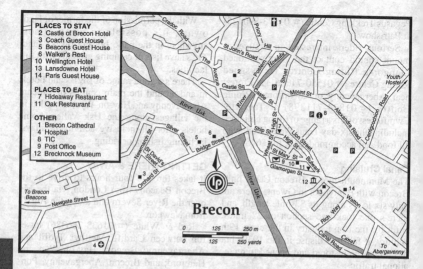

PLACES TO STAY
2 Castle of Brecon Hotel
3 Coach Guest House
5 Beacons Guest House
6 Walker's Rest
10 Wellington Hotel
13 Lansdowne Hotel
14 Paris Guest House

PLACES TO EAT
7 Hideaway Restaurant
11 Oak Restaurant

OTHER
1 Brecon Cathedral
4 Hospital
8 TIC
9 Post Office
12 Brecknock Museum

Brecon

began to grow. The local Welsh chieftain was overthrown by Bernard de Newmarch, the Norman lord who built the castle and church.

This sober, grey-stoned town seems an unlikely venue for a music festival of any kind, but on one weekend in mid-August, multicoloured awnings and flags transform the place for the Brecon Jazz Festival. This has become one of Europe's leading jazz festivals and it attracts crowds of literally thousands for what is essentially one long party. One famous jazz name you may see in town is George Melly, who lives nearby.

Orientation

Brecon is a compact town with everything within walking distance. There's no railway or bus station – most buses leave and arrive at the Bulwark in the centre, close to the TIC. B&Bs are in two groups: around the Watton road and across Bridge St in Llan Faes, the western area of Brecon.

Information

The TIC (☎ 622485), open daily, is in the Cattle Market car park. The National Park Information Centre (☎ 623156) shares the same office and is open daily from Easter to October – at other times, the TIC can help with information. A good range of books, maps and other information is available here, including a useful free leaflet listing all types of accommodation in the park. The TIC will also change travellers' cheques.

For information on the Jazz Festival contact the festival office (☎ 625557).

Mountain bikes can be rented from Beacons Experience Mountain Bike Hire (☎ 636799), 2 Forest Lodge, Libanus – five miles from Brecon.

Brecon Cathedral

Built in the 11th century above the Honddu River in the north of Brecon, on the site of an earlier church, all that remains of the Norman building is parts of the walls of the nave. The tower, choir and transepts date from the 13th century. In the mid 1860s the church was restored by Sir Gilbert Scott. In the west end of the nave is a stone cresset (an ancient lighting device), the only one that exists in Wales. The 30 cups each held oil to illuminate the church lamps.

There's an exhibition about the cathedral in the heritage centre (☎ 625222), housed in the newly-restored tithe barn in Cathedral Close.

MID WALES

Brecknock Museum

Brecon was once the county town of Brecknockshire, an administrative district now absorbed into Powys. This is one of the more interesting county museums.

There's an old dugout canoe found in Llangorse Lake, a re-created Welsh kitchen, a complete Victorian assize court and the town stocks. There's also a collection of that peculiar Welsh utensil (now reborn as a tourist souvenir), the lovespoon. The museum is open Monday to Saturday from 10 am to 5 pm; admission is free.

Welsh Whisky Visitor Centre

It's a well-kept secret that Wales produces surprisingly drinkable whisky. At the distillery visitor centre (☎ 622926) you can sample not only Prince of Wales whisky, but also Glan Usk gin and Tafski vodka. On the outskirts of Brecon, by the A40/A470 roundabout, it's open daily from May to September, and on weekdays only for the rest of the year; entry is £2.50/1.

Walks

For information on walks and other activities see the earlier sections. The Monmouthshire & Brecon Canal and the Taff Trail both start in Brecon.

Places to Stay

Hostel The *Ty'n-y-Caeau Youth Hostel* (☎ 665270) is in a large country house, a 2½-mile walk east of Brecon. Open from April to October, it's closed on Sunday apart from bank-holiday weekends and in the middle of summer. The nightly charge is £6.75/4.60.

Three miles south-east of Brecon, there's bunkhouse accommodation in the tiny village of Cantref, at *The Held* (☎ 624646). Charges are £7.50 per person.

Camping *Brynich Caravan Park* (☎ 623325) is near the youth hostel and costs from £3.75 per person.

During the jazz festival, open areas around the town are turned into temporary camping grounds.

B&Bs & Hotels There are several places in the Bridge St area.

The *Walker's Rest* (☎ 625993), 18 Bridge St, charges £14 per person. The *Beacons Guest House* (☎ 623339), 16 Bridge St, has a large range of rooms, with singles/doubles from £19.50/33. The *Coach Guest House* (☎ 623803), Orchard St, is a highly commended B&B with doubles for £38, bathroom. Smokers are not welcome here.

Along the Watton, the *Paris Guest House* (☎ 624205), at No 28, has rooms from £16 per person. There are rooms with bath from £26.50/45.50 at the *Lansdowne Hotel* (☎ 623321), at No 39, and there are several other hotels and B&Bs in the Watton area.

Just off the Watton, peacefully located on the canal, there's *Ty Gardd* (☎ 623464) with just three rooms at £16/32 or £38 for the double with bath.

The *Wellington Hotel* (☎ 625225) is right in the centre of town on the Bulwark. It's a comfortable place with a good range of facilities, including a pub, coffee shop and wine bar. B&B is £29/49.

The only part of the Norman castle that you can visit has been incorporated into the *Castle of Brecon Hotel* (☎ 624611), although there's not much left of the old building. Rooms in the main hotel are £49/70 (attached bath with shower), and in the lodge nearby they're £39/60 (attached shower); there are discounts if you stay for more than one night.

The *Griffin Inn* (☎ 754241) at Llyswen (about eight miles from Brecon on the A470) is a good place to stay and an excellent place to eat. B&B costs around £30 per person. Distinctly superior pub grub includes wood pigeon, jugged hare, braised wild duck and partridge with game chips. Most main dishes are around £9.50.

Places to Eat

Fast-food options are limited to fish & chips and Chinese/Indian takeaways. Big-name fast-food joints seem to have been kept out. The *Cantonese Kitchen* is a Chinese takeaway by the *Brecon Fish Bar* on the north-south section of High St. The best

Indian restaurant is the *Brecon Tandoori Restaurant* (☎ 624653), Glamorgan St, with dishes from £3.95 to £5.95.

There are several tearooms that also do reasonably priced meals, but they close early in the evening. *Hideaway Restaurant & Tea Rooms*, High St, is the perfect place for a cream tea and it serves superb chocolate gateau, and light lunches. *Oak Tea Rooms* (☎ 625501), on the Bulwark, is a little more upmarket, with main dishes from £3 to £6.

The restaurant at the *Beacons Guest House* (☎ 623339) is open to nonresidents and the food is all home-made and very good. There's a three-course dinner for £10. The dining-room at the upmarket *Castle of Brecon Hotel* is more expensive but recommended.

The town has a good selection of pubs, including the cosy *Three Horseshoes* with a log fire and bar food that's good value. The *Sarah Siddons*, on the Bulwark, is named after one of the most famous actresses of the 18th century, who was born in Brecon.

Getting There & Away

Brecon is 167 miles from London, 45 from Cardiff, 48 from Bristol and 20 from Abergavenny. The nearest railway stations are at Abergavenny and Merthyr Tydfil (from Cardiff). Taxis charge about £14 to Merthyr Tydfil.

National Express (☎ 0990-808080) has daily links to Brecon from most parts of southern Britain via Cardiff (1½ hours, £2.40). Silverline (☎ 01685-382406) operates daily coaches between Brecon and Merthyr Tydfil (35 minutes) and Swansea (85 minutes).

The Kilvert Connection (☎ 01432-356201) operates along the scenic route between Brecon and Hereford via Hay-on-Wye, but only on Sunday and on bank-holiday Mondays. A day-return ticket between Brecon and Hereford (two a day, 1½ hours) costs £3.60, and there is limited space for bicycles if booked in advance.

BRECON TO ABERGAVENNY
Tretower Court & Castle

Three miles north-west of Crickhowell, Tretower combines a large, medieval manor house and, across the meadow, the 13th-century tower, part of the castle. The house has been considerably restored and was originally the home of the Vaughan family; the best-known member of the family was the metaphysical poet, Henry Vaughan.

Tretower Court (☎ 01874-730279; Cadw) is open daily except Sunday morning. Entry is £2.20/1.70 and there's an excellent Walkman tour included in the price.

Crickhowell

• *pop 2000* • ☎ *01873*

This little village on the bus route between Brecon and Abergavenny is another good walking base. The TIC (☎ 812105) is on Beaufort St, by the main A40.

There's a camping ground in the village, the *Riverside Caravan Park* (☎ 810397), New Rd; charges are £3 per tent, plus £1 per

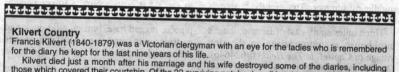

Kilvert Country

Francis Kilvert (1840-1879) was a Victorian clergyman with an eye for the ladies who is remembered for the diary he kept for the last nine years of his life.

Kilvert died just a month after his marriage and his wife destroyed some of the diaries, including those which covered their courtship. Of the 22 surviving notebooks, all but three were destroyed by a niece. The surviving volumes vividly depict the ups and downs of life in rural Radnorshire and Wiltshire.

Anyone planning a winter trip to Wales would do well to read Kilvert first. Heading for chapel one St Valentine's Eve, he describes his beard and moustache as so stiff with ice that he could barely open his mouth, while the cold managed to penetrate through two waistcoats, two coats, a scarf and a mackintosh. In the chapel itself the baby was christened in ice which was 'broken and swimming about in the font'. ∎

person. The most central B&B is *Mrs Morgan's* (☎ 811177), 2 Greenhill Villas, Beaufort St, with rooms from £18/30 for a single/double.

The *Bear Hotel* (☎ 810408) is the best place to stay in the town, and rates range from £42 to £55 for a single, £56 to £70 for a double. There's excellent bar food and a good restaurant. You can try Welsh laver bread here, served in the traditional way with cockles and bacon.

ABERGAVENNY (Y FENNI)
• *pop 10,000*   •   ☎ 01873

Standing by the eastern edge of the park, surrounded by hills, this busy market town styles itself as the 'Gateway to Wales'. It's a good base for walking in the Black Mountains, with a wide range of accommodation and, unlike Brecon, a railway station.

The town's history goes back 4000 years, when there was a Neolithic settlement here. The Romans established Gobarium Fort nearby and stayed from 57 to 400 AD; but Abergavenny only really began to grow after Hamelin de Ballon built his castle in 1090. Eventually falling into ruin, the keep was heavy-handedly restored by the Victorians and now houses a small **museum** of local history. The **Museum of Childhood** (☎ 850063), Market St, is of greater interest and amongst the numerous toys is a reputedly haunted dolls' house!

Amongst the former visitors who have enjoyed the town's rural position was Rudolf Hess in 1941. Although he wasn't here on holiday, his wardens did allow him a weekly hike up Pen-y-Fan.

The TIC (☎ 857588) is by the bus stand in Swan Meadow, and open year-round. In the same building is a national park visitors centre (☎ 853254).

Places to Stay
Two miles north of Abergavenny, in the village of Pantygelli, is *Smithy's Bunkhouse* (☎ 853432), down the farm track opposite the Crown Inn. There are two dormitories at this well-equipped bunkhouse; charges are £7 per person. There's a laundry, common

room and kitchen. The nearest HI youth hostel to Abergavenny is at Capel-y-Ffin, 15 miles north on the road to Hay-on-Wye.

In the north of the town, the 200-year-old *Aenon House* (☎ 858708), 34 Pen-y-Pound, is a very pleasant place to stay. Rooms are from £14 per person. Award-winning *Pentre House* (☎ 853435), Brecon Rd, is another good choice, with singles/doubles for £22/32. Evening meals are £10.

Halidon House (☎ 857855), 63 Monmouth Rd, is very centrally located, and just a short step from the bus and railway stations. It charges around £16 per person. Nearby on Holywell Rd is the similarly priced *Belchamps Guest House* (☎ 853204). There are several other B&Bs around the railway station.

At 36 Hereford Rd, *Park Guest House* (☎ 853715) is a Georgian building with six rooms at £18/32. The *Guest House* (☎ 854823), 2 Oxford St, is nearby, with comfortable rooms for £18.50/32, and evening meals.

The *Great George Hotel* (☎ 854230), Cross St, charges £30/40. The top place in town is the *Angel Hotel* (☎ 857121), also on Cross St. Rooms are £65/75 and there's no cheaper rate at weekends. There's a set three-course dinner in the restaurant for £16.95.

Places to Eat
On Market St there's *Market St Fish & Chips* (☎ 855791) for takeaways. The *Greyhound Vaults* (☎ 858549) is on the same street, opposite the Museum of Childhood. Lunchtime choices range from a salad roll at £1.55 to a steak for around £9, plus a few vegetarian dishes. It's also open for dinner.

Three miles north-east of Abergavenny at Llandewi Skirrid is the *Walnut Tree Inn* (☎ 852797), reputed to be the best restaurant in Wales. The chef is Italian, the cuisine international and the ingredients, as far as possible, Welsh. The menu might include anything from vincigrassi (pasta, béchamel, parma ham, ceps, truffles) to bubble and squeak. It's closed on Sunday and Monday, and very busy when it's open, so you must book. After a memorable dinner for two, including drinks and service, don't expect any change out of £80.

Getting There & Away

There's no direct National Express service from London; you must change at Hereford. Red & White (☎ 01633-266336) runs services to Brecon or Cardiff.

The railway station is just off Monmouth Rd, a 15-minute walk from the bus station and TIC. On Saturday there's a direct train from Bristol leaving at 9.52 am, reaching Abergavenny an hour later. There are services to Cardiff every hour (£6.40), and direct trains to Manchester. London requires a change at Newport. For information phone ☎ 0345-484950.

Getting Around

Park Taxis (☎ 858416) is just outside the station. You can rent bikes from Brook Bikes (☎ 857066), 9 Brecon Rd.

AROUND ABERGAVENNY
Blaenavon

Five miles south-west of Abergavenny, Blaenavon is home to the **Big Pit Mining Museum**, created inside a real mine which ceased production in 1980 – 100 years after the first miners began work there.

You can descend the 294 feet to the pit floor to inspect the tunnels and coalfaces in an old mine lift. Safety precautions are treated seriously, so you'll go down decked out in a hard hat and with a heavy power pack attached to your waist to light your helmet lamp. Some of the men who guide you round were once miners who cut coal here. It's not a trip for the claustrophobic. As well as the mine itself, you can also see the old pithead baths, the blacksmith's workshop and other colliery buildings.

The Big Pit (☎ 01495-790311) is open daily from 9.30 am to 5 pm, March to November, with hour-long underground tours (popular with school parties) from 10 am. It's cold at the bottom of the mine, and you should wear sturdy shoes. Entry is £5.50/3.50.

ABERGAVENNY TO HAY-ON-WYE
Llanfihangel Crucorney

Six miles from Abergavenny, off the road between Abergavenny and Hereford, this little village attracts lots of tourists. They mainly come to see the *Skirrid Mountain Inn* (☎ 01873-890258) which claims to be the oldest pub in Wales. From the early 12th century until the 17th century this was the courthouse, where almost 200 prisoners were hanged; the rope marks on one of the beams that was used can still be seen.

The most pleasant place to stay in the area is wonderful *Penyclawdd Court* (☎ 01873-890719), a tastefully-restored Tudor manor house below Bryn Arw mountain. B&B is around £30 per person and you must book ahead. Modern conveniences such as electricity are provided in the bedrooms, but not in the dining-room where delicious four-course meals are served by candlelight.

Llanthony

The ruins of the Augustinian priory church and the monastic buildings of **Llanthony Priory** (Cadw) are set in a beautiful location in the Ewyas Valley. There's a superb walk from the car park here up onto the bare ridge above, with excellent views. Offa's Dyke runs along the ridge.

The *Abbey Hotel* (☎ 01873-890487) is built into some of the surviving abbey buildings. Like Penyclawdd Court in Llanfihangel Crucorney, it's highly recommended for its atmosphere. There's a public bar in the vaulted crypt that serves basic meals. It's open daily from Easter to October, and on weekends in winter. Rooms are let only as doubles, and they're £43.50 during the week and £50 at weekends.

Capel-y-Ffin

Further up the valley, Llanthony Monastery was founded in 1870. Unoccupied by the 1920s, a commune was started in it by the artist and typographer Eric Gill. It's now a private residence.

Capel-y-Ffin Youth Hostel (☎ 01873-890650) is one mile north of the village, by the road to Hay-on-Wye. Its opening hours are complex – phone for details – but it's usually open daily in July and August and closed in December and January. The nightly charge is £6.75/4.60. There's a riding school by the hostel – this is excellent pony-trekking country. Offa's Dyke Path is 1½ miles from the hostel on the ridge. The walk to Hay is highly recommended.

HAY-ON-WYE
• pop 1600 • ☎ 01497

On 1 April 1977 Hay-on-Wye declared independence from Britain – just one publicity stunt this eccentric little bookshop town has used to draw attention to itself. Most of the publicity has been generated by bookseller Richard Booth, the colourful, self-styled King of Hay, who was largely responsible for Hay's evolution from just another market town on the Welsh-English border to the second-hand bookshop capital of the world.

A day browsing amongst the shops is definitely recommended. With its small centre made up of narrow sloping lanes, the town itself is also interesting, and the people it attracts certainly are. On the north-eastern corner of the national park, Hay makes an excellent base for the Black Mountains.

History
Most events in the history of Hay have been connected with its location as a Marches town, on the border of Wales and England. In fact, during the Norman period the town was administered as English Hay (the town proper) and Welsh Hay (the countryside to the south and west of the town).

A castle had already stood in the town before the construction of the present one, built in about 1200 by the treacherous William Breos II (one of the Norman barons, or Lords Marcher, granted vast tracts of land on border country to consolidate conquered territory). From then until the final acquisition of Wales by the English crown, Hay changed hands many times. It subsequently became a market town, employing a large number of people in the flannel trade during the 18th century. The first large-scale second-hand bookshop opened in 1961, the vanguard of a new industry.

The castle, complete with the Jacobean mansion built within its Norman walls, was purchased by Richard Booth in 1971 but a fire in 1977 left it in its present dilapidated state.

Orientation & Information
Hay's compact centre contains the castle and most of the bookshops, enclosed by a roughly square-shaped perimeter. The main central thoroughfare is Castle St, which links Oxford Rd with Lion St.

MID WALES

The Town of Books
There are now over 30 second-hand bookshops in Hay, containing literally hundreds of thousands of books – 400,000 in Richard Booth's Bookshop alone. Bear in mind that British publishers still churn out more than 80,000 new titles each year, and this country has a long history of publishing. According to the experts, quantity rather than quality is what you'll find in most places in Hay.

Some of these bookshops specialise in esoteric fields – for example, B & K Books (☎ 820386), Newport St, boasts the world's finest stock of books on apiculture. Rose's Books (☎ 820013), 14 Broad St, stocks rare and out-of-print children's books. Lion St Bookshop (☎ 820121), 36 Lion St, deals in militaria and anarchism. There's theology and church history at Marches Gallery (☎ 821451), Lion St. West House Books (☎ 821225), Broad St, does Celtica and women's studies. Legends (☎ 821855) stocks books on the occult, mysticism and the paranormal. You can also get tarot readings from the psychic here.

Many bookshops, however, cover everything – the most famous being Richard Booth's (☎ 820322), 44 Lion St, and the Hay Cinema Bookshop (☎ 820071), Castle St. Some shops will carry out searches to locate out-of-print books. Booksearch (Hay-on-Wye, Hereford HR3 5EA) deals only by post. There are regular book auctions at Y Gelli Auctions (☎ 821179), Broad St. ∎

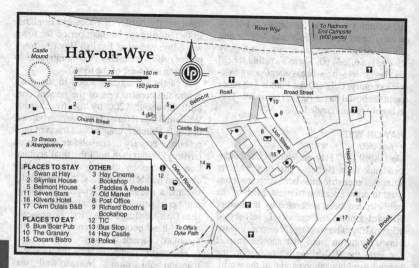

MID WALES

The TIC (☎ 820144), open every day, is on Oxford Rd, on the edge of town and just by the main car park. It's open from 11 am to 5 pm from Easter to November, and 11 am to 4 pm at all other times. It closes for lunch from 1 to 2 pm. Richard Booth operates an independent TIC (☎ 820164) from his Five Star Bookshop, Backfold.

Most bookshops stock the useful free town plan that locates and describes all the bookshops in Hay. The annual *Sunday Times* Festival of Literature (☎ 821299) takes place in May/June and is a very popular and entertaining affair.

Bikes can be hired from Paddles & Pedals (☎ 820604), Castle St, for £12.50 per day, £7.50 per half-day. They also hire out Canadian canoes (for two/three people).

Places to Stay

Hay has a fair number of B&Bs and hotels, but the nearest youth hostel is at Capel-y-Ffin, eight miles south. To stay at *Joe's Lodge* (☎ 01874-711845), Hay Rd, Talgarth, eight miles south-west of Hay, you need to book in advance. It's an independent hostel, and B&B costs £9.50. Also in Talgarth,

there's upmarket B&B at *Upper Trewalkin Farm* (☎ 01874-711349), Pengenffordd, for £19 per person. Meals here are excellent.

Back in Hay, *Radnors End Campsite* (☎ 820233) is 550 yards from the bridge over the Wye river, on the road to Clyro. The charge is £2.50 per person.

Belmont House (☎ 820718) is well located on Belmont Rd, with rooms for £18/30 (£36 for a double with bathroom attached). At *Cwm Dulais* (☎ 820640), Heoly-Dwr, also central, there are basic rooms for £18/30 and rooms with bath for £16/30.

Skynlas House (☎ 820368), on Church St, charges £17.50/33 for a single/double with attached bath. *Kilvert's Hotel* (☎ 821042) is right in the centre on the Bull Ring, with rooms at around £25 per person.

Two miles from Hay, at Llanigon and near Offa's Dyke Path, is the *Old Post Office* (☎ 820008), an excellent vegetarian B&B with rooms for £14 per person with shared bathroom, £19 with private bathroom.

Back in Hay, the *Seven Stars* (☎ 820886), Broad St, is an excellent place to stay. As well as comfortable rooms for £16.50 to £30 per person, it even has a swimming pool and sauna. The *Swan at Hay* (☎ 821188) is more conventionally luxurious and charges between £30 and £50 per person.

Places to Eat

For such a small place, there's a lot of variety. The *Sandwich Cellar* (☎ 8205890), Backfold Lane, is ideal for snacks. The *Old Stables Tea Rooms* (☎ 820563) is good for morning coffee as well as afternoon tea, although it's closed on Monday and Friday. For fish & chips (£3.70) and other cheap meals, there's the *Wine Vaults* (☎ 820409) on Castle St.

For something informal, yet substantial, the *Granary* (☎ 820790), Broad St, is an excellent and popular choice. A large steak & kidney pie costs £5.75, and there are good vegetarian dishes – Tibetan roast is recommended. It also has some interesting puddings, including the classic summer pudding, with raspberries and blackberries. It's open daily (during the day only in winter).

Oscars Bistro (☎ 821993), High Town, is central and offers very reasonably priced dishes (including vegetarian).

Pinocchio's (☎ 821166), 2 Broad St, is a good Italian restaurant with excellent pizza. It's closed on Sunday and Monday.

The tiny *Three Tuns*, on Broad St, is a wonderful old pub and cider house, popular with locals. The *Blue Boar* (☎ 820884), Castle St, has a wide selection of bar food. *Kilvert's Hotel* (☎ 821042) also has good pub food and an à la carte restaurant where main dishes are from £8 to £13.

Getting There & Away

The nearest railway station is in Hereford. There are six buses a day to Hereford (one hour, £2.90), Monday to Saturday, and three buses on Sunday. Departures are from Oxford Rd and there are additional services from the clocktower on Broad St. For Brecon (40 minutes), there are six buses a day, Monday to Saturday, and two on Sunday.

Offa's Dyke Path passes beside Hay.

Powys

Powys is a large and sparsely populated county, stretching from Brecon Beacons National Park in the south up to Snowdonia in the north. In the local government border reorganisation in 1974, Brecknockshire in the south, the central county of Radnorshire and Montgomeryshire in the north were combined to create the new county of Powys. The northern section is often still referred to as Montgomeryshire. There are few specific sights in the county – Powis Castle and the Centre for Alternative Technology are probably the main tourist attractions – but there's superb open walking country.

WALKS

There are some excellent walks in the area. The best-known is **Offa's Dyke Path**, the 168-mile national trail that runs the length of Wales, following the eastern border of Powys. See the Activities chapter at the start of this book for more information.

The 120-mile **Glyndŵr's Way** is through beautiful countryside and has the added interest of following in the footsteps of the Welsh hero. Contact the Planning Information Service, Powys County Council, County Hall, Llandrindod Wells, Powys LD1 6GG, for a series of leaflets covering the trail. There's also a guidebook: *Owen Glyndŵr's Way* by Richard Sale.

Glyndŵr's Way has now been designated a national trail. It takes six to nine days to walk from Knighton to Welshpool via Machynlleth, and the walk can be done in either direction. Some sections are along roads, which you could cut out by using public transport.

GETTING AROUND

Public transport in this area is limited. To visit the more remote areas, a certain amount of advance planning is necessary.

Bus

Crosville Cymru (☎ 01970-617951) operates

MID WALES

bus services to and from many areas in Mid Wales. It has a Crosville Rover ticket (£5.70) which allows unlimited travel for a day on its services.

In rural areas, bus services operate a 'Hail & Ride' system whereby a bus will stop anywhere on its route for a passenger as long as it is safe to do so.

Train

Rail services are sparse. One line runs through Shrewsbury and Machynlleth to terminate in Aberystwyth; another brushes across the south-east corner from Shrewsbury via Llandrindod Wells and Builth Wells and south to Swansea.

A useful ticket is the North & Mid Wales Rover, valid for seven days (£36/23.75) or for any three out of seven days (£23/15.20) on mainline services between Aberystwyth and Shrewsbury, Shrewsbury to Crewe and Crewe to Holyhead, and also on most bus services in the area. The Rover also entitles the holder to discounts on some of the private railways. However, it doesn't include services on the Shrewsbury-Llandrindod Wells-Swansea line.

LLANWRTYD WELLS
* *pop 500*   * ☎ *01591*

Llanwrtyd Wells was developed as a spa town in the 18th century when the health benefits of the local sulphur spring (still flowing) were discovered. This attractive little town is surrounded by beautiful countryside, with the Cambrian Mountains to the north west and the Mynydd Eppynt to the south east. As well as walking, mountain biking and pony-trekking, the town hosts a number of less orthodox events and pastimes – the World Bog-Snorkelling Championships (August bank holiday), for example. These involve swimming 120 yards underwater through a mud-filled trench. Why not?

There's a TIC (☎ 610666) on the square. The *Stonecroft Hostel* (☎ 610332) is a friendly self-catering guesthouse near the centre of town on Dol-y-coed Rd. It's a good place with dormitory accommodation for £8, and rooms from £10 per person. There's a

kitchen, riverside garden, and TV room. Breakfast (£2.50) is available next door at the *Stonecroft Inn*, which is also an excellent place for a pint and they do good pub grub. The *Neuadd Arms* (☎ 610236), on the square, does B&B for £22 per person (£25 in a room with bathroom attached). They rent mountain bikes for £12 per day.

LLANDRINDOD WELLS
* *pop 4300*   * ☎ *01597*

Roman remains at Castell Collen nearby show that people were here long before Llandrindod was reinvented as a spa town in the 18th and 19th centuries. The town's architecture – towers, balustrades, balconies – and ironwork reflect the tastes and style of the time. You can still take the water outside the Pump Room in Rock Park though no treatments are available. Once a year there's a Victorian Festival where the townspeople dress up in Victorian clothes.

The town is now the administrative centre for Powys. The TIC (☎ 822600) is in the Old Town Hall, Memorial Gardens, Temple St. The *Llanerch* (☎ 822086), Waterloo Rd, is a traditional pub known for its good-value bar food.

KNIGHTON

On the border with England, Knighton lies on Offa's Dyke, at the junction of two long distance footpaths – Offa's Dyke Path and Glyndŵr's Way.

The Offa's Dyke Centre & TIC (☎ 01547-528753), West St, is open daily from Easter to October. There are no plans to reopen the former youth hostel but there's accommodation from £9 at the *Plough Hotel* (☎ 01547-528041), Market St. A double with attached bath is around £35.

Knighton is on the Shrewsbury-Llandrindod Wells-Swansea railway line.

WELSHPOOL
* *pop 5000*   * ☎ *01938*

This town, situated in the Severn Valley, was originally called Pool, but the name was changed to avoid confusion with Poole in Dorset. Really the only reason to come here is to get to Powis Castle or ride the narrow-gauge railway.

The TIC (☎ 552043) is in the leisure centre on Salop Rd. There's a livestock market every Monday which dates back to 1263.

Things to See & Do

The **Welshpool & Llanfair Light Railway** (☎ 01938-810441) was originally built to take local people with their sheep and cattle to market. The line was closed in 1956 but reopened by enthusiasts in 1960. It runs on an eight-mile journey from Raven Square and operates between Easter and early October. Three trains run each way. The return fare is £7/3.50.

One mile south of Welshpool is **Powis Castle** (☎ 01938-554336; NT). The castle is an impressive sight with its red walls and beautiful terraced gardens. The museum contains treasures Clive of India brought back from India – his family married into the Herberts of Powis. The castle is open Wednesday to Sunday from early April to the end of October. In July and August it's also open on Tuesday. The gardens are open from 11 am to 6 pm, and the castle from 12 to 5 pm. Entry to the castle and gardens is £6/3, and to the gardens only it's £4/2.

Five miles south of Welshpool, at Berriew, is the **Andrew Logan Museum of Sculpture** (☎ 01686-640689), open May to October at weekends (Wednesday to Sunday in July and August), from 2 to 6 pm. Entry is £1.50/75p. Andrew Logan is one of Britain's top modern sculptors and this whacky, slightly camp collection is highly entertaining.

Getting There & Away

Welshpool is on the Shrewsbury to Aberystwyth line. From Shrewsbury to Welshpool takes 30 minutes (£4) with departures approximately every two hours Monday to Saturday, less often on Sunday.

MACHYNLLETH

- *pop 2000*   • ☎ *01654*

On the western edge of Montgomeryshire, Machynlleth (pronounced mahuncliff) holds an important place in Welsh history as it was here that Owain Glyndwr set up his parliament. In recent years it's become better known as a centre of green living, mainly owing to the influence of the Centre for Alternative Technology on the edge of the town.

Machynlleth is in the Dyfi Valley, and there's good cycling in this area. Bikes can

The Centre for Alternative Technology

If you're anywhere in the area don't miss the Centre for Alternative Technology (CAT; ☎ 01654-702400), three miles north of Machynlleth. Founded in 1975 by a group of environmentalists on a 40-acre site that was once a slate mine, it's now a self-sufficient working community. It's probably the most interesting eco centre in Europe.

There are working displays of wind, water and solar power, a low-energy self-built house and an organic garden, as well as an underground display on the world of the soil (complete with giant mole) and a transport maze. The displays manage to be interesting and fun yet also educational. There's a water-powered cliff railway (closed in the winter months in case of frost), bookshop and excellent vegetarian restaurant.

The centre is open daily from 10 am to 7 pm (last entry is 5 pm or at dusk if earlier). Entry is £4.50/2.50. Arrive by bike and entry is half-price. There are also discounted tickets available when you buy rail or bus tickets – inquire on buses or at the railway station.

CAT also runs residential courses throughout the year. Basic accommodation and meals are provided.

If you can't get there in person, you can always visit the Centre for Alternative Technology's home page on the world wide web: http://www.foe.co.uk/cat. Their e-mail address is cat@gn.apc.org. ∎

MID WALES

be hired from Greenstiles (☎ 703543), just behind the clock tower in the town centre, for £8 per day (£12 for mountain bikes).

The TIC is in the Canolfan Owain Glyndŵr Centre (☎ 702401).

Things to See & Do

The **Glyndŵr Parliament House** (☎ 702827) is open daily from April to September and has displays showing life in the Middle Ages in Wales, as well as on Owain Glyndŵr's fight for Welsh independence.

Celtica (☎ 702702), Y Plas, Aberystwyth Rd, is a new attraction that highlights Wales' Celtic roots. The main exhibition is a multimedia tour (£4.65/3.50), guided by a commentary relayed to your headset. There's a Celtic settlement, magic forest and a meeting with a Druid. It's actually rather more entertaining than it sounds. Also here is a good interpretive centre, bookshop, garden and 'historium' (resource centre for Celtic and Welsh history and culture). Celtica is open daily from 10 am to 6 pm (last entry is at 4.30 pm).

Places to Stay & Eat

At Corris, six miles north of Machynlleth, the energy-efficient *Corris Youth Hostel* (☎ 761686) is in the Old School. It's open daily from May to August, and daily except Monday in April, September and October. The nightly charge is £7.45/5.

In Machynlleth, five minutes from the clock tower, on Aberystwyth Rd, there's B&B for around £14 per person at *Haulfryn* (☎ 702206). It does excellent breakfasts.

Maenllwyd (☎ 702928) in Newtown Rd charges from £17.50 to £23 per person for B&B, and is a very pleasant place to stay; vegetarian breakfasts are served if required. *Pendre Guest House* (☎ 702088) in Maengwyn St has four rooms, two with attached bath, and charges from £15.50.

In Doll St try the *Glyndŵr Hotel* (☎ 703989); B&B is from £15 per person.

The excellent *Caeheulon* (☎ 703243) in Aberhosan has two rooms and charges £16.50 per person, less if you stay for three nights or more.

There's a good tea-room, *Y Lolfa Baned*, at the Celtica exhibition; they also do light lunches. The *Quarry Shop* (☎ 702624), 13 Maengwyn St, serves vegetarian food and uses organic ingredients where possible. *Café Maengwyn* (☎ 702126), located at 57 Maengwyn St, uses local produce including Welsh lamb. A vegetable bake (eg leek and potato pie) is £3.29.

Getting There & Away

Machynlleth is on the Shrewsbury to Aberystwyth line. Services from Shrewsbury (1½ hours, £10) operate almost every two hours. Crosville Cymru's (☎ 01970-617951) No 2 bus from Aberystwyth (40 minutes, £3.40) operates five times a day from Monday to Saturday, and twice a day on Sunday.

Ceredigion

Ceredigion (Cardiganshire) is the county that encompasses the southern coastal section of Cardigan Bay, and which extends inland to Powys. For three out of every five people who live here, Welsh is their first language.

The county includes 50 miles of coastline, much of which is protected by heritage coast status. The capital is the university town and classic seaside resort of Aberystwyth, certainly the most happening place in Ceredigion.

INFORMATION

Ceredigion's forward-looking TICs, and quite a few of its members, are all linked to the Internet. You can contact them directly on info@ceredigion.compulink.co.uk.

GETTING AROUND
Bus

Bus Dyfed's Rover ticket (£4) allows unlimited travel on its services for a day. Most other operators in the area will accept the ticket, but it's not valid on the postbus to Devil's Bridge. Crosville Cymru (☎ 01970-

617951) also operates bus services in Mid Wales. The Crosville Rover ticket (£5.70) allows unlimited travel for a day on its services.

Train

There are few lines in Ceredigion. The only mainline service is into Aberystwyth via Machynlleth from Shrewsbury. See the preceding Powys section. There's a popular private line, the Vale of Rheidol Railway which takes tourists from Aberystwyth up to Devil's Bridge.

CARDIGAN (ABERTEIFI)
- *pop 4000*   • ☎ *01239*

The former county town of Cardiganshire, the Welsh name refers to the town's position at the mouth of the Teifi. This was an important seafaring and trading centre until the harbour silted up.

The first competitive National Eisteddfod was held in the castle here in 1176. A strong local interest in the arts continues and the town has a good alternative theatre and arts centre, Theatr Mwldan (☎ 621200). The TIC (☎ 613230) is in the same building, on Bath House Rd. It's open Monday to Saturday from 10 am to 5 pm.

Places to Stay & Eat

The *Poppit Sands Youth Hostel* (☎ 612936) is four miles from Cardigan, by the start of the Pembrokeshire Coast Path. It's open from March to October, daily except some Mondays; beds are £7.45/5 in summer.

There are several good places to stay on Gwbert Rd, in the north of the town. *Maes-a-Môr* (☎ 614929), Park Place, Gwbert Rd, is opposite the King George V Park. B&B is £20/32 for a room with attached bath, cheaper off-season. No smoking is permitted. A few doors down is *Brynhyfryd Guest House* (☎ 612861), where B&B costs from £15 per person. If you're on the bus from Aberystwyth, it stops at the end of Gwbert Rd.

Situated on the cliffs, 2½ miles from Cardigan by the Teifi estuary, is the *Gwbert Hotel & Restaurant* (☎ 612638), an excellent place to stay – particularly for a romantic break. B&B is around £34.50 per person; all rooms have attached bathroom and satellite TV, and most have sea views. There's a set-menu dinner for £14.50 and the restaurant specialises in seafood.

Another comfortable place is the *Gwesty Penbontbren Farm Hotel* (☎ 810248), two miles from Cardigan Bay in Penbontbren. All rooms have attached bath and cost £40/68.

For a light meal, the *Theatr Mwldan Café*, in the theatre building, is excellent. A five-grain vegieburger costs £2.10 and there's a good range of herbal teas. The *Black Lion Hotel*, High St, pulls a reasonable pint and has good-value lunches on Sunday and bar food during the week. Round the back, on Black Lion Mews, *Go Mango Wholefoods* is a wholefood shop serving snacks to take away.

If the catering students are at Coleg Ceredigion you can taste their experiments at the *Gordon Edwards Restaurant* (☎ 612032), Park Place. Set lunches are around £4 and dinners cost about £7; it's very good value.

Getting There & Away

Cardigan is not accessible by rail. The easiest way to get there is to go to Aberystwyth and then take the No 550 bus service, which runs almost hourly, Monday to Saturday (two hours, £4 on a Dyfed Rover). There's only one service on Sunday. The route is covered by two operators – Richards Brothers (☎ 613756) and Crosville Cymru (☎ 01970-617951).

Alternatively, you could go to Haverfordwest or Carmarthen and take the hourly No 412 service via Fishguard to Cardigan (1½ hours, £2.75), which runs Monday to Saturday.

ABERYSTWYTH
- *pop 9000*   • ☎ *01970*

On the central coast of Wales, Aberystwyth combines the attractions of a traditional seaside resort with a lively university town.

Like many other towns in the area, it was

founded by Edward I when he started building a castle at the mouth of the River Rheidol in Ceredigion Bay in 1277. It was captured by Owain Glyndŵr in 1404 and destroyed by Cromwell's forces in 1649. By the beginning of the 19th century, the walls and gates had virtually disappeared. Now a pretty unimpressive ruin by day, it's quite attractive when floodlit at night.

The town developed a fishing industry, and silver and lead-mining industries were also important in the area. With the arrival of the railway in 1864, it began to develop into a fashionable resort. In 1872 Aberystwyth was chosen as the site of the first college of the University of Wales, and in 1907 it became home to the National Library of Wales.

The TIC (☎ 612125) is located at the junction of Terrace Rd and Bath St. It's open daily from 10 am to 6 pm during the summer.

Things to See & Do

The **Cliff Railway** (☎ 617642) is the longest electric cliff railway in Britain, running from the Promenade to the top of Constitution

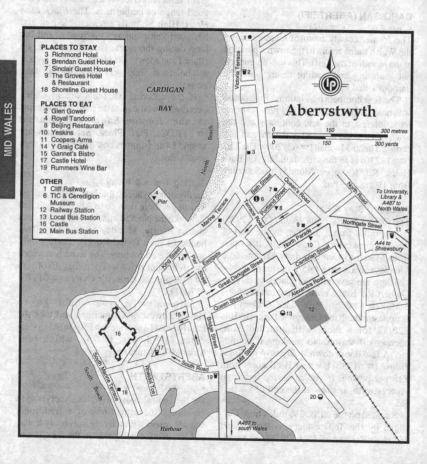

PLACES TO STAY
3 Richmond Hotel
5 Brendan Guest House
7 Sinclair Guest House
9 The Groves Hotel & Restaurant
18 Shoreline Guest House

PLACES TO EAT
2 Glen Gower
4 Royal Tandoori
8 Beijing Restaurant
10 Yeskins
11 Coopers Arms
14 Y Graig Café
15 Gannet's Bistro
17 Castle Hotel
19 Rummers Wine Bar

OTHER
1 Cliff Railway
6 TIC & Ceredigion Museum
12 Railway Station
13 Local Bus Station
16 Castle
20 Main Bus Station

Aberystwyth

CARDIGAN BAY

Hill. The hill offers good views over the bay and a **Camera Obscura** (a simple optical instrument like a projecting telescope) which almost gives you a peek at the inside of locals' houses. Trains depart daily every few minutes, Easter to October from 10 am to 6 pm; tickets cost £2/1 return.

The **National Library of Wales** (☎ 623816) holds over five million books in a variety of languages and various ancient manuscripts and pictures. It's open Monday to Friday from 9.30 am to 5 pm.

Ceredigion Museum (☎ 617911), is in the Coliseum, Terrace Rd, by the TIC. It has an entertaining collection of folk material based on the three main occupations of the people of Ceredigion – agriculture, seafaring and lead mining. There are also temporary exhibitions showing works by local artists. Entrance to the museum is free, and it's open Monday to Saturday from 10 am to 5 pm, and on Sunday during school holidays.

The **Vale of Rheidol Railway** (☎ 625819) runs from Aberystwyth to Devil's Bridge (see below), a journey of 11¾ miles, and is hauled by a narrow-gauge steam train. The railway was constructed to take the lead and timber from the Rheidol Valley, and the engines were built by the Great Western Railway in 1923.

The station is adjacent to Aberystwyth's mainline station and the ticket office opens at 10 am. The service operates daily from Easter to October, but there are no services on Friday in April and May, nor after the second Friday in September, nor on Friday, Saturday and Monday in October. Trains usually go twice a day in each direction (11 am and 2.30 pm from Aberystwyth, 1 and 4.30 pm from Devil's Bridge) but there are four a day on certain days in July and August. The return fare is £10/5.

Places to Stay

Borth Youth Hostel (☎ 871498) is nine miles to the north, near a wide sandy beach. It's fully open from April to August, and in March and September except on Sunday and Monday; the nightly charge is £8.25/5.55.

For B&B in Aberystwyth, three roads par-ticularly worth trying are Portland St, Marine Terrace (where most places overlook Cardigan Bay) and Rheidol Terrace.

Shoreline Guest House (☎ 615002), 6 South Marine Terrace, offers B&B from £14 per person. There are 11 rooms, all with satellite TV. It's a good place.

At 43 Portland St is the excellent *Sinclair Guest House* (☎ 615158), where B&B is £27.50/45 for a single/double with attached bath. The *Four Seasons Hotel* (☎ 612120), 50-54 Portland St, has 17 bedrooms, most with attached bath, £48/64. Another place nearby in Portland St is *Shangri-La* (☎ 617659), where B&B costs £15/28.

At 44-45 Marine Terrace is the *Richmond Hotel* (☎ 612201). Some rooms have attached bath and B&B is £38/55. *Brendan Guest House* (☎ 612252), also in Marine Terrace, charges £16.50/33 (£18.50/37 with bath attached). Most rooms have sea views.

The *Groves Hotel & Restaurant* (☎ 617623), 44 North Parade, has rooms at £42/55, all with attached bathroom. In the restaurant, there's a set three-course dinner for £16. Bar snacks are also available.

Places to Eat

The student presence ensures that there are plenty of good, cheap places to eat in Aberystwyth.

Y Graig, 34 Pier St, is a very popular wholefood restaurant for vegetarians, vegans and meat-eaters. Smoked mackerel with rice and salad is £3.95. There's a good range of herbal teas. It's also a good place to find out what's going on locally.

There are numerous Chinese restaurants and takeaways. The best is the *Beijing* on Portland St. The best of the several Indian restaurants is the *Royal Tandoori*, in an excellent location at the end of the pier.

Yeskins, on North Parade is a small family-run restaurant that has been recommended, with a range of main dishes from around £5. Next door is *Little Italy* (☎ 625707) with pasta from £5.25, pizzas at £4.50, and meat dishes including steak and chicken.

Gannet's Bistro (☎ 617164), 7 St James Square, does set lunches for £5. Main dishes

MID WALES

in the evening range from £5 to £10. It does some reasonable traditional food, such as Beef Wellington.

Entertainment

Rummers Wine Bar, Bridge St, is right by the river, and there are seats outside. It's open from 7 pm to midnight.

The *Castle Hotel* on Castle Terrace is a good traditional pub, and the *Coopers Arms* on Northgate St has live jazz some nights. The *Glen Gower*, Victoria Terrace, attracts students.

Getting There & Away

National Express (☎ 0990-808080) operates one service a day from London (seven hours, £24).

Crosville Cymru's bus No 701 connects Bangor with Cardiff and passes through Aberystwyth. There are two buses a day between Aberystwyth and Cardiff (3¾ hours, £9.70) and one a day to/from Bangor (three hours, £10.70).

Service No 550 runs between Aberystwyth and Cardigan (hourly Monday to Saturday, once on Sunday; two hours). Service No 2 goes between Aberystwyth and Caernarfon (change at Dolgellau) approximately every two hours. It's a three-hour trip and can be covered with a Crosville Day Rover (£5.70).

Aberystwyth is at the end of the Cambrian line from Shrewsbury (two hours, £13). There are departures every two hours,

Monday to Saturday, less frequently on Sunday.

See also the fares tables in the introductory Getting Around chapter.

AROUND ABERYSTWYTH
Devil's Bridge

Devil's Bridge is situated at the head of the Rheidol Valley in the Pumlumon Hills. The fast-flowing Mynach and Rheidol rivers meet in a gorge below the village. The Mynach river drops 100 yards in a series of spectacular waterfalls.

The Mynach is also notable for the three stone bridges which have been built on top of one another. The first is believed to have been built by the Knights Templars before 1188, the second in 1753 and the last is more recent.

The Rheidol Valley Steam Railway goes to Devil's Bridge (see Aberystwyth; Things to See & Do).

Places to Stay & Eat The *Ystumtuen Youth Hostel* (☎ 890693), Glantuen, is 1½ miles from Devil's Bridge and is open from Easter to October; the nightly charge is £5.50/3.75.

The excellent *Mount Pleasant Guest House* (☎ 890219) is 200 yards from the Rheidol Steam Railway. It charges £18/28, and breakfast is an extra £3.50. *Hafod Arms Hotel* (☎ 890232) is also about 200 yards from the railway and was originally a shooting lodge. B&B costs £25/36, or £32/50 with bathroom attached.

North Wales

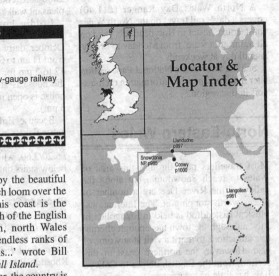

North Wales is dominated by the beautiful Snowdonia Mountains, which loom over the coastline. Unfortunately, this coast is the holiday playground for much of the English Midlands. 'From the train, north Wales looked like holiday hell – endless ranks of prison camp caravan parks...' wrote Bill Bryson in *Notes from a Small Island*.

Heading west from Chester, the country is flat, industrialised and uninteresting until you reach Llandudno. Llandudno is virtually contiguous with Conwy – either spot would make a good base. From Llandudno and Conwy you can catch buses or trains into the Snowdonia National Park. The park is also accessible from the bustling coastal market town of Porthmadog on the Ffestiniog Railway. From Porthmadog, you can loop back to Shrewsbury along the Cambrian coast.

The remote Llŷn Peninsula in the west escapes the crowds to a large extent; start from Caernarfon, with its magnificent castle, or Pwllheli. To the north is the island of Anglesey, joined to the mainland by bridges – Holyhead is one of the main ferry ports for Ireland. Near Porthmadog is whimsical Portmeirion, an entire village built in the Italianate style – very attractive but crowded in summer.

This section of Wales includes the counties of Caernarfonshire & Merionethshire and Anglesey (until 1996 administered together as Gwynedd), Aberconwy & Colwyn (formerly straddling Gwynedd and Clwyd), and Denbighshire, Flintshire and Wrexham (formerly Clwyd).

GETTING AROUND

The new county councils will presumably continue to coordinate public transport. A very useful *Public Transport Guide*, which includes the Llŷn Peninsula and all of Snowdonia is available from the Transport Unit (☎ 01286-679535). For Anglesey, phone ☎ 01248-752458. For the eastern half of North Wales, Flintshire County Council (☎ 01352-704035) produces timetables covering all the services within its area.

Rail services in North Wales include a line that runs along the north coast from Chester via Llandudno Junction, Conwy and Bangor, terminating by the ferry terminal at Holyhead. By using trains that cross Snowdonia (Conwy Valley line, Ffestiniog Railway and Cambrian Coast line), you can link with the

NORTH WALES

service that runs halfway along the Llŷn Peninsula to Pwllheli. Phone ☎ 0345-484950 for rail inquiries.

A North Wales Day Ranger (£11.40) covers a day's rail travel on the North Wales coast from Chester to Holyhead. It's valid on all trains after 9 am, from Monday to Friday, and all day at weekends.

See the Snowdonia National Park section later in this chapter for information on transport in that region.

North-Eastern Wales

Most travellers pass through this area of Wales to reach Snowdonia, but along the valley of the River Dee are a number of places worth stopping at. The International Musical Eisteddfod is held in Llangollen in July, although the town has enough alternative attractions to merit a visit at any time of year. However, the northern coast of this section, from the English border to Colwyn Bay, has little of great interest.

WREXHAM

- *pop 40,000*   • ☎ *01978*

The unappealing town of Wrexham is situated in the Clywedog Valley, near the border with England. The main reason for coming here is to see Erddig, the 17th-century stately home two miles to the south.

The TIC (☎ 292015) in Lambpit St is open all year.

Erddig

This house, inhabited by the Yorke family until 1973, gives probably the best insight in Britain into the 'upstairs-downstairs' relationship that existed between the upper classes and their servants. The Yorkes lived here for more than 200 years, and were known for the respect with which they treated their servants. Upstairs is a fine collection of furniture and an impressive state bed. Downstairs are photographs of servants through the ages and an interesting collection of household devices, such as the box

mangle, which was filled with heavy stones and rolled over the laundry. Outside is a 2000-acre country park, where there are pleasant walks.

Erddig house (☎ 313333; NT) and grounds are open from early April to early October, daily except Thursday and Friday, from 11 am to 6 pm for the grounds and from 12 to 5 pm for the house. Last admission to the house is at 4 pm. During October, the house is open from noon to 4 pm (last entry 3 pm).

Because Erddig is very popular, timed entry tickets may be issued. Entry to the grounds, family rooms and below stairs is £5.20/2.60, while entry to the grounds and below stairs only costs £3.40/1.70.

Places to Stay

If you want to stay in Wrexham, *Monfa Guest House* (☎ 354888), 65 Ruabon Rd, charges from £13 per person for B&B. *Abbotsfield Priory Hotel*, (☎ 261211), 29 Rhosddu Rd, offers B&B for £27/40 for a single/double.

Getting There & Away

National Express has one service a day from London. Crosville Cymru (☎ 363760) operates service No 1 from Chester to Wrexham, from Monday to Saturday every 15 minutes, and hourly on Sunday.

Wrexham is accessible by train from London via Shrewsbury, and also from Liverpool. There are departures every two hours from Shrewsbury (40 minutes, £4.10).

LLANGOLLEN

- *pop 2600*   • ☎ *01978*

Llangollen is famous for its International Musical Eisteddfod. The six-day music and dance festival attracts folk groups from around the world.

This attractive town makes an excellent base for outdoor activities, such as walks to ruined Valle Crucis Abbey and the Horseshoe Pass, horse-drawn canal-boat trips and canoeing on the River Dee.

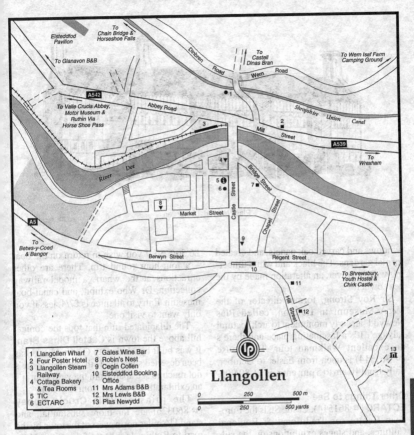

1 Llangollen Wharf
2 Four Poster Hotel
3 Llangollen Steam Railway
4 Cottage Bakery & Tea Rooms
5 TIC
6 ECTARC
7 Gales Wine Bar
8 Robin's Nest
9 Cegin Collen
10 Eisteddfod Booking Office
11 Mrs Adams B&B
12 Mrs Lewis B&B
13 Plas Newydd

Llangollen

NORTH WALES

Orientation & Information

Covering both banks of the River Dee, Llangollen is small enough to walk around. The TIC (☎ 860828), in the Town Hall, Castle St, is open daily from 10 am to 6 pm during the summer.

International Musical Eisteddfod

The International Musical Eisteddfod was first held in 1947. It now takes place in a purpose-built venue by the river over six days every July. It's a massive affair, with over 12,000 performers – choirs, musicians, folk singers and dancers – and crowds of more than 120,000. The occasion attracts famous names – Pavarotti in 1996, for example. Phone ☎ 860236 for details. The booking office is in the centre of town.

Plas Newydd

This was the home of the so-called Ladies of Llangollen, Lady Eleanor Butler and Sarah Ponsonby, who lived here from 1780 to 1829. In their own words, the women were 'seized with the oak-carving mania' and they set about transforming their house into a bizarre combination of Gothic and Tudor romantic styles. They added stained-glass

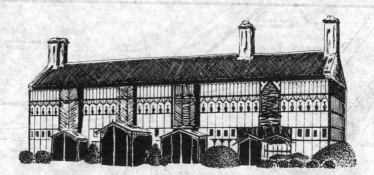

Plas Newydd, Llangollen

windows and carved oak panels, and created formal gardens. The black and white timbering was, however, an alteration made by the next owner.

Sir Roy Strong, former director of the V&A Museum in London, called Plas Newydd 'an early monument to architectural salvage'. It's a fascinating place and there's an excellent Walkman tour. The house (☎ 861314) is open from Easter to October, daily from 10 am to 5 pm; entry is £1.80/90p.

Other Things to See

ECTARC (☎ 861514), Castle St, is the European Centre for Traditional & Regional Cultures, and stages exhibitions on the cultures of lesser known European groupings. It's open daily from 10 am to 5 pm (11 am to 4 pm on Sunday); entry is free.

The **Llangollen Steam Railway** (☎ 860979) runs over a seven-mile line via Berwyn and the Horseshoe Falls to Glyndyrfrdwy and Carrog (£6/3), from April to October daily, and on weekends throughout the year.

Horse-drawn boats follow the canal from **Llangollen Wharf** (☎ 860702). Boats (£2.50/1.50) depart regularly for the 30-minute trip daily. There's also a two-hour trip over the Pontcysyllte Aqueduct (126 feet above the River Dee) for £5.50/4.50, or

£6.50/5.50 if you wish to return on the boat – a four-hour round trip. There are other attractions at the wharf, a model railway collection, Dr Who exhibit, and canal-boat museum. Entry to all three is £7/4, less if you only want to visit one.

The dilapidated ruin that tops the conical hill above the town is **Castell Dinas Bran**. It was built by Madoc ap Gruffydd and has been deserted since the 16th century. There's not much to see apart from the views but it's an exhilarating walk up from the town.

The ruins of **Valle Crucis Abbey** (☎ 860326) are far more substantial, and stand 1½ miles north-west of the town by the road to Ruthin. In a beautiful setting, Valle Crucis is rather like a smaller version of Tintern Abbey (see the South Wales chapter). In the care of Cadw, it's open daily from April to September, 10 am to 5 pm; entry is £1.70/1.20. Along the road out here you pass a small **Motor Museum**, open daily in summer.

Chirk Castle (☎ 01691-777701) is a magnificent Marcher fortress, five miles south-east of Llangollen and with superb views over the surrounding country. It was built in 1310, and adapted for more comfortable living from about the 16th century. It's open from April to September, daily except Monday and Saturday, and also in October

The Ladies of Llangollen

Lady Eleanor Butler and the Honorable Sarah Ponsonby, the Ladies of Llangollen, lived in Plas Newydd from 1780 to 1829 with their maid, Mary Carryl. They fell in love in Ireland where they were brought up in aristocratic Anglo-Irish families. Their families discouraged the relationship and, in a desperate bid to be allowed to live together, they eloped to Wales disguised as men. They set up home in Llangollen, to devote themselves to 'friendship, celibacy and the knitting of stockings'.

Their romantic friendship became well known yet respected, and they were visited by many literary and national figures of the day, including the Duke of Wellington, the Duke of Gloucester, Richard Brinsley Sheridan, Robert Southey, William Wordsworth and Sir Walter Scott. Wordsworth called them 'sisters in love, a love allowed to climb, even on this earth above the reach of time'. He was less accepting of Plas Newydd, which he called 'a low browed cot'.

Their relationship with their maid, Mary Carryl, was also close – most unusual for those days. She managed to buy the freehold of Plas Newydd and left it to them when she died. They erected a large monument to her in the graveyard at the Church of St Collen in Bridge St, where they are also buried. Lady Eleanor died in 1829, Sarah Ponsonby two years later. ■

on Sunday only, from 12.30 to 5 pm; entry is £4/2. There are buses to Chirk from Llangollen.

Activities

The two best walks in the area are along the canal to the Horseshoe Falls or up to Dinas Bran.

Llangollen is well known for canoeing and there are several centres. Jim Jayes (☎ 860763), Mile End Mill, Berwyn Rd, half a mile from Llangollen, charges from £6 to £12 per person per hour. You can also go white-water rafting, which costs £8 per person. There's bunkhouse accommodation here (see Places to Stay).

Places to Stay

There are plenty of places to stay, but for accommodation in July around the time of the Eisteddfod, you should book long in advance. If you're coming to Llangollen for the canoeing, some of the canoe centres also offer cheap accommodation.

The *Llangollen Youth Hostel & Activity Centre* (☎ 860330) is a Victorian manor house 1½ miles east of the centre. It's open daily from April to October, and the nightly charge is £8.25/5.55. The *Mill Café & Bunkhouse* (☎ 869043), Mile End Mill, Berwyn Rd, half a mile from Llangollen, charges £6 to £8 per person for dormitory accommodation.

Eirianfa Camp Site (☎ 860919) charges £5 for a tent and two people. It's about one mile from Llangollen, towards Betws-y-Coed. *Wern Isaf Farm* (☎ 860632) is across the river and to the east, half a mile from the school.

Mrs Lewis (☎ 860882), 1 Bodwen Villas, Hill St, offers B&B at around £16 per person and is centrally located. Also in Hill St is *Mrs Adams* (☎ 860770), at 3 Aberadda Cottages. B&B costs £15 in a room with bath attached.

Gales Wine Bar (☎ 860089), 18 Bridge St, has 15 very comfortable singles/doubles at £35/48 with bathroom. It's one of the most pleasant places to stay and is right in the centre of town. There's good-value food in the wine bar.

There's a company in town that deals in four-poster beds and keeps many of the hotels supplied with its product – affixed with a sticker that says 'Beds serviced by...', whatever that means. The *Four Poster Hotel* (☎ 861062), Mill St, specialises in four-posters, charging from £20 per person.

Places to Eat

Piersons Butchers, beside the TIC, is good for a snack, and sells hot barbecued chicken. The nearby delicatessen *James Bailey* does good home-made pies. Try a Welsh Oggie (meat, potato and onion pasty).

Cegin Collen (☎ 860091) on Castle St has quiche, home-made lasagne and apple pie

NORTH WALES

and cream, as well as lots of magazines to read while you eat. *Cottage Bakery & Tea Rooms* on Castle St do good cream teas.

Robin's Nest (☎ 861425) in Market St does jacket potatoes and light lunches. In the evening, main dishes cost from £5.25 to £9.50.

Gales Wine Bar (☎ 860089), 18 Bridge St, is an excellent place for a meal. Prices for dishes range from £1.50 for a jacket potato. Cranberry chicken is £6.25, fillet steak £8.25. The home-made ice cream is highly recommended.

Meals on wheels are available at weekends on the Llangollen Steam Railway (see the earlier section). A three-course lunch or dinner costs around £18.

Getting There & Away

Llangollen is 10 miles from Wrexham and there are frequent buses between these two places. There's a daily National Express bus to London.

Bryn Melyn (☎ 01978-860701) runs bus services from Ruabon and then on to Wrexham, hourly from Monday to Saturday. Public transport to Snowdonia is very limited. Bus No 94 runs to Dolgellau where you can pick up the No 2 for Aberystwyth.

The railway station here only serves the Llangollen Steam Railway; the nearest mainline station is at Ruabon, on the Shrewsbury to Chester main line. Services operate every two hours from Shrewsbury to Ruabon (30 minutes, £3.90). A taxi from Ruabon costs about £5 – contact Llangollen Taxis (☎ 861018).

Snowdonia National Park

Snowdonia is the second-largest national park in Britain, after the Lake District. Although the Snowdonia Mountains cover a fairly compact area, in the north they loom

over the coast and are undeniably spectacular.

The area around Mt Snowdon, at 3560 feet the highest peak in Britain south of the Scottish Highlands, is the busiest part of the park. About half a million people climb, walk or take the train to the summit each year. This was the area where members of the first successful attempt on Mt Everest trained, and it's been the training ground for many of Britain's best-known mountaineers since then.

The Welsh name for Snowdon is Yr Widdfa, which means 'great tomb' – legend says that a giant who was killed by King Arthur is buried on the summit. The English name is said to have been derived from an old word for snow, which crowns the peaks in winter.

As well as impressive mountains, the park contains a wide variety of other natural features – rivers, lakes, waterfalls, forests, moorlands, glacial valleys and a lovely coastline.

Despite the inhospitable nature of this rugged area, Snowdonia has provided both a home and a store of valuable natural resources for people since it was shaped by the retreating glaciers of the Ice Age. There are Stone-Age burial chambers at Dyffryn Ardudwy and Capel Garmon; Bronze-Age burial cairns at Bryn Cader Faner near Talsarnau; a hill fort at Pen-y-Gaer; Roman forts at Caerhun, Tomen-y-Mur and Caer Gai; and Welsh and Norman castles. The mountains sheltered Llywelyn ap Gruffydd in the 13th century and Owain Glyndŵr in the 15th, during their struggle to reclaim Wales from the English.

The remains of the huge mining and quarrying operations that were once a major industry can still be seen. There's now more money to be made from tourism, and so the former slate quarries and gold and copper mines are being turned into visitor attractions. Blaenau Ffestiniog now has two slate mines open to the public.

Snowdon and the nearby town of Llanberis form the main target for most visitors, but there's good mountain walking in

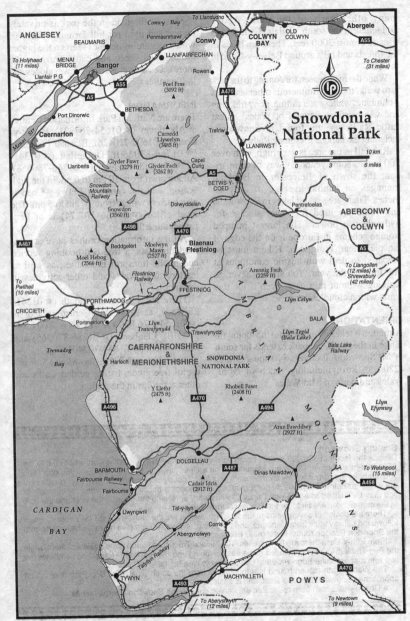

Snowdonia
National Park

many other parts of the park. Above Dolgellau in the south, Cadair (Cader) Idris rises to almost 3000 feet. There are hikes in the forests and hills around Betws-y-Coed in the east.

While the main reason for coming to the park is to walk, there are numerous other activities – climbing, white-water rafting, pony trekking and windsurfing. Several of Wales' 'Great Little Railways' are found in Snowdonia, including the famous Ffestiniog Railway.

Rainfall in the area is very high, with over 200 inches some years. By way of comparison, the town of Leicester in England manages an annual average of only 25 inches. There are several lakes in Snowdonia and some are used for water storage for hydroelectric power. The largest pumped storage scheme in Europe is on the edge of the park near Tanigrisau. Hikers must be prepared to deal with hostile conditions at any time of the year. You should never go walking without rain gear, even if the day starts with a cloudless sky.

ORIENTATION
Although it takes its name from the mountain range in the north, the park extends far south of Mt Snowdon. It covers 840 square miles (2200 sq km), including much of North Wales and parts of Mid Wales.

Most of the land in the park is privately owned and used for hill farming. Herds of wild goats are sometimes seen on the higher ground, and sheep and cattle graze on the more accessible grass of the lower slopes and in the valleys.

INFORMATION
There are National Park Information Centres at Aberdovey (☎ 01654-767321), Betws-y-Coed (☎ 01690-710426), Blaenau Ffestiniog (☎ 01766-830360), Dolgellau (☎ 01341-422888) and Harlech (☎ 01766-780658). All are open from 10 am to 6 pm in the high season, and the centre at Betws-y-Coed is also open in winter from 10 am to 5 pm. The head office (☎ 01766-770274) is at Penrhyndeudraeth.

All the information centres have accommodation lists, a free bed-booking service and public transport timetables, as well as leaflets about walks and other activities in the area.

There are TICs at Barmouth (☎ 01341-280787), at the Craft Centre in Corris (☎ 01654- 761244), Tywyn (01654-710070), Llanberis (☎ 01286-870765) and Machynlleth (☎ 01654-702401).

Available from TICs, *Snowdonia Star* is a useful free guide, listing guided walks and other activities in the region.

Scaling Snowdon
Despite the fact that 500,000 people tramp up Snowdon every year, it's still a worthwhile hike to the 3560-foot-high summit. Views are stupendous on a clear day, and even if it's cloudy you often find you're above the clouds – they swirl beneath your feet, occasionally clearing to give brief glimpses of the valley far below. It's probably not a great idea to choose a midsummer weekend for this walk or you may be inclined to agree with Prince Charles who, on seeing the crowds, the litter and the café at the summit, declared it to be the 'highest slum in Europe'.

There's a choice of seven paths to the top. The easiest are the Llanberis Path (5½ hours), which follows the railway track from Llanberis, and the Snowdon Ranger Path (five hours), which starts from the Snowdon Ranger Youth Hostel (near Beddgelert).

From Pen-y-Pass there are three routes. The Miners' Track (five hours) is the easiest of them, while the Pyg Track (5½ hours) includes some easy climbing and the Snowdon Horseshoe combines the two with a spectacular ridge walk that can take up to nine hours.

The Watkin Path (seven hours) is a tough walk from the south. The Rhyd Ddu Path (five hours) approaches Snowdon from the west, and is easier.

All these walks start from roads that are served daily by the Snowdon Sherpa bus. ∎

WALKS

The National Park publishes a useful series of leaflets (20p each) on many of the mountain walks, including one on each of the six routes up Snowdon. They're available from TICs and information centres.

Although there are walks of all grades, you should be aware that even some walks described as easy may follow paths that go near very steep slopes and over loose scree. Take the Pyg Path up Snowdon and you'll find yourself literally climbing parts of it. Inevitably, with so many people on the mountains, accidents happen – usually on the way down. Each year, an average of 70 serious incidents occur and about 10 people end their lives up here. Be properly equipped before setting out, with food, drink, warm clothing and waterproofs.

The National Park organises a wide variety of five to six-mile guided walks at various levels of difficulty. Charges are around £2.

CYCLE ROUTES

The high level of use of bridleways for off-road cycling to the summit of Snowdon has led to erosion and fears for walkers' safety. A ban is now in place and cycling is not allowed between 10 am and 5 pm, June to September.

In the Gwydyr Forest near Betws-y-Coed are two waymarked routes. The local information centre has details.

OTHER ACTIVITIES
Pony Trekking & Horse Riding

There are many stables offering escorted and unescorted rides. Snowdonia Riding Stables (☎ 01286-650342) is based at Waunfawr, on the western edge of the park near Caernarfon. It offers escorted rides only – one hour costs £10 and a full day £40. The stables are near the bus stop in Waunfawr, and the No 95 Sherpa bus service between Caernarfon and Llanberis stops here.

Meifod Isaf Riding & Trekking Centre (☎ 0341-247651), on the outskirts of Dyffryn Ardudwy, between Harlech and Barmouth, is open from early April to October and offers rides from £7.50 for one hour to £14 for an afternoon.

Narrow-Gauge Railway Journeys

One of the features of this area is the number of narrow-gauge railways. The Ffestiniog Railway runs from Porthmadog to Blaenau Ffestiniog, Snowdon Mountain Railway from Llanberis to the summit, and Talyllyn from Tywyn to Abergynolwyn. Shorter lines include the Llanberis Lake Railway, the Fairbourne Railway, the Bala Lake Railway and the Welsh Highland Railway. See the later sections of this chapter for details.

PLACES TO STAY

There are 11 youth hostels in the park, among them some of the best in the country.

Around Mt Snowdon, there are hostels at Pen-y-Pass (☎ 01286-870428), near Llanberis on the Pyg and Llyn Llydaw Miner's tracks up to the summit; Llanberis (☎ 01286-870280); Bryn Gwynant (☎ 01766-890251), Nant Gwynant, four miles from Beddgelert near the Watkin Path up Snowdon; Snowdon Ranger (☎ 01286-650391), five miles from Beddgelert at the starting point for the Ranger Path; and Idwal Cottage (☎ 01248-600225), Nant Ffrancon, near Bethesda.

There are also hostels at Capel Curig (☎ 01690-720225), five miles from Betws-y-Coed; Lledr Valley (☎ 01690-750202), on the main road between Betws-y-Coed and Ffestiniog; Rowen (☎ 01492-530627), five miles from Conwy; Llanbedr (☎ 01341-241287), Plas Newydd (near Harlech); Kings (☎ 01341-422392), Penmaenpool, near Dolgellau; and Bala (☎ 01678-520215).

In addition to the hostels, there are bunkhouses and camping grounds. To camp on a non-official site, you need to get the permission of the landowner.

Within the park, Betws-y-Coed has the most B&Bs and guesthouses; others are found in smaller villages and on farms.

GETTING THERE & AWAY

Bus

National Express (☎ 0990-808080) has services from London to Llandudno and Bangor twice daily, and from London to Aberystwyth once daily.

Crosville Cymru (☎ 01492-596969) operates a Trans-Cambria service (No 701) once daily from Cardiff through Machynlleth, Dolgellau and Caernarfon to Bangor.

Train

There's a regular InterCity service from London's Euston station via Crewe (where you may have to change) to Llandudno Junction and Bangor, with at least one train an hour. Change at Llandudno Junction for the Conwy Valley line, which connects Llanrwst, Betws-y-Coed, Pont-y-Pant and Blaenau Ffestiniog.

There's also an InterCity service from London via Birmingham to Shrewsbury, where you can take the line to Machynlleth for the scenic Cambrian Coast Railway via Harlech to Pwllheli.

For all rail inquiries phone ☎ 0345-484950.

GETTING AROUND

Despite the reorganisation of county boundaries, bus and rail information for the area continues to be produced in the useful *Gwynedd Public Transport Guide*, available from TICs. Phone ☎ 01286-679535 for information.

Many bus companies operate services in the area and several share a route, often with one company operating during the week and another at weekends. Red Rover passes allow unlimited travel for a day on routes within the park as well as from access points, such as Wrexham and Aberystwyth, for £4.20.

Two Snowdon Sherpa bus services operate in the area – these are particularly good for walkers and for people staying in youth hostels. The buses will stop on request at any safe place in the park, and they follow a round-the-mountain route so that walkers can go up one path and down another. Route 95 goes from Caernarfon to Beddgelert five times a day, and once a day on to Llanberis throughout the year (daily except Sunday). Route 19 goes from Llandudno via Llanrwst, Betws-y-Coed and Pen-y-Pass Youth Hostel to Llanberis. The service operates three times daily (seven times a day from Llandudno to Llanrwst) from Easter to October.

Apart from the narrow-gauge railways, there are three lines within the park that are useful for travellers – the Conwy Valley line, the Cambrian Coast line and the Ffestiniog Railway (see Getting There & Away).

If you plan to do a lot of travelling in one day, the North & Mid Wales Day Ranger allows travel on Bus Gwynedd and Crosville Cymru services (except the 700 series), and most trains, including the Ffestiniog Railway, with discounts on many of the private railways. Only available for travel after 9 am, the ticket costs £16 for one day's travel. There's also the North & Mid Wales Rover, with the same bus and train coverage and restrictions. This costs £38 for seven days travel, or £24.50 for three days within a seven-day period. Family tickets for two adults and up to four children are available and offer good value.

BETWS-Y-COED

- *pop 700* • ☎ *01690*

Betus (as it's known and pronounced) is a tourist village that styles itself as the eastern gateway to the park. The name means Chapel (or Prayer House) in the Wood, because of the 14th-century church here, and the village is still in an attractive woodland setting in the Gwydyr Forest.

Betws-y-Coed has been Wales' most popular inland resort since the Victorian days, and it gets very crowded in summer. There are walks to Swallow and Conwy Falls nearby, and pleasant hikes in the surrounding hills. It can make a reasonable base for walking in the Snowdon range, particularly if you have your own transport, but you may wish to stay in one of the villages closer to the mountains.

Orientation & Information

There are only two streets of note, so it's easy to find your way around.

The National Park Information Centre (☎ 710426) is in Royal Oak Stables, at the far end of the playing fields past the railway station.

On the High St, Climber & Rambler (☎ 710555) is an outdoor shop that also sells books and has information on walking, climbing and scrambling in the area.

Things to See & Do

There's little to do here except walk and take tea, which in this case is enough. There are two museums, neither of very great interest. **Betws-y-Coed Motor Museum** (☎ 710760) is a small collection near the information centre; entry is £1.30/80p. There's also the **Conwy Valley Railway Museum** (☎ 710568), which is adjacent to the railway station.

There's **pony trekking** at Ty Coch Farm (☎ 760248), Penmachno, six miles from Betws-y-Coed. Rides through the Gwydyr Forest cost from £8 for an hour. The farm also does a popular pub ride for £20, lasting around four hours.

Walks & Cycle Routes

The information centre has details of a number of walks in the surrounding area.

The popular Bridges & Rivers walk is an easy hike that takes two to three hours and starts from outside the information centre. You pass the meeting point of the Llugwy and Conwy rivers, the Waterloo Bridge, built in 1815 (of course) and decorated with leek, rose, shamrock and thistle. The next bridge is Pont-y-Pair – the Bridge of the Cauldron – which was built in the 15th century, and finally there's the Miners' Bridge.

Mountain bikes can be hired from Beics Betws (☎ 710766), Tan Lan, behind the post office. They charge £14 a day and can advise on routes.

Places to Stay

Betus has the largest number of beds in the park, and there are B&Bs and hotels to suit all budgets.

There are two youth hostels, both about five miles away. *Ledr Valley Youth Hostel* (☎ 01690-750202), Pont-y-Pant, is on the A470, and there's also the *Capel Curig Youth Hostel* (see the Capel Curig section).

In the High St, *Cross Keys Hotel & Restaurant* (☎ 710334) charges £20/25 for B&B (£35 for a double with attached bath). Next door is *Glan Llugwy* (☎ 710592), which is similarly priced, and non-smoking.

Closer to the centre, and also on the High St, the *Pont-y-Pair Hotel* (☎ 710407) charges around £15 per person. In the centre of town, on the High St near the green, is the *Plas Dderwen Hotel & Restaurant* (☎ 710388). B&B is around £17 per person.

There are several places on Llanrwst Rd, which is off the A470 heading to Llandudno and half a mile from Waterloo Bridge. The excellent *Bron Celyn Guest House* (☎ 710333) offers B&B at £16 for a basic single or £38 for a double with attached bath. *Bryn Bella Guest House* (☎ 710627), also on Llanrwst Rd, charges from £18/30. The proprietors of both guesthouses will pick you up from the railway station.

East of Betws-y-Coed in Capel Garmon is *Tan-y-Foes Country House* (☎ 710507). In a 16th-century stone building, it's a very comfortable non-smoking hotel. There are nine rooms, some with four-poster beds, and a swimming pool. B&B is from £55 per person but they also offer short-stay options.

Ty Gwyn (☎ 710383), south of the bridge in the village, is a 17th-century coaching inn, where B&B costs from £17.50 per person, rising to £27 for a room with attached bathroom or £35 per person for a four-poster bed. There's a good restaurant.

Places to Eat

Right beside the railway station is *Dil's Diner* (☎ 710346), where you can get a filling meal for between £3 and £5. Open from 8.30 am until around 8 pm, it is also licensed.

There are several teashops along the High St. The *Pont-y-Pair Hotel* does good bar

NORTH WALES

food. Three doors down is *Three Gables Restaurant*, where they do a three-course set lunch for under £9.

The top restaurant is at the *Ty Gwyn* (see Places to Stay). Prices are reasonable (£8.50 for pheasant in wild mushroom and wine sauce) and servings are generous. If you want to drink in the bar here the licence demands that you must also have a meal.

Getting There & Away

Betws-y-Coed is served by rail and bus from Llandudno Junction. There are six trains a day, Monday to Saturday, on the Conwy Valley line from Llandudno (25 minutes, £2.90).

Buses take about 10 minutes longer from Llandudno Junction to Betus. Snowdon Sherpa buses run from Llandudno to Conwy, Betws-y-Coed, Capel Curig and Pen-y-Pass (for the youth hostels), then on to Llanberis and Caernarfon.

CAPEL CURIG

Six miles west of Betws-y-Coed is a small village that is one of the oldest resorts in the area. It's a popular place with walkers, climbers and outdoor enthusiasts of all types.

The Plas Y Brenin National Mountain Centre (☎ 01690-720280) is on the edge of the village and has a bar and climbing wall. They run two-day courses in canoeing and abseiling, and most evenings at 8 pm there are lectures that are open to all. They can rent equipment and also offer some accommodation.

The *Capel Curig Youth Hostel* (☎ 01690-720225) is open daily from mid-February to mid-December. It's in the village, next to the garage. The nightly charge is £8.25/5.55.

In the evenings, everyone meets at the *Bryn Tyrch* (☎ 720223), a hotel with a busy pub, or at the bar at Plas Y Brenin.

The Snowdon Sherpa bus passes this way between Betws and Llanberis.

LLANBERIS
- *pop 2000*   • ☎ 01286

This tourist village lies at the foot of Mt Snowdon and becomes packed with walkers

and climbers. It makes an excellent base, although accommodation can be booked out in July and August.

Orientation & Information

It's bypassed by the A4086, which also separates the village from its two lakes, Llyn Padarn and Llyn Peris. The TIC (☎ 870765) is on the High St, opposite the post office. Almost all the accommodation and places to eat are strung out along this street – you can't get lost.

Snowdon Mountain Railway

Snowdon Mountain Railway (☎ 870223), Britain's only public rack-and-pinion railway, opened in 1896 and climbs more than 3000 feet from Llanberis to the summit of Snowdon, a five-mile journey that takes an hour.

Seven vintage steam locomotives and four modern diesel locomotives haul carriages up and down between mid-March and the end of October. Schedules are subject to the weather but trains usually start running at 9 am. The queues can be long during the main part of the season. If you can't be bothered walking to the top of Snowdon, you're made to pay for your laziness – a return ride is £14. It's sometimes also possible to buy a standby ticket down from the top for £6.

Other Things to See & Do

Across the bypass, the **Snowdonia Museum** adopts the Disney approach to Welsh history, with talking trees and a brief scattering of historical facts. The **Dinorwig Discovery** tour also starts here. Visits to this underground power station built deep inside the mountain are quite interesting. Dinorwig is a quick-response power station, constructed to deal with power surges on the national grid when half the population of Britain simultaneously puts the kettle on during the commercial breaks on TV. Combined tickets for the museum and power station are £5/2.50; they're both open daily from March to November.

The **Llanberis Lake Railway** (☎ 870549) runs beside Llyn Padarn between March and

October. The round trip takes 45 minutes and costs £3.90. The **Welsh Slate Museum** (☎ 870630) is on the site of the old Dinorwic Quarry, on the shore of Llyn Padarn. Visits to the old quarry workshops and demonstrations of the skills involved in splitting slate into tiles are interesting. The museum is open from April to September, 9.30 am to 5.30 pm; entry is £2.

Dolbadarn Castle (Cadw) is a 13th-century ruin that was built to guard Llanberis Pass. It's a pleasant walk south-east of the town.

Activities

Apart from hiking up Snowdon, there are numerous other outdoor activities in the area. The Dolbadarn Pony Trekking Centre (☎ 870277) operates from the Dolbadarn Hotel. It charges £10 per hour, hard hat included.

The Padarn Watersports Centre (☎ 870556), Llyn Padarn, offers a wide range of activities (kayaking, canoeing, raft building, climbing, abseiling and mountain walking) for groups of two to four people (or more). The charge for a group of five for half a day is £21 per person – whatever the activity.

Places to Stay

Hostels There's dormitory accommodation at the *Heights Hotel* (☎ 871179), 74 High St, from £7.50.

Surrounded by Welsh Black cattle, and with a good view over the top of the slate quarry, *Llanberis Youth Hostel* (☎ 870280) was originally a quarry manager's dwelling. It's half a mile south-west of the town and is open from April to August, daily. For the rest of the year it's open for most of the week – phone for opening days. The nightly charge is £8.25/5.55.

Pen-y-Pass Youth Hostel (☎ 870428) is superbly situated at the top of Llanberis Pass, 5½ miles from Llanberis. It was once a hotel popular with Victorian mountaineers. The hostel is open daily from January to October, and over the new year; a bed with a view costs £9.10/6.15.

Gwastadnant Bunkhouse (☎ 870356) is at Nant Peris, two miles out of Llanberis on the way to Pen-y-Pass. There's bunkhouse accommodation from £4 per person, camping for £2.50 and B&B from £13. Facilities include a coin-operated drying room, showers and cooker.

About three miles from Llanberis on the Bangor road, *Jesse James Bunkhouse* (☎ 870521), Penisarwaen, has been going since 1966 and is a popular walkers' base – non-smokers only. JJ is a mountain guide who offers accommodation from £6.50 to £12.

Camping Just past Llanberis Youth Hostel is *Hafodlydan Campsite*. They charge £1.50 a night per person. *Cae Gwyn Camp Site* (☎ 870718), at Nant Peris, two miles from Llanberis, charges £2.

B&Bs & Hotels *Beech Bank Guest House* (☎ 870414), at the far end of High St from the station, overlooking the lake, charges £13.50 per person. Also at the Caernarfon end of Llanberis is the *Alpine Lodge Hotel* (☎ 870294), 1 High St, which has doubles/triples from £35/45 and a small single for £15.

Padarn Lake Hotel (☎ 870260), at the other end of the High St, also charges £31/52 for singles/doubles. *Dolbadarn Hotel* (☎ 870277), opposite, has rooms for £18/36 (£40 for a double with attached bath). The hotel has a restaurant and bar, and there's a riding school (see Activities) beside it. Nearby, *Y Gwynedd Hotel* (☎ 870203) charges £24/44 for rooms with bath.

Pen-y-Gwyrd Hotel (☎ 870211) is seven miles from Llanberis, just beyond Pen-y-Pass on the junction of the A498 and A4086. The place doubles as a mountain-rescue post. B&B is from £20 per person. The 1953 Everest team used the inn as a training base – you can see their signatures on the ceiling. The residents sit down together for the evening meal in the dining room, and bar food is also available.

At Llanrug, five miles north-west of Llanberis along the A4086, Lakeside

NORTH WALES

(☎ 870065) offers B&B from £24 per person. It's set in delightful surroundings with peacocks and ornamental fowl in the grounds. You can even watch a pair of barn owls from a hide near the lake.

In Llanberis, the top place to stay is the *Royal Victoria Hotel* (☎ 870253), near the Snowdon Mountain Railway station. It has rooms with attached bathroom at £43 per person, including breakfast, or £46.50 for dinner, bed & breakfast. There may be reduced rates when business is slow. In the restaurant, there are two three-course set menus, one at £9.95 and the other at £14.95.

Places to Eat

Pete's Eats (☎ 870358) is a warm café where hikers swap information over large portions of healthy food. For walking fodder, try their Big Jim – a mixed grill with bacon, sausages, liver, chips etc for £7.95. There are good vegetarian choices and the place is open from Easter to October, 9 am to 8 pm on weekdays and 8 am to 8 pm at weekends. For the rest of the year, it's open from 9 am to 6.30 pm during the week and from 8 am to 8 pm at weekends. There's a useful notice board here.

In the evenings, climbers hang out in *The Heights* (☎ 871179), a hotel (see Places to Stay) with a pub that even has its own climbing wall. For takeaways, there's *Chico's Chinese Takeaway* (☎ 872205), but it's closed on Wednesday.

Y Bistro (☎ 871278) is the place to go for a splurge – Welsh produce with a French twist. They serve char from Llyn Padarn when available. It's open only in the evening, with set dinners from £19 to £25.

Getting There & Away

Llanberis is 13 miles from Bangor. From Bangor, take the No 77 bus which runs nine times a day (at irregular intervals) from Monday to Saturday (45 minutes, £1.30). From Caernarfon, take bus No 88, which runs about twice-hourly from Monday to Saturday (25 minutes, £1). This service continues to Nant Peris.

There are five No 95 Sherpa buses a day

from Caernarfon (1¼ hours), Monday to Saturday, and about three daily in the high season from Llandudno (two hours).

BEDDGELERT

This is one of the most attractive of the Snowdon villages, situated on the banks of the River Gwynant. The name means Gelert's Grave; and comes from a local legend that tells of Prince Llewlyn's dog Gelert, killed by its owner after he thought it had savaged his baby son, when the dog had in fact killed a wolf that was attacking the baby.

Just outside the village is the **Sygun Copper Mine** (☎ 01766-890595), mined from Roman times until it was turned into a tourist attraction. It's open daily and entry is £4.25/2.90.

Places to Stay

The *Snowdon Ranger Youth Hostel* (☎ 01286-650391) is five miles north of the village. Fully open from April to August (phone for other opening days), the nightly charge is £8.25/5.55.

The *Bryn Gwynant Youth Hostel* (☎ 01766-890251) is four miles from Beddgelert on the A498, in an idyllic location beside Llyn Gwynant. It's open daily from mid-March to August and from mid-September to October; a bed costs £8.25/5.55.

For B&B, *Ael-y-Bryn* (☎ 01766-890310), in the centre of the village, charges from £15 per person. The *Sygun Fawr Hotel* (☎ 01766-890258) is about a mile from Beddgelert, in an old house. Rooms have attached bathroom and cost £39/52 for a single/double.

Getting There & Away

Beddgelert is on the route of the Snowdon Sherpa bus. There are several services a day to Caernarfon and Llanberis.

BLAENAU FFESTINIOG

• *pop 5500*   • ☎ *01766*

Slate was the basis of the wealth in Snowdonia in the 19th century and Blaenau

Ffestiniog was the centre of the industry. Although slate mining continues here on a small scale, it's now a tourist town. The history of the slate industry, the Ffestiniog Railway (which has its northern terminus here) and the hydroelectric power station are the main tourist attractions.

Despite being in the centre of the park, the grey slate waste tips which surround Blaenau Ffestiniog prevented it from being officially included in the national park. The two main mines in the area are in the town – nearby is the smaller village of Ffestiniog.

The National Park Information Centre (☎ 830360) is in the High St, in the same building as the Ffestiniog Railway Office.

Ffestiniog Railway

A means of access as well as an attraction, the Ffestiniog Railway (☎ 512340) is a 13½-mile narrow-gauge line extending from Porthmadog on the coast.

Construction of the line began in 1832. In 1836, horse-drawn wagons started to take the slate from the mine down to Porthmadog, from where it was shipped to Europe and America. In the 1860s, steam locomotives were introduced and the line was opened up as a passenger service.

The railway is open daily from March to October, 9.15 am to 5 pm. A return trip on a steam train is £12, and one child aged under 16 goes free with each ticket-holder. The return fare going out by diesel and returning by any train is £10. A 1st-class ticket allowing you to sit in the observation car or in a traditional vintage coach is £5 extra for a return ticket. Seat reservations can be made for 50p for journeys from Porthmadog.

Slate Mines

The **Llechwedd Slate Caverns** (☎ 830306) are open all year from 10 am to 6 pm (shorter hours in winter). You can ride into the tunnels on the miners' tramway, dating from 1846, or descend into the Deep Mine on the steepest passenger railway in Britain. As you walk through vast underground chambers, a commentary explains what it was like to work down here. Tickets cost £5.95/4.20 for a single tour and £9.15/6.25 for both tours.

The **Gloddfa Ganol Slate Mine** (☎ 830664) claims to be the world's largest slate mine. Visitors walk half a mile into the mine to explore the underground workings. There's also a working mill, interesting restored quarrymen's cottages and museums. The mine is open from April to October, Monday to Friday, from 10 am to 5.30 pm, and on Sunday from mid-July to the end of August; entry is £5/2.50.

Places to Stay & Eat

Most of the people who visit Blaenau Ffestiniog do so on day trips on the train. If you want to stay, there's a small choice of accommodation.

Afallon (☎ 830468) in Manod Rd is a friendly place with three rooms; B&B is £12.50 per person. It's only half a mile from the station but they will meet you. Right by the railway station is *Dolawel* (☎ 830511), where B&B is from £14.50 per person.

The excellent *Ty Clwb* (☎ 762658) is a modernised 18th-century stone guesthouse in the square, offering B&B from £18 per person.

Tyddyn Du Farm (☎ 590281) is about six miles outside the town at Gellilydan. There are three rooms in the 17th-century farmhouse, where B&B is from £17 to £20 per person.

Five miles south of Blaenau in the village of Maentwrog is the *Old Rectory* (☎ 590305), where upmarket B&B costs £38/49 for a single/double in the house, £25/36 in the annex. All rooms have bathroom attached. Also in Maentwrog, is *Grapes* (☎ 590208), a pub and restaurant that does excellent meals. As well as soup and sandwiches there are good main courses for £5 to £9. They sometimes do spit-roasts on the open fire in the restaurant.

Getting There & Away

From Monday to Saturday there are hourly buses from Caernarfon to Blaenau Ffestiniog (1½ hours, £3). There are also services to Harlech, Barmouth and Pwllheli. Bus No 35 goes to Dolgellau three times a day, Monday to Saturday.

The Conwy Valley line goes from Llandudno or Llandudno Junction via Betws-y-Coed to Blaenau Ffestiniog, five times a day, Monday to Saturday (35 minutes, £3.80). From Porthmadog there's the Ffestiniog Railway (see preceding section).

Getting Around
Bus No 140 takes a circular route between Blaenau Ffestiniog and the slate mines five times a day (less often in winter), from Monday to Saturday. The Red Rover ticket is not valid on this service.

HARLECH
* pop 1300　　•　☎ 01766

Dramatically sited above the plains, the substantial ruins of Harlech Castle dominate this sleepy little town. There are superb views out to sea and some good beaches nearby.

The TIC (☎ 780658) is in the High St and is open daily from April to October. The railway station is on the plain below the castle.

Harlech Castle
The castle (☎ 780552; Cadw) is a World Heritage site, and rightly so. Another creation of Edward I, it was built between 1283 and 1289. The castle is rectangular with two concentric sets of walls, and is constructed of local grey sandstone.

Harlech is sometimes called the Castle of Lost Causes because it has been defended so many times to no avail. It was taken in 1404 by Owain Glyndŵr and became his stronghold until 1409. He was in turn besieged here by the future Henry V. It was the last castle to fall in the Wars of the Roses – attacks on the Lancastrians by the Yorkists continued from 1461 until 1468. By Elizabethan times, the castle was in ruins except for the massive twin-towered gatehouse and the outer walls, which are still intact. They make the place seem impregnable even now.

When it was built, the sea covered the plain below, and ships could sail right to the foot of the castle stairway that is still in use today. The castle is open daily; entry is £3/2.

Places to Stay & Eat
Llanbedr Youth Hostel (☎ 01341-241287), Plas Newydd, Llanbedr, is three miles south of Harlech. It's fully open from May to August; phone for other opening times. The nightly charge is £7.45/5.

You can camp at *Min-y-Don Caravan & Camping Site* (☎ 780286), situated by the beach below Harlech, for £2 per person.

Godre'r Graig (☎ 780905) on Morfa Rd (called 'the bottom road' because it's under the castle) charges around £14 per person for B&B. In the upper part of the town, in the High St next to the church, *Byrdir Hotel* (☎ 780316) does B&B from £14.50 per person, or £18 in a room with attached bath.

The *Lion Hotel* (☎ 780731), near the castle, charges from £16 per person. There's cheap pub grub in the bar.

The *Castle Hotel* (☎ 780529), Castle Square, has some rooms with superb views – No 3 is the best, and it's £58 for two people. Nearby *Castle Cottage* (☎ 780479) is a very comfortable place to stay, with singles/doubles with bathroom from £35/52. It also has a few singles without bath for £24. This is also the best place to eat in Harlech with set dinners from £17.

Plas Café (☎ 780204), in the High St, boasts the finest view of any place to eat in Harlech – across to the castle and down to the sea. You can also sit outside. They serve a variety of dishes from £5, steaks are £8.95, and there are good vegetarian choices.

Getting There & Away
Trains run from Machynlleth to Harlech seven times a day (1½ hours, £6.90). Bus No 38 operates from Barmouth to Harlech (25 minutes) nine times a day and continues to Blaenau Ffestiniog five times a day.

BARMOUTH
* pop 2200　　•　☎ 01341

Barmouth is a popular seaside resort with a long sandy beach, and there are some pleas-

NORTH WALES

ant walks in the area. You can hike up on the cliffs of Dinas Oleu above the town or across the estuary to Fairbourne.

The TIC (☎ 280787) is on Station Rd. There are numerous hotels and B&Bs. *Just Beds* (☎ 281165), Bryn Teify, King Edward St, offers accommodation from £9 per person. *Wavecrest Hotel* (☎ 280330), 8 Marine Parade, is a friendly sea-front hotel with comfortable accommodation from £18 to £25 per person. It's also noted for its food.

TYWYN
This little seaside town is best known for the Talyllyn Railway (☎ 01654-710472), which runs seven miles inland to Abergynolwyn. Trains run daily in summer and are all steam-hauled; tickets are £7.50/2. There's a small **railway museum** containing narrow-gauge locomotives by the station in Tywyn.

The Tywyn TIC (☎ 01654-710070) is in the High St.

DOLGELLAU
• *pop 2300*   • ☎ *01341*

Dolgellau (pronounced doll-geth-lie) is a market town that makes a good base for walks on Cadair Idris, the second-highest mountain in Snowdonia National Park.

In the 15th century, the town was Owain Glyndwr's capital, and his parliament was held here. The town has historical links with the Quaker movement, which established a community in the area. The TIC offers theme walks round the various Quaker sites in the summer. In the 18th century, Dolgellau was the centre of the prosperous Welsh wool industry; it's now the administrative centre for the region.

The National Park Information Centre (☎ 422888) is in Ty Meirion, Eldon Square. The centre is open daily in summer from 10 am to 6 pm.

Things to See
The **Gwynfynydd Gold Mine** is the only working gold mine open to the public; it's the main source of Welsh gold. Mining started here in the 1860s and it's been one of the most productive gold mines in Britain.

The mine's heyday was at the turn of the century. Tours start in the Welsh Gold Centre (☎ 423332), and you're then taken to the mine, six miles away. The mine is open daily from Easter to October, 9.30 am to 5 pm (4 pm in winter and closed on Sunday). They're obviously onto a gold mine here – the entry charge is a hefty £9.50/5!

No payment is necessary to see the interesting display at the **Quaker Heritage Centre**, above the TIC. It's open from March to October, 10 am to 6 pm.

Walks
The information centre has leaflets on local walks, including National Park descriptions of the trails up Cadair Idris. The standard route up Cadair Idris is the Pony Track from Ty Nant, a return trip of four to five hours. It can be wild up here if the weather comes down. Francis Kilvert wrote of his 1871 trip in *Kilvert's Diary*, describing it as 'the stoniest, dreariest, most desolate mountain I was ever on...It is an awful place in a storm. I thought of Moses on Sinai'. On a sunny summer's day, however, it's glorious.

The least energetic walk is the town trail. The Precipice Walk, which sounds rather more lethal than it actually is, starts near Llanfachreth and takes in wonderful views of the Mawddach Estuary.

Places to Stay
According to local legend, anyone who spends the night on top of Cadair Idris will wake either as a poet or go mad. Luckily there's a wide range of accommodation in the area.

There's a camping barn, camping ground and tearoom at *Ty Nant* (☎ 423433), Ffordd y Gader. The stone barn sleeps 12 (£3 per person) – all you need is a foam mat and sleeping bag. Gas cookers and cooking utensils are available. *Caban Cader Idris* (☎ 423178) is in a secluded valley at Islawrdref, about three miles south-west of Dolgellau. The nightly charge is £6 per person.

One mile out of Dolgellau is *Glynn Farm* (☎ 422286), with lovely views of the

Mawddach Estuary. B&B is from £14.50 per person, or £17 with attached bath. There's a small single for £13. The excellent *Tanyfron* (☎ 422638), Arran Rd, is half a mile from Dolgellau. B&B is £18 per person; non-smokers are preferred. There's also a camping ground, which costs from £6.50 per tent.

Ivy House (☎ 422535) is centrally located in Finsbury Square. B&B is from £18 per person; there's a bar and the restaurant serves good Welsh food. *Clifton House Hotel* (☎ 422554), Smithfield Square, is similarly-priced.

Dolserau Hall Hotel (☎ 422522) is 1½ miles outside Dolgellau. The hotel is open all year and charges from £39 per person for B&B. It's in a peaceful location and there are excellent views from the rooms.

Penmaenuchaf Hall Hotel (☎ 422129), two miles from Dolgellau at Penmaenpool, is the most luxurious hotel in the area, a peaceful retreat in 21-acre grounds. Charges are from £47.50 to £75 per person.

Places to Eat

Dylanwad Da Restaurant (☎ 422870), 2 Ffos-y-Felin, is a good place for dinner with main dishes from about £7 to £12. Lamb and apricot casserole is £9.60. There are several vegetarian choices. The *Old Country Gaol Restaurant* in the Clifton House Hotel serves good Welsh food.

Outside Dolgellau, in Penmaenpool, is the *George III* (☎ 422525), a pub that offers a wide range of reasonable food; daily specials are £4.75.

Getting There & Away

Crosville Cymru operates several services to Dolgellau. Bus No 2 from Caernarfon (1½ hours, £3.45) operates six times a day, Monday to Saturday, and twice a day on Sunday; the No 94 from Barmouth (22 minutes) operates six times a day, Monday to Saturday; and the No 34 from Aberystwyth/Machynlleth (35 minutes) operates six times a day from Monday to Saturday, twice a day on Sunday. Bus No 35

goes to Blaenau Ffestiniog three times a day, Monday to Saturday.

The No 780 runs from Shrewsbury three times a day on Monday, Tuesday, Friday and Saturday, and takes 1¾ hours. The No 794 goes once a day on Saturday from Chester and takes two hours.

BALA
• *pop 2000*   • ☎ *01678*

Bala is a small market town situated at the eastern end of Llyn Tegid, the largest natural lake in Wales. The lake is four miles long and almost three-quarters of a mile wide, and it's now the centre for a wide variety of water-based activities.

The Bala Adventure & Water Sports Centre (☎ 521059) offers introductory sessions in mountain biking, canoeing, raft building, windsurfing, sailing, rock climbing and abseiling. Sessions cost from around £16 per person. They will also rent equipment for all the above sports.

Canolfan Tryweryn (☎ 521083) offers a 20-minute white-water rafting trip for £10.

There's a TIC (☎ 521021) on Pensarn Rd, and *Bala Youth Hostel* (☎ 520215) is a mile from the lake at Rhos-y-Gwaliau, with beds for £7.45/5.

North-Western Wales

This section includes all of north-western Wales lying outside the Snowdonia National Park. Llandudno is a traditional seaside resort, Conwy and Caernarfon are dominated by spectacular castles and the particularly Welsh areas of Anglesey and the Llyn Peninsula see far fewer tourists than other parts of the country.

LLANDUDNO
• *pop 13,500*   • ☎ *01492*

As the largest seaside resort in Wales, Llandudno seethes with tourists, which in this instance seems entirely fitting. It was developed as an upmarket Victorian holiday town and it has retained its beautiful architecture and 19th-century atmosphere. There's a wonderful pier and promenade – and donkeys on the beach.

Llandudno is on its own peninsula, situated between two sweeping beaches, and is dominated by the spectacular limestone headland – the Great Orme – with the mountains of Snowdonia as a backdrop. The Great Orme, with its Bronze-Age mine, tramway, chair lift and superb views, is quite fascinating.

In its 19th-century heyday, Llandudno's visitors included many of the famous people of the day, such as Gladstone and Disraeli. In 1861, the Liddell family, whose daughter was Lewis Carroll's model for *Alice in Wonderland*, spent the summer in the house that is now the St Tudno Hotel. The Liddells later built a house on the other side of the town, which has since become the Gogarth Abbey Hotel.

Orientation & Information

The town fills the central section of the peninsula, with the Llandudno Bay beach to the north and the West Shore to the south-west. Mostyn St is the main shopping street. The tip of the peninsula is the Great Orme; the Little Orme is to the east.

The TIC (☎ 876413), 1 Chapel St, is open all year, daily from April to October, from 9.30 am to 6 pm. They stock a useful *Llandudno Walks* leaflet (25p).

Things to See & Do

There are superb views from the Great Orme and the headland is home to many species of flowers, butterflies and birds. Guided walks (free) are offered from May to September, and there's a café and gift-shop complex at the top.

The **Great Orme Tramway** (☎ 870870), at the top of Church Walks, takes you up in original 1902 tramcars. It operates daily from Easter to October, 10 am to 6 pm; tickets cost £3.40/2.40 return. The **Great**

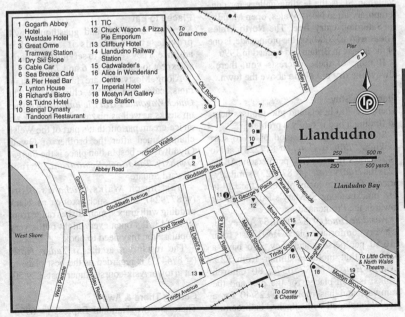

1 Gogarth Abbey Hotel
2 Westdale Hotel
3 Great Orme Tramway Station
4 Dry Ski Slope
5 Cable Car
6 Sea Breeze Café & Pier Head Bar
7 Lynton House
8 Richard's Bistro
9 St Tudno Hotel
10 Bengal Dynasty Tandoori Restaurant
11 TIC
12 Chuck Wagon & Pizza Pie Emporium
13 Cliffbury Hotel
14 Llandudno Railway Station
15 Cadwalader's
16 Alice in Wonderland Centre
17 Imperial Hotel
18 Mostyn Art Gallery
19 Bus Station

Llandudno

NORTH WALES

Orme Mine is a Bronze-Age copper mine halfway along the tramline. Open at the same time as the tram, entry is £4.40/2.60 – a combined ticket for the tramway and the mine is £6.50/4.50. There's also a cable car (☎ 877205) which operates, subject to the weather, from Happy Valley, above the pier. Tickets are £4.60/2 return.

Elegant Victorian **Llandudno Pier** stretches 2200 feet into the sea. The pier was first built in 1857 but it collapsed in a storm two years later. The current pier was started in 1877, and its main use was as a disembarkation point for passengers from the Isle of Man steamers.

The **Alice in Wonderland Visitors Centre**, alias The Rabbit Hole (☎ 860087), 3 Trinity Square, makes the most of the town's Alice connection with amateurish tableaux that will excite only the most ardent fans. It's open daily in summer and from Monday to Saturday in winter; entry is £2.50/1.95.

The **Mostyn Art Gallery** (☎ 879201), 12 Vaughan St, is the leading gallery for contemporary art in North Wales; open Monday to Saturday; entry free. The **North Wales Theatre** (☎ 872000), on the promenade, is one of the largest in Britain and opened in 1996.

If none of these interests you, there's always the **dry ski slope** above the town.

Places to Stay
There are 700 hotels and guesthouses here, so finding a bed is rarely a problem.

St David's Rd is a good place to start looking. *Cliffbury Hotel* (☎ 877224), at No 34, charges from £15.50 per person. At No 32 is the *Hilary Hotel* (☎ 875623), similarly-priced. There are many places in the £14 to £18 bracket along St Mary's Rd, one block towards the Promenade.

Westdale Hotel (☎ 877996), 37 Abbey Rd, is a very comfortable place. B&B costs from £16.50 per person, and they also have a package that includes dinner from £22. *Lynton House* (☎ 875057), 80 Church Walks, is well-placed for the pier and the tramway, and has rooms at £25/40 for a single/double, all with attached bathroom.

At the top end of the accommodation scale are some of the hotels along the Promenade, such as the *Imperial Hotel* (☎ 877466), an elegant Victorian building where B&B is £60/90 for a single/double. They offer discounts when business is slack.

The *St Tudno Hotel* (☎ 874411), North Parade, is a luxurious hotel that charges from £42.50 to £72.50 per person. It's notable in that out of the many awards it has won, it has several times received the accolade 'Best Hotel Loos in Great Britain'!

The other hotel with *Alice in Wonderland* connections is *Gogarth Abbey Hotel* (☎ 876211), West Shore. B&B is around £35 per person; there are 40 rooms, all with bathroom attached.

One of the top hotels in Wales, *Bodysgallen Hall* (☎ 584466), is three miles from the town, just off the A470. It's a luxurious country-house hotel where singles/doubles cost from £85/130. It does off-season two-day breaks for around £90 per person.

Places to Eat
Many of the B&Bs and guesthouses will provide evening meals if arranged in advance. They're used to serving them early, so expect to eat between 6 and 7 pm.

Along Mostyn St are fast-food restaurants, cafés and fish & chip places. The *Chuck Wagon & Pizza Pie Emporium* dishes up steaks as well as pizzas. *Cadwalader's* is an ice-cream parlour that's part of the Welsh chain named after the brother of Owain Glyndwr. The best Indian place is the *Bengal Dynasty Tandoori Restaurant*, Prince Edward Square.

On Church Walks, *Richard's Bistro* (☎ 877924), serves such exotica as black pudding with grapes; main dishes range from £9 to £13. It's open every night but is very popular: you may need to book.

The restaurant at the *St Tudno Hotel* (☎ 874411) is regarded as the best place to eat in town. A six-course dinner costs £29.50.

Getting There & Away
There are two National Express (☎ 0990-

NORTH WALES

808080) buses a day from London. Bus No 5 runs frequently between Llandudno, Bangor and Caernarfon.

The railway station at Llandudno Junction is on the main line from London's Euston, a 3½-hour journey. On average, there are three direct services a day. Services from Crewe (1¼ hours, £10.90) and Chester (50 minutes, £7.80) are fairly frequent throughout the year. Trains run on the Conwy Valley line to Betws-y-Coed and Blaenau Ffestiniog.

Llandudno itself is a short train journey (10 minutes, £1) from Llandudno Junction. Trains run frequently only from May to the end of September. At other times of the year you may have to take a bus – Nos 14, 15, 16 and 100 – for the eight-mile journey.

CONWY
- *pop 3800* • ☎ *01492*

Conwy has been revitalised since the through traffic on the busy A55 was consigned to a tunnel that burrows under the estuary of the River Conwy and the town. It's now a picturesque and interesting little place, dominated by the superb Conwy Castle, one of the grandest of Edward I's castles and a medieval masterpiece. As well as the castle, however, there are several other sights – 14th-century Aberconwy House, a virtually intact set of town walls and even a tiny building that claims to be the smallest house in Britain. Conwy is well worth a visit, and there's a new youth hostel on the outskirts of town.

The TIC (☎ 592248) is in the Conwy Castle Visitors Centre, not to be confused with the Conwy Visitors Centre by the railway station. It's open March to October, daily from 9.30 am to 6.30 pm, and Monday to Saturday for the rest of the year.

Things to See
Conwy Castle (☎ 592358; Cadw) looks every bit a castle, with eight massive crenellated towers. Its construction took just five years, from 1282 to 1287, and its shape was largely dictated by the rock on which it's built. The best view of the castle is from across the river, with the Snowdonia Moun-

tains providing a dramatic backdrop – on the rare occasion when they're not veiled in cloud.

Inside, the castle is largely a ruin, although there are some rooms that contain tableaux and exhibitions. The great hall is impressive, and the royal apartments and chapel are interesting. From the battlements there are good views across town and of Telford's suspension bridge, built in 1826. Reached by a bridge, the castle is open the same hours as the TIC; entry is £3/2.

Conwy's **town walls** make this one of the best examples of a medieval walled town in Europe. Still enclosing the town, they are three-quarters of a mile long, with 22 towers and three original gateways. You can walk along part of the walls.

Aberconwy House is a 14th-century timber-and-plaster house that has been restored by the NT. There are rooms furnished in period style and an interesting audiovisual presentation. The house (☎ 592246) is open daily except Tuesday, April to October, from 10 am to 5 pm; entry is £2/1. Nearby on the High St, Cadw is restoring an Elizabethan town house, **Plas Mawr**, which should be opening in June 1997.

The **Smallest House** is down on the quay, but not surprisingly there's little to see for your 50p/30p. There's also a **Teapot Museum** on Castle St.

A popular excursion from Conwy is to **Bodnant Garden** (☎ 650460; NT), eight miles south, one of the finest gardens in Britain. Entry is £4.20/2.10 and it's open daily, 10 am to 5 pm, from Easter to October. Bus Nos 25 and 65 pass close by.

Places to Stay
Conwy Youth Hostel (☎ 593571), Larkhill, Sychnant Pass Rd should now have opened. It's in a converted hotel, dorms are small and all have attached shower rooms. The hostel is a 10-minute walk from the centre, the nightly charge is £9.10/6.15, and they plan to be open year-round.

There are two cheaper HI youth hostels, both five miles from Conwy. *Colwyn Bay*

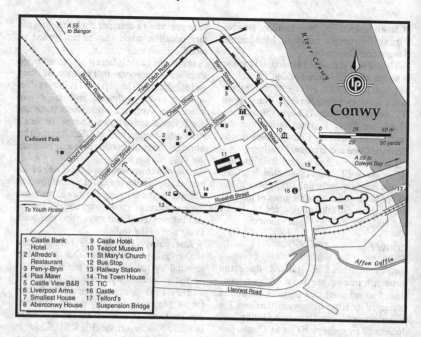

Conwy

Key to map:

1 Castle Bank Hotel
2 Alfredo's Restaurant
3 Pen-y-Bryn
4 Plas Mawr
5 Castle View B&B
6 Liverpool Arms
7 Smallest House
8 Aberconwy House
9 Castle Hotel
10 Teapot Museum
11 St Mary's Church
12 Bus Stop
13 Railway Station
14 The Town House
15 TIC
16 Castle
17 Telford's Suspension Bridge

Youth Hostel (☎ 530627), Foxhill, Nant-y-Glyn, Colwyn Bay is one mile inland and two miles from Colwyn Bay railway station. A bed costs £6.75/4.60 and it's fully open from May to August (phone for other opening times). For the more basic *Rowen Youth Hostel* contact the Colwyn Bay hostel for bookings.

Camping is possible at *Conwy Touring Park* (☎ 592856), 1½ miles south of Conwy; tent pitches cost from £4 to £9.95 per night.

Within the town walls there's the *Town House* (☎ 596454), Rosehill St, with B&B from £12 per person in a room with shared bath, £16 with private bathroom. *Castle View B&B* (☎ 596888), 3 Berry St, charges from £13 per person.

Pen-y-Bryn (☎ 596445) is an excellent guesthouse above the tearooms on the High St. B&B costs £16 per person (£19 in a room with bath).

Glan Heulog Guest House (☎ 593845) is a good place on Llanrwst Rd, to the south of the town but within walking distance. B&B is around £15 per person. The excellent *Castle Bank Hotel* (☎ 593888), Mount Pleasant, is west of the town. Non-smoking B&B costs from £25 per person.

The *Castle Hotel* (☎ 592324), High St, is dead central and rooms are from £60/70 for a single/double. It also has two-day leisure breaks, including dinner, for £59 per person per night.

Places to Eat

There are several tearooms dotted about the town, of which the best is *Pen-y-Bryn* (☎ 596445), where a full cream tea costs £4.70 and also includes bara brith and cake. It also does light lunches – pasta, soups, Welsh rarebit. The *Wall Place* on Chapel St does good vegetarian food.

Alfredo's Restaurant (☎ 592381), on the square, is an Italian place open each evening from 6 to 10 pm and also on Saturday for lunch. There's a set three-course dinner at the *Castle Hotel* (☎ 592324) for £15.95.

The *Conwy Frigate* (☎ 584468) is a fake Napoleonic frigate with bar and restaurant, moored by the town quay.

There are several pubs. The *Liverpool Arms*, down on the quay, is where the fishing crowd drinks.

Getting There & Away

Situated five miles west of Llandudno, and a mile from Llandudno Junction, Conwy is linked to both places by several buses an hour. There are frequent buses to Bangor (40 minutes, £2.05).

Conwy's railway station is now used only by regional trains. Llandudno Junction, a 15-minute walk from Conwy is the mainline station. There are only a few trains a day between Llandudno Junction and Conwy (three minutes, £1).

BANGOR

- *pop 12,000*   • ☎ *01248*

The town of Bangor is at its liveliest during the university terms. It's home to the University College of North Wales, which attracts students from all over Britain.

The first settlement on this site was probably the Celtic monastery established in 525 by St Deiniol, which would make Bangor the oldest diocese in Britain. The present **cathedral** was built in the 13th century, though much of it has been restored. Inside is the renowned early 16th-century carved figure known as the Mostyn Christ. The university's main building, up on the hill, is often mistaken for the cathedral, which is not surprising since that's what it was modelled on.

The renovated pier is worth seeing. It was built in 1896 and stretches 1500 feet into the Menai Strait. You get a good view of Thomas Telford's Menai Suspension Bridge, built in 1826 to link Anglesey to the mainland.

There's a TIC (☎ 352786), but it's a couple of miles out of the centre at the junction of the A5 and A55.

Places to Stay & Eat

Bangor Youth Hostel (☎ 353516), Tan-y-Bryn, is half a mile from the town centre and has good views of Penrhyn Castle. It's open daily from June to August (phone for other times); it charges £7.45/5 for a bed.

Tros-y-Waen Holiday Farm (☎ 364448), Pentir, is five miles south of Bangor on the road to Caernarfon. You can camp here from £2.50 per tent, and it also does B&B from around £13 per person.

The *University of Bangor* (☎ 371057) lets out student rooms on a B&B basis in July and August for £14.30 per person. It has special deals for longer stays.

Y Garreg Wen (☎ 353836), 8 Deiniol Rd, offers B&B for £12.50. There are only a few rooms but it's convenient for the station, and a very friendly place.

The British Hotel (☎ 364911) in the High St offers B&B from £20/40 for singles/doubles with attached bath. A three-course dinner is £12.50 and it also serves bar meals.

The excellent *Eryl Môr Hotel* (☎ 353789), 2 Upper Garth Rd, overlooking the pier and the Menai Strait, costs from £17 per person, or £29/43 for a room with attached bath.

The best place to stay is the comfortable *Menai Court Hotel* (☎ 354200), Craig-y-Don, which has rooms for £48/71 for a single/double, all with attached bathroom, and many with views. There's an excellent set dinner at £16.95. It's definitely the best place to eat in town.

There are several cheap restaurants and takeaways along Holyhead Rd, the main student area, and on the High St. The *Royal Tandoori* (☎ 364664), 111 High St, does restaurant meals and takeaways.

The *Fat Cat* (☎ 370445), 161 High St, has long been a popular place with students for its home-made burgers (£4.25), filled baguettes (£2.85) and steaks (£9.95). Vegetarian choices include spinach and walnut pasta (£4.95), and wine, beer and cocktails are available.

There's a bar at the university's *Students' Union* on Deiniol Rd, although it's supposed to be for students only. The best place in the area for live music is the *Victoria Hotel*, just across the bridge on Anglesey.

Getting There & Away

National Express (☎ 0990-808080) has two services a day from London to Bangor (£31).

Crosville Cymru (☎ 351879) operates bus services from Bangor to most places in the area. Most buses leave from Garth Rd. Services from Bangor operate to the following: Caernarfon (Bus Nos 5, 5A, 5B) every 20 minutes from Monday to Saturday and hourly on Sunday; Beaumaris (No 57) hourly and six (No 53) on Sunday; and Llanberis (No 77), from Bangor Plaza, about five times a day.

Bangor is on the InterCity line from London's Euston. There are about two trains a day direct to Bangor (4¼ hours), and many more services from Crewe to Bangor (1½ hours, £12.90). It's also on the North Wales coast line from Chester (1¼ hours, £9.80).

AROUND BANGOR

Penrhyn Castle

One and a half miles east of Bangor is Penrhyn Castle (☎ 01248-353084; NT). Unlike most other castles in the area it was not built by Edward I, nor is it a genuine Norman castle. It was constructed between 1820 and 1837 in the neo-Norman style, using a lot of local slate, by Thomas Hopper for Lord Penrhyn. It's certainly an impressive place, with the great hall modelled on Durham Cathedral and containing mock Norman furniture.

The castle is in a lovely setting and is worth a visit. It's open daily except Tuesday from April to the end of October, from 11 am to 5 pm during July and August, and from noon to 5 pm for the other months. Entry is £4.50/2.25.

CAERNARFON

- *pop 9400*   • ☎ 01286

In 1301, Edward made his son the first Prince of Wales and installed him in the mighty castle that still dominates this town. In 1911, in a bid to involve the crown more closely with his constituency in this part of Wales, Prime Minister David Lloyd George had the investiture ceremony for the heir to the throne transferred to the castle. It was an action that did not curry favour with the local people, for Caernarfon is at the heart of Welsh nationalist Wales, and a very depressed area that the royal link has done little to help. When Prince Charles was ceremonially invested here by his mother in 1969, there was an attempt to blow up his train.

Like Conwy, Caernarfon has a magnificent attraction in its castle and comparisons between the two towns are often drawn. While both are spectacular, Caernarfon is probably even more impressive from the outside, but perhaps a little too neat and tidy within.

Caernarfon was important for the Romans, who established a fort, Segontium, in the 1st century.

Orientation & Information

The castle stands by the river and there's a large car park below it. The TIC and the market square are immediately to the north and the town walls enclose a small area four blocks wide and two deep.

The friendly TIC (672232) is at Castle Pitch, Oriel Pendeitsh, Castle St. It's open daily from 10 am to 6 pm.

Early closing is on Thursday and on Saturday there's a market in the square.

Caernarfon Castle

Edward I wanted Caernarfon to be the most impressive of his Welsh fortresses, and it was modelled on the 5th-century walls of Constantinople. The castle was built between 1283 and 1301 as part of Edward's series of monumental forts constructed to keep the Welsh under control. It's particularly attractive at night, when the walls are floodlit.

Caernarfon was also designed to be a palace, and Edward's son was born here. Living quarters were contained in the towers, one of which is the Queen's Tower, named after Edward's wife Eleanor. This tower contains the regimental museum of the Royal Welsh Fusiliers, a regiment that seems to have produced quite a few poets and writers – Robert Graves and Siegfried Sassoon among them. The other towers contain exhibitions on the royal investiture in 1969, and on Edward I's campaigns.

The castle (☎ 677617; Cadw) is open from Easter to October, daily from 9.30 am to 6.30 pm, and until 4 pm for the rest of the year (afternoon only on Sunday). Entry is £3.80/2.80.

Other Things to See

The castle is very much the main attraction, but there's also a small **Maritime Museum** at Victoria Dock. The centrepiece is the SS *Seiont II*, a coal-fired steamship. The museum is open daily from June to September.

The foundations of the Roman fort **Segontium** are three-quarters of a mile east of the castle; there's also a museum. In the care of Cadw, it's open May to September, daily from 9.30 am to 6 pm (afternoon only on Sunday). In April and October it closes at 4 pm. Entry is £1.60/80p.

Places to Stay

Totters (☎ 672963), Plas Porth Yr Aur, 2 High St, offers cheap, friendly accommodation in the centre of town by the yacht club. A bed in a four or six-bed dorm costs £9 including bedding and breakfast.

Cadnant Valley Camping & Caravan Park (☎ 673196) is half a mile from the castle on Llanberis Rd. It's open March to October; tent pitches cost £4 for a tent and one person, £6 for two.

Cartref B&B (☎ 677392), 23 Market St, is only a couple of blocks north of the castle. It charges around £14 per person. One block east of the castle at 4 Church St is *Tegfan* (☎ 673703), which costs from £15/26 for a single/double.

The *Black Boy Inn* (☎ 673604), Northgate St, is an attractive old pub, centrally located. There are rooms without bathroom at £20/36 for a single/double and with bath for £23/40.

There are several guesthouses and hotels along North Rd, the road to Bangor. The *Menai Bank Hotel* (☎ 673297) is good and charges from £20/34. Also worth trying is the *Menai View Hotel* (☎ 674602), charging from £12.50 per person for a room with

shared bath, £16.50 with bath attached. At No 21 North Rd, there's *Gorffwysfa Guest House* (☎ 678981); B&B is from £13.50.

Closer to the centre, North Rd becomes Bangor St. Here, the *Prince of Wales Hotel* (☎ 673367) is a former coaching inn. There are 21 bedrooms and B&B is from £25.50 per person in a room with attached bath.

Places to Eat

The main places to eat are down Hole in the Wall St. *Stone's Bistro* is a reasonable place with main dishes at around £8, including vegetarian choices.

Near Stone's Bistro is a good pub, *Y Goron Fach* (☎ 673338), where they do bar meals every day, and evening meals from Monday to Thursday.

At the restaurant at the *Black Boy Inn* (☎ 673604), Northgate St, there's a set three-course dinner for £10.50. There's also good pub grub in the bar here.

The top place to eat is *Courtenay's Bistro* (☎ 677290), at 9 Segontium Terrace, close to the castle. It's also surprisingly inexpensive, with most main dishes in the £7 to £10 range. Rack of lamb is £7.75. Local produce is used as much as possible – mussels, sea trout, lamb and Welsh cheeses. It's closed on Sunday.

Getting There & Away

There are no train services to Caernarfon, nor are there direct coach services from London. It's best to go to Bangor and pick up a bus from there. Bus Nos 5, 5A and 5B run several times an hour (hourly on Sunday) from Bangor to Caernarfon (20 minutes, £1.30).

Caernarfon is a focal point for bus services to Snowdonia and the Llyn Peninsula.

ANGLESEY (YNYS MÔN)

Covering 276 square miles, Anglesey is the largest island in Wales and England, with a population of around 71,000. It has been connected with the mainland since 1826, when Thomas Telford built the Menai Bridge, the first heavy-duty suspension bridge to be constructed.

It's the flattest part of Wales, though there

NORTH WALES

are some rugged cliffs around the coast. It has an interesting coastline with some good sandy beaches. Most visitors, however, see little more than the countryside that surrounds the A5 on the route through to Holyhead and the ferries to Ireland.

Anglesey was a holy place to the ancient Celts and there are still many remains of ancient settlements. Inhabitants since then have relied on farming, smuggling, copper and coal mining and quarrying, as well as the sea, for their income. The land is very fertile and the island is referred to as Môn Mam Cymru – Mother of Wales – because it provides wheat, cattle and other farm produce for North Wales.

Llanfairpwllgwyngyllgogerychwyrndrobwllllantysiliogogogoch

The tour buses pour in to this little village simply because it's in the record books as having the longest name of any place in Britain, a sum total of 58 letters that are generally shortened to Llanfair PG or Llanfairpwll. The name means 'St Mary's Church in the hollow of the White Hazel near a rapid whirlpool and the Church of St Tysilio near the Red Cave', and was dreamt up in the 19th century to get the tourists in. It's a stop on the main line between Bangor and Holyhead and if you so wish you can buy a large platform ticket as a souvenir. At the TIC (☎ 01248-713177) in the knitwear shop nearby, they'll teach you how to pronounce it.

Plas Newydd

This is one of the most interesting stately homes in North Wales, an 18th-century house designed in the Gothic style for the marquess of Anglesey. There are superb views across to Snowdonia from the grounds. The house contains a celebrated mural by Rex Whistler. In the cavalry museum at the house is the state-of-the-art wooden leg designed for the marquess, who was field marshal at Waterloo.

Plas Newydd (☎ 01248-714795; NT) is open from April to September, daily except Saturday, and in October on Friday and

Sunday only; entry is £4/2. It's 1¾ miles from Llanfair PG railway station.

Beaumaris
• *pop 1500*   • ☎ *01248*

Beaumaris used to be the principal town and chief port of Anglesey. It's now known for the castle which James of St George built here for Edward I, and as a sailing and watersports centre.

Beaumaris Castle (☎ 810361; Cadw) is the last and largest of the castles built by Edward I. Construction started in 1295 on a site overlooking the Menai Strait. The flatness of the site meant the castle could be designed and built with geometrical symmetry – it's truly impressive and it's clear why it's a World Heritage site.

The castle is surrounded by a water-filled moat, then the outer walls, then evenly spaced towers, then more walls and towers, so it seems impregnable – though Owain Glyndwr did manage to conquer it. The castle last saw action in 1646 during the Civil War. Entry is £2.20/1.70.

Other things to see here include **Beaumaris Gaol** (☎ 810921), a model prison when it opened in 1829; the **Courthouse**, which can only be visited in summer when it's not being used as a magistrates' court; and the **Museum of Childhood** (☎ 810448), opposite the castle.

Cruises Several operators run summer cruises from Beaumaris pier to Puffin Island for the seabirds or along the Menai Strait. Try Beaumaris Marine Services (☎ 810746), which has a kiosk on the pier. Cruises are operated from April to October, from 12.30 pm. It costs £3/2 for an hour's cruise to Puffin Island; a 1½-hour Menai Strait cruise is £4.50/2.50.

Places to Stay There's little in the way of cheap accommodation in Beaumaris. *Swn-y-Don* (☎ 810794), 7 Bulkley Terrace, is open from April to November, and offers B&B for £18 per person. Some rooms overlook the Menai Strait; all have an attached bath.

Ye Olde Bulls Head Inn (☎ 810329),

Castle St, is the best place to stay. It has 11 rooms, all with attached bath, from £37.50 per room. The Bulls Head Inn dates back to 1472 – it was originally the posting house of the borough. The bedrooms are named after several of Dickens' characters, in honour of the author who once stayed in the hotel.

Getting There & Away Beaumaris is 10 miles from Bangor. Bus No 57 runs almost hourly Monday to Saturday from Bangor to Beaumaris (25 minutes, £1.45). On Sunday there are six services (No 53).

Holyhead
- *pop 12,700* • ☎ *01407*

Holyhead is a particularly grey and daunting ferry port. The only reason to come here would be to get to Ireland. The town is on Holy Island, which is separated by sand-banks and a narrow channel from the main island. If you're killing time waiting for a ferry, there's an RSPB **Nature Reserve** at South Stack, not far from the town.

The TIC (☎ 762622) is in the ferry terminal but it may be relocated in 1997. There's also a 24-hour information terminal in the railway station.

Places to Stay B&Bs are used to dealing with late ferry arrivals. Closest to the terminal is *Min-y-don* (☎ 762718). It's pleasant and has rooms for £14 per person.

An excellent place, though it only has three rooms, is *Hendre* (☎ 762929) in Porth-y-Felin Rd. B&B is from £20/35 for a single/double. The *Boathouse Hotel* (☎ 762094), Newry Beach, has B&B from £27.50 per person. *Tan-y-Cytiau Guest House* (☎ 762763), South Stack Rd, has seven rooms, at £17.50 per person.

About five miles south of Holyhead at Rhoscolyn, there's bunkhouse accommodation for £8.60 at *Outdoor Alternative* (☎ 860469), Cerrig-yr-Adar. It's beautifully situated, 300 yards from the beach.

Getting There & Away Both Irish Ferries (☎ 760222) and Stena Line (☎ 606606) run ferries to Ireland. See Getting There & Away at the start of this book. If you fancy a day-trip to Dublin, Irish Ferries sometimes have special offers from as little as £8 return.

There are hourly trains east to Llandudno, Chester, Birmingham and London, via Bangor (40 minutes, £4.90).

Crosville Cymru (☎ 01248-370295) operates bus service No 4 from Bangor to Holyhead (1¼ hours, £2.50) twice-hourly from Monday to Saturday.

LLŶN PENINSULA

This isolated peninsula is the most staunchly Welsh part of the country – in the villages you rarely hear a word of English spoken. It's a peaceful, predominantly undeveloped place with 70 miles of coastline, a few small fishing villages, some beautiful sandy beaches, good walks and quiet lanes for cycling.

The best beaches are at Abersoch, seven miles from Pwllheli, Aberdaron, from where you can catch a boat to Bardsey Island, and Nefyn, on the north coast.

Criccieth

This busy seaside town is the gateway to the Llŷn. **Criccieth Castle** dates from the early 13th century. Open standard Cadw hours, it's worth a visit and there are good views over the bay; entry is £2.20/1.70.

✝✝✝✝✝✝✝✝✝✝✝✝✝✝✝✝✝✝✝✝✝✝

The Bardsey Pilgrimage
A tiny island off the tip of the Llŷn peninsula, Bardsey was once known as the Isle of Twenty Thousand Saints. In the sixth century the obscure Saint Cadfan created a monastery here. At a time when journeys from Britain to Italy were long, perilous and beyond the means of most people, three pilgrimages to Bardsey came to have the same value as one to Rome. The twenty thousand were probably not so much saints as pilgrims who came here to die.

Most modern pilgrims to Bardsey are more prosaic seabird-watchers. although there are remains of a 13th-century abbey to mull over. The Bardsey Island Trust is in charge of visitor arrangements; phone ☎ 01766-522239 for more information. ∎

✝✝✝✝✝✝✝✝✝✝✝✝✝✝✝✝✝✝✝✝✝✝

Cricieth is on the railway line between Porthmadog and Pwllheli and there are lots of B&Bs and hotels here. Just over a mile from Cricieth on the B4411 Caernarfon road, there's bunkhouse accommodation for £4 at *Stone Barn* (☎ 01766-522115), Tyddyn Morthwyl. Book in advance.

Pwllheli

• *pop 5000*   • ☎ *01758*

The only place of any size on the peninsula is the market town of Pwllheli, of greatest interest to the visitor for its Welshness. It was here in 1925 that Plaid Cymru, the Welsh nationalist party, was formed. In the minds of many British people, however, the town is synonymous with the Butlins Holiday Camp, which is several miles from Pwllheli and has now been renamed Starcoast World.

The TIC (☎ 613000), opposite the railway station, has information on the Llyn Peninsula.

Places to Stay *Mrs Jones* (☎ 613172), 26 High St, does B&B from £12. *Gwynfryn Farm* (☎ 612536) is a working organic dairy farm one mile from Pwllheli, where B&B costs from £15. It also has flats for weekly rental from £94.

Getting There & Away Pwllheli is the last stop on the railway line from Shrewsbury (4¼ hours, £15.50). There are some direct trains during the summer but you'll probably have to change at Machynlleth.

It's also accessible by bus route No 12, operated by Clynnog & Trefor (☎ 01286-660208) from Caernarfon. The service runs hourly from Monday to Saturday (one hour, £1.40).

PORTHMADOG

• *pop 2000*   • ☎ *01766*

People come to this former slate port today for two reasons – to catch the Ffestiniog Railway to Blaenau Ffestiniog (see the Snowdonia National Park section) and to visit the nearby village of Portmeirion. The town makes a reasonable base for both.

The TIC (☎ 512981) in the High St is open daily from 10 am to 5 pm. In winter it closes for one day during the week, usually Tuesday or Thursday.

Places to Stay & Eat

Mrs Jones (☎ 513087), 57 East Avenue, offers B&B for £13.50 per person, though none of her rooms have attached bath. The B&B at *35 Madog St* (☎ 512843) is similarly priced, and *5 Glaslyn St* (☎ 514461) charges £15.

Tyddyn Llwyn Hotel (☎ 513903), Morfa Bychan Rd, is on the edge of Porthmadog in open countryside. It's a comfortable place with singles/doubles for £28.50/40, all with bath.

A good place to eat is the *Harbour Restaurant* (☎ 512471), 3 High St. Its set-price lunches (£6.95) are good value and sometimes include roast beef or lamb. There's an à la carte menu in the evening – Dover sole or T-bone steak for £11.50, half a lobster (when available) for a bargain £7.50. Alternatively there's the *Cantonese Restaurant* above the *Ship Inn* on Lombard St. The Ship is the best place in Porthmadog for a pint.

The top place to stay, *Hotel Portmeirion* (☎ 770228), is two miles from Porthmadog in the fantasy village of the same name (see Portmeirion section). Charges are £110 for a double room in the main building, or £75 for a room in one of the cottages in the village. Prices are based on two people sharing and breakfast is extra. The restaurant does set lunches from £10.50, set dinners from £20.

Getting There & Away

From Caernarfon, Express Motors (☎ 01286-674570) operates an hourly service (No 1), Monday to Saturday, to Porthmadog (45 minutes, £1.90). The service continues to Blaenau Ffestiniog. On Sunday the service is operated by Crosville Motors.

Porthmadog is on the railway line from Shrewsbury (four hours, £15.50). You usually have to change at Machynlleth. The service is not frequent but there's at least one train a day throughout the year.

PORTMEIRION

Two miles from Porthmadog, Portmeirion is an Italianate village (even the scenery is Mediterranean) created by the Welsh architect Sir Clough Williams-Ellis. It was built between 1925 and 1927 on a secluded peninsula five miles from his ancestral home. Sir Clough wanted to show that architecture could be fun, intriguing and interesting, and a visit to the village certainly fulfils all of these requirements, although in summer the crowds can detract from the pleasure.

There are 50 buildings around a central piazza; some of the buildings were brought to the site to save them from destruction elsewhere. Apart from the buildings, there's a restaurant, an ice-cream parlour, a hotel and seven shops, one of which sells seconds of the popular Portmeirion pottery line.

The perfect film set, Portmeirion was where the cult TV series *The Prisoner* was made in the 60s. It still draws the fans and there's even a Prisoner Information Centre.

Portmeirion (☎ 01766-770228) is open all year except January, daily from 9.30 am to 5.30 pm; entry is £3.20/1.60, and the charge is lower between November and March. There's a very good restaurant in the hotel here (see Porthmadog section).

NORTH WALES

CHANNEL
ISLANDS

The Channel Islands

HIGHLIGHTS

- Gerald Durrell's conservation zoo, Jersey
- The German Underground Hospital, Jersey
- Cycling on Alderney
- Sark – Europe's last feudal state

Locator & Map Index

LONDON

Channel Islands
p1012

Cherbourg

FRANCE

'Little bits of France dropped into the sea and picked up by Britain,' was how Victor Hugo described this small group of islands in the English Channel just off the coast of France's Normandy.

There are five main islands in the group – Jersey, Guernsey, Alderney, Sark and Herm. Their separation from mainland Britain is not merely geographical. Although British since 1066, the islands are not part of the UK and they're administered locally. Entry formalities are as for the UK: if you're visiting via Britain you don't need to show your passport.

Low rates of tax have made them something of a tax haven, and Jersey's capital, St Helier, is part buckets-and-spades beach-holiday resort, part international finance centre. The islands issue their own currency (exchangeable at par with the British pound) and postage stamps. There's no VAT on goods.

With reliable, sunny weather, sandy beaches and very low rates of crime, the Channel Islands are a good place for a holiday for families with young children. The islands are also popular with the yachting crowd and the marinas at St Helier and Guernsey's capital, St Peter Port, are packed with some of the world's most technically advanced sailing hardware – plus attendant beautiful people. Catering to this clientele are some excellent, though very pricey, seafood restaurants.

Although there are pleasant beaches, good walks and cycle rides on some islands, and

there's the famous conservation zoo started by Gerald Durrell on Jersey, compared to mainland Britain or the Scottish islands there's really not a lot to see and do. There are no youth hostels but there are several camping grounds.

GETTING THERE & AWAY
Air
Jersey & Guernsey There are numerous daily flights between Britain, Jersey and Guernsey. The biggest operator is British Airways/City Flyer Express (☎ 0345-222111) with up to 20 flights each day from Jersey and/or Guernsey to nine UK airports, mostly to London's Gatwick. British Midland (☎ 0345-554554) services the Midlands – mainly East Midlands airport. Jersey European (☎ 0345-676676) links Jersey and Guernsey with Gatwick, Exeter, Birmingham, Dublin, Belfast and Edinburgh. Air UK (☎ 0345-666777) links Jersey with Southampton and London's Stansted airport.

CHANNEL ISLANDS

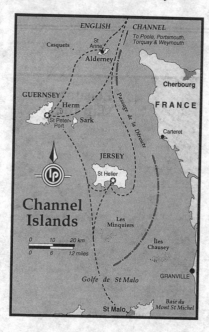

Channel Islands

Return air fares between Jersey/Guernsey and London on all these airlines range from around £70 up to £200. The cheaper deals usually require you to spend at least Saturday night in the Channel Islands. Theoretically tickets don't need to be bought in advance but the earlier you book your flight, the greater the chance of cheaper tickets being available.

Alderney All Alderney flights are operated by Aurigny Air Services (☎ 01481-822886) using tiny Trislanders painted an unmissable banana yellow. There are up to ten flights a day to and from Southampton (45 minutes, £60.50 one-way, £81 budget return). To France, it also operates flights between Jersey or Guernsey and Cherbourg or Dinard.

Boat
Condor (01534-601000) operates two fast ferries a day in each direction between Poole

in Dorset and Jersey via Guernsey. Return fares between Britain and Jersey (3½ hours) start at around £65 for a foot passenger, £175 for a car and driver. A day-return costs £29. It also runs a slower overnight ferry from Britain to Guernsey and Jersey; return foot passenger fares start at £50.

Ferry links to France are run by Emeraude (☎ 01481-711414) with services between Guernsey or Jersey and St Malo in Brittany; and also to Granville, Carteret and Diélette in Normandy.

JERSEY
• *pop 75,000* • ☎ 01534
Jersey is the largest of the Channel Islands, and the most popular destination for visitors. There are lots of safe clean beaches of all types, the best in the region. The main surf break is at St Ouen's Bay Watersplash.

Orientation & Information
Covering 45 sq miles, the island is roughly rectangular in shape; St Helier is on the south coast.

Jersey Tourism (☎ 500777) is on Liberation Sq, a short walk from the ferry terminal and opposite the bus station. It's open from 8.45 am to 8 pm daily in summer.

Landscapes of Jersey (£5.99), published by Sunflower, is a good pocket guide to walks and tours of the island.

Things to See
Of universal interest, the **Jersey Zoo** (☎ 864666), Les Augres Manor, Trinity, was started by writer and naturalist Gerald Durrell as a conservation and breeding centre for endangered species. It's a fascinating place to visit and is open daily from 9.30 am to 6 pm; entry is £5/3. Other things to see around the island include several castles, and the **German Underground Hospital**, dating from WWII when the Germans occupied the island. There are also lots of the types of attractions that appeal to families with young children.

St Helier, the capital, is not particularly attractive; it's an international finance centre that even boasts a few multi-storey buildings. Jersey Museum, near the TIC, has an interesting display on Jersey's history.

Places to Stay

Jersey Tourism operates a free booking service, Jerseylink (☎ 500888), and publishes a brochure listing over 300 places to stay.

There are camping grounds at St Martin, St Brelade and St Ouen. *Summer Lodge* (☎ 484089), St Ouen, charges £5 per person.

Cheap B&Bs in St Helier, charging around £13 per person, include *Corinthian* (☎ 878655), *Elysia* (☎ 33918) and *St Meloir des Ondes* (☎ 21165).

The *Golden Sands Hotel* (☎ 41241) is a modern hotel right on the beach at St Brelade's Bay. Rates range from £23 to £43 per person. The island's top hotel is the *Longueville Manor* (☎ 25501), St Saviour, where accommodation starts at £75 per person.

Places to Eat

There's a wide choice – everything from fish & chip shops to excellent seafood restaurants. In St Helier there's reasonable Thai food near the TIC at *Rodees* (☎ 32548) – £6.30 for all you can eat at lunchtime. The *Typsy Toad Town House* is an interesting pub on New St that has its own microbrewery and excellent pub grub.

For a special occasion, the *Longueville Manor* (☎ 25501), St Saviour, is one of the best places to eat on the island. Main dishes are around £19 and there are set menus up to £50.

Getting There & Away

For services to Britain and France, see Getting There & Away at the start of this section. Aurigny Air Services (☎ 43568) has 18 flights a day each way between Jersey and Guernsey (15 minutes, £26), and flights to Alderney. Emeraude (☎ 66566) runs one ferry in each direction between Jersey and Guernsey (one hour, £20). Condor ferries to Britain also link the two islands.

Getting Around

Between the airport and St Helier there's a choice of taxi (£5.50) or bus (£1.10). The journey takes 15 to 45 minutes depending on traffic.

Car hire is cheap – from £10 per day – but there are said to be 55,000 cars on the island so you may find yourself sitting in a jam. Try Holiday Autos (☎ 607072). It also rents motorcycles and bicycles.

GUERNSEY

- *pop 56,000*   • ☎ *01481*

More easy-going and peaceful than Jersey, Guernsey is, however, the most highly-populated of the Channel Islands. It's popular both with young families and elderly holiday-makers.

Orientation & Information

Guernsey is two-thirds the size of Jersey: roughly nine miles long by four wide. There are TICs at the airport and ferry terminal but the main office of Guernsey Tourism (☎ 723552) is on the waterfront in St Peter Port, opposite the Crown Pier.

Things to See

There are numerous **beaches**. **St Peter Port**, the capital, is one of the most attractive towns in the Channel Islands, looking out across the busy harbour to Sark and Herm. Victor Hugo, the French novelist, was exiled in 1855 and lived in St Peter Port until 1870. His house (entry £3/1.50) is a popular tourist attraction.

The Germans occupied Guernsey during WWII and their **underground hospital** and the **military museum** can be visited. Fortifications around the island bear witness to the fact that Guernsey has been of strategic importance from as long ago as Neolithic times.

Places to Stay

There are several camping grounds. *Fauxquets Valley Farm Campsite* (☎ 55460), Castel, has a heated pool, cycle hire and restaurant. Charges are from £3.70.

There are about 100 hotels and B&Bs. The

Hollies Guest House (☎ 725493), Hauteville, is a friendly place in St Peter Port with B&B from £14 per person. The *Midhurst House* (☎ 724391), Candie Rd, is an excellent small hotel in St Peter Port, with a quiet garden and good food. Rates are from £32/45. The *Old Government Hotel* (☎ 724921), formerly the official residence of the Guernsey governors, is a large old hotel with good views over St Peter Port and the harbour. Accommodation at the OGH ranges from £45 to £95 per person.

Places to Eat
For good vegetarian food visit *Mrs P's Kitchen*, up the side alley opposite Victoria Marina in St Peter Port. There's hamity pie for £1.10 and a great range of frozen yoghurts. There's good pub grub at the *Yacht Inn*, South Esplanade, St Peter Port. One of the top restaurants on the island is the *Café du Moulin* (☎ 65944), Rue de Quanteraine, St Peter Port. There are set lunches from £10.95, set dinners from £15.95, and separate menus for vegetarians.

Getting There & Away
See Getting There & Away at the start of this section for services to Britain and France. For inter-island services see the other islands. Condor (☎ 726121) runs a day-trip to Alderney in summer on Friday.

Getting Around
From the airport to St Peter Port there's a choice of taxi (10 minutes, £5.50) or bus (20 minutes, £1). Value (☎ 43547) rents cars from £14 per day with outlets at the airport and marina. Quay Cycle Hire (☎ 714146) is on the New Jetty in St Peter Port. It rents out bikes from £5 per day and has cycling maps of the island for 90p.

ALDERNEY
- *pop 2500*   •   ☎ *01481*

Although it's the third largest of the Channel Islands, Alderney is just 3½ miles by 1½ miles at its widest points. It's the quietest of all the Channel Islands – the day-trippers tend to head for Sark and Herm.

There are white sand beaches, cliff walks, and coastal forts dating from the 19th century and from the 1940s when the Germans occupied the island. There's a small museum in St Anne, the capital. The Alderney Railway operates in the tourist season, using old carriages from the London underground.

The majority of the population lives in St Anne, in the centre of the island less than a mile from the airport. Alderney Tourism Office (☎ 823737) is on QEII St in St Anne.

Places to Stay & Eat
There are about eight guesthouses on the island, with B&B from around £17 per person. Try *Saye Farmhouse* (☎ 822196), Mannez, on a sandy bay 1½ miles from St Anne.

There are more than a dozen hotels. The *Sea View* (☎ 822738) is by the beach in Braye, with B&B accommodation from £15 to £34 per person. There's more upmarket accommodation at *Hotel Chez André* (☎ 822777), Victoria St, St Anne.

The *Georgian House* (☎ 822471), Victoria St, St Anne, is known for seafood specialities. The *Divers Inn* at Braye Harbour is a popular pub.

Getting There & Away
Aurigny Air Services (☎ 822886) has two flights a day each way between Alderney and Jersey (15 minutes, £26.50), and eight a day each way to Guernsey (15 minutes, £26). See Getting There & Away at the start of this section for details of other flights. There are only one or two ferry links per week to Jersey or Guernsey in summer: contact the TIC for details.

Getting Around
For hire cars phone ☎ 822848, mopeds ☎ 822406 and bicycles ☎ 822294.

SARK
- *pop 550*   •   ☎ *01481*

Traffic-free Sark is probably best known as Europe's only feudal state. The Seigneur, currently Michael Beaumont, rules through a feudal constitution that dates back to Elizabethan times. Sark has no income tax, and maintains its own government and a collection of laws that includes such anomalies as the fact that no woman is entitled to divorce.

Three miles by 1½ miles but with a jagged coastline of over 30 miles, the island has beautiful scenery best appreciated after the crowds of day-trippers have departed. Sark is ideal for walkers who enjoy an unhurried pint – the pubs seem to remain open all hours.

Contact Sark Tourism (☎ 832345) for their island guide which gives details and prices of places to stay.

Places to Stay & Eat

On the west coast there's camping from £2.50 at *Falle's Beauregard Campsite* (☎ 832186). There's a pub here, the *Barn Bar*, known for its home-made sloe gin.

There are about 20 hotels and B&Bs. The cheapest is at *Le Pellon* (☎ 832289), from £13 per person. *La Sablonnerie* (☎ 832061) is a very comfortable hotel in the south of the island across the isthmus on Little Sark. Charges per person range from £37 to £62.50.

Founiais Restaurant (☎ 832626) on Harbour Hill is a good fish restaurant. There are several cafés and the larger hotels all have restaurants.

Getting There & Away

Isle of Sark Shipping (☎ 832450) has up to five sailings each way every day between St Peter Port in Guernsey and Sark (45 minutes, £17.50/8.75 return). The company also offers cheaper half-day excursions and special offers. Emeraude (☎ 01534-66566) operates a catamaran service to Jersey (45 minutes, £22/13 return), daily except Sunday.

Getting Around

There are no cars on the island, a tractor and trailer being the only motorised form of transport. There are horse-drawn carriage rides for £4 per hour. For cycle hire (£3.75 per day), purchase a voucher from Isle of Sark Shipping's Guernsey office to exchange for a bike on Sark.

HERM
* *pop 40* * ☎ 01481

A 20-minute boat trip across the bay from Guernsey, Herm is a pretty island half a mile wide by 1½ miles long. No cars, motorcycles or even bicycles are allowed, making this a walkers' mini-paradise, but it's one that's very popular with day-trippers from the larger Channel Islands.

Herm had been deserted for years when Major Wood bought a 99-year lease on the island in 1949. The island is now run by his daughter Pennie Hayworth and her family. It's an undeniably attractive place – white beaches famous for their variety of shells, clear sea and pleasant walks.

Places to Stay & Eat

Accommodation is booked through the administration office (☎ 722377). There's a choice between just one hotel – the upmarket *White House Hotel* (☎ 722159) from £48/96 for dinner, bed & breakfast – 18 self-catering cottages, and a camping ground.

For places to eat there's the *Mermaid Tavern*, the *Ship Restaurant* at the White House Hotel and two cafés.

Getting There & Away

Trident Travel (☎ 722377) runs up to eight trips in each direction between St Peter Port and Herm (20 minutes). Beat the crowds in summer and take the Milk Boat (£4/2 return) at 8.30 am. Other departures cost £6/3 return.

Getting Around

The only way to get around is on foot. It takes about two hours to walk right around the island.

Glossary

abe – estuary (Wales)

afon – river (Wales)

agister – someone paid to care for stock

auld – old (Scotland)

aye – yes/always

BABA – book-a-bed-ahead scheme

bach – small (Wales)

bailey – outermost wall of a castle

bairn – baby (Newcastle & Scotland)

banger – old, cheap car

bangers – sausages

bap – bun (northern England)

bar – gate (York)

ben – mountain (Scotland)

bent – not altogether legal

bevvied – drunk

bevvy – a drink (originally northern England)

bevvying – drinking

billion – a million million, not a thousand million

biscuit – cookie

bitter – beer

black pudding – a type of sausage made from dried blood (Scotland)

blatherskite – boastful or talkative person (northern England)

bloke – man

bodge job – poor-quality repairs

bothy – hut or mountain shelter (Scotland)

brae – hill (Scotland)

bridleway – path that can be used by walkers, horse riders and cyclists

broch – defensive tower (Scotland)

Brummie – Birmingham accent

bryn – hill (Wales)

BTA – British Tourist Authority

burgh – town (Scotland)

burn – creek (Scotland)

bus – local bus; *see also* coach

cadair – stronghold/chair (Wales)

caer – fort (Wales)

caff – cheap café

canny – good, great (Newcastle)

capel – chapel (Wales)

car bonnet – hood

car boot – trunk

carreg – stone (Wales)

ceilidh – pronounced kaylee, informal evening entertainment and dance (Scotland)

cheers – goodbye

chine – valleylike fissure leading to the sea

chips – French fries

close – entrance

clun – meadow (Wales)

coach – long-distance bus; *see also* bus

coaching inn – inn along a coaching route at which horses were changed

coch – red (Wales)

coed – forest/wood (Wales)

couchette – sleeping berth in a train or ferry

Corbett – mountain of between 2500 and 2999 feet in height

courgettes – zucchini

courts – courtyards

crack – good conversation (originally Ireland)

crannogh – artificial island settlement

crisps – potato chips

croft – plot of land with adjoining house worked by the occupiers

cromlech – burial chamber (Wales)

cwm – valley (Wales)

de – south (Wales)

dear – expensive

din (dinas) – fort (Wales)

DIY – do-it-yourself, as in handyman shop

dolmen – chartered tomb

donkey – engine

dosh – money

downs – rolling upland, characterised by lack of trees

du – black (Wales)

duvet – doona

EH – English Heritage

eisteddfod – festival in which competitions are held in music, poetry, drama and the fine arts (Wales)

Essex – derogatory adjective, as in Essex girl, meaning tarty, and identified with '80s consumerism

evensong – daily evening service (Church of England)

fag – cigarette; *also* a boring task

fagged – exhausted

fanny – female genitals, not backside

fawr – big (Wales)

fen – drained or marshy low-lying flat land

flat – apartment

ffordd – road (Wales)

firth – estuary (Scotland)

fiver – five-pound note

flip-flops – thongs

footpath – sidewalk

fussock – irritating woman (Yorkshire)

gaffer – boss or foreman

gate – street (York)

ginnel – alleyway (Yorkshire)

glan – shore (Wales)

glas – blue (Wales)

glen – valley (Scotland)

glyn – valley (Wales)

gobslutch – slovenly person (northern England)

grand – one thousand

greasy spoon – cheap café

gutted – very disappointed

guv, guvner – from governor, a respectful term of address for owner or boss, can be used ironically

gwyn – white (Wales)

gwyrdd – green (Wales)

haar – fog off the North Sea (Scotland)

hammered – drunk (northern England)

Hogmanay – New Year's Eve (Scotland)

hotel – accommodation with food and bar, not always open to passing trade

HS – Historic Scotland

Huguenots – French Protestants

inn – pub with accommodation

jam – jelly

jelly – jello

jumper – sweater

ken – know (Scotland)

kirk – church (Scotland)

kyle – narrow strait

lager lout – *see* yob

laird – estate owner (Scotland)

lands – multistoreyed apartment buildings (Scotland)

lass – young woman (northern England)

ley – clearing

lift – elevator

linn – waterfall (Scotland)

llan – enclosed place or church (Wales)

llyn – lake (Wales)

lock – part of a canal or river that can be closed off and the water levels changed to raise or lower boats

lolly – money; *also* candy on a stick (possibly frozen)

lorry – truck

love – term of address, not necessarily to someone likable

mad – insane, not angry

manky – low quality (southern England)

Martello tower – small, circular tower used for coastal defence

mate – a friend of any sex, or term of address for males

mawr – great (Wales)

merthyr – burial place of a saint (Wales)

motorway – freeway

motte – mound on which a castle was built

Munro – mountain of 3000 feet or higher (Scotland)

mynydd – mountain (Wales)

nant – valley/stream (Wales)

nappies – diapers

newydd – new (Wales)

NT – National Trust

NTS – National Trust for Scotland

NYMR – North Yorkshire Moors Railway

oast house – building containing a kiln for drying hops

offie – *see* off-license

off-license – carry-out alcoholic drinks shop

ogof – cave (Wales)

OS – Ordnance Survey
owlers – smugglers

pee – pence
pen – headland (Wales)
pend – arched gateway (Scotland)
pete – fortified houses
pint – beer
pissed – drunk (not angry)
pistyll – waterfall (Wales)
pitch – playing field
plas – hall/mansion (Wales)
ponce – ostentatious or effeminate male; *also* to borrow (usually permanently)
pont – bridge (Wales)
pop – fizzy drink (northern England)
postbuses – minibuses that follow postal delivery routes
pub – short for public house, a bar usually with food, sometimes with accommodation
punter – customer
pwll – pool (Wales)

quid – pound

ramble – to go for a short walk
reiver – warrior
rhiw – slope (Wales)
rhos – moor/marsh (Wales)
roll-up – roll-your-own cigarette
rood – alternative word for cross
RSPB – Royal Society for the Protection of Birds
rubber – eraser
rubbish bin – garbage can
rugger – rugby

sacked – fired
Sassenach – an English person or a lowland Scot (Scotland)
sett – tartan pattern
shout – to buy a group of people drinks, usually reciprocated
shut – partially covered passage
Sloane Ranger – wealthy, superficial, but well-connected young person, exemplified by Diana Spencer
snicket – alleyway (York)
snogging – kissing and cuddling

spondoolicks – money
sporran – purse (Scotland)
SSSI – Site of Special Scientific Interest
steaming – drunk (Scotland)
strath – valley (Scotland)
subway – underpass
sweet – candy

ta – thanks
thwaite – clearing in a forest
TICs – Tourist Information Centres
ton – one hundred
tor – Celtic word describing a hill shaped like a triangular wedge of cheese
torch – flashlight
traveller – nomadic, new-age hippy
tre – town (Wales)
tron – public weighbridge
twitchers – birdwatchers
twitten – passage, small lane
twr – tower (Wales)
ty – house (Wales)

underground – subway
uisge-bha – the water of life: whisky (Scotland)

VAT – value-added tax, levied on most goods and services
verderer – officer upholding law and order in the royal forests

way – a long-distance trail
wellied – drunk (originally Scotland)
wide boy – ostentatious go-getter, usually on the make
wold – open, rolling country
WTB – Wales Tourist Board
wynd – lane (Scotland)

yaya – plumby, upper-class twit
ynys – island (Wales)
yob – hooligan
ystwyth – winding (Wales)

For a glossary of definitions and terminology relating to churches, see the Architecture section of the Facts about England chapter.

Index

MAPS

TEXT

LONELY PLANET PHRASEBOOKS

Building bridges,
Breaking barriers,
Beyond babble-on

Nepali phrasebook

Ethiopian Amharic phrasebook

Latin American Spanish phrasebook

Ukrainian phrasebook

Greek phrasebook

Vietnamese phrasebook

Listen for the gems

Speak your own words

Ask your own questions

Master of your own image

- handy pocket-sized books
- easy to understand Pronunciation chapter
- clear and comprehensive Grammar chapter
- romanisation alongside script to allow ease of pronunciation
- script throughout so users can point to phrases
- extensive vocabulary sections, words and phrases for every situations
- full of cultural information and tips for the traveller

'...vital for a real DIY spirit and attitude in language learning' – Backpacker

'the phrasebooks have good cultural backgrounders and offer solid advice for challenging situations in remote locations' – San Francisco Examiner

'...they are unbeatable for their coverage of the world's more obscure languages' – The Geographical Magazine

---

Arabic (Egyptian)
Arabic (Moroccan)
Australia
  Australian English, Aboriginal and Torres Strait languages
Baltic States
  Estonian, Latvian, Lithuanian
Bengali
Burmese
Brazilian
Cantonese
Central Europe
  Czech, French, German, Hungarian, Italian and Slovak
Eastern Europe
  Bulgarian, Czech, Hungarian, Polish, Romanian and Slovak
Egyptian Arabic
Ethiopian (Amharic)
Fijian
French
German
Greek

Hindi/Urdu
Indonesian
Italian
Japanese
Korean
Lao
Latin American Spanish
Malay
Mandarin
Mediterranean Europe
  Albanian, Croatian, Greek, Italian, Macedonian, Maltese, Serbian, Slovene
Mongolian
Moroccan Arabic
Nepali
Papua New Guinea
Pilipino (Tagalog)
Quechua
Russian
Scandinavian Europe
  Danish, Finnish, Icelandic, Norwegian and Swedish

South-East Asia
  Burmese, Indonesian, Khmer, Lao, Malay, Tagalog (Pilipino), Thai and Vietnamese
Spanish
Sri Lanka
Swahili
Thai
Thai Hill Tribes
Tibetan
Turkish
Ukrainian
USA
  US English, Vernacular Talk, Native American languages and Hawaiian
Vietnamese
Western Europe
  Basque, Catalan, Dutch, French, German, Irish, Italian, Portuguese, Scottish Gaelic, Spanish (Castilian) and Welsh

---

LONELY PLANET JOURNEYS

JOURNEYS is a unique collection of travel writing – published by the company that understands travel better than anyone else. It is a series for anyone who has ever experienced – or dreamed of – the magical moment when they encountered a strange culture or saw a place for the first time. They are tales to read while you're planning a trip, while you're on the road or while you're in an armchair, in front of a fire.

JOURNEYS books catch the spirit of a place, illuminate a culture, recount a crazy adventure, or introduce a fascinating way of life. They always entertain, and always enrich the experience of travel.

THE GATES OF DAMASCUS
Lieve Joris
Translated by Sam Garrett

This best-selling book is a beautifully drawn portrait of day-to-day life in modern Syria. Through her intimate contact with local people, Lieve Joris draws us into the fascinating world that lies behind the gates of Damascus. Hala's husband is a political prisoner, jailed for his opposition to the Assad regime; through the author's friendship with Hala we see how Syrian politics impacts on the lives of ordinary people.

Lieve Joris, who was born in Belgium, is one of Europe's leading travel writers. In addition to an award-winning book on Hungary, she has published widely acclaimed accounts of her journeys to the Middle East and Africa. *The Gates of Damascus* is her fifth book.

'Expands the boundaries of travel writing' – Times Literary Supplement

---

KINGDOM OF THE FILM STARS
Journey into Jordan
Annie Caulfield

Kingdom of the Film Stars is a travel book and a love story. With honesty and humour, Annie Caulfield writes of travelling in Jordan and falling in love with a Bedouin. Her book offers fascinating insights into the country – from the traditional tent life of nomadic tribes to the first woman MP's battle with fundamentalist colleagues. *Kingdom of the Film Stars* unpicks some of the tight-woven Western myths about the Arab world, presenting cultural and political issues within the intimate framework of a compelling love story.

Annie Caulfield, who was born in Ireland and currently lives in London, is an award-winning playwright and journalist. She has travelled widely in the Middle East.

'Annie Caulfield is a remarkable traveller. Her story is fresh, courageous, moving, witty and sexy!' – Dawn French

LONELY PLANET TRAVEL ATLASES

Lonely Planet has long been famous for the number and quality of its guidebook maps. Now we've gone one step further and in conjunction with Steinhart Katzir Publishers produced a handy companion series: Lonely Planet travel atlases – maps of a country produced in book form.

Unlike other maps, which look good but lead travellers astray, our travel atlases have been researched on the road by Lonely Planet's experienced team of writers. All details are carefully checked to ensure the atlas corresponds with the equivalent Lonely Planet guidebook.

The handy atlas format means no holes, wrinkles, torn sections or constant folding and unfolding. These atlases can survive long periods on the road, unlike cumbersome fold-out maps. The comprehensive index ensures easy reference.

- full-colour throughout
- maps researched and checked by Lonely Planet authors
- place names correspond with Lonely Planet guidebooks
  – no confusing spelling differences
- legend and travelling information in English, French, German, Japanese and Spanish
- size: 230 x 160 mm

Available now:
Chile & Easter Island • Egypt • India & Bangladesh • Israel & the Palestinian Territories •Jordan, Syria & Lebanon • Kenya • Laos • Portugal • South Africa, Lesotho & Swaziland • Thailand • Turkey • Vietnam • Zimbabwe, Botswana & Namibia

---

LONELY PLANET TV SERIES & VIDEOS

Lonely Planet travel guides have been brought to life on television screens around the world. Like our guides, the programmes are based on the joy of independent travel, and look honestly at some of the most exciting, picturesque and frustrating places in the world. Each show is presented by one of three travellers from Australia, England or the USA and combines an innovative mixture of video, Super-8 film, atmospheric soundscapes and original music.

Videos of each episode – containing additional footage not shown on television – are available from good book and video shops, but the availability of individual videos varies with regional screening schedules.

Video destinations include: Alaska • American Rockies • Australia – The South-East • Baja California & the Copper Canyon • Brazil • Central Asia • Chile & Easter Island • Corsica, Sicily & Sardinia – The Mediterranean Islands • East Africa (Tanzania & Zanzibar) • Ecuador & the Galapagos Islands • Greenland & Iceland • Indonesia • Israel & the Sinai Desert • Jamaica • Japan • La Ruta Maya • Morocco • New York • North India • Pacific Islands (Fiji, Solomon Islands & Vanuatu) • South India • South West China • Turkey • Vietnam • West Africa • Zimbabwe, Botswana & Namibia

The Lonely Planet TV series is produced by:
Pilot Productions
The Old Studio
18 Middle Row
London W10 5AT UK

For video availability and ordering information contact your nearest Lonely Planet office.

Music from the TV series is available on CD & cassette.

PLANET TALK

Lonely Planet's FREE quarterly newsletter

We love hearing from you and think you'd like to hear from us.

When...is the right time to see reindeer in Finland?
Where...can you hear the best palm-wine music in Ghana?
How...do you get from Asunción to Areguá by steam train?
What...is the best way to see India?

For the answer to these and many other questions read PLANET TALK.

Every issue is packed with up-to-date travel news and advice including:

- a letter from Lonely Planet co-founders Tony and Maureen Wheeler
- go behind the scenes on the road with a Lonely Planet author
- feature article on an important and topical travel issue
- a selection of recent letters from travellers
- details on forthcoming Lonely Planet promotions
- complete list of Lonely Planet products

To join our mailing list contact any Lonely Planet office.

Also available: Lonely Planet T-shirts. 100% heavyweight cotton.

LONELY PLANET ONLINE

Get the latest travel information before you leave or while you're on the road

Whether you've just begun planning your next trip, or you're chasing down specific info on currency regulations or visa requirements, check out Lonely Planet Online for up-to-the-minute travel information.

As well as travel profiles of your favourite destinations (including maps and photos), you'll find current reports from our researchers and other travellers, updates on health and visas, travel advisories, and discussion of the ecological and political issues you need to be aware of as you travel.

There's also an online travellers' forum where you can share your experience of life on the road, meet travel companions and ask other travellers for their recommendations and advice. We also have plenty of links to other online sites useful to independent travellers.

And of course we have a complete and up-to-date list of all Lonely Planet travel products including guides, phrasebooks, atlases, Journeys and videos and a simple online ordering facility if you can't find the book you want elsewhere.

www.lonelyplanet.com
or
AOL keyword: lp

LONELY PLANET PRODUCTS

Lonely Planet is known worldwide for publishing practical, reliable and no-nonsense travel information in our guides and on our web site. The Lonely Planet list covers just about every accessible part of the world. Currently there are eight series: *travel guides, shoestring guides, walking guides, city guides, phrasebooks, audio packs, travel atlases* and *Journeys* – a unique collection of travel writing.

EUROPE

Amsterdam • Austria • Baltic States phrasebook • Britain • Central Europe on a shoestring • Central Europe phrasebook • Czech & Slovak Republics • Denmark • Dublin • Eastern Europe on a shoestring • Eastern Europe phrasebook • Estonia, Latvia & Lithuania • Finland • France • French phrasebook • Germany • German phrasebook • Greece • Greek phrasebook • Hungary • Iceland, Greenland & the Faroe Islands • Ireland • Italian phrasebook • Italy • Lisbon • Mediterranean Europe on a shoestring • Mediterranean Europe phrasebook • Paris • Poland • Portugal • Portugal travel atlas • Prague • Russia, Ukraine & Belarus • Russian phrasebook • Scandinavian & Baltic Europe on a shoestring • Scandinavian Europe phrasebook •Slovenia • Spain • Spanish phrasebook • St Petersburg • Switzerland •Trekking in Spain • Ukrainian phrasebook •Vienna •Walking in Britain • Walking in Switzerland • Western Europe on a shoestring • Western Europe phrasebook

Travel Literature: The Olive Grove: Travels in Greece

NORTH AMERICA

Alaska • Backpacking in Alaska • Baja California • California & Nevada • Canada • Florida • Hawaii • Honolulu • Los Angeles • Mexico • Miami • New England • New Orleans • New York City • New York, New Jersey & Pennsylvania • Pacific Northwest USA • Rocky Mountain States • San Francisco • Southwest USA • USA phrasebook • Washington, DC & the Capital Region

CENTRAL AMERICA & THE CARIBBEAN

Bermuda • Central America on a shoestring • Costa Rica • Cuba •Eastern Caribbean •Guatemala, Belize & Yucatán: La Ruta Maya • Jamaica

SOUTH AMERICA

Argentina, Uruguay & Paraguay • Bolivia • Brazil • Brazilian phrasebook • Buenos Aires • Chile & Easter Island • Chile & Easter Island travel atlas • Colombia • Deep South • Ecuador & the Galápagos Islands • Latin American Spanish phrasebook • Peru • Quechua phrasebook • Rio de Janeiro • South America on a shoestring • Trekking in the Patagonian Andes • Venezuela

Travel Literature: Full Circle: A South American Journey

ANTARCTICA

Antarctica

ISLANDS OF THE INDIAN OCEAN

Madagascar & Comoros • Maldives• Mauritius, Réunion & Seychelles

AFRICA

Africa - the South • Africa on a shoestring • Arabic (Moroccan) phrasebook • Cape Town • Central Africa • East Africa • Egypt • Egypt travel atlas• Ethiopian (Amharic) phrasebook • Kenya • Kenya travel atlas • Malawi, Mozambique & Zambia • Morocco • North Africa • South Africa, Lesotho & Swaziland • South Africa, Lesotho & Swaziland travel atlas • Swahili phrasebook • Trekking in East Africa • West Africa • Zimbabwe, Botswana & Namibia • Zimbabwe, Botswana & Namibia travel atlas

Travel Literature: The Rainbird: A Central African Journey • Songs to an African Sunset: A Zimbabwean Story

MAIL ORDER

Lonely Planet products are distributed worldwide. They are also available by mail order from Lonely Planet, so if you have difficulty finding a title please write to us. North American and South American residents should write to Embarcadero West, 155 Filbert St, Suite 251, Oakland CA 94607, USA; European and African residents should write to 10a Spring Place, London NW5 3BH; and residents of other countries to PO Box 617, Hawthorn, Victoria 3122, Australia.

NORTH-EAST ASIA

Beijing • Cantonese phrasebook • China • Hong Kong • Hong Kong, Macau & Guangzhou • Japan • Japanese phrasebook • Japanese audio pack • Korea • Korean phrasebook • Mandarin phrasebook • Mongolia • Mongolian phrasebook • North-East Asia on a shoestring • Seoul • Taiwan • Tibet • Tibet phrasebook • Tokyo

Travel Literature: Lost Japan

MIDDLE EAST & CENTRAL ASIA

Arab Gulf States • Arabic (Egyptian) phrasebook • Central Asia • Central Asia phrasebook • Iran • Israel & the Palestinian Territories • Israel & the Palestinian Territories travel atlas • Istanbul • Jerusalem • Jordan & Syria • Jordan, Syria & Lebanon travel atlas • Lebanon • Middle East • Turkey • Turkish phrasebook • Turkey travel atlas • Yemen

Travel Literature: The Gates of Damascus • Kingdom of the Film Stars: Journey into Jordan

ALSO AVAILABLE:

Travel with Children • Traveller's Tales

INDIAN SUBCONTINENT

Bangladesh • Bengali phrasebook • Delhi • Hindi/Urdu phrasebook • India • India & Bangladesh travel atlas • Indian Himalaya • Karakoram Highway • Nepal • Nepali phrasebook • Pakistan • Rajasthan • Sri Lanka • Sri Lanka phrasebook • Trekking in the Indian Himalaya • Trekking in the Karakoram & Hindukush • Trekking in the Nepal Himalaya

Travel Literature: In Rajasthan • Shopping for Buddhas

SOUTH-EAST ASIA

Bali & Lombok • Bangkok • Burmese phrasebook • Cambodia • Ho Chi Minh City • Indonesia • Indonesian phrasebook • Indonesian audio pack • Jakarta • Java • Laos • Lao phrasebook • Laos travel atlas • Malay phrasebook • Malaysia, Singapore & Brunei • Myanmar (Burma) • Philippines • Pilipino phrasebook • Singapore • South-East Asia on a shoestring • South-East Asia phrasebook • Thailand • Thailand's Islands & Beaches • Thailand travel atlas • Thai phrasebook • Thai audio pack • Thai Hill Tribes phrasebook • Vietnam • Vietnamese phrasebook • Vietnam travel atlas

AUSTRALIA & THE PACIFIC

Australia • Australian phrasebook • Bushwalking in Australia • Bushwalking in Papua New Guinea • Fiji • Fijian phrasebook • Islands of Australia's Great Barrier Reef • Melbourne • Micronesia • New Caledonia • New South Wales • New Zealand • Northern Territory • Outback Australia • Papua New Guinea • Papua New Guinea phrasebook • Queensland • Rarotonga & the Cook Islands • Samoa • Solomon Islands • South Australia • Sydney • Tahiti & French Polynesia • Tasmania • Tonga • Tramping in New Zealand • Vanuatu • Victoria • Western Australia

Travel Literature: Islands in the Clouds • Sean & David's Long Drive

THE LONELY PLANET STORY

Lonely Planet published its first book in 1973 in response to the numerous 'How did you do it?' questions Maureen and Tony Wheeler were asked after driving, bussing, hitching, sailing and railing their way from England to Australia.

Written at a kitchen table and hand collated, trimmed and stapled, *Across Asia on the Cheap* became an instant local bestseller, inspiring thoughts of another book.

Eighteen months in South-East Asia resulted in their second guide, *South-East Asia on a shoestring*, which they put together in a backstreet Chinese hotel in Singapore in 1975. The 'yellow bible', as it quickly became known to backpackers around the world, soon became *the* guide to the region. It has sold well over half a million copies and is now in its 9th edition, still retaining its familiar yellow cover.

Today there are over 240 titles, including travel guides, walking guides, language kits & phrasebooks, travel atlases and travel literature. The company is the largest independent travel publisher in the world. Although Lonely Planet initially specialised in guides to Asia, today there are few corners of the globe that have not been covered.

The emphasis continues to be on travel for independent travellers. Tony and Maureen still travel for several months of each year and play an active part in the writing, updating and quality control of Lonely Planet's guides.

They have been joined by over 70 authors and 170 staff at our offices in Melbourne (Australia), Oakland (USA), London (UK) and Paris (France). Travellers themselves also make a valuable contribution to the guides through the feedback we receive in thousands of letters each year and on our web site.

The people at Lonely Planet strongly believe that travellers can make a positive contribution to the countries they visit, both through their appreciation of the countries' culture, wildlife and natural features, and through the money they spend. In addition, the company makes a direct contribution to the countries and regions it covers. Since 1986 a percentage of the income from each book has been donated to ventures such as famine relief in Africa; aid projects in India; agricultural projects in Central America; Greenpeace's efforts to halt French nuclear testing in the Pacific; and Amnesty International.

'I hope we send people out with the right attitude about travel. You realise when you travel that there are so many different perspectives about the world, so we hope these books will make people more interested in what they see. Guidebooks can't really guide people. All you can do is point them in the right direction.'

– Tony Wheeler

LONELY PLANET PUBLICATIONS

Australia
PO Box 617, Hawthorn 3122, Victoria
tel: (03) 9819 1877 fax: (03) 9819 6459
e-mail: talk2us@lonelyplanet.com.au

USA
Embarcadero West, 155 Filbert St, Suite 251,
Oakland, CA 94607
tel: (510) 893 8555 TOLL FREE: 800 275-8555
fax: (510) 893 8563
e-mail: info@lonelyplanet.com

UK
10a Spring Place,
London NW5 3BH
tel: (0171) 428 4800 fax: (0171) 428 4828
e-mail: go@lonelyplanet.co.uk

France:
71 bis rue du Cardinal Lemoine, 75005 Paris
tel: 1 44 32 06 20 fax: 1 46 34 72 55
e-mail: 100560.415@compuserve.com

World Wide Web: http://www.lonelyplanet.com
or *AOL keyword: lp*